WEST'S LAW SCHOOL
ADVISORY BOARD

JESSE H. CHOPER
Professor of Law,
University of California, Berkeley

DAVID P. CURRIE
Professor of Law, University of Chicago

YALE KAMISAR
Professor of Law, University of Michigan
Professor of Law, University of San Diego

MARY KAY KANE
Chancellor, Dean and Distinguished Professor of Law,
University of California,
Hastings College of the Law

WAYNE R. LaFAVE
Professor of Law, University of Illinois

ARTHUR R. MILLER
Professor of Law, Harvard University

GRANT S. NELSON
Professor of Law, University of California, Los Angeles

JAMES J. WHITE
Professor of Law, University of Michigan

THE LAW OF MODERN PAYMENT SYSTEMS

By

Fred H. Miller
George Lynn Cross Research Professor
Kenneth McAfee Centennial Professor of Law
and Chair in Law
University of Oklahoma College of Law

Alvin C. Harrell
Robert S. Kerr, Sr. Professor of Law
Oklahoma City University School of Law

HORNBOOK SERIES®

THOMSON
WEST

Mat #18478080

West Group has created this publication to provide you with accurate and authoritative information concerning the subject matter covered. However, this publication was not necessarily prepared by persons licensed to practice law in a particular jurisdiction. West Group is not engaged in rendering legal or other professional advice, and this publication is not a substitute for the advice of an attorney. If you require legal or other expert advice, you should seek the services of a competent attorney or other professional.

Hornbook Series, *WESTLAW* and West Group are trademarks
registered in the U.S. Patent and Trademark Office.

COPYRIGHT © 2003 By WEST GROUP
610 Opperman Drive
P.O. Box 64526
St. Paul, MN 55164–0526
1–800–328–9352

All rights reserved
Printed in the United States of America

ISBN 0–314–26018–8

TEXT IS PRINTED ON 10% POST
CONSUMER RECYCLED PAPER

Preface

This book constitutes a current and comprehensive discussion of the law governing promissory notes and drafts and other means of payment, except for cash. Every provision in Articles 3 and 4 of the Uniform Commercial Code is discussed, including significant cases decided under those provisions. In relation to the law before the 1990 revision of and amendments to Articles 3 and 4, significant issues, and cases also are discussed as examples of the operation of the statute, and to show its deficiencies which led to the 1990 changes. Issues on which the present statute is unclear, or which are subject to a difference of opinion, also are discussed. Law beyond the Uniform Commercial Code that is related to matters governed by the Code, particularly in the consumer context, but also including relevant federal law, is at least mentioned, and is discussed in detail where a commercial rule is directly modified, such as in the area of holding in due course. Articles 3 and 4 were recently amended. This book discusses the amendments, which answer or clarify issues under the present law.

The treatment of other payment systems generally is less extensive. There is much less statutory and case law, and many of the rules are only in the contracts of the parties. Moreover, development in the field can make discussion in detail soon outdated and one of our goals for the book is to have it represent a degree of permanency. Other works cited are better suited for an in depth discussion as to credit cards and retail funds transfers and some emerging payment methods. However, Article 4A on funds transfers is discussed in detail, as well as some focus on previous law as found in the leading wholesale funds transfer cases. The discussion thus generally familiarizes the reader with these other systems, and permits a comparison between how problems are handled there as opposed to in the check system under the Uniform Commercial Code.

To the extent this book proves useful, the credit is not all ours. In part credit belongs to many who have taught and helped the authors, and to the families of the authors who have been patient while they were otherwise occupied. Deficiencies, however, are the responsibility of the authors alone.

FRED H. MILLER
ALVIN C. HARRELL

Norman, Oklahoma, December 2002
Oklahoma City, Oklahoma, December 2002

*

WESTLAW® Overview

The Law of Modern Payment Systems and Notes, by Fred H. Miller and Alvin Harrell offers a detailed and comprehensive treatment of legal principles and issues relating to payment systems and notes. To obtain supplemental information to the information contained in this book, you can access Westlaw, a computer-assisted legal research service of West Group. Westlaw contains a broad array of legal resources, including case law, statutes, expert commentary, current developments and various other types of information.

Learning how to use these materials effectively will enhance your legal research abilities. To help you coordinate the information in the book with your Westlaw research, this volume contains an appendix listing Westlaw databases, search techniques and sample problems.

The instructions and features described in this Westlaw overview are based on accessing Westlaw via westlaw.com® at **www.westlaw.com**.

THE PUBLISHER

*

Summary of Contents

	Page
PREFACE	iii
WESTLAW OVERVIEW	v

Chapter 1. The Law Governing Methods of Payment and Evidences of Debt ... **1**

¶ 1.01	Payment Transactions and Evidence of Debt	2
¶ 1.02	Uniform Commercial Code Article 3: The Primary Law	10
¶ 1.03	Governing Law When Article 3 Is Not Applicable	13
¶ 1.04	Negotiable Instruments in Context: Supplementary Governing Law	31

Chapter 2. Form Requirements for Negotiable Instruments ... **38**

¶ 2.01	Introduction	39
¶ 2.02	Form Requirements for Negotiable Instruments	47
¶ 2.03	Seals	79
¶ 2.04	Ambiguities and Omissions in Instruments	79
¶ 2.05	Incomplete Instruments	83

Chapter 3. Rights on Negotiable Instruments ... **86**

¶ 3.01	Issue and the Rights It Creates	87
¶ 3.02	Transfer and Negotiation	98
¶ 3.03	Holder in Due Course Status	115
¶ 3.04	Limitations on Holder in Due Course Status	146

Chapter 4. Liability on Negotiable Instruments: The Basic Obligors ... **155**

¶ 4.01	Introduction	156
¶ 4.02	Basis for Liability	156
¶ 4.03	The Drawer	165
¶ 4.04	The Drawee	176
¶ 4.05	The Maker	184
¶ 4.06	The Indorser	185

Chapter 5. Liability on Negotiable Instruments: Accommodation and Agency ... **192**

¶ 5.01	Introduction	192
¶ 5.02	Accommodation Parties	194
¶ 5.03	Agents	200

		Page
Chapter 6. Defenses to and Discharge of Liability on Negotiable Instruments		**207**
¶ 6.01	Introduction	208
¶ 6.02	Real Defenses, Including Discharge	213
¶ 6.03	Personal Defenses, Including Discharge	219
Chapter 7. Liability and Rights Not on the Instrument of Parties to Negotiable Instruments		**249**
¶ 7.01	Liability and Rights With Respect to the Underlying Transaction	250
¶ 7.02	Warranty	257
¶ 7.03	Other Bases for Liability and Rights	269
Chapter 8. Article 4: Provisional and Final Payment		**287**
¶ 8.01	Article 4: Scope and Key Concepts	289
¶ 8.02	The Payor Bank: Provisional Settlement Versus Final Payment	305
¶ 8.03	Final Payment and the Midnight Deadline for Collecting Banks	332
¶ 8.04	Funds Availability and Federal Reserve Regulation CC	346
¶ 8.05	Summary and Conclusions	377
Chapter 9. The Bank–Customer Relationship		**378**
¶ 9.01	When Is Payment of a Customer's Check Required, Permitted, or Prohibited?	380
¶ 9.02	Consequences of Wrongful Payment and Wrongful Dishonor	405
¶ 9.03	Rights and Obligations of Bank Customers	413
¶ 9.04	NOW and Share Drafts	438
¶ 9.05	The Basic Law of Bank Accounts	440
¶ 9.06	Banker's Lien, Setoff, Garnishment and Security Interests in Bank Accounts	451
Chapter 10. UCC Article 4A—Funds Transfers		**468**
¶ 10.01	Introduction and Scope—UCC Article 4A	469
¶ 10.02	Article 4A Definitions and Scope	470
¶ 10.03	Liability for Errors and Unauthorized Orders	474
¶ 10.04	Obligations of a Bank Accepting a Payment Order	477
¶ 10.05	Transmitting the Payment Order	482
¶ 10.06	Fees and Settlement	482
¶ 10.07	Payment	483
¶ 10.08	Miscellaneous Article 4A Issues	487
¶ 10.09	Unauthorized and Erroneous Orders	493
¶ 10.10	Summary and Conclusions—Implementing UCC Article 4A	496
¶ 10.11	Regulation J Subpart A: Collection of Checks Through Federal Reserve Banks	498
¶ 10.12	Regulation J Subpart B: Fedwire	500
¶ 10.13	Federal Choice of Law Provisions	503
¶ 10.14	Wire Transfer Monitoring Rules	504

	Page
¶ 10.15 The U.S. Treasury "Travel Rule"	506
¶ 10.16 Conclusion	507

Chapter 11. Non–UCC Payment Systems — 508
¶ 11.01 Introduction 508
¶ 11.02 The Law of Credit and Debit Cards 515
¶ 11.03 Applicable Law for Selected Other Non–UCC Payment Systems 525

Appendix: WESTLAW Appendix 535
Table of Cases 551
Table of Statutes 599
Index 657

Table of Contents

	Page
Preface	iii
Westlaw Overview	v

Chapter 1. The Law Governing Methods of Payment and Evidences of Debt 1

¶ 1.01 Payment Transactions and Evidence of Debt 2
    [1] Overview 2
    [2] Methods of Evidencing Debt and Making Payment 2
    [3] Prevalency and Uses of Negotiable Instruments 4
        [a] Consumer Transactions 4
        [b] Commercial Transactions 5
    [4] Definition of Negotiable Instrument 5
        [a] Order Paper: Drafts and Checks 6
        [b] Notes and Certificates of Deposit 7
        [c] Popular Name Instruments 9
        [d] Exclusions 10

¶ 1.02 Uniform Commercial Code Article 3: The Primary Law 10
    [1] Scope of Article 3 11
    [2] Instruments Not Payable to Order or to Bearer and Checks 11

¶ 1.03 Governing Law When Article 3 Is Not Applicable 13
    [1] Definitionary Exclusions From Article 3 13
        [a] Applicability of General Contract Law 13
        [b] Application of Article 3 by Analogy 14
    [2] Express Exclusions from Article 3 15
        [a] Money 15
        [b] Documents of Title 16
        [c] Investment Securities 16
        [d] Payment Orders 18
    [3] Choice of Law Exclusions 18
        [a] The Law of Another State 19
        [b] The Law of Another Country 20
        [c] International Law 21
        [d] Federal Law 24
            [i] Federal Common Law 24
            [ii] Federal Statutes or Regulations 29

¶ 1.04 Negotiable Instruments in Context: Supplementary Governing Law 31

			Page
	[1]	Uniform Commercial Code Article 4: Bank Deposits and Collections	31
	[2]	Regulation CC: Funds Availability	32
	[3]	Uniform Commercial Code Article 9: Secured Transactions	33
	[4]	General Provisions of Law Under the Uniform Commercial Code: Article 1	34
	[5]	General Provisions of Law Outside the Uniform Commercial Code: Section 1–103(b) of Article 1	35

Chapter 2. Form Requirements for Negotiable Instruments 38

¶ 2.01 Introduction 39
    [1] History of and Reasons for Form Requirements for Negotiable Instruments 39
    [2] Modern Critique of the Requirements 41
        [a] Erosion of Negotiable Status 41
        [b] Problems Where the Form of the Instrument Is Inadequate 42
        [c] Solutions 43
    [3] Indirectly Obtaining the Benefits of Article 3 45
        [a] General Inability to Invoke Rules of Article 3 by Agreement 45
        [b] Other Methods of Achieving Aspects of Negotiability 45

¶ 2.02 Form Requirements for Negotiable Instruments 47
    [1] Written Instrument 48
    [2] Signing 48
        [a] Creation of Liability on an Instrument 48
        [b] Definition of "Signed" 48
        [c] Weight Accorded to Signatures 49
    [3] Limited and Unconditional Promise or Order 50
        [a] Nature of Promise or Order 50
            [i] Informal Instruments 50
            [ii] Excessive Luggage Encumbering the Promise or Order 51
                [A] Provisions Relating to Collateral 52
                [B] Other Provisions 56
        [b] The Instrument in Relation to the Transaction Out of Which It Arose 57
            [i] References Versus Incorporation 57
                [A] Permitted References 57
                [B] References Not Permitted 61
            [ii] Other Agreements Affecting the Instrument 63
            [iii] Oral Parol Evidence 65
        [c] Limitations on Sources for Payment 67
        [d] Other Conditions 68
    [4] Sum Certain 68
        [a] Amount Ascertainable From the Instrument 68
        [b] Provisions Not Creating Uncertainty 71
    [5] Sum Payable in Money 71
        [a] Money Not Limited to Legal Tender 71
        [b] Instruments Payable in Foreign Money 72

				Page
	[6]	Payable on Demand or at a Definite Time		72
		[a] Instruments Payable on Demand		72
		[b] Instruments Payable at a Definite Time		73
	[7]	Payable to Order or to Bearer		75
		[a] Instruments Payable to Bearer		75
		[b] Instruments Payable to Order		77
¶ 2.03	Seals			79
¶ 2.04	Ambiguities and Omissions in Instruments			79
	[1]	Rules to Forestall Ambiguities		79
	[2]	Omissions Not an Impairment of Negotiability		83
¶ 2.05	Incomplete Instruments			83
	[1]	When an Instrument is Complete, Incomplete, or Not Within Article 3		83
	[2]	Authorized and Unauthorized Complete Instruments		84

Chapter 3. Rights on Negotiable Instruments — 86

¶ 3.01	Issue and the Rights It Creates			87
	[1]	An Instrument Is Not Effective Until Issued		87
	[2]	The Concept of Holder		89
	[3]	Rights of One Not a Holder of an Instrument		90
		[a] Remitters, Takers, Nonpossessors, and Creditors		90
		[b] Transferees and Shelter Rights		92
	[4]	Rights of the Holder of an Instrument		95
		[a] Introduction		95
		[b] Right to Enforce the Instrument or Discharge Parties on It		96
		[c] Right to Transfer or Negotiate the Instrument		97
¶ 3.02	Transfer and Negotiation			98
	[1]	Transfer		98
	[2]	Negotiation of a Bearer Instrument		98
	[3]	Negotiation of an Order Instrument		99
		[a] The Requirements of Indorsement and Delivery		99
		[b] Who May Indorse		102
			[i] Introduction	102
			[ii] Instruments Payable to More Than One Person	102
			[iii] Instruments Payable to Estates, Offices, and the Like	104
			[iv] Instruments with Misspelled Names, Accommodation Indorsers, and Unauthorized Indorsers	105
		[c] Types of Indorsements and Their Effect		106
			[i] Blank Indorsement	106
			[ii] Special Indorsement	107
			[iii] Restrictive Indorsement	108
				[A] Types of Restrictive Indorsements — 108
				[B] Effect of Restrictive Indorsements — 109
	[4]	Rescission of Negotiation and Reacquisition		112
		[a] Rescission		112
		[b] Reacquisition		114

				Page
¶ 3.03	Holder in Due Course Status			115
	[1]	Introduction		115
		[a]	The Reason and Need for Holder in Due Course Status	115
		[b]	Payee As a Holder in Due Course	117
	[2]	Elements of Proper Taking		120
		[a]	Value	120
		[b]	Good Faith and Lack of Notice	123
			[i] Relevant Time for Meeting Requirements	123
			[ii] Bad Faith or Knowledge of Agent	124
			[iii] Good Faith in General	124
			[iv] Notice in General	128
			[v] Specific Notice Provisions	132
		[c]	Burden of Proof	136
	[3]	Status of a Holder in Due Course		139
		[a]	Freedom from Claims and Defenses	139
			[i] Real and Personal Defenses	139
			[ii] Setoff (Claims in Recoupment)	140
			[iii] Claims	142
		[b]	Finality of Payment	144
¶ 3.04	Limitations on Holder in Due Course Status			146
	[1]	In the UCC		146
		[a]	Nonordinary Course Acquisitions	146
		[b]	Defenses and Claims of Persons With Whom the Holder Has Dealt	147
			[i] Defenses	147
			[ii] Claims	148
	[2]	Case Law Limits		150
	[3]	State Legislation		152
	[4]	Federal Rule		153

Chapter 4. Liability on Negotiable Instruments: The Basic Obligors 155

¶ 4.01	Introduction			156
¶ 4.02	Basis for Liability			156
	[1]	Signature		156
	[2]	Preclusion and Ratification		158
		[a]	Preclusion	158
		[b]	Ratification	163
	[3]	Liability and Capacity		164
¶ 4.03	The Drawer			165
	[1]	Description of Liability		165
	[2]	Conditions to Liability		165
		[a]	Dishonor	165
			[i] Presentment As a Condition to Dishonor	165
			[ii] Time of Presentment	168
			[iii] Manner of Presentment	169
		[b]	Notice of Dishonor	171

				Page
		[c]	Protest	173
		[d]	Discharge, Evidence, and Excuse	173
			[i] Discharge	173
			[ii] Evidence	173
			[iii] Excuse	174

¶ 4.04 The Drawee 176
    [1] Absence of Liability As Drawee 176
    [2] Liability As Acceptor 177
        [a] Acceptance and Certification 177
        [b] Consequences of Acceptance 179

¶ 4.05 The Maker 184

¶ 4.06 The Indorser 185
    [1] Description of Liability 185
    [2] Conditions to Liability 187
        [a] Dishonor and Notice of Dishonor 187
        [b] Discharge, Evidence, and Excuse 189
    [3] Order of Liability 190

Chapter 5. Liability on Negotiable Instruments: Accommodation and Agency 192

¶ 5.01 Introduction 192

¶ 5.02 Accommodation Parties 194
    [1] Definition and Determination of Status 194
        [a] Definition 194
        [b] Determination of Status 195
    [2] Liability to Taker of Instrument 197
    [3] Liability to and of Party Accommodated 198

¶ 5.03 Agents 200
    [1] Unauthorized Signatures 200
    [2] Authorized Signatures Creating Principal But Not Agent Liability 201
    [3] Authorized Signatures Creating Agent Liability Alone 202

Chapter 6. Defenses to and Discharge of Liability on Negotiable Instruments 207

¶ 6.01 Introduction 208
    [1] Relation Between Liability and Defenses 208
        [a] Procedural Considerations 208
        [b] Real and Personal Defenses 209
    [2] Use of Parol Evidence to Show Defenses 210
        [a] Introduction 210
        [b] Evidence the Instrument Is Not To Be Binding ... 211
        [c] Evidence of Conditions 212

¶ 6.02 Real Defenses, Including Discharge 213
    [1] Infancy and Other Incapacity 213
    [2] Duress 214
    [3] Illegality 214
    [4] Fraud 215
    [5] Discharge 216

			Page
	[6]	Forgery	216
	[7]	Alteration	217
¶ 6.03	Personal Defenses, Including Discharge		219
	[1]	In General	219
		[a] Personal Defenses Described	219
		[b] Jus Tertii (Defenses Based on the Better Right of a Third Party)	219
	[2]	"Counterparts" of Real Defenses	222
	[3]	Unauthorized Completion	224
	[4]	Nondelivery, Delivery for a Special Purpose, and Nonperformance of a Condition Precedent	226
	[5]	Want or Failure of Consideration	227
	[6]	Discharge	230
		[a] In General	230
		[b] Payment or Satisfaction and Tender of Payment	233
		[i] In General	233
		[ii] Payment or Satisfaction to the Holder	233
		[iii] Adverse Claims	235
		[iv] Tender of Payment	236
		[c] Cancellation and Renunciation	237
		[d] Impairment of Recourse or Collateral	240
		[i] Impairment of Recourse	240
		[ii] Impairment of Collateral	242
		[iii] Waiver of Defense	244
	[7]	Statute of Limitations	245

Chapter 7. Liability and Rights Not on the Instrument of Parties to Negotiable Instruments 249

¶ 7.01	Liability and Rights With Respect to the Underlying Transaction		250
	[1]	Relation Between the Instrument and the Transaction in General	250
		[a] Parity of Rights and Liabilities	250
		[b] Suspension of the Underlying Obligation	250
		[c] Effect of Dishonor or Payment of the Instrument	252
	[2]	Instruments on Which a Bank is Liable	253
	[3]	Accord and Satisfaction	254
¶ 7.02	Warranty		257
	[1]	Introduction	257
		[a] Nature of Warranty Obligations	257
		[b] Remedies and Limitations	259
	[2]	Warranties Made by a Transferor	260
	[3]	Presentment Warranties Made to an Acceptor or Payor	262
		[a] No Unauthorized Signature	263
		[b] No Forged Indorsements	265
		[c] No Alterations	268

			Page
¶ 7.03	Other Bases for Liability and Rights		269
	[1] In General		269
	[2] Negligence		270
	[3] Conversion		273
		[a] Owner's Basis for Suit	273
		[b] Defenses to Action Based on a Forged Indorsement	275
		[i] Effect of Failure to Follow Reasonable Commercial Standards	276
		[ii] Effect of Proceeds Remaining	278
		[c] Legally Irrelevant Forged Indorsements	279
		[i] Proceeds Are Correctly Paid	279
		[ii] Imposter, Fictitious Payee, and Padded Payroll Cases; Employer's Indorsements	280
		[A] In General	280
		[B] The Need for Proper Indorsement and Due Care	284
Chapter 8.	**Article 4: Provisional and Final Payment**		**287**
¶ 8.01	Article 4: Scope and Key Concepts		289
	[1] Scope of Article 4 and Choice of Law		289
		[a] Scope of Article 4	289
		[b] Choice of Law	292
	[2] Modification by Agreement and Preemption by Federal Rule		293
	[3] Definitions and Important Concepts		298
		[a] Item	298
		[b] Bank	299
		[c] Depository Bank	299
		[d] Payor Bank	299
		[e] Intermediary Bank	299
		[f] Collecting Bank	299
		[g] Customer	300
		[h] Agency	300
		[i] Banking Day	301
		[j] Midnight Deadline	301
		[k] Settle	301
		[l] Branches: Seperate Office of a Bank; Separate Data Processing Center	302
		[m] Types of Checks	302
		[n] Electronic Presentment	303
	[4] Bank Insolvency		304
¶ 8.02	The Payor Bank: Provisional Settlement Versus Final Payment		305
	[1] Settlement		306
		[a] Initial Settlement	306
		[b] Provisional Versus Final Settlement/Payment	308
		[c] Final Payment	312
	[2] Methods of Making Final Payment		314
		[a] Payment in Cash	314
		[b] Reserving the Right to Revoke	315

				Page
		[c]	The Midnight Deadline	316
	[3]	Final Settlement and Accountability Under Article 4		319
	[4]	Avoidance of Payment on Restitutionary Grounds		321
	[5]	Funds Availability Under Article 4		325
	[6]	Notice of Dishonor and Return of the Item		327
	[7]	Defenses and Excuses for Failure to Send Timely Notice of Dishonor		330

¶ 8.03 Final Payment and the Midnight Deadline for Collecting Banks 332
    [1] Introduction 332
    [2] Provisional Settlement by a Collecting Bank 333
    [3] Excuses for Failure to Meet the Midnight Deadline 339
    [4] Measure of Liability When a Collecting Bank Misses Its Midnight Deadline 340
    [5] Settlement by Remittance or Other Means 344

¶ 8.04 Funds Availability and Federal Reserve Regulation CC 346
    [1] Introduction 346
    [2] Regulation CC, Subpart B—Funds Availability Requirements 347
        [a] Funds Availability Schedules 347
        [b] Exceptions and Safeguards 348
        [c] Disclosure Requirements 351
        [d] Civil Liability 351
    [3] Regulation CC, Subpart C—Collection of Checks 352
        [a] Expeditious Return of Dishonored Checks 353
            [i] The Two-Day/Four-Day Test 354
            [ii] The Forward Collection Test 354
            [iii] Impact on Article 4—The Payor Bank 355
        [b] Identification of Returned Checks and Notice of Return—Duties of the Payor Bank 355
            [i] Notice of Return 355
            [ii] Notice of Nonpayment: Identifying the Depositary Bank 356
        [c] Duties of Returning Banks—Regulation CC Section 229.31 356
            [i] The Scope of Section 229.31 356
            [ii] Expeditious Return 357
            [iii] The Return Process: Comparison to UCC Article 4 357
            [iv] Settlement, Charges, and Other Notices 359
        [d] Duties of Depositary Banks 360
            [i] Acceptance by Depositary Banks 361
            [ii] Payment for Returned Items 361
            [iii] Notice to Customer 362
        [e] Warranties of Paying and Returning Banks 363
        [f] Truncation 367
            [i] Introduction 367
            [ii] Check Truncation 367
            [iii] Forward Collection Settlements Deemed Final; Impact on Article 4 367
        [g] Indorsements 368

				Page
	[4]	Conclusion: Impact of Regulation CC on UCC Articles 3 and 4		369
		[a]	The Mandatory Availability Rules and the Depositary Bank	370
		[b]	Impact of Regulation CC on the Midnight Deadline	371
		[c]	Provisional Settlement	372
		[d]	Direct Return of Dishonored Items	372
		[e]	Payable—Through Drafts	372
		[f]	Remote Data Processing Centers	372
		[g]	Truncation	373
		[h]	Indorsement	373
		[i]	Comparative Fault	373
		[j]	Variation by Agreement	373
		[k]	Standard of Care and Measure of Damages	374
		[l]	Good Faith	375
		[m]	Implications for the Future	376
¶ 8.05	Summary and Conclusions			377

Chapter 9. The Bank–Customer Relationship — 378

¶ 9.01	When Is Payment of a Customer's Check Required, Permitted, or Prohibited?			380
	[1]	The Concept of "Properly Payable"		380
	[2]	The 1990 Article 4 Revisions: Customer Overdrafts; Postdated Checks		383
	[3]	"Properly Payable" Under Article 4: A Partial Index to Relevant Provisions		384
	[4]	Stop-Payment Orders and Other "Legals"		385
		[a]	Stop Payment Orders	385
		[b]	Payment of an Altered Item Over a Stop Order: Good Faith and Ordinary Care	389
		[c]	Alternatives to Stopping Payment	391
		[d]	Can Payment be Stopped on a Cashier's or Similar Bank Check?	392
			[i] Can the Customer Stop Payment?	394
			[ii] Can the Bank Stop Payment?	394
			[iii] Bank Liability for Dishonor of a Cashier's or Similar Check	395
			[iv] Refusal to Pay a Cashier's or Similar Check: Measure of Liability	398
			[v] Lost, Destroyed, or Stolen Cashier's, Teller's, or Certified Checks	399
		[e]	Certification	400
	[5]	Receipt of Legal Process		400
	[6]	Death or Incompetence of the Drawer		402
	[7]	Final Payment, the "Four Legals," and the Bank's "Cutoff" Hour		403

		Page
¶ 9.02	Consequences of Wrongful Payment and Wrongful Dishonor	405
	[1] Introduction	405
	[2] Wrongful Dishonor	406
	[a] The Revision of Section 4–402	406
	[b] Limitations on Bank Liability for Wrongful Dishonor	408
	[3] Wrongful Payment—Bank Liability and the Right to Subrogation	410
	[4] Postdated Checks	412
¶ 9.03	Rights and Obligations of Bank Customers	413
	[1] The Bank–Customer Relationship	413
	[2] Does the Bank Have a Fiduciary or Other Special Duty?	414
	[a] Non–Code Consequences	414
	[b] Code Consequences	417
	[c] Regulation of Depositary Services Pricing	419
	[3] Modification by Agreement	420
	[4] Customer's Duties Under Section 4–406	423
	[a] Customer's Duty to Examine Checks	423
	[b] Impact of Revised Section 4–406	427
	[c] The New Role of Comparative Negligence and Good Faith	429
	[d] Other Revisions to Section 4–406	431
	[5] Payor Bank's Obligation to Examine Checks	433
	[6] Check Truncation and MICR Encoding	435
	[7] Conclusion	438
¶ 9.04	NOW and Share Drafts	438
¶ 9.05	The Basic Law of Bank Accounts	440
	[1] The Traditional Concept and Modern Variations of a "Bank Account"	440
	[2] Common Law Classifications of Deposit Accounts	442
	[a] General and Special Purpose Accounts	442
	[b] General or Special Purpose	443
	[3] The Basic Bank Account Relationship	444
	[a] Creating a Depositary Account	444
	[b] Nature of the Bank–Customer Relation	447
	[c] Fundamental Duties and Liabilities of the Bank	447
	[i] General Deposits	447
	[ii] Special Deposits	449
	[iii] Fiduciary Duty of Disclosure	449
	[iv] Duties of the Customer	450
	[v] Termination of the Relationship	450
	[vi] The Bank Secrecy Act	451
¶ 9.06	Banker's Lien, Setoff, Garnishment and Security Interests in Bank Accounts	451
	[1] Banker's Lien	451
	[2] Setoff	453

				Page
	[a]	Background and Legal Basis		453
	[b]	Maturity of the Debt		454
	[c]	Mutuality of Obligation		455
	[d]	Absence of Deposit Restrictions		456
	[e]	Competing Claims		456
		[i]	Wrongful Dishonor	457
		[ii]	Secured Creditor	458
		[iii]	Garnishing Creditor	459
		[iv]	Tax Claims and Internal Revenue Service Levies	460
		[v]	Depositor's Trustee in Bankruptcy	461
	[f]	Duty of Set-off		463
[3]	Garnishment			464
[4]	Security Interests in Deposit Accounts			465

Chapter 10. UCC Article 4A—Funds Transfers **468**

¶ 10.01 Introduction and Scope—UCC Article 4A 469
¶ 10.02 Article 4A Definitions and Scope 470
    [1] Fundamental Concepts 470
    [2] Scope—Payment Order Must Be Unconditional 472
¶ 10.03 Liability for Errors and Unauthorized Orders 474
    [1] Authority to Originate 474
    [2] Security Procedure 475
    [3] Commercially Reasonable Procedure Required 476
¶ 10.04 Obligations of a Bank Accepting a Payment Order 477
    [1] In General 477
    [2] Misdescription of Beneficiary 478
    [3] Preemption of Other State Law Claims 479
¶ 10.05 Transmitting the Payment Order 482
¶ 10.06 Fees and Settlement 482
¶ 10.07 Payment 483
    [1] Payment in General 483
    [2] Payment and Discharge Between Banks 484
    [3] Obligation of Beneficiary's Bank to Pay Beneficiary 485
    [4] Payment to the Beneficiary 486
    [5] Payment and Discharge 486
¶ 10.08 Miscellaneous Article 4A Issues 487
    [1] Variation by Agreement or Funds—Transfer Rule 487
    [2] Effect of Creditor Process or Injunction 488
    [3] The Bank–Customer Relation 489
    [4] Rate of Interest 489
    [5] Choice of Law 490
        [a] U.S. Transactions 490
        [b] Choice of Law and International Transactions 490
    [6] Statute of Limitations 492
¶ 10.09 Unauthorized and Erroneous Orders 493
    [1] Authorized and Unauthorized Orders 493
    [2] Erroneous Orders 494
    [3] Beneficiary Misdescription 494

			Page
	[4]	Cancellation	495
	[5]	Other	495
¶ 10.10	Summary and Conclusions—Implementing UCC Article 4A		496
	[1]	Summary	496
	[2]	Implementing Article 4A	496
¶ 10.11	Regulation J Subpart A: Collection of Checks Through Federal Reserve Banks		498
¶ 10.12	Regulation J Subpart B: Fedwire		500
	[1]	Scope of Subpart B	500
	[2]	Impact of Subpart B	501
¶ 10.13	Federal Choice of Law Provisions		503
¶ 10.14	Wire Transfer Monitoring Rules		504
¶ 10.15	The U.S. Treasury "Travel Rule"		506
¶ 10.16	Conclusion		507

Chapter 11. Non-UCC Payment Systems — 508

¶ 11.01	Introduction		508
¶ 11.02	The Law of Credit and Debit Cards		515
	[1]	Required Federal Disclosures and Documentation	516
	[2]	Error Resolution and Wrongful Dishonor	518
		[a] Error Resolution Under Federal Law	518
		[b] Wrongful Dishonor Under Federal and State Law	520
	[3]	Consumer Liability for Unauthorized Transfers Under Federal Law	521
	[4]	Federal Rules on Distribution of Access Devices	524
	[5]	State Law	524
	[6]	Arbitration Clauses	525
¶ 11.03	Applicable Law for Selected Other Non-UCC Payment Systems		525
	[1]	Smart Cards and Similar Products	525
	[2]	E-checks and Similar Products	531

APPENDIX: WESTLAW APPENDIX	535
TABLE OF CASES	551
TABLE OF STATUTES	599
INDEX	657

THE LAW OF MODERN PAYMENT SYSTEMS

Chapter 1

THE LAW GOVERNING METHODS OF PAYMENT AND EVIDENCES OF DEBT

Analysis

Para.
- ¶1.01 Payment Transactions and Evidence of Debt 2
  - [1] Overview 2
  - [2] Methods of Evidencing Debt and Making Payment 2
  - [3] Prevalency and Uses of Negotiable Instruments 4
    - [a] Consumer Transactions 4
    - [b] Commercial Transactions 5
  - [4] Definition of Negotiable Instrument 5
    - [a] Order Paper: Drafts and Checks 6
    - [b] Notes and Certificates of Deposit 7
    - [c] Popular Name Instruments 9
    - [d] Exclusions 10
- ¶1.02 Uniform Commercial Code Article 3: The Primary Law 10
  - [1] Scope of Article 3 11
  - [2] Instruments Not Payable to Order or to Bearer and Checks 11
- ¶1.03 Governing Law When Article 3 Is Not Applicable 13
  - [1] Definitionary Exclusions From Article 3 13
    - [a] Applicability of General Contract Law 13
    - [b] Application of Article 3 by Analogy 14
  - [2] Express Exclusions from Article 3 15
    - [a] Money 15
    - [b] Documents of Title 16
    - [c] Investment Securities 16
    - [d] Payment Orders 18
  - [3] Choice of Law Exclusions 18
    - [a] The Law of Another State 19
    - [b] The Law of Another Country 20
    - [c] International Law 21
    - [d] Federal Law 24
      - [i] Federal Common Law 24
      - [ii] Federal Statutes or Regulations 29
- ¶1.04 Negotiable Instruments in Context: Supplementary Governing Law 31
  - [1] Uniform Commercial Code Article 4: Bank Deposits and Collections 31
  - [2] Regulation CC: Funds Availability 32
  - [3] Uniform Commercial Code Article 9: Secured Transactions 33

Para.

¶1.04 Negotiable Instruments in Context: Supplementary Governing Law—Continued
    [4] General Provisions of Law Under the Uniform Commercial Code: Article 1... 34
    [5] General Provisions of Law Outside the Uniform Commercial Code: Section 1–103(b) of Article 1 35

¶ 1.01 Payment Transactions and Evidence of Debt

[1] *Overview*

Suppose that a person that has provided services or property is entitled to be paid. Further assume that person is under a legal obligation to repay a bank loan that was obtained to acquire the property sold. Finally, assume the person that has purchased the property or services from the seller owes payment of the price. In these, and in thousands of other transactions in which one person owes payment to another, how is payment to be accomplished? If an arrangement for credit was made, how is the debt to be evidenced before payment is due?

Suppose the person owed is paid by a check drawn on the debtor's bank in another city. Must the person who receives the check travel to that bank to get payment for the check, or can the check somehow be delivered, or crucial information on it forwarded, to the payor, and can return payment be mailed, or otherwise accomplished? What is the time frame for that?

In the case of the bank loan or the debt for the price, should the bank or the seller be satisfied with the oral agreement of the debtor to repay? If not, what kind of written evidence of the debt will the bank or seller want? Who must authenticate that evidence, and in what fashion, to obligate the debtor that is a corporation but not the person actually signing personally? Can the same evidence of debt be used in the purchase of consumer goods?

Could the property or services instead be purchased with a credit card? Could they be paid for by using a debit card? What does that mean?

In the case of the debt owed the seller of property or services, if the seller takes written evidence of debt and sells it to a bank so that the seller obtains immediate payment, what is the legal position of the bank? What if instead the seller arranges for a loan directly to the buyer from the bank; will that change legal rights?

These questions and hundreds of others related to how payment is made and to how indebtedness is evidenced are the subject of this book.

[2] *Methods of Evidencing Debt and Making Payment*

If one person owes payment to another, that debt, which is itself an intangible, may be evidenced by anything from an open account book entry to an accepted or unaccepted draft, or by a promissory note or a corporate bond. The promissory note is, however, a most common form to evidence a debt, and that type of instrument is the focus here, leaving evidences of debt that qualify as investment securities under Uniform Commercial Code Article 8 to other works.

There also are many ways in which payment of a debt may be made when it becomes due. The oldest method of payment is payment in kind; the debtor provides a negotiated amount of property or services to discharge the debt. Bartering is not worth discussion time here.

The simplest method of payment is payment in money because it involves no collection problem. It is also the riskiest. A dollar bill lost or stolen is likely gone forever. Primarily for that reason, the use of cash has long been "commercially irrelevant." Drawing on a letter of credit by presentment of a draft or other demand for payment is a method of obtaining payment for property sold in a commercial transaction as described in Uniform Commercial Code (UCC) §§ 2–325(2) and 5–108,[1] but this method also is left for treatment elsewhere. Giving a check, or in some cases a draft, is perhaps the most common method of accomplishing payment today. Currently, some forty-five billion checks are written annually, so the use of checks is prevalent. This method, of course, entails the necessity of collecting the draft or check.

Increasingly, because of modern technology, payment may be effected through the transfer of funds, actually debits and credits to accounts, popularly known as funds transfers, wire transfers, or "EFT." In fact, though there were only 56 million wire transactions in 1980, their dollar amount, because of large institutional transfers by this means, exceeded the amount for checks. Today commercial funds transfers in general run well over $1 trillion dollars per day; in February 1992, almost $860,000,000 was transferred through Fedwire, the Federal Reserve funds transfer system, and in January 1992, some $1,597,000,000 through CHIPS, the clearing house interpayments system of New York banks. There are a number of variants of this general method, including not only the large commercial funds transfers, but also retail debit card transactions, ACH transactions, transactions pursuant to so-called "stored value" or "smart cards," and so-called electronic checks and coins. Most persons also are familiar with the sending of money through Western Union; however, this method as a topic discussion will be eschewed as not of sufficient significance.

In summation, methods of evidencing debt by negotiable instruments will be discussed in this book if the evidence of debt is governed by UCC Article 3. Corporate bonds, some certificates of deposit, some commercial paper, and some government obligations may be governed by UCC Article 8 or other law, but this book does not discuss the law applicable to such investment securities. Methods for the payment of obligations using checks and drafts, debit and credit cards, and credit (as opposed to debit) funds transfer methods also will be discussed, along

---

¶ 1.01

1. All citations are to the Uniform Commercial Code Official Text as effective in 2002. When a previous version of Article 1, 3 or 4 is referred to, it is by citation to "old" Article 1, 3 or 4, or a particular section.

with discussion of newer electronic methods. Where collection of an instrument is necessary, that too will be discussed. Because the law concerning negotiable instruments and the collection of them is the most unified and highly developed law at the present time, that law will be the primary focus.

[3] Prevalency and Uses of Negotiable Instruments

A negotiable instrument continues to be perhaps the most prevalent means to make payment or to evidence debt. It thus accomplishes many important tasks in our economy, and is likely to do so for some time to come.

[a] Consumer Transactions

In a consumer transaction, when merchandise or a service of relatively small value is purchased, money is likely to be the medium of payment. When the property purchased or the service is of greater value, its cost may be charged to an account, or it may be "paid for" by a credit card. A credit card sales slip, or the slip used in a paper based debit card transaction, is not a negotiable instrument to the extent it states that it is subject to another agreement.[2] Nor are these slips "items" under Article 4 for the purpose of the bank collection process.[3] Increasingly, the property or service purchased may be paid for by a transfer of funds from the customer's account to the account of the merchant, triggered by a plastic "debit" card and the use of a personal identification number (PIN), by data on a check, or in some electronic manner.[4]

Nonetheless, a check, whether it is a personal check or a certified check, cashier's check or teller's check,[5] still remains an important means of payment. The check may be given for the cost of the property or service initially, or in settlement of the account to which the purchase may have been charged. Recent statistics show that a very large percent of all consumer payments still are made by check, and that billions of consumer and business checks are written nationally each year.

If the property or the service is even larger in value so that credit is arranged, or if the purchase is to be financed with the proceeds of a loan, another type of negotiable instrument may be given to evidence rather than to pay the purchase price. This instrument is the promissory note. Furthermore, today many consumers hold certificates of deposit covering funds currently not needed and on deposit to earn interest and for

---

2. §§ 3–104(a), 3–106(a). Even if it only makes reference to the cardholder agreement, it is likely to fail to meet other criteria, such as being payable to order or to bearer.

3. § 4–104(a)(9).

4. Such transfers are governed by the federal Electronic Fund Transfers Act, 15 U.S.C. § 1693 et seq., and its implementing Regulation E, 12 CFR pt. 205 (and interpretive Federal Reserve Board Commentary). The federal statute does not cover any transfer of funds originated by check, draft, or similar paper instrument, or payment made by check, draft or similar paper instrument at an electronic terminal. Regulation E § 205.3(c)(1). It is generally assumed the federal law governs when payment is made by an electronic check since only check data is used, or when made by electronic coins; this will be discussed *infra*.

5. Defined at § 3–104(g) and (h) and § 3–409(d).

safekeeping. The evidence of the obligation of the issuing financial institution may be a kind of negotiable instrument called a certificate of deposit. Normally, this is an instrument that, if covered under the UCC at all, will be covered under Article 3 rather than under Article 8.

[b] Commercial Transactions

Outside of the consumer context, purchases for commercial purposes on open account are common, with the funds transfer in payment occurring later by check or other means. Even though governmental funds transfers (involving such payments as direct deposits of Social Security benefits), corporate funds transfers for payroll and other purposes, and interinstitutional funds transfers increasingly are using electronic methods such as automated clearing houses and wire systems,[6] checks have not been displaced in this context.

Both domestic and international commercial sales transactions commonly involve a draft drawn by the seller on the buyer and accompanied by a document of title. The seller will send the draft for payment or acceptance by the buyer, or for payment by a bank pursuant to authority from the buyer[7] or, if arranged, for payment pursuant to a letter of credit,[8] and, if credit has not been arranged, payment will be a condition to the buyer's obtaining the document of title necessary to take delivery of the goods. If credit is involved, the draft instead will be presented for acceptance, and the resulting trade acceptance may be sold by the seller to a financing agency to eliminate the need for the seller to otherwise finance the purchase.[9]

Finally, both short-term and long-term notes are issued by commercial entities to evidence loans for business operations and to evidence loans made to acquire inventory, plant, and equipment,[10] and commercial funds, like consumer savings, may be invested and covered by certificates of deposit while awaiting other use.

The above discussion, of course, is only a brief and summary description of the modern uses of negotiable instruments. There are other uses, and new ones arise from time to time.

[4] Definition of Negotiable Instrument

UCC Article 3[11] covers "negotiable instruments." What is a "negotiable instrument" that may be used to make payment and to evidence

---

6. To illustrate, in Evra Corp. v. Swiss Bank Corp., 673 F.2d 951 (7th Cir.1982), *cert. denied*, 459 U.S. 1017, 103 S.Ct. 377, 74 L.Ed.2d 511 (1982), a corporation had chartered a ship. It made the first five payments by having its bank debit its account and send a telex message to a correspondent bank in Europe, which then advised the beneficiary's bank (the bank used by the charterer of the ship) to credit an account for the benefit of the charterer. The next two payments, on the other hand, were made by a check sent directly by the corporation to the bank of the ship charterer.

7. *See* State Bank & Trust v. First State Bank of Texas, 242 F.3d 390 (10th Cir. 2000).

8. *See* UCC § 2–325.

9. *See* UCC § 2–506.

10. These can be, but are not necessarily, governed by UCC Article 8. *See* §§ 8–103(d) and 3–102(a); Official Comment 2 to § 3–102.

11. The two sponsors of the UCC, the National Conference of Commissioners on Uniform State Laws (NCCUSL) and the American Law Institute (ALI), in 1990 com-

debt? Checks, notes, and drafts are kinds of negotiable instruments. Essentially, a negotiable instrument involves a writing calling for the payment of money.[12] Today, what is considered a negotiable instrument may be divided into two general classes.

[a] *Order Paper: Drafts and Checks*

The first class of negotiable instrument is "order" paper. Order paper involves a "drawer" who, by drawing the instrument, orders another party, called the "drawee," to pay a third party, called the "payee."[13] The UCC calls it a "draft" and if the draft is drawn on a bank and is payable on presentment, it is a particular form of draft known as a "check."[14] The draft is a method to make payment. So too are a retail or wholesale funds transfer, or a payment pursuant to a credit card, but these latter methods and other non-draft methods are discussed later.

As a payment method, the primary function of a draft is not to evidence an obligation to pay money that is a part of the underlying transaction giving rise to the draft. Rather it is a written message to the drawee to pay money in accordance with the order, and thus its primary function is to facilitate payment of an obligation. Samples of a check and a draft appear below. The reverse sides of these instruments usually are blank until indorsements are added in the process of transferring the instrument.

---

pleted work on a revision of UCC Article 3 and amendments to Article 4 to update former UCC Articles 3 and 4 (old Article 3 and old Article 4). The revision updated these laws for technological developments, changes in business practices, and to resolve ambiguities and different interpretations of the law. The revision of Articles 3 and 4 is the law in all states except New York and South Carolina. We do not encumber the discussion in this book with discussion of the old law for those two states, but only as desirable for historical background on some issues. Articles 3 and 4 were again modestly amended in 2002.

12. Neither federal nor state legislation that override writing and signature requirements override the requirements of Article 3. *See, e.g.*, Uniform Electronic Transactions Act ("UETA") § 3(b)(2); Electronic Signatures in Global and National Commerce Act ("E-sign"), 15 U.S.C. § 7003(a)(3).

13. *See* § 3–103(a)(6) defining "order," § 3–103(a)(2) and (3) defining "drawee" and "drawer," and § 3–104(a) and (e) through (i) defining "draft" and various types of "checks."

14. § 3–104(f) and (c).

Front of Check

```
[Name and Address      Date_____        CHECK NO. _____
  of Drawer]

Pay to the Order of _____  $_____
                      (Name of Payee)          (Amount in Figures)
_____DOLLARS
  (Amount in Words)

[Name of Drawee
   Bank]                              _____
                                         (Signature of Drawer)
Memo _____

MICR LINE
```

Front of Draft

```
$_____
  (Amount of Draft)     (Place Drawn)           (Date)

(Time for Payment) (In 30 days, at sight, etc.)

Pay to the Order of _____
                      (Name of Payee)

_____Dollars
  (Amount in Words)

to _____            _____
     (Name of Drawee)              (Signature of Drawer)
```

[b] Notes and Certificates of Deposit

The other class of negotiable instrument subject to UCC Article 3 consists of instruments in which a "maker" promises to pay another party called the "payee." This is a "promissory note" or, more concisely, just a "note."[15] A "certificate of deposit" is simply an acknowledgment by a bank of the receipt of money with a promise to repay it.[16] In short, it is a kind of note if it otherwise meets the requirements under Article 3 (which, often, it does not). Notes can be long and complex, or short and simple. A simple note is illustrated to show the necessary features that any note will have. A complex note usually will contain more terms from the underlying transaction.

---

15. *See* § 3–103(a)(9) defining "promise," § 3–103(a)(5) defining "maker," and § 3–104(a) and (e) defining "note."

16. § 3–104(j).

Front of Note

```
$ _____ _____        _____
  (Amount of Note)  (Place Drawn)                (Date)

_____ after date the undersigned promises to pay
(Time for Payment)  (In 90 days, on demand, etc.)

to the order of _____
                                    (Name of Payee)
_____ Dollars
              (Amount of Note in Words)
with interest at ___% per year until paid. The undersigned further promises to pay the expenses,
including attorney's fees, incurred in the collection or attempted collection of this note. If this note is
signed by more than one maker, they shall be jointly and severally liable.


                              _____
                                    (Signature of Maker)
```

Unlike in the case of the draft, the primary function of a note is to evidence an obligation to pay money that is a part of the underlying transaction giving rise to the note. Payment of that obligation is accomplished at maturity by other means, such as a check.

Given these different functions, one might expect some different applicable legal rules. However, by and large the same legal rules apply to each type of instrument with limited exceptions.[17] A number of those exceptions exist in recognition that to better accomplish their payment function today checks are processed by automation.[18] Further exceptions along this same line for checks[19] are created in Regulation CC,[20] the implementing regulation under the federal Expedited Funds Availability Act,[21] which substantially impacts on the provisions of Article 4 as discussed in a later chapter.[22]

---

17. One exception exists in § 3–503(2) on dishonor which is tied to the time for presentment. *Compare* § 3–502(a) for notes with § 3–502(b) and (c) for checks.

18. For example, a check is a negotiable instrument and can have a holder in due course even though it is not payable to order or to bearer and even though it contains a provision that it is not negotiable, because such provisions will not be noticed in automated processing. *See* § 3–104(c) and (d).

19. For the purposes of the UCC, and except as previously noted or as subsequently noted, a check is a draft, other than a documentary draft, payable on demand and drawn on a bank. § 3–104(f). The concept of check under Regulation CC may be somewhat broader; for example, payable-through demand drafts and traveler's checks are checks and so are United States Postal Service money orders. Regulation CC, 12 CFR § 229.2(k).

20. Regulation CC, 12 C.F.R. pt. 229.

21. 12 U.S.C. § 4001 et seq.

22. For example, Regulation CC in § 229.35 and in Appendix D to the regulation imposes elaborate requirements for and liability with respect to indorsements that have no counterpart in UCC Articles 3 and 4.

Articles 3 and 4 on their face for the most part do not explicitly recognize Regulation CC. Nonetheless, Regulation CC affects many of the provisions of Articles 3 and 4.

[c] Popular Name Instruments

Popular names for various kinds of drafts are in common use. For example, there is the "personal money order." This instrument at base is a "one-time" check; that is, it is an instrument purchased to make a specific payment. Under prior law its status was unclear; some cases treated it as an ordinary check[23] and others, because the instrument assertedly is viewed by the public as a "cash equivalent," treated it as an instrument accepted upon issuance so the drawee is liable and defenses to its payment cannot be raised.[24] Article 3 currently treats this "poor person's check" as an ordinary check, thus allowing payment to be stopped.[25] Given the experience in jurisdictions that follow this view under former law, it is doubtful its use will be impaired as this type of instrument does remove the insufficient funds risk since the instrument first must be purchased.

Another example of a popular name instrument is a "trade acceptance." A trade acceptance is essentially a draft that has been accepted by the drawee. Then there are "cashier's checks," "teller's checks" and "traveler's checks." Under Article 3 all of these instruments fundamentally are checks except a traveler's check can be a note if it is a promise and is payable at or through a bank.[26]

"Share drafts" and "negotiable orders of withdrawal" were names given to "checks" drawn on credit unions and thrift institutions in the days before such institutions gained checking account powers like commercial banks. Under Article 3, since the term "bank" now includes a savings and loan association or a credit union,[27] these instruments constitute checks.[28]

Thus in the last analysis popular-name instruments are not really a different type of negotiable instrument; virtually all of them fall within the class of order negotiable instruments.

---

23. *See, e.g.*, Garden Check Cashing Service, Inc. v. First Nat'l City Bank, 25 A.D.2d 137, 267 N.Y.S.2d 698 (1966), *aff'd* 18 N.Y.2d 941, 223 N.E.2d 566, 277 N.Y.S.2d 141 (1966).

24. *See, e.g.*, Sequoyah State Bank v. Union Nat'l Bank, 274 Ark. 1, 621 S.W.2d 683 (1981).

25. § 3–104(f). *But see* Official Comment 4 to § 3–104 noting the importance of its form.

26. § 3–104(f), (g), (h) and (i). A cashier's check, of course, is tantamount to a note of the bank. But because of commercial practice it is classified as a check even though the drawer's liability is equated to that of a maker. §§ 3–412, 3–414(a) and 3–104(f)(ii).

A teller's check is classified as a check even though it may not be drawn on a bank but only be payable at or through a bank. § 3–104(f)(ii) and (h).

A traveler's check only is a check if it is drawn on a bank, but the rules applicable to it essentially are the rules for orders if it is an order and is payable at or through a bank; if it is a promise, it is a note. *See* § 3–104(f) and (i) and Official Comment 4 to § 3–104.

27. § 3–103(c); § 4–105(1); Official Comment 4 to § 3–104. The definition does not preclude applying certain provisions to the activity of entities that are not banks but which operate like them. *See, e.g.*, Asian International, Ltd. v. Merrill Lynch, Pierce, Fenner & Smith, Inc., 435 So.2d 1058 (La.Ct.App.1983).

28. § 3–104(f)(i).

[d] Exclusions

A negotiable instrument must be a written instrument involving the payment of money.[29] The reason for this requirement and the details of it will be discussed later. For now, the statement suggests that money itself is not considered as a negotiable instrument. That is true. Nor should a payment order under UCC Article 4A be considered a negotiable instrument[30] because, even when a written payment order is involved,[31] the order goes to a bank to pay the payee rather than to the payee, who then initiates collection of the order, the appropriate legal rules may differ.[32]

At an earlier time, corporate bonds and similar investment securities were treated as a type of negotiable instrument similar to a note. The approach worked poorly at best, and under the Uniform Commercial Code they are no longer considered as subject to Article 3.[33]

¶ 1.02 Uniform Commercial Code Article 3: The Primary Law

The legal rules that resolve the problems that arise and that govern the relationships among the parties who may be involved with a negotiable instrument are found primarily in Article 3 of the Uniform Commercial Code. For instruments used to facilitate payment, such as checks, Article 4 of the Uniform Commercial Code also may become applicable when the instrument enters the collection process. Detailed discussion of Article 4 is postponed until later chapters. Of course, today, in addition to this state law structure, federal law under Regulation CC plays an important part with respect to checks. Detailed discussion of Regulation CC and its relation to the UCC is deferred until later.

---

29. Later in this book, so-called "electronic checks" will be discussed. Absent paper, they are not subject to Article 3 as a matter of law.

30. Note, however, that under law prior to Article 4A, the UCC often was looked to for guidance. Article 4 excludes as "items" payment orders under Article 4A. § 4–104(a)(9). Article 3 excludes payment orders from its scope in § 3–102(a). § 4A–103(a)(1)(iii) also excludes checks from the definition of "payment order." See also Official Comment 5 thereto.

31. Transmission of a payment order under Article 4A may be by letter or other written communication, oral communication or electronic communication. § 4A–103(a)(1) and § 4A–104, Official Comment 6.

Under the federal Electronic Fund Transfers Act, 15 U.S.C. § 1693 *et seq.*, as implemented by Regulation E, 12 CFR pt. 205, which governs consumer funds transfers instead of Article 4A (*see* § 4A–108), the transfer may be accomplished by a paper debit card slip. See Regulation E Commentary 2–21.5Q. The federal act specifically excludes any funds transfer originated by check, draft, or similar paper instrument. See Regulation E, 12 CFR § 205.2(g). The debit card slip would be excluded under § 3–104 as it normally recites it is subject to the cardholder agreement. Debit card slips also specifically are excluded from the definition of "item" under § 4–104(a)(9).

32. *For example,* banks in a funds transfer are not agents or subagents and a payment order itself does not embody rights and obligations. § 4A–212.

33. A discussion appears in W. Britton, Handbook of the Law of Bills and Notes § 17 (2d ed. 1961). Article 4, however, may apply to bonds and like instruments. See Official Comment 2 to § 3–102.

[1] Scope of Article 3

Article 3 applies only to written instruments;[34] there can be no orally agreed upon negotiable instrument. Moreover, the instrument must be signed by the maker or drawer;[35] and, except as provided for incomplete instruments,[36] it must contain an unconditional promise or order to pay a fixed amount of money;[37] it must be payable on demand or at a definite time;[38] and to order or to bearer;[39] and it must not contain any unauthorized terms.[40] An instrument meeting all of these requirements is a negotiable instrument within Article 3.[41] The importance of the consequence of this rule cannot be overemphasized; unless the writing meets the form requirements set out in Article 3, Article 3 *does not furnish, without more, the applicable legal rules*. In short, law *other than* Article 3 may govern. To illustrate, in one case[42] the decedent had purchased a money market certificate and named his stepdaughter as the pay-on-death beneficiary. When the decedent remarried, he orally told the bank to change the beneficiary to his new wife. When he died, both the stepdaughter and the wife claimed the instrument. The stepdaughter argued that because the instrument was payable to her, the only way her interest could be divested was if she had indorsed and delivered the instrument. For our purpose here, this might be a correct conclusion if Article 3 governed. The court ruled the promise in the instrument to pay the stepdaughter was conditioned upon the death of the decedent, and that the conditional promise destroyed negotiability and rendered Article 3 inapplicable. The court then found that under other law the wife should prevail.[43]

[2] *Instruments Not Payable to Order or to Bearer and Checks*

Nonetheless, former Article 3 did apply to some instruments that did not meet the criteria discussed above, so long as the only variance was that the instrument was not payable to order or to bearer and provided that the terms of the instrument did not preclude its transfer.[44] There, however, could not be a holder in due course of such an instru-

---

¶ 1.02

34. §§ 3–103(a)(6) and (9) and 3–104(a), and *see* note 29, *supra*. *But see* UETA § 16.

35. §§ 3–103(a)(6) and (9) and 3–104(a). The signature may be unauthorized, but no person is liable on an instrument unless its signature appears on the instrument, with one exception where an agent is authorized to sign for a principal. § 3–401(a).

36. § 3–115.

37. § 3–104(a).

38. § 3–104(a)(2).

39. § 3–104(a)(1). An exception exists for checks. § 3–104(c).

40. § 3–104(a)(3).

41. § 3–104(a) and (b). These requirements are discussed in detail in the next chapter.

42. West Greeley Nat'l Bank v. Wygant, 650 P.2d 1339 (Colo.Ct.App.1982).

43. Conversely, *see* Smith v. Haran, 273 Ill.App.3d 866, 210 Ill.Dec. 191, 652 N.E.2d 1167 (Ill.App.1995), where the appellate court overruled the trial court, which had found the instrument not to be negotiable and accordingly had applied contract law.

44. *See* the *Smith* case, *supra* note 43, and old UCC § 3–805. An example of such an instrument is a check "payable to John Doe" rather than "payable to the order of John Doe." At one time credit union share drafts commonly were of this nature.

ment.[45] This provision thus created an exception to the rule that Article 3 does not apply unless the writing fully meets its requirements.[46]

Probably the most prevalent example of such an instrument is the non-negotiable certificate of deposit payable to "John Doe" but not to "the order of John Doe."[47] The courts correctly decided that although old Article 3 might have been applicable, there could be no holder in due course of the instrument to take free of a defense asserted.[48]

Order instruments that fell within old UCC § 3–805 also are encountered from time to time. Three common examples were credit union share drafts,[49] drafts drawn by insurance companies on themselves and payable through designated banks to named payees but not to their order,[50] and so-called money orders payable through a designated bank to a named payee but not to his or her order.[51]

Current Article 3 mandates the requirement of "words of negotiability,"[52] as a dividing line.[53] On the other hand, given the traditionally broad reach of the term "item" used in defining the scope of Article 4,[54] and the fact that today many checks move through the collection process without any actual examination,[55] it seemed appropriate to retain the old rule as applied to checks, and even to expand that rule.[56] Accordingly, under § 3–104(c) not only is a check that is not payable to order or to bearer within Article 3, there can be a holder in due course of it.[57] Moreover, even if the check recites it is not negotiable or is not subject to Article 3, those words are not effective.[58]

---

45. *Id.*

46. The Official Comment to old § 3–805 made these points: the holder of a check reading "Pay A" establishes his or her case by production of the instrument and proof of signatures (*see* old UCC § 3–307); the indorser of such an instrument undertakes greater liabilities than those of an assignor (*see* old UCC § 3–414); and the rules as to alteration, accommodation parties, the liability of signing agents, discharge and the like apply to such an instrument (*see* old UCC §§ 3–407, 3–415, 3–403, and old Article 3, Part 6). These provisions essentially illustrate the differences between the rules of Article 3 and general contract law, the other significant difference being holder in due course status. *See* note 45, *supra*.

47. Often these instruments also provide that they are not transferable. In that circumstance, they were entirely outside of old Article 3.

48. *See, e.g.,* Continental Bankers Life Ins. Co. v. Bank of Alamo, 578 S.W.2d 625 (Tenn.1979) (so holding).

49. *See* § 3–104, Official Comment 2. *See* note 44, *supra*.

50. *See, e.g.,* Comet Check Cashing Serv., Inc. v. Hanover Ins. Group, 5 UCC Rep. Serv. 852 (N.Y.Civ.Ct.1968).

51. *See, e.g.,* Nation–Wide Check Corp. v. Banks, 260 A.2d 367 (D.C.App.1969).

52. *Compare* § 9–102(a)(47) defining "instrument" to include not only a negotiable instrument as defined in § 3–104 but also any other writing which evidences a right to the payment of money, that is not a security agreement or a lease, and that is of a type which is in the ordinary course of business transferred by delivery with any necessary indorsement or assignment.

53. *See* § 3–104, Official Comment 2. *See* Universal Premium Acceptance Corp. v. York Bank & Trust Co., 69 F.3d 695 (3d Cir.1995) (insurance draft reading "pay and deposit only to the credit of _____" was not negotiable in form). This would not have been fatal under old § 3–805 but under current Article 3 it is.

54. Neither old UCC § 4–104(1)(g) nor revised UCC § 4–104(a)(9) defining "item" are limited to negotiable instruments.

55. *See* § 3–103, Official Comment 4.

56. *See* § 3–104, Official Comment 2.

57. § 3–104(c).

58. § 3–104(d).

¶ 1.03 Governing Law When Article 3 Is Not Applicable

[1] Definitionary Exclusions From Article 3

[a] Applicability of General Contract Law

If an instrument does not meet the requirements of § 3–104 and is not saved from exclusion by § 3–104(c) or (d), it is not a negotiable instrument. If an instrument is not a negotiable instrument, it is not governed by the rules in Article 3.[59] What law then governs? A negotiable instrument is a contract. The contractual nature of a negotiable instrument is evident in the case of a promissory note, where there is an express promise to pay.[60] But it is also true of drafts, where the promise to pay is implied.[61] Nonetheless, a long time ago, rules known as the "law merchant," and different from those applicable to ordinary contracts, were worked out for contracts identified as negotiable instruments. For example, the holder of a negotiable instrument establishes a case by production of the instrument and proof of signatures.[62] The burden of proving any asserted defense of want of consideration is upon the obligor. For ordinary contracts, where consideration is required and is not presumed, the plaintiff must plead it as a factual condition of relief.[63] Negotiable instruments pass by indorsement and delivery or by delivery alone.[64] Words of assignment, as in the case of an ordinary contract, are unnecessary.[65] The indorser of a negotiable instrument normally undertakes greater liabilities than those of the assignor of an ordinary contract. Unless there is an express agreement, an assignor does not agree to perform if the obligor does not, but an indorser, unless the indorsement otherwise specifies by such words as "without recourse," does undertake to perform the obligation.[66] The holder of a negotiable instrument may have greater rights than the assignee of an ordinary contract. For example, if the holder is a holder in due course the holder is not subject to any claims to the instrument on the part of any person and is not subject to most defenses to the payment of the instrument, even if those defenses existed when the holder took the instrument or were inherent in the transaction underlying it.[67] These

---

§ 1.03

59. § 3–102(a) (this Article applies to negotiable instruments).

60. By definition, a note (and a certificate of deposit) must contain a promise or engagement to pay. §§ 3–103(a)(9) and 3–104(a), (e) and (j). § 3–412 states that the issuer of a note is obligated to pay the instrument according to its tenor at the time it was issued or as completed pursuant to § 3–115 on incomplete instruments, and also covers the obligation of the issuer of a cashier's check or other draft drawn on the drawer, which as to this point is treated as a promise of the issuer to pay even though § 3–104(f)(i) categorizes a cashier's check as a form of check for other purposes.

61. § 3–414(b). *But see* §§ 3–414(a) and 3–412 as to drafts drawn on the drawer.

62. § 3–308.

63. Old § 3–805, Official Comment.

64. § 3–201(b).

65. Official Comment to old § 3–805; L. Simpson, Handbook of the Law of Contracts § 125 (2d ed. 1965).

66. § 3–415. Both an indorser and an assignor impliedly make equivalent warranties, however, although those of the indorser also will run to successive parties taking the instrument. § 3–416. *See also* Simpson, *supra* note 65, § 135.

67. A holder in due course also is not subject to claims or defenses of the obligor that accrue after the holder takes the instrument and before the obligor receives notification of the change in obligees. *Compare* §§ 3–305 and 3–306 *with* Simpson,

examples do not exhaust the differences,[68] but they make the point.

Article 3 thus constitutes a special body of legal rules governing the particular kinds of contracts called negotiable instruments. If the instrument is not a negotiable instrument so as to be governed by these special rules of Article 3, then perhaps it logically should be governed by ordinary contract rules. To illustrate, in *von Frank v. Hershey National Bank*,[69] the issues were unauthorized completion, material alteration, and impairment of recourse. The instrument did not meet the requirements of old Article 3. The court held that the liability of the defendants was to be determined as a matter of simple contract law. Old Article 3 itself suggests that this is an appropriate resolution.[70] However, it would not seem this approach should be adopted without exception.

[b] *Application of Article 3 by Analogy*

A court, having to adjudicate the rights and responsibilities of parties to an instrument that is not within Article 3, might choose to turn to the Uniform Commercial Code by way of analogy, because otherwise the court could face applying case law likely to be of nineteenth-century vintage, spotty in coverage and dated in concept.[71] In *First National Bank v. Hull*,[72] the court may have done this. The court in that case applied the provisions of old Article 3 to a security agreement not within the definition of commercial paper under old Article 3. It is unclear, however, whether the court deliberately applied old Article 3 by way of analogy.

One may argue that this approach theoretically is inappropriate, as Article 3, by its very existence, stands for policies not present with respect to other contracts. Accordingly, if the instrument does not qualify as a negotiable instrument, the application of those policies would generally be inappropriate. The court in *In re Hein*,[73] a case involving facts similar to those in the *Hull* case, refused to treat a financing statement, completed as authorized, as effective by analogy to old §§ 3–115 and 3–407. The court criticized the *Hull* decision on the ground that applying the provisions of old Article 3 defeated the separate, and different, policy embodied in Article 9, which was applicable.[74]

---

supra note 65, § 133. Recall, however, that there can be a holder in due course of any check under § 3–104.

68. Others, such as the special rules of Article 3 as to alterations, filling in blanks, and accommodation, are mentioned in the Official Comment to old § 3–805.

69. 269 Md. 138, 306 A.2d 207 (Md. 1973).

70. Old § 3–805 Official Comment (a note containing an express condition is to be treated as a simple contract). *See also* Smith v. Haran, 273 Ill.App.3d 866, 210 Ill.Dec. 191, 652 N.E.2d 1167 (Ill.App.1995), where the lower court applied contract law when it erroneously concluded the instrument was not negotiable.

71. *See* E. Peters, Commercial Transactions 1421 (1971). *See also* Miller, Ballen, Davenport & Vergari, Commercial Paper, Bank Deposits and Collections, and Commercial Electronic Fund Transfers, 42 Bus. Law. 1269, 1292 n. 110 (1987), relating the fact of a non-Article 3 case won on the basis of a 1915 precedent. However, *see* Rogers, The Myth of Negotiability, 31 B.C. L. Rev. 265 (1990).

72. 189 Neb. 581, 204 N.W.2d 90 (Neb. 1973).

73. 20 UCC Rep. Serv. 745 (Bankr. W.D.Wis.1976).

74. *See also* European Am. Bank & Trust Co. v. Starcrete Int'l Indus., Inc., 613 F.2d 564 (5th Cir.1980), refusing to apply

On the other hand, too much should not be made from the argument against using Article 3 by analogy. The better approach is a careful analysis of the sense of applying Article 3 by analogy. For example, in another case,[75] the court had to apply UCC § 5–114(2)(a), which before Article 5 was amended in 1995 required the issuer of a letter of credit to pay pursuant to the credit notwithstanding certain difficulties in the transaction if the demand for payment was made by a person who acquired the right to make the demand under circumstances that would make the person a holder in due course (now see § 5–109(a)(1)). The court reasoned that the pleading and practice rules of old § 3–307 should be applicable in determining holder in due course status in this context as well as in the context of Article 3, particularly because UCC § 5–114(2)(a) expressly cited the holder in due course criteria of old § 3–302.

Whatever the merits of this debate in reference to old Article 3,[76] Official Comment 2 to § 3–104 repeats Official Comment 2 to old § 3–104 and then further states in pertinent part:

> . . . it may be appropriate, consistent with the principles stated in Section 1–102(2) [now § 1–103(a)], for a court to apply one or more provisions of Article 3 to the writing by analogy, taking into account the expectations of the parties and the differences between the writing and an instrument governed by Article 3. Whether such application is appropriate depends on the facts of each case.

[2] *Express Exclusions from Article 3*

Article 3 specifically excludes money and investment securities from coverage. It also excludes a payment order governed by Article 4A, and documents of title by definition.

[a] Money

The Uniform Commercial Code defines "money" as a medium of exchange authorized or adopted by a domestic or foreign government.[77] Thus, even though money may satisfy all the requirements of Article 3 and may be the best example of a negotiable instrument, Article 3 has nothing to do with money.[78] Money is governed by other law.[79]

---

the preclusion policy embodied in old § 3–404 to a guaranty not constituting a negotiable instrument on the ground that the preclusion policy was intended to enhance only the type of contract qualifying as commercial paper.

75. United Bank Ltd. v. Cambridge Sporting Goods Corp., 41 N.Y.2d 254, 360 N.E.2d 943, 392 N.Y.S.2d 265 (N.Y. 1976).

76. Official Comments 1 and 2 to old § 3–104 suggest that results akin to those reached under old Article 3 are appropriate in certain cases by judicial decision. This seems to reflect an approach similar to applying a provision of Article 3 by analogy, and reflects a philosophy articulated more than a hundred years ago in response to an argument an instrument was not payable in money and thus was not negotiable; the court responded that the law merchant was not fixed and might be expanded to meet the wants of trade and commerce. See Goodwin v. Roberts, L.R. 10 Ex. 76, *aff'd*, 10 Ex. 337 (1875).

77. UCC § 1–201(b)(24). The provision adds that "money" includes a monetary unit of account established by an intergovernmental organization or by agreement between two or more nations.

78. § 3–102(a).

79. See 31 U.S.C. § 5101 *et seq.*, and L. Rusch, Payment Systems 6–25 (West 2000).

[b] Documents of Title

Documents of title are not expressly excluded from Article 3, but since a negotiable instrument must contain a promise or order to pay money,[80] and the UCC defines a document of title as a receipt or order for the delivery of goods,[81] it would seem a document of title never would qualify as an instrument for the payment of money in any event.[82]

[c] Investment Securities

It is possible that an instrument may meet both the requirements for a negotiable instrument under Article 3 and the definition of a certificated security under UCC Article 8.[83] Indeed, under negotiable instruments law prior to the UCC, the application of that law to investment securities was an important topic.[84] A certificated security is a share, participation, or other interest in property of or an enterprise of the issuer ("stock"), or an obligation of the issuer ("bond"), that is represented by an instrument issued in bearer or registered form and that is of a type commonly dealt in on securities exchanges or markets or commonly recognized in any area in which it is issued or dealt in as a medium for investment and by its terms provides it is a security governed by Article 8. In addition, such a security is either one of a class or series, or by its terms is divisible into a class or series of shares, participation, interests, or obligations.

If the law applicable to an instrument could consist of rules from both Articles 3 and Article 8, a problem could arise because the rules that would govern the instrument are not necessarily the same.[85] The exclusion from Article 3 relating to investment securities[86] attempts to resolve any such problem by removing such instruments from the scope of Article 3. Article 8 then specifies the applicable law by providing that a writing that is a certificated security is governed by Article 8 and not by Article 3, even though the writing also meets the requirements of Article 3.[87] But one problem is only exchanged for another because this approach involves drawing a line that is not always easy to draw.[88]

To illustrate the nature of the problem, consider *Victory National Bank v. Oklahoma State Bank*.[89] This case involved a certificate of

---

80. § 3–104(a).

81. UCC § 1–201(b)(16). "Goods" are defined in UCC § 2–105(1) to exclude money.

82. § 3–102 Official Comment 2.

83. UCC § 8–103(d).

84. Rogers, The Myth of Negotiability, 31 B.C. L. Rev. 265, 318–19 (1990).

85. *See* Official Comment 2 to § 3–102 which points out that the issuer of a security may treat the registered owner as owner until the registration is changed under UCC § 8–207, but that the obligor of a negotiable instrument pays a person other than the actual holder at their peril under § 3–602 (with a slight exception in the case of a note).

86. § 3–102(a).

87. UCC § 8–103(d).

88. Official Comment 2 to § 3–102 suggests that the dividing line for non-bearer paper is whether the holder is registered on the issuer's records, and for bearer paper it depends upon economic function, for example, whether the note is an individual instrument or one of a series of an issue of commercial paper to raise capital. This is helpful, and seems to reflect what the courts have done.

89. 1973 OK 161, 520 P.2d 675 (Okla. 1973).

deposit that met the requirements of old § 3–805. Nonetheless, the court concluded that the issues in the case were controlled by Article 8 because the certificate of deposit was in registered form, was regarded as a medium for investment in Oklahoma, was serially numbered, and evidenced an obligation of the issuer.[90] Another court,[91] dealing with essentially the same kind of instrument, denied the applicability of Article 8 on the ground that it applied only to instruments issued in multiple transactions where all promises were in the same amount and due at the same time. The court believed Article 3 governed isolated transactions, as were present in the case. This latter view correctly reads the intent of the UCC, and, if the reasoning of the court is followed, instruments that are investment securities will be properly excluded from coverage under Article 3.[92] Of course, this does not mean in context that they are not negotiable instruments; it only means in context that they are negotiable instruments subject to a different set of rules.[93]

In some circumstances, however, Article 3 may have relevance to an instrument that is governed by Article 8. For example, some courts have demonstrated little reluctance in applying Article 3 in certain cases by analogy. The opinion of the court in *E. F. Hutton & Co. v. Manufacturers National Bank*[94] is an illustration. In that case, the court stated that once it is determined that a particular instrument is an investment security, Article 8 is the sole source of the law governing the rights of the parties to a transaction involving the instrument. The court believed, however, that where a particular issue could not be resolved solely on the basis of Article 8, it might be appropriate to look to Article 3 for guidance. It might be appropriate because an instrument in bearer form which is a negotiable instrument becomes subject to Article 8 as an investment security only if the instrument also is one of a series and is traded on an exchange. Thus the rights of the parties in a transaction involving such an instrument, absent a good reason, should not be markedly different under Article 8 from what they are under Article 3.[95] To the same effect is the opinion of another court,[96] concluding that one who purchases stock certificates at a judicial sale is not a bona fide

---

90. The certificate of deposit in the *Victory National Bank* case provided that it was transferable only on the books of the bank. For that reason, it may have been in registered form as the court determined. *See* UCC § 8–102(a)(13). Contrast the decision in Sanitary & Improvement Dist. No. 32 v. Continental Western Corp., 215 Neb. 843, 343 N.W.2d 314 (Neb. 1983), where it was argued that government warrants were investment securities. The court refused the argument as the warrants were not transferable only on the issuer's books. In the *Victory National Bank* case, however, the court's conclusion that the certificate of deposit was one of a series merely because it was upon a serially numbered form seems to be in error. In this sense, the court's decision in the *Jones* case, *infra* note 91, represents the sounder analysis.

91. Jones v. United Sav. & Loan Ass'n, 515 S.W.2d 869 (Mo.Ct.App.1974).

92. *See* Official Comment 15 to § 8–102.

93. *See* UCC § 8–103 Official Comment 5 (an Article 3 negotiable instrument may be a "financial asset" and, if so, the indirect holding system rules of Article 8 apply if it is held through a securities intermediary). *See also* Prefatory Note to Article 8, IV. B. 8., Prior Section 8–105.

94. 259 F.Supp. 513 (E.D.Mich.1966).

95. The logic of this, of course, ends where the statute does in fact prescribe different rights.

96. Mazer v. Williams Bros., 461 Pa. 587, 337 A.2d 559 (1975).

purchaser. Reliance was placed on the treatment accorded a holder in due course in Article 3, which denies that status in connection with the purchase of an instrument at a judicial sale or by taking under legal process.[97] The court believed similar policies were involved which necessitated similar interpretations.

Applying Article 3 to investment securities requires careful analysis, however.[98] For example, in one case[99] involving debentures that stated their maturity date only by the word "May" typed on the printed form without specifying any year, the court refused to apply old § 3–108, which deals with commercial paper payable on demand, and to treat the debentures as demand instruments because of their incomplete date. Instead the court cited a provision in Article 8[100] that provides that incomplete securities may be completed as authorized if the signatures necessary for their issue and transfer are present. The court is correct and, had it been needed, the correct parallel in Article 3 would have been §§ 3–115 and 3–407, which deal with the completion and alteration of instruments. Because Article 8 contained the governing provision,[101] no argument by analogy was necessary.

[d] Payment Orders

At the time Article 3 originally was prepared, funds transfers, except perhaps by Western Union,[102] were unknown and no real need to deal with them existed. Funds transfers today are a major payment method. To the extent they are governed by their own UCC Article,[103] they are not governed by Article 3.[104]

[3] Choice of Law Exclusions

If choice of law rules dictate the applicability of other law, Article 3 of the UCC as enacted by a particular jurisdiction may not be applicable even though the instrument involved in the litigation satisfies all the requirements of the jurisdiction's Article 3.[105]

---

97. § 3–302(c).

98. See note 95, supra.

99. Stoerger v. Ivesdale Co-op. Grain Co., 15 Ill.App.3d 313, 304 N.E.2d 300 (Ill. Ct.App.1973).

100. UCC § 8–206(a)(1).

101. Id.

102. Funds transfers over Western Union are not covered under UCC Article 4A, thus leaving them to other law. See UCC § 4A–103(a)(1) and Official Comment 2 to § 4A–104.

103. UCC Article 4A.

104. § 3–102(a) (this Article ... does not apply ... to payment orders governed by Article 4A). However, even to the extent a payment order is not governed by Article 4A, such as one by Western Union or one to or from a consumer account (see UCC § 4A–108), Article 3 should not govern for the reasons set out in Official Comment 5 to UCC § 4A–104; such orders are not like checks and they have their own law outside of the UCC in place. As to that law, see Baxter and Bhala, The Interrelationship of Article 4A with Other Law, 45 Bus. Law. 1485, 1491–93, 1499–1500 (1990). See also text prior to note 32, supra. Revised Article 4 also excludes as "items" payment orders under UCC Article 4A. § 4–104(a)(9).

105. This is a relatively unimportant issue since most states today have Article 3 and so choice of law issues are limited to non-uniform variances. Moreover, as it should be clear the choice of law provision in the UCC, § 1–301, only controls UCC issues, a court need not follow its guidance as to issues in transactions that are not governed by the UCC. See note 108, infra. Of course, to the extent one body of law

[a] The Law of Another State

The general rule for choice of law as to issues governed by the UCC is found in Article 1 of the UCC. Under that rule, with some limitation, whether or not a domestic transaction bears a reasonable relation to the forum state which enacted the UCC, the parties to the transaction may agree that either the law of the forum state or of another state shall govern their rights and duties.[106] Agreements as to the applicable law quite commonly appear in promissory notes. For example, in *Western Auto Supply v. Craig*,[107] the note, which was executed in Alabama to a payee whose principal place of business was in Missouri, provided that it should be governed by Missouri law. The court determined the agreement was effective.[108]

If the parties do not have an agreement on the applicable law, the forum state is directed to apply its conflict of laws principles.[109] *In re Estate of Voight*[110] may serve as an example. In that case the court had to decide whether a moral obligation was good consideration for notes. The transaction had contacts with both New Mexico (the maker resided there and the probate proceedings were there) and Illinois (the notes were signed there while the maker was on vacation). Failing an agreement on choice of law, the court ultimately chose the law of Illinois in which state the notes were executed and one of them was payable, instead of the law of New Mexico, where the maker's estate was being probated.

Of course, there is no choice-of-law problem if all aspects of the transaction are centered in only one state. That was the situation in one

---

should govern the entire transaction, a court may employ the principles of § 1–301. *See* Official Comment 3 to old § 1–105 and, *e.g.*, Davidson Oil Country Supply Co., Inc. v. Klockner, Inc., 908 F.2d 1238 (5th Cir. 1990) (applying contract choice citing old § 1–105 to usury issue not governed by the UCC). In addition, to the extent Article 3 does not change prior law but only sets out the preferred interpretation, the choice of law problem further is diminished, and much of current Article 3 is of that nature.

Article 4 has its own specific choice of law provision that is likely to minimize choice of law issues in that context. *See* UCC § 1–301(g)(3) and § 4–102(b).

106. UCC § 1–301(a)(1) and (c)(1). The same is true for an international transaction where the law of the forum state, or of another state or country, may be selected. UCC § 1–301(a)(2) and (c)(2). The limitations are (1) the specific choice of law rules in UCC § 1–301(g), (2) a fundamental public policy exception in UCC § 1–301(f), and (3) an exception when one of the parties to a transaction is a consumer. UCC §§ 1–301(e) and 1–201(b)(11).

107. 30 UCC Rep. Serv. (Callaghan) 1206 (S.D.Ala.1981).

108. If the issue is one the UCC does not regulate, such as a question of usury, the UCC choice of law rule should not govern, although it may be applied as an example of the appropriate rule. *See* Official Comment 1 to § 1–301, and First National Bank v. Whaley 168 W.Va. 327, 284 S.E.2d 618 (W.Va.1981) (issue of which state law controlled validity of provision for attorney's fees not controlled by old UCC § 1–105) and *In re* Cayer, 6 UCC Rep. Serv. 869 (Bankr.D.Me.1969) (interpretation of choice of law provision on usury issue). In the case of usury issues, however, often non-UCC debtor protection legislation either denies enforceability with respect to agreed charges that exceed what is permitted by the law of the forum when enforcement is sought in the forum, or invalidates choice of law provisions. *See, e.g.,* Unif. Consumer Cred. Code § 1.201 (1974). *Compare* Aldens, Inc. v. Ryan, 571 F.2d 1159 (10th Cir.1978) *with* Marquette Nat'l Bank v. First of Omaha Serv. Corp., 439 U.S. 299, 99 S.Ct. 540, 58 L.Ed.2d 534 (1978). In the latter case, the National Bank Act was held to preempt state regulation.

109. UCC § 1–301(d).

110. 95 N.M. 625, 624 P.2d 1022 (N.M.Ct.App.1981).

case where both parties to the note were Illinois corporations and the transaction occurred in Illinois.[111] In many other situations, the choice of law issue will be moot because Article 3 of the UCC is the law in all states, the District of Columbia, and the Virgin Islands. For example, in *First National Bank v. Jefferson Sales & Distributors, Inc.*,[112] the choice of law was immaterial because the UCC provisions relevant to the transactions involved were identical.[113]

However, it is necessary to recognize that the provisions of the Uniform Commercial Code are not always enacted uniformly and thus, any variance between them may make the choice of law important. This was true in *National Shawmut Bank v. International Yarn Corp.*[114] In that case, the New York federal court in which the action was brought ultimately applied Tennessee's uniform enactment of old § 3–804, rather than the New York variation of the section that mandated security for indemnification before suit could be brought on a lost or stolen instrument. The suit was by a Massachusetts bank on a lost check drawn on a Tennessee bank by a corporation with a factory and its principal place of business in Tennessee, and the check had been given in payment for goods shipped to Tennessee. The Official Comment 2 to old § 1–105 points out that the mere fact that suit is brought in a particular state does not make it appropriate to apply the substantive law of that state, and suggests that a choice between applying the law of the place of contracting and of the place of contemplated performance is appropriate. Furthermore, Official Comment 3 to old § 1–105 states that, in particular, where a transaction is governed in large part by the law of one state, application of other law to some detail of performance because of an accident of geography may violate the commercial understanding of the parties. Clearly, under these criteria the choice of law by the court was appropriate, and probably would still be under UCC § 1–301(d).

[b] The Law of Another Country

Important choice of law problems do arise when a transaction involves contacts with a foreign country because the Uniform Commercial Code is the law only in the United States.[115] UCC § 1–301 however

---

111. *In re* United East Coast Corp., 6 UCC Rep. Serv. 449 (E.D.N.Y.1969).

112. 341 F.Supp. 659 (S.D.Miss.1971), aff'd on other grounds, 460 F.2d 1059 (5th Cir.1972).

113. *But see* note 105, *supra*.

114. 322 F.Supp. 116 (S.D.N.Y.1970).

115. This observation is a principal motivation behind the United Nations Convention on International Bills of Exchange and International Promissory Notes discussed next. *See* Explanatory Comments on the Convention by Professor John A. Spanogle, Jr., appended to a Memorandum dated February 28, 1989 to Members of International Negotiable Instruments Study Group of the Secretary of State's Advisory Committee on Private International Law from Peter H. Pfund, Assistant Legal Advisor for Private International Law (copy in the files of the authors), at Comment 2:

> One [problem] is that the law governing the instrument may change as it travels from one state to another, and negotiable instruments laws of different legal regimes are quite different. For example, an unauthorized signature is effective as a necessary endorsement in many other nations but not in the United States.

Comment 7 explains the advantage of the Convention in this respect:

> Second, the determination of governing law will be more certain. * * * [A]s circu-

still purports to control the issue if the forum jurisdiction has enacted the UCC. In one of the cases expressly dealing with the issue,[116] suit was brought in Maryland on a draft drawn by the customer of the plaintiff. The plaintiff was a Swiss banking corporation. The draft had been accepted by the defendant Maryland corporation and discounted by the plaintiff in the ordinary course of its dealings with its customer. The main issue in the case centered on the need for and validity of an indorsement which had been placed on the draft by the plaintiff in Switzerland. Under Swiss law the indorsement was not valid, but its validity was not in question under Maryland law.

There is no doubt the transaction bore an appropriate relation to Maryland, which had enacted the UCC. Though this might be said to settle the choice of law issue under old § 1–105(1), which provides that the UCC applies to transactions bearing an appropriate relation to the enacting state absent agreement, the court refused to close the issue at this point. This analysis is even more appropriate under UCC § 1–301(d). The court noted that a foreign court, not bound by the full faith and credit clause of the United States Constitution, might elect not to honor a judgment produced through such an approach, when the transaction also involved significant contacts with another jurisdiction. The court found support for its analysis in Official Comment 3 to old § 1–105, which states that where a transaction has significant contacts with a state that has enacted the UCC, and also with other jurisdictions, the question of what relation is "appropriate" is left to judicial decision. Ultimately, the court applied Maryland law as the law of the place where the transfer of the instrument to the plaintiff occurred. Nonetheless, it seems the court was suggesting strongly, and properly, that the application of conflict of laws principles should be sensitive to the context of the litigation.[117]

[c] International Law

In international transactions, the possibility exists that United States law, and thus the UCC, will not apply. The applicability of the UCC in this context, absent applicable international law, was discussed above, and clearly involves an uncertain process, particularly in the absence of agreement, where, as in all commercial transactions, certainty is desirable.[118] Uniform international law may be increasingly applicable

---

lation between ... geographical areas and legal regimes increases, legal problems are likely to increase, especially where the parties draft their instruments assuming that party autonomy is available (e.g., as under the UCC), and the instrument then circulates to States that regard commercial paper law as mandatory law and disregard the parties directions.

116. United Overseas Bank v. Veneers, Inc., 375 F.Supp. 596 (D.Md.1973).

117. *See also* Israel Discount Bank, Ltd. v. Rosen, 59 N.Y.2d 428, 452 N.E.2d 1213, 465 N.Y.S.2d 885 (1983) (New York law rather than the law of Israel chosen when transaction largely within New York boundaries); Barclays Discount Bank, Ltd. v. Levy, 743 F.2d 722 (9th Cir.1984) (factors and issue indicating appropriate choice of California rather than Israeli law); and McNall v. Tatham, 676 F.Supp. 987 (C.D.Cal.1987) (same but selecting the law of Brazil rather than that of California).

118. *See* note 115, *supra*.

in the future. An international convention on international bills of exchange and international promissory notes has been completed. It applies to international bills of exchange and promissory notes, but not international checks, which expressly designate the convention as governing law and which on their face indicate that they will circulate between at least two nations, at least one of which is a convention signatory.[119] The United States has signed but has not yet ratified the convention. For this reason this book does not give more than the following overview of it.

On December 9, 1988, the United Nations General Assembly approved the Convention on International Bills of Exchange and International Promissory Notes ("Convention"). *See* Resolution 43–165 (A/RES/43–165). The text of the Convention is published unofficially in 28 INT'L LEGAL MATERIALS 176 (1989). The United States signed the Convention on June 30, 1990, but, as noted above, has not yet ratified it.

The Convention was drafted over a period of almost two decades by the United Nations Commission on International Trade Law to create a uniform law for a designated class of international transactions. As discussed above, the Convention applies to certain international bills of exchange and promissory notes, but does not apply to international checks. It provides for a new international negotiable instrument which the parties may choose to use in connection with international commerce.

The benefits of the Convention are several fold. When negotiable and other instruments are used in international transactions, the law governing the instrument may change as the instrument travels from one country to another. There also may be uncertainty as to which law governs particular circumstances. This problem is compounded by the fact that the legal regimes of various countries governing these instruments can be quite different.

In addition, many nations have not yet modernized their law on negotiable instruments. Under the law of certain of these countries, the types of instruments that are negotiable are quite restricted. When these laws are mandatory, the intent of the parties as expressed in the instrument may not be recognized, particularly with respect to persons not parties to the instrument.[120]

Legal uncertainty and impaired negotiability have associated economic costs. Negotiable instruments, for example, can circulate at a price closer to their stated value than can non-negotiable instruments, because the obligations of the parties to negotiable instruments are more completely defined and because many claims and defenses against such parties are cut off.

---

119. International Convention, Chapter I, Articles 1 and 2. Article 3 defines what is a bill of exchange and a promissory note in much the same terms as United States Law. A bill of exchange is a written instrument which contains an unconditional order whereby the drawer directs the drawee to pay a definite sum of money to the payee or to his order on demand or at a definite time, and which is dated and signed by the drawer. A promissory note is similarly defined except in terms of a promise.

120. *See* note 115, *supra*.

The Convention will allow many instruments with modern commercial terms, such as those with adjustable interest rates or that are payable in installments or units of account, and that are not now negotiable under the domestic law of many nations, to be negotiable in international commerce under the Convention.

Notwithstanding these advantages, the Convention applies only if an international bill of exchange or international promissory note specifies on its face that it is governed by the Convention. Accordingly, parties, in essence, can voluntarily "opt in" or contract into the Convention. This is a choice that requires careful consideration by an attorney who has concluded that otherwise the law of the United States might apply to the instrument to be used.

The Convention is an international agreement, and, as such, it represents numerous compromises and thus differences from the law of any one country. When compared to the UCC, the Convention differs in several significant respects. See scattered Official Comments added to UCC Articles 3 and 4 with the 2002 amendments to those Articles. The following are perhaps the most important.

The Convention provides that a forged indorsement is effective. The UCC, of course, with limited exceptions provides that a forged indorsement is not effective, and a person taking an instrument under a forged indorsement is not entitled to payment. The Convention establishes transfer warranties against forgeries and alterations of the instrument, but does not allow actions for breach of these warranties without prior dishonor. The UCC authorizes a holder to sue for breach of these warranties without prior dishonor.

A third difference is the Convention creates the concept of a protected holder. The UCC also provides for holders and holders in due course, both of which receive protection from the claims and defenses of other parties. But these protections are different than those accorded to a protected holder under the Convention. Finally, the Convention does not impose an obligation of prompt acceptance or dishonor. The UCC generally requires acceptance to occur before the close of the day of presentment.

Nonetheless, the Convention exchanges a set of standard principles of international commercial law for the uncertain system that presently exists. Parties whose countries are parties to the Convention should therefore carefully consider whether to be governed by it.

Another development is a UNCITRAL model law on electronic funds transfers.[121] This project was completed in 1992, and establishes rights and obligations of parties to an "international credit transfer." This is a funds transfer that results from a payment order being sent by a sending

---

121. Model Law, Art. United Nations General Assembly Official Records, Report of the United Nations Commission on International Trade Law on the Work of Its Twenty-Fifth Session, 47th Session, Supp. No. 17, at Annex I, United Nations Doc. A/47/17 [1992]. *See also* Permanent Editorial Board for the Uniform Commercial Code (PEB) Commentary No. 13 (February 16, 1994), discussing the Model Law in relation to UCC Article 4A.

bank in one country to a receiving bank in another country. Further limited discussion appears in PEB Commentary No. 13. The rules for determining applicable law absent applicability of international law also were discussed previously in this chapter.

[d] Federal Law

[i] Federal Common Law

When the instrument is one with which the federal government is involved, a different choice of law problem arises, but it is no less significant. If the federal government is a party to the instrument, its rights and duties are governed by federal rather than by state law.[122] The UCC does not govern because Congress has not enacted it for federal transactions and, absent a controlling federal statute or regulation, the federal presence makes the applicable law the federal common law and state law is not a choice.

In ascertaining the nature of the federal common law there is a choice, however, and some courts have drawn heavily upon the UCC because it does control most commercial transactions in the United States. For example, in *United States v. Wegematic Corp.*,[123] the court stated:

> The Code has been adopted by Congress for the District of Columbia [citation omitted], has been enacted in over forty states, and is thus well on its way to becoming a truly national law of commerce.... When the states have gone so far in achieving the desirable goal of a uniform law governing commercial transactions, it would be a distinct disservice to insist on a different one for the segment of commerce, important but still small in relation to the total, consisting of transactions with the United States.[124]

Moreover, as the court in another case recognized,[125] the purpose of the Uniform Commercial Code is to bring the body of commercial law into the contemporary world of business to meet the contemporary needs of a commercial society. The Supreme Court also has said that though the rights and duties of the United States on the commercial paper it issues are governed by federal rather than by local law, the United States, as drawee of commercial paper, stands in no different light than any other drawee and does business on business terms.[126]

---

122. Clearfield Trust Co. v. United States, 318 U.S. 363, 63 S.Ct. 573, 87 L.Ed. 838 (1943). *See also* D'Oench, Duhme & Co. v. FDIC, 315 U.S. 447, 62 S.Ct. 676, 86 L.Ed. 956 (1942). A more recent articulation of this philosophy came in an Article 9 context in United States v. Kimbell Foods, Inc., 440 U.S. 715, 99 S.Ct. 1448, 59 L.Ed.2d 711 (1979). Where an attorney prepared a tax return and received the refund check and forged his client's indorsement, however, the court held the UCC rule ought to apply in litigation between the client and the client's bank. Allen v. Crocker National Bank, 733 F.2d 642 (9th Cir.1984).

123. 360 F.2d 674 (2d Cir.1966).

124. United States v. Wegematic Corp., 360 F.2d 674, at 676 (2d Cir.1966).

125. General Elec. Credit Corp. v. R.A. Heintz Constr. Co., 302 F.Supp. 958 (D.Or. 1969).

126. *See* Clearfield Trust Co. v. United States, note 122, *supra.*

Nonetheless, Article 3 has not exerted an entirely uniform influence in litigation involving negotiable instruments to which the United States is a party. For example, in one case[127] where the payee's name on a Treasury check was furnished by two navy enlisted men who thereafter indorsed the payee's name and cashed the check, the court refused to apply the policy behind old § 3–405, which would have placed the loss on the United States and not on the cashing bank. The court may have reached this result because it believed itself bound by an earlier decision of the Supreme Court rendered at a time when the general law concerning negotiable instruments was otherwise on this issue. The same consideration also prompted the court in *United States v. Philadelphia National Bank*[128] to reject the UCC rule in a similar fact situation. But the court also noted that, beyond the precedent problem, there might be additional policy considerations different from those of the UCC, since the United States arguably might have more difficulty insuring against loss and in exercising control over its employees.[129]

Another context where the courts consistently have found a different policy to be applicable, and thus have not followed the UCC rules in fashioning federal common law, is where the negotiable instrument is being enforced by a federal financial institution insurance agency.[130]

The line of contrasting authority in this circumstance stems from *D'Oench, Duhme & Co. v. Federal Deposit Insurance Corp.*[131] In *D'Oench*, the FDIC brought suit on a renewal note executed by D'Oench, Duhme & Co. payable to Belleville Bank & Trust Co., which had been charged off by the bank. The company had sold the bank certain bonds, which later defaulted. The receipt for the note in question indicated the note

---

127. United States v. Bank of Am. Nat'l Trust & Sav. Ass'n, 438 F.2d 1213 (9th Cir.1971).

128. 304 F.Supp. 955 (E.D.Pa.1969).

129. *Compare* State v. Family Bank of Hallandale, 623 So.2d 464 (Fla.1993) (state warrant not negotiable notwithstanding definition in Article 3 as overriding policy to protect the public treasury from dishonest officials required protection from negotiability).

130. The cases mainly involve the Federal Deposit Insurance Corporation or the Federal Savings and Loan Insurance Corporation or its successor. As to the latter, *see* Milligan v. Gilmore Meyer Inc., 775 F.Supp. 400 (S.D.Ga.1991) (RTC as FSLIC's corporate successor may raise *D'Oench* doctrine). Also one case seems to involve the National Credit Union Administration. *See* Payne v. Mundaca Inv. Corp., 562 N.E.2d 51 (Ind.Ct. App.1990). *See also* Rhode Island Depositors Economic Protection Corp. v. Ryan, 697 A.2d 1087 (R.I.1997). *Generally see*, Miller and Meacham, The FDIC and Other Financial Institution Insurance Agencies as "Super" Holders in Due Course: A Lesson in Self–Pollinated Jurisprudence, 40 OKLA. L. REV. 621 (1987) (Miller and Meacham, *FDIC as HDC*). As noted in that article, the limitation on the protection afforded under the federal rule to the insurance agency in its corporate capacity rather than as receiver was diminishing. *See* Miller and Meacham, FDIC as HDC, at 622, note 7. *See also* Campbell Leasing, Inc. v. FDIC, 901 F.2d 1244 (5th Cir.1990) discussed at Note, Guarding the Fund: Holder in Due Course Status Extended to the FDIC as Receiver in Campbell Leasing, Inc. v. FDIC, 27 U.S. F. L. Rev. 653 (1993). *Cf.* Bell and Murphy and Associates v. Interfirst Bank Gateway, 894 F.2d 750 (5th Cir.1990), *cert. denied*, 498 U.S. 895, 111 S.Ct. 244, 112 L.Ed.2d 203 (1990). The dispute is moot after FIRREA which eliminated the distinction. It also should be recognized that a court may adopt the Code rule in this context if it believes it to be appropriate. The court did that in FDIC v. Blue Rock Shopping Center, Inc., 766 F.2d 744 (3d Cir. 1985) in a case that involved assertion of a "surety defense" under old § 3–606.

131. 315 U.S. 447, 62 S.Ct. 676, 86 L.Ed. 956 (1942), *reh'g denied*, 315 U.S. 830, 62 S.Ct. 910, 86 L.Ed. 1224 (1942).

was not to be called for payment because it and the predecessor notes to the renewal note had been executed only to enable the bank to avoid showing any past due bonds as assets. When sued, the company raised this defense. The court held the issue was governed by federal law, and that the proper legal rule, derived from the statutes governing the FDIC which evidenced a policy to protect the FDIC and the public funds that it administered against misleading appearances from undisclosed arrangements, was that a person executing an instrument in the form of a binding obligation is estopped to assert as a defense the fact that the parties simultaneously secretly agreed that the instrument should not be enforced.[132] The *D'Oench* doctrine, which arguably is limited to cases involving action with the taint of deceit and which many courts hold still survives as a common law principle,[133] later was codified in the federal statutes,[134] and the federal statutes have received a much broader[135] but, based on the legislative history,[136] inaccurate reading.

The substantial point of divergence of the federal common law rule from the UCC rule first occurred in *Federal Deposit Insurance Corporation v. Rockelman*,[137] where the court, without precedent or an accurate understanding of the legislative history, concluded:

> [T]he court concludes that, although the FDIC, in its corporate capacity, is not a holder in due course within the meaning of that term under the Uniform Commercial Code, Congress intended by means of section 1823 to clothe the Corporation with the protection afforded a holder in due course and shield the corporation against many defenses that would otherwise be available.[138]

With all due respect, there is a vast difference in the FDIC not being subject to a defense which poses the risk of unfair surprise, which type of defense is not valid even under state law against a mere holder,[139] and being accorded the rights of a holder in due course, even though a

---

132. The state law rule presumably would be the same, at least under the UCC. See § 3–117 Official Comment 2.

133. *But see* on the first point, note 130, *supra*, and Bowen v. FDIC, 915 F.2d 1013 (5th Cir.1990) (modern rule bars use of unrecorded agreements whether or not involving a specific obligation and whether or not malfeasance is involved); nonetheless *compare* Resolution Trust Corp. v. 1601 Partners, Ltd., 796 F.Supp. 238 (N.D.Tex. 1992) (inapplicable where subsequent assignment not contemplated). As to the second point, *see*, *e.g.*, *In re* Longhorn Securities Litigation, 573 F.Supp. 278 (W.D.Okla. 1983); Beighley v. FDIC, 868 F.2d 776 (5th Cir.1989); Harrison v. Wahatoyas, 253 F.3d 552 (10th Cir.2001). *But see* Murphy v. FDIC, 61 F.3d 34, 39 (D.C.Cir.1995); DiVall Insured Income Fund Ltd. Partnership v. Boatmen's First Nat'l Bank, 69 F.3d 1398 1402 (8th Cir.1995); FDIC v. Deglau, 207 F.3d 153, 171 (3d Cir.2000). *Also compare* Andrew D. Taylor Trust v. Security Federal Savings and Loan, 844 F.2d 337 (6th Cir. 1988) *with In re* Kanterman, 108 B.R. 432 (S.D.N.Y.1989) as to scope.

134. 12 U.S.C. § 1823(e) (banks, and since FIRREA, the RTC as successor to the federal savings and loan insurance agency— *see* Baumann v. Savers Fed. Sav. & Loan Ass'n, 934 F.2d 1506, 1515 (11th Cir.1991), *cert. denied*, 504 U.S. 908, 112 S.Ct. 1936, 118 L.Ed.2d 543 (1992)); 12 U.S.C. § 1787(p)(2) (credit unions).

135. Langley v. FDIC, 484 U.S. 86, 108 S.Ct. 396, 98 L.Ed.2d 340 (1987); FDIC v. Virginia Crossings Partnership, 909 F.2d 306 (8th Cir.1990).

136. Miller and Meacham, FDIC as HDC, *supra* note 130, at 626–28.

137. 460 F.Supp. 999 (E.D.Wis.1978).

138. *Id.*, at 1003.

139. *See* note 132, *supra*.

purchaser in bulk,[140] with the ability to take free of all claims to the instrument and all defenses to its payment other than real defenses.[141] Nonetheless, once postulated the doctrine, which probably is less an interpretation of § 1823(e) than one of federal common law, quickly grew, and today there perhaps is little room to argue that a federal financial institution insurance agency is not a holder in due course taking free of most defenses even if not arising from "an agreement," and even if UCC requirements for holding in due course are not met.[142] However, there still is unsettled law at the fringes.

First, a consumer case, where holder in due course status has not been the rule for decades, has not really been litigated.[143] It would seem the policy to protect consumer obligors, which is one of both state[144] and federal law,[145] is of more modern vintage and is more compelling than that of protecting the federal financial institution insurance agency, and that unless a federal statute controls[146] the consumer should prevail.[147]

Second, it is not completely clear whether the protection applies to obligations that are not evidenced by instruments on which there could be a holder in due course. The most common current example is a separate guaranty; numerous authorities have determined these are not negotiable.[148] Some authority exists that the protection applies, at least if § 1823 is applicable.[149]

---

140. A purchaser in bulk cannot be a holder in due course under the UCC. § 3–302(c)(ii). This includes a state agency that takes over and sells the assets of an insolvent institution. § 3–302, Official Comment 5. In addition, financial institution insurance agencies are unlikely to qualify as a holder in due course due to lack of indorsement, because the transfer is of an instrument in default, because there is notice of the claim or defense, or because the instrument is not negotiable. *See* Miller and Meacham, FDIC as HDC, *supra* note 130, at 623.

141. § 3–305(b).

142. *See, e.g.*, Campbell Leasing, Inc. v. FDIC, 901 F.2d 1244 (5th Cir.1990); Sunbelt Sav. v. Amrecorp Realty Corp., 742 F.Supp. 370 (N.D.Tex.1990); NCNB Texas National Bank v. Campise, 788 S.W.2d 115 (Tex.App.1990); FDIC v. Cremona Co., 832 F.2d 959 (6th Cir.1987), *cert. dismissed sub. nom.* Gonda v. FDIC, 485 U.S. 1017, 108 S.Ct. 1494, 99 L.Ed.2d 883 (1988); FDIC v. Leach, 772 F.2d 1262 (6th Cir.1985); FDIC v. Wood, 758 F.2d 156 (6th Cir.1985); and Gunter v. Hutcheson, 674 F.2d 862 (11th Cir.), *cert. denied* 459 U.S. 826, 103 S.Ct. 60, 74 L.Ed.2d 63 (1982). However, perhaps the future of the doctrine is not so clear after the restrictive opinion of the Supreme Court in another context in Atherton v. FDIC, 519 U.S. 213, 117 S.Ct. 666, 136 L.Ed.2d 656 (1997); only time will tell. *See* Comment, Alive, But Not Quite Kicking: Circuit Split Illustrates the Progressive Deterioration of the *D'Oench, Duhume* Doctrine, 42 St. Louis U. L.J. 945 (1998).

143. The probable reason is the amounts or the circumstances involved make litigation unlikely.

144. *See, e.g.*, Unico v. Owen, 50 N.J. 101, 232 A.2d 405 (N.J. 1967); 1974 Unif. Cons. Credit Code §§ 3.307, 3.403–3.405, 5.201.

145. Federal Trade Commission Trade Regulation Rule on Preservation of Consumers' Claims and Defenses, 16 CFR pt. 433; 15 U.S.C. § 1666i.

146. 12 U.S.C. § 1823(e); 12 U.S.C. § 1787(p)(2).

147. Given the expansive reading of § 1823(e) in Langley v. FDIC, *supra* note 135, however, the unfortunate consequence is that most consumer defenses will be eliminated by the statute. *But see* Patterson v. FDIC, 918 F.2d 540 (5th Cir.1990) (protection of homestead given by state law effective against bank which was charged with notice of the homestead character of the property, and against the FDIC).

148. *See, e.g.*, Gregoire v. Lowndes Bank, 176 W.Va. 296, 342 S.E.2d 264 (W.Va.1986) (guaranty).

149. FDIC v. Kratz, 898 F.2d 669 (8th Cir.1990) and FDIC v. Galloway, 856 F.2d 112 (10th Cir.1988) (guarantor); FDIC v.

Finally, there is some ambiguity about whether a concluded transaction or a claim that has been asserted can constitute a good defense. The cases are hard to reconcile. On the one hand, an accord and satisfaction has been recognized,[150] and in other cases not recognized.[151] It would seem the proper answer is that no asset exists to form the basis of suit.[152] In some cases notice of the defense has been found,[153] while in others the court has ignored notice arguments.[154]

To the extent the federal financial institution insurance agency is protected against claims and defenses, so too is any purchaser of the obligation from the agency under the shelter principle.[155]

Other than in the above two contexts, when not faced with a controlling decision the courts usually have adopted the UCC policy into the federal common law of negotiable instruments. For example, in *Bank of America National Trust & Savings Association v. United States*,[156] the court was confronted with facts similar to those in the prior cases discussed at notes 127 and 128, except that the payee on the instrument was fictitious and not an actual person whom the wrongdoers intended

---

Gulf Life Insurance Co., 737 F.2d 1513 (11th Cir.1984) (life insurance company's liability under policy for unearned premiums). *But see* Sunbelt Savings, FSB, Dallas, Texas v. Montross, 923 F.2d 353 (5th Cir. 1991) (variable rate note before UCC made such negotiable) and FDIC v. Percival, 752 F.Supp. 313 (D.Neb.1990) (guarantee).

150. FDIC v. Nemecek, 641 F.Supp. 740 (D.Kan.1986).

151. FSLIC v. Port Allen Dev. Corp., 684 F.Supp. 439 (M.D.La.1988). *See also* FDIC v. Manatt, 688 F.Supp. 1327 (E.D.Ark.1988), *aff'd*, 922 F.2d 486 (8th Cir.1991).

152. *See also* FDIC v. Prann, 694 F.Supp. 1027 (D.P.R.1988), *affirmed by* 895 F.2d 824 (1st Cir.1990) (canceled note) (*cf.* FDIC v. Byrne, 736 F.Supp. 727 (N.D.Tex. 1990) (debtor "recklessly" failed to obtain note after final payment, thus the case may be explicable as an application of estoppel)); FDIC v. Turner, 869 F.2d 270 (6th Cir. 1989) (real defense of fraud valid); *Patterson v. FDIC*, *supra*, note 147 (homestead exemption a real defense); Grubb v. FDIC, 868 F.2d 1151 (10th Cir.1989); First RepublicBank Fort Worth v. Norglass, 751 F.Supp. 1224 (N.D.Tex.1990), *aff'd*, 958 F.2d 117 (5th Cir.1992) and Thurman v. FDIC, 889 F.2d 1441 (5th Cir.1989) (judgment for debtor prior to bank's failure) (*cf.* FDIC v. Larsen, 793 S.W.2d 37 (Tex.App. 1990), *reversed on other grounds*, 835 S.W.2d 66 (Tex.1992) and FSLIC v. T.F. Stone–Liberty Land Associates, 787 S.W.2d 475 (Tex. App. 1990)); Campbell Leasing, Inc. v. FDIC, 901 F.2d 1244 (5th Cir.1990), FDIC v. Merchants Nat'l Bank of Mobile, 725 F.2d 634 (11th Cir.1984); Howell v. Continental Credit Corp., 655 F.2d 743 (7th Cir.1981) and Riverside Park Realty Co. v. FDIC, 465 F.Supp. 305 (M.D.Tenn.1978) (bilateral obligation breached by predecessor of federal insurance agency).

153. FDIC v. Bracero and Riveria, Inc., 895 F.2d 824 (1st Cir.1990) (FDIC bound by notice received by it in one capacity when purchasing a note in its other capacity). The case probably is explicable on the basis the note was discharged and thus is like the accord and satisfaction case in note 150, *supra*. *But see also* Sunbelt Sav. FSB, Dallas, Texas v. Amrecorp Realty, 742 F.Supp. 370 (N.D.Tex.1990) and Patterson v. FDIC, *supra*, note 147.

154. RSR Properties, Inc. v. FDIC, 706 F.Supp. 524 (W.D.Tex.1989) (an irrefutable presumption exists that records of the failed bank represent the true agreement between the parties). *See also* First City Nat'l Bank v. FDIC, 730 F.Supp. 501 (E.D.N.Y.1990) and Royal Bank of Canada v. FDIC, 733 F.Supp. 1091 (N.D.Tex.1990).

155. Sunbelt Savings, FSB, Dallas, Texas v. Cashin Constr., 737 F.Supp. 41 (E.D.Tex.1990); NCNB Texas Nat'l Bank v. Campise, 788 S.W.2d 115 (Tex.App.1990); Bell and Murphy and Associates v. Interfirst Bank Gateway, 894 F.2d 750 (5th Cir. 1990), *cert. denied*, 498 U.S. 895, 111 S.Ct. 244, 112 L.Ed.2d 203 (1990); FDIC v. Newhart, 713 F.Supp. 320 (W.D.Mo.), *aff'd* 892 F.2d 47 (8th Cir.1989). Dennis Joslin Co. v. Robinson Broadcasting, 977 F.Supp. 491 (D.D.C.1997), interpreting § 3–309 otherwise, is in error.

156. 552 F.2d 302 (9th Cir.1977).

to have no interest in the instrument. In this case the court applied the Uniform Commercial Code rule. In another case,[157] which involved a stolen postal money order on which the issuer's signature had been forged and which ultimately was paid to a bona fide purchaser, the court embraced the policy of finality of payment embodied in old § 3–418. It thus denied recovery of payment by the United States as against the bona fide purchaser for value of the instrument.[158]

The overwhelming weight of authority, both with respect to Article 3 and other articles of the UCC, is that their policies should be adopted as the federal common law, except in those very limited circumstances when it can be convincingly demonstrated that the UCC rule does not reflect important considerations involved in the federal context.

[ii] *Federal Statutes or Regulations*

If a federal statute or regulation, as opposed to federal common law, governs the issue, there is no choice of law problem. The statute or regulation simply supplants (or supplements) the UCC. Determining the extent of the preemption, however, may not be all that easy. In the context of checks, a major federal statute and regulation is the Expedited Funds Availability Act[159] and its implementing Regulation CC.[160] The impact of this law on when the prospective proceeds of a check (or an electronic payment or a cash deposit) must be made available in relation to the UCC rules[161] is clear enough, but its impact on the rules in UCC Article 4 for the return of dishonored checks is much more complicated.[162] An overview of this federal law as supplementary governing law is discussed briefly, *infra*, however.

In determining the applicability of a federal statute or regulation, there often is a choice of law to be made in a sense. An example of the kind of question encountered arose in a case[163] involving certain provisions of Federal Reserve Regulation J, dealing with the accountability of a payor bank for checks presented to it for payment and with settlement procedures. The federal provisions were not the same as comparable provisions contained in old Article 4 of the Uniform Commercial Code. The issue was whether the different federal rules were applicable to state banks that used Federal Reserve channels for collection.[164] The

---

157. United States v. First Nat'l Bank, 263 F.Supp. 298 (D.Mass.1967).

158. A similar case is A.C. Davenport & Son Co. v. United States, 538 F.Supp. 730 (N.D.Ill.1982), *aff'd*, 703 F.2d 266 (7th Cir. 1983), where the United States sued to recover a second payment it had made from a person in the position of a holder in due course. The double payment had been made because the first payment had gone to a copayee who had not properly allocated it and, since that person now was insolvent, the United States could not recover from it. The court mistakenly applied the UCC to find the second payment was final, but presumably would have reached the same result under federal law.

159. 12 U.S.C. § 4001 *et seq*.

160. 12 CFR pt. 229.

161. § 4–215(e) and (f); § 4A–404.

162. This matter is discussed later. *See also* note 22, *supra*; *infra* Chapter 8.

163. Community Bank v. Federal Res. Bank, 500 F.2d 282 (9th Cir.1974), *modified*, 525 F.2d 690 (9th Cir.1975).

164. As to the scope of present Regulation J, *see* 12 CFR §§ 210.3(b) and 210.2(g) (for "items," subpart A of Regulation J and

court applied the federal regulation, indicating that there was sufficient contact to apply it. In this case the UCC was not preempted, however, because under old Article 4[165] the effect of the provisions of that Article may be varied by agreement, and Federal Reserve regulations and operating letters have the effect of agreements[166] regardless of whether specifically assented to by all parties interested in items handled.[167]

An illustration of the kind of subtle questions that may arise between federal law, other than that involving funds availability, and the UCC and which the attorney who practices in the area of payments law must be alert for, is in connection with the use of a check cashing guarantee card to induce a merchant to accept a check that, when presented for payment, constitutes an overdraft and triggers the operation of a check credit arrangement. The guarantee card on these facts is a credit card[168] for purposes of the federal law that limits liability for the unauthorized use of a credit card to no more than $50.[169] On the other hand, under the UCC an unauthorized check is not properly payable by the drawee and no debit to the ostensible drawer's account may be made,[170] absent negligence on the part of the ostensible drawer that substantially contributes to the making of the unauthorized signature.[171] If we assume a theft of the guarantee card and a blank check form, the question would be resolved by applying the UCC rule alone,[172] but if we also hypothesize sufficient negligence on the part of the owner of the card with respect to the check form, the resolution of the question becomes a blend of federal and state law that results in no more than

---

subpart C of Regulation CC are binding on all parties interested in an item handled by any Reserve Bank), and §§ 210.27(b) and 210.26(c) (for "items" other than subpart A items, subpart B of Regulation J (wire transfers of funds) is binding on transferors, transferees, beneficiaries and other parties interested in the item). As to the scope of Regulation J after January 1, 1991, as to subpart B (funds transfers through Fedwire), *see* § 210.25. It should be noted that whatever the scope of Regulations J and CC at present, under § 609(c) of the Expedited Funds Availability Act, 12 U.S.C. § 4008(c), the Board of Governors of the Federal Reserve System may regulate *any aspect* of the payment system, including the receipt, payment, collection or clearing of checks, and *any related function* of the payment system with respect to checks (emphasis supplied). Nonetheless, doubt about the authority of the Federal Reserve to adopt rules that can bind check customers as opposed to banks given legislative history relevant to Regulation CC subject matter led to a proposal to repatriate relevant parts of Regulation CC in the UCC. *See* memorandum dated November 10, 2000, to the Council of the American Law Institute from the reporter and chair of the drafting committee formed to consider limited amendments to UCC Articles 3, 4 and 4A at page 1 (copy on file with authors). Ultimately, more doubts existed about the feasibility of that effort than concern about continuing to do business in doubt about the ability to bind third parties, and the proposal was dropped.

165. Old UCC § 4–103(1); current § 4–103(a) is the same.

166. § 4–103(b).

167. *Cf.* Kane v. American National Bank & Trust Co., 21 Ill.App.3d 1046, 316 N.E.2d 177 (Ill.App.1974), where the court determined that federal regulations were not applicable to the collection of items outside of Federal Reserve channels, and *see* note 164, *supra*.

168. *See* Commentary ¶ 226.2(a)(15)–2 under Regulation Z, 12 CFR § 226, the regulation implementing the Truth in Lending Act, 15 U.S.C. § 1601 *et seq.*

169. 15 U.S.C. § 1643.

170. § 4–401.

171. § 3–406.

172. Regulation Z, 12 CFR § 226.12(b)(4) provides that if state law imposes lesser liability, the lesser liability governs.

$50 liability.[173] Both results, then, are the consequence of a choice to superimpose an aspect of one system on a different system, perhaps with unintended consequences.

¶ 1.04 Negotiable Instruments in Context: Supplementary Governing Law

Negotiable instruments do not operate in a vacuum. Recognizing that a negotiable instrument represents only a part of the transaction that gave rise to it, and that the paper itself may become involved in yet other transactions, it is apparent that Article 3 is by no means the only law that is likely to apply to an instrument. Article 3 basically serves to define what is a negotiable instrument and to provide for the rights and responsibilities of parties on the instrument itself.[174] As has been seen, Article 3 is not necessarily complete even in that task, and other law may supplement or supplant its provisions.[175] Certainly Article 3 does not furnish the full governing law when a negotiable instrument becomes involved in other transactions, such as a note pledged as collateral for a loan,[176] but discussion of this other potential jurisprudence will be limited.[177] At this point, the focus will be only on some other major segments of law that may become involved in and to some extent govern aspects of transactions concerning negotiable instruments.

[1] *Uniform Commercial Code Article 4: Bank Deposits and Collections*

A check is a medium for the transfer of credit that the drawer has, by reason of a deposit or an agreement, with the drawee bank. Thus, checks, initially governed by Article 3, sooner or later become involved in the bank collection process governed by Article 4.[178] Logically enough, while checks are in this process they are additionally subject to the rules of Article 4. Moreover, the provisions of Article 3 are subject to the

---

173. 15 U.S.C. § 1643(a)(1)(B) states a cardholder may be liable for the unauthorized use of a credit card only if the liability is not in excess of $50 and the federal law would supplant inconsistent state law contained in § 3–406.

¶ 1.04

174. Article 3 also bears on the liability of parties to the instrument where the liability is not on the instrument. This includes liability on the underlying obligation and in warranty. Such liability is the major portion of the subject matter discussed later in this book.

175. *See, e.g.,* UCC Article 1, to be discussed, *infra*, and the discussion earlier. In particular, when the subject of defenses to liability on the instrument is taken up later in this book, there will be a number of good examples of other law supplementing the UCC.

176. UCC Article 9 would be involved.

177. An exception is the provisions of UCC Article 4 discussed later in this book. The alternative payment systems involving funds transfers and credit cards also will be discussed in some detail later.

178. Share drafts and negotiable orders of withdrawal under old Article 3 technically may not be "checks" because they arguably are not drawn on a "bank." Old § 3-104(2)(b) and old § 1-201(4). By and large, it makes little difference with respect to Article 3 because these instruments, if not a "check," are a "draft." Old § 3-104(2)(a). Under current Article 3, these instruments are checks since the definition of "bank" includes a savings and loan association and a credit union. §§ 4-105(1), 3-103(c), and 3-104(f). More-

provisions of Article 4 on bank deposits and collections.[179] Thus, in the case of a conflict between what Article 3 provides and what Article 4 provides, Article 4 governs.

Few, if any, instances of conflict exist between Articles 3 and 4. Some conflicts arguably did exist under the old Articles and, to the extent useful, those conflicts will be discussed in connection with the topic that perhaps gave rise to the conflict. A detailed discussion of the provisions of Article 4 will occur later.

[2] *Regulation CC: Funds Availability*

Regulation CC[180] has as its principal reason for existence the formulation of rules contained in Subpart B of the regulation to implement the Expedited Funds Availability Act[181] regarding the duty of banks[182] to make funds deposited into accounts[183] available for withdrawal.[184] In this regard, it affects the times provided in Article 4.[185] The regulation also contains rules creating exceptions to the otherwise required availability schedules,[186] requiring the payment of interest on deposits,[187] mandating the disclosure of funds availability policies,[188] regulating the relation of the federal rules to state law,[189] and implementing the imposition of liability of banks for failure to comply.[190]

Nonetheless, for the purpose of this book the far greater impact of Regulation CC is contained in Subpart C, which affects Parts 2 and 3 of Article 4 as to checks[191] in an attempt to speed up the return process for

---

over, checks drawn on credit lines rather than asset accounts also clearly are covered. § 4–104(a)(1).

179. §§ 3–102(b) and 4–102(a).

180. 12 CFR pt. 229.

181. 12 U.S.C. § 4001 *et seq.*

182. Regulation CC, 12 C.F.R. § 229.2(e). Commercial banks, savings and loan associations and credit unions, among other entities, are included in the term "bank." Regulation CC Official Commentary ¶ 229.2(e). The term is broader in scope for the purpose of Subpart C of the regulation than it is for the purpose of Subpart B.

183. *See* Regulation CC, 12 CFR § 229.2(a). Generally, the term "account" includes accounts at banks from which the account holder is permitted to make transfers or withdrawals by negotiable or transferable instrument, payment order of withdrawal, telephone transfer, electronic payment or other similar means for the purpose of making payments or transfers to third persons. The term does not include savings deposits or money market accounts even though they may have limited third party payment powers.

184. Regulation CC, 12 CFR §§ 229.10 (next day availability); 229.12 (permanent availability); and 229.19 (when funds are deposited, etc.).

185. § 4–215(e) and (f). Article 4A also is affected. § 4A–404.

186. *See* Regulation CC, 12 CFR § 229.13 (exceptions).

187. *See* Regulation CC, 12 CFR § 229.14.

188. *See* Regulation CC, 12 CFR §§ 229.15–229.18.

189. Regulation CC, 12 CFR § 229.20. The impact of this provision on Article 4 and its impact on Article 4A are discussed later.

190. Regulation CC, 12 CFR § 229.21.

191. Under Regulation CC, 12 CFR § 229.2(k), and for the purpose of Subpart C, the term "check" includes a negotiable or non-negotiable demand draft that is a cash item (*see* § 229.2(u) which defines "non-cash items," and *compare* §§ 3–104 and 4–104(1)(g) and 4–104(a)(9)) drawn on, or payable through or at, a U.S. office of a bank, one drawn on a Federal Reserve Bank, a Federal Home Loan Bank, the U.S. Treasury, or a state or local government, a U.S. Postal Service money order, and a traveler's check drawn on or payable through or at a bank. Credit card drafts and ACH debit transfers are not included but checks on credit lines are. Regulation CC Official Commentary ¶ 229.2(k); *compare* § 4–104(a)(9).

dishonored checks or otherwise to provide information of nonpayment to the depositary bank prior to the mandated time for funds availability so as to reduce potential losses from fraud or customer insolvency. Subpart C of Regulation CC accordingly mandates that:

(1) paying[192] and returning[193] banks expeditiously return a dishonored check to the depositary bank[194] and that the depositary bank accept returned checks,[195] and

(2) the paying bank send a notice of nonpayment to the depositary bank in the case of a dishonored check of $2,500 or more.[196]

Regulation CC Subpart C further provides for supporting warranties by paying and returning banks;[197] creates indorsement standards;[198] regulates the presentment and issuance of checks;[199] implements the imposition of liability for the failure of a bank to comply;[200] and deals with variation by agreement,[201] bank insolvency,[202] effect of merger,[203] exclusions,[204] and relation to state law.[205] These provisions, and particularly the impact of Regulation CC on Article 4, are discussed in a later chapter.

[3] Uniform Commercial Code Article 9: Secured Transactions

A negotiable instrument embodies valuable rights.[206] Therefore, it is a form of property. As property of value, it can be pledged as collateral for a loan.[207] A transaction of that kind would be a secured transaction governed by UCC Article 9.[208] Thus, a negotiable instrument used as collateral for a debt may also be subject to the rules of Article 9.[209]

In the event of conflict between Articles 3 or 4 and Article 9, the provisions of Article 9 will control.[210] Instances of conflict, if they exist at all, are rare. The case of *Jefferson v. Mitchell Select Furniture Co.*[211]

---

192. The term includes the drawee bank. Regulation CC, 12 CFR § 229.2(z), and *compare* §§ 3–103(a)(2) and 4–105(3).

193. A bank, other than the paying or depositary bank, handling a returned check or notice in lieu of return. Regulation CC, 12 CFR § 229.2(cc).

194. The first bank to which a check is transferred. Regulation CC, 12 CFR § 229.2(o). *Compare* § 4–105(2).

195. Regulation CC, 12 CFR § 229.32.

196. Regulation CC, 12 CFR § 229.33.

197. Regulation CC, 12 CFR § 229.34.

198. Regulation CC, 12 CFR § 229.35.

199. Regulation CC, 12 CFR § 229.36.

200. Regulation CC, 12 CFR § 229.38.

201. Regulation CC, 12 CFR § 229.37.

202. Regulation CC, 12 CFR § 229.39.

203. Regulation CC, 12 CFR § 229.40.

204. Regulation CC, 12 CFR § 229.42.

205. Regulation CC, 12 CFR § 229.41.

206. § 3–310(b).

207. The sale of a promissory note also is subject to Article 9. §§ 9–102(a)(65) and 9–109(a)(3).

208. In the bank collection process, if a bank makes an advance on or against an item, including credit withdrawable as of right or which is withdrawn, it acquires a security interest in the item and in any accompanying documents and in the proceeds of either by reason of statute and without the necessity for agreement under § 4–210(a). This security interest, however, is subject in some respects to Article 9. §§ 4–210(c) and 9–109(a)(6). A further discussion appears in a later chapter.

209. §§ 3–102(b) and 9–109(b).

210. § 3–102(b). As to Article 4, *see* § 4–210(c).

211. 56 Ala.App. 259, 321 So.2d 216 (Ala.Civ.App.1975).

might illustrate an instance of conflict. The secured party held a retail installment agreement and security interest that the court believed met the requirements of old § 3–104 so as to be governed by Article 3. The court nonetheless concluded that the agreement was not a negotiable instrument subject to Article 3; rather, it was governed by Article 9, and effect could be given to a consumer protection statute limiting holder-in-due-course status in accordance with old § 9–206 (now § 9–403), which expressly so provided. It would seem the court simply erred in reason but not in result because it is doubtful the agreement constituted a negotiable instrument. Even if it did, although old Article 3 does not contain a provision like old § 9–203 (now § 9–201) generally deferring to consumer protection legislation, consumer protection legislation that modifies the more general commercial law rules of Article 3 should be given effect on normal principles of statutory construction.[212]

[4] General Provisions of Law Under the Uniform Commercial Code: Article 1

Beyond Articles 3, 4 and 9 of the Uniform Commercial Code, the only other UCC Article likely to be of general applicability to transactions in negotiable instruments for the payment of money is Article 1, which contains general provisions applicable to all UCC articles.[213] Few of these principles seem to have had significant impact on the outcome of negotiable instrument cases. The most notable exception involves the cases applying old § 1–207 on performance under reservation of rights to checks tendered in full payment of disputed obligations.[214] These cases are discussed later.[215]

A variety of arguments have been made based on Article 1 provisions. To illustrate, in *Vedder v. Spellman*,[216] for example, the court determined that the rule of liberal construction, contained in old § 1–102(1) (now § 1–103(a)), did not operate to allow suit on an instrument given for an obligation barred by a state statute stipulating that a contractor may not sue for work done if the contractor was not licensed at the time the work was performed. In another case the court failed to find an absence of good faith as defined in old § 1–201(19) when a bank

---

212. § 3–302(g) does explicitly subject the holder in due course rules of Article 3 to consumer protection and any other limiting law. *See also* § 3–305(e) and (f), added by the 2002 amendments to Article 3.

213. § 3–103(d) specifically refers to Article 1 and states that it contains general definitions and principles of construction and interpretation applicable throughout Article 3. Article 1 was promulgated in revised and updated form in 2001. While the section numbers will change, most of the concepts mentioned here will not.

It may also be worth noting that the obligation of the issuer of a letter of credit to honor a proper presentation also may be triggered by the presentation of a draft, which need not, however, be negotiable under Article 3. Official Comment 11 to UCC § 5–102.

214. One other area of impact, however, is the obligation of good faith imposed in every contract or duty under the UCC by § 1–304. With the broader definition of good faith in § 3–103(a)(4) and § 1–201(b)(20), it is inevitable that some earlier results will change. *Compare, e.g.,* Official Comment 5 to § 9–331. This will be discussed *infra* as relevant.

215. The cases are treated in Chapter 7.

216. 78 Wn.2d 834, 480 P.2d 207 (Wash. 1971).

loaned money to a debtor evidenced by demand promissory notes, deposited the loan proceeds in the debtor's checking account, and then several days later called the notes due and set-off the debt against the checking account.[217] Finally, a prior transaction was not found to establish a course of dealing as defined in old § 1–205 (now § 1–303) so as to vary the necessity for a payor bank to comply strictly with the midnight deadline rule of old § 4–302.[218] Yet, in determining whether a collecting bank acted "reasonably" as required under old § 4–202[219] with respect to uncollected sight drafts that the bank failed to return or to otherwise act upon before its midnight deadline, a court did determine that course of dealing or custom and usage as defined in old § 1–205 were relevant.[220]

[5] General Provisions of Law Outside the Uniform Commercial Code: Section 1–103(b) of Article 1

The Uniform Commercial Code, including Article 3, relies on law outside of its confines to supplement its provisions. There are specific references of this nature in Article 3. For example, § 3–305(a)(1) refers to the law on incapacity to contract, duress, illegality, and fraud. The UCC also contains § 1–103(b); a general provision incorporating other law outside of the provisions of the UCC when that other law is not displaced.

Section 1–103(b) provides that, unless displaced by a particular provision of the Uniform Commercial Code, the principles of law and equity, including the law merchant and the law relative to capacity to contract, principal and agent, estoppel, fraud, misrepresentation, duress, coercion, mistake, bankruptcy, or other validating or invalidating cause shall supplement the UCC's provisions. The key issue in each case, of course, is whether the UCC rule has displaced the rule that otherwise would apply.[221] There are a number of illustrations of this in Article 3. For example, § 3–105(a) rejects decisions that prior to the UCC held that a recital in an instrument that it is given in return for an executory promise gives rise to an implied condition that the instrument is not to be paid if the promise is not performed, and that this condition destroys

---

217. Allied Sheet Metal Fabr., Inc. v. Peoples Nat'l Bank, 10 Wn.App. 530, 518 P.2d 734 (Wash.App.1974). Quere under the current broader Article 1 and 3 definitions which include the observance of reasonable commercial standards of fair dealing. Certainly a number of other "lender liability" type cases have since involved negotiable instruments, including First National Bank v. Twombly, 213 Mont. 66, 689 P.2d 1226 (Mont. 1984), Reid v. Key Bank, Inc., 821 F.2d 9 (1st Cir.1987), and Rodgers v. Tecumseh Bank, 1988 OK 36, 756 P.2d 1223 (Okla.1988). Some opinions have agreed with the *Allied Sheet Metal Fabricators* case, and some have not, but this book is a treatise on payment system rules and notes and not on lender liability so further discussion is left to other materials.

218. Sun River Cattle Co. v. Miners Bank, 164 Mont. 237, 521 P.2d 679 (Mont. 1974). The rule appears in current Article 4 at § 4–302.

219. Current § 4–202 is the same.

220. Marcoux v. Mid–States Livestock, Inc., 429 F.Supp. 155 (N.D.Iowa 1977), *modified* 572 F.2d 651 (8th Cir.1978).

221. There is some tension with § 1–103(a), which states the Code should be liberally construed and applied to promote its underlying purposes and policies. Revised Article 1 (see note 213, *supra*) attempts amelioration. *See* Official Comment 2 to § 1–103.

negotiability.[222] An example more difficult to discern because the displacement is not expressed in a single provision, occurred in *Bowling Green, Inc. v. State Street Bank & Trust Co.*[223] In the *Bowling Green* case, an action sought to hold the defendant bank as a constructive trustee of all or a part of funds that were the proceeds of a check. The check in question had been indorsed by the plaintiff to a corporation, and the corporation in turn had deposited the check in its checking account in the defendant bank. The court believed that because the action was within the scope of the UCC, the disposition of the action was governed not by general principles of equity but by particular provisions of the UCC that the court held to be governing. A similar case is *Brighton, Inc. v. Colonial First National Bank*,[224] in which the court determined that a drawer, whose signature was forged and who was barred by negligence from asserting the forgery in an action against the drawee, could not sue a collecting bank in negligence, conversion, or on a theory of money had and received even though the instrument also bore a forged indorsement. The court did believe an action based on actual complicity between the drawer's employee and an employee of the bank might not be displaced, however.[225]

If the UCC does not directly express itself on an issue, even though there is a closely related UCC provision, the outside rule generally will be considered applicable. For example, courts have held that provisions of state law other than the UCC supply the period of limitations for commencing an action for conversion under old § 3–419 and the elements constituting that tort.[226] Moreover, other courts have stated that if unauthorized indorsements other than forgeries or missing indorsements are not included within old § 3–419, which provides that an instrument is converted when it is paid on a forged indorsement, the law may reach the same result by general principles.[227]

Of course, if the UCC does not even contain an indirect expression and is thus completely silent on the matter, the determination is

---

222. § 3–106(a)(i) states a promise or order is unconditional unless it states an express condition to payment.

223. 425 F.2d 81 (1st Cir.1970), *affirmed* 86 N.J. 259, 430 A.2d 902 (N.J. 1981).

224. 176 N.J.Super. 101, 422 A.2d 433 (App.Div.1980).

225. A similar case involving a forged indorsement made effective under old § 3–405 is Merrill Lynch, Pierce, Fenner & Smith, Inc. v. Chemical Bank, 57 N.Y.2d 439, 442 N.E.2d 1253, 456 N.Y.S.2d 742 (N.Y.1982). These matters are discussed, *infra*, in Chapter 7.

226. *E.g.*, Bank of Am. Nat'l Trust & Sav. Ass'n v. Security Pac. Nat'l Bank, 23 Cal.App.3d 638, 100 Cal.Rptr. 438 (1972). The same is true for the elements of the tort under current § 3–420(a), but revised Article 3 now contains its own set of statutes of limitation. See § 3–118(g) on the point involved. *See also* Terry v. Kemper Insurance Co., 390 Mass. 450, 456 N.E.2d 465 (Mass. 1983), where an insurance settlement check, payable to the beneficiary of the insurance and his attorney, was misappropriated by the attorney who forged the client's indorsement. The court found that the insurance company had discharged its obligation by delivery of the check to the authorized agent under agency law, which had not been displaced by the Code in this regard. These matters are treated more extensively in terms of rights and liabilities in Chapter 7.

227. *E.g.*, Salsman v. National Community Bank, 102 N.J.Super. 482, 246 A.2d 162 (Law Div.1968), *aff'd* 105 N.J.Super. 164, 251 A.2d 460 (App.Div.1969). Current §§ 3–420(a) and 1–201(b)(41) agree.

relatively easy. In this context, the mere omission from the UCC of any exception covering the situation involved cannot, without more, be equated with a displacement of a rule of law that prevailed prior to the enactment of the UCC. Accordingly, in one case[228] the court held that the rule of prior law, which provided that a person who receives before maturity a note signed by the maker for the accommodation of another is not affected by the fact that it was made without consideration, continues after enactment of the UCC, notwithstanding the omission from old § 3–408 of any exception covering the situation.[229] Obviously, there are many illustrations of legal rules relevant to negotiable instruments that the UCC does not displace. Without attempting an exhaustive list, with respect to old Article 3 the courts have applied the principles relating to accord and satisfaction or novation,[230] parol evidence,[231] and mistake.[232]

228. Franklin Nat'l Bank v. Eurez Constr. Corp., 60 Misc.2d 499, 301 N.Y.S.2d 845 (Sup.Ct.1969).

229. *See, infra,* Chapters 5 and 6.

230. *E.g.,* Ampex Corp. v. Appel Media, Inc., 374 F.Supp. 1114 (W.D.Pa.1974).

231. *E.g.,* American Underwriting Corp. v. Rhode Island Hosp. Trust Co., 111 R.I. 415, 303 A.2d 121 (1973).

232. *E.g., In re* Country Club Casuals, Inc., 1 B.R. 274 (Bankr.S.D.Fla.1979); St. Regis Paper Co. v. Wicklund, 93 Wn.2d 497, 610 P.2d 903 (Wash.1980). The standard treatise on the subject is R. Hillman, J. McDonnell and S. Nickles, Common Law and Equity under the Uniform Commercial Code (1985). In some instances, current Article 3 explicitly refers to the law of mistake and restitution. *See* § 3–418. *See also* in Article 4A, § 4A–207(d).

Chapter 2

FORM REQUIREMENTS FOR NEGOTIABLE INSTRUMENTS

Analysis

Para.
¶2.01 Introduction 39
    [1] History of and Reasons for Form Requirements for
        Negotiable Instruments 39
    [2] Modern Critique of the Requirements 41
        [a] Erosion of Negotiable Status 41
        [b] Problems Where the Form of the Instrument Is
            Inadequate 42
        [c] Solutions 43
    [3] Indirectly Obtaining the Benefits of Article 3 45
        [a] General Inability to Invoke Rules of Article 3 by
            Agreement 45
        [b] Other Methods of Achieving Aspects of Negotiability 45
¶2.02 Form Requirements for Negotiable Instruments 47
    [1] Written Instrument 48
    [2] Signing 48
        [a] Creation of Liability on an Instrument 48
        [b] Definition of "Signed" 48
        [c] Weight Accorded to Signatures 49
    [3] Limited and Unconditional Promise or Order 50
        [a] Nature of Promise or Order 50
            [i] Informal Instruments 50
            [ii] Excessive Luggage Encumbering the Promise or
                Order 51
                [A] Provisions Relating to Collateral 52
                [B] Other Provisions 56
        [b] The Instrument in Relation to the Transaction Out of
            Which It Arose 57
            [i] References Versus Incorporation 57
                [A] Permitted References 57
                [B] References Not Permitted 61
            [ii] Other Agreements Affecting the Instrument 63
            [iii] Oral Parol Evidence 65
        [c] Limitations on Sources for Payment 67
        [d] Other Conditions 68
    [4] Sum Certain 68
        [a] Amount Ascertainable From the Instrument 68
        [b] Provisions Not Creating Uncertainty 71
    [5] Sum Payable in Money 71
        [a] Money Not Limited to Legal Tender 71
        [b] Instruments Payable in Foreign Money 72

Para.

¶2.02 Form Requirements for Negotiable Instruments—Continued
    [6] Payable on Demand or at a Definite Time 72
        [a] Instruments Payable on Demand 72
        [b] Instruments Payable at a Definite Time 73
    [7] Payable to Order or to Bearer 75
        [a] Instruments Payable to Bearer 75
        [b] Instruments Payable to Order 77
¶2.03 Seals 79
¶2.04 Ambiguities and Omissions in Instruments 79
    [1] Rules to Forestall Ambiguities 79
    [2] Omissions Not an Impairment of Negotiability 83
¶2.05 Incomplete Instruments 83
    [1] When an Instrument is Complete, Incomplete, or Not Within Article 3 83
    [2] Authorized and Unauthorized Complete Instruments 84

¶ 2.01 Introduction

[1] History of and Reasons for Form Requirements for Negotiable Instruments

The acceptability of a commodity, whether it is gold or a negotiable instrument, is determined in significant measure by the ease of ascertaining whether it is the "real thing." As discussed previously, a negotiable instrument obtains value from the fact that, even though it is a contract, it is governed by a special body of rules that confer particular benefits not available in an ordinary contract. For example, there is freedom from claims to it and many defenses to its payment, there are procedural advantages, and there may be recourse to one's assignor if the instrument is not paid, to name several. Thus some method must exist for distinguishing the contracts that are negotiable instruments from the contracts that are not. The method chosen by the common law for this purpose was a set of requirements as to the form of the instrument. If the instrument met the requirements, it was governed by special rules. If it did not, it was subject to the general rules that governed ordinary contracts. These form requirements today are contained in § 3–104 of Article 3, and are elaborated upon in subsequent sections of that Article.

The form requirements themselves originally were established principally to assure that the terms of the instrument would be certain.[1] Certainty was believed necessary to induce the prospective taker of a negotiable instrument to purchase it because, if the terms of the contract

---

¶ 2.01

1. The requirement that the instrument be signed, found in §§ 3–104(a) and 3–103(a)(6) and (9), goes to the contractual nature of the instrument rather than to the certainty of its terms. The requirement in § 3–104(a)(1) that the instrument be payable to order or to bearer relates to an intention for transfer. Of course, ease of transfer is the ultimate goal of the certainty requirements.

were uncertain, it would be difficult to value the contract,[2] and an asset of undeterminable value is not easily saleable, at least at something approaching par. In the years during which the form requirements were being fashioned, the law wished to promote the free transfer of negotiable instruments because negotiable instruments that passed from hand to hand in payment of debts were used to supplement the otherwise inadequate money supply.[3] Uncertainty as to the amount payable,[4] the time of payment,[5] or, worst of all, whether the instrument was absolutely payable without condition,[6] detracted from the goal of creating an easily enforceable right to the payment of money that was divorced from the transaction giving rise to the instrument and which was readily assignable. Ultimately the basic form requirements for negotiable instruments were formulated; legally, to be a negotiable instrument the instrument had to be a written unconditional promise or order to pay a fixed amount of money on demand or at a definite time to bearer or to the order of a named person.

Of course, negotiable instruments no longer are central to the function of supplementing the money supply. For a while it was asserted negotiable instruments performed another function; by promoting certainty and freedom from defenses and claims the market for credit obligations was enhanced. This "stock market" theory suggested that financing agencies therefore were more willing to finance transactions and, as a result, more persons could acquire property and services and upon better terms. The demise of the holder in due course doctrine in many consumer transactions without apparent devastation of the market for consumer paper seems to have at least raised a question about this analysis. One may thus ask, and a number have, who needs negotiability?

The simple answer is, a number of people perceive that negotiable instruments are still useful. For example, the Federal Home Loan Mortgage Corporation—Freddie Mac—endorsed the current version of Article 3 because it explicitly made variable rate notes negotiable, which

---

2. This thought also appears to be the genesis of the oft-quoted phrase that a negotiable instrument must be "a courier without luggage." Overton v. Tyler, 3 Pa. 346 (1846). Today, see § 3–104(a)(3) which, on pain of losing negotiability, prohibits including more than very limited obligations in the instrument beyond an obligation to pay money.

3. The origin of the requirement that the instrument be payable to order or to bearer apparently was to ensure that the parties intended transfer to be permissible. In Miller v. Race, 1 Burr. 452, 97 Eng. Rep. 398 (K.B. 1758), the instrument was a demand note of the Bank of England payable to bearer, something akin to a modern Federal Reserve Note except that, at the time, notes of the Bank of England were not legal tender. Lord Mansfield observed bank notes were treated as money, as cash, by the general consent of mankind, which gave them the credit and currency of money.

4. Under § 3–104(a), the amount of a negotiable instrument must be a fixed amount of money.

5. Under § 3–104(a)(2), a negotiable instrument must be payable on demand or at a definite time.

6. Under § 3–104(a), the promise or order to pay in a negotiable instrument must be unconditional. Overall certainty is further promoted by the requirement of a writing. See §§ 3–104(a) and 3–103(a)(6) and (9). Neither the Uniform Electronic Transactions Act ("UETA") or the Electronic Signatures in Global and National Commerce Act ("E–sign") override signature or writing requirements, as discussed in Chapter 1.

is believed to be of some value. Indeed, the New Payments Code[7] proposal to eliminate negotiability was not enthusiastically received, which again demonstrates that the concept of negotiability retains life. Thus, for better or for worse, Article 3 retains special rules for negotiable instruments, and the concept is likely to be with us for some time yet.

[2] Modern Critique of the Requirements

[a] Erosion of Negotiable Status

Nonetheless, the form requirements for negotiable instruments have not evolved and commercial practice and changes in the legal environment by-passed some of the requirements. Indeed, Article 3 itself, in some contexts, could be viewed as obsolete because, even following form requirements, it is no longer possible to achieve holder in due course status in most consumer transactions.[8] As a result, consumer notes often are now merged into combination forms containing a promise to pay, a security agreement, and a disclosure statement (to comply with the Truth in Lending Act[9]) and, of course, these combined documents do not qualify as negotiable instruments. Nonetheless, traffic in these documents as collateral or otherwise does not seem to have been appreciably diminished. It also is true that sales of promissory notes are included under Article 9 because such transactions have become common in securitizations, and in this context a distinction is not made between Article 3 and non-Article 3 instruments.

To further illustrate the point, it perhaps is sufficient to observe that it has been some time since many attorneys have seen a separate consumer or commercial note on which they would be willing to give an opinion that the instrument is negotiable.[10] Notwithstanding this point,

---

7. *See* Miller, A Report on the New Payments Code, 39 Bus. Law 1215 (1984).

8. Perhaps one of the best short discussions of the reason appears in Prefatory Note, 1974 Unif. Consumer Cred. Code, Consumer Oriented Changes and Additions, (1) Holder in Due Course; Sales Related Loans; Credit Cards. The matter is discussed in this book in Chapter 3.

9. 15 U.S.C. § 1601 *et seq..* The Truth in Lending Act requires a creditor to disclose information as to the cost and terms of credit to a consumer.

10. Today many notes call for a variable interest rate, which prior to 1990 most courts held destroys negotiability by rendering the sum uncertain. *See e.g.,* Doyle v. Trinity Sav. & Loan Ass'n, 869 F.2d 558 (10th Cir.1989), *vacated* at 940 F.2d 592 (10th Cir.1991); Taylor v. Roeder, 234 Va. 99, 360 S.E.2d 191 (1987); *In re* Gas Reclamation, Inc. Sec. Litig., 741 F.Supp. 1094 (S.D.N.Y.1990); Bankers Trust (Delaware) v. 236 Beltway Investment, 865 F.Supp. 1186 (E.D.Va.1994). *Cf.* Tanenbaum v. Agri–Capital, Inc., 885 F.2d 464 (8th Cir. 1989) and Goss v. Trinity Sav. & Loan Ass'n, 1991 OK 19, 813 P.2d 492 (Okla. 1991). In addition, in consumer notes the required Federal Trade Commission notice, which must appear in many notes and that evidences an agreement allowing the assertion of claims and defenses in consumer transactions, under old article 3 destroyed negotiability. *Cf.* current § 3–106(d) and § 3–305(e). *See* Official Comment 3 to § 3–106. In Henry v. Cobb Bank & Trust Co., 151 Ga. App. Ct. 725, 151 Ga.App. 725, 261 S.E.2d 459 (Ga.Ct.App.1979), the court held that a note, stating on its face that it was not negotiable, was not negotiable by reason of the agreement of the parties. *See also* Amarillo Nat'l Bank v. Dilday, 693 S.W.2d 38 (Tex.Ct.App.1985); First Nat'l Bank v. Duncan Sav. & Loan Ass'n, 656 F.Supp. 358 (W.D.Okla.1987), *aff'd,* 957 F.2d 775 (10th Cir.1992); and First State Bank v. Clark, 91 N.M. 117, 570 P.2d 1144

these separate promises to pay also continue to be transferred, and perhaps even are assumed to be governed by Article 3.

Overall many circumstances tend to make modern notes not negotiable. Notes taken in conjunction with real estate transactions commonly by their terms are made expressly subject to other agreements, such as mortgages and construction loan contracts, so as to incorporate events of default and other matters. If the promise of the note is thereby made conditional, negotiability is destroyed.[11] The problem is not limited to notes. Drafts and checks are equally open to the possibility of being nonnegotiable. For example, it can be argued that the legend "void after 90 days," which commonly appears on checks, impermissibly conditions a check's order with the result that the check is no longer a negotiable instrument.[12] Nevertheless, these instruments generally are treated by the parties and by the bank collection system without regard to their technical lack of negotiability.

[b] Problems Where the Form of the Instrument Is Inadequate

What problems result from the fact that a changed legal environment or different commercial practice have bypassed some of the requirements of Article 3 for negotiable instruments? First, to the extent the instrument is not negotiable in form, absent agreement (unusual in a negotiable instrument) no assignee of the right of payment that the instrument represents can take free of claims to the instrument and defenses to its payment; in short, there can be no holder in due course. However, although the achievement of holder in due course status may have been an original impetus for the special rules that Article 3 now embodies, this status may no longer be as important as it once was, if it is still important at all.[13]

Moreover, if the instrument is not negotiable, other consequences also follow. The main thing is that it is uncertain that the governing law

---

(1977). The rule is now reflected in § 3–104(d). Checks, however, are not within the rule.

Under Article 3, the inclusion of the required FTC notice, or a similar one mandated by state law, does not destroy negotiability, only the possibility of holder in due course status. § 3–106(d). However, even beyond these circumstances the complexity of modern commercial notes makes them particularly susceptible to an argument their terms do not meet the requirements for negotiability.

11. A promise is not unconditional if the instrument states that it is subject to or governed by any other agreement. §§ 3–104(a) and 3–106. The default issue will be discussed, *infra*, this chapter.

12. This point is discussed, *infra*.

13. One might argue it is important at least for checks because banks may not allow use of provisional credit unless they have the status to enforce the instrument if it is not paid. *See, e.g.*, Citizens Nat'l Bank v. Fort Lee Sav. & Loan Ass'n, 89 N.J.Super. 43, 213 A.2d 315 (Law Div.1965). It may be asked, why would a bank rely on the creditworthiness of a drawer or indorser it might not know, as opposed to the standing of its own customer? But it might be argued the doctrine is of greater importance since Regulation CC, 12 C.F.R. pt. 229, and mandated earlier funds availability. However, after Maine Family Fed. Credit Union v. Sun Life Assurance Company, 1999 ME 43, 727 A.2d 335 (Me.1999), which casts serious doubt on holder in due course status in that context, that argument may be weak. Nonetheless, whatever the true case, § 3–104 accords greater negotiability to checks than old Article 3 did.

for the instrument is Article 3; rather, it may be general contract law, which may be old, outdated, and unclear; in short, a much less certain legal structure may apply.[14] If certainty is a requisite for the acceptability of commercial paper, a significant problem may then exist.[15]

Finally, one should not overlook the potential loss of the other benefits of Article 3 beyond those mentioned here.[16] Thus, if it is assumed that negotiability is desirable, it is clear that the outdated nature of the requirements for negotiability needs to be addressed. The question then is, how may this be accomplished?

[c] Solutions

Ultimately amendments to the statute to conform the law to commercial practice and the modern legal environment are the only solution, and current Article 3 does that in a selective way, such as by including within its coverage variable rate notes and making it clear that a Federal Trade Commission notice to preserve consumer claims and defenses only has a limited impact on negotiability. In an earlier edition of this book, a more radical approach was suggested: a new definition of negotiable instrument to replace that of § 3–104(a), as follows and as updated:

(a) Subject to subsections (c) and (d), any writing to be a negotiable instrument within this article must be

   (a) signed by the maker or drawer;

   (b) for the payment, or evidence a right to the payment, of money; and

   (c) of a type which in the ordinary course of business is transferred by delivery with any necessary indorsement or assignment.[17]

This definition would remove any requirement that a negotiable instrument contain an unconditional promise or order to pay a fixed sum on demand or at a definite time and that it contain words of negotiability and not contain excessive other promises or orders.[18] If such an instrument is treated now in commercial practice as if it were a negotiable instrument, as is true under Article 9, there arguably is no reason why the law should treat it otherwise.[19] If the context in which the instrument arises or in which it will be used demands the additional certainty

---

14. Then, again, this perception may be equally a myth since the common law has developed. See the discussion, *supra*, in Chapter 1.

15. *Supra*, this chapter.

16. These are described in Chapter 1.

17. This definition is drawn from the definition of "item" in old § 4–104(1)(g) and the definition of "instrument" in § 9–102(a)(47). The definition represents a further extension of the development discussed in the comment to old § 3–805, and the development discussed immediately following in the text. Of course, other amendments to Article 3 also would be required, such as the revision of sections like §§ 3–106–3–109 which elaborate upon those parts of the definition of negotiable instrument that were being dropped.

18. Thus, § 3–104(a) and 3–103(a) would be substantially modified.

19. See UCC § 1–103(a). The UCC is designed to modernize commercial law and permit continued expansion through custom and agreement.

of an unconditional promise or order, a certain sum, a definite time for payment, or an instrument that is trim and without "luggage," the parties may contract accordingly.

This argument won some currency during the drafting process to revise old Article 3, and at one point the draft scope provision for Article 3 was considerably expanded, before being ultimately restricted to a scope that closely approximates that of old Article 3, but with some changes such as those already noted and others that are further described in this chapter. The argument for an expanded scope lost out for three principal reasons:

(1) the more the Article 3 door is opened to let additional contracts enter, the less justification exists for a separate body of rules to govern a less narrowly defined type of contract; and there also was some sentiment that the negotiable instrument rules were not that superior to the modern rules of contract law, or appropriate for chattel paper, and thus the present rules governing other contracts that would be included should not be displaced on a broader scale;

(2) the proposal would require proof of business practice in every case, as opposed to at least supposed ease of determination involving a bright line test and thus unduly complicate the analysis of negotiable instrument cases; this was thought to be undesirable given the experience with the similar test under UCC Article 9; and

(3) it was unclear what business practice actually was concerning the broader range of contracts that would be included, and thus just what was being authorized for the extraordinary rules of Article 3 such as holder in due course; for example, would the test authorize the assignee of a retail installment contract to take free of defenses to its payment even though arguably no commercial need for such a consequence had seemingly developed?

Of course, as to this latter point, the parties could provide for that result by agreement, through a so-called "waiver of defenses" clause, and also a court could reach that result without the mandate of Article 3. These observations, it was determined, should be emphasized by Article 3 and that, plus surgical-type amendments to address specific scope problems, would be adequate to update the statute.

Accordingly, Official Comment 2 to § 3–104 explicitly invites courts to continue the process in which some of them have been engaged under old Article 3. These courts apply the provisions of Article 3 by analogy, rather than ordinary contract law, to instruments that the parties treat as commercial paper, even though the instruments do not technically qualify as such.[20] Creating a common law by fashioning or borrowing rules from commercial and banking practice is nothing new for courts

---

20. The extent to which courts are presently using Article 3 by analogy was discussed in Chapter 1.

and is a task they are fully capable of performing.[21] This approach has several defects, however. One is the time consumed to complete it. Another is the many cases that must be consulted to ascertain the law. Ultimately, it is an uncertain process because the parties never can be sure a court will apply the rule they contemplate.[22] It was these very deficiencies that led to the codification of negotiable instruments law in the first place. Nevertheless, employing Article 3 by analogy is a process that, in a given case, can be useful.

The other method to allow Article 3 to keep pace with commercial practice and the modern legal environment is to employ the general ability of the parties to vary the effect of the provisions of the Uniform Commercial Code by agreement.[23] This is discussed below.

[3] Indirectly Obtaining the Benefits of Article 3

[a] General Inability to Invoke Rules of Article 3 by Agreement

The Uniform Commercial Code generally allows the effect of its provisions to be varied by agreement.[24] If an instrument is known not to meet the form requirements and therefore will not be governed by Article 3 (perhaps because it is subject to another agreement and the promise or order is not unconditional), can the parties simply agree that the instrument will be negotiable? In short, is it possible to contract into Article 3?

The parties to an instrument that does not qualify in form under Article 3 cannot directly invoke the benefits (or burdens) of Article 3 by agreement or conduct. Freedom of contract stops where the UCC otherwise provides,[25] and old § 3–104(1) stated at its inception that to qualify as a negotiable instrument, any writing must meet the requirements of that subsection.[26] Various comments to old § 3–104 made the message unmistakable.[27]

[b] Other Methods of Achieving Aspects of Negotiability

The denial of the benefits of Article 3 for instruments of improper form should not be construed to mean that the position the parties to an

---

21. This, of course, is how the law merchant, from which the Negotiable Instruments Law and then the Uniform Commercial Code were derived, was created. The process continued even after codification. Official Comment to old § 3–805.

22. See the discussion in Chapter 1.

23. See UCC § 1–302, generally allowing variation by agreement.

24. Id.

25. Id. For example, the obligations of good faith and care may not be disclaimed by agreement. See, e.g., Continental Airlines, Inc. v. Boatmen's National Bank, 13 F.3d 1254 (8th Cir.1994).

26. Instruments under old § 3–805 were the only exception. Current Article 3 reaches the same point, except not so explicitly. See §§ 3–102(a) and 3–104(a).

27. Official Comment 1 to UCC § 1–302 is equally pointed: "Thus, private parties cannot make an instrument negotiable within the meaning of Article 3 except as provided in Section 3–104...." See, for example, Ferguson Pontiac–GMC, Inc. v. Henson, 1994 OK CIV APP 179, 892 P.2d 657 (Okla.App.1994) (instrument not meeting requirements for a "check" was not a check even though labeled "certified banker's check").

instrument would have if it were governed by Article 3 cannot be reached other than through Article 3. Even before negotiability requirements were codified, the argument was made that unless the form was correct, all benefits of negotiability should be denied. The argument was found wanting. In *Goodwin v. Robarts*,[28] as against the argument that the instrument involved was not payable in money and thus was not negotiable, the court stated that this argument could not prevail because it was founded on the premise that the law merchant was fixed and incapable of being expanded and enlarged in order to meet the needs and requirements of trade in the varying circumstances of commerce.

Occasionally the *Goodwin* doctrine is forgotten,[29] but it is continued under the Uniform Commercial Code. An Official Comment declares that the language of § 3–104[30] leaves open the possibility that some writings may be made negotiable by judicial decision. Moreover, statutory examples exist within the UCC itself: documents of title, which may have the attribute of negotiability pursuant to Article 7;[31] certificated investment securities, which may have that attribute in accordance with Article 8;[32] and even ordinary contracts qualifying as security agreements under Article 9, if they contain a so-called "waiver of defenses" clause which, under ordinary contract rules of estoppel, operates to preclude the obligor from asserting a defense against a bona fide purchaser.[33]

As previously noted, creating negotiability by judicial decision for writings not negotiable under Article 3 is an uncertain process. However, if a form of holder in due course status, often considered the essence of negotiability, can be achieved by statutory authorization through a waiver of defenses clause, cannot other benefits of a negotiable instrument be achieved by agreement? In short, while the parties cannot contract directly into Article 3, there should be no general legal impediment to contracting for the various attributes of negotiability. If there was any doubt about this proposition, Official Comment 2 to § 3–104 makes it explicitly clear this is permitted. Nonetheless, two possible difficulties in resolving all matters in this manner exist.

The first is that the parties may fail to recognize the need to so contract, so no benefit is obtained. This is a risk about which little can be done. Second, even if the need to contract is perceived, the task of contracting for the individual benefits of Article 3 could be an extensive one and, if so, probably would require too much language even for the

---

28. L.R. 10 Ex. 76, *aff'd* 10 Ex. 337 (1875).

29. In Unico v. Owen, 50 N.J. 101, 232 A.2d 405 (1967), the court invalidated a clause attempting to invest a sale agreement with an attribute of negotiability on the ground the clause was opposed to the Negotiable Instruments Law. Under the UCC, *see* Fairfield Credit Corp. v. Donnelly, 158 Conn. 543, 264 A.2d 547 (1969). Compare these cases with Ashford v. Thomas Cook & Son (Bankers), Ltd., 52 Haw. 113, 471 P.2d 530 (1970) (travelers checks have acquired negotiable characteristics by established custom and public acceptance).

30. Official Comment 2 to UCC § 3–104.

31. *See* UCC §§ 7–104(1), 7–502, 7–504.

32. *See* UCC §§ 8–102(a)(4), 8–301, 8–303.

33. *See* UCC § 9–403. *See also*, UCC § 2A–407(3) ("hell or high water" clause).

most detailed forms of instruments.[34] Selective use of this approach, however, might involve coverage of one or several of the following points, as appropriate and as the parties are able to agree:

(1) The greater undertaking of an indorser as compared to an assignor under § 3–415, and transferor warranties similar to those of § 3–416;

(2) To the extent not prohibited by law, a waiver of defenses provision to grant to an assignee the greater ability to enforce the contract similar to the rights provided a holder in due course in § 3–305(b);

(3) The rules as to alteration and incomplete instruments of § 3–407;

(4) The rules as to the liability of accommodation parties and representatives, as set out in §§ 3–419 and 3–402;

(5) The rules as to discharge, particularly those contained in § 3–605; and

(6) The effect of the instrument on the underlying obligation, as set out in § 3–310.

On the other hand, if selective coverage is not bargained for, a general approach similar to incorporation should be valid, and the following provision should bind the parties and any other persons who assert rights with respect to an instrument with this language in it: "The parties agree that should a court determine that this instrument is not subject to Article 3 of the Uniform Commercial Code as enacted in _____ (Name of State), the parties agree that their rights and obligations, and those of other persons, with respect to this instrument shall be governed by the rules set forth in Article 3 of the Uniform Commercial Code as enacted in _____ (Name of State)." This clause may be viewed as nothing more or less than a form of choice of law clause which should be upheld absent contrary public policy, and no such policy would seem to exist.

¶ 2.02 Form Requirements for Negotiable Instruments

Absent agreement or application by analogy, to be a negotiable instrument under Article 3, with few exceptions an instrument must: be written; be signed by the maker or drawer; contain an unconditional promise or order to pay a fixed sum in money and no other undertaking or instruction given by the maker or drawer except as authorized in Article 3; be payable on demand or at a definite time; and be payable to order or to bearer.[35]

---

34. The list of differences between Article 3 and ordinary contract law is discussed in Chapter 1. *See also* the Official Comment to old § 3–805. One might argue that a simple clause could merely incorporate most sections of Article 3 by reference, but a court might treat this, albeit erroneously, the same as an attempt to contract directly into Article 3.

¶ 2.02

35. §§ 3–104(a) and 3–103(a).

[1] Written Instrument

To be within Article 3, the instrument must be written,[36] that is, intentionally reduced to tangible form by printing, typing, handwriting, or otherwise.[37] Although literally the instrument can be written on anything, at least for checks the necessity of handling large volumes of them exerts an important influence, making the writing uniform in style and form.

[2] Signing

[a] Creation of Liability on an Instrument

An instrument within Article 3 is a specialized form of written contract. Because assent is necessary to any contract, for a writing to be a negotiable instrument it must be signed by the maker or drawer to evidence that assent.[38] No person is liable on an instrument unless its signature appears thereon.[39]

[b] Definition of "Signed"

Signing an instrument includes using any symbol executed or adopted with the present intention to adopt or or accept a writing.[40] A signature may be made by the use of any name, including any trade or assumed name, on an instrument, or by any word or mark used in lieu of a written signature.[41] A signature may be handwritten, typed, printed, stamped, or may be made in any other manner, as by initials, by mark, by machine, or even by thumbprint. A complete signature is not necessary; it need not be subscribed; it may appear in the body of the instrument without any other signature, or on any part of the document, and in an appropriate case may be found in a billhead or letterhead.[42]

These provisions are extremely liberal. For example, the signatures of two of three partners were held to constitute the partnership's signature in accordance with an agreement to that effect.[43] A note signed in his own name by one of two partners, who also inserted beneath his

---

36. §§ 3–103(a)(6) and (9), 3–104(a). See also notes 6, *supra* and 64, *infra*. But see UETA § 16.

37. UCC § 1–201(b)(43). *Cf.* UETA § 16.

38. §§ 3–103(a)(6) and (9), 3–104(a). See also note 6, *supra*. In Central Bank v. Kaiperm Santa Clara Fed. Credit Union, 191 Cal.App.3d 186, 236 Cal.Rptr. 262 (6th Dist.1987), the issue was whether blank money order forms, which had been stolen, were governed by Article 3. The court held that inasmuch as in practice the bank did not require a drawer's signature to pay, the unauthorized completed forms did not qualify as negotiable instruments.

39. This rule does not prevent liability apart from the instrument, as discussed in Chapter 7. Issues of agency (*see* Chapter 5) and unauthorized signatures are discussed later (*see*, *infra*, Chapters 4, 6, and 7). The point considered here is the basic rule and what may be considered to be a signature.

Section 3–401(a) does allow an undisclosed principal to be bound by the personal signature of an agent. See §§ 3–401(a)(ii) and 3–402(a), Official Comment 1 to § 3–402.

40. UCC § 1–201(b)(37). *Cf.* §§ 3–602(f), 3–604(c).

41. Official Comment 37 to § 1–201 and § 3–401(b) and Official Comment 2 to that section.

42. *Id.* Other considerations also may be relevant, however. See, for example, 25 Okla. Stat. § 26.

43. Wolfe v. University Nat'l Bank, 270 Md. 70, 310 A.2d 558 (1973).

name the trade name of the partnership, "Desert Inn," and its address, was determined by the court, given evidence that the note was intended to cover a debt of the partnership, to have been signed by the partnership so that the other partner also was liable.[44] Invariably signatures involving an incorrect or imprecise corporate designation are upheld. Thus courts have validated "Steel Fabricators & Equipment, Inc.," for "Steel Fabricators and Erectors, Inc.;"[45] "Central American Steel," instead of "Central American Steel of Texas, Inc.,"[46] and, with the help of old § 3–307,[47] "Greenlaw and Sons" instead of "Greenlaw and Sons Roofing and Siding Co."[48]

On the other hand, no name, mark, or symbol will constitute a signature unless used with the present intention of adopting or accepting the writing. Thus in *Pollin v. Mindy Manufacturing Co.*,[49] the court held that a check, on which the name of a corporation was printed with two lines beneath it, neither of which were filled in, was not the executed instrument of the corporation. By similar reasoning, another court held that a form of certification impressed on a check by rubber stamp was not sufficient to constitute the bank's signature and thus an acceptance, where the form included a line for a signature but no signature was placed on the line.[50] In *Littky & Mallon v. Michigan National Bank*,[51] the court refused to permit a name imprinted at the top of a check to overcome an unauthorized written signature in the normal place. Finally, several cases under old Article 3 determined that money orders, issued by a bank and bearing its printed name as drawee, were ordinary checks, and the holder of the instrument had no right to compel payment from the drawee because its name on the money order was not a signature constituting a promise by the drawee to pay.[52]

[c] *Weight Accorded to Signatures*

The physical presence of what appears to be the signature of the maker or drawer (or any other party) on an instrument goes to the

---

44. McCollum v. Steitz, 261 Cal.App.2d 76, 67 Cal.Rptr. 703 (5th Dist.1968).

45. Atlas Steel Corp. v. Steel Fabricators & Erectors, Inc., 12 UCC Rep. Serv. 910 (Mass.Ct.App.1973).

46. Roland v. Republic Nat'l Bank, 463 S.W.2d 747 (Tex.Civ.App.1971), *writ ref. n. r. e.* (May 26, 1971).

47. Current § 3–308.

48. Watertown Fed. Sav. & Loan Ass'n v. Spanks, 346 Mass. 398, 193 N.E.2d 333 (1963).

49. 211 Pa.Super. 87, 236 A.2d 542 (1967).

50. Menke v. Board of Educ., 211 N.W.2d 601 (Iowa 1973).

51. 94 Mich.App. 29, 287 N.W.2d 359 (1979).

52. *See, e.g.*, Krom v. Chemical Bank New York Trust Co., 38 A.D.2d 871, 329 N.Y.S.2d 91 (1972); Garden Check Cashing Serv., Inc. v. First Nat'l City Bank, 25 A.D.2d 137, 267 N.Y.S.2d 698, *aff'd*, 18 N.Y.2d 941, 277 N.Y.S.2d 141, 223 N.E.2d 566 (N.Y. 1966). *But see* Sequoyah State Bank v. Union Nat'l Bank, 274 Ark. 1, 621 S.W.2d 683 (Ark. 1981); Interfirst Bank Carrollton v. Northpark Nat'l Bank, 671 S.W.2d 100 (Tex.Ct.App.1984). Section § 3–104 now settles the split in the cases; it adopts the better authority and basically treats a money order as an ordinary check. *See* § 3–104, Official Comment 4. On the other hand, in Jacoby Transp. Sys., Inc. v. Continental Bank, 277 Pa.Super. 440, 419 A.2d 1227 (1980), checks printed with the corporate name where a signature normally would go but with no signature line appearing were determined to be signed. Contrast this result with that in the *Central Bank* case, *supra* note 38.

purpose of adopting or accepting the instrument, but Article 3 also accords considerable emphasis to the function of attribution for a purported signature. Unless specifically denied in the pleading, each signature on an instrument is admitted.[53] Many makers and drawers who have filed a general denial to the complaint of the holder of the instrument have admitted their signatures under this rule.[54] Even if the effectiveness of a signature is put in issue, thereby avoiding this pleading pitfall, the signature is presumed to be genuine and authorized except in an action to enforce the obligation of a purported signer who has died or become incompetent.[55] Under this rule, most courts have determined that simply denying that a signature is valid is not enough to raise a defense.[56] Rather, something more is required, such as stating facts sufficient to support a finding that the signature was forged or unauthorized.[57] When signatures are admitted or established, production of the instrument entitles the holder to recover on it unless the defendant establishes a defense.[58]

[3] Limited and Unconditional Promise or Order

The policy of certainty as to the terms of an instrument, which is the original reason for the form requirements for a negotiable instrument, is strongly reflected in the rule that to be an instrument within the coverage of Article 3, the writing must contain a limited and unconditional promise or order.[59]

[a] Nature of Promise or Order

[i] Informal Instruments

The problem of informal instruments is not of major importance. Because anyone can draw an instrument, however, questions will arise as to whether the writing really is a draft or a note.

---

53. § 3–308(a). These rules are not limited to drawers and makers. The signature of an indorser or an acceptor would be included.

54. *See, e.g.*, Mechanics Nat'l Bank v. Shear, 7 Mass.App.Ct. 255, 386 N.E.2d 1299 (1979); Household Fin. Co. v. Watson, 522 S.W.2d 111 (Mo.Ct.App.1975); Holland v. First Nat'l Bank, 597 S.W.2d 406 (Tex.Civ. App.1980). *But see* Spurlock v. Commercial Banking Co., 151 Ga.App. 892, 260 S.E.2d 912 (Ga.Ct.App.1979) (under Georgia law denial of execution of contract is no longer a defense that must be affirmatively pled).

55. § 3–308(a).

56. *E.g.*, Burkett v. Finger Lake Dev. Corp., 32 Ill.App.3d 396, 336 N.E.2d 628 (Ill.Ct.App.1975); Virginia Nat'l Bank v. Holt, 216 Va. 500, 219 S.E.2d 881 (1975).

57. Under UCC § 1–201(b)(41) an "unauthorized" signature means one made without actual, implied or apparent authority and includes a forgery. *Compare* B & C Enter. v. Utter, 88 Nev. 433, 498 P.2d 1327 (1972) (proof that focused on whether there was a formal corporate authorization inadequate) *with* McCusker v. Fascione, 117 R.I. 478, 368 A.2d 1220 (1977) (denial by all three purported makers of notes that one of them had signed was sufficient as to that signature).

58. § 3–308(b). *See, e.g.*, Leopold v. Halleck, 106 Ill.App.3d 386, 62 Ill.Dec. 447, 436 N.E.2d 29 (1982); Tuttle v. Rose, 102 Ill. App.3d 865, 58 Ill.Dec. 414, 430 N.E.2d 356 (1981). Section 3–308(b) explicitly also includes a claim in recoupment. For this purpose, forgery and alteration also should be considered as defenses.

59. § 3–104(a).

To be a draft, there must be an "order."[60] An order is a direction to pay. It must be more than an authorization or a request.[61] The prefixing of words of courtesy to the direction is not fatal, but informal language, such as "I wish you would pay," will not suffice.[62] In drawing the line, it should be remembered that "homemade" instruments are of such little commercial importance, and would seem to have little need for the special rules of Article 3 as opposed to other contract law, so that bending the form requirement to any degree to accommodate them produces more uncertainty than it is worth. If a writing comes fairly within the requirements, informality will not disqualify it. Thus, "checks" written on envelopes rather than on regular forms may come within Article 3.[63] In another case, a telex communication, although not phrased in terms of a demand, was held to contain an order for the immediate payment of money.[64]

As for notes, a "promise" is an undertaking to pay and must be more than an acknowledgment of an obligation.[65] The word "promise" need not be used if a clear equivalent is found, such as "undertake." The requirement is intended to exclude mere IOUs and to deny negotiability to instruments merely stating that a certain amount is due to a specified person for value received, or which acknowledge a loan and state the money ought to be repaid within a specified period.[66]

[ii] *Excessive Luggage Encumbering the Promise or Order*

To facilitate the easy recognition of negotiable instruments and thus their easy transferability, it has been said that a negotiable instrument must be a "courier without luggage."[67] In so many words, it would appear the thought is that the more an instrument contains, the more difficult it is to distinguish it from an ordinary contract. The UCC continues this requirement in providing that an instrument, to be negotiable within Article 3, must contain no undertaking or instruction given by the maker or drawer, other than an unconditional promise or order to pay a fixed sum in money, except as authorized by Article 3.[68]

---

60. § 3–104(e).

61. § 3–103(a)(6).

62. Official Comment 2 to old § 3–102.

63. Wiley, Tate & Irby v. Peoples Bank & Trust Co., 438 F.2d 513 (5th Cir.1971).

64. Chase Manhattan Bank, N.A. v. Equibank, 394 F.Supp. 352 (W.D.Pa.1975), *vacated on other grounds*, 550 F.2d 882 (3d Cir.1977). *See also* TeleRecovery of Louisiana, Inc. v. Gaulon, 738 So.2d 662 (La. App. 1999), *writ denied*, 751 So.2d 224 (La.1999) (gambling markers held to be checks). On the other hand, the court in Houston Contracting Co. v. Chase Manhattan Bank, N.A., 539 F.Supp. 247 (S.D.N.Y.1982), found an unsigned telex was not a negotiable instrument. The Seventh Circuit in Evra Corp. v. Swiss Bank Corp., 673 F.2d 951 (7th Cir.1982), *cert. denied*, 459 U.S. 1017, 103 S.Ct. 377, 74 L.Ed.2d 511 (1982), the Fifth Circuit in Bradford Trust Co. v. Texas American Bank—Houston, 790 F.2d 407 (5th Cir.1986), and the Second Circuit in Delbrueck & Co. v. Manufacturers Hanover Trust Co., 609 F.2d 1047 (2d Cir.1979), plus other district courts, have all determined that a payment message in the form of an electronic funds transfer is not covered by Articles 3 and 4 of the Code. They are now governed by UCC Article 4A, discussed later in this book. *See* §§ 3–102(a) and 4–104(a)(9).

65. § 3–103(a)(9).

66. Official Comment 3 to § 3–103.

67. Overton v. Tyler, 3 Pa. 346 (1846).

68. § 3–104(a)(3).

The express exceptions authorized by Article 3 actually allow a fair amount of "luggage."[69] A number of other Article 3 provisions also hardly restrict the number of words that may appear in an instrument. An example was old § 3–105(1)(b), which allowed a statement of the consideration for the instrument or a reference to the transaction which gave rise to it.[70] Thus, strictly speaking, that an instrument contains language beyond that necessary to define it as a negotiable instrument under § 3–104 is not the test. The test is whether it contains another promise, order, obligation, or power beyond the payment of money and beyond the authorization of what is allowed in Article 3. Therefore, even if, as in one case, the writing contains a number of provisions set forth in approximately eighteen hundred words, theoretically the point is not the volume of the language but what the language does or does not provide.[71]

[A] Provisions Relating to Collateral

To be more specific as to what an instrument may contain without exceeding permitted limits, it may contain a statement that collateral has been or will be given to secure obligations, presumably either on the instrument or otherwise of an obligor on the instrument, or that in case of default on those obligations the holder may realize on or dispose of the collateral.[72] Although this provision essentially seems directed at authorizing a statement in the instrument that it is secured,[73] it also permits the inclusion of a clause authorizing the sale or disposition of collateral upon any default, whether in payment or otherwise. That, of course, would represent an additional power given by the maker or drawer in the instrument. In one case the provision was construed in that manner in connection with a premium finance agreement, to sanction a grant in the instrument of authority to the payee or assignee to cancel the insurance policy in the event of default and apply the return premiums against the unpaid balance.[74]

Other cases, however, which do not seem different in kind have been

---

69. See § 3–104(a)(3)(i) through (iii). No change in substance from prior law is intended. § 3–104 Official Comment 1.

70. § 3–106(a) clears away much of this legal underbrush as unnecessary but, again, no change in substance is intended. Official Comment 1 to § 3–106. However, the result is prior law that no longer is expressly reflected in the statute remains relevant. See also TeleRecovery of Louisiana, Inc. v. Gaulon, 738 So.2d 662 (La.App.1999), writ denied, 751 So.2d 224 (La.1999), where the instrument stated the drawer agreed to payment according to the terms of the Credit Payment Agreement previously executed, and the court construed this to be merely a reference to the Credit Payment Agreement and not a condition to payment.

71. See Akron Auto Fin. Co. v. Stonebraker, 66 Ohio App. 507, 35 N.E.2d 585 (1941). The case was decided before the UCC, but the point is the same. Not surprisingly, in with all the words, other promises rendering the instrument nonnegotiable were located by the court.

72. § 3–104(a)(3)(i) and (ii).

73. The court in Vinick v. Fourth Nat'l Bank, 1974 OK 145, 531 P.2d 327 (Okla. 1974), determined that a recital in a note, that a savings account passbook was deposited as collateral security for the payment of the note or any other indebtedness of the makers, did not affect the negotiability of the note.

74. Standard Premium Plan Corp. v. Hirschorn, 56 Misc.2d 687, 290 N.Y.S.2d 226 (N.Y.Civ.Ct.1968).

less liberal in their reading of the provision.[75] Probably the difference in result in these cases does not lie so much in differing interpretations of this provision as much as in the fact that the writings in the latter cases were sales contracts. These writings generally not only include a promise to pay money but also evidence the entire transaction between the seller and the buyer.[76] Accordingly, while the law never really has demanded a "bare-bones" instrument, the courts tend to approach writings, embodying an entire sales transaction, with its mutual obligations, with almost a presumption against negotiability,[77] and as a result invariably find somewhere in the language an impermissible "other promise or order" beyond what is allowed in negotiable instruments.[78] In *Pacific Finance Loans v. Goodwin*[79] and in *Geiger Finance Co. v. Graham*,[80] such a presumption was actually stated. The setting in which the writing is used, then, is helpful in understanding otherwise seemingly inconsistent results.[81]

The foregoing observation also helps to explain a number of additional older cases that otherwise seem difficult to reconcile with the statute. The words "obligations either on the instrument or otherwise of an obligor on the instrument," which appeared in old § 3–112(1)(b), were intended to recognize cross-collateral provisions that appear in collateral note forms used by banks and others, and to permit the use of these provisions without destroying negotiability. No reported case involving such a provision in the context of an otherwise negotiable note was located, but again, and notwithstanding the statute, in the context of a contract evidencing a sale, such a provision, or a clause of similar import, has contributed to a finding of nonnegotiability. For example, in

---

75. *E.g.*, All Lease Co. v. Bowen, 20 UCC Rep. Serv. 790 (Md.Cir.Ct.1975), where the writing allowed the seller to take possession of the goods pursuant to its security interest without judicial process, and the court held the contract was not negotiable. *See also* Ameritrust Company, N.A. v. White, 73 F.3d 1553 (11th Cir.1996), where the court determined that a provision stating that on non-payment any interest in the partnership interest for the price of which the note was given was forfeited rendered the note non-negotiable.

76. A true negotiable instrument is a simple promise to pay money without any strings attached and at most only references the transaction that gave rise to it. Discount Purchasing Co. v. Porch, 12 UCC Rep. Serv. 600 (Tenn.Ct.App.1973).

77. The mutual obligations could lead under normal contract law to an assumption of implied conditions, but this analysis clearly is not fully applicable in this context and is not enough to destroy negotiability per § 3–106(a)(i), which mandates an express condition.

78. Indeed, this observation is precisely the reason § 3–104(a)(3) retains this concept, as well as the requirement (except for checks) of "words of negotiability" in § 3–104(a)(1) and (c). *See* § 3–104 Official Comment 2.

79. 41 Ohio App.2d 141, 324 N.E.2d 578 (1974) (negotiability is a characteristic of such importance to commercial paper that any doubt is resolved against negotiability).

80. 123 Ga.App. 771, 182 S.E.2d 521 (Ga.Ct.App.1971) (where there is any doubt, the presumption is against negotiability).

81. A further part of that context also seems to be that some of the older cases involved consumer transactions. The courts seemed to believe that, if negotiability were denied, it either would open the door to other state legislation protecting consumers, or in itself would result in that protection. Today, this consideration is moot as §§ 3–302(g) and 3–305(e) and (f) explicitly defer to other protective law, which should be the result even absent such explicit deferral, and such other controlling law, as discussed *infra*, generally removes the need to strain to find a lack of negotiability.

one case an agreement that the terms of the contract might apply to subsequent sales was a factor in the court's denial of negotiability for the writing;[82] in another case a provision that the security interest would secure further or other indebtedness contributed to the court's decision that a retail installment contract and security agreement combined in one instrument did not constitute a negotiable instrument.[83]

Article 3 permits the inclusion in an instrument of an additional undertaking or instruction to maintain or protect collateral or to give additional collateral.[84] This provision was intended to operate in tandem with an acceleration clause, a provision broadly validated in § 3–108[85] and also by § 1–309. Again, no reported case involving such a clause in a "bare-bones" note was found, but clauses of this import in retail installment sale contracts have contributed to holdings denying negotiability.[86]

The ultimate question in connection with provisions authorizing undertakings and instructions in relation to collateral would be presented if the instrument itself contained a grant of a security interest together with customary accompanying terms. A respectable argument can be made that the slight additional step of including no more than a simple security agreement in an instrument is permissible. Once again, no reported case involving the issue of a security interest directly granted in a note alone was located,[87] but cases dealing with such clauses in retail installment sale contracts uniformly appear to find against negotiability.[88]

The observation that some courts seem to indulge in a presumption against negotiable status for sales contracts further helps to explain holdings denying negotiability in the retail installment sale context for

---

82. Geiger Fin. Co. v. Graham, 123 Ga. App. 771, 182 S.E.2d 521 (Ga.Ct.App.1971).

83. Wickware v. National Mortgage Corp., 1977 OK 81, 570 P.2d 330 (Okla. 1977). See also note 81, supra. Again, to the extent the fact the transaction was a consumer credit sale played a part, it is unlikely to be as important today. See, e.g., 1974 Unif. Consumer Credit Code §§ 3.301 through 3.303; Federal Trade Commission Credit Practices Rules, 16 CFR §§ 444.1 and 444.2(a)(4) (there are similar federal rules for banks and other financial institutions since the FTC does not have jurisdiction over them).

84. § 3–104(a)(3)(i).

85. § 3–108(b)(ii).

86. E.g., Geiger Fin. Co. v. Graham, 123 Ga.App. 771, 182 S.E.2d 521 (Ga.Ct.App. 1971) (the writing required the written consent of the holder for any transfer of the buyer's obligations and contained an application by the buyer for insurance); Insurance Agency Managers v. Gonzales, 578 S.W.2d 803 (Tex.Civ.App.1979) (the buyer promised to use the collateral primarily for consumer purposes and agreed it would remain in the buyer's possession). Some "consumer protection" against "due on transfer" clauses exists in real estate security law (see, e.g., G. Nelson & D. Whitman, Real Estate Finance Law §§ 5.21 through 5.26 (2d ed. 1985)), but has not been extended to personal property. But, then, real estate does not move.

87. But see In re Amex–Protein Devel. Corp., 504 F.2d 1056 (9th Cir.1974). Several cases decided prior to the UCC might be said to deny negotiability in this situation. See W. Britton, Handbook of the Law of Bills and Notes § 36 (2d ed. 1961). Whether this authority should carry over under the UCC is, however, perhaps another matter. See J. White & R. Summers, Handbook of the Law Under the Uniform Commercial Code pages 462–63 (1972).

88. E.g., Discount Purchasing Co. v. Porch, 12 UCC Rep. Serv. 600 (Tenn.Ct. App.1973) (that a retail installment contract granted security interest expressly cited in support of holding the instrument was not negotiable).

writings that involve other types of clauses that individually would be permissible. For example, in two cases the courts found objectionable a power in the holder to impose a delinquency charge for late payments.[89] Even if this clause were not insulated from question by the fact that the prohibition of § 3–104(a)(3) runs only to other undertakings[90] by the person promising,[91] the provision seems to fit squarely within the allowance of § 3–104(a) for other charges.[92] Several cases also have involved a waiver by the buyer of defenses that the buyer could have asserted against the seller,[93] or a provision for rebate of unearned finance charges.[94] The waiver clause should be allowable under § 3–104[95] permitting a term purporting to waive the benefit of any law intended for the advantage or protection of any obligor, and the rebate provision seems to fall within the protection that only other undertakings or instructions *by the person promising or ordering payment* are restricted.

These cases essentially represent a consistent line of authority suggesting that a combination of too many provisions, even if each alone may be valid, is harmful to negotiability. In short, at least in consumer transactions, the courts have been unwilling to find negotiability in cases involving writings that bear all the characteristics of other well-recog-

---

89. Geiger Fin. Co. v. Graham, 123 Ga. App. 771, 182 S.E.2d 521 (Ga.Ct.App.1971); All Lease Co. v. Bowen, 20 UCC Rep. Serv. 790 (Md.Cir.Ct.1975). This matter now is consistently regulated, as needed, by other law. *See e.g.*, 1974 Unif. Consumer Credit Code § 2.502 and Federal Trade Commission Credit Practices Rules, 16 CFR § 444.4.

90. Also instructions by the person ordering payment. § 3–104(a)(3).

91. *See* Universal C.I.T. Credit Corp. v. Ingel, 347 Mass. 119, 196 N.E.2d 847 (1964). In the *Ingel* case the court determined that a clause in a note containing a promise that the *holder* would obtain group credit life insurance on the maker did not affect negotiability. The court in Insurance Agency Managers v. Gonzales, 578 S.W.2d 803 (Tex.Civ.App.1979), overlooked the point that the promise must be by the maker when it objected to provisions authorizing the *holder* to waive particular remedies, to purchase insurance, and to pay taxes and demand payment. Of course, it can be argued that the power to impose a delinquency charge has two aspects because normally it must be agreed upon, and thus arguably perhaps it can be said to flow from a promise or power given by the maker.

The *Ingel* case is worthy of note in another respect. The court held that merely because the note and another document were "together" when executed (presumably they were part of the same package of forms, or perhaps were together on the same sheet separated by a perforated line) did not mean that they were "part of the same instrument" even though later separated. Thus an additional obligation in the other document was not permitted to render the note nonnegotiable. Any other holding would doom vast quantities of notes to nonnegotiable status, but this case must be distinguished from the retail installment sale contract situation where both the promise to pay and other provisions are contained in the same writing.

92. § 3–104(a), together with § 3–112, encompass in general terms the specific detail in old § 3–106, which is deleted. Except as explicit change is intended, as in the case of variable rate instruments, interpretations of the former provision should remain valid. A delinquency charge also seems the functional equivalent of a stated different rate of interest before or after default allowed in old § 3–106(1)(b).

93. Again, now regulated as necessary by other law. *See, e.g.*, 1974 Unif. Consumer Credit Code §§ 3.307, 3.404; Federal Trade Commission Rule on Preservation of Consumers' Claims and Defenses, 16 CFR pt. 433. Nonetheless, *see also* § 3–305(e) (and (f)); *compare* UCC §§ 9–403, 9–404.

94. Wickware v. National Mortgage Corp., 1977 OK 81, 570 P.2d 330 (Okla. 1977); Discount Purchasing Co. v. Porch, 12 UCC Rep. Serv. 600 (Tenn.Ct.App.1973). As to regulation of rebates under other law, *see, e.g.*, 1974 Unif. Consumer Credit Code § 2.510.

95. § 3–104(a)(3)(iii).

nized contract forms.[96] This may suggest that in practice the cases may have added a "volume of language" test to the "no other undertaking or instruction" test actually present in Article 3. If so, it probably is a different way of assuring that a negotiable instrument can readily be recognized without undue analysis of many or most of its provisions, a process that would slow and perhaps unduly dampen the goal of easy transferability. Suffice to say, it may be safely concluded that ordinary contracts are in no great danger of being treated and should not be treated as negotiable instruments.[97]

As noted,[98] current Article 3 radically simplifies the detail on what constitutes a negotiable instrument on the premise that the law is well settled enough that Article 3 no longer needs to serve as a "museum of antiquities."[99] This observation applies equally to the following discussion.

[B] Other Provisions

Other provisions that will not impair negotiability but that do not relate to collateral also are sanctioned by Article 3. A term purporting to waive the benefit of any law intended for the advantage or protection of an obligor is permitted.[100] The customary example of this provision is a waiver of notice of an extension of time or of a renewal,[101] or of presentment, protest, or notice of dishonor.[102] These are matters that relate to Article 3.[103] This provision, however, may apply to a waiver of the benefits of a law outside of Article 3, such as a homestead exemption[104] or a law for the advantage or protection of an obligor like an accommodation party.[105]

There is considerable litigation concerning old § 3–112(1)(d),[106] which sanctioned a term authorizing a confession of judgment on the instrument if it was not paid when due. However, essentially the cases merely point out the distinction made in a comment to that section. Such a clause does not affect negotiability if a confession of judgment is authorized only if the instrument is not paid when due; otherwise, it does. Thus, courts have approved notes containing an authorization for confession of judgment if the note is not paid at any stated or accelerated

---

96. This may represent a policy concern over the concept of negotiability in this context. If so, these cases may no longer be of much relevance. *See* note 81 et seq., *supra*.

97. § 3–104, Official Comment 2.

98. Notes 69, 70, and 92, *supra*.

99. Gilmore, Formalism and the Law of Negotiable Instruments, 13 CREIGHTON L. REV. 441 (1979).

100. § 3–104(a)(3)(iii).

101. Vinick v. Fourth Nat'l Bank, 1974 OK 145, 531 P.2d 327 (Okla.1974).

102. Community Nat'l Bank v. Dawes, 369 Mass. 550, 340 N.E.2d 877 (1976).

103. § 3–605 and Article 3, Part 5. These matters are discussed in Chapter 4 and in Chapter 6, *infra*.

104. The ability to waive such a protection may be restricted by other law. *See, e.g.,* Federal Trade Commission Credit Practices Rules, 16 CFR § 444.2(a)(2).

105. *See* §§ 9–102(a)(59) and 3–419, but, as to the ability to waive, also see § 9–602 and Official Comment 4 to that section.

106. Current § 3–104(a)(3)(ii). Given current consumer protection rules this matter should be mainly one of historical interest. *See* Federal Trade Commission Credit Practices Rules 16 CFR § 444.2(a)(1), and 1974 Unif. Consumer Credit Code § 3.306.

maturity.[107] On the other hand, notes that provide that judgment could be confessed "at any time after date,"[108] "as of any term,"[109] or which use similar language,[110] have been held not to be negotiable.

Finally, old Article 3[111] allowed a term in a draft providing that the payee, by indorsing or cashing it, acknowledges full satisfaction of an obligation of the drawer,[112] and also a statement in a draft drawn in a set of parts to the effect that the order is effective only if no other part has been honored.[113]

The authorizations in Article 3 as to other undertakings or instructions explicitly relate only to the negotiable or nonnegotiable status of the instrument and do not validate any term otherwise illegal.[114] These terms often are the subject of other laws as noted in this discussion.

[b] The Instrument in Relation to the Transaction Out of Which It Arose

[i] References Versus Incorporation

[A] Permitted References

A negotiable instrument is issued to evidence or facilitate the payment obligation in a larger, separate agreement. That agreement may constitute a sale of property or services, or a loan. This fact itself does not affect the negotiability of the instrument.[115] Indeed, the purpose of limiting a negotiable instrument to a basic promise or order to pay money[116] is to sever that aspect of the agreement, which can be easily evaluated by a prospective taker of the instrument, from the remainder of the agreement that gave rise to the instrument, which the prospective taker cannot so easily evaluate or perhaps even know about.

---

107. *E.g.*, Broadway Management Corp. v. Briggs, 30 Ill.App.3d 403, 332 N.E.2d 131 (1975).

108. *E.g.*, Marengo State Bank v. Meyers, 89 Ill.App.2d 421, 232 N.E.2d 75 (1967).

109. *E.g.*, von Frank v. Hershey Nat'l Bank, 269 Md. 138, 306 A.2d 207 (1973).

110. *E.g.*, Shatz v. Dunn, 18 Ill.App.3d 390, 309 N.E.2d 702 (1974).

111. Old § 3–112(1)(f).

112. *See* current § 3–311. The use of such a provision in context is discussed in Chapter 7.

113. Old § 3–112(1)(g). Current Article 3 omits old § 3–801, to which this provision relates, as a procedure that is no longer commercially relevant. Accordingly, this provision, which provides that the condition arising from such a statement, which but for this provision would presumably render the instrument nonnegotiable under § 3–104, also is no longer necessary. *See* old § 3–112, Official Comment 5, and old § 3–801, Official Comment 3.

114. Old § 3–112(2). Current Article 3 omits this and similar provisions, such as old § 3–106(2), as unnecessary to state the obvious.

115. Old § 3–119(2). *See, e.g.*, Northwestern Bank v. Neal, 271 S.C. 544, 248 S.E.2d 585 (1978) (note and separate conditional sales contract, executed together, were not merged in law so as to make note nonnegotiable). There is no similar explicit statement in current Article 3 but no change in the law is intended. *See* § 3–106(a)(i).

116. The promise or order to pay money is one prerequisite to negotiability under §§ 3–104(a) and 3–103(a)(6) and (9). *See* In re George and Four Other Cases, 85 Bankr. 133 (Bankr.D.Kan.1988), *aff'd*, 119 B.R. 800 (D.Kan.1990) (PIK certificates redeemable for commodities not Article 3 instruments).

Because a negotiable instrument does not embody the whole agreement of the parties to it, but only a promise or order to pay,[117] one might think that the promise or order to pay is subject to implied or constructive conditions arising out of the balance of the agreement which destroy the expressly unconditional promise or order otherwise contained in the instrument itself. This is not the law.[118] For example, a recital in an instrument that it is given in return for an unperformed promise does not necessarily give rise to a condition that the instrument is not to be paid if the promise is not performed, so as to destroy negotiability.[119]

Of course, if a condition is expressed in the instrument itself, the instrument is not negotiable. Thus in one case the court found that the existence of conditions precedent to payment expressed in a letter of credit precluded the letter of credit from being a negotiable instrument.[120] A similar result was reached where a check bore restrictive notations to the effect that the check would be dishonored unless an award and contract had been made pursuant to the bid with which the check was submitted.[121] It is not uncommon for the promise to pay in a certificate of deposit to be expressly conditioned upon the issuer's consent to assignment. This clause has been held to destroy the unconditional nature of the promise.[122]

In *West Greeley National Bank v. Wygant*,[123] the court determined that a certificate of deposit payable on death was not a negotiable instrument because the promise was conditional. It also would not seem to be payable at a definite time.[124] A more important point is the holding in *United National Bank of Miami v. Airport Plaza Ltd.*[125] that a nonrecourse note is non-negotiable because there is no unconditional promise to pay a sum certain in money. In fact, the court's real point is that the note is payable only from a particular fund or source, and while that would have made the instrument non-negotiable under old Article 3, it

117. §§ 3–104(a), 3–103(a)(6) and (9).

118. § 3–106(a)(i) states the rule in an affirmative way: a promise or order is unconditional unless it states an express condition to payment.

119. § 3–106(a), because it states the rule affirmatively, does not repeat the negations of this idea that appeared in old § 3–105(1). Official Comment 1 to § 3–106. A statement in a draft drawn in a set of parts that the order is effective only if no other part has been honored likewise does not impair negotiability. See note 113, *supra*.

120. Shaffer v. Brooklyn Park Garden Apartments, 311 Minn. 452, 250 N.W.2d 172 (1977). *See also* § 3–106, Official Comment 1. This also is the rule for payment orders. See § 4A–104, Official Comment 3.

121. Opinion of Comptroller General of United States, 4 U.C.C. Rep. Serv. 1176 (1968) (Nos. B–162984, B–162985, B–163056). *See also* Calfo v. D.C. Stewart Co., 717 P.2d 697 (Utah 1986) (due in full on final closing). *Cf.* City of Deerfield Beach v. Florida Nat'l Bank, 428 So.2d 779 (Fla. Dist.Ct.App.1983), where the drawer included language of accord and satisfaction on a check which was crossed out by the payee. In a suit against his bank for paying an "altered check," the court stated the bank need not pay attention to language intended to operate as an accord an satisfaction and then monitor changes in it because, to so require, would be "an unjustified impediment to the flow of commerce." As to accord and satisfaction under Article 3, *see* Chapter 7, *infra*. As to the effect of other information on a check, *see infra* this discussion.

122. Citizens Nat'l Bank v. Bornstein, 374 So.2d 6 (Fla.1979).

123. 650 P.2d 1339 (Colo.Ct.App.1982).

124. § 3–108. *See* the discussion, *infra*.

125. 537 So. 2d 608 (Fla.Dist.Ct.App. 1988), *review denied*, 547 So. 2d 1209 (Fla. 1989).

will not under current Article 3.[126] A final class of writings are guarantees which are excluded on the basis of a conditional promise as well as in most instances the lack of a sum certain and definite time for payment[127] because the obligation to pay is conditioned upon the prior default of the principal.[128]

On the other hand, a normal method to bind a lease in the oil and gas industry is for a lease broker to issue a draft to the person whose property is being leased payable some stated number of days after approval of the title to the property. This may seem to be an expressly conditional order to pay,[129] but even so such a draft passes without question commercially, as in *Clawson v. Berklund*.[130] A closer question is raised by drafts and checks marked "Void after 90 days," or the like. Though this legend could be viewed as making the order conditional, it seems more appropriate to consider it nothing more than a reflection of the policy that presentment for payment of an instrument should be within a reasonable time,[131] and the parties may by agreement determine what is a reasonable time.[132] An equally pertinent issue in these legends is the obligation, if any, of the drawee to comply with them when in the automated processing of checks the check may never be examined. One draft of the 1990 amendments to Article 4 employed an approach similar to that of the court in the *Deerfield Beach* case, *supra* note 121, for legends such as "void after 90 days" and "not good for over $1000," to recognize the automated processing of checks. This provision was deleted when the decision was made to basically amend Article 4 only so far as necessary to integrate it with the revision of Article 3. Thus financial institutions must still contend with these legends, which may not be seen, on the assumption they might make the instrument not properly payable. The issue should be addressed in bank-customer agreements.

A like-kind issue is raised for depositary banks under § 3–312, dealing with lost, destroyed or stolen bank obligations, and which recognizes a claim which may allow the issuer not to pay when the instrument is presented for payment after a period. Assuming the risk is perceived when the check is taken, perhaps because the issuer has legended the instrument "payment must be sought within 90 days of date" in order to advise holders that the issuer may not be responsible, it may be minimized by a call to the issuer or perhaps by invoking an

---

126. Old § 3–105(2)(b); current § 3–106(b)(ii). *See* discussion, *infra*.

127. *See* discussion, *infra*.

128. *See, e.g.*, Gregoire v. Lowndes Bank, 176 W.Va. 296, 342 S.E.2d 264 (1986) and Kordick v. Merchants Nat'l Bank & Trust Co., 496 N.E.2d 119 (Ind.Ct.App. 1986). *Cf.* Davis v. Timeshare Travel Int'l, 489 So.2d 47 (Fla.Dist.Ct.App.1986), where the point was not raised.

129. It also may appear to be an order not payable at a definite time, but this variation of payment on sight is treated as definite. *See* § 3–108(b); *infra* ¶ 2.02[6].

130. 188 Mont. 48, 610 P.2d 1168 (1980). The legal issue does not seem to have been raised, however.

131. § 3–414(f).

132. UCC § 1–302(b). Perhaps a similar type case is Triffin v. Dillabough, 448 Pa.Super. 72, 670 A.2d 684 (1996), where a legend on American Express money orders, stating they would not be paid if altered or stolen or if an indorsement was missing or forged so recourse against the customer of the person cashing the instrument was necessary, was held not to impair negotiability.

exception against the depositor's right to funds and availability under Regulation CC § 229.13(e) (but the latter is uncertain). Finally, in several other cases that involved checks issued by insurance companies which contained the words "upon acceptance pay to the order of" before the name of the payee, the courts considered the words not to impose a condition to the order for payment.[133]

Old Article 3 further provided that the negotiability of an instrument was not destroyed:

> (1) by a reference in the instrument to a separate agreement for rights as to prepayment or acceleration;[134]
>
> (2) by references to the consideration (whether performed or promised) for, or to the transaction which gave rise to, the instrument;[135] or
>
> (3) by statements in the instrument that the promise or order is made or the instrument matures in accordance with or "as per" the underlying transaction;[136] the instrument arises out of a separate agreement;[137] the instrument is drawn under a letter of credit;[138] or the instrument is secured (whether by mortgage, reservation of title, or otherwise).[139]

A variety of cases have interpreted these kinds of references. Courts have held that:

> the negotiability of a trade acceptance is not affected by the fact that the instrument referred to the underlying transaction of a purchase of goods by the acceptor from the drawer;[140]
>
> a check which bore the words, "This check is in payment of the following," is negotiable;[141]
>
> a prepared indorsement, which read, "Earnest money deposit on loan to be made ... on or before December 3, 1969, per

---

133. *See, e.g.,* Lialios v. Home Ins. Cos., 87 Ill.App.3d 740, 43 Ill.Dec. 193, 410 N.E.2d 193 (1980); Standard Fed. Sav. & Loan Ass'n v. Citizens Ins. Co., 99 Mich. App. 338, 297 N.W.2d 656 (Mich.Ct.App. 1980).

134. Old § 3–105(1)(c). This provision was not present in the enactments of old Article 3 in all states. It was added to Article 3 to deal with a particular problem that is discussed, *infra*. A similar provision appears at current § 3–106(b)(i) and should resolve the issue discussed, *infra*.

135. Old § 3–105(1)(b). General commercial understanding is that such references or statements are for the purpose of making a record or giving information and are not meant to condition payment. Current § 3–106(a) deletes this language as it only negates an implied condition. *See* § 3–106, Official Comment 1.

136. *Id.*

137. Old § 3–105(1)(c). Current § 3–106(a) deletes the provision as only negating an implied condition. *See* § 3–106, Official Comment 1, and § 3–106(a) (a reference to another writing does not of itself make a promise or order conditional).

138. Old § 3–105(1)(d). *See* note 137, *supra*, for the reason for deletion in current Article 3.

139. Old § 3–105(1)(e). *See* note 137, *supra*, for the reason for deletion in current Article 3.

140. Federal Factors, Inc. v. Wellbanke, 241 Ark. 44, 406 S.W.2d 712 (1966).

141. Anderson v. Consolidated Auto Wholesalers, Inc., 4 U.C.C. Rep. Serv. 205 (N.Y.Sup.Ct.1967).

agreement," did not affect a check's negotiability;[142]

the words "as per contract," which were contained in certain notes, had no impact on negotiability;[143]

a note, which recited it was secured by a mortgage on real property, was negotiable;[144] and

a notation on a check that the drawer agreed to payment according to the terms of the Credit Payment Agreement previously executed did not impair negotiability as it constituted only a reference.[145]

[B] References Not Permitted

If a reference to another agreement in the instrument goes further than being merely a reference and instead subjects the instrument to the other agreement, or if it provides that the instrument is governed by any other agreement or that rights or obligations with respect to the promise or order are stated in another writing, the promise or order in the instrument is conditional, and the instrument is not negotiable.[146] This is true whether the other agreement actually operates to condition the promise or order.[147] In *Holly Hill Acres, Ltd. v. Charter Bank*,[148] the court held that a promissory note that provided that the terms of the mortgage "are by this reference made a part hereof" did not qualify as a negotiable instrument.

This situation, where a note is secured by a mortgage or a security agreement, is particularly troublesome with respect to the rule against incorporation or subjugation. A note essentially will provide for one event of default allowing suit, and that is nonpayment. The mortgage or security agreement, on the other hand, will provide for many events of default ranging from nonpayment to a failure to insure the collateral or an attempt to sell the collateral without the creditor's consent. The issue is how to coordinate the note and the security instrument so that if the default is, for example, a failure to insure the collateral, the note will be due and the security may be foreclosed.

---

142. Meador v. Ranchmart State Bank, 213 Kan. 372, 517 P.2d 123 (1973).

143. D'Andrea v. Feinberg, 45 Misc.2d 270, 256 N.Y.S.2d 504 (Sup.Ct.1965).

144. First Nat'l Bank v. North Adams Hoosac Sav. Bank, 7 Mass.App.Ct. 790, 391 N.E.2d 689 (1979).

145. TeleRecovery of Louisiana, Inc. v. Gaulon, 738 So.2d 662 (La. App. 1999), *writ denied*, 751 So.2d 224 (La.1999) (not a condition to payment but only a reference). A similar case is DH Cattle Holdings Co. v. Reno, 196 A.D.2d 670, 601 N.Y.S.2d 714 (Sup.Ct. A.D.1993) (provision payments to be made as animals were sold was not a condition to payment but merely identified possible source of funds).

146. § 3–106(a)(ii) and (iii).

147. The intent of the provision is to render an instrument nonnegotiable unless the holder can ascertain all of its essential terms from its face. *See* United States v. Farrington, 172 F.Supp. 797 (D.Mass.1959) (if an instrument contains the phrase "subject to" the terms of another document, the reference is fatal to negotiability regardless of the actual provisions of the other document).

148. 314 So.2d 209 (Fla.Dist.Ct.App. 1975). A similar case is International Minerals and Chemical Corp. v. Matthews, 71 N.C.App. 209, 321 S.E.2d 545 (N.C.Ct.App. 1984), *review denied*, 313 N.C. 330, 327 S.E.2d 890 (1985).

There are several ways to achieve coordination between the note and the security instrument.[149] One way, of course, is to subject the note to the terms of the mortgage or security agreement. This will destroy negotiability.[150] Another possibility is to include the same events that trigger acceleration in the mortgage or in the security agreement in the note. This might impair negotiability as adding too much "luggage."[151] A third option is to provide in the note that the holder may accelerate payment or performance "at will," "when the holder deems itself insecure," or "when the holder believes the prospect of payment or performance is impaired." This language should not endanger negotiability but should allow enforcement of the note in every circumstance in which the mortgage or security agreement can be enforced.[152]

Under Article 3, a better solution is to rely on § 3–106(b)(i), which provides that a promise or order is not made conditional by a reference to another writing for rights as to collateral, prepayment or acceleration. While literally sanctioning something more than a mere reference, the proper interpretation of the provision would seem to be that subjecting the note to the mortgage or security agreement *for this limited purpose* is acceptable.[153]

A final solution often is overlooked. Between the obligor and that person's immediate obligee, or any transferee, an instrument may be modified or affected by the mortgage or security agreement if executed as a part of the same transaction.[154] Thus, if the security instrument provides that the obligation may be enforced in the event of nonpayment

---

149. *See* Note, Effect of Acceleration Clause in Mortgage or Security Agreement on Maturity Date of Note, 21 Okla. L. Rev. 50 (1968).

150. *See* Official Comment 1 to § 3–106 which provides illustrations of "subject to" situations.

151. *See* the discussion on excessive wording, *supra*. *But see* Official Comment 1 to § 3–106.

152. *See* UCC § 1–309. In Opinion of Att'y General, 3 UCC Rep. Serv. 183 (Iowa 1965) (No. 65-7-5), it was held that an acceleration clause reserving to the holder the power to declare the entire unpaid balance due when the holder considered that the indebtedness or the collateral was insecure did not render the instrument nonnegotiable. A clause of this nature, however, makes it more difficult to establish that the asserted circumstances permit acceleration than does a specific default clause. This in turn raises the prospect of lender liability, particularly given the good faith standard that applies to all issues involving Article 3. *See* UCC § 1–201(b)(20) and § 3–103(a)(4). Thus, in Bowen v. Danna, 276 Ark. 528, 637 S.W.2d 560 (Ark. 1982), it was asserted that the acceleration of the mortgagee was not in good faith. The court held that a good-faith requirement did not apply where there was default in a specific condition, as opposed to a right to accelerate at will. The decision probably is too unconditional, but certainly the fact a specific clause is breached is strong evidence of good faith. *See also* Karner v. Willis, 238 Kan. 246, 710 P.2d 21 (Kan. 1985). *Cf.* Smith v. Union State Bank, 452 N.E.2d 1059 (Ind.Ct.App.1983), where the court under the then law incorrectly applied an objective test of good faith. *See also* First Nat'l Bank v. Twombly, 213 Mont. 66, 689 P.2d 1226 (Mont. 1984), which awarded punitive damages for breach of the good faith standard, a questionable result if the standard merely determines how contract performance is to be measured. On that, *see* Permanent Editorial Board Commentary No. 10, February 10, 1994.

153. Official Comment 3 to old § 3–105 states that such a reference does not destroy negotiability even though it has mild aspects of incorporation by reference. Official Comment 1 to § 3–106 is more frank; a statement that rights and obligations with respect to the collateral are governed by the security agreement is permissible.

154. § 3–117. *See also* Metalcraft Inc. v. Pratt, 65 Md.App. 281, 500 A.2d 329 (Md. Ct.App.1985).

or any other specified default that allows foreclosure of the security, as between the parties coordination of the note and mortgage or security agreement is achieved. If the note and security instrument are assigned, no holder in due course is affected by any limitation of rights arising out of a separate agreement,[155] but coordinating the enforcement of the writings is an enhancement of and not a limitation on rights.

[ii] *Other Agreements Affecting the Instrument*

As long as an instrument remains in the hands of the original parties to it, it is unnecessary to any policy promoting certainty, and it would be patently unfair given that the instrument only evidences the payment portion of the agreement, for a court to limit its view of the agreement of the parties to what is represented by the negotiable instrument itself. The only pertinent consideration is one of the sanctity of the writing, that is, a parol evidence issue. As a result, where the entire agreement of the parties is written, as between the obligor and the immediate obligee or any transferee the terms of the instrument may be modified or affected by any other written agreement executed as a part of the same transaction.[156] The case of *Millman v. State National Bank*[157] illustrates how the rule works. There, a bank to which a note had been indorsed by the payee, brought an action against the payee and against the maker. The court held that the bank was entitled to summary judgment against the payee as indorser of the note. But it also held that the payee was not entitled to summary judgment on a cross-claim against the maker for the amount of any judgment rendered in favor of the bank because, as between the payee and the maker, the maker was entitled to assert defenses against the note, such as a failure of consideration by reason of the breach of the settlement agreement out of which the note had arisen.

A variety of other cases similarly have applied the rule to modify the otherwise unconditional terms of an instrument, including cases where the court: (1) construed a note and a security agreement, executed as part of the same transaction, together to defeat the action of the creditor to recover possession of the collateral, finding that the note was not due under the agreement read as a whole;[158] (2) gave effect to a provision in a written sales agreement making payment of the note contingent upon the receipt of a designated amount of sales income;[159] (3) determined that

---

155. § 3–117.

156. *See* § 3–117 and, *e.g.*, Perry v. Cain, 1978 OK 104, 581 P.2d 891 (Okla. 1978) (as between the immediate parties, a negotiable instrument is merely a part of an overall transaction). A "transferee," while not an original party to the transaction, is merely an assignee of the rights of one of those parties. § 3–203(b). § 3–117 does not limit itself to written agreements, specifically alludes to any separate parol evidence rule, and includes both agreements relied upon as well as those that are part of the same transaction, and thus obviates the difficulty discussed, *infra*, concerning oral parol evidence. Additional discussion appears in Chapter 6.

157. 323 A.2d 723 (D.C.1974).

158. Merchants Nat'l Bank v. Professional Men's Ass'n, 409 F.2d 600 (5th Cir. 1969), *cert. denied*, 396 U.S. 1009, 90 S.Ct. 567, 24 L.Ed.2d 501 (1970).

159. Texas State Bank v. Sharp, 506 S.W.2d 761 (Tex.Civ.App.1974), *writ. ref. n. r. e.* (Jul. 10, 1974).

a check, tendered in complete settlement of the parties' dispute but altered by obliteration of the language of release it bore on its reverse side before it was deposited, nonetheless resulted in an accord and satisfaction when considered with a letter by the drawer's attorney that accompanied it and that stated that the amount claimed was disputed, the check was offered in settlement, and that depositing it would constitute an acceptance of the offer;[160] (4) considered a written agreement, including parol evidence pertaining to the conditions of the sale, to determine whether a defense existed in an action on a note the defendant claimed was conditioned upon obtaining a Small Business Administration loan;[161] and (5) allowed a written contract limiting liability in connection with indorsements to restrict the unlimited indorser's contract appearing on the notes alone.[162]

Of course, if the agreement was not intended to modify or affect the terms of the instrument, it will not. For example, in one case,[163] in a written contract for the sale of real property, a provision was included to the effect that the broker would not be liable for damages by reason of acts, defaults, or other nonaction by, between, or upon the part of the purchasers or sellers. This provision was determined not to modify the broker's obligation on a note made separate from the real estate contract and which was executed and delivered by the broker to secure the purchasers against undisclosed debts that might become liens against the property.[164] If the intent of the parties is ambiguous, the court may construe the writing as not intended to affect the instrument at all. That was the result in *Pugh v. First National Bank*.[165] The court decided that a separate agreement for a method of payment of a note, which did not provide it was the exclusive method, did not relieve the maker of the obligation on the note when payment by that method was precluded. Finally, if there is outright contradiction between the agreement and the instrument, the instrument may be held to stand on its own and not be affected if there is no indication as to which writing the parties intended

---

160. A.G. King Tree Surgeons v. Deeb, 140 N.J.Super. 346, 356 A.2d 87 (N.J.Dist. Ct.1976). As to accord and satisfaction, *see* Chapter 7, *infra*.

161. Demaio v. Theriot, 343 So.2d 1143 (La.Ct.App.1977), *cert. denied*, 346 So.2d 218 (La.1977).

162. Gensplit Fin. Corp. v. Link Power & Machinery Corp., 36 UCC Rep. Serv. 588 (S.D.N.Y.1983). On the other hand, in Alves v. Baldaia, 14 Ohio App.3d 187, 470 N.E.2d 459 (Ohio Ct.App.1984), the court read old § 3–119 restrictively and determined that a written separate agreement could not modify an indorsement to a mere assignment because old § 3–119(1) did not apply to the terms of a conveyance of the instrument and parol otherwise could not contradict the writing. Under § 3–117, this restrictive reading should not be possible as the reference is not to "terms of the instrument" but to "the obligation of a party to an instrument to pay."

163. Brock v. Adams, 79 N.M. 17, 439 P.2d 234 (1968).

164. In West v. Turchioe, 144 N.H. 509, 761 A.2d 382 (1999), the note and written agreement were construed together so the integrated document elaborated on the language appearing in the note alone. *Contrast* Hunter v. McLelland, 143 Ga.App. 746, 240 S.E.2d 153 (Ga.Ct.App.1977) (amendment to land sales contract expressly stated it was made in consideration of note; failure to comply with the terms of contract thus discharged liability on note).

165. 130 Ga.App. 627, 204 S.E.2d 370 (Ga.Ct.App.1974).

to control.[166]

In order to modify the terms of the instrument, the asserted understanding must constitute an agreement and must be part of the same transaction or the instrument must have been issued or the obligation incurred in reliance on the asserted agreement. Thus where a letter of guarantee by individual defendants was executed prior to the date of the loans and the corporate notes given to evidence the loans and the letter were not between the same obligor and obligee, the court doubted the letter constituted an "other written agreement" executed as part of the same transaction giving rise to the notes.[167] In a New York case,[168] the execution of the note sued on by defendants was admitted, but it was conceded that the principal was not named and that there was no showing that the individual defendants had signed in a representative capacity. An enclosure letter stating that the defendants had signed the note as representatives of the principal and allegedly forwarded with the note was offered in evidence. The court did not consider that the letter constituted a separate agreement modifying the note because it was not an "agreement" within the meaning of that term as set forth in UCC § 1–201(b)(3).[169]

[iii] *Oral Parol Evidence*

Where the asserted other agreement entered into as part of the same transaction out of which the instrument arose or in reliance upon which the instrument is issued or the obligation is incurred is not written but is oral, a more difficult issue is presented as both the existence and the terms of that agreement may be in doubt.[170]

In *American Underwriting Corp. v. Rhode Island Hospital Trust Co.*,[171] the court reasoned that because Article 3 does not contain explicit rules as to when an instrument may be varied or affected by parol evidence, except to the extent Article 3 establishes certain rules of construction that cannot be altered by parol evidence other than in actions for reformation,[172] case law may determine under what circumstances parol modification of negotiable instruments is permissible pursuant to UCC § 1–103. Section 1–103(b) allows general principles of law to supplement the provisions of the UCC. This also was the view of the federal district court for the Southern District of Florida in *First*

---

166. Official Comment 3 to old § 3–119.

167. In any event, the defendants' liability was controlled by the guaranty and not Article 3 of the Code. Fewox v. Tallahassee Bank & Trust Co., 249 So.2d 55 (Fla.Dist.Ct.App.1971), *cert. denied*, 252 So.2d 799 (Fla.1971). *See also* McPherson v. Longview United Pentecostal Church, Inc., 540 S.W.2d 424 (Tex.Civ.App.1976), *writ ref. n. r. e.* (October 27, 1976).

168. Barden & Robeson Corp. v. Ferrusi, 52 A.D.2d 1061, 384 N.Y.S.2d 596 (1976).

169. The admissibility of this sort of parol evidence under § 3–402(b)(2) to establish representative capacity is discussed in Chapter 5.

170. § 3–117 allows any agreement, written or not, to modify, supplement or nullify the instrument, subject to any applicable parol evidence rule outside Article 3, but the existence and terms of any asserted agreement must be established.

171. 111 R.I. 415, 303 A.2d 121 (1973).

172. These rules formerly were collected in old § 3–118 but now are found in several sections of Article 3. *See* Cross Reference Table of Sections in old Articles 3 and 4 to revised Articles 3 and 4.

National City Bank v. Metal Trading Co.[173] This result is explicitly provided for in § 3–117.[174]

To illustrate the application of an applicable parol evidence rule, consider that the court in the *First National City Bank* case, above, further held that where an asserted defense in an oral agreement is offered to set up a different agreement that would alter, vary, or contradict the language of the written instrument, the evidence is not admissible. In short, the terms of the oral agreement may be shown consistent with general principles regulating the introduction of parol evidence, which will preclude the successful assertion of terms that contradict the writing. Thus in the *First National City Bank* case, when suit was brought on notes that neither made reference to another separate agreement nor contained anything other than the usual form language employed in printed notes, and the defendants alleged that the notes were executed as part of an oral joint-venture agreement with the plaintiff, that the notes were never to have been effective, and that they were only a sham for the purpose of "regularizing" the transactions, the court held the oral parol evidence was inadmissible.[175] The asserted prior oral agreement indicated the instruments were not to be enforceable, contrary to the terms of the notes themselves.[176] Likewise, in another case,[177] parol evidence of a contemporaneous oral agreement that the note sued on was not to be paid until after the exhaustion of other legal remedies was excluded on the ground it would operate to vary the time for payment beyond the one-year provision set forth in the note.[178]

---

173. 71 F.R.D. 363 (S.D.Fla.1976).

174. Official Comments 1 and 2 to § 3–117 provide this example: X applies for credit, which will be granted if X finds a co-maker. Y agrees to serve, if creditor also gets Z to be a co-maker. Creditor agrees and Y signs, but Z never signs. This agreement between creditor and Y can be shown in defense to suit by creditor, subject to law outside Article 3 regarding exclusion of proof of contemporaneous or previous agreements. As to that, *see* text, *infra*.

175. *See also* Hildebrandt v. Anderson, 180 Or.App. 192, 42 P.3d 355 (2002) (asserted condition to note where no condition appeared in the note or in the record did not make the note conditional and thus not governed by Article 3). *Compare* Official Comment 1 to old § 3–119, which indicates that a *written* agreement stating that upon certain conditions the instrument shall be discharged or not paid, or even that it is a sham and is not to be enforced at all, may modify the instrument. Current § 3–117 has no such comment but, as between the parties, their two writings should be construed together. The comment to old § 3–119 also cautions that nothing in the section is intended to validate any agreement that is fraudulent or void as against public policy, as in the case of a note given to deceive a bank examiner. *See* Cosmopolitan Fin. Corp. v. Runnels, 2 Haw.App. 33, 625 P.2d 390 (Haw.Ct.App.1981). Under § 3–117, *see* Official Comment 2. This same policy is behind the federal "holder in due course doctrine" for financial institution insurance agencies discussed in Chapter 1, *supra*. For an interesting discussion of the conflicts inherent here, *see* Jordan, "Just Sign Here—It's Only a Formality": Parol Evidence in the Law of Commercial Paper, 13 GA. L. REV. 53, 72–79 (1978).

176. *See also* Bank of Suffolk County v. Kite, 49 N.Y.2d 827, 404 N.E.2d 1323, 427 N.Y.S.2d 782 (1980); Wooldridge v. Groos Nat'l Bank, 603 S.W.2d 335 (Tex.Civ.App. 1980).

177. Foreman v. Melrod, 257 Md. 435, 263 A.2d 559 (1970).

178. Similar cases are Whiteside v. Douglas County Bank, 145 Ga.App. 775, 245 S.E.2d 2 (Ga.Ct.App.1978); Main Bank v. Baker, 86 Ill.2d 188, 56 Ill.Dec. 14, 427 N.E.2d 94 (1981). Other cases involving the same principle include Farmington National Bank v. Basin Plastics, Inc., 94 N.M. 668, 615 P.2d 985 (N.M. 1980) (asserted oral agreement to secure and perfect security interest; note did not require taking of se-

On the other hand, a series of cases have allowed asserted oral agreements to defeat recovery on the instrument where they are interpreted to create a condition precedent to enforceability rather than to contradict the terms of the instrument.[179] Presumably this escape can be foreclosed if the instrument contains a clause, similar to a merger clause, that stipulates no condition precedent to enforceability has been agreed upon.[180]

A distinguished authority on negotiable instruments once observed that it is elementary that most defenses necessarily rest in parol.[181] The accuracy of this observation is manifest. Further discussion of parol evidence in relation to defenses to negotiable instruments will be postponed to the points at which defenses to liability on the instruments are detailed.[182]

[c] *Limitations on Sources for Payment*

Under old Article 3, a promise or order contained in an instrument will not be unconditional and the instrument will not be negotiable unless the full resources of the obligor are placed behind the promise or order.[183] In one case the written agreement was to pay $5,000 "from the jobs now under construction." The court held this constituted a conditional promise.[184] A similar result was reached in *Hinckley v. Eggers*,[185] where the promissory note secured by real property provided for no personal liability and was limited to payment out of the proceeds of the sale of the property. On the other hand, the promise or order will not be considered conditional if the instrument only indicates a particular

---

curity); Evenson v. Hlebechuk, 305 N.W.2d 13 (N.D.1981) (unwritten agreement asserted to establish condition to unconditional promise to pay); *cf.* notes 159 and 175, *supra*; FDIC v. Borne, 599 F.Supp. 891 (E.D.N.Y.1984) (evidence of oral condition subsequent to liability precluded); and Brooks v. McCorkle, 174 Ga.App. 132, 329 S.E.2d 214 (Ga.Ct.App.1985) (parol evidence not admitted to contradict unconditional promise of note; the better analysis probably is the maker could not set off asserted defenses against third party against the payee).

179. Scott v. Wall, 55 Wn. App. 404, 777 P.2d 581 (Wash.Ct.App.1989); Scafidi v. Johnson, 420 So.2d 1113 (La.1982); Ketchian v. Concannon, 435 So.2d 394 (Fla.Dist. Ct.App.1983); Participating Parts Associates, Inc. v. Pylant, 460 So.2d 1299 (Ala. Civ.App.1984). *Cf.* Akin v. Dahl, 661 S.W.2d 914 (Tex.1983) (defense must go to enforceability of entire instrument and not contradict some terms), and, *supra*, note 161 (written agreement).

180. The alleged condition would then contradict the writing. *See, e.g.* Daly v. Del E. Webb Corp., 96 Nev. 359, 609 P.2d 319 (Nev.1980) (separate unconditional guarantee). A merger clause also is wise to defeat asserted "supplemental" agreements. See Official Comment 2 to § 3–117.

181. Britton, *supra*, note 87, at 121.

182. *See* Chapter 6. Parol evidence also plays a significant role in connection with accommodation and agent liability on instruments. Discussion of this aspect of parol evidence appears in Chapter 5. It further may have play in connection with the form requirements discussed, *infra*, and *see* note 175, *supra*.

Of course, none of any established defenses will be valid if the person enforcing the instrument is a holder in due course. See Chapter 3.

183. Old § 3–105(2)(b). *See* Peppertree Apartments, Ltd. v. Peppertree Apartments, 631 So.2d 873 (Ala.1993).

184. Webb & Sons, Inc. v. Hamilton, 30 A.D.2d 597, 290 N.Y.S.2d 122 (1968).

185. 587 S.W.2d 448 (Tex.Civ.App. 1979). *See also* United Nat'l Bank v. Airport Plaza Ltd. Partnership, 537 So.2d 608 (Fla.Dist.Ct.App.1988), *review denied*, 547 So.2d 1209 (Fla.1989).

account to be debited or a fund or source from which reimbursement is expected.[186] Under old Article 3 negotiability was not destroyed because the instrument was limited to payment out of a particular fund or the proceeds of a particular source if the instrument was issued by a government or governmental agency or unit, or because it was limited to payment out of the entire assets of a partnership, unincorporated association, trust, or estate by or on behalf of which the instrument is issued.[187] The purpose was to permit municipalities or other governments or governmental agencies to issue checks or other negotiable instruments in negotiable form even though payment was limited, for example, to the proceeds of a particular tax, and to allow negotiability for paper issued by commonly recognized entities like unincorporated associations, partnerships, trusts, and estates, even though member or fiduciary liability is excluded. Under this rule, a court found that a promissory note secured by a trust deed executed by a land trust trustee payable only out of the land trust *res* was a negotiable instrument.[188]

These results are changed under § 3–106(b)(ii). Current Article 3 entirely eliminates any qualification of this type as a consideration in determining negotiability.[189] Instead market forces will determine the marketability of instruments that are restricted as to payment sources.[190]

[d] Other Conditions

Consistent with its explicit inclusion of traveler's checks,[191] Article 3 provides that if a promise or order requires as a condition to payment a countersignature by a person whose specimen signature appears on the promise or order, the condition does not destroy negotiability but simply constitutes a personal defense.[192]

In the same vein, the required Federal Trade Commission notice to preclude holder in due course status, or any similar statutory or regulatory requirement under other law, does not destroy negotiability by rendering the promise or order conditional.[193]

[4] Sum Certain

[a] Amount Ascertainable From the Instrument

The same concern for certainty, which generated the rule that a negotiable instrument within Article 3 must contain an unconditional

---

186. Rothenberg v. Mellow Music, Inc., 291 So.2d 234 (Fla.Dist.Ct.App.1974). *See also* Bank of Viola v. Nestrick, 72 Ill.App.3d 276, 28 Ill.Dec. 469, 390 N.E.2d 636 (Ill.Ct. App.1979) (instrument payable from a designated contract was not payable solely from the contract).

187. Old §§ 3–105(1)(g), 3–105(1)(h). The latter provision was intended to affect only the negotiability of the instrument and was not intended to change the law as to the liability of a partner, a member of an association, a trustee, or a personal representative on the instrument. Official Comment 7 to old § 3–105.

188. Kitzer v. Kitzer, 20 Ill.App.3d 54, 312 N.E.2d 699 (Ill.Ct.App.1974).

189. §§ 3–104(a), 3–106(b)(ii).

190. § 3–106 Official Comment 1.

191. *See* Chapter 1, *supra*.

192. § 3–106(c) and Official Comment 2 to that section.

193. § 3–106(d) and Official Comment to that section.

promise or order, also produced the rule that basically the sum payable in an instrument must be a fixed amount of money, that is, a sum certain.[194] The formulation is that the instrument must be for a fixed amount of money with or without interest or other charges described in the instrument.[195] In Yin v. Society National Bank Indiana,[196] the note was issued for a line of credit not to exceed two million dollars and contained a promise to pay that amount but also contained a notation under the heading "disbursement" which stated "Draws to C/A #946009–372." The court denied negotiability. A concurring opinion, however, pointed out that the notation did not specify the note was issued in conjunction with a line of credit.[197]

The sum payable is certain even though the amount of the instrument is to be paid with stated interest or by stated installments, with stated different rates of interest before and after default or a specified date, or with a stated discount or addition if paid before or after the date fixed for payment. For example, that a note provides for 16 percent interest does not make the sum payable uncertain.[198] A less clear case is *Universal C.I.T. Credit Corp. v. Ingel*.[199] There a note contained a provision for "interest after maturity at the highest lawful rate." The

---

194. §§ 3–104(a) and 3–112. *See* Shepherd Mall State Bank v. Johnson, 1979 OK 135, 603 P.2d 1115 (Okla.1979) (a continuing guaranty is not a negotiable instrument because the amount payable is adjustable and not certain). Other cases denying negotiable status for a guaranty include T.O. Stanley Boot Co., Inc. v. Bank of El Paso, 847 S.W.2d 218 (Tex.1992); and Buckeye Fed. Savings & Loan Ass'n v. Guirlinger, 62 Ohio St.3d 312, 581 N.E.2d 1352 (Ohio 1991). *See, supra,* note 128 as well.

195. § 3–104(a). Section 3–112(b) provides that interest may be stated in the instrument as a fixed or variable amount of money or as a fixed or variable rate or rates. The amount or rate of interest may be stated or described in the instrument in any manner and may require reference to information not contained in the instrument. This rule is for the purpose of Article 3; it does not supersede any regulation of the formula or index provided by other law. § 3–112, Official Comment 2, and *see,* for example, 12 CFR pt. 34, Subpart B § 34.7 (national banks and subsidiaries may deal in adjustable rate mortgage loans and, if the loan is subject to 12 CFR § 226.19(b), the index must be readily available to and verifiable by the borrower and be beyond the control of the bank). *See also* note 212, *infra*.

The fact that § 3–112(b) provides a quite liberal standard should not obscure that if the amount of interest payable cannot be ascertained from the description in the instrument, to that extent the amount due cannot be determined. In that case, however, § 3–112(b) provides a back-up rule that interest is payable at the judgment rate in effect at the place of payment at the time interest first accrues. This rule will result in less interest than intended, but it is better than the alternative. A possible example of such a case is Tanenbaum v. Agri–Capital, Inc., 885 F.2d 464 (8th Cir.1989), where the note provided for the LIBOR rate or the highest rate authorized by law. Since the LIBOR rate is a spot rate and varies according to how long the dollars are borrowed, it is questionable the amount of interest could be ascertained from the note's description.

§ 3–112(a) specifies an instrument is not payable with interest unless provided for, and unless otherwise provided interest is payable from the date of the instrument.

196. 665 N.E.2d 58 (Ind.App.1996).

197. The case is erroneously decided; the promise to pay was two million and if less was advanced that would be a defense. *Distinguish* Resolution Trust Corp. v. Oaks Apartments Joint Venture, 966 F.2d 995 (5th Cir.1992), where the promise was to pay two million dollars or so much as may be advanced.

198. Mecham v. United Bank of Ariz., 107 Ariz. 437, 489 P.2d 247 (1971).

199. 347 Mass. 119, 196 N.E.2d 847 (1964). *See also* National Union Fire Ins. Co. v. Alexander, 728 F.Supp. 192 (S.D.N.Y. 1989).

court equated the instrument to one payable "with interest." The court then held that an instrument payable "with interest" is a negotiable instrument pursuant to old § 3–118(d), which provided that a provision "for interest" means interest at the judgment rate.[200] As confirmed by current § 3–112(b), the court's reasoning does no real violence to the policy behind the requirement of a sum certain, even though a reference to a source (the statute fixing the rate) outside the instrument is required because the source referred to is easily available and fixed. A similar situation would exist if the instrument provided for interest at a stated interest rate or at the maximum legal rate.[201] This sort of provision is designed to avoid usury if applying the agreed rate of interest would result in interest in excess of that permitted by law,[202] and ought not to destroy negotiability.[203]

On the other hand, clearly pushing these limits under old Article 3 is an instrument payable with interest "at the current rate"[204] or an instrument "with interest at bank rates."[205] Accordingly, in *DH Cattle Holdings Co. v. Reinoso*, a note that provided for a rate of 9 percent, but also that the amount of interest to be payable at maturity was to be determined, was not negotiable.[206] On the other hand, under § 3–112(b) if an instrument calls for interest, the amount of interest will always be determinable because interest then is payable at the judgment rate. Another example of a clause that previously went too far is one providing that the holder may pay taxes, assessments and insurance if the obligor fails to do so and then recover reimbursement.[207] Note, however, that if this provision appeared in a separate mortgage or security agreement securing the instrument, it would not affect the negotiability of the instrument[208] and under old § 3–119(1) (current § 3–117) the same result should obtain as if the provision were permissible and in the instrument. Current § 3–104(a), allowing other charges described, should directly allow this result.

An uncertainty as to the amount payable arising from a difference in the instrument between the amount expressed in figures and the amount expressed in words is not fatal to negotiability because the

---

200. Now *see* § 3–112(b), which clearly provides for this result.

201. *See* the *Tanenbaum* case, *supra* note 195.

202. The efficacy of a "savings clause" as to usury is not determined by the UCC. *See, e.g.*, Oklahoma Preferred Fin. & Loan Corp. v. Morrow, 1972 OK 36, 497 P.2d 221 (Okla.1972) (a savings clause will not relieve a creditor from penalties for usury).

203. Because of doubt, however, the Federal National Mortgage Association and the Federal Home Loan Mortgage Corporation Uniform Multifamily Notes at one time did not include a usury savings clause. *See* Murray & Judy, The Federal National Mortgage Association and Federal Home Loan Mortgage Corporation Uniform Multifamily Mortgage Instruments, 33 Bus. Law. 2303 (1978). Under §§ 3–104(a) and 3–112, this issue disappears.

204. Official Comment 1 to old § 3–106.

205. A. Alport & Son, Inc. v. Hotel Evans, Inc., 65 Misc.2d 374, 317 N.Y.S.2d 937 (Sup.Ct.1970). *See also* note 206.

206. 176 A.D.2d 1057, 575 N.Y.S.2d 203 (A.D.1991). Variable rate notes, negotiable under current §§ 3–104(a) and 3–112, are distinguishable since the interest rate must be readily ascertainable.

207. Hinckley v. Eggers, 587 S.W.2d 448 (Tex.Civ.App.1979), *writ ref. n. r. e. (Jan. 23, 1980)*.

208. Old § 3–119(2); current § 3–106(a).

statute itself resolves that ambiguity.[209] Nor is the fact that a rebate of any unearned finance charge may be due upon prepayment when the rebate, and thus the sum payable, will vary depending on when prepayment occurs.[210]

[b] *Provisions Not Creating Uncertainty*

Article 3 always allowed certain deviation from the basic principle that for the sum to be certain the amount payable must be determinable from the instrument itself. Thus, a sum is still certain even though it is to be paid with exchange or less exchange, whether at a fixed rate or at the current rate, and even though it is payable with costs of collection or an attorney's fee, or both, upon default.[211] These "exceptions" actually realistically reinforce the policy behind the sum certain requirement because they make the actual recovery to the holder the amount for which the instrument is written.

The rules as to certainty bear only on the negotiability of the instrument and do not validate any term which is otherwise illegal or regulated.[212] Thus a stated but usurious rate of interest is not sanctioned,[213] and the enforceability of a provision for the payment of an attorney's fee on default depends upon other law.[214]

[5] *Sum Payable in Money*

[a] *Money Not Limited to Legal Tender*

To be within Article 3, an instrument must be payable in money.[215] Money means a medium of exchange authorized or adopted by a domestic or foreign government as a part of its currency.[216] Money is not necessarily limited to what is legal tender, but does not include what

---

209. § 3–114. Ambiguities are discussed further, *infra*.

210. *See, e.g.,* Circle v. Jim Walter Homes, Inc., 535 F.2d 583 (10th Cir.1976) and Mortgage Assoc. v. Siverhus, 63 Wis.2d 650, 218 N.W.2d 266 (Wis. 1974). *But see* Walls v. Morris Chevrolet, Inc., 1973 OK CIV APP 11, 515 P.2d 1405 (Okla.Ct.App. 1973).

211. Old § 3–106(1)(d), (e). Current § 3–104(a) eliminates this detail in favor of a general principle of allowing other charges described in the instrument.

212. § 3–112, Official Comment 2.

213. Official Comment 5 to old § 3–106.

214. *Compare* Mammoth Cave Prod. Credit Ass'n v. Geralds, 551 S.W.2d 5 (Ky. Ct.App.1977) (a provision in a promissory note that the debtor pay the attorney fee arising as a result of the debtor's default is unenforceable as against public policy) *with* National Bank of North America v. Around the Clock Truck Serv., 58 Misc.2d 660, 296 N.Y.S.2d 606 (Sup.Ct.1968) (provision for a reasonable attorney's fee in a promissory note is enforceable and is not against public policy). This matter may be regulated by other statute. *See, e.g.,* 1974 Unif. Consumer Credit Code § 2.507.

215. §§ 3–104(a), 3–103(a)(6) and (9). *See* note 116, *supra*.

216. UCC § 1–201(a)(24). This includes a monetary unit of account established by an intergovernmental organization or by agreement between two or more nations. An instrument expressing the amount to be paid in sterling, francs, lira, or other recognized currency of a foreign government is negotiable even though payable in the United States. Official Comment 1 to § 3–104. The relevant time for determining what is "money" is when the instrument is made. If the instrument is payable in "currency" or "current funds," it is payable in money.

may be accepted as a medium of exchange in any particular locality at any particular time, such as gold dust.[217]

[b] Instruments Payable in Foreign Money

A question likely to arise is how a promise or order to pay in a foreign currency is to be performed. Unless a different medium of payment is specified in the instrument, under old Article 3 payment may be made of that number of dollars which the stated foreign currency will purchase at the buying sight rate for that currency on the day on which the instrument is payable or, if payable on demand, on the day of demand.[218] Current § 3–107 uses the language "current bank offered spot rate at the place of payment for the purchase of dollars on the day on which the instrument is paid." Thus, if a note is payable in Swiss francs, it could be paid in dollars on the basis of the bank spot rate for Swiss francs at the place of payment on the day on which the note was paid.[219]

But if the instrument specifies a foreign currency as the medium of payment, the instrument is payable in that currency.[220]

[6] Payable on Demand or at a Definite Time

To be a negotiable instrument within Article 3, an instrument either must be payable on demand or at a definite time.[221] The definite time requirement obviously reflects the desire for certainty that underlies all the special rules contained in Article 3 to govern contracts that are negotiable instruments. Nonetheless, an instrument payable on demand, seemingly the antithesis of one payable at a definite time, also is a negotiable instrument within Article 3, as was true at common law. The theory is that a demand instrument is due immediately, and that represents enough commercial certainty.

[a] Instruments Payable on Demand

Demand instruments include those payable at sight or on presentation and those in which no time for payment is stated.[222] A check is a good example, as is a sight draft. Notes lacking a due or maturity date are payable on demand. Indeed, if the date of payment of a note is originally left blank and subsequently the payee, without authorization, inserts the words "on demand," no issue as to alteration is raised because the instrument was payable on demand in any event.[223] Generally, matters extraneous to the basic terms of the instrument itself tend to

---

217. Official Comment 1 to old § 3–107. The reason for the rule is that gold dust, beaver pelts, or other goods, are necessarily of uncertain and fluctuating value. A note tied to a price index to increase the amount payable because of inflation likewise should not be negotiable under old Article 3. *But see* current § 3–112(b).

218. Old § 3–107(2). *See* under old Article 3, Lausen v. Federman, 9 UCC Rep. Serv. 866 (N.Y.Sup.Ct.1971).

219. § 3–107.

220. *Id.*

221. §§ 3–104(a)(2) and 3–108.

222. § 3–108(a).

223. Holliday v. Anderson, 428 S.W.2d 479 (Tex.Civ.App.1968).

be construed so as not to affect its characterization as a demand instrument. Thus, in one case, written instructions on the reverse side of a check limited the time for its deposit to a future date. Nevertheless, the instructions were found merely to request the payee to alter the express provisions on the face of the instrument, and not to preclude the check from being payable on demand.[224] In another case, there was an oral agreement between a debtor and a creditor that provided a demand note was to be paid only out of the proceeds from the sale of the debtor's building projects. The court stated the agreement did not contradict the terms of the instrument so as to make it not payable on demand, reasoning that demand notes are subject to the risk that the maker will be unable to pay upon presentment and, by contracting to restrict the source of funds for payment, the maker only increased that risk without changing the demand provision.[225]

Finally, an instrument stating that it is due at request with thirty days' notice is a demand instrument.[226] An instrument that states the maker promises to pay "at the earliest possible time" is not a demand instrument, however, and, because it cannot be construed to be payable at a definite time, it is not a negotiable instrument.[227]

[b] Instruments Payable at a Definite Time

An instrument is payable at a definite time, as opposed to on demand, if by its terms it is payable on a stated date or dates, at a fixed period after sight or acceptance, at a time or times readily ascertainable at the time the promise or order is issued, at a definite time subject to any prepayment or acceleration, at a definite time subject to extension at the option of the holder, or to extension to a further definite time at the option of the maker or acceptor, or automatically upon or after a specified act or event.[228] Optional instruments, such as a note stating that it is payable on demand but, if no demand is made, then at a stated date or in stated monthly installments beginning on a specified date (such instruments can be an alternative to a variable rate note), essentially are instruments that are payable at a definite time subject to

---

224. Silver Creations, Ltd. v. United Parcel Service, 133 N.J.Super. 543, 337 A.2d 641 (Law Div.1975). Usually in this situation a check is simply postdated. This does not impair negotiability. *See* old § 3–114(1); in this situation current Article 3 deletes this statement as unnecessary. *See* § 3–113, Official Comment. Ignoring the stated date may constitute improper payment, however. §§ 3–113(a) and 4–401(c), discussed later in this book.

225. Mozingo v. North Carolina Nat'l Bank, 31 N.C.App. 157, 229 S.E.2d 57 (App. 1976), *cert. denied*, 291 N.C. 711, 232 S.E.2d 204 (1977). The oral agreement, if admissible, under old Article 3 would appear to raise another issue relating to the negotiability of the note because of the limitations as to the source of payment. The court did not consider this point. No issue would arise under §§ 3–104(a) and 3–106(b)(ii). *But see also* notes 145 and 159, *supra*.

226. Shields v. Prendergast, 36 N.C.App. 633, 244 S.E.2d 475 (N.C.Ct.App. 1978). In Environics, Inc. v. Pratt, 50 A.D.2d 552, 376 N.Y.S.2d 510 (1975), the court treated a note payable thirty days after demand as a demand instrument. This case and the *Shields* case seem consistent, but both appear questionable in view of § 3–108(b), which treats an instrument payable at a fixed period after sight as one that is payable at a definite time.

227. Williams v. Cooper, 504 S.W.2d 564 (Tex.Civ.App.1973).

228. § 3–108(b).

acceleration upon demand and are not merely demand instruments.[229] Many decisions have upheld the negotiability of instruments payable at a definite time subject to any kind of acceleration, including a note containing a clause permitting acceleration in the event the holder deems itself insecure,[230] and notes that were given for the sale of real estate and that were made payable sixteen years after the date of their issuance but which permitted prepayment.[231]

On the other hand, an instrument which by its terms is payable only upon an act or event uncertain as to the time of occurrence is not payable at a definite time even though the act or event has occurred.[232] This language denies negotiability to post-obituary notes that anticipate an inheritance or a future interest.[233] Such notes find little or no use in general commerce. The language also will serve to deny negotiability to instruments not to be payable unless a contingency is met, such as a note which by its terms is payable "upon evidence of an acceptable permanent loan and upon acceptance of the loan commitment."[234] A case to be distinguished is *Smith v. Gentilotti*.[235] There a check for $20,000 was drawn and delivered in 1969, but was postdated to November 4, 1984. It also was indorsed by the drawer: "For Edward Joseph Smith Gentilotti My Son If I should pass away The amount of $20,000 Shall be taken from My Estate at death." The court held the check was payable on demand with reference to its 1984 date but subject to acceleration, and thus determined that the check was payable by the estate at the drawer's death in 1973.[236] But note that an undated instrument payable

---

229. Reese v. First Missouri Bank & Trust Co., 664 S.W.2d 530 (Mo.Ct.App. 1983); Corbin Deposit Bank & Trust Co. v. Mullins Enterprises, Inc., 641 S.W.2d 760 (Ky.Ct.App.1982); Seattle–First Nat'l Bank v. Schriber, 282 Or. 625, 580 P.2d 1012 (1978); C & Z, Inc. v. Oklahoma Tax Comm'n, 1969 OK 146, 459 P.2d 601 (Okla. 1969); Crown Mortgage Corp. v. Tarantino, 606 So.2d 29 (La.App.1992). Instruments of this nature bearing a fixed interest rate are in operation a type of variable rate note because if the market rate rises significantly over the note rate, the demand feature will be exercised, and a new interest rate will be negotiated to refinance the indebtedness due. § 3–108(c) specifically addresses these cases and treats the instrument as a demand instrument until the specified date; if no demand is made until then, it becomes payable on that date.

230. Broadway Management Corp. v. Briggs, 30 Ill.App.3d 403, 332 N.E.2d 131 (Ill.Ct.App.1975). *See* UCC § 1–309. *See also* note 152, *supra*.

231. Caruth v. United States, 411 F.Supp. 604 (N.D.Tex.1976), *rev'd on other grounds*, 566 F.2d 901 (5th Cir.1978).

232. § 3–108(b). Thus, for example in *In re* Boardwalk Marketplace Sec. Litigation, 849 F.2d 89 (2d Cir.1988), the court held that a note, with an estimated first payment date and which read that "Lender will notify me in writing of the first payment due date . . . ," was not a negotiable instrument. Note under § 3–108(b) the time for payment must be readily ascertainable at the time the promise or order is issued.

233. Official Comment 1 to old § 3–109. *See also* notes 123 and 124, *supra*.

234. Barton v. Scott Hudgens Realty & Mortgage Inc., 136 Ga.App. 565, 222 S.E.2d 126 (Ga.Ct.App.1975). Like cases are Krajcir v. Egidi, 305 Ill.App.3d 613, 238 Ill.Dec. 813, 712 N.E.2d 917 (Ill.Ct.App. 1999) (payable on the date HUD agreed to fund a project) and Regent Corporation U.S.A. v. Azmat Bangladesh, Ltd., 32 UCC Rep. Serv. 2d 900 (N.Y.Sup.Ct.1997) (payable specified number of days after a bill of lading date).

235. 371 Mass. 839, 359 N.E.2d 953 (1977).

236. Under § 4–405, there could be a question as to the authority of the drawee of the check to pay it because of the drawer's death. If suit was directly against the estate of the drawer and the applicable stat-

a certain number of days after date is not payable at a definite time, but is an incomplete instrument within § 3–115.[237]

[7] *Payable to Order or to Bearer*

When the special rules to govern negotiable instruments were being formulated, whether the parties intended transfer of the obligation represented by the instrument was an important concern. If they evidenced their intent by words in the instrument, this concern was satisfied. Over the years, "words of negotiability" became a requirement for a negotiable instrument. Thus, to be a negotiable instrument within Article 3, the writing must be payable to order or to bearer.[238]

[a] *Instruments Payable to Bearer*

An instrument is payable to bearer when by its terms it is payable to bearer or the order of bearer, a specified person or bearer, or "cash," the order of "cash," or otherwise does not state a payee or indicates that the person in possession is entitled to payment.[239] Thus the check commonly written to "cash" to withdraw money from a checking account is bearer paper. But an instrument payable to a named payee who is fictitious or nonexistent, or who is not intended to have an interest in the instrument, is not a bearer instrument under the UCC; rather, it is payable to order.[240] This rule suggests that often the significant issue is not whether an instrument is payable to bearer or to order to determine if it is governed by Article 3, but whether it is bearer paper or payable to order for the purpose of determining *how* it is governed by Article 3. In that respect, a bearer instrument is transferred by delivery alone.[241] An instrument payable to order in addition requires an indorsement.[242]

---

ute of wills was satisfied, however, the result of the case would seem a sensible resolution.

237. § 3–115, Official Comment 2, indicates that in all cases the instrument can be considered a demand instrument. Of course, if it is completed it is payable at a definite time and there is a defense or not based on whether the completion was as authorized. See § 3–115, Official Comment 2.

238. § 3–104(a)(1). An exception is made for checks in § 3–104(c). Under old Article 3 a broader exception for an instrument whose terms did not preclude transfer and which otherwise met the requirements for negotiability, but which was not payable to order or to bearer, existed. Old § 3–805. A case that illustrates that form "words of negotiability" still can be overcome by a negative intent against transferability is First State Bank v. Clark, 91 N.M. 117, 570 P.2d 1144 (1977). There the note bore a restriction that it could not be transferred without the maker's written consent. The court determined the restriction negated any implication of negotiability in the words "pay to the order of." See also note 10, *supra*.

239. § 3–109(a) and Official Comment 2 to that section. Of course, something less than the exact words of the statute will suffice, such as "Pay to holder." Note that an instrument where the name of the payee is left blank is bearer paper and also is an incomplete instrument governed by § 3–115. Davis v. Davis, 838 S.W.2d 415 (Ky.Ct.App.1992), Official Comment 2 to § 3–115, and Official Comment 2 to § 3–109. See also Waldron v. Delffs, 988 S.W.2d 182 (Tenn.Ct.App.1998), where the court held that a note with the blank space for the name of the payee mistakenly filled in with an account was bearer paper given § 3–109(a)(2).

240. Official Comment 2 to § 3–109. Nonetheless, the consequence is much the same. See the discussion of § 3–404 in Chapter 7.

241. § 3–201(b).

242. *Id. But again see* § 3–404(b), as applicable and noted in note 240, *supra*.

Under the law before the UCC, the rule was "once a bearer instrument, always a bearer instrument." In short, an instrument payable to bearer on its face could not be turned into one requiring a further indorsement by being specially indorsed. The UCC changes this rule. An instrument specially indorsed[243] becomes payable to the order of the special indorsee and may be further negotiated only by that person's indorsement.[244] By the same token, an instrument payable to order and then indorsed in blank[245] becomes payable to bearer and may thereafter be negotiated by delivery alone unless and until specially indorsed.[246]

Inevitably there are borderline cases. For example, suppose the instrument provides "Pay to the order of _____." Is this a bearer instrument, or something else? Under Article 3, the instrument is a bearer instrument when sent or delivered, and also is subject to the incomplete instrument rules.[247] A second common situation occurs when a drawer takes an ordinary blank check form on which the words "Pay to the order of" are preprinted and writes in the word "bearer" in the following blank. The instrument is intended as a bearer instrument and is so treated.[248] On the other hand, suppose the check form also had preprinted the words "or bearer" after the blank, and the name of a payee is inserted in the blank? It now appears the intent is for an order instrument, even though seemingly the instrument is payable to a specified person or bearer, which would make it bearer paper. Section 3–109(a) treats the instrument as bearer and under § 3–109(b) a bearer instrument cannot be an order instrument.[249]

A final example is when the drawer, intending the check for deposit, makes the check payable to the order of an account, such as "Depository Account No. 607." Is this a bearer instrument as not purporting to designate a specific payee? In *Frost National Bank v. Nicholas & Barrera*,[250] the court decided it was order paper under old § 3–110(1)(e), which provides in part that an instrument payable to the order of a fund

---

243. A special indorsement is an indorsement that specifies the person to whom or to whose order it makes the instrument payable. § 3–205(a). Note the indorsement need not contain the words "the order of"; "pay to" is adequate.

244. §§ 3–109(c) and 3–205(a).

245. A blank indorsement is an indorsement that specifies no particular indorsee and may consist of a signature alone. § 3–205(b).

246. §§ 3–109(c) and 3–205(b). An indorsement to a specified person and "its successors or assigns" is a special indorsement. The words "successors or assigns" do not operate to make the instrument thereafter payable to bearer. Security Pac. Nat'l Bank v. Chess, 58 Cal.App.3d 555, 129 Cal. Rptr. 852 (Cal.App.1976).

247. § 3–109, Official Comment 2 and *see* note 239, *supra*. Thus, if it is completed it becomes payable to the designated payee. § 3–115, Official Comment 2.

248. Official Comment 2 to § 3–109.

249. Official Comment 2 to § 3–109 indicates this changes old § 3–110(3), which is partly true for the reason the Official Comment gives, but on the example given in the Official Comment the instrument would be a bearer instrument under both old and current Article 3.

250. 500 S.W.2d 906 (Tex.Civ.App. 1973), *writ. ref. n. r. e.* (Jan. 30, 1974). Joffe v. United California Bank, 141 Cal.App.3d 541, 190 Cal.Rptr. 443 (Cal.App.1983) is a similar case. There the check was payable to "Continental Financial Systems—Wells Fargo Escrow Trust Account." The court used old § 3–110(1)(e) to determine the escrow trust was the designated payee and held the indorsement of the trust was necessary.

is an instrument payable to order. Current Article 3 reaches the same result.[251]

[b] Instruments Payable to Order

An instrument that is not payable to bearer is payable to order when by its terms it is payable to the order or assigns of an identified person, or to an identified person or order.[252] First note that an instrument "payable to John Doe," rather than "payable to the order of John Doe," will not qualify.[253] In fact, such an instrument, unless it is a check, is not within Article 3.[254]

Second, an instrument not otherwise payable to order but which recites that it is "payable upon its return properly indorsed," a provision that is common in certificates of deposit, is not payable to order even though this language seems to evidence an intention to make the instrument payable to an indorsee.[255] The reason is that the actual purpose of the language merely is to ensure the return of the instrument with an indorsement in lieu of a receipt.[256] An instrument is payable to order, however, when it conspicuously designates "exchange" or the like on its face and names a payee.[257]

To be payable to order, the person to whose order the instrument is payable[258] must be identified.[259] Article 3 itself resolves a number of "uncertainties" that might arise concerning the specification of the person to pay. Of course, an instrument may be made payable to the order of the maker, drawer, or drawee, as well as to the order of a payee who is none of those; to whom it is payable is determined by the intent of the person, whether or not authorized, signing as, or in the name or behalf of, the issuer.[260] It may be made payable to the order of two or more payees together or in the alternative.[261] Whether alternative payees

---

251. §§ 3–109(b), 3–110(c)(1).

252. § 3–109(b).

253. *See, e.g.*, Locke v. Aetna Acceptance Corp., 309 So.2d 43 (Fla.Dist.Ct.App. 1975) (notes where "buyer agrees to pay to seller" not negotiable instruments); Jones v. United Savings & Loan Ass'n, 515 S.W.2d 869 (Mo.Ct.App.1974) (savings certificate not payable to order or to bearer not negotiable). It is only an indorsement that need not contain the "order" language. *See* note 243, *supra*.

254. § 3–104(a)(1) and (c).

255. Old § 3–110(2). Current § 3–109(b) contains no such provision. Also old § 3–110(2) addresses an issue that has long ceased to be an issue; bearer certificates of deposit are a thing of the past for tax reasons.

256. Official Comment 5 to old § 3–110.

257. Old § 3–110(1). This codifies international usage which considers this language to evidence an intent for negotiability. Again, current § 3–109(b) does not pick up the archaic usage.

258. § 3–103(a)(6) states that an "order" may be addressed to one or more persons jointly or in the alternative, but not in succession. This provision has nothing to do with payees, but recognizes the practice of corporations issuing dividend checks that for commercial convenience name a number of drawees, usually in different parts of the country. Drawees in succession are not allowed, however, because the holder should not be required to make more than one presentment for payment or dishonor. See Official Comment 3 to old § 3–102.

259. § 3–109(b).

260. *See* old § 3–110(1)(a), (b), (c). Current § 3–109(b) dispenses with this redundancy. *See also* § 3–110(a). The balance of subsection (a), and subsection (b), deal with cases where the intent may not be clear.

261. § 3–110(d). Normally an instrument payable to "A and B" is intended to

are intended can be a problem.[262]

The use of the word "person" may appear to suggest the necessity of a legal entity as payee. This is not required. The UCC defines *person* to include organizations, and *organization* to include any legal or *commercial* entity, including a corporation, a government or a governmental subdivision or agency, a business trust, an estate, a trust, a partnership or an association, or two or more persons having a joint or common interest.[263] Thus an instrument may be made payable to the order of an estate, a trust, or an account, or to the order of a partnership or unincorporated association.[264]

---

be payable to the two parties as tenants in common and there is no survivorship in the absence of express language to that effect. *See* Fehling v. Cantonwine, 522 F.2d 604 (10th Cir.1975) (notes payable to the order of A and B and containing no language creating a right of survivorship between the payees were held by the payees as tenants in common). *Compare* Thomas v. Estate of Eubanks, 358 So.2d 709 (Miss.1978) (certificate of deposit payable to A or B with no reference to survivorship rights and in A's possession at her death was A's property and an asset of her estate).

262. *See* Kinzig v. First Fidelity Bank, N.A., 277 N.J.Super. 255, 649 A.2d 634 (Law Div.1994) (two payees whose names were separated by a virgule made instrument payable to them alternatively as a matter of law); J.R. Simplot, Inc. v. Knight, 93 Wn.App. 369, 973 P.2d 472 (Wash.Ct. App.1998), *rev'd*, 139 Wn.2d 534, 988 P.2d 955 (1999) (where payee's names separated by hyphen, to whom instrument payable was ambiguous); Bijlani v. Nationsbank of Florida, N.A., 25 UCC Rep. Serv. 2d 1165 (Fla.Cir.Ct.1995) (under § 3–110(d), an ambiguous multiple payee designation is treated as an alternative payee situation); Kenerson v. FDIC, 44 F.3d 19 (1st Cir.1995) (instrument payable to an estate, A & B Administrators, was payable to the administrators together (*see* § 3–110(c)(2)(i)) and under § 3–110(d) had to be negotiated or enforced by all together); and Piatt v. Medford Highlands, LLC, 173 Or.App. 409, 22 P.3d 767 (2001) (enforcement of a jointly payable note requires all payees to be made parties, a court may compel the joinder of a payee who refuses to participate as a plaintiff). *In* Ambassador Financial Services, Inc. v. Indiana Nat. Bank, 591 N.E.2d 1061 (Ind.Ct.App.1992), modified analysis at 605 N.E.2d 746 (Ind.1992), the check clearly was payable to both payees, but only one indorsed. The court applied the "intended payee defense," that is, there is no harm if the intended person received the proceeds.

See also employing equity to reach a similar result, Midwest Industrial Funding v. First National Bank, 973 F.2d 534 (7th Cir.1992). *Cf.* True v. Fleet Bank—NH, 138 N.H. 679, 645 A.2d 671 (N.H. 1994) (displacement of common law equitable defenses). *See also* the discussion in Chapter 3, *infra*.

263. UCC §§ 1–201(a)(25) and (27).

264. § 3–110(c). This provision determines who can deal with the instrument and does not necessarily determine ownership of the instrument or its proceeds. *See, e.g.,* Frost Nat'l Bank v. Nicholas & Barrera, 500 S.W.2d 906 (Tex.Civ.App.1973), *writ ref. n. r. e.* (Jan. 30, 1974), (instrument payable to the order of a specified deposit account was payable to order), note 250, *supra*, and § 3–110(c)(1). *Compare* West Penn Admin., Inc. v. Union Nat'l Bank, 233 Pa.Super. 311, 335 A.2d 725 (1975) (instrument payable to order of named bank with a particular account also designated was payable to the order of the bank unconditionally under old § 3–117(c) and not to the account, the account reference being merely descriptive) *with* Fireman's Fund Ins. Co. v. Security Pac. Nat'l Bank, 85 Cal.App.3d 797, 149 Cal.Rptr. 883 (1978) (check made out to a bank and an account number and name was not unconditionally payable to the bank as the words were intended to restrict payment). Current Article 3 covers old §§ 3–110 and 3–117 in § 3–110 and would confirm these cases.

What if the instrument is made out to the bank alone with no account designated? In J. Gordon Neely Enter., Inc. v. American Nat'l Bank, 403 So.2d 887 (Ala.1981), the court believed the instrument was payable to bearer as the bank itself was intended to have no interest. This analysis is in error. Under § 3–110(a) and, as applicable, § 3–404(b) the analysis is clearer. The resolution of these cases is discussed in Chapter 7; *see* Govoni & Sons Const. Co., Inc. v. Mechanics Bank, 51 Mass.App.Ct. 35, 742 N.E.2d 1094 (2001).

An instrument payable to an office or to an officer by his or her title as such is payable to the order of the principal.[265] Thus an instrument made payable to the order of "Treasurer of City Club" is not a bearer instrument, regardless of whether there is such an officer.[266]

¶ 2.03 Seals

At common law, a seal rendered an instrument, otherwise negotiable, nonnegotiable.[267] This is no longer true under the UCC, and sealed instruments are placed on the same footing as any other instruments as far as all sections of Article 3 are concerned, particularly with respect to the conclusiveness of consideration.[268]

¶ 2.04 Ambiguities and Omissions in Instruments

[1] Rules to Forestall Ambiguities

Certainty in terms is a goal of the law of negotiable instruments because it facilitates the free transferability of the instrument. Ambiguity is the antithesis of certainty. Moreover, if it were necessary to resolve ambiguity by resort to asserted other agreements of the parties to the instrument, even more uncertainty could result, leading to inadequate protection for holders of negotiable instruments that would discourage the free circulation of them. Accordingly, Article 3 states various rules of law that preclude a resort to parol evidence for any purpose under certain given circumstances, except the reformation of the instrument.[269]

When an instrument is payable to an estate, trust, or fund, it is payable to the order of the representative of such estate, trust, or fund, or his or her successors, and when payable to a partnership or association, it is payable to the partnership or association and may be indorsed or transferred by any person hereto authorized. § 3-110(c)(2)(i) and (iii). Note that an instrument payable to an estate, trust, or fund thus in essence is one which is payable to a named person with the addition of words describing him or her as a fiduciary for a specified person or purpose. Thus the instrument is payable to the individual and he or she may negotiate it, enforce it, or discharge it, but he or she remains subject to any liability for breach of his or her obligation as a fiduciary. *See also* the discussion, *infra*, in Chapter 3.

265. § 3-110(c)(2)(iv). But the incumbent of the office or his or her successors may act as if he, she or they were the holder. *See also* § 3-110(c)(2)(ii), which provides a like rule where an instrument initially is made payable to a named person with the addition of words describing him or her as agent or officer of a specified person. *See also* the discussion, *infra*, in Chapter 3.

266. Official Comment 3 to § 3-110.

¶ 2.03

267. Britton, *supra*, note 87, § 6.

268. *See* Venners v. Goldberg, 133 Md. App. 428, 758 A.2d 567 (Md.Ct.App.2000) and Bergren v. Davis, 287 F.Supp. 52 (D.Conn.1968). This rule was articulated in old § 3-113 but was not intended to affect any other statutes or rules of law relating to sealed instruments except to the extent they were inconsistent with Article 3. Thus a sealed instrument within old Article 3 could still be subject to a longer statute of limitations than a negotiable instrument not under seal, as old Article 3 did not contain a statute of limitations. Of course, since current Article 3 does in § 3-118, this example no longer holds. Indeed, current Article 3 leaves these issues to other law. *See* Cross Reference Table of Sections in old Articles 3 and 4 to Revised Articles 3 and 4.

¶ 2.04

269. The rules cannot be varied by any proof that any party intended the contrary, except as to reformation. Official Comment 1 to old § 3-118. The rules contained in old

Five common situations are dealt with in Article 3. The first is where there is doubt whether the instrument is a draft or a note, the holder may treat it as either.[270] A version of this arises where the drawer draws a draft on itself. Assume a bank issues a cashier's check. In form it is an order instrument, but practically it operates like a note issued by the bank. Suppose the bank now wishes to exercise a right to stop payment on the instrument. Where this issue has arisen, some cases used old § 3–118(a),[271] which in part provided that a draft drawn on the drawer is effective as a note, to deny that right.[272]

A second situation involves ambiguity among an instrument's terms and Article 3 provides that handwritten terms control typewritten and printed terms, and typewritten terms control printed ones.[273] To illustrate, a case resolved under the prior version of this rule is *Universal C.I.T. Credit Corp. v. Ingel*.[274] There the note provided that payment would commence on the 25th day of July, 1959, but the "ly" in July had been written over the "ne" in June. This might create an ambiguity as to when the note was payable, and create a problem as to negotiability.[275] But under the stated rule, the ambiguity is cured.

A third ambiguous situation is addressed by the rule that unless otherwise specified a provision for unascertainable interest means interest at the judgment rate at the place of payment and at the date interest first accrues.[276] The application of this rule was discussed in connection with the sum certain requirement and in reference to the *Ingel* case.

A fourth ambiguous situation is resolved by the rule that unless the instrument otherwise specifies, two or more persons signing as maker, acceptor, drawer, or anomalous indorser, or who indorse as a joint payee, are jointly and severally liable.[277] Case law also has dealt with what might be considered the converse ambiguity—where the instrument

---

§ 3–118 are dispersed in current Article 3, but this point should remain the same.

270. § 3–104(e).

271. *E.g.*, Banco Ganadero Y Agricola, S.A. v. Society Nat'l Bank, 418 F.Supp. 520 (N.D.Ohio 1976).

272. The court in *Banco Ganadero, supra* note 271, indicated that the issue really was not whether the bank had a right to stop payment on the instrument, but whether the bank was liable on the instrument as a maker; that is, whether it had any defense it could assert. This latter analysis is correct. This issue is discussed in Chapter 4 and in Chapter 9. Current Article 3 is much clearer. Because of commercial practice, cashier's checks are classified as checks but the drawer's liability is equated to that of a maker. *See* the discussion in Chapter 1, *supra*. The question of an ability to stop payment is explicitly addressed in § 3–411, discussed, *infra*, in this book.

273. § 3–114. § 3–114 also provides words prevail over numbers. *See* the discussion, *infra*, this chapter. For a case that did not even get that right, *see* France v. Ford Motor Credit Co., 323 Ark. 167, 913 S.W.2d 770 (Ark. 1996) (check had $8000 in numbers, $8 in words, and was encoded for $800).

274. 347 Mass. 119, 196 N.E.2d 847 (1964).

275. The time of payment would not be definite. §§ 3–104(a)(2) and 3–108(b).

276. § 3–112.

277. § 3–116(a). § 3–116(a) is more precise than prior law in stating the circumstances in which its rule applies, but less precise than old § 3–118(e) in that it does not state that the words "I promise to pay" are not a contradiction of the stated rule (but no difference in result from that under old § 3–118(e) is intended). § 3–116(b) and (c) deal with a right of contribution.

contains the words "we promise to pay." Generally several as well as joint liability is found in this instance.[278]

The resolution of another ambiguity was not carried over from old § 3–118(f),[279] which provided that unless otherwise specified consent to extension authorizes a single extension for not longer than the original period,[280] and, if expressed in the instrument, is binding on secondary parties[281] and accommodation makers.[282] A holder may not exercise the option over the objection of the maker, acceptor, or other party who properly tenders full payment when the instrument is due.[283]

The last ambiguous situation involves the internal conflict of terms, and is resolved by a provision[284] that states that words control figures except where the words are ambiguous; then figures control.[285] A case applying the provision is *Western Union Telegraph Co. v. Peoples National Bank*,[286] where the instrument stated $100 in words and $1,200 in figures. The court held $100 should have been paid.[287] A closer case is *United States v. Hibernia National Bank v. Rault*,[288] where the check had $244844.50 in figures and, on the line for the amount to be written in, "24844 DOLLARS/50 CENTS." The check was encoded and paid in the larger amount. The court held the depositary bank liable to the drawer. Query the application of § 3–114; *see* § 4–209.

Article 3 and Article 4 contain several other provisions in addition to those already discussed that statutorily resolve ambiguities. One of them is § 4–106.[289] The first part of that provision[290] specifies the meaning of

---

278. *See, e.g.*, Ghitter v. Edge, 118 Ga. App. 750, 165 S.E.2d 598 (Ga.Ct.App.1968). Where two or more persons execute a note as makers and are jointly and severally liable, the person who makes payment generally is entitled to contribution from the others. Grimes v. Grimes, 47 N.C.App. 353, 267 S.E.2d 372 (N.C.Ct.App.1980). § 3–116(b) now includes this rule.

279. Current Article 3 does not carry over this provision as the matters covered seem resolvable generally without resort to parol.

280. In Citizens State Bank v. Beermann Bros. Dehy, 188 Neb. 597, 198 N.W.2d 458 (Neb. 1972), the court held an extension for twenty-one days longer than the original period fell outside the consent authorized by the notes. *But see* Union Constr. Co., Inc. v. Beneficial Standard Mortgage Inv., 125 Ariz. 433, 610 P.2d 67 (Ariz.Ct.App.1980), where the court decided the provision in the note authorized multiple extensions of time.

281. Defined in old § 3–102(1)(d) to mean a drawer or an indorser. Current Article 3 does not use the term.

282. The expression in the instrument probably should appear in the body of the instrument on the front side. In a comparable situation, when a waiver of defenses based on extensions of time appeared on the reverse of a note, the court held an accommodation maker was not liable. Holcomb State Bank v. Adamson, 107 Ill. App.3d 908, 63 Ill.Dec. 704, 438 N.E.2d 635 (Ill.Ct.App.1982).

283. Tender of payment under § 3–603 is discussed in Chapter 6. *See, e.g.*, Taines v. Capital City First Nat'l Bank, 344 So.2d 273 (Fla.Dist.Ct.App.1977), *cert. denied*, 355 So.2d 517 (Fla.1978).

284. § 3–114. *See also* note 273, *supra*.

285. Note the rule in UCC § 4A–207 is different, but the operational context is different and the originator must appreciate the risk. In negotiable instruments, the opposite rule would entail undue risks as numbers are more easily altered than words as well as being subject to a greater incidence of mistake.

286. 169 N.J.Super. 272, 404 A.2d 1178 (1979).

287. *See also* Port City State Bank v. American Nat'l Bank, 486 F.2d 196 (10th Cir.1973).

288. 841 F.2d 592, *rehearing en banc denied*, 847 F.2d 840 (5th Cir.1988).

289. Three others are: § 3–204(a), discussed in Chapter 4; § 3–110(d), discussed, *supra*, note 262, and in Chapter 3; and

an instrument that states it is "payable through" a particular bank. This form of instrument is common in insurance, dividend, and payroll drafts. The language does not constitute the bank a drawee; it does not order or even authorize it to pay the instrument out of the drawer's account or any other funds of the drawer in its hands; and it does not require it to take the instrument for collection in the absence of a special agreement to that effect. It merely designates the bank as a collecting bank through which presentment is properly made to the drawee.[291] This distinction may be important in several instances. For example, it will keep a settlement made by the bank for the draft provisional in nature and the bank as the agent of the owner of the instrument until settlement is actually final.[292] Thus, if the draft is dishonored, the bank can demand repayment or charge back to the account of its customer.[293]

The other part of § 4–106 is drafted in the alternative.[294] Alternative A, which represents the commercial and banking practices of New York and surrounding states, treats a note or other instrument (§ 4–106(b) uses the more comprehensive term "item") made payable at a bank as the equivalent of a draft drawn on the bank. Thus the bank is ordered to make payment out of the account of the maker or acceptor when the instrument falls due without consulting the maker or acceptor. Even if the instrument states that it is payable at a bank, the bank cannot occupy the status of a payor bank unless the instrument is to fall due out of funds of the maker in current account or funds that are otherwise immediately available for the payment of the instrument.[295] And, if the bank pays the instrument despite a written and acknowledged stop-payment order, the instrument can be treated as a check in a resultant lawsuit.[296] Alternative B treats an item payable at a bank as merely designating a place of payment. The function of the bank is to notify the obligor that the instrument has been presented and to ask for instruc-

§ 3–111, which, except as provided for items under Article 4 (see Official Comment to § 3–111 and § 4–106(b), discussed, infra), determines the place of payment if not stated in the instrument. See also note 300, infra.

290. § 4–106(a).

291. Official Comment 1 to § 4–106(a).

292. In Berman v. United States Nat'l Bank, 197 Neb. 268, 249 N.W.2d 187 (Neb. 1976), where the instrument bore the designation "check" and simply had "through" in small print before the name of the bank, the court found the instrument was ambiguous and, based on what the parties had done over a long period, it determined the bank was a payor and thus accountable to the payee of the drafts after its midnight deadline had passed under § 4–302. Other similar cases include Southern Cotton Oil Co., Inc. v. Merchants Nat'l Bank, 670 F.2d 548 (5th Cir.1982); Horney v. Covington County Bank, 716 F.2d 335 (5th Cir.1983); and Reynolds–Wilson Lumber Co. v. Peoples Nat'l Bank, 1985 OK 32, 699 P.2d 146 (Okla.1985). § 4–106(c) explicitly addresses this issue, and generally would reverse these cases on the basis the bank is intended only to be a collecting bank where there is a non-bank drawee. See under § 4–106(c), Great Western Bank v. Steve James Ford, Inc., 915 F.Supp. 392 (S.D.Ga. 1996), so holding.

293. Manufacturers Nat'l Bank v. Sutherland, 16 Mich.App. 286, 167 N.W.2d 894 (Mich.Ct.App.1969). The provisions of Article 4 and Regulation CC are discussed in Chapter 8.

294. § 4–106(b).

295. Whitehall Packing Co. v. First Nat'l City Bank, N.A., 55 A.D.2d 675, 390 N.Y.S.2d 189 (1976).

296. Kupersmith v. Manufacturers Hanover Trust Co., 15 U.C.C. Rep. Serv. 696 (N.Y.Civ.Ct.1974).

tions. In the absence of specific instructions, the bank is not regarded as required or even authorized to pay. This reflects the custom in western and southern states. In a state adopting alternative B, a note payable at a bank is not equivalent to a check.[297]

[2] Omissions Not an Impairment of Negotiability

Although the negotiability of an instrument often will be affected by what it says, if it is negotiable in form it seldom will be affected by what it does not say.[298] Thus the omission of a statement of any consideration, or of the place where the instrument is drawn or payable, does not impair negotiability.[299] The negotiability of an instrument is not affected by the omission of a date.[300] However, this only means that the absence of a date in itself will not impair negotiability. Thus under old Article 3 an undated instrument providing that it is payable "thirty days after date" is not negotiable[301] unless the date is inserted, as provided for incomplete instruments under the rules discussed, *infra*.[302]

¶ 2.05 Incomplete Instruments

[1] When an Instrument is Complete, Incomplete, or Not Within Article 3

An instrument, incomplete with reference to the requirements for negotiability, is not enforceable in that form.[303] It may not be governed by Article 3 at all. For example, an incomplete writing that lacks an essential element or a complete writing that lacks an essential element for negotiability and which contains no blanks or spaces or any other

---

297. Don E. Williams Co. v. Commissioner, 527 F.2d 649 (7th Cir.1975), *aff'd,* 429 U.S. 569, 97 S.Ct. 850, 51 L.Ed.2d 48 (1977). For an illustration of the operation of the different alternatives, *see* Great Western Bank v. Steve James Ford, Inc., 915 F.Supp. 392 (S.D.Ga.1996) (failure to timely return draft subjected bank to only negligence liability under Alternative B rather than strict liability of a payor bank).

298. As a result, current UCC Article 3 omits many provisions of old Article 3 along these lines as unnecessary.

299. Old § 3–112(1)(a).

300. Old § 3–114(1) (deleted in current § 3–113 as unnecessary), and Carnival Leisure Industries, Ltd. v. Aubin, 830 F.Supp. 371 (S.D.Tex.1993), *rev'd,* 53 F.3d 716 (5th Cir.1995). Current § 3–113(b) stipulates the date if the instrument is undated. Section 3–113(a) also provides the rule if the instrument is antedated or postdated. *See* Staff Builders of Philadelphia, Inc. v. Koschitzki, 18 UCC Rep. Serv. 2d 228 (E.D.Pa.1992), *rev'd,* 989 F.2d 692 (3d Cir.1993) (a postdated check that is honored is payment on date borne by check absent contrary agreement). *See also* Commerce Bank, N.A. v. Rickett, 329 N.J.Super. 379, 748 A.2d 111, 41 UCC Rep. Serv. 2d 231 (App.Div. 2000), determining when check with mistaken date was overdue.

301. Official Comment 3 to old § 3–109 and Official Comment 2 to old § 3–114.

302. The result is different under current Article 3. *See* note 237, *supra*.

¶ 2.05

303. Distinguish instruments that appear to be incomplete but that are interpreted as legally complete. An example appears in Bryan v. Bartlett, 435 F.2d 28 (8th Cir.1970), *cert. denied sub. nom.* Edwards v. Bryan, 402 U.S. 915, 91 S.Ct. 1373, 28 L.Ed.2d 658 (1971), where the court held that a note in which the amount of the annual installment was left blank was not incomplete but rather was enforceable with the entire amount of the note being due one year from date.

indication that what is missing is to be supplied, does not fall within Article 3.[304]

On the other hand, Article 3 potentially may apply to the instrument even though at that point it does not fit the form requirements, if it can be determined the parties intended a negotiable instrument. For example, an instrument reciting "Pay to the order of _____" may be treated as an instrument intended to be completed.[305] So, too, an undated instrument payable "thirty days after date,"[306] instruments where the amount of the instrument is left out;[307] as noted, where the name of the payee is omitted;[308] and even where all of the instrument is left blank except for the signature of the maker or drawer.[309]

[2] *Authorized and Unauthorized Complete Instruments*

Under Article 3, when a paper is signed (by the maker or drawer) while still incomplete in any necessary respect,[310] but shows at the time of signing that it is intended (again by the maker or drawer) to become a negotiable instrument, it cannot be enforced until completed, but when it is completed in accordance with authority given, it is effective as completed and is governed by Article 3.[311] Moreover, enforcement is allowed even if the instrument is incomplete, as long as the requirements of § 3–104 then are met.[312] This is why, as previously discussed, a check without a payee can be enforced as a bearer instrument.[313] If an incomplete instrument is completed other than as authorized, it likewise is within Article 3 even though not delivered,[314] but is subject to the

---

304. Official Comment 3 to § 3–115 (which uses the illustration of an instrument with no amount filled in). *See, e.g.,* Hoss v. Fabacher, 578 S.W.2d 454 (Tex.Civ. App.1979) (signed form which stated no name of payee and contained no promise to pay any amount was not an instrument within the meaning of the Code). *See also* note 308, *infra.* But now see § 3–115, Official Comment 2, which indicates a check without the name of the payee filled in is a bearer instrument if not completed. *See* notes 239 and 247, *supra,* and discussion, *infra.*

305. *See* Gray v. American Express Co., 34 N.C.App. 714, 239 S.E.2d 621 (N.C.Ct. App.1977) and note 304, *supra.*

306. *See* notes 301 and 302, *supra.*

307. *E.g.,* In re Estate of Norris, 532 P.2d 981 (Colo.Ct.App.1974). *See* Official Comment 3 to § 3–115.

308. *See* § 3–115, Official Comment 2, and note 304, *supra.*

309. *E.g.,* First Nat'l City Bank v. American Broadcasting Co., 68 Misc.2d 861, 328 N.Y.S.2d 326 (Sup.Ct.1971).

310. "Necessary" means necessary to a complete instrument and will always include the promise or order, the designation of the payee, and the amount payable, and may include the time of payment. Official Comment 2 to old § 3–115 and Carnival Leisure Industries, Ltd. v. Aubin, 830 F.Supp. 371 (S.D.Tex.1993), *rev'd,* 53 F.3d 716 (5th Cir.1995). *But,* for example, *see* note 304, *supra.*

311. § 3–115(a) and (b) and *In re* Wegener, 186 B.R. 692 (Bankr.D.Neb.1995). The court in Milwaukee Petroleum Co. v. Glembin, 89 Wis.2d 174, 278 N.W.2d 471 (Wis.Ct.App.1979) stated that because old § 3–115 requires enforcement of an instrument as completed, in absence of proof that completion was unauthorized there is a presumption of authority to complete an incomplete instrument. On this point, *see* § 3–115(d).

312. § 3–115(b).

313. *See* Official Comment 2 to § 3–115, and note 304, *supra.*

314. §§ 3–115(a) and 3–105. This changes the rule prior to the UCC that an undelivered, incomplete instrument was not, when completed, a valid contract in the hands of any holder as against the person who signed it before delivery. *See* § 3–105(b), which provides non-issuance is

defense of material alteration.[315]

Most cases do not involve an incomplete instrument that is never completed[316] nor an argument that the paper was not intended to become an instrument when it was signed because the test for intent is objective.[317] Rather, the issue that is litigated concerns the unauthorized completion of the instrument. That issue is discussed in Chapter 6.

---

a defense (see Jones v. Phillips, 237 Ga. App. 24, 513 S.E.2d 241 (Ga.Ct.App.1999)), as is conditional issuance (delivery) or issuance for a special purpose. Establishing such may involve a parol evidence issue in some instances. See note 179, supra, and Herzog Contracting Corp. v. McGowen Corp., 976 F.2d 1062 (7th Cir.1992). See also the discussion in Chapter 3, infra.

315. § 3–115(c). Unauthorized completion and alteration still should be distinguished because § 3–407(c), which deals with the defense of material alteration against a subsequent holder in due course, provides different results depending on whether the instrument has been altered or completed otherwise than as authorized.

316. One case that did is Gray v. American Express Co., 34 N.C.App. 714, 239 S.E.2d 621 (N.C.App.1977), where the court determined that the plaintiff had the right to complete travelers checks he had taken in payment for goods by filling in his name as payee. However, because he did not, even though he had held them for nine years, the checks were incomplete and unenforceable against their issuer. See note 310, supra, but see § 3–115, Official Comment 2.

317. In re Wegener, 186 B.R. 692 (Bankr.D.Neb.1995) (secret intention not to be bound not controlling). But see Herdman v. First Nat'l City Bank, 3 UCC Rep. Serv. 628 (N.Y.Sup.Ct.1966), where in an action to recover the amount of a check allegedly signed, but with the name of the payee left blank, and then stolen and paid after having been made payable to cash, the court denied a motion for summary judgment, in part on the ground that a factual question existed as to whether the check was left in an incomplete form in a desk.

Chapter 3

RIGHTS ON NEGOTIABLE INSTRUMENTS

Analysis

Para.
¶3.01 Issue and the Rights It Creates 87
    [1] An Instrument Is Not Effective Until Issued 87
    [2] The Concept of Holder 89
    [3] Rights of One Not a Holder of an Instrument 90
        [a] Remitters, Takers, Nonpossessors, and Creditors 90
        [b] Transferees and Shelter Rights 92
    [4] Rights of the Holder of an Instrument 95
        [a] Introduction 95
        [b] Right to Enforce the Instrument or Discharge Parties on It 96
        [c] Right to Transfer or Negotiate the Instrument 97
¶3.02 Transfer and Negotiation 98
    [1] Transfer 98
    [2] Negotiation of a Bearer Instrument 98
    [3] Negotiation of an Order Instrument 99
        [a] The Requirements of Indorsement and Delivery 99
        [b] Who May Indorse 102
            [i] Introduction 102
            [ii] Instruments Payable to More Than One Person 102
            [iii] Instruments Payable to Estates, Offices, and the Like 104
            [iv] Instruments with Misspelled Names, Accommodation Indorsers, and Unauthorized Indorsers 105
        [c] Types of Indorsements and Their Effect 106
            [i] Blank Indorsement 106
            [ii] Special Indorsement 107
            [iii] Restrictive Indorsement 108
                [A] Types of Restrictive Indorsements 108
                [B] Effect of Restrictive Indorsements 109
    [4] Rescission of Negotiation and Reacquisition 112
        [a] Rescission 112
        [b] Reacquisition 114
¶3.03 Holder in Due Course Status 115
    [1] Introduction 115
        [a] The Reason and Need for Holder in Due Course Status ... 115
        [b] Payee As a Holder in Due Course 117
    [2] Elements of Proper Taking 120
        [a] Value 120
        [b] Good Faith and Lack of Notice 123

Para.			
¶3.03	Holder in Due Course Status—Continued		
	[i]	Relevant Time for Meeting Requirements	123
	[ii]	Bad Faith or Knowledge of Agent	124
	[iii]	Good Faith in General	124
	[iv]	Notice in General	128
	[v]	Specific Notice Provisions	132
[c]	Burden of Proof		136
[3]	Status of a Holder in Due Course		139
[a]	Freedom from Claims and Defenses		139
	[i]	Real and Personal Defenses	139
	[ii]	Setoff (Claims in Recoupment)	140
	[iii]	Claims	142
[b]	Finality of Payment		144
¶3.04	Limitations on Holder in Due Course Status		146
[1]	In the UCC		146
[a]	Nonordinary Course Acquisitions		146
[b]	Defenses and Claims of Persons With Whom the Holder Has Dealt		147
	[i]	Defenses	147
	[ii]	Claims	148
[2]	Case Law Limits		150
[3]	State Legislation		152
[4]	Federal Rule		153

¶ 3.01 Issue and the Rights It Creates

[1] An Instrument Is Not Effective Until Issued

A negotiable instrument within Article 3 is a contract to pay money made by its maker or drawer.[1] Unlike an ordinary contract, however, a negotiable instrument is not enforceable before it is issued.[2] Issue means

---

¶ 3.01

1. §§ 3-104(a), 3-103(a)(3), (5), (6) and (9), 3-412, and 3-414.

2. Official Comment 1 to § 3-420, § 3-105(a), and Jones v. Phillips, 237 Ga. App. 24, 513 S.E.2d 241 (Ga.Ct.App.1999). *See also* note 314 in Chapter 2, *supra*. This is not inconsistent with § 3-105(b), which states that an unissued instrument is binding, because § 3-105(a) defines "issue" as requiring "delivery" for the purpose of giving rights on it to a person, and under § 1-201(a)(15) "delivery" must be voluntary. Thus most instruments sought to be enforced have been "issued" or "delivered" only in the physical sense, and nonissuance in the legal sense is a defense. Under the law prior to the UCC, every contract on a negotiable instrument was incomplete and revocable until delivery of the instrument for the purpose of giving it effect. W. Britton, Handbook of the Law of Bills and Notes § 50 (2d ed. 1961). This is the same rule under the UCC under §§ 3-105(b) and 3-305(a)(2) as nondelivery is a defense. Several exceptions exist; nondelivery is not a defense against a holder in due course, and the contract of an acceptor under §§ 3-413 and 3-409(a) is activated by either delivery or notification. Two interesting (and perhaps debatable) cases may illustrate an exception of sorts. In both cases, checks were physically delivered to donees by a dying person. Even though they also were paid after the drawer's death (see § 4-405), the courts held there was no delivery until the funds were paid, and since payment occurred after death it was too late as either the order was revoked or a presentment warranty was breached when one check was filled in after authority to do so was revoked by death and so there was an alteration. Smart v. Woo, 20 UCC Rep. Serv. 2d 1288 (Va. Cir. Ct.1993), *aff'd*, 247 Va. 365, 442 S.E.2d 690 (1994) and DeLuca v. BancOhio Nat'l Bank, 74 Ohio App.3d 233, 598 N.E.2d 781 (Ohio Ct.App.1991).

the first delivery[3] of the instrument[4] to a holder or to a nonholder for the purpose of giving rights on the instrument to a person.[5] The case of *Rex Smith Propane, Inc. v. National Bank of Commerce*[6] furnishes an example of this rule. There a cashier's check was drawn at the request of a customer of the bank but was canceled by the bank before delivery to the payee when the bank learned its customer had gone bankrupt. The court denied the payee any rights in the check.[7]

For "issuance" to occur, delivery to the payee or to an agent of the payee of the instrument is sufficient.[8] Where delivery is made to the

---

3. "Delivery" is the voluntary transfer of possession. UCC § 1–201(a)(15).

4. "Instrument" is defined in § 3–104(b) as a negotiable instrument. Nonetheless, the definition of "issue" includes the delivery of an incomplete instrument. § 3–105(b). *But see* Gray v. American Express Co., 34 N.C.App. 714, 239 S.E.2d 621 (N.C.App. 1977) (incomplete checks were not enforceable).

5. § 3–105(a). The UCC does not define the term "nonholder" and old § 3–102(1)(a) used the term "remitter," which it did not define either. Section 3–103(a)(11) defines "remitter" as a person who purchases an instrument from its issuer (*see* § 3–105(c)) if the instrument is payable to an identified person other than the purchaser. Thus the meaning is the same as would be found in relation to old Article 3 as under other law "remitter" means the purchaser of an instrument and derives from the early practice where a debtor would purchase a draft drawn by A upon B and payable to a creditor to "remit" it to the creditor. Britton, *supra* note 2, § 75. A remitter then is one kind of nonholder. In essence, § 3–105(a) defines "issue" more broadly than old § 3–102(1)(a), and includes the first delivery to anyone by the drawer or maker for the purpose of giving rights to anyone on the instrument. § 3–105, Official Comment 1.

6. 372 F.Supp. 499 (N.D.Tex.1974). *See also* note 2, *supra*; note 7, *infra*; Walker v. Community Bank, 596 So.2d 886 (Ala.1992) (a negotiable instrument has no legal existence until it is delivered); and First Sec. Bank v. Goddard, 181 Mont. 407, 593 P.2d 1040 (Mont. 1979), where the issue was at what time a debtor became obligated on a note. Against the contention the payee could not enforce the note until it received it, the court determined the note was "issued" upon delivery, and delivery was effected when the note was mailed.

7. Another example arose in Winn v. First Bank, 581 S.W.2d 21 (Ky.Ct.App. 1978). In the *Winn* case, a mother drew a check payable to the local feed store where her son owed a considerable debt and delivered the check to the son. The son, however, forged the indorsement of the feed store and cashed the check. In the suit by the feed store, the court said the store had at best an expectancy in the check and could not recover. *See also:* Locks v. North Towne Nat'l Bank, 115 Ill.App.3d 729, 71 Ill.Dec. 531, 451 N.E.2d 19 (1983) (assignee of asserted beneficial owner of cashier's check had no standing when check was payable to and in possession of another); Da Silva v. Sanders, 38 UCC Rep. Serv. 270 (D.D.C. 1984) (plaintiff had no claim to check issued by bank to represent proceeds of plaintiff's property sold by bank and made payable to and delivered by bank to Small Business Administration to which plaintiff owed money); Sheiman v. Lafayette Bank & Trust Co., 4 Conn.App. 39, 492 A.2d 219 (Conn.Ct.App.1985) (heirs to whom a certificate of deposit had neither been issued or negotiated had no interest in the instrument); Bank of Waverly v. City Bank & Trust Co., 600 S.W.2d 630 (Mo.Ct.App. 1980) (lender to car dealer, even though it had a security interest in a check given to purchase an automobile, was a stranger to the instrument); Saloga v. Central Kansas Credit Union, 245 Kan. 668, 783 P.2d 339 (Kan. 1989) (even though cashier's check delivered to joint payee, when it was returned to other joint payee (who was the remitter) for indorsement, and the remitter instead returned it to the issuer, the issuer was entitled to rely on the fact that the check apparently had not been delivered); and Tuttle v. Rose, 102 Ill.App.3d 865, 58 Ill.Dec. 414, 430 N.E.2d 356 (1981); and Leopold v. Halleck, 106 Ill.App.3d 386, 62 Ill.Dec. 447, 436 N.E.2d 29 (1982) (person to whom instrument is payable and who is in possession need not allege and prove delivery to recover).

8. Eldon's Super Fresh Stores, Inc. v. Merrill Lynch, Pierce, Fenner & Smith, Inc., 296 Minn. 130, 207 N.W.2d 282 (Minn. 1973). *See also* Humberto Decorators, Inc. v. Plaza Nat'l Bank, 180 N.J.Super. 170, 434 A.2d 618 (App.Div.1981) (delivery to agent of payee established rights in payee).

person who purchased a cashier's check or a similar instrument, rather than to the payee, issue occurs upon delivery to the remitter.[9]

[2] The Concept of Holder

Issuance of an instrument to the payee of it, or in the case of bearer paper, to the person otherwise initially intended to have rights on it, will constitute that person a holder of the instrument. A holder is a person who is in possession of an instrument drawn or issued to the person or to the order of the person, or to bearer.[10] The doctrine of constructive possession is applicable under the UCC. Thus where the note of a corporation payable to A was left in the possession of one of the principals of the corporation in order to have the corporate seal impressed on the note, but the principal was holding the note for delivery to A, A was determined to be the holder of the note even though he had not taken actual possession of it.[11] Being a holder is important because, with the exceptions discussed, *infra,* in this chapter, only the holder of an instrument has any rights on it, or any ability to deal with it.[12]

A bearer instrument would be issued upon delivery to the person intended to have rights in it. § 3–105(a). *See also* 3–420(a) and Official Comment 1 to that section; and Crystaplex Plastics, Ltd. v. Redevelopment Agency, 77 Cal.App.4th 990, 92 Cal.Rptr.2d 197 (Cal.App.2000).

9. § 3–105(a). *See also* cases cited in note 7, *supra.* In this case, a debtor-creditor relationship arises between the remitter and the issuing bank; the remitter retains ownership of the instrument until delivery to the payee; and the remitter is entitled to return the instrument for cancellation. Gillespie v. Riley Mgmt. Corp., 59 Ill.2d 211, 319 N.E.2d 753 (1974). The court seems to have overlooked this rule in DiMonda v. Freedom Fed. Sav., 385 Mass. 1012, 434 N.E.2d 210 (Mass. 1982), where the remitter of a bank check, misappropriated by a third party so it did not reach the payee, was denied recovery against both the drawer and the drawee.

10. § 1–201(a)(21)(A) (stating this more generally).

11. Billingsley v. Kelly, 261 Md. 116, 274 A.2d 113 (Md. 1971). Similar cases are Midfirst Bank, SSB v. C.W. Haynes & Co., 893 F.Supp. 1304 (D.S.C.1994), *aff'd,* 87 F.3d 1308 (4th Cir.1996) (document custodian of residential mortgages pooled, securitized, and sold to investors was in constructive possession for holder in due course purposes), and Federal Deposit Ins. Corp. v. Linn, 671 F.Supp. 547 (N.D.Ill.1987) (in suit by FDIC against obligors, failed bank which retained notes held for FDIC as its agent). The *Linn* case demonstrates that "holder" status is not limited to persons to whom the instrument is initially issued. Later takers of the instrument may be holders because a "holder" also includes a person who is in possession of an instrument indorsed to that person or to that person's order, or to bearer, or in blank, or drawn to bearer. UCC § 1–201(a)(21)(A). *Compare* Lawson v. Gibbs, 591 S.W.2d 292 (Tex.Civ. App.1979) (indorsement and delivery of note constituted transferee a holder) *with* Wear v. Farmers & Merchants Bank, 605 P.2d 27 (Alaska 1980) (no indorsement, no holder status) and Ballengee v. New Mexico Fed. Sav. & Loan Ass'n, 109 N.M. 423, 786 P.2d 37 (N.M. 1990) (person in possession of unindorsed note not a holder). *See also* Lamb v. Opelika Prod. Credit Ass'n, 367 So.2d 957 (Ala.1979) (indorsement without delivery does not create holder status).

12. Old § 3–301; notes 7 and 11, *supra.* Current Article 3 deletes old § 3–301; the rights formerly stated there are specified in other sections. Official Comment to § 3–301. *See also,* Official Comment 1 to § 3–420. Instead, § 3–301 defines who is a "person entitled to enforce" the instrument and thus spells out what is discussed, *infra,* this chapter, and is not dealt with explicitly in old Article 3. Nonetheless, the most common person entitled to enforce an instrument is the holder of it (see § 3–301(i)); accordingly the discussion here often is presented using that term without intending necessarily to exclude other persons who may be entitled to enforce or otherwise deal with the instrument.

[3] Rights of One Not a Holder of an Instrument

[a] Remitters, Takers, Nonpossessors, and Creditors

There are several situations where a person may have rights on an instrument[13] but not be the holder of it. One example already noted is a remitter who is not a holder.[14] As the court in *Gillespie v. Riley Management Corp.*[15] stated, the remitter of an instrument retains ownership of it until delivery to the payee and is entitled to return it for cancellation. Another example would seem to be a person who has "taken" an instrument issued for value before it is due, and who may enforce the liability of an accommodation party.[16] This liability runs in favor of the taker even though that person is not a holder.[17]

Under old § 3–804 and current § 3–309, the person entitled to enforce an instrument that is lost, whether by destruction, theft, or otherwise,[18] is not a holder because of lack of possession, but may maintain an action in their own name and recover from any party liable on the instrument upon due proof of ownership, of the facts that prevent production of the instrument, and of the instrument's terms.[19]

---

13. A distinction is intended between "rights on the instrument" and "rights with respect to the instrument." There are many instances where a nonholder may have rights with respect to an instrument. For example, the owner of an instrument that has been stolen and the indorsement of the owner forged may sue in conversion. These other rights are discussed in Chapter 7. § 3–301 makes this distinction.

14. Munson v. American Nat'l Bank & Trust Co., 484 F.2d 620 (7th Cir.1973) (purchaser of cashier's check payable to a bank was neither a payee nor a holder). See supra note 9; § 3–301.

15. See note 9, *supra*.

16. Old § 3–415; no change is indicated in current § 3–419.

17. James Talcott, Inc. v. Fred Ratowsky Assocs., 2 UCC Rep. Serv. 1134 (Pa. Com.Pl.1965). Holder status may be absent because of the lack of indorsement. See §§ 1–201(a)(21)(A) and 3–201.

18. For example, the owner of an instrument lost during the collection process or a payee whose instrument has been taken and indorsement forged. See § 3–301(iii) and National Shawmut Bank v. International Yarn Corp., 322 F.Supp. 116 (S.D.N.Y.1970). But the instrument must have been delivered and then lost because an instrument never delivered is not "ownable." See, *supra*, note 7 and § 3–309(a).

19. See, *e.g.*, Laurel Bank & Trust Co. v. Sahadi, 32 Conn. Supp. 172, 345 A.2d 53 (Conn.Com.Pl.1975) (recovery allowed when copy of check was admitted without objection and was stipulated to be accurate and there was an explanation of loss). *But see* Brunswick Corp. v. Briscoe, 523 S.W.2d 115 (Mo.Ct.App.1975) (plaintiff's statement alone, where no executed or unexecuted copy of the instrument could be found and where there was no evidence that the mortgage securing the instrument ever was recorded, was found to be inadequate). *See also* Yanoff v. Muncy, 676 N.E.2d 765 (Ind. Ct.App.), *vacating*, 668 N.E.2d 1259 (Ind. App.1996) (failure to prove terms); Western Nat'l Bank v. Rives, 927 S.W.2d 681 (Tex. App.—Amarillo 1996), *writ denied* Feb. 21, 1977, *rehearing overruled*, 1996 WL 469677 (Tex.App.1996) (failure to have possession before instrument was lost and to explain what happened to note); *but see* New England Sav. Bank v. Bedford Realty Corp., 238 Conn. 745, 680 A.2d 301 (Conn. 1996) (foreclosures of mortgage without following § 3–309 procedure allowed when amount of debt could be proved). Section 3–309 is explicit and requires a person who was in possession and entitled to enforce the instrument when loss of possession occurred, a loss of possession that was not a result of a transfer or a seizure, and an inability to reasonably obtain possession because of destruction, another person's wrongful possession and the like. Presumably, a holder whose indorsement is forged (*see* note 18, *supra*), if suing under § 3–309(a), combines the action with a claim to obtain possession from the drawer so as to meet one or the other predicate for suit. *See also* § 3–309(b).

In Dennis Joslin Co. v. Robinson Broadcasting Corp., 977 F.Supp. 491 (D.D.C.

Another example of a nonholder who may have rights on an instrument is a creditor of a holder who acquires the instrument upon or pursuant to execution or like process. Unless the instrument is a bearer instrument, the creditor will not be a holder because the creditor has possession of the instrument but no appropriate indorsement. Nonetheless, the creditor may enforce or otherwise realize on the instrument. Under the law prior to the UCC, the purchaser of the instrument under an execution against the prior holder could enforce the instrument in their own name.[20] Under current Article 3 that purchaser, absent appro-

---

1997), the note was executed by Robinson to a bank, the bank failed and the FDIC acquired the instrument, and later sold it to plaintiff's assignor but did not deliver it as the note was lost. Plaintiff was denied recovery under § 3-309 because it was not in possession when the note was lost. The result of the case is wrong, as the FDIC was in possession when the note was lost and its rights ultimately were transferred to the plaintiff. *See* § 3-203(b) and Official Comment 5 to UCC § 9-109, which covers sales of promissory notes. Subsequent cases have not followed the *Joslin* case. *See* Beal Bank, S.S.B. v. Caddo Parish–Villas South, Ltd., 218 B.R. 851 (N.D.Tex.1998), *appeal dismissed*, 174 F.3d 624 (5th Cir.1999); NAB Asset Venture II v. Lenertz, Inc., 36 UCC Rep. Serv. 2d 474 (Minn.Ct.App.1998); Southeast Investments, Inc. v. Clade, 40 UCC Rep. Serv. 2d 255 (N.D.Tex.1999); Bobby D Associates v. DiMarcantonio, 751 A.2d 673, 41 UCC Rep. Serv. 2d 878 (Pa.Super.2000); and YYY Corp. v. Gazda, 145 N.H. 53, 761 A.2d 395, 41 UCC Rep. Serv. 2d 222 (N.H. 2000). A 2002 amendment to § 3-309(a)(1)(B) repudiates the result in the *Dennis Joslin* case. Amendment of the Official Comments to § 3-309 also clarify several other issues: whether the provision applies when an instrument is lost in transit; whether the provision alters rules that apply to the disposition of checks in connection with truncation; and whether a security interest may attach when the debtor is a person entitled to enforce the instrument but is not in possession of it. Official Comments 2 and 3 to § 3-309. Unfortunately, a somewhat similar case to the *Joslin* case is Strickler v. Marx, 246 Va. 384, 436 S.E.2d 447 (Va. 1993), where a business associate of one Davis acquired checks for which Davis was liable to his bank but was denied recovery on the ground he was not a holder since the checks had not been indorsed when he acquired them. Sections 3-309(b) and 3-308(b) would allow recovery on these facts since the plaintiff was a person entitled to enforce the instrument; moreover, so was the tranferor and thus the plaintiff by reason of § 3-203(b) (old § 3-201). *See also*

Piper v. Goodwin, 20 F.3d 216 (6th Cir. 1994).

A court may require security indemnifying the defendant against loss by reason of further claims on the instrument. This is in the discretion of the court, except in New York, where the giving of security is mandatory and the amount is fixed by statute. § 3-309 requires adequate protection, and is explicit on why flexibility is desirable. *See* Official Comment to § 3-309. Hopefully, New York will adopt the uniform version.

The New York non-uniform amendment has helped to expose, however, a practical problem in these provisions. Suppose, for example, a person puts his or her savings in a cashier's check, and it is lost in the mail? The bank cannot be sure it was not indorsed in blank and thus may come into the hands of a holder in due course. But the statute of limitations barring a claim may have years to run. In Santos v. First Nat'l State Bank, 186 N.J.Super. 52, 451 A.2d 401 (1982), the court resolved the dilemma as well as possible by putting the check proceeds in an escrow account, which protected the bank and preserved the interest, but not use of the principal, for the customer.

To meet this issue, New York enacted a statute preserving unimpaired payment of such bank obligations for a shorter period, after which the bank could be relieved of liability and the customer is liable. § 3-312 takes a similar tack. An asserted lost, destroyed or stolen cashier's, teller's or certified check is good against the bank for at least 90 days, the period empirical studies show is the period in which the overwhelming majority of such instruments are presented and paid. Thereafter, the bank may be relieved from liability by paying the amount of the instrument to a claimant who has filed with the bank an appropriate "declaration of loss." The provision furnishes an option to using § 3-309. *See* discussion *infra*.

20. Britton, *supra* note 2, at 184.

priate indorsement, may not be a holder,[21] but § 3–203(b), giving a transferee the rights of the transferor, in this context should allow the same result.[22]

Another case focused upon by § 3–301 is the person who must return the payment when an instrument has been accepted or paid by mistake; that person is entitled to enforce the instrument which is treated as dishonored.[23]

[b] Transferees and Shelter Rights

The most significant situation where the nonholder of an instrument may have rights on it is the case of a transferee of the instrument.[24] The transfer of an instrument vests in the transferee the rights the transferor has in it.[25] Moreover, unless otherwise

---

21. While it once was perhaps debatable whether the purchaser could be a holder even of a bearer instrument because there is authority that "delivery" does not include the transfer of certificates by a sheriff's sale since the transfer is not "voluntary" (Mazer v. Williams Bros. Co., 461 Pa.587, 337 A.2d 559 (Pa.1975),) *now see*: Good v. Good, 72 N.C.App. 312, 324 S.E.2d 43 (N.C.Ct.App.1985) (executor of estate of payee); Third Nat'l Bank v. Hardi–Gardens Supply, Inc., 380 F.Supp. 930 (M.D.Tenn. 1974) (holder in due course, which after default on note advertised and sold the note at a judicial sale at which it repurchased in its own name, did not diminish its status as a holder in due course); and by implication § 3–302(c)(i). *See also* current UCC § 3–201(a), and Official Comment 1 thereto, which allows negotiation by a voluntary or involuntary transfer.

22. Transfer of possession can be either voluntary or involuntary under § 3–201(a), and, given its purpose, the similar definition in § 3–203(a), but which focuses only on "delivery," is not seen as contradictory. *See* Official Comment 1 to § 3–203.

23. §§ 3–301(iii) and 3–418(d). *See also* § 4–201(b).

24. §§ 3–301(ii) and 3–203(a) and (b). Included also is a person who acquires the rights of a holder by subrogation. § 3–301, Official Comment, and *see* Federal Deposit Ins. Corp. v. Webb, 464 F.Supp. 520, 25 UCC Rep. Serv. 590 (E.D.Tenn.1978) (FDIC, as purchaser in bulk of part of the assets of a bank threatened with insolvency, was not a holder in due course but, as guarantor of the deposits of the bank, became subrogated to its rights). *See also*: the *Linn* case, *supra* note 11, which determined the failed bank held notes as agent of the FDIC; the discussion in Chapter 1, *supra*, of the status of the FDIC under federal law, which status a transferee of the instrument would acquire under 3–203(b); *but see* note 19, *supra*, concerning instruments lost by the FDIC and similar situations. On the other hand, as discussed, *infra*, a transferee by agreement may not be able to obtain holder status. Becker v. National Bank & Trust Co., 222 Va. 716, 284 S.E.2d 793 (Va. 1981). Also a person to whom the instrument is delivered for a purpose other than enforcement of the instrument is not a transferee; *e.g.*, a drawee. § 3–203, Official Comment 1. Finally, in Mandolfo v. Chudy, 253 Neb. 927, 573 N.W.2d 135 (Neb. 1998), the Mandolfos were guarantors with defendant Chudy of a note under a separate guarantee agreement. The Mandolfos paid the note and took an assignment of it, and then sued Chudy, not for contribution, but as a guarantor. The court ruled that the Mandolfos could proceed as creditors on the note, but the assignment did not alter their status as guarantors of the note and that the guaranty was neither part of the note nor a negotiable instrument itself.

25. § 3–203(b). *See* Mustin v. Citizens & Southern Nat'l Bank, 168 Ga.App. 549, 309 S.E.2d 822 (Ga.Ct.App.1983) (B, as A's transferee, acquired A's rights); and Fore v. Bles, 149 Ariz. 603, 721 P.2d 151 (Ariz.Ct. App.1986) (divorced spouse of holder awarded interest in note). This includes the transfer of a limited interest. §§ 3–203(d) and 3–204(c). *See also*: Federal Deposit Ins. Corp. v. West, 244 Ga. 396, 260 S.E.2d 89 (Ga. 1979); All Am. Fin. Co. v. Pugh Shows, Inc., 30 Ohio St.3d 130, 507 N.E.2d 1134 (Ohio 1987) (separate assignment as security "until such date as loan #1295 is paid in full" not a negotiation; the result is correct because of the separate assignment, but query the reason given that it was a mere partial assignment; Official Comment 2 to § 3–204); Illinois State Bank v. Yates, 678 S.W.2d 819 (Mo.Ct.App.1984). *But see* Man-

agreed,[26] a transfer for value gives the transferee the right to have the unqualified indorsement of the transferor.[27] Thus if the transferor was a holder, that person's transferee acquires those rights.[28]

A transferee, however, acquires no greater rights than the transferor had. Thus in *Stevens v. Bowie National Bank*,[29] where the transferor had waived the delinquency of certain payments on the note sold to a bank, the court held the bank acquired no greater rights in this respect than those possessed by its transferor. Despite this, the court determined the bank was not precluded from acceleration and foreclosure because, after the debtor learned the bank was attempting to accelerate the

---

ufacturers Hanover Trust Co. v. Robinson, 157 Misc.2d 651, 597 N.Y.S.2d 986 (Sup.Ct. 1993), where notes given to a partnership assertedly were induced by fraud, were negotiated to a bank as a holder in due course, and then under unexplained circumstances were negotiated back to the partnership, and later again to the bank. The court refused to treat the bank as having holder in due course rights as an asserted party to the fraud under § 3-203(b); this seems incorrect since originally the bank was a holder in due course and only sought to reassert rights that it once had. *See also* WAMCO, III, Ltd. v. First Piedmont Mortgage Corp., 856 F.Supp. 1076 (E.D.Va.1994) (assignee of RTC not entitled to longer statute of limitations of FIRREA applicable to actions brought by RTC in its status as receiver).

A transfer may include the surrender of an instrument to any person who pays it, even a stranger. Old § 3-603(2) (current Article 3 omits this provision as unnecessary). Thus, for example, when the executor of the estate of an indorser on a note paid the holder and received the instrument, the executor was allowed to sue the maker and an earlier indorser. Eikel v. Bristow Corp., 529 S.W.2d 795 (Tex.Civ.App.1975). *See also* the *Good* case, *supra* note 21.

Section 3-203(b) does provide an exception where earlier the transferee was a party to any fraud or illegality affecting the instrument or had notice of a defense or claim. *See* § 3-203; Official Comment 4, Examples; and the *Robinson* case, above, this note.

26. The agreement need not be express and may be implied from conduct, past practice, or the circumstances of the transaction. Official Comment 3 to § 3-203.

27. For example, in Pancoast v. Century Homes, Inc., 8 UCC Rep. Serv. 1289 (Okla. Ct.App.1971), the holders of a note tendered it indorsed "without recourse." The court held that because there was no agreement either way concerning the indorsement of the note which was transferred for value, an unqualified indorsement was required, the court had authority to order an indorsement in blank, and, if the indorsement was not made, the decree would operate as an indorsement. The rule does not apply to bearer paper, which needs no indorsement.

28. Cases cited at note 25, *supra*, and Perry & Greer, Inc. v. Manning, 282 Or. 25, 576 P.2d 791 (Or. 1978). The same is true if the transferor was a holder in due course; § 3-203(b) makes this clear. *But see* Lamson v. Commercial Credit Corp., 187 Colo. 382, 531 P.2d 966 (Colo. 1975), where the court denied to the transferee of dishonored checks, indorsed "Pay Any Bank," the rights of the transferor bank that had taken them for collection. Noting that the transferee was not the customer initiating collection and that the checks had not been specially indorsed to the transferee (who was not a bank), the court perceived a conflict between old § 3-201 and old § 4-201(2) (current § 4-201(b)). The latter section provided that, except where the transferee is the customer or takes under indorsement, after an item has been indorsed with the words "pay any bank" or the like, only a bank may acquire the rights of a holder. The court believed old § 4-201(2) controlled over old § 3-201. In truth, there was no conflict; old § 4-201(2) was only intended to deny a person outside of the bank collection chain "holder" rights *in their own behalf*. *See also* latter cases cited in note 25, *supra*.

Another questionable case is Lipkowitz & Plaut v. Affrunti, 95 Misc.2d 849, 407 N.Y.S.2d 1010 (Sup.Ct.1978), where a transferee of secured notes who was not a holder was denied the right to accelerate payment because this was a right given by the acceleration clause in the notes only to a "holder." Holder rights by transfer seem not to have been asserted.

29. 517 S.W.2d 686 (Tex.Civ.App.1974), *rev'd on other grounds*, 532 S.W.2d 67 (Tex. 1975).

unpaid balance of the note, the waiver was no longer in effect; the debtor had a duty to tender the delinquent amount, and the failure to do so under the terms of the note and deed of trust authorized foreclosure.

A transferee acquires the rights of the transferor but not the transferor's status.[30] In short, a transferee cannot improve its position after transfer. Under old Articles 3 and 4, this was an important distinction with respect to a bank to which a check has been transferred for collection. Thus, in *Bowling Green, Inc. v. State Street Bank & Trust Co.*,[31] because the provisions of Article 4 govern inconsistent provisions in Article 3[32] and because old §§ 4–201 and 4–205[33] recognize the common bank practice of accepting unindorsed checks for deposit and permit the bank to supply a missing indorsement, the court believed that a depositary bank that took an unindorsed check could be a holder by reason of old § 3–201 (current § 3–203(b)) if it took from a holder.[34] The probable better interpretation was that "to require a bank to make a mark on a paper to achieve certain rights is not inconsistent with enabling the bank to place the mark on the paper."[35] Under current § 4–205(1), however, the *Bowling Green* view is adopted by the statute, and if a customer delivers an item to a depositary bank for collection, the depositary bank becomes a holder of the item if its customer had that status, and may become a holder in due course.[36] The final point in these

---

30. Security Pac. Nat'l Bank v. Chess, 58 Cal.App.3d 555, 129 Cal.Rptr. 852 (1976) (old § 3–201 assures a transferee the rights of the transferor, but not the transferor's status as a holder).

31. 425 F.2d 81 (1st Cir.1970).

32. §§ 3–102(b), 4–102(a). These provisions do not contemplate a conflict with Article 5 on letters of credit. *But see* UCC § 5–116(d) and Official Comment 4 to § 5–116. In All Service Exportacao, Importacao Comercio, S.A. v. Banco Bamerindus Do Brazil, S.A., 921 F.2d 32 (2d Cir.1990), the court perceived a conflict did exist between old § 5–114(2) (current §§ 5–108 and 5–109) and old § 4–303(1)(a) (current § 4–303(a)(1)), and held Article 4 controlled. For a discussion of the use of old § 3–307 (current § 3–308) in conjunction with old § 5–114, *see* United Bank Ltd. v. Cambridge Sporting Goods Corp., 41 N.Y.2d 254, 392 N.Y.S.2d 265, 360 N.E.2d 943 (N.Y.1976).

33. Current §§ 4–201 and 4–205.

34. Alternatively, the bank may return the check for indorsement. § 3–501(b)(3)(i); Total Aviation Servs. Inc. v. United Jersey Bank, 39 UCC Rep. Serv. 969 (E.D.N.Y. 1984). An interesting case which interprets the term "bank" in reference to old § 4–205 is Asian Int'l, Ltd. v. Merrill Lynch, Pierce, Fenner & Smith, Inc., 435 So.2d 1058 (La.Ct.App.1983) (Merrill Lynch a "bank" for purpose of supplying indorsement; *see* current § 4–105(1)). See further discussion of this point later in this book.

35. United Overseas Bank v. Veneers, Inc., 375 F.Supp. 596 (D.Md.1973) (to hold that some provisions of the UCC enable the transferee of a holder to become, without a necessary indorsement, a holder who is then able, other conditions being met, to be a holder in due course would render other sections of the UCC nugatory). *See also* Marine Midland Bank, N.A. v. Price, Miller, Evans & Flowers, 57 N.Y.2d 220, 455 N.Y.S.2d 565, 441 N.E.2d 1083 (N.Y. 1982).

36. § 4–205(1). This rule better accords with modern practice. Many depositary banks receive unindorsed checks under lock-box arrangements from customers who receive a high volume of checks. No purpose is served by requiring a depositary bank to supply an indorsement. The safeguard function of an indorsement is covered by a warranty made by the depositary bank. § 4–205(2). *See* Barber v. United States Nat'l Bank, 90 Or.App. 68, 750 P.2d 1183 (Or.Ct.App.1988). This view allows a bank to avoid the debacle experience in Marine Midland Bank, N.A. v. Price, Miller, Evans & Flowers, 85 A.D.2d 903, 446 N.Y.S.2d 797 (App.Div. 4th Dept. 1981), *rev'd on other grounds*, 57 N.Y.2d 220, 455 N.Y.S.2d 565, 441 N.E.2d 1083 (N.Y. 1982), where the bank indorsed the check "credit to the account of payee herein named/Marine Midland Chautauqua Bank" but instead wired

cases, of course, is not whether the banks had holder rights in their own right or by transfer, but whether they had the rights of a holder in due course. They could not be holders in due course unless they first were holders in their own right, but alternatively could have such rights as transferee.

A transferee has the right to maintain an action on the instrument in the transferee's own name.[37] In *Waters v. Waters*,[38] the former husband of the daughter of the payee of a note had executed and delivered a demand note to his then father-in-law. Before his death, the father had delivered the note to his daughter, telling her that it was hers and that she could collect it. He did not indorse the note. In the action by the daughter against her former husband on the instrument, the court held the daughter was the owner of the note and was entitled to enforce it.[39] Under § 3–301(i), a holder also has the right to enforce payment in its own name. There is, nonetheless, a distinction of considerable importance: the transferee of an instrument not payable to bearer and not indorsed is not aided by any presumption that the transferee is entitled to recover on the instrument, and transferees must account for their possession by proving the transaction through which the transferee acquired the instrument.[40]

[4] Rights of the Holder of an Instrument

[a] Introduction

Subject to the previously discussed exceptions in § 3–301(ii) and (iii), the holder of an instrument is the only person who has any rights on it or any ability to deal with it. The holder of an instrument is the proper party to transfer or to negotiate an instrument and to discharge it or to enforce payment in their own name.[41]

The holder of an instrument need not be the owner of it.[42] Perhaps the most common example of the dichotomy between ownership and holder status involves a bank in possession of a check deposited by the owner of it for collection. That was the situation in *Citizens National*

---

the funds to another account as instructed and then, when the check was dishonored, was advised it could not be a holder in due course since it did not follow its own indorsement.

37. §§ 3–301(ii), 3–412 through 3–415.

38. 498 S.W.2d 236 (Tex.Civ.App.1973).

39. A corollary of the right to enforce payment is the right to retain payment made. *See* First Nat'l Bank v. Barrett, 141 Ga.App. 161, 233 S.E.2d 24 (Ga.Ct.App. 1977) (validating payment to a transferee).

40. *See* the *Tuttle* and *Leopold* cases cited in note 7, *supra*. *See also* Lawson v. Finance Am. Private Brands, Inc., 537 S.W.2d 483 (Tex.Civ.App.1976); § 3–203, Official Comment 2, and § 3–308(b). In the *Lawson* case, the proof consisted of testimony of the defendant that the payee's name was the former name of the plaintiff before a corporate reorganization.

41. The Official Comment to § 3–301 notes that section deals only with who can enforce an instrument, and explicitly recognizes others besides the holder may do so, and that other sections deal with the other matters; *e.g.*, transfer in § 3–203; discharge in Article 3, Part 6; and negotiation in § 3–201.

42. § 3–301 provides that a person may have the right to enforce an instrument *regardless of whether that person is the owner.*

Bank v. Fort Lee Savings & Loan Association.[43] The court noted that a holder is any person who is in possession of an instrument indorsed to its order or in blank. Accordingly, even if the bank took the check deposited by its customer solely for collection and with the right to charge it back against the depositor's account in the event it was dishonored, the bank is a holder of the check.[44] Another example where a holder, though having the legal title to an instrument, was not the beneficial owner of it arose in *Carter v. DeJarnatt.*[45] In that case, a note was executed to evidence a loan made by A but, because a printed form was used, the note instead named a bank as the payee. The bank indorsed the note to B, who in turn indorsed it to the plaintiff. The plaintiff brought suit as trustee for A. The court determined that A was not a necessary party to the action because the plaintiff was the holder of the note, and a holder may enforce payment in the holder's own name even though the holder is not the beneficial owner.

[b] Right to Enforce the Instrument or Discharge Parties on It

The basic rights of the holder of an instrument are to enforce it or to pass it on. Here the focus is on the right of the holder of an instrument to enforce payment in the holder's own name or to discharge the liability of parties on the instrument.

After establishing holder status,[46] a holder may recover on the instrument unless a defense is established.[47] Upon payment (or other satisfaction), the holder may discharge the liability of parties to the instrument.[48] An interesting case concerning the right to discharge, and illustrating a potential limitation on the right, is *Chenowith v. Bank of Dardanelle.*[49] In the *Chenowith* case, a depository bank that had allowed

---

43. 89 N.J.Super. 43, 213 A.2d 315 (Law Div. 1965).

44. *See also* Marine Midland Bank v. Graybar Elec. Co., 41 N.Y.2d 703, 395 N.Y.S.2d 403, 363 N.E.2d 1139 (N.Y. 1977) (depositor continuing to be the owner of checks and bank acting pursuant to § 4–201(a) as the depositor's agent for collection is not inconsistent with bank's status as holder).

45. 523 S.W.2d 88 (Tex.Civ.App.1975). A similar case is Good v. Good, 72 N.C.App. 312, 324 S.E.2d 43 (N.C.Ct.App.1985) (executor of estate).

46. *See* § 3–308(b); Russell v. Maxson Sales Co., 1979 OK 28, 591 P.2d 703 (Okla. 1979). In Lloyd v. Lawrence, 472 F.2d 313 (5th Cir.1973), the court denied an ostensible holder of instruments the right to enforce them on summary judgment because the copies of the notes attached to the complaint were not verified, no proof of possession was made nor claim that the instruments were lost or stolen, and the copies did not show the reverse side of the notes, and thus there was no evidence the notes had not been negotiated.

47. §§ 3–301(i) and 3–308(b). *See* the *Tuttle* and *Leopold* cases, *supra* note 7.

48. § 3–602(a). A 2002 amendment to § 3–602(b) modifies this rule in the case of a note, and provides a note is paid to the extent payment is made by or on behalf of a party obliged to pay the note to a person that formerly was entitled to enforce the note if at the time of the payment the party obliged to pay has not received adequate notification that the note has been transferred and that payment is to be made to the transferee. Subsection (c) then provides for discharge. See also subsection (d). The intent is to conform the Article 3 rule to the normal rule for contracts. *See* Restatement of Contracts (Second) § 338. While the change erodes one of the aspects of negotiability, the new rule accords with modern practice where notes are seldom examined nor installment payments noted upon them.

49. 243 Ark. 310, 419 S.W.2d 792 (Ark. 1967).

its customer to use the provisional credit given for certain checks, mistakenly returned the checks to the customer when they were dishonored by the drawee of them. The customer then settled with the drawer of the checks. The court held that when the bank had returned the checks to its depositor, the latter had become the holder so that he had the right to discharge the drawer's liability on the instruments, notwithstanding knowledge of the bank's claim to the checks by reason of his withdrawal of the credit given for them, because the bank had not supplied indemnity nor obtained an injunction against payment.[50]

Conversely, generally a person who is not the holder of an instrument may not enforce it or discharge it. Contrast the result in *In re United East Coast Corp.*,[51] where a secured party in possession of a note negotiated to the secured party was held to have the right as holder to collect the note at maturity even though the payee-debtor retained the actual title to the instrument, with the outcome in *Bank of Waverly v. City Bank & Trust Co.*,[52] where an inventory lender on a dealer's automobiles had sued a bank that had cashed a check given to the dealer in payment for a car rather than taking it for deposit. The lender was denied recovery despite its security interest in the check. The court said the lender was a stranger to the instrument and that one not in possession of an instrument cannot sue on it.

[c] Right to Transfer or Negotiate the Instrument

The holder of an instrument also may transfer or negotiate it.[53] For the purpose of Article 3, this right is not limited because the result of the transfer or negotiation may be a violation of law.[54] For example, in *Harvey v. Casebeer*,[55] the holder of four notes, originally payable to the trust of the daughter of the holder and negotiated by the holder, as sole trustee of that trust, to himself, brought suit on the notes. The court held that the possession of the notes properly indorsed entitled the plaintiff to holder status, and that if the negotiation of the notes to himself constituted a breach of fiduciary duty, it would be a claim to be enforced by the beneficiary of the trust and could not be raised by the party liable on the instruments.[56]

---

50. § 3–602(b)(1). Old § 3–301 expressly conditions the right to discharge on old § 3–603; current § 3–301, dealing only with enforcement, does not need to. § 3–602 is discussed in Chapter 6. The converse of the *Chenowith* case was presented in, for example, Investment Serv. Co. v. Martin Bros. Container & Timber Prods. Corp., 255 Or. 192, 465 P.2d 868 (Or. 1970), where the drawer made payment to the collecting bank. The court stated that payment to a prior holder does not operate as a discharge unless the prior holder has been authorized by the holder to receive payment. *But see* note 48, *supra*.

51. 6 UCC Rep. Serv. 449 (E.D.N.Y. 1969).

52. 600 S.W.2d 630 (Mo.Ct.App.1980).

53. §§ 3–201 and 3–203.

54. § 3–202.

55. 531 S.W.2d 206 (Tex.Civ.App.1975).

56. This is the *jus tertii* issue discussed in Chapter 6. Negotiation in violation of law is discussed further later in this chapter.

¶ 3.02 Transfer and Negotiation

[1] Transfer

Much of the purpose behind the special rules for negotiable instruments codified in Article 3 is to promote the free transferability of such paper. Thus a basic right of the holder of an instrument is to pass it on. That right is effectuated by transfer and, if additional requirements are met, by negotiation.

Transfer and negotiation differ in that transfer is the physical delivery of an instrument for the purpose of giving the recipient the right to enforce it.[57] Negotiation is a transfer of possession in a form that constitutes the transferee a holder.[58] In the case of a bearer instrument,[59] negotiation is the same thing as transfer, as above defined.[60] If the instrument is payable to order,[61] it is negotiated by delivery with any necessary indorsement.[62]

[2] Negotiation of a Bearer Instrument

Negotiation of a bearer instrument is accomplished simply by the transfer of possession of it.[63] The transfer of possession may be actual or constructive. A significant case allowing constructive possession is *Corporacion Venezolana de Fomento v. Vintero Sales Corp.*[64] In that case, a lender-payee of notes indorsed them in blank and delivered them to several banks in return for funds, which it then loaned to the maker of the notes. It further instructed the banks that had possession of the notes to issue certificates of participation in them which recited an irrevocable assignment of the amounts covered by the notes to third parties. The court held that there had been constructive delivery and thus the third parties were the holders of the notes, even though the banks still had actual physical possession of the instruments.[65]

¶ 3.02

57. "Transfer" is defined in § 3–203(a) as delivery by a person other than the issuer for the purpose of giving the person to whom delivery is made the right to enforce the instrument. This excludes delivery to the drawee for payment. Official Comment 1 to § 3–203. *See also* note 22, *supra*.

58. § 3–201(a).

59. A bearer instrument is one payable to bearer or indorsed in blank. §§ 3–109(a), 1–201(a)(5), 3–205(b).

60. Under § 3–201(b), if payable to bearer, an instrument is negotiated by transfer alone. *See also* Oscar Gruss & Son v. First State Bank, 582 F.2d 424 (7th Cir. 1978).

61. §§ 3–109(b), 3–205(a).

62. § 3–201(b). *See also* American Nat'l Bank & Trust Co. v. St. Joseph Valley Bank, 180 Ind.App. 546, 389 N.E.2d 379 (Ind.Ct.App.1979).

63. *See supra* note 60. Note the transfer can be involuntary; thus a stolen bearer instrument is negotiated to a thief. § 3–201, Official Comment 1. *See also* note 22, *supra*.

64. 452 F.Supp. 1108 (S.D.N.Y.1978).

65. *See also* note 11, *supra*. Apparently similar cases are Fore v. Bles, 149 Ariz. 603, 721 P.2d 151 (Ariz.Ct.App.1986) and Federal Deposit Ins. Corp. v. Linn, 671 F.Supp. 547 (N.D.Ill.1987). *See* Official Comment 1 to § 3–201. Other law also may be relevant or applicable to this fact pattern. *See* UCC § 9–109(a)(3) and Uniform Electronic Transactions Act § 16.

[3] Negotiation of an Order Instrument

[a] The Requirements of Indorsement and Delivery

The negotiation of an order instrument is accomplished by the transfer of possession of it with any necessary indorsement.[66] Thus with little exception the absence of either possession or a necessary indorsement will preclude negotiation. For example, in *Lamb v. Opelika Production Credit Association*,[67] a note payable to the association was prestamped with an indorsement to a bank, but it was never delivered. The court held the association and not the bank was the holder of the note and could sue on it. Negotiation does not take place, if ever, until the missing element is supplied.[68]

The absence of negotiation of an order instrument does not necessarily create a problem.[69] For example, in several cases where a bank has taken an unindorsed instrument and in return has issued a new instrument made payable in the same manner, the absence of negotiation because of the missing indorsement has not resulted in liability.[70] Similar results have been reached where a bank has otherwise correctly paid out funds on an unindorsed instrument.[71]

---

66. § 3–201(b). § 3–201 makes it clear, however, that a remitter can negotiate by transfer alone. *See* Official Comment 2. § 3–207 also makes it clear that the reacquirer of an instrument can be a holder without the indorsement of the former holder. *See* Official Comment to § 3–207 and Resolution Trust Corp. v. Juergens, 965 F.2d 149 (7th Cir.1992).

67. 367 So.2d 957 (Ala.1979). *See also* Russell v. Maxson Sales Co., 1979 OK 28, 591 P.2d 703 (Okla.1979) (check deposited by D in his bank with instructions to credit most of proceeds to a third party, which check was dishonored causing the bank to revoke the credit given, created no right of action in the third party against the drawer of the check because, never having had possession, the third party was not a holder entitled to enforce it). §§ 3–301(iii) and 3–418(d) would not seem applicable to change the *Russell* result, but arguably D would hold for the third party as his transferee under §§ 3–301(ii) and 3–203(b). *See* discussion in text prior to and note 65, *supra*.

68. Thus, in Cheshire Commercial Corp. v. Messier, 6 Conn. Cir. Ct. 542, 278 A.2d 413 (Conn.Cir.1971), where the plaintiff bought and took possession of a note in 1968, the court held it did not become a holder until the note was indorsed in 1970. *See* § 3–203, Official Comment 3.

69. But it generally will prevent holder in due course status and thus allow claims and defenses to be asserted. *See, e.g.*, National Bank v. Flushing Nat'l Bank, 72 A.D.2d 538, 421 N.Y.S.2d 65 (App.Div.1979) (bank was not a holder in due course of certificates of deposit held as security for a loan as they were never indorsed but only pledged by separate document) and Illinois State Bank v. Yates, 678 S.W.2d 819 (Mo. Ct.App.1984) (same). Holder in due course status is discussed, *infra*.

70. *See, e.g.*, Hays v. Friendly Nat'l Bank, 1979 OK CIV APP 9, 591 P.2d 1274 (Okla.Ct.App.1979) (drawee bank that issued cashier's check in return for its customer's personal check unindorsed by the payee was entitled to charge its customer's account).

71. *See, e.g.*, First National Bank v. Barrett, 141 Ga.App. 161, 233 S.E.2d 24 (Ga.Ct.App.1977) (a check payable to the order of a named payee and presented for payment through the collection chain without the payee's indorsement was properly paid entitling the payor bank to charge its customer's account where its proceeds went to the party to whom payment was intended to be made). *See also* Stratton v. Equitable Bank, 104 B.R. 713 (D.Md.1989), *aff'd*, 912 F.2d 464 (4th Cir.1990) (similar point). Similar results have been reached where an indorsement is forged and thus is legally missing. *See, e.g.*, American Nat'l Bank v. Seidel, 622 S.W.2d 19 (Mo.Ct.App.1981) and discussion in Chapter 2, *supra*, at note 262, and in Chapter 7, *infra*. But where there is an indorsement, it must be obeyed. *See, e.g.*, Marine Midland Bank, N.A. v. Price, Miller, Evans & Flowers, 57 N.Y.2d 220, 455 N.Y.S.2d 565, 441 N.E.2d 1083 (N.Y. 1982) (bank was not holder in due course

In two fact patterns the indorsement requirement for the negotiation of order paper causes recurring litigation. The first may be characterized as the "sloppily conducted negotiation." An example arose in a case where a note payable to a corporation was indorsed to a bank with only the signature of the authorized corporate individual followed by the designation "Sec.-Treas." The court upheld the negotiation even though the proper indorsement would have been the name of the corporate payee followed by the name and office of the authorized individual.[72] A similar case is *Watertown Federal Savings & Loan Association v. Spanks*,[73] where a note payable to "Greenlaw & Sons Roofing & Siding Co." was indorsed "Greenlaw & Sons by George W. Greenlaw."[74] The ultimate example of sloppy negotiation is where a necessary indorsement is missing entirely and is ignored. This will often occur where an instrument is taken as collateral for a loan and the focus primarily is on taking possession to perfect the security interest. It also occurs when a check is taken for deposit by a bank and the lack of indorsement is overlooked in the press of business or the lack is treated as not relevant given § 4–205. *Security Pacific National Bank v. Chess*[75] is an example of the first situation,[76] and *Bowling Green, Inc. v. State Street Bank & Trust Co.*[77] is an example of the second.[78]

Another instance where a missing indorsement may be overlooked is when the instrument is payable to joint payees and the absence of one indorsement is not obvious. For example, in *American National Bank & Trust Co. v. St. Joseph Valley Bank*,[79] the court held that the taker of a check made payable to a contractor and a husband and wife jointly could not qualify as a holder because the indorsement of the wife was absent.[80]

on a check it indorsed by a stamp that stated "Credit to the account of payee/Marine Midland Chautauqua Bank," where bank had wired funds as instructed, but the payee had no account at the bank and thus the bank acted contrary to the supplied indorsement).

72. American Nat'l Bank & Trust Co. v. Scenic Stage Lines, 2 Ill.App.3d 446, 276 N.E.2d 420 (1971). *Distinguish* Commonwealth Fed. Sav. & Loan Ass'n v. First Nat'l Bank, 513 F.Supp. 296 (E.D.Pa.1979), where the court held that a bank failed to follow reasonable commercial standards when it took a check payable to an organization indorsed with only an individual's signature.

73. 346 Mass. 398, 193 N.E.2d 333 (Mass. 1963).

74. The court used old § 3–307(1)(b) (current § 3–308(a)) to sustain the negotiation. That provision states that a signature on an instrument is presumed to be genuine or authorized except in two limited cases.

75. 58 Cal.App.3d 555, 129 Cal.Rptr. 852 (1976).

76. *See also* note 69, *supra*.

77. 425 F.2d 81 (1st Cir.1970).

78. *See* the discussion at and following note 31, *supra*.

79. 180 Ind.App. 546, 389 N.E.2d 379 (Ind.Ct.App.1979).

80. *See also* Southeastern Mun. Supply Co. v. Citizens First Nat'l Bank, 432 So.2d 753 (Fla.Dist.Ct.App.1983) (check payable to "Citrus Mechanical & Southeastern Municipal Supply Co." and indorsed only by Citrus Mechanical was improperly negotiated). A variation on the theme occurred in Morgan Guaranty Trust Co. v. Chase Manhattan Bank, N.A., 36 UCC Rep. Serv. 584 (N.Y.Sup.Ct.1983), where another payee's name was added in a different type style and then that person alone indorsed. The court held the check was not properly payable on the indorsement of the added payee only even given obvious alteration. Further discussion of the joint payee problem appears, *infra*, this chapter and at note 262, *supra*, Chapter 2.

Where an indorsement appears on the instrument is not inherently material. It may be written on the front or on the back,[81] and unless the instrument clearly indicates that a signature is made in some other capacity, it is an indorsement.[82] An indorsement need not even be on the instrument, but if it is not, it must be on a paper so firmly affixed to the instrument as to become a part of it, called an allonge.[83] Generally, a separate assignment of an instrument will not suffice as an allonge.[84] In *Estrada v. River Oaks Bank & Trust Co.*,[85] for example, the court held that the person in possession of four unindorsed promissory notes stapled to a single collateral assignment was not a holder of any of them. The single document could not serve as an indorsement of all of the notes because it could not be affixed to each so as to be an allonge to each, and, though it might be an indorsement of one of the notes, there was no way to determine which note.[86]

The second fact pattern where the indorsement requirement for negotiation of an order instrument leads to litigation is where there is an unauthorized indorsement. Negotiation fails in this circumstance because an unauthorized signature is inoperative and thus there legally is no indorsement.[87] The discussion of this problem appears in Chapter 7.

The absence of a necessary indorsement cannot be overcome by the agreement of the parties under Article 3. In one case, the payee of notes transferred them without an indorsement.[88] The notes contained a provision that the payee or its assignee could freely assign or negotiate the notes, however, and the argument was made the parties had varied the effect of the UCC rule on negotiation.[89] The court denied the

---

81. United States v. Tufi, 536 F.2d 855 (9th Cir.1976). Under § 3–204(a), however, location is one factor in determining if a signature is an indorsement.

82. This in essence is the § 3–204(a) rule, but the section allows other circumstances to indicate an indorsement is not intended. For example, the initials of an employee on the back of a check payable to a corporation to evidence receipt of cash would not be an indorsement. Nor is the counter signature of the owner of a traveler's check. § 3–204, Official Comment 1. This section also defines an indorsement in terms of purpose.

83. § 3–204(a). Whether lack of space on the instrument is a necessary predicate for the use of an allonge is not expressly stated in old Article 3. The cases suggest (Shepherd Mall State Bank v. Johnson, 1979 OK 135, 603 P.2d 1115 (Okla.1979)) or hold (Pribus v. Bush, 118 Cal.App.3d 1003, 173 Cal.Rptr. 747 (1981)) that an allonge is a paper annexed to an instrument on which to write indorsements for which there is no room on the instrument itself. § 3–204(a) rejects this view. *See* Official Comment 1 to that section.

84. Where the assignment is attached, under old § 3–202(4) (not repeated in current Article 3 as subsumed in other provisions, such as § 3–204(a)) the words of assignment, or words of condition, waiver, guaranty, limitation, or disclaimer of liability and the like, do not effect its character as an indorsement. Under § 3–203(d), however, negotiation occurs only when the entire instrument or any unpaid residue is conveyed, and anything less operates only as a partial assignment.

85. 550 S.W.2d 719 (Tex.Civ.App.1977).

86. *See also* note 25, *supra*. As to what degree of "affixation" is required for an "allonge," *see* Official Comment 3 to old § 3–202.

87. §§ 3–403(a), 3–201(a).

88. Becker v. National Bank & Trust Co., 222 Va. 716, 284 S.E.2d 793 (Va. 1981). *See also* note 23, *supra*.

89. Unless otherwise provided, the effect of provisions of the UCC may be varied by agreement. UCC § 1–302(a).

argument, saying that it was tantamount to allowing the parties to contract for the benefit of Article 3 without following the proper form.[90]

[b] Who May Indorse

[i] Introduction

An indorsement must be written by or on behalf of the holder.[91] This seemingly simple requirement harbors a number of subtle problem areas, one of which is that this rule prevents the further negotiation of an instrument that requires an indorsement but that bears an unauthorized indorsement. Since the "indorsement" is not that of the holder, it is not an indorsement and, without a necessary indorsement, there is no negotiation.[92] This problem will reoccur until discovery or until the instrument is paid.[93] Other problem areas follow.

[ii] Instruments Payable to More Than One Person

One of the most serious problems involves the instrument payable to the order of two or more payees together. If the instrument is payable to the order of them in the alternative, it is payable to any one of them and may be negotiated (or discharged or enforced) by the one who has possession.[94] But if the instrument is payable to their joint order, it is payable only to all of them and may be negotiated (or discharged or enforced) only by all of them.[95] The latter situation creates the difficulty because the "holder" is all of the payees and thus valid negotiation requires the indorsement of all of them.[96]

The difference is essentially between an instrument payable to "A *or* B," in which case the one who is in possession is the holder and that person may negotiate the instrument, and one payable to "A *and* B," in which case both must indorse in order to negotiate the instrument.[97] The root of a negotiation problem with an instrument payable to two or more persons often resides in the language of the instrument. A key indicator is the conjunction used. Instruments payable to the order of two or more payees may be payable to any one of them if the conjunction *or*, or other language suggesting payment in the alternative, is used, but an instrument payable to the order of more than one payee that uses the conjunction *and* requires the indorsement of all payees.[98] If both conjunc-

---

90. This question is discussed in more detail in Chapter 2; arguably agreement could afford a taker the rights of a holder but this is different than attempting to change the meaning of that term by agreement in contravention of Official Comment 1 to UCC § 1–302.

91. §§ 3–201(b) and 3–204(a).

92. § 3–201(a). This assumes the unauthorized indorsement is not made effective.

93. The rights of the various parties when an instrument bearing an unauthorized indorsement is paid or dishonored are discussed in Chapter 7.

94. § 3–110(d).

95. § 3–110(d). See also, supra, notes 71, 79 and 80; the discussion in Chapter 2 at note 262, supra; and Chapter 7, infra.

96. One payee, of course, could be authorized to sign for the others. Official Comment to old § 3–116.

97. Official Comment 4 to § 3–110.

98. Ford Motor Credit Co. v. United Servs. Auto. Ass'n, 11 UCC Rep. Serv. 361 (N.Y.Civ.Ct.1972) (check payable to "Lawrence W. Thompson and Ford Motor Credit Corp." can be negotiated only on the indorsement of both payees). See also notes

tions are used, the issue becomes more difficult. In *Leinert v. Sabine National Bank*[99] the court finally determined that a bank acted properly when it accepted for deposit in a joint account maintained by A and C a check without an indorsement payable to the bank "and A or B" and then allowed C to withdraw the deposit.[100]

In the absence of any conjunction, all the facts and circumstances must be considered. Several cases have held that the absence of the conjunction *or*, as where the instrument reads "John Smith–Mary Smith," itself determines that the instrument is not payable in the alternative.[101] On the other hand, cases have found instruments payable to two payees whose names are separated by a virgule, as "John Smith/Mary Smith," to be payable in the alternative.[102] Other cases present still other fact patterns, as in *Feldman Construction Co. v. Union Bank*,[103] where the payees on a check were identified by one name over the other on separate lines, the check was drawn by a contractor, the payees were a subcontractor and a supply company, and a statement on the back of the check provided that indorsement acknowledged payment of all material and labor on the building project as of that date. The court correctly held the indorsement of both payees was required.[104]

Even where the indorsements of all payees literally appear, instruments payable to the order of two or more persons often raise the problem of an unauthorized indorsement because one of the payees, without authorization, supplies the indorsement of the other payee. The invalid indorsement, of course, destroys negotiation.[105] In this situation, however, there may be an exception to the consequences of the rule that no negotiation occurs without all necessary indorsements if the intended person received the proceeds of the instrument. In *Gordon v. State Street Bank and Trust Co.*,[106] for example, A obtained a loan, the lender

---

71, 79 and 80, *supra*. The problem often is the instrument is ambiguous, as in the *Southeastern* case, *supra* note 80, and C.H. Sanders Constr. Co. v. Bankers Trust Co., 123 A.D.2d 251, 506 N.Y.S.2d 58 (N.Y. 1986). In the latter case, the court resolved the ambiguity in favor of the drawer in a suit by the drawer for improper payment. This result is inconsistent with the policy in § 3–406, and § 3–110(d) explicitly favors alternative payment where there is ambiguity. *Distinguish* Joffe v. United California Bank, 141 Cal.App.3d 541, 190 Cal.Rptr. 443 (Cal.Ct.App.1983), where the problem stemmed from a misinterpretation of who was the payee rather than from a joint payee instrument.

99. 541 S.W.2d 872 (Tex.Civ.App.1976).

100. The Official Comment to old § 3–116 describes an instrument payable to "A and/or B," which may be negotiated (or enforced, discharged or paid) by A, or by B, or by A and B together.

101. *E.g.*, Centre Le Corbusier v. Nabis Fine Arts, Inc., 13 UCC Rep. Serv. 500 (N.Y.Sup.Ct.1973) (where notes were payable to the order of "Centre Le Corbusier—Heidi Weber," Centre Le Corbusier and Heidi Weber were joint payees).

102. *E.g.*, L.B. Smith, Inc. v. Bankers Trust Co., 80 A.D.2d 496, 439 N.Y.S.2d 543 (App.Div.1981), *aff'd*, 55 N.Y.2d 942, 449 N.Y.S.2d 192, 434 N.E.2d 261 (N.Y. 1982). *See also* cases discussed in note 262, *supra*, Chapter 2.

103. 28 Cal.App.3d 731, 104 Cal.Rptr. 912 (1972).

104. *See also* Barden & Robeson Corp. v. Tompkins County Trust Co., 67 Misc.2d 587, 324 N.Y.S.2d 543 (Sup.Ct.1971); Swiss Baco Skyline Logging, Inc. v. Haliewicz, 18 Wn.App. 21, 567 P.2d 1141 (Wash.Ct.App. 1977).

105. *See, e.g.*, Perley v. Glastonbury Bank & Trust Co., 170 Conn. 691, 368 A.2d 149 (Conn. 1976) and note 92, *supra*.

106. 361 Mass. 258, 280 N.E.2d 152 (Mass. 1972). Another somewhat odd case making the same point is County Concrete

required A's wife also to sign the note, and the check for the loan proceeds was made payable to both A and his wife. A forged his wife's signature. In the resulting litigation, the court denied the lender recovery against its bank for improper payment when it determined the lender intended to make the loan to A, and had insisted on having the wife's name on the note only as additional security.[107] It also is true that the indorsement of a person who has no interest in the proceeds of the instrument is not required.[108] Thus in *Starkey Construction, Inc. v. Elcon, Inc.*,[109] a check representing a progress payment on a construction job was made payable to a subcontractor and one of its suppliers. The supplier's indorsement was forged, but the court held this did not hamper negotiability as even though the supplier's name had been placed on the check the supplier was not due any money on the construction project at the time. On the other hand, in *Trust Co. of Columbus v. Refrigeration Supplies, Inc.*,[110] the court found conversion when a check was paid without the indorsement of one of the payees the drawer intentionally designated, even though that payee was a materialman who could not have enforced the check against the drawer because the drawer in fact was under no obligation to pay the materialman nor to include the materialman as a payee on the check.[111] There was a strong dissent on the basis the materialman had suffered no legally cognizable loss.

[iii] *Instruments Payable to Estates, Offices, and the Like*

Another problem situation with respect to determining who is the holder of an instrument so as to be capable of indorsing it involves instruments payable to the order of an estate, a trust, or a fund, an office, an officer by his or her title as such, or a partnership or unincorporated association.[112] In the case of an instrument payable to an estate, a trust, or a person designated as a trustee or representative, or

---

Corp. v. Smith, 317 N.J.Super. 50, 721 A.2d 34 (App.Div.1998).

107. *See also* American Nat'l Bank v. Seidel, 622 S.W.2d 19 (Mo.Ct.App.1981) and discussion in Chapter 2 at note 262, *supra* and in Chapter 7, *infra*. Today this procedure probably would be in violation of Regulation B, § 202.7(d) (12 CFR pt. 202), the implementing regulation under the Federal Equal Credit Opportunity Act, 15 U.S.C. §§ 1691–1691f.

108. Conversely, an unauthorized indorsement is legally effective if the drawer or maker, or their employee supplying the name of payee, intends the payee to have no interest. §§ 3–404, 3–405. This matter is discussed in Chapter 7.

109. 248 Ark. 958, 457 S.W.2d 509 (Ark. 1970).

110. 241 Ga. 406, 246 S.E.2d 282 (Ga. 1978).

111. A similar case is Middle States Leasing Corp. v. Manufacturers Hanover Trust Co., 62 A.D.2d 273, 404 N.Y.S.2d 846 (App.Div.1978). In that case the drawer owed no money to A, who indorsed the check, but did to B, who did not indorse. The indorsing payee had persuaded the drawer to add his name because B owed A money. The court held on these facts all payees had to indorse.

112. Instruments payable to accounts also may generate problems. *See, e.g.*, Joffe v. United Cal. Bank, 141 Cal.App.3d 541, 190 Cal.Rptr. 443 (Cal.Ct.App.1983) (check payable to "Continental Financial Systems–Wells Fargo Escrow Trust Account" was payable to trust account and was not payable to joint payees). § 3–110(c)(1) more explicitly addresses this type of case. *See* the prior discussion concerning these matters in Chapter 2 at notes 263 through 266, *supra*.

to a fund, the instrument is payable to the order of the representative of the estate, trust, or fund, or to a successor.[113] In the case of an instrument payable to an office, or to a person described as holding the office it is payable to the named person, the incumbent of the office, or a successor.[114] In the case of an instrument payable to a partnership or an unincorporated association that is not a legal entity, it is payable to a representative of the members of the partnership or association.[115]

To illustrate an application of these provisions, in *Maplewood Bank & Trust Co. v. F.I.B., Inc.*,[116] with respect to a check made payable to the order of "X Atty. for Y," the court held that X was the payee and could negotiate or enforce the check.[117] In another case it was determined that a check payable to the order of X "as administrator of the estate of Y," which was indorsed by X in his own name without any indication of his capacity as administrator, was properly indorsed.[118] Finally, an instrument payable to a named person with words describing the person in any other manner is payable to the payee unconditionally.[119]

[iv] Instruments with Misspelled Names, Accommodation Indorsers, and Unauthorized Indorsers

A final potential problem situation concerning who may indorse an instrument is presented when an instrument is made payable to a person under a misspelled name or one other than that person's own.[120] Is the holder the named person or the person intended? The UCC permits the intended person to indorse in either the erroneous name or in their correct name, but indicates the proper and desirable form of indorse-

---

113. § 3–110(c)(2)(i) and (iii). *See also* notes 263–266, *supra*, Chapter 2.

114. § 3–110(c)(2)(iv). There is a similar rule for an instrument payable to an agent or similar representative of a named principal if the instrument is not handled by the principal. § 3–110(c)(2)(ii). Of course, the agent is liable for any breach of duty.

See also, notes 263–266, *supra*, Chapter 2.

115. § 3–110(c)(2)(ii). Other uniform acts (the Uniform Partnership Act and the Uniform Unincorporated Non-profit Associations Act) may make such organizations legal entities for this purpose, however.

Official Comment 1 to old § 3–117 (the provision in old Article 3 similar to § 3–110(c)(2)(ii)), indicates this was intended to cover the cases where the payee is specified as agent, as "John Doe, agent of Richard Roe," because in these cases the description is added, not for identification, but to make the instrument payable to the principal. *Contrast* "John Doe, agent," which is only descriptive. Official Comment 3 to old § 3–117. Of course, the agent is liable for any breach of duty.

See also notes 263–266, *supra*, Chapter 2.

116. 142 N.J.Super. 480, 362 A.2d 44 (App.Div.1976).

117. *See also* Bennett v. Cannon, 114 Ga.App. 479, 151 S.E.2d 828 (Ga.Ct.App. 1966), where the court decided that on a note made payable to the order of "A Atty. for B," B was entitled to enforce the note even though not indorsed by A. *See* § 3–110(c)(2)(ii).

118. Bates v. City of New York, 10 UCC Rep. Serv. 151 (N.Y.Sup.Ct.1971); § 3–110(c)(2)(i).

119. Old § 3–117(c); current § 3–110(c).

120. This discussion assumes that if Smith is in possession of an instrument payable to "Smythe" that Smith is the intended payee. But if the intended payee really is Smythe, then any indorsement by Smith is probably unauthorized. Moreover, even if the instrument is payable to "Smith", there could be a question, which Smith? As to this case, *see* Official Comment 1 to § 3–110 and Official Comment 3, Case #2, to § 3–406.

ment is in both names.[121] For example, in one case the insurance company erroneously issued a check in the son's name intending to pay the father.[122] The father simply indorsed the check. The court held the father had acted in accordance with law. Anyone who pays or takes an instrument for value or collection made to a person under a misspelled name or one other than the person's own name may require an indorsement in both the erroneous and also the actual name so as to avoid a later question as to title.[123]

There are two other situations that might be called exceptions to the rule that an indorsement must be written by or on behalf of the holder.[124] One involves a party who signs an instrument to lend their credit to another party to it. If the capacity in which the party signs is not clearly some other capacity, such as a maker or a drawer, the party is an indorser.[125] An indorsement showing that it is not in the chain of title, that is, not by a holder, is notice of its accommodation character.[126] This discussion is illustrated by the case of *Agfa–Gevaert, Inc. v. Bueding*,[127] where the signature of X appeared without further designation and was placed before the indorsement of the payee on the back of the note which X had signed on its face as president of the corporate maker. The court held that X was personally liable as an accommodation indorser.

The other exception may arise from § 3–403(a), which, after providing that any unauthorized signature is wholly inoperative as that of the person whose name is signed unless it is ratified or the person is precluded from denying the signature, states that the unauthorized signature will operate as the signature of the unauthorized signer in favor of a good faith payor or taker for value. Thus if an unauthorized signer indorses an instrument, the indorsement is not good, but the unauthorized signer may be liable as an indorser even though that person was not a holder.[128]

[c] *Types of Indorsements and Their Effect*

[i] *Blank Indorsement*

There essentially are three kinds of indorsements.[129] The first is the blank indorsement. An indorsement in blank specifies no particular

---

121. § 3–204(d).

122. Agaliotis v. Agaliotis, 38 N.C.App. 42, 247 S.E.2d 28 (N.C.Ct.App.1978).

123. § 3–204(d) (which also protects a party taking for collection).

124. See note 91, *supra*.

125. See note 82, *supra*.

126. §§ 3–205(d) and 3–419(c). The accommodation indorsement has nothing to do with negotiation and thus is made by a person not a holder. It is an "exception" to the rule only a holder may indorse. The function of an accommodation indorsement is to create liability for the accommodation indorser, a matter that is discussed in Chapter 5. Under § 3–204(a), "indorsement" is defined to explicitly recognize the point made here.

127. 11 UCC Rep. Serv. 794 (Md.Dist. Ct.1972).

128. See, by way of analogy, Griffin v. Ellinger, 538 S.W.2d 97 (Tex.1976) (a signer of a draft who has no authority to sign is liable upon the contract represented by the signature as drawer to any person who takes the instrument in good faith and for value).

129. The "qualified indorsement," described (but not by that name) in § 3–415(b), is not a separate type of in-

indorsee and may (and commonly does) consist of a mere signature.[130] Thus an instrument made out to John Jones and indorsed "John Jones" is indorsed in blank. The effect of a blank indorsement is to make an instrument payable to order into one payable to bearer so that it may be negotiated by transfer alone,[131] unless and until it is specially indorsed.[132]

Bearer paper, being negotiable by transfer alone, is subject to the risk that its holder may be deprived of the rights on it if, without authorization, it is taken and comes into the hands of a holder in due course.[133] Accordingly, the holder of the instrument may convert a blank indorsement into a special indorsement by writing over the signature of the indorser in blank any contract consistent with the character of the indorsement.[134] This protects the holder because the instrument then cannot be further negotiated without indorsement.[135]

[ii] *Special Indorsement*

The second kind of indorsement is the special indorsement. A special indorsement specifies the person to whom or to whose order it makes the instrument payable.[136] An instrument specially indorsed is payable to the order of the special indorsee and may be further negotiated only by that person's indorsement.[137] Thus the effect of a special indorsement is to allow the holder of an instrument to avoid the risk of the loss of rights on it that is associated with bearer paper.

---

dorsement but rather is a limitation on or disclaimer of indorser's liability. It is discussed in Chapter 4. *See, e.g.,* Gaetani v. Goss–Golden West Sheet Metal Profit Sharing Plan, 84 Cal.App.4th 1118, 101 Cal. Rptr.2d 432 (2000). § 3–204(a) can be said to include the anomalous indorsement as a fourth type. *See* note 126, *supra.*

130. § 3–205(b). Official Comment 2 to § 3–205 states that an indorsement "pay to _____" is a blank indorsement. Perhaps §§ 4–206 and 4–207(b) can be said to create versions of this type of indorsement, when they provide that any agreed method that identifies the transferor bank is sufficient and that a transferor who receives consideration makes a contract similar to that of an indorser.

131. § 3–201(b).

132. § 3–205(b). To have this effect the blank indorsement must be valid. *See, e.g.,* Sumiton Bank v. Funding Sys. Leasing Corp., 512 F.2d 774 (5th Cir.1975) (a bank was not the holder of a check on which the payee's indorsement was forged and on which another signature, presumably valid, was placed below the forged indorsement, as the forged indorsement was inoperative and the second signature (not being that of a holder) did not convert the check into bearer paper).

133. *See, e.g.,* M.G. Sales, Inc. v. Chemical Bank, 161 A.D.2d 148, 554 N.Y.S.2d 863 (App.Div.1990). This is discussed, *infra,* this chapter.

134. § 3–205(c). For example, the holder might insert "Pay to (name)."

135. §§ 3–201(b), 3–205(a).

136. § 3–205(a). An indorsement "pay to _____" is a blank indorsement, however. Official Comment 2 to § 3–205. The principles of § 3–110 on identification of the person to whom an instrument is payable are equally applicable here. § 3–205.

137. *Id. See also* Handel v. Manufacturers Hanover Trust Co., 16 U.C.C. Rep. Serv. 762 (N.Y.Sup.Ct.1975) (indorsement "Pay to the order of State Street Bank & Trust Co." was a special indorsement and absent the indorsement of that bank there could be no further negotiation of the instrument).

[iii] Restrictive Indorsement

[A] Types of Restrictive Indorsements

The last kind of indorsement is the restrictive indorsement. There are several types of restrictive indorsements, but their common denominator is that they purport to restrict further transfer of the instrument in some manner.[138] The kind of restrictive indorsement that purports to prohibit all further transfer of the instrument[139] is, however, completely negated by the UCC, which states that no restrictive indorsement prevents further transfer or negotiation of the instrument.[140] Thus an indorsement reading "Pay A only," or any other indorsement purporting to prohibit further transfer, is without effect for that purpose, and such an indorsement is given the same effect as an unrestricted indorsement.[141]

An indorsement stating that the instrument is for the benefit or use of the indorser or of another person is another kind of restrictive indorsement.[142] For example, the indorsement in *In re Quantum Development Corp.*[143] that read "For Deposit in Quantum Acct. Quantum bankruptcy Charles R. Joy" was held to be a restrictive indorsement of this kind.[144] The effect of this kind of restrictive indorsement is the same as that of the more common restrictive indorsement for the purpose of collection,[145] and, absent knowledge of breach of fiduciary duty, the duty to act consistently with the indorsement is limited to the first taker under it.[146]

A third kind of restrictive indorsement is the conditional indorsement, such as "Pay X when he completes painting my house."[147] This type of restrictive indorsement is treated like one purporting to prohibit further transfer, and thus it is treated as no restrictive indorsement at all.[148]

---

138. Thus a restrictive indorsement is a restrictive blank or special indorsement. Official Comment 2 to § 3–205.

139. § 3–206(a).

140. *Id.*

141. Official Comment 2 to § 3–206. That is, the indorsement is effective to negotiate the instrument and, as Comment 2 notes, it is not a restrictive indorsement.

142. § 3–206(d).

143. 397 F.Supp. 329 (D.V.I.1975), *aff'd on other grounds*, 534 F.2d 532 (3d Cir. 1976).

144. Other versions of this kind of restrictive indorsement are "Pay T in trust for B," "Pay T for B," "Pay T for account of B," and "Pay T as agent for B." *See* Official Comment 4 to § 3–206.

145. Discussed, *infra*, this chapter.

146. § 3–206(d). For example, if an instrument were indorsed "Pay T in trust for B," T, as the first taker, is subject to liability for any breach of the obligation as fiduciary. Beyond this, subsequent takers for value are not affected absent knowledge of breach of fiduciary duty. As to the latter point, *see* § 3–307. The trustee has power to negotiate the instrument and make the transferee a holder in due course, as the indorsement does not prevent further transfer or negotiation under § 3–206(a) and (e), and a later holder for value is neither given notice nor otherwise affected by the indorsement itself under § 3–206(d)(2). To the extent payment by an obligor on the instrument would be in violation of the indorsement, § 3–206(f) affords a defense to payment. *See also* § 3–602.

147. § 3–206(b). *See* Fairfax Bank & Trust Co. v. Crestar Bank, 247 Va. 356, 442 S.E.2d 651 (Va. 1994) ("By endorsing this check the payee agrees to record a first lien in favor [the bank]" held not to bind depositary bank).

148. *See* text at and note 141, *supra*, and § 3–206(b). Breach of the condition, however, does afford a defense or counter-

By far the most common kind of restrictive indorsement is the indorsement for the purpose of collection. This kind of indorsement is indicated by the words "for collection," "for deposit," "pay any bank," or like terms signifying a purpose of deposit or collection.[149] The effect of this kind of restrictive indorsement can be best understood in context.

[B] *Effect of Restrictive Indorsements*

This subject was considered above for the less common kinds of restrictive indorsements. Here the effect of an indorsement "For Deposit," "For Collection," or the like is considered. Suppose a check is written to a payee in exchange for property or services. The payee deposits the check in his or her bank under an indorsement "for collection" or "for deposit" for credit to his or her account. The bank, defined as the depositary bank,[150] forwards the check to a second bank, defined as an intermediary bank,[151] under the indorsement "pay any bank"[152] as a part of the process of collecting the check. The intermediary bank then presents the check to the drawee of it, defined as the payor bank,[153] for payment. The depositary and intermediate banks are agents or subagents of the payee, as the owner of the check, for the collection of the check, and the restrictive indorsements are evidence of this agency status.[154]

The credit that the depositary bank gave to the payee-owner of the check when it accepted it for deposit is provisional, that is, it is contingent upon the payment of the check by the payor bank and the receipt of settlement for the check by the depositary bank.[155] The credit may be revoked by the depositary bank, or used as a basis for charge back or refund against its customer, the payee-owner, if the depositary bank fails to receive a settlement for the check that is or becomes final because of the dishonor of the check by the payor bank or some other cause.[156] But the payee-owner of the check may wish, and may be allowed,[157] to utilize the credit by writing its own checks on the credit, or

---

claim between indorser and indorsee. Official Comment 2 to § 3–206.

149. §§ 3–206(c) and 4–201(b). *See, e.g.,* Chemical Bank New York Trust Co. v. Brand, 6 UCC Rep. Serv. 1078 (N.Y.Sup.Ct. 1969) ("for deposit only"). *See also* Stewart Office Suppliers, Inc. v. First Union Nat'l Bank, 97 N.C.App. 353, 388 S.E.2d 599 (1990), *rev'd* 328 N.C. 83, 399 S.E.2d 108 (1991), also noted at note 171, *infra*, where the dissent correctly questioned whether the indorsement "Stewart Office Suppliers For Deposit Only" was a restrictive indorsement since the payee's name preceded the restrictive words; the court assumed it was.

150. § 4–105(2).

151. § 4–105(4).

152. This is a similar type of restrictive indorsement. §§ 3–206(c)(i), 4–201(b). *But* *see* Regulation CC, 12 CFR § 229.35(c), Commentary.

153. § 4–105(3).

154. § 4–201.

155. *Id.* This, and the agency status of banks, are not changed by Regulation CC, 12 CFR pt. 229. *See* Regulation CC Commentary to §§ 229.32(b) and 229.36(d).

156. § 4–214. Article 4 stipulates the consequence if the depositary bank does not act in a timely manner. § 4–214(a); *see also* Appliance Buyers Credit Corp. v. Prospect Nat'l Bank, 708 F.2d 290 (7th Cir.1983). Further discussion appears later in this book.

157. And today, because of Regulation CC, the bank may be required to allow. *See* Regulation CC, 12 CFR §§ 229.10–229.13.

withdrawing it before the check for which it was given clears. In these circumstances, if the check for which the credit was given is dishonored, the depositary bank may desire to assume a status with respect to the check beyond that of agent for collection, in order to attempt to enforce payment of the check against a prior indorser or the drawer. It thus would have rights in addition to its rights of revocation, charge-back, or refund against its customer, the payee-owner. In short, the depositary bank may seek holder status to enforce payment in its own name,[158] and holder-in-due-course status so as to be free of possible claims and defenses if it took the check in good faith and without notice of any defense against or claim to it.[159]

Under law prior to the UCC, it was unclear whether a restrictive indorsee or any subsequent taker could become a holder in due course because of the notice of agency imparted by this type of restrictive indorsement. Under the UCC, the matter is clear. No such restrictive indorsement prevents further transfer or negotiation of the instrument.[160] An intermediary bank, and a payor bank which is not the depositary bank and which does not take the instrument for payment is neither given notice nor otherwise affected by such a restrictive indorsement of any prior person.[161] Except in those two cases, any transferee under an indorsement that includes the words "for collection," "for deposit," "pay any bank," or like terms, must pay or apply any value given for or on the security of the instrument consistently with the indorsement. To the extent this is done, the transferee becomes a holder, and may become a holder in due course if there is compliance with the requirements for that status.[162] Moreover, an intermediary bank or payor bank that is not a depositary bank and which does not take the instrument for payment over the counter from a person other than a collecting bank, is not liable in conversion solely by reason of the fact that the proceeds of an item restrictively indorsed are not paid or applied consistently with the restrictive indorsement.[163]

What is the net result of these provisions? It is simply that a non-bank purchaser or a payor bank that takes the instrument for immediate payment over the counter from a non-bank must see to the application of the proceeds of the instrument, and, in the most common case, a

---

158. § 3–301. An illustrative case is Citizens Nat'l Bank v. Fort Lee Sav. & Loan Ass'n, 89 N.J.Super. 43, 213 A.2d 315 (Law Div.1965). A holder also may transfer or negotiate the instrument. If the depositary bank revokes the credit, or is able to charge back against or obtain refund from its customer, the payee-owner, the bank will return the check to the payee-owner who, as the holder, then will enforce payment in their name. § 4–201(b)(1). The bank also may negotiate the check to a third party, who is not a bank, by special indorsement, and the third party will be a holder for the purpose of enforcing payment. § 4–201(b)(2).

159. See the Fort Lee case, supra note 158, and §§ 3–302(a) and (e), 4–211, 3–305(b) and 3–306, discussed, infra, this chapter.

160. § 3–206(a).

161. § 3–206(c)(4). See also § 3–206(d). The reason is such banks ordinarily handle instruments, especially checks, in bulk and have no practicable opportunity to consider the effect of restrictive indorsements.

162. § 3–206(e). See also § 3–206(b) and (c).

163. § 3–206(c)(4). See also § 3–206(d).

depositary bank (including a payor bank that is also the depositary bank) that ignores the restrictive indorsement of its customer made for the purpose of obtaining the collection of a check may be liable in conversion to the customer-owner of the instrument.[164] Otherwise, for the purpose of permitting items to move rapidly through banking channels, intermediary and payor banks are permitted to ignore such restrictive indorsements.[165] To illustrate how the rules work, in *Salsman v. National Community Bank*,[166] the court held that the depositary bank was liable in conversion when it credited to the account of an attorney the proceeds of a check that had been specially indorsed by the payee to an estate and then had been indorsed "for deposit" by the attorney, but without authorization. The court stated that even if the indorsement for the estate had been authorized, the bank still would be liable for failing to deposit the proceeds to the credit of the estate as required by that indorsement.[167] A similar result was reached in *Underpinning & Foundation Constructors, Inc. v. Chase Manhattan Bank, N.A.*,[168] where an employee falsified invoices from suppliers, stole the checks written in response, restrictively indorsed them, and deposited them to his own or confederates' accounts maintained with the defendant bank. The bank,

---

164. *See*, by implication, § 3–206(c)(1), (2) and (3). *See* Official Comment 3 to § 3–206 for an example involving a non-bank purchaser. A case similar to that in the Comment is Walcott v. Manufacturers Hanover Trust Co., 133 Misc.2d 725, 507 N.Y.S.2d 961 (Civ.Ct.1986), where the check was indorsed in blank, which indorsement included the payee's mortgage number and the mortgage company's mailing sticker, and mailed. It was cashed without the sticker by a check cashing service. The court held the indorsement with merely the mortgage number was not a restrictive one.

165. § 3–206(c)(4).

166. 105 N.J.Super. 164, 251 A.2d 460 (App.Div.1969).

167. In further illustration, *see* Travis v. La Junta State Bank, 694 P.2d 350 (Colo. Ct.App.1984), *rev'd en banc*, 727 P.2d 48 (Colo.1986) (payee's check indorsed for deposit deposited in other payee's account); Society Nat'l Bank v. Security Fed. Sav. & Loan, 71 Ohio St.3d 321, 643 N.E.2d 1090 (Ohio 1994) (check made out to Microtek, indorsed "For Deposit Only, John Vedrody" (Vedrody was president of Microtek), and deposited in the account of another corporation of which Vedrody also was president rendered depositary bank liable for paying funds inconsistently with the restrictive indorsement); State of Qatar v. First American Bank of Virginia, 880 F.Supp. 463 (E.D.Va.1995) (nothing in "fictitious payee" provision (§ 3–404) rids a depositary bank of its independent obligation to comply with a restrictive indorsement); Continental Airlines, Inc. v. Boatmen's National Bank of St. Louis, 13 F.3d 1254 (8th Cir.1994) (failure to follow restrictive indorsement lacks ordinary care as a matter of law); and Citizens Bank of Maryland v. Maryland Industrial Finishing Co., Inc., 338 Md. 448, 659 A.2d 313 (Md. 1995) (unauthorized omission by agent of restrictive language in an indorsement is sufficient to make the indorsement, which otherwise the agent was authorized to make, unauthorized). *Compare* Pazol v. Citizens Nat'l Bank, 110 Ga.App. 319, 138 S.E.2d 442 (Ga.Ct.App.1964) (depositary bank that permitted payee to withdraw the full amount of the check prior to any notice of dishonor applied value consistently with the indorsement "for deposit" by crediting the payee-depositor's account with the amount of the check and, presuming good faith, upon the dishonor of the check became a holder in due course of it) *with* Marine Midland Bank, N.A. v. Price, Miller, Evans & Flowers, 57 N.Y.2d 220, 455 N.Y.S.2d 565, 441 N.E.2d 1083 (N.Y. 1982) (bank that took unindorsed check and under authority of old § 4–205(1) stamped it "credit to the account of the payee herein named/Marine Midland Chautauqua Bank," and then wired the funds to a designated person, was not a holder in due course because the proceeds of the item were not deposited and thus were not applied consistent with the indorsement).

168. 46 N.Y.2d 459, 414 N.Y.S.2d 298, 386 N.E.2d 1319 (N.Y.1979).

by allowing such deposits, had applied the proceeds to credit accounts other than those indicated in the indorsements. The court believed old § 3–405(1)(c) (current § 3–405), discussed in Chapter 7, *infra*, which made the indorsements effective, was subject to the restrictive indorsement rule.[169] Moreover, in *Cairo Cooperative Exchange v. First National Bank*,[170] a bank that paid cash to the corporate agent rather than depositing restrictively indorsed corporate checks to the corporate account was held liable even though the bank argued the effect of the statute had been changed by an agreement with the corporate agent who, with seeming authority, had requested cash instead of deposit credit.[171]

[4] Rescission of Negotiation and Reacquisition

[a] Rescission

The negotiation of a negotiable instrument may involve a legal impediment or wrongdoing. For example, the instrument may have been transferred by an infant, a corporation exceeding its powers, or by another person without capacity. The instrument may have been obtained by fraud, duress, or mistake of any kind, or the negotiation of the instrument may have been a part of an illegal transaction, or may have been made in breach of a duty. Nonetheless, the negotiation is effective in all of these instances and no distinction is made between a deficiency such as lack of capacity or illegality, which may go to the essence of the transaction and make it entirely void, and a defect that merely renders the transaction voidable.[172]

As between the parties to the transaction, and even with respect to a third party who has no greater rights than one of the parties to the transaction, the negotiation is subject to rescission, the declaration of a constructive trust, or any other remedy permitted by law.[173] Normally

---

169. *See also* the *Qatar* case, *supra*, note 167.

170. 228 Kan. 613, 620 P.2d 805 (Kan. 1980), *modified as to judgment amount*, 229 Kan. 184, 624 P.2d 420 (1981).

171. *See also* Society Nat'l Bank v. Security Fed. Sav. & Loan, 71 Ohio St.3d 321, 643 N.E.2d 1090 (Ohio 1994), where the argument also failed (the question is not what might have been done, but the legal effect of what was done). A similar case is Rutherford v. Darwin, 95 N.M. 340, 622 P.2d 245 (N.M.Ct.App.1980). So too is Stewart Office Suppliers, Inc. v. First Union Nat'l Bank, 97 N.C.App. 353, 388 S.E.2d 599 (1990), *rev'd*, 328 N.C. 83, 399 S.E.2d 108 (1991) where, on appeal, the court allowed the jury to determine whether the bank acted properly when it allowed checks payable to Stewart Office Suppliers and indorsed "Stewart Office Suppliers For Deposit Only" to be deposited to another supplier's account under an agreement between the two suppliers under which the second supplier delivered the goods when Stewart was unable to. But as the dissent points out, the indorsement perhaps was not even a restrictive one. Arguably a restrictive indorsement should be subject to contrary authorized agreement. *See, e.g., infra* notes 180 and 185 and accompanying text. Official Comment 3 to § 3–206 makes it clear that the doctrine of waiver is not displaced by the UCC.

172. § 3–202. Distinguish the acquisition of the instrument by a thief and a transaction involving an unauthorized indorsement, neither of which qualify as a negotiation.

173. Official Comment 3 to § 3–202. In fact, as between the immediate parties an indorsement may be revoked by agreement, whatever the basis for it. For example, in L.H. Wagener, Inc. v. Kendall, 278 N.W.2d

the party whose rights on the instrument have been lost by the improper negotiation must assert the right to rescind the negotiation. For example, in *Harvey v. Casebeer*[174] the party liable on notes was not allowed to raise a breach of fiduciary duty against the defaulting trustee, who had indorsed the notes to himself and was admittedly the holder; the court stated that only the beneficiary of the trust could undo the negotiation.[175]

A negotiation thus is effective until it is undone due to the incapacity or the wrong. As a result, the taker of the instrument by the defective negotiation is a holder,[176] and that party may negotiate the instrument to a holder in due course. At that point the right of rescission or other remedy ceases because the improper negotiation creates a claim against the instrument,[177] but a holder in due course takes the instrument free from all claims to it on the part of any person.[178]

With respect to a void negotiation, this result is in sharp contrast with the result under another UCC section. Section 3–305(a)(1) makes many of the same defects, such as illegality and duress, when they are raised by the party sued, "real defenses" good against a holder in due course because the defect negates the contract sued upon. This difference at first seems troublesome. To illustrate, suppose an infant-payee of an instrument negotiates it to A, who then negotiates it to B, a holder in due course. B sues the infant on the indorser's contract under § 3–415(a), and the infant raises lack of capacity. Is this a "claim" by the infant, of which the holder in due course takes free under § 3–306, or is it a "defense," of which the holder does not take free under § 3–305(a)(1)? As the action is on the infant's indorser's contract, it should be considered a defense. This makes sense, even though the infant by an affirmative claim would have been unable to get the instrument or its proceeds from the holder in due course. The reason is the holder will have other rights against A as an indorser and against the maker or drawer of the instrument. Merely because the infant has lost rights on the instrument should not necessarily also mean that liability has accrued on the instrument for the infant. The justification then appears to be that the holder should be able to recover against any other parties on the instrument whose obligations are in no way affected by the subsequent defect in negotiation. In short, why should a maker benefit because a holder acquired the note by fraud?

---

18 (Iowa 1979), an accommodation indorser and the holder of a note, by a statement on the note, assigned all their right in the note without recourse (which negates indorser liability under § 3–415(a) and (b)) to plaintiff before delivery. The court held that while the accommodation indorser could not revoke liability to the holder after negotiation, the action here was sufficient to revoke the accommodation indorsement as to plaintiff.

174. 531 S.W.2d 206 (Tex.Civ.App. 1975).

175. *See* Official Comment 2 to § 3–202. A similar strong policy against a liable person being able to assert an initial defective negotiation as a defense to enforcement by a subsequent party appears in old § 3–413(3) (omitted as subsumed in other sections in current Article 3), which provided that by making, drawing, or accepting, the maker, drawer, or acceptor admits as against all subsequent parties, including the drawee, the existence of the payee and the payee's then capacity to indorse.

176. Official Comment 2 to § 3–202.

177. § 3–202(b).

178. § 3–306 and Official Comment 3 to § 3–202.

The kind of fact situation in which the issue can arise occurred in *Snyder v. Town Hill Motors, Inc.*[179] In that case, a minor, who had agreed to purchase an automobile from A for $1,000 and his own car in payment, went with A to an automobile dealer and indorsed and delivered a $1,000 check payable to the minor's order to the dealer to enable A to make a down payment on a new car. The court denied the right of the minor to rescind the negotiation of the check, holding that the minor had constructively delivered the check to A, who then constructively delivered it to the dealer, who took for value, without notice, and in good faith so as to be a subsequent holder in due course.

[b] Reacquisition

A different situation in which the negotiation of an instrument may be canceled is where the instrument is returned to or reacquired by a prior party.[180] In that circumstance, under § 3–207 the prior party may cancel any indorsement, and thus the negotiation of which it is a part, which is not necessary to title. In any event, any intervening party[181] is discharged as against the reacquiring party and subsequent holders not in due course.[182] And, if the indorsement of the intervening party has been canceled by the reacquiring party so as to give notice, the intervening party is discharged as against subsequent holders in due course as well.[183]

A common example of the application of this provision occurs when an instrument is deposited by its holder for collection, is not collected, and is returned to the holder.[184] In addition, in *United Credit Corp. v.*

---

179. 193 Pa.Super. 578, 165 A.2d 293 (1960).

180. § 3–207. § 3–207 makes it clear the reacquisition can be by negotiation, or by transfer in which case to do anything with the instrument intervening indorsements must be canceled. *See* Official Comment to § 3–207. The prior party must be one on the instrument. Thus where three notes made by a corporation were acquired by the executor of the estate of one of the indorsers in that person's representative capacity, the court held it did not constitute a reacquisition of the notes by a prior party. The executor was not a party to the notes and the decedent had never reacquired the notes so that the right of action on them could pass from the decedent to the estate. Eikel v. Bristow Corp., 529 S.W.2d 795 (Tex.Civ.App.1975).

181. An acceptor is not an intervening party. In Roswell Bank v. Atlanta Util. Works, Inc., 149 Ga.App. 660, 255 S.E.2d 124 (Ga.Ct.App.1979), a bank that certified checks for the payee argued the reacquisition by the payee of the checks after certification discharged the bank. This argument was promptly repudiated. Nor is a payor bank an intervening party. In Columbian Peanut Co. v. Frosteg, 472 F.2d 476 (5th Cir.1973), a bank the court found was in the position of payor and which paid checks on the forged indorsements of the payees argued that when the drawer had reacquired the checks, it was discharged as payor from responsibility. The argument was denied. § 3–207 is clear on this; *see* note 180, *supra*.

182. § 3–207. Otherwise, if the reacquiring party attempted to enforce the instrument against intervening parties on their indorsers' contracts, they would have an action back against the reacquiring party on the same basis. *See* the Official Comment to old § 3–208. Current § 3–207 seems to contemplate that an actual cancellation must occur for discharge, but the foregoing analysis should produce the result whether or not the indorsement is canceled. As note 180, *supra*, points out, a failure to cancel should be unusual.

183. *See* §§ 3–604(a), 3–601(b), 3–302(b), and Official Comment to § 3–207.

184. § 4–201(b)(1) limits holder rights in an item indorsed "pay any bank" or the like to a bank until the item has been returned to the customer initiating collec-

Necamp,[185] the court held that a finance company, to which the payee of a note had transferred it as security for an additional loan and which was restrictively indorsed "Pay to the order of any bank," was not affected by the restrictive indorsement and was a holder in due course when the note was returned to it by the bank to which it had been delivered for collection, as it could cancel the "pay any bank" indorsement.

Another example of the operation of § 3–207 is represented by *Schoonmaker v. Merchants National Bank & Trust Co.*[186] In that case the payee of an insurance check indorsed and delivered the check to the doctor who had treated his wife, and the doctor indorsed but did not deliver it to his bank. Rather, the doctor returned the check to the payee for return to the insurance company, as it was believed the insurance company was responsible for a larger payment. The payee, however, crossed out the doctor's indorsement, reindorsed the check, and the check was paid by the bank. In the suit by the doctor against the bank, the court decided that the bank had acted within the provisions of old § 3–208 and was not liable for conversion of the check.[187]

¶ 3.03 Holder in Due Course Status

[1] Introduction

[a] The Reason and Need for Holder in Due Course Status

The holder of a negotiable instrument and other parties entitled to enforce the instrument may transfer or negotiate an instrument, discharge it, or enforce payment of it.[188] In the last instance, what is being enforced is the contract liability of a party to the instrument[189] evidenced by the signature of that party.[190] As a contractual liability, it may be forestalled by a variety of defenses to payment, such as want or failure of consideration.[191]

In line with the normal contract rule, the assignee of commercial

---

tion, but upon return to the customer initiating collection of an item so indorsed, the indorsement may be canceled under § 3–207.

185. 19 UCC Rep. Serv. 1197 (Pa.Com. Pl.1976). A somewhat similar case is Resolution Trust Corp. v. Juergens, 965 F.2d 149 (7th Cir.1992).

186. 81 Misc.2d 967, 365 N.Y.S.2d 103 (N.Y.Co.Ct.1974).

187. The reacquiring party may negotiate the instrument. § 3–207. This is, however, no more than the right of that party as holder under § 3–301.

¶ 3.03

188. § 3–301 and other specific sections. *See* note 12, *supra*.

189. For a drawer or maker, this is stated in §§ 3–412, 3–414. The liability of an acceptor is the same as a maker. *See* § 3–413. The contract liability of an indorser is stated in § 3–415. An accommodation party is liable in whatever capacity in which the party signs under § 3–419. These liabilities are discussed in Chapter 4 and in Chapter 5.

190. No person is liable on an instrument unless that person's signature appears on the instrument. § 3–401(a). § 3–401, however, does allow an agent to bind an undisclosed principal.

191. §§ 3–305(a)(2) and (3), 3–303(b), 3–105(b).

paper acquires the rights of that person's assignor in the paper.[192] The most significant way in which a contract governed by Article 3 differs from an ordinary contract is that an assignee who qualifies as a holder of it sometimes may enforce the payment obligation represented by the paper without regard to most defenses assertable to the payment of the obligation and without regard to claims to the contract by other persons.[193] This extraordinary rule was developed long ago to facilitate the transferability of a negotiable instrument.[194] Because negotiable instruments still are transferred today, the rule continues,[195] although as will be seen, open to criticism and in a somewhat diminished state.[196]

The ability to enforce the obligation on a negotiable instrument without regard to claims and most defenses depends on holder in due course status.[197] Holder in due course status requires that the holder[198] must have taken the negotiable instrument[199] for value, in good faith, and without notice that it is overdue, or that it has been dishonored, or of any defense against or claim to it on the part of any person.[200]

The importance of the holder in due course rule should not obscure the fact that holder in due course status is only needed when there is a valid claim asserted or when a valid defense is established.[201] One does not need to be a holder in due course to withstand an invalid claim or to sue and recover upon an instrument where no defense exists.[202]

---

192. §§ 3–203(a) and (b), 1–201(b)(15).

193. §§ 3–305(b), 3–306. This and other differences from ordinary contracts were enumerated in Chapter 1. This difference in assignee rights did not exist where the instrument is governed by Article 3 by reason of old § 3–805; under current § 3–104 it exists for all instruments within Article 3. See § 3–104(a) and (c).

194. See the discussion in Chapter 2, supra.

195. But see the discussion in Chapter 2, supra, concerning the erosion of this status.

196. See, infra, this chapter. Article 3 also uses a form of holder in due course status to determine finality of payment. This different use is discussed, infra.

197. §§ 3–305(b), 3–306. Under §§ 3–305(a) and 3–306, any person who does not have the rights of a holder in due course takes the instrument subject to all valid claims to it on the part of any person, all defenses of any party which would be available in an action on a simple contract, and even what may be considered as several third-party defenses. See § 3–305(c) and (d).

198. A person in possession of the instrument with any necessary indorsement is a holder. UCC § 1–201(b)(21)(A). The matter was discussed, supra, this chapter.

199. If the instrument is not negotiable, Article 3 does not apply, or at least does not accord holder in due course status. See Chapter 1, supra.

200. § 3–302(a).

201. § 3–308(b). The status also may be needed to retain payment under § 3–418(c).

202. Until it is shown that a defense exists, the issue as to whether the holder is a holder in due course does not arise. In the absence of a defense, any holder or other person entitled to enforce the instrument under § 3–301 is entitled to recover. Even if a defense is asserted, the holder may elect to rebut the defense, in which case a verdict may be directed for either party or the issue may be for the jury. Official Comment 2 to § 3–308. Compare Perry & Greer, Inc. v. Manning, 282 Or. 25, 576 P.2d 791 (Or. 1978) (defendants having elected not to establish any of the defenses pleaded, it was unnecessary for plaintiffs to establish that they were holders in due course) with American State Bank v. Richendifer, 36 Or. App. 199, 584 P.2d 323 (Or.Ct.App.1978) (if defendant established either defense and plaintiff was unable to establish its status as a holder in due course, plaintiff would be subject to defenses). See also Tuttle v. Rose, 102 Ill.App.3d 865, 58 Ill.Dec. 414, 430 N.E.2d 356 (1981), and Leopold v. Halleck, 106 Ill.App.3d 386, 62 Ill.Dec. 447, 436 N.E.2d 29 (1982).

[b] Payee As a Holder in Due Course

The benefits of the holder in due course rule usually are available only if the instrument has been negotiated beyond the payee,[203] but not necessarily. First, one can acquire the benefit of the rule, even if not a holder in due course, if one's transferor was a holder in due course, because the transfer of an instrument vests in the transferee the rights the transferor had in it.[204] Perhaps more important, a payee may be a holder in due course.[205] Of course, when the issue arises, a payee normally will not qualify as a holder in due course because of notice of the facts which create the defense of the maker or drawer, or because the value given for the instrument will fail.[206] Under old Article 3, there was a further hurdle even if the payee was a holder in due course; the payee (or any holder in due course) could not take the instrument free from the defense of a person with whom the holder had "dealt."[207]

---

203. *See, e.g.*, Scott v. Wall, 55 Wn.App. 404, 777 P.2d 581 (1989), where buyers signed and delivered a note to sellers on the understanding it would not be enforceable unless a condition occurred. It did not, but sellers sued anyway. The court held sellers were not holders in due course and so the parol condition could be shown. It would indeed be unjust for sellers to be able to enforce the note when the parties had agreed otherwise. *See also* Ventures, Inc. v. Jones, 101 Idaho 837, 623 P.2d 145 (1981) and Evenson v. Hlebechuk, 305 N.W.2d 13 (N.D.1981). Moreover, the reason behind holder in due course status is to allow the taker of the instrument not to be subject to problems in the transaction about which the taker is ignorant. If the payee is a party to the transaction, this policy is irrelevant.

204. § 3–203(b). This simply preserves the market for the holder in due course; there is no prejudice to the obligor. If one had notice of a defense or claim as a prior holder, however, one cannot improve in position by taking from a later holder in due course.

205. Old § 3–302(2). Current § 3–302 deletes the statement as unnecessary; no change in result is intended. Official Comment 4 to § 3–302. Many cases so hold. *See, e.g.*, United States v. Second Nat'l Bank, 502 F.2d 535 (5th Cir.1974); First Nat'l Bank v. Creston Livestock Auction, Inc., 447 N.W.2d 132 (Iowa 1989); Chicago Title & Trust Co. v. Walsh, 34 Ill.App.3d 458, 340 N.E.2d 106 (1975).

206. *See*, note 203, *supra*, and *e.g.*, Mansion Carpets, Inc. v. Marinoff, 24 A.D.2d 947, 265 N.Y.S.2d 298 (App.Div. 1965) (payee of check issued for carpeting and floor covering installed by it was subject to defenses based on the original transaction); Dobbs–Maynard Co. v. Jumper, 388 So.2d 879 (Miss.1980) (where president and sole shareholder of corporation had promised maker that note payable to the corporation would not be enforced, corporation could not be holder in due course); Emery–Waterhouse Co. v. Rhode Island Hosp. Trust Nat'l Bank, 757 F.2d 399 (1st Cir. 1985) (payee of draft who was in control of seller was chargeable with defense of buyer known to seller and was not a holder in due course); Official Comment 4 to § 3–302 and Official Comment 2 to § 3–305. *See also* Kovash v. McCloskey, 386 N.W.2d 32 (N.D. 1986) (check in settlement payable to attorney and indorsed to client which bounced; attorney had defense of no consideration when sued by client).

207. Old § 3–305(2). This limitation accords with the policy behind holder in due course status. *See* note 203, *supra*. The limitation is discussed further, *infra*, this chapter but to illustrate the limitation here, in James Pair, Inc. v. Gentry, 134 Ga.App. 734, 215 S.E.2d 707 (Ga.Ct.App.1975), an employment agency was the payee of a note given by an employee for a job placement fee. Under the employee's agreement with the employer and the agency, the fee was refundable to the employee by the employer if the employee stayed with the employer more than six months. The employer breached this agreement. The court believed the breach constituted a defense to the debt represented by the note, held that even a holder in due course does not take the instrument free from defenses of a party with whom the holder has dealt, and determined that the parties had dealt with each other in the transaction out of which the employee's action for recovery of payments made on the note arose. It would seem that the correct analysis is either that no defense existed to the note, but that the

Current § 3–305 deletes this language as potentially productive of an erroneous result,[208] and as unnecessary if the case is properly analyzed.[209]

When may a payee be a holder in due course then? If the payee was not involved with the aspect of the transaction giving rise to the defense, and particularly if the payee was insulated from the maker or drawer by a third party, the payee may be able to take free of the asserted defense.[210] Official Comment 4 to § 3–302 contains several examples of when a payee may be a holder in due course. These may be taken to be examples of cases where the payee has given value, has taken in good faith and without notice, and has not dealt directly with the person asserting the defense.[211]

One of the examples most likely to occur involves an unfaithful agent of the maker or drawer, which can have several variations. In one case, *Saka v. Sahara–Nevada Corp.*,[212] a drawer signed a blank check and

employee had a claim against the employer, or, on the other hand, if there was a defense, it would seem the payee could not be a holder in due course as it would have notice.

208. As Official Comment 2 to § 3–305 states, suppose buyer fraudulently gets bank to issue a cashier's check to buyer's order and then buyer negotiates it to seller for a delivery of property or services. It is clear seller takes free of bank's defense. But what if the check was payable to seller and delivered directly to the seller? It could be argued the seller dealt with the bank and thus is subject to the defense, a wrong result. *See also* Official Comment 4, Case #1, to § 3–302; Village Motors v. American Fed. Sav. & Loan Assn., 231 Va. 408, 345 S.E.2d 288 (1986); and A.I. Trade Fin., Inc. v. Laminaciones de Lesaca, S.A., 41 F.3d 830 (2d Cir.1994) (court refused to apply language literally where plaintiff agreed to finance the sale and purchased buyer's note from seller). A similar case is Gentner & Co., Inc. v. Wells Fargo Bank, 76 Cal. App.4th 1165, 90 Cal.Rptr.2d 904 (Cal.Ct. App.1999), where the payee of a check presented it to Wells Fargo for payment and the bank issued a cashier's check notwithstanding a stop order on the check presented. When sued on the cashier's check, Wells Fargo asserted no consideration, and so the issue boiled down to whether plaintiff was a holder in due course even though plaintiff was the remitter. Perhaps uneasy about deciding the case on this basis given the plaintiff's status, the court alternatively held for plaintiff on the ground the cashier's check was payment that could not be recovered under § 3–418. *See also* § 3–411, discussed later in this book.

209. Official Comment 2 to § 3–305. *See also* American Bank & Trust Co. v. Sunbelt Envtl. Sys., Inc., 451 So.2d 1111 (La.Ct.App.1984) (want or failure of consideration cannot be a defense against a holder in due course who is a payee, or else the payee is not a holder in due course).

Some close analysis may be necessary, however. For example, in Turney v. Seale, 473 So.2d 855 (La.Ct.App.1985), the wife sought to enforce a note the former husband made payable to himself and indorsed to her in satisfaction of a debt for present and future alimony. The court held she was a holder in due course even though she later remarried, which would have constituted some failure of consideration. But clearly he then would have a claim against her pro tanto which could be set-off. *See also* § 3–305(b) and Official Comment 3. In Travelers Indem. Co. v. American Express Co., 559 F.Supp. 452 (S.D.N.Y.1983), a corporation had mistakenly paid both its American Express bill and that of an employee. The court held even if American Express was a holder in due course it had dealt with the corporation. Notice on the part of American Express also was argued, and that (or set-off as above) probably is the correct analysis. *See* § 3–307(b)(4) and Official Comment 5 to that section; *see also* Official Comment 4, Case #3, to § 3–302. *See* further illustrations, *infra*.

210. *Compare* note 207, *supra*, and *see* Kane v. Kroll, 196 Wis.2d 389, 538 N.W.2d 605 (Wis.Ct.App.1995).

211. Other examples beyond those discussed so far include A.C. Davenport & Son Co. v. United States, 538 F.Supp. 730, (N.D.Ill.1982), *aff'd*, 703 F.2d 266 (7th Cir. 1983) and First Nat'l Bank v. Creston Livestock Auction, Inc., 447 N.W.2d 132 (Iowa 1989). *See also*, *infra*.

212. 92 Nev. 703, 558 P.2d 535 (Nev. 1976). *Compare* Official Comment 4, Case #4, to § 3–302.

told a third party to cash it for $800 and give the money to the plaintiff in payment of a bill disputed between the third party and plaintiff. The check was instead made out to the plaintiff in the full amount it claimed, which was more than $3,000. As there was no competent evidence before the court concerning the merits of the dispute, the court stated no genuine issue of fact was raised as to plaintiff being a holder in due course in the resulting action on the check, on which the drawer had stopped payment because of the deviation from his instructions. In *Eldon's Super Fresh Stores, Inc. v. Merrill Lynch, Pierce, Fenner & Smith, Inc.*,[213] a check was delivered to the payee by the drawer's agent allegedly, according to the drawer, to purchase some stock for the drawer. The payee, ignorant as to this alleged purpose, took the check in payment for stock recently purchased by the agent individually. The court held that as the payee could have assumed the check had been given to the agent in payment for services that he rendered to the drawer, the payee was a holder in due course and not subject to the drawer's claim.

The *Eldon's* case is not entirely persuasive because this holding only disposed of the penultimate issue of whether a holder in due course existed under old Article 3, and a final issue of whether the payee dealt with the drawer was not discussed by the court. For the drawer to have had a claim, the agent must have been acting as such, and not on his own behalf with the check being payment for services performed by the agent. Thus, did not the payee deal with the drawer through the agent? This would seem to raise the final issue, but arguably this issue on the facts of the case is irrelevant because under old § 3–305(1) a holder in due course takes an instrument (and presumably its proceeds) free from all claims to it on the part of *any* person and there is no "having dealt with" limitation. On the other hand, if payment on the check had been stopped so that the payee had to sue the drawer, would the drawer then be able to raise the defense of delivery for a special purpose, because under old § 3–305(2) a holder in due course does not take free from *defenses* of a party *with whom he has dealt?*[214] Thus can the UCC be interpreted so as to produce a different result in some cases because of the mere chance of who is plaintiff? The answer is no, and the different language simply is because the UCC only deals with actions on an instrument and not claims to its proceeds. If a holder in due course can prevail over a defense, it should be able to use that status to resist a claim.[215] The court in the *Eldon's* case, while it did not deal with this question, on balance reached the correct result as indicated by Official Comment 2e to old § 3–302, once it determined that the payee really was a holder in due course, and under current Article 3 that would be the

---

213. 296 Minn. 130, 207 N.W.2d 282 (Minn. 1973). *Compare* Official Comment 4, Case #3, to § 3–302.

214. Old § 3–305(2).

215. *See, e.g.*, Nida v. Michael, 34 Mich. App. 290, 191 N.W.2d 151 (Mich.Ct.App. 1971)(a holder in due course takes free of personal defenses and, if already paid, can assert status as a defense in an action to recover back the payment). *See also* United States v. Mark Twain Bank–Kansas City, 771 F.2d 361 (8th Cir.1985). A further discussion appears, *infra*.

conclusive issue, since the "dealt with" language is deleted. Under current Article 3, the holder in due course issue in the case is treated in § 3–307, discussed, *infra*.[216]

[2] Elements of Proper Taking

[a] Value

To be a holder in due course, the holder must have given value.[217] In Article 3, value is a term of art and is not determined by the general definition of value appearing in the UCC.[218] Essentially, it is consideration that has been performed, as well as including the case where the instrument is taken in payment of or as security for an antecedent claim.[219] A holder should not be able to enforce the instrument over claims and defenses unless it is necessary to enable the holder to obtain reimbursement for value parted with or a change in position.[220]

In the bank collection process, a bank gives value to the extent that it has a security interest in an item.[221] A bank has a security interest in an item (and in any accompanying documents or the proceeds of either), in the case of an item deposited in an account, to the extent to which credit given for the item has been withdrawn or applied.[222] Thus, in *Falls Church Bank v. Wesley Heights Realty, Inc.*,[223] a bank, which had provisionally credited its depositor's account with a $1,400 check and then permitted him to withdraw $140, was determined to be a holder in due course to the amount of the $140 withdrawal.[224]

---

216. *See* § 3–302, Official Comment 4, Case #3. § 3–306 also covers the question of whether a holder in due course is protected as to the proceeds of an instrument. The section states a holder in due course is not subject to a claim of a property or possessory right in the instrument *or its proceeds* (emphasis supplied). *See* discussion, *infra*, this chapter.

217. § 3–302(a)(2)(i). The person giving value is normally under no duty to police the proper application of the value so given. Sherrill v. Frank Morris Pontiac–Buick–GMC, Inc., 366 So.2d 251 (Ala.1978). *But see* § 3–206(c)(1)–(3) and (d)(1) concerning restrictive indorsements, discussed, *supra*.

218. UCC § 1–204.

219. § 3–303(a).

220. Official Comment 2 to § 3–303.

221. § 4–211.

222. § 4–210(a)(1). Under § 4–210(a)(2), a bank has a security interest in the case of an item for which it has given credit available for withdrawal as of right to the extent of the credit given, whether it is drawn upon and whether there is a right of charge-back. Under § 4–210(a)(3), a bank has a security interest if it makes an advance on or against an item. § 4–210(b), sets up a first-in, first-out (FIFO) rule for determining when credits given are withdrawn. Essentially the security interest of a bank under these provisions is not subject to Article 9's requirements for a security agreement and filing. § 4–210(c) and §§ 9–203(c) and 9–309(7).

223. 256 A.2d 915 (D.C.1969).

224. The bank also must comply with the other requirements of § 3–302(a), being good faith and lack of notice, in order to be a holder in due course. In Seinfeld v. Commercial Bank & Trust Co., 405 So.2d 1039 (Fla.Dist.Ct.App.1981), where a depositor who was consistently overdrawn deposited $160,000 in checks and was allowed to withdraw the funds without even an inquiry to the bank, these requirements tripped the holder up. Perhaps the otherwise disturbing case of Maine Family Federal Credit Union v. Sun Life Assurance Company, 1999 ME 43, 727 A.2d 335 (Me.1999), where the court affirmed a jury verdict against holder in due course status under the broad good faith definition in § 3–103(a)(4), can be similarly explained, but perhaps the case instead represents a further attack on the negotiability concept because, on what may be viewed as less egregious facts, the courts usually hold for the depositary bank. Nati-

Aside from the above described particular rule for banks in the bank collection process, under Article 3 a holder takes an instrument for value to the extent that the agreed consideration has been performed or that the holder acquires a security interest in or a lien on the instrument otherwise than by legal process.[225] Value also is given when the instrument is taken in payment of or as security for an antecedent claim against any person, whether or not the claim is due,[226] and when a negotiable instrument is given for the instrument taken or an irrevocable commitment to a third person is made.[227] An executory promise is not value because, when the executory promisor learns of a defense against the instrument or of a defect in the title to it, the promisor simply may refuse to pay due to breach of a warranty by the transferor[228] and does not have to enforce the instrument to make itself whole.[229]

Most of the time, the application of these provisions is not difficult. For example, in one case no value was found because the instrument was taken only as provisional credit against a debt owed.[230] In *Bamberg v.*

onsbank of Virginia, N.A. v. Cookies, Inc., 22 UCC Rep. Serv. 2d 838 (Va.Cir.Ct.1993) (but no issue of good faith raised) and Isolano v. Chase Manhattan Bank, N.A., 25 UCC Rep. Serv. 2d 1174 (N.Y.Sup.Ct.1995). It is said that if it were not for this rule, depositary banks might refuse to permit withdrawal prior to the clearance of checks, to the hindrance of commercial transactions, because they could not prevail over defenses of other parties to the instrument and thus would only have practical recourse against their customer. Citizens Nat'l Bank v. Fort Lee Sav. & Loan Ass'n, 89 N.J.Super. 43, 213 A.2d 315 (Law Div.1965). The criticism is that it seems dubious that a bank should rely on the liability of a drawer or indorsers about which it may know nothing. Moreover, today, except as mandated by Regulation CC, 12 CFR pt. 229, many banks do not allow recourse to funds for periods of many days to make sure the funds actually are collected from the payor. The "funds availability" issue is further discussed later in this book. It would seem, however, that the *Maine* case requires a bank to go beyond what Regulation CC requires.

225. § 3–303(a)(1) and (2). *See* Carter & Grimsley v. Omni Trading, Inc., 306 Ill. App.3d 1127, 240 Ill.Dec. 187, 716 N.E.2d 320 (Ill.Ct.App.1999), *appeal denied*, 186 Ill.2d 566, 243 Ill.Dec. 560, 723 N.E.2d 1161 (Ill. 1999) (no value when services not yet performed for check given as retainer).

226. § 3–303(a)(3).

227. § 3–303(a)(4) and (5).

228. § 3–416(a)(4) provides a warranty that no defense of any party is good. This warranty is discussed in Chapter 7.

229. § 3–303, Official Comment 2, employs a slightly different analysis that reaches the same result using an example involving Article 2.

230. Wilson Supply Co. v. West Artesia Transmission Co., 505 S.W.2d 312 (Tex.Civ. App.1974). *Distinguish* St. Paul Fire & Marine Ins. Co. v. State Bank, 412 N.E.2d 103 (Ind.Ct.App.1980), where the bank took the check, credited its amount against notes, and surrendered the notes. Then, when payment on the check was stopped, the bank canceled the credits. The court determined the check was taken in payment of the notes and thus more than a provisional credit had been given. *See also* Peoria Sav. & Loan Ass'n v. Jefferson Trust & Sav. Bank, 81 Ill.2d 461, 43 Ill.Dec. 712, 410 N.E.2d 845 (Ill. 1980), finding that it is not necessary that a bookkeeping entry reducing the debt be accomplished before value is given if the facts otherwise disclose that the instrument was taken in payment of the debt; *but see* Godat v. Mercantile Bank, 884 S.W.2d 1 (Mo.Ct.App.1994), where plaintiff was told by an investment broker he had $500,000 in his account and so agreed to invest $200,000, the broker by fraud secured a cashier's check for that amount payable to plaintiff from defendant bank where the account was located, and then, when the fraud was discovered, the bank refused to pay. The court held that plaintiff had given no value as nothing existed in the account. *But quere*, if the broker owed plaintiff money, could it not be found plaintiff took the instrument for value in partial payment of an antecedent debt, and thus the bank could not raise the defense of failure of consideration against a holder in due course? *See* note 208, *supra*.

Griffin,[231] where the check in suit was given as an earnest money deposit in an uncompleted real estate transaction, value was held to be missing because of the completely executory nature of the consideration. *O. P. Ganjo, Inc. v. Tri–Urban Realty Co.*,[232] involved a promise to pay money that was partly executory and partly performed.[233] The holder of the instrument was found to be a holder in due course to the extent of the payment that had been made up to the time the holder could no longer become a holder in due course due to notice.

On the other hand, in some situations the application of the UCC rules for when value is given is more troublesome. For example, what about an executory promise to lease property or to perform services once performance is begun? In *Saka v. Mann Theatres*,[234] a check was given for a week's rental which already had commenced when notice of dishonor was received. The court found the check was taken for value on the basis that a division of the rental period was not required and the executory promise accordingly was performed. In *Korzenik v. Supreme Radio, Inc.*,[235] however, which involved notes taken by an attorney as a retainer one week after he had been retained and where the attorney had done some legal work, the court held the attorney was not a holder in due course. That probably is the correct decision under old Article 3 at least as to the executory services, and the *Saka* case may be explained on the ground the rental period would be over before the tenant could be ousted from possession. Under § 3–303(b), however, if an instrument is issued for a promise of performance, the issuer only has a defense to the extent performance of the promise is due and the promise has not been performed. *See also* § 3–302(d).

Questions of whether an irrevocable commitment has been made to a third party seem to be particularly troublesome. To illustrate, in *Crest Finance Co. v. First State Bank of Westmont*,[236] an agreement for the sale of corporate stock was consummated by the seller delivering the stock certificates to an escrow agent in return for cashier's checks. The seller also was to be relieved of his guarantees of the corporation's loans, and when he gave notice to the escrow agent that this had been accomplished, the stock certificates would be released. The court concluded that the seller had made an irrevocable commitment to the third-party escrow agent, and that accordingly he was a holder in due course of the

---

231. 76 Ill.App.3d 138, 31 Ill.Dec. 708, 394 N.E.2d 910 (1979).

232. 108 N.J.Super. 517, 261 A.2d 722 (Law Div.1969).

233. A $3,000 note had been purchased for a $200 discount, $1,000 having been paid and $1,800 having not yet been paid. The court found holder in due course status to the extent of $1,000, but also to the extent of $71.43 with respect to the discount. This latter part of the decision is in error as under old Article 3 under which the case was decided a holder in due course should not obtain any benefit of a discount unless the entire consideration has been performed. However, under § 3–302(d), the *Ganjo* result is adopted. *See* § 3–302, Official Comment 6, Case #5.

234. 94 Nev. 137, 575 P.2d 1335 (Nev. 1978).

235. 347 Mass. 309, 197 N.E.2d 702 (Mass. 1964). *See also* note 225, *supra*.

236. 37 Ill.2d 243, 226 N.E.2d 369 (Ill. 1967).

cashier's checks, the other elements for that status of good faith and no notice being met.[237]

[b] Good Faith and Lack of Notice

[i] Relevant Time for Meeting Requirements

To be a holder in due course, the holder must have taken the instrument in good faith[238] and without notice that it is overdue or has been dishonored, or of any defense against or claim to it on the part of any person.[239] In these respects, timing is important.

The crucial point is when value is given. A lack of good faith after that point or notice received after that time cannot impair the status obtained.[240] Conversely, a lack of good faith or notice obtained before that time will be fatal to holder in due course status, with two limited exceptions.[241] The first exception is that notice must be received at such time and in such manner as to give a reasonable opportunity to act on it.[242] The second exception concerns "forgotten notice," that is, notice once received which is then "forgotten." The UCC does not take any position whether such notice is still effective,[243] leaving it up to each jurisdiction to consider and apply the doctrine.[244]

There is another point worth noting in connection with the application of the timing rules of the UCC for holder in due course status. *Lazere Financial Corp. v. Crystal Mart, Inc.* is an illustrative case.[245] There the defendant defaulted on a series of notes held by plaintiff as a holder in due course. An arrangement was worked out whereby part payment was made and a new note issued to the plaintiff's assignor and

---

237. The decision seems questionable as, upon learning of the infirmities involving the cashier's checks, the seller should have been able to go to court for an order requiring the escrow agent to return the stock pursuant to a rescission of the sale. *See* Official Comment 3 to old § 3–303. A later, similar case from the same jurisdiction is Schranz v. I.L. Grossman, Inc., 90 Ill.App.3d 507, 45 Ill.Dec. 654, 412 N.E.2d 1378 (1980). Contrast the example used in Official Comment 5 to § 3–303—a letter of credit issued when an instrument is taken.

238. § 3–302(a)(2)(ii).

239. § 3–302(a)(1) and (2).

240. *See, e.g.*, McCook County Nat'l Bank v. Compton, 558 F.2d 871 (8th Cir. 1977); Chicago Title & Trust Co. v. Walsh, 34 Ill.App.3d 458, 340 N.E.2d 106 (1975); and American State Bank v. Northwest South Dakota Prod. Credit Assn., 404 N.W.2d 517 (S.D.1987).

241. If value is advanced both before and after notice, the holder will not be a holder in due course to the extent of the value given after the notice. American Exch. Bank v. Cessna, 386 F.Supp. 494 (N.D.Okla.1974). Note also that if at the time value is given the person providing it is not a holder because of a missing indorsement, that person cannot become a holder in due course until the indorsement is obtained. If at that time there is notice, the holder will not be a holder in due course notwithstanding the value given earlier. United Overseas Bank v. Veneers, Inc., 375 F.Supp. 596 (D.Md.1973).

242. § 3–302(f). Thus notice received by the president of a bank one minute before the bank's teller cashes a check is not effective to prevent the bank from becoming a holder in due course. Official Comment 12 to old § 3–304.

243. The time and circumstances under which a notice or notification may cease to be effective are not determined by this Act. UCC § 1–202 Official Comment: Changes from former law.

244. *See, e.g.*, First Nat'l Bank v. Fazzari, 10 N.Y.2d 394, 223 N.Y.S.2d 483, 179 N.E.2d 493 (N.Y. 1961).

245. 78 Misc.2d 379, 357 N.Y.S.2d 973 (Civ.Ct.1974).

indorsed to plaintiff to represent the balance due. In action on the new note, the defendant raised defenses to payment, and the court held that the arrangement had nullified the original obligation of which the plaintiff was a holder in due course and plaintiff's status as to the new note was to be determined by the circumstances existing at the time of its delivery.

[ii] Bad Faith or Knowledge of Agent

A holder may be bound by the conduct and knowledge of an agent or representative acting within the scope of that person's authority. In *Mid-Continent National Bank v. Bank of Independence*,[246] the bad faith or knowledge of an assistant cashier acting within the scope of her authority concerning the fraudulent procurement of a check taken by her bank employer resulted in denial of holder in due course status for the bank.[247] On the other hand, knowledge acquired by the vice chairman of the holder bank in his individual capacity as an accountant and not as an official of the bank, where the vice chairman had nothing to do with and had no knowledge of his bank accepting the instrument, was held not to be imputable to the bank.[248] In *Saale v. Interstate Steel Co.*[249] the holder also was not held to be barred by the acts of his agent in connection with a sale of goods, in the absence of evidence that the holder was a party to the fraudulent substitution of the goods by the agent or had notice of it.

[iii] Good Faith in General

Under UCC § 1–201(b)(20), good faith is honesty in fact and the observance of reasonable commercial standards of fair dealing. The first part of this definition was the standard that applied under old Article 3.[250] However, under current Articles 1, 3 and 4, the standard is honesty in fact *and the observance of reasonable commercial standards of fair dealing*.[251] Good faith thus demands, first, that a party have no actual knowledge of any material infirmity in the transaction out of which the

---

246. 523 S.W.2d 569 (Mo.Ct.App.1975).

247. Under Article 3, in determining whether notice of a breach of fiduciary duty exists, the actual knowledge of the person acting for the organization that takes the instrument is crucial. Under UCC § 1–202, knowledge of the organization is determined by the knowledge of the individual conducting the transaction. Official Comments 2–5 to § 3–307.

248. Millman v. State Nat'l Bank, 323 A.2d 723 (D.C.1974).

249. 27 A.D.2d 1, 275 N.Y.S.2d 532 (App.Div.1966), *aff'd*, 19 N.Y.2d 933, 281 N.Y.S.2d 340, 228 N.E.2d 397 (N.Y. 1967).

250. An illustrative case is Galatia Community State Bank v. Kindy, 307 Ark. 467, 821 S.W.2d 765 (1991), where the depositary bank received a check imprinted for $5550 but made out in handwriting for $6550. The intent of the drawer was to force the payor bank to call before paying, at which time he could stop payment if the goods for which the check was given had not been delivered. That happened, and when the check was returned to the plaintiff bank, it sued the drawer. *See* the discussion concerning restrictive indorsements, *supra*, this chapter. The court stated that since the depositary bank honestly believed the discrepancy was a mistake, when it credited its customer's account for the lesser amount it acted in good faith.

251. §§ 1–201(b)(20), 3–103(a)(4) and 4–104(c). The issue is not a question of ordinary care. Official Comment 4 to § 3–103, Halla v. Norwest Bank Minnesota, N.A., 601 N.W.2d 449 (Minn.App.1999), and San Tan Irrigation Dist. v. Wells Fargo Bank, 197 Ariz. 193, 3 P.3d 1113 (Ariz.Ct. App.2000).

instrument arose. A holder who had knowledge that the transaction was not a bona fide sale but was a pretended sale to cover a usurious transaction was found not to be a holder in due course.[252] To this extent the test is subjective, a "white heart and empty head" test, and lack of due care on the part of the holder is not sufficient to destroy good faith, nor is the presence of generally suspicious circumstances.[253] Nonetheless, in determining whether the subjective intent of the holder of the instrument amounted to good faith, the trier of fact may consider not only the testimony of the holder but also evidence of surrounding circumstances that inferentially illuminate the holder's honesty, such as, for example, paying an amount for the instrument far less than its face value.[254]

Given this observation, is the additional objective element of observance of reasonable commercial standards of fair dealing added by current Article 3 likely to change the outcome of any cases? Consider *McCarthy v. Kasperak*.[255] The defendant was offered a stolen bearer bond by her long-time accountant for a discount. She asserted she was told the bond was being sold for another client. She sought the advice of her banker nonetheless, who said that bearer paper was risky because of the possibility of theft and that better instruments existed. The defendant bought the bond anyway. The court allowed a jury verdict that denied holder in due course status on the ground the jury did not believe the defendant's explanation of the transaction. Perhaps that same result might more easily be reached on the basis of a lack of good faith, but not because the defendant might be considered to have acted negligently which, as Official Comment 4 to § 3–103 makes clear, is not the point.[256] Arguably the conduct of the defendant exhibited a lack of concern for another's possible rights and thus a lack of fairness akin to that in the examples in Official Comment 4 to § 3–311 (tendering an unreasonably

---

252. Mutual Home Dealers Corp. v. Alves, 23 A.D.2d 791, 258 N.Y.S.2d 786 (App.Div.1965). *See also* Frye v. Farmers & Merchants Bank, 561 S.W.2d 392 (Mo.Ct. App.1977), where the president of the bank insisted that corporate funds be used not only to pay a corporate note but also the personal note of the president of the corporation. The court held the bank did not receive the check in good faith and was not a holder in due course of it.

253. Breslin v. New Jersey Inv., Inc., 70 N.J. 466, 361 A.2d 1 (N.J.1976) (good faith is determined by looking into the mind of the particular holder, not by what the state of mind of a prudent man should have been); Riley v. First State Bank, 469 S.W.2d 812 (Tex.Civ.App.1971) (it is immaterial that the holder may have had notice of facts that would have put a reasonably prudent person on inquiry and which would lead to discovery of the circumstances surrounding the transaction); Northwestern Nat'l Ins. Co. v. Maggio, 976 F.2d 320 (7th Cir.1992) (neither a 50% discount paid for the instrument nor the number of notes involved, or both, triggered a duty of inquiry). But currently as to a duty of inquiry in at least one specific instance, *see* Official Comment 5 to § 9–331. *See also* Any Kind Checks Cashed, Inc. v. Talcott, 830 So.2d 160, 48 UCC Rep. Serv.2d 800 (Fla.App.2002) (concept of "fair dealing" includes not being an easy, safe harbor for the dishonest; larger than normal amount of check cashed by check cashing store, unusual for a business to conduct business not through a traditional bank, and need for speed in cashing large business check raised red flag).

254. Funding Consultants, Inc. v. Aetna Casualty & Surety Co., 187 Conn. 637, 447 A.2d 1163 (1982). *But see* the *Maggio* case, *supra*, note 253.

255. 3 Ohio App.3d 206, 444 N.E.2d 472 (1981).

256. *See* note 250, *supra*.

small insurance settlement check to a necessitous claimant or uniformly placing full settlement language on checks for less than the amount due even when no dispute exists).[257] Thus while the approach might vary in a given fact situation, case outcomes may not be changed. But it is too early to tell whether more may be involved. For example, is the result in the *Maine Family Federal Credit Union* case[258] merely facilitated by the broader definition, or were the facts there so ordinary and not egregious that the broader definition changed the result? Further, courts consistently have not found a lack of good faith in check kiting cases where banks have failed to disclose their assumption of a kite and have attempted to shift the loss to another bank. *See, e.g., First National Bank in Harvey v. Colonial Bank*, 898 F.Supp. 1220 (N.D.Ill.1995) and *Frost National Bank v. Midwest Autohaus, Inc.*, 241 F.3d 862 (7th Cir.2001). Can we assume the same analysis under a definition that in addition mandates the observance of *reasonable* commercial standards of *fair dealing* (emphasis supplied)? Perhaps the same result could be obtained if the court is willing to leave several equally culpable parties as it found them. And, of course, there may be yet other risks in these fact situations beyond an issue of good faith. *See, e.g., Lawyers Title Ins. Corp. v. United American Bank of Memphis*, 21 F.Supp.2d 785 (W.D.Tenn.1998) (tort "aiding and abetting" theory), and *International Finance Bank v. COFO Financial Group*, Case No. 98–30116 CA09 (Fla.Cir.Ct.2002) (on appeal) (violation of Regulation CC, 12 CFR §§ 229.30(d) and 229.33(b)(8); but also finding a lack of good faith on the facts present there).

One more specific caveat should be raised. Under old Article 3, there was no general legal duty in the good faith requirement to inquire into the real worth of the instrument or the underlying agreement even if some suspicious circumstances existed.[259] The reason is, if the holder of an instrument were required to investigate in each instance whether the contract had been completed satisfactorily or other extraneous facts before accepting the instrument, the burden placed on the free flow of negotiable paper would be almost insurmountable.[260] Does the obligation

---

257. *See* Dhiman v. Rockford Industries, Inc., 42 UCC Rep. Serv. 2d 767 (N.D.Ill.2000). *Compare* Woolridge v. J.F.L. Electric, Inc., 96 Cal.App. 4th Supp. 52, 117 Cal.Rptr.2d 771, 46 UCC Rep. Serv.2d 1059 (Super.Ct.2002).

258. *See* note 224, *supra*.

259. *See, e.g.,* Money Mart Check Cashing Center, Inc. v. Epicycle Corp., 667 P.2d 1372 (Colo.1983) (good faith, absent extremely suspicious circumstances, requires no inquiry). There are occasional aberrant decisions. *See, e.g.,* E. Bierhaus & Sons, Inc. v. Bowling, 486 N.E.2d 598 (Ind.Ct.App. 1985) (where matters are known that would put a reasonably prudent person on inquiry, inquiry must be made to obtain holder in due course status), and Strickland v. Kafko Mfg., Inc., 512 So.2d 714 (Ala.1987) (constructive knowledge is relevant in determining a lack of good faith).

260. Jaeger & Branch, Inc. v. Pappas, 20 Utah 2d 100, 433 P.2d 605 (Utah 1967). If a fair inquiry is made and no notification is received, it is an act of prudence and implies no knowledge of any impediment in the instrument. Central Bank & Trust Co. v. First Northwest Bank, 332 F.Supp. 1166 (E.D.Mo.1971), *aff'd*, 458 F.2d 511 (8th Cir. 1972). For example, the court found good faith in McCook County Nat'l Bank v. Compton, 558 F.2d 871 (8th Cir.1977), where a $10,000 discrepancy appeared on the face of the instrument but upon inquiry assurance was given that the instrument was valid for the larger amount.

to observe reasonable commercial standards of fair dealing now require an inquiry in suspicious circumstances? It is submitted that if the reason inquiry is not reasonable is to facilitate the flow of negotiable instruments, that policy has not changed, and thus reasonable commercial standards of fair dealing do not require inquiry where inquiry was not required before. This conclusion is supported by the explicit denial of a duty of inquiry stated in Official Comment 2 to § 3–307. Rather, the new duty of good faith would seem to impose a higher duty with respect to known facts to act as others would, as opposed to a new duty to discover facts. In short, the expanded definition in this context would seem to do no more than codify the case law gloss on the present definition that is represented by the following discussion.

Before turning to that discussion, however, a related development must be mentioned. In *In re Joe Morgan, Inc.*,[261] the relatively common problem of a junior secured party taking an instrument in payment from the debtor and resisting a claim by a senior secured party to it on the basis of asserted holder in due course status, was litigated. Employing the subjective test of good faith, the lower court found holder in due course status on the testimony of the junior secured party that it was new in the business, that the debtor had not disclosed any prior security interest, and that no security interest filing was known (constructive notice from a filing is not enough under § 9–331(c)). *See also* Permanent Editorial Board Commentary No. 7, March 10, 1990. This policy is difficult to accept, and the Eleventh Circuit did not, citing the *Strickland* case, *supra*, note 259, for the proposition that constructive knowledge is relevant in determining good faith. Perhaps that can be reconciled with the discussion below, but revised § 9–331, Official Comment 5, goes further and states in reference to this issue, and as an interpretation of Article 3 requirements, that " 'good faith' does not impose a general duty of inquiry . . . [but] there may be circumstances in which 'reasonable commercial standards of fair dealing' would require . . . a search." Once loose, it is questionable whether a little duty of inquiry can ever be again contained. *See* note 253, *supra*.

Notwithstanding the standard of "honesty in fact", less than actual knowledge has always negated good faith if the circumstances under which the instrument is taken are so suspicious that it must be concluded that anyone would have been aware of some potential material infirmity, and the holder avoided actual knowledge only by deliberately closing its eyes. In short, if a holder fails to make an inquiry for the purpose of remaining ignorant of facts which it believes would disclose a defect in the transaction, it may be found to have acted in bad faith.[262] In

---

261. 985 F.2d 1554 (11th Cir.1993), *aff'g in part and rev'g in part*, 130 B.R. 331 (Bankr.S.D.Ala.1991).

262. Mid–Continent Nat'l Bank v. Bank of Independence, 523 S.W.2d 569 (Mo.Ct. App.1975) (facts known to the holder were such that the failure to inquire disclosed a desire to avoid knowledge for fear it would reveal a defense to the instrument). *See also* Republic of Texas Sav. Ass'n v. First Republic Life Ins. Co., 417 So.2d 1251 (La. Ct.App.1982). Perhaps a case that illustrates the point is Farmers & Merchants State Bank v. Western Bank, 841 F.2d 1433 (9th Cir.1987), which involved a kiting scheme. If Western Bank did not actually

General Investment Corp. v. Angelini,[263] the finance company that purchased the note given for home improvements knew the extensive nature of the improvements and that the payment liability represented by the note was dependent upon completion of the work, but it took the note only ten days after the contract was executed under the contractor's assertion the work was done, and did not demand a certificate of completion nor inquire as to completion. The court denied recovery on the instrument.[264] A less satisfactorily reasoned opinion is *Norman v. World Wide Distributors, Inc.*,[265] where the court found an absence of good faith when the holder had purchased notes from a payee who had operated under three different names within a one-year period, the holder knew that the payee used a referral selling plan but not its details,[266] and the holder inquired of the makers before it took the instrument in question as to whether they were satisfied with the transaction and received no contrary notification. Nonetheless, on balance the court appears to have reached a correct result because the note, for a substantial consumer purchase of furniture, had been fraudulently completed to be payable in three days, and the holder never inquired about this extremely unusual aspect of the transaction.

[iv] Notice in General

Notice includes not only actual knowledge and the receipt of a notice or notification,[267] but also the situation where, from all the facts and circumstances known at the time in question, there is reason to know the facts from which the claim or defense arises.[268] The requirement of

---

know there was a kite (honesty in fact), it is pretty clear it strongly believed so, and acted in a calculated way to shift away from itself the probable loss resulting from its own acquiescence and assistance in the kite operation. The court refused to allow it to do so, stretching the old Article 3 use of good faith. Most cases under old Article 3 are not in accord. *See, e.g.,* Citizens Nat'l Bank v. First Nat'l Bank, 347 So.2d 964 (Miss.1977) and Alta Vista State Bank v. Kobliska, 897 F.2d 930 (8th Cir.1990). *But see* the *COFO Financial Group* case, *supra,* and discussion of the *Maine Family Federal Credit Union* case, *supra,* note 258. Again we see what may have been a hard case that made bad law, or at least pushed the envelope, turned into the law by an "improvement" in the law.

263. 58 N.J. 396, 278 A.2d 193 (N.J. 1971).

264. Note that knowledge by the finance company that the note was issued or negotiated in return for an executory promise or accompanied by a separate agreement itself does not give notice of a defense or claim under old § 3–304(4)(b) unless the purchaser has notice that a defense or claim has arisen from the terms of the transaction. This sort of listing of "fixes" for past cases was not continued in current Article 3, but no change in result should occur.

265. 202 Pa.Super. 53, 195 A.2d 115 (1963).

266. A referral selling plan is a variant of the chain letter where a seller promises to pay the buyer compensation for the referral by the buyer to the seller of customers or potential customers. The promised payments are independent of the buyer's obligation to pay for the merchandise, often the seller cannot be located when the buyer seeks payment, and, in any event, as more and more buyers are involved the chance of locating new referrals becomes increasingly difficult if not mathematically impossible. Consumer legislation normally prohibits referral sales if the compensation to the buyer is contingent upon events to occur after the consumer agrees to buy or lease. *See* Unif. Consumer Credit Code § 3.309 (1974).

267. UCC § 1–202(a)(1) and (2). This latter may not be the same as actual knowledge because "receipt" occurs upon due delivery whether the notice actually comes to the person's attention or not.

268. UCC § 1–202(a)(3).

notice thus differs from and goes beyond good faith.[269]

In applying the concept, often a very thin line separates notice from lack of notice. For example, in *Schneider Fuel & Supply Co. v. West Allis State Bank*,[270] although the bank that accepted checks for loan payments drawn by a contractor on his account with the bank did not know of the claims of a building materials supplier against the account which arose as the result of nonpayment by the contractor with respect to a sewer installation job for municipal corporations, it did know the source of the funds was the sewer project. The bank was held to know the state law which made funds paid to a contractor for public improvements a trust fund for the payment of claims, and the court therefore held the bank was not without notice of claims to the checks and could not be a holder in due course of them. In *In re Parkwood, Inc.*,[271] an insurance company purchased a note knowing that the loan was made at more than 6 percent interest, that the lender was a District of Columbia firm engaged in the mortgage banking business, that the note was payable in the District, and that the District of Columbia Loan Shark Act made it unlawful for a mortgage banker to loan money in excess of 6 percent without a license. The court denied holder in due course status. A later case of similar import is *Branch Banking & Trust Co. v. Creasy*,[272] where a bank that knew its customer was in financial difficulty and separated from his wife gave the customer a guaranty form for the wife to sign and

---

269. *See* Kaw Valley State Bank & Trust Co. v. Riddle, 219 Kan. 550, 549 P.2d 927 (Kan. 1976). It contains both subjective and objective elements (except in New York under a non-uniform amendment which makes notice only subjective. *See* DH Cattle Holdings Co. v. Smith, 195 A.D.2d 202, 607 N.Y.S.2d 227, 22 UCC Rep. Serv. 2d 799 (Sup.Ct. A.D.1994)). Of course, the definition of good faith also has an objective element. The definitions always tended to blur since notice involves not only what one knows but also what one should know, and good faith involves what one knows and, at its extreme, good faith also involves what one avoided knowing, and thus a person could be charged with what one should have known. *See* note 262, *supra*. To the extent good faith now also may involve inquiry (*see* text after note 261, *supra*), the two concepts diverge again, because notice does not involve inquiry. *Compare, e.g., In re* Military Circle Pet Center #94, Inc., 181 B.R. 282 (Bankr.E.D.Va.1994) (where outside counsel knew another firm had done legal work and was owed fees, it had reason to know of a lien on the note assigned) and Palmetto Leasing Co. v. Chiles, 235 Ill. App.3d 986, 176 Ill.Dec. 770, 602 N.E.2d 77 (1992) (holder of check knew drawer did not intend check to be paid unless specified funds delivered and that drawer had stopped payment; holder not holder in due course), *with* Doyle v. Resolution Trust Corporation, 999 F.2d 469 (10th Cir.1993) (FNMA bought loans in large numbers and routinely accepted notes with altered interest rates as long as borrower initialed change; if FNMA employees had compared initials on note with borrower's handwriting the forgery would have been detected, but under circumstances FNMA took without notice and was holder in due course) and Adamar of New Jersey, Inc. v. Chase Lincoln First Bank, 201 A.D.2d 174, 615 N.Y.S.2d 550, 24 UCC Rep. Serv. 2d 143 (N.Y.App.Div.1994) (casino which followed state gaming regulations and own internal procedures in verifying identity and validity of cashier's checks it cashed, was a holder in due course, even though the driver's license used was a temporary one without a photo, because regulations did not require a permanent photo license; quere the result under the new definition of good faith, however, given the *Maine Family Federal Credit Union* analysis, *supra*, note 258).

270. 70 Wis.2d 1041, 236 N.W.2d 266 (Wis. 1975). *See also In re Military Circle Pet Center #94, Inc., supra*, note 269.

271. 461 F.2d 158 (D.C.Cir.1971). *See also* the *Chiles* case, *supra*, note 269.

272. 44 N.C.App. 289, 260 S.E.2d 782 (N.C.Ct.App.1979), *rev'd*, 301 N.C. 44, 269 S.E.2d 117 (N.C. 1980).

then accepted it back without checking with the wife. The court determined that the bank took the guaranty subject to the wife's defense of nondelivery.[273] Another close case is *Ackmann v. Merchants Mortgage and Trust Corp.*,[274] where the court held an assignee had notice of the maker's defense of failure of consideration because it knew of the executory nature of the contract and the financial bind that the payee was experiencing.

Correctly analyzed, it is arguable that notice was not present in many of these cases because the total facts known do not quite add up to reason to know of the claim or defense asserted. In the *Schneider* case, for example, only if it also was known that the contractor had not paid some suppliers, in the *Parkwood* case if it also was known that the firm had no license, in the *Creasy* case if it also was known that the husband had not communicated with the wife, and in the *Ackman* case if it also was known the payee had no ability to perform its executory promise (*see* the discussion, *infra*), should notice be found. Thus the concept of notice technically probably was improperly applied in these cases, or the courts, without articulating it, went beyond the UCC and imposed an additional duty of inquiry which, when not performed, equated with what the inquiry would have produced.[275] Most courts have not stretched this far and have refused to include a duty of inquiry in notice.[276]

A group of more satisfactory decisions on the notice issue would include *Shaffer v. Brooklyn Park Garden Apartments*.[277] In that case, the holder of drafts under letters of credit that required certification by the beneficiary of the credit that funds drawn under the letter of credit were due and payable, knew of the severe financial difficulty of the beneficiary. The holder also knew the beneficiary was constructing an apartment complex, in connection with which the drafts were payable as capital contributions, and had received a letter from the attorney for the drawers of the drafts stating that the conditions of the letters of credit had not been and would not be fulfilled in the foreseeable future. Reason to know of the defense was found. In another case, a bank that knew the check sued upon was for a loan on receivables and that the payee was covering checks out of the credit given for it but was not depositing any proceeds of receivables, was denied holder in due course status.[278] Final-

---

273. On appeal, however, the decision was reversed on the ground there was no notice from these facts. Although a close call, this seems correct, but it seems unlikely that Article 3 should have been applied at all, however, because the guaranty should not qualify as a negotiable instrument. *See* Chapter 2, *supra*.

274. 659 P.2d 697 (Colo.Ct.App.1982), *rev'd en banc sub nom.*, Kopeikin v. Merchants Mortgage & Trust Corp., 679 P.2d 599 (Colo.1984).

275. Another improper pronouncement was made by the court in Wohlrabe v. Pownell, 307 N.W.2d 478 (Minn.1981), when it stated that, because of its character and the reliance upon it, more should be required in the way of notice to defeat the holder of a cashier's check than the holder of a regular check. The unnecessary confusion under old Article 3 concerning cashier's checks is discussed later in this book.

276. *See* note, 269, *supra*, and Frantz v. First Nat'l Bank, 584 P.2d 1125 (Alaska 1978) (absent actual knowledge or reason to know, there is no affirmative duty to inquire whether a defense exists).

277. 311 Minn. 452, 250 N.W.2d 172 (Minn. 1977).

278. Oklahoma Nat'l Bank v. Equitable Credit Fin. Co., 1971 OK 104, 489 P.2d 1331 (Okla.1971).

ly, in *A.C. Davenport & Son Co. v. United States*,[279] Davenport had supplied goods to another person who had a contract to resell the goods to the United States. By agreement the check of the United States in payment was to be delivered to Davenport so Davenport would be sure of payment. Instead, the check was sent by the United States to the seller and, when Davenport protested, the United States issued another check to Davenport and told Davenport that payment would be stopped on the first check. Nevertheless, the United States paid the first check and then claimed against Davenport to recover the payment it also made on the second check. The court refused recovery and held that Davenport had no notice of the claim when it took the second check because it could assume the stop order would be effective.

A common recurrent fact pattern on the notice issue appears to involve knowledge by the holder of the instrument of financial difficulty on the part of the person who negotiated the instrument. For example, a bank allows a consistently overdrawn customer to draw on the provisional credit given and then asserts holder in due course status to overcome the drawer's defense when the check is not paid and recovery from the bank's customer is not possible because of insolvency. In *Nicklaus v. Peoples Bank & Trust Co.*,[280] the court stated that although the defendant bank had knowledge that a grain dealer was in financial difficulty and had been dealing in spurious bills of lading, it was not chargeable with knowledge that the check had been procured by fraud. The most closely reasoned opinion on the point is *Bowling Green, Inc. v. State Street Bank & Trust Co.*[281] The court in *Bowling Green* held that even if the bank knew of the depositor's insolvency, and even though a loan officer of the bank was familiar with the depositor's affairs and was aware that the underlying transaction between the plaintiff and the depositor was executory, this did not require a finding that the bank had knowledge of facts and circumstances that would give it reason to know that the depositor had accepted the check in question from the plaintiff having no intention of performing its contract to deliver goods or that the depositor had taken the check with reckless disregard of its ability to perform.

Not all cases involving this fact pattern result in a win for the holder, however. *Seinfeld v. Commercial Bank & Trust Co.*[282] dealt with a customer who was overdrawn consistently and then deposited checks totaling a large sum and requested immediate clearance. This was given without even checking with the drawer's bank. When suit was necessary, the depositary bank attempted to establish holder in due course status

---

279. 538 F.Supp. 730 (N.D.Ill.1982), aff'd, 703 F.2d 266 (7th Cir.1983).

280. 258 F.Supp. 482 (E.D.Ark.1965), aff'd on other grounds, 369 F.2d 683 (8th Cir.1966).

281. 425 F.2d 81 (1st Cir.1970). Con- trast with Ackmann v. Merchants Mortgage & Trust Corp., 659 P.2d 697 (Colo.Ct.App. 1982), rev'd en banc sub nom., Kopeikin v. Merchants Mortgage & Trust Corp., 679 P.2d 599 (Colo.1984) *supra* note 274, where the court found notice merely because the executory nature of the contract and the financial bind of the payee were known to the holder at the time the instrument was taken.

282. 405 So. 2d 1039 (Fla.Dist.Ct.App. 1981). *See also* note 224, *supra*.

on the basis of an affidavit from a bank officer who had not participated in the transaction. The case leaves the impression that it is correctly decided but that the bank lost because of its cavalier inattention to proving its position more than because it had notice of the drawer's claim of defense.[283]

[v] *Specific Notice Provisions*

The UCC does not leave the resolution of the notice issue entirely up to a general standard. Old § 3–304(1), (2), and (3) provided guidelines, albeit general in nature, as to when the purchaser of the instrument would have notice. Current Article 3 carries some of these guidelines over without change, clarifies or makes modest changes to some, and deletes others as implicitly dealt with in other sections.[284] For example, a purchaser is not a holder in due course if the instrument is so incomplete, or bears such apparent evidence of forgery or alteration, or is otherwise so irregular as to call into question its authenticity.[285] A purchaser also had notice of a claim or defense under old Article 3 if there was notice that the obligation of any party is voidable in whole or in part, or that all parties have been discharged.[286]

To illustrate how these tests have been or may be applied, consider the facts in *New Waterford Bank v. Morrison Buick, Inc.*[287] In that case, that a check bore two signature lines, only one of which was signed, was held not to be notice of a defect. In *National State Bank v. Kleinberg*,[288] the alternation of the figure of the final installment in a note from $41,000 to $42,000 was held not to give notice of an infirmity where the language in the note clearly indicated that the parties intended the final payment to be $42,000. The court in *J. Gordon Neely Enterprises, Inc. v. American National Bank*[289] found that even though some checks involved visible minor erasures or other minor irregularities, whether to pay them was a judgment call under all the circumstances. But in *First National Bank v. Otto Huber & Sons, Inc.*,[290] the court determined that where a

---

283. If so, the case is much less cause for concern than the *Maine Family Federal Credit Union* case, *supra*, note 224, where the court allowed the result to be controlled under the broader definition of good faith.

284. *See* §§ 3–302(a)-(c), and (f), 3–304(b) and 3–307.

285. § 3–302(a)(1). Under old § 3–304(1)(a), there was notice of a claim or defense. As to why the different approach, *see* Official Comment 1 to § 3–302.

286. Old § 3–304(1)(b). Notice that *one* party having been discharged is not notice of an infirmity in the obligations of other parties who remain liable. Thus a purchaser with notice that an indorser has been discharged takes subject to that discharge as provided in old §§ 3–602 and 3–305(2)(e), but is not prevented from taking the obligation of the maker in due course. Current Article 3 omits a provision like that of old § 3–304(1)(b) as unnecessary. *See* §§ 3–601(b) and 3–302(b).

287. 3 UCC Rep. Serv. 426 (Pa.Com.Pl. 1965).

288. 4 UCC Rep. Serv. 100 (N.Y.Sup.Ct. 1967).

289. 403 So.2d 887 (Ala.1981). A similar approach was taken in Adamar of New Jersey, Inc. v. Chase Lincoln First Bank, N.A., 201 A.D.2d 174, 615 N.Y.S.2d 550, 24 UCC Rep. Serv. 2d 143 (N.Y.Sup.Ct. A.D.1994) (misspelling of payee's name) and in Doyle v. Resolution Trust Corp., 999 F.2d 469 (10th Cir.1993).

290. 394 F.Supp. 1284 (D.S.D.1975).

note was susceptible of at least two interpretations as to its due date, the irregularity prevented holder in due course status.[291]

A person will have notice of a claim against the instrument if the person has actual knowledge[292] that a fiduciary has dealt with the instrument in payment of or as security for the fiduciary's own debt or in any transaction for the fiduciary's own benefit, or otherwise in breach of duty.[293] Thus where the purchaser of notes payable to X as attorney for Y made its check for the notes payable to X individually and discharged X's personal debt to a bank in return for the notes, the purchaser was charged with notice.[294] By the same token, where a bank allowed a guardian to deposit a check payable to him as guardian in his individual account the bank was not a holder in due course.[295]

Knowledge of the fact any person negotiating the instrument is or was a fiduciary does not of itself give the purchaser notice of a defense or claim.[296] Thus, a bank that cashed two checks drawn by a corporation, made out to "cash" and signed by an individual who was the sole stockholder and chief executive of the corporation, for its customer, a liquor store, which had taken the checks in trade, was held to be a holder in due course.[297] A similar result was reached in *Merchants*

---

291. This result is consistent with § 3–302(a)(1). *See* Official Comment 1 to that provision.

292. UCC § 1–202(b). Even if the circumstances would have induced a prudent banker to investigate more thoroughly, that is not enough to constitute actual knowledge. Chemical Bank v. Haskell, 51 N.Y.2d 85, 432 N.Y.S.2d 478, 411 N.E.2d 1339 (N.Y. 1980). Moreover, the actual knowledge of the person acting for the organization that takes the instrument is determinative. *See* note 247, *supra*.

293. § 3–307(b).

294. Maber, Inc. v. Factor Cab Corp., 19 A.D.2d 500, 244 N.Y.S.2d 768 (App.Div. 1963).

295. Smith v. Olympic Bank, 103 Wn.2d 418, 693 P.2d 92 (Wash.1985). *See also* Maley v. East Side Bank, 361 F.2d 393 (7th Cir.1966) (bank knowingly engaged in transaction in violation of bank resolutions and thus with actual knowledge of action in excess of authority); Nashville City Bank & Trust Co. v. Massey, 540 F.Supp. 566 (M.D.Ga.1982) (bank knew terms of partnership agreement and extent of partner's authority, but still took notes made by limited partners for benefit of partnership as security for personal loan to general partner); Trenton Trust Co. v. Western Surety Co., 599 S.W.2d 481 (Mo.1980) (guardian with knowledge of agent of bank, pledged certificates of deposit purchased with minor's funds as collateral for a personal loan); and Swiss Baco Skyline Logging, Inc. v. Haliewicz, 18 Wn.App. 21, 567 P.2d 1141 (Wash.Ct.App.1977) (check payable to corporation used to purchase personal certificate of deposit by former president). *But see* Knox v. Columbia Banking Fed. Sav. & Loan Ass'n, 64 N.Y.2d 434, 488 N.Y.S.2d 146, 477 N.E.2d 448 (N.Y. 1985) (bank that cashed check payable to individual as guardian was not liable when money was later deposited to the individual's account). Under current Article 3, the results would be similar, except the result in the *Knox* case is rejected, and *compare In re* Broadview Lumber Co., Inc., 118 F.3d 1246 (8th Cir.1997) (reaching same result as in *Knox* but under non-uniform § 3–307(b)(2) enacted in Missouri (deletes § 3–307(b)(2)(iii)). *See* § 3–307(a) and (b)(2). Cases involving checks payable to a business entity and then appropriated by an agent also are involved here. *See* Official Comment 3 to § 3–307. These cases are discussed, *infra*, in Chapters 4 and 7. The provision is not applicable if there is no negotiation so that the assignee is subject to the claim of breach of duty. First Nat'l Bank v. Munns, 602 S.W.2d 910 (Mo.Ct.App.1980) (assignment of trust certificate evidencing trust savings account by trustee to bank contested by beneficiaries of account).

296. § 3–307(b).

297. McConnico v. Third Nat'l Bank, 499 S.W.2d 874 (Tenn.1973). *See* § 3–307(b)(3). *But see* Heilig Trust & Beneficiaries v. First Interstate Bank, 93 Wn. App. 514, 969 P.2d 1082 (Wash.Ct.App. 1998) (checks drawn by trustee on trust

National Bank & Trust Co. v. United States,[298] where the United States took checks in payment of taxes with notice that plaintiff had taken and perfected a security interest in the drawer's accounts receivable and their proceeds.[299] Finally courts often refuse to find notice where the holder takes a check of the principal made out to the holder in payment of the debt of the agent of the principal.[300] Without notice of improper action, the agent could have been in essence a remitter in connection with a debt owed to the agent by the principal as, for example, for salary, and recipients of routine checks in the due and normal course of business are not required to make searching inquiries in depth before accepting payment.[301]

Section 3–307(b) probably tightens up but does not necessarily change the result in these types of cases when it provides that the taker has notice of the breach of fiduciary duty if the instrument is taken in payment of or as security for a debt known by the taker to be the personal debt of the fiduciary. Official Comment 2 to the section indicates that where the individual who receives and processes the instrument on behalf of the organization that is the taker is a clerk who has no knowledge of any fiduciary status of the person from who the instrument is received, § 3–307 does not apply.[302] Furthermore, the person acting for the organization must have knowledge of facts that indicate a breach of fiduciary duty; in this instance, that the instrument is taken in payment or as security for a personal debt of the fiduciary or for the personal benefit of the fiduciary. *See also* Official Comment 5 to § 3–307.[303]

Old § 3–304(4) and (5) provide fairly specific statements of what

---

account payable to trustee personally either cashed or deposited into personal account; could be in payment for services rendered); *see also* New Jersey Title Ins. Co. v. Caputo, 163 N.J. 143, 748 A.2d 507 (N.J. 2000) (lawyer drew checks on trust account payable to himself and deposited them into his business account and then made ATM withdrawals from the business account in large amounts from a terminal at a casino; lawyer was a known gambler; court allowed jury to consider whether bank in bad faith in the sense contemplated in note 261, *supra*).

298. 12 UCC Rep. Serv. 902 (Ct.Cl. 1973).

299. *See* Valley Nat'l Bank v. Porter, 705 F.2d 1027 (8th Cir.1983) (IRS was holder in due course of third-party checks accepted for taxes even though they were collateral subject to perfected security interest). Under § 3–302(b), the filing or recording of a document like a financing statement to perfect a security interest does not of itself constitute notice to a person who would otherwise be a holder in due course. *See also* UCC § 9–331. An interesting similar case is Resolution Trust Corp. v. Gill, 960 F.2d 336 (3d Cir. 1992), where, if the IRS levy on the bank account occurred after the checks were issued and the checks were in the hands of a holder in due course, the IRS would lose, but not if the levy occurred before issuance of the checks.

300. *See, e.g.,* Eldon's Super Fresh Stores, Inc. v. Merrill Lynch, Pierce, Fenner & Smith, Inc., 296 Minn. 130, 207 N.W.2d 282 (Minn. 1973).

301. Hartford Accident & Indem. v. American Express, 74 N.Y.2d 153, 544 N.Y.S.2d 573, 542 N.E.2d 1090 (N.Y. 1989).

302. *See In re* Broadview Lumber Co., Inc., 118 F.3d 1246 (8th Cir.1997).

303. Cases involving checks payable to a bank which the bank has permitted to be deposited in the personal account of an employee of the drawer are also involved here. *See, e.g.,* Federal Ins. Co. v. First Nat'l Bank of Boston, 633 F.2d 978 (1st Cir.1980) and Govoni & Sons Constr. Co., Inc. v. Mechanics Bank, 51 Mass.App.Ct. 35, 742 N.E.2d 1094 (2001). These cases are covered in § 3–307(b)(4). *See* Official Comments 2 and 5 to the section. These cases are noted, *infra*, in Chapter 7.

other facts alone will not give a purchaser notice of a defense or claim.[304] Merely knowing that an instrument was antedated or postdated, or that it was issued or negotiated in return for an executory promise or accompanied by a separate agreement, unless the purchaser has notice that a defense or claim has arisen from the terms of the agreement, does not give notice of a defense or claim.[305] Thus where a series of six postdated checks was given to a payee in payment for legal services to be performed, and the checks later were purchased by plaintiff, that the checks were postdated and were issued for an executory promise was determined not to be enough to defeat the claim of plaintiff as a holder in due course.[306] In another case, knowledge by a bank to which a note had been pledged that the agreement underlying the note was executory and subject to rescission, which might later create liability on the part of the payee to refund an investment, did not constitute notice where no breach had occurred at the time of the negotiation.[307] But the payee of a check given in partial payment for a lot was not allowed to recover from the drawers who had declined to complete the purchase and who had stopped payment because the payee had notice that the check was postdated and that the sale might not be completed if the terms of payment could not be worked out.[308]

Knowledge that a party has signed for accommodation does not give notice of a defense or claim,[309] and knowledge that an incomplete instrument has been completed does not give the purchaser notice of a defense or claim unless the purchaser also has notice of any improper completion.[310] In *Saka v. Sahara–Nevada Corp.*,[311] for example, the court held that the fact a check was completed in handwriting different from the signature was not enough for notice, absent knowledge that the check was completed by a party acting in excess of authority.

To be a holder in due course, a holder also must take the instrument without notice that it is overdue or that it has been dishonored.[312] Old § 3–304(3) provided that a purchaser had notice that an instrument was overdue if the purchaser had reason to know that any part of the principal amount was overdue;[313] or there is an uncured default in

---

304. As these provisions are implicit in the general rules and are unnecessary detail today because they primarily are responses to prior litigated points now long settled, current Article 3 omits these provisions for the most part. No change in result is intended.

305. Old § 3–304(4)(a) and (b).

306. Financial Assoc. v. Impact Mktg., Inc., 90 Misc.2d 545, 394 N.Y.S.2d 814 (Civ. Ct.1977).

307. Ocean First Nat'l Bank v. Baird, 9 UCC Rep. Serv. 1092 (N.Y.Sup.Ct.1971).

308. Briand v. Wild, 110 N.H. 373, 268 A.2d 896 (N.H. 1970). Arguably, the *Chiles* case, *supra* note 269, is similar. *See also* Salter v. Vanotti, 42 Colo.App. 448, 599 P.2d 962 (Colo.Ct.App.1979) (knowledge from documents delivered with note of a right to rescind because of failure to deliver required document); Kaw Valley State Bank & Trust Co. v. Riddle, 219 Kan. 550, 549 P.2d 927 (Kan. 1976) (information appearing in an accompanying document delivered with a note may disclose a defense so as to prevent holder in due course status).

309. Old § 3–304(4)(c).

310. Old § 3–304(4)(d).

311. 92 Nev. 703, 558 P.2d 535 (Nev. 1976).

312. § 3–302(a)(2)(iii).

313. Old § 3–304(3)(a); Hane v. Exten, 255 Md. 668, 259 A.2d 290 (Md. 1969) (doubtful whether holder can be a holder in due course taking a note in the belief no

payment of another instrument of the same series;[314] or acceleration of the instrument has been made;[315] or a demand instrument is being taken after demand has been made or more than a reasonable time after its issue.[316] However, knowledge that there has been default in payment of interest on the instrument, or in the payment of any other instrument except one of the same series, does not of itself give notice.[317]

[c] Burden of Proof

The result of the application of the rules for determining good faith and lack of notice, no matter how specific the rules are, ultimately turns on the particular facts of an individual case. The question is generally one for the trier of fact unless only one inference from the evidence is possible.[318] Moreover, after it is shown that a defense exists,[319] a person claiming the rights of a holder in due course has the burden of establishing[320] that the claimant, or some person under whom the claimant claims,[321] is in all respects[322] a holder in due

---

payments have been made at a time when eleven monthly payments should have been made). *But see* Yahn & McDonnell, Inc. v. Farmers Bank, 708 F.2d 104 (3d Cir.1983) (taking certificate of deposit due in 1976 in 1978 not necessarily fatal). In current Article 3, *see* § 3–304(b)(1) and (2). *See also* Commerce Bank, N.A. v. Rickett, 329 N.J.Super. 379, 748 A.2d 111 (App.Div. 2000) (when check with mistaken date overdue).

314. § 3–302(a)(2)(iii).

315. § 3–304(b)(3).

316. § 3–304(a). It is not conclusive that the instrument was in fact overdue when it was negotiated if the holder takes without notice that it is overdue. Unadilla Nat'l Bank v. McQueer, 27 A.D.2d 778, 277 N.Y.S.2d 221 (App.Div.1967) (where note as originally executed was overdue at time of negotiation but alteration of due date was not noticeable, holder could claim status as holder in due course).

A domestic check is presumed stale after thirty days under old § 3–304(3)(c). Thus the court in County Trust Co. v. Pascack Valley Bank & Trust Co., 93 N.J.Super. 252, 225 A.2d 605 (App.Div.1966) held that a bank that cashed a check ten months old was not a holder in due course. Under current § 3–304(a), the rule is 90 days. As to a note, *see* Official Comment 1 to § 3–304.

317. § 3–304(c). *See also* Central State Bank v. Kilroy, 57 A.D.2d 940, 395 N.Y.S.2d 78 (App.Div.1977) (bank that cashed two checks drawn on insufficient funds and that had been stolen and completed without authorization was not on notice merely because one check was returned before the other was cashed).

318. *See, e.g.,* Manufacturers & Traders Trust Co. v. Murphy, 369 F.Supp. 11 (W.D.Pa.1974), *aff'd*, 517 F.2d 1398 (3d Cir. 1975); Peoples Bank of Aurora v. Haar, 1966 OK 252, 421 P.2d 817 (Okla.1966); Favors v. Yaffe, 605 S.W.2d 342 (Tex.Civ. App.1980).

319. *See* Seigel v. Merrill Lynch, Pierce, Fenner & Smith, Inc., 745 A.2d 301 (D.C. 2000) (failure to establish a defense to enforcement of checks cashed by casinos).

320. The burden of persuading the trier of fact that the existence of a fact is more probable than its nonexistence. UCC § 1–201(b)(8). A preponderance of the credible evidence is required. United Bank, Ltd. v. Cambridge Sporting Goods Corp., 41 N.Y.2d 254, 392 N.Y.S.2d 265, 360 N.E.2d 943 (N.Y. 1976).

Several courts have stated a holder is presumed to be a holder in due course until a defense is shown. *See, e.g.,* Ritz v. Karstenson, 39 Ill.App.3d 877, 350 N.E.2d 870 (1976) and Jonwilco, Inc. v. C.I.T. Financial Servs., 662 S.W.2d 664 (Tex.Ct.App.1983). Since, in the absence of a defense, any holder is entitled to recovery, there is no reason to presume a holder to be a holder in due course.

321. *See* § 3–203(b) (the "shelter" doctrine).

322. In addition to establishing that the instrument was taken for value, in good faith, and without notice, holder status also must be established, which includes the proper form of the instrument and negotiation. *See, e.g.,* Bank of Statesville v. Blackwelder Furniture Co., 11 N.C.App. 530, 181

course.[323] As a result, and even though the burden initially is only a slight one because it involves precluding proof of a negative fact,[324] procedural considerations may play a large part in the decisions with respect to these cases. In the end, prediction is difficult. In that regard, *Wohlrabe v. Pownell*,[325] is illustrative. In that case, an accountant had embezzled money from a clinic and a profit-sharing trust but purportedly had purchased a note for the clinic and the trust as an investment with the money. When the attorney for the clinic and the trust could not find the note, the accountant was asked about it. After delay and excuses, he could not produce the note. The attorney then indicated he would report his suspicion of embezzlement to his clients and the proper authorities. At that point, the accountant defrauded a friend to obtain the money to buy a cashier's check. He gave the check to the attorney for the clinic and the trust, and the attorney then delivered the check to the clients in satisfaction of the debt. The majority of the appellate court reversed the trial court and held the check was taken in due course because, even if there was a good reason to suspect that the accountant had attempted to defraud the clinic and the trust, there was no reason to suspect he also had defrauded others in order to repay. The dissent observed that the check was received with knowledge that something was wrong, that men of business experience know that hard-pressed debtors turn sharp corners, and that the trial court, as the trier of the facts, was justified in concluding the check was received with notice.

Procedural considerations particularly will weigh heavily in the extreme case where the holder testifies that the instrument was taken in

S.E.2d 785 (N.C.Ct.App.1971); Foremost Ins. Co. v. First City Sav. & Loan Ass'n, 374 So.2d 840 (Miss.1979). Delivery, nonpayment, consideration and holder status need not be alleged or proven where the instrument comes within Article 3 as to form, is produced, is payable to the claiming party, and no defense is established. Tuttle v. Rose, 102 Ill.App.3d 865, 58 Ill.Dec. 414, 430 N.E.2d 356 (1981); and Leopold v. Halleck, 106 Ill.App.3d 386, 62 Ill.Dec. 447, 436 N.E.2d 29 (1982).

323. § 3–308(b) and Godat v. Mercantile Bank, 884 S.W.2d 1 (Mo.App.1994). Under these provisions for this purpose, alteration may be thought of as a defense, as may forgery. Technically, *see* § 3–302(a)(2)(iv) and Official Comment 2 to that section. As to forgery, *see* § 3–308(a) (which also deals with the liability of the undisclosed principal). *See* Official Comment 1 to § 3–308. The claim of a third party also may be available as a defense to a limited extent. § 3–305(c). *See* Maine Family Fed. Credit Union v. Sun Life Assurance Co., 1999 ME 43, 727 A.2d 335 (Me.1999). *Jus tertii* will be discussed later in Chapter 6.

324. That is, that the holder had notice or was in bad faith. First Int'l Bank of Israel, Ltd. v. L. Blankstein & Son, Inc., 59 N.Y.2d 436, 465 N.Y.S.2d 888, 452 N.E.2d 1216 (App.1983). The court held that testimony of the holder that it did not know of a defense put the person asserting the lack of holder in due course status to the task of rebuttal. In establishing holder in due course status, however, mere averments of holder in due course status should not be adequate. *See, e.g.*, Patterson v. First Nat'l Bank, 47 Ala.App. 98, 251 So.2d 230 (Ala. Ct.App.1971); Daric Constr. Corp. v. Radice Constr. Corp., 4 UCC Rep. Serv. 763 (N.Y.Sup.Ct.1967). Affirmative proof is required. United Bank, Ltd. v. Cambridge Sporting Goods Corp., 41 N.Y.2d 254, 392 N.Y.S.2d 265, 360 N.E.2d 943 (1976). *But see* Jonwilco, Inc. v. C.I.T. Financial Servs., 662 S.W.2d 664 (Tex.Ct.App.1983) (pleading holder status plus a presumption of holder in due course status sufficed; again, there seems no basis for a presumption here—*see* note 320, *supra*).

Note that where the use of a concept like holder in due course is involved in connection with finality of payment under § 3–418, the provisions of § 3–308 cannot literally be applied.

325. 307 N.W.2d 478 (Minn.1981).

the usual course of business, for value, in good faith and without notice, that there were no apparent irregularities, and that the instrument was taken before maturity and perhaps even after inquiries that disclosed no problem. If the obligor presents no evidentiary facts to support an allegation that the instrument was taken in bad faith or with notice, some courts will find for the holder.[326] Others will not disturb a trier of fact denial of holder in due course status because, though the evidence may indicate that the plaintiff was in good faith and had no knowledge of a defense, reasonable persons might differ as to this conclusion because the plaintiff's evidence is indirect and consists only of testimony by the plaintiff itself. In short, there is still the credibility issue.[327] In summary, the court in *Arnd v. Aylesworth*[328] put it well some years ago:

> It is ordinarily to be expected, in these cases, that the purchaser will testify to his good faith and want of notice, and that defendant is compelled to rely on circumstantial evidence to rebut such showing. Whether plaintiff has sufficiently satisfied the burden resting upon him and made good his claim to be an innocent purchaser is therefore a question for the jury, save in those instances where the testimony is not only consistent with the good faith of such purchase, but is such that no fair-minded person can draw any other inference therefrom. A categorical denial of notice or knowledge is something which in many, if not in most, instances cannot be opposed by direct proof; and the credibility of the witnesses, their interest in the case, the reasonableness or unreasonableness of their statements, the time, place, and manner of the transaction, its conformity to or its departure from the ordinary methods of business, and all the other facts and circumstances which, though of slight moment in themselves, yet, when taken together, give character and color to the purchase under inquiry, constitute a showing which the court cannot properly pass upon as a matter of law.... Uncontradicted evidence is not sufficient to command a directed verdict where the inferences to be drawn from all the circumstances are open to different conclusions by reasonable men.[329]

---

326. *E.g.*, First Int'l Bank of Israel, Ltd. v. L. Blankstein & Son, Inc., 59 N.Y.2d 436, 465 N.Y.S.2d 888, 452 N.E.2d 1216 (N.Y.App.1983).

327. *Compare* Peoples Bank v. Haar, 1966 OK 252, 421 P.2d 817 (Okla.1966) (issue in these circumstances properly left to trier of fact) *with* Favors v. Yaffe, 605 S.W.2d 342 (Tex.Civ.App.1980) (unequivocal and uncontradicted testimony as to good faith established holder in due course status). In this context, the presence of a "deep" discount has nonetheless been held by numerous courts to be evidence of bad faith. *See, e.g.*, O.P. Ganjo, Inc. v. Tri-Urban Realty Co., 108 N.J.Super. 517, 261 A.2d 722 (Law Div.1970) (unreasonably large discount) and note 254, *supra*.

328. 145 Iowa 185, 123 N.W. 1000, 1002–03 (Iowa 1909).

329. There is no inherent inconsistency between a subjective standard of good faith and a reasonable inquiry into circumstances surrounding the purchase of negotiable paper. The trier of fact may consider not only the testimony of the holder but also evidence of surrounding circumstances that inferentially illuminate the holder's honesty. Funding Consultants, Inc. v. Aetna Casualty & Surety Co., 187 Conn. 637, 447 A.2d 1163 (Conn. 1982), discussed in text at note 254, *supra*.

[3] Status of a Holder in Due Course

[a] Freedom from Claims and Defenses

[i] Real and Personal Defenses

To the extent that a purchaser is a holder in due course, under Article 3, by statute and without the necessity of agreement for this result,[330] the purchaser takes the instrument free from all property or possessory claims to it or its proceeds on the part of any person[331] and all defenses of any party to the instrument (with whom the purchaser has not dealt[332]), except so-called "real defenses"[333] including any discharge in insolvency proceedings.[334] Conversely, a person who does not have the rights of a holder in due course[335] takes the instrument subject to real defenses and also subject to all valid property or possessory claims to it on the part of any person[336] and all defenses of any party which would be available in an action on a simple contract, including the defenses of want or failure of consideration, nonperformance of any condition precedent, nondelivery, and delivery for a special purpose.[337] Thus the rights

---

330. *Compare, e.g.,* UCC § 9–403(b).

331. § 3–306. § 3–306 makes it clear that the protection extends to the instrument *and* its proceeds. *See* text at and notes 215 and 216, *supra*.

332. This concept is omitted in current Article 3 as unnecessary. *See* notes 208 and 209, *supra*.

333. "Real defenses," good even against a holder in due course, are, as listed in § 3–305(a)(1), infancy, incapacity, duress, illegality (*see* Carnival Leisure Industries, Ltd. v. Aubin, 830 F.Supp. 371 (S.D.Tex. 1993) (validity of gambling debt), *rev'd*, 53 F.3d 716 (5th Cir.1995)) and Kedzie & 103rd Currency Exchange, Inc. v. Hodge, 156 Ill.2d 112, 189 Ill.Dec. 31, 619 N.E.2d 732 (Ill. 1993) (check used to pay for work by unlicensed plumber)), fraud in the factum and discharge in insolvency proceedings. Forgery and alteration as provided in §§ 3–403(a) and 3–407(c) technically are not defenses as no obligation exists. However, they may be thought of as such. *See* note 323, *supra*. Defenses are discussed in Chapter 6, *infra*.

334. § 3–305(a)(1)(iv). Under § 3–302(b), notice of any other discharge which leaves other parties liable on the instrument does not prevent the purchaser from becoming a holder in due course. As to the other parties, the purchaser may be a holder in due course, but takes the instrument subject to the discharge of which there was notice. If the purchaser is without notice, the discharge is not effective under § 3–601(b). *See* Official Comment 3 to § 3–302, and Official Comment to § 3–601. An example is the cancellation of an indorsement, which leaves the maker and prior indorsers liable. *See* § 3–207. Another example is certification of a check which discharges a prior indorser. *See* Official Comment 3 to § 3–302. *See* also § 3–602(d).

335. This includes a person who has not qualified in their own right as a holder in due course and who has not acquired, pursuant to § 3–203(b), the rights of a holder in due course by transfer.

336. § 3–306. Again, § 3–306 makes it clear that the claim is good against both the instrument and its proceeds. A "claim" includes the right to rescind a negotiation and recover the instrument or its proceeds, but not a defense based on the same facts. *See, e.g.,* Maine Family Fed. Credit Union v. Sun Life Assurance Company, 1999 ME 43, 727 A.2d 335 (Me.1999) (involving *jus tertii* where defense of fraud asserted but not to rescind negotiation). *See also* Resolution Trust Corp. v. Gill, 960 F.2d 336 (3d Cir. 1992) (tax lien). The provisions of Article 3 may be supplemented under UCC § 1–103(b) by the principles of law and equity. In Cheltenham Nat'l Bank v. Snelling, 230 Pa.Super. 498, 326 A.2d 557 (1974), the court held that the maker of a note would be precluded from asserting defenses against the assignee of it if the facts warranted an equitable estoppel.

337. § 3–305(a)(2) and Official Comment 2 to § 3–305. Claims in recoupment under § 3–305(a)(3) are discussed, *infra*. At times this apparently disadvantageous position may be beneficial. *See, e.g.,* United States v. Kellerman, 729 F.2d 281 (4th Cir. 1984), where a bank president successfully

of a holder in due course of an instrument governed by Article 3 differ radically from those of the assignee of an ordinary contract, who takes the contract subject to all the terms of the contract and any defense or claim arising out of it, and also to any other defense or claim against the assignor which accrues before notification of the assignment.[338]

[ii] Setoff (Claims in Recoupment)

The defenses of which a holder in due course of the instrument takes free include not only defenses arising out of the contract in connection with which the instrument was given,[339] but also any other defenses arising out of the transaction that gave rise to the instrument. Article 3 calls these "claims in recoupment"[340] and the example given in Official Comment 3 involves a note issued by a buyer to a seller for the price of goods sold which have been accepted but which are defective, and raise a breach of warranty claim in recoupment.

To illustrate, in *Martin Management Corp. v. Farner*,[341] the action was by an assignee who was the president and sole stockholder of the corporation to which the instruments had been issued and which owed a debt to the issuer of the instruments. The court held the issuer of the instruments was not entitled to set-off against its admitted liability on the instruments the debt owing to it by the corporation where there was evidence sufficient to support a finding that the plaintiff was a holder in due course.

---

defended a criminal action because an assignee had not acquired holder in due course status and thus the court said an assertable defense rendered the instrument without value.

338. *See, e.g.*, C. Rohwer & A. Skroki, Contracts in a Nutshell § 12.8 (5th ed. 2000). If the contract contains an agreement by the obligor not to assert any claims or defenses that may exist against the assignor against the assignee if the contract is assigned, the assignee may acquire a status similar to that of a holder in due course. *See, e.g.*, Chicago City Bank & Trust Co. v. Davidson, 42 Ill.App.3d 386, 1 Ill.Dec. 128, 356 N.E.2d 128 (1976). But although the presence of a "waiver of defenses" clause has the effect of imparting some of the characteristics of negotiability to an otherwise nonnegotiable contract, the holder of the contract is not actually a holder in due course. This rule is codified in the UCC for security agreements in Article 9. *See* UCC §§ 9–403, 9–404. It also is subject to limitation in consumer transactions as discussed, *infra*. Further, under an amendment promulgated in 2002 to 3–305, in a consumer transaction an instrument is treated as if it contained a required statement in accordance with the Federal Trade Commission rule at 16 C.F.R. Part 433, even if it does not, and thus is consistent with the qualification on the general rule for consumers contained in UCC §§ 9–403(d) and 9–404(d). In addition, another amendment to § 3–602 provides that a note is paid to the extent payment is made by or on behalf of a party obligated to pay the note to a person that formerly was entitled to enforce the note if at the time of payment the party obligated to pay has not received adequate notification that the note has been transferred and that payment is to be made to the transferee. *See* § 3–602(b), (c), (d) and (f). This amendment eliminates one aspect of negotiability for notes, and conforms the rule to the ordinary contract rule (*see* Restatement of Contracts § 338(1)) and UCC § 9–406(a), as well as reflects modern practice. The latter amendment also leaves the application of traditional rules of agency in place.

339. For example, fraud and failure of consideration. *See, e.g.*, Illinois Valley Acceptance Corp. v. Woodard, 159 Ind.App. 50, 304 N.E.2d 859 (Ind.Ct.App.1973).

340. § 3–305(a)(3).

341. 124 Ga.App. 552, 184 S.E.2d 597 (Ga.Ct.App.1971).

One might expect, in contrast, that a nonholder in due course would be subject to set off as well as defenses arising out of the contract in connection with which the instrument was given. But the *Farner* court stated that, even as to one not a holder in due course, set-off is a defense only as to those equities existing between the original parties that grow out of the same transaction. This limitation is perhaps unwarranted as a matter of normal contract law concerning the status of an assignee, and old Article 3 was not clear on the matter.[342] The statement in the *Farner*[343] case itself is explained by another Georgia statute that the court construed as reflecting the intention of the legislature to limit set-off to demands in some way connected with the debt sued upon or the transaction out of which the debt sued upon arose.[344] Under old Article 3, courts have not dealt with the question consistently. For example, in *Goldberg v. Rothman*,[345] the court reasoned that a set off or counterclaim was not strictly a "defense," which was the word used by old Article 3, but in *In re Johnson*[346] the court said this was irrelevant because the right to set off, even if not a defense to the instrument, constituted a defense to liability because it operated to reduce the remedy even if not to defeat the debt. This point of view seems desirable as it tends to eliminate multiple lawsuits,[347] but also undesirable to the extent it exposes a holder to a wide range of possible off-sets and thus reduces the negotiability of instruments.[348]

Current Article 3 specifically deals with this issue, and subjects a nonholder in due course only to claims in recoupment of the obligor against the original payee of the instrument if the claim arose from the transaction that gave rise to the instrument.[349] Thus a holder is exposed to breach of warranty claims,[350] but not to wholly unrelated claims (as determined under local procedural law).[351]

---

342. See text, *infra*, this chapter.

343. See note 341, *supra*.

344. *Id*. The court in *Farner* also held that a holder is disqualified from holder in due course status only by notice of defenses against the instrument and not by notice of those stemming from separate and distinct transactions. This appears correct.

345. 66 Misc.2d 981, 322 N.Y.S.2d 931 (Civ.Ct.1971).

346. 552 F.2d 1072 (4th Cir.1977).

347. *See also* Bisson v. Eck, 430 Mass. 406, 720 N.E.2d 784 (1999) (an obligor should not be deprived of the right to raise a set off claim because of a subsequent assignment of the instrument) and Trueheart v. Braselton, 875 S.W.2d 412 (Tex.Ct.App.1994).

348. Official Comment 3 to § 3–305.

349. § 3–305(a)(3). No affirmative recovery is allowed, however. This is consistent with interpretation of UCC § 9–404(b).

See also, Michelin Tires (Canada) Ltd. v. First Nat'l Bank, 666 F.2d 673 (1st Cir. 1981).

350. Official Comment 3 to § 3–305 states that if a note is taken for the price of goods which are not delivered, nondelivery (failure of consideration) is a defense, but if the goods are delivered and accepted but are defective the damages constitute a claim in recoupment.

351. Such as a debt owed from a prior and unrelated transaction. *Compare* UM-LIC-TEN Corp. v. Jones, 41 UCC Rep. Serv. 2d 1187 (Conn.Super.Ct.2000) (claim for waste allowable in enforcement of note secured by mortgage on land subject to asserted waste) *with* Zener v. Velde, 135 Idaho 352, 17 P.3d 296 (Idaho Ct.App.2000) (enforcement of note given for price of land sold not subject to claim for damage due to logging several months after sale).

[iii] Claims

Claims cut off by a holder in due course include legal title,[352] liens,[353] equitable claims such as a claim of a beneficial interest in a constructive trust,[354] claims for rescission of a prior negotiation in accordance with § 3–207,[355] delivery for a special purpose,[356] and conditional delivery.[357]

The claim, defense or claim in recoupment of a third person[358] to the instrument is not available as a defense to a party liable on the instrument against any person entitled to enforce the instrument, however, unless the third person defends the action for the liable party,[359] the defense is that the person seeking to enforce the instrument or a person through whom that person holds the instrument acquired it by theft,[360] payment or satisfaction to the holder would be inconsistent with the terms of a restrictive indorsement,[361] or the defense or claim in recoupment is one of the accommodated party (except for discharge in insolvency proceedings, infancy, and lack of legal capacity) and the action is to enforce the obligation of the accommodation party.[362] The policy behind this rule is twofold. First, the contract of the obligor is to pay the holder of the instrument, and the claims of other persons against the holder are generally not of concern.[363] Second, the obligor usually will

---

352. *E.g.*, Watkins v. Sheriff of Clark County, 85 Nev. 246, 453 P.2d 611 (Nev. 1969) (theft of check indorsed in blank).

353. *E.g.*, Commercial Discount Corp. v. Milwaukee W. Bank, 61 Wis.2d 671, 214 N.W.2d 33 (Wis. 1974) (checks written on account into which proceeds of collateral deposited). *See also* note 298, *supra*.

354. *E.g.*, Capital Inv. Co. v. Estate of Morrison, 484 F.2d 1157 (4th Cir.1973) (claim of constructive or resulting trust due to nonpayment for asset). *See also* Bowling Green, Inc. v. State Street Bank & Trust Co., 425 F.2d 81 (1st Cir.1970).

355. Official Comment to § 3–306.

356. *E.g.*, Eldon's Super Fresh Stores, Inc. v. Merrill Lynch, Pierce, Fenner & Smith, Inc., 296 Minn. 130, 207 N.W.2d 282 (Minn. 1973) (delivery of check to purchase stock instead used to pay debt of agent).

357. *E.g.*, D. Nelsen & Sons, Inc. v. General Am. Dev. Corp., 6 Ill.App.3d 6, 284 N.E.2d 478 (1972) (certificate of deposit to be held until a certain event occurred at which time it was to be used for a particular purpose). Current Article 3 is somewhat more explicit than old Article 3. *Compare* old §§ 3–305(1) and 3–306(a) *with* § 3–306.

358. A "claim" indicates certain rights in the instrument on which a suit may be based, rather than a reason why the alleged debtor is not liable. *See* note 336, *supra*, and Fulton Nat'l Bank v. Delco Corp., 128 Ga.App. 16, 195 S.E.2d 455 (Ga.Ct.App. 1973), Official Comment 2 to § 3–201 and Official Comment 4 to § 3–305. Thus breach of warranty is a defense or claim in recoupment and not a claim unless it is sufficient to allow rescission of negotiation under § 3–202, and that remedy is invoked. *See* Official Comment 3 to § 3–305 and Official Comment to § 3–306. Incapacity, fraud, duress, mistake, illegality, or breach of trust or duty on which a rescission of a negotiation is based also may give rise to either a claim or a defense. *See, e.g.*, the *Maine Family Federal Credit Union* case, *supra*, note 336 and Duxbury v. Roberts, 388 Mass. 385, 446 N.E.2d 401 (1983) (maker's defense that payee, as trustee, breached trust when note assigned could not be asserted unless the trust joined the action and defended the suit itself).

359. § 3–305(c).

360. § 3–305(c).

361. § 3–305(c) does not explicitly mention this exception because it is unnecessary; the liable party need not pay in contravention of the contract of which the restrictive indorsement is part. *Compare* old § 3–306(d).

362. § 3–305(d). This point was not explicitly covered in old Article 3 but presumably the same result would have been reached. *See* Official Comment 5 to § 3–305.

363. § 3–305(c). *See also* note 356, *supra*, § 3–602(a), and Lakeshore Commercial Fin. Corp. v. Bradford Arms Corp., 45 Wis.2d 313, 173 N.W.2d 165 (Wis. 1970) (investor-owners of mortgaged property,

have no satisfactory evidence on the issue, and so the provision that the claim may not be set up is as much for the obligor's protection as for that of the holder.

This does not mean that the claim may not be raised, however. The claimant can intervene in the holder's action against the obligor, or defend the action for the latter and assert the claim in the course of the intervention or defense. Any interpleader, deposit in court, or other available procedure under which the defendant may bring the claimant into court, or be discharged without litigating the claim as a defense is also appropriate. The circle of protection for the obligor and the holder is completed by the rule that allows the obligor to discharge the obligor's liability on the instrument by payment (or satisfaction) to the holder, even though it is made with knowledge of the claim of another person to the instrument, unless prior to the occurrence of payment (or satisfaction) the claimant either supplies indemnity to the obligor (not available in the case of a bank obligation under § 3–602) or has payment (or satisfaction) enjoined in an action in which the claimant and the holder are parties, or unless the claim is theft or the payment would be inconsistent with a restrictive indorsement.[364]

In *Fulton National Bank v. Delco Corp.*[365] these provisions were invoked to deny to a bank as the drawer of a draft by way of defense to its drawer's liability the claim of the bank's customer to the draft. The bank had drawn the draft payable to the plaintiff at the request of its customer for the customer to use as a down payment, and had stopped payment on the draft and refunded its customer's money when the customer called off the transaction with the plaintiff because financing could not be obtained. The court recognized the claim, however, because the customer defended the action on the bank's behalf.[366] Distinguish *Nawas v. Holmes*,[367] where the payee of a note sued the maker of the note that had been delivered to guarantee payment of the debt of the maker's travel agency to the payee. The maker was allowed to set up the payment of the note by the travel agency as a defense. Finally, in *Klomann v. Sol K. Graff & Sons*,[368] the holder sued the maker of certain notes that had been made payable to a payee, specially indorsed by the payee and delivered to another person, returned by that person to the payee for collection, and then the payee had crossed out that person's name, inserted the holder's name and delivered the notes to the holder.

---

who are not parties to the note and who neither assumed nor guaranteed it, precluded from asserting an alleged misapplication of funds in an action to foreclose the mortgage on the basis that they have no claim to the note and are not parties to the transaction). The UCC rules on *jus tertii* are further discussed in Chapter 6. If it is the claim of the person asserting the claim, that person, of course, may assert it. § 3–306.

364. § 3–602. *See also* note 359, *supra*. The matter from this perspective is discussed in Chapter 6.

365. 128 Ga.App. 16, 195 S.E.2d 455 (Ga.Ct.App.1973).

366. Article 3 specifically addresses this factual situation in an attempt to make a cashier's check and like instruments more in accord with the perception of their legal status. This is discussed *infra* in this book.

367. 541 S.W.2d 283 (Tex.Civ.App. 1976).

368. 22 Ill.App.3d 572, 317 N.E.2d 608 (1974).

The court stated the holder had no interest in the notes and allowed the maker to raise that as a defense. The result of the case seems sensible and is perhaps not inconsistent with the law because a form of theft was involved.[369]

[b] Finality of Payment

A concept like that of holder in due course plays a second role under the UCC not involving the cutting off of claims and defenses. This role relates to protection of payment, thus better assuring the goal of finality of payment.[370]

Except in relation to bank payments under Article 4 and liability for breach of warranty on presentment under § 3–417,[371] payment or acceptance[372] of an instrument is final in favor of a person who took the instrument in good faith and for value, or a person who has in good faith changed position in reliance on the acceptance or payment.[373] The reason is that it is highly desirable to end the transaction on an instrument when it is paid (or accepted), rather than reopen the matter and upset a series of commercial transactions at a later date when some objection to the payment (or acceptance) arises.[374] This, of course, is true, but given the exceptions for various cases in Article 3 it appears that the real principle at work is that losses from improper payment should fall upon the person who is best able to have prevented them, and that, if that person is the payor, the loss ought not to be shifted by a recovery by the payor from the person paid. The UCC comments thus say the rule is consistent with the case of *Price v. Neal*.[375] That case placed the loss from an unauthorized signature of the drawer on the drawee, as the drawee was in a superior position to detect the forgery because it is expected to know and compare its customer's signature. The UCC uses the same reasoning to place a loss from an overdraft payment on the drawee, who should best know the state of its customer's account.[376] But because

---

369. § 3–305(c) precludes the claim of a third person generally being used as a defense but not where the claim is the holder acquired the instrument by theft.

370. § 3–418(c) and (d) and text after note 371, *infra*.

371. The holder in due course concept not only plays a protective role in warranty liability under § 3–417(1) but also in connection with preclusion from asserting an alteration or lack of an authorized signature under § 3–406. These matters are discussed in Chapters 4 and 7, *infra*. The reference to Article 4 is essentially a reference to § 4–208, which basically is the same section as § 3–417, except that it controls in the check-collection context, and to the finality of payment provisions of Article 4, §§ 4–215, 4–301 and 4–407. The relevant provisions of Article 4 also are discussed in Chapter 8.

372. Acceptance is the drawee's signed engagement to honor the draft as presented. It must be written on the draft and becomes operative when completed by delivery or notification. Certification of a check is acceptance. § 3–409(a) and (d). The matter is discussed in Chapter 4, *infra*. Basically, an acceptor must pay, and so it is the close equivalent of payment itself.

373. § 3–418(c). *See* Gentner & Co., Inc. v. Wells Fargo Bank, 76 Cal.App.4th 1165, 90 Cal.Rptr.2d 904, (Cal.App.1999) (recovery of payment by cashier's check by mistake over stop order denied).

374. Official Comments 1 and 2 to old § 3–418.

375. 3 Burr. 1354, 97 Eng. Rep. 871 (K.B. 1762).

376. The same is true, at least initially, for a payment made over a valid stop payment order. *See* §§ 4–401, 4–407.

under the UCC erroneous payments of instruments that have been materially altered or on which necessary unauthorized indorsements appear are recoverable,[377] which is consistent with the principle of *Price v. Neal* but not with finality of payment,[378] it appears that the principle of *Price v. Neal* is the real basis for the UCC position.

In any event, where the payor bank sues the depositary bank after paying a forged instrument, the cases protect the latter and payment is held to be final.[379] In fact, in several cases protection has been extended even when there was a double forgery of both the instrument and indorsements.[380]

There are only a handful of transactions that fall outside of the finality of payment rule. That is why Official Comment 1 to § 3–418 can continue to state the UCC rule is consistent with the rule of *Price v. Neal* even though § 3–418(a) explicitly provides for restitutionary recovery where payment or acceptance occurs by mistake because a stop payment order or forged drawer's signature is overlooked,[381] and § 3–418(b) explicitly allows for recovery in other cases[382] to the extent

---

377. § 3–417(a)(1) and (2).

378. The warranty as to the drawer's signature in § 3–417(a)(3) normally is not breached as it only is one of no knowledge. Since there is no breach of warranty and payment is final, the drawee, who should recognize its customer's signature, bears the loss. The continued viability of this analysis is discussed later in this book. *See for now*, Ballen et al., Commercial Paper, Bank Deposits and Collections, and Other Payment Systems, 46 Bus. Law. 1521, at 1541 (1991). Several jurisdictions have also changed this result in the case of so-called "demand drafts" as discussed, *infra*, in this book, and an amendment promulgated in 2002 now changes the rule in Article 3 for "demand drafts" drawn on consumer accounts. *See, e.g.*, § 3–416(a)(6). On the other hand, an unauthorized indorsement or a material alteration will breach the warranties of § 3–417(a)(1) and (2). This permits recovery of payment. A drawee normally has no ability to detect an unauthorized indorsement or a skillful alteration of the instrument.

The emphasis on culpability in § 3–418 also explains why finality exists only in favor of a person who gave value in good faith. The person paid is favored when there is only negligence on his or her part, and the payor is favored where there is bad faith or notice on the part of the person paid which prevents good faith or holding in due course.

379. Except as noted in note 378 for demand drafts, *supra. See, e.g.*, Perini Corp. v. First Nat'l Bank, 553 F.2d 398 (5th Cir. 1977); First Israel Bank & Trust Co. v. Franklin Nat'l Bank, 9 UCC Rep. Serv. 861 (N.Y.Sup.Ct.1971). The depositary bank attains holder in due course status under §§ 4–210 and 4–211.

380. *E.g.*, Perini Corp. v. First Nat'l Bank, 553 F.2d 398 (5th Cir.1977). The courts have reasoned that the principal cause of the loss in a double forgery case is the forged instrument. In the *Perini Corp.* case, the court also stated that the final payment rule would protect depositary and collecting banks against claims by the drawer whose signature had been forged, as well as against claims of the drawee or other payor. But the court suggested that common law negligence liability might follow if a forged check loss could be tied to a holder's unreasonable conduct. § 3–404 essentially codifies this analysis and is discussed, *infra*, in Chapter 7, as well as negligence theories in the context of commercial paper.

381. Official Comment 2 to § 3–418 furnishes an elaborate example involving a check issued to pay for goods to be delivered where the bank overlooks a stop payment order and issues a cashier's check to the seller in return for the drawer's check. If the goods are not delivered, the bank may recover from seller or set-off. If the goods were delivered, bank may not recover under this section but may have rights under § 4–407. *See also* note 371, *supra*.

382. According to Official Comment 3 to § 3–418, the most likely case is insufficient funds. If the insufficient funds check was a gift, restitutionary recovery could be had. However, in most other cases the remedy of restitution is not likely to be available.

permitted by the law governing mistake and restitution; finality occurs where payment is made or acceptance runs to a person who took the instrument in good faith and for value or a reliance payee.[383]

To illustrate the narrowness of exceptions to finality, in *Maplewood Bank & Trust Co. v. F.I.B., Inc.*,[384] a check made payable to the attorney for the seller of property, as a deposit on the executory contract of purchase, was deposited by the attorney in a trust account and paid by the drawee even though the drawer had insufficient funds. In the suit by the drawee to recover the payment, the court held the attorney did not come within the protection of § 3–418 because the client was the real holder of the check and, as to the client, the executory contract was not value and there was no reliance.[385] In *Rockland Trust Co. v. South Shore National Bank*,[386] a bank was allowed to undo its certification of a check where the check was written on an account into which the proceeds of a loan secured by stock and made by the bank had gone, when it discovered the stock was stolen and notified the holder of the check before that holder had given value for it.[387]

¶ 3.04 Limitations on Holder in Due Course Status

[1] In the UCC

[a] Nonordinary Course Acquisitions

Not all holders who take an instrument for value, in good faith and without notice, are entitled to holder in due course status. A holder does not become a holder in due course of an instrument by the purchase of it at a judicial sale, or by taking it under legal process,[388] or by acquiring it in taking over an estate,[389] or by purchasing it as part of a bulk transaction not in the regular course of business of the transferor.[390]

---

383. Official Comment 1 to § 3–418.

384. 142 N.J.Super. 480, 362 A.2d 44 (App.Div.1976).

385. Under current § 3–418(b), any recovery would be governed by the law of mistake and restitution.

386. 366 Mass. 74, 314 N.E.2d 438 (Mass. 1974).

387. Under current § 3–418(b), this result would be determined by the law of mistake and restitution.

¶ 3.04

388. § 3–302(c)(i). *See, e.g.*, Mazer v. Williams Bros. Co., 461 Pa. 587, 337 A.2d 559 (Pa. 1975) (purchaser at judicial sale does not become holder in due course).

389. § 3–302(c)(iii). *See, e.g.*, Wyatt v. Mount Airy Cemetery, 209 Pa.Super. 250, 224 A.2d 787 (1966) (one who had received instruments as a legatee through another was not a holder in due course).

390. § 3–302(c)(ii). In Federal Deposit Ins. Corp. v. Webb, 464 F.Supp. 520, 25 UCC Rep. Serv. 590 (E.D.Tenn.1978), the court held that the FDIC, as purchaser in bulk of part of the assets of a bank threatened with insolvency, was not a holder in due course, but as guarantor of the deposits of the bank became subrogated to its rights and took subject to defenses assertable against the bank. As discussed in Chapter 1, *supra*, later cases have determined that the federal common law on this topic should not follow the UCC rule, and this limitation has not been applied to federal financial institution insurance agencies. *See* Official Comment 5 to § 3–302. For a case interpreting the limitation as state law, *see* First Alabama Bank v. Hunt, 402 So.2d 992 (Ala. Civ..App.1981), where the court held this provision was limited to transfers incident to the cessation, liquidation, or reorganization of the transferor's business and did not bar a bank that bought a batch of notes sold to raise operating capital from holder

However, such holders will not lose prior rights held,[391] and succeed to prior rights, which may be those of a holder in due course.[392]

A purchaser of a limited interest is a holder in due course only to the extent of the interest purchased.[393] This limitation normally arises in connection with the pledge of an instrument for security. Thus in *Wood v. Willman*[394] the court held that a purchaser of notes assigned to him as security for a loan could enforce the notes over the defenses of the maker only to the extent of the unpaid balance due on the loan, and defenses good against the pledgor of the notes remained available insofar as the pledgor retained an equity in the instruments.[395]

[b] Defenses and Claims of Persons With Whom the Holder Has Dealt

[i] Defenses

Under old Article 3, a holder in due course will not take an instrument free from defenses of a party to it with whom the holder has dealt.[396] An example of a case where the limitation was applied is the case of *Estate of Lucas v. Whiteley*.[397] The name of a mental incompetent was signed to a note by his agent acting under a power of attorney executed during the incompetency. The note was taken from the agent by the holders of it in good faith and without notice and for value. But, even though under the applicable state law the defense of incompetency was not a real defense, the court held the holders took the note subject to the defense as they had dealt with the incompetent having the defense through his agent. Another similar case is *James Pair, Inc. v. Gentry*,[398] which involved a note given to an employment agency for a job placement fee where there also was an agreement among the agency, the employer, and the employee that if the employee worked six months for the employer the placement fee would be refunded. The note was held not to be enforceable by the agency over this defense. And in *Coplan Pipe & Supply Co. v. Ben-Frieda Corp.*,[399] the court held that a corporation that had negotiated and arranged the underlying transaction, and to

---

in due course status. That same reasoning has resulted in decisions upholding holder in due course status in securitizations where mortgage notes have been purchased in volume. Bankers Trust (Delaware) v. 236 Beltway Investment, 865 F.Supp. 1186 (E.D.Va.1994) and Midfirst Bank, SSB v. C.W. Haynes & Co., 893 F.Supp. 1304 (D.S.C.1994), *aff'd*, 87 F.3d 1308 (4th Cir. 1996).

391. Third Nat'l Bank v. Hardi-Gardens Supply, Inc., 380 F.Supp. 930 (M.D.Tenn.1974) (holder in due course, which after default on note advertised and sold the note at a judicial sale at which it repurchased in its own name, did not diminish its status as a holder in due course).

392. Official Comment 5 to § 3-302 and § 3-203(b). This rule has been applied to protect purchasers from a federal financial institution insurance agency. *See* discussion in Chapter 1, *supra*.

393. § 3-302(e).

394. 423 P.2d 82 (Wyo.1967).

395. This is the same example given in Official Comment 6, Case #6, to § 3-302.

396. Old § 3-305(2). *See also* the prior discussion beginning at note 207, *supra*.

397. 550 S.W.2d 767 (Tex.Civ.App. 1977).

398. 134 Ga.App. 734, 215 S.E.2d 707 (Ga.Ct.App.1975).

399. 256 So.2d 218 (Fla.Dist.Ct.App. 1972).

which the funds were ultimately paid, was not a holder in due course with respect to the maker of the note, even though the note had been executed to a third person and assigned to the corporation.

On the other hand, in *Chicago Title & Trust Co. v. Walsh*,[400] even though the bank holding an escrow account funded by the debtor with a forged certified check had dealt with creditors of the debtor by issuing drafts to them and taking release documents issued to the debtor, the court held the creditors were holders in due course of the drafts issued by the bank as their dealings with the drawer of the drafts had nothing to do with the disbursing arrangement reached between the bank and the debtor.

As discussed earlier in this chapter,[401] current Article 3 does not incorporate the "dealt with" concept as potentially productive of an erroneous result and unnecessary if a proper analysis of the facts is made. The *Gentry* case was discussed there; as to the other cases the analysis in the applicable comments to §§ 3–302 and 3–305 again should be reviewed. *See also* the policy reflected in § 3–203(b).

[ii] *Claims*

A similar limitation (that one does not take free of claims of a party with whom one has dealt) does not expressly appear with respect to claims in old Article 3.[402] One might assume the reason is that a claim, as the converse of a defense, generally would not arise until after the instrument is paid, and thus would not be a claim *to the instrument*. Though that assumption is technically true, the cases litigate whether holder in due course status on the instrument may be used to resist a claim to its proceeds. For example, in *Snyder v. Town Hill Motors, Inc.*[403] a minor had agreed to purchase an automobile from a friend. The friend in turn was purchasing a new car from a dealer. A check made payable to the minor, as well as the minor's old car, were delivered directly to the dealer at the instruction of the friend to serve as the friend's down payment. When the minor discovered the lien on the friend's car secured a larger amount due than had been represented, he sought to get his money back from the dealer. This claim was denied by the court on the ground the dealer was a holder in due course. A close analysis of the opinion, however, shows that the court did not rule that a holder in due course takes free of claims even though they are made by one with whom the holder has dealt because the court specifically found the dealer had not dealt with the minor in relation to the transaction out of which the claim arose. It considered that the check had been negotiated first to the friend and then by the friend to the dealer as a subsequent holder in due

---

400. 34 Ill.App.3d 458, 340 N.E.2d 106 (1975).

401. Beginning at note 207, *supra*.

402. Under old § 3–305(1), a holder in due course takes free of all claims to the instrument on the part of *any* person.

403. 193 Pa.Super. 578, 165 A.2d 293 (1960).

course by constructive delivery. As such, the case is similar to the examples of when a payee may be a holder in due course.[404]

A case that does expose the issue of whether claims and defenses should be treated alike because they may be the same assertion separated only by time is *Eldon's Super Fresh Stores, Inc. v. Merrill Lynch, Pierce, Fenner & Smith, Inc.*[405] In that case, the agent of the plaintiff, who owed a stockbroker for securities purchased, applied a check made out to the stockbroker in the amount owed by the agent and allegedly given to the agent to purchase stock for his principal, to payment of his own debt. The court determined that the stockbroker payee of the check was a holder in due course, having taken the check for value and without notice of the plaintiff's claim that the agent negotiated it in breach of his duty.[406] Certainly, the case should not come out differently if the asserted defalcation of the agent had been discovered earlier, and the stockbroker had to sue the drawer and face the asserted claim as a defense to payment rather than as a claim after the instrument was paid.[407] This case and the next case were also discussed earlier in this chapter.[408]

One reported case under old Article 3 did seemingly impose the same limitation with respect to claims as old Article 3 imposed with respect to defenses. This case is *James Pair, Inc. v. Gentry*.[409] There a new employee gave a note to an employment agency. There was an agreement among the agency, the employee, and the employer that if the employee worked for the employer for six months the employer would pay the fee. After the employee made two monthly payments on the note, the employer breached the agreement by stating it would not pay the fee. The employee then sued to recover the payments made, in essence claiming a better right to the note and its proceeds than the agency had. The court held that even a holder in due course does not take the instrument free from defenses of a party to the instrument with whom the holder has dealt, the breach of the agreement would operate as a defense, and the parties had dealt with each other in the transaction out of which the employee's cause of action for recovery of the payments made on the note arose. In stating it this way, the court recognized the apparent incongruity of a different rule for claims than for defenses; the suit just as easily could have been the agency to recover on the note, in which case the UCC clearly would have allowed the breach of contract as a defense because the parties had dealt with each other. The court is correct as to result.[410]

---

404. Official Comment 2 to old § 3–302.

405. 296 Minn. 130, 207 N.W.2d 282 (Minn. 1973).

406. A payee may be a holder in due course under old § 3–302(2). One must have actual knowledge that a fiduciary has negotiated the instrument in breach of duty before notice of such a claim exists under old § 3–304(2). Under current Article 3, *see* § 3–307(b)(4).

407. As to the asserted defalcation of the agent, it would appear that the payee did not deal with the party asserting it either as a claim or as a defense through the agent. *See* Official Comment 2 to old § 3–302, Example e.

408. Notes 213 and 396, *supra*.

409. 134 Ga.App. 734, 215 S.E.2d 707 (Ga.Ct.App.1975); note 396, *supra*.

410. Another case where the court ignored the different language between old

[2] Case Law Limits

In addition to limitations on holder in due course status in the UCC, in the consumer area and, under some cases in the small business area, restrictions have been imposed outside the statute both by case law[411] and by statute or regulation.[412]

The type of limitation by case law is illustrated by *Unico v. Owen*.[413] That case involved the credit sale of a stereo record player and 140 record albums to be delivered over a several years' period to the consumer buyers. Their note was immediately negotiated to a financing agency which claimed holder in due course status when the seller became insolvent and failed to deliver most of the records for whose price the note was given. The court stated that the basic philosophy of holder in due course status is to encourage free negotiability of commercial paper by removing certain anxieties of one who takes the paper as an innocent purchaser knowing no reason why the paper is not as sound as its face would indicate. The court thought it followed, therefore, that the more the holder knew about the underlying transaction, and particularly the more the holder controlled or participated or became involved in it, the less the holder fit the role of a good faith purchaser for value. In short, the closer the holder's relationship or connection is to the underlying transaction that is the source of the instrument, the less need there is for giving holder in due course rights. The court concluded that if it appears from the totality of the arrangements between the dealer and the financier that the financier has had a substantial voice in setting standards for the underlying transaction, or has approved the standards established by the dealer, and has agreed to take all, or a predetermined, or a substantial quantity of the negotiable paper that is backed by such standards, the financier should be considered a participant in the original transaction and therefore not entitled to holder in due course status.

The *Unico* case articulates a judge-made overlay to the UCC (and prior law) called the "close-connectedness" doctrine. The doctrine has been adopted by the courts in a number of states to limit the ability of a

---

§§ 3–305(1) and (2) is Travelers Indem. Co. v. American Express Co., 559 F.Supp. 452 (S.D.N.Y.1983). There, a corporation mistakenly paid both its American Express bill and the personal American Express bills of employees, and the court held that even if American Express was a holder in due course of the check it could not take free of the corporation's claim for reimbursement because it had dealt with the corporation.

411. See, *infra*, this chapter.

412. § 3–302(g), which defers to any law limiting status as a holder in due course in particular classes of transactions. However, even if not explicitly recognized, other consumer protection statutes should prevail. *Compare, e.g.,* § 3–602 *with* Unif. Consumer Credit Code § 3.204 (1974). For the purpose of this discussion, a consumer transaction is one in which an individual obtains credit primarily for a personal, family, or household purpose. *See, e.g.,* Unif. Consumer Credit Code §§ 1.301(12), (15) (1974). In Saint James v. Diversified Commercial Fin. Corp., 102 Nev. 23, 714 P.2d 179 (Nev. 1986), the court also extended protection to a small business person who had given notes to evidence the purchase of a business. *But see* Bankers Trust Co. v. Crawford, 781 F.2d 39 (3d Cir.1986). The small business cases involve agriculture primarily. *See* Arcanum Nat'l Bank v. Hessler, 69 Ohio St.2d 549, 433 N.E.2d 204 (Ohio 1982) and Valmont Credit Corp. v. McIlravy, 344 N.W.2d 691 (S.D.1984). *See also* the 2002 amendments to §§3–305, and to 3–602, *supra* note 338, and *infra*.

413. 50 N.J. 101, 232 A.2d 405 (N.J. 1967).

seller in a consumer credit transaction to separate the consumer's obligation to pay from the seller's obligation to perform by the negotiation of the consumer's note to an asserted holder in due course, who can then claim to hold the instrument free from personal defenses like failure of consideration, breach of warranty, and fraud in the inducement.[414] The philosophy behind the doctrine is that financing institutions have close relations with sellers from whom notes are acquired, and that these institutions are better able than consumers to police sellers and require them to adopt reasonable standards of performance. The doctrine generally is effective because the elements on which it is based (preparation of standard forms, checks or approvals of standards for buyers, and volume assignment of paper) are precisely those upon which the relationship between most sellers and a reputable financiers are based.[415]

Some courts took other approaches or perhaps added a different spin to the "close connection" analysis. As suggested in Chapter 2, various courts, perhaps stretching, found the writing was not a negotiable instrument so that holder in due course status could not arise. Other courts found that because of a close connection the seller was the agent of the financing institution and thus the institution was responsible for the seller's conduct.[416] Still other courts said the close connection between transferor and transferee resulted in a lack of good faith or in the presence of notice in what generally must be recognized as strained applications of those concepts.[417] Finally, some courts reasoned that the

---

414. As note 412 indicates, the doctrine has not always been limited to consumer transactions. This was true even pre-Code. *See, e.g.,* Mutual Fin. Co. v. Martin, 63 So.2d 649 (Fla.1953) (transferee which prepared and furnished payee's forms that contemplated assignment, investigated and approved the credit of buyers from the payee, and took the notes contemporaneously was not a holder in due course even when the purchase for which the notes were given was for a business purpose). For discussion of the doctrine, *see, e.g.,* White v. Gilliam, 244 Va. 113, 419 S.E.2d 247 (Va. 1992) (generally not recognizing the doctrine) and Vitols v. Citizens Banking Co., 10 F.3d 1227 (6th Cir.1993) (recognizing doctrine but not finding requirements met). An untested issue, given § 3–302(g) which restricts the holder in due course doctrine as provided in other law in contemplation of the Federal Trade Commission "Holder" rule and various state statutes as discussed *infra,* is whether this doctrine still is viable. Official Comment 7 to § 3–302, however, seems broad enough to include it.

415. Any other procedure probably would have the financing institution purchasing lawsuits in almost the same volume as it is purchasing paper. Of course, a deep enough discount coupled with a blind faith purchase might make that alternative approach look profitable and cases evidence that some financing institutions use this approach, but the discount will make it difficult for the financiers to achieve holder in due course status. *See, e.g.,* United States Fin. Co. v. Jones, 285 Ala. 105, 229 So.2d 495 (Ala. 1969).

416. *See, e.g.,* Kaw Valley State Bank & Trust Co. v. Riddle, 219 Kan. 550, 549 P.2d 927 (Kan. 1976) (a holder of a negotiable instrument may be prevented from assuming holder in due course status when so closely aligned with the transferor that the transferor may be considered an agent of the holder so that the transferee is charged with the actions and knowledge of the transferor).

417. *See, e.g.,* White v. Gilliam, 244 Va. 113, 419 S.E.2d 247 (Va. 1992); Vasquez v. Superior Court, 4 Cal.3d 800, 484 P.2d 964, 94 Cal.Rptr. 796 (Cal. 1971); Timeplan Corp. v. Fuxa, 9 UCC Rep. Serv. 262 (Okla. Ct.App.1971) (one who takes with notice of a defense against an instrument is not a holder in due course). In the *Timeplan* case, the court said that a financial institution may be denied holder in due course status because of its close connection with the seller; there is some suggestion that the close connection in essence caused the financing institution to deal with the consumer buyer.[418] In some of these cases, the close connection doctrine was extended to a financing agency that loaned the consumer the money to purchase the goods or services involved, rather than taking an assignment of a note from the seller.[419]

[3] *State Legislation*

The legislatures of a number of states also dealt with both the assigned paper and the direct loan situations.[420] One form of this legislation takes the approach of requiring that the note refer to the installment agreement in such a manner that its negotiability in essence is destroyed.[421] Another similar type of legislation mandates a legend, such as "Consumer Note," which renders the instrument nonnegotiable under the statute.[422] A more direct approach prohibits the taking of a note.[423] Most statutes provide that if the instrument is taken in violation of the statute, whatever its approach, and the assignee knows this, the assignee cannot be a holder in due course.[424] More modern statutes like § 3.404 of the 1974 Uniform Consumer Credit Code deny this status irrespective of knowledge, and often, in addition, impose a penalty for violation.

---

finance company was merely a straw man to shield the seller from liability for its breach. *See also* as to this, Courtesy Fin. Servs., Inc. v. Hughes, 424 So.2d 1172 (La. Ct.App.1982) (seller and lender essentially same entity).

418. *See, e.g.*, Jones v. Approved Bancredit Corp., 256 A.2d 739 (Del.1969) (finance company was more an original party to the transaction than a subsequent purchaser of the paper), and Bank One of Columbus, N.A. v. Myers, 14 Ohio App.3d 196, 470 N.E.2d 485 (Ohio Ct.App.1984).

419. *See* notes 415 and 416, *supra*. Absent a close connection with the seller, a lender should be able to enforce the loan transaction without regard to problems in a separate sales transaction. But where the seller and the lender essentially are the same entity, the lender should be subject to defenses to payment arising from the sales transaction as the court held in Courtesy Fin. Serv., Inc. v. Hughes, *supra* note 417. *See also* Educational Beneficial, Inc. v. Reynolds, 67 Misc.2d 739, 324 N.Y.S.2d 813 (Civ.Ct.1971). The court in the *Reynolds* case stated that the relationship between the lender and the seller was such as to render them indistinguishable in legal contemplation because the sole reason for the lender's existence was to serve as a financing resource to which the seller could direct its prospective customers. In Waterbury Sav. Bank v. Jaroszewski, 4 Conn. Cir. Ct. 620, 238 A.2d 446 (Conn.Cir.Ct.1967), on similar facts, except that the lender was not a captive of the seller, the doctrine was not applied.

420. State legislation also commonly deals with the related problem of a waiver of defenses clause, eliminating or limiting its operation. *See, e.g.*, 14A Okla. Stat. § 2–404; Unif. Consumer Credit Code § 3.404 (1974). Federal legislation in Section 170 of the Fair Credit Billing Act, 15 U.S.C. § 1666i, subjects credit card issuers to claims and defenses good against sellers honoring the credit card under designated circumstances. *See* the discussion later in this book.

421. A provision of this nature was applied in Kennard v. Reliance, Inc., 257 Md. 654, 264 A.2d 832 (Md. 1970).

422. A case applying a statute like this is Alcoa Credit Co. v. Nickerson, 5 UCC Rep. Serv. 152 (Mass.App.Div.1968) which, interestingly enough, involved a note that apparently was not actually within the requirements of the statute.

423. *See, e.g.*, Circle v. Jim Walter Homes, Inc., 535 F.2d 583 (10th Cir.1976), construing such a statutory provision. *See also* Unif. Consumer Credit Code §§ 3.307, 3.404 (1974).

424. *See, e.g.*, 14A Okla. Stat. § 2–403 (holder is not a holder in good faith if the negotiable instrument is taken with notice that it is issued in violation of the statute). § 3–302(g) and § 3–305(f) defer to such laws.

[4] Federal Rule

State law dealing with holder in due course rights in consumer transactions generally was superseded when the Federal Trade Commission promulgated a trade regulation rule[425] in 1975 dealing with the preservation of consumers' claims and defenses (the holder rule).[426] The holder rule requires that in connection with any purchase money loan[427] or any sale or lease[428] of goods or services[429] in or affecting commerce, the

---

425. However, a transaction subject to the federal rule still is subject to state law restricting holder in due course status to the extent that the state law is at least as protective of consumers. *See, e.g.*, FTC Staff Advisory Letter, Oct. 12, 1976 [Transfer Binder–Decisions 1974–1980] Consumer Cred. Guide (CCH) ¶ 98, 284. This is particularly important with respect to the remedy for violation. The sanction for a violation of the federal rule is that for committing an unfair or deceptive act or practice under Section 5 of the FTC Act (15 U.S.C. § 45). This may involve an FTC proceeding for a cease and desist order including a civil penalty of up to $10,000 or more per day. But private enforcement is probably not available. *See* Holloway v. Bristol-Myers, 485 F.2d 986 (D.C.Cir.1973). Thus if the federal rule is not complied with, the assignee may still be a holder in due course. *See, e.g.*, Capital Bank & Trust Co. v. Lacey, 393 So.2d 668 (La.1980) *(but see infra)*. Accordingly, a state restriction on due course rights may still be important. For this reason, for example, in UCC Article 9 the federal rule is incorporated by reference. UCC §§ 9–102(a)(3) and 9–404 through 9–406. The same is now true in § 3–305(e), which codifies the holdings in two cases where the federal rule was not complied with but the court treated the holder as if the legend required by the rule was present. Associates Home Equity Services, Inc. v. Troup, 343 N.J. Super. 254, 778 A.2d 529 (App.Div. 2001) and Gonzalez v. Old Kent Mortgage Company and Quality Builders, Inc., 2000 WL 1469313 (E.D.Pa.2000) (lender should not avoid the consequences of the required legend by its own illegal failure to include the holder notice in loan documents). This reasoning turns the federal rule into a substantive amendment of state law, which is beyond the power of the Federal Trade Commission, but while state legislative action in adopting § 3–305(e) renders that issue moot, it creates another one, since the next subsection of § 3–305, subsection (f), subjects § 3–305 to law other than Article 3 which establishes a different rule for consumer transactions. If the state has a provision like that cited in note 424 *supra*, does a holder who takes a note without the legend from the original lender take subject to defenses of the maker, or under the state rule made applicable by § 3–305(f) and § 3–302(g) take free if in good faith and without notice? Hopefully, legislators will consider this issue in the enactment process of the 2002 amendments to Articles 3 and 4.

426. 16 CFR § 433. In late 1979, the Federal Trade Commission approved in substance amendments to the rule to extend its coverage to lenders, but withheld final promulgation pending public comment on certain language changes. *See* 44 Fed. Reg. 65, 771 (Nov. 15, 1979). Later these amendments were abandoned as unnecessary. 53 Fed. Reg. 44,456 (Nov. 3, 1988).

427. Defined in 16 CFR pT. 433.1(d) as a cash advance received by a consumer in return for a finance charge as defined by the Truth in Lending Act (15 U.S.C. § 1601 *et seq.*) and Regulation Z, which is applied in whole or substantial part to a purchase of goods or services for personal, family, or household use, from a seller who refers consumers to the lender or who is affiliated with the lender by common control or business arrangement.

Note that the application of the holder rule in this context depends on what the consumer does with the loan, and not on what he or she says he or she will do. This presents some risk. For guidance as to what loans are covered, *see* FTC Staff Guidelines, Consumer Cred. Guide (CCH) ¶ 11,399 *et seq.*

Note also that all purchase money loans are not covered. There must be a referral or common control or business arrangement. A number of questions concerning these and other general terms are answered in the FTC Staff Guidelines on the rule at Consumer Cred. Guide (CCH) ¶ ¶ 11,380 *et seq. See also* Statement of Enforcement Policy, Consumer Credit Guide (CCH) ¶ 10,190 *et seq.*

428. The leases covered are only those which are "disguised" sales, and not "true" leases. *See* FTC Staff Guidelines, Consumer Cred. Guide (CCH) ¶ 11,397. Thus protection in the case of a true lease must reside, if at all, in state law. *See* Miller, Consumer Leases Under Uniform Commercial Code Article 2A, 39 Ala. L. Rev. 957 (1988).

429. Creditors should consider home improvement transactions and those involv-

seller[430] include in the consumer credit contract[431] the following provision in at least ten-point, bold-face type: "Any holder of this consumer credit contract is subject to all claims and defenses which the debtor could assert against the seller of goods or services obtained pursuant hereto or with the proceeds hereof. Recovery hereunder by the debtor shall not exceed amounts paid by the debtor hereunder."[432]

The theory of the notice requirement is that the provision serves as a part of the agreement to allow contractually what otherwise might not result. It also serves as a notice to the consumer of at least the rights provided through the rule under the agreement. The provision can appear anywhere in the contract, even by incorporation by reference, and in connection with open-end credit, even outside of the contract.[433] This uniform federal regulation finally should substantially lay to rest one of the most hotly debated issues in the law of commercial paper.[434]

---

ing mobile homes as covered and not as excluded because real estate is involved. The same approach would include swimming pools, pre-fab and other home packages, and perhaps even home-building itself as opposed to finished real property transactions. *See* FTC Staff Guidelines, Consumer Cred. Guide (CCH) ¶ 11,397.

430. "Seller" is defined in 16 CFR § 433.1(j) as a person who, in the ordinary course of business, sells or leases goods or services to consumers.

431. Defined in 16 CFR § 433.1(i) as any instrument which evidences or embodies a debt arising from a purchase money loan transaction or a financed sale. When a loan is involved, the seller cannot, without violating the rule, accept the proceeds of the loan unless the required notice is in the loan contract and note. 16 CFR § 433.2(b).

432. 16 CFR § 433.2(a). The notice for the loan document differs slightly. Essentially the rule operates as a shield and not as a sword. Thus a consumer was only allowed to set-off against the amount owed the assignee of the contract the amount of actual damages awarded under state law, and not punitive and treble damages. Hardeman v. Wheels, Inc., 56 Ohio App.3d 142, 565 N.E.2d 849 (Ohio Ct.App.1988). Moreover, affirmative damages are not recoverable. Ford Motor Credit Co. v. Morgan, 404 Mass. 537, 536 N.E.2d 587 (1989) and Stewart v. Credithrift of America Consumer Discount Co., 93 B.R. 878 (Bankr. E.D.Pa.1988). One case denied recovery of amounts paid on the contract. Cuchine v. H.O. Bell, Inc., 210 Mont. 312, 682 P.2d 723 (Mont. 1984). The opinion appears questionable. *See* FTC Staff Guidelines, Consumer Cred. Guide (CCH) ¶ 11,394. As to what claims and defenses may be asserted, *see* Vietnam Veterans of Am., Inc. v. Guerdon Indus., Inc., 644 F.Supp. 951 (D.Del. 1986). There also is a split of authority over whether the rule expands assignee liability under the Truth in Lending Act. *Compare* the *Vietnam Veterans* case, above, *with* Cox v. First Nat'l Bank of Cincinnati, 633 F.Supp. 236 (S.D.Ohio 1986). The weight of authority clearly refutes the expansion of the statute by the rule. *See, e.g.,* Taylor v. Quality Hyundai, Inc., 150 F.3d 689 (7th Cir.1998) and Walker v. Wallace Auto Sales, Inc., 155 F.3d 927 (7th Cir.1998). Generally, *see* Greenfield & Ross, Limits on a Consumer's Ability to Assert Claims and Defenses Under the FTC's Holder in Due Course Rule, 46 Bus. Law. 1135 (1991).

433. FTC Staff Guidelines, Consumer Cred. Guide (CCH) ¶ 11,406.

434. But it may have created problems of its own. For example, assume an automobile financed with the dealer and which secures its unpaid debt. Suppose it has some of the all too common minor problems. The consumer by inference is told under the holder rule that he or she may withhold payment from the assignee, but under state law which controls the remedy his or her remedy may be only repair or replacement under a limitation of remedy clause if there are insufficient defects to revoke the acceptance. The withholding of payment thus may trigger a default, and that may lead to the loss of the car and any trade-in, and even to a deficiency. So, too, may the incorporation of the rule into state law. *See* note 425, *supra*.

Chapter 4

LIABILITY ON NEGOTIABLE INSTRUMENTS: THE BASIC OBLIGORS

Analysis

Para.

¶4.01	Introduction		156
¶4.02	Basis for Liability		156
	[1]	Signature	156
	[2]	Preclusion and Ratification	158
		[a] Preclusion	158
		[b] Ratification	163
	[3]	Liability and Capacity	164
¶4.03	The Drawer		165
	[1]	Description of Liability	165
	[2]	Conditions to Liability	165
		[a] Dishonor	165
		[i] Presentment As a Condition to Dishonor	165
		[ii] Time of Presentment	168
		[iii] Manner of Presentment	169
		[b] Notice of Dishonor	171
		[c] Protest	173
		[d] Discharge, Evidence, and Excuse	173
		[i] Discharge	173
		[ii] Evidence	173
		[iii] Excuse	174
¶4.04	The Drawee		176
	[1]	Absence of Liability As Drawee	176
	[2]	Liability As Acceptor	177
		[a] Acceptance and Certification	177
		[b] Consequences of Acceptance	179
¶4.05	The Maker		184
¶4.06	The Indorser		185
	[1]	Description of Liability	185
	[2]	Conditions to Liability	187
		[a] Dishonor and Notice of Dishonor	187
		[b] Discharge, Evidence, and Excuse	189
	[3]	Order of Liability	190

¶ 4.01 Introduction

Chapter 3 discusses those persons who have rights on negotiable instruments. This chapter considers against which persons those rights are assertable and the details of the rights. Briefly, it addresses who is liable on a negotiable instrument and under what circumstances. Specialized aspects of the subject in connection with accommodation and agency are discussed in Chapter 5.

¶ 4.02 Basis for Liability

[1] Signature

Liability on a negotiable instrument is a matter of contract. It cannot arise without the signature of the party asserted to be liable affixed to the writing because no person is liable on an instrument unless their signature appears on it.[1]

The chief application under old Article 3 of the rule that a person is not liable on an instrument unless the person signed it appears in cases holding that a principal whose name does not appear on the instrument signed by an agent is not liable on the instrument even though the payee knew when the instrument was issued that it was intended to be the obligation of the one who did not sign.[2] An example is a case where individuals signed their own names preceded by the word "by," but their corporations were not mentioned; the court held it was error to enter judgment against the corporations on the note.[3]

¶ 4.02

1. *See* also the discussion in Chapter 1 and in Chapter 2. There is an exception in § 3–401(a) for the undisclosed principal. This rule applies to all the parties who may be liable on a negotiable instrument; that is, a maker, a drawer, an indorser, and an acceptor. This rule appears in § 3–401(a). Legal principles outside the UCC may define that liability, however. *See, e.g.*, First W. Bank & Trust Co. v. Bookasta, 267 Cal.App.2d 910, 73 Cal.Rptr. 657 (Cal.App. 1968) (even if corporate note was not signed by an individual who dominated the affairs of the corporation that was a framework for his manipulations, he could be held liable under the alter ego theory).

2. A signature may be made by the use of any name adopted by a person with present intention to authenticate a writing. § 3–401(b). An odd case employing this rule is Community National Bank v. Channelview Bank, 814 S.W.2d 424 (Tex.Ct.App. 1991), where one Brink purchased a cashier's check payable to L.B. Foster, apparently a name Brink used "for his own convenience" and then indorsed it under that name and his own to Woods, who sought to get payment from the bank. The bank questioned Woods' right, but the court held the indorsement valid. Official Comment 2 to old § 3–401. Official Comment 2 to old § 3–403 also states that even though an agent is authorized to sign, the principal is not liable on the instrument unless the instrument names the principal and clearly shows that the signature is made on the principal's behalf. Current § 3–401(a)(ii) changes this rule. The reason is stated in Official Comment 1 to § 3–402.

While UCC Articles 3 and 4 are "exempt" from the Uniform Electronic Transactions Act and "E-sign" (*see* UETA § 3(b)(2), E–sign § 7003(a)(3)), amendments to Articles 3 and 4 in 2002 contemplate electronic records in certain instances (*e.g.*, § 3–119: notice of litigation in a "record"), and distinguish between manual signatures and electronic signatures (*e.g.*, § 3–602(f): "signed," with respect to a record that is not a writing, includes the attachment to or logical association with the record of an electronic symbol, sound, or process to or with the record with the present intent to adopt or accept the record).

3. Dynamic Homes, Inc. v. Rogers, 331 So.2d 326 (Fla.Dist.Ct.App.1976). *See also* Ness v. Greater Ariz. Realty, Inc., 21 Ariz. App. 231, 517 P.2d 1278 (Ariz.Ct.App.1974)

Other applications of the rule occur though, such as where it is asserted that a signature is unauthorized. An unauthorized signature is wholly inoperative as that of the person whose name is signed.[4] In this context, the litigation often is not to fix liability on the basis of the signature but rather to allocate the loss stemming from the inoperative nature of the unauthorized signature. For example, the drawer of a check may be asserting that the drawee bank should not have paid the check because the drawer's signature was unauthorized.[5] The issue of whether a party has signed the instrument is fundamentally the same in any context, however.

The rule of no liability without signature operates only in connection with liability on the instrument. It is not intended to prevent liability arising apart from the instrument itself,[6] as on the original obligation for which the instrument was given,[7] for breach of an agreement to sign, in tort for misrepresentation or negligence,[8] on an oral guaranty of payment where the statute of frauds is satisfied, or under any separate writing.[9]

A party may be found to have signed the instrument under the normal rules of agency.[10] A party also may be estopped to deny the

(a complaint alleging only that a note was signed by the agent of defendants with full authority to bind them and was delivered by the agent acting for defendants failed to state a cause of action because it did not show that the names of the defendants appeared on the note). *See also* 626 Joint Venture v. Spinks, 873 S.W.2d 73 (Tex.Ct. App.1993) (undisclosed principal of note signed only "Don Bizzell, Trustee" not liable on instrument; the principal was found to be liable on the transaction, however) and Carelli v. Hall, 279 Mont. 202, 926 P.2d 756 (Mont. 1996) (same). In Security Pac. Nat'l Bank v. Chess, 58 Cal.App.3d 555, 129 Cal.Rptr. 852 (1976), which involved notes indorsed to a corporation and further indorsed in the name of an individual who was president of the corporation, some of the signatures being followed by "Pres.," the question was not whether the corporation was liable but whether the indorsement was effective to negotiate the instruments. The court held the notes were indorsed by the corporation because there was no question of the authority of the individual.

4. § 3–403(a).

5. If true, the check would not be properly chargeable to the drawer's account. § 4–401(a). *See* the discussion later in this book. *See* as illustrating the principle but applying it under UCC Article 8 in the case of a securities account (*see* UCC §§ 8–107 and 8–507), Powers v. American Express Financial Advisors, Inc., 40 UCC Rep. Serv. 2d 597 (D.Md.2000).

6. *See* note 3 and the *Spinks* case, *supra*.

7. *See, e.g., In re* Eton Furniture Co., 286 F.2d 93 (3d Cir. 1961). *See also* § 3–310.

8. *E.g.,* Sabin Meyer Regional Sales Corp. v. Citizens Bank, 502 F.Supp. 557 (N.D.Ga.1980) (bank's oral representation that drawer's account contained sufficient funds to cover certain checks not an acceptance but raised a question of negligent reporting of the status of the account). Further *see* the discussion, *infra*, concerning liability of a drawee.

9. *See, e.g.,* Wenke v. Norton, 120 Ga. App. 70, 169 S.E.2d 663 (Ga.Ct.App.1969) (agreement to assume unpaid balance of note). *But see* Abby Fin. Corp. v. Margrove Mfg. Co., 5 UCC Rep. Serv. 1088 (N.Y.Sup. Ct.1968) (allegation that corporation was "successor in interest" to maker of notes was not enough to show liability of the corporation for the notes).

10. *See* § 3–402 and, *e.g.*, Wiley v. Manufacturers Hanover Trust Co., 6 UCC Rep. Serv. 1083 (N.Y.Sup.Ct.1969); W.R. Grimshaw Co. v. First Nat'l Bank & Trust Co., 563 P.2d 117 (Okla.1977) (power to sign for another may be established as in other cases of representation and parol is admissible to prove or deny it). *See also* First Rome Bank v. Reese Oil Co., 206 Ga.App. 667, 426 S.E.2d 384 (Ga.Ct.App.1992) (employee who misused indorsement stamp nonetheless was authorized to use it).

signature, as where the instrument is purchased in good faith reliance on an assurance that a forged signature is genuine,[11] or where the deposit agreement grants authority to rely on a facsimile or other signature and no further precaution is taken in connection with the particular signature.[12]

[2] Preclusion and Ratification

[a] Preclusion

The negligence of a party may prevent the denial of an unauthorized signature that otherwise would not be effective. This is because under old Article 3 an unauthorized signature is inoperative as that of the person whose name is signed unless that person is precluded from denying it.[13] Moreover, § 3–406 provides that any person whose failure to exercise ordinary care[14] substantially contributes to the making of an

---

11. *See* old § 3–404, Official Comment 4, which recognizes the possibility of an estoppel against the person whose name is signed, as where he or she expressly or tacitly represents to an innocent purchaser that the signature is genuine. Current § 3–403(a) drops the preclusion language that appeared in old § 3–404(1) for the reason discussed in Official Comment 1 to § 3–403. However, estoppel as a general doctrine still is available through UCC § 1–103(b) to the extent it would not overlap and thus be displaced by § 3–406. *See also* note 13, *infra*. In Willey v. Mayer, 876 P.2d 1260, 23 UCC Rep. Serv. 2d 1003 (Colo. 1994), the trial court found that the failure to revoke a power of attorney to sign precluded denial of the principal's unauthorized signature made by the agent. On appeal, the majority of the Supreme Court instead found authorization under the power even though the agent signed without the principal's knowledge and for his own benefit. An estoppel may apply with respect to one other than the person whose signature is forged. *See, e.g.,* as to forged indorsements and a drawer, IFCO of South Carolina, Inc. v. Southern Nat'l Bank, 42 N.C.App. 499, 256 S.E.2d 825 (1979).

12. *Compare* Aimco Imports, Ltd. v. Industrial Valley Bank & Trust Co., 291 Pa.Super. 233, 435 A.2d 884 (1981) (upholding agreement) *with* Cumis Ins. Soc'y, Inc. v. Girard Bank, 522 F.Supp. 414 (E.D.Pa. 1981) (in dicta questioning agreement). *See also* Perini Corp. v. First Nat'l Bank, 553 F.2d 398 (5th Cir.1977); Wilmington Trust Co. v. Phoenix Steel Corp., 273 A.2d 266 (Del.1971). Official Comment 2, Case #4 to § 3–404 appears to settle any argument that might exist concerning the enforceability of such agreements as a general proposition. *See also* Official Comment 3, Case #1, to § 3–406 for a like result. In agreement is Spear Insurance Co., Ltd. v. Bank of America, N.A. 40 UCC Rep. Serv. 2d 807 (N.D.Ill. 2000) and *compare* Inn Foods, Inc. v. Equitable Co-operative Bank, 45 F.3d 594 (1st Cir.1995) (corporate resolution authorizing conduct). *But see* Federal Insurance Co. v. NCNB National Bank of North Carolina, 958 F.2d 1544 (11th Cir.1992) (corporation resolution allowed one manual and one facsimile signature on lesser checks; negligence determined when larger checks so drawn were paid). As to attribution in the case of an electronic signature, *see* Uniform Electronic Transactions Act § 9.

13. Old § 3–404(1). Thus, negligence may preclude denial of a signature. Official Comment 4 to old § 3–404. As previously stated in note 11, *supra*, current § 3–403 drops this provision, leaving only § 3–406. Of course, also as previously noted, other conduct may operate as a preclusion. *See*, for example, estoppel discussed in note 11, *supra*, and laches as discussed in Johnstown School Employees Fed. Credit Union v. Mock, 7 UCC Rep. Serv. 311 (Pa.Com.Pl. 1969) (delay of three years did not raise laches where assurances were made that the matter would be straightened out). *See also* Swiss Credit Bank v. Chemical Bank, 422 F.Supp. 1305 (S.D.N.Y.1976) (remaining silent when under a duty to speak). An unauthorized signature does operate as the signature of the unauthorized signer in favor of any person who in good faith pays the instrument or who takes it for value. § 3–403(a).

14. § 3–103(a)(7) in part sets a standard for ordinary care. This standard does not require a bank to physically examine each item (Karmin Door Co. v. BankBoston, N.A., 41 UCC Rep. Serv. 2d 1191 (Mass.Su-

forged signature[15] is precluded from asserting the lack of authority against a holder in due course, or against a drawee or other payor who pays the instrument or a person who takes it for collection in good faith.[16]

Both old § 3–406 and old § 3–404 contemplated that negligence could preclude a person asserting that a signature was unauthorized, but the provisions were not the same. Old § 3–406 required negligence that substantially contributed to the unauthorized signature and only raised the preclusion in favor of certain persons. Old § 3–404 was silent on these points. There was sound authority, however, that coordinated the two provisions. In *Trust Co. of Georgia Bank, N.A. v. Port Terminal & Warehousing Co.*,[17] the court held that a payor, who could not invoke a preclusion under old § 3–406 because it was not in good faith or had failed to adhere to reasonable commercial standards, also should not be able to raise the preclusion under old § 3–404.[18] To remove this confusion, current Article 3 deletes the preclusion language in the revised

---

per.2000) and The Guardian Life Ins. Co. of America v. Weisman, 223 F.3d 229, 42 UCC Rep. Serv. 2d 1 (3d Cir. 2000)), and rejects prior cases such as Medford Irrigation Dist. v. Western Bank, 66 Or.App. 589, 676 P.2d 329 (1984). Decisions applying the standard include Stowell v. Cloquet Co-op Credit Union, 557 N.W.2d 567 (Minn.1997); Story Road Flea Market, Inc. v. Wells Fargo Bank, N.A., 42 Cal.App.4th 1733, 50 Cal. Rptr.2d 524 (1996); Travelers Indemnity Co. v. Stedman, 910 F.Supp. 203 (E.D.Pa. 1995), modified, 925 F.Supp. 345 (E.D.Pa. 1996); and, with respect to a depositary bank (but which also was the drawer), Simcoe & Erie General Insurance Co. v. Chemical Bank, 770 F.Supp. 149 (S.D.N.Y.1991). *See also* The Guardian Life Insurance Co. of America v. Weisman case, *supra* this note, suggesting review of payee indorsements should be accomplished by depositary bank as best able to verify, and *In re* McMullen, 251 B.R. 558 (Bankr.C.D.Cal. 2000) (depositary bank negligent for accepting checks for deposit without payee indorsement; quere given § 4–205, perhaps an assertion of negligence liability for violation of § 3–307 is a sounder theory). Use of a processing system to handle a high volume of checks also does not involve an issue of good faith. Halla v. Norwest Bank Minnesota, N.A., 601 N.W.2d 449, 39 UCC Rep. Serv. 2d 1104 (Minn.App.1999). *Further see* American Bankers Association, Deposit Account Fraud Committee, Signature Verification White Paper, 9 Clarks' Bank Deposits and Payments Monthly 1 (July 2000).

15. *See* Official Comment 2 to § 3–406. § 3–406 also covers material alterations.

Discussion of this aspect of the provision appears in Chapter 6.

16. § 3–406. *See* Official Comment 1 § 3–406.

One may argue that §§ 3–404 and 3–405, create a similar rule in connection with certain situations involving unauthorized indorsements, and that it is a rule of conclusive negligence. Discussion of these sections is deferred until Chapter 7. Section 4–406 is another section of the UCC that raises a preclusion with respect to an unauthorized signatures (and alterations) premised upon negligence. Section 4–406 is discussed later in this book.

17. 153 Ga.App. 735, 266 S.E.2d 254 (1980). *See also In re* Lou Levey & Sons Fashions, Inc. Litigation, 988 F.2d 311, 19 UCC Rep. Serv. 2d 1107 (2d Cir.1993).

18. Good faith should be required in both instances, in the case of old § 3–404 that requirement arising under UCC § 1–203 (now § 1–304). Thus, the significance of the decision is the imposition of a requirement to act in accordance with reasonable commercial standards under old § 3–404(1). This requirement had no application in a case where ratification was the issue. *See, e.g.*, American Travel Corp. v. Central Carolina Bank & Trust Co., 57 N.C.App. 437, 291 S.E.2d 892 (1982). Under current § 3–103(a)(4) "good faith" now includes the observance of reasonable commercial standards of fair dealing. The obligation of good faith, even if imposed through Article 1, involves the Article 3 standard, including the observance of rea-

section that replaces old § 3–404.[19]

Examples of negligence that may constitute a preclusion in connection with a signature abound and derive from virtually unlimited contexts.[20] However, some of the more obvious ones are: a drawer who makes use of a signature stamp or other automatic signing device and is negligent in looking after it;[21] a payee who has notice that forgeries of his or her signature have occurred and is negligent in failing to prevent further forgeries by the same person;[22] a drawer who delivers or mails a check to one of two interested parties without notifying the other co-payee;[23] and a drawer who hires an employee without making basic

---

sonable standards of fair dealing, in the context of Article 3.

19. *See* note 11, *supra*.

20. *See also* Official Comment 1 to § 3–406; note 14, *supra*; Webb Carter Construction Co. v. Louisiana Central Bank, 922 F.2d 1197 (5th Cir.1991) (cashing corporate checks for employee not authorized to cash checks by corporate resolution); *c.f.* Simcoe & Erie General Insurance Co. v. Chemical Bank, 770 F.Supp. 149 (S.D.N.Y. 1991); New Jersey Steel Corp. v. Warburton, 139 N.J. 536, 655 A.2d 1382 (failure to follow own procedures). Section 3–406 also may preclude raising an alteration because of negligence. The clearest example is leaving excessive spaces when drawing the instrument. *See, e.g.*, Owensboro Nat'l Bank v. Crisp, 608 S.W.2d 51 (Ky.1980); HSBC Bank USA v. F & M Bank Northern Virginia, 246 F.3d 335 (4th Cir.2001); discussion in Chapter 6, *infra*; and Official Comments 1 and 3 (Case #3) to § 3–406.

21. *See* § 3–406, Official Comment 3, Case #1, and First Nat'l Bank & Trust Co. v. Cutright, 189 Neb. 805, 205 N.W.2d 542 (Neb. 1973). *See by analogy* Zambia National Commercial Bank v. Fidelity International Bank, 855 F.Supp. 1377 (S.D.N.Y.1994), *amended in part on a different issue*, 1994 WL 440717 (S.D.N.Y.1994) (using same source to print blank checks and assemble signature list equivalent to leaving one's checkbook and signature stamp unguarded; however, no link between this conduct and actual forgeries). On the other hand, no fault was found when blank checks and a protectograph were stolen from a locked office in a locked building. Fred Meyer, Inc. v. Temco Metal Prods. Co., 267 Or. 230, 516 P.2d 80 (Or. 1973). *But see* Savemart, Inc. v. Bowery Sav. Bank, 117 Misc.2d 947, 461 N.Y.S.2d 144 (N.Y.Sup. App.Term 1982), where the court refused summary judgment in favor of the ostensible drawer when a thousand blank tellers check forms were lost or stolen and a forged one came into the hands of the plaintiff. The court suggested there was an issue of fact as to possible negligence. *See also* Michaeli v. Greater New York Sav. Bank, 129 Misc.2d 1096, 498 N.Y.S.2d 90 (N.Y.Sup. App.Term 1985) and Dubin v. Hudson County Probation Department, 267 N.J.Super. 202, 630 A.2d 1207 (Law Div.1993).

22. *See, e.g.*, Cooper v. Union Bank, 9 Cal.3d 371, 107 Cal.Rptr. 1, 507 P.2d 609 (Cal. 1973). A related kind of negligence might involve failure to notify a person who had cashed previous instruments. *See* Hartford Accident & Indem. Co. v. Dean's Shop–Rite, Inc., 48 N.C.App. 615, 269 S.E.2d 282 (1980). *But see* Chicago Heights Currency Exchange, Inc. v. Par Steel Prods. & Serv. Co., 123 Ill.App.3d 1054, 79 Ill.Dec. 275, 463 N.E.2d 829 (1st Dist. 1984). Along the same lines, *see* Union National Bank v. Daneshvar, 33 Ark.App. 171, 803 S.W.2d 567 (Ark.Ct.App.1991) (failure to promptly provide affidavit of loss concerning missing checks).

23. *E.g.*, Fidelity & Deposit Co. v. First Nat'l Bank, 98 Wis.2d 474, 297 N.W.2d 46 (Wis.Ct.App.1980). *See also* Koerner & Lambert v. Allstate Ins. Co., 374 So.2d 179 (La.Ct.App.1979). A variation of this fact situation is mailing a check to the wrong one of two persons with the same name. *See* § 3–406, Official Comment 3, Case #2. *See* Park State Bank v. Arena Auto Auction, Inc., 59 Ill.App.2d 235, 207 N.E.2d 158 (2d Dist. 1965). But the somewhat similar situation of picking a faithless agent to whom the instrument is delivered usually is not considered to involve negligence. *Compare* Florida Bar v. Allstate Ins. Co., 391 So.2d 238 (Fla.Dist.Ct.App. 3d Dist.1980) *and* Tormo v. Yormark, 14 UCC Rep. Serv. 962 (D.N.J.1974) (no negligence) *with* Hutzler v. Hertz Corp., 39 N.Y.2d 209, 383 N.Y.S.2d 266, 347 N.E.2d 627 (N.Y. 1976) (the unwise selection of an agent raises a preclusion). *See also* Terry v. Kemper Ins. Co., 390 Mass. 450, 456 N.E.2d 465 (Mass. 1983) (special statute excusing insurance company for payment to agent authorized to receive check). Current § 3–405(a)(3) is unlikely to influence these results. *See also* Official Comment 2 to § 3–406.

inquiries that would have disclosed past indiscretions and who then gives the employee free access to write checks with virtually no supervision.[24]

Ordinary negligence will suffice to raise the preclusion; gross negligence is not required.[25] Whether the negligence must directly and proximately cause the unauthorized signature, or whether the correct test is that it be a substantial factor was a matter of some dispute under old Article 3. To illustrate, in one case, a court held that the breach by a stockbroker of the New York Stock Exchange rule to "know your customer" constituted negligence that contributed to the loss when the customer's indorsement on the check made out to him was forged, even though the breach of the rule was not the proximate cause of the loss.[26] On the other hand, in another case the failure to conduct a customer investigation pursuant to the rules of the New York Stock Exchange, which led to checks payable to the plaintiff individually and as guardian of her minor children having the indorsement forged on them by her attorney, was characterized as negligent conduct leading merely to the unwarranted issuance of the checks, and was not held to be the proximate cause contributing to the forgery itself.[27] Overall, a substantial number of cases hold that in appropriate circumstances negligence in the conduct of the business of the issuer of the instrument may result in a preclusion. For example, a failure to verify loan applications that were fraudulent is negligence that will raise a preclusion to asserting forged indorsements on the instruments later issued.[28] The "substantially con-

---

24. *E.g.*, Commercial Credit Equip. Corp. v. First Ala. Bank, N.A., 636 F.2d 1051 (5th Cir.1981). *See also* Ashley–Hall Interiors, Ltd. v. Bank of New Orleans, 389 So.2d 850 (La.Ct.App. 4 Cir.1980); K & K Manufacturing, Inc. v. Union Bank, 129 Ariz. 7, 628 P.2d 44 (Ariz.Ct.App.1981); Atlantic Mutual Insurance Co. v. The Provident Bank, 79 Ohio Misc.2d 5, 669 N.E.2d 901 (Ohio Mun.Ct.1996).

25. *E.g.*, West Penn Admin., Inc. v. Union Nat'l Bank, 233 Pa.Super. 311, 335 A.2d 725 (1975) (a finding of gross negligence is not required). Current Article 3 uses a "failure to exercise ordinary care." *See* note 14, *supra*.

The negligent party is not made liable in damages because of the negligence but rather is precluded from questioning the signature. Otherwise the extent of the loss would involve the possibility of recovery from the wrongdoer, and that cannot be determined at the time of the litigation. Thus the decision would have to be made on the unsatisfactory basis of burden of proof. Official Comment 1 to § 3–406. *See also* White Sands Forest Products, Inc. v. First National Bank of Alamogordo, 132 N.M. 453, 50 P.3d 202 (2002). *But note* §§ 3–404(d) and 3–405(b).

26. Fidelity & Deposit Co. v. Chemical Bank New York Trust Co., 65 Misc.2d 619, 318 N.Y.S.2d 957 (Sup.Ct.1970), *aff'd without opinion*, 39 A.D.2d 1019, 333 N.Y.S.2d 726 (App.Div. 1972). *See also* Dominion Constr., Inc. v. First Nat'l Bank, 271 Md. 154, 315 A.2d 69 (Md. 1974) (former standard of "proximate cause" has been replaced with the "substantial factor" test).

27. Bagby v. Merrill Lynch, Pierce, Fenner & Smith, Inc., 491 F.2d 192 (8th Cir. 1974). An unusual case of a similar nature is Ed Stinn Chevrolet, Inc. v. National City Bank, 28 Ohio St.3d 221, 503 N.E.2d 524 (Ohio 1986), where the dealer's employee stole cash from the cash box and then forged checks to replace it. The court did not consider the dealer's failure to supervise proximately relevant to the forgeries.

28. *E.g.*, Fidelity & Cas. Co. v. Constitution Nat'l Bank, 167 Conn. 478, 356 A.2d 117 (Conn. 1975) (finance company manager failed to verify information which would have revealed fraudulent loan applications); Prudential Ins. Co. v. Marine Nat'l Exch. Bank, 55 F.R.D. 436, 11 UCC Rep. Serv. 129 (E.D.Wis.1972) (failure to verify loan applications that turned out to be false). *See also* United Bank v. Mesa N.O. Nelson Co., 121 Ariz. 438, 590 P.2d 1384 (Ariz. 1979) (laxness in the conduct of business relations with the forger raises a preclusion); Thompson Maple Prods., Inc. v. Citi-

tributes" test is used by current § 3–406 rather than a "direct and proximate cause" test.[29]

Section 3–406 raises the preclusion in favor of a person who in good faith pays the instrument or takes it for value or for collection, but if the person raising the preclusion itself fails to exercise ordinary care in paying or taking the instrument and that failure substantially contributes to loss, the loss is allocated between the person precluded and the person asserting the preclusion according to the extent to which the failure of each to exercise ordinary care contributed to the loss.[30] Thus, it is not an all or nothing situation, and, subject to the "substantially contributes" threshold,[31] cases under old Article 3 could still be relevant. However, cases under old Article 3 are not especially clear with respect to what will constitute a failure to act in accordance with ordinary care or reasonable commercial standards. A failure to determine the lack of authority of the party negotiating the instrument appears as the most prevalent reason why a person paying the instrument may lose the benefit of the preclusion to some extent. Courts, however, have not employed this reason in a uniform manner. For example, in one case where a depositary bank had accepted for deposit checks payable to an entity and indorsed to the depositor by an unrestricted indorsement that was rubber-stamped, the failure to investigate the authenticity of the indorsement was held to raise an issue of fact as to whether the payor had acted in accordance with reasonable commercial standards.[32] On the

---

zens Nat'l Bank, 211 Pa.Super. 42, 234 A.2d 32 (1967) (drawer's negligent conduct of business but for which the checks would not have been issued was sufficient to preclude). *But see* East Gadsden Bank v. First City Nat'l Bank, 50 Ala.App. 576, 281 So.2d 431 (Ala.Civ.App.1973) and Commonwealth v. National Bank & Trust Co., 469 Pa. 188, 364 A.2d 1331 (Pa. 1976) (mere laxity in the conduct of business affairs is not such negligence as will raise a preclusion).

29. Official Comment 2 to § 3–406; Vectra Bank of Englewood v. Bank Western, 890 P.2d 259 (Colo.Ct.App.1995) (applying "substantially contributes" test); *compare* with City Check Cashing, Inc. v. Jul–Ame Constr. Co., 326 N.J.Super. 505, 742 A.2d 141 (App.Div.1999) (applying proximate cause analysis under old Article 3).

30. § 3–406(b). Because "good faith" requires the observance of reasonable commercial standards of fair dealing under § 3–103(a)(4), and "ordinary care" under § 3–103(a)(7) means the observance of reasonable commercial standards prevailing in the area in which the person is located with respect to the business in which the person is engaged, it would appear some overlap in standards could exist since under UCC § 1–304 good faith is involved in every contract or duty under the UCC. Nonetheless, the two are not the same, and "ordinary care" should constitute a broader standard. See § 3–104, Official Comment 4. This standard settles the issue litigated in Travelers Ins. Co. v. Jefferson Nat'l Bank, 404 So.2d 1131 (Fla.Dist.Ct.App. 3d Dist.1981), as to whether more than the bank's own standards were involved.

31. This threshold should prevent cases like Owensboro Nat'l Bank v. Crisp, 608 S.W.2d 51 (Ky.1980) where the bank's negligence, if any there was, surely was too slight to have "substantially" contributed to the loss. *But see* Lichtenstein v. Kidder, Peabody & Co., 840 F.Supp. 374 (W.D.Pa. 1993), where the plaintiff's conduct was characterized as "perhaps irresponsible", but not negligent so as to invoke the comparison. On the application of the "substantially contributes" standard, *see* The Bank/First Citizens Bank v. Citizens & Assocs., 44 UCC Rep. Serv.2d 1072 (Tenn.Ct.App. 2001), *rev'd on other grds.*, 82 S.W.3d 259 (Tenn.2002).

32. Continental Bank v. Wa–Ho Truck Brokerage, 122 Ariz. 414, 595 P.2d 206 (Ariz.Ct.App.1979). The burden of establishing the matter as a defense rests upon the person asserting it. United States v. Bankers Trust Co., 17 UCC Rep. Serv. 136 (E.D.N.Y.1975). Note that cases on either side of this example are easier to decide.

other hand, in *Aetna Casualty & Surety Co. v. Hepler State Bank*,[33] the court stated that a bank that fails to inquire concerning an individual cashing or depositing a check made payable to a business entity and then indorsed engages in an unreasonable commercial practice as a matter of law.[34]

[b] Ratification

An unauthorized signature, including a forgery, also may be made good by ratification.[35] Ratification with knowledge[36] retroactively[37] validates the unauthorized signature on the instrument by making it the signature of the ratifying party. It does not, however, relieve the actual signer from liability to the person whose name is signed,[38] and the

---

See, e.g., Brite Lite Lamps Corp. v. Manufacturers Hanover Trust Co., 34 UCC Rep Serv. 1221 (N.Y.Sup.Ct.1982) (violation of restrictive indorsement) (*but see* Spielman v. Manufacturers Hanover Trust Co., 60 N.Y.2d 221, 469 N.Y.S.2d 69, 456 N.E.2d 1192 (N.Y. 1983) (restrictive indorsement which specified account of culprit was no notice)); Matco Tools Corp. v. Pontiac State Bank, 614 F.Supp. 1059 (E.D.Mich.1985) (check payable to both corporation and individual, and individual had authority generally to indorse); and Thompson v. Lake County Nat'l Bank, 47 Ohio App.2d 249, 353 N.E.2d 895 (Ohio Ct.App.1975) (forged check paid over valid stop order). *See also* Halla v. Norwest Bank Minnesota, N.A., 601 N.W.2d 449, 39 UCC Rep. Serv. 2d 1104 (Minn.App.1999) (failure to have a policy against accepting for deposit checks that name a business as a payee related to question of ordinary care, not good faith).

33. 6 Kan.App.2d 543, 630 P.2d 721 (Kan.Ct.App.1981).

34. *See also* American Machine Tool Distribs. Ass'n. v. National Permanent Fed. Sav. & Loan Ass'n., 464 A.2d 907 (D.C. 1983); Continental State Bank v. Miles General Contractors, Inc., 661 S.W.2d 770, 38 UCC Rep. Serv. 243 (Tex.Ct.App.1983); Pargas, Inc. v. Estate of Taylor, 416 So.2d 1358 (La.Ct.App. 3 Cir.1982), where a district manager diverted corporate checks into his personal account by indorsing them in blank with a rubber stamp and the court found the bank did not act in a commercially reasonable manner; Allied Insurance Center v. Wauwatosa Savings & Loan Association, 200 Wis.2d 369, 546 N.W.2d 544 (Wis.Ct.App.1996); and Martin Glennon, Inc. v. First Fidelity Bank, N.A., 279 N.J.Super. 48, 652 A.2d 199 (App.Div.1995). *But* in Hartford Accident & Indem. Co. v. Dean's Shop–Rite, Inc., 48 N.C.App. 615, 269 S.E.2d 282 (N.C.Ct.App.1980), the court believed that a person who routinely cashes checks for its customers and who knows the person for whom a check is cashed acts reasonably. *See also* American Nat'l Ins. Co. v. Fidelity Bank, N.A., 691 F.2d 464 (10th Cir.1982), where a bank was held to have acted properly in accepting for deposit almost three hundred checks payable to an insurance company and indorsed in blank by a rubber stamp to the account of an agent for the company. The insurance company had been grossly negligent in not checking out the agent before utilizing him, however, and never checked on or supervised the agent thereafter. Perhaps it is unfortunate that it was all or nothing under old § 3–406 and that comparative negligence did not have a place. Under current § 3–406(b), where it does, the expectation is that litigation will decrease. This also is likely because current Article 3 substantially alters the loss allocation plan for this recurrent fact situation. This is discussed in Chapter 7, *infra*. An exhaustive discussion of this area, at least with respect to old § 3–419(3), appears in Official Comment, Forged Indorsements, Depositary Banks, and the Defense of Section 3–419(3), 18 HOUS. L. REV. 103, 185–88 (1980).

35. § 3–403(a) and UCC § 1–201(b)(41).

36. *E.g.*, United Bank v. Mesa N.O. Nelson Co., 121 Ariz. 438, 590 P.2d 1384 (Ariz. 1979) (no ratification where plaintiff unaware of the forgeries). *See also* Martin Glennon, Inc. v. First Fidelity Bank, N.A., 279 N.J.Super. 48, 652 A.2d 199, 25 UCC Rep.Serv.2d 842 (App.Div.1995).

37. Official Comment 3 to § 3–403.

38. § 3–403(c). Obtaining judgment against the unauthorized signer by the person whose name is signed does not itself constitute a ratification. This is true even when there is a partial recovery from the unauthorized signer, at least to the extent of the loss not recovered. Twellman v. Lindell Trust Co., 534 S.W.2d 83 (Mo.Ct.App.

ratification does not cure a violation of the criminal law.[39]

Ratification can occur in a variety of ways. It can stem from conduct as well as from express statements, including the retention of benefits received in the transaction with knowledge of the unauthorized signature.[40] Another example of ratification occurred in a case where a contractor, who became aware that four checks payable to it had been collected by a subcontractor without authority on unauthorized indorsements, agreed to forego collecting its interest in the checks because the subcontractor had a 75 percent interest in the proceeds of the checks;[41] in foregoing an objection, the contractor would keep a good business relationship with the subcontractor. But objection to a note bearing an unauthorized signature is not precluded merely because the corporate maker has paid other notes also bearing unauthorized signatures by the same signers after knowledge of the problem.[42]

[3] Liability and Capacity

The nature of the contractual liability of a party on an instrument is determined by the capacity in which the party signs the instrument. On a draft or a check, the person who issues it will sign it and will be liable as a drawer.[43] The person to whom the draft or check is delivered, the payee, if that person negotiates the instrument with an indorsement, will be liable as an indorser,[44] and all later indorsers also may have liability.[45] The drawee[46] does not sign and is not liable on the instrument, unless the drawee accepts it.[47] Finally, the person signing a note and undertaking to pay, the maker, is liable on the instrument as a maker,[48]

1976); and Hennesy Equip. Sales Co. v. Valley Nat'l Bank, 25 Ariz.App. 285, 543 P.2d 123 (Ariz.Ct.App.1975).

39. § 3–403(c).

40. *E.g.*, Guaranty Bank & Trust Co. v. Federal Reserve Bank, 454 F.Supp. 488 (W.D.Okla.1977), *superseded on another point by a change in the law as stated in* State Bank & Trust, N.A. v. First State Bank of Texas, 39 UCC Rep. Serv.2d 191 (N.D.Okla.1999), *rev'd on other grounds*, 242 F.3d 390 (10th Cir.2000) (retention of benefits is a major element in finding ratification); Starkey Constr., Inc. v. Elcon, Inc., 248 Ark. 958, 457 S.W.2d 509 (Ark. 1970) (materialmen who accepted payments due from proceeds of checks on which indorsements were forged held to have ratified the indorsements); Eutsler v. First Nat'l Bank 639 P.2d 1245 (Okla.1982) (payee whose indorsement forged by his brother indicated to bank that it would be worked out with brother); Stella v. Dean Witter Reynolds, Inc., 241 N.J.Super. 55, 574 A.2d 468 (1990) (intent to allow broker who forged indorsement on check for proceeds of sale to have proceeds to invest). *But see* Carpenter v. Payette Valley Coop., 99 Idaho 143, 578 P.2d 1074 (Idaho 1978) (no ratification where the manager of a cooperative without authority guaranteed a member's note by indorsing it in the name of the cooperative, even though a part of the proceeds were used to pay a debt owed to the cooperative and another part was used to purchase property in which the cooperative acquired a security interest).

41. Thermo Contracting Corp. v. Bank of New Jersey, 69 N.J. 352, 354 A.2d 291 (N.J. 1976).

42. Eggleston v. George Braun Packing Co., 470 S.W.2d 69 (Tex.Civ.App.1971).

43. § 3–414. *See also* § 3–103(a)(3) defining "drawer." Under § 3–412, however, the liability of the drawer of a cashier's check (§ 3–104(g)) or other draft drawn on the drawer is that of a maker.

44. § 3–204(b).

45. § 3–415.

46. § 3–103(a)(2).

47. §§ 3–408 and 3–413. *See also* § 3–103(a)(1) defining "acceptor."

48. § 3–412. *See also* § 3–103(a)(5) defining "maker" and note 43, *supra*.

and the liability of an indorser of a note is the same as in the case of an indorser of a draft or check.[49]

¶ 4.03 The Drawer

[1] Description of Liability

The drawer of a draft or check is the person who signs the instrument to order payment.[50] The liability of the drawer of an instrument, if any,[51] derives from the drawer's signature, which by statute constitutes an engagement that upon dishonor of the instrument and any necessary notice of dishonor or protest, the drawer will pay the amount of the instrument to the holder or to any indorser who takes it up.[52] The drawer's liability on the instrument is conditional, and for that reason a drawer under old Article 3 was characterized as a "secondary party;"[53] current Article 3 does not use the term "secondary party."

[2] Conditions to Liability

[a] Dishonor

[i] Presentment As a Condition to Dishonor

Because by drawing the draft the drawer has ordered the drawee to pay, the refusal of the drawee to pay, and the resultant dishonor of the instrument,[54] is a condition to the liability of the drawer on the instrument.[55] Of course, to determine what the action of the drawee will be, presentment of the instrument to the drawee normally must be made. Presentment is a demand for acceptance or payment made upon the

---

49. An agent who properly signs an instrument has no liability on it; the principal is the liable party. An agent that does incur liability is liable in the capacity in which the signature appears. An accommodation party is liable in the capacity in which the signature appears. These matters are discussed in Chapter 5. Other liability of any party beyond the instrument, such as on the underlying obligation or in warranty, is discussed in Chapter 7.

¶ 4.03

50. § 3–103(a)(3).

51. A drawer may disclaim drawer's liability by drawing without recourse. § 3–414(e) (except on a check). "Check" is defined in § 3–104(f).

52. § 3–414(b). If the instrument when signed was incomplete, it can be enforced as completed in accordance with authority. § 3–115(b). Thus, a check is a promise of future payment at the time of presentation. Estate of Kohlhepp v. Mason, 25 Utah 2d 155, 478 P.2d 339 (Utah 1970). Section 3–414 divides drawer's liability into two categories. Liability on an unaccepted draft essentially is as above. Liability on a draft accepted by a bank is discharged. § 3–414(c). The reason is the holder is not relying on the drawer. The liability of the bank as acceptor is substituted. § 3–413 and Quistgaard v. EAB European American Bank & Trust Co., 182 A.D.2d 510, 583 N.Y.S.2d 210 (App.Div. 1st Dep't 1992). If the drawer's liability is important, the holder can obtain a guaranty or an indorsement. Official Comment 3 to § 3–414. Liability on a draft accepted by a person other than a bank is the same as that of an indorser. A "bank" is defined in §§ 3–103(c) and 4–105(1).

53. Old § 3–102(1)(d).

54. In certain instances, such as where the draft itself so provides, a refusal to accept as opposed to pay the instrument also may constitute dishonor. What constitutes dishonor is discussed, *infra*, under this heading.

55. §§ 3–414(b) and (d) and 3–502(b) and (d). *But see*, as to the drawer of a cashier's check or like instrument, §§ 3–414(a) and 3–412.

maker, acceptor, drawee, or other payor by or on behalf of the holder.[56] To illustrate the concept, in one case a collecting bank thought a draft was payable through a bank rather than being drawn upon it.[57] It therefore did not contemplate that the bank would make payment when it forwarded the draft to the bank.[58] Nevertheless, the court held that because any item sent for collection is sent for eventual payment, presentment had been made.[59]

An instrument is dishonored when either a necessary or optional presentment is duly made and due acceptance or payment is refused or cannot be obtained within the prescribed time,[60] or presentment is

---

56. § 3–501(a).

57. Engine Parts v. Citizens Bank, 92 N.M. 37, 582 P.2d 809 (N.M. 1978).

58. A bank with respect to which an instrument is payable through is a collecting bank. § 4–106(a).

59. *But see* Western Air & Refrigeration Inc. v. Metro Bank of Dallas, 599 F.2d 83 (5th Cir.1979) (agreement between payor bank and payee to leave check until funds came into drawer's account to pay it was not a presentment or demand for payment). To the same effect is Bank of Miami v. Banco Industrial Y Ganadero Del Beni, S.A., 515 So.2d 1038 (Fla.Dist.Ct.App. 3d Dist. 1987) (such items are "collection" items; that is, demand items not presented for immediate payment but delivered with the understanding that the bank will pay the item if and when sufficient funds are deposited in the drawer's account to cover the amount of the item). *See also* Regulation CC, 12 CFR § 229.2(u) and Official Commentary concerning noncash items.

60. Under § 3–502, dishonor of instruments is categorized and comprehensive rules are stated. A demand note is dishonored when presented and not paid. § 3–502(a)(1). A time note payable at or through a bank or whose terms require presentment is dishonored if presented and not paid. § 3–502(a)(2). Otherwise the note is dishonored if it is not paid when due. § 3–502(a)(3).

An unaccepted non-documentary draft that is a check is dishonored if presented for payment otherwise than for immediate payment over the counter when returned or notice of dishonor or nonpayment is sent or when the bank becomes accountable under §§ 4–301 and 4–302. Thus, a refusal by the payor bank to pay a check delivered to it with a request for payment and a return of it to the presenter constitutes a dishonor. Merriman v. Sandeen, 267 N.W.2d 714 (Minn.1978). If not a check, or if a check is presented over the counter there is dishonor if presentment is made and payment is refused. If the draft is a time draft, dishonor occurs if it is not paid when presented and due or later when presented, or if it is not accepted when presented. § 3–502(b). The rules for unaccepted documentary drafts are similar except payment or acceptance may be delayed for up to three business days. § 3–502(c). *But see* UCC §§ 5–108 and 5–116(d).

Accepted demand drafts are dishonored if presented and not paid and time drafts are dishonored if not paid when presented and due or later when presented. § 3–502(d).

The Official Comments to § 3–502 elaborate on the changes made from old Article 3 and the reason: essentially to modernize the rules.

There is authority that invoking a right of setoff constitutes a dishonor. *See* abstract of opinion in Joseph v. United of America Bank, 131 Ill.App.2d 434, 266 N.E.2d 438 (1st Dist. 1970) (digest of opinion at 131 Ill.App.2d 434, 266 N.E.2d 438, 8 UCC Rep. Serv. 1098) stating that a setoff of proceeds of cashier's checks payable to a payee against alleged obligations of the payee to the bank constitutes dishonor of the instruments. There is some authority that charging a service fee on presentment might constitute dishonor. Your Style Publications, Inc. v. Mid Town Bank & Trust Co., 150 Ill.App.3d 421, 103 Ill.Dec. 488, 501 N.E.2d 805 (1st Dist.1986). In its Federal Register Notice accompanying its proposal on same day settlement (RIN 7100–ABOI, Docket No. R–0723, Proposed amendment of Regulation CC, 12 CFR pt. 229), however, the Federal Reserve Board remarked that the UCC does not explicitly sanction or prohibit barriers to same-day settlement and thus the payment of presentment fees to obtain same-day settlement has become a common business practice. Moreover, inasmuch as only the drawer has standing to assert wrongful dishonor (the court in the *Your Style Publications* case, however, found the holder of the instrument qualified as a third party beneficiary of the deposit contract

excused[61] and the instrument is not duly accepted or paid.[62] Return of the instrument for lack of a proper indorsement is not a dishonor.[63] Moreover, if the draft or an indorsement of it permits representment of the draft after a dishonor, the holder may elect to treat the draft as not dishonored without affecting the liability of any secondary party (drawer or indorser) bound by the term in order to present it again up to the end of the permitted time period.[64] If there is such a term in the draft, this would allow a collecting bank to represent the draft for payment in the instance where the draft arrives before a covering deposit. This is done on occasion anyway, but at some risk, as discussed later in this book.[65]

An acceptance by the drawee which varies the draft as presented in any manner may be treated by the holder as a dishonor.[66] The types of variances covered include conditional acceptances, acceptances for part of the amount, acceptances to pay at a different time from that required by the draft, acceptance by less than all of the drawees, or any other engagement that changes the essential terms of the draft.[67] The common acceptance, "Payable only as originally drawn and when properly indorsed," is not an acceptance which varies the draft.[68] The terms of a draft also are not varied by an acceptance to pay at any particular bank or place in the United States unless the acceptance states that the draft is to be paid only at such bank or place.[69] Upon dishonor and subject to any necessary notice of dishonor and protest, the holder has an immediate right of recourse against the drawers and indorsers.[70]

Presentment for payment, unless excused, is necessary to charge any

between the drawer and the bank, but even under that theory the holder would be in the same position as the drawer), a provision allowing the fee in the deposit agreement should settle the matter. *See also* Moorehouse v. Chase Manhattan Bank, 76 S.W.3d 608 (Tex.Ct.App.2002) (check cashing fee alleged to result in dishonor of check; while conceded such a claim belonged only to drawer, argued conversion alternatively, and fraud in non-disclosure did not intend to pay full amount; alternative claims rejected). A variation on the theme occurred in Messing v. Bank of America, 143 Md.App. 1, 792 A.2d 312 (Md. Ct.Spec.App.2002), *cert. granted*, 369 Md. 301, 799 A.2d 1262 (2002), where a "thumbprint signature" was required and, when the check holder refused, wrongful dishonor was argued, and rejected on the basis there was no dishonor as no proper presentment occurred. *Further see* the following text as to what may or may not constitute dishonor.

61. § 3–504, discussed, *infra* in the case of the drawer.

62. § 3–502(e).

63. § 3–501(b)(3)(i). *See also* note 60, *supra*.

64. Current Article 3 leaves this to contract; compare § 3–504.

65. In the case of a check, such a provision would be inconsistent with the availability schedules in Regulation CC, 12 CFR pt. 229, unless the check qualifies as a noncash item. Regulation CC, 12 CFR § 229.2(u). *But see* Regulation CC, 12 CFR § 229.13(c).

66. § 3–410(a). If the election is to treat the acceptance as dishonoring the draft, the drawee is entitled to have the variant acceptance canceled. On the other hand, if the holder assents to the variant acceptance, each drawer and indorser who does not affirmatively assent is discharged under § 3–410(c).

67. Official Comment 1 to § 3–410.

68. Rockland Trust Co. v. South Shore Nat'l Bank, 366 Mass. 74, 314 N.E.2d 438 (Mass. 1974).

69. § 3–410(b).

70. § 3–414(b) and (d). The liability of the drawer of a cashier's check or other draft drawn on the drawer is governed in § 3–412. This matter is discussed, *supra*, in Chapter 2, as well as in this chapter.

drawer.[71] Presentment for acceptance will result in dishonor only if the draft is presented for acceptance before it is payable and is not accepted, or its date of payment depends on presentment for acceptance and it is not accepted when presented.[72] Thus, presentment for acceptance is optional in other cases and, accordingly, a refusal to certify[73] an ordinary check is not a dishonor of it.[74]

[ii] Time of Presentment

A duly made presentment would seem to involve one that is timely.[75] Current Article 3 omits the detailed timing rules in old § 3–503 in favor of allowing collection of instruments in ways that make sense commercially without having to be concerned about a formal presentment on a given day and because the old rules often were inconsistent with practice that seldom involves face to face dealings.[76] Thus, § 3–502 on dishonor in essence incorporates the times for presentment in describing when dishonor occurs,[77] and, in addition, other sections, to maintain the liability of a secondary party (drawer or indorser), require presentment for payment or collection within 30 days after that party becomes liable on the instrument.[78] Presentment must be made at a reasonable hour and, if at a bank, during the banking day.[79]

If an act is a condition precedent to a right of action against the drawer, the drawer is not liable and cannot be sued without the act,

---

71. §§ 3–414(b) and 3–502(b). *But see* note 70, *supra*, as to the drawer of a cashier's check or other draft drawn on the drawer.

72. § 3–502(b)(3) and (4) deal with when presentment for acceptance will result in dishonor under Article 3. *See* Official Comment 4 to that section.

73. Certification is a form of acceptance. § 3–409(d). Once a check is stamped "CERTIFIED" and signed, a bank cannot claim a check was not certified because the bank had not completed its established procedure. Quistgaard v. EAB European American Bank & Trust Co., 182 A.D.2d 510, 583 N.Y.S.2d 210 (App. Div., 1st Dept.1992). *See also* the *Messing* case, *supra* note 60, where it also was argued the bank accepted the check because it processed it prior to demanding further identification; this argument failed.

74. § 3–409(d). *But see* Gallinaro v. Fitzpatrick, 359 Mass. 6, 267 N.E.2d 649 (Mass. 1971) (two requests by payee of a check for certification which were refused constituted sufficient presentment to revive the underlying obligation). §§ 3–502(b) and 3–409(d) would seem to prevent this result under current law.

75. Other elements are listed in § 3–501(b), such as the proper place and means and what must be done. § 3–501(b) also describes what may be required by the person to whom presentment is made.

76. Official Comments 2 and 3 to § 3–502.

77. § 3–502(a) for notes; § 3–502(b) for unaccepted non-documentary drafts, including for checks the applicable rules in UCC Article 4; § 3–502(c) for unaccepted documentary drafts; § 3–502(d) for accepted drafts; and § 3–502(e) for other cases. *See also* § 3–502(f).

78. §§ 3–414(f) and 3–415(e). *See, e.g., In re* Lindenbaum's, Inc., 2 UCC Rep. Serv. 495 (Bankr.E.D.Pa.1964), applying the similar former presumption where the check was deposited for collection two weeks after its issuance.

79. 3–501(b)(4). Section 4–104(a)(3) defines "banking day" as that part of the day when the bank is open to the public to carry on most of its banking functions. *See also* § 4–108. As banks carry on more of their functions on Saturday, this definition becomes more difficult of application. Compare Regulation CC, 12 CFR § 229.2(f) and (g). For an interesting case determining that the Federal Reserve Bank of Chicago was deemed to have a twenty-four hour banking day, *see* Oak Brook Bank v. Northern Trust Co., 256 F.3d 638 (7th Cir.2001).

however long delayed, occurring, unless excused.[80] Given that a "dishonor" is defined in terms of a duly made presentment,[81] and presentment involves timing considerations,[82] it might appear that an unexcused delay in presentment is fatal to preservation of liability because the delay frustrated a condition to the liability.[83] However accurate an analysis that may be for a complete failure to present, nonetheless a failure to make proper presentment in a timely manner discharges the drawer only as provided in the Code,[84] a point discussed, *infra*.

[iii] *Manner of Presentment*

A duly made presentment is one that is made in an appropriate manner.[85] A presentment is sufficient, and the instrument is dishonored by nonacceptance or nonpayment, even though the party making presentment may be liable for improper collection methods.[86] Presentment may be made by any commercially reasonable means,[87] including through a clearing house,[88] or, in the case of an item not payable by, through, or at a bank, unless otherwise instructed, by sending to the party to accept or pay a notice in record form that the collecting bank holds the item for acceptance or payment.[89] These methods are permissive and other possible methods are not foreclosed.[90]

Presentment should be made at the place of acceptance or payment specified in the instrument, or, if there is none, at the place of business or residence of the party to accept or pay.[91] An instrument made payable at a bank in the United States must be presented at such bank,[92] except that, in view of the increase in presentment at centralized bookkeeping centers and electronic processing centers maintained or used by payor banks, many of which are at locations other than the locations of the banks themselves, presentment may be made at a place requested by the

---

80. § 3–414(b).

81. § 3–502.

82. § 3–502.

83. § 3–414(b) and (d) (§ 3–415(a) for indorsers).

84. § 3–414(f). In the case of an indorser, this inquiry would not seem to matter as to result. § 3–415(e).

85. Notes 60, 75 and 79, *supra*.

86. For example, in the pre-Code case of Minneapolis Sash & Door Co. v. Metropolitan Bank, 76 Minn. 136, 78 N.W. 980 (Minn. 1899), the court held that mailing the check to the drawee was not the exercise of reasonable care. § 4–202(a)(1) also requires a collecting bank to use ordinary care in presenting an item or sending it for presentment, but § 4–204(b)(1) allows a collecting bank to send any item direct to the payor bank.

87. § 3–501(b)(1). This may not include by telephone. Kirby v. Bergfield, 186 Neb. 242, 182 N.W.2d 205 (Neb. 1970). *But see* § 3–501(b)(1) (oral communication, if reasonable).

88. § 3–501(b)(1). "Through a clearing house" means that presentment is not made when the demand reaches the clearing house, but when it reaches the obligor or the obligor's designee. *See* Capital City First Nat'l Bank v. Lewis State Bank, 341 So.2d 1025 (Fla.Dist.Ct.App. 1st Dist.1977), where the court held that presentment through the clearing house to a bank by a member of the clearing house with whom the payor had contracted for computer services was presentment to the payor even though the payor bank was not a signatory to a local clearing house agreement.

89. §§ 3–501(b)(1), 4–212. *See* Batchelder v. Granite Trust Co., 339 Mass. 20, 157 N.E.2d 540 (Mass. 1959).

90. Official Comment 4 to old § 4–204. As to truncated checks, *see* § 4–110 and Regulation CC, 12 CFR § 229.36(c).

91. §§ 3–501(b)(1) and 3–111.

92. § 3–501(b)(1).

payor.[93] Presentment may be made to any one of two or more makers, acceptors, drawees or other payors,[94] or to any person who has authority to make or refuse the acceptance or payment.[95]

The party to whom presentment is made may require the exhibition of the instrument; reasonable identification of the person making presentment and evidence of the person's authority to make it if made for another;[96] and that the instrument be indorsed as necessary and be presented for acceptance or payment in accordance with its terms, any applicable agreement or applicable law; or, absent such direction, at any place reasonable in the circumstances, and may require a signed receipt on the instrument for any partial or full payment and its surrender upon full payment.[97] A demand for compliance with any or all of these requirements will not constitute a dishonor, as a failure to comply with any requirement invalidates the presentment and thus due acceptance or payment is not refused.[98]

Presentment in a legal sense may be deferred without dishonor until the next business day following the presentment if actual presentment is made after an established cut off hour,[99] payment or acceptance without dishonor may be delayed for up to three business days in the case of an unaccepted documentary draft, and a person entitled to acceptance may

---

93. §§ 3–501(b)(1), 3–111 and 4–204(c). *Compare* Capital City First Nat'l Bank v. Lewis State Bank, 341 So.2d 1025 (Fla.Dist. Ct.App. 1st Dist.1977) (delivery of a check to bank C pursuant to an arrangement whereby bank C performed computer services for the payor and other banks constituted presentment to the payor bank as it was the place or person designated by the payor bank for receipt of presentment) *with* Catalina Yachts v. Old Colony Bank & Trust Co., 497 F.Supp. 1227 (D.Mass.1980) (delivery to a bank other than the payor bank of a check for computer processing pursuant to an agreement between the banks was not presentment to the payor bank). The *Catalina Yachts* decision distinguishes the *Capital City* case on the basis of the agreement of the parties. *See, e.g.,* Miller & Scott, Commercial Paper, Bank Deposits and Collections, and Commercial Electronic Fund Transfers, 38 Bus. Law. 1129, 1164–66 (1983). Subsequent cases are not entirely consistent but authority is in favor of finding presentment. *See, e.g.,* Idah–Best, Inc. v. First Security Bank, N.A., 101 Idaho 402, 614 P.2d 425 (Idaho 1980) (no presentment); Central Bank of Alabama, N.A. v. Peoples Nat'l Bank, 401 So.2d 14 (Ala.1981) (presentment); South Sound Nat'l Bank v. First Interstate Bank, 65 Or.App. 553, 672 P.2d 1194 (Or.Ct.App. 1983) (presentment); and Chrysler Credit Corp. v. First Nat'l Bank & Trust Co., 582 F.Supp. 1436 (W.D.Pa.1984), *aff'd*, 746 F.2d 200 (3d Cir.1984) (presentment). Regulation CC, 12 CFR § 229.36(b) now settles the matter in favor of presentment for checks. *See also* Los Angeles National Bank v. Bank of Canton, 31 Cal.App.4th 726, 37 Cal.Rptr.2d 389, 25 UCC Rep. Serv. 2d 873 (2d Dist.1995) (receipt of check occurred when check was available for pickup at clearing house by processing agent).

94. § 3–501(a) and (b)(1). *See, e.g.,* Horney v. Covington County Bank, 716 F.2d 335 (5th Cir.1983).

95. § 3–501(b)(1).

96. Reasonable identification depends on the circumstances. If the person making presentment is known, no requirement of identification may be reasonable. Official Comment 2 to old § 3–505. *See also* the *Messing* case, *supra* note 60.

97. § 3–501(b)(2) and (3). *See also* § 4–110 and Official Comment to § 3–501.

98. Old § 3–505(2). Current Article 3 omits this rule as implicit in the dishonor provisions. *See* the *Messing* case, *supra* note 60. The person presenting has a reasonable time in which to comply, however, and the time for acceptance or payment runs from the time of compliance. Like most other UCC rules, the effect of this rule can be varied by agreement. Official Comment to § 3–501.

99. § 3–501(b)(4).

agree to late acceptance.[100] Payment may be deferred without dishonor pending reasonable examination to determine whether the instrument is properly payable, but the general rule is payment or settlement must be made before the close of business on the day of presentment.[101]

[b] *Notice of Dishonor*

Unless excused, notice of the dishonor of the instrument may be given to any person who may be liable on the instrument, and it must be given to an indorser and to the drawer of a draft accepted by other than a bank if the acceptor dishonors.[102] Thus, under current Article 3, the liability of the drawer of an unaccepted draft is treated as a primary liability and notice of dishonor is necessary only with respect to indorser's liability.[103]

Notice of dishonor may be given by or on behalf of the holder of the instrument or any party who has received notice, or any other party who can be compelled to pay the instrument.[104] Any necessary notice of dishonor must be given by a bank before its midnight deadline[105] and with, respect to an instrument in collection, by any other person before 30 days after receipt of notice of dishonor.[106] The notice may be given in

---

100. § 3–502(c) and (f). *But see* UCC §§ 5–108 and 5–116(d).

101. § 3–502. Presentment occurs upon receipt of the demand for payment or acceptance. Official Comment to § 3–501. Part 5 of Article 3 generally is subject to provisions in Article 4. *See* §§ 3–502(b)(1), 4–109(a) (which does not extend to checks in light of Regulation CC), 4–212 (*see* note 89, *supra*), and 4–502.

102. §§ 3–414(d), 3–415(c), and 3–503(a). Under old §§ 3–508(1), 3–501(2)(b), 3–413(2) notice of dishonor was a condition to the liability of the drawer. Under current Article 3, the drawer remains liable on a draft accepted by a non-bank, but in that case the drawer's liability is identical to that of an indorser and is stated that way. A drawer's liability is released on a draft accepted by a bank because holders normally do not rely on the drawer to guarantee the bank's solvency. § 3–414(c). If the holder wishes to hold the drawer, the specific guaranty of payment of the drawer should be obtained, or the drawer's indorsement. Official Comment 3 to § 3–414.

103. §§ 3–414(b), 3–415(c), and 3–503(a).

104. § 3–503(b). Under § 4–202(a)(2), a collecting bank must use ordinary care in sending notice of dishonor or nonpayment or in returning an item other than a documentary draft to the bank's transferor (or directly to the depository bank) after learning that the item has not been paid or accepted. *See, e.g.*, Sun Bank/Miami, N.A. v. First Nat'l Bank, 698 F.Supp. 1298 (D.Md. 1988). Notice operates for the benefit of all parties who have rights on the instrument against the party notified. § 3–503(b). Notice of dishonor may be given to an agent of the person entitled to it. Old § 3–508(1) stated in the bank collection context that notice could be given to the principal or customer or to another agent or bank from which the instrument was received. Under old § 3–508(6), notice may be given either to the insolvent person or to the representative of the estate when any party is in insolvency proceedings instituted after the issue of the instrument. And under old § 3–508(7), notice could be sent to the last known address of a dead or incompetent party or given to a personal representative. These latter points are not explicitly covered in current § 3–503(a).

105. § 3–503(c)(i). *See also* §§ 4–202(b), 4–214, 4–301 and 4–501. These matters are discussed in more detail later in this book. In Lufthansa German Airlines v. Bank of America Nat'l Trust & Sav. Ass'n, 478 F.Supp. 1195 (N.D.Cal.1979), *aff'd*, 652 F.2d 835 (9th Cir.1981), the court noted under old § 4–212(1) (current § 4–214(a)), that the midnight deadline for giving notice of charge back is deferred until the collecting bank "learns the facts," and thus that the timing for a notice of dishonor is not necessarily the same as for notice of charge back.

106. § 3–503(c)(ii). Otherwise, notice is due within 30 days of dishonor. As in the case of a delay in presentment, a question

any reasonable manner.[107] A Federal Reserve operating circular may set the requirements,[108] as may a clearing house rule.[109] A notice that states the obligor of the instrument, the date and amount of the instrument, the payee and persons to whom notice was given, and that the instrument was presented, is unpaid, and has been protested, is sufficient.[110] Notice of dishonor may be given in oral, electronic, or written form.[111] Section 4–301, however, requires a payor bank to send written notice of dishonor or nonpayment if the item is held for protest or is otherwise unavailable for return in order to revoke a settlement for the item.[112] Substantively the two provisions are not in conflict because the payor bank is not seeking to hold the drawer on the drawer's contract, but rather is asserting a right to charge back to avoid payment or accountability. In *Available Iron & Metal Co. v. First National Bank*,[113] the court recognized this, but, in addition, resolved any perceived conflict in favor of the requirement of written notice in this context by reference to the predecessor section to § 4–102(a), which provided that in the event of conflict the provisions of Article 4 control those of Article 3. Sending the instrument bearing a stamp, ticket, or writing stating that acceptance or payment has been refused, or sending a notice of debit with respect to the instrument, will be sufficient in any event.[114]

---

arises as to the effect of a delayed notice of dishonor, since notice of dishonor purports to be a condition precedent to liability. Old § 3–501(2)(b) provided that a failure to give timely notice discharged a drawer only as stated in old § 3–502(1)(b). Under Article 3, *see* §§ 3–503(a) and 3–415(c) The point is discussed, *infra*.

107. § 3–503(b).

108. Bank of Wyandotte v. Woodrow, 394 F.Supp. 550 (W.D.Mo.1975). *See* §§ 3–503(b) and 3–102(c).

109. Security Trust Co. v. First Nat'l Bank, 79 Misc.2d 523, 358 N.Y.S.2d 943 (Sup.Ct.1974). *See* § 3–503(b).

110. First Stroudsburg Nat'l Bank v. Nixon, 10 UCC Rep. Serv. 852 (Pa.Com.Pl. 1971). Specifically, the notice must reasonably identify the instrument and indicate that it has been dishonored or has not been paid or accepted. Return of an instrument given to a bank for collection is a sufficient notice. *See also* § 3–505(a)(2). As to checks, *see* Regulation CC, 12 CFR § 229.30(d) (reason for return required). A misdescription that does not mislead the party notified should not invalidate notice. As to the consequence if it does, *compare* Frost National Bank v. Midwest Autohaus, Inc., 241 F.3d 862 (7th Cir.2001) (item returned stamped "uncollected funds" rather than "insufficient funds" misled and breached Regulation CC, thus rendering one liable for damages for negligence). *Compare also* Regulation CC § 229.33 (notice of nonpayment).

111. § 3–503(b): notice may be given by any commercially reasonable means, including an oral, written, or electronic communication. Under old § 3–508(4), written notice is given when sent although it is not received. Under current § 3–503 the rule is no different since the requirement is notice be given. UCC § 1–202. Telephone notice has been held to satisfy old § 3–508(3). Wells Fargo Bank v. Hartford Nat'l Bank & Trust Co., 484 F.Supp. 817 (D.Conn.1980). *But see* discussion, *infra*, in the check collection system.

112. §§ 4–215(a)(3), 4–302. Neither the Uniform Electronic Transactions Act nor the federal "E-sign" act impact on this, but federal Regulation CC does as described in the Official Comments and later in this book. A 2002 amendment to § 4–301 now substitutes record notice for written notice and also allows return of an image of the item if there is an agreement so authorizing. § 4–301(a).

113. 56 Ill.App.3d 516, 13 Ill.Dec. 940, 371 N.E.2d 1032 (1st Dist.1977).

114. § 3–503(b) and 3–505(a)(2). *See also* note 110, *supra*. The point is discussed further in a later chapter.

[c] Protest

The last condition under old Article 3 to the drawer's contract of liability on the instrument in some instances was any necessary protest of dishonor.[115] A protest is a certificate identifying the instrument and certifying dishonor.[116] If utilized, it generally is due by the time that notice of dishonor is due.[117]

[d] Discharge, Evidence, and Excuse

[i] Discharge

To charge the drawer, the instrument must have been dishonored and where required in the case of a draft accepted by a non-bank, notice of dishonor[118] given. Even if the applicable conditions of the drawer's contract have not been properly met because of delay, the drawer is not discharged from contractual liability on the instrument, except to the extent that the drawer is deprived of funds maintained with the drawee or payor bank to pay the instrument because the drawee or payor bank became insolvent during the period of delay.[119] In that event only, the drawer will be pro tanto discharged upon giving an assignment to the holder of the instrument of the drawer's rights against the drawee or payor bank in respect of the funds.[120] Thus, in one case where uncertified checks were held by the payee for more than thirty days after their date of issue and when finally presented for payment were returned for insufficient funds, the drawer who asserted the unexcused delay was held not to be per se discharged because the record did not show that the drawee bank became insolvent during the delay.[121]

[ii] Evidence

A drawer may avoid liability on the drawer's contract because of inadequacies of proof with respect to the establishment of the drawer's liability. For example, a concurring opinion in *Valley Bank & Trust Co. v. First Security Bank, N.A.*[122] emphasized the insubstantial proof that notice of dishonor had occurred. In this respect, the following evidence is admissible and creates a presumption of dishonor and of any notice of dishonor therein shown:[123]

---

115. Old §§ 3–413(2), 3–501(3). The requirement essentially only applied with respect to international drafts. But it also still is generally required by foreign law. Official Comment 6 to old § 3–501. A collecting bank under old § 4–202(1)(d) must use ordinary care in making or providing for any necessary protest in order to avoid liability on its own account. Current § 4–202 deletes this provision as protest is eliminated as a requirement in current Article 3. However, protest may still be relevant in some contexts. For example, *see* notes *infra*, and Official Comment to § 3–505.

116. § 3–505(b).

117. Old § 3–509(4).

118. §§ 3–414(b) and (d), § 3–503(a) and (c). *But see* § 3–414(a) and (c).

119. § 3–414(f).

120. *Id.*

121. Grist v. Osgood, 90 Nev. 165, 521 P.2d 368 (Nev. 1974). Under § 3–414(f), *see* Official Comment 6 to § 3–414.

122. 538 P.2d 298 (Utah 1975).

123. § 3–505.

(1) a document regular in form in accordance with the statutory requirements which purports to be a protest;[124]

(2) the purported stamp or writing of the drawee, payor bank, or presenting bank on the instrument or accompanying it stating that acceptance or payment has been refused for reasons consistent with dishonor;[125]

(3) any book or record of the drawee, payor bank, or any collecting bank kept in the usual course of business which shows dishonor, even though there is no evidence of who made the entry.[126]

[iii] *Excuse*

Any deficiency in meeting the conditions of the drawer's contract may be excused. The provision on excuse is § 3–504.[127]

Under old Article 3, delay could be excused when the party was without notice that presentment, protest, or notice of dishonor was due.[128] This might occur, for example, where an instrument has been accelerated without the party's knowledge.[129] Absent an explicit rule, delay also is excused when the delay is caused by circumstances beyond the control of the party and reasonable diligence is exercised after the cause of the delay ceases to operate.[130]

Any of the requirements of the drawer's contract themselves may be excused when the party to be charged has waived them (or any of them) expressly or by implication either before or after they are due.[131] The

---

124. § 3–505(a)(1). This provision recognizes that the only function of protest is that of proof of dishonor. Thus, even where it is not required, protest may have definite benefits, for example, where process does not run to another state and the taking of depositions is a slow and expensive matter. Official Comment 6 to old § 3–501.

125. § 3–505(a)(2). This is one of two substitutes for protest as proof of dishonor provided by old § 3–510. Reasons that are satisfactory evidence of dishonor consistent with due presentment include insufficient funds, account garnished, no account, and payment stopped. Reasons that are not evidence of dishonor but merely of justifiable refusal to pay or accept are indorsement or signature missing, signature illegible, forgery, payee or date altered, postdated, and not drawn on us. Official Comment 2 to old § 3–510. *See also* note 110, *supra*.

126. § 3–505(a)(3).

127. Old Article 3 had other provisions, like old § 3–504(2)(c). Current Article 3 has no similar explicit statement; the prior statement provided in part that if neither the party to accept or pay nor anyone authorized to act for that party is present or accessible at the place of acceptance or payment specified in the instrument or at the place of business or residence of the party to accept or pay, presentment is excused. *See also* old § 3–416(5) (when words of guaranty are used, presentment, notice of dishonor, and protest are not necessary to charge the user). Current § 3–419(b) and (c) address this by stating that words of guaranty are indication of accommodation status as maker, indorser or other liability capacity.

128. Old § 3–511(1). Consistent with its approach to state general rules to resolve not only past issues but also future ones, current § 3–504 does not have an explicit statement but considering all sections together, including the reduced circumstances where these requirements exist and the approach of current Article 3, no different result should be reached. Official Comment to § 3–504.

129. Official Comment 2 to § 3–511.

130. § 3–504(c). Alleged unforeseen and unavoidable employee absenteeism was held to raise a triable issue of fact in Rich v. Franklin Sav. Bank, 18 UCC Rep. Serv. 451 (N.Y.Sup.Ct.1975).

131. § 3–504(a)(iv) and (b)(ii); Fred Shearer & Sons, Inc. v. Prendergast, 152 Or.App. 657, 955 P.2d 324 (Or.Ct.App. 1998), rev'd on other grounds, 152 Or.App. 657, 955 P.2d 324 (1998).

waiver may be express or implied, oral or written, and may be given before or after the proceeding waived is due. It may be, and often is, a term of the instrument when it is issued.[132] For example, see the language in the sample form of note in Chapter 1. The requirements also should be deemed excused when the party has dishonored the instrument, has countermanded payment,[133] or otherwise has no reason to expect nor right to require that the instrument be accepted or paid.[134] For example, evidence that the drawer had insufficient funds on deposit to pay checks will support a finding that presentment is excused because the drawer would have no reason to expect or to require that the checks be paid.[135] Last, the requirements should be deemed excused when, notwithstanding reasonable diligence, the presentment or protest cannot be made nor the notice given.[136] Where a draft has been dishonored by nonacceptance, a later presentment for payment and any notice of dishonor and protest for nonpayment are excused unless in the meantime the instrument has been accepted.[137]

If any unmet but applicable conditions of the drawer's contract have been excused, or if any delay is excused, the drawer is liable on the instrument. Recovery against the drawer will be granted unless a defense is established,[138] and, even if one is established, recovery still will be granted if the holder is a holder in due course.[139] Thus in *Hebel v. Ebersole*,[140] the court determined that the holder in due course of the check had a right of action against the drawer, who had stopped

---

132. Where the waiver is embodied in the instrument itself, it is binding upon all parties, but where it is written above the signature of an indorser, it binds that person only. Old § 3–511(6) (omitted in revised § 3–504 as unnecessary but no change in result should occur). A waiver of protest is also a waiver of presentment and of notice of dishonor even though protest is not required. *See* § 3–504(b) and Official Comment to § 3–505. A waiver of presentment is also a waiver of notice of dishonor. § 3–504(b).

133. § 3–504(a)(ii), (iv) and (v). § 3–504(b) on notice of dishonor is not explicit. The drawer of a check who has stopped payment on it is not entitled to notice of dishonor from the collecting bank. Klein v. Tabatchnick, 418 F.Supp. 1368 (S.D.N.Y.1976), *modified on other grounds*, 610 F.2d 1043 (2d Cir.1979).

134. *See* note 131, *supra*. Section 3–504(a)(ii) explicitly states an excuse for presentment exists if a maker or acceptor is dead or is in insolvency proceedings. Since prompt payment or acceptance in these cases is unlikely, presentment is excused so immediate recourse to others can be pursued, and they can file any necessary claim in the probate or insolvency proceedings. But this should not displace other law that, for example, may require a claim to be made to an estate. *See also* § 4–216 dealing with bank insolvency and preference. Section 3–504(a)(iii) and (b)(i) also recognize the terms of the instrument may excuse either presentment or notice.

135. Canal–Randolph Anaheim, Inc. v. Wilkoski, 78 Cal.App.3d 477, 143 Cal.Rptr. 789 (1978) superseded on another point by legislation as noted in WDT—Winchester v. Nilsson, 27 Cal.App.4th 516, 32 Cal.Rptr.2d 511 (1994). *See also* the *Prendergast* case, *supra* note 131, as to liability as an indorser.

136. § 3–504(a)(i). Again, § 3–504(b) is not explicit.

137. § 3–502(f). Some courts concluded the comparable provision in old Article 3 excused notice of dishonor for a check once presented and dishonored and re-presented in the hope covering funds have arrived. *See, e.g.*, Reynolds–Wilson Lumber Co. v. Peoples Nat'l Bank, 699 P.2d 146 (Okla. 1985), overruling an earlier case, Goodman v. Norman Bank of Commerce, so holding. This is discussed in a later chapter.

138. § 3–308(b).

139. § 3–305(b). Of course, a real defense would preclude recovery.

140. 543 F.2d 14 (7th Cir.1976).

payment, free of any defense the drawer might assert against the person who had indorsed the check to the holder.

¶ 4.04 The Drawee

[1] *Absence of Liability As Drawee*

Even though ordered by the drawer in the draft to pay it, the drawee of a draft has no liability on the instrument to the holder of it for a failure to do so.[141] A drawee is not liable on the instrument until the drawee accepts it.[142] In essence, this proposition is nothing more than a restatement of the rule that no person is liable on an instrument unless the person has signed the instrument.[143] A drawee does not sign a draft, unless the draft is accepted by the drawee's signed engagement on the draft, which is an acceptance.[144]

¶ 4.04

141. The drawee may have liability to the drawer, however, for the failure to pay a properly payable draft. § 4–402. Liability for wrongful dishonor is discussed in a later chapter. *But see also* note 60, *supra*; specifically the *Your Style Publications* case.

142. § 3–408. *E.g.*, Brown v. South Shore Nat'l Bank, 1 Ill.App.3d 136, 273 N.E.2d 671 (1971).

143. § 3–401(a), discussed, *supra*.

144. § 3–409(a) and *see* note 73, *supra*. A drawee, however, may incur liability to the holder in other ways, such as under § 4–302 for the late return of an item. Old § 3–409(2) also stipulates that nothing in old § 3–409 shall affect any liability in contract, tort, or otherwise arising from an obligation or representation which is not an acceptance. Current § 3–408 omits this provision as unnecessary. § 3–408, Official Comment. Considerable litigation occurs on this point for obvious reasons; much of it is not successful. *See, e.g.*, Outdoor Technologies, Inc. v. Allfirst Financial, Inc., 44 UCC Rep.Serv.2d 801 (Del.Super.Ct. 2001) (no evidence of false statement); Sabin Meyer Regional Sales Corp. v. Citizens Bank, 502 F.Supp. 557 (N.D.Ga.1980) (oral representation of bank officer to payee that drawer's account would contain necessary funds was not an acceptance, but the bank might be liable for negligence in reporting the status of the account); Carroll v. Twin City Pontiac Used Cars, Inc., 397 So.2d 42 (La.Ct.App. 2 Cir.1981) (breach of promise to honor drafts); Bigger v. Fremont Nat'l Bank & Trust Co., 215 Neb. 580, 340 N.W.2d 142 (Neb. 1983) (statement possibly created an estoppel); First Nat'l Bank v. Anderson Ford–Lincoln–Mercury, Inc., 704 S.W.2d 83 (Tex.Ct.App.1985) (negligent assurances); Hansman v. Imlay City State Bank, 121 Mich.App. 424, 328 N.W.2d 653 (1982) (right of bank to set off funds deposited for payment of checks questioned); First Georgia Bank v. Webster, 168 Ga.App. 307, 308 S.E.2d 579 (Ga.Ct.App.1983) (negligent statement check was good); North Carolina Nat'l Bank v. McCarley & Co., 34 N.C.App. 689, 239 S.E.2d 583 (N.C.Ct.App.1977) (a drawee is liable in conversion for paying a check on an unauthorized indorsement); note 8, *supra;* and Mitchell Buick & Oldsmobile Sales, Inc. v. McHenry Savings Bank, 235 Ill.App.3d 978, 176 Ill.Dec. 662, 601 N.E.2d 1360 (2d Dist.1992) (statement if buyer deposited $10,000 or more bank would pay the check only enforceable as to funds actually collected by bank). On the other hand, *see, e.g.*, Atlantic Cement Co. v. South Shore Bank, 730 F.2d 831 (1st Cir. 1984) (no third party beneficiary theory); Happy Cattle Feeders, Inc. v. First Nat'l Bank, 618 S.W.2d 424 (Tex.Civ.App.1981) (bank can pay items from account in order convenient even if knows holder of check sold goods which were resold and proceeds deposited in account); Galaxy Boat Mfg. Co. v. East End State Bank, 641 S.W.2d 584 (Tex.Ct.App.1982) (oral promise to pay check not enforceable); Schaller v. Marine Nat'l Bank, 131 Wis.2d 389, 388 N.W.2d 645 (Wis.Ct.App.1986) (course of dealing cannot establish a duty); Thiele v. Security State Bank, 396 N.W.2d 295 (N.D.1986) (bank's practice of honoring overdrafts did not create an obligation to do so; *but see* Spencer Companies v. Chase Manhattan Bank, N.A., 81 B.R. 194 (D.Mass.1987) (longstanding policy of paying overdrafts terminated without notice of change in policy stated cause of action)); Barber v. United States Nat'l Bank, 90 Or.App. 68, 750 P.2d 1183 (1988); Total Aviation Servs. Inc. v. United Jersey Bank, 39 UCC Rep. Serv. 969 (E.D.N.Y.1984) (ability to refuse to pay an

Moreover, the drawee is not liable to the holder of a draft even if the drawer has on deposit with the drawee sufficient funds to enable the payment of the draft, or the drawee otherwise owes the drawer more than the amount of the draft. A check or other draft does not of itself operate as an assignment of any funds in the hands of the drawee available for its payment.[145] This is because in a number of states the first assignee of a right to payment prevails over a second assignee even if the latter collects first, and the problem for a drawee that might technically have notice of the assignment, were the UCC rule otherwise, is thus obvious.[146] However, an assignment may appear from additional facts and, when an intent to make an assignment is clear, the check may be the means by which the assignment is effected.[147]

[2] Liability As Acceptor

[a] Acceptance and Certification

A drawee does become liable on an instrument if the drawee accepts the instrument,[148] but the liability is as an acceptor and not as drawee.[149]

---

unindorsed check: on this, *see* § 4–205); and Green Property Corp. v. O'Callaghan, Saunders & Stumm, P.C., 177 Ga.App. 686, 340 S.E.2d 652 (1986) (bank not liable to payee of check for loss of interest on funds).

145. § 3–408. *See, e.g.*, Rex Smith Propane, Inc. v. National Bank of Commerce, 372 F.Supp. 499 (N.D.Tex.1974). An incident of this rule are the cases that litigate when a check constitutes payment or a transfer for a variety of issues. For example, in Smart v. Woo, 20 UCC Rep. Serv. 2d 1288 (Va. Cir. Ct.1993), *aff'd*, 247 Va. 365, 442 S.E.2d 690 (1994), the issue was whether there was sufficient delivery of checks written and delivered to the payee by the dying drawer. The court, citing this rule, held no. A similar analysis where a discount depended on payment was used in Staff Builders of Philadelphia, Inc. v. Koschitzki, 18 UCC Rep. Serv. 2d 228 (E.D.Pa.1992), *rev'd*, 989 F.2d 692 (3d Cir.1993), and where the issue was whether there was a preference in bankruptcy under Bankruptcy Code § 547 by the Supreme Court in Barnhill v. Johnson, 503 U.S. 393, 112 S.Ct. 1386, 118 L.Ed.2d 39 (1992). *But see* In re Lee & Ota, 108 F.3d 239 (9th Cir.1997) as to § 547(c)(4). On the other hand, on appeal in the *Staff Builders* case, the court of appeals determined the appropriate date was delivery (or the date of the check if postdated) assuming the check was paid, an analysis that seems consistent with § 3–310(b). Staff Builders of Philadelphia, Inc. v. Koschitzki, 989 F.2d 692 (3d Cir. 1993). Likewise the analysis of the court in Hall–Mark Electronics Corp. v. Sims (*In re* Lee), 179 B.R. 149, 26 UCC Rep. Serv. 2d 386 (9th Cir. BAP 1995), where the instrument was a cashiers check, as to the cashiers check.

146. *See* Note, Assignment by Check, 60 YALE L.J. 1007, 1022–25 (1951). The no-assignment rule has other consequences. For example, it will determine whether a garnishment is successful. *See, e.g.*, State Bank v. Stallings, 19 Utah 2d 146, 427 P.2d 744 (Utah 1967) (garnishments placed against drawer's account before checks presented to drawee for payment were entitled to priority). As noted in note 145, *supra,* it determines whether a preferential transfer in bankruptcy has occurred. *See also In re* Sportsco, 12 B.R. 34 (Bankr.D.Ariz.1981); 11 U.S.C. § 547(c)(2); *In re* Roehrich, 107 B.R. 675 (Bankr.D.N.D.1989); and Matter of Kimball, 16 B.R. 201, 33 UCC Rep. Serv. 627 (Bankr.M.D.Fla.1981) (preference period begins on delivery not payment of a cashier's check as no right to stop payment exists and customer's funds are transferred at issuance).

147. *In re* Schenck's Estate, 63 Misc.2d 721, 313 N.Y.S.2d 277 (Sur.Ct.1970); Fourth Street Bank v. Yardley, 165 U.S. 634, 17 S.Ct. 439, 41 L.Ed. 855 (1897). This sort of liability beyond the instrument is discussed in Chapter 7, *infra*.

A debit of the drawer's account by the drawee pursuant to a letter of advice of an international sight draft, as allowed by old § 3–701(2), does not effect an assignment to the holder of the draft. Official Comment 2 to old § 3–701. Current Article 3 omits Part 7 of old Article 3 as outdated and addressing practice outside the United States.

148. §§ 3–408 and 3–413.

149. § 3–413. An acceptor engages that the acceptor will pay the instrument ac-

An acceptance is the drawee's signed engagement to honor the draft as presented.[150] It must be written on the draft,[151] but it may consist of a signature alone.[152] As a signature is whatever symbol a party executes or adopts with the present intention to authenticate a writing,[153] the signature must amount to more than merely the name of the drawee printed on the instrument. Cases that have considered the status of money orders that bear a bank's printed name have divided on this issue; the better reasoned ones have determined they are equivalent to ordinary checks and that the name of the bank imprinted on the instrument does not constitute an acceptance.[154] Certification of a check is acceptance.[155]

Customarily the drawee's signature for acceptance is written vertically across the face of the instrument but, since the drawee has no reason to sign for any other purpose, a signature in any other place, even on the back of the instrument, is sufficient. Moreover, no particular words such as "accepted" or "certified" need appear, but words indicating an intent to refuse to honor the instrument are not an acceptance.[156] The signature need not be dated, but where the draft is payable at a fixed period after sight and the acceptor fails to date the acceptance, the

---

cording to its tenor at the time the engagement is made or as completed pursuant to § 3–115. Section 3–413(a)(i) clarifies that this is so even though the acceptance limits the obligation to the draft as originally drawn. This can be important if the instrument is raised after issuance. *See also* § 3–413(b).

150. § 3–409(a).

151. § 3–409(a). Local custom or usage whereby the failure to return a re-presented item within ten days amounts to an agreement to pay it will not suffice as an acceptance. Bank of America v. Security Pac. Nat'l Bank, 23 Cal.App.3d 638, 100 Cal.Rptr. 438 (1972). Acceptance for honor, virtual acceptance by a written promise to accept drafts to be drawn, and collateral acceptance by a separate writing are eliminated by the UCC as obsolete. Thus even though a check guarantee plan might not be obsolete, a bank's liability under it is a matter of other law and is not an acceptance. Which is to say, as noted in note 144, *supra*, that a drawee may, however, have liability in contract, tort, or otherwise arising from the separate writing or any other obligation or representation. Finally, while acceptance by delay or refusal to return the instrument is eliminated, a drawee may be liable in such a case for conversion under the general law of conversion under § 3–420, Official Comment 1. *See, e.g.*, Messing v. Bank of America, 143 Md.App.

1, 792 A.2d 312 (Md.Ct.Spec. 2002), *cert. granted*, 799 A.2d 1262 (2002).

152. § 3–409(a).

153. UCC § 1–201(b)(37).

154. *See, e.g.*, Krom v. Chemical Bank New York Trust Co., 38 A.D.2d 871, 329 N.Y.S.2d 91 (App.Div. 3d Dep't 1972); Garden Check Cashing Serv., Inc. v. First Nat'l City Bank, 25 A.D.2d 137, 267 N.Y.S.2d 698 (App.Div. 1st Dep't 1966), *aff'd*, 18 N.Y.2d 941, 277 N.Y.S.2d 141, 223 N.E.2d 566 (N.Y. 1966). Cases to the contrary are Sequoyah State Bank v. Union Nat'l Bank, 274 Ark. 1, 621 S.W.2d 683 (Ark. 1981), and Interfirst Bank Carrollton v. Northpark Nat'l Bank, 671 S.W.2d 100 (Tex.Ct.App. 1984). These cases find acceptance in the drawee's name and emphasize that these instruments are widely regarded as the equivalent of cashier's checks. Current Article 3 settles this issue and treats ordinary money orders as regular checks. The discussion appears in Chapter 1, *supra*. *See also*, *infra*, Chapter 8.

155. § 3–409(d).

156. Official Comment 2 to § 3–409. Once a check is stamped "CERTIFIED" and signed, a bank cannot claim the check was not certified because procedures were not completed. Quistgaard v. EAB European American Bank & Trust Co., 182 A.D.2d 510, 583 N.Y.S.2d 210 (App.Div. 1st Dept. 1992).

holder may complete it by supplying a date in good faith.[157] An acceptance becomes operative when completed by delivery or notification.[158]

The liability of the drawee as an acceptor of the instrument is to pay the instrument according to its tenor at the time of the acceptance or as completed pursuant to the provisions on incomplete instruments.[159] Thus acceptance of a draft in effect makes the draft the note of the acceptor.[160] For that reason, under Article 3, if a draft is accepted by a bank, the drawer is discharged regardless of when or by whom acceptance was obtained,[161] and prior indorsers are discharged.[162] If a bank certifies a check before returning it for lack of proper indorsement, the drawer is discharged.[163]

An acceptor admits the genuineness of the drawer's signature[164] and the existence of the payee and the payee's then capacity to indorse, but not the genuineness or the presence of the signature of the payee or the indorsers.[165] Further, in practical effect a bank certifying a check represents that the drawer has sufficient funds on deposit to pay the check and that the funds will not be permitted to be withdrawn to the prejudice of the holder of the check because the acceptor is liable even if it has failed to set aside and hold funds belonging to the drawer.[166]

[b] Consequences of Acceptance

The certification of a drawer's check terminates the ability to stop payment on it by the drawer.[167] The bank, in certifying the check,

---

157. § 3–409(c).

158. § 3–409(a). Acceptance is thus an exception to the usual rule that no obligation on an instrument is effective until delivery of the instrument. *See* the discussion in Chapter 3, *supra*.

159. § 3–409(c). A mistaken acceptance may be subject to withdrawal, but it must relate to the account balance or genuineness of a signature. *See* § 3–418 and Quistgaard v. EAB European American Bank & Trust, 182 A.D.2d 510, 583 N.Y.S.2d 210 (App.Div. 1st Dept.1992). Incomplete instruments are dealt with in § 3–115. A draft may be accepted although it has not been signed by the drawer or is otherwise incomplete or is overdue or has been dishonored. § 3–409(b).

160. *E.g.*, Program Aids Co. v. W.R. Bean & Son, Inc., 4 UCC Rep. Serv. 210 (N.Y.Sup.Ct.1967) (in an action to collect on trade acceptances drawn by plaintiff upon defendant, payable to the order of plaintiff, and accepted by defendant, defendant's liability was to be determined as if the instruments were negotiable notes).

161. § 3–414(c). As Official Comment 3 explains, holders that have a bank obligation do not normally rely on the drawer. A holder who wishes to may obtain a guaranty or an indorsement of the drawer.

162. § 3–415(d).

163. § 3–414(c).

164. This is the end result under § 3–418, which makes payment final, and § 3–417, which does not allow a drawee to recover if payment is made on a forged instrument.

165. Old § 3–413(3); current § 3–413 omits this provision. C. Norton, Law of Bills and Notes 147–148 (2d ed. 1896) tells us when the drawee accepts a bill the drawee assents to what the drawer holds out—that there is a payee to whom the instrument is issued and that the payee may order it paid to another. Moreover, while a drawee is estopped if there is failure to detect a forged drawer's signature, the same cannot be true for that of the payee. These propositions exist either in § 3–418 or as a general rule through UCC § 1–103(b), and no need exists to perpetuate the archaic expression of them.

166. *See* § 3–411 and, *e.g.*, Wallach Sons, Inc. v. Bankers Trust Co., 62 Misc.2d 19, 307 N.Y.S.2d 297 (Civ. Ct. 1970). Of course, normally a debit is made to the drawer's account and a credit to the certified check account of a bank. In some circumstances, however, an acceptor may have a defense against one not a holder in due course or reliance payee. This is discussed, *infra*, later in this book.

167. §§ 4–403(a) and 4–303(a)(1).

obligates itself to a person entitled to enforce the instrument to pay the amount for which the check is drawn.[168] In an effort to reach the same result for cashier's checks, some courts have held that a cashier's check is *accepted* by its drawee-drawer in advance by the act of issuance and therefore it is not subject to countermand.[169] The difficulty with this analysis, other than it being entirely unnecessary and not reaching the real issue which is must the drawer pay, is that the implication in its rule sometimes creates a problem for which an exception must then be created. For example, in *Anderson, Clayton & Co. v. Farmers National Bank*,[170] the bank refused to honor its cashier's check on the ground the consideration for it had failed. The court allowed the defense when the check was presented by a party to the instrument with whom the bank had dealt.[171] When this sort of an exception is not recognized, one may get a result as in *Florida Frozen Foods, Inc. v. National Commercial Bank & Trust Co.*,[172] where the court allowed the holder of a cashier's check, issued in exchange for checks payable to the holder and drawn by a depositor of the bank that the holder knew was filing bankruptcy, to recover on the basis the bank could not stop payment.[173] Thus, the

---

168. §§ 3–413(a); 3–418. *See also* § 3–413(b). The obligation is to the person entitled to enforce the instrument under § 3–301 or the drawer or indorser that pays it, but acceptance only is final in favor of a person who took the instrument in good faith and for value or in good faith changed position in reliance.

169. *E.g.*, Laurel Bank & Trust Co. v. City Nat'l Bank, 33 Conn.Supp. 641, 365 A.2d 1222 (1976); Abilities, Inc. v. Citibank, N.A., 87 A.D.2d 831, 449 N.Y.S.2d 242 (App.Div. 2d Dep't 1982) (a cashier's check is considered accepted when issued); Wertz v. Richardson Heights Bank & Trust, 495 S.W.2d 572 (Tex.1973); Yukon Nat'l Bank v. Modern Builders Supply, Inc., 686 P.2d 307 (Okla.Ct.App.1984); Bank One, Merrillville, N.A. v. Northern Trust Bank/DuPage, 775 F.Supp. 266 (N.D.Ill.1991); Quistgaard v. EAB European American Bank & Trust Co., 182 A.D.2d 510, 583 N.Y.S.2d 210 (App. Div. 1st Dept., 1992). A similar result might be reached under another analysis as well; *see, e.g.*, Adamar of New Jersey, Inc. v. Chase Lincoln First Bank, N.A., 201 A.D.2d 174, 615 N.Y.S.2d 550 (App.Div. 4th Dep't 1994), where the court held the bank was estopped from asserting a defense when its negligence led to the theft and unauthorized completion of the cashiers checks. The issue can arise over a teller's check (a check drawn on another bank) as well. *Compare* Meritor v. Duke, 22 UCC Rep. Serv. 2d 833 (Va. Cir. Ct.1993) (able to stop payment if holder not holder in due course) *with* Guaranty Fed. Sav. & Loan Ass'n v. Horseshoe Operating Co., 748 S.W.2d 519 (Tex.Ct.App. 1988). Additional discussion occurs later in this book. As recognizing that the current Code rejects this analysis and thus abrogates the rule in the *Wertz* case, *supra*, see Associated Carriages, Inc. v. International Bank of Commerce, 37 S.W.3d 69 (Tex. Ct. App. San Antonio 2000), *rehearing overruled* 2001, and Flatiron Linen, Inc. v. First American State Bank, 1 P.3d 244 (Colo. App. 1999), *rev'd* (unfortunately) 23 P.3d 1209 (Colo. 2001).

170. 624 F.2d 105 (10th Cir.1980).

171. A like case is Banco Di Roma v. Merchants Bank, 92 A.D.2d 42, 459 N.Y.S.2d 592 (App.Div. 1st Dep't 1983) where the check was procured by fraud and enforcement was sought by a party not a holder in due course.

172. 81 A.D.2d 978, 439 N.Y.S.2d 771 (App.Div. 3d Dep't 1981).

173. Even if the bank is bound to pay, it should be able to invoke the liability of the holder to it, as applicable, in fraud, in warranty, or as an indorser on the checks given for the bank's check, and use its right of setoff. A holder in due course, however, should prevail. *See, e.g., In re* Henrickson, 14 B.R. 474, 32 UCC Rep. Serv. 902 (Bankr. D.Minn.1981). Cases like the *Florida Frozen Foods* case include: Hotel Riviera, Inc. v. First Nat'l Bank & Trust Co., 768 F.2d 1201 (10th Cir.1985) (holder of cashier's check given to pay unenforceable gambling debt allowed to recover over defense of no consideration); First Nat'l Bank v. United

proper analysis in the above situation where the bank has a claim or defense of its own is simply that it may refuse to perform its drawer's contract against anyone but a holder in due course (with whom it did not deal).[174]

A number of courts have used that analysis.[175] So does current Article 3. It provides that if an obligated bank wrongfully refuses to pay a cashier's or certified check or stops or refuses payment of a teller's check,[176] the person asserting the right to enforce the check is entitled to compensation for expenses and loss of interest resulting from the non-payment, and may recover consequential damages if the obliged bank refuses to pay after receiving notice of particular circumstances giving rise to the damages, unless the obligated bank asserts a claim or defense of the bank it has reasonable grounds to believe is available against the person entitled to enforce the instrument.[177]

States, 41 UCC Rep. Serv. 1583 (Cl.Ct. 1985); and Hill v. Mercantile First Nat'l Bank, 693 S.W.2d 285 (Mo.Ct.App.1985) (cashier's check constituted payment of check given for it and could not be stopped).

On the point in the *Hill* case concerning payment of the check given for it by the cashier's check, Official Comment 2 to § 3–418 agrees. *See also* Gentner & Co. v. Wells Fargo Bank, 76 Cal.App.4th 1165, 90 Cal.Rptr.2d 904, 40 UCC Rep. Serv. 2d 38 (2d Dist. 1999). However, Official Comment 3 to § 4–215 and § 4–215(a)(1), cited for the payment rule, only deal with cash, and § 4–213(a)(1) and (c) do not seem to equate cash and a cashier's check. Indeed, *see* Official Comment 8 to § 4–215; of course, the bank may be accountable, but it already is. Official Comment 8 suggests the item given for the cashiers check may be paid under § 4–215(a)(2) (settled with no right to revoke). This may be true considering only § 4–301(a), but is not necessarily so given that a right to revoke may exist by agreement. Of course that right to revoke would be subject to the rights of the holder of the cashier's check which would be superior if that party is a holder in due course. *See* §§ 3–305(b) and 3–306.

Even if the item given for the cashier's check is paid, the analysis earlier in this note is confirmed by Official Comment 2 to § 3–418, which indicates the bank may have a right of recovery; in the case posited in the Official Comment, a right of restitution under § 3–418(a). If not, it would be because the holder was a holder in due course; under any analysis the bank's defense or claim would not be good in that instance.

174. Current Article 3 does not employ the "dealing with" concept. *See* the discussion, *supra*, in Chapter 3.

175. *See, e.g.*, Rezapolvi v. First Nat'l Bank, 296 Md. 1, 459 A.2d 183 (Md. 1983) (cashier's check issued in return for customer's assertedly invalid check). In this particular fact situation the court decided the check given for the cashier's check was paid when the cashier's check was issued since the check was drawn on the same bank. The court concluded the bank could use old § 4–407 to refuse payment on the cashier's check. *See also* note 173, *supra*. Other cases include Pulaski Chase Co–operative v. Kellogg–Citizens Nat'l Bank, 130 Wis.2d 200, 386 N.W.2d 510 (App.1986), except as noted in Gentner and Company, Inc. v. Wells Fargo Bank, 76 Cal.App.4th 1165, 90 Cal.Rptr.2d 904 (1999), the analysis relied upon to preserve a defense that the holder had dealt with the party asserting the defense is no longer tenable under current Article 3. *See also* note 169, *supra*.

176. These same issues have arisen with certified and teller's checks. § 3–418 makes the rule relatively clear for certified checks but there was confusion in the case of teller's checks. *See, e.g.*, Guaranty Fed. Sav. Bank v. Horseshoe Operating Co., 793 S.W.2d 652 (Tex.1990) (right to stop payment), *reversing in part the appellate decision*, 748 S.W.2d 519 (Tex.Ct.App.1988), going the other way, and note 168, *supra*.

177. § 3–411. Expenses and consequential damages also are not recoverable if nonpayment occurs because the bank suspends payments, has reasonable doubt about the person to pay, or payment is legally prohibited. Note the allowance of consequential damages, thus superseding UCC § 1–305, which furnishes a strong inducement to pay. The circumstances when refusal to pay is valid include insolvency and illegality as well, and are discussed in Official Comment 3. *See* Associated Carriages, Inc. v. Interna-

A number of the cases involve the refusal of the bank to pay at the behest of its customer.[178] These cases need not be resolved on an "acceptance upon issuance" analysis either.[179] The more appropriate analysis of them is that the purchaser of a cashier's check never has the right to stop payment on it, but the bank, as drawer, may stop payment. When sued by the holder on its drawer's contract, however, the bank will be unable to use any claim of the purchaser of the instrument in defense unless the purchaser joins the action and asserts the claim (§ 3–305(c)) or the adverse claim procedure under § 3–602(e)(1)(i) is employed, or the holder acquired the instrument by theft or through one who so acquired it, or payment would not be consistent with a restrictive indorsement of the instrument.[180] These cases will be resolved in this manner under current § 3–411 for cashier's, certified and teller's checks, as the only relevant exceptions from liability on the instrument plus expenses or consequential damages are the bank has a reasonable doubt whether the person demanding payment is entitled to enforce the instrument or payment is prohibited by law.[181] Aside from these cases where a claim or defense of a third party, not asserted by that party, might be involved, the third party will have to defend, absent a case of theft and attempted enforcement by a non-holder in due course,[182] where the liability of an obligated party is not discharged by payment with knowledge it should not be made.[183]

Another set of problems in connection with the liability of an acceptor may arise when a draft is raised in amount by its payee, and then acceptance by the drawee is sought. A wise drawee will condition any acceptance to the draft "as originally drawn."[184] But if the instrument after acceptance is negotiated to a holder in due course, who obtains full payment, may payment in excess of the original tenor of the

tional Bank of Commerce, 37 S.W.3d 69 (Tex.Ct.App.—San Antonio 2000), rehearing overruled 2001, and Godat v. Mercantile Bank of Northwest County, 884 S.W.2d 1, 24 UCC Rep. Serv. 2d 385 (Mo.Ct.App.1994) (cashier's check obtained under false pretenses sought to be enforced by holder who failed to establish holder in due course status).

178. *See, e.g.*, Fur Funtastic, Ltd. v. Kearns, 104 Misc.2d 1030, 430 N.Y.S.2d 27 (Civ.Ct.1980) and Warren Fin., Inc. v. Barnett Bank, 552 So.2d 194, *corrected*, 14 Fla. L.W. 574 (Fla. 1989).

179. *See, e.g.*, Bank of New York v. Welz, 118 Misc.2d 645, 460 N.Y.S.2d 867 (N.Y.Sup.Ct.1983) and further discussion in a later chapter, *infra*.

180. § 3–602(e)(2). *See, e.g.*, Fulton Nat'l Bank v. Delco Corp., 128 Ga.App. 16, 195 S.E.2d 455 (Ga.Ct.App.1973) (the question is not whether the bank has a right to stop payment on the instrument, but whether the bank is liable on the instrument, which depends on whether its customer's claim is both good and available under old § 3–306(d) to the bank).

181. § 3–411(c)(iii) and (iv). *See, supra*, note 176, and DRP, Inc. v. Burgess, 730 So.2d 474 (La.Ct.App. 4 Cir.1999).

182. § 3–305(c).

183. § 3–602(a) and (e)(1)(i) and (2). Note where these type of checks are involved, indemnity can no longer justify nonpayment. Thus banks should not take indemnity. If they do, and refuse to pay, the indemnity had better cover their complete exposure to the party seeking payment. If indemnity is taken and payment is made, a bank may be liable under other law for breach of the indemnity agreement. Official Comment to § 3–602.

184. A drawee is entitled to condition its certification of a check "payable only as originally drawn and when properly indorsed." Rockland Trust Co. v. South Shore Nat'l Bank, 366 Mass. 74, 314 N.E.2d 438 (Mass. 1974). *But see* § 3–413(a)(i), which appears to override this contract provision notwithstanding UCC § 1–302.

instrument be recovered by the drawee? A holder in due course may keep the entire payment because it is final, and no warranty made to the payor bank by the holder is breached.[185] This accords with the perception of the worth of a certified check; one would not expect to be subject to a risk of alteration on such a check.[186] But suppose the drawer has objected to the excessive debit to the drawer's account before the draft is presented to the drawee so that the drawee refuses to pay the draft. This will force the holder in due course to sue. Suit can only be on the acceptor's contract, which is conditioned to the check "as originally drawn." Old § 3–413(1) contained no language that negated the contractual condition limiting responsibility to the draft's original tenor. This literal difference in result should be avoided, the liability of the acceptor should be consistent with the result when payment has been made,[187] and this is the result under current § 3–413(a)(i).[188]

The case of *Wallach Sons, Inc. v. Bankers Trust Co.*[189] illustrates another variation of the alteration problem. In the *Wallach* case, the drawer obtained certification on a check drawn and payable to her for $29; she raised the amount of the check to $2,900 and negotiated it to a jeweler in payment for a ring. The bank refused payment and, when sued, prevailed, even though the jeweler obviously had relied upon the certification. The court refused to accept the argument that the certification should have shown its amount. The decision seems correct absent a specific rule. Section 3–413(b) now provides such a rule and thus accepts the argument not accepted in the decision.

The contract of an acceptor is not conditioned on any notice of dishonor and protest, as the contract of a drawer in some respects is. Nonetheless, presentment for payment and notice of dishonor is necessary in the case of the acceptor of a draft payable at a bank.[190] Because the same rules apply in the case of the liability of a maker on an instrument, this discussion is deferred.

---

185. §§ 3–418, 3–417.

186. The payor bank will be able to debit the drawer's account for the original tenor of the draft and will have a cause of action for the remainder in warranty against a prior transferor who does make a warranty that the instrument has not been materially altered. Thus the effect of the Code is to preserve the validity of an accepted instrument in the hands of a holder in due course who relies on the acceptance and who pays value consistent with the appearance of the altered instrument, but to otherwise allocate the loss to the culprit or the party who dealt with the culprit. Revised Articles 3 and 4 are the same as to this result. *See* §§ 4–401(d)(1), 3–418(c), 3–417(d) and 4–208(d), and Official Comment 4 to § 3–417.

187. The Comment to old § 3–413 in part so suggested by stating that old § 3–413(1) applied to all drafts (including checks) the rule that the acceptance relates to the instrument as it was at the time of acceptance and not (in the case of alteration before acceptance) to its original tenor. The problem arose because the effect of the UCC presumably could be varied by agreement unless otherwise provided under old UCC § 1–102(3). There is no reported case, but for dicta as to the result suggested, *see* Brower v. Franklin Nat'l Bank, 311 F.Supp. 675 (S.D.N.Y.1970).

188. Of course, even now one must read the words "except as otherwise provided in this Act" in § 1–302(a) liberally in order to allow § 3–413(a)(i) to be read as a mandatory rule.

189. 62 Misc.2d 19, 307 N.Y.S.2d 297 (N.Y.Civ.Ct.1970).

190. §§ 3–413, 3–414, 3–415(e), 3–501(a) and 3–502(d).

¶ 4.05 The Maker

Unlike the contract of the drawer, which is statutorily defined as implicit from the signature alone, the contract of the maker of an instrument is set out in the instrument as well as by the statute. A maker, both by agreement and by statute, promises to pay the instrument according to its terms at the time of issue or when it first comes into the possession of a holder, or as completed pursuant to § 3–115 on incomplete instruments.[191] A maker may make whatever contract the parties agree upon, however, and thus may vary the effect of the statutory obligation by agreement.[192]

The contract of the maker is not conditional upon any of dishonor after presentment or notice of dishonor or protest.[193] Accordingly, a demand for payment normally is not necessary to charge the maker of a promissory note,[194] and is not a prerequisite to the institution and maintenance of a suit on the note or other action against the maker.[195] Where the holder wishes to accelerate the debt, however, the absence of a requirement that demand be made upon the maker for payment does not displace any common law rule requiring demand for payment of the past-due installments prior to the exercise of rights under an optional acceleration clause.[196] No demand for payment prior to acceleration is necessary, though, where the instrument contains a provision waiving "presentment for payment, demand, protest, notice thereof and dishonor and diligence in collecting."[197]

Presentment for payment and notice of dishonor seem to be required to hold the maker in one case. If a note is payable at a bank, what sometimes was called "domiciled paper,"[198] there is an agreement to keep funds on deposit until demanded. This is the same situation as with a check, and as the contract of the drawer of a check is conditioned on the refusal of a demand (dishonor), this same concept was carried over to other types of instruments payable at banks.[199]

¶ 4.05

191. § 3–412. Under Revised § 3–412, the issuer of a cashier's check or other draft drawn on the drawer also has primary liability. *See also* § 3–412, Official Comment 1, and § 3–414(a). *See, e.g.*, Philadelphia Bond & Mortgage Co. v. Highland Crest Homes, Inc., 235 Pa.Super. 252, 340 A.2d 476 (1975) (an individual who signed a note which stated that "the undersigned ... jointly and severally promise to pay" made the contract of a maker).

192. UCC § 1–302. But in Pugh v. First Nat'l Bank, 130 Ga.App. 627, 204 S.E.2d 370 (1974), the court found that a separate agreement for a method of payment of a note, which did not provide that it was the exclusive means of payment, when not followed did not relieve the maker of his primary obligation entered into by signing the note.

193. § 3–412. Thus the maker, like an acceptor, is not a secondary party. *See* old § 3–102(1)(d). The term "secondary party" is not used in current Article 3.

194. *See, e.g.*, Commerce Union Bank v. Davis, 581 S.W.2d 142 (Tenn.Ct.App.1978) and Official Comment 2 to § 3–502.

195. *See, e.g.*, Allen Sales & Servicenter, Inc. v. Ryan, 525 S.W.2d 863 (Tex.1975). However, *see* § 3–502(a) as to dishonor for the purpose of an indorser's liability.

196. *See* the *Ryan* case, *supra*, note 195.

197. Sylvester v. Watkins, 538 S.W.2d 827 (Tex.Civ.App.1976). *See also* § 3–502, Official Comment 2.

198. Old § 3–501, Official Comment 4. The term included a draft payable at a bank as well.

199. §§ 3–412, 3–415, 3–501(a) and 3–502(a). An example of a note payable at *a bank* is a certificate of deposit. § 3–104(j). As previously noted, presentment for pay-

Delay beyond the time when it is due, without excuse, of any necessary presentment or notice of dishonor discharges a maker only to the extent of a deprival of funds during the delay because of the insolvency of the bank.[200] A delay in presentment or notice of dishonor may be excused, and in some cases the requirements themselves may be excused, as applicable, under § 3–504. By far the most common excuse in the case of a note is that the party to be charged has waived presentment and notice expressly or by implication either before or after it is due.[201] For example, in one case the court stated that because the signed note contained a statement that the makers and indorsers severally waived demand for payment, notice of dishonor, protest, and notice of protest, presentment of the note for payment was entirely excused.[202]

¶ 4.06 The Indorser

[1] Description of Liability

The remaining party who may be liable on an instrument is an indorser.[203] The indorser generally will be the payee who has negotiated the instrument, or some subsequent holder who has passed the instrument on.[204] Like that of the drawer, the liability of an indorser on an instrument[205] is conditional. An indorser engages, unless the indorsement otherwise specifies such as by words like "without recourse,"[206] that upon dishonor and any necessary notice of dishonor, the indorser will pay the instrument according to its tenor at the time of the

---

ment and notice of dishonor also are required to charge an acceptor of a draft payable at a bank. An example of this kind of instrument would be a certified check. Thus the rule applies to all makers and acceptors of domiciled—"payable at a bank"—paper but not as to "undomiciled" paper. *See* Table of Dispositions of Sections in Former Article 3, Former § 3–501(1)(c) carried over to current §§ 3–414(f), 3–415(e).

200. §§ 3–414(f) and 3–415(e). The time for presentment, how it must be made, the rights of the party to whom it is made, the time allowed for acceptance or payment, and how notice of dishonor must be given, have been previously discussed in connection with the liability of the drawer and are applicable here. *See* Article 3, Part 5.

201. § 3–504(a)(iv) and (b)(ii).

202. Riley v. First State Bank, 469 S.W.2d 812 (Tex.Civ.App.1971).

¶ 4.06

203. Defined in § 3–204(b). The drawer of a draft accepted by a non-bank also is treated as an indorser in terms of liability. § 3–414(d).

204. The term "indorser," however, includes an accommodation indorser. § 3–204(a) and (b). Such a person who guarantees collection rather than payment has a modified indorser's liability. §§ 3–415(a) and 3–419(d). Under § 3–419(f) an accommodation party also is not liable to the party accommodated. *See* Rahall v. Tweel, 186 W.Va. 136, 411 S.E.2d 461 (W.Va.1991).

205. An indorser also may have liability with respect to the underlying transaction out of which the transfer of the instrument arises, and in warranty. Discussion of liability with respect to the underlying obligation and in warranty appears in Chapter 7. A bank handling a check for collection or return also may have liability under Regulation CC, 12 CFR § 229.35(b).

206. § 3–415(b). A "without recourse" indorsement is a qualified indorsement and absolves the indorser from liability on the instrument. Wolfram v. Halloway, 46 Ill. App.3d 1045, 5 Ill.Dec. 264, 361 N.E.2d 587 (1st Dist. 1977). *See also* Gaetani v. Goss-Golden West Sheet Metal Profit Sharing Plan, 84 Cal.App.4th 1118, 101 Cal.Rptr.2d 432 (1st Dist. 2000) ("assigns and transfers all right, title and interest" equals "without recourse"). Since the disclaimer varies the written contract of indorsement, the disclaimer itself must be written on the instrument and cannot be proved by parol. Official Comment 1 to old § 3–414.

indorsement[207] to the person entitled to enforce the instrument or to any subsequent indorser who takes it up, even though the indorser who takes it up was not obligated to do so.[208] Indorser liability on an instrument is separate from the liability of the drawer, maker, or acceptor[209] and, because of the right to presentment and dishonor and notice of dishonor, under old Article 3 an indorser was classified as a secondary party.[210]

Normally the capacity in which a party signs an instrument, which determines the contractual liability of that party, is not difficult to ascertain. For example, where the president of a corporation signed a note on behalf of the corporation, and also signed it personally beneath a typed notation which read "personal indorsement," the court held he was clearly an indorser and not the maker of the note.[211] And in *O'Grady v. First Union Nat'l Bank*,[212] a court had little difficulty in determining that a person who signed a note in the bottom right-hand corner was a maker and not an indorser. In other situations, however, the determination may not be as simple. In those instances, any ambiguity[213] as to the capacity in which a signature is made must be resolved by a rule of law that it is an indorsement.[214] To illustrate, the court in *United States v. Tufi*[215] held that the purported signature of the payee appearing on the front of the check rather than on the back did not mean the signature

---

207. If a person indorses an altered or incomplete instrument, liability as indorser is assumed on the instrument as altered or completed. § 3–415(a), Official Comment 3 to old § 3–414. An indorser's liability is coextensive with all the terms of the instrument. Therefore, when a note contains a stipulation for the payment of attorney's fees or costs of collection, it is part of the tenor of the note in accordance with which an indorser is statutorily liable. Paragon Buying Serv., Inc. v. Sylbay Realty Corp., 3 UCC Rep. Serv. 67 (N.Y.Sup.Ct.1966).

208. § 3–415(a) and Official Comment 1. Under § 4–207(a) and (b), each customer who transfers an item and receives a settlement or other consideration by statute makes certain warranties, and also engages that upon dishonor it will take up the item. This engagement is identical in substance to that provided in § 3–415, and arises automatically as a part of the bank-collection process, notwithstanding the absence of a written indorsement, for the purpose of simplification and speeding up the bank-collection process. Indorsement liability should be distinguished from the right of a collecting bank to charge back under § 4–214. *See* Laurel Bank & Trust Co. v. Sahadi, 32 Conn.Supp. 172, 345 A.2d 53 (Conn.Com.Pl.1975) (even though bank did not exercise its right to charge-back after the check was dishonored by the drawee bank, it was entitled to proceed in an action on the instrument under old § 3–414(1)).

209. The liability of an indorser is independent from that of another liable party on the instrument, such as the maker of the note. Allyn–Mason, Inc. v. Kuehl, 10 UCC Rep. Serv. 675 (N.Y.Sup.Ct.1972) (maker bankrupt). If the instrument is secured, the indorser's contract does not require that the holder proceed against the collateral before proceeding against the indorsers. Central State Bank v. Baccara Restaurant, Inc. 9 UCC Rep. Serv. 488 (N.Y.Civ.Ct. 1971).

210. Old § 3–102(1)(d). Current Article 3 does not employ the term. Official Comment 2 to § 3–414.

211. Tampa Bay Bank v. Loveday, 526 S.W.2d 480 (Tenn.Ct.App.1974). The signature on behalf of the corporation in a representative capacity bound the corporation but not the individual personally.

212. 296 N.C. 212, 250 S.E.2d 587 (N.C. 1978).

213. Evidence as to the purpose of the signature may be used to prevent ambiguity as long as the evidence appears in the instrument. Thus, if the signature is followed by a designation, "witness," the signer is not liable at all. Official Comment to old § 3–402. *See* § 3–204, Official Comment 1 for a further discussion.

214. § 3–204(a).

215. 536 F.2d 855 (9th Cir.1976).

was not an indorsement. The issue is to be determined from the face of the instrument alone, and parol evidence is not admissible to show any other capacity.[216]

[2] Conditions to Liability

[a] Dishonor and Notice of Dishonor

The indorser's contract is conditioned upon dishonor,[217] precipitated by a necessary or optional presentment duly made and due acceptance or payment being refused,[218] or, if presentment is excused, by a failure of due acceptance or payment.[219] The indorser's contract also is conditioned upon any necessary notice of dishonor.[220] These are the same conditions as in the case of the drawer's contract, and have been discussed earlier in this chapter.[221] Presentment for payment is necessary to charge any indorser,[222] and notice of any dishonor is required unless excused.[223] Protest of dishonor is unnecessary, and even under old Article 3 it was only necessary to charge indorsers of a draft which on its face appeared to be drawn or payable outside of the United States and its dependencies.[224] Neither presentment nor notice of dishonor are necessary to charge an indorser who has indorsed the instrument after maturity.[225]

---

216. See also note 213, supra. Parol is admissible, however, for the purpose of reformation of the instrument as permitted under the rules of the particular jurisdiction. Moreover, the application of the restriction by the courts has been flexible. See, e.g., Standard Premium Plan Corp. v. Hirschorn, 56 Misc.2d 687, 290 N.Y.S.2d 226, 5 UCC Rep. Serv. 163 (N.Y.Sup.Ct. 1968) (holding that even though premium finance agreement was a note and the assigning insurance broker an indorser, the broker was not liable as an indorser unless the terms of recourse were spelled out, as a result more consonant with the realities of the situation); Jamaica Tobacco & Sales Corp. v. Ortner, 70 Misc.2d 388, 333 N.Y.S.2d 669 (Civ.Ct.1972) (where defendant, to induce plaintiff not to levy on goods of a debtor, agreed to guarantee the debt, and then indorsed notes by the debtor before delivery to plaintiff, defendant was a principal obligor on the same level as the maker of the notes).

217. § 3–415(a).

218. § 3–502. Dishonor also may occur when due acceptance or payment cannot be obtained within the prescribed time or, in the case of bank collections, the instrument is seasonably returned by the midnight deadline.

219. § 3–502(e). For example, a telephone call from a co-maker of a note to the holder advising of a refusal to pay unless certain things were done by the payee was held to be a dishonor. First Pa. Banking & Trust Co. v. De Lise, 186 Pa.Super. 398, 142 A.2d 401 (1958).

220. §§ 3–415(c) and 3–503(a). Protest has been deleted as a requirement. § 3–505 Official Comment.

221. Notice of dishonor is a more general requirement in the case of an indorser, however. § 3–503(a).

222. §§ 3–415(a), 3–502. Presentment for acceptance is only necessary under old § 3–501(1)(a) to charge indorsers of a draft where the draft so provides, or is payable elsewhere than at the residence or place of business of the drawee, or its date of payment depends upon such presentment. The holder may, at the holder's option, present for acceptance any other draft payable at a stated date. See current § 3–502.

223. §§ 3–415(c) and 3–503(a).

224. Old § 3–501(3).

225. Old § 3–501(4). This removed a trap that existed under the law prior to the UCC. Under that law, an instrument indorsed when overdue became payable on demand as to the indorser. The indorser would then be discharged by the delay unless the instrument was promptly presented for payment. Presentment of such overdue paper would not be the normal commercial

Presentment is made in the same manner as to charge a drawer;[226] the rights of the party to whom presentment is made are the same;[227] the same time is allowed for acceptance or payment;[228] and the rules on notice of dishonor operate similarly in both situations.[229]

Certain rules on notice of dishonor nonetheless are particular to the indorser's liability, there are differences in the indorser's situation from that of the drawer that are worth noting, and certain of the rules are worth emphasizing. Thus, though notice of dishonor normally is given by the holder of the instrument or by an indorser who has received notice, any party who may be compelled to pay the instrument may notify any party who may be liable on it. Accordingly, an indorser may notify another indorser who is not liable to the indorser giving notice, even when the latter person has not received notice from any other party to the instrument.[230] Except in the case of a bank, the time within which necessary notice must be given is 30 days.[231] This time is set as the estimated period necessary to ascertain what is required and to get out an ordinary business letter.[232] *Nevada State Bank v. Fischer*,[233] can be used to illustrate the operation of these rules. In that case, the court concluded that a bank that cashed a check drawn on an out-of-state bank and indorsed by plaintiff, that initiated collection within one day of the indorsement, and that notified plaintiff of dishonor within one day of receipt of notice of dishonor by the bank, was nonetheless not entitled to debit the plaintiff's account when ninety days had elapsed between the date of the original transaction and the date on which the plaintiff was given notice of dishonor. The remedy for the bank, of course, was against the other bank in the chain of collection that had been guilty of unreasonable delay in itself giving notice of dishonor.[234]

Important differences between the situations of a drawer and an indorser arise in several instances. One instance is in connection with the rules on time of presentment.[235] In the case of a check, this time, with respect to the drawer, is thirty days after date,[236] but in the case of an indorser, the time is thirty days after indorsement within which to present for payment or to initiate bank collection.[237] To illustrate, under old Article 3, where the time for an indorser was presumed to be seven days, and where the indorsee made no demand on the indorser for payment within seven days or any other reasonable time after indorsement, the indorsee could not recover from the indorser for a check

---

practice, however. Under current Article 3, see §§ 3–502 and 3–415(e).

226. § 3–501.
227. *Id.*
228. § 3–502.
229. § 3–503(b) and (c).
230. § 3–503(b).
231. § 3–503(c)(ii). A bank has until its midnight deadline. § 3–503(c)(i). *But see* § 4–214(a) for the right of charge back.

232. Official Comment 2 to old § 3–508 (which only allowed three days). Clearly current Article 3's longer period reflects the increased volume of business today (or less efficiency?).
233. 93 Nev. 317, 565 P.2d 332 (Nev. 1977).
234. *See* § 3–503(a) and (c).
235. § 3–414(f), 3–415(e).
236. § 3–414(f).
237. § 3–414(e).

dishonored for insufficient funds.[238]

[b] Discharge, Evidence, and Excuse

Another significant difference between the situation of an indorser and that of the drawer is that an unexcused delay in making a necessary presentment,[239] or in giving notice of dishonor,[240] will discharge any indorser. To illustrate the latter rule, in *Dozier v. First Alabama Bank, N.A.*[241] the court held under old Article 3 that a six-day delay in giving notice of dishonor[242] completely discharged the liability of the indorser on the check. The reason for the stricter rule, compared to the case of the drawer,[243] is that a discharge will not give an indorser a windfall, unlike in the case of the drawer.[244] Also, the goal behind these rules of inducing the prompt collection of checks can be effectuated with these differences.[245]

There are no significant differences between the rules for a drawer and for an indorser with respect to evidence of dishonor[246] or with respect to waived or excused delay or default in presentment, protest (to the extent relevant), or notice of dishonor.[247] But in this respect, while a waiver of presentment, notice and protest[248] embodied in the instrument itself is binding on all parties, where it is written above the signature of an indorser it binds the indorser only.[249] Furthermore, an indorser who is involved with the instrument in more than one capacity may as a result have one or more of the conditions to their indorser's liability on the instrument excused. For example, in one case,[250] the same person was the only person who had signed as the maker and as the indorser of notes. The court held that lack of presentment was not a defense as the defendant was the only one who would make any payment, and it was he

---

238. Official Comment 4 to § 3–415 and Dluge v. Robinson, 204 Pa.Super. 404, 204 A.2d 279 (1964). Also, as previously discussed, the consequences of delay in relation to discharge are dramatically different. *See, infra*, this chapter.

239. § 3–415(e) and note 238, *supra*.

240. § 3–415(e).

241. 363 So.2d 781 (Ala.Civ.App.1978).

242. Old § 3–508(2) only permitted two or three days; § 3–503(c) permits 30 days except in the case of a bank.

243. The drawer only is discharged where its liability is deemed that of an indorser. §§ 3–503 and 3–414(d).

244. A purpose of the limited discharge rule in the case of a drawer is to avoid unjust enrichment of the drawer or other party who normally has received goods or other consideration for the issue of the instrument. Official Comment 2 to old § 3–502. Of course, an indorser also has normally received goods or other consideration for the transfer of the instrument, but the indorser usually will have given consideration to obtain the instrument; thus a discharge results in a neutral position.

245. The drawer, who has itself issued the check and normally expects to have it paid, is reasonably required to stand behind it to a greater extent than the indorser, who has normally merely received the check and passed it on, who does not expect to have to pay it, and who is entitled to know promptly whether it is to be dishonored in order that the indorser may have recourse against the person with whom the indorser has dealt. Even so, current Article 3 somewhat minimizes the differences.

246. § 3–505(a).

247. § 3–504.

248. § 3–504(a)(iv) and (b)(ii).

249. Old § 3–511(6). Current § 3–504 omits this statement, apparently as a self-evident truth. *See* Table of Disposition of Sections in Former Article 3, old § 3–511(6) reference to "omitted."

250. Rourke v. Angelis, 12 UCC Rep. Serv. 526 (N.Y.Sup.Ct.1973).

who had defaulted.[251] It is not apparent in the case what counsel hoped to accomplish with the argument as to lack of presentment, since liability as a maker would exist in any event, but there are many similar cases where the issue is real because the persons who are indorsers have otherwise signed the instrument only in a representative capacity for the maker.[252]

[3] *Order of Liability*

The person who holds a dishonored instrument normally will seek recourse against the indorser with whom they dealt. The law permits this course of action. Unless they otherwise agree, indorsers are liable to one another in the order in which they indorse, which is presumed to be the order in which their signatures appear on the instrument.[253] Parol evidence is admissible to show that they in fact indorsed in another order, or that they otherwise agreed as to their liability to one another.[254]

The basic rule on order-of-indorser liability is inappropriate where an instrument, such as a note, is indorsed by one or more persons as an accommodation. In this instance, successive liability is not intended. Accordingly, the rule which provides in pertinent part that unless the instrument otherwise specifies, two or more persons who sign as anomalous indorsers are jointly and severally liable should be applied.[255] The court so held in one case where individuals and corporations signed notes made by another corporation as accommodation indorsers.[256] The court determined the indorsers were jointly and severally liable following the maker's default, and that two indorsers who received no benefit and suffered detriment not shared by the remaining indorsers nonetheless had signed in the same capacity as the other indorsers. The court also stated that the order in which the signatures appeared did not constitute evidence of any other agreement.[257]

---

251. The court cited old § 3–511(2)(b) (current § 3–504(a)(iv)), which excuses the conditions when the party to be charged has no reason to expect that the instrument will be accepted or paid, in support of its decision.

252. *E.g.*, Makel Textiles, Inc. v. Dolly Originals, Inc., 4 UCC Rep. Serv. 95 (N.Y.Sup.Ct.1967) (deciding that a principal officer, who signed both for the corporation and as indorser and who knew the notes could not and would not be paid from corporate funds, was liable). *See also* Schenectady Trust Co. v. Estate of Sciocchetti, 82 Misc.2d 1075, 371 N.Y.S.2d 36 (Sup.Ct. 1975) (notice of dishonor to indorser of corporate note who was officer of and actively engaged in corporation and fully cognizant of its financial affairs would be redundant act).

253. § 3–415 drops this statement, which appeared in old § 3–414(2), as superfluous. Official Comment 1 to § 3–415. *See also*, as qualifying the general rule, § 3–419(d) and (f) with respect to accommodation parties. *See also* § 3–116.

254. Official Comment 4 to old § 3–414.

255. Section 3–116(a) (which also treats indorsers who indorse as joint payees similarly). Note the rule of § 3–116(a) makes successive accommodation indorsers subject to contribution rather than reimbursement unless otherwise agreed. §§ 3–116 and 3–419(f).

256. Zapp Nat'l Bank v. Metropolitan Planning & Redevelopment Corp. 242 N.W.2d 96 (Minn. 1976).

257. *Distinguish* Niebergall v. A.B.A. Contracting & Supply Co., 24 A.D.2d 799, 263 N.Y.S.2d 589 (App.Div. 3d Dep't 1965), where a person indorsed a note as an accommodation to a later indorser of the note to facilitate bank acceptance of a loan. The later indorser redeemed the note, and upon his death his estate brought suit against the prior indorser. The court found an understanding between them that the prior indorser would not be liable to the accommodated party in case of default and rendered judgment accordingly. *See* old § 3–415(5) (current § 3–419(f)), discussed in Chapter 5.

Chapter 5

LIABILITY ON NEGOTIABLE INSTRUMENTS: ACCOMMODATION AND AGENCY

Analysis

Para.
¶5.01 Introduction 192
¶5.02 Accommodation Parties 194
    [1] Definition and Determination of Status 194
        [a] Definition 194
        [b] Determination of Status 195
    [2] Liability to Taker of Instrument 197
    [3] Liability to and of Party Accommodated 198
¶5.03 Agents 200
    [1] Unauthorized Signatures 200
    [2] Authorized Signatures Creating Principal But Not Agent Liability 201
    [3] Authorized Signatures Creating Agent Liability Alone 202

¶ 5.01 Introduction

In Chapter 4, the liability on an instrument of a party to it (drawer, acceptor, maker, or indorser) was discussed. This chapter deals with particular aspects of the liability of a person signing in one of those capacities.

A party who signs in one of the above capacities, but who signs as a surety for another party to the instrument, is called an accommodation party. An accommodation party is a person who signs the instrument for the purpose of incurring liability on the instrument without being a direct beneficiary of the value given for the instrument.[1] For example, in *Smith v. Singleton*,[2] a person added his signature to a note made by

---

¶ 5.01

1. § 3–419 (a). In Rahall v. Tweel, 186 W.Va. 136, 411 S.E.2d 461 (W.Va.1991), decided under old § 3–415, the court held the trial court was in error in instructing that a party who signs a note but receives no direct benefit was an accommodation party. This result would be changed under current § 3–419. *See* Official Comment 1 to § 3–419. *See also In re* Robinson Brothers Drilling, Inc. (ABB Vecto Gray, Inc. v. First National Bank of Bethany), 9 F.3d 871 (10th Cir.1993) (discussion of burden of proof as to direct benefit and what constitutes).

2. 124 Ga.App. 394, 184 S.E.2d 26 (Ga. Ct.App.1971).

another person which was given to evidence the unpaid price for the purchase of equipment. The signature was added after the purchase transaction had otherwise been completed and for the purpose of inducing a financing agency to approve the note. The court held the person so signing was an accommodation party.

An accommodation party is always a surety[3] (which includes a guarantor[4]), and that is the only distinguishing feature from another party to the instrument. An accommodation party differs from other sureties only in that the party's liability must be on the instrument and the party must be a surety for another party to the instrument.[5] An accommodation party's obligation is therefore determined by the capacity in which the party signs.[6] There is one peculiarity in the case of an accommodation indorser. Generally, an indorsement must be written by or on behalf of a holder.[7] An accommodation indorser may not meet this test because the indorser will not be a holder.[8] Nevertheless, an accommodation indorser has liability in an indorser's capacity.[9]

A party who signs in the capacity of drawer, acceptor, maker, or indorser as a representative of another person,[10] if authorized and if the

---

3. The status of an accommodation party is that of a surety whether the person is primarily liable on the paper or secondarily liable. Anna Nat'l Bank v. Wingate, 63 Ill. App.3d 676, 21 Ill.Dec. 84, 381 N.E.2d 19 (1978).

4. UCC § 1–201(b)(39) ("surety" includes guarantor). Under Article 3, there basically is no difference (*see* § 3–419(c) and Official Comment 4). Note, however, the liability of a guarantor for collection is conditioned on unsatisfied collection. Section 3–419(d). As amended in 2002, § 3–419(e) now also states the liability of a party that guarantees payment.

5. Official Comment 1 to old § 3–415. In addition to those defenses available to the principal (*see* § 3–305(d), but excluding discharge in bankruptcy, infancy and incapacity), under Article 3 an accommodation party has certain defenses under § 3–605, dependent upon the accommodation status. These are discussed in Chapter 6, *infra*. An accommodation party's liability being governed by Article 3 rather than other law may be significant. For example, in Halpin v. Frankenberger, 231 Kan. 344, 644 P.2d 452 (Kan. 1982), the court found that a guaranty separate from a note did not qualify as a negotiable instrument and, accordingly, that old § 3–606 was not available to discharge the guarantor when the holder released collateral for the debt without the consent of the guarantor. As a result, any defense would have to be found in other law. Other law may be different from the UCC. For example, an unconsented-to extension of time may discharge a compensated surety only to the extent of actual harm and not as a matter of law, as may be the case otherwise. *See, e.g.*, A/C. Elec. Co. v. Aetna Ins. Co., 251 Md. 410, 247 A.2d 708 (Md. 1968). The UCC rule of unconditional discharge draws no such distinction in old § 3–606(1)(a). *But see* current § 3–605(b). Permanent Editorial Board Commentary No. 11, February 10, 1994, discusses extensively the provisions of §§ 3–116, 3–305, 3–415, 3–419, and 3–605 in relation to Restatement of the Law Third, Suretyship, which may furnish applicable rules beyond Article 3. Amendment of § 3–605 in 2002, however, generally brings § 3–605 more closely in line to the Restatement, thus lessening the chances that applicable state law outside of Article 3 and § 3–605 may produce different results depending on the form of contract.

6. *E.g.*, Wohlhuter v. St. Charles Lumber & Fuel Co., 25 Ill.App.3d 812, 323 N.E.2d 134 (2 Dist.), *aff'd*, 62 Ill.2d 16, 338 N.E.2d 179 (1975) (an accommodation maker's basic liability is identical to that of any other maker although the surety status will give special defenses unavailable to the general maker). *See* § 3–419(b).

7. § 3–205(a) and (b).

8. § 3–205(d).

9. §§ 3–204(a)(iii) and 3–205(d).

10. Under UCC § 1–201(b)(33), a "representative" includes an agent, an officer of a corporation or association, a trustee, an executor or administrator of an estate, or any other person empowered to act for an-

signer executes the instrument in the correct manner, incurs no personal liability.[11] The signature, of course, binds the principal in the capacity in which it was made.[12] On the other hand, when the signature is not in the correct form, the signer may incur individual liability, again in the capacity in which the signature is made.[13] Thus the issue is whether the principal or the representative is liable in whatever capacity the signature is made.

¶ 5.02 Accommodation Parties

[1] Definition and Determination of Status

[a] Definition

As previously noted, an accommodation party is a person who signs the instrument as maker, drawer, acceptor, or indorser for the purpose of incurring liability on the instrument without being a direct beneficiary of value given for the instrument; *i.e.*, for the benefit of another party to the instrument.[14] Accordingly, even if the intent of the party in signing is for accommodation, unless the party accommodated is also a party to the instrument, the signer is not an accommodation party within Article 3. For example, in one case,[15] where a bank as payee and A and B as makers were the only parties to a renewal note given after a corporation failed to pay an earlier note given to the bank for its benefit by A and B, the court held that A and B were not accommodation makers, although the bank knew that the proceeds for which the original note was given were for the corporation. The reason was the corporation was not a party to the instrument; A and B and the bank were the only parties. By the same token, if the signature of the accommodation party is not on an instrument, the rules of Article 3 also do not govern the relationship created.[16]

The liability of an accommodation party on the instrument signed is determined by the capacity in which the party signs.[17] For example, a co-

---

other. For the purpose of this chapter, "agent" is used as well as "representative."

11. § 3–402(b)(1). *See* discussion, *infra*, this chapter.

12. §§ 3–401(a), 3–402(a). *See* the discussion, *supra*, in Chapter 2.

13. §§ 3–402(b)(2), 3–403(a). Again, *see* the discussion, *infra*, this chapter.

¶ 5.02

14. §§ 3–419(a) and 3–204(a)(iii).

15. Bank of America v. Superior Court of San Diego County, 4 Cal.App.3d 435, 84 Cal.Rptr. 421 (1970).

16. *E.g.*, Fewox v. Tallahassee Bank & Trust Co., 249 So.2d 55 (Fla.Dist.Ct.App. 1971); Chemical Bank v. PIC Motors Corp., 87 A.D.2d 447, 452 N.Y.S.2d 41 (App.Div. 1982), *aff'd*, 58 N.Y.2d 1023, 462 N.Y.S.2d 438, 448 N.E.2d 1349 (1983) (where guarantee of loans evidenced by notes stemmed from letter of guarantee that was not a negotiable instrument, Article 3 was inapplicable). *See also* cases discussed, *supra*, in Chapter 2 and Official Comment 2 to § 3–605 as amended in 2002.

Official Comment 3 to § 3–605 as amended in 2002 also points out that the accommodation rules in Article 3 apply in three other situations where the liability is functionally similar to that of a "secondary obligor" (*see* § 3–103(a)(17) as amended in 2002): a "regular" indorser, the drawer of a draft that is accepted by a party that is not a bank, and a co-maker of an instrument even when the co-maker does not qualify as an accommodation party.

17. § 3–419(b). *See* D'Annolfo v. D'Annolfo Construction Co., Inc., 39 Mass.App. Ct. 189, 654 N.E.2d 82 (1995) (liability of

maker may be an accommodation maker.[18] If the party also uses words of guaranty, liability is further determined by the language used. A guarantor differs as to liability only because the guarantor has added some words to the signature and thus may have altered the liability the guarantor would have had if the guarantor had simply put the signature on the instrument as an ordinary accommodation party.[19]

A guarantor either guarantees payment or collection, depending on the words used. "Payment guaranteed" or equivalent words added to a signature mean the signer will pay the instrument if it is not paid when due without a need for the holder to resort to another party.[20] "Collection guaranteed" means resort must first be had to others.[21] Words of guaranty that do not otherwise specify guarantee payment.[22] No words of guaranty added to the signature of a sole maker or acceptor will affect that person's liability on the instrument as a maker or acceptor, but words of guaranty added to the signature of one of two or more makers or acceptors create a presumption that the signature is for the accommodation of the others.[23] Words of guaranty under old Article 3 waived any necessity of presentment, notice of dishonor, and protest to charge the user;[24] under current Article 3, the user is liable in the capacity in which the signature appears.[25] Thus under old but not under current Article 3, an indorser who guarantees payment waives not only presentment, notice of dishonor, and applicable protest, but also all demand upon the maker or drawee, and the liability of the indorser becomes indistinguishable from that of a maker.[26]

[b] *Determination of Status*

The question of whether a person signing as a maker, drawer, acceptor, or indorser is an accommodation party is determined by

---

guarantor of payment is indistinguishable from that of a co-maker).

18. *E.g.*, Murphy v. Bank of Dahlonega, 151 Ga.App. 264, 259 S.E.2d 670 (Ga.Ct.App.1979). *But see* Nester v. O'Donnell, 301 N.J.Super. 198, 693 A.2d 1214 (App.Div. 1997), where a note signed in a corporate name and by two individuals, which stated the undersigned jointly and severally promise to pay, was held to preclude accommodation status. The court seems to have unduly relied on language that was less than carefully drawn for the exclusion of evidence that might have established accommodation status. The case perhaps illustrates the risk current Article 3 took when, as it so often does, it abandoned specific rules in favor of more general ones and clarifying expressions as unnecessary because the matter was self-evident; old § 3–415(3) explicitly stated that in cases not involving a holder in due course without notice of the accommodation, oral proof of accommodation was allowable.

19. J. White & R. Summers, Handbook of the Law Under the Uniform Commercial Code 578 (3rd ed. 1988); § 3–419(c), (d) and (e).

20. § 3–419(b) and (e). *See* Cusimano v. First Maryland Savings and Loan, Inc., 639 A.2d 553 (D.C.Ct.App.1994).

21. § 3–419(d).

22. § 3–419(d) and (e). *See, e.g.*, Cusick v. Ifshin, 70 Misc.2d 564, 334 N.Y.S.2d 106 (Civ.Ct.1972), *aff'd*, 73 Misc.2d 127, 341 N.Y.S.2d 280 (Sup.Ct.1973) ("personally guarantee the obligation" is a guaranty of payment). *See also* the *Cusimano* case, *supra*, note 20.

23. § 3–419(c). This specific provision in old § 3–416(4) is asserted to be absorbed in the more general rule of § 3–419(c). Table of Disposition of Sections in Former Article 3, old § 3–416(4) referred to current § 3–419(c).

24. Old § 3–416(5).

25. § 3–419(b); Official Comment 4 to § 3–419.

26. Official Comment to old § 3–416.

ascertaining the intent of the parties.[27] In ascertaining that intent, an indication of accommodation status sometimes may be obtained from the instrument and the signature of the party. There is a presumption that words of guaranty added to the signature of one of two or more makers or acceptors makes the signature one for the accommodation of the others.[28] Also, an indorsement that shows it is not in the chain of title is notice of accommodation.[29] Thus in a Maryland case,[30] the court held that a person, whose signature appeared without further designation and before the indorsement of the payee on the back of a note which the person had signed on its face as president of the maker corporation, was personally liable on the note as an accommodation indorser.[31]

If the instrument does not disclose the intent of the parties as to accommodation, parol evidence may be used to show it. Oral (and presumably evidence in a record as Article 3 draws no distinction) proof of accommodation status may not be used against a holder in due course without notice of the accommodation for the purpose of giving the accommodation party the benefit of discharges dependent on the accommodation character as such,[32] but in other cases the accommodation character may be shown.[33] For example, in *Lee Federal Credit Union v. Gussie*,[34] the court held that where the payee, who was a holder in due course, knew of the accommodation, oral evidence as to accommodation status was properly admitted. And in *Gehrig v. Ray*,[35] as against a nonholder in due course, the court admitted parol evidence to show that the defendants had executed the note as accommodation makers.

In determining accommodation status where the intent of the parties is not clear, various factors have been considered by the courts. The courts primarily have looked at whether the claimed accommodation party received benefits from the transaction. The receipt of benefits generally is considered to be inconsistent with accommodation status.[36] Whether the party claiming accommodation status was compensated for

---

27. *E.g.*, Kerney v. Kerney, 120 R.I. 209, 386 A.2d 1100 (R.I. 1978).

28. § 3–419(c). Other words, such as "accommodation party" after a signature, presumably would do as well. The intent of the parties also may prevent accommodation status. *See, e.g.*, Wohlhuter v. St. Charles Lumber & Fuel Co., 62 Ill.2d 16, 338 N.E.2d 179 (Ill. 1975) (where corporate note provided that all signers were principals, individual co-makers were not accommodation parties). *But see* note 18, *supra*, and the *Nester* case discussed there.

29. §§ 3–205(d) and 3–419(c).

30. Agfa–Gevaert, Inc. v. Bueding, 11 UCC Rep. Serv. 794 (Md.Dist.Ct.1972).

31. *But see* Schaeffer v. United Bank & Trust Co., 32 Md.App. 339, 360 A.2d 461 (Md.Ct.Spec.App. 1976), *aff'd* 280 Md. 10, 370 A.2d 1138 (Md. 1977) (person who signed blank reserve side of note to enable makers to obtain loan was an accommodation maker as the note provided that all signers were to be deemed makers).

32. Old § 3–415(3); current §§ 3–419(c) and 3–605(e). *See* note 18, *supra*. Those defenses are discussed in Chapter 6.

33. *Id.*

34. 542 F.2d 887 (4th Cir.1976).

35. 332 So.2d 703 (Fla.Dist.Ct.App. 1976).

36. The burden is on the signer to prove that no benefits were received from the proceeds of the instrument and therefore the signer was an accommodation party. Riegler v. Riegler, 244 Ark. 483, 426 S.W.2d 789 (Ark. 1968). *Compare* Hanson v. Cheek, 251 Ark. 897, 475 S.W.2d 526 (Ark. 1972) (possibility accommodation indorsers of corporate note might receive compensation from corporation for arranging permanent financing not sufficient) *and* Oak Park Currency Exch., Inc. v. Maropoulos, 48 Ill. App.3d 437, 6 Ill.Dec. 525, 363 N.E.2d 54

the signature is irrelevant,[37] however, and it also is irrelevant whether the instrument is negotiated subsequent to the signing.[38]

[2] Liability to Taker of Instrument

When an instrument is taken for value before it is due,[39] an accommodation party on it is liable in the capacity in which that party signed, even though the taker[40] knows of the accommodation.[41] Any other rule would negate the reason for the accommodation party signing in the first place. The consideration for the obligation of the accommodation party is that which supports the obligation of the principal.[42] Thus an accommodation maker or acceptor is bound on the instrument without any resort to the principal, and an accommodation indorser is liable after presentment and notice of dishonor.[43] The liability deriving from the capacity in which an accommodation party signs, however, may be increased or decreased by the instrument,[44] but liability stemming from that capacity may not be varied by an agreement beyond the instrument unless entered into with the taker of the instrument.[45] In particular, a

---

(1977) (accommodation indorsement as a favor to a friend) *with* Commerce Union Bank v. Davis, 581 S.W.2d 142 (Tenn.Ct. App.1978) (receipt of proceeds from the instrument or other direct benefit generally is inconsistent with accommodation status) *and* Common Wealth Ins. Sys., Inc. v. Kersten, 40 Cal.App.3d 1014, 115 Cal.Rptr. 653 (1974) (signers of corporate note who were among principal stockholders of corporation and where loan to corporation was essential to the preservation of their interest were not accommodation makers). *See also* note 1, *supra*. § 3–419(a) generally codifies the first three decisions. *See* Official Comment 1 to the section.

37. *See* § 3–419(b) and Official Comment 2.

38. Darden v. Harrison, 511 S.W.2d 925 (Tex.1974) (accommodation status does not require that the instrument be negotiated to a third party who then extends credit to the accommodated party). *See* § 3–419(b).

39. The limitation "before it is due" is one of suretyship law, by which the obligation of the surety is terminated at the specified time, unless in the meantime the obligation of the principal has become effective by issuance. Official Comment 3 to old § 3–415. The principle should apply under current Article 3 through UCC § 1–103(b).

40. The taker (a person entitled to enforce or an indorser who paid the instrument) need not be a holder. James Talcott, Inc. v. Fred Ratowsky Assocs., Inc., 2 UCC Rep. Serv. 1134 (Pa.Com.Pl.1965). *See* § 3–301.

41. § 3–419(b).

42. *See, e.g.*, American Viking Contractors v. Scribner Equip. Co., 745 F.2d 1365 (11th Cir.1984) and Burke v. Burke, 89 Ill.App.3d 826, 45 Ill.Dec. 71, 412 N.E.2d 204 (1980). § 3–419(b) is in accord. *See* Official Comment 2. Distinguish, however, Deep South Servs., Inc. v. Wade, 248 Ga. 80, 281 S.E.2d 561 (Ga. 1981), where consideration was promised to the accommodation parties and was not carried out. The court allowed a defense. The ostensible tension between § 3–303(b) and § 3–419(b) on these facts can be resolved by assuming liability in the accommodation party but with a corresponding set off in the same amount for breach of the promise of consideration.

43. § 3–419(b). A case involving an accommodation party signing in the capacity of a drawer is National Bank v. Beinhorn, 10 UCC Rep. Serv. 847 (N.Y.Sup.Ct.1972).

44. *E.g.*, L.H. Wagener, Inc. v. Kendall, 278 N.W.2d 18 (Iowa 1979) (an accommodation indorsement was revoked by a signed statement typed on the note that assigned rights to plaintiff without recourse and which was made before the instrument was negotiated to plaintiff); Warren v. Washington Trust Bank, 19 Wn.App. 348, 575 P.2d 1077 (Wash.Ct.App.1978), *modified*, 92 Wn.2d 381, 598 P.2d 701 (Wash.1979) (an accommodation indorser of a note that stated the indorser was "bound thereon as a principal and not as surety" was primarily liable as well as retaining the rights of a surety to the maker of the note).

45. *E.g.*, Philadelphia Bond & Mortgage Co. v. Highland Crest Homes, Inc., 221

guarantee that accompanies the signature of an accommodation party on the instrument may vary the liability the party otherwise would have in the capacity in which the party signed.[46] But where words of guarantee were absent, in *Still v. Citizens Bank*[47] the court stated that if the accommodation party had an agreement that he would be liable only for any deficiency, the law required him to write "collection guaranteed" or equivalent words in connection with his signature and, absent such words, he was liable as an accommodation party for the unpaid balance of the note.[48] An accommodation party is bound by the terms of the instrument signed[49] and generally has available the same defenses to liability as the principal does.[50]

[3] *Liability to and of Party Accommodated*

An accommodation party is not liable to the party accommodated.[51] This provision in essence qualifies the otherwise applicable rule that an accommodation party is liable in the capacity in which the party has signed.[52] For example, where the accommodation party executed two notes so that the payee of the notes could make up a financial statement with which to obtain a loan, the court held the accommodation party as the maker was not liable to the payee who was the party accommodated and the plaintiff's decedent.[53] It is often important to determine who was

Pa.Super. 89, 288 A.2d 916 (1972) (where the holder/payee of a note induced the maker to become an accommodation party by agreeing he should not be held liable as a principal, parol evidence is admissible to show that the maker signed as an accommodation party). Other circumstances may eliminate the liability. *See, e.g.,* Schaeffer v. United Bank & Trust Co., 32 Md.App. 339, 360 A.2d 461 (Md.Ct.Spec.App. 1976), *aff'd* 280 Md. 10, 370 A.2d 1138 (Md. 1977) (accommodation maker not liable when he reasonably thought he was signing only as a character reference). Because in some cases the accommodation character of a signature may be shown by oral proof, that does not necessarily mean that the signer may by oral testimony modify any capacity in which the person signed. *See, e.g.,* Perfect Picture Frames, Inc. v. Consolidated Fine Arts, Ltd., 9 UCC Rep. Serv. 283 (N.Y.Sup.Ct. 1971) (agreement that notes were not to be presented for payment was a parol variation of their terms and of no effect). As to these matters, *see* § 3–117.

46. § 3–419(d).

47. 6 UCC Rep. Serv. 813 (Okla.Ct.App. 1969).

48. The UCC does not provide that an accommodation party is discharged when notice is given to the creditor to sue the principal debtor and the creditor fails to do so. Thus the pre-Code doctrine of Pain v. Packard, 13 Johns. 174 (N.Y.1816), prevailing in some eighteen states, cannot be invoked by an accommodation party. Only a guarantor of collection has the right under the UCC to require that collection first be attempted against the principal. Philadelphia Bond & Mortgage Co. v. Highland Crest Homes, Inc., 235 Pa.Super. 252, 340 A.2d 476 (1975). *See also* Rassette v. Jacobson, 39 Mich.App. 172, 197 N.W.2d 330 (1972) (holder has no duty to resort to either collateral or any other party before seeking payment from guarantors), and § 3–419(e).

49. *E.g.,* Warner–Lambert Pharmaceutical Co. v. Sylk, 471 F.2d 1137 (3d Cir.1972) (clauses allowing acceleration and attorney's fees bound indorser even though they were not referred to in the contract of guarantee).

50. *E.g.,* A.J. Armstrong Co. v. Janburt Embroidery Corp., 97 N.J.Super. 246, 234 A.2d 737 (1967). A guarantor may still be bound even though the instrument is forged. *See, e.g.,* Universal Metals & Mach., Inc. v. Bohart, 539 S.W.2d 874 (Tex.1976). *Now see* § 3–305(d). An accommodation party also may have defenses particular to that status. *See* § 3–605, discussed in Chapter 6.

51. § 3–419(f). *See also* § 3–116.

52. § 3–419(b). *See also* § 3–116.

53. Darden v. Harrison, 511 S.W.2d 925 (Tex.1974). *See also* Ridings v. Motor Vessel "Effort," 387 F.2d 888 (2d Cir.1968) (ac-

the accommodated party. For example, in *T.W. Sommer Co. v. Modern Door & Lumber Co.*,[54] a company had sustained a fire loss and was in liquidation. It owed debts to two companies owned by Sommer, who was a friend of the principal owner of the company in liquidation. The company in liquidation executed notes payable to the companies owed, and the principal owner indorsed them. The notes were then indorsed by the payee companies to a bank to secure a loan by the bank to Sommer. When the notes were not paid, the payee companies had to pay them and brought suit against the principal owner, who had indorsed them. The defense was the companies were the parties accommodated, and not the maker company. The court agreed, as it could perceive no reason for the accommodation party to assume a debt owed by a company in liquidation. Contrast a Colorado case where the defendants, at the request of the bank, indorsed a renewal note of a corporation as security for a debt owed to the bank.[55] The court held the maker and not the bank was the accommodated party. For this purpose, as against the accommodated party, the accommodation party may offer oral proof of the accommodation status.[56]

If the accommodation party pays the instrument, there is a right of recourse on the instrument against the party accommodated.[57] Traditionally, a surety has three rights. The first, the right of exoneration whereby the surety may compel the principal debtor to pay the creditor, thus relieving the surety, originally was not covered by the UCC but should not be considered to be displaced. It is now covered. Neither was the right of reimbursement resting upon the debtor's express or implied promise to indemnify the surety, as it is not a right on the instrument.[58] The statute restates the third right of a surety which is the right to be subrogated to the rights of the person paid against the accommodated party in that party's capacity on the instrument.[59] It thus is inappropriate to think of the instrument as paid by the accommodation party. That would remove the basis for suit. What has been discharged by the accommodation party's payment is the liability of the accommodation party, and there is no effect on the remaining liability of the accommodated party.[60] The accommodation party's right also will normally carry with it rights with respect to any security for the instrument.[61]

commodated party was still subject to this rule even though it purchased instruments from holder).

54. 293 Minn. 264, 198 N.W.2d 278 (Minn. 1972).

55. State Bank of Greeley v. Owens, 31 Colo.App. 351, 502 P.2d 965 (Colo.Ct.App. 1972).

56. § 3–419(c); T. W. Sommer Co. v. Modern Door & Lumber Co., 293 Minn. 264, 198 N.W.2d 278 (Minn. 1972); Darden v. Harrison, 511 S.W.2d 925 (Tex.1974).

57. § 3–419(f).

58. It, too, now is covered. Both exoneration and reimbursement, not involving liability on the instrument, are outside the scope of this chapter. Indeed, whether they survived to an accommodation party on commercial paper outside of old Article 3 was unclear. See White & Summers, *supra* note 19, § 13–18. Now see § 3–419(f).

59. § 3–419(f) and Official Comment 5.

60. Anna Nat'l Bank v. Wingate, 63 Ill. App.3d 676, 21 Ill.Dec. 84, 381 N.E.2d 19 (1978) (also holding subrogation is not the surety's only recourse).

61. *E.g.*, Bruer v. Sanford Atl. Nat'l Bank, 247 So.2d 764 (Fla.Dist.Ct.App.1971). *See also* old § 3–603(2), deleted as unnecessary under current Article 3; § 3–605, Offi-

What of rights among accommodation parties themselves? Since accommodation parties are liable in the capacity in which they sign, the same rules as where no accommodation party is involved are applicable. For example, if the accommodation parties are indorsers, the rule is that, in the absence of a contrary agreement, they are liable to one another in the order in which they indorse,[62] unless the situation falls within the rule providing that two or more persons who sign as makers, acceptors, drawers, indorsers who indorse as joint payees, or anomalous indorsers are jointly and severally liable.[63] In *Zapp National Bank v. Metropolitan Planning & Redevelopment Corp.*,[64] the court determined that the latter rule controlled, and held that individuals and corporations which signed guarantee agreements on the back of notes made by another corporation were jointly and severally liable as they had signed at the same time as part of the same transaction. On the other hand, in *Brown v. Arcuri*,[65] where A, the accommodated party, and B and C, the accommodation parties, all executed the note, the court held B could recover full indemnity from C because it found B would not have signed without C's signature guaranteeing him payments.[66]

¶ 5.03 Agents

[1] Unauthorized Signatures

If a representative signs an instrument for another person without authority to do so,[67] the signature has the effect of an unauthorized signature.[68] As an unauthorized signature, it is ineffective as that of the person whose name is signed, absent ratification or preclusion,[69] and the

---

cial Comment 5. Permanent Editorial Board Commentary No. 11, February 10, 1994, extensively discusses a number of issues in relation to old Article 3, current Article 3, and the Restatement of Suretyship; amendments to Article 3 now bring the discussion into the statute and comments.

62. No different result should occur under current Article 3 even though old § 3-414(2), so stating, is deleted as superfluous. § 3-415 Official Comment 1.

63. § 3-116(a). In some infrequent cases a right to reimbursement will be reduced to one of contribution (for example, where there are successive anomalous indorsers).

64. 308 Minn. 309, 242 N.W.2d 96 (Minn. 1976).

65. 43 A.D.2d 993, 352 N.Y.S.2d 254 (App.Div.1974).

66. Normally an accommodation maker only has a right of contribution from a co-accommodation maker. Fithian v. Jamar, 286 Md. 161, 410 A.2d 569 (Md. 1979). See § 3-116.

¶ 5.03

67. *See* UCC § 1-201(b)(33) and note 10, *supra*. An interesting case dealing with the issue of authority is Willey v. Mayer, 876 P.2d 1260 (Colo.1994) (agent who signed for principal under general power of attorney for own benefit ultimately determined to be authorized).

68. Official Comment 1 to § 3-403. An unauthorized signature also includes a signature of an organization when one or more required agent's signatures are missing. § 3-403(b). This resolves a split of authority under old Article 3. *Compare* Far West Citrus, Inc. v. Bank of America, 91 Cal. App.3d 913, 154 Cal.Rptr. 464 (1979) (not an unauthorized signature), superseded by statute as stated in Edward Fineman Co. v. Superior Court, 66 Cal.App.4th 1110, 78 Cal.Rptr.2d 478 (2 Dist. 1990), with Pine Bluff National Bank v. Kesterson, 257 Ark. 813, 520 S.W.2d 253 (1975) (is an unauthorized signature).

69. As provided in Article 3 or 4. *See* § 3-403(a) discussed in Chapter 4.

person whose name is signed is not liable on the instrument.[70] However, the unauthorized representative is bound in the capacity in which he or she signed in favor of any person who in good faith pays the instrument or takes it for value.[71]

The authority of an agent to sign for a principal on an instrument may be established as in other cases of representation. No particular form of appointment is necessary to establish the authority.[72] It may be by express authority,[73] by authority implied in law or in fact,[74] or may rest upon apparent authority.[75] Parol evidence is admissible to prove or to deny the agent's authority.[76] Moreover, unless specifically denied in the pleadings, each signature on an instrument is admitted,[77] and, even when put in issue, the signature is presumed to be genuine or authorized except where a purported signer has died or become incompetent.[78]

[2] *Authorized Signatures Creating Principal But Not Agent Liability*

If an agent is authorized to sign for the principal, the principal, but not the agent, will be liable in the capacity in which the signature appears if the form of the signature shows unambiguously that the signature is made on behalf of the principal who is identified in the instrument.[79] Thus the proper way to make a signature in a representa-

---

70. § 3–401(a).

71. § 3–403(a).

72. § 3–402(a). The substantive law on this issue is left to law outside the UCC.

73. *E.g.*, Meador v. Ranchmart State Bank, 213 Kan. 372, 517 P.2d 123 (Kan. 1973) (undisputable evidence that signer was agent and attorney of organization with authority to act for it). *See also* note 67, *supra*.

74. *E.g.*, Hartford Accident & Indem. Co. v. South Windsor Bank & Trust Co., 171 Conn. 63, 368 A.2d 76 (Conn. 1976) (insurance agent had no implied authority to indorse check payable to insurance company where agent had no express authority, only one check was involved, and power to indorse was neither necessary or incident to agent's performance of duties).

75. *E.g.*, Senate Motors, Inc. v. Industrial Bank, 9 UCC Rep. Serv. 387 (D.C. Super Ct. 1971) (although car salesman had neither express nor implied authority to indorse checks payable to car dealer, where in ninety-five prior transactions with knowledge of the dealer he had indorsed checks payable to the dealer, dealer had a duty to speak or to permit bank reasonably to retain impression that salesman had authority); W. R. Grimshaw Co. v. First Nat'l Bank & Trust Co., 563 P.2d 117 (Okla.1977) (where business had appearance of family business and son had authority to pick up checks, solicit jobs and make bids, make deposits, sign business letters, evidence was sufficient to raise question of fact as to whether son had authority to indorse checks).

76. Official Comment 1 to old § 3–403.

77. § 3–308(a). *See, e.g.*, Modern Free & Accepted Masons v. Cliff M. Averett, Inc., 118 Ga.App. 641, 165 S.E.2d 166 (Ga.Ct. App.1968) (as no issue as to authority was raised in the pleadings or on trial, the obligation was that of the organization).

78. § 3–308(a).

79. § 3–402(b)(1) and Official Comment 2. A different result may be otherwise established, however, where there is ambiguity. *See* § 3–402(b)(2). Thus, in Kroll v. Crest Plastics, Inc., 142 Mich.App. 284, 369 N.W.2d 487 (Mich.Ct.App.1985), even though the signature evidenced representative capacity, parol was admitted when the note stated "we" promise to pay and the corporation was not in existence. In FDIC v. Woodside Construction, Inc., 979 F.2d 172 (9th Cir.1992), the note bore the agent's signature above the name of the principal followed by the agent's signature with a designation of representative capacity. The court held the agent personally liable and refused parol evidence to the contrary against the FDIC, which was not the payee. *See* § 3–402(b)(2). In Marek Interior Systems, Inc. v. White, 230 Ga.App. 518, 496 S.E.2d 749 (Ga.Ct.App.1998), the note

tive capacity is to name the principal and set forth representative capacity. For example, where a note was signed by individuals with the name of a corporation and with their titles by their signatures, the court held that the note was signed in a representative capacity and the individuals were not personally liable on the note.[80] In another case,[81] a note bearing an individual signature with title, followed by the name of a corporation underneath it, also was determined to be a corporate responsibility.[82]

[3] *Authorized Signatures Creating Agent Liability Alone*

Under Article 3, an authorized agent who signs his or her own name to an instrument may be personally obligated if the form of the signature does not show unambiguously that the signature is made in a representative capacity or if the instrument does not identify the person represented.[83] For example, if Pat Pringle is the principal and Ann Adams is the agent, and the instrument is simply signed "Ann Adams," the agent is personally obligated as against a holder in due course and parol evidence is inadmissible to disestablish her obligation.[84] This is the rule

---

was signed with the name of the principal followed by the signature of the agent preceded by the word "By" and followed by a line for the agent's title, but the note read that (names of individuals) promised to pay. The court found ambiguity and allowed conflicting parol evidence. *Compare* Fred Shearer & Sons, Inc. v. Prendergast, 152 Or.App. 657, 955 P.2d 324 (Or.Ct.App. 1998), where the facts were similar except Prendergast's signature without indication of representative capacity appeared below his signature that did indicate representative capacity but the note also read that Prendergast & Associates, Inc., promises to pay. The court denied co-maker liability, but did leave open indorser liability. *See* §§ 3-204 and 3-419. In Grotz v. Jerutis, 13 Ill.App.3d 543, 301 N.E.2d 60 (1973), the court allowed parol evidence to show that the loans purportedly evidenced by corporate notes signed by defendant in a representative capacity were personal loans that defendant had orally promised to repay, saying the notes were not a complete integration of the loan agreement. *See also* Edward A. Kemmler Memorial Foundation v. 691/733 East Dublin–Granville Road Co., 62 Ohio St.3d 494, 584 N.E.2d 695 (Ohio 1992), where the court considered all documents executed by a partnership in a mortgage transaction in resolving the question of personal liability, and Harris v. Reitz, 649 S.W.2d 228 (Mo.Ct.App.1983), a similar case to the *Grotz* case, *supra*, this note, but the corporate officer escaped liability. And in Zagoria v. DuBose Enter., Inc., 163 Ga. App. 880, 296 S.E.2d 353 (Ga.Ct.App.1982), rev'd 250 Ga. 844, 302 S.E.2d 674 (Ga. 1983), the court refused to hold a nonsigning law partner or a properly signing one in light of the professional corporation statute.

80. First Nat'l Bank v. C & S Concrete Structures, Inc., 128 Ga.App. 330, 196 S.E.2d 473 (Ga.Ct.App.1973). *See also* Official Comment 2 to § 3-402, as "P, by A, Treasurer."

81. Karr v. Baumann, 3 UCC Rep. Serv. 180 (N.Y.Sup.Ct.1966).

82. *But see* Williamson v. Bertino, 685 So.2d 93 (Fla.Dist.Ct.App.1997). The case should be decided differently today. *See also* Official Comment 3 to old § 3-403 which suggested two other methods of signature that should not bind the agent. Thus, assuming that Peter Pringle is the principal and Arthur Adams is his agent, the signature "Peter Pringle" made by Adams will not bind Adams if authorized, and if the instrument reads "Peter Pringle promises to pay" and is signed "Arthur Adams, Agent," Adams should also not be bound. *See* Official Comment 2 to § 3-402.

83. § 3-402(b)(2). This rule is absolute in situations involving a holder in due course without notice that the agent was not intended to be liable, and in other cases the agent must establish a lack of intent by the original parties for representative liability.

84. Official Comment 2, Case #1, to § 3-402. *See also* Schwartz v. Disneyland Vista Records, 383 So.2d 1117 (Fla.Dist.Ct.

even if the person represented is named on the face of the instrument or there is an indication of representative capacity. However, if the person enforcing the instrument is not a holder in due course or had notice that the agent was not intended to be liable, parol evidence of the intent of the original parties is admissible.[85] Thus when a note recited the corporation promised to pay, an individual shareholder who had not indicated representative capacity was able to escape personal liability.[86]

As certainty is an important goal in the law of commercial paper, many courts have tended to construe the rule strictly. For example, in one case the court held that where the name of the corporation was followed by the word "by" before the individual's signature and the individual had signed again on the next line which had the word "debtor" under it, the individual was personally liable as a matter of law.[87] On occasion, very harsh results have been reached. In a New York case,[88] the court assumed the plaintiff had full knowledge that the individuals intended signing in a representative capacity, but it nonethe-

App.1980); Thomas v. McNeill, 448 N.W.2d 231 (S.D.1989); City Bank & Trust Co. v. White, 434 So.2d 1299 (La.Ct.App.1983); Mid–America Real Estate & Inv. Corp. v. Lund, 353 N.W.2d 286 (N.D.1984); Shipp v. First Alabama Bank, 473 So.2d 1014 (Ala. 1985); Campion v. Wynn, 486 N.E.2d 543 (Ind.Ct.App.1985); United Burner Serv., Inc. v. George Peters & Sons, Inc., 5 UCC Rep. Serv. 383 (N.Y.Sup.Ct.1968); Thomas v. McNeill, 448 N.W.2d 231 (S.D.1989) (even though the payee was not a holder in due course and knew the signer was an agent); FDIC v. Trans Pacific Industries, Inc., 14 F.3d 10 (5th Cir.1994) (agent signed with no indication of representative capacity but court decided an identification box at top of note that stated the corporation was the borrower was adequate to prevent personal liability; query if under § 3–402(b)(2) that even is enough to demonstrate ambiguity as the agent could have been a surety without being the borrower); and Tampa Bay Economic Development Corp. v. Edman, 598 So.2d 172 (Fla.Dist.Ct. App.1992) (officers signed with each indicating their title but corporation not named and note stated the undersigned jointly and severally promised; held unambiguous and personal liability; a somewhat dubious result that exposes the vagueness in the § 3–402 test). The rule only applies with respect to liability on the instrument. It would not apply, for example, to an action by a bank on a debt created by overdrafts. Note § 3–402(b)(2) qualifies the above cases to the extent they impose strict liability to one who is not a holder in due course. Note also § 3–402(a) makes an undisclosed principal liable on the instrument.

85. Under § 3–402(b)(2), the agent must prove the intent for the agent not to be liable. C.F. Williamson v. Bertino, 685 So.2d 93 (Fla.Dist.Ct.App.1997). As to what evidence is required *see* Burrus v. Farmers Bank, 938 S.W.2d 889 (Ky.Ct.App.1997).

86. § 3–402(b)(2). *See* Wurzburg Bros. v. Coleman, 404 So.2d 334 (Ala.1981). *See also* First Nat'l Bank v. Blackhurst, 176 W.Va. 472, 345 S.E.2d 567 (W.Va.1986). *Compare* Southern Oxygen Supply Co. v. De Golian, 230 Ga. 405, 197 S.E.2d 374 (Ga. 1973), where the note contained the corporate name in a part of the note that was designated for addresses, only the signature of an individual appeared in the part designated for signatures, and the court decided the principal was not named, and Yeomans v. Coleman, Meadows, Pate Drug Co., 167 Ga.App. 646, 307 S.E.2d 121 (Ga.Ct.App. 1983), where the note recited "I promise to pay," was signed with an individual name, and a corporate name was typed at the bottom; even though the court did not rule the instrument named the corporation as the person represented, it admitted parol in an attempt by the individual to establish signing in a representative capacity, *with* cases in note 84, *supra*. Note the rule is subject to the rights of a remote holder. § 3–402(b)(2); Bankers Turst Co. v. Javeri, 105 A.D.2d 638, 481 N.Y.S.2d 362, 39 UCC Rep. Serv. 1346 (N.Y.App.Div.1984).

87. Phenix Girard Bank v. Cannon, 414 So.2d 926 (Ala.1982). *But see* as contra, Maine Gas & Appliances, Inc. v. Siegel, 438 A.2d 888 (Me.1981).

88. United Burner Serv., Inc. v. George Peters & Sons, Inc., 5 UCC Rep. Serv. 383 (N.Y.Sup.Ct.1968).

less found individual liability.[89] On the other hand, on similar facts the court in *First Bank & Trust Co., Palatine v. Post*[90] refused to impose personal liability, saying that it would create an injustice to apply the rule strictly. Even more to this point is the decision of the court in *St. Regis Paper Co. v. Wicklund*,[91] where the agent signed alone and there was evidence personal liability was intended, but the court allowed parol to show only corporate liability was intended under the assertion the form of the signature was a mutual mistake. In contrast, current Article 3 tends to shy away from harsh results in favor of more equitable individual results where usually mistake and sometimes fraudulent inducement may exist.[92] Also, as discussed, *infra*, a direct attack is made in the case of checks where some courts previously reached very harsh results.[93]

Thus if the instrument identifies the person represented but does not unambiguously show that the agent signed in a representative capacity,[94] or if the person represented is not identified, still the authorized representative is not necessarily personally obligated if the instrument is not held by a holder in due course without notice the agent was not intended to be liable and if the agent proves that the original parties did not intend for the agent to be personally bound.[95] The cases appear to divide essentially into three categories. Indorsements by an officer of the payee or holder are leniently treated because the issue commonly is not one of indorser liability but rather is whether the indorsement is effective to negotiate the instrument. For example, in a California case where notes had been indorsed to a corporation, the court had little trouble in determining that handwritten indorsements in the name of an individual, some of which were followed by the designation "Pres.," constituted the signature of the corporation to further indorse the notes.[96]

The second category does involve liability and concerns checks. Some opinions evidenced the belief that no personal liability should be

---

89. *See also* cases cited in note 84, *supra*.

90. 10 Ill.App.3d 127, 293 N.E.2d 907 (1973).

91. 93 Wn.2d 497, 610 P.2d 903 (Wash. 1980).

92. § 3–402 Official Comment 2.

93. § 3–402(c).

94. *See* Official Comment 2, Case #3, to § 3–402. *See also* Case #1 and Case #2 where the principal is not named. The difference between "named" used in old Article 3 and "identified" is to reverse the cases where the principal's legal name is not used. Official Comment 2 to § 3–402.

95. § 3–402(b)(2). If parol is admissible between the maker and the payee as immediate parties to show that an agent signed only as a representative, it also is admissible when a surety sues the signer as the surety stands in the shoes of the payee-creditor. Moore v. White, 603 P.2d 1119 (Okla.1979).

96. Security Pac. Nat'l Bank v. Chess, 58 Cal.App.3d 555, 129 Cal.Rptr. 852 (1976). *Also see* discussion in Chapter 3, *supra*. Distinguish, however, cases where the indorsement is anomalous so that the issue is liability and not negotiation, and there is no clear indication of representative capacity. In such cases, liability is normally found, subject to a different understanding being established by parol between the immediate parties. *See, e.g.*, Wolfram v. Halloway, 46 Ill.App.3d 1045, 5 Ill.Dec. 264, 361 N.E.2d 587 (1977) (as note indorsed "Duane S. Wolfram (Manager)" showed a possible representative capacity but did not name the person represented, parol is admissible between the immediate parties).

found with respect to a check, the nature of the instrument itself establishing that personal liability was not intended. Current § 3–419(c) adopts this view. Thus, in a New York case the court stated that the name and address of the business was printed at the top of the checks and there was nothing on the face of the checks to show that it was necessary for the manager of the business to indicate that he was signing in a representative capacity.[97] However, other courts treated a check like any other instrument and found personal liability,[98] unless a different understanding was established between the immediate parties. In that latter regard, one court found no individual liability when the signer testified that she never intended to sign in an individual capacity and there was no contradictory evidence,[99] but the mere assertion the signer intended to sign as a representative is not enough.[100] No personal liability was found in *St. Croix Engineering Corp. v. McLay*,[101] when the check was issued in response to an invoice sent to the corporation that the creditor knew was operated by the individual signer of the check.

The third and last category relates to promissory notes. Corporate notes commonly are also individually signed by corporate principals in order to enable corporations of weak creditworthiness or minimal capital to obtain credit. Accordingly, where the note of a corporation shows a signature that is not clearly made in a representative capacity, the cases tend to be, and should be, quite rigorous in refusing to disallow individual liability,[102] again unless a clear understanding to the contrary between the original parties can be shown.[103] Thus, in *Kuhns v. Coussement*[104] the president of a corporation was found personally liable on a note that recited the corporation promised to pay, but which was signed in a way that did not evidence his representative capacity. The president introduced parol evidence that he intended to sign as a corporate officer, that

---

97. Jenkins v. Evans, 31 A.D.2d 597, 295 N.Y.S.2d 226 (App. Div. 1968). Similar cases are Valley Nat'l Bank v. Cook, 136 Ariz. 232, 665 P.2d 576, 36 UCC Rep. Serv. 578 (Ariz.Ct.App.1983); and Pollin v. Mindy Mfg. Co., 211 Pa.Super. 87, 236 A.2d 542 (1967).

98. *E.g.*, American Exch. Bank, Collinsville, Okl. v. Cessna, 386 F.Supp. 494 (N.D.Okla.1974); Financial Assocs. v. Impact Mktg., Inc., 90 Misc.2d 545, 394 N.Y.S.2d 814 (Civ. Ct. 1977); Griffin v. Ellinger, 538 S.W.2d 97 (Tex.1976); Colonial Baking Co. of Des Moines v. Dowie, 330 N.W.2d 279 (Iowa 1983); In re Turner, 49 B.R. 231 (Bankr.D.Mass.1985); Braden Corp. v. Citizens National Bank of Evansville, 661 N.E.2d 838 (Ind.Ct.App.1996); A.L. Jackson Chevrolet, Inc. v. Oxley, 564 P.2d 633 (Okla.1977); Serna v. Milanese, Inc. 643 So.2d 36 (Fla.App.1994); Cooper v. Emery & Sons, 829 S.W.2d 642 (Mo.Ct.App. 1992).

99. Speer v. Friedland, 276 So.2d 84 (Fla.App.1973).

100. § 3–402(b)(2). *See, e.g.*, A.L. Jackson Chevrolet, Inc. v. Oxley, 564 P.2d 633 (Okla.1977); Ex Parte Coussement, 412 So.2d 783 (Ala.1982).

101. 304 N.W.2d 912 (Minn.1981).

102. *E.g.*, Factors & Note Buyers, Inc. v. Green Lane, Inc., 102 N.J.Super. 43, 245 A.2d 223 (Law Div.1968); Rotuba Extruders, Inc. v. Ceppos, 46 N.Y.2d 223, 413 N.Y.S.2d 141, 385 N.E.2d 1068 (N.Y. 1978).

103. Personal liability will be found, of course, in the absence of any parol evidence. Legg. v. Kelly, 412 So.2d 1202 (Ala. 1982). In Berryfast, Inc. v. Zeinfeld, 714 F.2d 826 (8th Cir.1983), evidence that earlier notes, where individual liability was intended, were signed differently, only the corporation had paid, and that later credit had been extended to the corporation, was found adequate. *See also* note 85, *supra*.

104. *See* note 100, *supra*.

the debt was that of the corporation, and that corporate checks for installment payments previously had been accepted. The court stated the necessary showing was that the other party knew he was signing in a representative capacity. On the other hand, the court reached a different conclusion in *Leahy v. McManus*,[105] where payment was not demanded from the individual signer during the life of the payee even though the note became due some four years prior to the payee's death. The court believed the evidence supported the conclusion that the parties regarded the instrument as signed in a representative capacity only.

Note cases also have arisen where the instrument does not name the person represented but does show that the representative signed in a representative capacity. An example would be where Peter Pringle is the principal, Arthur Adams is the agent, and the instrument is signed "Arthur Adams, Agent."[106] Some of the anomalous indorser cases also fall into this category.[107] A like example occurred in a case[108] where the note bore individual signatures followed by the word "trustee." Individual liability will be found unless a clear contrary understanding between the immediate parties can be and is established.[109]

---

105. 237 Md. 450, 206 A.2d 688 (Md. 1965).

106. § 3–402, Official Comment 2, Case #2.

107. *See* note 96, *supra*.

108. Uptown Fed. Sav. & Loan Ass'n v. Collins, 105 Ill.App.2d 459, 245 N.E.2d 521 (1969).

109. § 3–402(b)(2).

Chapter 6

DEFENSES TO AND DISCHARGE OF LIABILITY ON NEGOTIABLE INSTRUMENTS

Analysis

Para.
¶6.01 Introduction 208
    [1] Relation Between Liability and Defenses 208
        [a] Procedural Considerations 208
        [b] Real and Personal Defenses 209
    [2] Use of Parol Evidence to Show Defenses 210
        [a] Introduction 210
        [b] Evidence the Instrument Is Not To Be Binding 211
        [c] Evidence of Conditions 212
¶6.02 Real Defenses, Including Discharge 213
    [1] Infancy and Other Incapacity 213
    [2] Duress 214
    [3] Illegality 214
    [4] Fraud 215
    [5] Discharge 216
    [6] Forgery 216
    [7] Alteration 217
¶6.03 Personal Defenses, Including Discharge 219
    [1] In General 219
        [a] Personal Defenses Described 219
        [b] Jus Tertii (Defenses Based on the Better Right of a Third Party) 219
    [2] "Counterparts" of Real Defenses 222
    [3] Unauthorized Completion 224
    [4] Nondelivery, Delivery for a Special Purpose, and Nonperformance of a Condition Precedent 226
    [5] Want or Failure of Consideration 227
    [6] Discharge 230
        [a] In General 230
        [b] Payment or Satisfaction and Tender of Payment 233
            [i] In General 233
            [ii] Payment or Satisfaction to the Holder 233
            [iii] Adverse Claims 235
            [iv] Tender of Payment 236
        [c] Cancellation and Renunciation 237
        [d] Impairment of Recourse or Collateral 240
            [i] Impairment of Recourse 240
            [ii] Impairment of Collateral 242

Para.	
¶6.03	Personal Defenses, Including Discharge—Continued
	[iii] Waiver of Defense 244
[7]	Statute of Limitations 245

¶ 6.01 Introduction

[1] Relation Between Liability and Defenses

[a] Procedural Considerations

The production of an instrument, once signatures on it are admitted or established,[1] entitles the holder of the instrument to recover its amount, unless a defense is established.[2] Since, unless specifically denied in the pleadings, each signature on an instrument is admitted and, even if in issue, is presumed to be authentic and authorized as a general rule,[3] defenses concerned with signatures may be procedurally lost if not properly raised or established. For example, in *National Equipment, Ltd. v. David Jones Sales*,[4] an alleged defense of forgery was lost when it was not specifically raised as a defense. Other procedural missteps also may result in lost liability.[5] And, while a few opinions are perhaps overly generous to the party asserted to be liable as to what constitutes the "establishment" of a defense,[6] most opinions disallow the claimed defense unless it is made out by a preponderance of the total evidence. Merely asserting the claimed defense or presenting some evidence is not enough. For example, in *Calvert Credit Corp. v. Humble*,[7] the court held mere allegations of defenses, without more, did not establish the defenses, and in *Newby v. Armour Agricultural Chemical Co.*,[8] the court stated that because the evidence with respect to the defense was in conflict, a finding for the holder of the instrument was proper. Of course, a defense also may fail because the facts, as established, do not legally constitute a defense.[9]

The proving of a defense will preclude liability unless the holder is a holder in due course and the defense is not one of those good against a

---

¶ 6.01

1. As liability on an instrument is a function of signature, the absence of a signature or an unauthorized signature is a defense to asserted liability. §§ 3–401(a), 3–403. This is discussed in Chapters 2 and 4 and in this chapter.

2. § 3–308(b).

3. § 3–308(a).

4. 268 S.C. 551, 235 S.E.2d 125 (S.C. 1977).

5. *See, e.g.*, Medi–Fi Two, Inc. v. Riordan, 71 Ill.App.3d 491, 28 Ill.Dec. 19, 390 N.E.2d 1 (1979) (introduction of ledger sheets showing unpaid balance not sufficient where entries contained a number of errors and were contradictory as to amount due).

6. *E.g.*, Peoples Bank v. Haar, 421 P.2d 817 (Okla.1966) (evidence indicating the "possibility" of a defense was sufficient). Section 3–308(b) requires the defense be "proved."

7. 249 A.2d 518 (D.C.1969).

8. 119 Ga.App. 650, 168 S.E.2d 652 (Ga. Ct.App.1969).

9. *See, e.g.*, Cissna Park State Bank v. Johnson, 21 Ill.App.3d 445, 315 N.E.2d 675 (1974) (signature requested and obtained on note without explanation of legal significance did not establish fraud).

holder in due course.[10] A person claiming the rights of a holder in due course has the burden of establishing that he or she or some person under whom he or she claims is in all respects a holder in due course.[11] This burden may determine the outcome of the case as the issue normally is a question of fact,[12] and, where the evidence is conflicting or is not sufficiently persuasive, the result will go against the party having the burden of proof and thus liability will be determined by procedural considerations.

[b] *Real and Personal Defenses*

A defense that a party on the instrument is able to establish may prevent liability to the holder of the instrument. To the extent the holder is a holder in due course, however, the holder takes the instrument free from all defenses or claims in recoupment of any party to it and property or possessory claims of others to the instrument or its proceeds, with certain exceptions.[13] On the other hand, a person who is not a holder in due course takes the instrument subject to defenses and claims in recoupment of the obligor, although the claim of a third person to the instrument or its proceeds may not be raised as a defense except in limited circumstances.[14]

Most defenses are the product of the normal rules of contract law and equity.[15] Certain of these defenses, known as real defenses, are good against even a holder in due course. In the main, real defenses are those which deny the existence of any valid contract stemming from the signature on the instrument.[16] A real defense will defeat liability on the

---

10. § 3–305(a) and (b).

11. § 3–308(b); Godat v. Mercantile Bank, 884 S.W.2d 1, 24 UCC Rep. Serv. 2d 385 (Mo.Ct.App.1994).

12. The existence of elements constituting holder in due course status are questions of fact to be determined by the jury. Northside Bank v. Investors Acceptance Corp., 278 F.Supp. 191 (W.D.Pa.1968). *Compare* Peoples Bank v. Haar, 421 P.2d 817 (Okla.1966) (even though there was no evidence of bad faith or knowledge of the defense and there was evidence of good faith and no knowledge, it is best for the jury to determine the question) *with* Favors v. Yaffe, 605 S.W.2d 342 (Tex.Civ.App.1980) (where plaintiff testified unequivocally as to good faith and there was no contradictory evidence, holder in due course status was established).

13. §§ 3–305(b) and 3–306. Holder in due course status is discussed in Chapter 3, *supra*.

14. §§ 3–305 and 3–306. A claim in recoupment of the obligor against the original payee must arise from the transaction that gave rise to the instrument and the claim of the obligor may be asserted against a transferee only in reduction of the amount owing. *See* Official Comment 3 to § 3–305 and *compare* Trueheart v. Braselton, 875 S.W.2d 412 (Tex.Ct.App.1994) (decided under old Article 3).

15. Many, but by no means all, defenses are enumerated or referred to in §§ 3–305 and 3–306. For example, want or failure of consideration, nonperformance of any condition precedent, nondelivery, delivery for a special purpose, incapacity, duress, illegality, and fraud are mentioned or referred to. Other defenses are mentioned in other provisions of Article 3. *See, e.g.,* § 3–601(b), providing that discharge is a personal defense, and § 3–407(b) and (c), providing defenses in the case of alteration. Not all defenses are the product of contract law or equity. A discharge in an insolvency proceeding like bankruptcy, for example, is a defense. § 3–305(a)(1)(iv).

16. Thus "real" defenses include infancy to the extent it is a defense to a simple contract, incapacity, duress, illegality and fraud in the factum. § 3–305(a)(1). Forgery and alteration technically are not defenses because no obligation against which a defense exists is created. This seems a very fine distinction given the nature of other "real defenses," and forgery and alteration

instrument no matter who holds the instrument. The balance of possible defenses to the liability of a party on an instrument are known as "personal defenses." The nature of the defense involved is important, however, only when the holder of the instrument is able to establish holder in due course status.

[2] Use of Parol Evidence to Show Defenses

[a] Introduction

Because of the abbreviated form required for a negotiable instrument,[17] only infrequently will a defense be evident from the instrument itself.[18] Consequently, normally any defense must be shown by parol evidence. Article 3 contains no parol evidence rule as such. Rather the rule, as it exists outside of Article 3, is applicable with respect to negotiable instruments.[19]

Overall, the parol evidence rule causes little real difficulty with respect to showing a defense to liability on a negotiable instrument. Part of the reason is that only a few defenses, however established, will be good because in many cases the holder will be a holder in due course or a person who is a transferee of the rights of a holder in due course. Thus the question does not arise in every case.[20] Second, those defenses that are real defenses do not invoke the operation of the parol evidence rule because they do not attempt to rewrite any term of the contract, but rather seek to show that what appears to be a contract is not one,[21] or that any contract has been discharged,[22] or that any contract for other reasons should not be enforced.[23] Finally, under old Article 3, as between the parties to the instrument or as between the person who has the defense and a holder who is not a holder in due course, the terms of the

---

may, and for some purposes need to, be considered as "real defenses" under Article 3. See Chapter 3, supra.

17. The instrument may only contain an unconditional promise or order to pay a fixed sum in money on demand or at a definite time to order or to bearer and no other promise, order, obligation, or power given by the maker or drawer except as sparingly authorized in Article 3. § 3–104(a). These requirements are discussed in Chapter 2. Thus a negotiable instrument evidences the gist of but one side of the transaction that gave rise to it.

18. One example of a defense that would be evident on the face of the instrument is a badly done alteration.

19. Pursuant to § 1–103(b). See § 3–117. This point is discussed in Chapter 2.

20. Under § 3–308(b), holder in due course status only needs to be proved once a defense or claim in recoupment is established. Therefore, procedurally the existence of holder in due course status does not moot the issue of whether parol may be used to establish a defense because a determination of holder in due course status need not be undertaken until the parol evidence issue is settled and the defense is or is not established. Most cases, however, do not proceed on this literal a basis and, if holder in due course status is clear, the issue of parol evidence will not arise. See, e.g., Franklin Nat'l Bank v. Sidney Gotowner, Inc., 4 UCC Rep. Serv. 953 (N.Y.Sup.Ct. 1967) (oral condition to negotiation of instrument not questioned when suit was by holder in due course as it was not available as a defense).

21. As in the case of forgery (§§ 3–403(a) and 3–401(a)), and alteration (§ 3–407(c)).

22. As in the case of a bankruptcy discharge or a discharge of which the holder had notice. §§ 3–305(a)(1) and 3–302(b).

23. As in the case of infancy and other incapacity, duress, illegality, and fraud in the factum. § 3–305(a)(1).

instrument may be modified or affected by any other written agreement executed as a part of the same transaction.[24] Thus the question of whether a particular defense may be established by parol evidence usually only comes up where the defense seeks to rewrite one or more terms of the instrument. In that circumstance parol evidence may be barred.

[b] *Evidence the Instrument Is Not To Be Binding*

The most extreme example of a defense to be established by parol is an alleged agreement that the signer of the instrument is not to be bound at all. In one such case[25] the court refused to admit evidence of a prior oral agreement that the notes were not to be effective and were only for the purpose of "regularizing" the transaction,[26] even though it noted that a written agreement executed as part of the same transaction, providing that the instruments should not be enforced at all, could modify or affect the instruments.[27] If the evidence is offered to establish fraud or want or failure of consideration, however, two defenses that must and can be established by parol, it becomes admissible.[28] The bottom line is an extremely fine one. Thus in *First National Bank & Trust Co. v. Thompson*,[29] a bank officer allegedly assured the corporate officer there would be no personal liability and the bank would look only to the corporation for payment. The court found no fraud. In *Town North National Bank v. Broaddus*,[30] the court held that a mere representation by the payee to the maker that the maker would not be liable did not amount to fraud in the inducement. On the other hand, in *Wool-*

---

24. Old § 3–119(1). Current § 3–117 is both more and less explicit and suggests that the above statement might read old § 3–119(1) too literally. Probably few actual results should differ under either version. *But see* text, *infra* this chapter. These provisions also are discussed in Chapter 2 and in Official Comments 1 and 2 to § 3–117.

25. First Nat'l City Bank v. Metal Trading Co., 71 F.R.D. 363, 20 UCC Rep. Serv. 701 (S.D.Fla.1976).

26. Other cases of similar nature are Bank of Suffolk County v. Kite, 49 N.Y.2d 827, 427 N.Y.S.2d 782, 404 N.E.2d 1323 (N.Y. 1980) and Perfect Picture Frames, Inc. v. Consolidated Fine Arts, Ltd., 9 UCC Rep. Serv. 283 (N.Y.Sup.Ct.1971) (that agreement notes were not to be presented for payment was parol variation and of no effect).

27. Official Comment 1 to § 3–117 indicates that any distinction between oral and written agreements should disappear under § 3–117, but Official Comment 2 and the application of the parol evidence rule suggest little real change, if any, will occur. Moreover, such an agreement that is fraudulent or void as against public policy, as in the case of a note given to deceive a bank examiner, is not validated by the provision. *Compare* § 3–117 Official Comment 2 *with* Cosmopolitan Fin. Corp. v. Runnels, 2 Haw. App. 33, 625 P.2d 390 (Hawai'i.Ct.App.1981).

This discussion indicates that the UCC would produce the same result as reached under federal law in D'Oench, Duhme & Co. v. FDIC, 315 U.S. 447, 62 S.Ct. 676, 86 L.Ed. 956 (1942), and thus perhaps illustrates how ill—premised is the federal holder in due course doctrine discussed, *supra*, in Chapter 1.

28. *E.g.*, First Nat'l City Bank v. Metal Trading Co., 71 F.R.D. 363, 20 UCC Rep. Serv. 701 (S.D.Fla.1976) (parol evidence rule does not preclude the defense of lack or failure of consideration); Lewis v. Citizens & Southern Nat'l Bank, 139 Ga.App. 855, 229 S.E.2d 765 (Ga.Ct.App.1976) (ordinarily proof of a contemporaneous oral agreement never to enforce a note is inadmissible except where the defense asserted is that of fraud).

29. 240 Ga. 494, 241 S.E.2d 253 (Ga. 1978).

30. 569 S.W.2d 489 (Tex.1978).

dridge v. Groos National Bank,[31] the court allowed extrinsic evidence to show fraud in the inducement when a representation as to nonenforcement involved a pattern of deceit to induce belief that prior arrangements would also apply to this instrument. *See also* Official Comment 1 to § 3–117 which recognizes there may be a condition to enforceability.

[c] *Evidence of Conditions*

Another distinction exists between an oral agreement that a signer is not to be bound upon the happening of a condition subsequent to the instrument becoming effective, which may not be shown by parol as contradictory to the instrument,[32] and an agreement that the signer will not become bound until the satisfaction of a condition precedent, which may be shown by parol as precluding any obligation at all.[33] Thus, in a Georgia case the court characterized an agreement that the note would be transferred to a corporation organized to carry on the business ventures of the individual makers as one which did not relate to the creation of a valid obligation, but rather to restrictions upon one that had come into existence.[34] Yet in another case, the court admitted parol evidence to show that the note was delivered for the special purpose of assuring that an individual would work for a partnership and would be canceled when this was performed.[35] It would seem that the agreement in the first case could be construed just as well as creating no liability until an event occurs, and the agreement in the second case as discharging an obligation if an event occurs. Perhaps a wise course of action, as Official Comment 2 to § 3–117 suggests, is to draft a merger or integration clause into instruments, including a statement that no condition to enforceability was agreed upon.

Generally, evidence that contradicts any of the specific terms of an instrument will be refused. Accordingly, courts have denied evidence of agreements that attempt to condition otherwise unconditional liability. For example, in *Main Bank of Chicago v. Baker*[36] the note clearly obligated its makers to make monthly payments until the note was paid, and the court denied admissibility of evidence of oral agreements making the receipt of lease payments a condition to the note payments.[37] Courts

---

31. 603 S.W.2d 335 (Tex.Civ.App.1980).

32. *E.g.,* La Voie v. Celli, 61 Misc.2d 126, 304 N.Y.S.2d 671 (Sup. Ct. 1969) (parol evidence may not be used to show a condition subsequent).

33. Official Comment 1 to § 3–117; *e.g.,* Kelley v. Carson, 120 Ga.App. 450, 171 S.E.2d 150 (Ga.Ct.App.1969) (delivery on condition that proceeds would enlarge working capital of corporation and that four other persons simultaneously contribute a like amount); Brames v. Crates, 399 N.E.2d 437 (Ind.Ct.App.1980) (parol evidence may be used to show delivery for a special purpose only); Long Island Trust Co. v. International Institute for Packaging Education, Ltd., 38 N.Y.2d 493, 381 N.Y.S.2d 445, 344 N.E.2d 377 (N.Y. 1976) (only four out of five required indorsers had signed); Nawas v. Holmes, 541 S.W.2d 283 (Tex.Civ.App. 1976) (note delivered to be enforced only if debt owed by travel agency not paid).

34. Tatum v. Bank of Cumming, 135 Ga.App. 675, 218 S.E.2d 677 (Ga.Ct.App. 1975).

35. Chera v. The Shores, 145 N.J.Super. 19, 366 A.2d 994 (App.Div.1976).

36. 86 Ill.2d 188, 56 Ill.Dec. 14, 427 N.E.2d 94 (Ill. 1981).

37. *See also* Texas Export Dev. Corp. v. Schleder, 519 S.W.2d 134 (Tex.Civ.App. 1974) (oral understanding that payees would look solely to expected oil profits for

also have avoided contradictory evidence bearing on the time that the instrument would otherwise be due. Thus in *La Voie v. Celli*,[38] parol evidence that a note due by its terms ninety days after its date would be due only upon the commencement of a building or within six years whichever occurred first, was excluded.[39] Ultimately, there are as many possible fact situations that may raise the parol evidence issue as there are provisions in instruments.[40]

¶ 6.02 Real Defenses, Including Discharge

[1] Infancy and Other Incapacity

Infancy, to the extent that it is a defense to a simple contract, and other incapacity as renders the obligation of the signing party a nullity, constitute real defenses.[41] Law other than the UCC determines when infancy is available as a defense and the conditions under which it may be asserted.[42] For example, in *Trenton Trust Co. v. Western Surety Co.*,[43] the court held infancy under the circumstances involved in that case was a real defense because a state statute provided that no contract pledging the assets of a minor was binding without court approval. Other law also determines what is covered by the category of incapacity. Generally it includes mental incompetence, guardianship, ultra vires acts or lack of corporate capacity to do business, any remaining incapacity of married women, or any other incapacity apart from infancy.[44] Other law also determines what is necessary to establish the defense. For example, in *Katski v. Boehm*[45] the court determined that incompetency was not established by the evidence the signer of the instrument was nervous, distraught, and under strain. Infancy is a real defense even though its effect is only to render the instrument voidable and not void, but incapacity is not a real defense if under local law its effect is merely to render the obligation voidable at the election of the obligor.[46]

---

reimbursement could not be shown). *But see* Scafidi v. Johnson, 420 So.2d 1113 (La. 1982) (oral understanding note to be paid only from earnings of company could be shown); Mozingo v. North Carolina Nat'l Bank, 31 N.C.App. 157, 229 S.E.2d 57 (N.C.App.1976) *cert. denied* 291 N.C. 711, 232 S.E.2d 204 (N.C. 1977) (agreement note to be paid only out of proceeds from sale of building projects could be shown).

38. 61 Misc.2d 126, 304 N.Y.S.2d 671 (Sup. Ct. 1969).

39. *See also* Chaplin v. Milne, 555 S.W.2d 161 (Tex.Civ.App.1977) (oral agreement that on its due date note would be renegotiated not admissible).

40. To illustrate only an additional two: Factors & Note Buyers, Inc. v. Green Lane, Inc., 102 N.J.Super. 43, 245 A.2d 223 (Law Div.1968) (agreement not to discount notes); Farmington Nat'l Bank v. Basin Plastics, 94 N.M. 668, 615 P.2d 985 (N.M.

1980) (agreement to secure and perfect a security interest where note did not require the taking of any security and there was a consent to exchange or releases of any collateral).

¶ 6.02

41. §§ 3–305(a)(1)(i) and (ii) and (b).

42. Official Comment 1 to § 3–305.

43. 599 S.W.2d 481 (Mo.1980).

44. Official Comment 1 to § 3–305. *See, e.g.*, Ryan v. Ryan, 298 A.2d 343 (Del.Super.Ct.1972) (disability to contract due to marriage).

45. 249 Md. 568, 241 A.2d 129 (Md. 1968).

46. Official Comment 1 to § 3–305. *See, e.g.*, Estate of Lucas v. Whiteley, 550 S.W.2d 767 (Tex.Civ.App.1977) (under Texas law, obligation of incompetent is not void).

[2] Duress

Duress sufficient to render the obligation of the signing party a nullity is a real defense.[47] Duress is a matter of degree. It must be sufficient to void the signature to constitute a real defense and if it only renders the signature voidable, the defense is personal and may be cut off by a holder in due course.[48] In this light, unconscionability, which is a defense resulting from more than inequality in bargaining power but less than duress,[49] would not be a real defense.

[3] Illegality

Illegality of the transaction that renders the obligation of the signing party a nullity qualifies as a real defense.[50] The effect of any illegality is determined under law other than the UCC, and must be sufficient to make the obligation entirely null and void or else the defense will be only a personal one.[51] For example, in *Bankers Trust Co. v. Litton Systems, Inc.*,[52] though the contract was induced by commercial bribery, which was a criminal offense, the court determined the bribery only rendered the contract voidable rather than void, and thus the instrument involved was enforceable by a holder in due course.[53]

The mere fact that a negotiable instrument stems from a transaction that is prohibited by statute or from a transaction that is contrary to public policy should not necessarily result in a refusal to enforce the instrument in the hands of a holder in due course.[54] Thus in one case where a note was obtained by a corporation as part of a transaction that violated an injunction and then was sold to a holder in due course, the court allowed enforcement of the note because the illegality of the corporation's entering into the transaction did not render the note obligation a nullity, and no statute existed to make the note void and

---

47. § 3–305(a)(1)(ii) and (b).

48. Official Comment 1 to § 3–305. The issue is for the trier of fact. Ralls v. First Federal Sav. & Loan Assoc., 422 So.2d 764 (Ala.1982). In Quazzo v. Quazzo, 136 Vt. 107, 386 A.2d 638 (Vt. 1978), the court did not determine if the duress employed rendered the obligation void as the holder was not a holder in due course and therefore was subject to any defense of duress which would be available in an action on a simple contract.

49. This characterization derives from Official Comment 1 to UCC § 2–302, which indicates the principle is one of the prevention of oppression and unfair surprise and not of disturbance of allocation of risks because of superior bargaining power.

50. § 3–305(a)(1)(ii) and (b).

51. Official Comment 1 to § 3–305.

52. 599 F.2d 488 (2d Cir.1979).

53. *See also* AgriStor Credit Corp. v. Lewellen, 472 F.Supp. 46 (N.D.Miss.1979)

(usury statute calling for forfeiture of interest, or interest and principal, makes the obligation merely voidable). *Compare* Vedder v. Spellman, 78 Wn.2d 834, 480 P.2d 207 (Wash. 1971) (state statute barring compensation for work done by unlicensed contractor precluded suit on check by nonholder in due course) with Kedzie & 103rd Currency Exchange, Inc. v. Hodge, 156 Ill.2d 112, 189 Ill.Dec. 31, 619 N.E.2d 732 (Ill. 1993) (real defense of illegality limited to situations where statute makes void the instrument arising from the contract).

54. Of course, if the instrument is not actually associated with an illegal transaction, no defense exists. *See, e.g.*, North Cent. Kansas Production Credit Ass'n v. Boese, 19 UCC Rep. Serv. 179 (D.Kan.1976) (check merely cashed by Las Vegas casino). *But see* Carnival Leisure Industries, Ltd. v. Aubin, 830 F.Supp. 371 (S.D.Tex.1993), *rev'd* 53 F.3d 716 (5th Cir.1995).

unenforceable.⁵⁵ Where a strong public policy is involved, however, the illegality of the transaction will taint the instrument and make it void. To illustrate, in a Nevada case⁵⁶ the court held that checks to cover gambling losses by statute were void and could not be enforced by a holder in due course.⁵⁷

[4] *Fraud*

Misrepresentation that induces a party to sign the instrument with neither knowledge nor reasonable opportunity to obtain knowledge of its character or its essential terms is a real defense.⁵⁸ The fraud must negate any intent to enter into the contract upon which liability is sought,⁵⁹ and where there is actual intent, albeit induced by fraud, there is no real defense but only a personal defense.⁶⁰ The common illustration of the real defense of fraud is where the party is tricked into signing the instrument in the belief that it is merely a receipt or some other document.⁶¹ The defense does extend to an instrument signed with knowledge that it is a negotiable instrument if the signing party is without knowledge of its essential terms.⁶²

According to the Official Comments, the real defense of fraud may be lost, and reduced to a personal defense, if the signer's ignorance of the character or contents of the instrument is not excusable. In making that determination, all relevant factors should be taken into account, including the age and sex of the signing party; the party's intelligence, education, business experience, and ability to read or to understand English; the representations made and the reason for relying on them or for having confidence in the person making them; the possibility of obtaining independent information; and the apparent need for acting without delay. Thus in *Equitable Discount Corp. v. Fischer*,⁶³ the defendant knew he was signing three obligations that he would be required to pay on their due dates and that they were like checks, with which he was familiar, but he made no effort to learn from an outside source the meaning or implication of the instruments. The court denied the real defense of fraud with respect to his liability on the trade acceptances. On

---

55. New Jersey Mortgage & Inv. Corp. v. Berenyi, 140 N.J.Super. 406, 356 A.2d 421 (App.Div.1976).

56. Sandler v. Eighth Judicial District, 96 Nev. 622, 614 P.2d 10 (Nev. 1980). *But see* note 54, *supra*.

57. *See also* Pacific Nat'l Bank v. Hernreich, 240 Ark. 114, 398 S.W.2d 221 (Ark. 1966) (notes executed pursuant to contract made by unlicensed foreign corporation in violation of statute prohibiting foreign corporations from doing business without compliance with requirements were void ab initio).

58. § 3–305(a)(1)(iii) and (b).

59. Official Comment 1 to § 3–305.

60. *See, e.g.*, Citizens Nat'l Bank v. Brazil, 141 Ga.App. 388, 233 S.E.2d 482 (Ga.Ct. App.1977) (check given on false representation that materials for construction were already purchased was subject to only personal defense even if the crime of theft by deception was committed).

61. Official Comment 1 to § 3–305. An illustrative pre-Code case is First Nat'l Bank v. Fazzari, 10 N.Y.2d 394, 223 N.Y.S.2d 483, 179 N.E.2d 493 (N.Y. 1961) (maker signed note believing it was a wage statement).

62. *Id*.

63. 1 UCC Rep. Serv. 245 (Pa.Com.Pl. 1957).

the other hand, in *United Bank & Trust Co. v. Schaeffer*,[64] the court allowed the real defense of fraud when the party sued was almost illiterate and the character of the instrument signed was misrepresented to him as a character reference by his friend and supervisor at work. The most common excuses offered are a failure to read the instrument and signing it in blank. Both commonly are rejected.[65]

[5] Discharge

A discharge in insolvency proceedings, such as bankruptcy, is a real defense.[66] Aside from recognizing the paramount nature of the federal Bankruptcy Code,[67] this provision is necessary to prevent the massive increase in the use of commercial paper that would result if a holder in due course could cut off this kind of defense to the obligation and thus impair the fresh-start concept of bankruptcy.

Another kind of discharge that was stated to be a real defense in old Article 3 was any discharge of which the holder had notice when the instrument was taken.[68] This provision was a housekeeping one. Under old § 3–602, no discharge of any party provided by Article 3 was effective against a subsequent holder in due course unless the holder in due course had notice of it when the instrument was taken. Old § 3–304(1)(b) by implication provided that notice of a discharge of one party, which left other parties liable on the instrument, did not prevent holder in due course status. But holder in due course status technically allowed the holder in due course to take free of all defenses except real defenses. Thus, to preserve the rule of old § 3–602, this exception technically was needed, even though its character was distinctly different from that of other real defenses. Current Article 3 does not treat this type of discharge as a real defense, but states that notice of it does not defeat holder in due course status although the discharge is effective against any person with notice of it.[69]

An example of the defense would be the cancellation of an indorsement, which under § 3–604(a) discharges the indorser but leaves the maker and prior indorsers liable. As to such parties, a purchaser of the instrument may be a holder in due course, but the purchaser takes the instrument subject to the discharge of the indorser of which there was notice from the instrument.[70]

[6] Forgery

An unauthorized signature is ineffective as that of the person whose

---

64. 280 Md. 10, 370 A.2d 1138 (Md. 1977).

65. Failure to read: Exchange Int'l Leasing Corp. v. Consolidated Business Forms Co., 462 F.Supp. 626 (W.D.Pa.1978). Signing in blank: Lynric Assocs., Inc. v. Moroh, 3 UCC Rep. Serv. 181 (N.Y.Sup.Ct. 1966).

66. § 3–305(a)(1)(iv) and (b).

67. Official Comment 8 to old § 3–305.

68. Old § 3–305(2)(e).

69. §§ 3–302(b) and 3–601(b); also § 3–602(d).

70. Official Comment 9 to old § 3–305. *See also* old § 3–304, Official Comment 4, and old § 3–602, Official Comment.

name is signed.[71] Because no person is liable on an instrument unless their signature appears on it,[72] an unauthorized signature that is not ratified[73] constitutes what amounts to a real defense if there is no preclusion against raising the issue.[74] Thus in the simple case of a forged check, the ostensible drawer is not liable upon it if the drawee refuses to pay it and the ostensible drawer is then sued by the holder. The ostensible drawer is not liable for the amount of the check even if the drawee does pay it because it is not properly payable under § 4–401(a). Further ramifications of allocating loss from a forgery are discussed in Chapter 3 and in Chapter 7.

[7] Alteration

The final matter that amounts to a real defense is alteration.[75] No holder who alters an instrument or who takes an instrument subsequent to an alteration has an unqualified right to enforce the instrument otherwise than in accordance with its original tenor.[76] Thus in *Wallach Sons, Inc. v. Bankers Trust Co.*,[77] the court held that a check altered after it was certified was good only for the amount originally certified. If an ordinary check is altered and then is not paid by the drawee, the drawer is not liable to the holder beyond the original tenor of the item. Nor is the drawer liable for more than the original tenor if the drawee does pay the altered check. Under § 4–401(d)(1), a bank that pays an altered item may only charge the account of its customer according to the original tenor of the altered item. Further ramifications of allocating loss from an alteration are discussed in Chapter 7.

An altered instrument may be enforced as altered, however, when the alteration was assented to.[78] For example, in *Bluffestone v. Abrahams*[79] a note signed by the maker was altered by the holder to add monthly payment and attorney fee provisions with the consent of the maker's father and brother, who then signed the note. The court held

---

71. § 3–403(a). It is effective as that of the signer in favor of a person who in good faith pays the instrument or takes it for value.

72. § 3–401(a). Current law does allow an agent to bind an undisclosed principal. § 3–401(a)(ii).

73. Under § 3–403(a), an unauthorized signature may be ratified for all purposes of Article 3 and then becomes valid on a retroactive basis so far as its effect as a signature is concerned.

74. *See* note 16, *supra*. Preclusion includes the possibility of an estoppel and negligence preventing a denial. *See* § 3–406(a). Thus negligence does not reduce this real defense to a personal one as in the case of fraud, but rather removes it entirely. *But note* § 3–406(b) if both parties are negligent. Preclusion is discussed in Chapter 4, *supra*.

75. *See* note 16, *supra*. Distinguish unauthorized completion discussed *infra*.

76. A person not a subsequent holder in due course may enforce an instrument that has not been fraudulently altered according to its original tenor. A subsequent holder in due course or a person that paid the instrument may enforce any altered instrument according to its original tenor. § 3–407(b) and (c).

77. 62 Misc.2d 19, 307 N.Y.S.2d 297 (N.Y. Civ. Ct. 1970).

78. § 3–407(b). So too when the alteration has been ratified. § 3–407(b). *See*, *e.g.*, Teratron Gen. v. Institutional Inv. Trust, 18 Wn.App. 481, 569 P.2d 1198 (Wash.Ct. App.1977).

79. 125 Ariz. 42, 607 P.2d 25 (Ariz.Ct. App.1979).

the change was binding upon the father and brother as consenting parties.

An altered instrument also may be enforced as altered if the party whose contract is changed is precluded from asserting the defense.[80] A number of cases concerning a preclusion against raising an alteration have been litigated. The classic case is where a person, by leaving spaces, so negligently draws an instrument as to facilitate its material alteration. In this situation, the negligence will be held to have substantially contributed to the alteration, and the person will be precluded from asserting the alteration against a person who has in good faith paid the instrument, or taken it for value or for collection.[81] Exactly this arose in *Farmers State Bank v. Ray*,[82] where the amount line of the check was not fully filled in, the payee raised it from $1.50 to $1,851.50, and the drawee bank paid it. The trial court, perhaps on the basis that the drawer was an innocent bumpkin and the payee was a persuasive slicker, found no negligence on the part of the drawer. The court of appeals properly reversed this, but the Texas Supreme Court reinstated the finding of the trial court. Hard cases do make bad law, but these kinds of cases also seem to be uniformly decided. The court in *Owensboro National Bank v. Crisp*[83] reached virtually the same result by shifting the loss to the bank after finding some failure to follow reasonable commercial standards on its part. Such cases should be amenable to more reasonable results under current § 3–406(b), where the negligence of each party is taken into account on a proportional basis, except that the bank's negligence must at least substantially contribute before any balancing occurs.

As the above discussion demonstrates, the circumstances under which an altered instrument may be enforced as altered are essentially the same circumstances under which an instrument bearing an unauthorized signature may be enforced, as discussed in Chapter 4. This should not be surprising as an altered instrument is, to the extent of the alteration, without authorization.[84]

If an alteration of an instrument is fraudulent,[85] any party whose obligation is thereby affected is discharged as against the party enforcing the instrument, absent assent or a preclusion to raise the defense.[86] However, a subsequent holder in due course or payor takes free of any

---

80. §§ 3–407(b), 3–406. Section 4–406 on the failure of a customer of a bank to report the alteration after examining the bank statement also may be applicable and is discussed in Chapter 9.

81. *See* Official Comments 1 and 3, Case #3 to § 3–406. Distinguish HSBC Bank USA v. F & M Bank–Northern Virginia, 246 F.3d 335, 44 UCC Rep. Serv. 2d 319 (4th Cir.2001) (drawer used adequate care even though spaces left).

82. 565 S.W.2d 103 (Tex.Civ.App.1978), *rev'd*, 576 S.W.2d 607 (Tex.1979). A similar case but involving forgery rather than alteration is Lichtenstein v. Kidder, Peabody & Co., Inc., 840 F.Supp. 374 (W.D.Pa.1993).

83. 608 S.W.2d 51 (Ky.1980).

84. *See* the discussion on this point in Chapter 4.

85. Under old § 3–407(2)(a), the alteration had to be both fraudulent and material, but under § 3–407(1) virtually all alterations were material. Current § 3–407 more directly states the rule and § 3–407(a) defines alteration. *See* Official Comment 1 to § 3–407. Spoliation by a meddling stranger should not affect the rights of the holder.

86. § 3–407(b). An innocently made alteration does not discharge any party and the instrument may be enforced according to its original tenor. Official Comment 1 to § 3–407; Willis v. Willis, 30 UCC Rep. Serv.

defense of discharge based on alteration.[87] Thus, this defense stemming from an alteration is only a personal defense and must be distinguished from the real defense of alteration. The personal defense of alteration is treated, *infra*.

¶ 6.03 Personal Defenses, Including Discharge

[1] In General

[a] Personal Defenses Described

Under § 3–305(a)(2) and (b), a person who does not have the rights of a holder in due course takes the instrument subject to all defenses under Article 3 and to those of any party that would be available in an action on a simple contract. Defenses that are good against all but a holder in due course are known as personal defenses. Personal defenses largely stem from the general law of contract and equity. They thus include matters ranging from want or failure of consideration to discharge. There also are defenses stemming from the fact that a negotiable instrument is property, such as the defense of nondelivery, and defenses resulting from a number of policies that may affect the contract, such as an illegal purpose, but which do not go so far as to void it and thus constitute a real defense. Many personal defenses are created or referenced in Article 3.[88] Many others arise outside of Article 3 and are not referred to except indirectly through UCC § 1–103(b), which makes law outside of Article 3 generally applicable. Examples would be estoppel,[89] waiver,[90] and setoff.[91] This chapter will limit itself to discussion of some of the more common personal defenses as judged from the litigated cases.

[b] Jus Tertii (Defenses Based on the Better Right of a Third Party)

A person who does not have the rights of a holder in due course also takes the instrument subject to all valid claims of a property or possesso-

---

1332 (D.D.C.1980), *aff'd in part, rev'd in part* 655 F.2d 1333 (D.C.Cir.1981) (alteration made with benevolent motive). *See also* Liberty State Bank & Trust v. Hemisphere Development Group, Inc., 98 Mich.App. 285, 296 N.W.2d 241 (Mich.Ct.App.1980) (alteration of loan ledger card not alteration of instrument).

87. § 3–407(b) and (c). *See* Official Comment 2 to § 3–407 as to this, and, as to the further discharge of any party who had a right of recourse against the party discharged, *see* Official Comment 1.

¶ 6.03

88. The list ranges throughout Article 3 from § 3–118, providing statutes of limitations, through § 3–605, dealing with discharge of accommodation parties and others. *See* § 3–305(a)(2) and Official Comment 2, which furnishes a list of many of the sections in Article 3 stating defenses, and mentions the more prevalent common law defenses. Also § 3–305(d) deals with what defenses of the principal may be raised by an accommodation party.

89. *E.g.*, Commonwealth Bank & Trust Co. v. Plotkin, 371 Mass. 218, 355 N.E.2d 917 (Mass. 1976).

90. *E.g.*, Munson v. American Nat'l Bank & Trust Co., 484 F.2d 620 (7th Cir. 1973).

91. *E.g.*, Bank of Wyandotte v. Woodrow, 394 F.Supp. 550 (W.D.Mo.1975). Article 3 itself now clarifies the ability of an obligor to set off against the person enforcing the instrument, and deals with the issue as one involving a claim in recoupment. § 3–305(a)(3), Official Comment 3, and discussion, *supra*.

ry right to it or its proceeds on the part of any person.[92] Literally applied, this rule would permit a nonholder in due course seeking to enforce the liability of a party to the instrument to be defeated in that effort, not only by reason of a defense belonging to the party sued, but also by reason of that party using the claim of a third person as a defense. In short, recovery against the party sued might be denied because the holder might not be the proper person to enforce the instrument.

The concept of a claim is not synonymous with that of a defense.[93] For example, failure of consideration is not a claim.[94] Still, a great number of matters are includable within the category of claims.[95] Consequently, without more a nonholder in due course would be exposed to a considerable risk that enforcement of the instrument would be defeated. A consequence would be discouragement of the assignability of negotiable instruments. Moreover, it would be a questionable policy to allow or require strangers to a claim to litigate it. Suppose the claim stems from a negotiation of a note made by an incapacitated person. The maker wants to use this claim to defeat liability to the holder, but the person with the claim may be perfectly satisfied and may not wish to return what was given for the note. Even more to the point, if use of the claim is allowed and in the suit by the holder the claim is not established and liability is found, may not liability also be found to the claimant when the claimant sues the maker because the claimant is not bound by the prior litigation to which the claimant was not a party?[96] Alternatively, if the claimant does not sue, why should the maker obtain a windfall by also denying the holder recovery?[97]

Section 3–305(c), with minor exception,[98] expressly disallows jus tertii (a defense based on the better right of a third party). The section provides that the defense, claim in recoupment or claim of any third person to the instrument is not available as a defense to any party liable on the instrument unless the third person actually defends the action for the liable party. The presence of the claimant removes the objections to the use of the third-party claim and, indeed, serves judicial economy by

---

92. § 3–306. Included is a claim to rescind a negotiation and recover the instrument or its proceeds.

93. Fulton Nat'l Bank v. Delco Corp., 128 Ga.App. 16, 195 S.E.2d 455 (Ga.Ct.App. 1973).

94. *But see* Capital Inv. Co. v. Estate of Morrison, 484 F.2d 1157 (4th Cir.1973), *cert. denied*, 440 U.S. 981, 99 S.Ct. 1790, 60 L.Ed.2d 241 (1979) (transfer without consideration asserted to give rise to claim of constructive or resulting trust).

95. Claims would include claims of legal title, lien, constructive trust, or other equity, and other claims of right against the instrument or its proceeds stemming from rescission of a negotiation, whether based on incapacity, fraud, duress, mistake, illegality, breach of trust or duty, or any other reason, or from conditional delivery or delivery for a special purpose. § 3–306 Official Comment. Section 3–306 also includes the claim of a person who was wrongfully deprived of possession. Claims in recoupment are different, however, and are dealt with in § 3–305(a)(3).

96. Official Comment 5 to old § 3–306 observes that the obligor usually will have no satisfactory evidence of its own as to the claim, and so a provision that the obligor may not use it is as much for the obligor's protection as for that of the holder.

97. *See, e.g.,* Landscape Design & Constr., Inc. v. Warren, 598 S.W.2d 38 (Tex. Civ.App.1980).

98. For example, § 3–305(d) clarifies this does not bar an accommodation party using a principal's defenses.

settling all litigation at once. The claimant may appear by intervening in the holder's action against the obligor, or by defending the action for the latter and asserting the claim in the course of the intervention or defense. Moreover, any interpleader, deposit in court, or other available procedure, like vouching-in under which the liable party may bring the claimants into court or be discharged without litigating the claim as a defense, will satisfy the rule.[99] Otherwise, the claim cannot be used. Thus in *Federal Deposit Insurance Corp. v. Moore*,[100] the maker of a note upon which the FDIC brought suit asserted that the FDIC had acquired the note illegally in taking over the assets of a bank in receivership. The court held that under old § 3–306(d) the party liable on the instrument could not assert the alleged illegality as a defense.

There is a purported exception to the rule that a third party's claim cannot be used; a person that does not have the rights of a holder in due course is subject to the defense that he or she or a person through whom he or she holds the instrument acquired it by theft.[101] Even though not explicitly stated, it also is assertable that payment or satisfaction to the holder would be inconsistent with the terms of a restrictive indorsement.[102] A refusal to pay because payment would be contrary to a restrictive indorsement really is a defense belonging to the party sued based on the failure of the suing party to establish that party's own contractual right to recover, and thus not a jus tertii case at all. Of course, to the extent the theft and loss exception normally will involve a missing or unauthorized indorsement,[103] this claim also could be viewed as a defense belonging to the party sued that there is no contractual obligation to pay the suing party who is not a holder,[104] rather than that the suing party should not be paid because of the better right of another party from whom the instrument was stolen. In any event, whether a personal defense or a claim of a third person that may be raised, loss or theft and payment in contravention of a restrictive indorsement, as well as any defense belonging to the party sued, may be asserted against one not a holder in due course.[105]

---

99. Official Comment 4 to § 3–305. *See, e.g.*, Fulton Nat'l Bank v. Delco Corp., 128 Ga.App. 16, 195 S.E.2d 455 (Ga.Ct.App. 1973) where the claim was allowed to be asserted because the claimant was involved in the litigation. *But see* Duxbury v. Roberts, 388 Mass. 385, 446 N.E.2d 401 (Mass. 1983), where it was not because the person having the claim had not joined the action and defended the suit itself.

100. 448 F.Supp. 493 (D.S.C.1978).

101. Section 3–305(c) also contains this exception for loss.

102. *See* old § 3–306(d). Current § 3–305(d) does not so state for the reason discussed immediately following in the text.

103. If not, the instrument would have to be a bearer instrument and not be held by a holder in due course, a very rare case. Nonetheless, in such a case the analysis immediately following in the text would not be available, and an exception is necessary.

104. No person taking with an unauthorized indorsement in the chain, or one that is missing, can be a holder under §§ 3–403(a), 3–201(b), 3–204(a). Essentially, the only person entitled to payment is a holder or a person with the rights of a holder. §§ 3–412, 3–413(a), 3–414(b), 3–415(a), 3–301, 3–602(a).

105. *See also* discussion in Chapter 3, *supra*. Isolated other situations that may be viewed as a variation of the jus tertii issue exist, for example, the ability of a surety to use a defense of the principal, discussed in Chapter 5. *See also* Chemical Bank v. Haskell, 68 A.D.2d 347, 417 N.Y.S.2d 541 (N.Y.App.Div.1979), *rev'd on other grounds*,

[2] "Counterparts" of Real Defenses

Some of the real defenses discussed previously have a counterpart that is only a personal defense.[106] For example, any discharge other than in insolvency proceedings of which the holder *does not have* notice when the instrument is taken is a personal defense.[107] Another is fraud in the factum, which loses its character as a real defense and becomes a personal defense if the person asserting the defense did not utilize a reasonable opportunity to obtain knowledge as to the character or essential terms of the instrument.[108] Finally, any incapacity or duress or illegality other than infancy, that does not render the obligation of the party a nullity but only voidable, is a defense even though not a real one.[109]

Related to the real defenses of fraud in the factum and alteration are the personal defenses of fraud in the inducement and discharge due to a fraudulent alteration.[110] The essential distinction between the real defense of fraud in the factum and the personal defense of fraud in the inducement is that, for the former, the person must not have intended to sign an instrument such as the one signed at all;[111] for the latter, there was an intent to sign but it was fraudulently induced.[112] An example is where the payee of a check obtained it by falsely representing that he had already purchased the materials to be used in performing a contract to make improvements on the drawer's home. The court held the defense of fraud was personal, even though the payee might be guilty of the crime of theft by deception.[113]

As a general proposition and as discussed earlier in this chapter, no unauthorized alteration of an instrument may be enforced by any holder,

---

51 N.Y.2d 85, 432 N.Y.S.2d 478, 411 N.E.2d 1339 (N.Y. 1980), where the court allowed the limited partners of a partnership to assert, when sued on their individual notes given to the partnership and transferred to the bank, the claim of the partnership, which was not a party to the action, that the general partner had breached its duty to the partnership in transferring the notes to the bank, which was asserted not to be a holder in due course. The court believed old § 3–306(d) was not intended to bar this type of defense. Actually, the case may simply illustrate the line of reasoning described in the above text: that the bank had no ability to enforce the notes in its own right because the court characterized the indorsement of the partnership necessary to give the bank holder status as unauthorized and thus wholly inoperative.

106. Some do not. Thus infancy is a real defense or no defense at all. Likewise, discharge in insolvency proceedings is only a real defense. Forgery and alteration viewed as defenses also are only real defenses because any negligence on the part of the party seeking to assert the defense under §§ 3–406 and 4–406 is relevant but does not operate to recharacterize the defense.

107. § 3–601(b).

108. § 3–305(a)(1)(iii) and Official Comment 1.

109. § 3–305(a)(1)(ii). *See, e.g.*, Estate of Lucas v. Whiteley, 550 S.W.2d 767 (Tex. Civ.App.1977) (under Texas law the obligation of an incompetent is not void but merely voidable and the defense of incompetency will be cut off if the holder is a holder in due course who has not dealt with the party to the instrument having the defense).

110. The former defense arises outside of Article 3. The latter is created by § 3–407(b) to discourage the alteration of instruments.

111. Official Comment 1 to § 3–305.

112. Citizens Nat'l Bank v. Brazil, 141 Ga.App. 388, 233 S.E.2d 482 (Ga.Ct.App. 1977) (fraudulent misrepresentations which induce the execution of an otherwise valid contract render it voidable but not void).

113. *Id.*

even a holder in due course. In addition, an alteration of an instrument by the holder of it that is fraudulent is a complete defense to all liability on the instrument of any party whose obligation is affected by the alteration as against the person making the alteration.[114] Any alteration is material because any change in the contract of any party in any respect is material.[115] This includes the addition of one cent to the amount payable or advancing the date of payment by as little as one day.[116] Specifically under old § 3–407(1), a change in the number or relations of the parties or adding to or removing any part of the writing was a material alteration.[117] To illustrate, in *Silvia v. Industrial National Bank*[118] a check payable to the "Internal Revenue Service" was held to be altered when the words by "John J. Mahoney" were added to the payee line.[119] Raising the amount of an instrument is an obvious material alteration. Many cases, including *Owensboro National Bank v. Crisp*,[120] so decide.

The alteration must be of the contract represented by the instrument, however. It is not relevant whether an unaltered instrument and what is done with it alters or deviates from the underlying agreement of the parties.[121] Moreover, additions to the instrument that have no bearing on the contract of any party are not alterations. Thus noting the rate at which a note was discounted is not an alteration of the note.[122] A closer case arose in *Epstein v. Paskow & Epstein*,[123] where a note was for a sum "with interest," and the words "at 6%" were added. The court concluded there was no alteration because 6 percent was the judgment

---

114. *See* note 110, *supra*; § 3–407(b). Anyone whose contract is not affected cannot assert the defense, but the contract of a party is necessarily affected by the discharge of any party against whom the party has a right of recourse on the instrument. § 3–407, Official Comment 1, *but compare* § 3–605. In Peppers v. Citizens & Southern Nat'l Bank, 127 Ga.App. 16, 192 S.E.2d 409 (Ga.Ct.App.1972), the court held that a guarantor under a guaranty contract on the back of a note was discharged by a material alteration on the face of the note even though the guaranty contract language itself had not been altered.

115. Old § 3–407(1) required materiality. Current Article 3 is the same, as § 3–407(a) directly limits the concept of "alteration" to "material" changes. § 3–407, Official Comment 1.

116. Official Comment 1 to old § 3–407 and to current § 3–407.

117. Old §§ 3–407(1)(a), and (c). The result should not be different under the more general standard of § 3–407(a)(i). The unauthorized completion of an instrument also is made a material alteration in § 3–407(a)(ii). This aspect of the defense is discussed, *infra*.

118. 121 R.I. 810, 403 A.2d 1075 (R.I. 1979).

119. The facts of each case are important. For example, no alteration was found in Holliday v. Anderson, 428 S.W.2d 479 (Tex.Civ.App.1968), where the word "at" was inserted after the word "Anderson" in a note reading pay "to the order of Mary and Robert L. Anderson The Harlingen National Bank at its Banking House in Harlingen, Texas" because the court did not believe any change in the contract as written, if properly interpreted, had occurred.

120. 608 S.W.2d 51 (Ky.1980).

121. Thus it is not relevant if other evidence of the arrangement of the parties is altered. *See, e.g.*, Liberty State Bank & Trust v. Hemisphere Dev. Group, Inc., 98 Mich.App. 285, 296 N.W.2d 241 (Mich.Ct. App.1980) (alteration of sum due on ledger card for loan in no way altered sum due on note). Such conduct may raise a different defense, however.

122. Sterling Nat'l Bank & Trust Co. v. Fidelity Mortgage Inv., 510 F.2d 870 (2d Cir.1975).

123. 4 UCC Rep. Serv. 1066 (N.Y.Sup. Ct.1968).

rate that would have applied in the absence of the addition.[124]

No alteration discharges a party, however, unless it also is made for a fraudulent purpose. Thus an alteration to correct a mistake or to conform the instrument to the agreement of the parties does not affect enforcement of the instrument as altered. For example, the substitution of a correct due date as indicated from the written portion of the instrument was held permissible,[125] and in *National State Bank v. Kleinberg*,[126] the addition of $1,000 to the amount to correct a mistake and conform the instrument to the agreement did not result in a discharge. Changes favorable to the obligor are unlikely to be made with a fraudulent intent. Thus where notes were changed from demand instruments to being payable one and two years after their dates, no discharge was warranted in the opinion of the court.[127] Nor was a discharge found in *Bluffestone v. Abrahams*,[128] where the holder altered a note to add monthly payment and attorney fee provisions; the court held that the alteration was not fraudulent because it was made with a misguided rather than a dishonest or deceitful purpose. The same result was reached in *Willis v. Willis*,[129] where a father signed a renewal note of a note signed by his daughter and her former husband with an intent to substitute himself and assist his daughter. Nonetheless, given the possibility of discharge, any tinkering with an instrument poses some risk and the best rule is "hands off."

[3] *Unauthorized Completion*

The Code makes unauthorized completion of an instrument a variation of the personal defense of fraudulent alteration. Where the contents of a paper at the time of signing show that it is intended to become an instrument, and the paper is signed while still incomplete in any necessary respect and then is completed not in accordance with authority given, the resulting instrument is treated as altered to permit a personal defense.[130] The requirement that the paper be incomplete in some

---

124. *See also* Holliday v. Anderson, 428 S.W.2d 479 (Tex.Civ.App.1968) (addition of words on demand when date of payment originally left blank is permissible). See § 3–115, Official Comment 2, Case #1. A case that is probably too generous is Placido v. Citizens Bank & Trust Co., 38 Md.App. 33, 379 A.2d 773 (Md. 1977), where the alteration of the date of a demand note from late 1971 to early 1973, which legally extended the period of liability of the parties to the note, was held not to be a material alteration in view of the fact that an action on the note was commenced within the applicable limitations period from the original date.

125. Zara Constr. Co. v. De Lillo Const. Co., 2 UCC Rep. Serv. 277 (N.Y.Sup.Ct. 1964).

126. 4 UCC Rep. Serv. 100 (N.Y.Sup.Ct. 1967). A case of like import but where the alterations created the agreement is *In re Estate of Pickard*, 97 A.D.2d 61, 468 N.Y.S.2d 264 (N.Y.App.Div.1983). There the holder of a note kept increasing the rate to keep up with the market even though the note was not a variable rate note, but the court found agreement when the maker knowingly kept paying the higher rates. *See* § 3–407(b).

127. Hutcheson v. Herron, 131 Ill. App.2d 409, 266 N.E.2d 449 (1970).

128. 125 Ariz. 42, 607 P.2d 25 (App. 1979).

129. 30 UCC Rep. Serv. 1332 (D.D.C. 1980), *aff'd in part, rev'd in part*, 655 F.2d 1333 (D.C.Cir.1981).

130. §§ 3–115(c), 3–407(a)(ii), (b) and (c). That is, a payor or a person who took the instrument for value, in good faith and without notice of the alteration may enforce

necessary respect precludes any enforcement until completion.[131] Incomplete in any necessary respect includes a missing essential date, the absence of a promise or order, and a blank left as to the amount payable or time of payment. However, the date of issue is not essential unless the instrument is made payable at a fixed period after that date.[132]

If the paper is completed in accordance with authority given, it is effective as completed and no defense exists.[133] If it is completed in an unauthorized manner, however, any party whose obligation is thus purported to be modified with fraudulent intent is discharged as against any person other than a subsequent payor or holder in due course,[134] unless the party having the defense assents to the change or is precluded from asserting the defense.[135] Unauthorized completion thus is not a real defense, as in the case of the alteration of a completed instrument, because a subsequent payor or holder in due course may enforce the instrument as completed whether in accordance with authorization or not.[136] The reason for the difference is that an alteration of a completed instrument is beyond the control of the party whose liability is being enforced, while control of the partially completed instrument is not.[137] Thus an unauthorized completion is a personal defense.[138]

---

the instrument according to its terms as completed. Of course, one cannot be a holder in due course if the instrument is so incomplete as to call into question its validity. § 3–302(a)(1) and Official Comment 4 to § 3–115.

131. § 3–115(b). If an incomplete instrument is nonetheless an instrument, it can be enforced in that form. § 3–115(a).

132. *See* Hoss v. Fabacher, 578 S.W.2d 454 (Tex.Civ.App.1979) (form without payee or promise to pay any amount not enforceable). Under § 3–115(b) a blank as to the payee does not make an instrument incomplete. *See* § 3–115, Official Comments 2 and 3, and the discussion in Chapter 2, *supra*.

133. § 3–115(b); and Carnival Leisure Industries, Ltd. v. Aubin, 830 F.Supp. 371 (S.D.Tex.1993), *rev'd on other grds.*, 53 F.3d 716 (5th Cir.1995). Even if the instrument is not completed as authorized, if the deviation is by mistake, old § 3–407(2)(b) provided that an instrument completed other than as authorized but not fraudulently (as, for example, where a blank is filled in the honest belief that it is as authorized), may be enforced, but only according to the authority given. Current § 3–407(b) is the same. For example, in Bank of New Effington v. Thompson, 502 P.2d 978 (Colo.Ct.App.1972), a note by agreement to be due in two years was mistakenly completed to provide for installments, the last of which was due in about a year and a half. The court held the note could be enforced according to authority given, but that suit instituted ten months prior to the authorized maturity was premature.

134. § 3–407(b) and (c)(ii). *See also* the discussion in Chapter 2, *supra*.

135. *Id.* and *see* National Loan Investors, L.P. v. Martin, 488 N.W.2d 163 (Iowa 1992) (notes completed in excess of authority enforceable as completed in hands of holder in due course). In Fairfield County Trust Co. v. Steinbrecker, 5 Conn.Cir.Ct. 405, 255 A.2d 144 (Conn.Cir.A.D.1968), however, assent was found.

136. § 3–407(c)(ii). The payor or holder, of course, also may elect to enforce the instrument according to authority given. Official Comment 4 to old § 3–407.

137. Official Comment 4 to old § 3–407 and Official Comment 2 to old § 3–406. If the alteration is not beyond the control of the party, as where negligence substantially contributes to the making of the alteration, then a preclusion may arise under § 3–406. *See also* Official Comment 1 to § 3–407.

138. This is true even when the instrument is stolen and completed after the theft. Official Comment 2 to § 3–407. This situation raised a real defense under prior law because theft was not negligence. Since neither nondelivery nor unauthorized completion are real defenses under the Code, there is little logic that the two together should be a real defense. *See* Official Comment 5 to old § 3–115. Moreover, a holder in due course will see the same paper whether completed in an unauthorized

In many instances, the extent of the authority of the person who completed the instrument will be a key issue. The statute places the burden of establishing that any completion is unauthorized on the party so asserting.[139] For example, in *Newby v. Armour Agricultural Chemical Co.*,[140] the court allowed recovery when the evidence as to authority for the completion was in conflict. In fact, a number of cases state that the UCC confers a right to complete blanks and there is a presumption that such completion is in accordance with authority.[141]

[4] Nondelivery, Delivery for a Special Purpose, and Nonperformance of a Condition Precedent

The trio of related personal defenses comprised of nondelivery or non-issuance, delivery for a special purpose, and nonperformance of a condition precedent, shows that the law of negotiable instruments not only draws its concepts from contract law but also from property law. Absent a special agreement, no rule of contract law requires that a written contract be delivered to be effective. From the property law aspect of negotiable instruments, which views a negotiable instrument as embodying valuable rights in the writing, the notion arises that delivery of the instrument is a condition precedent to the existence of the contract it reflects.[142] The defense of nondelivery or nonissuance is, however, a personal and not a real defense.[143] Thus in one case[144] where the party sued (plaintiff's husband) was able to show that plaintiff was only a nominal payee, the court allowed the defense that the notes were never delivered but were taken from the husband's dresser drawer when marital strife caused a separation.[145]

It is but a short step from nondelivery to delivery for a special purpose and to delivery subject to the performance of a condition precedent. These personal defenses[146] spring from the contract law on

---

manner before it is stolen or completed afterward. Thus to promote negotiability, the holder should not bear the loss in either case.

139. § 3–115(d).

140. 119 Ga.App. 650, 168 S.E.2d 652 (Ga.Ct.App.1969). Another case involving authority worth noting even though it did not arise in exactly the context under discussion is Willey v. Mayer, 876 P.2d 1260, 23 UCC Rep. Serv. 2d 1003 (Colo.1994).

141. *E.g.*, Flushing Nat'l Bank v. Brightside Mfg. Co., 59 Misc.2d 108, 298 N.Y.S.2d 197 (N.Y.Sup.Ct.1969).

142. Section 3–105 uses the term "issuance" and defines "issue" as the first delivery. *See* Official Comments 1 and 2. A contract on a negotiable instrument is incomplete and revocable until delivery of the instrument for the purpose of giving effect to it. Ryan v. Ryan, 298 A.2d 343 (Del.Super.Ct.1972); Jones v. Phillips, 237 Ga.App. 24, 513 S.E.2d 241 (Ga.Ct.App.1999). This is discussed in Chapter 3, *supra*.

143. § 3–105(b) and Official Comment 2 to § 3–305; First Nat'l City Bank v. American Broadcasting Co., 68 Misc.2d 861, 328 N.Y.S.2d 326 (N.Y.Sup.Ct.1971).

144. Silverglit v. Borsil Realty Corp., 2 UCC Rep.Serv. 408 (N.Y.Sup.Ct.1965).

145. The court allowed the lack of delivery to be shown by parol evidence. The parol evidence rule is not a bar since the defense goes to the absence of a contract rather than to contradicting one. *See* the discussion, *supra*.

146. § 3–105(b) and Official Comment 2 to § 3–305; National State Bank v. Kleinberg, 4 UCC Rep. Serv. 100 (N.Y.Sup.Ct.1967); Franklin Nat'l Bank v. Sidney Gotowner, Inc., 4 UCC Rep. Serv. 953 (N.Y.Sup.Ct.1967).

conditions.[147] Nonperformance of a condition precedent and delivery for a special purpose are specifically mentioned as personal defenses in old § 3–306(c) to make it clear that the party sued has the burden of establishing them under old § 3–307 (current § 3–308).[148] Illustrative cases include *American Underwriting Corp. v. Rhode Island Hospital Trust Co.*,[149] where the court found that a draft had been indorsed and delivered for a special purpose and accordingly held that the indorser was not liable beyond the scope of that purpose, and *Briand v. Wild*,[150] where the defense that the check was delivered on the condition that the sale for which it was given be consummated (which did not occur) was allowed.[151] On the other hand, the court in *First International Bank of Israel, Ltd. v. L. Blankstein & Son, Inc.*[152] refused to accept as evidence to avoid liability that a note was delivered to be held as collateral for future performance. The court believed the condition was a subsequent one and not a condition to the note becoming binding.

[5] Want or Failure of Consideration

One of the most commonly raised personal defenses[153] is want or failure of consideration.[154] Want of consideration means a total lack of any valid consideration, and failure of consideration is the neglect, refusal, or failure of one of the parties to furnish what was agreed upon.[155]

---

147. Parol evidence may be used to establish delivery for a special purpose or a condition precedent to liability, as the parol goes to whether any obligation came into existence rather than to contradict the terms of the instrument. Ventures, Inc. v. Jones, 101 Idaho 837, 623 P.2d 145 (Idaho 1981).

148. Official Comment 4 to old § 3–306. The same is true for the defense of nondelivery. Presumably, after 40 years the relegation of this point to Official Comment 2 to § 3–305 should not be of moment, particularly since specific mention was redundant.

149. 111 R.I. 415, 303 A.2d 121 (R.I. 1973).

150. 110 N.H. 373, 268 A.2d 896 (N.H. 1970).

151. *See also* Chemical Bank v. Haskell, 68 A.D.2d 347, 417 N.Y.S.2d 541 (App.Div. 1979), *rev'd on other grounds*, 51 N.Y.2d 85, 432 N.Y.S.2d 478, 411 N.E.2d 1339 (N.Y. 1980) (negotiation conditioned on completion of a certain percentage of construction); Long Island Trust Co. v. International Institute for Packaging Ed., Ltd. and Rochman, 38 N.Y.2d 493, 381 N.Y.S.2d 445, 344 N.E.2d 377 (N.Y. 1976) (condition to effective delivery that note have five named indorsers).

152. 88 A.D.2d 501, 449 N.Y.S.2d 737 (N.Y.App.Div.1982), *aff'd*, 59 N.Y.2d 436, 465 N.Y.S.2d 888, 452 N.E.2d 1216 (N.Y. 1983).

153. The defense of want or failure of consideration is not good against a holder in due course. Ampex Corp. v. Appel Media, Inc., 374 F.Supp. 1114 (W.D.Pa.1974); Official Comment 2 to § 3–305.

154. §§ 3–303(b), 3–419(b); *see* Venners v. Goldberg, 133 Md.App. 428, 758 A.2d 567 (Md.Ct.App.2000) (neither language of note "For money received" or fact it was under seal precluded defense). The defense is specifically mentioned in old § 3–306 to make it clear that either want or failure of consideration is a defense which the defendant has the burden of establishing under old § 3–307. This approach obviates the need for a presumption of consideration as existed in prior law, and it emphasizes a difference between the rules that govern negotiable instruments and those that govern ordinary contracts. As discussed in Chapter 1, the holder of a negotiable instrument need not plead consideration as a factual condition of relief. *See* note 148, *supra*.

155. Holm v. Woodworth, 271 So.2d 167 (Fla.Dist.Ct.App.1972). Partial failure of consideration is a defense pro tanto whether the failure is in an ascertained or a liquidated amount. § 3–303(b).

Under the UCC, however, an exception exists and no consideration is necessary for an instrument or obligation on an instrument that is given in payment of or as security for an antecedent obligation of any kind.[156] The purpose of this exception is to do away with the necessity for new consideration where a note is renewed or secured by a substitute note or other obligation entered into by the original payor or others.[157] The provision was correctly applied in *Blake v. Coates*[158] where renewal notes, even though no new funds were advanced, were held valid as instruments given in payment of or as security for an antecedent obligation.[159]

The exception that no consideration is necessary for an instrument or obligation taken as payment or security for an antecedent debt also specifically renders invalid one aspect of the often-used argument that an accommodation party who receives no compensation is not bound. This argument, of course, also is made in situations not involving the exception. It is not a valid one in that context. The essential fact is that the accommodation party is a surety, and not that the signature of the accommodation party is gratuitous. The obligation of a surety is supported by any consideration for which the instrument is taken before it is due.[160] Thus, in *Franklin National Bank v. Eurez Construction Corp.*,[161] the court held that a corporate note indorsed by the individual defendant as an accommodation to its payee and delivered to a bank by the payee for a loan was not subject in the hands of the bank to the defense of want of consideration raised by the accommodation party.

In *Deep South Services, Inc. v. Wade*,[162] the court may have applied the exception that no consideration is necessary in the case of an antecedent debt too narrowly. In the *Wade* case, a promise was made to accommodation parties to induce their signatures. The promise was not carried out and, when sued, they raised *failure* of consideration as a defense. The court noted that the exception only states that *no* consideration is necessary and allowed the defense. Perhaps the opinion can be regarded as merely expressing the probable end result of the litigation; liability on the instrument completely setoff by liability for breach of the promise made to the liable parties.

---

156. §§ 3–303(a)(3) and (b) (*see also* Official Comment 1, Case #1) and § 3–419(b). Section 3–303 actually states the matter a little differently; an instrument is issued or transferred for value if it is issued or transferred as payment of or security for an antecedent claim, and if issued for value, the instrument also is issued for consideration.

157. Official Comment 2 to old § 3–408.

158. 292 Ala. 351, 294 So.2d 433 (Ala. 1974).

159. The court also held in any event that the extension of time given was sufficient consideration. *See also* Official Comment 4 to § 3–303.

160. § 3–419(b). This provision is specifically intended to change decisions holding that there is no sufficient consideration when an accommodation party signs an instrument after it is in the hands of a holder for value and there is no extension of time or other concession, consistent with the more general provision of old § 3–408 as to antecedent obligations as consideration. *See* Official Comment 2 to § 3–419.

161. 60 Misc.2d 499, 301 N.Y.S.2d 845 (N.Y.Sup.Ct.1969).

162. 248 Ga. 80, 281 S.E.2d 561 (Ga. 1981). The case would seem to be more easily resolved under § 3–303(b) and § 3–419(b). *See also* discussion in Chapter 5, *supra*.

Article 3, beyond the exception with respect to an antecedent debt, does not otherwise displace regular contract law on consideration. For example, with respect to the necessity or sufficiency of consideration, generally obligations on an instrument are subject to the ordinary rules of contract law.[163] Thus, a note given for particular kindness to the maker and members of the family is unenforceable for lack of consideration.[164] Nor does the Code displace any doctrine under which a promise is enforceable notwithstanding lack or failure of consideration.[165]

There have been a large number of cases in which the defense of want or failure of consideration has been raised, but few are worth mentioning. One of the more interesting cases is *Rago v. Cosmopolitan National Bank*,[166] in which the court held that the evidence that a mortgage was part of a plan to perpetuate a love affair, and that no payment was ever intended, established the defense of failure of consideration. Another case involved an attempted suit on a draft erroneously issued by an insurance company where no obligation was owed to the insured under the insurance contract.[167] The court held that the draft was without consideration. Most cases fall into certain fact patterns. These include: the contract out of which the instrument arose was breached by the other party;[168] a warranty on the sale for which the instrument was given was breached;[169] the consideration for which the instrument was given was never delivered;[170] the instrument was delivered for an instrument on which payment was stopped or with respect to which there were insufficient funds;[171] the consideration for which the instrument was given was inadequate or was never performed;[172] and the consideration for the instrument went only to a third party or the instrument was gratuitously taken.[173]

---

163. § 3–303(b).

164. *In re* Estate of Wetmore, 36 Ill. App.3d 96, 343 N.E.2d 224 (1976).

165. Promissory estoppel or any other equivalent or substitute for consideration is to be recognized as in other contract cases. Official Comment 3 to old § 3–408. *Compare* UCC § 2–203.

166. 89 Ill.App.2d 12, 232 N.E.2d 88 (1967).

167. Criterion Ins. Co. v. Fulgham, 219 Va. 294, 247 S.E.2d 404 (Va. 1978).

168. *E.g.*, Mecham v. United Bank, 107 Ariz. 437, 489 P.2d 247 (Ariz. 1971) (note given for agreement to procure a permanent first mortgage loan commitment, which was not obtained). *See also* § 3–303, Official Comment 1, Case #3.

169. *E.g.*, Northern Plumbing Supply v. Gates, 196 N.W.2d 70 (N.D.1972) (with respect to note given for purchase of personal property, claim of breach of warranty equivalent to a plea of failure of consideration). Under § 3–305, the analysis is different but the result is the same. *See* Official Comment 3.

170. *E.g.*, Illinois Valley Acceptance Corp. v. Woodard, 159 Ind.App. 50, 304 N.E.2d 859 (Ind.Ct.App.1973) (failure to deliver goods represented by trade acceptance). *See also* § 3–305, Official Comment 3.

171. *E.g.*, United States v. Second Nat'l Bank, 502 F.2d 535 (5th Cir.1974) *cert. denied* 421 U.S. 912, 95 S.Ct. 1567, 43 L.Ed.2d 777 (1975) (IRS could collect on bank money orders issued in return for checks on which payment stopped if IRS was a holder in due course). *See also* § 3–303, Official Comment 2.

172. *E.g.*, Hardy v. Brookhart, 259 Md. 317, 270 A.2d 119 (Md. 1970) (note given pursuant to agreement for future legal services). *See also* § 3–303, Official Comment 1, Case #2.

173. *E.g.*, Unruh v. Nevada Nat'l Bank, 88 Nev. 427, 498 P.2d 1349 (Nev. 1972) (defense of makers that they had received no consideration in that check had been issued to third party was without merit; a bargained-for consideration may be given to the promisor or to some other person);

[6] Discharge

[a] In General

The personal defense[174] of discharge has many variations. Discharge by reason of a fraudulent alteration was discussed earlier.[175] Generally speaking, any party is discharged from liability on an instrument to another party by any act or agreement with the party that would discharge a simple contract for the payment of money.[176] To illustrate, in one case[177] the court held that an agreement between the principal makers of a note, whereby one maker would assume the entire liability on the instrument, operated as between them to discharge the other principal maker, but did not insulate from any liability as an accommodation maker.[178] On the other hand, a premature attempt to enforce the instrument is not a repudiation of the contract and does not result in a discharge;[179] a release of one co-maker for a money payment does not

---

Quazzo v. Quazzo, 136 Vt. 107, 386 A.2d 638 (Vt. 1978) (note which was given gratuitously after expenditures made rather than in exchange for them was subject to defense of lack of consideration). See also § 3–419(b) and Official Comment 2.

174. § 3–601(b) states that no discharge of any party is effective against a subsequent holder in due course unless the holder in due course has notice of it when the instrument is taken. Thus the discharge of the liability on an instrument of a party is a personal defense of the party which is cut off when a subsequent holder in due course takes the instrument without notice of the defense. See also § 3–302(b).

Note that not all discharges are personal defenses. Thus a discharge in insolvency proceedings under § 3–305(a)(1)(iv) is a real defense. This is discussed earlier in this chapter. See also § 3–602(d).

175. A listing of relevant sections appeared in old § 3–601(1). Current Article 3 does not repeat such laundry lists but rather provides general rules. See § 3–601(a). Other specific kinds of discharge besides fraudulent alteration, such as discharge by reason of acceptance of the instrument and unexcused delay in presentment, have been previously discussed. See Chapter 4. Further specific variations are discussed, infra. Still further variations, such as discharge by accord and satisfaction, will be discussed in later chapters. See, e.g., Chapter 7.

176. § 3–601(a).

177. Fithian v. Jamar, 286 Md. 161, 410 A.2d 569 (Md.Ct.App.1979).

178. As to the accommodation party point, see former § 3–605(b) and Official Comment 3. Of particular relevance to that Comment as it explains the change to old § 3–606, see Matthews v. Saleen, 812 P.2d 1186 (Colo.Ct.App.1991). See also Litwin v. Barrier, 6 Kan.App.2d 128, 626 P.2d 1232 (Kan.Ct.App.1981), where a co-maker paid the note and took an assignment of it. The court held the payment discharged the other co-maker since the paying party was not a surety, but that a right of contribution did exist. Siegler v. Ginther, 680 S.W.2d 886 (Tex.App.1984) is the same, but see Roark v. Hicks, 234 Va. 470, 362 S.E.2d 711 (1987) (same except for rights lost through procedural mistakes). On that, see § 3–116(b) and (c). As to a surety, see also former § 3–419(e) (now § 3–419(f)) and Transamerica Commercial Finance Corp. v. Naef, 842 P.2d 539 (Wyo.1992), where the payee loaned money to the husband and as part of an established policy had the wife sign the note as a co-obligor even though the husband's credit status supported the loan. The court refused to enforce the wife's obligation on the note because of the lender's blanket, illegal and unreasonable policy of requiring spousal signatures. See federal Regulation B, 12 CFR § 202.7(d)(1). Former § 3–605(b) was amended in 2002 and, with a shift in policy, is now § 3–605(a). As to the change in policy, see Official Comment 4 to § 3–605 as amended; the provision, as before, is designed to facilitate negotiated workouts, so long as they are not at the expense of the surety who has not consented—compare Official Comment 3 to former § 3–605 which states former subsection (b) was designed to allow a creditor to settle with the principal debtor without risk of losing rights against sureties. See also Official Comment 3 to § 3–605 as amended.

179. Mechanics Nat'l Bank v. Shear, 7 Mass.App.Ct. 255, 386 N.E.2d 1299 (Mass. App.Ct.1979).

discharge the other co-maker, absent evidence that the other co-maker was a surety known to the holder of the instrument;[180] and a bank examiner-ordered write-off is not a discharge of the maker of the note ordered written off.[181]

A negotiable instrument, of course, is merely a piece of paper bearing writing. It thus is incapable of being discharged. Rather it is the parties to the instrument who are discharged from liability on their contracts on the instrument.[182] As a result, the Code states that it is the liability of parties to the instrument and not the instrument that is discharged, and this analysis must be kept in mind to avoid confusion.

A discharge of all parties to the instrument will occur when any party who has no right of action or recourse on the instrument either reacquires the instrument in that party's own right or is discharged under any provision of Article 3, except as otherwise provided with respect to discharge for impairment of recourse or of collateral.[183] This rule says nothing more than that all parties to an instrument are discharged when no party is left with rights against any other party on the paper. For example, when an indorser reacquires an instrument in his or her own right, his or her own prior liability as an indorser is discharged, and any intervening indorsee to whom he or she was liable in that prior capacity is also discharged.[184] If he or she is left with no right of action against any prior party, all parties obviously are discharged.[185] However, even if all parties are discharged, the instrument is not extinct. It can be reissued or renegotiated with a new and further liability, and, if it reaches the hands of a holder in due course without notice of the prior discharge, it may even be enforced without regard to the discharge which is a personal defense.[186]

An interesting interpretation of the application of these latter rules was made by the court in *Columbian Peanut Co. v. Frosteg*.[187] In that case, checks written by the plaintiff to various peanut growers were taken by the plaintiff's agent and the indorsements of the growers were forged. The checks were then presented through the normal collection process and paid. Upon discovery of the problem, the plaintiff paid the

---

180. Fall River Sav. Bank v. Lebel, 33 UCC Rep. Serv. 1041 (Mass.App.Div.1982). *But note* former § 3–605(b), and *see* Deese v. Mobley, 392 So.2d 364 (Fla.Dist.Ct.App. 1981) (there is a discharge to the extent of one half of the obligation). *See* now § 3–605(a).

181. Federal Deposit Ins. Corp. v. Manning, 608 S.W.2d 270 (Tex.Civ.App.1980).

182. Official Comment 2 to old § 3–601.

183. Old § 3–601(3). Current Article 3 does not explicitly so state, but the result is the same pursuant to § 3–207.

184. § 3–207. These provisions are discussed in Chapter 3, *supra*.

185. *See* note 183, *supra*. Another example is that under § 3–605, discussed *infra*, this chapter, the discharge of a party discharges those who have a right of recourse against that party, except in certain cases involving an accommodation party or a failure to give notice of dishonor. *See* former § 3–605(b), and Official Comment 3 to former § 3–605. But now *see* § 3–605 as amended, particularly Official Comment 4. Thus a discharge of one who has himself or herself no right of action or recourse on the instrument may discharge all parties.

186. Official Comment to § 3–207 and Official Comment to § 3–601.

187. 472 F.2d 476 (5th Cir.1973); *cert. denied* 414 U.S. 824, 94 S.Ct. 126, 38 L.Ed.2d 57 (1973).

peanut growers. The plaintiff then had the growers indorse the purloined checks, which had been returned to plaintiff, "pay to the order of plaintiff." Plaintiff then sued the banks that wrongfully had paid the checks. The court denied a defense based on plaintiff's reacquisition of its own checks and held that old §§ 3–208 and 3–601(3) were intended to prevent circuity in responsibility and should not have the effect of depleting the rule of strict responsibility for a bank that pays a check over a forged indorsement.[188] A less satisfactory and more literalistic result was initially reached by the Arizona Court of Appeals in *Best Fertilizers v. Burns*,[189] where the maker of a note secured by a mortgage, who had sold the real estate to another party on a subject to the mortgage basis, paid the note to avoid foreclosure and took an assignment of the note and mortgage. The court held the reacquisition by the maker discharged the note, which released the mortgage and allowed a second lien on the property to advance its priority.[190]

A situation that involves a question of discharge in a context uncommon to most persons arises in the case of a draft drawn in a set of parts.[191] Drafts in sets (that is, two to four copies of a draft) apparently came into use largely in foreign transactions so that the payee could send several orders for acceptance or payment with the likelihood being that at least one would arrive. The use of the device has diminished today with different and better communication.[192] A draft in a set is treated as one draft. Thus a taker of one of the parts may become a holder in due course of the whole, and a person liable is liable to the holder in due course who acquires title first if there is more than one holder in due course.[193] But as against the drawee of the draft, the first presented part is entitled to acceptance or payment and, as to the holder and drawer, payment of a subsequently presented part amounts to payment over a valid stop order.[194] When any part of a draft drawn in a set is discharged, it discharges the whole draft.[195]

---

188. Under § 4–401, the result should be the same.

189. 117 Ariz. 178, 571 P.2d 675 (Ariz. Ct.App.1977), *rev'd*, 116 Ariz. 492, 570 P.2d 179 (1977).

190. *Compare* § 3–419(f), which gives an accommodation party a right of recourse in somewhat similar circumstances to that in which the maker found himself. Indeed, the maker might be considered as an accommodation party. *See* former § 3–605, Official Comment 6, and note 178 *supra*. Arguably, a closer reading of the UCC could have prevented the litigation in both the *Frosteg* and *Burns* cases as an action on the instrument was not involved in the former case and in connection with the latter case the discharge of parties does not render the instrument extinct. Most courts are sensitive to a sensible reading of the Code. Thus in Warren v. Washington Trust Bank, 92 Wn.2d 381, 598 P.2d 701 (Wash.1979), where the bank returned the note of an accommodated party stamped "canceled" after it had been paid by the plaintiff's certificate of deposit, which had been put up as security, the court held old §§ 3–605(1)(a) and 3–601(3)(a) did not deprive the plaintiff, who was an accommodation party, of the right to recover on the note. *See* §§ 3–604(a)(i), 3–419(f) and 3–207 and the discussion as to cancellation, *infra*, this chapter.

191. Old § 3–801.

192. Current Article 3 omits old § 3–801 as outmoded and involving matters, like protest, not of concern to domestic law.

193. Old § 3–801(1), (2).

194. Old § 3–801(3).

195. Old § 3–801(4).

[b] Payment or Satisfaction and Tender of Payment

[i] In General

A specific example of the defense of discharge is payment or other satisfaction. The contract of a party to a negotiable instrument is to pay money to the holder of the instrument or other person entitled to enforce it.[196] Accordingly, payment of the amount of the instrument in money or in an agreed upon satisfaction to the holder will satisfy the contract and discharge the liability of the party under it.[197] For example, the drawer's liability on checks will be discharged when payment is made on the drawer's behalf by the drawee bank.[198] Payment of less than the amount of the instrument, if pursuant to valid agreement, also may fully discharge a party's liability.[199]

The liability of a party to the instrument may be discharged by other satisfaction to the holder.[200] What constitutes satisfaction is not specified by the statute. An accord and satisfaction is the obvious example,[201] but any agreement whereby the obligation is deemed to be satisfied will suffice. For example, in one case a renewal note given for the original note, which was marked "paid," was held to be taken in satisfaction of the obligation on the original note,[202] and another case determined that the drawer's liability on a check was satisfied when the goods purchased were returned and accepted.[203]

[ii] Payment or Satisfaction to the Holder

No discharge will eventuate from a payment or satisfaction if the payment or satisfaction is made other than to the holder of the instru-

---

196. §§ 3–412 through 3–415.

197. § 3–602(a). Payment or other satisfaction discharges only the liability of the person making it. That discharge may, however, operate to discharge the liability of other parties when the discharge of the payor discharges others who have a right of recourse against the payor (*but see* § 3–605); when reacquisition of the instrument discharges intervening parties under § 3–207; and when the one discharged has no right of recourse and other parties are discharged as stated in old § 3–601.

Payment of less than the full amount may be a discharge if there is an accord and satisfaction, discussed *infra*, Chapter 7.

198. Schneider Fuel & Supply Co. v. West Allis State Bank, 70 Wis.2d 1041, 236 N.W.2d 266 (Wis. 1975).

199. *E.g.*, Russell v. Maxson Sales Co., 591 P.2d 703 (Okla.1979) (holder of a check for $29,290.86 was held to have discharged it by accepting, as agreed, another check for $13,288.52). Otherwise, part payment only discharges pro tanto.

200. Old § 3–603(1). Section 3–602(a) does not mention satisfaction but the same result would occur under § 3–601(a).

201. *E.g.*, Wood v. Willman, 423 P.2d 82 (Wyo.1967), where, because of a failure of consideration in the underlying transaction, an accord and satisfaction was entered into between the maker and the payee stipulating that the notes were to be considered paid in full. Accord and satisfaction is discussed in Chapter 7.

202. Cipra v. Seeger, 215 Kan. 951, 529 P.2d 130 (Kan. 1974). Usually a renewal note will not be taken in satisfaction of the obligation on the original note, but it depends on the intent of the parties. *See, e.g.*, First Pa. Bank v. Triester, 251 Pa.Super. 372, 380 A.2d 826 (1977) (in absence of proof of agreement, renewal note only suspended original obligation). *See also* Williams v. Illinois Trust & Sav. Bank, 109 Ill.App.3d 828, 65 Ill.Dec. 499, 441 N.E.2d 412 (1982).

203. Duilio v. Senechal, 7 UCC Rep. Serv. 222 (Mass.App.Div.1969).

ment.[204] Payment to a prior holder generally will not suffice. Because any discharge resulting from payment or satisfaction is only a personal defense,[205] if the original holder has negotiated the instrument without notice to the party liable upon it, that party, except as noted in the case of a note, may have to pay twice if the instrument is not exhibited at the first payment. This point was cogently made in a Florida case[206] under prior law where the maker of notes, who neither required a notation of the payments made on the notes nor demanded their surrender by the original holder, was required to make a second payment in full to a holder in due course to whom the original holder had negotiated the instruments. A similar problem can arise if the drawer of a dishonored check settles with the person to whom the check was given but the check is in the hands of a bank that has allowed withdrawal of the uncollected funds represented by the check.[207] Moreover, payment to only one of two joint payees will not suffice.[208] And if payment is made to a person holding under a necessary forged or missing indorsement, it will not result in a discharge because the party paid will not be a holder.[209]

Payment or satisfaction need not be made by the drawer or maker, or even by an indorser who takes up the instrument. With the consent of the holder, payment or satisfaction may be made by any person, including a stranger to the instrument.[210] This rule therefore rejects, for example, decisions under prior law that an accommodation indorser who pays the instrument cannot recover on it; in this context it reaches the same result as under § 3–419(f).[211] When a person does pay the instru-

---

204. § 3–602(a). Section 3–602(a) literally requires payment to a person entitled to enforce the instrument. But as that usually is the holder, this discussion often uses that term alone. See § 3–301. For example, in Champion International Corp. v. Union Nat'l Bank, 73 N.C.App. 147, 325 S.E.2d 656 (N.C.Ct.App.1985), the authorities seized three certificates of deposit payable to an employee who allegedly had embezzled the funds. The bank nonetheless paid the employee, an action the court found to be improper. See also Lambert v. Barker, 232 Va. 21, 348 S.E.2d 214 (Va. 1986). As amended in 2002 this rule was changed for notes so it accords with the normal contract rule illustrated, for example, in UCC § 9–406(a). Thus in certain circumstances payment to a prior holder can discharge.

205. § 3–601(b).

206. Bank of Miami v. Florida City Express, Inc., 367 So.2d 683 (Fla.Dist.Ct.App. 1979).

207. E.g., Chenowith v. Bank of Dardanelle, 243 Ark. 310, 419 S.W.2d 792 (Ark. 1967).

208. E.g., Feldman Constr. Co. v. Union Bank, 28 Cal.App.3d 731, 104 Cal.Rptr. 912 (1972); § 3–110(d). But see Kenerson v. FDIC, 44 F.3d 19, 25 UCC Rep. Serv. 2d 401 (1st Cir.1995) (discharge of drawer under rule of Restatement (Second) Agency § 178(2) applicable through UCC § 1–103; if an agent is authorized to receive a check and forges the principal's name, the drawer is relieved of liability when the check is paid).

209. The resolution of who bears the risk of loss with respect to a check paid on a forged indorsement is discussed in Chapter 7. See Cooper v. Union Bank, 9 Cal.3d 371, 107 Cal.Rptr. 1, 507 P.2d 609 (Cal. 1973), however, where the indorsements of the payee were forged but because of the payee's negligence the forgeries were precluded from being asserted and the court thus concluded the forger was a holder for the purpose of receiving payment to discharge liability. This is the result under § 3–405(b).

210. Old § 3–603(2). Current § 3–602 omits this rule as redundant, and the payor should obtain an assignment in the absence of old § 3–603(2). See §§ 3–203 and 3–419(f).

211. E.g., Collection Control Bureau v. Weiss, 50 Cal.App.3d 865, 123 Cal.Rptr. 625 (Cal.App.1975) (under old § 3–415(5) an accommodation party who paid the instrument had a right of recourse on it against

ment, the surrender of the instrument to that person gives the person the rights of a transferee, which means the rights of the transferor of the instrument.[212] Thus in one case where a mother paid her son's note, the court stated that she became a transferee of it vested with all the transferor's rights including the mortgage securing it.[213] In another case,[214] a note executed by a corporation, and by the plaintiff as an accommodation maker, was paid by the plaintiff. The court held the plaintiff was entitled to pay the note under old § 3–603(2), that upon payment he had a right of recourse against the corporation under old § 3–415(5), and, because the holder had assigned the note to him and there was no issue of fraud or illegality, that he succeeded to the holder's rights under old § 3–201 and could sue on the note. No different result would obtain under current Article 3.

[iii] Adverse Claims

Under law prior to the Uniform Commercial Code, in order for a payment to discharge the liability of a party the payment had to be made by the party in good faith and without notice that the title of the holder of the instrument might be defective. This rule put the party to pay in a difficult position because that party normally had no way of knowing whether a claim adverse to the holder's title was good.[215] The UCC eliminated the requirement that payment be made in good faith and without notice.[216] The liability of any party may be discharged by payment (or other satisfaction) made by or on behalf of the party obligated to pay to the party entitled to enforce the instrument, even though it is made with knowledge of a claim of another person to the instrument.[217] Thus to prevent a discharge by a payment or other satisfaction, the person making the adverse claim must either, with one exception, supply indemnity deemed adequate by the party seeking the discharge or have payment or other satisfaction enjoined by order of a court of competent jurisdiction in an action in which the adverse claimant and the holder are parties.[218]

The adverse claim must be a property or possessory claim to the instrument. A claim arising from a basis only involving damages, as

---

the party accommodated, and under old § 3–603(2) even a stranger to an instrument who paid it, and to whom it was surrendered, had the rights of a transferee).

212. § 3–203.

213. Griffith v. Griffith, 250 Ark. 845, 467 S.W.2d 737 (Ark. 1971).

214. Simson v. Bilderbeck, Inc., 76 N.M. 667, 417 P.2d 803 (N.M. 1966).

215. See Official Comment 3 to old § 3–603.

216. § 3–602(c).

217. Id.

218. § 3–602(e)(1). To better assure the payment of bank obligations such as cashier's, certified and teller's checks and thus preserve their worth, § 3–602(e)(1) excepts the indemnity option in relation to such instruments. Thus the bank still must pay, or face liability pursuant to § 3–411, even if it has taken indemnity. As a result, if it takes indemnity the indemnity had better be sufficient to cover not only the amount of the item and legal fees, but also possible consequential damages, which, of course, probably is not feasible. If indemnity is taken and payment is made, liability for breach of the indemnity contract is not governed by Article 3. § 3–602, Official Comment.

might be the case with a breach of warranty, is not sufficient.[219] The UCC provides little detail to guide an adverse claimant. For example, how much indemnity must be supplied and in what manner? The only restriction appears to be that the demand for indemnity be in good faith consistent with UCC former § 1–203 (now § 1–304), which presumably would require some reasonable estimate as to the expenses likely to be incurred by the liable party while the identity of the person to be paid is litigated, and reasonableness as to the form the indemnity might take (presumably cash in advance would be unreasonable). The application of the indemnity rule also is unclear where the person liable and the person to make payment are not the same party. An example is a draft written by one party upon another party as to which the customer of the drawer has asserted an adverse claim. Arguably the Code should be construed to allow the adverse claim to be presented to the drawer, which then would legally be required to stop payment to effectuate the purpose in this particular context.[220] Since teller's checks are not subject to the indemnity option under § 3–602(e)(1)(ii), this issue as a practical matter largely has disappeared.[221] If the party liable to pay chooses to refuse to pay and stand suit, even though not indemnified or enjoined, under § 3–305(c) the payor still must rely on the third-party claimant to litigate the issue because the payor may not defend on the ground of the claim.[222]

There is one explicit exception under Article 3 to the rule that a payment or other satisfaction results in the discharge of the liability of a party. That is where the party in bad faith pays or satisfies a person in possession of the instrument who acquired the instrument by theft, or who, unless having the rights of a holder in due course, holds through one who so acquired it.[223] A second explicit exception under old Article 3 and inherent under current Article 3 is where the party seeking discharge, other than an intermediary bank or a payor bank which is not a depositary bank, pays or otherwise satisfies the holder of an instrument which has been restrictively indorsed in a manner not consistent with the terms of the restrictive indorsement.[224]

[iv] Tender of Payment

Tender of payment, as opposed to payment or satisfaction, normally

---

219. Fulton Nat'l Bank v. Delco Corp., 128 Ga.App. 16, 195 S.E.2d 455 (Ga.Ct.App. 1973). § 3–602(c) makes it clear claims in recoupment are not included.

220. *See, e.g.,* Fur Funtastic, Ltd. v. Kearns, 104 Misc.2d 1030, 430 N.Y.S.2d 27 (N.Y.Civ.Ct.1980) suggesting this interpretation.

221. *See* note 218, *supra*.

222. *E.g.,* FDIC v. Moore, 448 F.Supp. 493 (D.S.C.1978) (if FDIC illegally acquired instrument, bank in receivership might be a third-party claimant, but the maker when sued by the FDIC cannot assert the illegality as a defense to suit on the instrument). *See also* Bank of New York v. Welz, 118 Misc.2d 645, 460 N.Y.S.2d 867 (N.Y.Sup.Ct. 1983), where the court allowed the drawer of a teller's check to stop payment on it, but observed it might not do the drawer much good if it was merely trying to accommodate its customer at whose instance the check was issued and who had the defense. Jus tertii is discussed, *supra,* this chapter.

223. § 3–602(e)(2).

224. Old § 3–603(1)(b). As stated, current § 3–602 does not explicitly articulate this exception as unnecessary since payment other than as authorized cannot be compelled. Note these provisions track the jus tertii exception(s) in § 3–305(c), discussed *supra,* this chapter.

will not discharge a party's liability to pay on an instrument.[225] However, any party making tender[226] of full payment to a holder when or after it is due[227] is discharged from subsequent liability for interest, costs, and attorney's fees.[228]

[c] Cancellation and Renunciation

The liability of a party on an instrument also may be specifically discharged by the person entitled to enforce the instrument, without consideration, by any intentional voluntary act or an agreement not to sue or otherwise renouncing rights against the party by a signed record.[229] Examples include intentionally and voluntarily canceling the instrument or the party's signature by destruction or mutilation, or by striking out the party's signature.[230] As noted, further a party may be discharged without consideration by an agreement not to sue or by

---

225. § 3–603(a). Under § 3–603(b), however, the refusal of tender by the holder wholly discharges any party who has a right of recourse against the party making the tender. This might include an indorser or an accommodation party. *But see* Taines v. Capital City First Nat'l Bank, 344 So.2d 273 (Fla.Dist.Ct.App.1977) *cert. denied*, 355 So.2d 517, where the court held that the holder of either a demand or a time note is not required to accept tender of payment if there is an option to extend the note; that the holder may instead elect to exercise the option, and this does not prejudice the rights of accommodation indorsers who are bound pursuant to old § 3–118(f) (the subject of this provision is left to agreement in current Article 3) as, upon the maturity of the original note and notwithstanding their prior consent to any extension or renewal, they could have made full tender of the balance outstanding and been discharged to the extent of subsequent liability for interest, costs, and attorney's fees. A holder may not exercise an option to extend, however, over the objection of a maker or acceptor who tenders full payment.

226. Where the maker or acceptor of an instrument payable otherwise than on demand is able and ready to pay at every place of payment specified in the instrument when it is due, it is equivalent to tender. § 3–603(c). A proper tender must be kept open if refused, generally by paying the full amount due into court. Stockwell v. Bloomfield State Bank, 174 Ind.App. 307, 367 N.E.2d 42 (Ind.Ct.App.1977), *overruled as to another point*, Farner v. Farner, 480 N.E.2d 251 (Ind.Ct.App.1985). A tender that is qualified or conditioned will not suffice. *E.g.*, Still v. Plaza Marina Commercial Corp., 21 Cal.App.3d 378, 98 Cal.Rptr. 414 (1971).

227. In the absence of agreement or an applicable statute, an obligor does not have a right to prepay. Thus a tendered prepayment will not result in a discharge as it is not made "when or after it is due." *E.g.*, Kohlenberg v. American Plumbing Supply Co., 82 Wis.2d 384, 263 N.W.2d 496 (Wis. 1978).

228. § 3–603(c). Such discharge will not occur if the tender is of no more than another promise to pay. Fleet Real Estate Funding Corp. v. Frampton, 812 P.2d 416 (Okla.Ct.App.1991).

229. § 3–604(a). Because UCC Article 3 is exempt from the Uniform Electronic Transactions Act and the federal E-sign act, this requirement is not overridden. As amended in 2002, however, § 3–604 allows a "signed record." As used in the amendment, "signed" includes the attachment to or logical association with the record of an electronic symbol, sound, or process with the present intent to adopt or accept the record. *See also* UCC §§ 3–103(d) and 1–201(b)(37).

230. § 3–604(a)(i); G.E. Capital Mortgage Services, Inc. v. Neely, 135 N.C.App. 187, 519 S.E.2d 553, 39 UCC Rep. Serv. 2d 1170 (N.C.App.1999) (cancellation and surrender due to clerical error or mistake does not discharge); FirsTier Bank, N.A. v. Triplett, 242 Neb. 614, 497 N.W.2d 339 (Neb. 1993) (same); *see also* Winkel v. Erpelding, 526 N.W.2d 316, 25 UCC Rep. Serv. 2d 852 (Iowa 1995) (possession of notes by the debtor raises a presumption of discharge); Dluge v. Robinson, 204 Pa.Super. 404, 204 A.2d 279 (1964) (surrender of checks by indorsee to indorsor without payment or a demand for payment indicates an intention to discharge).

renunciation of the holder's rights by a writing signed and delivered.[231] The act effectuating the discharge either must be completed before the person entitled to enforce the instrument acquires the instrument or with the concurrence of that person.[232] The discharge is not effective against a later holder in due course without notice.[233]

Cancellation or renunciation is not effective if procured by fraud. Thus where a cosigner obtained the cancellation and surrender of the original notes by fraud, no party was granted a discharge.[234] Nor is cancellation or renunciation effective if it is a result of mistake. In *Gibraltar Savings Association v. Watson*,[235] a note was marked as paid due to a mistake in crediting the makers with more than they had paid. The court found no discharge. However, the failure of the party canceling the instrument to appreciate the legal consequences that will flow from cancellation or surrender does not constitute a mistake negating the cancellation or surrender. In *Peterson v. Crown Financial Corp.*,[236] the holder asserted that there had been no intent to alter the terms of an old note when it intentionally was canceled and returned in exchange for a new note which the court interpreted to represent a lesser indebtedness. The court refused to admit evidence on the point because it would impair the certainty of the writing. The court's point that allowing parol evidence to contradict a new writing is different from permitting it to show that an old writing should not be extinguished appears to be valid.[237]

Since there must be an intent to discharge a party as well as the act, neither cancellation nor surrender without accompanying intent is effective. One of the more common fact patterns where no intent to discharge is found involves the payment of the instrument by an accommodation party. Often the holder will mark the instrument paid or canceled or the like before delivering it to the accommodation party. When the accom-

---

231. § 3–604(a)(ii). *But see* note 229, *supra*. An example is Farmers & Merchants State Bank v. Lloyd, 99 Idaho 416, 582 P.2d 1094 (Idaho 1978) (affidavit of holder that notes were canceled and no debt was owed); *see also* KAM, Inc. v. White, 675 S.W.2d 459 (Mo.Ct.App.1984) (bill of sale providing for assumption of loan by buyer assented to by holder).

232. *E.g.*, L.H. Wagener, Inc. v. Kendall, 278 N.W.2d 18 (Iowa 1979), where the court held that an accommodation indorsement was effectively revoked when the accommodation party and the first transferee of the note each signed a statement typed on the note that they assigned all their right and interest to plaintiff without recourse before the note was negotiated to plaintiff. *See also* the *KAM, Inc.* case, *supra*, note 231.

233. §§ 3–601(b), 3–302(b). Nor will cancellation or renunciation without surrender of the instrument affect the title to it. § 3–604(b).

234. Citizens Fidelity Bank & Trust Co. v. Stark, 431 S.W.2d 722 (Ky.1968).

235. 624 S.W.2d 650 (Tex.App.1981). *See also* cases cited in note 230, *supra*, and First Galesburg Nat'l Bank & Trust Co. v. Martin, 58 Ill.App.3d 113, 15 Ill.Dec. 603, 373 N.E.2d 1075 (1978) (debtor on note stamped "paid" and returned to the debtor by mistake at the time the account was written off as a bad debt is not discharged). Distinguish Williams v. Illinois Trust & Savings Bank, 109 Ill.App.3d 828, 65 Ill. Dec. 499, 441 N.E.2d 412 (1982) (where notes on which one maker had died reduced to "zero balance" on books of bank and other maker executed new notes, no discharge of estate occurred as no delivered writing or surrender of notes).

236. 661 F.2d 287 (3d Cir.1981).

237. *See also* Merchants Nat'l Bank v. Blass, 282 Ark. 497, 669 S.W.2d 195 (Ark. 1984).

modation party sues the accommodated party,[238] the courts uniformly conclude that the only discharge that occurred is of the liability of the accommodation party to the holder, and the accommodated party is still liable with respect to the instrument to the accommodation party.[239] Another situation where the issue often arises is where a party seeks to establish that a renewal note was intended to discharge an earlier note. In *Cipra v. Seeger*,[240] the court held that when the maker of a note gave a renewal note at a time when the maker was solvent, and the original note also was marked "paid," it had to be assumed the renewal note was accepted as satisfaction of the obligation on the original note.[241]

The intent to discharge a party must be a present intention and not a future intent.[242] However, a present intent for future action is acceptable,[243] as is a provision in a duly executed will renouncing the testator's interest in certain notes.[244]

Several cases have held that an instrument cannot be discharged by an oral statement.[245] The reasoning is that the Code provides that a renunciation must be by a record; otherwise marking or mutilating, the surrender of the instrument, or the like is required. This analysis overlooks that the Code also provides that a party may be discharged by any act or agreement that would discharge a simple contract for the payment of money.[246] Thus a negotiable instrument may be discharged by an oral release or an agreement entered into for valuable consideration, and a record is required only when there is a gratuitous discharge.[247]

---

238. § 3–419(f).

239. *E.g.*, K & S Int'l, Inc. v. Howard, 249 Ark. 901, 462 S.W.2d 458 (Ark. 1971).

240. 215 Kan. 951, 529 P.2d 130 (Kan. 1974).

241. *See also* note 237, *supra*. But on the whole courts are slow to find discharge in this context. *See, e.g.*, Gullette v. FDIC, 231 Va. 486, 344 S.E.2d 920 (Va. 1986). *Compare* Bowles v. City Nat'l Bank & Trust Co., 537 P.2d 1219 (Okla.Ct.App.1975) (original notes were neither surrendered nor in any manner canceled or mutilated). As the issue is one of intent, the parties should expressly provide whether the old note is discharged. *See, supra*, note 202.

242. *E.g.*, Gorham v. John F. Kennedy College, Inc., 191 Neb. 790, 217 N.W.2d 919 (Neb. 1974) (notes not discharged by a written renunciation signed and delivered by the holder stating he would surrender, as the words connoted future action and were not an outright renunciation as of the time the writing was executed).

243. *E.g.*, First Nat'l Bank v. Cobler, 215 Va. 852, 213 S.E.2d 800 (Va. 1975) (turning over note to maker with intention to relinquish it and abandon the ownership of it effective upon the death of the holder resulted in a surrender on the designated event).

244. *E.g.*, Cantonwine v. Fehling, 582 P.2d 592 (Wyo.1978) (also holding that delivery of the will to the makers during the holder's lifetime was unnecessary). *But see* Greene v. Cotton, 457 S.W.2d 493 (Ky.1970) (release of balance of note signed by holder but not executed as a will found in his lockbox at bank upon death not effective).

245. *E.g.*, Community Nat'l Bank & Trust Co. v. Gold, 45 A.D.2d 947, 359 N.Y.S.2d 118 (N.Y.App.Div.1974), *aff'd*, 37 N.Y.2d 831, 378 N.Y.S.2d 29, 340 N.E.2d 465 (N.Y. 1975).

246. § 3–601(a). For a case where an oral agreement was held to discharge a guaranty, *see* Fidelity Nat'l Bank v. Reid, 180 Ga.App. 428, 348 S.E.2d 913 (1986).

247. Brannon v. Langston, 375 So.2d 231 (Miss.1979); Brunswick Corp. v. Briscoe, 523 S.W.2d 115 (Mo.Ct.App.1975). "Record" does not include an oral statement, and is defined at UCC § 3–103(a)(14) or § 1–201(b)(31).

[d] Impairment of Recourse or Collateral

[i] Impairment of Recourse

A final specific manner in which the liability of some parties on an instrument may be discharged under Article 3 is by impairment of "recourse".[248] These are defenses available to any party who is in the position of a surety or an indorser (including a drawer who is treated like an indorser under § 3–414(d)) having a right of recourse either on the instrument or under other law.[249] There are two basic categories of defenses. The first discussed here is that the person entitled to enforce an instrument may discharge any party to it to the extent that without that party's consent[250] the person, without preserving recourse in the release or extension[251] releases in whole or in part or, agrees not to sue

---

248. § 3–605(a), (b) and (c). Thus former § 3–606(1)(a) on release of the debtor is now covered in § 3–605(a) discussed *infra* this chapter. But Article 3 does not apply unless the discharge is with respect to liability on an instrument. *See* Official Comment 2 to § 3–605. For example, in National Bank v. Alford, 65 Mich.App. 634, 237 N.W.2d 592 (Mich.Ct.App.1975), the court held that the parties to a separate guaranty agreement were not discharged pursuant to Article 3 by an unjustifiable impairment of the collateral for a loan. *See also* the *Reid* case, *supra*, note 246, where Article 3 was held to be inapplicable to a guaranty.

The 2002 amendments to Article, 3, however, better conform the rules in § 3–605 to those in the Restatement of Suretyship, to that degree narrowing differences between rules governing a negotiable instrument in Article 3 and those governing a non-negotiable instrument like a guaranty in other law. *Compare* T.O. Stanley Boot Co., Inc. v. The Bank of El Paso, 847 S.W.2d 218, 19 UCC Rep. Serv.2d 514 (Tex.1992) (guarantors could not raise impairment defense under Article 3 but could raise that defense as it exists at common law).

249. An indorser of a note is included as, unless without recourse, under § 3–415(a) the liability is that of a guarantor of payment. In addition, § 3–605 also covers a drawer of a draft that is accepted by a party that is not a bank; an indorser of a check; and co-makers of instruments. UCC § 3–103(a)(17) and Official Comment 3. Inclusion of a non-accommodation party co-maker settles a major controversy in this regard. There was a split of authority under old § 3–606 as to whether a co-principal can raise the defense of unjustifiable impairment of collateral. *Compare* Godfrey State Bank v. Mundy, 90 Ill.App.3d 142, 45 Ill. Dec. 549, 412 N.E.2d 1131 (1980) (defense does not extend to a co-maker not a surety) *with* American Express Int'l Banking Corp. v. Sabet, 512 F.Supp. 463, 30 UCC Rep. Serv. 271 (S.D.N.Y.1980) (nonsurety co-maker may assert defense) and Crimmins v. Lowry, 691 S.W.2d 582 (Tex.1985) (co-maker with right of recourse may assert suretyship defense). The defenses provided are available to any party who has a right of recourse and are not limited to parties who are commonly recognized as secondarily liable. Thus, this includes an accommodation maker or an acceptor known to be so. In any event, a person entitled to raise these Article 3 defenses also may be able to raise other applicable surety defenses under law outside the UCC. *See, e.g.*, First Nat'l Bank v. Hargrove, 503 S.W.2d 856 (Tex.Civ.App. 1973).

250. Consent or waiver of discharge may be given in advance and incorporated in the instrument, or it may be given afterward. It requires no consideration. § 3–605(f); Official Comment 9 to § 3–605. Consent in the instrument is discussed *infra*. A case finding consent other than in the instrument is London Leasing Corp. v. Interfina, Inc., 53 Misc.2d 657, 279 N.Y.S.2d 209 (N.Y.Sup.Ct.1967). Consent by the principal obligor to an act that would lead to a discharge also constitutes consent by the secondary obligor if the secondary obligor controls the principal obligor or deals as its agent. § 3–605(f).

251. An express reservation of rights under old Article 3 made the binding nature of a release, an agreement not to sue, or an extension of time conditional upon the consent of the surety, and thus theoretically there could not be prejudice to the rights of the surety without the surety's consent. But the surety was not required to be notified. *Compare* Stanley v. Ames, 378 Mass. 364, 391 N.E.2d 908 (Mass. 1979), where

or to suspend enforcement against any person against whom the party has, to the knowledge of the holder,[252] a right of recourse.[253] For example, the acceptance of a postdated check by the holder of a delinquent note may discharge accommodation parties on the note as an extension of the time to pay,[254] but a mere failure to enforce the instrument when it is due cannot be equated with an agreement not to sue.[255] The discharge operates whether the surety was compensated or not. Under § 3–605(a) and (b), there is a discharge only to the extent[256] the secondary party proves that the extension caused loss to that party with respect to the right of recourse.[257] To be discharged, however, the holder must know the person was in the position of a surety, and a latent surety is excluded from a discharge.[258]

Section 3–605(c) extends coverage to any other modification of the instrument, but a complete discharge does not occur unless the second-

the holder extended the time for payment by an agreement that also provided that the forbearance would not waive any of the terms of the original note. The court found the provision was an express reservation of rights. Current § 3–605 deletes the express reservation of rights exception in old Article 3, but in § 3–605(g) allows the release or extension to preserve the secondary obligor's recourse, such as by the person entitled to enforce the instrument retaining the right to do so against the secondary obligor. No "magic words" are necessary. Official Comments 4, 5 and 10. No notice to the secondary obligor is required, but if notice is not given there are limitations on the effectiveness of the release or extension. Official Comments 4 and 5 to § 3–605. Also no reason exists why the same result cannot be obtained by agreement, as in *Stanley*. Thus, the bottom line is under current § 3–605 the principal will not be misled as he or she might be by the nonunderstandable legalistic formula of a reservation of rights.

252. § 3–605(e). No rational creditor will partially or fully release a debtor or extend more time to pay if the surety also will be released. Thus the knowing creditor will first get the surety's consent; the surety is likely to consent if the settlement will induce the debtor to make a partial payment or better enable payment and the surety is not harmed. These provisions thus promote settlement and reduce uncontemplated results by allowing (with some exceptions) a release or extension without risk of losing rights under circumstances where a surety is unlikely to be harmed and is likely to benefit. Official Comments 4 and 5 to § 3–605 and § 3–605(h) and (i).

253. § 3–605(a) and (b).

254. Lee Fed. Credit Union v. Gussie, 542 F.2d 887 (4th Cir.1976).

255. FDIC v. Vara, 28 UCC Rep. Serv. 114 (Mass.App.Div.1979). In North Bank v. Circle Inv. Co., 104 Ill.App.3d 363, 60 Ill. Dec. 105, 432 N.E.2d 1004 (1982), the court held that the mere making of an agreement was enough to discharge even though the agreement was not enforceable because of lack of consideration. *See also* First Nat'l Bank v. Egbert, 663 P.2d 85 (Utah 1983). Current § 3–605(b) agrees.

256. Under prior Article 3, it was not always necessary to establish prejudice. *See* Philco Fin. Co. v. Patton, 248 Or. 310, 432 P.2d 686 (Or. 1967). But a failure or delay in effecting any required presentment, protest, or notice of dishonor with respect to the principal does not discharge the surety if presentment, protest, or notice of dishonor is effective or unnecessary as to the surety. Old § 3–606(1)(a). Current § 3–605 does not repeat this truism.

257. §§ 3–605(a)(3), (b)(2), (h) and (i). Official Comments 4 and 5 to § 3–605 explain that in most cases a release or an extension of time to pay is beneficial and thus the change reflects what the parties probably would have done by agreement. One may question this premise, but the rule the surety should have to prove loss is probably the sounder rule.

258. *See* note 252, *supra*, and § 3–605(e). *See e.g.*, Wohlhuter v. Saint Charles Lumber & Fuel Co., 25 Ill.App.3d 812, 323 N.E.2d 134 (1975), aff'd, 62 Ill.2d 16, 338 N.E.2d 179 (Ill. 1975). For example, an accommodation maker, where there is nothing in the instrument to show that he or she has signed for accommodation and the holder is ignorant of the accommodation, will not be discharged.

ary obligor proves that loss was caused by the modification.[259]

[ii] *Impairment of Collateral*

The second category of defense is that the person entitled to enforce an instrument discharges any party to it to the extent that, without that party's consent,[260] the holder unjustifiably impairs the value of any interest in collateral for the instrument given by or on behalf of the party or any person against whom he or she has a right of recourse.[261] The defense is not an absolute discharge but merely operates as a discharge pro tanto according to the value of the lost security.[262] Without satisfactory evidence of the value of the security, there is no way to measure the extent of loss, and there may be no discharge.[263]

Generally a release of collateral without substitution or debt reduction is an unjustified impairment.[264] A failure to use ordinary care to preserve the collateral also will result in a discharge.[265] A failure to

---

259. There was no apparent reason why old § 3–606 did not extend to all modifications; § 3–605(c) now does. The base rule concerning discharge is the same as in the cases of release or extension even though it is perhaps less likely a modification in general will presumptively be of benefit. However, this removes the difference between the discharge rule in prior § 3–605(c) and (d), which could be interesting when both provisions were involved, such as an extension of time with an agreed upon increase in interest. *See* Official Comment 5, Case #3, to prior § 3–605.

260. There can be no agreement preserving rights with respect to this ground because impairment cannot be conditionally done. The same rule applies to modifications under § 3–605(c).

261. § 3–605(d). Even if this defense were not available to one who puts up collateral but who is not a surety (*see* note 249, *supra*), that party should have a cause of action against the creditor for unjustifiable impairment if caused by the creditor, and to that extent a similar result would be reached. *See* cases cited in note 264, *infra*. Under § 3–605(d), a non-accommodation party co-maker is explicitly given a discharge defense to the extent the impairment would cause that party to pay more than if impairment had not occurred. Official Comment 7 to current and prior § 3–605 illustrates how the provision works. Assume X and Y sign a note for $1000 as co-makers. X puts up collateral worth more than the debt, but the creditor does not perfect. X goes bankrupt. Had the security interest been perfected, Y could have paid and have been subrogated to the creditor's rights in the collateral to secure the right of contribution. The discharge is equal to that right of $500 assuming a no asset bankruptcy. The same result occurs if Y is an unknown accommodation maker; the right of reimbursement is treated as a right of contribution.

262. This is spelled out in § 3–605(d).

263. *E.g.*, Van Balen v. Peoples Bank & Trust Co., 3 Ark.App. 243, 626 S.W.2d 205 (Ark.Ct.App.1981). Under § 3–605(d) and (h), the burden of proving impairment is on the party seeking discharge. However, the rule in Langeveld v. L.R.Z.H. Corp., 74 N.J. 45, 376 A.2d 931 (N.J. 1977), is codified; that is, if impairment can be measured in monetary terms, that will ordinarily establish the extent of discharge, but if prejudice can be established but not its extent in terms of monetary loss, the surety will normally be completely discharged. § 3–605(i).

264. *E.g.*, Beneficial Fin. Co. v. Husner, 82 Misc.2d 550, 369 N.Y.S.2d 975 (N.Y.Sup. Ct.1975). *But see* Still v. Citizens Bank of Drumright, 6 UCC Rep. Serv. 813 (Okla.Ct. App.1969) (no evidence released mortgage had any value). Section 3–605(d) provides a non-exclusive list of kinds of impairments, including this ground.

265. *E.g.*, First Nat'l Bank v. Helwig, 464 S.W.2d 953 (Tex.Civ.App.1971) and § 3–605(d). But a general decline in real estate values in the area due to vandalism is not an impairment causing discharge. FDIC v. Kirkland, 272 S.C. 310, 251 S.E.2d 750 (S.C. 1979). Nor is deterioration of property not in the control or possession of the creditor. Buckeye Federal Sav. & Loan Ass'n v. Guirlinger, 62 Ohio St.3d 312, 581 N.E.2d 1352 (1991).

properly dispose of the collateral,[266] to insure the collateral, or to collect or properly use insurance proceeds from the collateral, may be held to be an impairment resulting in a discharge.[267] That the collateral is not repossessed,[268] that an insurance claim is not pursued,[269] that another claim to the collateral is not removed,[270] or that the secured party did not object to being listed as unsecured in the debtor's bankruptcy,[271] without more, will not be an unjustified impairment. Moreover, what is an unjustified impairment may depend upon the agreement of the parties.[272]

The cases and now § 3–605(d) also cover unjustified impairment of recourse to collateral. Thus a misdescription in the financing statement filed to perfect a security interest resulting in an unperfected interest may result in an impairment and a discharge.[273] Many cases reach the conclusion that there is an unjustified impairment where no perfection at all is accomplished[274] or maintained.[275]

The defense of impairment of recourse or of collateral is available to any party who is in the position of a surety.[276] But there is a difference of opinion as to whether the defenses are available to a party that contracts as a principal and who only subsequently assumes a suretyship position by reason of the sale of the collateral. For example, assume the maker of a note secured by a mortgage (a principal) sells the mortgaged property

---

266. § 3–605(d). Thus, for example, if a secured party's improper disposition prevents recovery against the debtor under UCC Article 9, the liability of the surety is lost as well.

267. *E.g.*, Godfrey State Bank v. Mundy, 90 Ill.App.3d 142, 45 Ill.Dec. 549, 412 N.E.2d 1131 (1980). Much will depend on the agreement of the parties in this respect.

268. American Discount Corp. v. Glover, 391 So.2d 853 (La.Ct.App.1980) (creditor failed to prevent removal of collateral by debtor but note was not in default and debtor denied an intent to move out of state); Salter v. AmSouth Bank, N.A., 487 So.2d 927 (Ala.Civ.App.1985).

269. *E.g.*, Liberty Nat'l Bank & Trust Co. v. Interstate Motel Dev., 346 F.Supp. 888 (S.D.Ga.1972).

270. *E.g.*, Residential Indus. Loan Co. v. Brown, 559 F.2d 438 (5th Cir.1977).

271. *E.g.*, Chemical Bank v. Valentini, 84 A.D.2d 801, 444 N.Y.S.2d 154, 32 UCC Rep. Serv. 901 (N.Y.Sup.Ct.1981). If the secured claim was prejudiced, however, the result should be different.

272. *E.g.*, Family Provisioners, Inc. v. Columbia Acceptance Co., 274 Or. 303, 545 P.2d 1379 (Or. 1976) (alleged wrongful conduct had to be measured against terms of reserve agreement which set rights and duties with regard to the collateral). *See also In re* Alcock, 50 F.3d 1456, 26 UCC Rep. Serv. 2d 376 (9th Cir.1995) (what is "unjustified" is determined from perspective of the guarantor, not that of the debtor).

273. *E.g., In re* Estate of Voelker, 252 N.W.2d 400 (Iowa 1977) (omission of legal description required by former UCC § 9–402(1) of real estate on which crops were grown).

274. *E.g.*, Beneficial Fin. Co. v. Lawrence, 301 N.W.2d 114 (N.D.1980) and § 3–605(d). But the court found no discharge because otherwise prior interests had exhausted any value of the collateral. *See also* Schauss v. Garner, 590 P.2d 1316 (Wyo.1979) (stock was void and as a result had no value as collateral).

275. Mitchell v. Ringson, 169 Ga.App. 88, 311 S.E.2d 516 (Ga.Ct.App.1983) and § 3–605(d). An odd case of this type occurred in Americana State Bank v. Jensen, 353 N.W.2d 652 (Minn.Ct.App.1984), where the court determined that an anti-deficiency statute that protected the debtor also resulted in discharge of the guarantor. In a sense, collateral was lost even though the loss was not due to the creditor's act. For this reason, a proper agreement should result in an ability to hold the guarantor.

276. Section 3–605 explicitly extends the defenses to indorsers and co-makers. Official Comment 3 to § 3–605 and note 249, *supra*. With respect to the defense of impairment of collateral, there was dispute under old Article 3 as to whether persons in a principal status were included.

to a buyer who, as part of the consideration, agrees to assume and pay the mortgage. As between the parties, the maker is now a surety and the buyer is the principal. If the secured party should then unjustifiably impair the collateral or extend the time for payment without the consent of the maker, should the maker be discharged? Opinions from Tennessee deny the discharge.[277] Other cases disagree.[278] If the discharge is limited to situations where the secured party knows of the transfer, the better view would seem to permit a discharge. Current § 3–605 does not address this issue.[279]

[iii] *Waiver of Defense*

A discharge due to impairment of recourse or of collateral may be avoided if the secondary obligor consents to the event or conduct that would otherwise constitute a discharge or waives the discharge.[280] In a large number of cases, the consent or waiver is incorporated in the instrument in advance.[281] However, where the provision, fairly read, cannot be interpreted to cover the action involved, a discharge will result. For example, in *First Bank & Trust Co. v. Post*,[282] the court held that a provision consenting to extensions for payment or performance did not cover an impairment of collateral. Moreover, several cases have interpreted common provisions in such a way that it reflects not so much a fair reading of them as an attitude that boilerplate clauses do not indicate actual consent and should not always be enforced. Thus in one case the court refused to find that a provision consenting to the exchange or surrender of collateral covered a failure to file to perfect the security interest.[283]

---

277. Commerce Union Bank v. Davis, 581 S.W.2d 142 (Tenn.Ct.App.1978); Commerce Union Bank v. May, 503 S.W.2d 112 (Tenn.1973).

278. *E.g.*, Smiley v. Wheeler, 602 P.2d 209 (Okla.1979) (involving personal property).

279. § 3–605, Official Comment 2. The reason is there is no discharge of the obligation of a "principal obligor." § 3–103(a)(11).

280. § 3–605(f) (as to both impairment of recourse and of collateral).

281. § 3–605(f). *See, e.g.*, Indianapolis Morris Plan Corp. v. Karlen, 28 N.Y.2d 30, 319 N.Y.S.2d 831, 268 N.E.2d 632 (N.Y. 1971); Abby Fin. Corp. v. Weydig Auto Supplies Unlimited, Inc., 4 UCC Rep. Serv. 858 (N.Y.Sup.Ct.1967). In Holcomb State Bank v. Adamson, 107 Ill.App.3d 908, 63 Ill.Dec. 704, 438 N.E.2d 635 (1982), a preprinted consent to extensions of time appeared on the back of a note. The court held it did not bind an accommodation maker who had signed on the front. *Compare* old § 3–511(6) (no counterpart in current Article 3 as the provision only makes an obvious statement). Section 3–605(f) is quite generous, allowing waiver either by specific or general language, but it does not explicitly address the point in the *Adamson* case. Nor would it necessarily solve the problem in Citizens Bank of Smithville v. Lair, 687 S.W.2d 268 (Mo.Ct.App.1985), where, despite broad language of waiver, the court found that the creditor did not act in good faith when it applied the proceeds of the collateral to older loans and extended the time on the loan in question.

As to whether a surety can waive rights and duties under Article 9 in a secured transaction, *see* § 9–602 and Official Comment 4 to § 9–602 and Official Comment 9 to § 3–605. The issue is no less clear if the collateral is real estate not governed by Article 9.

282. 10 Ill.App.3d 127, 293 N.E.2d 907 (1973).

283. First New Haven Nat'l Bank v. Tirkot, 25 UCC Rep. Serv. 795 (Conn.Super.Ct.1978). *But see* Executive Bank v. Tighe, 66 A.D.2d 70, 411 N.Y.S.2d 939 (N.Y.App.Div.1978), *rev'd*, 54 N.Y.2d 330, 445 N.Y.S.2d 425, 429 N.E.2d 1054 (N.Y.

[7] Statute of Limitations

A statute of limitations is a personal-type defense to the liability of a party on a negotiable instrument. The classification of the statute of limitations as a personal-type defense, rather than as a defense good against any holder of the instrument, at first may seem puzzling. Certainly the statute of limitations is assertable against any holder of the instrument. However, because under § 3–302(a)(2)(iii) it is most unlikely there can be a holder in due course of an instrument overdue long enough to bring into play any statute of limitations, and if having acquired an instrument not overdue, a holder in due course allows the statute of limitations to run, the issue is no different from the case of any other defense assertable between the immediate parties involved even if one of them is a holder in due course, classifying the defense as a personal-type defense seems the most appropriate approach.

Old Article 3 contained no statute of limitations. Thus, resort was necessary to law outside the Code for the appropriate statute of limitations.[284] Old Article 3 did stipulate, however, when a cause of action accrued on an instrument in various contexts for the purpose of the running of the applicable statute of limitations.[285] This resulted in considerable confusion and no uniformity. To clarify the area, § 3–118 provides statutes of limitations.[286] For notes, the period is six years after

---

1981), holding a consent to a release includes a failure to file.

284. UCC § 1–103(b). The applicable outside law includes not only the statute of limitations but also what tolls it. *See, e.g.,* Guild v. Meredith Village Sav. Bank, 639 F.2d 25, 30 UCC Rep. Serv. 1021 (1st Cir. 1980).

285. Old §§ 3–122(1), (2), (3). Old § 3–122(4) controlled the date for the measurement of interest at the judgment rate or a rate provided in the instrument.

286. § 3–118. The purpose is similar to that articulated in the Official Comment to UCC § 2–725 on the statute of limitations for sales contracts. In Article 3, however, the starting points for the running of the statutes of limitations may be found in the various substantive provisions. Official Comment 1 to § 3–118 and *see, e.g.,* § 3–412 on the liability of the issuer of a note or a cashier's check. Section 3–118 is not exhaustive; for example, it leaves the subject of tolling to law outside of Article 3 pursuant to UCC § 1–103(b). *See* Guild v. Meredith Village Sav. Bank, 639 F.2d 25, 30 UCC Rep. Serv. 1021 (1st Cir.1980) (payment of interest tolls statute) and Premier Capital, Inc. v. Gallagher, 144 N.H. 284, 740 A.2d 1047, 39 UCC Rep. Serv. 2d 951 (N.H. 1999) (payments or acknowledgment of liability will toll the statute but will not ordinarily diminish a guarantor's defense of staleness). *See also* Karlton v. Jenkins, 86 Md.App. 556, 587 A.2d 580 (Md.Ct.App. 1991), *cert. granted,* 323 Md. 214, 592 A.2d 505 (Md. 1991); *decided* Jenkins v. Karlton, 329 Md. 510, 620 A.2d 894 (Md. 1993). Another tolling case, but one involving only federal law (FIRREA) which was applicable under the circumstances to the note involved, is SMS Fin., L.L.C. v. ABCO Homes, Inc., 167 F.3d 235 (5th Cir.1999).

Presumably all instruments issued before the effective date of § 3–118 are governed by the previously applicable statute of limitations. However, this issue has prompted considerable litigation. If the former law would bar the claim, courts have so held. McNeal Constr. Co. v. Wilson, 271 Ga. 540, 522 S.E.2d 222 (Ga. 1999). If § 3–118 would bar the claim but it is not barred under the former law, the former law also has been applied. Hill v. Mayall, 886 P.2d 1188 (Wyo. 1994). Otherwise, the tendency has been to apply § 3–118 retroactively as a procedural matter where the claim is not barred under the former statute. Lenders Collection Corp. v. Harris, 900 P.2d 1022 (Okla.Ct. App.1995); Emerson v. Zagurski, 3 Neb. App. 658, 531 N.W.2d 237 (1995); Motley v. Motley, 60 F. Supp. 2d 380 (D.N.J.1999). As to the relation between the statute of limitations and the common law doctrine of presumed payment, *see* Wool v. Nations-Bank, N.A., 248 Va. 384, 448 S.E.2d 613 (1994).

the due date or dates (including any accelerated due date) or demand (if no demand is made, action is barred ten years after the last payment of principal or interest).[287] Action on an unaccepted draft must be commenced within three years of dishonor or ten years after date, whichever period expires first.[288] An action against the acceptor of a certified check or the issuer of a teller's, cashier's or traveler's check must be begun within 3 years of demand.[289] For an accepted draft other than a certified check, the period is six years after the due date of an acceptance payable at a definite time or after the date of acceptance otherwise.[290] An action on a certificate of deposit must be commenced within six years after demand, or any due date and demand.[291] Finally, there is a residual provision for conversion, money had and received, and the like; breach of warranty; and other obligations arising under Article 3 of three years after the cause of action accrues, as determined by the substantive provision.[292]

Under old Article 3, as against the maker of a demand note[293] (and the acceptor of a check or a sight draft),[294] the instrument is due on its date or, if no date is stated, upon issue, and thus an action could be

---

287. § 3–118(a) and (b). The latter provision is designed for intra-family notes. In Fallimento C. Op. M.A. v. Fischer Crane Co., 995 F.2d 789, 20 UCC Rep. Serv. 2d 944 (7th Cir.1993), a buyer executed a note to evidence the purchase price of goods. Nearly 10 years later, seller sued and the 4 year statute of limitations of § 2–725 for sales of goods was raised as a defense. The seller argued the 10 year statute for notes, then outside of Article 3, applied. The court applied the 4-year period of § 2–275 because the statute for notes so directed. § 3–118(a) does not speak to the point, but it would seem clear it, and not § 2–725, should apply in a similar case. In WAMCO, III, Ltd. v. First Piedmont Mortgage Corp., 856 F.Supp. 1076 (E.D.Va.1994), the assignee of a note from the Resolution Trust Corporation as receiver for the original lender argued it got the benefit of the statute of limitations in the federal act. The court held the assignee only received the rights the lender had and was subject to the state law statute of limitations. *See also* Fisher v. First Citizens Bank, 302 Mont. 473, 14 P.3d 1228, 43 UCC Rep. Serv. 2d 344 (Mont. 2000) (demand note with final maturity date where no demand is made is governed by § 3–118(a) on notes payable at a definite time).

288. § 3–118(c). The relation between this statute and perhaps a longer statute on the underlying obligation is not stated in Article 3, but as § 3–118 provides a defense and not a discharge within § 3–310, suit on the underlying obligation may still be possible. *See also* the *Fallimento C. Op. M.A.* case, *supra* note 287.

289. § 3–118(d). Thus note the statute may never run, but such instruments often are kept as a form of savings.

290. § 3–118(f).

291. § 3–118(e). *See* note 289, *supra*, and Landreth v. First National Bank of Cleburne County, 45 F.3d 267, 25 UCC Rep. Serv. 2d 1167 (8th Cir. 1995) (statute does not begin to run until demand for payment is made, which need not be within any particular time). *See also* Penagos v. Capital Bank, 766 So.2d 1089, 42 UCC Rep. Serv. 2d 751 (Fla.App.2000) (same).

292. § 3–118(g). As to that point, *see* E.S.P., Inc. v. Midway Nat'l Bank, 447 N.W.2d 882 (Minn.1989). *See also* Menichini v. Grant, 995 F.2d 1224, 20 UCC Rep. Serv. 2d 959 (3d Cir. 1993); and Husker News Co. v. Mahaska State Bank, 460 N.W.2d 476 (Iowa 1990) (as to when a cause of action for conversion of a negotiable instrument accrues).

293. An instrument in which no time for payment is stated. Harris & Harris v. Tabler, 232 Va. 75, 348 S.E.2d 241 (Va. 1986).

294. A check and a sight draft both are demand instruments. §§ 3–104(e) and (f), 3–108(a). The liability of an acceptor is the same as that of a maker. §§ 3–412, 3–413. Literally, the running of the statute of limitations appears not to be delayed until the acceptance contract is effective under old § 3–410(1), *but see* § 3–118(d) and (f).

brought immediately without demand.[295] The same rule applied with respect to the guarantor of a demand instrument.[296] If the instrument was a demand certificate of deposit, however, the cause of action against the obligor as maker accrued only upon demand.[297] Finally, a cause of action against a drawer of a draft or an indorser of any instrument accrued upon demand following dishonor of the instrument, and notice of dishonor constituted a demand.[298]

The different points for the accrual of a cause of action against the acceptor and the drawer of a check under old Article 3 could create an interesting comparison. The matter is illustrated by the case of *First National Bank v. Allison*.[299] In that case, the bank issued cashier's checks in 1953, but they were not presented for payment until 1968, when they were dishonored. Suit was begun in 1970, and the court had to determine whether the action was barred by the six-year New Mexico statute of limitations. The action would not be if the drawer rule for checks, that is, the cause of action does not accrue until demand after dishonor, was applicable. The court held the statute had begun to run upon the issuance of the checks under the theory that a cashier's check is accepted upon issuance. A better analysis to reach that result would be that under old § 3–118(a) a draft drawn on the drawer was effective as a note. This would produce the same result because a cause of action on a demand instrument accrues against an acceptor or a maker on the date of issue. Otherwise, the result reached by the court seems arguably sensible because a holder ought not to be able to delay the running of the statute

---

295. Old § 3–122(1)(b). *See, e.g.*, Jenkins v. Karlton, 329 Md. 510, 620 A.2d 894 (Md. 1993); Environics, Inc. v. Pratt, 50 A.D.2d 552, 376 N.Y.S.2d 510 (N.Y.App.Div. 1975) (note payable thirty days after demand); Seifert v. Seifert, 708 S.W.2d 150 (Mo.Ct.App.1985) (cashier's check accepted upon issuance). *Compare* § 3–118(b) and (d) (demand necessary to start the six or three year period). In Tepper v. Citizens Fed. Sav. & Loan Ass'n, 448 So.2d 1138, 38 UCC Rep. Serv. 528 (Fla.Dist.Ct.App.1984), the court refused to treat a teller's check like a certified or cashier's check (accepted instruments), and required dishonor to start the statute of limitations.

296. Ligran, Inc. v. Medlawtel, Inc., 86 N.J. 583, 432 A.2d 502 (N.J. 1981).

297. Old § 3–122(2); current § 3–118(e) agrees. The same rule applies to a time certificate of deposit, but demand on a time certificate may not be made until or after the date of maturity. § 3–118(e). The reason for the demand, which is not required in the case of other demand instruments under old § 3–122 (current § 3–118 is to the contrary), is the expectation that in this context a demand will be made before any liability is expected. In addition, certificates of deposit are often held for a considerable length of time, which in many instances could exceed the period of a statute of limitations commencing upon the date or issuance of the instrument. *See* Notes 289 and 291, *supra*.

298. Old § 3–122(3). The old Article 3 rule was in conformity with the underlying contract of these parties, it being conditioned upon dishonor and any necessary notice of dishonor or protest under old §§ 3–413(2) and 3–414(1). *But see* current §§ 3–414, 3–415 and 3–118(c), and Official Comment 2. Further under old Article 3, because an indorser that guarantees payment incurs a liability that is like that of a co-maker under old § 3–416, the statute of limitations began for an indorser who guaranteed payment at the same time as for the maker of the instrument. Bank of New York v. Bersani, 90 A.D.2d 302, 457 N.Y.S.2d 142 (N.Y.App.Div.1982). The court further suggested that the same rule should apply for an indorser who waived presentment, notice of dishonor and protest. *See also* Silk v. Merrill Lynch, Pierce, Fenner & Smith, Inc., 437 So.2d 112 (Ala.1983) (involving an indorser where notice of dishonor was excused).

299. 85 N.M. 511, 514 P.2d 30 (N.M. 1973).

by neglecting to present the instrument for payment.[300] Moreover, the rule is thus the same for cashier's checks and certified checks, which serve the same function.[301] Under current Article 3, the rule for all bank obligations is the same,[302] but it is different than determined by courts under old Article 3 in that demand for payment is necessary.[303]

A cause of action against a maker or an acceptor of a time instrument under old Article 3 accrued on the day after maturity.[304] For example, a note due on May 30, 1977 could not be sued upon until May 31, 1977.[305] Some cases, however, were not so easily decided. In one case the agreement of the parties set the due date of the note at two years, but the seller without authorization filled in the instrument for payment in installments.[306] The court held suit instituted on the basis of the unauthorized terms and prior to the authorized maturity date should be dismissed without prejudice. What if the note had been an actual installment note? The statute of limitations in that instance began to run against each installment on the day following the date on which the installment became due.[307] But all properly drafted installment notes have an acceleration clause allowing the entire debt to be called due upon an event of default.[308] Acceleration avoids a series of suits as each installment becomes due. In this instance, it would appear that the rule as to when a cause of action accrued should apply with respect to each installment until notice that the entire note is due is given, and then the statute should run on the remaining debt from that point.[309]

---

300. In the case of a regular check, a holder delayed presentment at some risk under old §§ 3–503(2) and 3–502(1).

301. The function of a certificate of deposit, however, is different, as is the rule. Old § 3–122(2) and note 297, *supra*.

302. § 3–118(d) and (e); the limitations period is shorter for checks, however, which are payment instruments.

303. Official Comments 3 and 4 to § 3–118 explain why. *Compare* notes 289, 291 and 295, *supra*. Note the rule for drawers essentially is the same also. § 3–118(c).

304. Old § 3–122(1)(a). *See* current § 3–118(a), (c) and (f)(i) in relation to the applicable substantive provisions; no different conclusion seems warranted.

305. Milgrim v. Moses, 19 UCC Rep. Serv. 541 (N.Y.Sup.Ct.1976). *See also* Marine Midland Bank v. Graybar Elec. Co., 41 N.Y.2d 703, 395 N.Y.S.2d 403, 363 N.E.2d 1139 (1977) (no setoff on due date of note); Artistic Greetings, Inc. v. Sholom Greeting Card Co., Inc., 36 A.D.2d 68, 318 N.Y.S.2d 623 (N.Y.App.Div.1971) (judgment not available on notes not due until after commencement of action even though it was clear none of notes would be paid in accordance with their terms).

306. Bank of New Effington v. Thompson, 502 P.2d 978 (Colo.Ct.App.1972).

307. Oklahoma Brick Corp. v. McCall, 497 P.2d 215 (Okla.1972).

308. In Central Home Trust Co. v. Lippincott, 392 So.2d 931 (Fla.Dist.Ct.App. 1980), the court determined that a bookkeeping charge off did not constitute acceleration.

309. *See, e.g.*, Premier Capital, Inc. v. Doucette, 797 A.2d 32, 47 UCC Rep.Serv.2d 1409 (Me.2002) and the *Lippincott*, case, *supra* note 308, determining that a bookkeeping charge-off did not constitute acceleration and the statute thus had run only from the due date of each installment; Mechanics Nat'l Bank v. Killeen, 377 Mass. 100, 384 N.E.2d 1231 (Mass. 1979) (holding the debtor was not in default on notes where the holder had accelerated them pursuant to a clause deeming itself insecure but had not notified the debtor). *See* current § 3–118(a).

Chapter 7

LIABILITY AND RIGHTS NOT ON THE INSTRUMENT OF PARTIES TO NEGOTIABLE INSTRUMENTS

Analysis

Para.

¶7.01 Liability and Rights With Respect to the Underlying Transaction 250
    [1] Relation Between the Instrument and the Transaction in General 250
        [a] Parity of Rights and Liabilities 250
        [b] Suspension of the Underlying Obligation 250
        [c] Effect of Dishonor or Payment of the Instrument 252
    [2] Instruments on Which a Bank is Liable 253
    [3] Accord and Satisfaction.................................... 254

¶7.02 Warranty.. 257
    [1] Introduction... 257
        [a] Nature of Warranty Obligations 257
        [b] Remedies and Limitations.............................. 259
    [2] Warranties Made by a Transferor 260
    [3] Presentment Warranties Made to an Acceptor or Payor........ 262
        [a] No Unauthorized Signature 263
        [b] No Forged Indorsements 265
        [c] No Alterations 268

¶7.03 Other Bases for Liability and Rights 269
    [1] In General 269
    [2] Negligence 270
    [3] Conversion 273
        [a] Owner's Basis for Suit 273
        [b] Defenses to Action Based on a Forged Indorsement 275
            [i] Effect of Failure to Follow Reasonable Commercial Standards 276
            [ii] Effect of Proceeds Remaining 278
         [c] Legally Irrelevant Forged Indorsements 279
            [i] Proceeds Are Correctly Paid 279
            [ii] Imposter, Fictitious Payee, and Padded Payroll Cases; Employer's Indorsements 280
                [A] In General................................... 280
                [B] The Need for Proper Indorsement and Due Care 284

¶ 7.01 Liability and Rights With Respect to the Underlying Transaction

[1] *Relation Between the Instrument and the Transaction in General*

[a] Parity of Rights and Liabilities

Chapters 3 through 6 of this book discuss the rights and liabilities of parties on a negotiable instrument. However, a negotiable instrument does not arise in a vacuum. It normally is either given to evidence an obligation, such as a debt owed for the purchase price of property, or to transfer funds (by way of debits and credits to accounts) to satisfy an obligation, such as to repay a loan. This underlying obligation also will involve rights and liabilities. What is the relationship between the instrument and the obligation?

Generally speaking, the issuance of an instrument generates no greater rights or liabilities on it than exist with respect to the transaction out of which it arises. For example, in *Criterion Insurance Co. v. Fulgham*,[1] an insurance company erroneously issued a check to pay a claim for medical expenses that were not covered by the policy. When the company discovered the error and dishonored the instrument, suit was brought on the instrument. As the plaintiff was not a holder in due course, the court upheld the defense of the insurance company that the instrument was without consideration because there was no valid obligation underlying it.[2] An exception may exist, however, where an instrument is given to evidence an obligation and the issue is the appropriate statute of limitations. In this instance, a court held that while the statute of limitations had run on the obligation to pay for the goods sold, the note given to evidence the debt was not governed by that statute.[3]

[b] Suspension of the Underlying Obligation

Unless otherwise agreed, and except as to bank obligations, the taking of an instrument suspends the underlying obligation for which it is taken pro tanto until the instrument is due or, if it is payable on

---

¶ 7.01

1. 219 Va. 294, 247 S.E.2d 404 (Va. 1978).

2. *See also* Vedder v. Spellman, 78 Wn.2d 834, 480 P.2d 207 (Wash. 1971) (instrument taken for obligation that is barred because payee not licensed is not enforceable).

3. O'Neill v. Steppat, 270 N.W.2d 375 (S.D.1978). Fallimento C. Op. M.A. v. Fischer Crane Co., 995 F.2d 789, 20 UCC Rep. Serv. 2d 944 (7th Cir.1993) is not to the contrary as the statute of limitations for the instrument deferred to the statute of limitations for the sale. The result in the *O'Neill* case should be clear given § 3–118, which for the first time creates a uniform statute of limitations for negotiable instruments. Section 3–118 should not be applied to an instrument issued prior to the effective date of § 3–118. If the § 3–118 limitation period expires before that on the underlying obligation, it should make no difference as liability on the instrument is not discharged but is merely subject to a defense. *See* § 3–310(b) and discussion in Chapter 6, *supra*.

There also may be certain advantages to suing on an instrument as opposed to suing on the underlying obligation. Some of these are discussed in Chapter 1. *See also* Humble Oil & Ref. Co. v. Copley, 213 Va. 449, 192 S.E.2d 735 (Va. 1972) (plaintiff could not be required to proceed on account, which would deprive it of the right to attorney's collection fees provided in the note).

demand, until its presentment.[4] Thus taking the instrument is a surrender of the right to sue on the obligation until the instrument is due.[5] Accordingly, the running of the statute of limitations on the obligation is suspended,[6] but the taking of a regular check does not constitute an extension of time on the underlying obligation so as to discharge a surety.[7] The suspension of the obligation may result in other consequences. In *Kirby v. Bergfield*,[8] a check was delivered in connection with a contract to purchase property even though there were then insufficient collected funds in the drawer's bank account to pay the check. The holder learned this fact and did not present the check for payment. Suit eventuated over whether the contract was still in force. The court held the obligations of the underlying contract were suspended until presentment and dishonor of the check. As a result, the court determined that the contract had not terminated prior to the time a second and good check had been given.[9]

Taking an instrument, however, unless otherwise agreed, does not constitute actual payment of the underlying obligation.[10] Thus in *Cullotta v. Kemper Corp.*[11] the court held that a loss sustained between when a check to renew insurance coverage was given and the time the check was dishonored was not covered by insurance unless the parties had agreed the check was taken in payment for the insurance renewal. And in

---

4. § 3–310(b) and (c)(ii). *See* Quigley v. Acker, 288 Mont. 190, 955 P.2d 1377 (Mont. 1998). Bank obligations are treated in § 3–310(a) and (c)(i) and discussed later in this chapter and in Chapter 9.

The "taking" of a check treats the underlying obligation as paid for certain purposes at the time of receipt by the payee, but if the check is dishonored, the underlying obligation is revived; if the check is honored, the underlying obligation is discharged and the discharge relates back. *See* Gallant Ins. Co. v. Amaizo Federal Credit Union, 726 N.E.2d 860 (Ind.Ct.App.2000) (issue on breach of insurance contract dependent on when check paid); Staff Builders of Philadelphia, Inc. v. Koschitzki, 989 F.2d 692 (3d Cir. 1993) (issue of whether additional amount due under contract dependent on when check paid). *See also In re* Lee & Ota (Hall–Mark Electronics Corp. v. Sims), 179 B.R. 149, 26 UCC Rep. Serv. 2d 386 (9th Cir. BAP 1995) *affirmed*, 108 F.3d 239 (9th Cir.1997) (transfer for preference purposes in case of a bank obligation occurs on date of delivery). *But see* the *Staff Builders* case (postdated check pays debt on date of check); Barnhill v. Johnson, 503 U.S. 393, 112 S.Ct. 1386, 118 L.Ed.2d 39 (1992) (transfer for preference purposes does not occur until check is paid by drawee bank); Crystaplex Plastics, Ltd. v. Redevelopment Agency, 77 Cal.App.4th 990, 92 Cal.Rptr.2d 197, 40 UCC Rep. Serv. 2d 784 (Cal.App. 2000) (joint payee check where one payee's indorsement forged not paid for purpose of suit by that payee against drawer); and Smart v. Woo, 20 UCC Rep. Serv. 2d 1288 (Va. Cir. Ct.1993), *aff'd*, 247 Va. 365, 442 S.E.2d 690 (1994) (delivery of checks in anticipation of death did not constitute a gift causa mortis, check must be paid by the bank).

5. Official Comment 3 to old § 3–802.

6. *Id.*

7. Old § 3–802(2). Current Article 3 apparently assumes this is self–evident and omits the provision.

8. 186 Neb. 242, 182 N.W.2d 205 (Neb. 1970).

9. On the other hand, in Canal-Randolph Anaheim, Inc. v. Wilkoski, 78 Cal. App.3d 477, 144 Cal.Rptr. 474 (1978), the court decided that where there were insufficient funds on deposit almost consistently from the date of issuance of the checks until trial, presentment could be excused under old § 3–511(2)(b) (current § 3–504(a)), and therefore that old § 3–802, providing for suspension of the underlying obligation until presentment, would not bar suit.

10. Official Comment 3 to old § 3–802. *But see* note 4, *supra*.

11. 78 Ill.2d 25, 34 Ill.Dec. 306, 397 N.E.2d 1372 (Ill. 1979).

Merriman v. Sandeen,[12] where the check given to extend an option was dishonored upon presentment, the court held the option had only been extended until the presentment of the check and, upon the dishonor of the check, the option had expired.

[c] Effect of Dishonor or Payment of the Instrument

If an instrument taken for the underlying obligation is dishonored, an action may be maintained on either the instrument or on the obligation.[13] In essence the right to sue on the obligation is "revived." For example, if a check is not paid because of a stop order, a cause of action exists on it or on the obligation.[14] A security interest given to secure the obligation continues.[15] If, however, reliance by a third party has been placed upon a release of lien that occurred in return for the instrument, if the instrument is dishonored the lienholder will be estopped from reasserting the lien. Thus in *Mountain Stone Co. v. H. W. Hammond Co.*,[16] where mechanics lienors released their liens in return for payment by the landowner to the contractor, who then delivered checks to the lienors, when the checks given by the contractor were dishonored the court would not allow the liens to be reasserted.

If the instrument taken for the underlying obligation is not dishonored and is paid (or certified in the case of an uncertified check), the

---

12. 267 N.W.2d 714 (Minn.1978).

13. § 3–310(b)(3). However, if the person entitled to enforce the instrument is one other than the obligee, as where the obligee has sold the instrument, then the obligee cannot enforce the obligation as the only right that survives is the right to enforce the instrument. Official Comment 3 to § 3–310 and § 3–310(b)(4). *See also* note 14, *infra*.

14. *See* note 4, *supra*, and *e.g.*, David Graubart, Inc. v. Bank Leumi Trust Co., 48 N.Y.2d 554, 423 N.Y.S.2d 899, 399 N.E.2d 930 (N.Y.App.1979) (right of payee of check to sue on debt revived when check dishonored); § 3–310(b)(3) and Official Comment 3.

Where an instrument is not paid because it is lost or stolen and payment is not made to the former holder, suit may be brought under old § 3–804, permitting an action by the owner of a lost instrument. National Shawmut Bank v. International Yarn Corp., 322 F.Supp. 116 (S.D.N.Y.1970). *See* Guttman v. National Westminster Bank, 146 Misc.2d 391, 550 N.Y.S.2d 812 (N.Y.Sup.Ct. 1990), as to whether the section applies to a mailed check that allegedly never got there. Under § 3–309, *now see* Crystaplex Plastics, Ltd. v. Redevelopment Agency Barstow, 77 Cal.App.4th 990, 92 Cal.Rptr.2d 197, 40 UCC Rep. Serv. 2d 784 (Cal.App.2000). Under old Article 3, however, some debate existed as to whether this was so if there had been no presentment for dishonor, and as to whether suit on the obligation was possible or whether it still was suspended. Section 3–310(b)(4) settles the matter, allowing suit on the instrument as dishonor has occurred under §§ 3–504(a)(i) and 3–502(e) but denying suit on the obligation. § 3–310, Official Comment 4. But § 3–309(a)(iii) must be read "cheerfully" in that context. Another issue under § 3–309 developed when the assignee of an instrument from the FDIC sued on the instrument under § 3–309 because it was lost by the FDIC before the assignment. In Dennis Joslin Co., LLC v. Robinson Broadcasting Corp., 977 F.Supp. 491 (D.D.C.1997), the court read § 3–309 to deny recovery as the assignee never was in possession as required by § 3–309(a)(i). This view, of course, overlooks the "shelter" principle applicable through § 1–103(b) and § 3–203(b), and has been rejected by later cases, Official Comment 5 to revised § 9–109, and a 2002 amendment to § 3–309(a), which allows suit if the person seeking to enforce the instrument either was so entitled when possession was lost, or directly or indirectly acquired ownership from a person so entitled. *See also* Official Comment 3 to § 3–309.

15. *In re* Hayman, 6 UCC Rep. Serv. 928 (W.D. Okla. 1969).

16. 39 Colo.App. 58, 564 P.2d 958 (Colo. Ct.App.1977).

underlying obligor is not only discharged on the instrument but also is discharged on the obligation itself.[17] In context, the point at which payment occurs may be important. For example, in a Delaware case a check was delivered to the insurer after the expiration of the policy period but before an accident.[18] The check was ultimately paid by the drawee after being dishonored twice for insufficient funds after the accident had occurred. The court held that under an insurance statute using the standard "actually received," payment had not been actually received before the accident and thus the insurer was not liable.[19]

The parties may agree that the giving of the instrument will constitute a discharge of the underlying obligation.[20] The question is one of fact for the jury,[21] and the burden is on the party asserting that it was intended that the instrument constitute payment.[22] Thus in an Illinois case the court stated that the fact an insurance policy was reinstated upon the receipt of a check without any condition being expressed, when other factors were considered raised the question of whether the check was taken in payment so as to provide insurance coverage even though the check was ultimately dishonored.[23]

[2] Instruments on Which a Bank is Liable

Where a bank[24] is the drawer, maker, or acceptor of the instrument taken, the rule that no discharge of the underlying obligation occurs from the taking of the instrument is reversed, and, unless otherwise agreed, the obligation is pro tanto discharged if there is no recourse on the instrument against the underlying obligor.[25] Recourse may be present if the check is payable to the customer and then is indorsed. It may

---

17. § 3–310(b)(1) and (2) and (c)(ii). The rule also applies where discharge is through a process other than payment under old § 3–802(1)(b). The same result is proper under § 3–310(b), but it must be read "cheerfully" to reach that result. For example, in Chandler Motors, Inc. v. Dunham, 127 N.J.Super. 320, 317 A.2d 386 (App.Div.1974), the holder of a draft failed to give an indorser notice of dishonor. This discharged the indorser on the instrument (old § 3–502(1)(a)), and also on the obligation between them under old § 3–802(1)(b). Current § 3–310(b)(3) is the same. See Official Comment 3. Certification of a check also results in discharge under § 3–310(b)(1). See also §§ 3–414(c) and 3–415(d).

18. Moore v. Travelers Indem. Ins. Co., 408 A.2d 298 (Del.Super.Ct.1979).

19. See also notes 4 through 12, supra. Section 4–215 determines when the drawee bank pays an instrument. This is discussed in Chapter 8. Amended Official Comment 4 to § 3–502 discusses the relationship between payment of a check by a bank and dishonor of the check.

20. § 3–310(b) and (c)(ii).

21. Official Comment 2 to old § 3–802.

22. E.g., United States ex rel. D'Agostino Excavators, Inc. v. Heyward–Robinson Co., 430 F.2d 1077 (2d Cir.1970) cert. denied, 400 U.S. 1021, 91 S.Ct. 582, 27 L.Ed.2d 632 (1971).

23. Cullotta v. Kemper Corp., 78 Ill.2d 25, 34 Ill.Dec. 306, 397 N.E.2d 1372 (Ill. 1979). See also note 11, supra.

24. "Bank" is defined in UCC § 1–201(b)(4) as any person engaged in the business of banking, and the term is specifically stated to include a savings bank, savings and loan association, credit union and trust company. See also §§ 4–104(d) and 3–103(d).

25. § 3–310(a) and (c)(i); American Federal Sav. & Loan Assn. v. Madison Valley Properties, Inc., 288 Mont. 365, 958 P.2d 57 (Mont. 1998); and Neve–Welch Enters. v. Twelves, 27 UCC Rep. Serv. 1071 (Bankr. D.Utah 1979). Discharge occurs even if there is recourse under § 3–310(a), but any right of recourse on the instrument, such as on an indorsement, is preserved.

be absent in a number of other situations. As procuring certification by the holder will make the bank an acceptor of a check and discharge the drawer and prior indorsers,[26] a certified check is one example.[27] Other common examples are cashier's checks[28] or teller's checks[29] obtained by the customer of the bank and made payable to the person to whom they are to be delivered in payment.[30]

If the bank instrument is not accepted by the person to whom it is tendered, there will be no discharge. Thus where the beneficiaries under a will received cashier's checks in accordance with the terms of the will and, instead of cashing them, they instituted a will contest, the court held that there was no bar to the contest action.[31]

[3] Accord and Satisfaction

The receipt and collection of an instrument may have a significant effect with respect to an underlying obligation that is unliquidated or in dispute. The tender of partial payment by instrument upon the condition

---

26. §§ 3–414(c) and 3–415(d). For this reason, Article 3 makes it difficult for a bank obligation to be dishonored. As discussed in Chapter 6, basically a bank cannot dishonor and use a customer's defense to its liability. See §§ 3–602(e), 3–305(c), 3–411(b), 4–403(a) and DRP, Inc. v. Burgess, 730 So.2d 474 (La.Ct.App.1999). Some courts have held that a bank cannot refuse payment even if it has its own defense. See Flatiron Linen, Inc. v. First American State Bank, 23 P.3d 1209 (Colo.2001); and Hotel Riviera, Inc. v. First National Bank & Trust, 768 F.2d 1201 (10th Cir.1985). This analysis, however well intentioned, logically does not hold up, and § 3–411 should be read to reject it as § 3–411(c)(ii) clearly allows a bank to assert a claim or defense of the bank. The better reasoned cases came out this way, even under old Article 3. See Godat v. Mercantile Bank, 884 S.W.2d 1, 24 UCC Rep. Serv. 2d 385 (Mo.Ct.App.1994). Thus, the normally key questions are: (1) does the bank have a good defense that can prevail because the person enforcing the instrument cannot establish holder in due course status (see the Godat case—there the defense was fraud and plaintiff could not establish value for holder in due course status); or (2) does the bank have reasonable doubt whether the person seeking payment is a person entitled to enforce the instrument (see Associated Carriages, Inc. v. International Bank of Commerce, 37 S.W.3d 69, 43 UCC Rep. Serv. 2d 489 (Tex. Ct. App. 2000) petition for review denied (2001)). Note also that if the bank refuses payment due to mistake, for example, and the person seeking to enforce the instrument did not take it for value or in good faith, the bank may escape liability pursuant to § 3–418. See State Bank & Trust v. First State Bank of Texas, 242 F.3d 390 (Table) (10th Cir.2000). There is further discussion in Chapter 9, infra.

These rules place a premium on the availability of an effective remedy if a bank obligation is lost or destroyed. For that reason, § 3–312 goes beyond § 3–309 in affording effective relief. See, e.g., Clarks' Bank Deposits and Payments Monthly, Vol. 9, No. 7, January 2001, page 5.

27. Under § 3–414(c), discharge occurs no matter who procures certification. If the holder is worried about bank insolvency, an indorsement or guarantee may be obtained. § 3–414, Official Comment 3.

28. § 3–104(g).

29. A "teller's check" is a name used to describe a check drawn by one bank on another. See § 3–104(h).

30. Even with their expanded powers to make loans and pay out on demand instruments similar to checks, a savings and loan association or a credit union would probably not qualify under old Article 3 as a bank for the purpose of old § 3–802(1)(a). Inasmuch as their instruments are similar to those of banks, however, a court could find an agreement by custom to treat those instruments like bank instruments for the purpose of old § 3–802(1). See UCC § 1–201(b)(3). Other problems with instruments like checks drawn on savings and loan associations and credit unions are discussed in Chapter 9. This issue is removed under current Articles 3 and 4. See note 24, supra.

31. Tennant v. Satterfield, 158 W.Va. 917, 216 S.E.2d 229 (W.Va.1975).

that its acceptance will discharge the disputed or unliquidated debt, when accepted on this condition, will discharge the entire obligation.[32]

Section 1–308(a) of the UCC provides that a party who with explicit reservation of rights, such as by using the words "without prejudice," "under protest," or the like, performs or promises performance or assents to performance in a manner demanded or offered by the other party does not thereby prejudice the rights reserved. As a result, some courts under the prior provision (§ 1–207) held that a party receiving an instrument submitted in partial payment on a disputed obligation may avoid the application of the accord and satisfaction rule by indorsing the instrument using language which reserves the right to collect the disputed balance.[33] For example, in one case[34] the court held that an indorsement "under protest and with reservation of all their rights" produced this result.[35] If the payee has the check certified before indorsing it and submitting it for collection, however, the reservation of rights may come too late. Courts hold the procurement of the certification itself indicates

---

32. *E.g.*, Kilander v. Blickle Co., 280 Or. 425, 571 P.2d 503 (Or. 1977). This is an accord and satisfaction. The same conclusion may be reached even though the creditor crosses out language of release appearing on the tendered check when the accompanying letter makes the condition clear. A. G. King Tree Surgeons v. Deeb, 140 N.J.Super. 346, 356 A.2d 87 (Dist.Ct. 1976); N.H. Boring, Inc. v. Adirondack Environmental Associates, Inc., 145 N.H. 397, 762 A.2d 1036, 42 UCC Rep. Serv. 2d 1086 (N.H. 2000) (statement in accompanying letter and not on check); and Hardison v. Jackson, 45 Ark.App. 49, 871 S.W.2d 410, 23 UCC Rep. Serv. 2d 136 (Ark.App.1994) (scratched out "paid in full" language and substituted "not paid in full"). The rule is not applicable where there is no dispute as to liability. Ampex Corp. v. Appel Media, Inc., 374 F.Supp. 1114 (W.D.Pa.1974); Wickman v. Kane, 136 Md.App. 554, 766 A.2d 241, 43 UCC Rep. Serv. 2d 1046 (Md. App.2001) *cert. denied*, 364 Md. 462, 773 A.2d 514 (Md. 2001). *See* Official Comment 4 to § 3–311. Merely holding the check will not invoke the rule if the ground for retention is explained to the debtor. Kelly v. Kowalsky, 186 Conn. 618, 442 A.2d 1355 (Conn. 1982).

33. *See*, *e.g.*, Horn Waterproofing Corp. v. Bushwick Iron & Steel Co., 66 N.Y.2d 321, 488 N.E.2d 56, 497 N.Y.S.2d 310 (1985). The reservation may occur without a notation on the instrument if the circumstances make it clear that acceptance was with a reservation of rights. Northern Helex Co. v. United States, 455 F.2d 546 (Ct. Cl.1972). *See also* note 32, *supra*. But there is no need for an indorsement that reserves rights if there is no notice that the instrument is submitted in full payment. Holley v. Coggin Pontiac, Inc., 43 N.C.App. 229, 259 S.E.2d 1 (N.C.Ct.App.1979), *review denied*, 298 N.C. 806, 261 S.E.2d 919 (N.C. 1979).

The rule works both ways. Thus full payment under protest will reserve rights. Peterson v. Crown Fin. Corp., 476 F.Supp. 1155 (E.D.Pa.1979), *modified on other grounds*, 661 F.2d 287 (3d Cir.1981).

34. Miller v. Jung, 361 So.2d 788 (Fla. Dist.Ct.App.1978). A decision by another Florida court of appeals goes the other way. Eder v. Yvette B. Gervey Interiors, Inc., 407 So.2d 312 (Fla.Dist.Ct.App.1981). A similar division exists in New York. Compare Gimby v. Frost, 84 A.D.2d 806, 444 N.Y.S.2d 143 (N.Y.App.Div.1981) *with* Braun v. C.E.P.C. Distrib., 77 A.D.2d 358, 433 N.Y.S.2d 447 (N.Y.App.Div.1980) and *see* the *Horn Waterproofing* case, *supra* note 33. Enactment of revised Article 3 cured the problem in Florida, but New York has yet to enact the revised Article.

35. Merely deleting language on the instrument that acceptance will constitute full payment or indorsing without recourse will not be sufficient. *E.g.* Wilcox Press, Inc. v. Beauty Fashion, Inc., 73 A.D.2d 988, 423 N.Y.S.2d 565 (N.Y.App.Div.1980). *See also* cases cited in note 32, *supra*. In City of Deerfield Beach v. Florida Nat'l Bank, 428 So.2d 779 (Fla.Dist.Ct.App.1983), where the payee crossed out the restrictive language on the check, indorsed with a reservation of rights, and the bank paid the check, the drawer sued the bank for paying a different check than written. The court denied the action.

acceptance of the offer of part payment.[36]

There was far from a consensus that UCC former § 1–207 was applicable to an instrument submitted in full settlement. Several courts thought the provision should not be applicable if the underlying obligation was outside the Code, such as a contract for services.[37] More courts refused to apply UCC former § 1–207 on the grounds there was no intent to change the common law.[38] The most persuasive argument against application, however, was that accepting the proffered check under a reservation of rights is not assenting to performance in a manner demanded or offered by the other party, which is necessary for application of UCC former § 1–207.[39] Current Article 3 settles the issue in conjunction with § 1–308(b).

The real problem in many of these cases is that the full settlement check is deposited by a clerk in an organization that does not appreciate the consequences, or is handled by automated means through a lock box arrangement where the offer is never noticed.[40] Current Articles 3 and 1 first adopt the majority position that UCC former § 1–207 does not change the common law.[41] Organizational creditors can protect against inadvertent accord and satisfaction by notifying customers that full satisfaction checks must be sent to a designated location which is set up to deal with the matter, and by proving any check submitted in full satisfaction was not sent there.[42] For creditors who do not wish to periodically notify customers (the notice must be within a "reasonable

---

36. *E.g.*, Lange–Finn Constr. Co. v. Albany Steel & Iron Supply Co., 94 Misc.2d 15, 403 N.Y.S.2d 1012 (N.Y.Sup.Ct.1978).

37. *E.g.*, Blottner, Derrico, Weiss & Hoffman v. Fier, 101 Misc.2d 371, 420 N.Y.S.2d 999 (N.Y. Civ. Ct. 1979) (contract for legal services). *But see* Hardison v. Jackson, 45 Ark.App. 49, 871 S.W.2d 410, 23 UCC Rep. Serv. 2d 136 (Ark.App.1994) (applied in a painting contract dispute). *See also* the *Horn Waterproofing* case, *supra* note 33.

38. *E.g.*, Chancellor, Inc. v. Hamilton Appliance Co., 175 N.J.Super. 345, 418 A.2d 1326 (Dist.Ct.1980); Milgram Food Stores, Inc. v. Gelco Corp., 550 F.Supp. 992 (W.D.Mo.1982); Air Van Lines, Inc. v. Buster, 673 P.2d 774 (Alaska 1983). In Scholl v. Tallman, 247 N.W.2d 490 (S.D.1976), the outcome was influenced by a statute outside the UCC. Statutes bearing on this issue do exist in some states. *See, e.g.*, Cal. Civ. Code § 1526(a) (no accord and satisfaction if check cashed under protest); *but see* Directors Guild of America v. Harmony Pictures, Inc., 32 F. Supp. 2d 1184 (C.D.Cal. 1998) (holding enactment of revised Article 3 impliedly repealed this statute).

39. *E.g.*, Barber v. White, 46 N.C.App. 110, 264 S.E.2d 385 (1980) and Hearst Corp. v. Laurer, Markin & Gibbs, Inc., 37 Ohio App.3d 87, 524 N.E.2d 193 (1987).

40. *See, e.g.*, Slavenburg Corp. v. Kenli Corp., 36 UCC Rep. Serv. 8 (E.D.Pa.1983) (handled by clerk); John Grier Constr. v. Jones Welding & Repair, Inc., 238 Va. 270, 383 S.E.2d 719 (Va. 1989) (notation on check not noticed); McMahon Food Corp. v. Burger Dairy Co., 103 F.3d 1307 (7th Cir. 1996) (employee only handled checks and not the whole transaction).

41. UCC § 1–308(b) and § 3–311(a) and (b).

42. § 3–311(c)(1). If the check is nonetheless knowingly processed, accord and satisfaction will result. § 3–311(d). However, the person tendering the full settlement check must do so in good faith, and much of the litigation under § 3–311 has centered on this requirement, with the cases negating perceived sharp dealing. *See, e.g.*, McMahon Food Corp. v. Burger Dairy Co., 103 F.3d 1307 (7th Cir.1996); Fremarek v. John Hancock Mutual Life Ins. Co., 272 Ill.App.3d 1067, 209 Ill.Dec. 423, 651 N.E.2d 601 (Ill.Ct.App.1995); Commonwealth of Virginia v. Wills, 27 UCC Rep. Serv. 2d 926 (Va. Cir. Ct.1995); Webb Business Promotions, Inc. v. American Electronics, 617 N.W.2d 67, 42 UCC Rep. Serv. 2d 534 (Minn.2000); Dhiman v. Rockford Industries, Inc., 42 UCC Rep. Serv. 2d 767 (N.D.Ill.2000).

time" before tender) or set up a special office, where it probably will receive some misdirected checks from customers who do not read carefully, an inadvertent accord and satisfaction can be averted if, once the nature of the check is discovered, repayment is tendered within 90 days after payment of the instrument.[43] This solution is not perfect; for example, a creditor may not press a customer for payment owed and find out about the full satisfaction check until after 90 days due to minimum payments in open end credit or grace allowed before collection efforts are begun, but it seems reasonable and fair overall no matter which side a person finds itself on. And, as Official Comments 1 and 3 to § 3–311 indicate, the provision may be employed both in consumer and in commercial contexts, and by both sides to a dispute.

¶ 7.02 Warranty

[1] Introduction

[a] Nature of Warranty Obligations

In addition to evidencing a contract, an instrument under Article 3 is property embodying valuable rights.[44] As property, its transfer carries with it certain implied warranties beyond the contract liability of the parties on the instrument.[45]

Five implied warranties are imposed upon the transfer of a negotiable instrument for consideration.[46] The warranties are given by any person who transfers the instrument for consideration. Several cases

---

43. § 3–311(c)(2). Again, § 3–311(d) will not allow a knowing acceptance of the check. *See* Moncrief v. Williston Basin Interstate Pipeline Co., 880 F.Supp. 1495 (D.Wyo.1995), *aff'd in part, rev'd in part on other matters*, 174 F.3d 1150 (10th Cir. 1999).

¶ 7.02

44. *See, e.g.*, Official Comment 2 to old § 3–419, declaring that a negotiable instrument is property and a thing of value. *See also* People v. Marques, 184 Colo. 262, 520 P.2d 113 (Colo. 1974), where a conviction for taking property with a value in excess of $100 was sustained in a case where checks having an aggregate face value of more than $900 were stolen.

45. The warranties are specified in §§ 3–416 and 3–417. Sections 4–207 and 4–208 are like provisions for items (which under § 4–104(a)(9) include a negotiable instrument) in the bank collection process. Since the warranties created under Article 4 are, in core coverage, substantially the same as those created under Article 3, no independent general discussion of the Article 4 warranties appears here. One difference, however, is that Article 4 includes encoding and retention warranties to facilitate automated processing and check truncation. § 4–209 and, *e.g.*, U.S. Bank National Ass'n v. First Security Bank, 44 UCC Rep. Serv.2d 1088 (D.Utah 2001) (effect of delay in raising claim for breach of warranty) and First Union National Bank v. Bank One, 47 UCC Rep.Serv.2d 645 (E.D.Pa. 2002) (allocation of encoding error). Another difference is that Article 4 warranties carry an indorsement contract that cannot be eliminated. *See* § 3–415(b), 3–416, and 4–207(b). Discussion of those warranties in context appears both in this chapter and in Chapter 8; the latter discussion also relates these warranties to those under Regulation CC.

46. § 3–416. In addition, Article 4, as noted in note 45, *supra*, in § 4–209, creates warranties as to encoding and electronic presentment. Further, amendment of §§ 3–416, 3–417, 4–207 and 4–208 in 2002 created a transfer and also a presentment warranty that the person on whose account a remotely created consumer item was drawn authorized the issuance of the item in the amount for which it was drawn. §§ 3–416(a)(6), 3–417(a)(4), 4–207(a)(6), 4–208(a)(4), 4–104(c) and 3–103(a)(2) and (16). The purpose is to permit a payor bank on what have been called consumer "demand drafts" (a check drawn by a third party, such as a telemarketer, and not signed by the consumer, on a consumer's

have held that an accommodation indorser does not make a warranty.[47] The warranties extend to the transferee of the instrument and, if the transfer includes an indorsement, the warranty extends to any subsequent transferee who takes the instrument in good faith.[48] Consequently, where there is an indorsement, the warranty of the transferor-indorser also runs with the instrument as does the indorsement. As a result, a remote holder may sue the transferor-indorser directly in warranty and avoid a multiplicity of suits. The holder also may avoid a loss which might otherwise occur because of the insolvency of the holder's intermediate transferor.[49]

Somewhat different and fewer warranties are made by a person who obtains payment or acceptance and by any prior transferor to a person who in good faith pays or accepts the instrument.[50] And because of a different policy, the warranty as to the authorized nature of signatures differs here from that made upon the transfer for consideration of the instrument.[51] Accordingly, the latter warranties do not run to payors or acceptors.[52]

Warranty liability clearly is not contractual liability on the instrument. Warranty liability is imposed upon a transferor even if there is no

---

bank account, but which assertedly was not authorized, or authorized in the amount drawn, by the consumer) to use a warranty claim to absolve itself of responsibility for honoring an unauthorized item. Official Comment 8 to § 3–416. As such, these provisions constitute a limited rejection of the result in Price v. Neal, 97 Eng. Rep. 871 (K.B.1762), and follow, but somewhat less expansively, non-uniform amendments to the UCC in a number of states, such as Texas and California, that address this kind of check fraud. Since in the commercial context other methods exist to address fraud, like positive-pay arrangements, and the parties are perhaps more sophisticated, the narrower approach of the UCC amendments seems warranted.

47. *E.g.*, Oak Park Currency Exch., Inc. v. Maropoulos, 48 Ill.App.3d 437, 6 Ill.Dec. 525, 363 N.E.2d 54 (1977). Under old § 3–417(4), a selling agent or broker, as opposed to an agent for collection, who does not disclose his or her status gives full warranties, but if he or she does disclose his or her status, he or she warrants only his or her good faith and authority. Current § 3–416 omits this statement as unnecessary.

48. § 3–416(a) and (b).

49. Official Comment 1 to § 3–416. If any indorsement is forged, however, there can be no later indorsement and thus no later holder. §§ 3–201(b), 3–205. In that event, under old § 3–417(2) it would appear that suit would have to proceed between each transferee and transferor, multiple suits would be required, and an insolvent transferor could not be skipped. It is unlikely the statute intended this unique exception to the otherwise general rule. Insofar that in the bank collection process under old § 4–207(2) the warranties run with the instrument without need for an indorsement, the described exception probably is less troublesome than it otherwise might be. Of course, current § 4–207 is the same as old § 4–207, and current § 3–416(a), by stating "if the transfer is by indorsement, to any subsequent transferee," would seem to have cured the problem.

50. § 3–417.

51. *Compare* § 3–416(a)(2) *with* § 3–417(a)(3). The reason for the difference is discussed, *infra*, this chapter. The demand draft warranty (*supra* note 46), however, applies under both sections. Moreover, note the applicability of each provision is refined in Article 4 since "transfer" excludes "presentment." § 3–203(a).

52. Dozier v. First Ala. Bank, 363 So.2d 781 (Ala.Civ.App.1978). There normally is no consideration involved in a transfer to a payor or an acceptor, and only a person who receives consideration makes the warranties under § 3–416(a). The same is not true with respect to § 4–207(a) as it uses the phrase "settlement or other consideration."

Several courts extended the warranties imposed by old § 3–417(1) to persons who were not "payors," however. This is discussed, *infra*, this chapter.

indorsement[53] and, if an indorsement without recourse is made so that the indorser has no liability on the instrument,[54] the only effect under old Article 3 on warranty liability is to change the warranty that no defenses are good against the transferor from an unqualified one to one of no knowledge.[55] Nor is warranty liability related to liability on the underlying transaction. For example, if liability on the instrument is discharged, and thus also liability on the underlying obligation,[56] it has no necessary impact on any warranty liability.

[b] Remedies and Limitations

While old Article 3 is silent as to what remedies may exist for breach of a warranty, a monetary recovery certainly is available,[57] and current Article 3 expressly allows damages for breach of warranty.[58] Recovery of attorneys fees is left to other state law.[59] In addition, rescission should be available where a warranty is breached.[60] Indeed, as Article 3 does nothing more than statutorily impose defined warranties, all the usual rules of law applicable to warranties should be employed as to details not covered in the UCC, including the necessity of reliance in good faith on the warranty.[61] Accordingly, as Articles 2 and 2A of the Code may be

---

53. §§ 3–416, 3–417. *See also* §§ 4–207, 4–208.

54. § 3–415(b).

55. Old § 3–417(3). There is no effect under current § 3–416. *See* § 3–416, Official Comment 3, and note 45, *supra*. The inability to disclaim in the case of checks also suggests a non-contractual analysis. §§ 3–416(c), 3–417(e), 4–207(d) and 4–208(e).

56. § 3–310.

57. Official Comment 1 to old § 3–417. A case granting a damage recovery for breach of warranty is Sun 'n Sand, Inc. v. United Cal. Bank, 21 Cal.3d 671, 148 Cal. Rptr. 329, 582 P.2d 920 (Cal. 1978) (measure of recovery in the case of altered checks is difference between raised amount and original amount). Enactment of current § 3–405 rejected another point in the *Sun 'n Sand* case. *See* Lee Newman, M.D., Inc. v. Wells Fargo Bank, 87 Cal.App.4th 73, 104 Cal.Rptr.2d 310 (2001) (§ 3–405 precludes common law negligence action as to its subject matter). *See also* § 7.03[2].

58. §§ 3–416(b), 3–417(b) and (d)(2). *See also* §§ 4–207(c) and 4–208(b) and (d).

59. §§ 3–416, Official Comment 6, and 3–417, Official Comment 5. In Perkins State Bank v. Connolly, 632 F.2d 1306 (5th Cir.1980), the court included recovery of attorney's fees as damages for breach of warranty. However, in Christensen Aviation, Inc. v. State Bank, N.A., 20 P.3d 170, 44 UCC Rep. Serv. 2d 213 (Okla. Civ. App. 2001), the court determined that attorney fees were not recoverable as "expenses" in an action based on transfer and presentment warranties under §§ 4–207 and 4–208 in light of Oklahoma's strict application of the American rule and the failure of the legislature to address the issue. *See also* Vectra Bank of Englewood v. Bank Western, 890 P.2d 259, 25 UCC Rep. Serv.2d 862 (Colo.Ct.App.1995) (same result); and State Bank & Trust, N.A. v. First State Bank of Texas, 43 UCC Rep. Serv. 2d 1206 (10th Cir.2000) (same).

60. Official Comment 1 to old § 3–417.

61. *Id*. The good faith requirement, for example, should preclude one who takes an instrument knowing that it is forged from relying on the transferor's warranty that it is genuine. Arguably, the learning with respect to the good faith test for holder in due course status, discussed in Chapter 3, might be applied here. Other examples might include E.S.P., Inc. v. Midway National Bank, 447 N.W.2d 882 (Minn.1989) (determining that the statute of limitations [now § 3–118(g)(ii)] begins to run when loss is sustained; *e.g.*, when the claimant has reason to know of the breach per §§ 3–416(d) and 3–417(f); *see also* §§ 4–207(e) and 4–208(f)); Bidwell & Co. v. National Union Fire Ins. Co., 44 UCC Rep. Serv. 2d 221 (D.Or.2001) (where person receiving payment for checks breached transfer warranty to bank, bank could properly use common law right of set off to recover sums from person's account); and Comerica Bank v. Michigan National Bank, 211 Mich.App.

considered to embody the usual rules of law applicable to warranties, an ability to disclaim the warranties generally should exist if done properly.[62] The section in Article 2, for example, governing disclaimer is UCC § 2–316. By analogy to it, language that in common understanding calls attention to the exclusion of warranty would be necessary, including being conspicuous if the disclaimer is in writing. It would seem that to be effective the disclaimer would have to appear in the form of the indorsement, as parol proof of an "agreement otherwise" would not bind later parties without notice of it.[63] Perhaps an agreement to limit remedies by analogy to, for example, UCC § 2–719 could be an alternative to a disclaimer. How far the usual rules from Article 2 actually can be applied is not entirely free from doubt. For example, by stating that a disclaimer occurs by agreement between the immediate parties, Official Comment 1 to old § 3–417 perhaps suggests that a disclaimer will not necessarily be good against those not in privity but who nonetheless may sue on a warranty. That result, if that is the way the statute should be read (which is doubtful), would not always be consistent with the outcome of this issue under Article 2.[64]

[2] *Warranties Made by a Transferor*

A person who transfers an instrument for consideration warrants the right to enforce the instrument.[65] This concept is similar enough to

---

534, 536 N.W.2d 298, 27 UCC Rep. Serv. 2d 547 (Mich.Ct.App.1995) (intended payee defense allowable in action for breach of warranty as to indorsements).

62. Sections 3–416(c), 3–417(e), 4–207(d) and 4–208(e) expressly address this issue but only in part. *See* § 3–416, Official Comment 5, and § 3–417, Official Comment 7. The warranties cannot be disclaimed with respect to checks as any disclaimer might not be noticed in automated processing. Otherwise a disclaimer consistent with the policies of Articles 2 and 2A may be effective.

63. *See* Official Comment 5 to § 3–416. Official Comment 1 to old § 3–417 perhaps indicates parol proof would be inadmissible even between the immediate parties. But there is nothing on this in the statute itself, and the parol normally would not contradict the writing as opposed to the obligation imposed on the writing. Thus the Comment should be read in relation to later parties. Official Comment 5 to current § 3–416 is much the same.

64. *See* Official Comment 1 to UCC § 2–318, which indicates that exclusions and modifications of warranties in a sales contract are effective against beneficiaries of those warranties who are not parties to the sales contract. UCC § 2A–216 explicitly so states in the statute. Official Comment 5 to § 3–416 seems more clearly to support the conclusions reached in the text above, but is not entirely free from ambiguity either.

65. § 3–416(a)(1). There is a similar presentment warranty. § 3–417(a)(1). *See also* § 4–207(a)(1). Essentially this is a warranty of good title, that is, no missing or unauthorized indorsements, or that the transfer is otherwise rightful. In The Guardian Life Ins. Co. of America v. Weisman, 223 F.3d 229, 42 UCC Rep. Serv.2d 1 (3d Cir.2000), in connection with a drawee bank's defense under § 3–406, the court stated a drawee bank receives presentment warranties from the depositary bank and, given these warranties, there is little reason for the drawee to inquire into the validity of payee indorsements; it is reasonable that review take place at the depositary bank. The court in Mandelbaum v. P & D Printing Corp., 279 N.J.Super. 427, 652 A.2d 1266 (App.Div.1995), followed this reasoning even though the instrument was an insurance draft where the insurance company drawer-drawee had the opportunity itself to spot the missing indorsement before it accepted the draft, but § 3–417(b) seems to agree; the right of a drawee to recover damages is not affected by any failure of the drawee to exercise ordinary care in making payment (as warranty liability is strict liability). *See* Official Comment 5 to § 3–417.

that in UCC § 2–312 to suggest that the warranty should be considered breached not only by a failure of title but also by a substantial cloud upon it. To avoid a breach of the title warranty in Article 2, the title must be a good, clean title transferred in a rightful manner so that the buyer will not be exposed to a lawsuit in order to protect it.[66] A transferor also warrants that all signatures are authentic and authorized,[67] and that the instrument has not been materially altered.[68]

These three warranties are the ones that operate in the first instance to place the loss from an instrument bearing a forged signature or one that is materially altered upon the person who dealt with the culprit. For example, if the payee of a check raises its amount, and

---

66. *Compare* § 3–416, Official Comment 3, indicating one should not have to purchase a lawsuit, *with* Official Comment 1 to UCC § 2–312. Thus a holder subjected to an adverse claim under § 3–602, should be able to invoke a breach of warranty rather than litigate, or be able to rely on the breach to recover any loss after litigation.

67. § 3–416(a)(2). *See also* § 4–207(a)(2). The presentment warranty is different except in the case of a remotely created consumer item. §§ 3–416(a)(2) and (6) and 3–417(a)(3) and (4). *See also* §§ 4–207, 4–208. There has been much litigation over whether a signature is authorized. Strong authority upholds agreements as to this matter. *See, e.g.,* Spear Insurance Co., Ltd. v. Bank of America, N.A., 40 UCC Rep. Serv. 2d 807 (N.D.Ill.2000) (resolution authorizing bank to pay checks bearing facsimile signatures that "resemble[d]" the signatures of bank officials protected bank when it paid counterfeit checks). This can cut both ways. *See* Federal Insurance Co. v. NCNB Nat'l Bank, 958 F.2d 1544 (11th Cir.1992) (checks with one hand and one facsimile signature not in compliance with resolution requiring two hand signatures). As to remotely created consumer items, *see* Federal Trade Commission Telemarketing Sales Rule, 16 C.F.R. § 310.3(a)(3). Properly drafted agreements can be particularly useful in litigation over unauthorized indorsements, as discussed *infra*. *See, e.g.,* Western Assurance Co. v. Star Financial Bank of Indianapolis, 3 F.3d 1129 (7th Cir. 1993); Inn Foods v. Equitable Co-operative Bank, 45 F.3d 594 (1st Cir.1995); American Parkinson Disease Ass'n v. First National Bank, 584 N.W.2d 437 (Minn.Ct.App.1998); First Rome Bank v. Reese Oil Co., 206 Ga.App. 667, 426 S.E.2d 384 (Ga.Ct.App. 1992). Moreover, an agent's authority to indorse checks for a principal is not invalidated by the agent's later deposit of those checks to the agent's own account, unless making deposits to the principal's account was also required. Citizens Bank of Maryland v. Maryland Industrial Finishing Co., Inc., 338 Md. 448, 659 A.2d 313 (Md. 1995), limited by opinion in Hartford Fire Insurance Co. v. Maryland National Bank, N.A., 341 Md. 408, 671 A.2d 22 (Md.Ct. App. 1996). *See also In re* McMullen, 251 B.R. 558 (Bankr.C.D.Cal.2000) and *In re* Bartoni–Corsi Produce, Inc., 130 F.3d 857 (9th Cir.1997). Ultimately the issue may be one of interpretation of authority, and that issue particularly presents itself where the instrument is jointly payable to an attorney and the client, and the attorney indorses without the actual indorsement of the client. In Hunt v. Clark, 41 UCC Rep. Serv. 2d 541 (Mass. Super. Ct. 2000), no authority in the attorney was found because the court read the power of attorney very closely. A similar approach was taken by the court in Tifton Bank & Trust Co. v. Knight's Furniture Co., 215 Ga.App. 471, 452 S.E.2d 219 (1994) and True v. Fleet Bank–NH, 138 N.H. 679, 645 A.2d 671, 24 UCC Rep. Serv. 2d 598 (N.H. 1994).

An interesting aspect of these cases is when the authorized person nonetheless obtains moneys that person should not have due to some negligence on the part of the bank (*see* the *First Rome Bank* and *Hartford Fire Insurance Co.* cases, above). The Code seems not to cover the issue since there is no unauthorized indorsement. Nonetheless, usually there is negligence on the part of both parties, and a comparative negligence approach would seem appropriate utilizing an analysis similar to that in §§ 3–404 through 3–406. *See Hartford Fire Insurance Co., supra* (dictum).

68. § 3–416(a)(3). There is a similar presentment warranty. § 3–417(a)(2). *See also* § 4–207(a)(3). Presumably the standard is that of § 3–407, and includes any change of the contract in any respect without regard to intent. Similar warranties of a right to enforce the instrument and with respect to alteration are created under federal Regulation J. 12 CFR §§ 210.5(a)(2) and 210.6(b).

negotiates it to a third person, who deposits the check in his or her bank for collection but it is dishonored by the payor bank because the alteration is detected, the warranty against material alteration will be breached along the line,[69] ultimately allowing recovery against the person who took the check from the payee, whose only recourse is against the payee.

A person who transfers an instrument for consideration further warrants that no defense or claim in recoupment of any party is good against him or her,[70] and that he or she has no knowledge of any insolvency proceeding instituted with respect to the maker or acceptor of the instrument, or with respect to the drawer of an unaccepted instrument.[71] Note, however, that the transferor of a check makes no warranty that the drawer of the check has sufficient funds on deposit to cover it,[72] and there is no warranty against difficulties of collection generally, or against impairment of the credit of the obligor, or even against insolvency.[73]

[3] Presentment Warranties Made to an Acceptor or Payor

The warranties under old Article 3 made to a good faith acceptor or payor of a negotiable instrument by a person that obtains payment or acceptance and any prior transferor are:

1. There is a good title to the instrument or authorization to obtain payment or acceptance on behalf of one who has a good title.[74]

2. There is no knowledge that the signature of the maker or drawer is unauthorized (except the warranty is not given by a holder in due course acting in good faith in certain situations).[75]

3. The instrument has not been materially altered (except, again, this warranty is not given by a holder in due course acting in good faith in certain situations).[76]

---

69. Actually, in this example the appropriate provision would be § 4–207(a)(3), where bank collection is involved. The terms of the warranties are the same.

70. § 3–416(a)(4). There is no similar presentment warranty. *See also* § 4–207(a)(4). In the absence of a contrary understanding, the warranty is implied because a buyer does not undertake to purchase an instrument incapable of enforcement. The defense does not have to be good for the warranty to be breached. Official Comment 3 to revised UCC § 3–416. *See also* note 66, *supra*. If the transfer is "without recourse," the warranty under old § 3–417(3) was limited to one that the transferor had no knowledge of the defense, but current § 3–416 eliminates this. *But see* Hartford Life Ins. Co. v. Title Guarantee Co., 520 F.2d 1170 (D.C.Cir.1975) (payee who indorsed without recourse, but who was aware of facts upon which it was subsequently found that the note was unenforceable because of the illegality of the underlying loan, breached the warranty even if ignorant of the law).

71. § 3–416(a)(5). There is no similar presentment warranty. *See also* § 4–207(a)(5).

72. Kirby v. First & Merchants Nat'l Bank, 210 Va. 88, 168 S.E.2d 273 (Va. 1969).

73. Official Comment 4 to § 3–416. If insolvency proceedings have been instituted and the transferor knows it, the concealment amounts to a fraud, and the warranty provides a remedy.

74. Old § 3–417(1)(a). *See also* old § 4–207(1)(a).

75. Old § 3–417(1)(b). *See also* old § 4–207(1)(b).

76. Old § 3–417(1)(c). *See also* old § 4–207(1)(c).

Current § 3–417 makes no real substantive change but substantially reorganizes the rules for clarity. Thus these presentment warranties are separated from the transfer warranties,[77] and the warranties made with respect to an undishonored, unaccepted draft are separated from those made with respect to other types of instruments.[78]

[a] No Unauthorized Signature

When made to an acceptor or payor, as opposed to a transferee, the warranty concerning authorized signatures is not unqualified but rather is limited to an undertaking that the transferor has no knowledge of an unauthorized signature of the drawer.[79] The reason for the limitation in this context is the principle established in *Price v. Neal*[80] that a payor or acceptor is in a superior position to detect a forgery because that person has the drawer's signature and is expected to know and compare it. Thus if the holder of an instrument presents it knowing that the signature of the maker or drawer is forged or unauthorized, an obvious fraud is committed upon the party to whom presentment is made and the warranty is breached; otherwise, the person paying or accepting, being in a superior position to prevent the loss, should bear it, or at least share it.[81]

---

77. *See* § 3–416 (transfer warranties) and § 3–417 (presentment warranties). The same is true in Article 4. *See* § 4–207 (transfer warranties) and § 4–208 (presentment warranties).

78. § 3–417(a) and (d). *See also* § 4–208(a) and (d). This change permits deletion of the exceptions as a matter of form that appeared in old §§ 3–417(1)(b) and (c) and 4–207(1)(b) and (c). The warranty as to remotely created consumer items is in § 3–417(a)(4).

79. Under §§ 3–417(a)(3) and 4–208(a)(3) this warranty is made only to the drawee of an unaccepted draft as to the drawer's signature, and thus the exceptions in old §§ 3–417(1)(b) and 4–207(1)(b) for makers, drawers and acceptors are not necessary. This also is true for the warranty as to a remotely created consumer item. Moreover, the analysis that the warranties in subsection (a) can be made to a drawer, which was the result in Sun 'n Sand, Inc. v. United California Bank, 21 Cal.3d 671, 148 Cal. Rptr. 329, 582 P.2d 920 (Cal. 1978), is rejected. § 3–417, Official Comment 2; Steinroe Income Trust v. Continental Bank N.A., 238 Ill.App.3d 660, 179 Ill.Dec. 671, 606 N.E.2d 503 (1992). That the drawer can otherwise sue the depositary bank, also a holding of the *Sun 'n Sand* case, also is rejected. Official Comment 1 to § 3–420. *Cf.* Hartford Fire Insurance Co. v. Maryland National Bank, N.A., 341 Md. 408, 671 A.2d 22 (Md.Ct.App.1996). In Cassello v. Allegiant Bank and Royal Banks of Missouri, 288 F.3d 339 (8th Cir.2002), the federal court had to determine whether under Missouri law a person who asserted he was fraudulently induced to write certain checks could recover against the bank of deposit that assertedly was negligent in accepting the checks for deposit. The court correctly denied a claim under the UCC on the basis a breach of warranty claim is denied to a drawer, but then held that a common law negligence claim existed. To what extent the UCC displaces such claims under § 1–103(b) is a difficult issue, which again will be discussed *infra*.

80. 3 Burr. 1354, 97 Eng. Rep. 871 (K.B. 1762).

81. Old § 3–417, Official Comment 4, and old § 3–418, Official Comment 1. *See also* Official Comment 3 to § 3–417. Official Comment 1 to old § 3–418 suggests that a less fictional basis for the result is that it is desirable to finalize commercial transactions upon payment and not to reopen them. *See also* Official Comment 1 to current § 3–418. However that may be, the broader picture, including how issues on instruments bearing forged indorsements and on altered instruments are resolved and the fact this warranty is not changed even though banks do not always examine checks (*see* § 3–103(a)(7)) and many checks are truncated (*see* § 4–110), strongly suggests that the rule represents a combination of the principle established in *Price v. Neal*, that the party best able to prevent

The warranty concerning an unauthorized signature of the drawer made to the person accepting or paying the instrument must be read in conjunction with § 3–418, which was discussed in Chapter 3. Section 3–418 makes payment or acceptance final in favor of a person who took the instrument in good faith and for value or who in good faith changed position in reliance on the payment or acceptance, except, as applicable, for liability for breach of warranty on presentment. The tandem operation of these provisions is illustrated by *Dime Savings Bank v. Chase Manhattan Bank*.[82] There a forger presented a paper, probably not even governed by Article 3 because of its form, to Chase Manhattan Bank. The writing ordered a savings bank to pay $15,000 out of an account that the forger purportedly had with it to Chase to be deposited to an account with Chase. The paper was forwarded to the savings bank,

---

the loss should bear it, and finality. It should be noted that some erosion of finality in favor of the *Price v. Neal* concept in fact exists in § 3–406(b). *See* Official Comment 3 to § 3–404. The same is true in the case of the warranty claim for an unauthorized remotely created consumer item in §§ 3–416, 3–417, 4–207 and 4–208; there is a limited rejection of *Price v. Neal*, and the premise for the warranty is that monitoring by depositary banks can control for the type of fraud involved more effectively than practices available to payor banks. Official Comment 8 to § 3–416. Note also no finality principle can control a contrary federal policy. *See* FDIC v. McKnight, 769 F.2d 658 (10th Cir.1985); *infra* Chapter 8.

Because of truncation, the fact banks routinely do not examine all checks, and the sophistication of modern check counterfeiting methods, a product called "Positive Pay" is often utilized. Some 54.5% of large banks market the service to customers. In a positive pay arrangement, the drawer of checks, say a company, submits a list of all checks written (a check report). If a check drawn on the drawer's account is presented but is not on the report, it is called an "exception check." A list of exception checks is sent to the drawer. Depending on the agreement, the bank will either pay an exception check unless the drawer objects (within the midnight deadline) or not pay the exception check unless within that same time period the drawer grants permission.

Positive pay can significantly prevent fraud losses due to forged or altered (if the information is sufficient) items and it furnishes a basis for limiting the warranty as to remotely created consumer items to that context (*see* note 46, *supra*), but it raises a number of interesting issues, including some very basic issues. It is an agreement that generally can change the statutory rights of customers (*see* UCC § 1–302), but to what extent (*compare* Spear Insurance Co., Ltd. v. Bank of America, N.A., 40 UCC Rep. Serv. 2d 807 (N.D.Ill.2000) (upholding agreement protecting bank which paid counterfeit checks) *with* UCC §§ 1–302(b) and 4–103(a)), and at what cost to relations if the customer does not understand the ramifications? Moreover, once imaging becomes available, it may hold promise for detection of problems in connection with indorsements as well. *See infra* Chapter 9

Other approaches to check fraud also exist. An American Bankers Association White Paper (*see* Clarks' Bank Deposits and Payments Monthly, Vol. 9, No. 1, July 2000, page 1) indicates that verifying signatures of items exhibiting a high probability of fraud is a risk-based alternative to random signature verification that is cost effective (losses reduced $16–$20 per dollar spent).

Arguments made that the check system should adopt a structure akin to that which governs electronic checks under federal Regulation E (*see* Clarks' Bank Deposits and Payments Monthly, Vol. 9, No. 10, March 2001, page 3) to prompt the development of superior technology to prevent check fraud generally have not been accepted to date. Experience in that area, discussed in a later chapter of this book, may however yet inform legal developments for paper checks. *See infra* Chapters 9 and 11.

82. 16 UCC Rep. Serv. 171 (N.Y.Sup.Ct. 1974). UCC §§ 3–418 and 4–208 also operate together. A case that illustrates the operation of § 3–418 where no breach of warranty is involved is Gentner & Co., Inc. v. Wells Fargo Bank, 76 Cal.App.4th 1165, 90 Cal.Rptr.2d 904, 40 UCC Rep. Serv. 2d 38 (Cal.App.1999) (cashier's check issued by mistake for a check subject to a stop payment order). As to the right of the bank to refuse to pay the cashier's check, *see* § 3–411, discussed *supra* in Chapters 4 and 6 and *infra* Chapter 9.

which complied. In the ensuing litigation, the court did not believe Article 3 applied or, even if it did, that Chase breached any warranty because, in the final analysis, the loss of the savings bank was due to its own negligence in failing to spot the forgery in the first instance. Without a warranty breached by Chase, the payment to it by the savings bank was final.[83]

The principle of *Price v. Neal* also explains the exceptions to the warranty on unauthorized signatures under old Articles 3 and 4. A holder in due course acting in good faith[84] did not make the warranty to a maker with respect to the maker's own signature,[85] or to a drawer with respect to the drawer's own signature, whether or not the drawer was also the drawee.[86] Nor did a holder in due course acting in good faith make the warranty to an acceptor of a draft, if the holder in due course took the draft after the acceptance or obtained the acceptance without knowledge that the drawer's signature was unauthorized.[87]

[b] No Forged Indorsements

The principle of *Price v. Neal* also dictates that the other two warranties, that is, entitlement to enforce the instrument,[88] and against

---

83. This assumes Chase was a holder in due course or a reliance payee. If not, under § 3–418(a)(ii), payment might be recoverable. The savings bank would not be able to charge its customer for the payment either under § 4–401 and so, in accordance with *Price v. Neal*, it would bear the loss. If the funds represented by the forged instrument actually accrue to the use of the purported drawer, however, no basis for recovery by the purported drawer against the drawee exists. *E.g.*, Davis Aircraft Prods. Co. v. Bankers Trust Co., 36 A.D.2d 705, 319 N.Y.S.2d 379 (N.Y.App.Div.1971).

84. Under old § 3–302(1), the holder cannot have known of the forgery at the time of taking the instrument. Thus to breach the "no knowledge" warranty of old § 3–417(1)(b), the holder must have learned of the forgery after the instrument was taken. To then present the instrument knowing of the forgery commits an obvious fraud even if the maker or drawer is also negligent. It is unclear how this can be reconciled with the requirement of good faith on the part of the holder in due course. But it is clear that the intent of the statute was that a holder in due course made no warranty that was breached in this instance. Official Comment 4 to old § 3–417. Old § 4–207 was the same.

85. Old § 3–417(1)(b)(i). *See also* old § 4–207(1)(b)(i).

86. Old § 3–417(1)(b)(ii). *See also* old § 4–207(1)(b)(ii).

87. Old § 3–417(1)(b)(iii). *See also* old § 4–207(1)(b)(iii). The acceptor is the drawee, who is bound to know the signature of its drawer. There is the additional policy reason of protecting the worth of certified checks that mandates there should be no warranty where a holder in due course takes the draft relying on the acceptance and, if the holder in due course procured the acceptance without knowledge of the forgery, unless he or she thereafter is relieved of the warranty if he or she obtains knowledge, his or her earlier obtained rights with respect to the acceptance will be valueless.

As to the structure under current § 3–417, where these exceptions are not necessary, *see* Official Comment 4 to § 3–417.

88. Old § 3–417(1)(a). *See also* old § 4–207(1)(a). In current § 3–417(a)(1) (*see also* § 4–208(a)(1)), this warranty is stated as one of entitlement to enforce the draft or authorization to obtain payment or acceptance of the draft on behalf of a person entitled to enforce the draft. It is, in effect, a warranty that there are no unauthorized or missing indorsements. This warranty also is made to the drawer or indorser of a dishonored draft and to a party obligated to pay any other instrument as well as to the drawee of an undishonored, unaccepted draft.

Distinguish the case where the drawer sues the person paid in conversion; here recovery should be denied. *See* Simmons v. Lennon, 139 Md.App. 15, 773 A.2d 1064, 44 UCC Rep.Serv.2d 772 (2001) and the discussion, *infra*, this chapter.

material alteration,[89] made to a payor or acceptor[90] be unqualified so that the person to whom the warranty is made, who does not know the persons who may have indorsed or the original nature of the instrument, may recover from the person paid if there is a necessary unauthorized indorsement or an alteration of the instrument. The same reasoning further lies behind the exceptions in old Articles 3 and 4 to the warranty concerning material alteration.[91]

The warranty of good title or entitlement to enforce the instrument normally is breached when an instrument bearing an unauthorized indorsement is accepted or paid.[92] A missing indorsement likewise will

---

89. Old § 3–417(1)(c); current § 3–417(a)(2). *See also* old § 4–207(1)(c); current § 4–208(a)(2). This warranty only is made to the drawee of an undishonored, unaccepted draft.

90. *See supra* notes 88 and 89 as to precisely to whom these warranties extend under current Articles 3 and 4.

91. Old § 3–417(1)(c)(i), (ii), (iv). *See also* old § 4–207(1)(c)(i), (ii), (iv). The exception in old § 3–417(1)(c)(iii) is to allow a holder in due course to rely on an acceptance to preserve the worth of a certified check and is discussed in Chapter 4. Because this warranty extends only to the drawee of an unaccepted draft, the exceptions are unnecessary under current §§ 3–417 and 4–208. Official Comment 4 to § 3–417.

92. Under UCC § 1–201(b)(41), an "unauthorized" signature (as amended, § 1–201(b)(41) deletes "or indorsement" to clarify that the term "signature" includes an indorsement) means one made without actual, implied, or apparent authority, and includes a forgery. *See* South Rayne Water Corp. v. Bank of Commerce & Trust Co., 619 So.2d 158 (La.Ct.App.1993) (an unauthorized signature is encompassed within the concept of forgery for purposes of old § 3–419 (current § 3–420)); and Citizens Bank v. Maryland Industrial Finishing Co., 338 Md. 448, 659 A.2d 313 (Md. 1995). However, not all courts agreed. *See* White County Bank v. Noland Co., 214 Ga.App. 780, 449 S.E.2d 325 (Ga.Ct.App.1994). The language of § 3–420 clearly now resolves the issue.

The warranty does not apply in the case of bearer paper. Sun 'n Sand, Inc. v. United California Bank, 21 Cal.3d 671, 148 Cal. Rptr. 329, 582 P.2d 920 (1978). Nor does it apply if no forged indorsement is involved. For example, in Gabovitch v. Coolidge Bank & Trust Co., 29 UCC Rep. Serv. 1313 (Mass.App.Div.1980), the court held the mere fact the check was payable to "Scotch Whiskey, Ltd." and indorsed "Scotch Whiskey, Inc." did not establish a forgery given the presumption of signature validity in old § 3–307 (current § 3–308) and the provisions of old § 3–203 (current § 3–204(d)) on wrong and misspelled names.

Further, in Federal Ins. Co. v. Groveland State Bank, 37 N.Y.2d 252, 372 N.Y.S.2d 18, 333 N.E.2d 334 (N.Y. 1975), an employee of the drawer bank embezzled its funds by getting the bank to draw checks on itself payable to another bank at which the employee had an account, which were then collected by the second bank and the funds placed in the employee's account. Similar cases are Federal Ins. Co. v. First Nat'l Bank, 633 F.2d 978 (1st Cir.1980); *Fireman's Fund Ins. Co. v. Security Pac. Nat'l Bank*, 85 Cal.App.3d 797, 149 Cal.Rptr. 883 (Cal.App.1978); and Govoni & Sons Const. Co., Inc. v. Mechanics Bank, 51 Mass.App. Ct. 35, 742 N.E.2d 1094 (2001). These cases represent an alternative type of scheme to the kind of fraud situations that often involve an unauthorized indorsement, but do not involve the warranty and given appropriate facts may be resolved against the drawer or against the bank which did not check on the intended use, as the case may be, by allocation to the person best able to prevent the problem in an analysis like that behind §§ 3–404 and 3–405, discussed, *infra*, this chapter. *See also* § 3–307(b)(4). *But see* Southwest Bank v. Information Support Concepts, Inc., 85 S.W.3d 462, 48 UCC Rep. Serv.2d 675 (Tex.Ct.App.2002) (comparative fault not applicable where indorsement missing rather than forged since UCC does not so provide). This analysis is criticized in 11 *Clarks' Bank Deposits and Payments Monthly* at 5–6 (Nov. 2002). Note, however, that adding the wrong lock box number to the name of the payee does not change to whom the instrument is payable. Continental Airlines, Inc. v. Boatmen's National Bank of St. Louis, 13 F.3d 1254, 22 UCC Rep. Serv. 2d 841 (8th Cir.1994). Note also that a preclusion because of negligence

result in a breach of the warranty.[93] As mentioned, the reason this warranty is unqualified is that while the acceptor or payor at least theoretically is in a position to verify the maker's or drawer's signature by comparison, there ordinarily is no opportunity to verify an indorsement; nonetheless the warranty is still breached even when the problem is apparent, as in the case of a missing indorsement as opposed to an unauthorized indorsement.[94] Where there has been a double forgery of the instrument and of an indorsement most courts have held that the primary cause of the loss is the forgery of the instrument, and thus the payor may not recover payment made.[95]

The breach of the warranty of good title or entitlement to enforce the instrument will allow the payor to recover the payment made.[96] In *East Gadsden Bank v. First City National Bank*[97] the court held that the collecting bank was liable on its warranty of indorsement to the drawee bank, and that the defense that the negligence of the drawer had substantially contributed to the forgery was not available to the collecting bank except through third-party practice.[98] The drawer of the instrument on which an unauthorized indorsement appears may not be charged with the payment.[99] Thus the loss from the unauthorized indorsement will pass down the collection chain until the person who took

in effect may make an unauthorized indorsement valid. *See, e.g.,* Tormo v. Yormark, 398 F.Supp. 1159 (D.N.J.1975) and § 3–406. Finally, under §§ 3–404 and 3–405, discussed *infra* this chapter, certain indorsements by faithless employees and others that are forged are nonetheless validated so as to remove the basis for breach of this warranty, but the protection of old § 3–405 does not extend to a false representation of agency status. *See* Thieme v. Seattle–First Nat'l Bank, 7 Wn.App. 845, 502 P.2d 1240 (Wash.Ct.App.1972). *See* Official Comment 1 to § 3–404 which changes this last rule.

93. *E.g.,* Insurance Co. v. Atlas Supply Co., 121 Ga.App. 1, 172 S.E.2d 632 (Ga.Ct. App.1970); Official Comment 2 to § 3–417.

94. Official Comment 3 to § 3–404 and *see* note 65, *supra.*

95. *E.g.,* Perini Corp. v. First Nat'l Bank, 553 F.2d 398 (5th Cir.1977); First Israel Bank & Trust Co. v. Franklin Nat'l Bank, 9 UCC Rep. Serv. 861 (N.Y.Sup.Ct. 1971); Banco Mercantil De Sao Paulo, S.A. v. Nava, 120 Misc.2d 517, 466 N.Y.S.2d 198 (N.Y.Sup.Ct.1983); Winkie, Inc. v. Heritage Bank, 99 Wis.2d 616, 299 N.W.2d 829 (Wis. 1981); National Credit Union Admin. v. Michigan Nat. Bank, 771 F.2d 154 (6th Cir.1985); Travelers Indemnity Co. v. Stedman, 895 F.Supp. 742 (E.D.Pa.1995), *modified*, 925 F.Supp. 345 (E.D.Pa.1996); Bank of Glen Burnie v. Loyola Federal Savings Bank, 336 Md. 331, 648 A.2d 453 (Md. 1994). Current § 3–404(b) agrees; *see* Official Comment 2, case #5, to the section. *But also* note, as applicable, § 3–404(d).

96. *See* §§ 3–417(a)(1), (b) and (d), 4–208(a)(1), (b) and (d), and 3–418. The right of the drawee to recover is not affected by any failure of the drawee to exercise ordinary care in making payment. §§ 3–417(b) and 4–208(b) codify the result in Hartford Accident & Indem. Co. v. First Pennsylvania Bank N.A., 859 F.2d 295 (3d Cir.1988). *See also* note 65, *supra.*

97. 50 Ala.App. 576, 281 So.2d 431 (Ala. Civ.App.1973).

98. If that negligence had been established, it could have precluded liability on the part of the drawee. § 3–406. This would mean the ultimate loss should rest on the drawer and not on the collecting bank, but that the collecting bank must bring the drawer into the action to achieve that resolution. *See infra* note 120. Under §§ 3–417(c) and 4–208(c), a warrantor may defend by proving that the indorsement is effective under §§ 3–404 or 3–405, or the drawer is precluded as to the indorsement or an alteration under §§ 3–406 and 4–406.

99. § 4–401 and, *e.g.,* Perley v. Glastonbury Bank & Trust Co., 170 Conn. 691, 368 A.2d 149 (Conn. 1976) (as between the drawer of a check and the drawee, the drawee is bound to determine the genuineness of indorsements and, if the drawer is free from negligence warranting a preclusion, the drawee cannot charge the drawer's

the instrument from the culprit is reached. That person normally will bear the loss.[100]

What of the person whose indorsement was forged, normally the payee of the check? The warranty of good title or right to enforce the instrument does not extend to the payee whose indorsement was forged and thus the indorsement is not effective.[101] The payee does have a remedy though, discussed, *infra*, this chapter. There was a division of authority under old Articles 3 and 4 as to whether the warranty of good title extended to the drawer of the instrument on the thought that the drawer is the actual payor.[102] This question is part of a larger issue as to how losses from instruments bearing forged indorsements should best be allocated, which is discussed, *infra*, this chapter.

[c] No Alterations

The warranty in favor of a good faith payor or acceptor (the drawee) under §§ 3–417(a)(2) and 4–208(a)(2) that the instrument has not been materially altered is breached without regard to the knowledge of the party presenting the instrument.[103] The reason is that the drawee is in no better position to detect an alteration "than the person presenting the instrument for payment or acceptance."[104] Nonetheless under old

---

account for a check paid bearing a necessary forged indorsement).

100. In this procedure, the "vouching in" provision of § 3–119 may be employed, whereby a later party sued for breach of warranty may be bound by a determination of fact in prior litigation that is common to the two litigations. *See* Bank of St. Helens v. Clayton Bank, 502 S.W.2d 449 (Mo.Ct. App.1973) (letter from drawee sued in connection with forged indorsement to remitting bank notifying it of suit and requesting that it assume the defense was sufficient notice under old § 3–803).

101. National Sur. Corp. v. Citizens State Bank, 41 Colo.App. 580, 593 P.2d 362 (Colo.Ct.App.1978), *aff'd on other grounds*, 199 Colo. 497, 612 P.2d 70 (Colo. 1980); §§ 3–417(a)(1) and (d), 4–208(a)(1) and (d).

102. *Compare* Nida v. Michael, 34 Mich. App. 290, 191 N.W.2d 151 (Mich.Ct.App. 1971) (warranties on presentment or transfer do not run in favor of drawer of check) *with* Insurance Co. v. Atlas Supply Co., 121 Ga.App. 1, 172 S.E.2d 632 (Ga.Ct.App.1970) (drawer of checks whose account is debited is a "payor" who may claim benefit of warranty). Under §§ 3–417 and 4–208, there is no warranty made to the drawer when presentment is made to the drawee. Official Comment 2 to § 3–417, rejecting Sun 'n Sand, Inc. v. United California Bank, 21 Cal.3d 671, 148 Cal.Rptr. 329, 582 P.2d 920 (Cal. 1978). *But see* note 79, *supra*, and Commonwealth v. National Bank & Trust Co., 469 Pa. 188, 364 A.2d 1331 (Pa. 1976), where the drawee banks actually assigned their rights against a collecting bank to the drawer, and §§ 3–417(d)(1) and 4–208(d) and Official Comment 2 to § 3–417.

103. § 3–417(a)(2). *See also* § 4–208(a)(2).

104. But where payment had been stopped on an altered item and the bank paid anyway, recovery was denied under warranty. Savings Banks Trust Co. v. Federal Reserve Bank, 738 F.2d 573 (2d Cir. 1984). *See* §§ 3–417(b) and 3–418(a)(i) and discussion, *infra*, Chapter 9. *And see* Barber v. United States Nat'l Bank of Oregon, 90 Or.App. 68, 750 P.2d 1183 (Or.Ct.App. 1988), where a raised check was deposited without indorsement and paid and, in the drawer's suit against the bank, summary judgment for the bank was reversed. Clearly the fact the bank paid even though the payee had not indorsed should not preclude recovery in warranty to the extent warranted against the presenting bank. *See* §§ 3–417(b), 4–208(b), and 4–205.

A payor bank that paid a raised check and then recredited its customer's account even though the negligence of the drawer had facilitated the alteration was, however, denied recovery against the depositary and intermediary banks on the ground it had a valid defense against the drawer's claim. Canadian Imperial Bank v. Federal Reserve Bank, 64 Misc.2d 959, 316 N.Y.S.2d 507 (N.Y.Sup.Ct.1970). *But compare* old

Articles 3 and 4, a holder in due course acting in good faith does not make the warranty against material alteration to the maker of a note, the drawer of a draft (even if the drawer is also the drawee), or to the acceptor of a draft with respect to alteration made after the acceptance.[105] Consistent with the principle of *Price v. Neal*, these persons should know the form and amount of the instrument they have signed. The format of current §§ 3–417(a)(2) and (d) and 4–208(a)(2) and (d) makes such exceptions unnecessary.

¶ 7.03 Other Bases for Liability and Rights

[1] In General

In addition to contractual liability on the instrument and rights and liabilities with respect to the underlying transaction and warranty, law outside of Article 3 continues to be applicable as a basis for creating and defining the rights and liabilities of parties to a negotiable instrument unless displaced by the particular provisions of the UCC.[106] For example, it is law outside the UCC that provides content for the limitation on the rights of a transferee who has been a party to any fraud or illegality affecting the instrument.[107] It is outside law and not Article 3 that defines the rights of a holder of the instrument under the provisions of the UCC referring to other state law for what constitutes incapacity, and illegality,[108] or the defenses available in an action on a simple contract.[109] Various provisions of the UCC rely heavily on the law of agency to define rights and liabilities of parties to negotiable instruments.[110]

Outside law may create as well as define rights and liabilities. For example, even though a check or other draft does not of itself operate as an assignment,[111] an assignment may appear from other facts that establish an agreement for assignment under ordinary contract law.[112] Moreover, results similar to that reached on an assignment theory may be reached on yet other theories of "special deposit" or the like outside the Code.[113] Therefore, equally as important as the use of law beyond the Code to define the rights and liabilities of parties to a negotiable instrument is the use of that law to create rights and liabilities.

§ 3–406 *with* old § 4–406(5). *See contra* Mellon Nat'l Bank & Trust Co. v. Merchants Bank, 15 UCC Rep. Serv. 691 (S.D.N.Y.1972). Current Articles 3 and 4 follow the *Canadian Imperial Bank* case in §§ 3–417(c), 4–208(c).

105. Old § 3–417(1)(c)(i), (ii), (iv). *See also* old § 4–207(1)(c)(i), (ii), (iv).

¶ 7.03

106. UCC § 1–103(b).

107. § 3–203(b).

108. § 3–305(a)(1)(ii).

109. § 3–305(a)(2).

110. §§ 3–401(a), 3–402(a), and 3–403(a).

111. § 3–408, and *see* Outdoor Technologies, Inc. v. Allfirst Financial, Inc. 44 UCC Rep. Serv. 2d 801 (Del.Super.Ct.2001) 3–408 does not provide a basis for action by check payee against the bank on an unaccepted check).

112. The rule is discussed, but no assignment was found, in State Bank v. Stallings, 19 Utah 2d 146, 427 P.2d 744 (Utah 1967). *See* the discussion in Chapter 4, *supra*.

113. *See, e.g.,* Mid–Continent Cas. Co. v. Jenkins, 431 P.2d 349 (Okla.1967) (loan

[2] Negligence

The UCC also uses negligence to define rights and liabilities, and at times as an affirmative basis for action.[114] This has been true for some time. To illustrate, in *Maley v. East Side Bank*[115] the trustee in bankruptcy of a corporation sued a bank to recover amounts of checks payable to the corporation, but which the bank had allowed the corporation's president to cash or deposit for his own benefit. The court indicated that liability might stem from the bank so acting with actual knowledge of the president's lack of authority, but that evidence of negligence also had a proper place in the action.[116] A similar analysis was used in a New York case to find liability on the part of a negligent bank to its customer whose checks to its suppliers were deposited by the customer's bookkeeper to the bookkeeper's own account with forged indorsements.[117] And several cases have suggested or allowed a cause of action in negligence by a drawer against a bank where a dishonest employee of the drawer has caused the drawer to draw checks to the bank which the bank has then allowed the employee to deposit in a personal account or to otherwise deal with for the employee's own benefit.[118] Suit also has been authorized in the other direction, as evidenced by a decision[119] that permitted a collecting bank, which was bound on its warranty of good title, to recover from the drawer of the instrument in negligence where the drawer had contributed to the

was to be handled as a special fund and bank was obligated to honor check).

114. *E.g.*, §§ 3–404, 3–405, and 3–406, which consider negligence of a party in connection with an unauthorized signature or an alteration. A case illustrating the operation of § 3–406 is The Bank/First Citizens Bank v. Citizens & Associates, 44 UCC Rep. Serv. 2d 1072 (Tenn.Ct.App.2001), *rev'd*, 82 S.W.3d 259 (Tenn. 2002) (comparing lack of due care of drawer and depositary bank). The concept plays a role in § 4–406, as well; *see e.g.*, § 4–406 (c) and (d) (duty to examine statements for alterations and forgeries and preclusion), § 4–406(e) (loss allocation due to negligence), and § 4–406(f) (strict one year preclusion); Stowell v. Cloquet Co–op Credit Union, 557 N.W.2d 567 (Minn. 1997) (ability to define reporting period by contract); and Halifax Corp. v. Wachovia Bank, N.A., 41 UCC Rep. Serv. 2d 897 (Va. Cir. Ct.2000), *aff'd sub. nom.* Halifax Corp. v. First Union National Bank, 262 Va. 91, 546 S.E.2d 696 (2001) (inapplicability of good faith requirement to one year preclusion); c.f. Falk v. Northern Trust Co., 327 Ill.App.3d 101, 261 Ill. Dec. 410, 763 N.E.2d 380, 46 UCC Rep. Serv.2d 302 (2001). The UCC terminology is failure to exercise ordinary care rather than negligence. See § 3–103(a)(7). *Also see* previous discussion in Chapter 4, *supra*, at ¶ 4.02[2][a].

As to the standard for measuring whether ordinary care has been exercised, *see* Expresso Roma Corp. v. Bank of America, N.A., 100 Cal.App.4th 525, 124 Cal.Rptr.2d 549, 48 UCC Rep.Serv.2d 265 (2002). As to whom a duty to exercise ordinary care may be owed, *see,* Eisenberg v. Wachovia Bank, N.A., 301 F.3d 220 (4th Cir.2002).

115. 361 F.2d 393 (7th Cir.1966).

116. *See* note 114, *supra*, and *infra*, this chapter, particularly the discussion of § 3–405(b).

117. Titan Air Conditioning Corp. v. Chase Manhattan Bank, 61 A.D.2d 764, 402 N.Y.S.2d 12 (N.Y.App.Div.1978). See §§ 3–404(d) and 3–405(b), discussed, *infra*.

118. Govoni & Sons Constr. Co. v. Mechanics Bank, 51 Mass.App.Ct. 35, 742 N.E.2d 1094 (2001); Sun 'n Sand, Inc. v. United Cal. Bank, 21 Cal.3d 671, 148 Cal. Rptr. 329, 582 P.2d 920 (Cal. 1978); Fireman's Fund Ins. Co. v. Security Pac. Nat'l Bank, 85 Cal.App.3d 797, 149 Cal.Rptr. 883 (1978); Bank of Southern Maryland v. Robertson's Crab House, 39 Md.App. 707, 389 A.2d 388 (Md. 1978). *See also* note 92, *supra*, and *compare* §§ 3–404(c) and (d), 3–405(b) and (c) and Official Comment 3, Case #4, to § 3–405.

119. Girard Bank v. Mount Holly State Bank, 474 F.Supp. 1225 (D.N.J.1979).

forgery.[120]

In context, the issue under Article 3 is whether the provisions of the UCC displace the asserted cause of action based on negligence. Thus in a case that essentially involved an attempt to establish a claim predicated in part on negligence that would have made a bank liable, notwithstanding the rule that a check is not an assignment, while the majority of the court found that an issue as to the bank's liability was raised, the dissent believed the UCC controlled the issue and no cause of action should exist.[121] But in another case,[122] the court denied recovery to a drawer, whose signature was forged on an instrument that also bore a forged indorsement, but where the drawer was barred from recovery against the drawee under the UCC because of negligence, and was also barred from recovery from a collecting bank in conversion, money had and received, or in negligence.[123] However, the court did suggest recovery

---

120. Under old Articles 3 and 4, the negligence may not be a defense the bank always can use in connection with the breach of its warranty. Under current Articles 3 and 4, it is a defense. *See* note 98, *supra*. *Also see* Official Comment 3 to § 3–404 indicating a cause of action exists as well as a defense for failure to exercise ordinary care.

121. Livingston Indus., Inc. v. Walker Bank & Trust Co., 565 P.2d 1117 (Utah 1977). *But see* old § 3–409(2) and the discussion in Chapter 4, *supra*.

122. Brighton, Inc. v. Colonial First Nat'l Bank, 176 N.J.Super. 101, 422 A.2d 433 (App.Div.1980), *aff'd*, 86 N.J. 259, 430 A.2d 902 (N.J.1981).

123. *See* Official Comment 2, Case numbers 4 and 5, to § 3–404, and §§ 3–420(a)(i) and 3–417(a)(1). Other cases include City Check Cashing, Inc. v. Manufacturers Hanover Trust Co., 166 N.J. 49, 764 A.2d 411 (2001), where a check cashing service contacted the bank before cashing a large check under suspicious circumstances but cashed it anyway after waiting only two hours for a reply from the bank. The court held the bank had no duty to respond under the circumstances involved prior to its midnight deadline and in any event two hours was not a reasonable time for the bank to respond. In Halifax Corp. v. First Union National Bank, 262 Va. 91, 546 S.E.2d 696 (2001), a company tried to get around the strict preclusion of § 4–406(f) by theories of negligence and breach of contract. The court denied the claims on the basis that Article 4 comprehensively governs the relationships between a bank and its customers. Likewise in Bank Polska Kasa Opieki, S.A. v. Pamrapo Savings Bank, S.L.A., 909 F.Supp. 948 (D.N.J.1995), the court stated that allowing a common law negligence action would upset the loss allocation scheme contemplated by the UCC on the facts of that case, which involved a forged indorsement and a suit by the drawer against the depositary bank. True v. Fleet Bank—NH, 138 N.H. 679, 645 A.2d 671, 24 UCC Rep. Serv. 2d 598 (N.H. 1994) reaches a similar conclusion when a joint payee whose indorsement was forged sued the depositary bank; common law defenses that might have been available are displaced. A similar case is Hartford Fire Ins. Co. v. Cavallo, 27 UCC Rep. Serv. 2d 35 (N.Y.Sup.Ct.1995) (conversion action has supplanted common law negligence action in action by payee whose indorsement was forged against depositary bank). *See also* note 128, *infra*.

As discussed *infra*, there often may be substantial line drawing necessitated in this context, but ultimately in some instances perhaps the cases simply cannot be reconciled. To illustrate, in Cassello v. Allegiant Bank and Royal Banks of Missouri, 288 F.3d 339 (8th Cir.2002), the Eighth Circuit was faced with two seemingly contradictory Missouri decisions in the litigation before it involving a drawer who was defrauded into writing checks that were deposited in the defendant banks either without proper indorsements or to accounts other than the accounts of the payees. In City of Wellston v. Jackson, 965 S.W.2d 867 (Mo.Ct.App. 1998), the court held that a common law negligence claim in a case like the one at hand should not be allowed, but in Dalton & Marberry, P.C. v. NationsBank, N.A., 982 S.W.2d 231 (Mo.1998), the Missouri Supreme Court allowed a common law negligence claim against a bank that failed in a duty of inquiry (*see* Govani & Sons Construction Co. v. Mechanics Bank, *supra* note 92: where a bank accepts a check for deposit that is made payable to the bank, it has a duty to inquire whether the depositor

might be had if actual complicity between the drawer's employee and an employee of the bank could be shown, since the UCC rules did not contemplate actual collusion.[124]

Often there will be substantial line drawing involved in determining whether the Code displaces the basis for action. For example, under old Article 3 the New York Supreme Court was persuaded that a drawer stated a cause of action in negligence against the drawee, even though the drawer was barred from recovery against a collecting bank under old § 3–405, in a case where the drawee dealt with checks payable to a corporation that were indorsed in blank and deposited in accounts other than those of the corporate payee.[125] The New York Court of Appeals correctly reversed on the ground the cause of action was not compatible with old § 3–405.[126] Nonetheless, in *Underpinning & Foundation Constructors, Inc. v. Chase Manhattan Bank*,[127] the court of appeals had allowed an action by a drawer, where the checks were good but the

---

has authority to receive the proceeds) when an employee repeatedly exchanged her employer's checks drawn on the bank for money orders or cashier's checks. The Eighth Circuit found no UCC displacement, even though it concluded the UCC precluded a direct action by a drawer against the depositary bank in a case like this because the drawer's remedy instead was against the drawee for improper payment.

In Heche v. Chase Manhattan Bank, 45 UCC Rep.Serv.2d 549 (Conn.Super.Ct.2001), the Connecticut court allowed a common law conversion claim by a person whose signature was forged on a series of checks by a dishonest employee even though a conversion claim pursuant to UCC § 3–420 is denied to an issuer. Directly contrary is White Sands Forest Products, Inc. v. First National Bank of Alamogordo, 132 N.M. 453, 50 P.3d 202 (App.2002), which held § 3–420 displaces all common law claims. *See also* Gallagher v. Santa Fe Federal Employees Federal Credit Union, 132 N.M. 552. 52 P.3d 412, 48 UCC Rep. Serv.2d 655 (App.2002) and Southwest Bank v. Information Support Concepts, Inc., *supra* note 9 (but the latter case does suggest an answer as to how fault apportionment should occur if a common law action outside the UCC is recognized).

When UCC § 1–103 was revised in connection with the revision of Article 1, the displacement issue was not specifically clarified, but the revision does emphasize that in determining whether or not law outside the UCC is displaced, the UCC does preempt principles of the common law and equity that are inconsistent with either UCC provisions *or the purposes and policies of the UCC* (emphasis supplied). Official Comment 2 to § 1–103.

124. That is, bad faith. *See* Official Comment 2 to § 3–405. *But see* Oki Semiconductor Co. v. Wells Fargo Bank, N.A., 298 F.3d 768 (9th Cir.2002) (acts of employee not within course and scope of employment). That also could explain Midwest Industrial Funding v. First National Bank of Lockport, 973 F.2d 534 (7th Cir.1992), where plaintiff with a technically correct argument tried to take advantage of an innocent mistake to unjustly recover from another.

125. Merrill Lynch, Pierce, Fenner & Smith, Inc. v. Chemical Bank, 82 A.D.2d 772, 440 N.Y.S.2d 643 (N.Y.App.Div.1981).

126. Merrill Lynch, Pierce, Fenner & Smith, Inc. v. Chemical Bank, 57 N.Y.2d 439, 456 N.Y.S.2d 742, 442 N.E.2d 1253 (N.Y.App.1982). Current § 3–405(b) removes this tension.

127. 46 N.Y.2d 459, 414 N.Y.S.2d 298, 386 N.E.2d 1319 (N.Y. 1979). *See also* Davis v. Committee for First Home Owners, Inc., 180 Misc.2d 425, 692 N.Y.S.2d 882 (N.Y. Civ. Ct. 1997), (citing *Underpinning*). Distinguish also Insurance Co. of Pennsylvania v. Citibank, 145 A.D.2d 218, 537 N.Y.S.2d 519 (N.Y.App.Div.1989), *appeal denied*, 74 N.Y.2d 607, 545 N.Y.S.2d 103, 543 N.E.2d 746 (N.Y. 1989), where the checks were forged and the restrictive indorsements were not effective so the drawer thus had a claim against the drawee, and then consider Olean Area Camp Fire Council, Inc. v. Olean Dresser Clark Fed. Credit Union, 142 Misc.2d 1049, 538 N.Y.S.2d 905 (N.Y.Sup. Ct.1989), which followed the *Underpinning* case even though, like in the *Citibank* case, the checks were forged, but, unlike in *Citibank*, the indorsements were effective. As to treatment under current Article 3, *see* note 128, *infra*.

unauthorized nature of the indorsement was again precluded from being shown under old § 3–405, because, in addition, the indorsements were restrictive ("for deposit only") and the bank, by allowing deposit to accounts in names other than those of the named payees, had not followed the indorsements.[128] Perhaps all that can be predicted is that a court may well allow a tort cause of action if it believes the Code has left an inequitable gap and that the permitted action would advance what it considers as basic UCC policies.[129] For this reason, the issue is less likely to prove troublesome under current Article 3, which overall leaves fewer gaps because, for example, §§ 3–404, 3–405, 3–406 and 4–406 incorporate consequences for failure to exercise ordinary care into their scheme.

[3] Conversion

[a] Owner's Basis for Suit

Perhaps the most extensive employment of law outside the UCC to create rights and liabilities in parties to negotiable instruments occurs through the theory of conversion. Conversion, but not its details, is expressly incorporated in Article 3,[130] including use of the theory of

---

128. However, it would not appear that the *Underpinning* result could obtain pursuant to a conversion theory under current Article 3 which, in § 3–420(a)(i), denies an action in conversion to the issuer of the instrument. While Official Comment 1 to § 3–420 makes it clear that the rule has a forged indorsement case and not a restrictive indorsement case in mind (*see* § 3–206(c)(2), which states violation of this type of restrictive indorsement constitutes conversion), the point seems the same: the drawer has an adequate remedy against the payor bank for recredit of the drawer's account, or does not for a policy reason that permitting recovery would perhaps undermine. On the other hand, since under §§ 3–404(d) and 3–405(b) the person bearing the loss in part may recover from a person failing to exercise ordinary care, if the action in failing to abide by the restrictive indorsement constitutes negligence, and it would seem to under §§ 3–103(a)(7) and 3–206(c)(2), the *Underpinning* result might still obtain, at least in part. *See, e.g.*, Hartford Fire Insurance Co. v. Maryland National Bank, N.A., 341 Md. 408, 671 A.2d 22 (Md.Ct.App.1996) and discussion, *supra*, notes 92 and 123.

For an interesting case of what may constitute a restrictive indorsement, *see* Stewart Office Suppliers, Inc. v. First Union National Bank, 97 N.C.App. 353, 388 S.E.2d 599 (Ct.App.1990) (dissent questioned whether name of payee *followed by* words "For Deposit Only" was actually a restrictive indorsement), *reversed* by reasons stated by dissent, 328 N.C. 83, 399 S.E.2d 108 (1991).

129. *See* Girard Bank v. Mount Holly State Bank, 474 F.Supp. 1225 (D.N.J.1979) and note 123, *supra*.

130. *See* § 3–206 (restrictive indorsement) and § 3–420(a) (forged, unauthorized and missing indorsements). *See also* cases noted at note 123, *supra*. The elements of the conversion claim, however, are found in those principles of law and equity which supplement Article 3. *E.g.*, Yeager & Sullivan, Inc. v. Farmers Bank, 162 Ind.App. 15, 317 N.E.2d 792 (Ind.Ct.App.1974). There was a difference of opinion under old Article 3 over the applicable statute of limitations. *Compare* Continental Cas. Co. v. Huron Valley Nat'l Bank, 85 Mich.App. 319, 271 N.W.2d 218 (Mich.Ct.App.1978) (applying three year statute for conversion) *with* Hechter v. New York Life Ins. Co., 46 N.Y.2d 34, 412 N.Y.S.2d 812, 385 N.E.2d 551 (N.Y. 1978) (applying the six-year contract period of limitations on ground state law outside the UCC alternatively permitted suit in contract). *See also* Insurance Co. of N. Am. v. Manufacturers Bank of Southfield N.A., 127 Mich.App. 278, 338 N.W.2d 214 (Mich.Ct.App.1983) (applying 3 year statute for injury to property). Current § 3–118(g)(i) imposes a uniform 3 year statute whether the theory is conversion, money had and received or like action. As to when the statute commences to run, see the discussion in Chapter 6, *supra*; *see also* Menichini v. Grant, 995 F.2d 1224 (3d Cir. 1993) (cause of action accrues when wrongful dominion exercised).

conversion to complete the structure for resolving problems in connection with instruments bearing unauthorized indorsements.[131]

The measure of liability in a conversion action normally is the face amount of the instrument.[132] As a consequence, Article 3 provides the owner of an instrument whose indorsement has been forged with an

---

[131]. § 3–420(a). Payment on a forged indorsement, even though made in good faith, is an exercise of dominion and control over the instrument inconsistent with the rights of the owner and results in liability for conversion. Old § 3–419, Official Comments 2 and 3. *But see* Franklin v. Safeco Ins. Co. of Am., 303 Or. 376, 737 P.2d 1231 (Or. 1987) (insurance drafts on which one payee forged indorsements of others and which were paid were not converted by depositary bank as that bank did not "pay on a forged indorsement"). *See also* Bursey v. CFX Bank, 145 N.H. 126, 756 A.2d 1001, 42 UCC Rep. Serv. 2d 187 (N.H. 2000) (payment requires more than acceptance by the depositary bank); *but compare* Whalen v. Chase Manhattan Bank, N.A., 43 UCC Rep. Serv. 2d 614 (S.D.N.Y.2000), *affirmed*, 14 Fed.Appx. 120 (2d Cir.2001) (suit against depositary bank for conversion implicitly assumes that bank holds the proceeds of the instrument). This latter analysis is discussed further, *infra*. The formulation under § 3–420(a) precludes such confusion. Old §§ 3–419(1)(a) and (b) also provided that an instrument was converted when a drawee to whom it was delivered for acceptance refuses to return it on demand or when any person to whom it was delivered for payment refused on demand either to pay or to return it. These latter provisions are deleted from § 3–420(a) as better left to other law. Official Comment 1 to § 3–420. Morrow v. First Interstate Bank of Oregon, N.A., 118 Or.App. 164, 847 P.2d 411, 20 UCC Rep. Serv. 2d 206 (Or.Ct.App.1993); and Hecker v. Ravenna Bank, 237 Neb. 810, 468 N.W.2d 88 (Neb. 1991) (refusal to return as used for set-off; quere if exercise of set-off proper).

There is authority under old Article 3 that a missing indorsement is tantamount to one that is forged for the purpose of a suit in conversion. *See, e.g.,* FDIC v. Marine Nat'l Bank, 431 F.2d 341 (5th Cir.1970); and Commonwealth Fed. Sav. & Loan Assn. v. First Nat'l Bank, 513 F.Supp. 296 (E.D.Pa.1979). There was perhaps some difference of opinion on this point. *See* Drug House, Inc. v. Keystone Bank, 272 Pa.Super. 130, 414 A.2d 704 (1979). These cases are covered under § 3–420. Official Comment 1 to § 3–420.

[132]. § 3–420(b). Under old § 3–419(2), the measure of liability in an action against a drawee was stated to be the face amount of the instrument. Thus, in Thornton & Co. v. Gwinnett Bank & Trust Co., 151 Ga.App. 641, 260 S.E.2d 765 (1979), the court refused to allow the bank that paid a negotiable instrument over a forged indorsement to show that the draft had been issued by the drawer upon a fraudulent application and was not based upon any obligation. The court did limit the liability of the bank to the amount not returned to the drawer by the forger. For a similar result in relation to forged checks, *see* SCCI, Inc. v. United States Nat'l Bank, 78 Or.App. 176, 714 P.2d 1113 (1986). A less satisfactory opinion on the latter point is Smith v. General Cas. Co., 75 Ill.App.3d 971, 31 Ill.Dec. 602, 394 N.E.2d 804 (1979), where the court refused to consider a partial reimbursement made by a bar association client security fund. *See also* Bryant Heating & Air Conditioning Co. v. United States Nat'l Bank, 216 Neb. 107, 342 N.W.2d 191 (Neb. 1983) (recovery of some funds from forger does not preclude suit against depositary bank); and Lawyers' Fund for Client Protection of the State of New York v. Bank Leumi Trust Co. of New York, 94 N.Y.2d 398, 706 N.Y.S.2d 66, 727 N.E.2d 563, 40 UCC Rep. Serv. 2d 930 (N.Y.App.2000). In an action against one other than a drawee, the liability only is presumed to be the face amount of the instrument and evidence is admissible to show that the obligation is worth less because of insolvency, the existence of a defense, or some other reason. Old § 3–419, Official Comments 2 and 4. Section 3–420(b) states a presumption in all cases that the measure of liability is the amount payable on the instrument, but explicitly limits recovery to the amount of the plaintiff's interest in the instrument. This codifies, for example, the result in Southern Cal. Permanente Medical Group v. Bozinovski, 148 Cal.App.3d 503, 196 Cal.Rptr. 150 (Cal.Ct.App.1983), where the court allowed the bank that had paid a joint payee check over the forged indorsement of one payee to deduct from the recovery the amount it had paid to the forger in accordance with the intention of the drawer, and rejects decisions like Stapleton v. First Security Bank, 219 Mont. 323, 711 P.2d 1364 (Mont. 1985). While this approach may create some proof problems, overall it is fairer than imposing further risk of loss upon the bank. *See* Official Comment 2 to § 3–420.

alternative to suing the drawer.[133] The alternative is a suit in conversion against the payor.[134] Under § 3–420(c), generally suit also may be maintained against a depositary bank, as discussed below.

[b] Defenses to Action Based on a Forged Indorsement

The owner of an instrument paid on a forged indorsement may wish to bring suit in conversion directly against the person who may be ultimately liable, the person who dealt with the forger, which often, perhaps usually, is the depositary bank. In that circumstance, a person forging a payee's indorsement will be depositing the checks in accounts opened in one or two banks even though the checks may be drawn on numerous banks. Thus suit against the depositary bank(s) is more efficient than against the payors. However, old § 3–419(3) in that event

---

133. The theory is that because, where there is a necessary unauthorized indorsement, there never can be a holder of the instrument, payment of the instrument does not discharge the liability of the party to pay under old § 3–603(1) and current § 3–602(a). Thus suit still should be maintainable on the instrument using old § 3–804, current § 3–309. If the instrument is not paid, there also is no discharge of the obligation for which it was given under old § 3–802 and current § 3–310. But there were arguments to the contrary. Current Article 3 finally clears up this basic issue. Under § 3–310(b)(4), the payee is limited to suit on the instrument in accordance with §§ 3–309 (read liberally) and § 3–414(b), and dishonor has occurred under §§ 3–504(a)(i) and 3–502(e). The underlying obligation remains suspended. §§ 3–602(a) and 3–310(b)(3) and (4). *See* Official Comment 4 to § 3–310.

134. § 3–420(a). *See* notes 131 and 123, *supra*. To have an action in conversion, generally the instrument must have come into the hands of a person entitled to seek recovery. Under old Article 3, one issue was the right of a payee who did not gain possession of the instrument. *See* Humberto Decorators, Inc. v. Plaza Nat'l Bank, 180 N.J.Super. 170, 434 A.2d 618 (App.Div. 1981) (delivery to agent was delivery to owner); State of New York v. Barclays Bank of New York, 76 N.Y.2d 533, 561 N.Y.S.2d 697, 563 N.E.2d 11 (N.Y. 1990) (possession of check required); and Drug House, Inc. v. Keystone Bank, 272 Pa.Super. 130, 414 A.2d 704 (1979) (payee who never received check misdirected to third party denied suit). Some cases, however, allowed the payee who did not receive possession to sue. *See, e.g.,* Lund v. Chemical Bank, 665 F.Supp. 218 (S.D.N.Y.1987), *reh'g denied*, 675 F.Supp. 815 (S.D.N.Y.1987), *rev'd on other grounds*, 870 F.2d 840 (2d Cir.1989), *dismissed on basis of Barclay's Bank decision*, 1990 WL 17711 (S.D.N.Y.1990) (WESTLAW). *See also* Sony Corp. of America v. American Express Co., 115 Misc.2d 1060, 455 N.Y.S.2d 227 (N.Y. Civ. Ct. 1982) (payee as assignee of rights of purchaser of money order). Section 3–420(a)(ii) resolves the issue in favor of the majority rule and Official Comment 1 to § 3–420 indicates in that case the payee's right on the obligation is unimpaired.

Another issue was the right of a remitter (*see* § 3–103(a)(11)) to recover. In DiMonda v. Freedom Fed. Sav. and Loan, 32 UCC Rep. Serv. 492 (Mass.App.Div., Boston Mun. Ct. 1981), *aff'd*, 385 Mass. 1012, 434 N.E.2d 210 (Mass. 1982), recovery was denied. *See also* C.A.L., Inc. v. Worth, 813 S.W.2d 12 (Mo.Ct.App.1991) (on basis check belongs to the payee, not the remitter). It was allowed in Lawrence v. Central Plaza Bank & Trust Co., 469 So.2d 201 (Fla.Dist. Ct.App.1985). Article 3 would seem to contemplate recovery. *See* Official Comment 1 to §§ 3–420 and §§ 3–105(a) and 3–312.

At times, persons other than the instrument's owner have tried suit. In Stockton v. Gristedes Supermarkets, Inc., 177 A.D.2d 425, 576 N.Y.S.2d 267 (N.Y.App.Div.1991), the drawer sued the payee of a forged check. The court responded that the indorsement of the payee was not forged. Perhaps similar motivation has more commonly led drawers to sue depositary banks, and on occasion this has been successful even though the drawer has no interest to convert as the drawer's account cannot be debited. *Compare* Wymore State Bank v. Johnson International Co., 873 F.2d 1082 (8th Cir.1989) *with* Bank of Polska Kasa Opieki, S.A. v. Pamrapo Savings Bank, S.LA., 909 F.Supp. 948 (D.N.J.1995) and Hartford Fire Insurance Co. v. Maryland National Bank, N.A., 341 Md. 408, 671 A.2d 22 (Md.Ct.App.1996). Section 3–420(a) closes down such suits. Official Comment 1 to § 3–420; *but see* note 128, *supra*.

provided, subject to the provisions concerning restrictive indorsements, that a representative, including a depositary or collecting bank, that has in good faith and in accordance with the reasonable commercial standards applicable to its business, dealt with the instrument or its proceeds on behalf of one who was not the true owner was not liable in conversion or otherwise to the true owner beyond the amount of any proceeds remaining in the account. Pursuant to this defense, a Pennsylvania court found that a depositary bank was liable only to the extent of cash and other value it had recovered from the forger's assets.[135] Full liability was found by another court where stolen checks had been restrictively indorsed by the forger and deposited to his own or to a confederate's accounts, but the failure of the bank to be insulated from liability can be attributed to the failure to abide by the restrictive indorsements.[136] Thus a direct conversion action against other than the payor contemplated by old § 3–419(3) basically was limited to the situation where the forger had left all or a portion of the ill-gotten gains on deposit, which of course was a very unlikely occurrence.[137] As is discussed below, however, under a number of theories that limitation also worked out to be fairly rare. Under current Article 3, this defense for a depositary bank is deleted in accordance with the discussion in the court's opinion in the leading case on the issue under old Article 3, *Knesz v. Central Jersey Bank & Trust Co.*[138]

[i] Effect of Failure to Follow Reasonable Commercial Standards

A representative will be liable under old Article 3 without regard to any proceeds remaining if it has not followed reasonable commercial standards. In that event, the defense granted by old § 3–419(3) is lost.[139]

---

135. West Penn Admin., Inc. v. Union Nat'l Bank, 233 Pa.Super. 311, 335 A.2d 725 (1975).

136. Underpinning & Foundation Constr., Inc. v. Chase Manhattan Bank, 46 N.Y.2d 459, 414 N.Y.S.2d 298, 386 N.E.2d 1319 (N.Y. 1979). *See also* Brite Lite Lamps Corp. v. Manufacturers Hanover Trust Co., 34 UCC Rep. Serv. 1221 (N.Y.Sup.Ct.1982); State of Qatar v. First American Bank of Virginia, 885 F.Supp. 849 (E.D.Va.1995); Hartford Fire Insurance Co. v. Maryland National Bank, N.A., 341 Md. 408, 671 A.2d 22 (Md.Ct.App.1996).

137. *E.g.,* Jackson Vitrified China Co. v. People's Am. Nat'l Bank, 388 So.2d 1059 (Fla.Dist.Ct.App.1980); Denn v. First State Bank, 316 N.W.2d 532 (Minn.1982); Coulter Electronics, Inc. v. Commercial Bank, 727 F.2d 1078, 38 UCC Rep. Serv. 239 (11th Cir.1984). Suit on a different basis than conversion is theoretically possible, but should lack motivation under current Article 3 because a direct action now is authorized. For example, in Lewittes Furniture Enter., Inc. v. Peoples Nat'l Bank, 82 Misc.2d 1013, 372 N.Y.S.2d 830 (N.Y.Dist. Ct.1975), the payee sued as an assignee of the warranty of good title the collecting bank had made to the drawee. Warranty liability is not conditioned on proceeds remaining in the hands of the warrantor. *See also* Hydroflo Corp. v. First Nat'l Bank, 217 Neb. 20, 349 N.W.2d 615 (Neb. 1984) (upholding old § 3–419(3) as a defense, but seemingly following the theory of *Cooper v. Union Bank* discussed, *infra*, in relation to a money had and received theory).

138. 97 N.J. 1, 477 A.2d 806 (N.J. 1984). *See also* Peerless Ins. Co. v. Texas Commerce Bank, 791 F.2d 1177 (5th Cir. 1986). *See* § 3–420(c) and Official Comment 3 to that section.

139. This requirement is deleted under § 3–420(c), which also denies the defense to depositary, as opposed to collecting, banks. Bad faith also will remove the defense. Persons other than the depositary bank may be liable. For example, in Ickes v. Bache Halsey Stuart Shields, Inc., 133 Ariz. 300, 650 P.2d 1282 (Ariz.Ct.App.1982), a brokerage

For example, where stolen checks were restrictively indorsed by the forger and deposited to his own or a confederate's account, the court held not only that the bank had failed to abide by the restrictive indorsements but also that the bank's conduct violated standards of care for depositary banks.[140] In *Federal Deposit Insurance Corp. v. Marine National Bank*,[141] the bank simply admitted a failure to comply with relevant standards.[142] And in *Handel v. Manufacturers Hanover Trust Co.*, the deviation consisted of an indorsement that was entirely missing.[143] But courts in other cases presenting less damaging facts, presumably induced by the perceived efficiency of the direct action,[144] worked hard to find a failure to follow reasonable standards so as to remove the defense to conversion liability. A number of courts hold that a bank that fails to inquire concerning an individual cashing or depositing a check made payable to a business entity, such as a corporation, and which is then indorsed, engages in an unreasonable commercial practice as a

---

firm lost when it presented no evidence as to what constituted reasonable commercial standards for that business.

A memorandum from the reporter and chair of the drafting committee to make the 2002 amendments to UCC Articles 3 and 4, addressed to the Council of the American Law Institute, dated November 14, 2000, observed there are a number of provisions in Articles 3 and 4 that provide for proportionate allocation of fault among a payor bank, drawer and depositary bank, but they do not adequately deal with cases where there is negligence by all three, nor in relation to § 3–307 and the interaction between warranty and §§ 3–304 and 3–405. Support for clarification in these respects, however, was not itself adequate to continue the work to make arguably desirable changes, and thus the Code scheme remains apparently incomplete and perhaps inconsistent in treating similar situations. Accordingly, one can predict litigation will continue to be the solution, with its attendant costs and inefficiencies, as noted in note 123, *supra*.

Perhaps an ambiguity also is present here, in the change from old § 3–419 and the deletion of the requirement to follow reasonable commercial standards. One may say, the defense is gone so why not also a condition to it? But if the depositary bank now is liable in conversion, is that to say any negligence of one of the other parties is irrelevant? One would think not, but how then for comparative fault purposes is the fault of the bank liable in conversion to be measured? Perhaps the cases under old § 3–419 may yet have utility? *Also compare*, The Bank/First Citizens Bank v. Citizens & Associates, 44 UCC Rep. Serv. 2d 1072 (Tenn.Ct.App.2001), *rev'd*, 82 S.W.3d 259 (Tenn.2002).

140. Underpinning & Foundation Constr., Inc. v. Chase Manhattan Bank, 46 N.Y.2d 459, 414 N.Y.S.2d 298, 386 N.E.2d 1319 (N.Y. 1979). *See also* Continental Airlines, Inc. v. Boatmen's National Bank of St. Louis, 13 F.3d 1254, 22 UCC Rep. Serv. 2d 841 (8th Cir.1994).

141. 431 F.2d 341 (5th Cir.1970).

142. The test is the reasonable commercial standards in the locale or industry, and not the commercial standards of the particular representative. Travelers Ins. Co. v. Jefferson Nat'l Bank, 404 So.2d 1131 (Fla. Dist.Ct.App.1981). A bank that fails to follow its own procedures also is likely to be in trouble. *See* Torino Construction Corp. v. Ensign Federal Credit Union, 111 Nev. 1515, 908 P.2d 702 (Nev. 1995).

143. 16 UCC Rep. Serv. 762 (N.Y.Sup. Ct.1975). That, along with checks made out to a corporate payee being deposited to an individual account, was important in American Parkinson Disease Ass'n v. First National Bank, 584 N.W.2d 437 (Minn.Ct.App. 1998).

144. A suit by the payee directly against the person who dealt with the forger is obviously more efficient than a suit by the payee against the payor, who then must sue in warranty, as others also may have to do, to place the loss ultimately upon the same person. Moreover, a payee who has more than one instrument taken may face suits against many payors and in different jurisdictions, while it is unlikely the forger dealt with more than one, or at most two, persons close to home. *See, e.g.*, Knesz v. Central Jersey Bank & Trust Co., 97 N.J. 1, 477 A.2d 806 (1984) and Official Comment 3 to § 3–420. *See also* the inadequacies noted in note 139, *supra*.

matter of law.[145]

[ii] Effect of Proceeds Remaining

Some courts emasculated the defense of old § 3–419(3) to reach a direct result; presumably this will not occur under current § 3–420(c) since depositary banks are not accorded the defense. The leading case under old Article 3 is *Cooper v. Union Bank*.[146] In that case the payee of a number of checks, on which his secretary had forged his indorsement and then cashed or deposited the checks for collection, brought suit against the collecting and drawee banks in conversion. All amounts had been withdrawn and the trial court found no liability with respect to the collecting banks. On appeal, the California court held that the suit ratified payment by the drawees to the collecting banks, but that since, as a legal matter, those banks could only have paid out their own funds and not the proceeds to which the forger was not entitled, the proceeds still remained and old § 3–419(3) did not preclude liability. This result, of course, virtually eliminated the defense provided in old § 3–419(3). Nonetheless, the banks in the *Cooper* case did not bear the full brunt of the loss because the court determined the negligence of the payee contributed to the loss. This often is the situation in these cases and, indeed, current § 3–405, discussed, *infra*, this chapter, creates a liability rule initially without regard to negligence in those circumstances.

Some courts also did not stop with a direct action against the depositary bank. The most direct placement of loss from a forged indorsement would involve a suit by the obligor on the instrument, such as the drawer, against the person who should ultimately bear the loss, who is the person who took the instrument from the forger.[147] A number

---

145. The same standard is discussed in Chapter 4 in connection with preclusion. Of course, the issue extends beyond this context. For a general rule, *see* J. Gordon Neely Enterprises, Inc. v. American Nat'l Bank, 403 So.2d 887 (Ala.1981) (checks contained visible minor erasures or other minor irregularities; payment of anything other than a pristine instrument cannot itself be considered a violation of reasonable commercial standards). *See also* Martin Glennon, Inc. v. First Fidelity Bank, N.A., 279 N.J.Super. 48, 652 A.2d 199 (App.Div.1995); Allied Insurance Center, Inc. v. Wauwatosa Sav. & Loan Assn., 200 Wis.2d 369, 546 N.W.2d 544 (Wis.Ct.App.1996); American Parkinson Disease Ass'n v. First National Bank, 584 N.W.2d 437 (Minn.Ct.App.1998); *In re* Lou Levy & Sons Fashions, Inc. Litigation, 988 F.2d 311, 19 UCC Rep. Serv. 2d 1107 (2d Cir.1993).

146. 9 Cal.3d 371, 107 Cal.Rptr. 1, 507 P.2d 609 (Cal. 1973). Other courts followed the lead. *See, e.g.*, Justus Co. v. Gary Wheaton Bank, 509 F.Supp. 103 (N.D.Ill.1981); Averon v. First Nat'l City Bank, 23 UCC Rep. Serv. 402 (N.Y.Sup.Ct.1978) (perhaps limited to where the check is cashed); Whalen v. Chase Manhattan Bank, N.A., 43 UCC Rep. Serv. 2d 614 (S.D.N.Y.2000), *aff'd*, 14 Fed.Appx. 120 (2d Cir.2001) (suit against depositary bank in conversion implicitly assumes that bank holds the proceeds of the instrument).

147. Otherwise the obligor would have to force a recredit of the account and the payor would have to sue the depositary bank. However, efficiency is unlikely to be the obligor's motive. The reasons an obligor may sue, as opposed to the payee, are no doubt many. The payee may not be able to sue because a person who never receives delivery of the instrument so as to acquire ownership cannot sue in conversion. *See* City Nat'l Bank v. Wernick, 368 So.2d 934 (Fla.Dist.Ct.App.1979) *cert. denied*, 378 So.2d 350 (Fla.1979) and, *supra*, note 134. The obligor may not be able to force the payor to recredit his or her account because of negligence. *See, e.g.*, Stone & Webster Eng'g Corp. v. First Nat'l Bank & Trust Co., 345 Mass. 1, 184 N.E.2d 358 (Mass. 1962). If a direct action is allowed, however,

of cases denied a suit by the obligor against a depositary bank on the ground that the obligor is not a proper party,[148] and that to allow the suit may short-circuit defenses the payor or some other person may have to liability.[149] Other courts nonetheless allowed the suit.[150] Current Article 3 was intended to preclude suit by the issuer or acceptor against the depositary bank.[151]

[c] Legally Irrelevant Forged Indorsements

[i] Proceeds Are Correctly Paid

There are two related situations, not involving issues of agency, ratification (*see Stella v. Dean Witter Reynolds, Inc.*, 241 N.J.Super. 55, 574 A.2d 468 (App.Div.1990) and *Fulka v. Florida Commercial Banks*, 371 So.2d 521 (Fla.Dist.Ct.App.1979)), or preclusion based on negligence, where the loss from a forged indorsement is not placed upon the party who took the instrument from the forger. The first is where, notwithstanding the unauthorized signature, the proceeds of the instrument come into the hands of the intended party. Thus in one case[152] where a

---

normally the defendant will be accorded the benefit of the same defenses against the drawer that the payor would have had. Sun 'n Sand, Inc. v. United Cal. Bank, 21 Cal.3d 671, 148 Cal.Rptr. 329, 582 P.2d 920 (Cal. 1978). Under current Article 3, *see* § 3–420(a)(i), *but see* note 123 *supra*.

148. The obligor can force the payor to recredit the account and thus has lost nothing with respect to the instrument. Stone & Webster Eng'g Corp. v. First Nat'l Bank & Trust Co., 345 Mass. 1, 184 N.E.2d 358 (Mass. 1962). *See also* Sunbelt Factors, Inc. v. Bank of Gonzales, 481 So.2d 648 (La.Ct. App.1985); and Kings Premium Serv. Corp. v. Manufacturers Hanover Trust Co., 115 A.D.2d 707, 496 N.Y.S.2d 524 (N.Y.App.Div. 1985), as well as note 134, *supra*.

149. Stone & Webster Eng'g Corp. v. First Nat'l Bank & Trust Co., 345 Mass. 1, 184 N.E.2d 358 (Mass. 1962). *But see* Sun 'n Sand, Inc. v. United Cal. Bank, 21 Cal.3d 671, 148 Cal.Rptr. 329, 582 P.2d 920 (Cal. 1978), and note 147, *supra*.

150. Note 134, *supra* and e.g., International Indus., Inc. v. Island State Bank, 348 F.Supp. 886 (S.D.Tex.1971); Prudential Ins. Co. v. Marine Nat'l Exch. Bank, 315 F.Supp. 520 (E.D.Wis.1970); Justus Co. v. Gary Wheaton Bank, 509 F.Supp. 103 (N.D.Ill.1981); Wymore State Bank v. Johnson Int'l Co., 873 F.2d 1082 (8th Cir.1989). Sometimes the theory is not conversion. For example, in Allied Concord Fin. Corp. v. Bank of Am. Nat'l Trust & Sav. Ass'n, 275 Cal.App.2d 1, 80 Cal.Rptr. 622 (Cal.App. 1969), the court held that the drawer was a third party beneficiary of the warranty of good title made by the bank. And in Sun 'n Sand, Inc. v. United Cal. Bank, 21 Cal.3d 671, 148 Cal.Rptr. 329, 582 P.2d 920 (Cal. 1978), the person who pays and to whom the warranty of good title is made was interpreted in a nontechnical sense to include a drawer. Section 3–417 rejects this analysis. *See* Official Comment 2 to § 3–417.

151. § 3–420(a)(i) and *see* Official Comment 1 to the section; *but see* notes 123, 128, 134, and 139, *supra*.

152. Gordon v. State Street Bank & Trust Co., 361 Mass. 258, 280 N.E.2d 152 (Mass. 1972). *See also* Clemens v. First Nat'l Bank, 286 Ark. 290, 692 S.W.2d 222 (Ark. 1985) (proceeds of check where wife's indorsement forged actually deposited in joint checking account); Gallagher v. Santa Fe Federal Employees Federal Credit Union, 132 N.M. 552, 52 P.3d 412, 48 UCC Rep.Serv.2d 655 (App.2002) (same in dicta); County Concrete Corp. v. Smith, 317 N.J.Super. 50, 721 A.2d 34 (App.Div.1998); Hall v. Mid–Century Insurance Co., 248 Kan. 847, 811 P.2d 855 (Kan. 1991); Ambassador Financial Services, Inc. v. Indiana National Bank, 605 N.E.2d 746 (Ind.1992). But in another case where the proceeds, after being deposited in the payee's account were allowed to be withdrawn, the defense that the intended person actually received the proceeds of the instrument was held not to be applicable. Kosic v. Marine Midland Bank, 76 A.D.2d 89, 430 N.Y.S.2d 175 (N.Y.App.Div.1980). A similar case is Bursey v. CFX Bank, 145 N.H. 126, 756 A.2d 1001, 42 UCC Rep. Serv. 2d 187 (N.H.

check evidencing a loan was issued to both the husband and the wife, but only the husband had actually applied for the loan, the wife's unauthorized indorsement was held to be immaterial.[153] A similar result is reached if the unauthorized signature has no relevance because the party was intended to have no interest. For example, where an individual was named as a payee on a check issued to cover a fire insurance claim but was not a named insured on the policy and had no claim to the proceeds of the check, the court held that no recovery from a depositary bank that had cashed the check over that person's unauthorized indorsement was warranted.[154]

[ii] Imposter, Fictitious Payee, and Padded Payroll Cases; Employer's Indorsements

[A] In General

The other situations where a forged indorsement may be legally irrelevant include instances involving an imposter, a fictitious payee, and a padded payroll, and also the case where a responsible employee forges the employer's indorsement. Under old Article 3 an indorsement by any person in the name of a named payee was effective if:

(1) an imposter,[155] by the use of the mails or otherwise, induced the maker or drawer to issue the instrument to him or her or to his or her confederate in the name of the payee;[156]

(2) a person signing as or on behalf of a maker or drawer[157]

2000). *See also* Atlantic Bank v. Israel Discount Bank, Ltd., 108 Misc.2d 342, 441 N.Y.S.2d 315, 31 UCC Rep. Serv. 1057 (N.Y. App. Term 1981), where the borrower forged the car dealer's indorsement on the loan check but then paid the car dealer from the funds. But the car dealer, had it received the check, would have had a perfected a security interest, and this was not done because of the borrower's action. The court found a ground for objection to the extent of loss due to non-perfection. And in Eatinger v. First Nat'l Bank, 199 Mont. 377, 649 P.2d 1253 (Mont. 1982), even though the intended payee (a lumber company) did get the proceeds, the forged indorsement led the payee to apply the proceeds to a debt owed to it rather than to the price of materials purchased by the drawer from it, as the drawer intended, and the rule also was held inapplicable. *See also* Ambassador Financial Services, Inc. v. Indiana National Bank, 605 N.E.2d 746 (Ind.1992) (that the intended payee received the funds is not a defense if improper payment proximately caused other harm to drawer).

153. Similar cases where a new instrument payable in the same manner is issued for an unindorsed instrument are discussed in Chapter 3, *supra*.

154. Tette v. Marine Midland Bank, 78 A.D.2d 383, 435 N.Y.S.2d 413 (N.Y.App.Div. 1981). *See also* American National Bank v. Seidel, 622 S.W.2d 19 (Mo.Ct.App.1981) and the discussion in Chapter 3, *supra,* and in this chapter, *infra*.

155. "Imposter" under old Article 3 referred to impersonation and did not extend to a false representation that the party was the authorized agent of the payee. § 3–404(a) eliminates this qualification. *See* Official Comment 1 to § 3–404 and note 92, *supra*.

156. Old § 3–405(1)(a); current § 3–404(a).

157. In Perini Corp. v. First Nat'l Bank, 553 F.2d 398 (5th Cir.1977), an unknown person forged checks payable to nonexistent payees and indorsed them. The court held the indorsements were effective because whoever drew the checks intended the named payees to have no interest in them. The case seems an expansive reading of old § 3–405(1)(b), given the policy behind it discussed below. Nonetheless, current Article 3 carries it forward. *See* Official Comment 2, Case #5, to § 3–404 and note 95, *supra*.

intended the payee to have no interest in the instrument;[158] or

(3) an agent or employee of the maker or drawer supplied the maker or drawer with the name of the payee, intending the latter to have no such interest.[159]

Current Article 3 adds a fourth category of case—that where a responsible employee forges the indorsement of the employee's employer as payee of the check.[160]

These provisions reflect the policy that an obligor should bear the loss resulting from an undetected impersonation and that an employer obligor or payee should bear the loss from a dishonest employee as a risk of business. The obligor or payee in these circumstances normally is in a better position to prevent the forgeries, and negotiability is promoted.[161] If the otherwise forged indorsement is made effective,[162] any person dealing with the instrument has not done so inconsistently with the direction of the person drawing the instrument, and thus there is no cause of action in conversion or to recredit the account, and the maker or drawer or payee must recoup directly or indirectly from the forger or bear the loss.[163]

To illustrate how the imposter provision[164] works, in *Fair Park National Bank v. Southwestern Investment Co.*,[165] the court stated that if an instrument is made payable to A and B due to X's impersonation of A, and is delivered to X, then X or anyone else[166] can make effective

---

158. Old § 3–405(1)(b); current § 3–404(b). The pre-Code rule required a "fictitious or nonexisting person." The rule under old § 3–405(1)(b) was different because the existence or nonexistence of the named payee was not decisive and was important only as it might bear on an intent that the payee have no interest. Indeed, the old "fictitious person" approach seemed foreclosed by old § 3–413(3), which provided that by making, drawing, or accepting the party admitted, as against all subsequent parties including the drawee, the existence of the payee and his then capacity to indorse. Since fully applying this reasoning would substantially eliminate the need for old § 3–405(1)(b), it may be concluded that old § 3–413(3) should be construed as speaking only to "capacity" and should not bear on "genuineness." *See, e.g.*, Phoenix Assurance Co. v. Davis, 126 N.J.Super. 379, 314 A.2d 615 (Law Div.1974). Current § 3–404(b) includes both the "no intent" rule in § 3–404(b)(i) and the "fictitious payee" rule in § 3–404(b)(ii), and eliminates old § 3–413(3). *See* Official Comment 2 to § 3–404, which illustrates with five example cases.

159. Old § 3–405(1); current § 3–405(b).

160. § 3–405(b).

161. *See* Official Comment 4 to old § 3–405.

162. The effect imparted to the indorsement by these provisions does not preclude criminal or civil liability of the person making the indorsement. § 3–403(c).

163. The maker or drawer or payee may insure against the loss. *See, e.g.*, Delmar Bank v. Fidelity & Deposit Co., 428 F.2d 32 (8th Cir.1970) (bank's blanket indemnity bond treated checks with indorsements effective under old § 3–405 as bearing forged indorsements).

164. Old § 3–405(1)(a); current § 3–404(a). *See also* the illustrative cases in Official Comment 2 to § 3–404; Franklin Nat'l Bank v. Shapiro, 7 UCC Rep. Serv. 317 (N.Y.Sup.Ct.1970); Covington v. Penn Square Nat'l Bank, 545 P.2d 824 (Okla. Ct. App. 1975); Shube v. Cheng, 157 Misc.2d 255, 596 N.Y.S.2d 335 (N.Y.Sup.Ct.1993), *aff'd*, 208 A.D.2d 606, 618 N.Y.S.2d 226 (1994); Murray Hill Investments, Inc. v. Adas Yereim, Inc., 205 A.D.2d 512, 612 N.Y.S.2d 679 (1994) (imposter organization).

165. 541 S.W.2d 266 (Tex.Civ.App. 1976).

166. The indorsement need not be made by the imposter or other fraudulent actor. If someone steals it from that person, no reason to reverse the policy of the section exists. Official Comment 1 to old § 3–405.

indorsements in the names of both A and B. An extension of this concept occurred in *Philadelphia Title Insurance Co. v. Fidelity–Philadelphia Trust Co.*,[167] where the drawer did not deal directly with the imposter and the communication between them was through representations of third persons. Nonetheless the court believed that the language "by use of the mails or otherwise" was broad enough to cover the case.[168]

The main issue with respect to the unintended or fictitious payee provision seems to be whether the person whose intent determines to whom the instrument is payable in accordance with § 3–110 intended the payee to have an interest.[169] To understand the issue, consider spouse A who applies for a loan and the other spouse also signs the application. The check for the loan proceeds is made out to both, but A, without authority, indorses for both. In *Gordon v. State Street Bank & Trust Co.*,[170] the unauthorized signature was held to be irrelevant as the lender never intended the other spouse to have an interest and required that person's obligation on the loan only to avoid any later collection problems.[171] But on similar facts the court in *Perley v. Glastonbury Bank and*

---

167. 419 Pa. 78, 212 A.2d 222 (Pa. 1965).

168. This language was intended to reject distinctions between face to face imposture and imposture by mail; that is, where A induces a drawer to issue a check, not by misrepresenting his or her identity in a face to face meeting, but by delivering a letter in which A misrepresents himself or herself to be a well known and respected person. Extending this analysis, one could conclude, as did the court, that further line drawing is not sensible. On the other hand, there should be an imposter in the picture. Nonetheless, in Minster State Bank v. Baybank Middlesex, 414 Mass. 831, 611 N.E.2d 200 (Mass. 1993), where a husband applied for a loan for both he and his wife and signed her name to the documents mailed in and then forged her indorsement on the check, the court applied the imposter rule, saying he had done more than merely misrepresent that he could act for her. But what more, since he never claimed to be her, but only that she was involved? Several cases, however, have used this analysis, in essence determining that using the mail to deliver forged documents qualifies. *See* Dominion Bank, N.A. v. Household Bank, F.S.B., 827 F.Supp. 463 (S.D.Ohio 1993); and Intelogic Trace Texcom Group, Inc. v. Merchants National Bank, 626 N.E.2d 839 (Ind.Ct.App. 1993).

The need for an imposter is key to understanding another application of the rule; the rule covers posing as an agent, but not a misrepresentation of authority. Thus, in King v. White, 265 Kan. 627, 962 P.2d 475 (Kan. 1998), the court correctly held there must be impersonation of an actual agent, not merely an agent who misrepresents his or her authority. The courts generally have gotten this right. Valley Bank v. Monarch Investment Co., 118 Idaho 747, 800 P.2d 634 (Idaho 1990), *rev'd in part on other grounds,* 120 Idaho 733, 819 P.2d 1133 (1991); Title Insurance Co. v. Comerica Bank–California, 27 Cal.App.4th 800, 32 Cal.Rptr.2d 735 (1994).

In North Side State Bank v. Board of County Commissioners, 894 P.2d 1046 (Okla.1994), the court drew an arguably improper line involving an instrument issued by a governmental entity pursuant to a court order. The court held the imposter had never dealt with the actual issuer of the instrument but had fooled the court which issued the order but not the instrument, and thus the defense did not apply.

169. Old § 3–405(1)(b); current § 3–404(b). If the payee is fictitious that speaks for itself. *See* Kansas Bankers Surety Co. v. Bank of Odessa, 386 F.Supp. 555 (W.D.Mo. 1974); In re Western Iowa Farms Co., 135 F.3d 1257 (8th Cir.1998). There is a dispute as to the application of this rule to instruments involving rights and liabilities of the United States. A discussion of that dispute appears in Chapter 1.

170. 361 Mass. 258, 280 N.E.2d 152 (Mass. 1972).

171. As such, the lender today might violate Regulation B, 12 CFR § 202.7(d) under the Equal Credit Opportunity Act, 15 U.S.C. § 1691 *et seq.*, which prohibits automatically requiring the signature of an applicant's spouse or other person on a credit instrument.

Trust Co.[172] determined that both husband and wife were intended to have an interest. Thus the court must have found that either they both initially applied for the loan or the one spouse was necessary to support the creditworthiness of the other. Consequently, a proper result depends on a careful assessment of the facts.[173]

Finally, the padded payroll provision, and the additional provision under current Article 3 making an employer liable for its employee's forgery of its indorsement on instruments on which it is the payee, also require a careful assessment of the facts.[174] For example, suppose a

---

172. 170 Conn. 691, 368 A.2d 149 (Conn. 1976).

173. *See also* Dayton, Price & Co., Ltd. v. First Nat'l City Bank, 64 A.D.2d 563, 406 N.Y.S.2d 823 (N.Y.App.Div.1978); and McConnico v. Third Nat'l Bank, 499 S.W.2d 874 (Tenn.1973), as to intent where the payee is an existing creditor with a valid claim against the drawer. However, this makes little difference under current Article 3, which is sounder policy. Official Comment 1, Case #2, to § 3–404. The rule also has been applied where the drawer and the payee are the same, and the culprit generated the instruments to remove funds from an account over which the culprit did not have control to one over which control existed. Sybedon Corp. v. Bank of Leumi Trust Co., 224 A.D.2d 320, 638 N.Y.S.2d 50 (N.Y.App.Div.1996) (mem.).

In Getty Petroleum Corp. v. American Express Travel Related Services Co., 90 N.Y.2d 322, 660 N.Y.S.2d 689, 683 N.E.2d 311 (N.Y. 1997), computer generated checks that were never intended to be issued but which were only drawn for internal bookkeeping purposes were stolen and used to pay the culprit's bills. The procedure was adopted to save costs. The court correctly allowed the defense, and held under old Article 3 that the negligence of the persons paid by the checks was irrelevant. Most cases so held on this last point. Stone Manufacturing Co. v. NCNB of South Carolina, 308 S.C. 287, 417 S.E.2d 628 (S.C.Ct.App. 1992); Shearson Lehman Brothers, Inc. v. Wasatch Bank, 788 F.Supp. 1184 (D.Utah 1992); *but see* State of Qatar v. First American Bank of Virginia, 880 F.Supp. 463, 26 UCC Rep. Serv. 2d 284 (E.D.Va.1995), *additional opinion*, 885 F.Supp. 849 (E.D.Va. 1995), where the bank failed to follow restrictive indorsements. Of course, now under § 3–404(d), the negligence of the persons paid is relevant, as it generally should be. But where the procedure, albeit risky, is adopted as worth the risk due to cost savings, should the benefit be even further enhanced by shifting some of the risk to another party, even recognizing that party was negligent?

174. Old § 3–405(1)(c); current § 3–405(b). The former provision, of course, is not limited to adding names to payrolls although that situation is covered. *See* Official Comment 3, Case #7, to § 3–405. *See also*, *e.g.*, May Dept. Stores Co. v. Pittsburgh Nat'l Bank, 374 F.2d 109 (3d Cir. 1967) (false invoices); and Delmar Bank v. Fidelity & Deposit Co., 428 F.2d 32 (8th Cir.1970) (fraudulent loan); Witten Productions, Inc. v. Republic Bank & Trust Co., 102 N.C.App. 88, 401 S.E.2d 388 (N.C.Ct. App.1991); Guardian Life Ins. Co. of America v. Chemical Bank, 94 N.Y.2d 418, 705 N.Y.S.2d 553, 727 N.E.2d 111, 40 UCC Rep. Serv. 2d 923 (N.Y.App.2000).

As in the case of the unintended and fictitious payee rule discussed, *supra*, negligence of the bank was irrelevant under old Article 3, unless it was so "commercially outrageous" as to amount to bad faith. McAdam v. Dean Witter Reynolds, Inc., 896 F.2d 750 (3d Cir.1990); Prudential–Bache Sec., Inc. v. Citibank, 73 N.Y.2d 263, 536 N.E.2d 1118, 539 N.Y.S.2d 699 (1989). Negligence now is relevant under § 3–405(b) (and § 3–406(b)). Moreover, it is not only negligence in relation to the instrument that may be relevant; negligence in relation to the account also is relevant. Official Comment 4 to § 3–405. However, the negligence must "substantially contribute" to loss resulting from the fraud, and that will not be the case if there is an insufficient link between the negligence and the forgery. Zambia Nat. Commercial Bank Ltd. v. Fidelity International Bank, 855 F.Supp. 1377 (S.D.N.Y.1994), *amended in part on a different issue*, 1994 WL 440717 (S.D.N.Y. 1994). *See also* The Bank/First Citizens Bank v. Citizens & Assocs., 82 S.W.3d 259 (Tenn.2002).

The additional provision in current Article 3 applies to fact situations like that in *Cooper v. Union Bank, supra* note 146, where the employee of an attorney took numerous client checks written on diverse banks, forged the attorney's indorsement, and deposited or cashed the checks at her bank.

dishonest employee takes checks prepared for bona fide creditors of the drawer that are based on submitted invoices and forges the indorsements of the payees. Some courts held this situation was not covered by the provision in old Article 3.[175] However, where a dishonest employee, in no way involved with the preparation or execution of checks, initiated the process that ultimately produced the checks by false sell orders, the court held the distance between the culprit and the preparation of the checks, involving many departments of the drawer, did not preclude finding that the culprit supplied the name of the payee.[176]

[B] The Need for Proper Indorsement and Due Care

The first of two other issues involving considerable litigation under old § 3–405 is what constitutes "an indorsement by any person in the name of a named payee". For example, in *Western Casualty & Surety Co. v. Citizens Bank*[177] the court held that an indorsement that misspelled "Greater" as "Grater" in the name of the payee was not fatal. On the other hand, when the payee was named as "Longview Fibre Co." and the indorsement read "Longview Fibre Products," the court found that old § 3–405 was not applicable.[178] Such analysis seems too strict, but against

---

175. Snug Harbor Realty Co. v. First Nat'l Bank, 105 N.J.Super. 572, 253 A.2d 581 (App.Div.1969), aff'd, 54 N.J. 95, 253 A.2d 545 (1969). Other decisions drew no distinction from the situation where the payees were fabricated. Texas Stadium Corporation v. Savings of America, 933 S.W.2d 616 (Tex.App.Dallas 1996, writ denied); Verde America, Inc. v. Bank of New York, 24 UCC Rep. Serv. 2d 154 (N.Y.Sup.Ct. 1994); Aetna Cas. & Surety Co. v. Bank of New York, 22 UCC Rep. Serv. 2d 813 (N.Y.Sup.Ct.1993). The problem is the same as noted in note 173, *supra*: did the employee intend to take the check before it was signed so the section applies, or only after so that the indorsement should be regarded as forged and the situation is governed under old § 3–406 on the basis of any negligence? *See, e.g.*, Girard Bank v. Mount Holly State Bank, 474 F.Supp. 1225 (D.N.J. 1979); Firemen's Ins. Co. v. Chase Manhattan Bank, N.A., 102 Misc.2d 613, 424 N.Y.S.2d 83 (N.Y. Sup. Ct.1979); Danje Fabrics Div. v. Morgan Guaranty Trust Co., 96 Misc.2d 746, 409 N.Y.S.2d 565 (N.Y.Sup.Ct. 1978). The issue disappears under current § 3–405. *See* Official Comment 3, Case number 6.

176. New Amsterdam Cas. Co. v. First Pa. Banking & Trust Co., 451 F.2d 892 (3d Cir.1971); *see also* Knight Publishing Co. v. Chase Manhattan Bank, N.A., 125 N.C.App. 1, 479 S.E.2d 478 (N.C.Ct.App.1997). One can argue that no line drawing is warranted in the application of this provision. On the other hand, one can argue the absolute liability it imposes should only accrue for employees involved with checks, against whom the drawer can reasonably guard. Liability for conduct by extraneous persons, like a janitor, would then be based on negligence in guarding the check writing process. This is the position taken in § 3–405, which defines its scope through the concept of an "employee" (*see* current § 3–405(a)(1)) with "responsibility" (*see* § 3–405(a)(3)). Janitors are excluded. Official Comment 3, Case #1, to the section. Bookkeepers and clerks involved in the check handling process are included. Official Comment 3, Case numbers 3, 5 and 7, to the section.

177. 676 F.2d 1344 (10th Cir.1982). *See also* Basse Truck Line, Inc. v. First State Bank, 949 S.W.2d 17 (Tex.App.1997, writ denied).

178. First Nat'l Bank v. Security Nat'l Bank, 32 UCC Rep. Serv. 926 (D.Mass. 1981). *See also* Seattle–First Nat'l Bank v. Pacific Nat'l Bank of Washington, 22 Wn. App. 46, 587 P.2d 617 (1978); and Twellman v. Lindell Trust Co., 534 S.W.2d 83 (Mo.Ct.App.1976); American Title Insurance Co. v. Shawmut Bank of Rhode Island, N.A., 812 F.Supp. 301 (D.R.I.1993) (Michael DiChiro, Jr. v. Michael DiChiro too imprecise).

In Guardian Life Ins. Co. of Am. v. Weisman, 30 F. Supp. 2d 720 (D.N.J.1998), the court also refused to accept the defense where the indorsement was not legible. Illegible indorsements would seem common enough not to raise suspicion, and so the

what standard should the indorsement be measured? The standard used by the court in *Western Casualty* was whether the instrument presented a normal appearance. Perhaps uniformity would have been better served by adoption of the same standard of irregularity that would provide sufficient notice to prevent holder in due course status.[179]

Current § 3–405(c) (and § 3–404(c)) deals with this issue, and the provision applies if the indorsement is in a name substantially similar to the name of the person to whom the instrument is payable[180] or the instrument, whether or not indorsed, is deposited to an account in a name substantially similar to the name of that person.[181] This rule should substantially reduce litigation and, to the extent the cases under old § 3–405 were influenced by the next issue, the way Article 3 addresses that issue also should assist in this context.

The other issue is whether the rules of old § 3–405 were conclusive; that is, may conduct by the other party that does not conform to reasonable commercial standards influence the result? It is clear that actual bad faith is relevant.[182] Beyond that, most courts concluded the provision imposed an absolute loss allocation and left no room for consideration of negligence.[183] There was some authority to the contrary. For example, in a case[184] where a bank cashed checks of a corporation drawn over a four year period made out to fictitious payees or payees

---

decision seems questionable. On appeal, Guardian Life Insurance Company of America v. Weisman, 223 F.3d 229 (3d Cir. 2000), the court thought review of payee indorsements was the responsibility of the depositary rather than the payor bank; the case was remanded.

179. *See* old § 3–304(1)(a), discussed in Chapter 3.

180. *See* note 177, *supra*. This should change the results of cases cited in note 178, *supra*. *See also* Knight Publishing Co. v. Chase Manhattan Bank, N.A., 125 N.C.App. 1, 479 S.E.2d 478 (N.C.Ct.App. 1997) (Graphic Image v. Graphic Color Prep. not substantially similar). If the culprit indorses in the culprit's own name, the provision would not apply unless the instrument was made so payable. Travco Corp. v. Citizens Fed. Sav. & Loan Ass'n, 42 Mich. App. 291, 201 N.W.2d 675 (1972). Even if the indorsement is good, if it is restrictive the loss may be reallocated. Underpinning & Foundation Constructors, Inc. v. Chase Manhattan Bank, N.A., 46 N.Y.2d 459, 414 N.Y.S.2d 298, 386 N.E.2d 1319 (N.Y. 1979) and Spielman v. Manufacturers Hanover Trust Co., 60 N.Y.2d 221, 469 N.Y.S.2d 69, 456 N.E.2d 1192 (N.Y. 1983).

181. *See* Kraftsman Container Corp. v. United Counties Trust Co., 169 N.J.Super. 488, 404 A.2d 1288 (Law Div.1979). A similar provision appears at § 3–404(c).

182. *See* notes 173 and 174, *supra*; UCC § 1–304; Prudential Ins. Co. v. Marine Nat'l Exch. Bank, 371 F.Supp. 1002 (E.D.Wis.1974). Under §§ 3–404 and 3–405, good faith is explicitly required, and it is the broad standard of § 3–103(a)(4) (and, now, § 1–201(b)(20)). Under old § 3–405, some courts stretched to determine bad faith. *See, e.g.*, McAdam v. Dean Witter Reynolds, Inc., 896 F.2d 750 (3d Cir.1990), which probably only involved gross negligence.

183. Notes 173 and 174, *supra*, Western Cas. & Surety Co. v. Citizens Bank, 676 F.2d 1344 (10th Cir.1982); Merrill Lynch, Pierce, Fenner & Smith, Inc. v. Chemical Bank, 57 N.Y.2d 439, 456 N.Y.S.2d 742, 442 N.E.2d 1253 (N.Y. 1982); Prudential–Bache Securities, Inc. v. Citibank, N.A., 4 UCC Rep. Serv. 2d 533 (N.Y.Sup.Ct.1987), *aff'd*, 529 N.Y.S.2d 983, 141 A.D.2d 353 (1988), *and aff'd*, 73 N.Y.2d 263, 539 N.Y.S.2d 699, 536 N.E.2d 1118 (N.Y. 1989) (the case also discusses whether the acts of its employees could be attributed to the bank in relation to the adverse agent principle); McCarthy, Kenney & Reidy, P.C. v. First Nat'l Bank, 402 Mass. 630, 524 N.E.2d 390 (1988); City of Phoenix v. Great Western Bank & Trust Co., 148 Ariz. 53, 712 P.2d 966 (Ariz.Ct. App.1985). *See also* note 124, *supra*.

184. Kraftsman Container Corp. v. United Counties Trust Co., 169 N.J.Super. 488, 404 A.2d 1288 (Law Div.1979).

intended to have no interest and the checks were either not indorsed or indorsed illegibly, the court perceived bad faith in a consistent failure by the bank to monitor and investigate a series of irregular transactions and indicated it thus might be liable to the drawer.[185]

The *Kraftsman* case[186] well represents the tension present in the entire area of allocating losses due to forgery and alteration under old Articles 3 and 4. The decision seems right, but note that in addition to overriding the presumed conclusive fault of the drawer, which underlies the rules in old § 3–405, a finding of liability against the bank, in this case the drawee, would also cancel the conclusive rule in old § 4–406(4)[187] that precludes raising an unauthorized indorsement without regard to care or lack of care more than three years after the bank has made a statement of the account or the items available to its customer. Current Articles 3 and 4 eschew this tension.[188] In context, §§ 3–404(d) and 3–405(b) both allow any failure to exercise ordinary care by the person paying the instrument or taking it for value or for collection to be taken into account in allocating the loss from forgery or alteration on a comparative negligence basis.[189] This change is designed to reduce the litigation in this area since where both parties may bear some responsibility a negotiated settlement seems more likely than litigation arguing over the exact percentage, and should promote efficiency since due care will be prompted thus reducing the overall losses the system must bear.

---

185. *See also* Dykstra v. National Bank of South Dakota, 328 N.W.2d 862 (S.D. 1983) (negligence of payor bank in allowing joint payee to indorse in name of both payees (one of whom was nonexistent) in presence of bank officer, made bank liable to drawer notwithstanding old § 3–405) and E.F. Hutton & Co., Inc. v. City Nat'l Bank, 149 Cal.App.3d 60, 196 Cal.Rptr. 614 (Cal. Ct.App.1983).

186. *See, supra,* note 184.

187. Current § 4–406(f) omits this rule; it now is covered in § 4–111. *See* Official Comment 5 to § 4–406.

188. This also is true with respect to § 3–406, discussed in Chapter 4 and § 4–406, discussed in Chapter 9.

189. The negligence first must substantially contribute to the loss, and then must relate to paying or taking the instrument. *See* note 174, *supra.* Official Comment 4 to § 3–405 indicates this phrase is to be broadly construed to encompass all the facts relating to a bank's conduct with respect to collection of the check, including opening the account, the deposit of the check, and withdrawal of funds from the account. *Compare* Official Comment 4 to § 3–405, Official Comment 4 to § 3–406, and Official Comment 3 to § 3–404 *with* City of Phoenix v. Great Western Bank & Trust, 148 Ariz. 53, 712 P.2d 966 (Ariz.Ct.App.1985), discussing negligence in opening an account and in connection with withdrawals from it. *See also* Apcoa, Inc. v. Fidelity Nat'l Bank, 906 F.2d 610 (11th Cir.1990). *But see* again discussion in notes 92 and 123, *supra.*

Chapter 8

ARTICLE 4: PROVISIONAL AND FINAL PAYMENT

Analysis

Para.

¶8.01 Article 4: Scope and Key Concepts 289
    [1] Scope of Article 4 and Choice of Law 289
        [a] Scope of Article 4 289
        [b] Choice of Law 292
    [2] Modification by Agreement and Preemption by Federal Rule ... 293
    [3] Definitions and Important Concepts 298
        [a] Item 298
        [b] Bank 299
        [c] Depositary Bank 299
        [d] Payor Bank 299
        [e] Intermediary Bank 299
        [f] Collecting Bank 299
        [g] Customer 300
        [h] Agency 300
        [i] Banking Day 301
        [j] Midnight Deadline 301
        [k] Settle 301
        [*l*] Branches; Separate Office of a Bank; Separate Data Processing Center 302
        [m] Types of Checks 302
        [n] Electronic Presentment 303
    [4] Bank Insolvency 304
¶8.02 The Payor Bank: Provisional Settlement Versus Final Payment 305
    [1] Settlement 306
        [a] Initial Settlement 306
        [b] Provisional Versus Final Settlement/Payment 308
        [c] Final Payment 312
    [2] Methods of Making Final Payment 314
        [a] Payment in Cash 314
        [b] Reserving the Right to Revoke 315
        [c] The Midnight Deadline 316
    [3] Final Settlement and Accountability Under Article 4 319
    [4] Avoidance of Payment on Restitutionary Grounds 321
    [5] Funds Availability Under Article 4 325
    [6] Notice of Dishonor and Return of the Item 327
    [7] Defenses and Excuses for Failure to Send Timely Notice of Dishonor 330
¶8.03 Final Payment and the Midnight Deadline for Collecting Banks 332
    [1] Introduction 332
    [2] Provisional Settlement by a Collecting Bank 333

Para.

¶8.03 Final Payment and the Midnight Deadline for Collecting Banks—Continued
- [3] Excuses for Failure to Meet the Midnight Deadline 339
- [4] Measure of Liability When a Collecting Bank Misses Its Midnight Deadline 340
- [5] Settlement by Remittance or Other Means 344

¶8.04 Funds Availability and Federal Reserve Regulation CC 346
- [1] Introduction 346
- [2] Regulation CC, Subpart B—Funds Availability Requirements .. 347
  - [a] Funds Availability Schedules 347
  - [b] Exceptions and Safeguards 348
  - [c] Disclosure Requirements 351
  - [d] Civil Liability 351
- [3] Regulation CC, Subpart C—Collection of Checks 352
  - [a] Expeditious Return of Dishonored Checks 353
    - [i] The Two–Day/Four–Day Test 354
    - [ii] The Forward Collection Test 354
    - [iii] Impact on Article 4—The Payor Bank 355
  - [b] Identification of Returned Checks and Notice of Return—Duties of the Payor Bank 355
    - [i] Notice of Return 355
    - [ii] Notice of Nonpayment: Identifying the Depositary Bank 356
  - [c] Duties of Returning Banks—Regulation CC Section 229.31 356
    - [i] The Scope of Section 229.31 356
    - [ii] Expeditious Return 357
    - [iii] The Return Process: Comparison to UCC Article 4 357
    - [iv] Settlement, Charges, and Other Notices 359
  - [d] Duties of Depositary Banks 360
    - [i] Acceptance by Depositary Banks 361
    - [ii] Payment for Returned Items 361
    - [iii] Notice to Customer 362
  - [e] Warranties of Paying and Returning Banks 363
  - [f] Truncation 367
    - [i] Introduction 367
    - [ii] Check Truncation 367
    - [iii] Forward Collection Settlements Deemed Final; Impact on Article 4 367
  - [g] Indorsements 368
- [4] Conclusion: Impact of Regulation CC on UCC Articles 3 and 4 369
  - [a] The Mandatory Availability Rules and the Depositary Bank 370
  - [b] Impact of Regulation CC on the Midnight Deadline 371
  - [c] Provisional Settlement 372
  - [d] Direct Return of Dishonored Items 372
  - [e] Payable—Through Drafts 372
  - [f] Remote Data Processing Centers 372
  - [g] Truncation 373
  - [h] Indorsement 373
  - [i] Comparative Fault 373
  - [j] Variation by Agreement 373
  - [k] Standard of Care and Measure of Damages 374

Para.

¶8.04 Funds Availability and Federal Reserve Regulation CC—Continued
    [*l*] Good Faith 375
    [m] Implications for the Future 376

¶8.05 Summary and Conclusions 377

¶ 8.01 Article 4: Scope and Key Concepts

[1] Scope of Article 4 and Choice of Law

[a] Scope of Article 4

The Uniform Text of Uniform Commercial Code (UCC or the Code) Article 4 was revised in 1990 and the revised text had been adopted in all but two states as of June, 2001.[1] Article 4 governs the deposit, collection and payment or dishonor of items in the bank collection system. It specifies standards governing such transactions, and provides remedies when those standards are not met.

Generally, Article 4 will apply any time an "item" is deposited or sent for collection or presented for payment to or through a bank.[2] "Bank" is defined broadly at § 4–105(1) to include any "person" (*see* UCC § 1–201(30)) engaged in the banking business, including banks, savings and loan associations, credit unions, and trust companies.

Article 4 governs bank deposits, payments, and collections with respect to "items," a concept that extends beyond but includes Article 3 negotiable instruments.[3] For example, the term "item" included non-

---

¶ 8.01

1. The exceptions are New York and South Carolina. While these two states are important in terms of banking transactions, the 1990 revisions are evolutionary and essentially codify the better view or majority rules in the case law. Therefore, the revised text is useful even in those two states.

References herein to Article 3 or 4 sections, or the Comments thereto, refer to the 1990 revised uniform text. Sometimes these are also referred to as "current" or "revised" in order to distinguish them from the "old" Code. References to "old" Article 3 or 4 refer to the uniform text prior to the 1990 revisions. At the 2002 Annual Meeting of the National Conference of Commissioners on Uniform State Laws (NCCUSL) on July 26–August 2, 2002, further amendments to the uniform text of Articles 3 and 4 were approved. These will be referred to as the 2002 amendments.

2. *See* §§ 4–104 and 4–105 (definitions), and 4–201 (scope).

3. Old § 4–104(1)(g) defined "item" as any instrument for the payment of money whether or not negotiable. Tally v. American Sec. Bank, 35 U.C.C. Rep. Serv. 215 (D.D.C.1982) concluded that a savings account withdrawal slip was an "item" and, as a result, applied § 4–406, discussed *infra* in Chapter 9 at ¶ 9.03[4], against the account holder. *See also* Shaw v. Union Bank and Trust Co., 640 P.2d 953 (Okla.1981) (bank's refusal to honor a savings withdrawal order was wrongful dishonor of an item under old § 4–402), and discussion of the definition of "item" *infra* at ¶ 8.01[3][a].

Section 4–104(a)(9) contains a similar definition of "item," except that it is broadened somewhat beyond the concept of an "instrument," to include any "instrument or a promise or order to pay money handled by a bank for collection or payment." This confirms cases like *Tally* and *Shaw* that treated savings withdrawal orders as "items," and makes clear that Article 4 covers such promises and orders even if they do not qualify as an "instrument" under Article 3. "Instrument" is defined for purposes of Article 3 at old § 3–104, revised § 3–104(a), (b).

As a result, an investment security (such as a bond) being collected through the banking system is an "item" governed by

negotiable drafts, drafts drawn by the payee, drafts "payable through" a bank (*see* section 4–106 and Article 4 Part 5), and drafts or notes within the broad definition of "instrument" in revised UCC Article 9, § 9–102(a)(47). Thus, an instrument that is excluded from Article 3 because it is non-negotiable in form under § 3–104, and is therefore not an "instrument" for purposes of Article 3, could nonetheless be an "instrument" under Article 9 and an "item" under Article 4 and covered by the UCC to that extent. Article 4 is consistent with the stated purposes of the UCC, to provide simple, clear and modern rules to govern transactions and to facilitate the expansion of commercial practices through recognition of custom, usage, and private agreements.[4] This not mere boilerplate but a statement of philosophy that runs throughout the UCC. Thus, while of necessity providing specific rules governing such things as finality of payment,[5] Article 4 extensively defers to custom and usage in the banking industry, and private agreements such as the bank-customer agreement.[6] It is generally the purpose of Article 4 to encourage and recognize the development of commercial practices, *e.g.*, to accommodate emerging technologies, within the context of traditional UCC standards.

In the event of a conflict between the provisions of Article 4 and other UCC articles, the provisions of Article 4 are subject to those of Article 8 (Investment Securities), but the provisions of Article 4 control over Article 3 (Negotiable Instruments).[7] For example, in determining whether a bank gave value for the purpose of holder in due course status, in *Rockland Trust Co. v. South Shore National Bank*[8] the court

---

Article 4 even though it is not an "instrument" under Article 3 or Article 9. *See* § 3–102(a) and Comment 2 (for purposes of Article 3 "instrument" does not include investment securities as defined in UCC Article 8 at § 8–102); Comment 1 to § 3–104; revised § 9–102(a)(47) (Article 9 "instrument" does not include investment property); and *supra* this text ¶ 1.03[2][c].

Although the 1990 revisions broadened the definition of "item" generally, as noted above, the definition is also narrowed in a specific manner: "The term does not include a payment order governed by Article 4A or a credit or debit card slip." *See* § 4–104(a)(9). The exclusion of Article 4A payment orders is designed to establish a dividing line and avoid conflicts between Articles 4 and 4A. The exclusion of debit and credit card slips is apparently designed to avoid problems that might arise from efforts to apply Article 4 provisions such as the stop payment rules in the context of credit and debit card transactions.

An automated teller machine (ATM) transaction does not involve an "item" and is not covered by Article 4. Heritage Bank v. Lovett, 613 N.W.2d 652 (Iowa 2000). An "IOU" is a mere acknowledgement of a debt and is not an an instrument under Article 3 or an item under Article 4. *See supra* this text ¶ 2.02[3][a][1]. However, gambling "markers" have been held to be checks under Article 3 for purposes of "bad check" laws. Nguyen v. The State of Nevada, 116 Nev. 1171, 14 P.3d 515 (2000).

4. UCC § 1–102(2). In effectuating these purposes the UCC is to be liberally, not strictly, construed. UCC § 1–102(1).

5. *See* §§ 4–215, 4–301, and 4–302; *infra* this text ¶ 8.02.

6. *See, e.g.*, §§ 3–103 (ordinary care), 4–103 (variation by agreement), 4–104(a)(3) ("Banking day"), 4–108 (time of receipt), 4–109 (delays), 4–110 (electronic presentments), 4–202 (collecting bank responsibilities), among many other examples. *Cf.* §§ 4–215, 4–301, and 4–302 (finality of payments), providing less flexibility. *See infra* ¶ 8.02 for discussion of final payment.

7. *See* § 4–102(a). The primary difference between Article 4 and Article 8 concerns transfer rules that might conflict if a bank handled bonds for collection. *See* Comment 1 to § 4–102.

8. 366 Mass. 74, 314 N.E.2d 438 (Mass. 1974).

looked primarily to old § 4–208(1) rather than to old § 3–303.⁹ In *Bowling Green, Inc. v. State Street Bank and Trust Co.*,¹⁰ the court determined that the requirement of an indorsement for holder status under old § 3–202(1) was superceded by old § 4–205, which allows a bank in the collection process to supply the indorsement of its customer necessary for title. Article 4 now reaffirms this position at § 4–205(a) and, in order to facilitate automatic processing of items, carries it a step further by providing that the depositary bank becomes a holder of an item it receives for collection if its customer was a holder, with or without an indorsement.¹¹

There do not appear to be any recognizable areas of conflict between Article 4 and Articles 5 or 7. Finally, problems of conflicts between Article 4 and Article 9 on security interests is resolved by (§ 4–210(c)), governing the creation and priority of a bank's security interest in the collection and deposit of items.¹²

---

9. The rules on taking for value for purposes of holder in due course status appear at § 3–303 in both versions, but old § 4–208 is now § 4–210. Among other things, the revisions to this provision specify that only a collecting bank can have an Article 4 security interest in an item. *See* § 4–210(a). Of course any bank or other secured party may have a security interest in any item as proceeds of an Article 9 security interest, pursuant to §§ 9–102(a)(64), 9–203(f), 9–315, and various other provisions of revised Article 9 and other law. If the proceeds item is deposited into a bank account, the Article 9 secured party may follow that deposit and claim a security interest in the bank account as proceeds. Such a security interest may represent a priority claim to the item or deposit account, quite aside from the rules of Article 4. *See, e.g.*, Bowling Green, Inc. v. State Street Bank and Trust Co., 425 F.2d 81 (1st Cir.1970); Smith v. Mark Twain Nat'l Bank, 805 F.2d 278 (8th Cir.1986); Alvin C. Harrell, Security Interests in Deposit Accounts: A Unique Relationship Between the UCC and Other Law, 23 U.C.C. L.J. 153, 154–55, 163–65 (1990).

The Uniform Text of Article 9 was revised in 1998 (subject to some subsequent technical amendments) with a uniform effective date of July 1, 2001. All 50 states enacted the revisions before July 1, 2001, though a few adopted a slightly delayed effective date. For more information, *see* the NCCUSL website, http://www.ccusl.org/nccusl/default.asp. Revised Article 9 for the first time allows a direct security interest in deposit accounts, except in a consumer transaction. *See* revised § 9–109(d)(13); §§ 9–104, 9–203(b)(3)(D), 9–304, 9–312, 9–314, and 9–327; Ben Carpenter, Security Interests in Deposit Accounts and Certificates of Deposit Under UCC Article 9, 55 CONSUMER FIN. L.Q. REP. 123 (2001); *infra* this text ¶ 9.06. *Cf.* old § 9–104(*l*) (no direct Article 9 security interest in deposit accounts); old §§ 9–203(1)(a), 9–305, 9–308, 9–309; and revised §§ 9–203(b)(3), 9–313, 9–330, 9–331, 9–332 (possessory security interests in instruments and chattel paper and claims of transferees of money under Article 9).

10. 425 F.2d 81 (1st Cir.1970). *See also* Perini Corp. v. First Nat'l Bank of Habersham County, 553 F.2d 398 (5th Cir.1977).

11. *See* revised § 4–205(1) (also providing that such a bank may be a holder in due course if it meets the other requirements of § 3–302). *Cf.* old § 4–205(1) (which merely authorized the depositary bank to supply a missing endorsement and did not address the holder in due course issue). In this respect the revisions substantively reject the rationale of cases like United Overseas Bank v. Veneers, Inc., 375 F.Supp. 596 (D.Md.1973). The comment to revised § 4–205 cites Marine Midland Bank, N.A. v. Price, Miller, Evans & Flowers, 85 A.D.2d 903, 446 N.Y.S.2d 797 (N.Y. App. Div. 4th Dept. 1981), *rev'd*, 57 N.Y.2d 220, 455 N.Y.S.2d 565, 441 N.E.2d 1083 (N.Y. 1982), as evidence of the divergent views resolved by the revision to § 4–205. *See also* discussion of indorsements *infra* at ¶ 8.04[3][g].

12. *See supra* note 4 and, *e.g.*, revised § 4–102, Comment 1; Anderson on the Uniform Commercial Code § 4–102:4 (1971); UCC §§ 9–203(1), 9–312(1); Harrell, Security Interests in Deposit Accounts: A Unique Relationship Between the UCC and Other Law, *supra* note 9. Regarding conflicts with the Bankruptcy Code, *see, e.g.*, F. Miller and A. Harrell, The ABCs of the UCC Related Insolvency Law (Am. Bar Assoc. 2002).

Article 4 governs issues concerning the deposit, collection, and payment of items via the banking system. Even so, it does not govern or control all such matters. For example, in one case a cutting torch was used to rob a bank's night depository. A customer whose deposit was stolen sued the bank. As a defense, the bank invoked a clause in the deposit contract, providing that the risk was on the customer until the bank began to process the deposit. Because the customer's deposit had not been processed, the court held that Article 4 did not apply and contract law controlled. Under the terms of the deposit contract, the bank won.[13] As noted again *infra* at ¶ 8.01[2], Article 4 is frequently subject to modification by agreement of the parties, clearing-house rules, or federal law.

Article 4 does not purport to define or regulate every aspect of the bank-customer relation, or to resolve every related consumer protection issue.[14] Article 4 is supplemented by state and federal consumer protection law, and Article 4 must be read in conjunction with other applicable laws and regulations.[15] For example, the official comment to § 4–101 suggests that consumers may be unaware that § 4–401(c) permits immediate payment of a postdated check unless the drawer gives certain notification to the payor bank.[16] As a result it is possible that an unscrupulous person could induce a consumer to issue a postdated check with the mistaken belief that this would protect the consumer from payment by the payor bank before the check date.[17] Absent the required notice from the customer[18] the payor bank is authorized to pay such an item upon presentment, at any time, and Article 4 does not address related issues pertaining to the potential for fraud claims between the drawer and payee of the item, leaving such to other law.

[b] Choice of Law

Section 4–102(b) states the basic choice of law rule for Article 4:

The liability of a bank for action or non-action with respect to an item handled by it for purposes of presentment, payment or collection is governed by the law of the place where the bank is located. In the case of action of non-action by or at a branch or separate office

---

13. Valley Nat'l Bank of Arizona v. Tang, 18 Ariz.App. 40, 499 P.2d 991 (1972). *See also* § 4–103; and Employers Ins. of Wausau v. Chemical Bank, 117 Misc.2d 601, 459 N.Y.S.2d 238 (Civ. Ct. 1983). In Orrico v. Beverly Bank, 109 Ill.App.3d 102, 64 Ill. Dec. 701, 440 N.E.2d 253 (Ill.App.1982), a bank disregarded a court order appointing a conservator and permitted a mentally incompetent depositor to withdraw a large sum in cash.

14. *See* Comment 3 to § 4–101, and *infra* ¶ 9.03[1], [2], ¶ 9.03 [7], and ¶ 9.05.

15. *Id.* Perhaps the most important example is Federal Reserve Regulation CC, discussed *infra* at ¶ 8.04. *See also* Comment 1 to § 4–102, noting that Regulation CC effectively supercedes Article 4 for some purposes by converting provisional settlements between collecting banks into final settlement (Regulation CC, 12 CFR § 229.36(d)), and by permitting extension of the midnight deadline in limited circumstances (Regulation CC, 12 CFR § 229.30(c)).

16. *See* Comment 3 to § 4–101, § 4–401(c), and discussion *infra* at ¶ 9.02[4].

17. *See* Comment 3 to § 4–101. *Cf.* 15 U.S.C. § 1692f(4) (unfair practice under Fair Debt Collection Practices Act).

18. *See* § 4–401(c) and *infra* ¶ 9.02[4].

of a bank, its liability is governed by the law of the place where the branch or separate office is located.[19]

Comment 2 to § 4–102 notes three "vexatious" conflicts of laws issues that are addressed and resolved by this section: the need to have a single choice of state law for the collection and payment activities of a given bank (rather than, for example, applying the laws of the places where different checks were issued or indorsed);[20] the adoption of essentially a tort theory for choice of law, consistent with the duty of a collecting bank to use ordinary care;[21] and the extension of this choice of law rule to all aspects of the collection process from deposit through forwarding, presentment, payment and remittance or credit of proceeds.[22] In essence any action or non-action of a collecting bank with regard to the handling of an item for deposit, collection, or payment will be governed by the law of the state where the bank or branch handling the item is located.[23] The Code does, however, recognize the ability of the parties to make a contractual choice of law, within certain limitations.[24]

[2] Modification by Agreement and Preemption by Federal Rule

The effect of the provisions of Article 4 may be varied by agreement between or among the parties, except that no agreement can be used to avoid a bank's duties of good faith and due care.[25] For example, in *David*

---

19. *See* § 4–102(b). *Cf.* revised UCC Article 9 § 9–304 (location of bank and choice of law governing security interests in deposit accounts).

20. Comment 2a to § 4–102.

21. *See* Comment 2b to § 4–102. Generally the Article 4 rights and obligations of collecting banks are stated in terms of the duties of agency, good faith and ordinary care. *See, e.g.*, §§ 4–103(a)-(e), 4–201, 4–202(a), 4–207(c), 4–208(a); *infra* ¶ 8.03 and 8.04[4][d]; and *infra* ¶ 9.03[7]. In contrast, the rules in revised Article 9 governing security interests in deposit accounts are largely contractual in nature, and therefore extensively defer to choice of law provisions in the deposit contract or other agreements of the parties. *See* revised § 9–304; *infra* ¶ 9.06.

22. *See* Comment 2c to § 4–102, noting that this rejects the conflicts rules of older cases, such as Weissman v. Banque De Bruxelles, 254 N.Y. 488, 173 N.E. 835 (1930), and St. Nicholas Bank of New York v. State Nat'l Bank, 128 N.Y. 26, 27 N.E. 849 (1891). Regarding security interests in deposit accounts, *see supra* notes 9, 12, 19 and 21; *infra* ¶ 9.06.

23. Comment 2c to § 4–102; First National Bank of Lewisville, Ark. v. First National Bank of Clinton, Ky., 258 F.3d 727 (8th Cir.2001) (dishonor of cashier's check payable to an out-of-state payee did not subject the issuing bank to jurisdiction in the payee's state).

24. *See* Comment 2d to § 4–102, referring to UCC § 1–105 and § 4–103(a); *In re Kemper* (Anderson v. Chainani), 263 B.R. 773 (Bankr.E.D.Tex.2001) (promissory note); Sun Forest Corp. v. Shvili, 152 F.Supp.2d 367 (S.D.N.Y.2001) (loan transaction—choice of New York law was reasonable where loan was closed and payments were to be received there). *See also* Evans v. Harry Robinson Pontiac-Buick, Inc., 336 Ark. 155, 983 S.W.2d 946 (1999); Alvin C. Harrell, Case Note: Evans v. Harry Robinson Pontiac-Buick and UCC Choice of Law in Consumer Sales Transactions, 53 CONSUMER FIN.L. Q.REP. 198 (1999); *infra* ¶ 8.01[2], ¶ 8.04[4][d], ¶ 9.03[3], and ¶ 9.05. In addition, law outside the Code, such as a consumer protection statute, may impose limitations. For example, Unif. Cons. Credit Code § 1.201(8) (1974). *See also supra* notes 16–18; *infra* ¶ 8.01[2]. Revisions to the uniform text of UCC Article 1, adopted by NCCUSL in 2002, may affect a choice of law analysis conducted under the new Article 1. *See* revised § 1–301 (2002 uniform text).

25. *See* § 4–103(a). *See generally* Arrow Industries, Inc. v. Zions First National Bank, 767 P.2d 935, 937 (Utah 1988) (bank

Graubart, Inc. v. Bank Leumi Trust Co.,[26] the court concluded that the bank's deadline to decide to pay or dishonor an item was governed by an "advice to customer" slip, which constituted a collection agreement between the parties, and which gave the bank additional time beyond its midnight deadline.[27] Furthermore, the court found that the Code concept of "agreement" is broad enough to encompass custom and usage in the industry,[28] and that the bank's adherence to standards created by custom, usage, and the contract precluded liability for violation of the midnight deadline under Article 4. In *Sun River Cattle Co. v. Miners Bank of Montana*,[29] however, the court reached a different result on the basis that the bank had failed to establish the existence of an agreement to supercede the normal midnight deadline. It was not enough to demonstrate a past practice of missing the deadline and an understanding by a bank officer that the items were to be held for collection. The Comment to § 4–103 indicates subsequent support for the broad interpretation of the *Bank Leumi* case.[30]

Within limits, the effect of Article 4 also may be varied by local clearing house rules or Federal Reserve System operating circulars and regulations.[31] Generally such rules and regulations impose additional

---

has a duty to act in good faith and exercise ordinary care); *infra* ¶ 8.04[4][d] and ¶ 9.03[3], and ¶ 9.04[5]. While a bank must follow the instructions that accompany a collection item, it is not bound by instructions written on the "memorandum" portion of the face of the check. This is not a part of the contract and does not bind the bank or the parties to the instrument. See Woods v. Bank of New York, 806 F.2d 368 (2d Cir.1986). *See also infra* ¶ 8.04[3][g] (indorsements); § 3–206 (restrictive indorsements); and § 4–203 ("effect of instructions").

26. 48 N.Y.2d 554, 423 N.Y.S.2d 899, 399 N.E.2d 930 (N.Y.App.1979). *Bank Leumi* is also discussed *infra* at notes 131, 115, and 134. *See also* SOS Oil Corp. v. Norstar Bank of Long Island, 76 N.Y.2d 561, 561 N.Y.S.2d 887, 563 N.E.2d 258 (N.Y. 1990).

27. *Bank Leumi*, 399 N.E. 2d at 934–36. *See* discussion beginning *infra* at note 25. *See also* Wolverton Farmers Elevator v. First American Bank of Rugby, 851 F.2d 223 (8th Cir.1988) (ambiguous "advice form" was sufficient to excuse the midnight deadline). As discussed *infra* this section, this rationale is probably limited to individual items and could not be used to circumvent the midnight deadline in general. *See also infra* ¶ 8.04[4][d] and ¶ 9.03[3]

28. *Id.* at 934, *citing* UCC §§ 1–201(3), 1–205. This is also supported, *e.g.*, by §§ 3–103(a)(7), and 4–103(c).

29. 164 Mont. 237, 521 P.2d 679 (Mont. 1974). This matter also is discussed *supra* in Chapter 1 at ¶ 1.04[4]. *See also* Iverson v. First Bank of Billings, 219 Mont. 283, 712 P.2d 1285 (Mont. 1985).

30. "Legends on deposit tickets, collection letters and acknowledgements of items, coupled with action by the affected party constituting acceptance, adoption, ratification, estoppel or the like, are agreements if they meet the tests of the definition of 'agreement.'" § 4–103, Comment 2 (citing § 1–201(3) and various cases). Time periods for taking action, such as those for reporting unauthorized items under § 4–406, generally are subject to variation by agreement in the deposit contract or by other reasonable means, so long as there is no effort to disclaim the bank's duties of good faith or ordinary care. National Title Insurance Corporation Agency v. First Union National Bank, 263 Va. 355, 559 S.E.2d 668 (2002); Canfield v. Banc One, Texas, N.A., 51 S.W.3d 828 (Tex.App.2001) *But see infra* this text and notes 44–46.

31. *See* § 4–103(b); Federal Reserve Regulation J, 12 CFR §§ 210.3(a), (b), 210.5(a). *See also, e.g.*, West Side Bank v. Marine Nat'l Exch. Bank, 37 Wis.2d 661, 155 N.W.2d 587 (Wis. 1968). For example, the Federal Reserve Banks formerly limited their liability for failure to use ordinary care in handling an item to the "immediate sender." *See, e.g.*, First National Bank of Gatlinburg v. RepublicBank Dallas, 676 F.Supp. 128 (N.D.Tex.1987), *construing* 12 CFR § 210.6(a)(1). Section 210.6(a)(1) was revised in 1988 to extend this liability to "the owner, to the sender, to a prior collecting bank, or to the deposit bank's customer

requirements but do not excuse liability under the requirements of Article 4. However, the relationship between Article 4 and these competing rules and regulations is often unclear. For example, any theory based on contract requires privity and therefore can be enforced only against parties to the contract. In addition, courts may have some hesitancy about interpreting contract language to overturn the clear meaning of a statute that is subject to public reliance. For example, in a 1976 Oklahoma case a payor bank was excused from complying with certain requirements for dishonor under a Federal Reserve Bank Operating Letter.[32] In *Colorado National Bank v. First National Bank & Trust Co.*,[33] however, a federal district court in Michigan refused to interpret a similar operating circular "as altering the acts or action which constitute final payment under the UCC in the absence of language clearly indicating such an intent on the part of the Federal Reserve."[34] There was little question that the operating circular could have governed the transaction, as old § 4–103(2) (now § 4–103(b)) provided that such rules "have the effect of agreements ... whether or not specifically assented to...."[35] But the *Colorado National Bank* court concluded that the circular did not directly address the issue of final payment, and found no evidence that the Federal Reserve intended to alter the UCC rule. The Comment to Article 4 supports the view that all parties are bound by Federal Reserve operating circulars and similar agreements, "on the principle that collecting banks acting as agents have authority to make binding agreements with respect to items being handled.[36] But, under § 4–201, collecting banks are agents only of the owner of the item, not prior parties to the instrument who may be liable on and have rights relating to the instrument. Absent separate assent such parties would not be bound the deposit agreement, operating circulars or clearing-house

with respect to a check...." See 12 CFR § 210.6(a)(1) (1991); 53 Fed. Reg. 21984 (June 13, 1988). *See also infra* ¶ 9.03[7]. *See* discussion below, this text at notes 37–43, regarding the impact of Federal Reserve Regulation CC.

32. Security Bank & Trust Co. v. Federal Nat'l Bank & Trust of Shawnee, 554 P.2d 119 (Okla. App. 1976). *See also* Wolverton Farmers Elevator v. First American Bank of Rugby, 851 F.2d 223 (8th Cir.1988); Lockhart Sav. & Loan Ass'n. v. RepublicBank Austin, 720 S.W.2d 193 (Tex. Ct. App. 1986) (clearinghouse rule can alter the midnight deadline). The court also reached this result in Wells Fargo Bank v. Hartford National Bank & Trust Co., 484 F.Supp. 817 (D.Conn.1980), but it is dubious whether the court interpreted the intent of the circular correctly. This is the point of the next case discussed in the text.

33. 459 F.Supp. 1366 (W.D.Mich.1978). *See also* Reynolds–Wilson Lumber Co. v. Peoples Nat'l Bank, 699 P.2d 146, 154 (Okla.1985).

34. *Id*. at 1372. *Accord*: Northwestern Nat'l Ins. Co. v. Midland Nat'l Bank, 96 Wis.2d 155, 292 N.W.2d 591 (Wis. 1980).

35. *See also* discussion *infra* at ¶ 9.03[3] on "Modification by Agreement," and *infra* ¶ 9.03[7] (effect on prior parties).

36. § 4–103, and Comment 2. *See generally infra* ¶ 9.03[7]. However, that authority does not absolve the bank of liability for making agreements prejudicial to the rights of other parties. *See also* § 4–201(a) (collecting bank is agent or sub-agent of the owner of the item). "This conclusion was assumed but was not flatly decided in Federal Reserve Bank of Richmond v. Malloy, 264 U.S. 160, 44 S.Ct. 296, 68 L.Ed. 617, ... 31 A.L.R. 1261 (1924)." § 4–103, Comment 3. Regarding the effect of Federal Reserve Operating Circulars, *see generally* Sharon A. Sweeney and Jane Anne Schmoker, Federal Reserve Bank and the Payment System: Regulation J, Regulation CC, Operating Circulars, and Other Deposit Account Issues, 51 Consumer Fin. L.Q. Rep. 204 (1997).

agreements. This may have an effect on banks' ability to use check truncation agreements to authorize destruction of checks and substitute electronic processing.

Beyond their effect as agreements, certain regulations and operating circulars can directly preempt state law. Perhaps the most significant example of preemption is Federal Reserve Regulation CC, which implements the federal Expedited Funds Availability Act.[37] Regulation CC preempts any inconsistent UCC provision, "but only to the extent of the inconsistency."[38] Determining the extent and effects of such preemption remains a challenging task, due to the imprecise relationship between the UCC and Regulation CC.[39] This chapter discusses the impact of Regulation CC in the context of the Article 4 provisions governing provisional and final payment (at ¶ 8.02 and ¶ 8.03) and also describes Regulation CC separately (at ¶ 8.04). These issues are also noted extensively in the Federal Reserve Commentary to Regulation CC and in the Official Comments to Article 4. In addition, Federal Reserve Regulation J[40] governs the collection of checks and other items through the Federal Reserve System.[41] For a bank that has entered into a collection agreement with a Federal Reserve Bank to facilitate processing and collection of such items, Regulation J may provide additional requirements or even supercede the provisions of Article 4.[42] Those provisions of Regulation J which are by their own terms applicable upon presentment to or by a Federal Reserve Bank may not be applicable to the collection of items

---

37. 42 U.S.C. §§ 4001 et seq.; 12 CFR §§ 229.1–229.42. See generally further discussion infra ¶ 8.04.

38. 12 CFR § 229.41. See also infra ¶ 8.04[4]; Oak Brook Bank v. Northern Trust Co., 256 F.3d 638 (7th Cir.2001) (relation of Regulation CC and Article 4; dishonor was timely under Article 4 due to extended operating hours of Federal Reserve Bank.).

39. See, e.g., § 4–102, Comment 1. Efforts to reconcile these two important laws have come to naught. See, e.g., Alvin C. Harrell, UCC Article 4 and Regulation CC: Can They Ever Be Reconciled?, 54 CONSUMER FIN. L.Q. REP. 236 (2000); Alvin C. Harrell, NCCUSL Article 3, 4, and 4A Drafting Committee Highlights Current Payment System and Negotiable Instrument Issues, 54 CONSUMER FIN. L.Q. REP. 351 (2000); infra ¶ 9.03[7].

40. 12 CFR pt. 210.

41. 12 CFR § 210.1. For a discussion of the part played by the Federal Reserve System in the payments system and related developments, see the Annual Surveys of the Law of Commercial Paper, Bank Deposits and Collections, and Commercial Electronic Fund Transfers, in *The Business Lawyer* starting at 39 BUS. LAW. 1333 (1984).

Note that Regulation J only applies where the specific item involved is being collected through a Federal Reserve Bank. See 12 CFR § 210.3. Courts have not always recognized this limitation. See, e.g., Community Bank v. Federal Reserve Bank of San Francisco, 500 F.2d 282 (9th Cir.1974), modified, 525 F.2d 690 (1975), cert. denied, 419 U.S. 1089, 95 S.Ct. 680, 42 L.Ed.2d 681 (1974). The same limitation does not apply to Regulation CC, which governs all checks being collected or returned between banks through the banking system. See 12 CFR § 229.1(b)(3). However, note that Regulation CC is limited to the collection and return of checks between banks, and does not apply to checks outside the banking system or to other types of items being handled by banks. Id.

42. See, e.g., Community Bank v. Federal Reserve Bank of San Francisco, 500 F.2d 282 (9th Cir.1974), cert. denied, 419 U.S. 1089, 95 S.Ct. 680, 42 L.Ed.2d 681; Colonial Cadillac, Inc. v. Shawmut Merchants Bank, N.A., 488 F.Supp. 283 (D.Mass.1980); Universal C.I.T. Credit Corp. v. Farmers Bank of Portageville, 358 F.Supp. 317 (E.D.Mo. 1973). However, the previous Regulation J return item requirements at § 210.12(a) have been deleted in favor of a reference to the Regulation CC requirements. See 12 CFR § 210.12(a), and infra ¶ 8.04[3].

transferred directly between private banks or to other issues and transactions not involving the Federal Reserve. As noted, however, this limitation has not always been recognized by the courts.[43]

There are limits to a bank's or a system's ability to modify the Article 4 duties. Section 4–103(a) precludes any disclaimer of a "bank's responsibility for its own lack of good faith or failure to exercise ordinary care," and prohibits any limitation on the measure of damages for failure to meet these standards. The definition of "ordinary care" at § 3–103(a)(7) (defined to include "observance of reasonable commercial standards, prevailing in the area in which that person is located") makes it more important than ever to distinguish between that duty (which cannot be waived, under § 4–103(a)) and other statutory duties, which generally are subject to modification by agreement under § 4–103(a). It is also important to distinguish between the duty of "good faith" (defined at § 3–103(a)(4) to include "observance of reasonable commercial standards of fair dealing") and other statutory duties in Article 4, since under § 4–103(a) the latter can be waived but the former is not subject to modification by agreement.

For example, in *Sunshine v. Bankers Trust Co.*,[44] a payor bank attempted to revoke a settlement after it negligently exceeded its midnight deadline. After unsuccessfully attempting to apply old § 4–212 (that section—now § 4–214—is limited to collecting banks and does not apply to payor banks), the bank argued that the deposit contract with its customer modified the provisions of Article 4. Specifically, the bank contended that the provisions of the deposit contract extended the bank's midnight deadline and permitted revocation of the settlement in that case. The court, however, stated flatly that: "To the extent that either of the agreements attempts to extend the period during which the Bank can charge back a depositor's account in a situation such as the one before us now, they are invalid."[45] Given the facts in the case, the court's conclusion arguably can be justified under old § 4–103(1) (now § 4–103(a)) as invalidating a bank's efforts to disclaim responsibility for its own bad faith or failure to exercise ordinary care. The problem with this rationalization is that the payor bank's liability for missing the midnight deadline is statutory (*see* § 4–302) and is not dependent on whether good faith or ordinary care was exercised. Therefore, a bank's effort to avoid an Article 4 time period by contract should not be prohibited by § 4–103(a), and should be a proper subject for agreement between the parties.[46]

---

43. *See supra* note 41, and Kane v. American Nat'l Bank & Trust Co., 21 Ill. App.3d 1046, 316 N.E.2d 177 (Ill.App.1974).

44. 34 N.Y.2d 404, 358 N.Y.S.2d 113, 314 N.E.2d 860 (N.Y.App.1974). These duties are discussed further, *infra* at ¶ 8.02, ¶ 8.03, ¶ 8.04[4][d], ¶ 9.03[1], [2], and ¶ 9.03[4][c].

45. *Id.* at 863.

46. Nonetheless, there may be good faith and public policy implications if a bank seeks to arbitrarily extend a commonly relied-on statutory rule such as the Article 4 midnight deadline, *e.g.*, on a blanket basis through an adhesion contract. Agreements that are enforceable generally under contract law may be subject to greater scrutiny if inserted quietly in a form contract so as to constitute an unfair surprise. *See, e.g.*, Green Tree Financial Corp. v. Randolph,

[3] Definitions and Important Concepts

Because Article 4 is a statute dealing with specialized banking matters, there are several banking terms and concepts that are consistently employed. One purpose of Article 4 is to codify these concepts, and the drafters of the Code incorporated some of the most common ones in Article 4 as definitions. These include:

> **[a] Item:** Under § 4–104(a)(9), "item" is defined as "an instrument or a promise or order to pay money handled by a bank for collection or payment," except an Article 4A payment order or a credit or debit card slip.[47]

---

531 U.S. 79, 121 S.Ct. 513, 148 L.Ed.2d 373 (2000) (arbitration clause); Badie v. Bank of America, 67 Cal.App.4th 779, 79 Cal. Rptr.2d 273 (1998) (arbitration clause). *Green Tree* generally upheld the use of arbitration clauses in consumer contracts, based on the strong federal policy evidenced in the Federal Arbitration Act, 9 U.S.C § 2. *Badie* denied enforceability of an arbitration clause, on grounds that a "change of terms" notice in a "statement stuffer" was not a sufficient consensual basis to modify a fundamental contract term. For further discussion of these issues, *see* A. Daniel Woska, Arbitration Clauses in Consumer Retail Installment Sales Contracts After the Green Tree Financial v. Randolph Decision, 55 Consumer Fin. L.Q. Rep. 107 (2001). See *also* David Graubart, Inc. v. Bank Leumi Trust Co., 48 N.Y.2d 554, 423 N.Y.S.2d 899, 399 N.E.2d 930 (N.Y.App.1979), discussed *supra* at note 26 and *infra* this text starting at note 161. *See also* the cases collected at Bell, The Payor Bank and Its Customer: An Analysis of Recent Cases, 6 U. Tol. L. Rev. 110 (1974); *supra* note 30. *But see infra* ¶ 9.03, ¶ 9.05.

A related issue is whether otherwise applicable common law duties are displaced by specific UCC provisions. Under UCC § 1–103, common law principles supplement the UCC unless displaced by a particular provision. *See, e.g.,* Cassello v. Allegiant Bank and Royal Bank of Missouri, 288 F.3d 339 (8th Cir.2002) (no displacement of negligence claim); Heche v. Chase Manhattan Bank, 45 UCC Rep.Serv.2d 549 (Conn. Sup.Ct.2001) (UCC § 3–420 does not displace common law negligence claim); White Sands Forest Products, Inc. v. First National Bank of Alamogordo, 132 N.M. 453, 50 P.3d 202 (N.M.App.2002) (contra); Mutual Service Cas. Co. v. Elizabeth State Bank, 265 F.3d 601 (7th Cir.2001) (bank had common law duty to guard against misapplication of funds); Lee Newman, M.D., Inc. v. Wells Fargo Bank, 87 Cal.App.4th 78, 104 Cal. Rptr.2d 310, 43 UCC Rep.Serv.2d 912 (2001) (§ 3–405 precludes common law negligence claim); Moody Nat. Bank v. Texas City Development, Ltd. Co., 46 S.W.3d 373 (Tex.Ct.App.2001) (loss allocation rules of Article 4A supercede common law negligence claim). *See also infra* ¶ 8.02[4].

47. *See* § 4–104(a)(9). Under old § 4–104(1)(g), "item" was defined as any instrument for the payment of money (including both negotiable and non-negotiable instruments but not money), deposited and/or being collected through the banking system. As noted *supra* at note 3, this definition always has been broader than the definition of negotiable instrument in Article 3. As a result, many nonnegotiable orders and promises to pay are "items" governed by Article 4 although they are excluded from Article 3. *Cf.* § 3–104 *and see* discussion *supra* Chapter 2. The cases reflect this broad definition, holding for example that a savings withdrawal slip is an "item" subject to Article 4. *See* First National Bank of Nocona v. Duncan Savings & Loan Association, 656 F.Supp. 358 (W.D.Okla.1987), *aff'd,* 957 F.2d 775 (10th Cir.1992); Tally v. American Sec. Bank, 35 U.C.C. Rep. Serv. 215 (D.D.C.1982); Shaw v. Union Bank and Trust Co., 640 P.2d 953 (Okla.1981). Article 4 embraces this broad view, with the specific exception of Article 4A payment orders and debit/credit card slips.

The comment to Article 4 notes that bonds and "like instruments constituting investment securities under Article 8 may also be handled by banks for collection purposes." In that case UCC Articles 4 and 8 may both apply, but Article 8 will control in the case of a conflict. *See* § 4–102, Comment 1. *See also supra* ¶ 8.01[1]; *supra* note 3; revised Article 9 § 9–102(a)(47) (broad definition of "Instrument" to include nonnegotiable instruments).

An ATM transaction does not involve an "item." Heritage Bank v. Lovett, 613 N.W.2d 652 (Iowa 2000). *See also supra* this

[b] Bank: "[A] person engaged in the business of banking, including a savings bank, savings and loan association, credit union, or trust company."[48]

[c] Depositary Bank: The "first bank to take an item even though it is also the payor bank, unless the item is presented for immediate payment over the counter."[49]

[d] Payor Bank: The drawee (the bank on which a draft is drawn).[50]

[e] Intermediary Bank: A bank that transfers the item between the depositary and payor banks.[51]

[f] Collecting Bank: Any bank other than the payor bank.[52]

---

chapter note 3, and *supra* Ch. 2 ¶ 202[3][a][1].

48. § 4–105(1). Essentially the same definition appears in revised Article 9 at § 9–102(a)(8). This definition resolves uncertainties regarding the status of savings institutions, credit unions, and other bank-like organizations. Note that the definition is sufficiently broad ("any person engaged in the business of banking") to possibly include a brokerage or other institution that offers checking accounts or other banking services for perhaps some purposes. *Cf.* Asian International, Ltd. v. Merrill Lynch, Pierce, Fenner and Smith, Inc., 435 So.2d 1058 (La.Ct.App.1983) (Merrill Lynch treated as a "bank" for indorsement purposes under § 4–205(1)); Merrill Lynch, Pierce, Fenner & Smith, Inc. v. Van Kylen, 98 B.R. 455 (Bankr.W.D.Wis.1989) (Merrill Lynch "Cash Management Account" not a "deposit account" under old § 9–105(1)(e)). *See* discussion in Mendelson, Investment Securities Review, 45 Bus. Law. 2461, 2470–2472 (1990). *Cf.* The definition of "Deposit account" at revised Article 9 § 9–102(a)(29) ("a demand, time, savings, pass book, or similar account maintained with a bank. The term does not include investment property or accounts evidenced by an instrument."). *See generally infra* ¶ 9.05, ¶ 9.06.

49. § 4–105(2); old § 4–105(a) was similar but did not include the final phrase excluding payment over the counter.

50. § 4–105(3). Old § 4–105(b) defined payor bank as the "bank by which an item is payable as drawn or accepted." The 1990 revision clarified this by relating it to the term "drawee." *See also* § 4–105, Comment 4. "Drawee" is defined at § 4–104(a)(8) as "a person ordered in a draft to make payment." *See also* § 4–104(c) (incorporating the Article 3 definition of "order" at § 3–103).

51. § 4–105(4). "The term 'intermediary bank' includes the last bank in the collection process if the drawee is not a bank." § 4–105, Comment 5. *See also* § 4–105(6) (presenting bank).

52. § 4–105(5). If there is an ambiguity as to whether the bank named on a draft is a collecting bank (*e.g.,* directed to make presentment to a nonbank drawer), or a drawee (payor bank), the bank is deemed a collecting bank. *See* § 4–106(d). Among other things, the distinction between payor and collecting banks is important because a payor bank is accountable for the amount of an item not returned within its midnight deadline (§ 4–302), while a collecting bank is obligated only to exercise ordinary care (§ 4–202) and upon presentment to a nonbank drawee the latter has 30 days to pay or dishonor. *See* §§ 3–503(d)(ii), 4–202, and 4–214. Moreover, absent bad faith the collecting bank is liable only for actual damages caused by a failure to exercise ordinary care, up to the amount of the item. *See also* § 4–103(e); *cf.* § 4–302 (payor bank). *See infra* ¶ 8.02 [3], [4], and [7]; ¶ 8.03.

The distinctions are illustrated by State Bank & Trust, N.A. v. First State Bank of Texas, 242 F.3d 390, 43 UCC Rep. Serv.2d 1206 (10th Cir.2000) (unpublished). Documentary drafts totaling $87,750 were deposited by the payee in its account at Bank of Texas. Bank of Texas treated the drafts as cash items and gave its depositor immediate credit, which was then withdrawn. The drafts were sent to State Bank (the bank named on the face of the drafts), which acted as a collecting bank and made presentment to its customer as a nonbank drawee. This nonbank drawee dishonored the drafts, and State Bank returned them unpaid to Bank of Texas. If State Bank was a payor bank, this return would be untimely for purposes of dishonor under § 4–301, and State Bank would be accountable for the amount of the item under § 4–302. But if State Bank was a collecting bank, it met

Notice that this term includes both depositary and intermediary banks. This is important for purposes of §§ 4–202 and 4–214, governing the bank's right of charge-back, among other provisions.

[g] Customer: Any person having an account with a bank or for whom a bank has agreed to collect items. The term includes a bank carrying an account with another bank.[53]

[h] Agency: The depositary bank and all collecting banks, prior to final settlement, are agents or subagents of the owner of the item. The payor bank is an agent of the drawer.[54]

---

its duty of ordinary care under §§ 4–202 and 4–214, and the nonbank drawee's notice of dishonor was timely under § 3–503(c). Thus, the crucial question was whether State Bank was acting as a payor or collecting bank.

The *State Bank* court noted that the 1990 revisions to the uniform text of Article 3 reversed the rule of Reynolds–Wilson Lumber Co. v. Peoples National Bank, 699 P.2d 146 (Okla.1985) by creating a presumption of collecting bank status where the face of the item is ambiguous. 43 UCC Rep. Serv.2d at 1212, n.4. Where the items were documentary drafts accompanied by collection letters, and the bank named on the drafts was not authorized to make payment without its customer's approval, the bank's status was at least ambiguous and it was deemed to be acting as a collecting bank. Thus, the returns were timely. For a depositary bank, this case illustrates the danger of treating ambiguous drafts as cash items worthy of immediate credit.

Note that Federal Reserve Board Regulation CC is *contra* on this issue. *See infra* 8.04 [3] [f].

53. § 4–104(a)(5). In determining whether a person is a "customer" of a bank, a court may consider "all material circumstances surrounding the opening of the account, the acknowledged intent of the parties ..., the bank's knowledge of that intent, and the nature of the bank's transactions with the parties." Schoenfelder v. Arizona Bank, 165 Ariz. 79, 796 P.2d 881 (Ariz. 1990) (concluding that an individual required as a signatory on a corporate account was a customer of the bank). *Schoenfelder* rejected Loucks v. Albuquerque Nat'l. Bank, 76 N.M. 735, 418 P.2d 191 (N.M. 1966), discussed *infra* at ¶ 9.02[2][b], and similar cases holding that corporate officers and individual partners are not "customers" as to a corporate or partnership account. Despite this case, *Loucks* remains the majority view and the view adopted by the 1990 Article 4 revision. But whether an officer or a partner may sue in the case of wrongful dishonor is another matter. *See* Comment 5 to § 4–402. *See also* Dodd v. Citizens Bank of Costa Mesa, 222 Cal. App.3d 1624, 272 Cal.Rptr. 623, 12 U.C.C. Rep. Serv. 2d 465 (Cal.Ct.App.1990) (non-account customer not a customer). *See generally infra* ¶ 9.05.

One court held that a person cashing a check at a bank where he does not have an account is not a "customer" of the bank, and therefore does not make the warranties at old § 4–207(1). First Nat'l Bank in Eureka v. Giles, 225 Mont. 467, 733 P.2d 357 Mont. 1987), *overruled on other grounds*, 276 Mont. 55, 915 P.2d 799 (Mont.1996). This is consistent with the new rules on privacy under the federal Gramm–Leach–Bliley Act, Pub. L. No. 106–102, 113 Stat. 1338 (1999), which define "customer" as excluding a non-account holder who merely uses an ATM or cashes a check at the bank. *See* 16 CFR § 313.3(h); Symposium on Privacy, 55 Consumer Fin. L.Q. Rep. 4 (2001). However, such a person might qualify as a person collecting an item through a bank, within the definition at § 4–104(a)(5). In Central Bank v. Kaiperm Santa Clara Fed. Credit Union, 191 Cal.App.3d 186, 236 Cal. Rptr. 262 (Cal.App. 6 Dist.1987), the court held that a credit union selling personal money orders as an agent of a bank was not a "customer" of the bank under old § 4–104 because it did not carry an account at that bank. *See generally infra* ¶ 9.05.

54. § 4–201(a). This agency status is extremely important. *See* Comments 2–4 to § 4–201. The subagency point also is of significance. *See, e.g.*, § 4–202(c) and Comment 4. *See also* Regulation J, 12 CFR § 210.6(a); Colonial Cadillac, Inc. v. Shawmut Merchants Bank, N.A., 488 F.Supp. 283 (D.Mass.1980). *But see* Regulation CC, 12 CFR § 229.36(d) and Commentary thereto.

Among other things, agency status means that a bank presenting a documentary draft drawn on a customer of the bank is acting as the agent of the owner of the draft, not as agent of the drawee/customer. As a

[i] **Banking Day:** That part of a day during which substantially all departments of the bank are open to the public for business.[55]

[j] **Midnight Deadline**: Midnight of the banking day immediately following the banking day in which an item was received.[56] For example, if an item (*e.g.*, a check) is deposited at the drive-in window at 5:30 P.M. (after the main bank has closed and the "banking day" has ended) on Tuesday, this item is received during the "banking day" on Wednesday. Therefore, the "midnight deadline" is midnight Thursday (midnight of the banking day following the banking day of receipt), assuming no intervening holidays. Or, suppose that an item (a check) is deposited at the drive-in window of the payor bank on Friday evening after the main bank has closed. Assume that Saturday is not a "banking day," as the primary bookkeeping, commercial, and other operational banking departments are not open—only the teller's windows and drive-ins conduct business. The banking day of receipt is the following Monday, and the midnight deadline is midnight Tuesday.[57]

[k] **Settle:** Old Article 4 provided that "settle" meant to pay in cash, by clearing house settlement, in a charge or credit, by

---

result such a bank owes its primary duty to the owner of the draft rather than to the drawee, even though the drawee may be the bank's regular customer. *See also* § 4–106 (payable through draft generally designates bank as a collecting bank) and § 4–503(2), and Alta Vista State Bank v. Kobliska, 897 F.2d 930, 934 (8th Cir.1990) (payor bank is not an agent of depositary bank). *See also infra* ¶ 9.03[7].

55. §§ 4–104(a)(3), 4–108; *see, e.g.*, United Bank of Crete–Steger v. Gainer Bank, N.A., 874 F.2d 475, 480 (7th Cir. 1989) (Saturday is not a banking day unless substantially all departments of the bank are open).

In Oak Brook Bank v. Northern Trust Co., 256 F.3d 638 (7th Cir.2001), the court held that, for purposes of processing returned checks, a Federal Reserve Bank is open 24 hours each day, and therefore its banking day is 24 hours. This was based on the court's conclusion that "a federal reserve bank is open to the public for substantially all of its banking functions whenever the check-processing department is open for the receipt of checks, which in the case of the Federal Reserve Bank of Chicago is 24 hours of every day that the bank is open." *Id.* at 641. Therefore, an expedited return item delivered to the Reserve Bank at 4:46 p.m. (apparently after the reserve bank was closed to the general public) was nonetheless received on that banking day and therefore timely. The decision was specifically limited to Federal Reserve Banks. *Id.*

56. §§ 4–104(a)(10), 4–108.

57. *See, e.g., United Bank*, 874 F.2d 475. *See supra* note 55. The midnight deadline begins to run on "the banking day on which [the bank] receives the relevant item or notice or from which the time for taking action commences to run, whichever is later." *See* § 4–104(a)(10). Lufthansa German Airlines v. Bank of Am., 478 F.Supp. 1195 (N.D.Cal.1979), interpreted this to mean that the deadline begins to run when the bank receives the item or notice, whichever comes *first*, unless other law provides for a later date. Under this view a collecting bank that receives such notice cannot wait for receipt of the item before notifying affected parties. Since the revisions did not alter the relevant statutory language, the *Lufthansa* interpretation continues to represent a potential risk for banks. *See also* Wells Fargo Bank v. Hartford National Bank & Trust Co., 484 F.Supp. 817 (D.Conn.1980) (telephonic notice adequate, bank not entitled to wait for dishonored check); and Appliance Buyers Credit Corp. v. Prospect National Bank, 708 F.2d 290 (7th Cir.1983) (depositary bank liable for failure to notify customer that it received notice of nonpayment); Regulation CC,12 CFR § 229.33, and *infra* ¶ 8.04[3]; *infra* ¶ 9.03[7]. Nonetheless, the language of § 4–104(a)(10) provides the basis for a strong argument contrary to *Lufthansa*.

remittance, or otherwise as instructed. Current Article 4 is the same except that "instructed" was changed to "agreed."[58] Under Article 4, settlement may be either provisional (subject to revocation) or final. For example, when a depositary bank takes a check for collection, Article 4 provides that any credit given the depositor normally will be provisional. If payment is made by the payor bank, that credit will then become final and the depositary bank changes from being an agent to being the debtor of the depositor. *See* discussion *infra* ¶ 8.02[1][b]. However, this has now been significantly impacted by Regulation CC, as discussed *infra* at ¶ 8.04[3].

[*l*] Branches; Separate Office of a Bank; Separate Data Processing Center: A bank may have branch offices. Are these separate banks for the purposes of computing time limitations such as the midnight deadline? Both old and current Article 4 allow a separate office or branch to be treated as a separate bank for purposes of computing the time allowed and the place for taking certain required action or receiving certain notices relating to the collection, payment or dishonor of items, in certain circumstances. In effect, under this provision a branch is treated as a separate bank.[59] The status of a separate data processing center has now been clarified, both under federal regulation and case law, in favor of treating delivery of items to the data processing center as presentment to the payor bank for purposes of triggering the required time limits for dishonor and return of the dishonored item.[60]

[m] Types of Checks: By incorporating the Article 3 definitions, Article 4 provides specific definitions for different types of checks, to help categorize these items for purposes of determining their specific legal attributes. For example, a cashier's check is defined as a draft drawn by a bank on itself, and a teller's check is defined as a draft drawn by a bank on another bank or payable at or through a bank.[61] A traveler's check is an instrument denoted as

---

58. Old § 4–104(1)(j); revised § 4–104(a)(11).

59. Old § 4–106; revised § 4–107. But, of course, not for all purposes. *See* Comments 3 and 4. The 1990 revision deleted previously optional language relating to the maintenance of separate ledgers by each bank, rendered obsolete by centralized computer processing. *See* revised § 4–107, Comment 5. *Cf.* Regulation CC, 12 CFR §§ 229.32(a), 229.33(c), 229.36(b) (designation of offices for receipt of notices, returned checks, etc.). *See also* revised Article 9 § 9–304.

60. *See, e.g.*, Regulation CC, 12 CFR § 229.36(b) ("A check is considered received by the paying bank when it is received . . . [a]t a location to which delivery is requested by the paying bank. . . ."); Regulation CC, Commentary § 229.36(b)–1 ("the processing center acts as the agent of the paying bank . . ."), citing old § 4–204(3); Sass Trucking, Inc. v. Security Bank and Trust Co., 737 P.2d 113 (Okla. 1987) (delivery to data processing center constitutes presentment to payor bank); Chrysler Credit Corp. v. First National Bank & Trust Co., 582 F.Supp. 1436 (W.D.Pa.1984), *aff'd*, 746 F.2d 200 (3d Cir. 1984) (as designated place of presentment, receipt of item at data processing center commenced running of the midnight deadline). *See also* § 4–204(c) and discussion *supra* Chapter 4; *infra* ¶ 8.02[2][c] and notes 141–143; ¶ 8.02[2][d]; and *infra* ¶ 8.04.

61. *See* § 4–104(c) and § 3–104(g), (h), and discussion *supra* Chapter 1, ¶ 1.01[4][c]. All of these definitions are consistent with prior law and banking practice. In Roberts Fertilizer, Inc. v. Steinmeier, 748 S.W.2d 883 (Mo.App.1988), a "Bank Disbursement Check" was deemed not to

such and requiring a countersignature on its face by the drawer.[62] A certified check is a check accepted by the bank on which it is drawn.[63] In contrast a money order is treated as an ordinary check (and therefore, *e.g.*, is subject to a stop payment order), unless it otherwise qualifies as a cashier's check, teller's check, or certified check.[64]

Generally under Articles 3 and 4 a cashier's check, teller's check, or certified check is not subject to a stop payment order issued by the customer who purchased the check,[65] while an ordinary check or money order would be subject to such an order.[66] This resolved some residual uncertainty under prior law.[67]

[n] Electronic Presentment: Article 4 § 4–110 specifically authorizes presentment by way of "an image of the item or information describing the item ('presentment notice') rather than delivery

---

be a cashier's check and therefore could be dishonored by the bank without liability. Disclaimers on the face of the check indicated that it should not be treated as cash, and it was properly dishonored and returned before the bank's midnight deadline. See also *infra* ¶ 9.01[4][d], and *infra* notes 62–67. *Cf.* §§ 3–312, 3–411, and 3–412 (obligations of issuer of cashier's check). Many banks are inserting language on the face of their cashier's checks stating that a bond will be required before a replacement check will be issued, in order to limit the potential for customer abuses under § 3–312.

62. See § 3–104(i). See also § 3–106(c) (requirement of countersignature does not render instrument nonnegotiable).

63. See § 4–104(c) and § 3–409(d). See also § 3–409(a) (acceptance defined as the drawee's signed agreement to pay the draft as presented).

64. See, e.g., § 3–104(f) and First National Bank of Nocona v. Duncan Savings & Loan Association, 656 F.Supp. 358 (W.D.Okla.1987), aff'd, 957 F.2d 775 (10th Cir.1992) (teller's check labeled "Money Order"). Under current Article 4 this item would be treated as a teller's check despite the label. *See also infra* notes 59–61. It has been held that a money order which does not require the signature of the purchaser is not a negotiable instrument. *See* Central Bank v. Kaiperm Santa Clara Fed. Credit Union, 191 Cal.App.3d 186, 236 Cal.Rptr. 262 (Cal.App. 6 Dist.1987). *Cf.* §§ 3–104(a), 3–103(a), (b).

65. See discussion *supra* Chapter 4 and *infra* Chapter 9 at ¶ 9.01[4][d]; Behavioral Health and Wellness, Inc. v. FDIC, 802 So.2d 374 (Fla.Dist.Ct.App.2001).

66. See infra ¶ 9.01[4]; §§ 3–104(f), 4–403, and discussion *supra* in Chapter 1.

67. Compare poorly reasoned cases like Unger v. NCNB National Bank, 540 So.2d 246 (Fla.Dist.Ct.App.1989) (money order is akin to a cashier's check; issuing bank liable for payment even though it never signed the instruments), with better decisions such as: Adam Int'l. Trading, Ltd. v. Manufacturers Hanover Trust Co., 150 A.D.2d 294, 542 N.Y.S.2d 1 (N.Y.App.Div.1989), *appeal dismissed*, 74 N.Y.2d 844, 546 N.Y.S.2d 560, 545 N.E.2d 874 (N.Y. 1989) (bank had no liability on stolen money orders because they were the "legal equivalent of unaccepted checks"); Duggan v. State Bank of Antioch, 184 Ill.App.3d 699, 133 Ill.Dec. 245, 540 N.E.2d 1111 (1989), *appeal denied*, 127 Ill.2d 614, 136 Ill.Dec. 584, 545 N.E.2d 108 (Ill. 1989) (money order subject to stop payment order of remitter just like personal check); Garden Check Cashing Service, Inc. v. First National City Bank, 25 A.D.2d 137, 267 N.Y.S.2d 698 (1966), *aff'd on opinion below*, 18 N.Y.2d 941, 277 N.Y.S.2d 141, 223 N.E.2d 566 (1966) (money order is like personal check and is subject to the stop payment order of a purchaser); McLaughlin v. Franklin Society Federal Savings & Loan Assn., 6 UCC Rep. 1183 (N.Y. Civ.Ct. 1969) (customer entitled to stop payment of money order); First National Bank of Nocona v. Duncan Savings & Loan Association, 656 F.Supp. 358 (W.D.Okla.1987), *aff'd*, 957 F.2d 775 (10th Cir.1992), properly concluded that a money order is not the equivalent of cash but rather is a "check" under the UCC, and therefore is subject to a stop payment order. The *Nocona* court rejected Sequoyah State Bank v. Union National Bank of Little Rock, 274 Ark. 1, 621 S.W.2d 683 (Ark. 1981) and other cases to the contrary. The Article 4 revisions adopt the *Nocona* view.

of the item itself," pursuant to an agreement between the parties.[68] This is designed to facilitate truncation and other automated collection arrangements.[69] Regulation CC permits and even encourages such arrangements.[70]

[4] Bank Insolvency

Article 4 contains a provision dealing with the impact of bank insolvency on items being collected through the banking system.[71] The rules stated in this provision are derived from the American Bankers Association Bank Collection Code.[72] The Official Comment to § 4–216 notes that other state law may supplement these rules,[73] and recognizes that § 4–216 does not apply to national banks.[74] Still, the Article 4 rules reflect widely accepted principles regarding the impact of bank insolvency on bank deposits and collections, and apply to institutions where no conflict with federal law exists.

The basic principle stated in § 4–216 has four parts: (1) if an item is delivered to a collecting or payor bank and the bank is declared insolvent or otherwise suspends payments before the item has been paid, the item must be returned by the bank's receiver to the transferor or presenting bank;[75] (2) if a payor bank has made final payment under Article 4,[76] and the bank suspends payments before making settlement, the person entitled to settlement has a "preferred claim" against the payor bank;[77] (3) if a payor or collecting bank gives or receives a provisional settlement and thereafter suspends payments, the suspension does not prevent the settlement from becoming final if that happens automatically after a certain period of time or upon a specific event;[78] (4) if a collecting bank receives settlement and then suspends payments without making a required settlement with its customer, the customer has a preferred claim against the bank.[79]

As noted, federal law relating to bank insolvency will preempt state law to the extent of any inconsistency.[80] However, Regulation CC[81]

---

68. § 4–110(a).

69. Id. See also § 4–101, Comment 3.

70. See 12 CFR § 229.36(c) and Article 4 § 4–110, Comment 2. See also infra ¶ 8.04 [3][f] and infra ¶ 9.03[6].

71. § 4–216.

72. "[B]ut with the abandonment of any theory of trust." § 4–216, Comment 2.

73. § 4–216, Comment 2, citing Note, Uniform Commercial Code: Stopping Payment of an Item Deposited with an Insolvent Depositary Bank, 40 OKLA. L. REV. 689 (1987).

74. § 4–216, Comment 3, citing Jennings v. United States Fidelity and Guaranty Co., 294 U.S. 216, 55 S.Ct. 394, 79 L.Ed. 869 (1935). See generally F. Miller and A. Harrell, The ABCs of the UCC Related Insolvency Law (Am. Bar Assoc. 2002).

75. § 4–216(a). "Suspends payments" is defined at § 4–104(a)(12) as meaning closure by supervisory authorities, appointment of a public officer (e.g., a receiver), or refusal to make payments in the ordinary course of business.

76. See infra ¶ 8.02 and ¶ 8.03.

77. "Preferred claim" is not defined.

78. § 4–216(c).

79. § 4–216(d). "Preferred claim" is not defined.

80. See generally, Lofts, Querio, & Jensen, Financial Institutions Receiverships Before and After the Financial Institutions Reform, Recovery and Enforcement Act of 1989, 45 CONSUMER FIN. L. Q. REP. 158 (1991); and Note, Uniform Commercial Code: Stopping Payment of an Item Deposited with an Insolvent Depositary Bank, supra note 73. See also discussion of the impact of federal law on the holder in the course rule, supra Chapter 3 ¶ 3.04.

81. See, e.g., infra ¶ 8.04[3][g].

follows § 4–216 by prescribing similar rules to govern settlement for checks by or to an insolvent bank.[82]

Like Article 4, Regulation CC provides a four-part rule:[83] (1) if a check is in the possession of a bank that suspends payments, and is not paid, it must be returned to the bank or customer who delivered the check to the insolvent bank;[84] (2) if a paying or depositary bank makes final payment but suspends payments before completing the settlement, the bank entitled to settlement has a preferred claim against the bank that owes settlement;[85] (3) if a collecting, paying, or returning bank receives final settlement, and suspends payments without making final settlement in favor of a party entitled to such, that party has a preferred claim against the bank;[86] (4) if a paying or depositary bank gives, or a collecting, paying, or returning bank gives or receives, a settlement and then suspends payments, the suspension does not prevent the settlement from becoming final if such finality occurs automatically after a certain time or upon a specific event.[87]

¶ 8.02 The Payor Bank: Provisional Settlement Versus Final Payment

If an item deposited or sent for collection has been paid under § 4–215(a) or (c), the payor bank has paid or owes settlement to the owner of the item, and any collecting bank that receives such final settlement similarly owes settlement to its customer under § 4–215(d). Upon final payment the drawer and all other parties on the instrument are discharged, under Article 3 §§ 3–601 and 3–602. *See* the discussion *supra* Chapter 6. If the item is not paid, earlier parties on the item may have to respond to later parties on it; due to their liability on the instrument under Article 3 Parts 4 and 5. *See* the discussion *supra* in Chapters 4 and 7. And, if the payor delays too long in deciding whether to pay, it may become accountable for the amount of the item regardless of whether the item is properly payable; that is, it may owe the owner whether or not the payor bank can debit its customer's account.[88] This is

---

82. *See* 12 CFR § 229.39 and the Commentary. Regulation CC also provides that any bank that handles a check for either forward collection or return processing is liable to any subsequent bank to the extent that it does not receive payment due to bank insolvency. 12 CFR § 229.35(b). This creates a system similar to the Article 4 warranty system, protecting subsequent parties against the insolvency of prior banks in the collection or return process. *See* Regulation CC Commentary § 229.35(b).

83. The Regulation CC Commentary states that 12 CFR § 229.39 is derived from old § 4–214 which is now § 4–216; the rules appear to be essentially similar.

84. 12 CFR § 229.39(a). By its terms this would apply to the forward collection as well as the return item process. This is similar to old § 4–214(1) and current § 4–216(a).

85. 12 CFR § 229.39(b). "Paying bank" is defined at 12 CFR § 229.2(z), to include payor and payable-through banks. This rule is similar to old § 4–214(2) and revised § 4–216(b). "Preferred claim" is not defined.

86. 12 CFR § 229.39(c). This is similar to old § 4–214(3) and revised § 4–216(c).

87. 12 CFR § 229.39(d). This is similar to old § 4–214(4) and revised § 4–216(d).

¶ 8.02

88. *See* § 4–302; § 4–215, Comment 8; and discussion *infra* at ¶ 8.02[3]. *See also* Regulation CC, 12 CFR §§ 229.30 and 229.38, which may extend the midnight

a primary function of the midnight deadline. In the context of a banking transaction, all of these issues revolve around the process of settlement, as discussed below.

[1] Settlement

[a] Initial Settlement

When an item is presented to a payor bank (defined at § 4–105 as the bank on which the item is drawn), either through a collecting bank[89] or by the owner in person, under §§ 4–215, 4–301, and 4–302 the payor bank must, except in the cases of documentary drafts or drafts presented for immediate payment over the counter, either make settlement or dishonor the item within its midnight deadline. Dishonor occurs when an instrument is properly presented and payment is refused.[90] Settlement occurs if the payor pays or allows some form of credit for the item.[91] Section 4–302(a)(1) requires at least initial provisional settlement by midnight of the banking day of receipt (except where the payor is also the depositary bank). The payor then must either make final payment or dishonor the item before midnight of the next banking day after the banking day of receipt.[92] Regulation J similarly requires a payor bank using the Federal Reserve System for collection to make settlement by the close of the banking day of receipt and to revoke before the end of the next banking day.[93] If the payor bank refuses either to dishonor or to settle for the item, this is conversion[94] and, for a payor bank, the measure of damages for such a conversion may be the face amount of the instrument.[95]

---

deadline and/or impose additional duties and liabilities, as discussed *infra* at ¶ 8.04[3][a].

89. "Collecting bank" is also defined at § 4–105, as any bank except the payor bank. Permissible methods of presentment by a collecting bank are detailed at § 4–204. The duty of the collecting bank in this respect is stated at § 4–202(a)(1), (b), and (c). Section 4–202(b), defining the duty of a collecting bank to exercise ordinary care by reference to the midnight deadline, was completely rewritten for clarity in the 1990 revisions but without apparent substantive change. *See also* discussion *infra* at ¶ 8.03. The time and proper place for presentment of checks are also governed by Regulation CC. *See* 12 CFR §§ 229.36(b) and 229.41; Revised § 4–204, Comment 4, and discussion *infra* at ¶ 8.04[3].

90. Article 3, Part 5. Presentment and dishonor are discussed *supra* in Chapter 4. For checks being collected through the banking system, the Regulation CC rules on presentment also will apply. *See* 12 CFR § 229.36, and discussion *infra* at ¶ 8.04[3]. *See also* 12 CFR § 229.31(c) (settlement by returning banks for returned checks). However, in many cases the issues will be outside the scope of Regulation CC and therefore governed by the UCC.

91. §§ 4–104(a)(11), 4–213, and 4–215. For returned checks, *see* Regulation CC, 12 CFR § 229.31(c) (settlement by returning banks), and *infra* ¶ 8.04[3][c]. *See also* the definition of "settle" at § 4–104(a)(11), discussed *supra* at ¶ 8.01[3][k].

92. §§ 4–302(a)(1), 4–301(a), (b). *See also* § 4–215 (final payment); *also* Comment 2 to old § 4–301. For checks, *see also* 12 CFR § 229.30, and discussion *infra* at ¶ 8.04[3][a], [b].

93. *See, e.g.*, Community Bank v. Federal Reserve Bank of San Francisco, 500 F.2d 282 (9th Cir.1974), *cert. denied*, 419 U.S. 1089, 95 S.Ct. 680, 42 L.Ed.2d 681 (1974); 12 CFR §§ 210.9(a), 210.12(a).

94. § 3–420 refers to the general law of conversion, but is governed by the more specific rule at § 4–302. *See* § 4–102(a).

95. *Id.*; § 3–420(b). *See also* § 4–302(a) (payor bank is "accountable" for the amount of the item if it is not dishonored before the midnight deadline, subject to certain defenses at § 4–302(b)).

As discussed *infra* at ¶ 8.04, Regulation CC additionally requires that a dishonored check be returned in an "expeditious manner," pursuant to either a "two day/four day test" or a "forward collection test."[96] Although Regulation CC preempts Article 4 to the extent of any inconsistency,[97] from the standpoint of the payor bank the Regulation CC expeditious return requirements for the most part merely supplement, and do not displace, the Article 4 rules governing final payment, the midnight deadline, and the accountability of the payor bank.[98] Indeed, most of the litigation on this issue continues to be under Article 4, not Regulation CC.

Nonetheless, Regulation CC provides its own system for determining the liability of a payor bank that fails to meet the Regulation CC expeditious return requirements,[99] and such liability may accrue independently of whether the bank has met its obligations under Article 4. Thus banks must endeavor to comply with the return item and final payment requirements of both Article 4 and Regulation CC.[100]

The primary purpose of Article 4 § 4–301 is to determine when and how an initial settlement can be revoked.[101] There are three basic prerequisites for revocation of settlement under § 4–301: (1) the item must be a demand item other than a documentary draft; (2) it must not have been presented over the counter for immediate payment; and (3) the payor bank must return the item (unless it is unavailable for return) before final payment and the midnight deadline.[102] Regulation CC may preempt this for checks in some cases, by extending the deadline, finalizing payment, and/or permitting notice in lieu of return.[103]

Universal C.I.T. Credit Corp. v. Farmers Bank of Portageville[104] is a classic example of how the Article 4 rules on initial settlement work in

---

96. 12 CFR § 229.30(a). These tests are described *infra* at ¶ 8.04[3][a]. The impact on Article 4 is discussed further at ¶ 8.04[4].

97. *See* 12 CFR § 229.41, and discussion *infra* at ¶ 8.04[3].

98. *See* the Commentary to Regulation CC §§ 229.30 and 229.38(d). While under Regulation CC settlements are final so the right of charge back may be lost, a payor bank still may recover upon dishonor. One exception to § 4–301 and § 4–302 is 12 CFR § 229.30(c), which may extend the Article 4 midnight deadline where the payor bank uses certain types of expedited return systems.

99. *See, e.g.,* 12 CFR § 229.38(a) (damages for failure to exercise ordinary care); 12 CFR § 229.38(b) (no double liability under Regulation CC and Article 4); 12 CFR § 229.38(c) (comparative negligence). *See also infra* ¶ 8.04[4].

100. *Id.* 12 CFR § 229.38(b) specifies that where an action violates both § 229.30(a) and the Article 4 midnight deadline, the bank will be liable under Regulation CC or Article 4, but not both. *See infra* ¶ 8.04[3][a], and ¶ 8.04[4]. *See generally* Oak Brook Bank v. Northern Trust Co., 256 F.3d 638 (7th Cir.2001), discussed *supra* at note 55.

101. *See* § 4–301, Comment 2.

102. *Id.* In Wells Fargo Bank v. Hartford National Bank & Trust Co., 484 F.Supp. 817 (D.Conn.1980), the court erroneously held that the old federal requirement of wire advice of nonpayment preempted this provision. *See* currently Regulation CC, 12 CFR § 229.33 and its Commentary.

103. *Id.,* citing 12 CFR §§ 229.31(f) and § 229.33, discussed *infra* ¶ 8.04[3][b], ¶ 8.04[4]. Also Regulation CC makes settlement final for checks, but allows recovery where a check is properly returned. *See* Commentary to Regulation CC, 12 CFR § 229.36(d).

104. 358 F.Supp. 317 (E.D.Mo.1973). *See also* Anderson, Clayton & Co. v. First American Bank of Erick, 614 P.2d 1091, 1094 (Okla.1980).

the context of a deferred posting procedure. Deferred posting merely means that the payor need not make a final decision to pay or dishonor on the day it receives the item, but can make a provisional settlement in the form of an initial posting to each account, while deferring the final decision on payment until the resulting account balances can be reviewed at a later time. Deferred posting is necessary because of the enormous volume of checks being handled. It permits automated handling of checks and posting received in "batches," without the need to make a prior decision on the payment of each item. For example, in *Universal C.I.T.*, the payor bank received the checks in question on January 15 but did not make a decision on payment until the following day. This is typical of a deferred posting system, whereby items presented during one banking day are "batched" together and posted in production-line fashion, subject to possible revocation at a later time.[105]

When the payor bank in *Universal C.I.T.* subsequently refused payment of the disputed checks, the owner of the checks sought to recover under old §§ 4–301(1) and 4–302(a). Those provisions required the payor bank (other than a depositary bank) to settle for an item by midnight of the banking day of receipt, and made the bank "accountable" for the item upon a failure to do so. Current §§ 4–301(a) and 4–302(a)(1) are similar. Since in *Universal C.I.T.* the payor bank failed to affirmatively make settlement by midnight of January 15, it might appear that the bank would be liable. In addition, a Federal Reserve Bank of Saint Louis Operating Letter 9A also required the payor bank to make settlement by midnight of the banking day of receipt.[106] This, again, would suggest bank liability.

Fortunately for the bank, it was not quite that simple. "Settle" was defined at old § 4–104(1)(j) as payment "in cash, by clearing house settlement, in a charge or credit or by remittance, or otherwise as instructed." Current § 4–104(a)(11) is similar, except that "instructed" is changed to "agree." In *Universal C.I.T.*, the court found that the operating agreement signed by the payor bank and the Federal Reserve Bank of Saint Louis described an "automatic charge date" providing for settlement by the second banking day. This agreement provided "a method of provisional settlement which eliminated the necessity of any formal action on the part of the payor bank (defendant) except to protest, prior to the midnight deadline, in the event the items were not acceptable. Such prior authorization was the functional equivalent of a provisional settlement . . . prior to midnight of the banking day of receipt."[107]

[b] *Provisional Versus Final Settlement/Payment*

Under Article 4, when a payor bank makes an initial settlement, it

---

105. Such a system is described in *Universal C.I.T.*, 358 F. Supp. at 321. *See also* Comment 4 to § 4–402.

106. *Universal C.I.T.*, 358 F. Supp. at 322.

107. *Id.* at 323. *See also* § 4–213(a); § 4–103; discussion *supra* at ¶ 8.01[2].

may be either provisional or final.[108] If the settlement is provisional, it may be revoked by the payor bank up to the earlier of the time of the final payment or the bank's midnight deadline.[109] But if the settlement is or has become final, or payment has been made, the payor bank owes or has paid the amount of the item.[110] In that event the payor bank cannot revoke the settlement (except for limited reasons such as breach of warranty or fraud or other restitutionary remedies, as noted *infra* or as allowed under § 3–418 or § 4–302(b)) and therefore the payor bank generally must bear any loss caused by the uncollectability of the instrument (for example, due to forgery, alteration, insufficient funds, etc.).[111] Under Article 4 the only exceptions outside of § 3–418 are the possibility of an action for breach of warranty[112] or circumstances involv-

---

108. § 4–104(a)(11). *See also* §§ 4–213 and 4–215(a), Comment 4 to § 4–215, and discussion *infra*. As noted *infra* at ¶ 8.04, Regulation CC preempts Article 4 to some extent by making all settlements by collecting banks final in the collection of checks, except between the depositary bank and its customer. *See* 12 CFR §§ 229.31(c), 229.32(b), and 229.36(d). *See also* § 4–102, Comment 1; § 4–201, Comment 4; § 4–302, Comment 1. Nonetheless, Regulation CC does not generally preempt the midnight deadline for payor banks under Article 4, though it may extend the payor bank midnight deadline in order to allow more expeditious return of dishonored items. *See* 12 CFR § 229.30 and *infra* ¶ 8.04[3][a], [b], and [4].

109. § 4–301(a). *But see* Regulation CC §§ 229.31(c), 229.32(b), and 229.36(d), discussed *infra* at ¶ 8.04 (all settlements for checks are final, except as between the depositary bank and its customer). Nonetheless, Regulation CC allows recovery where a check is properly returned (*see* note 97, *supra*) and does not preempt, though it may extend, the payor bank midnight deadline as the deadline for return of dishonored items. *See* 12 CFR § 229.30, and *infra* ¶ 8.04[3][a], [b], and [4].

110. § 4–215(a) and (b). *See, e.g.,* Kimberly A. Allen Trust v. FirstBank of Lakewood, N.A., 989 P.2d 203 (Colo.Ct.App. 1999) (failure to dishonor item before the payor bank's midnight deadline is equivalent to final payment and payor bank becomes accountable for amount of item, precluding subsequent revocation of settlement for the item). When settlement occurs because final payment is made, the payor bank's obligation to pay is discharged. Note that § 4–215(b) and Comment 2 to § 4–302 clarify the relation between payment and accountability. *See also* Comment 3 to § 4–301 and Comments 6–10 to § 4–215; *infra* ¶ 8.02 [3], [4], and [7], *e.g., infra* note 156.

111. In these instances, the payor bank may be unable to charge its customer's account because the item is not properly payable under § 4–401(a), or may not be able to collect from its customer because his or her account has insufficient funds. Typically this leaves the payor bank with a very limited recourse against the party who presented the item for payment, under § 4–302(b) and § 3–418(c). *See* § 4–301, Comment 7, and § 4–302, Comment 3. This point is discussed *infra* this text and notes immediately following and also *infra* at ¶ 8.02[3]. In addition the payor bank may have rights against both the party it paid and its customer, by way of subrogation under § 4–407, as discussed *infra* at ¶ 9.02[3]. *See infra* ¶ 8.02 [7].

112. *See, e.g.,* First National Bank & Trust Co. of the Treasure Coast v. Belmont National Bank, 43 UCC Rep.Serv.2d 666, 2001 WL 15937 (Ohio App. 2001) (omission of required joint indorsement is breach of warranty that allows the payor bank to revoke the settlement and return the item after the midnight deadline); Lawyer's Fund for Client Protection v. Gateway State Bank, 273 A.D.2d 565, 709 N.Y.S.2d 243 (N.Y.App.Div.2000) (effect of forged indorsement); Georgia R.R. Bank & Trust Co. v. First Nat'l Bank & Trust Co. of Augusta, 139 Ga.App. 683, 229 S.E.2d 482 (Ga.App. 1976), *reh. denied* (Sept. 29, 1976), *aff'd*, 238 Ga. 693, 235 S.E.2d 1 (Ga. 1977); Northwestern Nat'l Ins. Co. v. Midland Nat'l Bank, 96 Wis.2d 155, 292 N.W.2d 591 (Wis. 1980). Under § 4–208(a), a payor bank is given three warranties as to each item presented for payment: (1) the title to the instrument is good (it bears no unauthorized or missing indorsements), (2) no knowledge exists as to a lack of authorization for the drawer's signature, and (3) the item has not been materially altered. Thus in the case of a forged or missing indorsement or an alteration, a payor, even after final payment, may recover payment made

ing fraud.[113]

An unresolved question under the old version of the Code was whether the payor bank owes a duty of final payment or accountability under the midnight deadline rule to any presenter of the item, or whether restrictions elsewhere in the Code limit the bank's liability to specified parties. The issue centers on the relationship with § 3–418. The latter section provides a final payment rule similar to that at §§ 4–215, 4–301, and 4–302, except that it operates only in favor of a party who takes an instrument in good faith and for value or a person who in good faith has changed position in reliance on the payment. Does the qualification at § 3–418 limit the protection of the § 4–215 final payment rule? Some cases decided under old Article 3 held that it does not and that a payor bank becomes liable to any holder.[114]

(or resist liability), but the payor may bear the loss for payment on an unauthorized drawer's signature or payment of an item drawn on insufficient funds, absent a presentment with guilty knowledge. *See also* § 4–302(b), discussion *infra* ¶ 8.02 [4] and ¶ 8.02 [7]. Each customer and collecting bank makes equivalent warranties, except that these parties make an unqualified warranty that all signatures are genuine, under § 4–207(a). Sections 4–207 and 4–208 are similar except for this latter point. There are also misencoding and truncation warranties under § 4–209. *See infra* ¶ 9.03[6]. In addition there are warranties under Regulation CC. *See infra* ¶ 8.04[3][e]. As a result, any party dealing with an item in the bank collection system may have recourse against prior parties if there is a breach of warranty. This issue is also discussed *supra* in Chapter 7; and *infra* this text, *e.g.*, at note 127.

113. For example, under old Article 4, in Bank Leumi Trust Co. v. Bally's Park Place, Inc., 528 F.Supp. 349 (S.D.N.Y.1981), a gambler wrote a $60,000 check to the casino. He then died, leaving only a $5,000 estate. Discovering that the estate was insolvent, the casino decided to deposit the check for presentment to the payor bank. The fondest hopes of the casino were realized when the payor bank missed its midnight deadline. The court, however, permitted the bank to rescind the settlement on grounds that old §§ 3–418, 4–301, and 4–302 were limited to interbank settlement procedures and did not preclude restitutionary remedies. As explained immediately *infra* in this text and notes, and discussed again *infra* at ¶ 8.02[3], the Article 4 revisions approve this result on these facts. *See also infra* this text at note 115; ¶ 8.02 [4] and ¶ 8.02 [7]; and *infra* notes 161 and 167.

In addition the result in *Bank Leumi* can be seen as an application of supplementary equitable principles under UCC § 1–103; indeed, the casino's position is hardly one that evokes sympathy. But this case was criticized for deemphasizing the plain and compelling purpose of the old Article 4 final payment provisions; *i.e.*, to provide an ascertainable point of finality. *See, e.g.*, old § 3–418, Comment 1. The obvious risk after *Bank Leumi* was that the Article 4 finality of payment rules would be ignored outside of interbank settlement cases, leading to great uncertainty as to the final payment of other items. The better view of *Bank Leumi* is that it should be interpreted as precluding the casino from enforcing its Article 3 and Article 4 rights because it violated its UCC § 1–203 obligation to enter the transaction in good faith. This view prevailed in the revision of Article 4. Current § 4–302(b) specifically permits a payor bank to rescind final payment where the item was presented "for the purpose of defrauding the payor bank," thus codifying while also limiting the rule in the *Bank Leumi* case. *See infra* ¶ 8.02 [4] and ¶ 8.02 [7]; *supra* note 46.

114. *E.g.*, Northwestern Nat'l Ins. Co. v. Midland Nat'l Bank, 96 Wis.2d 155, 292 N.W.2d 591 (Wis. 1980). *See, e.g.*, Miller, Commercial Paper, Bank Deposits and Collections, and Letters of Credit, 37 Bus. Law. 973, 992 (1982).

See also §§ 4–210, 4–211; Citizens Nat'l Bank v. Fort Lee Sav. & Loan Ass'n, 89 N.J.Super. 43, 213 A.2d 315 (Law Div. 1965). To the extent banks are limited in their ability to put holds on funds availability (*see infra* ¶ 8.02[3] and ¶ 8.04[2]), the issue may become more important, because a collecting bank may be required to allow withdrawal of uncollected funds. This places great importance on that bank's ability to collect a subsequently dishonored item as a holder in due course. In addition

Current §§ 3–418 and 4–215 were revised in 1990 in ways that address these uncertainties. Section 3–418(d) specifically refers to § 4–215 and the comments, particularly § 3–418 Comment 2, makes it clear that the sections are to be read together. Thus, as discussed in more detail *infra* at ¶ 8.02 [4] and ¶ 8.02 [7], revocation of settlement by the payor bank may be allowed under § 3–418(a), as an exception to the final payment and accountability rules of §§ 4–215, 4–301, and 4–302, subject to the limitations at § 3–418(c) (protecting good faith for value and reliance parties).

In addition, § 4–302(b) permits a payor bank to defend against accountability under § 4–302(a), if there has been a breach of a presentment warranty (*see* § 4–208), or upon "proof that the person seeking enforcement of the liability presented or transferred the item for the purpose of defrauding the bank." This latter language permits a defense by the bank to the money owed (or recovery of money paid) as part of an Article 4 settlement, in cases like *Bank Leumi Trust Co. v. Bally's Park Place, Inc.*, which allowed restitutionary recovery by the payor bank where the presentment was made with knowledge that the check was bad.[115] In effect, as discussed further *infra* at ¶ 8.02 [4] and ¶ 8.02 [7], under the 1990 revisions § 3–418 operates with §§ 4–215, 4–301, and 4–302, even though § 4–302(b) specifies defenses of its own.

Obviously payor banks prefer to keep settlement provisional and thereby delay final payment as long as possible, until they have processed the item. In most cases this deferred payment is recognized by statute[116] (§§ 4–301 and 4–302[117]), but it also may be done by contract.[118]

---

such a bank's holder in due course status may be affected by the new definition of "good faith" at § 3–103(a)(4). *See supra* ¶ 3.03. Note that even if there is no holder in due course, a reliance payee also may keep payment under § 3–418. There is little law under the Code on what constitutes reliance. Your authors believe it should require irrevocably parting with the payment received, rather than a mere detriment that could be set off against recovery. This is consistent with the traditional Article 3 concept of "value," which excludes an executory consideration. *See* § 3–303. On the applicability of § 3–418 in Article 4 cases, *see infra* this text at ¶ 8.02[3] and [4].

115. *See Bank Leumi*, 528 F.Supp. 349, discussed *supra* at note 113. *See also* First National Bank and Trust Co. of the Treasure Coast v. Belmont National Bank, 43 UCC Rep. Serv.2d 666, 2001 WL 15937 (Ohio Ct. App. 2001) (improper indorsement constitutional breach of warranty allowing late return); Copple v. Boatmen's First Nat. Bank of Okla., 958 P.2d 820 (Okla. Civ. App. 1998) (check returned more than six months after final payment, due to breach of warranty). Section 4–302(b) essentially codifies the *Bank Leumi* rationale, which was questionable under the statutory language in then–applicable old Article 4. *See also* discussion *infra* at ¶ 8.02 [1] [c], ¶ 8.02[3], ¶ 8.02[4], ¶ 8.02[7]. Note that language at old § 4–213(1), indicating that upon final payment the payor bank is accountable for the amount of the item, was deleted from § 4–215(a), eliminating this as a source of confusion. If final payment has been made under § 4–215, there is no continuing accountability under § 4–302 because the obligation to pay has been discharged. Thus, generally speaking §§ 4–215 and 4–302 are mutually exclusive alternatives, although there remains some overlap. *See supra* notes 108 and 110; *infra* ¶ 8.02[3] and note 156, ¶ 8.02 [4], and ¶ 8.02 [7]; *infra* this text at notes 124–128.

116. § 4–215(a)(2). *See also infra* note 119.

117. *See* §§ 4–301(a), (b). *See also* discussion *supra* at ¶ 8.02[1]. Note that under old §§ 4–213(1)(b) and 4–301 provisional settlement depended on the lack of a final payment while the lack of a final payment depended on provisional settlement. A contract provision was therefore wise. § 4–215(a)(2) provides that final payment occurs only if the bank has no right to

Thus, many deposit slips will include language to the effect that "items are credited subject to final payment."

[c] Final Payment

Under Article 4, the determination of what constitutes a provisional settlement and when it becomes final payment basically is controlled by §§ 4–215 and 4–301.[119] Under § 4–301(a) any authorized settlement made before midnight of the banking day of receipt for a demand item other than a documentary draft and one presented for immediate payment over the counter is provisional and may be revoked prior to the earlier of the payor bank's midnight deadline or the time the settlement becomes final payment under § 4–215(a). The process of posting (old § 4–213(1)(c)) was eliminated as a method of making final payment, as part of the 1990 revisions. Old § 4–213(1) provided that settlement by the payor bank became final payment when the bank did any of four things, whichever was first: paid the item in cash;[120] settled for the item without reserving or otherwise having a right to revoke the settlement;[121] completed the process of posting;[122] or failed to revoke the provisional settlement and send the item or notice of dishonor before the midnight deadline as provided at § 4–301.[123] As noted, current § 4–215(a) is similar except that the process of posting was eliminated as a means of making final payment. This and other revisions to the final payment rules are also discussed *infra* at ¶ 8.02.

Upon a final payment under these provisions, under old Article 4 the payor bank "shall be accountable for the amount of the item."[124] In

---

revoke a provisional settlement under statute, clearing-house rule, or agreement. § 4–301(a) in turn provides that a payor bank may revoke such a settlement if it returns the item before the midnight deadline and before final payment. In terms of circular reasoning, this represents a modest improvement but a contractual provision may still be helpful. *See also infra* ¶ 8.02[2][b].

118. Old § 4–213(1)(b) stated that payment was final if settlement was made without reserving a right to revoke by rule or agreement and without the bank having such a right under statute. Current § 4–215(a)(2) is similar but clarifies the rule by specifying that a right to revoke can be provided by statute regardless of whether there is any other right to revoke.

119. *See, e.g.*, § 4–215 and Comments 1, 3, and 4. As noted *supra* and discussed *infra* at ¶ 8.04[3] and [4], this is subject to partial preemption by Regulation CC with regard to the collection of checks. Regulation CC provides that with regard to checks, all settlements between collecting banks are final, except as between the depositary bank and its customer. *See* 12 CFR §§ 229.31(c), 229.32(b), and 229.36(d); § 4–102, Comment 1; § 4–201, Comment 4; and § 4–302, Comment 1. Regulation CC does not relieve the payor bank of its obligation to meet the Article 4 midnight deadline, except in limited circumstances where the deadline may be extended for purposes of expeditious return under Regulation CC, nor does it preclude recovery by the payor bank of the amount of a returned check under Article 3 and 4; if the check is returned within applicable UCC limits. *See* 12 CFR §§ 229.30, 229.31, 229.38, and discussion *infra* at ¶ 8.04[3][a], [b], and [4].

120. Old § 4–213(1)(a); current § 4–215(a)(1).

121. Old § 4–213(1)(b); current § 4–215(a)(2).

122. Old § 4–213(1)(c); as noted in the text, this provision was deleted as a part of the revisions to current § 4–215(a). *See also* discussion *infra* this text and at ¶ 8.02[2][c].

123. Old § 4–213(1)(d); current § 4–215(a)(3); *see* Merrill Lynch, Pierce, Fenner & Smith, Inc. v. Devon Bank, 832 F.2d 1005, 1008–09 (7th Cir.1987) (effect when bank failed to give notice of dishonor by its midnight deadline).

124. Old §§ 4–213(1), 4–302; current § 4–302(a)(1). Note that similar language was deleted from current § 4–215(a) (for-

current Article 4 this language was deleted "as an unnecessary source of confusion."[125] It is unnecessary because under current Article 4 the payor bank either pays the item under § 4–215, dishonors and returns it before the midnight deadline under § 4–301, or becomes accountable for the amount of it under § 4–302. These are intended to be mutually exclusive alternatives, although some overlap remains, *e.g.*, between §§ 4–215 and 4–302 (as discussed *infra* at ¶ 8.02[3], [4] and [7]). Thus, there is no need to include a statutory rule of accountability with the rules on payment at § 4–215. In contrast, in old Article 4 the rule arguably was needed (at old § 4–213) because a payor bank could become accountable by completing the process of posting under old § 4–213(1)(c). With the deletion of that provision there is no need for a specific accountability rule outside of § 4–302.[126]

The basic Article 4 scheme for payor banks is straightforward. A settlement that is provisional can be revoked until the payor bank does any of the applicable things described above. If any of the above means of settlement occurs, the payor bank makes payment or becomes liable to do so. If the payor bank neither pays nor returns the item within its midnight deadline, it becomes accountable for the amount of the item under § 4–302.[127] In addition, as noted *infra*, for checks, Regulation CC

---

merly § 4–213(1)), in order to reduce confusion between the separate concepts of final payment (§ 4–215) and accountability (§ 4–302), and as not needed since any accountability is discharged by payment, particularly now that posting is deleted as a point of payment. *See, e.g.*, § 4–215 Comment 6 and § 4–302 Comment 3, as well as the discussion *infra* at ¶ 8.02[2][c] and notes 140–141.

125. *See Id.*

126. *Id. See also* the 2002 revision to Cmt. 4 of the uniform text § 3–502; *supra* note 115; *infra* note 156.

127. *See* § 4–215, and Comment 6; §§ 4–301 and 4–302. *See also* Kimberly A. Allen Trust v. FirstBank of Lakewood, N.A., 989 P.2d 203 (Colo.Ct.App.1999) (failure to dishonor item before the payor bank's midnight deadline is equivalent to final payment and payor bank becomes accountable for amount of item, precluding subsequent revocation of settlement for the item). This is subject to payor bank defenses, *e.g.*, breach of warranty and fraud. *See infra* ¶ 8.02 [4], [7]; § 4–302(b). For example, in First National Bank and Trust Co. of the Treasure Coast v. Belmont National Bank, 43 UCC Rep. Serv.2d 666, 2001 WL 15937 (Ohio Ct. App. 2001), a check was deposited without the required indorsement of a joint payee. It was sent through the banking system to the payor bank, which gave provisional credit and did not dishonor the item or revoke the credit within its midnight deadline (thereby losing the right to dishonor it under § 4–301 and becoming accountable for the amount of the item under § 4–302).

When the missing indorsement was discovered, the payor bank returned the item to the depositary bank and revoked credit for the item, on grounds of breach of warranty. The depositary bank had paid out the funds to its depositor, who was now bankrupt, and the depositary bank sued the payor to recover the payment under the midnight deadline rule at § 4–302. The court correctly concluded that recovery under § 4–302 was barred by the payor bank's counter-claim (asserted as a defense) for breach of warranty due to the lack of a required indorsement. *See also* Copple v. Boatmen's First National Bank of Okla., 958 P.2d 820 (Okla.Civ.App. 1998) (check returned more than six months after final payment, due to an improper indorsement constituting breach of warranty).

The transfer and presentment warranties, at §§ 3–416 and 3–417, and §§ 4–207(c) and 4–208(d), allow the breach of warranty claimant to recover damages up to the amount of the item plus "expenses and loss of interest." A recent Oklahoma Court of Appeals decision held that these provisions do not allow recovery of attorney fees. Christensen Aviation, Inc. v. State Bank, 20 P.3d 170 (Okla. Civ. App. Div. 2, 2001) (statutory language does not expressly provide for attorney fees, as do other UCC sections where that is intended). The court noted that there is a split of authority on this issue.

may modify and even extend the midnight deadline in some cases.[128]

[2] Methods of Making Final Payment

[a] Payment in Cash

If a payor bank takes a check from the holder, drawn on the payor bank, and gives the holder cash, it has made final payment of the check.[129] Normally this would occur only if the holder personally makes presentment at the payor bank and the payor bank is able to review the status of the drawer's account before making the payment.

Problems can arise, however, as illustrated by the classic case of *Kirby v. First & Merchants National Bank*.[130] In this case Mrs. Kirby, the holder of a check for $2,500, presented it to the payor bank for deposit but received a deposit slip crediting her account at the same bank with $2,300, listed on the line for cash deposit. In effect, this deposit slip was completed so as to indicate that the check was cashed, that $2,300 in cash was deposited, and that $200 in cash was retained by Mrs. Kirby.

Note that the presentment warranties do not include a warranty that the drawer's signature is genuine, only a warranty that the presenter has no knowledge to that effect. Thus, the drawee (*e.g.*, the payor bank) generally bears the burden (and loss) of any forged drawer signatures discovered after the item has been paid. The drawee cannot charge the customer's account for an improperly paid item, and cannot recover for breach of warranty from an innocent presenting party. *See, e.g.*, Decibel Credit Union v. Pueblo Bank & Trust Co., 996 P.2d 784, 43 UCC Rep.Serv.2d 941 (Colo.Ct. App. 2000).

128. *See* 12 CFR §§ 229.30 and 229.38, discussed *infra* at ¶ 8.04[3], and revised § 4–215, Comment 7.

129. § 4–215(a)(1) and Comments 3 and 8. Hill v. Mercantile First National Bank, 693 S.W.2d 285 (Mo.Ct.App.1985), held that payment of a personal check by issuance of a cashier's check constituted final payment in cash under old § 4–213(1)(a). This is not correct, unless one indulges in the fiction that cash was paid and then used to purchase the cashier's check, even though Comment 2 to § 3–418 states that in these circumstances payment has occurred by cash, because a cashier's check is not cash and therefore settlement by cashier's check is not payment by cash under § 4–215(a)(1). *See* § 4–213(a) and (c), and § 4–215 Comment 3. It would be more accurate to treat this as final settlement without reserving a right to revoke under § 4–215(a)(2), since § 4–301(a) does not deem the settlement provisional when an item is presented over the counter for immediate payment. *See* § 4–301(a), and Comments 4 and 8 to § 4–215 which so state. However, because the form of payment in such a case (a cashier's check) represents an obligation to pay rather than payment, a bank could reserve the right to revoke or assert a right of setoff, at least against the payee. So settlement by cashier's check could be either final or provisional, depending on the circumstances. *See, e.g.*, Gentner & Co., Inc. v. Wells Fargo Bank, 76 Cal. App.4th 1165, 90 Cal.Rptr.2d 904 (Cal.Ct. App.1999) (bank erroneously paid a customer's check over a valid stop payment order, by issuing a cashier's check to the payee. This constituted final payment under § 4–215 and a novation under § 3–310; the court erroneously concluded that this also cut off the bank's rights of subrogation under § 4–407). *See also infra* note 132; *infra* ¶ 8.02 [3]. *See* discussion *supra* in Chapter 4 at ¶ 4.04[2][b]. In any event, once final payment has been made, the payor bank's rights regarding revocation of settlement under § 4–301 terminate. *See* § 4–301(a), and Comment 2. This does not however preclude other forms of restitutionary recovery under § 3–418 or § 4–302(b). *See, e.g.*, § 4–301, Comment 7, citing National Savings and Trust Co. v. Park Corp., 722 F.2d 1303 (6th Cir.1983), *cert. denied*, 466 U.S. 939, 104 S.Ct. 1916, 80 L.Ed.2d 464 (1984) as a correct statement of the law; discussion *supra* at ¶ 8.02[1][b]; *infra* ¶ 8.02[4] and ¶ 8.02[7].

130. 210 Va. 88, 168 S.E.2d 273 (Va. 1969). While hardly a recent case, *Kirby* remains a classic in terms of illustrating the perils of final payment.

When it was subsequently discovered that the $2,500 check deposited by Mrs. Kirby was drawn on insufficient funds (the bank had not made Mrs. Kirby wait while it checked the account, perhaps because the check was drawn on a different branch), the bank was unable to charge back the insufficient check because the court concluded that the bank had made final payment in cash. The case is subject to obvious criticism because in all likelihood the check was deposited and $200 was withdrawn, no matter what the deposit slip showed, but it serves as a stark reminder of the importance of final payment, and careful bank teller training.[131]

[b] *Reserving the Right to Revoke*

Article 4 has long provided (at old § 4–213(1)(b)) that any settlement is final unless the payor bank reserves the right to revoke (or has it by clearing house rule or statute). Current § 4–215(a)(2) continues this rule, and expands it slightly by providing that settlement is final where the bank settles "without having a right to revoke . . . under statute, clearing-house rule, or agreement." This clarifies the bank's right to revoke settlement by agreement, or under the statute even in the absence of a contractual provision.[132] Most deposit contracts and deposit

---

131. The fundamental point is that once final payment has been made, the payor bank loses its right to revoke the settlement under § 4–301. In *Kirby* this resulted in large part from the teller's failure to make sure that the deposit slip reflected a deposit of the check rather than a cash transaction. *See* § 4–215, and Comment 8; § 4–301(a), and Comment 2. However, as noted *supra*, this remains subject to a possible restitutionary recovery. *See, e.g.,* § 4–301, Comment 7; §§ 3–418 and 4–302(b); *supra* ¶ 8.02[1][b]; *infra* ¶ 8.02[4] and ¶ 8.02[7].

132. § 4–215(a)(2). Comment 8 to § 4–215 suggests that this provision makes a cashier's check final payment of an "on-us" item given for it because § 4–301(a) does not apply. But that ignores the obvious distinctions between cash and a draft (*see* § 3–412; *supra* note 129, *infra* ¶ 8.02[3]), and the distinctions drawn between cash and cashier's checks for purposes of settlement at § 4–213(a) and (c), not to mention the probable effect of a contractual provision. *See also* § 3–411; *infra* ¶ 9.01[4][d].

The relation between stop payment orders and cashier's checks (or like instruments) can produce interesting results under § 4–407. In Gentner & Co., Inc. v. Wells Fargo Bank, 76 Cal.App.4th 1165, 90 Cal. Rptr.2d 904 (Cal.Ct.App.1999), the bank erroneously paid a customer's check despite a valid stop payment order, by issuing a cashier's check to the payee. This constituted final payment of the customer's check under §§ 3–418 and 4–215, and substituted the liability of the bank on the cashier's check for that of the drawer on the customer's check, under § 3–310.

While normally a bank that issues a cashier's check cannot assert claims or defenses of the remitter as a defense against the bank's liability to the holder of the cashier's check (*see* § 3–305(c)), in the *Gentner* scenario § 4–407 specifically subrogates the bank to the rights of the customer who stopped payment on the check written by that customer. To the extent the customer has a defense against the payee of the customer's check, the bank also can assert that defense under § 4–407. In *Gentner* the bank properly argued that the payee was not entitled to immunity against such defenses as a holder in due course under § 3–305(c), because the payee dealt directly with the bank that was asserting the defense.

In *Gentner* the bank should have won on these issues, but instead the court reprimanded the bank (and its lawyer) for interfering with the customer's expectations regarding the stop payment order. The court focused on final payment of the customer's check and § 3–418 as precluding rescission of that transaction. As far as it goes, this analysis of § 3–418 may have been correct, but even if that payment was final, the crucial question is whether the bank could assert its customer's rights under § 4–407 as a defense to liability on the subsequent cashier's check. The *Gentner* court errone-

receipt forms contain language specifying that the deposit credited is provisional and subject to revocation, and this constitutes a contractual authorization. Some deposit slips simply refer to the deposit contract (usually contained on the signature card), which normally contains a similar provision. Some form of reservation may be advisable, as suggested *supra* at note 117 and for other reasons as well, because while the Code in § 4–301 constitutes a statute that reserves the right to revoke, the statutory language indicating that the right to revoke cannot exist after final settlement and may lead a court to conclude that an unintended final settlement has occurred. A clear contractual provision may reduce the risk of such confusion.

Occasionally a customer will assert that the language on a deposit slip indicates an intent that settlement constitute final payment. Since the deposit slip usually is drawn with an opposite intent in mind, these efforts generally have not been successful.[133] Section 4–215(a)(2) should put such concerns to rest, by permitting the bank to rely on its right to revoke under § 4–301 prior to the midnight deadline, without regard to a reservation of rights under contract law.

[c] The Midnight Deadline

Section 4–215(a)(3) provides that a provisional settlement becomes final payment if the payor bank fails to revoke the settlement "in the time and manner permitted by statute, clearing house rule or agreement." This essentially refers to and incorporates the midnight deadline rule of § 4–301.[134] Section 4–301(a) and (b) allow a payor bank (whether

---

ously concluded that because the customer's liability on the customer's check was discharged under § 3–310, allowing the bank to assert a defense against liability on the cashier's check would leave the payee without a remedy; but this would merely allow the bank to assert the customer's position so as to resolve the dispute between the customer and payee. It is a means of resolving such disputes, not eliminating remedies; in its effort to preserve the payee's remedies, the *Gentner* court effectively eliminated the bank's remedy under § 4–407, even though § 3–418(c) (relied on by the court) specifically preserves these rights under § 4–407. See also *infra* ¶ 8.02[7].

133. See, e.g., Pracht v. Oklahoma State Bank, 592 P.2d 976 (Okla.1979).

134. See old § 4–215, Comment 7. Generally this only applies to items deposited for handling through regular bank collection channels, and not to items delivered to a bank for special handling or subject to a separate collection arrangement. See, e.g., Bank of Miami v. Banco Industrial Y Ganadero Del Beni, S.A., 515 So.2d 1038 (Fla. Dist.Ct.App.1987) (checks delivered to payor with instructions to hold for sufficient funds; instructions superseded the midnight deadline); David Graubart, Inc. v. Bank Leumi Trust Co., 48 N.Y.2d 554, 423 N.Y.S.2d 899, 399 N.E.2d 930 (N.Y.App. 1979) (discussed *supra* at note 25, and *infra* at note 213 and accompanying text); and Idaho Forest Indus., Inc. v. Minden Exch. Bank & Trust Co., 212 Neb. 820, 326 N.W.2d 176 (Neb. 1982) (depositary bank, after initial dishonor, re-delivered checks to payor with instruction to hold them for collection). See also discussion *supra* at ¶ 8.01[2] and *infra* at ¶ 9.03[3].

Moveover, if a clearing house rule were to provide a shorter or longer period, it could control. See, e.g., West Side Bank v. Marine Nat'l Exch. Bank, 37 Wis.2d 661, 155 N.W.2d 587 (Wis. 1968), discussed *supra* ¶ 8.02[2][c]; Western Air & Refrigeration v. Metro Bank of Dallas, 599 F.2d 83 (5th Cir.1979), discussed *infra* this text; and Springhill Bank & Trust Co. v. Citizens Bank & Trust Co., 505 So.2d 867 (La.Ct. App.1987). *Cf.* Merrill Lynch, Pierce, Fenner & Smith, Inc. v. Devon Bank, 832 F.2d 1005 (7th Cir.1987), *cert. denied*, 485 U.S. 1008, 108 S.Ct. 1473, 99 L.Ed.2d 702 (1988) (earlier deadline under clearing house rule

it is also the depositary bank or not) to revoke a provisional settlement if it returns the item or (if the item is unavailable for return) sends written notice of dishonor[135] before its midnight deadline.[136]

For payor banks the midnight deadline does not begin to run until actual presentment is made.[137] For example, in *Western Air & Refrigeration v. Metro Bank of Dallas*,[138] a check was left with the bank pending deposit of sufficient funds in the drawer's account; this did not constitute presentment so as to start the clock on the midnight deadline. A similar issue arose in *Pracht v. Oklahoma State Bank*,[139] where the parties disagreed over the date on which the deadline began to run. The customer argued that the check was received during business hours on the day in question, so that the deadline began to run on that date. But the court accepted the testimony of the bank president that it was received after the end of the banking day, and so the period for calculating the midnight deadline did not begin to run until the following banking day. The customer also objected to the order in which the items presented were paid and dishonored, but the court recognized that old § 4–303(2) allowed the bank to pay items in any order convenient to the bank. Current § 4–303(b) is similar, simply permitting payment "in any order" (the words "convenient to the bank" were deleted as unneces-

---

did not supersede the midnight deadline). The *Merrill Lynch* result is questionable, but was apparently based on the court's conclusion that the clearing house rule did not indicate an intent to override the midnight deadline. Lockhart Savings & Loan Association v. RepublicBank Austin, 720 S.W.2d 193 (Tex. Ct. App. 1986), represents a more customary analysis (clearing house rule requiring earlier return overrides midnight deadline; payor bank cannot choose between the two deadlines). *See also* Wolverton Farmers Elevator v. First American Bank of Rugby, 851 F.2d 223 (8th Cir.1988) (ambiguous "advice form" excused the midnight deadline); the definition of the midnight deadline at § 4–104(a)(10); interpretation of old § 4–104(1)(h) in Lufthansa German Airlines v. Bank of Am., 478 F.Supp. 1195 (N.D.Cal.1979), discussed *infra* at ¶ 8.03[4] and *supra* at note 57; § 4–109(a). *See generally* the discussion of modification by agreement, *supra* at ¶ 8.01[2] and *infra* at ¶ 9.03[3].

In addition the midnight deadline may be subject to extension under Regulation CC, if the payor bank expedites delivery of the returned item by a means that would ordinarily result in delivery by the receiving bank's next banking day after the otherwise applicable deadline. This deadline can be extended even further by use of a "highly expeditious means of transportation." *See* 12 CFR § 229.30(c), and discussion *infra* at ¶ 8.04[3][a][3].

135. Of course, the dishonor must also come before the bank has made final payment under any of the other provisions of § 4–215(a). *See* §§ 4–215(a) and 4–301(a). Note that where the payor bank is also the depositary bank, there is a partial exclusion from the initial settlement requirement at § 4–301(a). *See* § 4–301(b). *See* Comment 4 to § 4–301. *See also* SOS Oil v. Norstar Bank of Long Island, 76 N.Y.2d 561, 561 N.Y.S.2d 887, 563 N.E.2d 258 (N.Y. 1990) (§ 4–302 defeats bank's defenses in encoding error).

136. *See* § 4–301, Comment 2. As noted *supra* and discussed *infra* at ¶ 8.04[3][a] and [b], Regulation CC may preempt these rules by permitting notice in lieu of return and/or extending the midnight deadline in limited circumstances. *See* 12 CFR §§ 229.31(f) and 229.33 (notice of return); § 229.30(c) (extension of midnight deadline).

137. As noted *infra*, this raises questions regarding the time and place of presentment. On presentment, *see* § 3–501; 12 CFR § 229.36; *supra* ¶ 8.01[3][*l*], [n]; *infra* ¶ 8.04[3][f].

138. 599 F.2d 83 (5th Cir.1979). *See also* Reynolds–Wilson Lumber Co. v. Peoples Nat'l Bank, 699 P.2d 146 (Okla.1985), discussed *supra* at note 52.

139. 592 P.2d 976 (Okla.1979). *See also* Third Century Recycling Inc. v. Bank of Baroda, 704 F.Supp. 417 (S.D.N.Y.1989).

sary, but without intent to make a substantive change).[140]

Other problems can arise when items are presented via branch banks or through a data-processing center. In *Idah-Best, Inc. v. First Security Bank*,[141] items were routed to the payor bank via a check-processing center that performed various bookkeeping functions before delivery of the checks to the payor. Did presentment occur and the midnight deadline begin to run upon delivery to the data-processing center, or only upon the subsequent delivery to the payor bank itself? In *Idah-Best* the court applied a functional test and the data-processing center was treated as a collecting bank, so that presentment was made only when the item was actually delivered to the payor bank. A number of other courts reached similar conclusions in cases where a collecting bank additionally was providing data-processing services for the payor bank.[142] However, as noted below and *supra* at ¶ 8.01[3][*l*], there are important cases to the contrary and the trend was running in the other direction even before *Idah-Best* was essentially rejected in the 1990 revisions. For example, in *Central Bank v. Peoples National Bank*,[143] a separate data-processing center was treated as an integral part of the bank branch on which the item was drawn, making delivery to the center a presentment to the branch. While, under Article 4, presentment means a demand for payment made on the payor,[144] and the traditional definition of the process of posting[145] indicates that both processing and the decision to pay are essential elements of payor bank status and therefore that mere processing functions are suggestive of collecting bank status, current § 4–204(c) confirms *Central Bank* by making clear that the time begins to run if the bank requests presentment at a data processing center. Under § 4–204(c), presentment may be made where requested by the payor bank.[146] Thus, in these circumstances it is

---

140. See § 4–303, Comment 7: "No priority rule is stated ... [t]he drawer has no basis for urging one should be paid before another; and the holders have no direct right against the payor bank.... [T]he bank has the right to pay items for which it is itself liable ahead of those for which it is not." See also Shelley v. AmSouth Bank, 2000 WL 1121778 (S.D. Ala.), *affd*, 247 F.3d 250 (11th Cir.2001) (denial of class certification); Union Planters Bank, N.A. v. Watson, 2001 WL 336055 (Ala.), *replacing* 2000 WL 1841875 (Ala. 2000) (judgment affirmed without opinion). The best case from a bank's perspective is Hill v. St. Paul Federal Bank, 329 Ill.App.3d 705, 263 Ill.Dec. 562, 768 N.E.2d 322 (2002) (rejecting good faith and deceptive practices claims against a bank for maximizing its overdraft fees).

141. 99 Idaho 517, 584 P.2d 1242 (Idaho 1978) (subsequent history at 101 Idaho 402, 614 P.2d 425 (Idaho 1980)). See also Sass Trucking, Inc. v. Security Bank and Trust Co., 737 P.2d 113 (Okla.1987), and other authorities cited *infra* notes 142–143;

and *supra* ¶ 8.01[3][*l*], at note 60. See also discussion *supra* in Chapter 4.

142. Catalina Yachts v. Old Colony Bank & Trust Co., 497 F.Supp. 1227 (D.Mass.1980); Bon Bon Productions, Ltd. v. Xanadu Productions, Inc., 32 U.C.C. Rep. Serv. (Callaghan) 253 (D. Mass. 1981). See also the discussion *supra* in Chapter 4 at ¶ 4.03[2][a][iii].

143. 401 So.2d 14 (Ala.1981). See also Chrysler Credit Corp. v. First Nat'l Bank & Trust Co., 582 F.Supp. 1436 (W.D.Pa.1984); and *Sass Trucking*, 737 P.2d 113.

144. § 3–501(a).

145. See old § 4–109; as noted *supra* at ¶ 8.02[2][c], current Article 4 deletes this concept as unneeded, and unsuitable for a system of automated check collection or electronic presentment. But the definition remains useful in this context.

146. See also Regulation CC, 12 CFR § 229.36(b), and other authorities cited *supra* at note 60.

prudent to act on the basis that presentment may occur before the check arrives (if it ever does) at the payor bank,[147] and payor banks need to be sure that dishonored items are being properly returned under § 4–301 within a midnight deadline that commences to run upon any requested delivery of the item to a designated processing center.

[3] Final Settlement and Accountability Under Article 4

As noted *supra* at ¶ 8.02[1][c], under Article 4 there are three possibilities upon presentment of an item: (1) it may be paid, under § 4–215; (2) it may be dishonored by return within the midnight deadline, under § 4–301; or (3) the payor bank may become accountable for the amount of the item under § 4–302. These are separate and mutually exclusive possibilities with potentially different consequences, and should be distinguished from one another.

While the relation between §§ 4–215, 4–301, and 4–302 may trigger some complex issues, the basic structure of the Code is clear: (1) Section 4–215 determines whether an item has been paid and, if so, the consequences under Article 4; (2) § 4–301 determines whether an item has been dishonored and, if so, the consequences under Article 4; and (3) § 4–302 is the residual provision that makes the payor bank accountable for the amount of the item if neither of the other sections applies because the bank has failed to either pay or dishonor the item before its midnight deadline. But sometimes identifying the precise dividing lines between these sections and the transactions they cover can be a challenge.

For example, if the payor bank makes a provisional settlement of an item under § 4–301, and the settlement later becomes final under a clearing house agreement,[148] this constitutes final payment under § 4–215(a)(3). In contrast, if the item is returned before the bank's midnight deadline pursuant to an agreement or under § 4–301(a)(1), then any provisional settlement may be revoked pursuant to that section.[149] Finally, if the payor bank makes a provisional settlement, *e.g.*, by remitting a cashier's or teller's check through the bank collection system under § 4–215(a)(3) (not an over-the-counter payment under § 4–215(a)(2)), and that settlement fails to become final under § 4–213(c)(1) (*e.g.*, because the check is not paid), then the payor bank becomes accountable under § 4–302(a).[150] Note, however, that where the

---

147. This also is true for the time limits under Regulation CC, 12 CFR § 229.36(b). However, it should be noted that Regulation CC does not necessarily govern presentment for purposes of Article 4. *See* 12 CFR § 229.38(a), § 229.36(b).

148. *See* § 4–215, Comment 4.

149. *See also* § 4–215, Comment 7. Regulation CC also imposes requirements and potential liabilities on the payor bank in these circumstances. *See* 12 CFR §§ 229.30 and 229.38, discussed *infra* ¶ 8.04[3][a], [b]; and § 4–215, Comment 7. *See also infra*

¶ 8.04[3][c] (duties of returning banks). Regulation CC essentially eliminates provisionality of settlement for banks, but leaves the distinctions between provisional settlement and final payment in effect for depositary banks. *Id.*, and *infra* ¶ 8.04 [3] [b], [c], and [d].

150. *See, e.g.*, § 4–215(a)(3) and (b), and Comment 8. This is subject to various defenses at §§ 3–418 and 4–302(b), and at common law to the extent available between the parties, as discussed *infra* at ¶ 8.02[4]. *See also* §§ 1–103, 3–411; *infra*

payor bank fails to revoke a provisional settlement under § 4–301, this may be treated as a final settlement and payment of the item under § 4–215(a)(3), and not accountability under § 4–302.[151]

As stated in Comment 8 to § 4–215, § 4–215(b) is a limited exception to the final payment rule at § 4–215(a)(3). Section 4–215(b) provides that: "[i]f provisional settlement for an item does not become final, the item is not finally paid."[152] Thus if, a payor bank makes provisional settlement under § 4–215(a)(3), *e.g.*, by cashier's check, and that settlement fails to become final, *e.g.*, under § 4–213(c), then § 4–215(b) specifies that payment has not occurred, thereby triggering the accountability rule at § 4–302 rather than the final payment rule of § 4–215. But if settlement has occurred and is not effectively revoked, *e.g.*, under § 4–215(a)(2) or (3) by reason of clearing house rule or over-the-counter payment by cashier's check, § 4–215(b) does not apply because there has been final payment under § 4–215(a). Final payment under § 4–215(a) generally "firms up" all prior, provisional settlements,[153] and entitles the party who presented the item and the owner of the item to withdrawal of the funds as a matter of right subject to time limitations and defenses.[154]

If final payment has occurred in the form of a settlement under § 4–215(a)(2) or (3) (*e.g.*, by a cashier's check taken over-the-counter or clearing house rule or agreement), and that settlement fails (*e.g.*, under § 4–213(c)(2)), the payment is nonetheless final and the risk is on the party receiving the settlement, as explained at § 4–215 Comment 8. Where the provisional settlement does not become final, as under § 4–215(b) and § 4–301, the payor bank becomes accountable for the item under § 4–302(a), and there is created a statutory liability subject to applicable defenses.[155] Thus there may be a distinction in the analysis in some instances, depending whether the settlement remained provisional (§§ 4–215(b), 4–301, and 4–302)), or was revoked (§ 4–301), or final payment was made (§ 4–215(a).[156] In addition, Regulation CC may

¶ 8.02[7]. *See also infra* ¶ 8.03[5] (Settlement by Remittance or Other Means).

151. *Id.* and § 4–215, Comment 7. *See also* discussion *infra* at ¶ 8.02[4] and [7]; § 3–502, Comment 4 (2002 uniform text); and further discussions below. The courts do not always recognize this distinction. *See, e.g.*, Channel Equipment Co., Inc. v. Community State Bank, 996 S.W.2d 374 (Tex.Ct.App.1999).

152. § 4–215, Comments 7 and 8. *See also* § 4–301, Comment 3.

153. § 4–215(c).

154. *See* §§ 4–215(d), (e), 4–214(a), 4–213, and 3–418, and § 4–215, Comments 9 through 11. This is subject to exceptions where the final payment was made by remittance instrument. *See infra* ¶ 8.03[5].

155. *See* § 4–302(a), (b), and Comments 2 and 3; *infra* ¶ 8.02[4]. *See, e.g.*, Channel Equipment Co., Inc. v. Community State Bank, 996 S.W.2d 374 (Tex.Ct.App.1999).

156. *See, e.g.*, § 4–215, Comment 8 and § 4–301(a), noting that if there has been a final payment in cash or otherwise "over the counter" under § 4–215(a)(1) or (2), then the settlement is immediately final and the §§ 4–301 and 4–302 provisions on settlement, accountability, and revocation do not apply. *See supra* ¶ 8.02[1][b]. It is also possible that § 3–418 applies only after payment under § 4–215(a), and that § 4–302(b) applies only upon accountability under § 4–302(a). This would represent another distinction between payment under § 4–215 and accountability under § 4–302. Logically the same range of claims and defenses should be applicable in both cases. *See also supra* ¶ 8.02[1][c]. *But see infra* ¶ 8.02[4], [7].

The distinctions between final payment (§ 4–215), dishonor (§ 4–301), and accountability (§ 4–302) are further discussed in the 2002 amendments to § 3–502 (the Article 3 dishonor rule) at Comment 4.

impose additional requirements and/or liabilities on the parties in these circumstances.[157]

Note that settlement by cashier's check can be either final payment under § 4–215(a)(2) (as in payment of an item presented over-the-counter), or provisional settlement under § 4–215(a)(3) which is subsequently revoked because it does not become final under §§ 4–213(c) and 4–215(b) (as in an agreed remittance between banks). Clearing-house settlements could similarly be final under § 4–215(a)(2) or provisional under § 4–215(a)(3). A significance of the distinction is that settlements under § 4–215(a)(2) are final payment and cannot be revoked, while settlements under § 4–215(a)(3) become final payment only if they are not revoked or don't otherwise fail to become final (*e.g.*, under § 4–213(c)). Thus settlements by cashier's checks or clearing house rule may constitute final payment under § 4–215(a)(2), or be a prelude to a revocation or failure of provisional settlement under § 4–215(a)(3) and (b), leading not to final payment under § 4–215 but rather to accountability under § 4–302(a).

[4] *Avoidance of Payment on Restitutionary Grounds*

As noted, *Kirby v. First and Merchants National Bank*[158] is a classic case illustrating the limitations on a payor bank's ability to rescind final payment on equitable or other grounds. In seeking to recover a final payment erroneously made to Mrs. Kirby, the bank sought to recover the funds on equitable grounds, including theories of mistake and estoppel. The check was paid to Mrs. Kirby by mistake—despite insufficient funds—and in part the bank had failed to dishonor the check within its midnight deadline due to the Kirby's telephone assurances that they would cover the check, giving rise to an equitable estoppel argument. This raised issues that were unclear under old Article 4, regarding the ability of a payor bank to revoke Article 4 final payment on equitable restitutionary grounds.[159]

In *Kirby* the bank's arguments were unsuccessful,[160] but cases such as *Bank Leumi Trust Co. v. Bally's Park Place, Inc.*[161] allowed the payor bank to avoid accountability under § 4–302 on a restitutionary theory.

---

157. *See* 12 CFR §§ 229.30, 229.38, discussed *infra* at ¶ 8.04[3][a]. *See also* discussion *supra* at ¶ 8.02[1][b], and *infra* at ¶ 8.02[4] and ¶ 8.02[7].

158. 210 Va. 88, 168 S.E.2d 273 (Va. 1969), discussed *supra* this text at notes 130–131 and accompanying text, and *infra* this text at notes 159–171. *See also supra* ¶ 8.02[1][b]. *See also* National Savings and Trust Co. v. Park Corp., 722 F.2d 1303 (6th Cir.1983); *supra* ¶ 8.02[1][c] and [3].

159. *See e.g.*, Hill, A Drawee's Right to Restitution under Articles 3 and 4 of the UCC: A Plea for Clarification, 7 J.L. & Com. 293 (1987) and *supra* this text at notes 114–115.

160. In *Kirby* the dissenting opinion approved of the estoppel argument. *See Kirby*, 168 S.E.2d 273, at 279 (Harrison, J. dissenting).

161. 528 F.Supp. 349 (S.D.N.Y.1981), discussed *supra* notes 113 and 115 and accompanying text. *See also* National Savings & Trust Co. v. Park Corp., 722 F.2d 1303 (6th Cir.1983), *cert. denied*, 466 U.S. 939, 104 S.Ct. 1916, 80 L.Ed.2d 464 (1984); Morgan Guaranty Trust Co. v. American Sav. & Loan Ass'n, 804 F.2d 1487 (9th Cir.1986), *cert. denied*, 482 U.S. 929, 107 S.Ct. 3214, 96 L.Ed.2d 701 (1987); National Bank of Canada v. Artex Industries, Inc., 627 F.Supp. 610 (S.D.N.Y.1986).

One primary obstacle to such a recovery has always been the language at § 4–302 making the payor bank "accountable" for the amount of an item upon a failure to either pay or dishonor the item.[162] For example, Professors White and Summers initially followed the reasoning of Fairfax Leary that old §§ 4–213 and 4–302 "cut off" the payor bank's right to restitution after the midnight deadline.[163] In the third edition of their hornbook, however, Professors White and Summers recanted, on grounds that restitutionary remedies should not be cut off under the language of old § 4–302.[164] Section 4–302(b) now states that the accountability of a payor bank under § 4–302(a) is subject to the bank defenses of breach of a presentment warranty or fraud, and final payment under § 4–215 is clearly subject to revocation on restitutionary grounds under § 3–418.[165] This codification is consistent with the later White and

---

162. Similar language appears at the end of old § 4–213(1), but was deleted from current § 4–215(a). See *supra* notes 124–126, and 134–136, and 148–154; discussion *supra* ¶ 8.02[1][c].

163. See, e.g., J. WHITE & R. Summers, Uniform Commercial Code § 16–4, and 594, n. 131 (1972); Leary & Schmitt, Some Bad News and Some Good News From Articles Three and Four, 43 OHIO ST. L.J. 611 (1982); Northwestern Nat'l Ins. Co. v. Midland Nat'l Bank, 96 Wis.2d 155, 292 N.W.2d 591 (Wis. 1980); State & Savings Bank v. Meeker, 469 N.E.2d 55 (Ind.Ct.App.1984) (UCC displaces the doctrine of equitable restitution); National Savings & Trust Co. v. Park Corp., 722 F.2d 1303 (6th Cir.1983), cert. denied, 466 U.S. 939, 104 S.Ct. 1916, 80 L.Ed.2d 464 (1984). Even so, some courts found other theories to get around this argument. See e.g., *Meeker*, 469 N.E.2d 55 (bank may have benefit of other recovery by holder) and Starcraft Co. v. C.J. Heck Co., 748 F.2d 982 (5th Cir.1984) (subrogation to claim of customer of bank against person asserting § 4–302). See *infra* this text ¶ 9.02[3]. See *also supra* ¶ 8.02[1][b] and ¶ 8.02[3].

164. See J. White & R. Summers, Uniform Commercial Code § 17–2 (3d Ed. 1988). The statutory language of old § 4–302 makes the bank's accountability subject to "a valid defense," arguably including a restitutionary recovery. As noted *supra* at ¶ 8.02[1][b] and *infra* this text, this language is modified by the Article 4 revision to expressly recognize a fraud defense. See *also supra* notes 108–115, 124–126, and 134–156, and ¶ 8.02[1][c].

165. See § 4–301, Comment 7. See *supra* ¶ 8.02[1][b] and [3]; *infra* ¶ 8.02 [7]. See generally Kimberly A. Allen Trust v. First-Bank of Lakewood, N.A., 989 P.2d 203 (Colo.Ct.App.1999) (failure to dishonor item before the payor bank's midnight deadline is equivalent to final payment and payor bank becomes accountable for the amount of item, precluding subsequent revocation of settlement for the item). But this accountability is subject to a payor bank claim for breach of warranty. If breached, the presentment warranties at § 4–208 allow the payor bank to return an item after the midnight deadline.

For example, in First National Bank and Trust Co. of the Treasure Coast v. Belmont National Bank, 43 UCC Rep. Serv.2d 666, 2001 WL 15937 (Ohio Ct. App. 2001), a check was deposited without the required indorsement of a joint payee. It was sent through the banking system to the payor bank, which gave provisional credit and did not dishonor the item or revoke the credit within its midnight deadline (thereby losing the right to dishonor it under § 4–301 and becoming accountable for the amount of the item under § 4–302).

When the missing indorsement was discovered, the payor bank returned the item to the depository bank and revoked credit for the item, on grounds of breach of warranty. The depository bank had paid out the funds to its depositor, who was now bankrupt, and the depository bank sued the payor bank to recover the payment under the midnight deadline rule at § 4–302. The court correctly concluded that recovery under § 4–302 was barred by the payor bank's counter-claim (asserted as a defense) for breach of warranty due to the lack of a required indorsement. Summary judgement for the payor bank was properly affirmed.

Note, however, that the presentment warranties do not include a warranty that the drawer's signature is genuine, only a warranty that the presenter has no knowledge to that effect. Thus, the drawee (e.g., the payor bank) generally bears the burden (and loss) of any forged drawer signatures

Summers view and cases such as *National Savings & Trust Co. v. Park Corp.*,[166] which allowed restitution on grounds of mistake. The statute also confirms the result of cases like *Bank Leumi*,[167] where the item was fraudulently presented for payment with knowledge that the drawer had died leaving an insolvent estate. Thus, Article 4 now explicitly permits restitutionary recoveries on grounds of fraud, even where the bank has made final payment under § 4–215 or is otherwise accountable under § 4–302.[168]

Moreover, even where a payor bank is accountable under § 4–302 or has made final payment under § 4–215, it may have the benefit of other theories of recovery, and may be subrogated to the rights of its customer (the drawer of the item) under § 4–407 so as to enable the bank to assert as a defense to liability any other recovery by the asserting party and any rights the bank's customer may have against the payee or other holder of the item.[169] In effect these theories represent other avenues of

---

discovered after the item has been paid: The drawee cannot charge the customer's account for an improperly paid item, and cannot recover for breach of warranty from an innocent presenting party. *See, e.g.,* Decibel Credit Union v. Pueblo Bank & Trust Co., 996 P.2d 784, 43 UCC Rep. Serv.2d 941 (Colo.Ct.App. 2000).

166. 722 F.2d 1303 (6th Cir.1983), *cert. denied,* 466 U.S. 939, 104 S.Ct. 1916, 80 L.Ed.2d 464 (1984). This case is cited at § 4–301, Comment 7, as a correct statement of the law.

167. 528 F.Supp. 349 (S.D.N.Y.1981), discussed *supra* notes 113, 115 and 161, and infra note 168 and accompanying text.

168. *See* § 4–302(b), and Comment 3, citing *Bank Leumi* with approval. *See also* Sayan v. Riggs Nat'l Bank of Washington, D.C., 544 A.2d 267 (D.C. 1988) (customer who intentionally withdraws uncollectible funds may be guilty of bank fraud under 18 U.S.C. § 2113(b)); Charles R. Cravens, Jr., U.S. v. Morgenstern: Forgery Deterrent, 46 Consumer Fin. L.Q. Rep. 46 (1992).

169. *See, e.g.,* State & Savings Bank v. Meeker, 469 N.E.2d 55 (Ind.Ct.App.1984) and Starcraft Co. v. C.J. Heck Co., 748 F.2d 982 (5th Cir.1984). Section 4–407 also may enable the bank to recover from the customer by way of subrogation to the rights of the payee or holder. *See* § 4–407(1), (2); Pulaski State Bank v. Kalbe, 122 Wis.2d 663, 364 N.W.2d 162 (Wis.Ct.App.1985). Section 4–407 makes clear that a payor bank has this right even after the account has been closed. *See* discussion *infra* at ¶ 9.02[3]. If the bank is subrogated to the rights of a holder in due course the bank may be entitled to charge the customer's account with immunity to certain defenses that would otherwise be available to the drawer to preclude this. *See* Valley Bank of Nevada v. JER Management Corp., 149 Ariz. 415, 719 P.2d 301 (Ariz.Ct.App.1986). For a discussion of holder in due course status, *see supra* Chapter 3. These subrogation rights are in addition to any rights the bank may have in its own right. Notice that even if the prior holder otherwise qualifies as a holder in due course, it will fail to so qualify if it took the item more than a reasonable time after its issue date. For a check governed by old Article 3 a reasonable time was deemed to be 30 days. *See* old § 3–304(3)(c); and American State Bank v. Northwest S.D. P.C.A., 404 N.W.2d 517 (S.D. 1987). Under current Article 3 the time period is 90 days. *See* §§ 3–302(a)(2) and 3–304(a)(2).

The relation between stop payment orders, cashier's checks (or like instruments), and the final payment rules can produce interesting results under § 4–407. In Gentner & Co., Inc. v. Wells Fargo Bank, 76 Cal.App.4th 1165, 90 Cal.Rptr.2d 904 (Cal. Ct.App.1999), the bank erroneously paid a customer's check despite a valid stop payment order, by issuing a cashier's check to the payee. This constituted final payment of the customer's check under §§ 3–418 and 4–215, and substituted the liability of the bank on the cashier's check for that of the drawer on the customer's check, under § 3–310.

While normally a bank that issues a cashier's check cannot assert claims or defenses of the remitter as a defense against the bank's liability to the holder of the cashier's check (*see* § 3–305(c)), in the *Gentner* scenario § 4–407 specifically subrogates the payor bank to the rights of the customer who stopped payment on the check written

defense against liability for accountability or final payment, not specified at §§ 4–302(b) or 3–418. And of course the bank may have other rights, such as common law set-off or recoupment rights, that arise outside of Article 4. Subrogation under § 4–407 in essence constitutes an exception to the general rule, stated at § 4–407 and at § 3–305(c), that no party can assert any claim or defense of another person.[170] The final payment and accountability rules at §§ 4–215 and 4–302 are designed to provide finality of payment with respect to matters relating to the bank payment system and Article 4, not to immunize parties using that collection system from liability for fraud or other wrongdoing in the same or unrelated transactions. Thus, for example, other claims of the bank against the customer can be set off against the bank's accountability under § 4–302. As discussed here and *infra* at ¶ 8.02[7], §§ 4–215(a) and 4–302(a) should not be construed so broadly as to cut-off the bank's non-Article 4 claims. In this respect, the *Kirby* rationale has been rejected.

None of this, however, resolves the related questions of whether the payor bank's defenses and rights under § 3–418 are limited to final payment scenarios under § 4–215, and whether the payor bank's defenses at § 4–302(b) are limited to accountability claims under § 4–302(a). Logically the full range of defensive rights based on equitable concepts like fraud and mistake should be available in both payment and accountability cases, rather than limiting mistake to a defense against or claim to recover payment (§ 3–418) and limiting fraud (or breach of warranty) to a defense against accountability (§ 4–302(b)). It is possible that the drafters intended a broad applicability of equitable defenses in both

---

by that customer. To the extent the customer has a defense against the payee of the customer's check, the payor bank also can assert that defense under § 4–407. In *Gentner*, the bank properly argued that the payee was not entitled to immunity against such defenses as a holder in due course under § 3–305(c), because the payee dealt directly with the bank that was asserting the defense.

In *Gentner*, the bank should have won on these issues, but instead the court reprimanded the bank (and its lawyer) for interfering with the customer's expectations regarding the stop payment order. The court's focus on final payment of the customer's check and § 3–418 may have been correct, but even if that payment was final, the crucial question is whether the bank could assert its customer's rights under § 4–407 as a defense to liability on the subsequent cashier's check. The *Gentner* court erroneously concluded that because the customer's liability on the customer's check was discharged under § 3–310, allowing the bank to assert a defense against liability on the cashier's check would leave the payee without a remedy; but this would merely allow the bank to assert the customer's rights so as to resolve the dispute between the customer and payee. It is a means of resolving such disputes, not eliminating remedies; in its effort to preserve the payee's remedies, the *Gentner* court effectively eliminated the bank's remedy under § 4–407, even though § 3–418(c) (relied on by the court) specifically preserves these rights under § 4–407.

Of course, the party seeking to hold the bank accountable under § 4–302 cannot use that rule to achieve a double recovery. In Channel Equipment Co., Inc. v. Community State Bank, 996 S.W.2d 374 (Tex.Ct.App. 1999) the bank dishonored the checks after the midnight deadline, becoming accountable under § 4–302. However, the dishonored checks were returned to the depositor, and the depositor was able to recover from the drawer on the checks. When the depositor sought to recover again from the payor bank under § 4–302, the court rejected this claim to a double recovery. *See also* Union Bank of Benton v. First National Bank of Mt. Pleasant, 621 F.2d 790 (5th Cir.1980); State & Savings Bank of Monticello v. Meeker, 469 N.E.2d 55 (Ind.App.1984); First Nat'l. Bank in Harvey v. Colonial Bank, 898 F.Supp. 1220 (N.D.Ill.1995).

170. *See also* Comment 5 to § 4–407 on yet other possible defenses.

payment and accountability scenarios, simply focusing on the most likely scenarios for each Code section (as noted *infra*). But for whatever reason, the statutory language recognizes separate payor claims and defenses at §§ 3–418 and 4–302(b); perhaps this merely recognizes that it is more likely an erroneous payment will involve an affirmative mistake under § 3–418 while the more passive concept of accountability under § 4–302(a) is more likely to trigger a defense based on fraud or breach of warranty under § 4–302(b) rather than a claim based on mistake by the payor. Indeed, in a broad sense accountability under § 4–302(a) will often result from mistake so a broad statutory exception for mistake at § 4–302(b) might swallow the accountability rule at § 4–302(a). Thus, we believe that §§ 3–418 and 4–302(b) normally should be read together as exceptions to the rules of final payment and accountability (§§ 4–215(a) and 4–302(a)) and as supplementary to the otherwise broad doctrine of mistake (§ 1–103). Within logical limits, either § 3–418 or § 4–302(b) should be applicable in a payment or accountability scenario. The inherent overlap between §§ 4–215, 4–301, and 4–302, together with the broad scope of § 1–103, makes this a plausible reading despite the Article 4 distinctions between payment and accountability. But unless and until this issue is finally clarified, the conservative position may be to recognize that in some instances § 3–418 could be limited to § 4–215, and § 4–302(b) could be limited to § 4–302(a).[171]

[5] *Funds Availability Under Article 4*

Where the depositary bank is not both the depositary and the payor bank,[172] and settlement was made for the item through a clearing house

---

171. Thus, for example, if a bank pays an item by mistake over a stop payment order, it may have a claim under § 3–418, while if the bank merely misses the midnight deadline it is accountable under § 4–302 absent fraud or breach of warranty. In the latter scenario the bank cannot avoid accountability merely because the delay was accidental (and in that sense a mistake). But if the failure to meet the midnight deadline qualifies as payment under § 4–215(a) (3) (*see supra* ¶ 8.02 [2]), and the payor bank acted in a mistaken belief that there was no stop payment order, the bank should be entitled to revoke the settlement under § 3–418. In other words, if the delay causing the bank to miss the midnight deadline also involved a mistake under § 3–418, the bank should have a defense against § 4–302(a) accountability under § 3–418 (subject to the § 3–418(c) rights of a holder in due or reliance party), independently of § 4–302(b). If the drawer's signature is forged, the bank may have a defense against payment under § 3–418 (again, subject to the § 3–418 rights of a holder in due course or reliance party) and may also have a defense under § 4–302(b) if there was fraud or a breach of warranty. But note that in this scenario (a forged drawer's signature), the payor bank receives only a limited warranty regarding the drawer's signature, at § 4–208(a)(3). Essentially this warrants only a lack of guilty knowledge. *See supra* ¶ 7.02. This codifies the old English case of Price v. Neal, which is also consistent with § 3–418. Thus, an appropriately innocent party will not be subject to a claim or defense of the payor under either § 3–418 or § 4–302(b), though the theory in each of these sections is somewhat different (under § 3–418 a forged signature is treated as genuine after final payment to an innocent party; under § 4–302 the midnight deadline accountability rule is enforced absent an exception at § 4–302(b)). But a party who is not innocent (*e.g.*, who participated in the forgery) will be subject to revocation of payment under § 3–418 and claims for fraud and breach of warranty under § 4–302(b). *See also infra* ¶ 8.02[1][c], ¶ 8.02[7]; 2002 revisions to § 3–502, Comment 4 (2002 uniform text); *supra* note 156.

172. The rule where the payor also is the depositary bank is set out in

or by debits or credits in accounts at each step as the item proceeded through the collection chain, when the payor bank finally pays the item the settlements become final under § 4–215(c) seriatim between the presenting and payor banks and between the presenting and successive prior collecting banks. As discussed *infra* at ¶ 8.04, Federal Reserve Board Regulation CC preempts this to some extent by deeming settlements for checks between banks to be final when made. Under Article 4 § 4–215(d), upon final settlement each collecting bank is accountable to its customer, but the funds from the collected check are not available to a depositor as "of right," even though the check has been paid, until the depositary bank has had a reasonable time to learn that the settlement by the payor bank is final.[173] However, as recognized at § 4–215(e), and as discussed *infra* this text at ¶ 8.04, the customer may have a right to earlier funds availability under other state law or, more probably, under Regulation CC.[174]

Under Article 4 Part 2, the depositary bank may allow its customer to draw against credit for a deposited item before payment of that item is final, and doing so will not preclude the bank from charging the item back to the customer's account if the item is not paid. Of course, allowing a customer to draw against uncollected funds poses a risk to the depositary bank if the amount of collected funds in the account is insufficient to bear the charge-back and the customer is not creditworthy, because the item ultimately may be dishonored by the payor and returned unpaid. Prior to Regulation CC, depositary banks often delayed funds availability by contract, until a deposited item should have been paid or notice of dishonor received from the payor and, as a general rule, such contracts were valid under Article 4.[175] However, as noted *infra* at ¶ 8.04, such contracts are now limited by Regulation CC as regards the collection of checks.

The waiting time to learn of final disposition (payment or dishonor) may be a considerable time from the date of deposit of the item. A depositary bank only learns that settlement is final by not getting back a dishonored item or notice of dishonor, and as a practical matter it can only be sure that this will not occur by waiting a sufficient time. The amount of time that is sufficient is a function of the normal time it will take the item to arrive at the payor bank, plus the time it should take for the item to be returned or notice to be given to the depositary institution

§ 4–215(e)(2). The rule for a deposit of money is set out in § 4–215(f).

173. More accurately under § 4–215(e)(1), the requirement is that sufficient time for the item's return has passed.

174. *See* Regulation CC, Subpart B, 12 CFR §§ 229.10–229.21, described *infra* at ¶ 8.04 [2]. In addition, Regulation CC, Subpart C, makes all settlements for checks between banks final but within appropriate deadlines the depositary bank can still recover payment for a returned check. The result is essentially the same as under Article 4, except that under Regulation CC the settlements between banks are final so that forward collection and return paths need not be the same. *See* Comments 4 to §§ 4–214 and 4–215 and *see infra* ¶ 8.04[3].

175. *See, e.g.*, Rapp v. Dime Savings Bank, 48 N.Y.2d 658, 421 N.Y.S.2d 347, 396 N.E.2d 740 (N.Y.App.1979), *aff'd*, 64 A.D.2d 964, 408 N.Y.S.2d 540 (App. Div. 1978), with respect to agreements allowing 6 busi-

if the item is dishonored.[176] Return times for dishonored items generally are much longer than forward collection times because return processing is not automated to the same extent as is forward collection processing. As noted *infra* at ¶ 8.04[3], Regulation CC has sought to speed up the return process. However, this has met with only limited success.

Regulation CC was prompted in part by complaints about banks' "hold" periods for deposited items. Some viewed these as an attempt by banks to capture float benefits from consumers. Others recognized other reasons for the holds but complained that some banks waited longer than necessary before recognizing that final settlement had taken place. States, including New York and California, enacted legislation to deal with the delayed availability issue. California and New York amended old § 4–213(4)(a) to require regulators to specify what is a "reasonable amount of time" to wait before giving check depositors availability as of right. The statutes also required depositary institutions to disclose availability policies to their customers. These were important nonuniform amendments and represented the first time that regulatory implementation of UCC provisions had occurred.[177] As discussed *infra* at ¶ 8.04, Regulation CC has now largely preempted this field.

[6] *Notice of Dishonor and Return of the Item*

If the payor bank determines not to pay the item, and if the bank is to avoid being held accountable for the amount of that item, it must return the item in a timely manner or (in limited circumstances) send notice of dishonor.[178] Section 4–301(a)(1) provides the primary requirement to return the item. Under the 1990 revisions, sending notice of dishonor, without returning the dishonored item, continues to be an

---

ness days for local items and 15 business days for other items.

176. Of course, the check actually could take less time, or more time, in cases of MICR fraud. *See, e.g,* Miller, Ballen, Davenport and Vergari, Commercial Paper, Bank Deposits and Collections, and Commercial Electronic Fund Transfers, 42 BUS. LAW. 1269, 1279–1283 (1987). Regulation CC, 12 CFR § 229.33, requires notice of nonpayment for checks in the amount of $2,500 or more as one attempt to address this sort of problem.

177. New York Banking Law § 14–3; California Financial Code §§ 866–866.9. The New York regulations became part of the General Regulations of the Banking Board, part 34 (effective Mar. 8, 1984). The California Regulations were at § 10.190401 *et seq.* Because hold periods reflect a balance between risk to the bank and convenience to the customer, this was traditionally considered an issue to be determined between banks and their customers, as with other account terms. Therefore, there was understandable need for consistency and to decide the issue by statutory rule in Article 4. In retrospect, addressing the issue in Article 4 might have precluded partial federalization of the bank collection system in Regulation CC, with all of the attendant inconsistencies between state and federal law (which remain unresolved even to this day). *See generally* Alvin C. Harrell, UCC Article 4 and Regulation CC: Can They Ever be Reconciled?, 54 CONSUMER FIN. L.Q. REP. 236 (2000). Nonetheless, those who were hesitant to resolve such issues by statute in Article 4 may have reason to feel vindicated by the apparent increases in fraud losses by depository banks in the aftermath of the mandatory funds availability rules in Regulation CC.

178. *See* §§ 4–301(a), 4–302(a). Section § 4–402(c) permits the payor bank to dishonor an item based on an initial determination that it is drawn on insufficient funds, even if the drawer subsequently makes a deposit to cover the item. *See* discussion *infra* ¶ 9.02[2]. Regulation CC

alternative under § 4–301(a)(2) only if the item unavailable for return.[179] However, the 2002 amendments to the Uniform Text added a new § 4–301(a)(2) to allow a payor bank to return an image of the returned item, if this comports with an agreement between the payor bank and the party to whom the image is returned.[180] Thus, under the 1990 uniform text, written notice should be used as a substitute for return of the item only if the item is unavailable for return. Oral notice such as telephone notice is not permitted as a means of dishonor by a payor bank under Article 4.[181] Generally, where notice of dishonor is permitted as a substitute for return of the item by the payor bank, under the 1990 uniform text, the notice must be written[182] and the provision in Article 3 permitting notice of dishonor "in any reasonable manner"[183] generally is not applicable as a means to avoid accountability in Article 4 cases.[184] As noted, the 2002 amendments to § 4–301(a) may change this. A provision of Regulation CC, § 229.33, permitting telephone or wire notice, supplements Article 4 and permits other than written notice, but only for

imposes additional requirements. *See infra* ¶ 8.04[3][a], [b].

179. *See* § 4–301(a)(2); Northwestern Nat'l Ins. Co. v. Midland Nat'l Bank, 96 Wis.2d 155, 292 N.W.2d 591 (Wis. 1980) (applying old § 4–301(1)(b)). *See* Comment 2 to § 4–301 (check truncation), and *infra* ¶ 8.04[3][f] and ¶ 9.03[6] (same). For checks, the Article 4 rules may be preempted by Regulation CC, which permits notice to be sent in lieu of returning the item, in certain circumstances. *See* 12 CFR § 229.30(f), § 229.33, and discussion *infra* ¶ 8.04[3][b].

180. This 2002 amendment is designed to facilitate electronic check processing by protecting the payor banks from claims that it violated the midnight deadline by returning only an electronic image. *See* amended § 4–301, Comment 8. However, note that this does not resolve related issues with respect to claims by the owner of the items (*e.g.*, the depositor); for example if the item is destroyed, does this discharge the liability of parties on the instrument? *Id. See also*, Alvin C. Harrell. Electronic Checks, 55 Consumer Fin. L. Q. Rep. 283 (2001).

181. *But see* Wells Fargo Bank v. Hartford National Bank & Trust Co., 484 F.Supp. 817 (D.Conn.1980), where such notice sufficed as the court erroneously believed it was authorized by a predecessor rule to Regulation CC, 12 CFR § 229.33, which it thought preempted the Article 4 rule. The better view is that Regulation CC preempts Article 4 only to the extent necessary to effectuate Regulation CC; with narrow exceptions (*see supra* notes 174, 178, and 179), this would not include § 4–301.

In contrast to the rules for payor banks, a collecting bank is required only to return the item or "send notification of the facts." § 4–214(a). As a result for some purposes a collecting bank can give either oral or written notice of dishonor as an alternative to returning the dishonored item. *See, e.g.*, Yoder v. Cromwell State Bank, 478 N.E.2d 131 (Ind.Ct.App.1985); *infra* ¶ 9.03[7]. This permits the collecting bank to retain the item as security for any claim against its customer for an overdraft caused by dishonor of the item. *See* §§ 4–210, 4–211; *infra* ¶ 8.03[2]. However this also means that for purposes of returning a dishonored item the midnight deadline of a collecting bank may begin to run upon receipt of telephone or other informal notice of dishonor. *See, e.g.*, Lufthansa German Airlines v. Bank of Am., 478 F.Supp. 1195 (N.D.Cal.1979), discussed *supra* at notes 57 and 134. In contrast, as noted *supra* at ¶ 8.02[2][d], the midnight deadline for payor banks commences only upon presentment. *See supra* notes 135–136, and 179–181 and accompanying text; *infra* ¶ 9.03[7]. *See also* the Regulation CC notice requirements, discussed *infra* at ¶ 8.04[3][b].

182. § 4–301(a)(2). *Cf.* discussion of Regulation CC, *infra* at ¶ 8.04[3][b].

183. § 3–503(b); discussion *infra* this text at notes 184–188.

184. *But see* the 2002 amendments at § 4–301(a)(2), (3), allowing other forms of notice for some purposes. *See also* the cases collected at Wells Fargo Bank v. Hartford Nat'l Bank, 484 F.Supp. 817, 821 n. 9 (D.Conn.1980). *See also* the discussion *supra* in Chapter 4 at ¶ 4.03[2][b]; discussion *infra* this text at notes 185–188.

purposes of complying with that regulation.[185]

Of course, returning the dishonored item with a notation that payment has been refused is a form of written notice of dishonor.[186] Thus it can be said that the 1990 uniform text of § 4–301 requires notice of dishonor, and that this is to be accomplished by return of the item or, in limited circumstances, by sending some other form of written notice. But the result is that under the 1990 uniform text a payor bank cannot properly retain presented items and send some other form of notice as an ordinary procedure. The 2002 amendments at § 4–301(a)(2) change this to permit return of an electronic image as an alternative, for purposes of meeting the Article 4 midnight deadline rule, but do not address other issues relating to the impact on the liability of parties to the instrument.

Even under the 1990 uniform text, the payor bank may send some other form of written notice where the item is unavailable for return. This could be the case if the item was lost or has been destroyed.[187] In this situation the payor bank would be required only to give timely written notice of dishonor in order to avoid accountability under the midnight deadline rule. If the item has been destroyed pursuant to a truncation arrangement, this provision arguably applies. However, once again, this does not address related issues such as the impact on the holder rights of the item's owner or the possible discharge of liability on the instrument. This could create liability in favor of parties who have not agreed to the truncation, under either the 1990 or 2002 Uniform Text.

Regardless of the form that notice of dishonor takes, to avoid accountability under Article 4 the payor bank must act before its midnight deadline. This requirement appears at § 4–301(a) and is defined at § 4–104(a)(10). Section 4–301(d) determines the effective time of return. Under § 4–301(d), return occurs:

> (1) as to an item presented through a clearing house, when it is delivered to the presenting or last collecting bank or to the clearing house or is sent or delivered in accordance with clearing-house rules; or

---

185. *See* discussion *infra* at ¶ 8.04[3][b] and ¶ 9.03[7]. This supercedes a previous Regulation J wire notice requirement. *See Wells Fargo Bank*, 484 F. Supp. at 821–22. *See also* §§ 3–502(b) and 3–503. If a bank timely returns the item, it is not accountable under § 4–302 even if it failed to give wire advice of nonpayment to the presenting bank as required by Regulation CC. Remedies for some violations of Regulation CC are found at 12 CFR § 229.21 (Civil Liability). However, a violation may also stem from a lack of due care for which there may be liability for a resulting loss under Regulation CC and Article 4. *See, e.g.*, Whalen & Sons Grain Co. v. Missouri Delta Bank, 496 F.Supp. 211 (E.D.Mo. 1980). *See also* 12 CFR § 229.38(a) and discussion *infra* ¶ 8.04[4].

186. § 3–503(b). *See also* Comment 2 to § 4–301 and discussion *infra* at ¶ 8.04[3][f], ¶ 9.03[6] and ¶ 9.03[7] on check truncation.

187. *See* § 3–309. *See also* Regulation CC, 12 CFR § 229.30(f) and its Commentary. Regulation CC supercedes Article 4 to the extent of the form and content of the notice.

(2) in all other cases, when it is sent or delivered to the bank's customer or transferror or pursuant to instructions.[188]

In connection with the requirement that the dishonored item be "sent," it may be relevant to consider the general Code definition of "send." "Send" is defined at UCC § 1–201(38) as follows:

> Send in connection with any writing or notice means to deposit in the mail or deliver for transmission by any other usual means of communication with postage or cost of transmission provided for and properly addressed and in the case of an instrument to an address specified thereon or otherwise agreed, or if there be none to any address reasonable under the circumstances. The receipt of any writing or notice within the time at which it would have arrived if properly sent has the effect of a proper sending.

Note that 2002 revisions to the uniform text of UCC Article 1 include a slightly different definition of "send," at revised § 1–201(b)(36).

[7] Defenses and Excuses for Failure to Send Timely Notice of Dishonor

The "strict liability" of a payor bank that has made final payment under § 4–215(a), or has become accountable for the item under § 4–302(a) due to a failure to return the item or to send an appropriate notice of dishonor by the midnight deadline under § 4–301, is not absolute. For example, *see* discussion *supra* at ¶ 8.02[3], and discussion of the payor bank's rescissionary remedies, *supra* at ¶ 8.02[4]. There may be other statutory defenses, such as fraud or breach of presentment warranty (under § 4–302(b)). As a result, the presentment warranties at § 4–208 may allow the payor bank to return an item after the midnight deadline. For example, in *First National Bank and Trust Co. of the Treasure Coast v. Belmont National Bank*,[189] a check was deposited without the required indorsement of a joint payee. It was sent through the banking system to the payor bank, which gave provisional credit and did not dishonor the item or revoke the credit within its midnight deadline (thereby losing the right to dishonor it under § 4–301 and becoming accountable for the amount of the item under § 4–302(a)).

When the missing indorsement was discovered, the payor bank returned the item to the depositary bank and revoked credit for the item, on grounds of breach of warranty. The depositary bank had paid out the funds to its depositor, who was now bankrupt, and the depositary bank sued the payor bank to recover the payment under the midnight deadline rule at § 4–302. The court correctly concluded that recovery under § 4–302 was barred by the payor bank's counter claim (asserted as a

---

188. § 4–301(d)(1), (2). The 1990 revisions changed the word "received" to the current term "presented," apparently to make clear the rule applies only after presentment to the payor.

189. 43 UCC Rep. Serv.2d 666, 2001 WL 15937 (Ohio Ct. App. 2001). *See also supra* ¶ 8.02[4] and note 165.

defense) for breach of warranty due to the lack of a required indorsement.

In *Copple v. Boatmen's First Nat'l Bank of Okla.*,[190] a bank depositor sued her bank (the depositary bank) and the payor bank for charging back to her account a check she had previously deposited, after the check was returned to the depositary bank by the payor bank due to a missing or improper indorsement.

The check was returned more than six months after it had been paid by the payor bank; the return was at the request of the drawer, on grounds the check was not properly payable due to an improper indorsement. This return was well after the payor bank's midnight deadline (§ 4–104) and thus the check could not be dishonored by the payor bank under § 4–301. However, §§ 3–418 and 4–302 allow a late return in limited circumstances, including mistake and breach of warranty. Upon allegations by its customer (the drawer) of an improper indorsement constituting a breach of warranty, the payor bank recredited the drawer's account, charged the depositary bank's account, and returned the check to the depositary bank. *See also* § 4–208 (presentment warranties).

In addition, there may be valuable rights of subrogation under § 4–407. The relation between stop payment orders, cashier's checks (or like instruments), accountability and final payment can produce challenging results under § 4–407. For example, in *Gentner & Co., Inc. v. Wells Fargo Bank*,[191] the bank erroneously paid a customer's check despite a valid stop payment order, by issuing a cashier's check to the payee. This constituted final payment of the customer's check under §§ 3–418 and 4–215, and substituted the liability of the bank on the cashier's check for that of the drawer on the customer's check (a novation), under § 3–310.

While normally a bank that issues a cashier's check cannot assert claims or defenses of the remitter as a defense against the bank's liability to the holder of the cashier's check (*see* § 3–305(c)), in the *Gentner* scenario § 4–407 specifically subrogates the bank to the rights of the customer who stopped payment on the check written by that customer. To the extent the customer has a defense against the payee of the customer's check, the bank also can assert that defense under § 4–407. In *Gentner*, the bank properly argued that the payee was not entitled to immunity against such defenses as a holder in due course under § 3–305(c), because the payee dealt directly with the bank that was asserting the defense. The bank should have won on these issues, but the court apparently did not understand this and instead reprimanded the bank (and its lawyer) for interfering with the customer's expectations regarding the stop payment order. The court focused on final payment of the customer's check and § 3–418 as precluding rescission of that transaction. But the crucial question was whether the bank could assert its customer's rights under § 4–407; because the liability on the customer's check was discharged under § 3–310, allowing the bank to assert a defense against liability on the cashier's check would not have

---

190. 958 P.2d 820 (Okla.Civ.App. 1998). *See also supra* note 115.

191. 76 Cal.App.4th 1165, 90 Cal. Rptr.2d 904 (Cal.Ct.App.1999). *See also supra* notes 129 and 132.

left the payee without a remedy; it would merely allow the bank to assert the customer's position against the payee so as to resolve the dispute between the customer and payee. It is a means of resolving such disputes, not eliminating remedies; in its effort to preserve the payee's remedies, the Gentner court improperly eliminated the bank's remedy under § 4–407, even though § 3–418(c) (relied on by the court) specifically preserves these rights under § 4–407.

¶ 8.03 Final Payment and the Midnight Deadline for Collecting Banks

[1] Introduction

As noted *supra* at ¶ 8.01[3][f], under § 4–105(5) a "collecting bank" is any "bank handling an item for collection except the payor bank." By its terms this includes a depositary bank (defined at § 4–105(2)) unless it is also the payor, and all intermediary banks (as defined at § 4–105(4)).[192] A bank handling an item for collection must exercise caution to assure that it is not deemed to be a payor bank for purposes of the more stringent final payment and accountability rules applicable to payor banks.[193]

Generally speaking, a collecting bank is an agent of the owner of the item, and has a duty to use ordinary care in forwarding the item or notice of the action taken to the next bank or party in the forward collection or return process; this duty is *per se* met if the bank acts before its midnight deadline.[194] But the specifics of this duty in various circumstances, and the consequences of a violation, can be more complex than this simple statement indicates.[195] The subject is best approached by dividing the various situations into two categories: those where the

---

¶ 8.03

192. *See also infra* ¶ 8.04[3][d] (duties of depositary banks under Regulation CC); ¶ 8.04[3][c] (duties of returning banks).

193. *See, e.g.,* Reynolds–Wilson Lumber Co. v. Peoples National Bank, 699 P.2d 146 (Okla.1985) (bank treated as "co-payor" of collection draft). *Cf.* Southern Cotton Oil Co. v. Merchants National Bank, 670 F.2d 548 (5th Cir.1982); Harper v. K & W Trucking Co., 725 P.2d 1066 (Alaska 1986). Section 4–106 states that a "payable through" bank is a collecting bank, rejecting the *Reynolds–Wilson* rationale. *See also infra* ¶ 8.04[3][f] (payable through drafts under Regulation CC); *supra* note 52 and *infra* note 205.

194. *See* §§ 4–201(a), 4–202, 4–204, 4–212, 4–213, 4–214(a), 3–503(c). *See also* § 4–201, Comment 3: "The prima facie agency status of collecting banks is consistent with prevailing law and practice today. . . . [However, the related] right of charge-back with respect to checks is limited by Regulation CC." *See* 12 CFR § 226.36(d), discussion *infra* ¶ 8.04 [3][c], and § 4–202, Comment 4. As a result, in a given case Regulation CC may preempt Article 4 as to the finality of settlement during the forward collection process and with regard to the time and place of presentment, as well as with regard to the return path of dishonored checks. *See* 12 CFR §§ 229.31, 229.36(b), (d); § 4–202, Comment 4; § 4–204, Comment 4; and *infra* ¶ 8.04[3][c]. However, the depository bank's right of charge-back under Article 4 §§ 4–202 and 4–214 is largely unaffected by Regulation CC. *See infra* ¶ 8.04[3][d]. The agency status of collecting banks is specifically recognized at § 4–201(a), and in Federal Reserve Regulation J, which provides that every "Reserve Bank shall act only as agent or subagent of the owner with respect to the item." *See* 12 CFR § 210.6(a)(1). *See infra* ¶ 9.03[7].

195. *See* §§ 4–103, 4–109, 4–202, 4–203, and 4–204. If it is asserted that a bank has violated its duty of care (or other statutory duties) with regard to an item not properly payable, the bank may assert against the claimant a preclusion on grounds the claim-

collecting bank has granted provisional credit for the item, and those where it has not. In the latter case, such as where the collecting bank is handling the item for collection pursuant to a separate agreement (not as a cash item), or makes settlement by remittance draft as discussed at ¶ 8.03[5], the bank need only be concerned with avoiding liability for damages as a result of breaching the contract or its failure to meet its duty of ordinary care or the midnight deadline.[196] But if the bank has granted provisional credit, it must additionally be concerned with possible loss of the right to revoke the credit. As discussed *infra* at ¶ 8.03[2], the 1990 Article 4 revisions impacted the latter issue. Furthermore, as discussed *infra* throughout this text and more specifically at ¶ 8.04, Regulation CC may impact Article 4 issues with regard to return of dishonored checks.

[2] *Provisional Settlement by a Collecting Bank*

Demand items like checks that are deposited in a bank other than the payor bank are normally treated as "cash items," that is, the transferor is given provisional credit under § 4–201(a) while the item is sent through the banking system to the payor bank for payment. The depositary bank may forward a batch of such checks to its correspondent bank, clearing house, or Federal Reserve Bank, which will then forward

---

ant's actions contributed to the loss. For example, such a preclusion generally means the item will be treated as properly payable, thereby eliminating many grounds for liability on the part of any bank that processed or paid the item. However, in such case the claimant then may argue that the bank failed to exercise ordinary care and that this failure substantially contributed to the loss. If this is established, the loss will be apportioned between the parties on the basis of their comparative negligence. The purpose and effect is to encourage settlements where both the bank and claimant contributed to the loss, which often seems to be the case, by making it unlikely that either will prevail on a motion for summary judgment and likely that any trial will result in an apportionment of liability.

This is illustrated in the companion cases of Gina Chin & Associates, Inc. v. First Union Bank, 260 Va. 533, 537 S.E.2d 573 (Va. 2000), and Gina Chin & Associates, Inc. v. First Union Bank, 256 Va. 59, 500 S.E.2d 516 (Va. 1998). In these cases, a teller at the depositary bank had conspired with an employee of the drawer, to accept for deposit stolen and forged checks drawn on the drawer's (employer's) account. The employee stole blank checks for the employer's account, forged the employer's signature, and with the help of the teller deposited the checks into an account controlled by one of the conspirators at the depositary bank.

As between the banks involved, the checks were the responsibility of the depositary bank due to the latter's breach of warranty (*see* § 3–416). In *Gina Chin* the depositary bank sued the employer on whose account the checks were drawn, seeking a preclusion under §§ 3–404 and 3–405 for failure to adequately monitor its checkbook and supervise its employee. The employer countered that the depositary bank failed to exercise ordinary care due to its teller's fraud. While the trial court essentially concluded that the teller's fraud was outside the scope of employment and therefore not imputed to the depositary bank, granting summary judgment to the bank, the Supreme Court of Virginia reversed and allowed the case to go forward for trial on the issue of comparative negligence and the scope of the teller's employment.

196. *See infra* ¶ 9.03[7]. This discussion is directed primarily toward checks and other demand items deposited or presented for immediate credit. If an item is sent for collection, banks handling the item may be subject to special instructions or other duties. *See, e.g.,* Bar–Ram Irrigation Products v. Phenix–Girard Bank, 779 F.2d 1501 (11th Cir.1986) (collecting bank liable for failure to obtain signature on drafts before releasing title documents). *See also* Article 4, Part 5 (Collection of Documentary Drafts); *infra* ¶ 8.04[3][f]; *infra* ¶ 9.03[7].

them to the payor or to another correspondent bank in the vicinity of the payor. The items ultimately will be presented for payment to the payor. Under Article 4, each bank in this chain will, upon receipt of the item, give its transferor provisional credit for the amount of the item.[197]

The credit or "settlement"[198] is provisional under Article 4 because the Article 4 makes it so unless Regulation CC intervenes or a contrary intent clearly appears.[199] It is an important point because, to the extent the settlement is provisional, upon notification that the item has been dishonored the collecting bank may revoke the credit.[200] This rule is subject to certain qualifications, excuses, and clarifications that are to be discussed. These issues are clarified under the 1990 revision to Article 4, as discussed *infra*.

For intermediary banks, issues relating to provisional settlement for checks have been extensively preempted by Regulation CC; but for

---

197. As noted *infra* and as discussed more fully at ¶ 8.04, such settlements are regarded as final under Regulation CC, 12 CFR §§ 229.31(c), 229.32(b) and 229.36(d). See also § 4–214, Comment 2.

A good case describing this process, and the effects of a Magnetic Ink Character Recognition (MICR) encoding error, is First Union National Bank v. Bank One, 47 U.C.C. Rep. Serv.2d 645 (E.D.Pa. 2002).

Subject to separate funds availability requirements in Federal Reserve Board Regulation CC (*see infra* ¶ 8.04), cashier's checks and similar instruments are treated like any other items by depository banks under Article 4. Deposit of a cashier's check is provisional settlement that can be revoked under Article 4 Part 2 as with any other item. For example, a fraudulent cashier's check that is deposited in a collecting bank, and later dishonored by the payor bank, can be charged-back to the depositor's account and any resulting overdraft can be collected from the depositor. *See, e.g.*, Chitty v. Bank One, N.A., 42 U.C.C. Rep. Serv.2d 799 (Ohio Ct. App. 2000); *infra* ¶ 9.01[4][d].

198. *See, e.g.*, § 4–104(a)(11).

199. § 4–201(a). Note the potential preemptive effect of Regulation CC, with regard to checks. 12 CFR §§ 229.31(c), 229.32(b), and 229.36(d) provide that, for checks, all settlements between banks are final. *See also* § 4–201, Comment 4; § 4–214, Comment 2; and *infra* ¶ 8.04[3][a], [b], [c], and [4]. However, the precise extent and effect of such preemption remains unclear, and may be limited to narrow Regulation CC issues. *See generally infra* ¶ 9.03[7].

200. § 4–214(a). As discussed *infra* this text, § 4–214(a) specifies that such revocation may occur after the midnight deadline or a longer reasonable time but the bank is liable for any loss resulting from the delay. Thus, a failure of the collecting bank to meet its midnight deadline or duty of ordinary care (§ 4–202) or its duties under a collection agreement (§§ 4–103, 4–203, 4–204) does not preclude that bank from charging-back a returned item or otherwise revoking provisional settlement, though the bank may be liable for damages. *See* §§ 4–103(5), 4–214(a).

Subject to separate funds availability requirements in Federal Reserve Board Regulation CC, cashier's checks and similar bank instruments are treated like any other items by depository banks under Article 4. Deposit of a cashier's check is provisional settlement that can be revoked under Article 4 Part 2 as with any other item. For example, a fraudulent cashier's check that is deposited in a collecting bank, and later dishonored by the payor bank, can be charged-back to the depositor's account and any resulting overdraft can be collected from the depositor.

As noted, Regulation CC preempts these Article 4 rules to some extent. *See, e.g,* 12 CFR §§ 229.31(c), 229.32(b), and 229.36(d), and *infra* ¶ 8.04[3]. However, Regulation CC does not affect the collection of items other than checks, and does not affect the right of a bank to recover payment from the bank to which the item is returned or that of the depositary bank to charge back a returned check to its customer's account. *See* 12 CFR §§ 229.1(b)(3), 229.2(cc) (Regulation CC applies to the return of checks to, not by, the depositary bank), and §§ 229.31(c) and 229.32(b). *See also* 12 CFR § 229.33(d) (requiring notice of a returned check to the customer); § 4–202; and Appliance Buyers Credit Corp. v. Prospect National Bank, 708 F.2d 290 (7th Cir.1983) (duty of depositary bank to notify customer upon receiving notice of nonpayment).

depositary banks this is not the case. Several of the resulting issues are illustrated by the facts of *First Security Bank v. Ezra C. Lundahl, Inc.*[201] The Lundahls deposited a check in their account at First Security Bank, and received provisional credit. First Security then sent the check to the payor for payment. The payor subsequently notified First Security that the check was drawn on insufficient funds, and advised that the check would be held for possible collection later unless otherwise instructed. This was held to constitute notice of dishonor since the item was not available for return, and First Security then had a duty to send notice of dishonor to the Lundahls before its midnight deadline.[202] First Security, however, failed to give this notice of dishonor to the Lundahls until a month and a half later, when the check was returned by the payor unpaid and charged back to the Lundahls' account. The Lundahls then claimed that this revocation of settlement was improper because notice was not given within the midnight deadline.[203] While the *Lundahl* court correctly concluded that the bank's notice of dishonor was not timely, it is important to note that under current law (as discussed below) the result is not loss of the bank's right to revoke the settlement.

The *Lundahl* court discussed First Security's duty as a collecting bank under Article 4, and the extent and nature of its liability for a violation of that duty. Old § 4–202(1)(b) was applicable, and provided in part: "A collecting bank must use ordinary care in . . . sending notice of dishonor or non-payment or returning an item . . . to the bank's transferor . . . after learning that the item has not been paid. . . ." Current § 4–202(a)(2) is substantially the same. Old § 4–202(2) then provided that: "A collecting bank taking proper action before its midnight deadline following receipt of an item, notice or payment acts seasonably; taking proper action within a reasonable longer time may be seasonable but the bank has the burden of so establishing." Current § 4–202(b) was rewritten for clarity but in substance is essentially the same. Regulation CC is applicable where the item is $2,500 or more, and is similar, requiring a depositary bank to give notice to its customer "by midnight of the banking day following the banking day on which it received the

---

201. 22 Utah 2d 433, 454 P.2d 886 (Utah 1969).

202. Old §§ 4–202(1)(b) and (2) and 4–212(1); Current §§ 4–202(a)(2), (b) and 4–214(a). Section 4–202(b) was rewritten for clarity as part of the 1990 revisions. *See also* § 4–104(a)(10) (definition of "midnight deadline"); and Regulation CC, 12 CFR § 229.33(d) (as applicable, (for items of $2,500 or more) requiring notice to the customer by midnight of the banking day after receipt of the returned item or notice); and discussion *infra* ¶ 8.04[3][c], [d], [4]. *See also Appliance Buyers,* 708 F.2d 290.

203. *See* old §§ 4–201(1), 4–212, and 4–213; current §§ 4–201(a), 4–214, 4–215. "Unless a contrary intent clearly appears" and prior to the time that a settlement given by a collecting bank for an item is or becomes final, the bank is an agent or subagent of the owner of the item and any settlement given for the item is provisional. *See* § 4–201. Old § 4–212(1) permitted revocation in general up to the midnight deadline of the collecting bank. Old § 4–212(4)(b) contradicted this permitting charge back despite a failure to use ordinary care, while noting the potential liability for damages. Current § 4–214(a) resolves this conflict by specifying that revocation of provisional settlement is permitted after the end of the midnight deadline, but the bank is liable for any loss caused by the delay. *See also* §§ 4–103, 4–109, 4–203.

returned check or notice, *or within a longer reasonable time.*"[204] Thus a collecting bank can discharge its duty of ordinary care by acting within its midnight deadline, but also can demonstrate that a longer time was reasonable.[205] This flexibility is specified at § 4–214(a), which describes the right of the collecting bank to rescind the provisional credit given for an item that is subsequently dishonored:

> If a collecting bank has made provisional settlement with its customer for an item and itself fails ... to receive [final settlement], the bank may revoke the settlement given by it, charge back the amount of any credit given for the item to its customer's account or obtain refund from its customer ... *if by its midnight deadline or within a longer reasonable time after it learns the facts it returns the item or sends notification of the facts.*[206]

Current § 4–214(a) also includes the following language added in the 1990 revisions:

> If the return or notice is delayed beyond the bank's midnight deadline or a longer reasonable time after it learns the facts, the bank may revoke the settlement, charge back the credit, or obtain

---

204. 12 CFR § 229.33(d). *See also infra* ¶ 8.04[3][d]. This only applies to depositary banks. Intermediary banks handling returned checks are subject to a more strict regimen under Regulation CC. *See* 12 CFR § 229.31 and *infra* ¶ 8.04[3][c]. *See also infra* ¶ 8.04[3][f] and 12 CFR § 229.38(a), (b).

205. *See, e.g.*, §§ 4–202, 4–204, 4–109; Southern Cotton Oil Co. v. Merchants Nat'l Bank, 670 F.2d 548 (5th Cir.1982). In the *Southern Cotton* case, the bank delayed sending notice of dishonor for 52 days. The court held that since it was a collecting bank rather than a payor bank its duty was to act seasonably, and it was not limited to the midnight deadline. A previous course of dealing led the court to conclude that the bank acted seasonably in delaying notice. *Cf.* United Ky. Bank, Inc. v. Eagle Mach. Co., 644 S.W.2d 649 (Ky.App.1983), where the court determined that 48 days was too long.

In these circumstances it is crucial to the bank's argument that the collecting bank not be characterized as a drawee/payor bank, as that will subject the bank to strict liability (subject to limited exceptions) for missing the midnight deadline, under § 4–302. *See, e.g.*, Horney v. Covington County Bank, 716 F.2d 335 (5th Cir.1983) (collecting bank liable as drawee because its name followed that of private drawee); Reynolds–Wilson Lumber v. Peoples Nat'l Bank, 699 P.2d 146 (Okla.1985) (collecting bank incorrectly characterized as payor and subjected to the absolute "accountability" standard of § 4–302). *See also* discussion *supra* at ¶ 8.02[1][c], ¶ 8.02[1][b], ¶ 8.02[2][d], ¶ 8.02[3], [4], and [7], and *supra* notes 52 and 193. The result in *Reynolds–Wilson* and *Horney* is repudiated at § 4–106(a). *See also infra* ¶ 8.04[3][f]; the excuses for delay at § 4–109, discussed *infra* ¶ 8.03[3]; the definitions *supra* at ¶ 8.01[3][c]–[f]; and the standards of care in Regulation CC, 12 CFR § 229.38(a), discussed *infra* at ¶ 8.04[3][f] and ¶ 8.04[4].

Regulation CC, 12 CFR § 229.36(d), states that all settlements of checks between banks in the forward collection process are final. This may have an impact on intermediary banks but generally does not affect the depositary bank's right of chargeback. *See* § 4–202, Comment 4, and *infra* ¶ 8.04[3][a]–[d], [f]; *infra* ¶ 9.03[7].

206. Emphasis added. The italicized language could be read to indicate that the right to rescind provisional settlement terminates if the collecting bank misses its midnight deadline or fails to return the item or send notice of dishonor within a "longer reasonable time." As noted *supra* note 203–205, and *infra* this note, this view is rejected in subsequent language, as noted below. *But see* Lufthansa German Airlines v. Bank of Am., 478 F.Supp. 1195 (N.D.Cal. 1979), discussed *supra* at notes 57, 134, and 181. As discussed *infra* at ¶ 8.03[4], the view that the right to revoke settlement is lost is clearly rejected at § 4–214(a). *See also infra* ¶ 9.03[7].

refund from its customer but is liable for any loss resulting from the delay.

This makes clear that in a case like *Lundahl*, the depositary or other collecting bank does not lose its right of charge-back as a result of missing its midnight deadline, although it remains liable for any loss caused by the delay.[207]

In addition, unlike payor banks, which generally are required to give notice of dishonor by returning the item,[208] collecting banks are allowed to either return the item or send "notification of the facts."[209] This permits a collecting bank to give notice by any reasonable means, including oral or telephone notice.[210]

Among other things, this permits the depositary bank to retain the item as security for any overdraft in the customer's account caused by charge-back of the dishonored item.[211] One risk in this for collecting banks is that an informal, telephone or oral notice from another collecting bank may trigger the running of the midnight deadline, before the dishonored item has been received.[212] If the depositary bank waits until it has received the item before giving notice of dishonor to prior parties, it may violate its midnight deadline.[213]

In addition to charge-back under Article 4, in a case like *Lundahl*, the bank may be able to hold its customers (or other parties to the instrument) liable as indorsers. The Article 4 rules are consistent with the provisions of Article 3. Section 3–415(a) provides that upon dishonor by the payor and (under § 3–503) and upon any necessary notice of dishonor, the holder of a dishonored instrument has recourse against the indorsers.[214] Sections 3–503(a) and 3–415(c) provide that notice of dis-

---

207. *See* §§ 4–103, 4–109, 4–202, 4–203, 4–204, and 4–214. *See also* Regulation CC, 12 CFR § 229.31 (responsibilities of returning banks) and 12 CFR § 229.32 (responsibilities of depositary banks), discussed *infra* at ¶ 8.04[3][c] and [d]; 12 CFR § 229.33(d) (notice by depositary bank to its customer), and 12 CFR § 229.38(a), discussed *infra* at ¶ 8.04[4]. *See, e.g.*, Appliance Buyers Credit Corp. v. Prospect Nat'l Bank, 708 F.2d 290 (7th Cir.1983).

The bank's right of charge-back has priority over a competing levy against the account by a competing creditor. DNI Nevada, Inc. v. Medi-Peth Medical Lab, Inc., 337 N.J.Super. 313, 766 A.2d 1197 (App.Div. 2001).

208. This issue has been impacted by the 2002 amendments to the uniform text. *See* the 2002 amendments to § 4–301(a), and discussion *supra* at ¶ 8.02[6].

209. § 4–214(a). *See also* § 4–202(a)(2); Regulation CC, 12 CFR § 229.31(f) (notice in lieu of return), discussed *infra* ¶ 8.04[3][c].

210. *See* § 3–503(b); definition of "send" at § 1–201(38); Yoder v. Cromwell State Bank, 478 N.E.2d 131 (Ind.Ct.App. 1985). This represents a danger to the recipient of such notice, whose own midnight deadline may be commenced by receipt of telephone notice. *See* Lufthansa German Airlines v. Bank of Am., 478 F.Supp. 1195 (N.D.Cal.1979), and discussion *supra* at notes 57, 134, 181, and 206; Wells Fargo Bank v. Hartford Nat'l Bank, 484 F.Supp. 817 (D.Conn.1980). *See also* 12 CFR § 229.31 (responsibilities of returning banks under Regulation CC), discussed *infra* at ¶ 8.04[3][c].

211. *See* §§ 4–210, 4–211.

212. *See Lufthansa*, 478 F.Supp. 1195. Such notice also may be permitted or required under Regulation CC. *See* 12 CFR § 229.31(f) (notice in lieu of return), and 12 CFR § 229.33 (notice of nonpayment), discussed *infra* at ¶ 8.04[3][b], [c]. *But see infra* ¶ 9.03[7].

213. *See, e.g., supra* notes 57, 134, 181, and 206; ¶ 8.02[6].

214. Section 3–415 describes the indorser's basic contract, and conditions indorser liability on "dishonor," which is defined at

honor is necessary to charge any indorser. Section 3–503(c) requires that any necessary notice of dishonor must be given by a bank before its midnight deadline. These issues are also discussed *supra* this text in Chapters 3 and 4. Where the dishonored item is charged back to the customer's account and this creates an overdraft, the depositary bank also may recover this overdraft under § 4–401 or (typically) under the terms of the deposit contract with its customer, and may be able to assert holder in due course status as against parties liable on the instrument.[215]

Thus, a collecting bank's failure to give timely notice of dishonor does not preclude revocation of settlement or other forms of recovery. However, as further discussed below, while a depositary bank's right to revoke provisional credit on a dishonored item does not always depend on the bank giving notice of dishonor within its midnight deadline, giving notice within the midnight deadline is the clearest way to meet the bank's duty of care under § 4–202 and may be necessary to hold the customer liable as an indorser under § 3–415. In a case like *Lundahl*, it

---

§ 3–502; under § 3–503 this liability is also conditioned on notice of dishonor, subject to § 3–504. See also First Security Bank v. Ezra C. Lundahl, Inc., 22 Utah 2d 433, 454 P.2d 886 (Utah 1969), discussed *supra* at notes 201–213.

215. On the latter point, see §§ 3–104, 3–201, 3–302—3–305, 4–205, 4–210, and 4–211. The higher standard of good faith (including observance of reasonable commercial standards of fair dealing), included at § 3–103(a)(4) as part of the 1990 revisions to the uniform text of Article 3, has begun to be a factor in the cases on this point. Two recent cases illustrate the importance of this in diverse scenarios.

San Tan Irrigation Dist. v. Wells Fargo Bank, 197 Ariz. 193, 3 P.3d 1113 (Ariz.Ct. App. 2000) involved a check that had been deposited with an indorsement forged by one of the plaintiff's employees. When sued for conversion under § 3–420, the depository bank sought to claim a preclusion against the plaintiff for negligence contributing to the loss, because of the failure of the plaintiff to adequately supervise its employee, under §§ 3–405 and 3–406. But this preclusion is available only if the depository bank acted in good faith. See § 3–405(b), § 3–406(a). In *San Tan*, the plaintiff argued that the bank was careless and therefore did not meet the new standard of good faith at § 3–103(a)(4), and this was sufficient for summary judgment to be awarded against the bank; on appeal this was held relevant only to the duty of care, a very different thing from good faith. The case was remanded for a trial on the issue of the bank's good faith, a better though hardly attractive result for the bank.

In Maine Family Federal Credit Union v. Sun Life Assurance Co., 727 A.2d 335 (Me. S.Ct. 1999), the court held that the credit union (a "bank" under § 4–105) was not a holder in due course when it took an item for deposit because it did not meet the new standard of good faith at § 3–103(a)(4). The court concluded that the credit union met the former standard of "honesty in fact," and noted that under this traditional standard of good faith depository banks have routinely qualified as holders in due course of deposited items. But the new standard also requires observance of reasonable commercial standards of fair dealing; illustrating the dangers of this concept, the *Maine Family Credit Union* court allowed the jury to conclude that it was not reasonable for the credit union to allow immediate credit to its depositor for three $40,759.35 checks drawn on a major out-of-state insurance company. The jury concluded it would have been better for the credit union to place a "hold" on the funds in these circumstances, and therefore the credit union failed the good faith test at § 3–103(a)(4) and was not a holder in due course.

These cases illustrate the potential dangers of the expanded UCC concept of good faith. See also Govoni and Sons Construction Co., Inc. v. Mechanics Bank, 51 Mass. App.Ct. 35, 742 N.E.2d 1094 (2001).

However, even without holder in due course status, the depositary bank's right of charge-back has priority over competing lien creditors, *e.g.*, a competing levy. See, *e.g.*, DNI Nevada, Inc. v. Medi-Peth Medical Lab, Inc., 337 N.J.Super. 313, 766 A.2d 1197 (App.Div.2001).

would be clear that the collecting bank failed to give this notice within the midnight deadline and would then be appropriate to determine whether notice was given within "a longer reasonable time."[216] As discussed immediately below at ¶ 8.03[3], determining the precise results of this type of failure requires an additional step in the analysis. But even if the bank loses on these issues, as discussed *infra* at ¶ 8.03[4], it should only be liable for resulting damages.

[3] *Excuses for Failure to Meet the Midnight Deadline*

A collecting bank that misses its midnight deadline has two basic arguments before bearing any consequence for the failure. First, as noted *supra* at ¶ 8.03[2], a collecting bank's midnight deadline is not an absolute standard. The basic responsibility of a collecting bank is to exercise ordinary care under § 4–202(a); under § 4–202(b), meeting the midnight deadline is one way to satisfy this duty. Moreover, the midnight deadline rule for collecting banks is flexible. Notice of dishonor must be sent or the item returned within the midnight deadline "or within a longer reasonable time."[217] The collecting bank has the burden of establishing that a longer time was reasonable. Hence, the immediate effect of a collecting bank missing its midnight deadline is that the burden shifts to the bank to prove that the delay was reasonable. If the bank succeeds, it will avoid liability.[218]

Even if the collecting bank cannot demonstrate that the delay was reasonable, it may yet escape liability. There are several provisions that may excuse the delay. Paramount is the provision at § 4–109(b), which excuses any delay caused by "interruption of communication or computer facilities, suspension of payments by another bank, war, emergency conditions, failure of equipment, or other circumstances beyond the control of the bank, [provided] the bank exercises such diligence as the circumstances require."[219] The Comments to § 4–109 refer to §§ 4–202(b), 4–214, 4–301, and 4–302, indicating that the bank has the burden of proving that it acted with diligence if it goes beyond the midnight deadline.[220] As noted, Regulation CC has a similar provision

---

216. *See* §§ 4–202, 4–214.

217. *See* §§ 4–202(a) and 4–214(a); discussion *supra* ¶ 8.03[2]; Regulation CC, 12 CFR §§ 229.31, 229.32, 229.33, and *infra* ¶ 8.04[3]. Section 4–214(a) adopts the view of Appliance Buyers Credit Corp. v. Prospect National Bank, 708 F.2d 290 (7th Cir. 1983) (failure of a collecting bank to meet its midnight deadline does not affect its right of charge back against the customer's account, but bank is liable for any loss caused from the delay). *See* § 4–214, Comments 3, 5 and 6. The Regulation CC Commentary also cites *Appliance Buyers*. *See* Commentary § 229.33(d). *See also* §§ 4–203 and 4–204.

218. *See, e.g.*, Southern Cotton Oil Co. v. Merchants Nat'l Bank, 670 F.2d 548 (5th Cir.1982), and discussion *supra* at ¶ 8.03[2]. As noted *supra*, the right of charge-back survives a failure to meet the midnight deadline, but the collecting bank remains potentially liable for losses caused by the delay. *See* § 4–214, Comments 3, 5, and 6.

219. *See* § 4–109(b). Section 4–109(b) expanded this list as part of the 1990 revisions, to include interruption of computer facilities and failure of equipment. This is consistent with Regulation CC, which uses similar language. *See* 12 CFR § 229.38(e), and § 4–109, Comment 3.

220. *See* § 4–109, Comment 1. The requirement of diligence is in addition to the usual duties of good faith (UCC § 1–203) and ordinary care (§ 4–202), neither of which can be disclaimed (*see* § 4–103(a)).

with language nearly identical to § 4–109(b).[221]

Section 4–109(b) applies to collecting banks and payor banks. Many of the cases interpreting that section involve payor banks. For example, in *Blake v. Woodford Bank & Trust Co.*,[222] two posting machines malfunctioned and an employee missed work because of illness, just as check-processing volume reached a peak during the Christmas holidays. As a result the payor bank was late in returning dishonored items and the midnight deadline was missed. The court found that such events were foreseeable and reversed the trial court, concluding that these were not "circumstances beyond the control of the bank" within the meaning of old § 4–108. The 1990 revisions (now at § 4–109) certainly chip away at this decision, by listing "interruption of communication or computer facilities" as excuses for delay at § 4–109(b); however, this revision, while seemingly aimed at cases like *Blake* does not necessarily reject the rule of that case, because of the *Blake* court's conclusion that the circumstances were not beyond the bank's control and could have been avoided by greater diligence.

Compare *Port City State Bank v. American National Bank*,[223] where the shift from a manual to a computerized bookkeeping system led to chaos after the old system was gone and the new one did not work. The U.S. Court of Appeals for the Tenth Circuit found that this constituted circumstances beyond the control of the bank and that on the facts it had used due diligence, thus excusing liability under old § 4–108 for failure to meet the midnight deadline. The 1990 revisions to old § 4–108(2) (now § 4–109(b)) and the Comments approve this result and at least cast doubt on cases like *Blake*.

[4] *Measure of Liability When a Collecting Bank Misses Its Midnight Deadline*

Just as the midnight deadline for collecting banks appears to be less strict than for payors, the measure of liability when the deadline is violated by a collecting bank is less severe than for a similar violation by a payor bank. An unexcused failure to meet the midnight deadline by a payor bank will cause that bank to become "accountable for" (that is, liable for) the amount of the item subject only to limited defenses.[224] Moreover, the payor bank, having been forced to pay the owner of the instrument, may be left with no subsequent recourse against its custom-

---

On payor bank liability, *see* § 4–302, discussed *supra* at ¶ 8.02[2][d] and ¶ 8.02[3].

221. *See supra* ¶ 8.03[2].

222. 555 S.W.2d 589 (Ky.App.1977). A similar case is First Wyoming Bank v. Cabinet Craft Distrib., Inc., 624 P.2d 227 (Wyo. 1981). *See also* National Savings and Trust Co. v. Park Corp., 722 F.2d 1303 (6th Cir. 1983).

223. 486 F.2d 196 (10th Cir.1973). The *Port City* rule is incorporated into Revised § 4–109(b) and the case is cited with approval in Comment 3.

224. *See* § 4–302(a)(1), (b); discussion *supra* at ¶ 8.02[1][b], ¶ 8.02[2], ¶ 8.02[3], and ¶ 8.04[4]. *See also* Ahmann v. American Federal Savings and Loan Assoc., 235 Mont. 184, 766 P.2d 853, 858 (Mont. 1988), *overruled on other grounds,* Allers v. Riley, 273 Mont. 1, 901 P.2d 600 (Mont.1995); *supra* ¶ 8.03[3].

er because it can only charge the customer's account if the item is properly payable.[225] This can be viewed as a form of strict liability.

Under Article 4 the risk for a collecting bank that violates the midnight deadline is far lower. This is appropriate, as collecting banks are essentially mere couriers with no economic stake in (or knowledge about) the underlying payment transaction. The low level of risk for collecting banks is reflected in the low cost of collecting items through the banking system. This low cost depends on the efficiencies of bulk processing systems, made possible by the low level of legal risk associated with handling such items. If collecting banks faced significant or "strict" liability (the way payor banks do at, *e.g.*, § 4–302) as a result of performing their collection function, the cost and pricing structure for customer bank accounts would look very different than it does today.

The applicable provisions for collecting banks are §§ 4–202, 4–103, and 4–214. Section 4–202 imposes on collecting banks a duty of ordinary care that can be met by meeting the midnight deadline.[226] Section 4–103(e) then specifies the measure of damages for violation of this standard: "The measure of damages for failure to exercise ordinary care in handling an item is the amount of the item reduced by an amount that could not have been realized by the use of ordinary care. If there is also bad faith it includes any other damages suffered as a proximate consequence."[227]

---

225. *See* § 4–401(a). Additionally, final payment discharges the liability on the instrument of all secondary parties because their liability is conditioned upon dishonor by the payor. *See* §§ 3–414, 3–415, 3–501, 3–504. They in turn may be discharged on the underlying obligation as well. *See* § 3–310; discussion *supra* Chapters 3 and 4 of this text. However, the payor may be able to assert the rights of prior parties by subrogation or have certain other defenses. *See* § 4–407; discussion *supra* at ¶ 8.02[4] and [7], and discussion *infra* at ¶ 9.02[3].

226. *See also* Regulation CC, 12 CFR § 229.31 (responsibility of returning banks for return of checks); 12 CFR § 229.32 (responsibility of depositary bank to accept returned checks); 12 CFR § 229.33(d) (responsibility of depositary bank to notify customer of returned check within the midnight deadline or a longer reasonable time); 12 CFR § 229.38(a) (duty of ordinary care and good faith; liability for actual damages). *Cf.* §§ 4–103(e), 4–202, 4–214.

227. § 4–103(e) is similar to old § 4–103(5) but has been reworded slightly. Under old § 4–103(1) and current § 4–103(a), this measure of liability cannot be limited by agreement. Old § 4–103, Comment 6; current § 4–103, Comment 6. *Cf.* the similar language at Regulation CC, 12 CFR §§ 229.37, 229.38(a). *See also* 12 CFR § 229.38(b), (c). *See infra* ¶ 8.04[3][c], [d], and [4]; *infra* ¶ 9.03[7].

If it is asserted that a bank has violated its duty of care (or other statutory duties) with regard to an item not properly payable, the bank may assert against the claimant a preclusion on grounds the claimant's actions contributed to the loss. For example, such a preclusion may be asserted under §§ 3–404, 3–405, 3–406, 3–407, or 4–406. If effective, such a preclusion generally means the item will be treated as properly payable, thereby eliminating many grounds for liability on the part of any bank that processed or paid the item. However, in such case the claimant may argue that the bank failed to exercise ordinary care and that this failure substantially contributed to the loss. If this is established, the loss will be apportioned between the parties on the basis of their comparative negligence. The purpose and effect is to encourage settlements where both the bank and claimant contributed to the loss, which often seems to be the case, by making it less likely that either will prevail on a motion for summary judgment and more likely that any trial will result in a roughly equal apportionment of liability.

This is illustrated in the companion cases of Gina Chin & Associates, Inc. v. First Union Bank, 260 Va. 533, 537 S.E.2d 573

In the absence of bad faith, liability is limited to actual damages, with a ceiling of the amount of the item. In the latter case, the maximum recovery is the amount of the item and this is reduced by the amount of any loss that would have been suffered even if due care had been used.[228] Damages beyond the amount of the item are allowed only if the bank was guilty of bad faith. Consider the impact where a bank sues its customer as an indorser under Article 3 but has not given proper notice of dishonor. In that instance the failure to give timely notice of dishonor to the indorser may discharge the bank's claim and the indorser may not be liable as such, regardless of good or bad faith.[229] But the bank may

---

(Va. 2000), and Gina Chin & Associates, Inc. v. First Union Bank, 256 Va. 59, 500 S.E.2d 516 (Va. 1998). In these cases, a teller at the depositary bank had conspired with an employee of the drawer, to accept for deposit stolen and forged checks drawn on the drawer's (employer's) account. The employee stole blank checks for the employer's account, forged the employer's signature, and with the help of the teller deposited the checks into an account controlled by one of the conspirators at the depositary bank.

As between the banks involved, the checks were the responsibility of the depositary bank due to the latter's breach of warranty. The depositary bank sued the employer on whose account the checks were drawn, seeking a preclusion under §§ 3–404 and 3–405 for failure to adequately monitor its checkbook and supervise its employee. The employee countered that the depositary bank failed to exercise ordinary care due to its teller's fraud. While a trial court essentially concluded that the teller's fraud was outside the scope of employment and therefore not imputed to the depositary bank, granting summary judgment to the bank, the Supreme Court of Virginia reversed and allowed the case to go forward for trial on the issue of comparative negligence and the scope of the teller's employment.

Another example of these defenses is Sebastian v. D & S Express, Inc., 61 F.Supp. 2d 386 (D.N.J.1999), where corporate employees (including the President) had issued 87 corporate checks payable to fictitious payees over a seven year period, and cashed them at a local bank after indorsing them in the names of the fictitious payees. The checks were purportedly for maintenance work, which was not performed. When the fraud was discovered, the corporation sued the bank that had cashed the checks. The bank defended that the indorsements were valid under the fictitious payee rule at § 3–404(b), and the corporation countered with a comparative negligence claim on grounds the bank failed to exercise ordinary care under § 3–404(d).

The court held that the corporation's § 3–404(d) comparative negligence claim was barred by the statute of limitations at § 3–118(g) because § 3–404(d) seeks enforcement of a duty; the claims more than three years old were barred. The corporation's claims for conversion under § 3–420 were also dismissed, on grounds that § 3–420(a) bars such an action by the issuer. The corporation's common law negligence claims were barred as superceded by § 3–404. Thus, the effect of §§ 3–118 and 3–404(b) was to prevent the corporation from shifting its loss (caused by its own president and employees) to the bank, subject to comparative negligence claims asserted within three years under § 3–404(d).

228. In United Ky. Bank, Inc. v. Eagle Mach. Co., 644 S.W.2d 649 (Ky.App.1983), the court followed this analysis when the bank failed to properly notify its customer of the dishonor of a check given as a down payment, with the result that the customer delivered the goods to the drawer. The court did not discuss whether an attempt to get the goods or obtain payment had failed. In Royal Trust Bank of Orlando v. All Florida Fleets, Inc., 431 So.2d 1043 (Fla.App. 1983), the court overturned a summary judgment against the bank on the ground the bank had raised a question of fact as to whether the customer could recover from the drawer. The customer has the burden of proof to establish some loss. Wertling v. Manufacturers Hanover Trust Co., 118 Misc.2d 722, 461 N.Y.S.2d 157 (Civ. Ct. 1983) and Comment 6 to § 4–103. *Cf.* Regulation CC, 12 CFR § 229.38(a), discussed *infra* ¶ 8.04[4]. *See infra* ¶ 9.03[7].

229. *See* §§ 3–415(c), 3–502, 3–503, 3–504. The indorser also will be discharged on the underlying obligation. *See* § 3–310. Note that even under old Article 4 the customer's obligation to permit the bank to charge back or to refund a provisional credit pursuant to old § 4–212(1) was not considered an "underlying obligation" dis-

still be able to revoke any provisional settlement and recover from its customer under § 4-214 and the deposit contract, subject to an offset in favor of the customer for any damages caused by the delayed notice. This is not an inconsistency; it is simply separate treatment of two different issues that may arise in the same context.

The 1990 revisions eliminated any ambiguity on this issue in old § 4–212 by specifying that where a collecting bank fails to receive final payment of an item, it may revoke any provisional settlement, charge back any credit, and obtain a refund of any uncollected funds drawn by its customer, whether or not it has returned the item or given notice within its midnight deadline, or otherwise met its duty of ordinary care, although as always the bank remains liable for any loss resulting from the delay.[230] This effectively confirms the better view under old § 4–212.[231]

While the 1990 revisions to Articles 3 and 4 (and the provisions of Regulation CC) provide for comparative negligence as a means to allocate losses due to forgery or alteration,[232] the revisions to old § 4–212 (at

---

charged under old § 3–802; the instrument is not taken for that obligation by the customer. This view is further supported by current § 4–214(a), which specifically includes a provision permitting a collecting bank to charge-back a dishonored item even if the bank has failed to give timely notice to the customer. *See* discussion *supra* at ¶ 8.03[2].

230. *See* § 4–214(a). Similarly, 12 CFR § 229.33(d) requires that notice be given by the depositary bank to its customer by midnight of the banking day following the banking day of receipt. This is the same timeframe as the bank's midnight deadline under § 4–104(a)(10). 12 CFR § 229.38(a) then provides an actual damages rule similar to that at § 4–103(e). *But see* discussion *infra* ¶ 8.04[4], and 12 CFR § 229.38(b), (c). The right of charge-back has priority over a competing levy. DNI Nevada, Inc. v. Medi-Peth Medical Lab, Inc., 337 N.J. Super. 313, 766 A.2d 1197 (App.Div.2001).

231. *See, e.g.*, Northpark National Bank v. Bankers Trust Co., 572 F.Supp. 524 (S.D.N.Y.1983), and *supra* ¶ 8.03[1], [2]. *But see* Pandol Brothers, Inc. v. NCNB National Bank, 450 So.2d 592, 38 U.C.C. Rep. Serv. 944 (Fla.Dist.Ct.App.1984) (right of charge-back is not lost by failure of bank to use ordinary care, but may be lost if bank was negligent in delaying notification); First Georgia Bank v. Webster, 168 Ga.App. 307, 308 S.E.2d 579 (Ga.Ct.App.1983) (right of chargeback lost because bank was negligent in telling customer that the check was good, and customer relied on that representation). *See also* § 4–202(b) (collecting bank exercises ordinary care if it meets its midnight deadline; missing the deadline may still constitute ordinary care but the bank has the burden of proof); discussion *infra* at ¶ 8.04[4], and ¶ 9.03[1], [2].

232. *See* §§ 3–404(d), 3–405(b), 3–406(b), and 4–406(e); 12 CFR § 229.38(c). Conversion actions against depository banks may also involve claims of contributory negligence. *See, e.g.*, Govoni and Sons Construction Co., Inc. v. Mechanics Bank, 51 Mass.App.Ct. 35, 742 N.E.2d 1094 (2001). *Govoni* was decided under old Article 3 and involved an accountant who diverted payroll tax checks from his small business client to his own use, by depositing the checks in his personal account without a proper indorsement. In *Govoni*, the depositary bank was the defendant in the lawsuit brought by the victim (the small business drawer who hired the crooked accountant).

The business victim (the drawer) sued the depositary bank alleging conversion and negligence. The trial court held that the unendorsed checks were not properly payable and that the depositary bank was negligent in accepting the unendorsed checks for deposit. The depositary bank sought a preclusion or comparative negligence allocation of damages under old § 3–406 on grounds of the plaintiff's negligence in hiring the crooked accountant.

The trial court applied a comparative negligence standard and found the small business to be 25% negligent. On appeal this was reversed on grounds that a comparative negligence standard was not available to the bank due to the bank's failure to observe reasonable commercial standards, and on grounds the UCC preclusion at old

revised Section 4–214) apparently follow the case law and reject the use of comparative negligence concepts in relation to charge back and delayed return of dishonored items.[233]

[5] Settlement by Remittance or Other Means

Although less common than other forms of settlement, payment by means of a remittance authority or instrument is specifically permitted by Article 4.[234] Under old Article 4, collecting banks had long been authorized to accept such as a means of settlement, and a collecting bank had no liability for accepting a remittance instrument so long as it either forwarded or dishonored the instrument within its midnight deadline.[235]

These rules were generally carried forward in the 1990 revisions at § 4–213, but the language of old § 4–212 was rewritten with some significant changes. Section 4–213(a) now recognizes that in most instances the type of settlement will be determined by Federal Reserve System regulations or circulars, clearinghouse rules, or agreement.[236] In other cases the medium of settlement normally is to be cash or by credit to an account in a Federal Reserve Bank or as specified by the recipient.[237] If the tender of settlement is by a means not authorized according to these rules, no settlement occurs until the attempted settlement is accepted by the intended recipient.[238] For example, if a payor bank attempts to make settlement by cashier's check, without a prior agree-

---

§ 3–406 did not apply to a strict liability claim for negligence. The fictitious payee rule (with its potential preclusion against the drawer) was deemed inapplicable because there was no fraudulent indorsement. The small business (drawer) was allowed to recover 100% of the damages.

The *Govoni* court appears to have misinterpreted the intended effect of § 3–406, even under the old version applicable to this case. The result should clearly be different under revised Article 3, which specifies a comparative negligence standard. *But see* San Tan Irrigation Dist. v. Wells Fargo Bank, 197 Ariz. 193, 3 P.3d 1113 (Ariz.Ct. App.2000); and Maine Family Federal Credit Union v. Sun Life Assurance Co., 727 A.2d 335 (Me.Sup.Ct.1999) (effect of new, higher standard of good faith at § 3–103(a)(4)). *See also In re* McMullen Oil Co., 251 B.R. 558 (Bankr.C.D.Cal.2000) (depositary bank liable for deposit of improperly indorsed checks by corporate president, after the debtor had filed bankruptcy depriving the president of authority to indorse the checks).

Under former Article 3 § 3–419, the liability of a depositary bank for conversion was limited to the proceeds of the check held by the bank. But under revised § 3–420(c), this is limited to parties other than depositary banks, thus apparently reversing the result of some depositary bank cases decided under old § 3–419.

See Lawyers' Fund for Client Protection v. Gateway State Bank, 273 A.D.2d 565, 709 N.Y.S.2d 243 (N.Y.App.Div.2000) (forged indorsement); Bursey v. CFX Bank, 145 N.H. 126, 756 A.2d 1001 (N.H. 2000) (missing indorsement).

233. *See, e.g.*, Comment 5 to § 4–214 for the reason; *see also* and United States Fidelity & Guaranty Co. v. Federal Reserve Bank of New York, 590 F.Supp. 486 (S.D.N.Y.1984), and 620 F.Supp. 361, 41 U.C.C. Rep. Serv. 1153 (S.D.N.Y.1985).

234. Old § 4–211. This section was significantly rewritten as current § 4–213 to cover settlement generally. *Cf.* Regulation CC, 12 CFR § 229.31(c) (settlement for returned checks by same means as used during forward collection); 12 CFR § 229.32(b) (payment by depositary bank).

235. Old § 4–211(1), (2); *cf.* current § 4–213(a), (b).

236. *See* current § 4–213(a), and Comment 1. *See also* § 4–103 (variation by agreement); discussion *supra* ¶ 8.01[2]; and discussion of Regulation CC, *infra* ¶ 8.04.

237. Current § 4–213(a)(1) and Comment 1.

238. Current § 4–213(b).

ment, the recipient may reject the settlement by returning the check, or may accept it as settlement.[239]

If settlement is made by a cashier's or teller's check, and the recipient presents or forwards the check for collection before its midnight deadline, then under current Article 4 settlement is final when the check is finally paid.[240] But if the recipient fails to present or forward the check before its midnight deadline, then under current Article 4 the settlement becomes final at the midnight deadline of the recipient.[241] In effect the recipient of the settlement can minimize the risk of nonpayment by presenting or forwarding the check before its midnight deadline.[242] On the other hand, if settlement is by means of authority to charge the account of the bank giving settlement, that settlement is final when the charge is made, if the account contains sufficient funds.[243] It should be noted again, however, that neither settlement by check nor by authority to charge an account is an authorized form of settlement in the absence of an agreement, clearinghouse rule, or similar authorization.[244]

Revised Article 4 also provides rules governing the time of settlement.[245] These rules provide generally that a settlement occurs when cash (or a cashier's or teller's check) is sent or delivered, or when a credit to an account is made, or when payment by funds transfer is made pursuant to Article 4A § 4A–406(a).[246]

Under Regulation CC all settlements for checks, in both the forward collection and return process, are final.[247] Regulation CC preempts Article 4 where both are directly applicable (*i.e.*, for some aspects of settlement and the return of checks), to the extent of any inconsistency.[248] Regulation CC provides that a returning bank must settle for checks sent to it by the same means that it would use to settle for a check in the forward collection process.[249]

Thus, while Regulation CC generally does not preempt Article 4 as to the means used to effect settlement in the forward collection process,

---

239. *See* current § 4–213, Comment 1.

240. Current § 4–213(c)(1). Thus, the risk of nonpayment remains with other parties if the collecting bank meets its midnight deadline, as under old Article 4. *See* current § 4–213, Comment 2; *cf.* old § 4–211(2), (3).

Subject to separate funds availability requirements in Regulation CC, deposits of cashier's checks and similar instruments are treated like any other item by depository banks under Article 4. Deposit of a cashier's check is provisional settlement that can be revoked under Article 4 Part 2 as with any other item. For example, a fraudulent cashier's check that is deposited in a collecting bank, and later dishonored by the payor bank, can be charged-back to the depositor's account and any resulting overdraft can be collected from the depositor. *See* §§ 4–201—4–214; Chitty v. Bank One, N.A., 42 U.C.C. Rep. Serv.2d 799 (Ohio Ct. App. 2000).

241. Current § 4–213(c)(2). Again, this is similar to old Article 4. *See* old § 4–211(3)(c).

242. Current § 4–213, and Comment 3; *cf.* old § 4–211(2), (3).

243. § 4–213(d).

244. *See* § 4–213, Comment 3.

245. *See* § 4–213(a)(2).

246. *Id.*

247. *See* 12 CFR §§ 229.31(c), 229.32(b), and 229.36(d), discussed *infra* at ¶ 8.04[3][c], [d], [4].

248. *See* 12 CFR §§ 229.1(b)(3), 229.41 (scope of Regulation CC and preemption of state law). *But see* 12 CFR § 229.37 (variation by agreement).

249. 12 CFR § 229.31(c).

the focus of Regulation CC being on the return item process after the item has been dishonored,[250] Regulation CC does preempt Article 4 in the forward collection of checks to the extent of making all settlements final, thereby prohibiting revocation of provisional settlement by collecting banks upon dishonor of a check. As a result, the mechanisms of settlement at § 4–213 are not preempted, but the nature and revocation of the resulting settlement under § 4–214 are affected, as to settlements for checks between banks.[251] In effect, "a paying or collecting bank does not ordinarily have a right to charge-back against the bank from which it received the returned check, although it is entitled to settlement [under Regulation CC] if it returns the returned check to that bank...."[252]

¶ 8.04 Funds Availability and Federal Reserve Regulation CC

[1] Introduction

In 1987, Congress passed the federal Expedited Funds Availability Act (EFAA),[253] giving the Federal Reserve Board a broad mandate to preempt UCC Article 4 (and other state law) by creating federal regulations to govern the deposit, collection, payment, and return of items through the banking system. The Federal Reserve Board (the "Federal Reserve") responded by promulgating Federal Reserve Regulation CC[254] to implement the EFAA. Regulation CC has two primary subparts,[255] governing funds availability and the collection/return of checks.

Regulation CC was drafted with some regard for its relationship to UCC Article 4. Nonetheless, there are a number of uncertainties and conflicts arising from the relationship between Regulation CC and Article 4, which have yet to be resolved.[256] As discussed *infra* this part, most of the resulting problems fall into four broad areas: (1) Regulation CC imposes a series of expedited return requirements, generally on top of (not as a replacement for) the Article 4 midnight deadline rules; (2) Regulation CC modifies (and to that extent, preempts) the return item process of Article 4, by providing that an item need not be returned by the same route as in the forward collection process; and (3) in order to separate the forward collection and return processes to expedite returns, Regulation CC preempts the Article 4 rules on provisional settlement in the forward collection process. This was deemed necessary because provisional settlements granted in the forward collection process cannot

---

250. See *infra* ¶ 8.04[3].

251. Regulation CC Commentary § 229.31(c); article 4 § 4–214, Comment 4.

252. Regulation CC Commentary § 229.31(c). As a result, if the return path is the same as the forward collection path, the results may be similar under both Article 4 and Regulation CC.

¶ 8.04

253. 12 U.S.C. §§ 4001–4010 (1987).

254. Regulation CC appears at 12 CFR Part 229.

255. Subparts B and C. Subpart A contains general provisions and definitions.

256. See *generally*, Alvin C. Harrell, UCC Article 4 and Regulation CC: Can They Ever Be Reconciled?, 54 Consumer Fin. L.Q. Rep. 236 (2000); Alvin C. Harrell, NCCUSL Article 3, 4, and 4A Drafting Committee Highlights Current Payment System and Negotiable Instrument Issues, 54 Consumer Fin. L.Q. Rep. 351 (2000).

be revoked if the item is returned by a different route; therefore Regulation CC deems all settlements for checks between banks to be final when made.[257] Finally, (4) the Regulation CC funds availability schedules may have preemptive effects on the bank-customer relationship as it exists under Article 4. Each of these issues is discussed more thoroughly *infra*.

The 1990 Article 4 revisions note the points of intersection between Article 4 and Regulations CC, but do not for the most part detail the consequences. Many, but not all, of the differences are noted in Article 4 or its Official Comments.[258] In addition many differences are noted in the Regulation CC Commentary. Any person studying an Article 4 check collection issue should consider the impact of Regulation CC and should review the Article 4 Official Comments and Regulation CC Commentary for references to possible conflicts. Regulation CC issues are also noted through-out this chapter, in addition to the general overview that follows.

[2] Regulation CC, Subpart B—Funds Availability Requirements

[a] Funds Availability Schedules

Regulation CC Subpart B describes the required schedule for availability of funds deposited in a bank.[259] This schedule mandates a specific availability for deposited funds, based on the nature of the item deposited. In contrast Article 4 does not require that deposited funds be made available for withdrawal at any particular time, except that a deposit of cash must be made available at the opening of the next banking day after the day of receipt.[260]

Regulation CC § 229.10(a) and (b) essentially require next day availability of funds deposited in cash or by electronic payments.[261] In addition, under § 229.10(c), other types of deposits generally are entitled to next day availability: U.S. Treasury checks that have been deposited in the payee's account;[262] U.S. Postal money orders and Federal Reserve Bank checks or Federal Home Loan Bank checks deposited in person in the payee's account;[263] state and local government checks deposited in person to a bank employe in the payee's account in a bank located in the

---

257. *See* Regulation CC, 12 CFR § 229.31(c), § 229.32(b), § 229.36(d), and Commentary, § 229.31(c) and § 229.36(d).

258. *See, e.g.,* § 4–102, Comment 1, noting the deference to Regulation CC at § 4–215(e) and (f) (as "applicable law stating a time for availability of funds"). *See also* § 4–215, Comment 11, recognizing the primacy of Regulation CC; § 4–103, Comment 3.

259. "Bank" is defined to include commercial banks, savings banks, credit unions, savings institutions, and other insured depositories. *See* 12 CFR § 229.2(e). Article 4 is similar. *See* § 4–105(1).

260. § 4–215(f). *See generally supra* ¶ 8.01 [1] and *infra* ¶ 8.04[3][d].

261. Such funds must be made "available for withdrawal not later than the business day after the banking day on which the [cash is deposited or electronic payment is received]." *See* 12 CFR § 229.10(a), (b). *See also* § 4–215(f).

262. 12 CFR § 229.10(c)(1)(i).

263. *Id.* § 229.10(c)(1)(ii), (1)(iii).

same state as the governmental unit;[264] cashier's, certified, and teller's checks deposited in person to a bank employee in an account of the payee using a specially designated deposit slip where required;[265] checks drawn on the same or another branch of the depositary bank if both are in the same state or check processing region;[266] and the first $100 of any other checks deposited.[267] If the deposited check falls into one of these categories except that it does not meet the requirement of being deposited in person to a bank employee, then the funds must be made available not later than the second business day after the banking day of receipt.[268]

Since September 1, 1990, depositary banks have been required to make other deposited funds available not later than the second business day following the banking day of deposit, to the extent the deposit consists of: local checks and, if not governed under § 229.10(c), U.S. Treasury checks, U.S. Postal Service money orders, local checks drawn by a Federal Reserve Bank, a Federal Home Loan Bank, or a state or local government, or a local cashier's, certified, or teller's check.[269] Prior to September 1, 1990, a "temporary availability schedule" called for such funds to be available somewhat later.[270]

After September 1, 1990, funds from deposits of non-local checks must be made available for withdrawal not later than the fifth business day following the banking day of receipt.[271] This covers deposited items of the following types: nonlocal checks;[272] Federal Reserve Bank and Federal Home Loan Bank checks, checks drawn by state and local governments, and cashier's, certified and teller's checks, that are nonlocal checks and are not covered by § 229.10(c).[273]

[b] *Exceptions and Safeguards*

In the context of current check collection and processing times, the Regulation CC funds availability schedule may require the depositary bank to make funds available to the depositor for withdrawal before the deposited items have been paid by the payor. This may leave the depositary bank susceptible to loss where the customer withdraws funds drawn on a deposited item that is subsequently returned unpaid.[274]

---

264. *Id.* § 229.10(c)(1)(iv).

265. 12 CFR § 229.10(c)(1)(v); § 229.10(c)(3) permits the depositary bank to require a special deposit slip where next day availability use is required for the deposit of a cashier's, certified, or teller's check (also state or local government checks).

266. 12 CFR § 229.10(c)(1)(vi).

267. *Id.* § 229.10(c)(1)(vii).

268. 12 CFR § 229.10(c)(2). This applies to the checks covered by § 229.10(c)(1)(ii), (iii), (iv), and (v). *Id.*

269. 12 CFR § 229.12(b). Most of these terms are defined at 12 CFR § 229.2. For example, "Local check" is defined as one drawn on a payor located in the same check processing region as the depositary bank. *See* 12 CFR § 229.2(r), (s).

270. Former 12 CFR § 229.11 (repealed; now "Reserved").

271. 12 CFR § 229.12(c).

272. 12 CFR § 229.12(c)(1)(i). Essentially defined as any check not within the definition of a "Local check." *See* 12 CFR § 229.2(r), (s), (v), (w).

273. *See* 12 CFR §§ 229.10(c), 229.12 (c)(1)(ii).

274. Public awareness that the bank will be required to allow withdrawals of cash on uncollected deposits may have contributed to an increased level of fraudulent bank deposits. *See, e.g.,* Gullo, Bad Checks

Regulation CC addresses this concern by providing a series of exceptions to the mandatory funds availability schedule.[275] The exceptions allow a depositary bank to delay making funds available for withdrawal, beyond the mandatory funds availability schedule, for certain exceptional transactions. These are:

New accounts: A new account is one that has been open for 30 days or less.[276] Cash and electronic payments deposited to a new account must be made available for withdrawal on the business day following the banking day of receipt;[277] however, the availability requirements at 12 CFR § 229.10(c)(1)(i) through (v) and § 229.10(c)(2) (for government checks, cashier's checks, etc.)[278] apply only to the first $5,000 deposited on any one banking day.[279] The balance of such a deposit must be made available not later than the ninth business day following the banking day of deposit.[280] The exception to the required availability schedule for deposits to new accounts supersedes the otherwise applicable rules for deposits as described at §§ 229.10(c)(1)(vi) (personal checks drawn on the same bank) and (vii), 229.11, and 229.12 (personal checks and other checks outside the parameters of § 229.10(c)).[281]

Large Deposits: The required funds availability schedule does not apply to deposits that aggregate more than $5,000 in any one banking day.[282] For purposes of this rule, the bank may aggregate multiple accounts of the same account holder and limit the withdrawal to the maximum of $5,000, "even if the customer is not the sole holder of the accounts and not all of the holders of the accounts are the same."[283]

Redeposited Checks: The required funds availability schedule does not apply to checks that have been dishonored by the payor and are redeposited by the customer.[284] However, this exception does not apply to checks that are returned by the payor due to a missing indorsement or because postdated if no longer postdated when redeposited.[285]

Repeated Overdrafts: The required funds availability schedule does not apply to any customer whose account has been "repeatedly overdrawn."[286] "Repeatedly overdrawn" is defined to mean that checks were

---

Surged Last Year; Bankers Blame Fed's New Rules, AM. BANKER, Aug. 20, 1991, at 1.

275. *See* 12 CFR § 229.13. In addition to the safeguards discussed *infra* this part, this concern is addressed by the provisions requiring expedited return of dishonored items, as discussed *infra* at ¶ 8.04[3].

276. 12 CFR § 229.13(a)(2). Of course, a problem with this kind of rule is that persons wishing to abuse it may simply avoid the rule by opening an account and then waiting more than 30 days to perpetrate their fraud. Banks may therefore wish to be vigilant as to new accounts that have been open more than 30 days.

277. 12 CFR § 229.13(a)(1)(i).

278. *See supra* this text at notes 320–328.

279. 12 CFR § 229.13(a)(1)(ii).

280. *Id.*

281. *Id.* at 229.13(a)(1)(iii).

282. 12 CFR § 229.13(b).

283. *Id.*

284. 12 CFR § 229.13(c). In contrast the Article 4 midnight deadline and other requirements for timely presentment, dishonor, and notice of dishonor generally apply to redeposited items. *See supra* ¶ 8.02[7].

285. 12 CFR § 229.13(c)(1), (2). On redeposited checks, *see generally supra* ¶ 8.02[7].

286. 12 CFR § 229.13(d).

presented for payment on insufficient funds on six or more banking days during the preceding six months, or that on two or more banking days during the preceding six months a check was presented which would overdraw the account by $5,000 or more if paid.[287] Once this exception to the funds availability requirements is triggered, it applies for a period of six months following the last such overdraft.

Reasonable Cause to Doubt Collectability: "If a depositary bank has reasonable cause to believe that the check is uncollectible ...," the required availability schedules do not apply.[288] "Such belief shall not be based on the fact that the check is of a particular class or is deposited by a particular class of persons."[289] The bank generally must notify the depositor at the time of deposit of the reason for the bank's belief that the check is not collectible.[290] If such notice is not given, the bank may be precluded from assessing any fees for any overdraft or insufficient funds check that is returned as a result of the unavailability of the deposited funds.[291]

Emergency Conditions: The required availability schedules do not apply if there is an "interruption of communications or computer or other equipment facilities; [a] suspension of payments by another bank; [a] war; or [a]n emergency condition beyond the control of the depositary bank, if the depositary bank exercises such diligence as the circumstances require."[292]

Notice of Exception: When a depositary bank invokes one of the exceptions to the required availability schedules, it must provide the customer a written notice that includes: the account number, date and amount of deposit, amount of the deposit that is being delayed, the reason for the exception, and the date the funds will be available for withdrawal (the latter requirement need not be met if the date is unknown due to emergency conditions.)[293] The notice must be given to the customer "at the time of deposit, unless the deposit is not made in person to an employee of the depositary bank" or the facts justifying the delay are not known to the bank at the time of the deposit.[294] In such cases the notice must be mailed to the customer "as soon as practicable, but no later than the first business day following the day the facts become known to the depositary bank, or the deposit is made, whichever is later."[295] The bank must maintain a record of such notices, together

---

287. 12 CFR § 229.13(d)(1), (2). It does not matter whether the check was paid. It is enough that the requisite number of checks have been presented and, if paid, they would have overdrawn the account.

288. 12 CFR § 229.13(e)(1). The Regulation CC provides examples of what may constitute reasonable cause; an obvious one is notice the check is being returned.

289. *Id*. For example, the exception cannot be invoked on the basis of national origin.

290. *Id*. *See also* 12 CFR § 229.13(g) (form and content of the required notice).

291. 12 CFR § 229.13(e)(2).

292. 12 CFR § 229.13(f). *Cf.* Article 4 § 4–109(b) (using similar language), discussed *supra* this text at ¶ 8.03[3].

293. 12 CFR § 229.13(g)(1).

294. *Id*. at § 229.13(g)(2).

295. *Id*.

with a "brief statement of facts" describing the reason for the exception.[296]

Length of Delay Due to Exceptions: When a depositary bank invokes an exception to the required availability schedule, it may delay the availability of funds for a "reasonable period of time."[297] An extension of time up to five business days for local checks and six for non-local checks generally is deemed to be a reasonable period.[298] "A longer extension may be reasonable, but the bank has the burden of so establishing."[299]

[c] Disclosure Requirements

Every bank is required to provide to its customers a clear, conspicuous, written disclosure describing the bank's funds availability policy.[300] This disclosure must be provided to potential new customers before the account is opened, and was required to be given to all existing account holders between September 1, 1988 and October 31, 1988.[301] In addition, all preprinted deposit slips must contain a notice that deposits may not be available for immediate withdrawal, and a notice listing the bank's funds availability schedule must be posted "in a conspicuous place in each location where its employees receive deposits to consumer accounts."[302] Disclosures must also be posted at ATM locations, and must be given to any person upon request.[303]

The bank must send notice of any change in policy that would further delay funds availability, to all affected account holders, at least 30 days prior to effectuating the change.[304]

[d] Civil Liability

A bank that violates the foregoing Regulation CC Rules is liable for any actual damages resulting from the violation, plus (in an individual action) statutory damages of not less than $100 but not more than $1,000, and in a class action up to the lesser of $500,000 or one percent of the net worth of the institution.[305] The successful plaintiff can also recover court costs and reasonable attorney fees.[306]

The bank is not liable for the violation if it "demonstrates by a preponderance of the evidence that the violation was not intentional and [that it] resulted from a bona fide error, notwithstanding the maintenance of procedures reasonably adapted to avoid any such error."[307]

---

296. *Id.* at § 229.13(g)(3).

297. *Id.* § 229.13(h)(1).

298. *Id.* at § 229.13(h)(4).

299. *Id.*

300. 12 CFR § 229.15(a), § 229.16(a).

301. *Id.* § 229.17(a), (b). This notice must be "in a form that the customer may keep." 12 CFR § 229.15(a).

302. *Id.* § 229.18(a), (b).

303. *Id.* at § 229.18(c),(d).

304. *Id.* § 229.18(e).

305. *Id.* § 229.21(a)(1), (2). Violations of Regulation CC, Subpart C–Collection of Checks, are discussed *infra* at ¶ 8.04[3].

306. 12 CFR § 229.21(a)(3).

307. *Id.* § 229.21(c). 12 CFR § 229.21(e) also provides a defense for good faith conformity with the regulation, Commentary or model form even if the regulatory articulation is held to be invalid at a later date.

[3] *Regulation CC, Subpart C—Collection of Checks*

Subpart C of Regulation CC[308] focuses on the return of dishonored checks that have been presented through the banking system. It is this part of Regulation CC that provides the greatest potential for conflict with Article 4, and therefore the greatest potential for preemption of the Article 4 rules. The Expedited Funds Availability Act[309] gives the Federal Reserve Board broad authority to regulate the check collection and processing system, "including the receipt, payment, collection, or clearing of checks and any related function of the payment system...."[310] Until recently, however, the Federal Reserve Board had acted cautiously in terms of preempting Article 4, in an apparent effort to minimize disruption of the banks collection system. Regulation CC remains interstitial and therefore to date has had only a minimal effect on Article 4 issues and litigation. However, on December 17, 2001 the Federal Reserve Board submitted to Congress a proposed federal Check Truncation Act, which would significantly increase federal preemption of UCC Articles 3 and 4. *See, e.g.*, Alvin C. Harrell, Eletronic Checks, 55 Consumer Fin. L.Q. Rep. 283, 287-89 (2001).

Moreover, the precise relationship between Regulation CC and Article 4 as to a number of issues remains unclear, as is the extent of preemption of the latter by the former. Article 4 is preempted to the extent of any inconsistency with Regulation CC,[311] but Regulation CC does not always attempt to clarify the extent of or reconcile those inconsistencies.[312] To some extent the Official Comments to Article 4 reference potential inconsistencies, but some of these simply can't be resolved under current law.[313] In addition the impact of Federal Reserve

---

308. 12 CFR §§ 229.30–229.42.

309. 12 U.S.C. §§ 4001–10 (1987).

310. *See, e.g.,* Fred H. Miller, Expedited Funds Availability and Other Payment System Developments, 42 Consumer Fin. L.Q. Rep. 103 (1988) at 103, citing 12 U.S.C. § 4008(c)(1). This article also notes the federalization of payment system issues that results when an insolvent banking institution is taken over by the FDIC and that agency imposes federal rules to supercede the state laws that previously governed the bank's check collection and processing functions. *Id.,* text and note 6, citing Federal Deposit Insurance Corporation v. McKnight, 769 F.2d 658 (10th Cir.1985); Miller & Meachem, The FDIC and Other Financial Institution Insurance Agencies as "Super" Holders in Due Course: A Lesson in Self–Pollinated Jurisprudence, 40 Okla. L. Rev. 621 (1987). Subsequent developments have reinforced this and have broadened the preemption of state law by federal banking laws and regulations. *See, e.g.,* Lofts, Querio, & Jensen, Financial Institutions Receiverships Before and After the Financial Institutions Reform, Recovery and Enforcement Act of 1989, 45 Consumer Fin. L. Q. Rep. 158 (1991).

311. 12 CFR § 229.41.

312. There are summaries of the preemptive effects of Regulation CC in the Commentary, at § 229.30(a) (payor banks) and § 229.31(a) (for collecting banks). These are discussed *infra*. Regulation CC was formulated prior to the Revised Article 4 but the references to Article 4 in the Regulation CC Commentary have been updated to reflect the 1990 Article 4 revisions. The Commentary was updated in 1995, 1997, and 1999. *See* Regulation CC, 12 CFR Pt. 229, Appendix E (Commentary).

313. *See, e.g.,* § 4–102, Comment 1; § 4–103, Comment 3. Efforts to reconcile these inconsistencies within the statute have not received the support needed to be successful. *See, e.g.,* Alvin C. Harrell, UCC Article 4 and Regulation CC: Can They Ever Be Reconciled?, 54 Consumer Fin. L.Q. Rep. 236 (2000); Alvin C. Harrell, NCCUSL Articles 3, 4, and 4A Drafting Committee Highlights Current Payment System and Negotiable Instrument Issues, 54 Consumer Fin. L.Q. Rep. 351 (2000).

Regulation J must be considered.[314] While these issues are noted throughout this chapter, this part will describe in more detail the impact and requirements of Regulation CC, Subpart C.

[a] Expeditious Return of Dishonored Checks

Subpart C of Regulation CC, § 229.30 applies to a bank in its capacity as payor of checks drawn by the bank's customers on their accounts at the bank. Regulation CC refers to this as a "paying bank."[315] It requires that a paying bank, dishonoring a check presented through the banking system, return the dishonored check to the depositary bank "in an expeditious manner."[316] "Expeditious manner" is defined as meeting one of two tests provided under Regulation CC: the two-day/four-day test or the forward-collection test.[317] Generally, a check is returned expeditiously if the return process is as fast as the forward-collection process."[318] If a payor bank misses both the midnight deadline under Article 4 and the deadlines imposed for expeditious return under Regulation CC,[319] the bank may be held liable under Regulation CC or Article 4, but not both.[320]

---

314. *See* 12 CFR Part 210, and discussion *supra* at ¶ 8.01[2]. The relationship between Regulation CC and Regulation J is noted periodically in the Regulation CC Commentary. *See, e.g.,* Commentary § 229.30(c). *See also* discussion *infra*.

315. "Paying bank," is defined to include payable-through-the-bank and payable-at-the-bank transactions. *See* 12 CFR § 229.2(z). The definition is therefore somewhat broader than the Article 4 definition of payor bank. *Cf. supra* ¶ 8.01[3][d]. *See also* Article 4 § 4–105(3). In contrast, Subpart B of Regulation CC, discussed *supra* this text at ¶ 8.04[2], applies to the bank in its capacity as depositary bank, *e.g.*, in regard to checks deposited by the bank's customers.

316. 12 CFR § 229.30(a).

317. *Id.* § 229.30(a)(1), (a)(2). *See also id.* § 229.32(a), discussed *infra* this text at notes 415–16, and ¶ 8.04[3][d].

318. Regulation CC Commentary § 229.30(a). This means the process similarly situated banks would use for the forward collection of a check drawn on the depositary bank. *See* discussion *infra*.

319. *See* Regulation CC Commentary § 229.30(a)–(c), and discussion *supra* at ¶ 8.01[2]. The Regulation CC Commentary at § 229.30(a) and (c) briefly reference Article 4 provisions affecting payor banks that are also affected by Regulation CC. Primarily these references note that §§ 4–301 and 4–302 continue to apply (*see supra* ¶ 8.02), along with §§ 3–418 and 4–215 on final payment, although the Article 4 deadlines can be extended in limited circumstances by the Regulation CC expeditious return requirements. The Commentary at § 229.30(a) ¶ 10. identifies Article 4 § 4–301(a) and (d) as provisions affected by Regulation CC: § 4–301(d) may be preempted as to when and how an item is to be returned; § 4–301(a) may be affected by the Regulation CC requirement of expeditious return. In addition, Article 4 § 4–214(b) (return of dishonored item to bank's customer or transferor or pursuant to its instructions) may be preempted by the Regulation CC rule at § 229.30(a)(2) that permits direct return of dishonored checks to the depositary bank. *See* Regulation CC Commentary to § 229.30(a). *Cf.* §§ 4–214(b), 4–301(d), and 4–301(a). However, it is clear that a payor bank remains liable for meeting its midnight deadline under Article 4, unless that is specifically extended under Regulation CC. *See* Regulation CC Commentary §§ 229.30(a).

320. *See* 12 CFR § 229.38(b) and the Commentary to §§ 229.30(a), (b), (c), and 229.38(b). "[Regulation CC] does not relieve a paying bank from the requirement for timely return (i.e., midnight deadline) under U.C.C. 4–301 and 4–302, which continue to apply." Regulation CC Commentary § 229.30(a) ¶ 9.a. *See also* the Commentary § 229.30(b), (c). The Regulation CC Commentary also mentions Regulation J, 12 CFR Part 210, as a deadline rule that may be applicable. Generally the stricter liability under Article 4 would be the utilized approach in private litigation.

[i] The Two-Day/Four-Day Test

This is the more certain test for expeditious return; it is met if the item is returned "in a manner such that the check would normally be received by the depositary bank not later than 4:00 p.m. . . . of the second business day following [the banking day of presentment]," for local checks, or by the fourth business day following the banking day of presentment for nonlocal checks.[321]

[ii] The Forward Collection Test

This test for expeditious return is met if the paying bank returns the item in a manner similar to the way "a similarly situated bank would normally handle a check . . . [o]f similar amount . . . [d]rawn on the depositary bank [and] [d]eposited for forward collection" by noon of the banking day after presentment.[322] In effect, this test is met if the bank returns the check by the same route that it uses for checks being sent to another bank for payment, or "forward collection."[323]

There are two basic methods described in Regulation CC for meeting this "forward collection" test: (1) the paying bank may return the check directly to the depositary bank;[324] or (2) it may return the check via any other bank that has agreed to return checks expeditiously under 12 CFR § 229.31(a),[325] including a Federal Reserve Bank.[326]

In returning the check, the paying bank also must decide whether to return the item as is, or to convert it to a "qualified returned check." This is defined as one that has been prepared for automated return "by placing the check in a carrier envelope or placing a strip on the check and encoding the strip or envelope in magnetic ink."[327] In effect this permits automatic processing as if the check was being processed for forward collection, a much more rapid and efficient process than the less-automated return system for other checks. Converting a check to "qualified return" status should help the bank satisfy its duty of expeditious return, but is not required.

Meeting the duty of expeditious return under Regulation CC does not relieve the bank from its responsibilities under other law, such as the midnight deadline and other requirements in Article 4 and Federal Reserve Regulation J, except as noted below and in the Regulation CC Commentary.[328] Unless the Article 4 requirements are preempted by

---

321. 12 CFR § 229.30(a)(1). *See also* 12 CFR § 229.32(a), discussed *infra* this text at notes 415-16 and ¶ 8.04[3][d].

322. 12 CFR § 229.30(a)(2).

323. *See* 12 CFR § 229.2(q) ("Forward collection means the process by which a bank sends a check on a cash basis to the paying bank for payment").

324. This method of return may preempt § 4-214(b), otherwise calling for return to the bank's customer or transferor or pursuant to its instructions, as noted *infra* at ¶ 8.04[3][c] and [4].

325. Discussed *infra* at ¶ 8.04[3][c].

326. 12 CFR § 229.30(a)(2).

327. 12 CFR § 229.2(bb). The encoding must include the routing number of the depositary bank, the amount of the check, and a specified return item identifier (the number "2") in the 44th position of the MICR line. *See* 12 CFR § 229.30(a)(2).

328. *See* 12 CFR § 229.30(a)(2). *See also* Regulation CC Commentary §§ 229.30(a), (b), (e), 229.31(b), and 229.38(b).

Regulation CC or other law,[329] they still apply, and the bank should avoid being so preoccupied with Regulation CC that it inadvertently violates an Article 4 requirement. Despite the impact of Regulation CC, UCC Article 4 remains the most significant source of potential liability for payor banks.[330]

[iii] Impact on Article 4—The Payor Bank

The paying bank's midnight deadline under Article 4 (and Federal Reserve Regulation J)[331] may be extended through preemption by Regulation CC.[332] The Article 4 midnight deadlines may be extended if the paying bank, "in an effort to expedite delivery of a returned check . . . , uses a means of delivery that would ordinarily result in the returned check being received by the bank to which it is sent on or before the receiving bank's next banking day following the otherwise applicable deadline."[333] For example, an expeditious return that would ordinarily result in receipt of the returned check on or before the banking day following the payor's midnight deadline will satisfy the midnight deadline even though the specific requirements of Article 4 are not met. An example would be where the paying bank uses a courier that leaves after midnight to deliver its forward collection checks.

Additionally, the midnight deadline is "extended further" by return of a check using a "highly expeditious means of transportation" even if it "would ordinarily result in delivery after the receiving bank's next banking day."[334]

[b] Identification of Returned Checks and Notice of Return—Duties of the Payor Bank

[i] Notice of Return

The payor bank returning a dishonored check must "clearly indicate on the face of the check that it is a returned check and the reason for return."[335] If the check is unavailable for return, the bank may send a

---

329. See supra ¶ 8.01[2].

330. See supra ¶ 8.02 and infra ¶ 8.04[3][a] and ¶ 8.04[4].

331. See supra ¶ 8.02[2][d].

332. See 12 CFR § 229.30(c) and the Commentary to § 229.30(c). This applies only to paying banks and not to returning banks. See generally, Oak Brook Bank v. Northern Trust Company, 256 F.3d 638 (7th Cir.2001) (extended midnight deadline for expeditious return under Regulation CC).

333. 12 CFR § 229.30(c)(1). See also 12 CFR § 229.32(a), discussed infra this text at notes 415–16, and ¶ 8.04[3][d]. See generally, Oak Brook Bank v. Northern Trust Company, 256 F.3d 638 (7th Cir.2001) (extended midnight deadline for expeditious return under Regulation CC).

334. 12 CFR § 229.30(c)(1). This permits a payor bank that has missed its midnight deadline to use a "highly expeditious" means of delivery (such as a courier) to satisfy both Regulation CC and Article 4 by returning the item for expected receipt on the following day, even though it is received after the close of the receiving bank's banking day. See 12 CFR § 229.30(c)(1) and the Commentary; Oak Brook Bank v. Northern Trust Company; 256 F.3d 638 (7th Cir. 2001). Among other things, Oak Brook held that a federal reserve bank has a 24 hour "banking day" for purposes of timely return under this rule. See supra ¶ 8.01[3][i].

335. 12 CFR § 229.30(d). "Refer to Maker" remains a permissible reference "in appropriate cases." Commentary § 229.30(d). The Commentary does not

copy of the front and back of the check or, if no copy is available, a written notice of nonpayment containing the information noted below.[336] The copy or notice must clearly state that it is a "notice in lieu of return."[337] The copy or notice will be treated as a returned check for purposes of the expeditious return requirements and other requirements of Regulation CC, Subpart C.[338]

[ii] *Notice of Nonpayment: Identifying the Depositary Bank*

When the payor bank dishonors a check in the amount of $2,500 or more, *in addition to* all other requirements, direct notice must be given by the payor bank to the depositary bank to be received by 4:00 p.m. local time on the second business day following the banking day of presentment to the payor bank.[339] The notice can be given by "any reasonable means, including the returned check, a writing (including a copy of the check), telephone, Fedwire, telex, or other form of telegraph."[340] If the second business day following the day of presentment is not a banking day for the depositary bank, receipt of notice on the next banking day will be considered timely.[341] The required contents of the notice are described at 12 CFR § 229.33(b), and are the same as the requirements for a notice in lieu of a returned check under § 229.30.[342]

[c] Duties of Returning Banks—Regulation CC Section 229.31

[i] *The Scope of Section 229.31*

Regulation CC § 229.31 applies to "returning banks." "Returning bank" is defined as any bank other than a paying bank or depositary bank that handles a returned check or notice in lieu of return.[343] The Regulation CC definition states that "[a] returning bank is also a collecting bank for purposes of UCC 4–202(b)."[344] In effect a returning

---

elaborate as to what those cases might be. *Id.*

336. 12 CFR § 229.30(f). *See also* discussion *infra* ¶ 8.04[3][f] and ¶ 9.03[6] (check truncation). *But see infra* ¶ 9.03[7].

337. *Id.* These requirements will supercede any contrary provisions of § 4–301. *See* the Regulation CC Commentary to § 229.30(f).

338. *Id.* The notice must be directed to a location of the depositary as provided at 12 CFR § 229.32(a), discussed *infra* this text at notes 429–431 and ¶ 8.04[3][d].

339. 12 CFR § 229.33(a) and Commentary.

340. *Id.*

341. *Id.*

342. *See* text *supra* at ¶ 8.04[3][b].

343. 12 CFR § 229.2(cc). *See generally,* Oak Brook Bank v. Northern Trust Company, 256 F.3d 638 (7th Cir.2001) (Federal Reserve Banks as returning banks).

344. *Id. Cf.* Article 4 § 4–202(b). This may be somewhat misleading, in the sense it suggests that the Regulation CC definition of "returning bank" is the same as the Article 4 definition of "collecting bank" at § 4–105(5). The Article 4 definition of "collecting bank" includes all banks except the payor, and therefore includes both intermediary and depositary banks, while the Regulation CC definition of "returning bank" includes only Article 4 intermediary banks and not depositary banks. *See* Article 4 § 4–105(4), (5). In effect the Regulation CC definition of "returning bank" is more closely akin to the Article 4 definition of "intermediary bank." *Cf.* 12 CFR § 229.2(cc) with Article 4 § 4–105(4). Nonetheless, since all Article 4 "intermediary banks" (and Regulation CC "returning banks") are within the broader category of

bank is any bank that handles a returned check between the payor bank and the depositary bank.[345] The Regulation CC duties of a returning bank are described at § 229.31, as outlined below.

[ii] Expeditious Return

Returning banks are subject to essentially the same deadlines for expeditious return as are payor banks, under the two-day/four-day and forward collection tests.[346] However, returning banks can extend the time for expeditious return under the forward collection test (as well as the return deadlines under Article 4 and Regulation J) by a period of one business day, if the returning bank converts the returned check to a "qualified returned check"(QRC).[347] This extension does not apply to the two-day/four-day test or where the payor returns the check directly to the depositary bank, because QRC status would add nothing to the return process in that context.[348]

[iii] The Return Process: Comparison to UCC Article 4

Regulation CC differs from UCC Article 4 in terms of the legal regime it prescribes for the return of dishonored checks.[349] Thus, the potential for preemption of state law is significant.[350]

Under Article 4, each collecting bank in the forward collection process is an agent or subagent of the owner of the item.[351] Hence each bank in the forward collection chain has an obligation to handle the check as a returned item upon its dishonor under § 4–202. In addition,

---

Article 4 "collecting banks," the Regulation CC reference is technically correct.

345. Again this is essentially the same as an Article 4 "intermediary bank," and is within the larger Article 4 definition of "collecting bank." *See* Article 4 § 4–105 and *supra* note 423. *See generally*, Oak Brook Bank v. Northern Trust Co., 256 F.3d 638 (7th Cir.2001) (Federal Reserve Banks as returning banks).

346. *See* 12 CFR § 229.31(a)(1), (2), and discussion *supra* ¶ 8.04[3][a]. The Regulation CC Commentary § 229.31(a) contains several examples.

347. *See* 12 CFR § 229.31(a)(2), and the Commentary. This does not apply to payor banks. *See also supra* this text and note 393. *See also*, Oak Brook Bank v. Northern Trust Company, 256 F.3d 638 (7th Cir. 2001) ("Banking day" is 24 hours for Federal Reserve Bank acting as a returning bank, where checks are processed around-the-clock).

348. *Id. See also supra* this text at notes 408–409, for discussion of the "qualified return check" process.

349. "The expeditious return requirement for a returning bank in this regulation is more stringent in many cases than the duty of a collecting bank to act seasonably under U.C.C. 4–202 in returning a check." Regulation CC Commentary § 229.31(a), ¶ 7; *see also* Oak Brook Bank v. Northern Trust Company, 256 F.3d 638 (7th Cir.2001).

350. Regulation CC Commentary § 229.31(a), ¶ 10. describes the preemption of three Article 4 provisions that affect collecting banks: (1) § 4–202(b) is preempted to the extent that Regulation CC modifies the time limits for return of such checks by intermediary banks; and (2) § 4–214(a) is preempted by the Regulation CC provision at § 229.31(c) governing settlement for returned checks and the time limits for an expeditious return. Regulation CC Commentary § 229.31(a), ¶ 10. The Commentary formerly noted that old § 4–212(2) (revised § 4–214(b)) is preempted by the Regulation CC provision at § 229.31(a) permitting direct return of dishonored checks; this seems still to be the case though the Commentary no longer says so. Other examples are discussed *infra*. For a similar summary of the preemptive effects as regards payor banks, *see* Regulation CC § 229.30(a) and Commentary; discussion beginning *supra* at note 392.

351. *See* § 4–201(a).

the collecting bank may have a direct interest in doing so, in order to rescind the provisional credit it provided its transferor during the forward collection process.[352] As a result, under Article 4 prior to Regulation CC the return process for a dishonored item essentially was the reverse of the forward collection process, with each collecting bank having a right to revoke the prior provisional settlement and a duty of ordinary care that could be met by returning the item within the bank's midnight deadline.[353]

Regulation CC changes this. Under Regulation CC all settlements for checks between banks are final in both the forward and return process.[354] Under Regulation CC the check can be returned via any means that satisfy an expeditious return test.[355] This may result in return by a path that is the same as the forward collection process in reverse, in which case final settlements are offset as if they were provisional under Article 4, though it must also meet the requirements of Regulation CC. But often, under Regulation CC, dishonor will mean return through a returning bank or banks different from the banks which handled the check for forward collection; indeed, under Regulation CC the check does not even have to be returned to the same branch of the depositary bank that initially handled the item.[356] Under Regulation CC it is intended that some banks (including the Federal Reserve Banks) will specialize in expeditious returns and will charge a fee for the service. Unlike Article 4, Regulation CC does not impose a duty on any bank other than the depositary bank to handle returned items.[357] Under Regulation CC, the returning bank is an agent or subagent of the paying bank, and a subagent of the depositary bank for the purpose of returning the check, and may be liable to the depositary bank and its customer or other party to the check but generally has no responsibility for the actions of other banks in the chain of collecting or returning banks.[358] Despite the expeditious return requirements in Regulation CC, and the collecting bank midnight deadline in Article 4 § 4–214, Regulation CC may allow an extra day to return a "qualified returned check."[359] However, in other respects the specific duties relating to expeditious return that are imposed on intermediary banks under Regulation CC § 229.31 generally are more onerous than the less rigid requirements at

---

352. See, e.g., § 4–214, and the discussion *supra* at ¶ 8.03.

353. See § 4–202, and *supra* ¶ 8.03.

354. See 12 CFR §§ 229.31(c), 229.32(b), and 229.36(d). This preempts Article 4, *e.g.*, §§ 4–201, 4–202, and 4–214, to some extent. This is recognized in the Official Comment to Article 4. See e.g., § 4–201, Comment 3 and 4; § 4–202, Comment 4; and § 4–214, Comment 4.

355. See 12 CFR §§ 229.30(a), 229.31(a).

356. The check must be returned to the location as described at 12 CFR § 229.32(a).

See discussion *supra*, text and notes 319–328, and *infra* ¶ 8.04[3][d].

357. See Regulation CC Commentary § 229.31(a). Cf. Article 4 § 4–202(a)(2) (duty of collecting bank to return an item); 12 CFR § 229.31(d) (returning bank may impose a charge for handling a returned check).

358. See Regulation CC Commentary to § 229.31(a), § 229.38(a).

359. See 12 CFR § 229.31(a) and the Commentary, and discussion *supra* at text and notes 327–328 and 347–348.

Article 4 § 4–202, even considering the effective incorporation of the midnight deadline into the latter standard.[360]

Under Regulation CC, the returning bank may be subject to liability for encoding errors due to negligence under Regulation CC § 229.38.[361] Under Article 4, a bank that encodes information on an item may be liable for breach of warranty to any subsequent party for any encoding error.[362] The encoding required by Regulation CC to convert a check to a "qualified returned check" thus also may carry with it some risk of liability under these provisions.[363]

[iv] *Settlement, Charges, and Other Notices*

Under Regulation CC, the rules governing identification of the depositary bank and proper delivery of returned checks are essentially the same for returning banks as for payor banks.[364] A returning bank must settle for returned checks with the payor bank in the same way that the bank would settle for a similar item during forward collection.[365] This applies regardless of whether the same banks handled the check during forward collection.[366] The method of settlement may vary according to the agreement between the parties but, however settlement is effected, under Regulation CC it is considered final when made.[367]

The mechanical differences between Article 4 and Regulation CC with regard to settlement in the forward collection and returned item processes are dramatic. Article 4 treats settlements in the forward collection process as provisional, essentially requiring that returned items retrace the forward collection process in order to allow revocation of the provisional credit granted at each stage of the forward process.[368] Under Article 4, "[t]he guiding principle is that settlements should be final [only] when the presenting person has received usable funds."[369] In contrast, Regulation CC seeks to bypass the relatively slow return process of Article 4 in favor of a more "expeditious return."[370] In order to

---

360. *Cf.* 12 CFR § 229.31(a), and discussion *supra* this text at notes 339–346, *with* § 4–202(b), discussed *supra* at ¶ 8.03[2].

361. 12 CFR § 229.38. *See also infra* ¶ 9.03[6].

362. § 4–209(a). *See also infra* ¶ 9.03[6].

363. *See* 12 CFR § 229.31(a).

364. *Cf.* 12 CFR §§ 229.31. *See also* discussion *supra* ¶ 8.04[3][b].

365. 12 CFR § 229.31(c).

366. *See* discussion *supra* ¶ 8.04[3][c] for comparison of the Regulation CC and Article 4 return systems.

367. *See* 12 CFR § 229.31(c) and the Commentary thereto; *cf.* Article 4 § 4–201(a) (settlement between banks is provisional); § 4–213 ("Medium and Time of Settlement by Bank"); § 4–214 (right to charge back provisional settlement). *See supra* ¶ 8.03[2],[5]. The Official Comment to § 4–201 recognizes that for checks governed by Regulation CC §§ 229.31(c), 229.32(b), and 229.36(d), "all settlements between banks are final." *See* § 4–201, Comment 4. § 4–213(a) is similar to Regulation CC § 229.31(c) in allowing settlement by any means agreed to by the parties. *See supra* ¶ 8.03[5].

368. *See* revised §§ 4–201, 4–213, 4–214, and 4–215, and discussion *supra* at ¶ 8.03[2].

369. Revised § 4–201, Comment 4.

370. *See* 12 CFR §§ 229.30(a), 229.31(a), and discussion *supra* this text at ¶ 8.04[3][a], [c].

bypass the Article 4 system and permit return by the most expeditious means, Regulation CC must also bypass the system of revoking provisional credit at each stage of the return process, as contemplated under Article 4. Regulation CC does this by making all settlements final during the forward collection process, thus preempting the Article 4 provisional settlement rules as to checks.[371] The result, however, is that banks handling the item for forward collection receive final settlement as well as give final settlement, and may collect payment for a returned item they agree to handle because they must finally settle for that item.[372] This essentially eliminates the concept of provisional settlement for banks except for depositary banks.[373] However, since the settlement is owed by another, there may be some risk for collecting banks.[374]

As noted *supra*, returning banks may impose charges for performing a return service.[375] Much like payor banks, returning banks may be entitled to send a notice of nonpayment in lieu of returning the check, and may rely on the depositary bank's routing number as it appears in the depositary bank's indorsement or as encoded on a qualified returned check.[376]

[d] Duties of Depositary Banks

Regulation CC describes the duties of depositary banks at § 229.32.[377] "Depositary bank" is defined as the first bank to which a check is transferred "even though it is also the paying bank or the payee."[378] In order to facilitate the acceptance by depositary banks of direct or expeditious returns from banks with which the depositary bank may have no prior relationship, Section 229.32 provides rules to govern such acceptance.

---

371. *See* revised § 4–201, Comment 4, and 12 CFR § 229.31(c) and Commentary. *See also* 12 CFR §§ 229.31(c), 229.32(b), and 229.36(d). *Cf.* discussion of the Article 4 system, *supra* at ¶ 8.03[2].

372. *See* 12 CFR §§ 229.31(c);

373. For payor banks, *cf.* Article 4 §§ 4–215, 4–301, and 4–302 *with* Regulation CC, 12 CFR §§ 229.30, 229.31(c) and 229.33; *see also* Regulation CC Commentary § 229.30(a) at ¶ 9 and ¶ 10 (Regulation CC does not relieve payor bank of Article 4 duty of timely return although mechanics of return may be affected and the midnight deadline may be extended in limited circumstances under Regulation CC § 229.30(c).). For depositary banks, *cf.* Article 4 §§ 4–201, 4–202, and 4–214, *with* Regulation CC, 12 CFR § 229.32; *see also* Regulation CC Commentary § 229.32(b) at ¶ 6 (Regulation CC does not affect depositary bank's right to revoke provisional settlement from its customer for a check that is returned). *See also* Regulation CC, 12 CFR § 229.38(a), (duty of ordinary care, consistent with Article 4); § 229.38(b) (no double recovery under both Article 4 and Regulation CC). *See also infra* ¶ 8.04[3][d] (Duties of Depositary Banks); *infra* ¶ 9.03[7].

374. The ramifications in the context of insolvency or other suspension of payments are described at 12 CFR §§ 229.35(b) and 229.39.

375. *See* 12 CFR § 229.31(d), and discussion *supra* this text and notes 452–458.

376. *See* 12 CFR §§ 229.31(f), (g), and discussion *supra* at ¶ 8.04[3][b].

377. 12 CFR § 229.32. *See also* 12 CFR § 229.33(d) (duty of depositary bank to send notice of dishonor to customer), discussed *infra* ¶ 8.04[3][d].

378. 12 CFR § 229.2(*o*). Article 4 defines "depositary bank" similarly, as "the first bank to take an item even though it is also the payor, unless the item is presented for immediate payment over the counter." Article 4 § 4–105(2).

[i] Acceptance by Depositary Banks

As noted *supra*, the depositary bank must accept returned checks and written notices of nonpayment at four locations but normally two locations control:[379]

1. The depositary bank must accept returns (or an appropriate notice in lieu thereof) at "a location at which presentment of checks for forward collection is requested by the depositary bank."[380]

2. The depositary bank must also accept returns at a "branch, head office, or other location consistent with the name and address of the bank in its indorsement on the check...."[381]

There follows at Regulation CC § 229.32(a)(2) a series of back-up rules for cases where the information required for the second location is not available.[382] These rules permit delivery of returns (or appropriate notices in lieu thereof) at: (1) a branch or head office associated with the depositary bank's routing number, where the bank's address is unavailable; (2) at any location consistent with the address in the indorsement and at a branch or head office associated with the routing number in the depositary bank's indorsement, where the address and routing number in the indorsement are in different check processing regions, or (3) at any branch or head office of the depositary bank, where no routing number or address appears in the indorsement stamp.[383]

The depositary bank is entitled to require that returned items be separated from forward collection items delivered to it.[384]

[ii] Payment for Returned Items

A depositary bank that receives a returned check must pay the returning or payor bank the amount of the check by the close of business on the banking day of receipt (called the "payment date" in Regulation CC).[385] This payment must be by means of (1) a debit to the account of the depositary bank at the returning or payor bank, (2) cash, (3) wire transfer, or (4) any other form of payment acceptable to the returning or payor bank.[386] These methods are allowed only if the proceeds are

---

379. *See* discussion *supra* at ¶ 8.04[3][b].

380. 12 CFR § 229.32(a)(1). This location is always available to returning or paying banks, because every depositary bank has a location at which presentment during forward collection is requested, usually a processing center. Note, however, that "presentment" is not a defined term in Regulation CC. *Cf.* § 3–501 (UCC definition of "presentment").

381. *See* 12 CFR § 229.32(a)(2)(i), and discussion *supra* this text and notes 415–16.

382. The indorsement standards at 12 CFR § 229.35 and Appendix D are designed to assure that the information called for at § 229.32(a)(2)(i) will be available as a part of the depositary bank's indorsement stamp. However, the back-up rules noted *infra* this text are designed to be applicable in those cases where that data is missing.

383. *See* 12 CFR § 229.32(a)(2)(ii), (iii), and (iv).

384. 12 CFR § 229.32(a)(2).

385. 12 CFR § 229.32(b). The day of receipt is determined pursuant to Article 4 § 4–108. *See* Regulation CC Commentary § 229.32(b).

386. 12 CFR § 229.32(b)(1)–(4). *Cf.* § 4–213 ("Medium and Time of Settlement by Bank"). Unlike Regulation CC, old Article 4 allowed settlement by cashier's check or other remittance draft without consent

available to the returning or payor bank as of the payment date.[387] If the payment date is not a banking day for any of the banks involved, payment by the next banking day will suffice.[388] In addition, the returning or payor bank may agree to accept payment at a later date, *e.g.*, where it determines that the amount involved does not warrant the cost of same-day payment by means of a wire transfer.[389] If the payment cannot be made before the close of the banking day (as determined under Article 4 § 4–108), *e.g.*, if the returned check is received after the returning or payor bank has closed or after Fedwire has closed, payment may be made the next banking day.[390] All payments are final when made.[391]

[iii] *Notice to Customer*

It should be noted again that the Regulation CC rules making settlement between banks final[392] do not apply to settlements between the depositary bank and a nonbank customer, so that any provisional settlement given for such a deposit remains subject to revocation and charge-back pursuant to Article 4.[393] Similarly, the Regulation CC funds availability requirements do not affect depositary bank policies relating to such things as the standards for acceptance of checks for deposit (or for cash), standards for revocation or charge back of provisional credit, and notices relating thereto.[394] However, the depositary bank is precluded from charging a presentment or processing fee for accepting and paying checks being returned to it.[395] If the depositary bank fails to give notice of the return to its customer within the midnight deadline or within a longer reasonable time, it is liable for damages.[396]

---

of the recipient. *See* old § 4–211(1)(a), (b). In contrast, Regulation CC allows such a means of payment only upon the agreement of the parties. *See* 12 CFR § 229.32(b). The 1990 Article 4 revisions essentially embraced the Regulation CC position. *See* § 4–213(a), (b). However, Article 4 contains specific provisions regarding settlement by cashier's check or teller's check, where such an instrument is used. *See* § 4–213(c) and Comment 3, and discussion *supra* at ¶ 8.03[5].

387. 12 CFR § 229.32(b), and the Commentary.

388. *Id.*

389. *See* 12 CFR § 229.32(b), and Commentary.

390. 12 CFR § 229.32(b). This could be the case, for example, where the depositary bank is a west coast bank that remains open to receive checks after the east coast returning bank has closed. *See* the Commentary to § 229.32(b).

391. 12 CFR § 229.32(b). As noted *supra*, this conflicts with the provisional settlement rules of Article 4. *See* Article 4 §§ 4–201, 4–213, 4–214, and discussion *supra* at ¶ 8.03[2].

392. *See* 12 CFR §§ 229.31(c), 229.32(b), and 229.36(d).

393. *See* Article 4 § 4–214(a) and Comment 4; Regulation CC, 12 CFR § 229.33(d); and the Commentary to § 229.32(b). *See also* discussion *supra* ¶ 8.03[2] and ¶ 8.04[3][c] and *infra* ¶ 9.03[7]; and *compare* Regulation CC, 12 CFR § 229.19(c)(2)(ii).

394. 12 CFR § 229.19(c)(2) and the Commentary. Furthermore the depositary bank may qualify as a holder in due course for purposes of collecting the check. *See supra* Chapter 3 at ¶ 3.03. *But see infra* ¶ 9.03[7].

395. 12 CFR § 229.32(d). *Cf.* § 229.31(d) (returning bank [often a Federal Reserve Bank] may impose charges—unlimited by Regulation CC—for handling a returned check).

396. *See* 12 CFR §§ 229.33(d) (required notice to customer) and 229.38(a), (c). *Cf.* Article 4 §§ 4–103(e), 4–202, and 4–214; discussion *supra* at ¶ 8.03[4], and *infra* at

If a check is returned in error to a bank that is not the depositary bank, the receiving bank must promptly send the check to the depositary bank, either directly or by means of a returning bank that agrees to handle the returned check expeditiously under Regulation CC § 229.31(a).[397]

[e] Warranties of Paying and Returning Banks

Every paying[398] and returning bank that transfers a returned check and receives a settlement or other consideration warrants to the transferee, to any subsequent returning bank, to the depositary bank, and to the owner of the check, that:

1. The paying bank returned the check within the appropriate deadline under Article 4 and Regulation J or Regulation CC Section 229.30(c);[399]

2. the paying or returning bank is authorized to return the check;[400]

3. the check has not been materially altered;[401]

4. if the bank is returning a notice in lieu of return of the item, the original check has not and will not be returned.[402]

These warranties are not made with regard to checks drawn on the U.S. Treasury, U.S. Postal money orders, or checks of a local or state government not payable at or through a bank.[403] These warranties also do not include a warranty that the bank has complied with the expeditious return requirements of Regulation CC.[404] It should also be empha-

¶ 8.04[4] and ¶ 9.03[7]. The Regulation CC Commentary states that the notice requirement at § 229.33(d) is "similar" to the Article 4 requirement as interpreted in Appliance Buyers Credit Corp. v. Prospect National Bank, 708 F.2d 290 (7th Cir. 1983). See Regulation CC Commentary § 229.33(d).

397. 12 CFR § 229.32(c), referencing 12 CFR § 229.31(a) (discussed *supra* at ¶ 8.04[3][d]).

398. Paying bank is defined at 12 CFR § 229.2(z) to include banks "through which a check is payable and to which it is sent for payment or collection." *Cf.* the definition of "Payor bank" at Article 4 § 4-105(3) ("a bank that is the drawee of a draft"). The Regulation CC definition of paying bank includes both payor and "payable at or through" banks. The definition of "bank" at 12 CFR § 229.2(e) includes virtually any type of regulated depository institution, e.g., banks, thrifts, and credit unions. *Cf.* Article 4 § 4-105(1) (similar broad definition).

399. If a check is payable by one bank but is payable through another bank (credit union share drafts are commonly handled in this manner), this warranty is made by the bank by which the check is payable. 12 CFR § 229.34(a)(1). On the midnight deadlines, *see supra* ¶ 8.01[2] and ¶ 8.02[2][d].

The Regulation CC warranty at § 229.34(a) includes a warranty that the Regulation J return deadline has been met. Regulation J subsequently was revised to delete a specific deadline in favor of a reference to the deadlines imposed under Article 4, Regulation CC, and Federal Reserve Bank operating circulars. See Regulation J, 12 CFR § 210.12(a).

400. 12 CFR § 229.34(a)(2).

401. 12 CFR § 229.34(a)(3). *Cf.* Article 4 § 4-207(a)(3) (Article 4 warranty of no alteration by customer and collecting banks). *See also* UCC Article 3 §§ 3-406, 3-407, 3-416, discussed *supra* this text at Chapter 7, ¶ 7.02.

402. 12 CFR § 229.34(a)(4). *See generally infra* ¶ 9.03[7].

403. 12 CFR § 229.34(a).

404. The warranty is as to compliance with 12 CFR § 229.30(c), not (a). See Commentary 229.34(a), referring to the return

sized that by the terms of Regulation CC § 229.34(a), these warranties are limited to paying and returning banks, and therefore do not apply in the forward collection process. Warranty issues in the forward collection process remain within the scope of Article 4 §§ 4–207, 4–208, and 4–209.

In addition, each paying bank that gives a notice of nonpayment pursuant to 12 CFR § 229.33[405] warrants to the transferee, to any subsequent transferee bank, to the depositary bank, and to the owner of the check, that:

1. the paying bank returned or will return the check within the Article 4, Regulation J, and Regulation CC § 229.30 (c) deadlines;[406]
2. the bank is authorized to send the notice;[407] and
3. the check has not been materially altered.[408]

Like the other Regulation CC warranties, these warranties are not made with regard to state or local government checks not payable at or through a bank.[409]

Damages for breach of these warranties are limited to the consideration received by the warrantor, plus finance charges and expenses "related to the returned check, if any."[410] The Regulation CC Commentary states that this expands the warranty damages rule of Article 4 § 4–209(a) by providing that all banks that transfer or present or return a check make the encoding warranty. (In contrast, § 4–209(a) is limited to the encoder and hence essentially to the forward collection process.)[411] The warranties at Regulation CC § 229.34(b) do *not* include a warranty that the notice is accurate and timely under § 229.33. Such issues are instead subject to the general liability provisions of Regulation CC § 229.38.[412]

Article 4 does not provide an equivalent system of warranties for returned items, perhaps in part because Article 4 envisions a returned item path just the reverse of the forward collection system, giving each party recourse under the prior relationship thereby created including, as

---

requirements at §§ 229.30(a) and 229.31(a). The liability rules are different. *See* 12 CFR § 229.34(c), § 229.38.

405. *See supra* ¶ 8.04[3][b].

406. 12 CFR § 229.34(b)(1). As noted *supra*, where the check is payable by one bank but through another, the bank which will pay makes this warranty. *See supra* note 382. The Regulation CC deadline subject to this warranty is the § 229.30(c) extended midnight deadline for expedited return. *See supra* ¶ 8.04[3][a]. Once again there is no warranty of expedited return under § 229.30(a). *See* the Regulation CC Commentary § 229.34(a).

The Regulation CC warranties at § 229.34(a) and (b) include a warranty that the Regulation J return deadlines were met; however, these were deleted in a subsequent revision of Regulation J, in favor of a reference to the Regulation CC expedited return requirements, the Article 4 midnight deadline, and Federal Reserve Bank operating circulars. *See* 12 CFR § 210.12(a).

407. 12 CFR § 229.34(b)(2).

408. *Id.* § 229.34(b)(3). *See also supra* note 499.

409. 12 CFR § 229.34(b).

410. *See* 12 CFR § 229.34(c), and the Commentary.

411. Regulation CC Commentary § 229.34(c). *Cf.* Article 4 § 4–207(c).

412. *See* the Regulation CC Commentary §§ 229.33(a), 229.34(b).

necessary, the forward transfer warranties.[413] Because Regulation CC often creates a new returned item path, banks handling the item for the first time may need the warranty protection afforded under Regulation CC. It is arguable that the Article 4 transfer warranties in some circumstances may apply to the transfer of a returned check by a paying or returning bank.[414] It would not seem they are needed, however, since any dishonored check will ultimately be returned to the depositary bank which must settle for it under Regulation CC § 229.32(b).

The substantive scope of the Regulation CC warranties is somewhat similar to that of the Article 4 warranties.[415] The Article 4 warranties protect primarily against unauthorized indorsement and alteration.[416] The Regulation CC warranties at § 229.34 also protect against (presumably later) alteration, and unauthorized return.[417] As noted *supra*, the Regulation CC warranty only applies to transfers of returned checks, that is, transfers after dishonor by the payor bank, while the Article 4 warranties are designed to protect the parties to transfers in the forward collection process.[418] In effect the Article 4 warranties provide warranty protection against actions of parties prior to presentment of the check for payment, while the Regulation CC warranties provide protection against actions of parties subsequent to dishonor.

---

413. *See* UCC §§ 3–416, 4–207, and discussion *supra* this text in Chapter 7, at ¶ 7.02[2].

414. *See* Article 4 §§ 4–104(a)(5) and 4–105(5). UCC § 3–203(a) defines "transfer" as delivery "by a person other than its issuer for the purpose of giving to the person receiving the delivery the right to enforce the instrument." Transfer of a returned check is not primarily for the purpose of enabling the transferee to enforce the instrument; however each transferee does in fact have such a right as holder of the instrument. *See* UCC § 3–203(b), (c).

415. *Cf.* 12 CFR § 229.34, *with* UCC §§ 3–416 and 4–207.

416. *See* Article 4 §§ 4–207 and 4–208. If breached the Article 4 warranties allow the payor bank to return an item after the midnight deadline (The midnight deadline is discussed *supra* at ¶ 8.02). On the Article 4 warranties, *see also supra* ¶ 7.02.

A typical case is First National Bank and Trust Co. of the Treasure Coast v. Belmont National Bank, 43 UCC Rep. Serv.2d 666, 2001 WL 15937 (Ohio Ct. App. 2001), where a check was deposited without the required indorsement of a joint payee. It was sent through the banking system to the payor bank, which gave provisional credit and did not dishonor the item or revoke the credit within its midnight deadline (thereby losing the right to dishonor it under § 4–301 and becoming accountable for the amount of the item under § 4–302).

When the missing indorsement was discovered, the payor bank returned the item to the depositary bank and revoked credit for the item, on grounds of breach of warranty. The depositary bank had paid out the funds to its depositor, who was now bankrupt, and the depositary bank sued the payor to recover the payment under the midnight deadline rule at § 4–302. The court correctly concluded that recovery under § 4–302 was barred by the payor bank's counter claim (asserted as a defense) for breach of warranty due to the lack of a required indorsement.

Note that the presentment warranties do not include a warranty that the drawer's signature is genuine, only a warranty that the presenter has no knowledge to that effect. Thus, the drawee (*e.g.*, the payor bank) generally bears the burden (and loss) of any forged drawer signatures discovered after the item has been paid: The drawee cannot charge the customer's account for an improperly paid item, and cannot recover for breach of warranty from an innocent presenting party. *See, e.g.*, Decibel Credit Union v. Pueblo Bank & Trust Co., 996 P.2d 784 (Colo.Ct.App. 2000).

417. 12 CFR § 229.34(a)(2) and (3), (b)(2) and (3).

418. *Cf.* 12 CFR § 229.34(a), (b), with UCC §§ 3–416 and 4–207. The Article 4 presentment warranty in § 4–208 only applies, of course, where the drawee pays or accepts, as opposed to dishonors.

Thus, the Regulation CC warranties include a warranty that the transferor has met its midnight deadline,[419] something not included in the Article 4 warranties, with their focus on the forward collection process.[420] Similarly, Regulation CC includes a warranty that the payor or returning bank has authority to return the item[421] and, where a notice in lieu of return is used, that the original will not be returned.[422] The Article 4 has no counterpart to the latter provision but, as noted, there is a warranty that there is a right to enforce the item.[423]

To some extent the Regulation J obligation is patterned after the Regulation CC warranty.[424] However, the scope of Regulation CC is much broader, as Regulation J is limited to items being processed through the Federal Reserve System,[425] while Regulation CC applies to the return of any check by a banking institution.[426]

As a result of this matrix of warranties, a bank may have rights and liabilities under a variety of theories. For example, if a payor bank misses the Article 4 midnight deadline by failing to return the item by midnight of the banking day after the banking day of presentment, the bank may be liable for violations of duty under Article 4, Regulation J, and Regulation CC.[427] A similar matrix of duties applies to collecting and returning banks.[428] Thus, missing the Article 4 midnight deadline may trigger: (1) liability for up to the amount of the item under Article 4 §§ 4–214 or 4–302; (2) liability for violation of Regulation J § 210.12;[429] or liability for breach of warranty under Regulation CC § 229.34. The recovery for breach of warranty under Regulation CC could include attorney fees, court costs, and other "expenses related to the returned check."[430]

---

419. 12 CFR § 229.34(a)(1), (b)(1). The Regulation CC warranties include a warranty that the Article 4 midnight deadline has been met (or excused under Regulation CC § 229.30(c)), but no warranty that the Regulation CC expeditious return requirements have been met. *See* Regulation CC Commentary § 229.34(a). Similarly, there is no warranty that the notice of return requirements at Regulation CC § 229.33 have been met. Such issues are covered by the liability rules of § 229.38. *See* Regulation CC Commentary § 229.34(b). Note if the paying bank does not meet its deadline, its liability under Article 4 may be greater than under Regulation CC, but the liability for a returning bank should be similar under both Regulation CC and Article 4. *See infra* note 518.

420. The Article 4 collection process includes something of a midnight deadline for collecting banks, at § 4–202(a) and (b), and the liability for breach would seem to be similar under §§ 4–202 and 4–103(e) or 12 CFR § 229.34(c).

421. 12 CFR § 229.34(a)(2), (b)(2).

422. *Id.* § 229.34(a)(4).

423. *See* UCC §§ 3–416 and 4–207.

424. 12 CFR § 210.12(c).

425. *See id.* § 210.1.

426. *See* 12 CFR § 229.1(b)(3); § 229.2(e), (z), and (cc); *id.* §§ 229.30(a), and 229.31(a).

427. *See* UCC § 4–104(a)(3) and (10); §§ 4–215(a)(3), 4–301, and 4–302; discussion *supra* ¶ 8.02[2][d]. *See also* Regulation J, 12 CFR § 210.12, and Regulation CC, 12 CFR § 229.34.

428. *See* UCC § 4–105(1), (5), 4–212; 12 CFR § 229.34(a).

429. Regulation J requires timely return under Article 4 and Regulation CC. 12 CFR § 210.12(a)–(c).

430. 12 CFR § 229.34(d), and the Commentary; *cf.* Comment 6 to UCC § 3–416(b). The Regulation CC Commentary states that this incorporates, for the Regulation CC § 229.34 warranties, the

¶ 8.04 FEDERAL RESERVE REGULATION 367

The liabilities recognized in Regulation CC presumably do not in any way preclude a party's alternative liability under the UCC.[431] However, if because of the same violation a bank has failed to comply with the requirements of Article 4, Regulation J, and/or Regulation CC, the bank presumably can be held liable under only one of those laws.[432]

[f] Truncation

[i] Introduction

Regulation CC § 229.36 provides authority for truncation of checks.[433]

[ii] Check Truncation

The Expedited Funds Availability Act and Regulation CC specifically authorize and even encourage truncation of checks, pursuant to an agreement of the parties.[434] Articles 3 and 4 also specifically authorize check truncation.[435] A former rule in Regulation CC, providing that the truncation agreement could not extend the expeditious return requirements in a manner affecting the rights of anyone not a party to the truncation agreement, has been deleted.[436]

[iii] Forward Collection Settlements Deemed Final; Impact on Article 4

As noted,[437] a major difference between Regulation CC and Article 4 with regard to the check collection process is that Article 4 generally regards settlements as provisional until the item has been finally paid,[438] while Regulation CC treats all settlements for checks between banks as final.[439] However, Regulation CC makes clear that a collecting bank

---

damages rules of § 4–207(c) and UCC § 4A–506(b).

431. Compare 12 CFR § 229.38(a).

432. Compare id. § 229.38(b).

433. 12 CFR § 229.36(c). So does UCC § 3–501 (presentment) and § 4–110 (electronic presentment). See supra ¶ 8.01[3][n] (electronic presentment); infra 9.03[6] (truncation).

434. See 12 U.S.C. § 4008(b)(2), § 4008(f); 12 CFR § 229.36(c). See also infra ¶ 9.03[6], [7]. The term "truncation" can include a wide variety of procedures whereby the check is destroyed or otherwise removed from the collection process and the information represented thereby is subsequently handled electronically. See infra ¶ 9.03[6], [7].

435. See §§ 3–501(b)(1) and 4–110, and discussion infra ¶ 9.03[6].

436. See 12 CFR § 229.36(c) (now Reserved). Regulation CC Commentary formerly noted that:

This paragraph allows truncation by agreement with the paying bank; however, such agreement may not prejudice the interests of prior parties to the check. For example, a truncation agreement may not extend the paying bank's time for return as such an extension could damage the depositary bank, which must make funds available to its customers under mandatory availability schedules.

Former Regulation CC Commentary § 229.36(c). (now Reserved). Despite the deletion of this language, there remains doubt in some quarters whether a truncation agreement between banks can bind those not a party to the agreement. This appears to be a matter of contract law; in other words, the former § 229.36(c) and its Commentary may have simply stated the obvious, in which case the deletion of that language has no significant effect.

437. See supra ¶ 8.03.

438. See UCC §§ 4–201, 4–202, and 4–215; supra ¶ 8.02[1].

439. 12 CFR § 229.36(d). Note that this is limited to checks, defined at 12 CFR § 229.2(k) as a negotiable demand draft drawn on a bank or the U.S. Treasury, and

handling an item for forward collection may still be liable for negligence to prior parties, including the depositary bank and its customer, under Article 4.[440] Thus Regulation CC contemplates continuing duties for collecting banks under Article 4, such as the duty of ordinary care and related midnight deadline obligations under §§ 4–202, 4–214, and 4–103. To the extent that it is applicable, however, Regulation CC preempts inconsistent Article 4 rules on provisional settlement, since those rules are inconsistent with the Regulation CC final settlement rule; but as noted Regulation CC does not otherwise preempt the Article 4 forward collection liability system.[441]

As a result, for checks, all settlements given during both the forward collection and return processes are final, and cannot be revoked unless otherwise permitted (perhaps on some additional legal basis), despite the general rules to the contrary in Article 4.[442] As noted *supra*,[443] the purpose is to permit dishonored checks to be returned by the most expeditious route even if that is different from the forward collection path. Nonetheless, Regulation CC recognizes a continuing agency relationship and duty of care in the forward collection system under Article 4, so that a collecting bank has recourse against prior parties in the collection chain for damages suffered as a result of the failure to meet the Article 4 duty of care.[444]

And the Regulation CC § 229.36(d) provision, deeming settlements for checks between banks final when made, does not preempt the Article 4 rules on final payment and accountability of payor banks under §§ 4–215 and 4–302 (except possibly to allow expeditious return after the midnight deadline under § 229.30(c)). Regulation CC § 229.36(f) largely replicates Article 4 §§ 4–301 and 4–302, and the Commentary to § 229.36(f) indicates that Regulation CC does not preempt the final payment rules of Article 4 at § 4–215 or "[o]ther provisions of the U.C.C. not superceded by [Regulation CC Subpart C]." With the possible exception of § 229.30(c), Regulation CC § 229.30 (return of checks) similarly does not preempt the Article 4 rules at §§ 4–215, 4–301, and 4–302.[445]

[g] Indorsements

Every bank (except the payor bank) that handles an item during forward or return collection must "legibly indorse" the instrument in accordance with the standards set forth in Appendix D to Subpart C of Regulation CC.[446] These rules create strict indorsement standards, as

---

thus does not preempt Article 4 as to other items.

440. 12 CFR § 229.36(d), and the Commentary. *See also supra* ¶ 8.03.

441. *See* § 4–201(a), and Comment 4; 12 CFR § 229.36(d) and the Commentary.

442. *See* § 4–201 and Comment 4; § 4–214(b) and Comment 4. "Thus owing to the federal preemption, this subsection [§ 4–214(b)] applies only to noncheck items." *Id.*

443. *See supra* ¶ 8.04[3][a].

444. *See* 12 CFR § 229.36(d) and Commentary; §§ 4–201(a), 4–202.

445. *See also* 12 CFR § 229.38(a), and (b), and Commentary.

446. 12 CFR § 229.35(a). *Cf.* UCC § 3–201(b) (negotiation of order instrument requires indorsement); §§ 3–205—3–206 (special, blank, and restrictive indorsements); § 3–301 (persons entitled to enforce

noted below. In contrast, Articles 3 and 4 always have allowed a variety of indorsements, and the 1990 revisions to Articles 3 and 4 continue in this respect.[447]

Regulation CC requires that all depositary bank indorsements must contain: (1) the bank's nine-digit routing number, set off with arrows; (2) the bank's name and location; and (3) the indorsement date. This information must appear all in dark purple or black ink, and must be placed on the back of the check in the space between three inches from the leading edge and one and a half inches from the trailing edge of the check.[448]

Indorsements by subsequent collecting banks may not include more than (1) the bank's nine-digit routing number, set off without arrows, and (2) the indorsement date (a trace/sequence number is optional). This information must be in a color of ink other than purple, and must be placed within a three inch band along the leading edge of the check.[449]

Each returning bank must stamp its indorsement using ink that is not purple in color, outside the area between three inches from the leading edge to the trailing edge.[450]

These indorsement standards eliminate the traditional "PEG" (previous endorsements guaranteed) portion of the collecting bank indorsement stamp. "PEG" has long been superfluous because the UCC provides for such a guarantee as a matter of law.[451]

[4] Conclusion: Impact of Regulation CC on UCC Articles 3 and 4

The relationship between Regulation CC and UCC Articles 3 and 4 remains complex and to some degree unsettled.[452] A primary concern is

---

the instrument); § 4–205 (depository bank deemed holder of an unindorsed item); § 4–206 (any agreed method of transfer permitted between banks); §§ 4–207 and 4–208 (transfer and presentment warranties).

447. See references *supra* note 446. *See also supra* this text Chapter 3, ¶ 3.02.

448. 12 CFR § 229.35(a) and Appendix D–1. Optional information includes a branch identifier, trace/sequence number, telephone number (for receipt of notice of nonpayment), and other data not affecting readability of the indorsement.

449. 12 CFR § 229.35(a) and Appendix D–2.

450. 12 CFR § 229.35(a) and Appendix D–3.

451. See § 4–208(a)(1). *See also* Chilson v. Capital Bank, 10 Kan.App.2d 111, 692 P.2d 406 (Kan.Ct.App.1984). Under Regulation CC, "collecting-bank indorsements may not include this [P.E.G.] language." Commentary § 229.35(a).

452. *See generally* Alvin C. Harrell, NCCUSL Articles 3, 4, and 4A Drafting Committee Highlights Current Payment System and Negotiable Instrument Issues, 54 Consumer Fin L.Q. Rep. 351 (2000); Alvin C. Harrell, UCC Article 4 and Regulation CC: Can They Ever be Reconciled?, 54 Consumer Fin. L.Q. Rep. 236 (2000); Thomas C. Baxter, Jr., Stephanie A. Heller, and Ana G. Rodriguez, Finality of Payment: Articles 3, 4, and 4A of the Uniform Commercial Code, 51 Consumer Fin. L.Q. Rep. 200 (1997); Sharon A. Sweeney and Jane Anne Schmoker, Federal Reserve Bank and the Payment System: Regulation J, Regulation CC, Operating Circulars, and other Deposit Account Issues, 51 Consumer Fin. L.Q. Rep. 204 (1997); Conni L. Allen, The New Rules Governing Collection and Payment of Checks in the Banking System: Impact of Regulation CC, 47 Consumer Fin. L.Q. Rep. 129 (1993). Fred H. Miller, Expedited Funds Availability and Other Payment System Developments, 42 Consumer Fin. L. Q. Rep. 103 (1988).

that the differences between these state and federal laws result in preemption issues, potentially misleading parties who rely on the UCC, which remains the primary source of law governing these issues.[453] Regulation CC preempts any "inconsistent" provision of the UCC (or any other state law), "but only to the extent of the inconsistency."[454] This leaves a somewhat murky relationship between these important laws. The simple solution is that banks and other affected parties should try to comply with the requirements of both state and federal law, to the extent possible. But of course that does not answer the more difficult questions that may arise when the two laws conflict. Nor does it address the compliance issues inherent in an effort to satisfy the requirements of disparate statutes in complex daily transactions.

These issues are dealt with throughout Chapter 8 of this text, and particularly at ¶ 8.04. This discussion will provide an overview and summary of some of the main issues.

[a] The Mandatory Availability Rules and the Depositary Bank

The Regulation CC mandatory rules impose limits on the hold periods for deposited funds that can be imposed by depositary banks.[455] The maximum hold periods in general are two days for local checks and five days for nonlocal checks.[456] As a result, depositary banks may be required to make funds available for withdrawal by the customer before the items deposited have been paid and the funds collected. This rather significantly increases the risks for depositary institutions; if a deposited item is dishonored by the payor (*e.g.*, due to insufficient funds, forgery, or alteration), the depositary bank may find that the customer has withdrawn the funds before the depositary bank received notice of the dishonor. Expedited return provisions and the provision that requires wire notice for items of $2,500 or more are designed to prevent this but may not always be effective.[457] It is possible that this legal regime is partly responsible for the increased fraud losses suffered by banks in such transactions in recent years.

These risks increase the importance of the depositary bank qualifying as a holder in due course, as this status may be essential to collection of the dishonored item.[458] To some extent the 1990 revisions to Article 3 benefit the depositary bank by expanding the scope of Article 3 to allow

---

453. To a much lesser extent, similar issues result from the relationship between Federal Reserve Regulation J, 12 CFR Pt. 210, and the UCC. However, Regulation J is much more closely patterned after Article 4, so there are fewer conflicts and preemption issues. *See supra* ¶ 8.01[2], and Miller, *supra* note 452.

454. 12 CFR § 229.41.

455. *See* 12 CFR § 229.12 and discussion *supra* at notes ¶ 8.04[2].

456. 12 CFR § 229.12(b), (c). *See generally* Miller, *supra* note 452.

457. *See* 12 CFR § 229.30; Rapp v. Dime Savings Bank, 64 A.D.2d 964, 408 N.Y.S.2d 540 (App. Div. 1978), *aff'd*, 48 N.Y.2d 658, 421 N.Y.S.2d 347, 396 N.E.2d 740 (1979); Guelo, Bad Checks Surged Last Year; Bankers Blame Fed's New Rules, AM. BANKER, Aug. 20, 1991, at 1.

458. *See* UCC §§ 3-302—3-308, and discussion *supra* Chapter 3.

any check to qualify as a negotiable instrument.[459] At the same time, however, the definition of good faith (a prerequisite to holder in due course status under § 3–302(a)(2)) was tightened by a requirement that it include "observance of reasonable commercial standards of fair dealing."[460] This has made it significantly more difficult for a depositary bank to qualify as a holder in due course. *See, e.g.*, Maine Family Federal Credit Union v. Sun Life Assurance Co., 727 A.2d 335 (Me.1999) (depositary bank failed to meet the new "good faith" test because it allowed deposit of a large check drawn by an out-of-state insurance company without invoking a "hold" under Regulation CC). This case seems clearly wrong, as holder in due course status does not require a hold on every large insurance claims payment, but the analysis illustrates the danger of the new good faith standards.

[b] Impact of Regulation CC on the Midnight Deadline

The Regulation CC expeditious return requirements[461] are imposed on top of the Article 4 midnight deadline, not as a replacement. As a result, banks continue to be liable under Article 4 for missing the midnight deadline, just as before.[462] Thus, although Regulation CC essentially abolishes the concept of provisional settlement for banks, it probably does not abolish the Article 4 midnight deadline rules as a potential source of liability for any bank.

Generally, the Regulation CC requirements are imposed in addition to the Article 4 duties. For example, the Regulation CC funds availability and notice requirements are related to the time the item or notice is received by the depositary bank, rather than the time of return by the returning bank as under Article 4.[463] In addition Regulation CC codifies the direct wire notification requirement for large items, previously provided by Federal Reserve Operating Letters and later by Regulation J.[464] Thus banks must seek to comply with both Article 4 and Regulation CC. Notably, under Regulation CC some return methods will result in extension of the Article 4 midnight deadline.[465] Regulation CC also provides a warranty that every transferor bank has met its midnight deadline.[466] This could result in recovery of attorney fees under Regulation CC, for violation of an Article 4 midnight deadline rule.[467]

---

459. *See* UCC § 3–104(c).

460. *See* UCC § 3–103(a)(4), and discussion *supra* Chapter 3, at ¶ 3.03[2][b].

461. *See* 12 CFR §§ 229.30 and 229.31 and discussion *supra* at ¶ 8.04[3][a].

462. *See* §§ 4–202(b), 4–214, 4–215, 4–301, 4–302, and discussion *supra* at ¶ 8.02[2][d] and ¶ 8.03. However, expeditious return under Regulation CC may extend the Article 4 midnight deadline. *See, e.g.*, Oak Brook Bank v. Northern Trust Company; 256 F.3d 638 (7th Cir.2001).

463. 12 CFR §§ 229.12, 229.30, and 229.31, and discussion *supra* ¶ 8.04[2] and [3][a].

464. *See* 12 CFR § 229.33, discussion *supra* at ¶ 8.04[3][b], and Miller, *supra* note 452, at 109.

465. *See* 12 CFR § 229.30(c), and discussion *supra* at ¶ 8.04[3][a]; Oak Brook Bank v. Northern Trust Company, 256 F.3d 638 (7th Cir.2001).

466. *See* 12 CFR § 229.34(a) and discussion *supra* at ¶ 8.04[3][e].

467. *See* 12 CFR § 229.34(c); Revised § 4–207(c), Revised § 3–416, Comment 6. This may resolve a split in the cases. For example, Riedel v. First National Bank, 287 Or. 285, 598 P.2d 302 (1979), held that Comment 5 to current Section 4–207 was

[c] Provisional Settlement

Regulation CC differs fundamentally from Article 4 in that it considers all settlements in the collection process between banks to be final;[468] in contrast Article 4 treats the settlements as provisional except in stipulated circumstances.[469] As a practical matter, this affects primarily intermediary banks. The Regulation CC Commentary at § 229.32(b) recognizes that Regulation CC does not interfere with the depositary bank's right of charge-back under Article 4; and the Regulation CC Commentary at § 229.30(a) recognizes that Regulation CC does not in most instances interfere with the Article 4 rules on payment, dishonor provisional settlement and accountability for payor banks at §§ 4–215, 4–301, and 4–302.

[d] Direct Return of Dishonored Items

Old Article 4 did not provide for mandatory direct return of dishonored items; Regulation CC specifically authorizes such.[470] The 1990 revisions to Article 4 revised the previous rule (now at § 4–214(b)) but still provide only for return to the bank's customer or by agreement, thereby conflicting with Regulation CC.[471]

[e] Payable—Through Drafts

Under Regulation CC, payable-at and payable-through banks are treated as paying banks for purposes of the expeditious return and notice of dishonor requirements.[472] Article 4 treats a "payable-through" bank as a presenting bank for purposes of this notice and midnight deadline requirements and has a similar alternative for "paying-at" banks.[473]

[f] Remote Data Processing Centers

Under old Article 4 it was not clear whether delivery of an item to a remote data processing center constituted presentment to the payor bank for purposes of the Article 4 midnight deadline.[474] In contrast, Regulation CC expressly provides that delivery to an off-premises pro-

---

not sufficient to change the American rule, which does not permit recovery of attorney fees in these cases. In contrast Guaranty Bank & Trust Co. v. Federal Reserve Bank of Kansas City, 454 F.Supp. 488 (W.D.Okla. 1977), allowed recovery of attorney fees in a warranty case.

468. 12 CFR §§ 229.31(c), 229.32(b), 229.36(d).

469. See §§ 4–201, 4–215, 4–301; cf. 12 CFR § 229.36(d) and Regulation CC Commentary. See also supra ¶ 8.03[2]; ¶ 8.04[3][c] and [4]; ¶ 8.04[3][f].

470. Cf. 12 CFR § 229.30(a) and old § 4–212(2). See also supra ¶ 8.04[3][c]. Old Article 4 was later amended to allow for direct return in optional, bracketed language, with a cautionary legislative note indicating disagreement on the issue.

471. The 1990 revision is at § 4–214(b). cf. old § 4–212(2). See also supra ¶ 8.04[3][a]. Official Comment 4 to § 4–214 recognizes that Regulation CC § 229.31 preempts but § 4–214(b) still applies to items other than checks.

472. See 12 CFR §§ 229.36(a) and 229.2(z)(2); discussion supra at ¶ 8.04[3][f].

473. See § 4–106. See also Article 4 Part 5.

474. See, e.g., Sass Trucking, Inc. v. Security Bank & Trust Co., 737 P.2d 113 (Okla.1987). See also supra ¶ 8.01[3][l] and ¶ 8.02[2][d].

cessing center constitutes presentment to the payor bank.[475] Current § 4–204 is consistent with Regulation CC on this point.

[g] Truncation

Regulation CC expressly authorizes truncation.[476] The 1990 Article 4 revisions move firmly in that direction.[477]

[h] Indorsement

Regulation CC provides strict indorsement standards.[478] Old Article 4 allowed a variety of indorsements, and in this respect current Article 4 is little changed.[479]

[i] Comparative Fault

Regulation CC introduced the concept of comparative fault into the check collection process.[480] In contrast, Old Articles 3 and 4 placed all of the loss on one party or another, based on a hierarchy of rules tied to negligence.[481] Current Articles 3 and 4 substantially base the amount of liability on comparative fault.[482] The result is a system of absolute liability for payor banks missing the midnight deadline under Article 4, with a mixed system of comparative fault and liability for actual damages for other issues under Article 4 and Regulation CC.[483]

[j] Variation by Agreement

It is a guiding principle that the UCC may be modified by agreement of the parties, except that the obligations of good faith, diligence, reasonableness and care may not be disclaimed.[484] This is specifically reinforced in Article 4, which provides that:

---

475. See 12 CFR § 229.36(b), and discussion *supra* at ¶ 8.01[3][*l*] and ¶ 8.04[3][f]. § 4–204(c) should provide the same rule.

476. See 12 CFR § 229.36(c), and discussion *supra* ¶ 8.04[3][f].

477. See §§ 4–110 and 4–406, and discussion *supra* at ¶ 8.04[3][f], and *infra* at ¶ 9.03[6]. Further such revisions may be in the offing. See, *e.g.*, Alvin C. Harrell, NCCUSL Articles 3, 4, and 4A Drafting Committee Highlights Current Payment System and Negotiable Instrument Issues, 54 CONSUMER FIN. L.Q. REP. 351 (2000).

478. See 12 CFR § 229.35(a). See *supra* ¶ 8.04[3][g].

479. See § 4–206. The Article 3 provisions are likewise very liberal. See §§ 3–201—3–206; and discussion *supra* at ¶ 8.04[3][g].

480. See 12 CFR § 229.38(c). See *supra* ¶ 8.03[1].

481. See, *e.g.*, old §§ 3–405, 3–406, 4–406.

482. See §§ 3–404(d), 3–405(b), 3–406(b), and 4–406(e), *supra* ¶ 8.03[1], and discussion *infra* this text at Chapter 9, ¶ 9.03[4][c]. These rules may be supplemented by case law refining a state's other comparative negligence rules. For example, Oklahoma's comparative negligence law is explained in Boyles v. Oklahoma Natural Gas Co., 619 P.2d 613 (Okla.1980), and Laubach v. Morgan, 588 P.2d 1071 (Okla. 1978).

483. See §§ 4–302, 4–214, 3–404, 3–405, 3–406, and 4–406; 12 CFR §§ 229.34(c) and 229.38(c) and the Regulation CC Commentary. See *infra* Chapter 9, ¶ 9.03[4][c], for further discussion in the context of UCC § 4–406. See also *supra* ¶ 8.03[4] and *infra* ¶ 8.04[4].

484. See Article 1 § 1–102(3), Article 4 § 4–103(a). However, "the standards by which the performance of such obligations is to be measured" may be set by agreement if not "manifestly unreasonable." *Id.* See *supra* note 30; *infra* Ch. 9 ¶ 9.03[3].

The effect of the provisions of this Article may be varied by agreement, but the parties to the agreement cannot disclaim a bank's responsibility for its lack of good faith or failure to exercise ordinary care or limit the measure of damages for the lack or failure. However, the parties may determine by agreement the standards by which the bank's responsibility is to be measured if those standards are not manifestly unreasonable.[485]

Regulation CC also provides that it may be varied by agreement,

"except that no agreement can disclaim the responsibility of a bank for its own lack of good faith or failure to exercise ordinary care, or can limit the measure of damages for such lack or failure.[486]

[k] Standard of Care and Measure of Damages

Article 4 imposes a duty of ordinary care on collecting banks in handling an item for collection, presentment, or return, and in settling for an item and sending any required notice,[487] but the payor bank's specific duties are stated in terms of the midnight deadline, rather than a duty of care.[488] Article 4 also provides for a general duty of ordinary care applicable to collecting banks, at § 4–202(a).

Under Regulation CC, banks in the check collection process must "exercise ordinary care and act in good faith in complying with the requirements" of Subpart C of Regulation CC.[489] A bank that violates this duty is liable to the depositary bank, that bank's customer, the owner of the check, or any other party to the check, for actual damages.[490] The measure of damages is the amount of the loss, up to the amount of the check, reduced by the amount of loss that would have been suffered even if the bank had exercised ordinary care.[491] However, if

---

485. Article 4 § 4–103(a). Old § 4–103(1) is very similar. The equivalent Regulation CC provision (12 CFR § 229.37) is likewise "similar to U.C.C. 4–103." Regulation CC Commentary § 229.37. See also supra note 46; supra ¶ 8.02[4].

486. 12 CFR § 229.37. Like the UCC, Regulation CC allows the parties to set the standards by which their responsibilities are to be measured, where not "manifestly unreasonable." Id. Cf. UCC § 1–102(3). The Commentary to § 229.37 states that this is "similar" to UCC § 4–103. See supra.

487. § 4–202(a). Old § 4–202(1) is similar. Meeting the midnight deadline satisfies this test. See § 4–202(b); old § 4–202(2); supra ¶ 8.03[4]. See also §§ 4–103, 4–109, 4–214.

488. See §§ 4–215, 4–301, 4–302; old §§ 4–213, 4–301, 4–302; supra ¶ 8.02. The Regulation CC Commentary to § 229.38(a) makes clear that the obligation to comply with Regulation CC does not relieve the payor bank of liability under Article 4.

489. 12 CFR § 229.38(a). Subpart C contains the check collection rules. The Regulation CC Commentary to § 229.38(a) stresses that this standard of care is "similar" to the good faith and ordinary care requirements of the UCC, and that these duties apply to all of the requirements of Regulation CC:

Thus, the standard of care applies to a paying bank under §§ 229.30 and 229.33, to a returning bank under § 229.31, to a depositary bank under §§ 229.32 and 229.33, to a bank erroneously receiving a returned check or written notice of nonpayment as depositary bank under § 229.32(d), and to a bank indorsing a check under § 229.35. The standard of care is similar to the standard imposed by U.C.C. 1–203 and 4–103(1) and includes a duty to act in good faith, as defined in § 229.2 (nn) of [Regulation CC] . . . .

490. 12 CFR § 229.38(a). Regulation CC Commentary § 229.38(a), ¶ 1.

491. Id. The Regulation CC Commentary describes this as follows:

Under this measure of damages, a depositary bank or other person must show

the bank did not act in good faith, it may be liable for other damages suffered as a "proximate consequence."[492]

As noted, the Regulation CC measure of damages provisions[493] are similar to the Article 4 provision measuring the damages for a failure to exercise ordinary care in handling an item:

> The measure of damages for failure to exercise ordinary care in handling an item is the amount of the item reduced by an amount that could not have been realized by the exercise of ordinary care. If there is also bad faith it includes any other damages the party suffered as a proximate consequence.[494]

However, as noted, in Article 4 the duty of ordinary care is primarily important with regard to collecting banks; the duties of payor banks are stated in more absolute terms.[495] Regulation CC specifically states that it does not affect the liability of a payor bank to its customer under the UCC or other law.[496]

[l] Good Faith

The Regulation CC requirement of good faith is imposed at § 229.38(a) ("a bank shall exercise ordinary care and act in good faith in complying with the requirements of this subpart.") and defined at § 229.2 (nn) ("*Good faith* means honesty in fact and observance of reasonable commercial standards of fair dealing"). Its relationship to the UCC is unclear,[497] particularly with respect to the role of good faith in Articles 3 and 4.[498] Indeed, the precise effects of the recent change in the

---

that the damage incurred results from the negligence proved. For example, the depositary bank may not simply claim that its customer will not accept a chargeback of a returned check, but must prove that it could not charge back when it received the returned check and could have charged back if no negligence had occurred, and must first attempt to collect from its customer. (*See* Marcoux v. Van Wyk, 572 F.2d 651 (8th Cir. 1978); Appliance Buyers Credit Corp. v. Prospect Nat'l Bank, 708 F.2d 290 (7th Cir. 1983)). Generally, a paying or returning bank's liability would not be reduced because the depositary bank did not place a hold on its customer's deposit before it learned of nonpayment of the check. Commentary § 229.38(a). *Cf.* Article 4 § 4–103(e), discussed below.

492. 12 CFR § 229.38(a). Apparently this is a reference to consequential damages, and not punitive damages. *See also* the Regulation CC definition of good faith at § 229.2 (nn).

493. The Regulation CC standard is at 12 CFR § 229.38(a).

494. Article 4 § 4–103(e); old § 4–103(5) is similar. *See also* Article 4 provisions on a bank's liability for wrongful dishonor (§ 4–402) and failure to honor a stop payment order (§ 4–403), discussed *infra* ¶ 9.01[1] and ¶ 9.02. The similarity to Regulation CC is noted in the Commentary at § 229.38(a).

495. *Cf.* § 4–202 (duty of collecting banks to use ordinary care) *with* §§ 4–215, 4–301, and 4–302 (final payment and accountability for payor banks). *See also supra* ¶ 8.02 and ¶ 8.03.

496. 12 CFR § 229.38(a). The Regulation CC Commentary also states that a payor bank which fails to meet both the Article 4 and Regulation CC return requirements will be liable under Article 4 or Regulation CC, but not both. 12 CFR § 229.38(b). *See also supra* notes 30 and 46; *supra* ¶ 8.02[4]; *infra* ¶ 9.03[3] (importance of common law issues).

497. 12 CFR § 229.38(a).

498. The definition of "good faith" in Article 3 now requires the "observance of reasonable commercial standards of fair dealing." *See* § 3–103(a)(4), and *supra* Chapter 3. This definition is recognized in Article 4. *See* § 4–104(c). It has already been problematical in banking transactions.

UCC definitions of good faith, *e.g.*, at § 3–103(a)(4), are themselves unclear. The traditional UCC obligation of good faith in Article 1 was applicable in old Article 3 and 4 transactions. It was defined to require only "honesty in fact" and did not impart any additional, special duties.[499] But this has since been superceded to some extent by the expanded definition at § 3–103(a)(4). It appears that the current Regulation CC obligation of good faith[500] is intended to encompass the broader Article 3 concept, for general application as to Regulation CC, Subpart C issues. Of course, if Article 1 in a given state is revised to conform to Article 3 in this respect, any remaining disparity on this issue will go away, at least in that state, but until then there is still an argument that some aspects of the transaction could be subject to the former UCC Article 1 definition of good faith at §§ 1–201(19) (honesty in fact) and common law principles under § 1–203 while other aspects come under the Regulation CC and the Article 3 definition. In the meantime, while there is no indication that Congress or the Federal Reserve Board intended to overturn the then-existing legal regime in this context, it remains to be seen whether this Regulation CC obligation of good faith for collecting and payor banks will be used by courts to impose a new standard on check collection and processing activities.[501] Some courts have demonstrated an undue propensity to use concepts such as good faith as the basis for revising the economic bargain of the parties.[502]

Both the UCC and Regulation CC make clear that whatever the duty of good faith in banking transactions, it cannot be disclaimed.[503] Regulation CC also makes clear that it does not affect any additional duties of a payor bank under Article 4, although in some cases there is an express bar to double recovery.[504]

[m] Implications for the Future

Potential solutions for federal and state law interrelationship and preemption problems range from arguments that the entire system should be federalized in order to resolve the conflicts and uncertainties, to proposals that Regulation CC be grafted onto state law as a part of Article 4 in order to create a comprehensive bank collection code as existed for most of the 20th century prior to Regulation CC. There is also precedent for the latter approach in the context of modern consumer protection law, *e.g.*, the system of deference by federal to state law where

---

See, e.g., Maine Family Federal Credit Union v. Sun Life Assurance Co., 727 A.2d 335 (Me. S.Ct. 1999).

499. UCC §§ 1–203, 1–201(19). The more comprehensive definition clearly applies where the term "good faith" is used in Article 4, such as in §§ 4–103(e) (converse of good faith) and 4–406(e), but whether it is of general applicability in Article 4 pursuant to UCC § 1–203 is less clear; some believe it would make little sense to conclude otherwise.

500. 12 CFR §§ 229.2 (nn) and 229.38(a).

501. There is no evidence of such to date.

502. *See* discussion *infra* at ¶ 9.03[1], [2]; *Maine*, 727 A.2d 335. *See also supra* notes 30, 46, and *supra* ¶ 8.03[2].

503. *See* UCC § 1–102(3); § 4–103(a); 12 CFR § 229.37, § 229.38(a).

504. 12 CFR §§ 229.38(a), (b). *See also* Commentary § 229.38(a), (b), reproduced *supra* at notes 489 and 491.

the state in question has a qualifying equivalent to the Regulation Z Truth in Lending disclosure requirements.[505]

Neither the 1990 Article 4 revisions nor the 2002 amendments attempt to resolve these issues. The drafters and sponsoring organizations concluded that the issues were not ready to be resolved at this stage by Article 4 revisions. As a result the uniform text of Article 4 is an evolutionary product which focuses on resolving ambiguities, responding to case law developments, and recognizing changes in technology and business practices. As such, it is a sound product and represents clear improvements in the law. However, it leaves banks, practitioners, and the courts to conduct their own analyses to resolve the conflicts and preemption issues on a case-by-case basis.

¶ 8.05 Summary and Conclusions

Consistent with other Code Articles, Article 4 provides a general backstop of definitions, concepts, and rules to govern the bank deposit and collection process. Article 4 resolves a number of gaps and ambiguities that have surfaced over the past 50 years, and hence is relevant in resolving these issues even in the few jurisdictions where the revisions have not been enacted. Beyond the statute, express agreements between the bank and its customer and customary bank practices supplement the statute and vary its effect, so they must be considered in order to reach a correct conclusion. So too, where appropriate, must Regulations J or CC or rules of the Federal Reserve Board collection system and those established by clearing houses.

---

505. So far the necessary banking industry support for such reform has been missing. *See, e.g.*, Alvin C. Harrell, UCC Article 4 and Regulation CC: Can They Ever be Reconciled?, 54 CONSUMER FIN. L.Q. REP. 236 (2000); Alvin C. Harrell, NCCUSL Articles 3, 4, and 4A Drafting Committee Highlights Current Payment System and Negotiable Instrument Issues, 54 CONSUMER FIN. L.Q. REP. 351 (2000).

Chapter 9

THE BANK–CUSTOMER RELATIONSHIP

Analysis

Para.
¶9.01 When Is Payment of a Customer's Check Required, Permitted, or Prohibited? 380
   [1] The Concept of "Properly Payable" 380
   [2] The 1990 Article 4 Revisions: Customer Overdrafts; Postdated Checks 383
   [3] "Properly Payable" Under Article 4: A Partial Index to Relevant Provisions 384
   [4] Stop-Payment Orders and Other "Legals" 385
      [a] Stop Payment Orders 385
      [b] Payment of an Altered Item Over a Stop Order: Good Faith and Ordinary Care 389
      [c] Alternatives to Stopping Payment 391
      [d] Can Payment be Stopped on a Cashier's or Similar Bank Check? 392
         [i] Can the Customer Stop Payment? 394
         [ii] Can the Bank Stop Payment? 394
         [iii] Bank Liability for Dishonor of a Cashier's or Similar Check 395
         [iv] Refusal to Pay a Cashier's or Similar Check: Measure of Liability 398
         [v] Lost, Destroyed, or Stolen Cashier's, Teller's, or Certified Checks 399
      [e] Certification 400
   [5] Receipt of Legal Process 400
   [6] Death or Incompetence of the Drawer 402
   [7] Final Payment, the "Four Legals," and the Bank's "Cutoff" Hour 403
¶9.02 Consequences of Wrongful Payment and Wrongful Dishonor 405
   [1] Introduction 405
   [2] Wrongful Dishonor 406
      [a] The Revision of Section 4–402 406
      [b] Limitations on Bank Liability for Wrongful Dishonor 408
   [3] Wrongful Payment—Bank Liability and the Right to Subrogation 410
   [4] Postdated Checks 412
¶9.03 Rights and Obligations of Bank Customers 413
   [1] The Bank–Customer Relationship 413
   [2] Does the Bank Have a Fiduciary or Other Special Duty? 414
      [a] Non–Code Consequences 414

Para.

¶9.03 Rights and Obligations of Bank Customers—Continued
        [b] Code Consequences 417
        [c] Regulation of Depositary Services Pricing 419
    [3] Modification by Agreement 420
    [4] Customer's Duties Under Section 4–406 423
        [a] Customer's Duty to Examine Checks 423
        [b] Impact of Revised Section 4–406 427
        [c] The New Role of Comparative Negligence and Good Faith 429
        [d] Other Revisions to Section 4–406 431
    [5] Payor Bank's Obligation to Examine Checks 433
    [6] Check Truncation and MICR Encoding 435
    [7] Conclusion 438

¶9.04 NOW and Share Drafts 438

¶9.05 The Basic Law of Bank Accounts 440
    [1] The Traditional Concept and Modern Variations of a "Bank Account" 440
    [2] Common Law Classifications of Deposit Accounts 442
        [a] General and Special Purpose Accounts 442
        [b] General or Special Purpose 443
    [3] The Basic Bank Account Relationship........................ 444
        [a] Creating a Depositary Account.......................... 444
        [b] Nature of the Bank–Customer Relation................. 447
        [c] Fundamental Duties and Liabilities of the Bank 447
            [i]   General Deposits 447
            [ii] Special Deposits 449
            [iii] Fiduciary Duty of Disclosure 449
            [iv] Duties of the Customer 450
            [v] Termination of the Relationship 450
            [vi] The Bank Secrecy Act 451

¶9.06 Banker's Lien, Setoff, Garnishment and Security Interests in Bank Accounts... 451
    [1] Banker's Lien 451
    [2] Setoff... 453
        [a] Background and Legal Basis 453
        [b] Maturity of the Debt................................... 454
        [c] Mutuality of Obligation 455
        [d] Absence of Deposit Restrictions 456
        [e] Competing Claims 456
            [i]   Wrongful Dishonor 457
            [ii] Secured Creditor................................. 458
            [iii] Garnishing Creditor 459
            [iv] Tax Claims and Internal Revenue Service Levies 460
            [v] Depositor's Trustee in Bankruptcy 461
        [f] Duty of Set-off... 463
    [3] Garnishment 464
    [4] Security Interests in Deposit Accounts 465

¶ 9.01 When Is Payment of a Customer's Check Required, Permitted, or Prohibited?

As noted *supra* at ¶ 8.02, under UCC §§ 4–215 and 4–301 a payor bank must either pay or return a customer's check (an "item" under Article 4 § 4–104), before its midnight deadline, or be held accountable for the amount of the item under § 4–302. When it makes final payment, under § 4–401(a) the payor bank can debit the customer's account for that amount, if the item was properly payable. However, this simple statement merely describes the result of a process that in many cases is not simple. For example, in some circumstances a payor bank is required to make final payment, and failure to do so can lead to liability. In other cases, a payor bank is prohibited from making payment, and payment will lead to liability. In still other cases, the payor bank may exercise its own discretion and should do so based on its own prospects for recovering reimbursement. Therefore, it is important to understand the nature and the extent of a payor bank's authority and duty to pay or dishonor items presented to it.

As in the previous chapter, a reference to "old" Article 4 means the uniform text prior to the 1990 revisions; "revised" or "current" Article 4 refers to the 1990 revisions; and the "2002 amendments" refers to the amendments to the uniform text approved in July–August 2002.

[1] The Concept of "Properly Payable"

The starting point of the analysis is the payor bank's statutory authority to charge its customer's account for an item that is presented in "properly payable" form. Section 4–401(a) states: "A bank may charge against the account of a customer an item that is properly payable from that account even though the charge creates an overdraft."[1] Section 4–401(a) also defines a "properly payable" item as one that "is authorized by the customer and is in accordance with any agreement between the customer and bank." All versions of Article 4 are consistent with the contractual basis for the relationship between the bank and its customer, but the 1990 revisions clarify that relationship and make it more explicit. The origin of the contractual relationship is the deposit contract, under which the customer authorizes the bank to charge the customer's account for any item that is properly payable from

---

¶ 9.01

1. In the event the bank's payment creates an overdraft, the bank's payment creates a debt of the bank's customer and invokes an implied promise by the customer to repay the bank. *See* Comment 1 to old § 4–401, and Comment 1 to revised § 4–401. While this principle remains a part of Article 4, the rules governing customer liability for an overdraft were significantly revised in the 1990 revisions. *See infra* ¶ 9.01[2]. Among other things, the 1990 revisions make clear that a customer is not liable for an overdraft unless that person either signed the item that created the overdraft or benefitted by it. *See* § 4–401(b), § 4–401 Comment 2, and discussion *infra* at ¶ 9.01[2]. References herein to Articles 3 or 4, or the Comments thereto, refer to the uniform text as revised in 1990 unless otherwise stated. Some references to "current" or "revised" sections are also used to emphasize distinctions from the "old" Code. References to "old" Article 3 or 4 refer to the uniform text prior to the 1990 revisions.

that account.[2] Conversely, of course, the bank has no authority to charge the customer's account for any item that is not "properly payable." This rule is a slightly modified version of the common law case of *Hall v. Fuller*.

Of course, this simple rule does not directly answer many crucial questions about whether a particular item is "properly payable." The definition at old § 4–104(1)(i) was scarcely helpful, and was deleted in the revision of Article 4. But it is clear that the term "properly payable" at least incorporates the requirements and conditions precedent to payment contained in the deposit contract and Article 4, as well as UCC Article 3 and any other law or contract governing enforcement of the item in question. That would include the applicable provisions concerning enforcement of negotiable instruments in UCC Article 3, *e.g.*, the rules governing execution, negotiation and defenses such as alteration and forgery. The Article 3 provisions are covered in previous chapters of this text; however, under § 4–102 they serve as a backdrop to the requirements contained in Article 4.

Determining whether a particular item is "properly payable" can sometimes be difficult, particularly in view of the large volume of items being handled in the banking system (at this writing generally estimated at around 75 billion per year). Several cases illustrate the point. For example, in *Cumis Insurance Society, Inc. v. Girard Bank*,[3] the deposit agreement allowed the bank to honor checks bearing or purporting to bear facsimile signatures with the same effect as if the signatures were manual. The court concluded that the agreement did not protect the bank from a claim involving forged instruments, on the ground the bank would not be protected in that instance if a manual signature had been forged. The court reached this conclusion even though it is clear that this result was the exact opposite of what the parties' agreement intended.[4] Under old Article 4, the courts were split on whether a

---

2. The signature card, account agreement, related customer corporate resolutions, and monthly account statements all form parts of the contract between the payor bank and its customer, and should be reviewed periodically by both parties to assure consistency and that these documents reflect the intended agreement. For example, in Reliance Ins. Co. v. Bank of America Nat'l. Trust & Sav. Ass'n., 43 UCC Rep. Serv.2d 946 (N.D.Ill. 2001), the account agreement, customer's corporate resolutions, and monthly statements established 30 days as a reasonable time period for customer examination of the monthly account statements. The parties were bound by this agreement.

Although the basis for the relationship is the deposit contract, the relationship itself, and the duties and liabilities arising from it, also are governed by banking codes and other statutes, as well as the law of property, torts and of course UCC Article 3. *See*, *e.g.*, Shaw v. Union Bank & Trust Co., 640 P.2d 953 (Okla.1981); *infra* ¶ 9.03; and *infra* ¶ 9.05 and ¶ 9.06.

3. 522 F.Supp. 414 (E.D.Pa.1981). *See also generally* the discussion *supra* at notes 1 and 2.

4. The court also indicated that even if the agreement were interpreted to protect the bank, it could not stand as a matter of public policy. This is a dubious pronouncement, despite the limitations of § 4–103(a) (none of which were implicated in *Cumis*). *See supra* ¶ 4.02[1], *supra* ¶ 8.01[2] and 8.04[4], and *infra* ¶ 9.03[3]. Note that where a drawer's signature is forged by use of a facsimile machine, the perpetrator may also forge the payee's indorsement in an effort to avoid detection, thus creating a "double forgery." Under old Article 4 the majority rule was that this "double forgery" should be treated as a forged drawer's signature and not as a forged indorse-

postdated check was properly payable before its date; this has been resolved in favor of permitting payment unless the customer gives certain notice to the bank.[5]

In *City of Deerfield Beach v. Florida National Bank*,[6] the issue was whether a bank properly paid a check on which some language added by the drawer had been altered by the payee. The drawer had submitted a check to its payee with language of accord and satisfaction. The payee crossed out this language and indorsed the check with a reservation of rights. The drawer sued the payor bank for paying an "altered" item. There is no question that paying a check that has had its amount altered is improper,[7] but the court in this case ruled that the payor need not pay attention to and monitor language intended to operate as an accord and satisfaction, or as a compromise or release. While this result is compelling in view of the need for automated processing of large volumes of checks, policy questions remained about where the line should be drawn. For example, if the drawer specified that the check was not to be paid if the restrictive language is changed, should that be binding if in the contract of the check itself? Moreover, what should be done about legends on the instrument such as "void after 90 days" or "not good for over $100"? Under old Article 4, these issues remained unanswered in the statute, and therefore needed to be addressed in the deposit contract.

Revised § 3–311 answers some of the questions on accord and satisfaction by making clear that Article 4 does not displace the law of accord and satisfaction. Old UCC § 1–207 authorized a reservation of rights and some courts had held that this permitted a payee to reserve his or her rights by scratching out accord and satisfaction language above the payee's indorsement.[8] Revised § 3–311 amended § 1–207 to reject these cases and provide that an accord and satisfaction discharges such a claim if the item "or an accompanying written communication contained a conspicuous statement to the effect that the instrument was tendered as full satisfaction of the claim."[9] There is an exception where the claimant has previously notified the drawer that any such instru-

---

ment, although this view was criticized. *See* Perini Corp. v. First Nat'l Bank of Habersham County, 553 F.2d 398 (5th Cir.1977), *reh'g denied*, 557 F.2d 823 (5th Cir.1977); Graybill, Reconsidering an Old Conundrum: The Case for Indorsement Liability on Double Forgeries, 83 Comm. L.J. 61(1987). Revised Articles 3 and 4 recast these issues by introducing the concept of comparative negligence and also providing that in double forgery cases the perpetrator may make an effective indorsement. *See* §§ 3–110, 3–404(b), (d), 3–405(b), and 3–406, and discussion *supra* Chapter 7.

5. *See, e.g.*, Siegel v. New England Merchants National Bank, 386 Mass. 672, 437 N.E.2d 218 (Mass. 1982) (not properly payable until date on item); Allied Color Corp. v. Manufacturers Hanover Trust Co., 484 F.Supp. 881 (S.D.N.Y.1980) (bank held accountable for payment of postdated check received and not dishonored prior to item date); revised § 4–401(c); discussion *infra* at ¶ 9.01[2], ¶ 9.02[4].

6. 428 So.2d 779 (Fla.App.1983).

7. Old § 4–401(2)(a); revised § 4–401(d).

8. *See, e.g.*, Scholl v. Tallman, 247 N.W.2d 490 (S.D.1976), where the payee scratched out "settlement in full" language and added a reservation of rights against the drawer before indorsing the check. This was deemed an effective reservation of rights under § 1–207, negating the intention of the drawer. As noted in this text *infra* at note 9, this is rejected in the 1990 revisions.

9. § 3–311(b).

ment must be sent to a designated "person, office, or place" and the instrument was not sent as instructed, or if the claimant did not know the instrument was tendered in full satisfaction and returns the disputed payment within 90 days of receipt.[10] In view of these rules, an alteration of accord and satisfaction language on the item by the holder/claimant prior to deposit should not alter the drawer's intended settlement of the claim. As a result the drawer should have no reason for objecting to payment of such an item. This effectively confirms the result in *City of Deerfield Beach*. *See* the further discussion *supra* in Chapter 7.

[2] The 1990 Article 4 Revisions: Customer Overdrafts; Postdated Checks

Issues relating to customer liability for an overdrawn account and bank liability for postdated checks received considerable attention in the 1990 revision of Article 4. Section 4–401 now reads as follows:

(a) A bank may charge against the account of a customer an item that is properly payable from the account even though the charge creates an overdraft. An item is properly payable if it is authorized by the customer and is in accordance with any agreement between the customer and bank.

(b) A customer is not liable for the amount of an overdraft if the customer neither signed the item nor benefited from the proceeds of the item.

(c) A bank may charge against the account of a customer a check that is otherwise properly payable from the account, even though payment was made before the date of the check, unless the customer has given notice to the bank of the postdating describing the check with reasonable certainty. The notice is effective for the period stated in Section 4–403(b) for stop payment orders, and must be received at such time and in such manner as to afford the bank a reasonable opportunity to act on it before the bank takes any action with respect to the check described in Section 4–303. If a bank charges against the account of a customer a check before the date stated in the notice of postdating, the bank is liable for damages for the loss resulting from its act. The loss may include damages for dishonor of subsequent items pursuant to Section 4–402.

(d) A bank that in good faith makes payment to a holder may charge the indicated account of its customer according to:

(1) the original terms of the altered item; or

(2) the terms of the completed item, even though the bank knows the item has been completed unless the bank has notice that the completion was improper.

---

10. § 3–311(c)(1), (2). This was designed to accommodate "lock box" arrangements and to protect claimants from inadvertently assenting to an accord and satisfaction in large volume transactions.

Among other things, these provisions mean that where there are joint account holders (*e.g.*, more than one person is authorized to draw on an account) only the person who signed the item creating the overdraft will be liable for that overdraft, unless the other joint account holder (or holders) benefited from the payment of that item.[11] As a result of this provision, banks may need to make overdraft decisions based on the credit-worthiness of the party who signed the check, rather than the status or history of the account. In addition, banks may decide to provide in the deposit contract for an allocation of any losses resulting from checks drawn by one of multiple or joint account holders.[12]

Postdated checks received attention in the 1990 revisions because automated processing means that banks may not be able to review each check's date when large volumes of checks are presented. Section 4–401(c) (reproduced in the preceding paragraph) permits the bank to pay a postdated check and to charge the customer's account, before the date of the check, unless the customer has provided notice to the bank under rules similar to those for stop payment orders.[13] In effect a customer wishing to issue a check, but seeking to postpone payment of the check until a later date, must give the bank notice similar to a stop payment order. Otherwise the bank is entitled to pay the instrument upon presentment regardless of its date. If the customer properly notifies the bank of a postdated check, and the bank nonetheless pays it before the appropriate date, the bank is liable for any resulting loss including damages for wrongful dishonor of other items that are dishonored as a result of depletion on the account by payment of the post-dated check, under § 4–402. These issues are discussed more fully *infra* at ¶ 9.02[4]. Whether the customer may have a claim against the person who presented the check early is governed by other law. In such cases the rules and cases dealing with stop payment orders should present helpful analogies.

[3] *"Properly Payable" Under Article 4: A Partial Index to Relevant Provisions*

Article 4 contains a number of specific provisions that either permit or prohibit the payment of an item and thus serve to help define the

---

11. This confirms the rule of Williams v. Cullen Center Bank & Trust, 685 S.W.2d 311 (Tex.1985) (joint account holder not liable for overdraft created by the other account holder, unless that other holder was contractually liable, benefitted from payment of the item, or ratified the transaction or overdraft). On ratification, *see* Eutsler v. First Nat'l Bank, 639 P.2d 1245 (Okla.1982); Guaranty Bank & Trust Co. v. Federal Reserve Bank of Kansas City, 454 F.Supp. 488 (W.D.Okla.1977).

12. Otherwise, a credit-worthy account held by a long-time customer may suddenly become a problem if a less credit-worthy joint account holder is added or begins to write checks that overdraw the account. For cases on contractual liability and ratification, *see supra* note 11.

13. *Compare* § 4–401(c) with § 4–403(a), discussed *infra* ¶ 9.01[4][a]. *See also* § 3–113(a). The 1990 revision resolved an apparent split of authority on whether a postdated check could be properly payable before the date on the item. *Cf.* Allied Color Corp. v. Manufacturers Hanover Trust Co., 484 F.Supp. 881 (S.D.N.Y.1980) (bank held accountable for item paid prior to item date); Siegel v. New England Merchants National Bank, 386 Mass. 672, 437 N.E.2d 218 (Mass. 1982) (postdated item not properly payable until item date); *see also infra* ¶ 9.02[4].

general concept of "properly payable." The provisions prohibiting payment or permitting nonpayment (dishonor) include:

(Mandatory Dishonor)
    Section 4–401 (Item not properly payable);
    Section 4–403 (Stop payment order);
    Section 4–303 (Receipt of legal process), and
    Section 4–405 (Death or incompetence of the drawer under certain circumstances).

(Permissible Dishonor)
    Section 4–303 (Bank's right of setoff); and
    Section 4–404 ("Stale" check more than six months old).

An item that is properly payable is by definition outside the mandatory dishonor provisions and may be charged to the customer's account without liability on the part of the bank. Indeed, if a payor bank refuses to pay and (dishonors) an item that is properly payable, it may be liable for wrongful dishonor under § 4–402, unless it has some additional defense or excuse. Conversely, a payor bank must dishonor an item covered by the "mandatory dishonor" provisions and, if the bank pays an item that is not properly payable, it has exceeded its authority, generally cannot charge the item to the customers account, and may suffer the loss.[14] Each of the statutory bases for mandatory dishonor will be considered separately in this chapter. The reader is also referred to *supra* ¶ 8.02 and ¶ 8.03 regarding payor and collecting bank responsibilities with regard to settlement and payment.

[4] Stop-Payment Orders and Other "Legals"

[a] Stop Payment Orders

In Article 4 the right to stop payment is provided in § 4–403. The 1990 revised uniform text provides that:

> (a) A customer or any person authorized to draw on the account if there is more than one person may stop payment of any item drawn on the customer's account or close the account by an order to the bank describing the item or account with reasonable certainty received at a time and in a manner that affords the bank a reasonable opportunity to act on it before any action by the bank with respect to the item described in Section 4–303. If the signature of more than one person is required to draw on an account, any of these persons may stop payment or close the account.

> (b) A stop-payment order is effective for six months, but it lapses after 14 calendar days if the original order was oral and was not confirmed in writing within that period. A stop-payment order may

---

14. *See* § 4–401(a); § 4–302; *supra* this text ¶ 8.02. *See also* G & R Corp. v. American Sec. & Trust Co., 523 F.2d 1164 (D.C.Cir.1975). *Note also* § 4–303(b), and Comment 7, allowing the bank to pay items in any order it wishes, even if the bank chooses to maximize its overdraft charges; Hill v. St. Paul Federal Bank, 329 Ill.App.3d 705, 263 Ill.Dec. 562, 768 N.E.2d 322 (2002) (same).

be renewed for additional six-month periods by a writing given to the bank within a period during which the stop-payment order is effective.

(c) The burden of establishing the fact and amount of loss resulting from the payment of an item contrary to a stop-payment order or order to close an account is on the customer. The loss from payment of an item contrary to a stop-payment order may include damages for dishonor of subsequent items pursuant to Section 4–402.

The 2002 amendments change § 4–403(b) to read as follows:

(b) A stop-payment order is effective for six months, but it lapses after 14 calendar days if the original order was oral and was not confirmed in a record within that period. A stop-payment order may be renewed for additional six months periods by a record given to the bank within a period during which the stop-payment order is effective.

These same rules govern the closure of an account. Notice four limitations. The right to stop payment is exercisable: (1) only by a "customer" or a person "authorized to draw on the account" (any person authorized to draw on the account also may stop payment of any item drawn on that account); (2) the stop payment order must describe the item or account with reasonable certainty; and (3) the stop payment order must be received "at such time" and (4) "in such manner" as to allow the bank to act on it before the payor bank has made final payment or otherwise has become bound under § 4–303.[15] "Customer" is defined as any "person having an account with a bank or for whom a bank has agreed to collect items...."[16] The 2002 amendments to § 4–403(b) substitute the term "record" for the previous "writing" requirement, and are designed to facilitate electronic communications.

As noted, Article 4 also makes clear that where more than one person is authorized to draw on an account, "any person authorized to draw on the account" can stop payment of any item drawn on that account.[17] Furthermore, Article 4 allows any party authorized to draw on such an account to close the account:[18]

If the signature of more than one person is required to draw on an account, any of these persons may stop payment or close the account.[19]

"Account" is defined at § 4–104(a)(1) as "any deposit or credit account with a bank [including] a demand, time, savings, share draft, or like account, other than an account evidenced by a certificate of depos-

---

15. *Compare* the similar language for notice of postdating at revised § 4–401(c), discussed *supra* ¶ 9.01[2]. *See also* §§ 4–215, 4–301, and 4–302, and discussion of final payment *supra* this text at ¶ 8.02.

16. § 4–104(a)(5). Thus, for a partnership account, the partnership and not the partners is the customer. Loucks v. Albuquerque Nat'l Bank, 76 N.M. 735, 418 P.2d 191 (N.M. 1966). *See* more extensive discussion of this definition *supra* at ¶ 8.01[3][g], and discussion *infra* at ¶ 9.02[2][b]. A payee or an indorsee has no right to stop payment. *See* Comment 2 to § 4–403.

17. § 4–403(a). In other words, a joint account holder can stop payment of an item drawn by the other joint account holder.

18. § 4–403(a).

19. *Id.*

it." This underscores the contractual basis for the bank-customer relationship, although the liabilities that result also may be of another nature.[20]

"At such time" means that the stop payment order must be given in time to allow the bank to act on the order before the check is accepted or paid.[21] One and a half hours has been held to be sufficient notice, and once the requirement of timely notice is established, it is not necessary to prove that the bank was negligent in order for the customer to recover.[22]

"In such manner" and the requirement to describe the item with reasonable certainty relate to the need for a stop payment order to be in a form sufficient to allow the bank to identify the item being stopped. Article 4 does not, however, specify the information a stop order must contain. Comment 5 to § 4-403 states that in the absence of contrary agreement the customer must supply information that allows the bank under existing technology to identify the item with reasonable certainty. Litigation has ensued when the customer provides inaccurate or insufficient information, as where the amount designated in the stop order is not the same as the amount of the check. The trend of authority suggests that where the stop order contains a slight error as to the amount of the check, the order may be found to be sufficient if other information given is sufficient to identify the check.[23] Article 4 follows these cases; however, it is not clear, if the bank programs for an exact amount, whether a requirement for precision is permissible if technology would allow programming a range. Seemingly the deposit agreement can resolve this issue. Other errors in the stop order probably will not be significant. Thus in *Thomas v. Marine Midland Tinkers National Bank*,[24] the customer's stop payment order contained an erroneous digit in the stated check number. This error did not render the stop order inadequate and did not preclude bank liability when the check was paid. In

---

20. *See supra* note 2, and *infra* ¶ 9.03. Note that this is very different from the definition of the same term in UCC Article 9, at § 9-102(a)(2). For discussion about the right of noncustomers to recover for wrongful payment or wrongful dishonor, *see infra* ¶ 9.02.

21. §§ 4-403(a), 4-303(a). Clearly a stop payment order issued after the bank has made final payment comes too late. *See* First National Bank v. Continental Bank, 138 Ariz. 194, 673 P.2d 938 (Ariz.Ct.App. 1983). Section 4-303(a)(5) permits a payor bank to establish a "cutoff" time for receipt of a stop payment order during a banking day. *See* discussion *infra* at ¶ 9.01[7].

22. Tusso v. Security Nat'l Bank, 76 Misc.2d 12, 349 N.Y.S.2d 914 (Dist. Ct. 1973).

23. *See, e.g.*, Parr v. Security Nat'l Bank, 680 P.2d 648 (Okla. App. 1984) (stop payment order effective notwithstanding 50¢ error in amount). In Delano v. Putnam Trust Co., 33 UCC Rep. Serv. 635 (Conn.Super.1981), the court held that a stop-payment order was effective even though it misstated the amount of the check by $100, because the order correctly described the check in other ways. But in Poullier v. Nacua Motors, Inc., 108 Misc.2d 913, 439 N.Y.S.2d 85 (Sup. Ct. 1981), a $40 error rendered the order ineffective because the bank had advised the customer that an exact figure was required. *See also* Kunkel v. First National Bank of Devils Lake, 393 N.W.2d 265 (N.D.1986) (adequacy of stop payment order description is question of fact). The basic questions in these cases should be: (1) did the bank specify the information needed for its system to identify the item; and (2) did the customer accurately supply that information?

24. 86 Misc.2d 284, 381 N.Y.S.2d 797, 18 UCC Rep.Serv. 1273 (N.Y. Civ. Ct. 1976).

Sherrill v. Frank Morris Pontiac–Buick–GMC, Inc.,[25] however, a stop order that misstated both the name of the payee and the date of the check was held to be ineffective. This result is correct if the bank's system uses that information to identify items subject to such orders.

Several courts have concluded that a bank waived its right to a proper description of the check by accepting a stop order without advising the customer that a better description was needed. In *Rimberg v. Union Trust Co.*,[26] a teller accepted the stop payment order knowing that the customer was unsure of the exact amount and without advising the customer that the exact amount was needed. The court found that this constituted a waiver of the bank's rights under old § 4–403(1). A pre-Article 4 case reached the same result where a teller accepted an oral stop order without advising the customer that the statute then in effect required a written order.[27] The 1990 Article 4 revisions do not specifically address this issue so presumably cases like these basically remain good law and emphasize the need, as § 4–403 Comment 5 suggests, to deal with this issue in the deposit agreement, subject to the general duty of good faith and other applicable limitations. *See also* Comment 7 to § 4–403.

A customer has a right to stop payment for any reason, even if there are not sufficient funds in the account to cover the check.[28] However, questions have arisen concerning the right of a bank to refuse a stop payment order upon nonpayment of any fee it may seek to charge for that service. Article 4 does not deal with the fee issue (*see* Comment 3 to § 4–401), but it seems unlikely that a bank can impose an unreasonable fee as a prerequisite to honoring a stop order given the philosophy expressed in Comment 1 to § 4–403. On the other hand, Article 4 clearly does not bar a reasonable fee. What is reasonable or unreasonable? An opinion by the attorney general of Michigan states that a fee may be charged for a stop payment order if the agreement with the customer clearly and specifically provides.[29]

---

25. 366 So.2d 251 (Ala.1978).

26. 12 UCC Rep. Serv. 527 (D.C. Super. Ct. 1973). *See also supra* note 25.

27. Article 4 provides that an oral order is binding upon the bank only for 14 calendar days unless confirmed in writing within that period. Section 4–403(b) was rewritten in 1990 for clarity but the substance of the rule was unchanged. There is no requirement for a bank to advise a customer when an oral order is taken that it is good for only 14 days.

28. *See* Dynamite Enterprises v. Eagle National Bank, 517 So.2d 112 (Fla.Dist.Ct. App. 1987). This is because the bank could pay the overdraft. Also, in effect a customer without sufficient funds to cover a check can order payment stopped as a means of avoiding dishonor for insufficient funds.

29. Michigan Att'y Gen. Op. No. 5947, 33 UCC Rep. Serv. (Callaghan) 1445 (1981). Presumably any fee pursuant to such an agreement is reasonable subject to the requirements of good faith and substantive unconscionability. Comment 3 to § 4–401. *See also infra* ¶ 9.03. Note, in this context, the potential impact of the new definition of good faith at § 3–103(a)(4). Efforts to attack bank practices relating to imposition of fees and charges for cashing checks have generally not been successful. *See, e.g.*, Hayes v. First Commerce Corp., 763 So.2d 733 (La.Ct.App.2000); Batten v. Bank One, N.A., 2000 WL 1364408 (N.D.Ill. 2000). Absent extraordinary circumstances, it seems likely that attacks on stop payment fees will meet a similar fate. After all, if the customer does not like the fee, he or she can simply close the account. *See infra* ¶ 9.01 [4] [c].

There is always some risk for a bank that accepts and then fails to honor a stop payment order. Section 4–403(c) specifies that if a failure to honor a binding stop payment order results in wrongful dishonor of other checks, the bank will be liable for damages under § 4–402.[30] This has long been the rule established by case law, but § 4–403 makes it explicit.[31] Also, as noted *supra,* Article 4 makes it clear that if more than one person is authorized to draw on an account, "any person authorized to draw on the account" can stop payment of any item drawn on that account.[32] It is also made clear that any party authorized to draw on the account may close the account.[33] These rules represent potential liabilities for a bank that fails to adjust its procedures accordingly.[34]

Under § 4–403(b), an oral stop payment order is binding for only 14 days unless confirmed during that period, and after confirmation a stop payment order is effective for only six months unless properly renewed during that period.[35] The 1990 uniform text requires confirmation and renewal in "writing"; the 2002 amendments instead require only a "record."[36]

Among other things, this makes clear that a written or record stop payment order is effective for six months after receipt; however, if the written order or record is confirming an earlier oral stop payment order, and is received within 14 calendar days, the written order is effective for six months after the earlier oral stop payment order was received.[37] A renewal of the stop order must be in writing or a record and must be received by the bank during the effective period of the prior order. If payment occurs after a stop order has expired, it may not be wrongful.[38] Article 4 also makes clear that if wrongful payment over a valid stop payment order results in depletion of the account so as to cause wrongful dishonor of other items, the loss from the wrongful payment may include damages for wrongful dishonor of the other items under § 4–402.[39]

[b] Payment of an Altered Item Over a Stop Order: Good Faith and Ordinary Care

When an item is paid contrary to a stop payment order because the item has been altered and no longer matches the stop order, special questions may arise regarding the good faith and ordinary care of the payor. This is what happened in *Hartford Accident & Indemnity Co. v.*

---

30. § 4–403(c).

31. *See generally* Comment 7 to § 4–403.

32. § 4–403(a). In other words, a joint account holder can stop payment of an item drawn by the other joint account holder. *See supra* text at note 17.

33. § 4–403(a). *See supra* this text at note 18.

34. *See infra* ¶ 9.02[2], [3].

35. § 4–403(b).

36. *Id.* "Record" is defined in UCC Article 1, at § 1–201(b)(31) of the 2002 uniform text, and may also be defined in Article 3 § 3–103(a)(14) in some states. *See also* Uniform Electronic Transactions Act § 2(13).

37. *Id. See also* § 4–403, Comment 6.

38. Hartford Accident & Indem. Co. v. First Pennsylvania Bank, N.A., 859 F.2d 295 (3d Cir.1988).

39. *See* § 4–403(c). *See also* discussion of stop payment orders generally, *supra* this text and discussion of liability *infra* at ¶ 9.02[3].

First Pennsylvania Bank, N.A.,[40] with the added twist that it was alleged the check was paid in bad faith because it was "stale" (more than one year old). Normally in such circumstances the item is not properly payable (both as a result of the alteration and the stop payment order), and the bank must recredit the customer's account.[41] The payor bank may, however, be able to recover for breach of warranty from the depositary bank or any other party who made presentment.[42] This, however, may be subject to assertion of a defense on grounds that the payor bank failed to exercise ordinary care or good faith. For example, in *Hartford* the depositary bank (which had presented the item) asserted as a defense that the item was paid in bad faith because it was stale and was paid contrary to a stop payment order. However, the court noted that the stop payment order had expired, and concluded that the bank's payment of a stale item, although possibly careless, was not bad faith.

Under § 3–103(a)(4), "good faith" requires "observance of reasonable commercial standards of fair dealing."[43] This might suggest that payment of a stale item or payment over a stop payment order would not be payment in good faith if done negligently, a conclusion that could have adverse consequences for the bank that paid the item.[44] Absent extraordinary circumstances, this would be a misuse of the good faith concept, but the expansion of that concept in the UCC suggests some new litigation risks.

However, as Comment 4 to § 3–103 makes clear, good faith is not equivalent to ordinary care; good faith is concerned with the fairness of conduct rather than the care with which an act is performed. A bank's

---

40. 859 F.2d 295 (3d Cir.1988). *See also* Farmers & Merchants State Bank v. Western Bank, 841 F.2d 1433 (9th Cir.1987) (depositary bank took check with notice of "check kiting" operation; this constituted bad faith and the payor bank was able to assert this as a defense to liability on a cashier's check issued to the depositary bank as payment). *See also* discussion of good faith *infra* ¶ 9.03[2]; Dunnigan v. First Bank, 217 Conn. 205, 585 A.2d 659, 13 U.C.C. Rep. Serv. 2d 1196 (1991) (no loss resulted from bank's failure to follow stop order); Maine Family Federal Credit Union v. Sun Life Assurance Co., 727 A.2d 335 (Me. S.Ct. 1999) (impact of new § 3–103(a)(4) definition of good faith)..

41. This is subject to the bank's various rights (*see* Comment 7 to § 4–403) including the right of subrogation under § 4–407, discussed *infra* at ¶ 9.02[3]. *See also* discussion *supra* at note 33 and ¶ 9.01[4][a] and *infra* ¶ 9.02[3]. However, subrogation to the rights of a party to an altered instrument is not likely to be very helpful. *See* § 3–407, discussed *supra* in Chapter 6 and *infra* ¶ 9.02[3]. But the bank's right of recourse for breach of warranty under § 4–208(a)(2) may be helpful. In short, the bank often will have either a subrogation or a breach of warranty claim. As discussed *infra*, the bank also may be able to preclude the customer from asserting the alteration, under § 4–406, if the bank has exercised ordinary care. *See infra* ¶ 9.03[4].

42. *See* §§ 3–417 and 4–208; discussion *supra* at note 43; and *supra* Chapter 7. *See generally*, First National Bank and Trust Co. of the Treasure Coast v. Belmont National Bank, 43 U.C.C. Rep. Serv.2d 666 (Ohio Ct. App. 2001) (breach of warranty).

43. § 3–103(a)(4), incorporated into Article 4 at § 4–104(c). *See also supra* Chapter 3; ¶ 3.03[2][b] *supra*. Chapter 8 notes 44–46, 114, 215, and 497–504; ¶ 9.03[2].

44. For example, the customer may allege that this violates the bank's duty of good faith under § 1–203, § 3–103(a)(4), and § 4–406(e), so as to deprive the bank of its § 4–406 preclusion defense (*see infra* ¶ 9.03[4]), or that it violates the requirement of good faith at § 4–404. *See also Maine*, 727 A.2d 335, discussed *supra* Chapter 8 at note 215, and *infra* at notes 124, 167, and 188.

duty of ordinary care under Article 4[45] is described at § 3–103(a)(7) as follows:

> (7) "Ordinary care" in the case of a person engaged in business means observance of reasonable commercial standards, prevailing in the area in which that person is located, with respect to the business in which that person is engaged. In the case of a bank that takes an instrument for processing for collection or payment by automated means, reasonable commercial standards do not require the bank to examine the instrument if the failure to examine does not violate the bank's prescribed procedures and the bank's procedures do not vary unreasonably from general banking usage not disapproved by this Article or Article 4.

Thus, a bank should be able to pay an altered or stale item, as in *Hartford*, without violating its duty of ordinary care, as long as the payment is done by automated means or otherwise in accordance with general banking practices in that area and pursuant to the bank's internal procedures. The bank also should be able to either charge its customer's account (for a stale item) or recover in warranty (for an altered item) and perhaps to preclude customers who did not reasonably discover the alteration from asserting the alteration, under § 4–406, as discussed *infra* at ¶ 9.02[3]. Section 4–208(b) makes clear that the payor bank's right to recover from the party making presentment, for breach of warranty, is "not affected by any failure of the [payor bank] to exercise ordinary care in making payment." In effect, Articles 3 and 4 recognize the right of a payor bank to recover from prior parties for breach of warranty (where such an action is otherwise appropriate) regardless of whether the bank used ordinary care and as long as it paid in good faith. This is consistent with the analysis and result in *Hartford*.[46]

[c] *Alternatives to Stopping Payment*

Customers sometimes seek to avoid the expense, procedures and limitations of stop payment orders by using other means to prevent payment of an item. One course of action sometimes considered an alternative is for the customer to withdraw enough funds from the account that the check will be dishonored for insufficient funds.[47] Of course, there is the risk that the bank may pay the item anyway, creating an overdraft, which it then may collect from its customer.[48] And

---

45. *See* § 4–406(e). *See also* § 4–104(c). Beyond Article 4, *see* Regulation CC, 12 CFR § 229.38(a) (duty of ordinary care and good faith in complying with Regulation CC, Subpart C—collection of checks), discussed *supra* ¶ 8.04[3].

46. On the warranties, *see* Comment 5 to § 3–417, and *supra* Chapter 7. On the § 4–406 preclusion, *see infra* ¶ 9.03[4]. *But see supra* notes 43–44 (impact of new good faith standard).

47. *See, e.g.*, Continental Bank v. Fitting, 114 Ariz. 98, 559 P.2d 218, 20 UCC Rep.Serv. (Callaghan) 1263 (Ariz. App. 1977).

48. *See* § 4–401(a), and Comment 1; *see also supra* ¶ 9.01[1]; and City Bank of Honolulu v. Tenn., 52 Haw. 51, 469 P.2d 816 (Haw.1970). Moreover, if otherwise permitted by contract, the bank may collect a service charge for paying the overdraft. Hoffman v. Security Pac. Nat'l Bank, 121

this strategy is sure to fail if the bank has instituted some type of overdraft protection plan designed to avoid such dishonors.

Another alternative is to close the account, thus revoking the bank's authority to charge or to pay any items. However, if the customer has checks outstanding, this approach could result in unwanted dishonor of such checks, and even criminal prosecution.[49] A third possible alternative is the adverse claim procedure, which allows an adverse claim against the instrument to serve as a basis for dishonor *if* the claimant supplies "indemnity deemed adequate by the person seeking the discharge or enjoins payment or satisfaction by order of a court of competent jurisdiction in an action in which the claimant and holder are parties...."[50] The adverse claim procedure does not make much sense when the drawer is asserting the claim, and it becomes important primarily where the customer or other adverse claimant has no right to stop payment, as in the case of a cashier's check.[51]

[d] Can Payment be Stopped on a Cashier's or Similar Bank Check?

In transactions where the payee will not accept the drawer's personal check, the drawer may have the check certified or, more commonly, obtain a cashier's or teller's check.[52] The drawer who purchases such a check is sometimes called the remitter.[53] If the remitter then becomes dissatisfied with the transaction, he or she may seek to stop payment of the certified, cashier's, or teller's check. For purposes of this analysis all of these instruments are treated the same, representing in each case a primary obligation of the issuing bank under §§ 3–409 through 3–414.[54]

Cal.App.3d 964, 176 Cal.Rptr. 14 (1981). A topic of litigation under the old Article 4 was whether one joint account holder could be liable for an overdraft of the other. *See, e.g.*, United States Trust Co. v. McSweeney, 91 A.D.2d 7, 457 N.Y.S.2d 276 (App. Div. 1982). This was resolved in the 1990 revisions to Article 4 by limiting liability to those who signed the instrument or benefitted from its proceeds. *See* § 4–401(b); discussion *supra* at ¶ 9.01[2]; and discussion *supra* ¶ 9.01[1], [2], and [4][a].

49. *See, e.g.*, 21 Okla. Stat. §§ 1541.3, 1541.4 (1981). Could a bank go ahead and pay the outstanding checks after the account is closed, as an accommodation? There is some authority that it may not. *See, e.g., MJZ Corp. v. Gulfstream First Bank & Trust, N.A.*, 420 So.2d 396 (Fla. App.1982). This seems unduly restrictive. But even if the *MJZ Corp.* case is good law, it would seem a bank and its customer could agree to an "open account after closure."

50. *See* § 3–602, discussed *supra* at ¶ 6.03[6][b][iii].

51. *See* Comment 4 to § 4–403, and discussion *infra* ¶ 9.01[4][d].

52. For definitions of these terms, *see* § 1–104 and *supra* ¶ 8.01[3][m]. It is also possible that the payee or other holder will present the drawer's check and request payment in the form of a cashier's check. While in many ways the functional equivalent of the remitter scenario described in the text, this scenario is less likely to involve an effort of the bank customer to stop payment after the cashier's check has been issued. However, this scenario can yield its own problems, as where the cashier's check is erroneously issued in payment of a customer's check that is subject to a valid stop payment order: *See, e.g.*, Gentner & Co., Inc. v. Wells Fargo Bank, 76 Cal.App.4th 1165, 90 Cal.Rptr.2d 904 (Cal.Ct.App.1999) (erroneously depriving the payor bank of its § 4–407 subrogation rights).

53. *See* § 3–103(a)(11). The purchaser is a remitter only if the check is payable to someone other than the purchaser. *Id.*

54. See § 3–104(f)–(h); § 3–412. In contrast a money order signed by the customer as drawer is treated as a personal check under Articles 3 and 4, and therefore represents an obligation of the customer subject

Several issues may arise from an effort to stop payment of such an instrument. Suppose, for example, a customer of a financial institution requests a teller to issue a check drawn by the institution on its account with another bank (a "teller's check" under § 3–104(h)), as payment for goods being purchased by the customer. At the customer's request the teller makes the check payable to a seller.[55] The customer is thus the remitter. The customer/remitter then delivers this check to the seller as payment for goods or services. When a disagreement subsequently arises concerning the sale, the customer/remitter directs the institution to stop payment on the check. If the institution complies, and the check is dishonored when it is presented to the drawee, the seller may then sue the drawer (the bank that issued the check).

The check in this hypothetical was a draft drawn by the institution on its funds held in an account at another bank.[56] As noted, the legal and practical effects in this context are the same as in the case of a cashier's check. Like a cashier's check, the teller's check is signed by the customer's bank as drawer; thus that bank became liable "on the instrument."[57] And like a cashier's check, the check was intended to be and was taken as a substitute for cash, based on the independent liability of the drawer bank.[58]

---

to a stop payment order under § 4–403. *See* §§ 3–104(f) and 3–408, and *supra* ¶ 8.01[3][m] and ¶ 9.01[4][a].

55. A cashier's check is functionally the same in this context, for most purposes. *See* §§ 3–104 and 3–412. The example in the text resembles the facts of a number of cases, reflecting the relatively common nature of this type of transaction. *See, e.g.,* Malphrus v. Home Savings Bank, 44 Misc.2d 705, 254 N.Y.S.2d 980 (Co. Ct. 1965); Dziurak v. Chase Manhattan Bank, N.A., 58 A.D.2d 103, 396 N.Y.S.2d 414 (1977), *aff'd*, 44 N.Y.2d 776, 406 N.Y.S.2d 30, 377 N.E.2d 474 (1978); Fulton National Bank v. Delco Corporation, 128 Ga.App. 16, 195 S.E.2d 455 (Ga. Ct. App.1973). This example is also similar to the scenario described at § 3–411, Comment 1, discussed *infra* at ¶ 9.01[4][d][iv]. As noted here and explained in the text *supra* at note 54 and again *infra*, for purposes of the customer's right to stop payment, it makes no difference whether this is a teller's or a cashier's check.

56. As noted *supra* at notes 52–55, under the revisions this would be called a "teller's check." *See* § 3–104(h). In most respects relevant to this scenario, this is similar to a "cashier's check." *See* § 3–104(g). *See also* § 3–412 (obligation of issuer). Sometimes a teller's check is also called a "bank draft." *See* Note, Personal Money Orders and Teller's Checks: Mavericks Under the UCC, 67 COLUM. L. REV. 524 (1967), and discussion *supra* ¶ 8.01[3][m].

57. Old § 3–118 stated that "A draft drawn on the drawer [*e.g.*, a cashier's check] is effective as a note." Although this language reflects the primary obligation of the bank that issues a cashier's check (as opposed to the secondary liability of other drawers—*see* § 3–412 and *compare* § 3–414), it is inconsistent with the customary treatment of cashier's checks as drafts rather than notes. As a result the quoted language was deleted from revised Article 3. In the words of Comment 2 to revised § 3–103:

> Former Section 3–118(a) treated a cashier's check as a note. It stated "a draft drawn on the drawer is effective as a note." Although it is technically more correct to treat a cashier's check as a promise by the issuing bank to pay rather than an order to pay, a cashier's check is in the form of a check and it is normally referred to as a check. Thus, revised Article 3 follows banking practice in referring to a cashier's check as both a draft and a check rather than a note.

Nonetheless, the liability of the bank that issues the check remains that of a maker under § 3–412.

58. There is thus a novation under § 3–310(a). *See also* Crunk v. State Farm Fire & Cas. Co., 106 Wn.2d 23, 719 P.2d 1338 (1986) (policy covering cash theft loss

For purposes of this discussion, the basic question of whether payment may be stopped will be subdivided into three, more narrow questions: Does the customer who procures the check have authority to order payment stopped? Does the bank have the authority to stop payment? If the bank refuses or prevents payment, what are the consequences?

[i] Can the Customer Stop Payment?

Under old § 4–403(1), a "customer" could order "his bank to stop payment of any item payable for his account." This clearly authorizes a customer to stop payment of a check written by the customer on that customer's account, for any reason (or for no reason). Note, however, that under old Article 4 the right to stop payment is limited to a "customer" and is further limited to items payable "for his account." As discussed *supra* at ¶ 9.01[4][a], under revised § 4–403(a) any party authorized to sign checks on an account can order payment of any item drawn on that account to be stopped. "Customer" was defined at old § 4–104(1)(e) as: "any person having an account with a bank or for whom a bank has agreed to collect items and includes a bank carrying an account with another bank." The definition in revised Article 4 is essentially the same: "carrying an account" was changed to read "maintaining an account at another bank."[59] So clearly the customer can order payment stopped as to his own check, before it is paid.

However, as to a teller's check or cashier's check, the customer of the drawer bank has no right to stop payment of the check because the check is not drawn by or payable on the account of the customer, and the customer is not authorized to draw on the account from which the check is payable. Rather, a teller's check or cashier's check is payable from the bank's own funds, from an account on which only the bank can draw. A teller's check is drawn on the account of the drawer bank held at another bank. This other bank is the drawee, and the drawer or customer as to this account is not the person who originally procured the teller's check, but rather the drawer is the bank from which the check was procured. A cashier's check is the same, except that it would be drawn by the bank on itself.[60] This result is stated clearly at Comment 1 to § 3–411. Thus, once the customer's check has been paid by issuance of a cashier's or teller's check, it is too late for the customer to stop payment.

[ii] Can the Bank Stop Payment?

As explained above, it is clear that the bank's customer has no right to stop payment of a teller's check or cashier's check. But if the drawer bank is the customer (as to a teller's check), can the drawer bank order another bank as drawee of the teller's check to stop payment, or itself simply refuse to pay in the case of a cashier's check? It is clear that a

---

covered cashier's check), and revised § 3–412.

59. Revised § 4–104(a)(5). *See also supra* ¶ 8.01[3][g].

60. *See* revised § 3–104(g),(h), and *supra* ¶ 8.01[3][g],[m]. *See also* Comment 4 to revised § 4–403.

customer may stop payment of any item payable for his or her account without regard to reason or purpose.[61] With regard to a teller's check or a cashier's check, the drawer bank is the customer as to the account, and therefore the drawer bank has an unqualified right to order the drawee to stop or refuse payment under § 4–403, whether the drawee bank is itself or another bank. Cases to the contrary overlook the fact that in every such case the bank has successfully caused dishonor of the check by either refusing to make payment or ordering payment stopped, forcing the case into court where the various competing rights and liabilities can be resolved. Thus there can be no doubt that the drawer bank can stop or refuse payment; the only real question is the appropriate legal consequences of that action. If the drawer bank is ultimately held liable, it is because of other applicable rights and liabilities, not because the bank had no authority to refuse payment of a cashier's check or to stop payment on a teller's check.[62] The 1990 revisions at § 3–411 further clarify this, by distinguishing between proper and wrongful dishonor of a cashier's check. In this regard the ability of a bank to stop payment on its own checks is no different from that of any other "customer" under Article 4. To the question, can the bank stop payment?, the answer must be "yes." However, that does not address the more difficult question: What are the legal consequences that result?

[iii] Bank Liability for Dishonor of a Cashier's or Similar Check

Although the drawer bank may have the ability to prevent payment of the check upon presentment, as noted above, this does not resolve the question of the bank's ultimate liability on the instrument. As with the dishonor of any instrument, dishonor of a cashier's check or a teller's check merely invokes the liability of the drawer "on the instrument."[63] Therefore, if the customer of the bank who procures a cashier's check or a teller's check convinces the drawer bank to stop or otherwise prevent payment of the check upon its initial presentment, this merely requires the holder of the check to proceed against the bank as drawer, under § 3–412. If it is necessary to proceed in court, the drawer bank's liability will be established by its signature on the instrument, under § 3–308, subject to any defenses that it can raise against the holder.[64]

The narrow issue then becomes: What defenses can the drawer bank raise against the holder? This is the real crux of such a case. Under a proper reading of Articles 3 and 4, it seems clear that if the holder is a holder in due course and has not dealt with the drawer bank in relation to the defense, then the drawer bank can assert against the holder only the real defenses; but if the holder of the check does not have the rights

---

61. See § 4–403 and discussion *supra* at ¶ 9.01[4][a].

62. See ¶ 9.01[4][d][iii] and (iv) *infra*; Associated Carriages, Inc. v. International Bank of Commerce, 37 S.W.3d 69 (Tex. App.-San Antonio 2000); Behavioral Health and Wellness, Inc. v. FDIC, 802 So.2d 374 (Fla.Dist.Ct.App.2001).

63. § 3–412; *cf.* § 3–414(b); Article 3 Pt.5. *See also supra* Chapter 4.

64. § 3–412; § 3–308. This is also discussed *supra* in Chapter 6 at ¶ 6.01[1][a].

of a holder in due course (under §§ 3–201, 3–203, and 3–302), or has dealt directly with the drawer bank under § 3–305(b), then any personal defenses of the drawer bank (but, with limited exceptions, none of the remitter) may be raised. In other words, as between the drawer bank and a holder of the item, the same rules should apply that govern the liability of any drawer of a draft.[65]

An illustrative case is *TPO, Inc. v. FDIC*.[66] In that case the president of a bank issued cashier's checks to TPO for the purchase of securities, ostensibly for the account of the bank. As the result of a scheme between the bank president and certain TPO employees, however, the securities were diverted to the personal benefit of the conspirators. When the bank became insolvent the FDIC was appointed receiver and refused to pay the cashier's checks.

The trial court held that the bank (or its receiver) could not refuse payment of the cashier's checks on the ground that a bank could not stop payment of a cashier's check under old § 4–303. On appeal the court of appeals stated that a cashier's check represents an independent, unconditional, primary obligation of the bank, and that this contractual and statutory liability is not countermanded by the bank's ability to stop or refuse payment upon presentment. In other words, the bank cannot simply refuse to pay at its own discretion, without a further reason. The *TPO* court also recognized, however, that as against any holder not in due course the bank could assert any defenses that would be available to the bank on a simple contract. There were, then, two requisite elements that permitted the bank successfully to refuse payment of the checks. First, the holder/payee of the checks had dealt directly with the bank through its president, and therefore could not have the immunities of a holder in due course. Second, the holder's participation in the scheme to defraud the bank through its employees gave the bank its own claims and defenses against the holder, independent of any rights of other parties.[67] These defenses allowed the bank to refuse payment of its cashier's check. In effect, as with any drawer, the bank's ability to stop or refuse payment on its check does not alter its contractual and statutory liability on the instrument, in this case under § 3–412. Instead, stopping or refusing payment of a teller's or cashier's check merely forces the parties to reconcile their conflicting claims, if necessary taking the matter into court for a determination of that liability under the normal rules of Article 3 and other, *e.g.*, contract law. This

---

65. *See supra* ¶ 4.03; Associated Carriages, Inc. v. International Bank of Commerce, 37 S.W.3d 69 (Tex.App.—San Antonio 2000); Behavioral Health and Wellness, Inc. v. FDIC, 802 So.2d 374 (Fla.Dist.Ct. App.2001).

66. 487 F.2d 131 (3d Cir.1973).

67. *See also* Pulaski Chase Co–operative v. Kellogg–Citizens National Bank, 130 Wis.2d 200, 386 N.W.2d 510 (Wis.Ct.App. 1986) (no reason to deprive bank of defenses against holder of cashier's check); Farmers & Merchants State Bank v. Western Bank, 841 F.2d 1433 (9th Cir.1987) (holder of cashier's check failed to qualify as holder in due course because check was purchased in an effort to avoid loss from customer's check kiting scheme). *But see* Gentner & Co., Inc. v. Wells Fargo Bank, 76 Cal. App.4th 1165, 90 Cal.Rptr.2d 904 (Cal.Ct. App.1999) (bank erroneously deprived of § 4–407 claims and defenses because cashier's check was issued); *supra* Chapter 8 at note 169; *infra* note 68.

remains the law today, and the clear meaning of revised §§ 3–411 and 3–412, although not all courts have recognized this basic point.[68]

Some of the more confused cases dealing with this type of situation involve efforts of the issuing bank to assert defenses that might be available to the customer of the bank who procured the cashier's check or teller's check, perhaps arising out of a transaction between that customer and the holder of the cashier's check. Generally the bank, like any obligor, can assert its own claims and defenses but not those of other parties. This is a fundamental rule of law and is codified in Article 3 at § 3–305(c), subject of course to the law of assignment as codified at § 3–203 (which is normally not implicated in the cashier's check cases). Most of the cases on this issue are correct in refusing to allow the bank to assert defenses of its customer because of § 3–305(c), or its predecessor, old § 3–306(d), but sometimes misstate the point by holding that a bank is not entitled to stop payment on a cashier's or teller's check. This obviously overstates the point. These cases should be distinguished from others like *TPO* where the bank is asserting its own defense. The point should be clear: there is no reason why a bank should not be able to assert its own defense against the holder of a cashier's or teller's check, subject to the holder in due course rules. But if the customer who procures the check and delivers it to the payee or a holder has a claim or

---

68. The best recent case is Associated Carriages, Inc. v. International Bank of Commerce, 37 S.W.3d 69 (Tex.App.—San Antonio 2000). *Associated Carriages* is important because it considers the impact of the revised (1990) provisions at § 3–411, noting that these provisions emphasize the distinctions between proper and wrongful dishonor of a cashier's check under Article 3 and contemplate cases where an issuing bank may have defenses to liability that justify dishonor. *See also* Behavioral Health and Wellness, Inc. v. FDIC, 802 So.2d 374 (Fla.Dist.Ct.App.2001). *Cf.* Abilities, Inc. v. Citibank, N.A., 87 A.D.2d 831, 449 N.Y.S.2d 242 (N.Y. Sup. Ct. 1982) (payment cannot be refused on a cashier's check); Yukon National Bank v. Modern Builders Supply, 686 P.2d 307 (Okla. App. 1984) (same); Hotel Riviera, Inc. v. First Nat'l Bank & Trust Co. of Okla. City, 768 F.2d 1201 (10th Cir.1985) (same); First National Bank v. United States, 41 UCC Rep. Serv. 1583 (Ct.Cl.1985) (same); Wertz v. Richardson Heights Bank & Trust, 495 S.W.2d 572 (Tex.1973)(same). These cases are clearly incorrect and should be considered rejected by revised §§ 3–411 and 3–412. *See also* Crunk v. State Farm Fire & Casualty Co., 106 Wn.2d 23, 719 P.2d 1338 (Wash. 1986) (cashier's check treated as equivalent to cash); Hill v. Mercantile First National Bank, 693 S.W.2d 285 (Mo.Ct.App.1985). *Crunk* and *Hill* are noted and criticized in Miller, Ballen, Davenport & Vergari, Commercial Paper, Bank Deposits and Collections, and Commercial Electronic Fund Transfers, 42 Bus. Law. 1269, 1302–03(1987). *TPO and Pulaski* represent the better view, now validated by §§ 3–411 and 3–412, § 4–403, and cases like *Associated Carriage*. *See also* Farmers & Merchants State Bank v. Western Bank, 841 F.2d 1433 (9th Cir.1987) (bank could assert defenses to liability on cashier's check).

An interesting variation on the theme occurred in Santos v. First Nat'l State Bank, 186 N.J.Super. 52, 451 A.2d 401 (App.Div.1982) where the remitter claimed the cashier's check was lost. He was unable to establish that the check had not been indorsed in blank (if it were, it could come into the hands of a holder in due course), but nonetheless he wanted his money back. The court had the bank issue a certificate of deposit in the name of the remitter, but allowed the bank to hold the certificate for security until the statute of limitations on the cashier's check had run. *See also* Diaz v. Manufacturer's Hanover Trust Co., 92 Misc.2d 802, 401 N.Y.S.2d 952 (1977). Another case where a less favorable result occurred is Guttman v. National Westminster Bank, 146 Misc.2d 391, 550 N.Y.S.2d 812, 10 UCC Rep. Serv. 2d 1297 (N.Y. 1990). This issue also is discussed in Chapter 4 at ¶ 4.04[2][b]. This problem is addressed at current § 3–312, discussed *infra* at ¶ 9.01[4][d][iv], [v], or alternatively under § 3–309.

defense arising out of the transaction with the payee or a holder, it is equally clear that the drawer bank cannot assert that claim or defense against the holder if the bank refuses to pay the check and is sued.

Thus a drawer bank cannot assert claims or defenses that are personal to the bank's customer, any more than any other drawer can do so.[69] The bank is not a party to the transaction between its customer (who procured the check) and the holder of the check. Having issued the check as drawer in return for payment, the bank has become liable to the holder "on the instrument" as an independent obligation of the bank. And, as stated at old § 3–306(d): "The claim of any third person to the instrument is not otherwise available as a defense to any party liable thereon unless the third person himself defends the action for such person."[70] Revised Section 3–305(c) and (d) are similar.

[iv] Refusal to Pay a Cashier's or Similar Check: Measure of Liability

Revised § 3–411 seeks to define the liability of a bank upon its wrongful refusal to pay a cashier's or certified check, or after it has wrongfully stopped payment of a teller's check. Note that this section triggers liability only upon a bank's *wrongful* refusal to pay or stopping of payment. In other words, it sets the parameters for a bank's liability where the bank has stopped or refused payment without an adequate defense. Comment 3 to § 3–411 states this clearly: "Subsection (b) applies only if the refusal to honor the check is wrongful. If the bank is not obligated to pay there is no recovery. The bank may assert any claim or defense that it has." Thus the fact of liability must be determined

---

69. This is true in any transferee situation; this prohibition on the use of another party's defense is not limited to banks, but applies to all drawers. *See, e.g.*, Security State Bank v. Morlock, 355 N.W.2d 441 (Minn.App.1984), discussed ¶ 6.03[1][b]. In *Morlock*, an insurance draft was delivered to a bank as security but the customer convinced the insurance company to stop payment and to reissue a second draft directly to the customer. When sued by the bank (as holder of the draft) the insurance company had to pay, even though it had already paid its customer on the second draft. While the court analyzed the issues under contract law, it is clear that under old § 3–306(d) and revised § 3–305(c) (which makes this point even more clearly) the insurance company (as obligor) could not assert against the bank (as holder) any defense or claim of the customer (or any other third party). Having no defense of its own, the insurance company was obligated to pay the draft.

However, there are qualifications to this basic principle. For example, a bank may be subrogated to the rights of third parties under § 4–407. For a case that incorrectly barred these rights because the cashier's check was issued in a payment subject to § 3–418, *see* Gentner & Co., Inc. v. Wells Fargo Bank, 76 Cal.App.4th 1165, 90 Cal. Rptr.2d 904 (Cal.Ct.App.1999), discussed *supra* at note 67 and *supra* Chapter 8 at note 169. *Gentner* is particularly inexplicable because it relied on § 3–418, which specifically recognizes remedies provided under § 4–407. Of course, if rights are assigned they become the rights of the assignee. This is also basic contract law, codified at § 3–203. Oddly, this simple point continues to escape some courts. The two worst cases are Triffin v. Bridge View Bank, 330 N.J.Super. 473, 750 A.2d 136 (App.Div. 2000); and Dennis Joslin Co., LLC v. Robinson Broadcasting Corp., 977 F.Supp. 491 (D.D.C.1997). These cases are rejected in the 2002 amendments.

70. Old § 3–306(d). There are two exceptions generally not applicable in the context being discussed, where the instrument was stolen or payment would be contrary to a restrictive indorsement. As noted, revised § 3–305(c) and (d) make this point even more clearly.

after consideration of any claims or defenses assertable by the bank under the normal rules of Article 3, as noted *supra* at ¶ 9.01[4][d][iii]. If it appears that the bank had no legitimate basis for stopping or refusing payment, liability for the amount of the check exists on the drawer's or acceptor's contract and additional or reduced liability may then exist under § 3–411.

Under § 3–411(b), the bank that has wrongfully stopped or refused payment of a cashier's, teller's, or certified check is liable for "compensation for expenses and loss of interest resulting from the nonpayment," and for consequential damages where the bank had notice of the particular circumstances giving rise to such. But under § 3–411(c), expenses and consequential damages cannot be recovered from the bank if the refusal to pay resulted from a suspension of payments, assertion of a defense of the bank that the bank had reasonable grounds to believe was available against the party seeking payment, a reasonable doubt that said person was entitled to enforce the instrument, or a prohibition of law.

In effect, these provisions entitle a bank to refuse or stop payment on a cashier's or similar check, on grounds of a reasonably perceived defense or claim of the bank against the holder, with potential liability limited to the amount of the item plus interest should the bank not prevail in court. This effectively rejects the thrust of cases like *Hotel Riviera, Inc. v. First Nat'l Bank & Trust Co. of Okla. City*, noted *supra* at 9.01[4][d][iii], holding that a bank has no right to refuse payment of a cashier's check despite the existence of a valid defense. Of course § 3–411(c) would not provide a shield against expenses or consequential damages where the bank refuses or stops payment on the basis of a spurious defense, as where the bank is seeking to assert a personal defense against a holder in due course.

[v] *Lost, Destroyed, or Stolen Cashier's, Teller's, or Certified Checks*

A new § 3–312 was added to Article 3 in the 1990 revisions and as an alternative to the customer's remedy at § 3–309, which may involve an expensive bond. If a cashier's, teller's or certified check has been lost, stolen, or destroyed, the drawer, payee, or remitter (the "claimant") may deliver a "declaration of loss" (described at § 3–312(a)(3)) to the issuing bank. If this declaration is received by the bank "at a time and in a manner affording the bank a reasonable time to act on it before the check is paid," then under § 3–312(b) the claimant's claim becomes enforceable at the later of: (1) the time the claim is asserted; or (2) the 90th day following the date of the cashier's or teller's check or certification.

Under § 3–312(b)(2), the bank is entitled to pay or allow payment of the check at any time up to the 90th day, to any person entitled to payment, and such payment will discharge the bank under § 3–602, despite the declaration of loss. But if the check is presented after the claim has become enforceable (as described above and at § 3–312(b)(1)), the bank is not obligated to pay the check and such payment will not discharge the bank's liability to the claimant. When the claim becomes enforceable, if the bank has not previously paid the check to a person entitled to enforce the check, it is obligated to do so to the claimant, and in turn this will discharge the bank's liability on the check, pursuant to § 3–312(b)(4).

If the check is then later presented for payment by a holder in due course, the claimant is obligated to pay the holder or to reimburse the bank if the bank makes payment, under § 3–312(c). Section 3–312(d) makes clear that a person may assert rights under § 3–312 or, where appropriate, § 3–309 ("Enforcement of Lost, Destroyed, or Stolen Instrument"). Thus in the right circumstances, these provisions represent alternative remedies. These revisions are in apparent response to cases like *Santos v. First Nat'l State Bank*, discussed *supra* at note 68, and which are also discussed *supra* this text at ¶ 3.01[3][a].

One effect of this provision is to make cashier's and similar checks unenforceable after 90 days, absent a holder in due course, where a declaration of loss is filed during the 90 day period. If no declaration of loss is filed, such a check should continue to be enforceable after 90 days, as under prior law. Section 3–312 also creates some new risks for banks, *e.g.*, where the banks pay on a declaration of loss and then the cashier's check is presented after the 90th day by a holder in due course. To guard against this, some banks are including protective language on the face of their cashier's checks, such as "void after 90 days."

[e] *Certification*

Section 4–403(a) provides that any right to stop payment terminates when the payor bank accepts or certifies the check or takes any of the actions listed in § 4–303. These are basically the same actions that constitute final payment under § 4–215 (*see supra* ¶ 8.02). Section 4–403(a) was reworded slightly for clarity but is substantively the same as old § 4–403(1).[71] Since certification of a check is acceptance under § 3–409(a),(d), and acceptance creates an obligation of the acceptor to pay under §§ 3–409 and 3–413, the effect of a certified check is similar to that of a cashier's check.[72] Thus certification will end a customer's right to stop payment, and a bank that refuses payment of its certified check will nonetheless remain liable "on the instrument."[73]

[5] *Receipt of Legal Process*

If a payor bank receives legal process that prohibits the transfer of funds from a certain account, this will prevent the bank from paying any items drawn on that account as long as the legal process was received in

---

71. Except that the process of posting has been eliminated as a means of making final payment. With respect to checks, however, within limits the bank can set a cut off point in replacement. *See* § 4–303(a)(5) and Comment 4 to that section. *See also* § 4–108, and *supra* ¶ 8.02[2][c].

72. *See* old §§ 3–411(1), 3–802(1)(a); revised §§ 3–414(c), 3–415(d) and 3–310(a). *See supra* ¶ 8.01[3][m], ¶ 9.01[4][d].

73. *See also* § 4–403, and Comment; discussion *supra* this text at ¶ 9.01[4][d].

time to allow the bank to act before acceptance or before payment of the item became final. Conversely, the events that constitute final payment will effectively cut-off the effects of any subsequent legal process or stop payment order. Those things that constitute "final payment" for this purpose under Article 4 are listed in § 4–303(a):

(2) payment of the item in cash;

(3) settlement for the item without reserving a right to revoke the settlement and without having such right under statute, clearing house rule or agreement;[74] or

(4) accountability for the item under § 4–302. The reference to accountability in old § 4–213 is deleted in revised § 4–215, but is in revised §§ 4–302 and 4–303(a)(4), dealing with the payor bank's responsibility for late return of items.[75]

(5) In addition to final payment, the bank may establish a cut-off time to bar subsequent legal process or stop payment orders, under § 4–303(a)(5).

"Legal process" is not defined in the UCC, but it presumably includes any order of a state court of competent jurisdiction, such as a garnishment summons or order of attachment or execution. An Internal Revenue Service levy would qualify, as would notice of the drawer's bankruptcy. Because the latter are governed by federal law, problems can arise with regard to the relationship between federal and state law.[76] For example, in *Bank of Marin v. England*,[77] the payor bank paid items after the drawer had declared bankruptcy, but before the bank had received notice of the proceeding. The drawer's trustee in bankruptcy

---

74. Under old § 4–303(1)(d), completion of the process of posting was a fourth means to make final payment. Action short of completion of posting could suffice as long as a decision to pay had been made. This rule and old § 4–303(1)(d) was deleted from revised Article 4, eliminating the process of posting (and a related decision to pay) as a means of final payment. A companion revision at § 4–215(a) likewise eliminated the process of posting as a means of determining whether final payment has been made. Old § 4–109, illustrating the process of posting, was also eliminated. These revisions reflect a judgment that the process of posting is too vague a standard to use in defining finality of payment and is unsuitable for a system of automated check collection or electronic presentment. *See* § 4–215, Comment 5; § 4–303, Comment 4; and discussion of final payment, *supra* ¶ 8.02[1],[2][c]. *See*, however, *supra* note 71.

75. *Cf.* § 4–303(a) and § 4–215(a) (final payment). *See supra* ¶ 8.02. Under old Article 4, the rules on final payment at old § 4–213 were consistent with, and referred to, the rules making a payor bank "accountable" for an item upon final payment, at old §§ 4–302. As noted *supra* in Chapter 8, the 1990 revisions largely severed the overlap between payment and accountability, maintaining a separation between the two concepts. Revised § 4–303(a)(4) (on accountability) refers only to § 4–302, because the 1990 revisions eliminated the "accountability" language from revised § 4–215(a) (on final payment). A change was made to accommodate the elimination of the process of posting, so that § 4–302 is the only source of the "accountability" rule, in order to avoid possible confusion between different sections of Article 4. Revised § 4–302 also clarifies and specifies exceptions to the "accountability" rule. *See* § 4–215, Comment 6, § 4–302, Comments 3 and 5, and discussion *supra* ¶ 8.02.

76. *See, e.g.*, Harrell, Miller, & Woodward, Update on UCC–Other Law Conflicts, 45 Consumer Fin. L. Q. Rep. 335 (1991). For related rules involving funds available in relation to a funds transfer, *see* UCC §§ 4A–502, 4A–503 and 4A–504; *infra* Chapter 10.

77. 385 U.S. 99, 87 S.Ct. 274, 17 L.Ed.2d 197 (1966).

claimed the payment was wrongful because the filing of the bankruptcy petition vested all of the drawer's property in the trustee.[78] Because bankruptcy law preempts inconsistent state law,[79] it was claimed that the bankruptcy petition revoked the bank's authority to pay items from the drawer's account, even though the bank was without notice. The U.S. Supreme Court concluded, however, that under equitable principles applicable to a bankruptcy proceeding, the bank's authority to pay continued until it received notice of the bankruptcy proceeding.

Today, this position is incorporated in the Bankruptcy Code. The current bankruptcy statute allows the payor bank to pay items in good faith until it receives actual notice or knowledge of the bankruptcy proceeding.[80] The drawer's trustee, however, may be able to recover the money paid to the recipient as a voidable preference, unless the recipient received the item in payment of a debt incurred in the ordinary course of business.[81]

[6] *Death or Incompetence of the Drawer*

The death or incompetence of the drawer creates issues similar to those confronted upon bankruptcy of the drawer, but here state law controls. Section 4–405 provides that neither death nor incompetence of the drawer revokes the bank's authority to pay items "until the bank knows of the fact of death or of an adjudication of incompetence and has reasonable time to act on it."[82] Moreover, even with such knowledge a

---

78. Today this would be asserted under 11 U.S.C. § 541; in *Bank of Marin* it was governed by § 70a of the old Bankruptcy Act. *See* §§ 362 (automatic stay) and 541 (bankruptcy estate) of the current Bankruptcy Code, 11 U.S.C. §§ 362, 541, continuing this basic principle.

79. *See* U.S. Const. Art. I, § 8. *See also* Harrell, Miller, & Woodward, *supra* note 76.

80. Section 542(c) of the Bankruptcy Code, 11 U.S.C. § 542(c). *See* Comment 2 to Article 4 § 4–303. The automatic stay at 11 U.S.C. § 362 still creates potent pitfalls for a creditor who exercises any remedies after receiving notice of the bankruptcy, including set-off of a deposit account. However, subject to some limits the bank is entitled to impose an administrative freeze on the account to preserve the status quo and protect its right of set-off. *See* Citizens Bank v. Strumpf, 516 U.S. 16, 116 S.Ct. 286, 133 L.Ed.2d 258 (1995); Alvin C. Harrell and Fred H. Miller, The Law of Personal Property Secured Transactions Under The Uniform Commercial Code and Related Laws Ch. 21 (2001), Fred H. Miller and Alvin C. Harnell, The ABCs of the UCC Related Insolvency Law 46–52 (Am. Bar Assoc. 2002).

81. Section 547(c)(2) of the Bankruptcy Code, 11 U.S.C. § 547(c)(2). *See also* 11 U.S.C. § 549(b). In Union Bank v. Wolas, 502 U.S. 151, 112 S.Ct. 527, 116 L.Ed.2d 514 (1991), the U.S. Supreme Court held that interest payments on a long-term loan as well as those on short-term debt could be made in the ordinary course of business, and therefore were not preferential transfers that could be recovered by the bankruptcy trustee from the creditor recipient. On a related issue, there was a split of authority over whether, for purposes of the bankruptcy preference rules, a payment made by check occurs on the date it is honored by the drawee bank, or upon issue or delivery of the check to the payee. *See In re* Antweil, 931 F.2d 689 (10th Cir.1991). The view payment occurs on the later date is generally consistent with the UCC. *See* old § 3–409(1), revised § 3–408. A number of cases, however, adopt an earlier time. *See, e.g., In re* Belknap, Inc., 909 F.2d 879 (6th Cir.1990); Global Distr. Network, Inc. v. Star Expansion Co., 949 F.2d 910, 16 UCC Rep.Serv. (Callaghan) 2d 394 (7th Cir. 1991). The issue was ultimately decided by the Supreme Court, which concluded that the preference period begins when the check is honored and not when it is received. Barnhill v. Johnson, 503 U.S. 393, 112 S.Ct. 1386, 118 L.Ed.2d 39 (1992). *See also supra* Chapter 4, ¶ 4.04[1].

82. § 4–405(a).

bank may for ten days after the date of death pay or certify checks drawn on or prior to that date unless ordered to stop payment by a person claiming an interest in the account.[83] Section 4–405 is for the protection of the bank only and does not prevent the personal representative or an heir of the decedent from proceeding against the recipient of payment.[84] One effect of this provision is to give any surviving relative, creditor, or other interested party a right to order the bank not to pay a particular check, or any checks at all, even during the ten day period following the drawer's death.[85]

Section 4–405 merely allows a bank to make payment in the stated circumstances; it does not permit payment once made to be rescinded. This is illustrated by *Sunshine v. Bankers Trust Co.*[86] Oscar Sunshine was president of a corporation that maintained a checking account at Bankers Trust. Shortly before his death, he signed and delivered a corporate check to his wife. She indorsed and deposited this check to her account at the same bank. A short time later he died and Oscar's son from a previous marriage, Melvin, succeeded his father as president of the corporation. Melvin executed a stop-payment order against the check his father had written to his stepmother. Two or three banking days had elapsed since the stepmother had deposited the check and received provisional settlement. The midnight deadline had passed and thus the settlement received by the stepmother had become final payment (*see supra* this text at ¶ 8.02). Despite this, apparently as an accommodation to the new president of a valued corporate customer, the bank revoked the credit given the stepmother and returned the funds to the corporate account. She objected and sought return of the funds to her account. The court affirmed a summary judgment in favor of the stepmother on the issue of final payment, subject to any claims or defenses arising from the circumstances surrounding issuance of the check that might be asserted by the bank as subrogee of the corporation under § 4–407.[87]

[7] *Final Payment, the "Four Legals," and the Bank's "Cut-off" Hour*

Stop payment, legal process, and the bankruptcy, death, or incompetence of the customer are three categories of the so-called "four legals." The "four legals" are the four traditional bases requiring dishonor of an item.[88] The fourth "legal" is the bank's exercise of its

---

83. § 4–405(b).

84. § 4–405, Comments 2 and 3. *See generally* Black v. Hart, 301 So.2d 787 (Fla. App.1974).

85. *See* § 4–405, Comment 3; *see also* Comment 2 to § 4–405. The bank has no duty to determine the validity of such a claim or "even whether it is 'colorable'," and is entitled to honor a no-payment direction by any person claiming an interest in the decedent's account. *Id.* The bank, however, must act in good faith. *See* § 1–203 and §§ 3–103(a)(4) and 4–104(c).

86. 34 N.Y.2d 404, 358 N.Y.S.2d 113, 314 N.E.2d 860 (N.Y.App.1974).

87. *See* discussion of § 4–407, *infra* ¶ 9.02[3].

88. *See, e.g.,* D. King, C. Kuenzel, T. Lauer, N. Littlefield & B. Stone, Commercial Transactions Under the Uniform Commercial Code 11–62 & 11–63 (3d ed. 1981), *citing* W. Hawkland, A Transactional Guide to the UCC 398 (A.L.I./A.B.A. 1964).

right of setoff.[89] Each of these "legals" is a basis for dishonor only if it occurs before acceptance or what amounts to final payment of the check. Thus, the "four legals" typically involve the issue of final payment and a determination of when that event occurs.[90]

A new provision introduced in the 1990 revisions to Article 4, § 4–303(a)(5), permits a payor bank to establish a "cutoff" time after which any of the four legals comes too late to affect the bank's right to pay the item in question. This "cutoff hour" can be "no earlier than one hour after the opening of the next banking day after the banking day on which the bank received the check and no later than the close of that next banking day."[91] If the bank has not established such a cutoff time, then a statutory time is provided: "the close of the next banking day after the banking day on which the bank received the check."[92]

It is important to understand the relationship between this new cutoff hour and the bank's regular cutoff hour for other purposes under § 4–108, and the rules on final payment. This relationship is explained in Comment 4 to § 4–303:

> In the usual case settlement for checks is by entries in bank accounts. Since the process-of-posting test has been abandoned as inappropriate for automated check collection, the determining event for priorities is a given hour on the day after the item is received. (Paragraph (5) of subsection (a).) The hour may be fixed by the bank no earlier than one hour after the opening on the next banking day after the bank received the check and no later than the close of that banking day. If an item is received after the payor bank's regular Section 4–108 cutoff hour, it is treated as received the next banking day. If a bank receives an item after its regular cutoff hour on Monday and an attachment is levied at noon on Tuesday, the attachment is prior to the item if the bank had not before that hour taken the action described in paragraphs (1), (2), and (3) of subsection (a). The Commentary to Regulation CC Section 229.36(d) ex-

---

89. Article 4 does not define the right of setoff. In some states, an overt act is required. *In re* McCormick, 5 B.R. 726 (Bankr.N.D.Ohio 1980). In other states, setoff is virtually automatic. Pittsburgh Nat'l Bank v. United States, 657 F.2d 36 (3d Cir.1981). Thus Article 4 § 4–303 is less uniform than it appears. *See also* Alvin C. Harrell, Security Interests in Deposit Accounts: A Unique Relationship Between the UCC and Other Law, 23 U.C.C. L.J. 153 (1990). But revised UCC Article 9 reverses prior law in many states by generally giving priority to a bank's right of set-off, as against prior security interests, unless the secured party has "control" of the deposit account. *See* revised Article 9 §§ 9–104, 9–109(d)(10), 9–203, 9–327, and 9–340. This may have reintroduced greater uniformity with respect to this issue.

90. *See* §§ 4–215(a), 4–302, 4–303; discussion *supra* ¶ 8.02 and ¶ 9.01[5]. A leading case is West Side Bank v. Marine Nat'l Exch. Bank, 37 Wis.2d 661, 155 N.W.2d 587 (Wis. 1968), discussing old § 4–213(1)(c) and (d) and the process of posting. As noted *supra*, the process of posting was deleted from revised § 4–215(a). *See supra* ¶ 8.02[2][c]. *Cf.* H. Schultz & Sons, Inc. v. Bank of Suffolk County, 439 F.Supp. 1137 (E.D.N.Y.1977). As to old § 4–213(1)(a), revised § 4–215(a)(1), *see* Kirby v. First & Merchants Nat'l Bank, 210 Va. 88, 168 S.E.2d 273 (Va. 1969), and discussion *supra* at ¶ 8.02[2]. As to old § 4–213(1)(b), revised § 4–215(a)(2), *see* Douglas v. Citizens Bank of Jonesboro, 244 Ark. 168, 424 S.W.2d 532 (Ark. 1968).

91. Revised § 4–303(a)(5).

92. *Id.*

plains that even though settlement by a paying bank for a check is final for Regulation CC purposes, the paying bank's right to return the check before its midnight deadline under the UCC is not affected.

In other words, the banking day of receipt of the item will be determined under § 4–108 for purposes of the midnight deadline and final payment rules. Then if notice of one of the four legals is received after the item is received but before acceptance or final payment, the timeliness (and hence the effectiveness) of that notice will be determined by whether it was received before the "cutoff hour" under § 4–303(a)(5).

For example, in *Yandell v. White City Amusement Park, Inc.*,[93] a restraining order was served on the bank at 2:15 p.m. on August 1, 1960. On July 29, the bank had received some checks for payment from the account affected by the restraining order. A bank officer had authorized payment and made a notation on the ledger card to that effect on July 29. The checks were stamped in a manner that signified payment, but because it was late in the day, the items were not posted and thus were not finally paid until August 2. The court held that even though final payment had not been made before the restraining order was received, the order was too late to prevent the payment because under old § 4–303(1)(d) any of the "legals" was too late once a decision to pay has been made and there is evidence of it.[94] Under revised Article 4, the process of posting (and hence the decision to pay) has been eliminated as a factor relevant to final payment, so revised § 4–303(a)(5) is intended to preserve a time line short of the midnight deadline and thus an equivalent of the *Yandell* rule. Revised § 4–303(a)(5) establishes a reasonable point in time, by which the order or notice must be received in order to be effective in preventing final payment.

¶ 9.02 Consequences of Wrongful Payment and Wrongful Dishonor

[1] Introduction

As discussed in greater detail *supra* in Chapter 8, when an item is presented to the bank on which it is drawn for payment (the payor bank), the bank must either pay the item or dishonor it, within its midnight deadline. Settlement must be given pending completion of the process of handling the check for payment or dishonor, but eventually the midnight deadline requires either dishonor or final payment of the item. Failing this, the payor bank becomes accountable under § 4–302. These issues are discussed *supra* at ¶ 8.02. If the item is paid, any parties who are adversely affected by that payment may claim that the payment was wrongful. For example, if an indorsement was forged or the item was altered, it is not properly payable under § 4–401 and the drawer may object. If the item was dishonored, parties who are adversely affected, including again the drawer, may claim that the dishonor was

---

93. 232 F.Supp. 582 (D.Mass.1964).   **94.** Old § 4–303(1)(d) and Comment 3.

wrongful. Each time a bank pays or dishonors an item, it faces the possibility that those who are adversely affected will object. Therefore, it is important to clearly outline the rights and duties of the bank in these circumstances. This discussion will cover these issues, except as already discussed in Chapter 7 with respect to forgery and alteration.

[2] Wrongful Dishonor

[a] The Revision of Section 4–402

The basic principle of wrongful dishonor was codified at old § 4–402 as follows:

> A payor bank is liable to its customer for damages proximately caused by the wrongful dishonor of an item. When the dishonor occurs through mistake, liability is limited to actual damages proved. If so proximately caused and proved damages may include damages for an arrest or prosecution of the customer or other consequential damages. Whether any consequential damages are proximately caused by the wrongful dishonor is a question of fact to be determined in each case.

While this remains a succinct statement of the law, in 1990 § 4–402 was significantly revised, to provide greater specificity on these issues, as follows:

> (a) Except as otherwise provided in this Article, a payor bank wrongfully dishonors an item if it dishonors an item that is properly payable, but a bank may dishonor an item that would create an overdraft unless it has agreed to pay the overdraft.
>
> (b) A payor bank is liable to its customer for damages proximately caused by the wrongful dishonor of an item. Liability is limited to actual damages proved and may include damages for an arrest or prosecution of the customer or other consequential damages. Whether any consequential damages are proximately caused by the wrongful dishonor is a question of fact to be determined in each case.
>
> (c) A payor bank's determination of the customer's account balance on which a decision to dishonor for insufficiency of available funds is based may be made at any time between the time the item is received by the payor bank and the time that the payor bank returns the item or gives notice in lieu of return and no more than one determination need be made. If at the election of the payor bank, a subsequent balance determination is made for the purpose of reevaluating the bank's decision to dishonor the item, the account balance at that time is determinative of whether a dishonor for insufficiency of available funds is wrongful.

The 1990 Article 4 revisions to § 4–402 address three important issues. First, revised § 4–402(a) specifies that if a payor bank dishonors an item and payment of that item would have been proper, it creates an action in its customer for wrongful dishonor.[95] While this was already inferred under old Article 4, having it spelled out in the statute should minimize frivolous allegations to the contrary.

Second, revised § 4-402(b) is intended to make clear that "[l]iability [for wrongful dishonor] is limited to actual damages proved."[96] This reinforces the rejection by most courts under prior law of the so-called "trader rule," under which a court might impose liability on payor banks without proof of damages. As discussed *infra* this text, the old version of Article 4 likewise could be interpreted to repudiate the "trader rule," but some cases found ambiguities in the statutory language that permitted continuation of the rule. Revised § 4-402(b) was intended to finally put this issue to rest.[97]

Third, revised § 4-402(c) represents an important codification of the practice applicable to dishonor of items drawn on insufficient funds. This revision addresses the problem of items that are returned for insufficient funds at or shortly after the time the drawer has made a deposit to cover the NSF check. Revised § 4-402(c) specifies that a payor bank is entitled to make an initial determination as to whether an item is drawn on sufficient funds, at any time after receipt but before dishonor of the item, and is then entitled to act on that determination by returning or otherwise dishonoring the item, regardless of any subsequent deposit by the customer. The bank is not required to reevaluate the account at any time after this initial determination, although if it does so it is bound by such reevaluation. This permits the bank to make an initial determination, and then later to act on it, even if the customer has made a deposit during the interval.

Note that wrongful dishonor is a separate issue that normally does not involve due care, final payment, or the midnight deadline. Liability for wrongful dishonor is governed by § 4-402, not §§ 4-103, 4-215, or 4-302.[98]

¶ 9.02

95. *See* § 4-402, Comment 1. Note that is is not wrongful dishonor or otherwise improper for a bank to impose a fee for a noncustomer to cash a check. *See* Moorehouse v. Chase Manhattan Bank, 76 S.W.3d 608 (Tex.Ct.App.2002); Hayes v. First Commerce Corp., 763 So.2d 733 (La.Ct.App. 2000); Batten v. Bank One, N.A., 2000 WL 1364408 (N.D.Ill.2000); Wells Fargo Bank Texas, N.A. v. James, 184 F.Supp.2d 588 (W.D.Tex.2001), *aff'd* 321 F.3d 488 (5th Cir. 2003); Office of the Comptroller of the Currency (OCC) Interpretive Letters 932, 933, and 934 (referencing 12 U.S.C. § 24(7) and 12 CFR § 7.4002).

96. § 4-402(b).

97. *See* § 4-402, Comments 1 and 3.

98. *See* revised § 4-402, Comment 2. Thus negligence or contract damages should measure liability where wrongful dishonor is not involved. *See, e.g.,* Wright v. Commercial & Savings Bank, 297 Md. 148, 464 A.2d 1080 (Md.1983) (breach of contract); and Johnson v. Grant Square Bank, 634 P.2d 1324 (Okla.App. 1981), criticized in Note, Banks and Banking: Wrongful Dishonor Under the UCC—Does It Apply In The Case Of A Rightful Dishonor With A Wrongful Notice?, 35 OKLA. L. REV. 590. Notice also that the holder of the item has no action for any dishonor because a drawee is not liable on the instrument until the drawee accepts it. *See* § 3-408; Chapter 4; and *supra* Chapter 4 ¶ 4.04.

[b] Limitations on Bank Liability for Wrongful Dishonor

Old § 4–402 contained language limiting a bank's liability to actual damages when the wrongful dishonor occurred through mistake. As noted in Comment 1 to revised § 4–402, this "implied that the bank was liable for some other form of damages other than those proximately caused by the dishonor if the dishonor was other than by mistake." By adopting a very narrow definition of mistake (sometimes effectively limiting it to cases where there was a clerical error), some courts routinely held banks liable for wrongful dishonor without regard to actual damages. In effect this resurrected the "trader rule," despite the intended rejection of that rule by the drafters of Article 4.[99] As discussed in revised § 4–402 Comment 1, the 1990 revisions to § 4–402 eliminated the reference to mistake, thereby making clear that the only remedy for wrongful dishonor is actual damages, regardless of the reason for the dishonor. This revision rejects the cases that narrowly limited the concept of mistake and thereby allowed recovery of punitive damages where anything more than a clerical error was involved.

For example, in *Yacht Club Sales & Service, Inc. v. First National Bank of North Idaho*,[100] the bank put a hold on the account of the plaintiff after receiving a writ of garnishment against another corporation with a similar name. This caused the wrongful dishonor of several of the plaintiff's checks. The plaintiff operated its yacht club on land owned by the other corporation, the names were similar, and bank officials apparently thought that the two corporations were the same. In the court's view this was not a mere mistake so as to limit the bank's liability to actual damages. Rather, the court emphasized that the bank intentionally took action to put a hold on the account and dishonor the checks. Indeed, the court thought this action was enough to permit recovery of punitive damages.[101] This result went clearly beyond the

---

99. *See* revised § 4–402, Comment 1.

100. 29 U.C.C. Rep. Serv. 1340 (Idaho 1979), *on reh.*, 101 Idaho 852, 623 P.2d 464 (Idaho 1980). *Cf.* Elizarraras v. Bank of El Paso, 631 F.2d 366 (5th Cir.1980) (mistake of law may constitute mistaken dishonor, since the standard is the bank's good faith). *But see infra* this text and notes. In contrast where an item is paid on a forged indorsement the true owner may have an action against collecting banks that handled the item, for conversion. *See, e.g.*, § 3–420; in Bursey v. CFX Bank, 145 N.H. 126, 756 A.2d 1001 (N.H. 2000), a former husband deposited checks payable to him and his former wife, obtained by improper withdrawals from their joint account. He also deposited jointly payable insurance checks issued in payment for damage to a jointly owned vacation home. In both cases the checks were payable to the former husband *and* former wife, and were deposited by the former husband without the required indorsement of his co-payee (the ex-spouse).

The checks were not properly payable due to lack of the required indorsement, and the depositary bank avoided liability for conversion under old § 3–419 (revised § 3–420) as to the first check only because it was dishonored by the drawee and therefore the depositary bank received no proceeds to convert. Note that under revised § 4–320(d) this is no longer a defense for a depositary bank. *See* Lawyer's Fund for Client Protection v. Gateway State Bank, 709 N.Y.S.2d 243 (N.Y.App.Div.2000) (forged indorsement). *See also* Cooper v. Union Bank, 9 Cal.3d 371, 107 Cal.Rptr. 1, 507 P.2d 609 (Cal. 1973), discussed *supra* Chapter 7 at ¶ 7.03(3)(b)(ii).

101. A similar case is Morse v. Mutual Fed. Sav. & Loan Ass'n, 536 F.Supp. 1271 (D.Mass.1982). The *Morse* case also raises the question of whether consequential damages can include mental distress. Recovery was allowed. *See also* Shaw v. Union Bank & Trust, 640 P.2d 953 (Okla.1981), and

recognized constraints of the applicable law. As noted, revised § 4–402 clearly rejects this approach and the *Yacht Club* rationale.

A second limitation on liability limits the class of parties who can recover. Section 4–402 limits a bank's liability for wrongful dishonor only to its customer. "Customer" is defined at § 4–104(a)(5) as "any person having an account with a bank or for whom a bank has agreed to collect items and includes a bank carrying an account with another bank."[102] Therefore, the only person entitled to sue a bank for wrongful dishonor under § 4–402 is the person who has a deposit or other contract with the payor bank.[103]

Note also that wrongful dishonor may flow from an earlier wrongful payment, if the earlier payment reduced the account balance so as to cause subsequent items to be dishonored for insufficient funds. For example, in *In re Brandywine Associates*,[104] the bank was held liable for the funds that it wrongfully paid from the account, and again for the resultant dishonor of subsequent items. Revised Article 4 adopts this rule.[105] Wrongful dishonor may also result from a wrongful setoff, if that setoff depletes the account.[106]

Buckley v. Trenton Savings Fund Soc., 111 N.J. 355, 544 A.2d 857 (N.J. 1988). For a case that properly limits consequentials to those that are foreseeable, *see* Larstone Corrugated Carton Co. v. First Seneca Bank & Trust Co., 39 UCC Rep.Serv. 1397 (Pa. Com.Pl.1984). Query whether § 4–402 displaces this concept as it would apply under principles of contract law, to the extent Article 4 authorizes proximately caused consequentials. It would seem not, as § 4–402 appears to incorporate the law of damages except as that law is expressly limited. *See also* UCC § 1–103. The Code also nowhere specifically authorizes punitive damages for wrongful dishonor. The only possibility, then, for punitives is to bring in state law under UCC § 1–103, to the extent not displaced by § 4–402. *See* UCC § 1–106(1). Because § 4–402 does not adopt a theory of liability (tort or contract), and covers the entire range of mistaken and deliberate dishonor cases, a strong argument exists that § 4–402 displaces any ground for punitive damages. But there is also an argument that, if a basis exists outside the Code, § 4–402 does not bar punitive damages. *See* Shaw v. Union Bank & Trust Co., 640 P.2d 953 (Okla.1981), and Twin City Bank v. Isaacs, 283 Ark. 127, 672 S.W.2d 651 (1984).

102. In revised § 4–104(a)(5) the term "carrying" was changed to "maintaining." *See also supra* ¶ 8.01[3][g].

103. *See, e.g.,* Koger v. East First Nat'l Bank, 443 So.2d 141 (Fla.App.1983). *See also,* Green Property Corp. v. O'Callaghan, Saunders & Stumm, 177 Ga.App. 686, 340 S.E.2d 652 (Ga.App.1986) (bank was not liable to payee of wrongfully dishonored check for loss of interest or other damages); § 4–402, Comment 5, citing First American National Bank v. Commerce Union Bank, 692 S.W.2d 642 (Tenn.App.1985).

104. Hooper v. Bank of New Jersey v. Hooper 30 UCC Rep. Serv. (Callaghan) 1369 (Bankr.E.D.Pa.1980).

105. *See* revised § 4–403(c). It does not address, however, the case where a refusal under Article 4A results in wrongful dishonor. Comment 2 to revised § 4–402.

106. *See, e.g., infra* ¶ 9.06; Smith v. Citizens State Bank of Hugo, 732 P.2d 911 (Okla.App. 1986) (bank's "wanton, oppressive, and deceptive" wrongdoing in making setoff against customer's account meant that subsequent dishonor of items drawn on that account constituted wrongful dishonor). *See also* Morse v. Mutual Fed. Sav. & Loan Ass'n, 536 F.Supp. 1271 (D. Mass. 1982 (discussed *supra* at note 101); and Hansman v. Imlay City State Bank, 121 Mich.App. 424, 328 N.W.2d 653 (1982), discussing a virtual laundry list of possible errors committed by the bank in making a setoff that led to the alleged subsequent wrongful dishonor. Among other things, in *Hansman* the deposit may have been a special (rather than general) deposit, therefore not subject to set-off; the checks may have been dishonored prior to the setoff (while the account still contained sufficient funds); the funds may have belonged in part to the debtor's spouse (who did not owe the debt to the bank); and the debt may have been setoff before it was due. Any of these things

[3] Wrongful Payment—Bank Liability and the Right to Subrogation

Suppose a bank pays an item that it should not have paid; for example, it pays despite a valid stop payment order, or an item that is improperly drawn, indorsed, or presented, or has been altered within the meaning of § 3–407. Regardless of the reason, if the bank pays an item that is not properly payable, the bank has no authority to charge that item to the drawer's account.[107] This is the initial principle in determining liability for wrongful payment. Moreover, § 4–303(b) reinforces the initial principle by permitting payment of checks "in any order" convenient to the bank (*see also* old § 4–303(2) as similar), subject to the provisions of § 4–303(a) governing death of the drawer, stop-payment

---

would make the setoff (and any resultant dishonor) wrongful. *See also* Twin City Bank v. Isaacs, 283 Ark. 127, 672 S.W.2d 651 (Ark. 1984) (actual and punitive damages due to bank's refusal to recredit account); Larstone Corrugated Carton Co. v. First Seneca Bank & Trust Co., 39 UCC Rep. Serv. (Callaghan) 1397 (Pa.Com.Pl. 1984) (setoff of funds in special account as basis for consequential damages, including lost profits and damages to reputation beyond actual damages proved). *See generally* Alvin C. Harrell, Security Interests in Deposit Accounts: A Unique Relationship Between the UCC and Other Law, 23 U.C.C. L.J. 153, 155–165 (1990).

107. *See* § 4–401(a). The original amount of an altered item or a completed item can be charged as noted *infra. See* § 3–407; § 4–401(d)(1). Alteration is discussed *supra* in Chapter 6. Stop payment orders are discussed *supra* at ¶ 9.01[4][a]. If the item was paid over a valid stop payment order, and that payment depletes the account resulting in wrongful dishonor of other items, the bank will be liable for wrongful dishonor under § 4–402. *See* §§ 4–402 and 4–403(c), and discussion *supra* ¶ 9.02[2]. In addition, § 4–401(c) provides similar rules for wrongful payment of a post-dated check. *See supra* ¶ 9.01 [2].

If the instrument was paid on a forged indorsement, the true owner may have an action against one or more banks for conversion. *See* § 3–420; Cooper v. Union Bank, 9 Cal.3d 371, 107 Cal.Rptr. 1, 507 P.2d 609 (Cal. 1973); and discussion *supra* Chapter 7 at ¶ 7.03[3]. If breached, the presentment warranties allow the payor bank to return an item after the midnight deadline; this may allow the payor bank to recover from the presenting party if the item was not properly payable. The midnight deadline is discussed *supra* at ¶ 8.02. On the Article 4 warranties, *see supra* ¶ 7.02.

The result of applying § 3–309 in *Crystaplex* was that the drawer was liable to the joint payee whose indorsement was missing when the check was paid. Generally, the obligation to assure an item is properly indorsed is on the first party to take the item (*e.g.*, the depositary bank), not the drawer, and a drawer is not obligated to pay an unindorsed instrument (*see* § 3–501(b)(2), (3)). Even if one views the *Crystaplex* decision as some sort of rough justice, the court had to stretch the scope of § 3–309 to get there. Section 3–420 and a conversion action against the depositary bank (if the aggrieved payee was deemed to have received the check), or an action against the drawer on the underlying obligation (if the payee was deemed not to have received the check), would be more appropriate. On the latter point, *see* § 3–310.

The result of making the drawer liable to the aggrieved joint payee in these circumstances, either under § 3–309 or on the underlying obligation, is that the drawer can proceed to recover from the payor bank (if the item was paid by the payor bank and charged to the drawer's account) on grounds the item was not properly payable. The payor can then recover from the depositary bank for breach of warranty, thus creating a circuitous route of remedies that will impose ultimate liability on the depositary bank that took the check without a required indorsement. In appropriate cases, § 3–420 permits this net result by direct action by the aggrieved payee against the depositary bank, resulting in increased judicial efficiency. But note that § 4–407 may allow the payor bank to assert the rights of the payee as against the drawer, thus allowing the payor bank to assert § 3–309 and the *Crystaplex* rationale as a defense to an allegation by the drawer that the item was not properly payable. This would effectively require the drawer to proceed directly against the depositary bank under § 3–420, which is the correct result anyway.

orders, receipt of legal process, setoff, and so on.[108] In effect, the right to charge the customer's account depends on compliance with the rules on proper payment and terminates if such rules are violated.

Another Article 4 provision qualifies the issue. Section 4–401(d) provides that: "A bank that in good faith makes payment to a holder may charge the indicated account of its customer according to: (1) the original terms of his altered item; or (b) the terms of the completed item ... unless the bank has notice that the completion was improper."[109] This section thus operates as a limitation on the initial principle that a bank may not charge its customer's account unless the item is properly payable.

If the payment asserted to be wrongful occurs other than because of an overlooked stop payment order, the same § 4–407 analysis as in the stop payment cases should be employed. For example, in *Cooper v. Stock Yards Bank of Oklahoma City*,[110] a bank customer sued his bank for wrongfully paying $33,151.37 worth of corporate checks. The checks were drawn and signed by a bookkeeper who allegedly did not have proper authority to do so. Although the decision was based partially on estoppel (resulting from the customer's failure to review his bank statements or to protest the checks), the fact that the unauthorized checks were used to pay bona fide debts of the customer also was a factor in the court's decision. The court's reasons for denying the customer recovery for wrongful payment included: "First, Customer failed to prove he was damaged; conversely, Bank proved all disputed checks were paid to legitimate creditors."[111] This is consistent with the view that no

---

108. *See also* UCC §§ 4A–502 and 4A–504 for comparable rules under Article 4A.

109. § 4–401(d), old § 4–401(2) is similar. Comment 4 to § 4–401 recognizes this as an equivalent of the § 3–407 provision protecting a holder in due course against the defenses of material alteration or unauthorized completion of an instrument. "It adopts the rule of cases extending the same protection to a drawee who pays in good faith." Section 3–407 is discussed *supra* in Chapter 6.

110. 644 P.2d 123 (Okla. App. 1981).

111. *Id*. A similar case involving a funds transfer is Gatoil (U.S.A.), Inc. v. Forest Hill State Bank, 1 UCC Rep. Serv. (Callaghan) 2d 171 (D. Md. 1986).

A party who issues an instrument to an imposter or fictitious payee may be precluded from asserting the forged indorsement that results, as against a party who takes or pays the instrument in good faith, under § 3–404. The theory is that the issuer has created the problem and should not be allowed to shift the loss to an innocent party; but if the latter failed to exercise ordinary care there may be an apportionment of the loss based on contributory negligence.

A typical example is Sebastian v. D & S Express, Inc., 61 F.Supp. 2d 386 (D.N.J. 1999), where corporate employees (including the President) had issued 87 corporate checks payable to fictitious payees over a seven year period, and cashed them at a local bank after indorsing them in the names of the fictitious payees. The checks were purportedly for maintenance work, which was not performed. When the fraud was discovered, the corporation sued the bank that had cashed the checks. The bank defended that the indorsements were valid under the fictitious payee rule at § 3–404(b), and the corporation countered with a comparative negligence claim on grounds the bank failed to exercise ordinary care under § 3–404(d).

The court held that the corporation's § 3–404(d) comparative negligence claim was barred by the statute of limitations at § 3–118(g) because § 3–404(d) seeks enforcement of a duty; the claims more than three years old were barred. The corporation's claims for conversion under § 3–420 were also dismissed, on grounds that § 3–420(a) bars such an action by the issuer. The corporation's common law negligence claims were barred as superseded by

recredit should be maintainable without proof of loss. It also is consistent with the § 4–407 subrogation theory; the bank was subrogated to the position of the parties it paid and was able to use the rights of these parties as a defense to the drawer's claim. Indeed, § 4–407 is essentially a codification of general principles of common law and equity. Certainly the answers should be the same whether the wrongful payment is due to a stop order or some other reason. In effect the cases involving stop-payment orders suggest the proper reading of § 4–407 in the non-stop payment cases.

[4] Postdated Checks

Under old Article 4, a check was not properly payable until the date on the face of the check. Under old § 3–114, and under revised § 3–113(a), a postdated check can be a negotiable instrument, but it generally will not be considered payable until the stated date. As a result, such an item was not considered properly payable under old § 4–401(1) until the date stated on the face of the instrument. Under old Article 4, a payor bank that paid such an item before the stated date probably made a wrongful payment and could be required to reimburse the drawer's account, subject to the bank's right of subrogation to the position of the party it paid (discussed immediately above).[112]

This rule was troublesome for banks in an age when the volume of checks requires automated processing, because the processing equipment commonly in use does not provide for automated review of the date of the check. Recognizing that the old rule created an impediment to automated processing, the 1990 revisions include a new § 4–401(c) that addresses the issue.

Revised § 4–401(c) requires an order similar to a stop payment order as a prerequisite to an enforceable postdating of a check. Under the revision, if a customer wishes the payor bank to recognize the postdated feature of a check, the customer must notify that bank using a procedure similar to that for stopping payment. In turn, the payor bank can properly charge the customer's account for a postdated check, prior to its date, "unless the customer has given notice to the bank of the postdating describing the check with reasonable certainty."[113]

The required notice is effective for the same duration as a stop payment order (under § 4–403(b)), and like a stop payment order it must be received "at such time and in such manner as to afford the bank a reasonable opportunity to act on it...."[114] A bank paying over such a

---

§ 3–404. Thus, the effect of §§ 3–118 and 3–404(b) was to prevent the corporation from shifting its loss (caused by its own president and employees) to the bank, subject to comparative negligence claims asserted within three years under § 3–404(d).

112. See § 4–407; and Siegel v. New England Merchants National Bank, 386 Mass. 672, 437 N.E.2d 218 (Mass. 1982) (postdated item not properly payable until item date); cf. Allied Color Corp. v. Manufacturers Hanover Trust Co., 484 F.Supp. 881 (S.D.N.Y.1980) (bank held accountable for item presented prior to its date). See also discussion supra ¶ 9.01[1], [2], and ¶ 9.02[3].

113. Revised § 4–401(c). See also supra ¶ 9.01[2].

114. Id. See also supra ¶ 9.01[2], [4].

notice is liable for actual damages, including damages for wrongful dishonor of subsequent items under § 4–402.[115] Cases involving wrongful payment over a valid stop payment order should be relevant in establishing standards of reasonableness for the notice required under § 4–401(c), although such cases will not necessarily be relevant in terms of the appropriate damages for wrongful payment.[116]

¶ 9.03 Rights and Obligations of Bank Customers

[1] The Bank–Customer Relationship

For purposes of Article 4, the bank-customer relationship normally is initiated when the customer and the bank enter into a deposit contract. This is typically incorporated into the signature card the bank requires the customer to sign, but it is possible that the arrangement could be less formal. Article 4 defines "customer" as "a person having an account with a bank or for whom a bank has agreed to collect items, including a bank that maintains an account at another bank."[117] This very general description potentially could include a variety of informal arrangements, including an oral agreement to honor or collect drafts. For example, in *Columbian Peanut Co. v. Frosteg*,[118] the bank orally had

---

115. *Id. See supra* ¶ 9.02 [2]. Note that while a bank has a right of subrogation under § 4–407 in the circumstances, it may be of little use in the circumstances; for example, it will be irrelevant that the payment discharged a lawful debt if damages were caused by a *premature* payment that resulted in wrongful dishonor of other items. On the other hand, aside from this wrongful dishonor issue, premature payment seems unlikely to cause significant loss.

116. *Id. See* discussion of stop payment orders, *supra* ¶ 9.01[4], and discussion of wrongful payment, *supra* ¶ 9.02[3]. As noted, a major difference is that improper payment of a postdated check may result in premature payment of a lawful debt, depleting the account and resulting in wrongful dishonor of other items. In these circumstances, unlike the stop payment order cases, the bank's subrogation to the position of the drawer's creditor may not be very helpful, since it was not the payment itself but the timing of that payment that caused damages to the drawer.

¶ 9.03

117. § 4–104(a)(5). The 1990 revisions changed "any person" to "a person" and "carrying an account" to "maintains an account." *See also supra* ¶ 8.01[3][g]. The term "customer" may, however, be defined differently for different purposes. *Cf., e.g.,* the Article 4 definition at § 4–104 with the federal law definition for purposes of the Gramm–Leach–Bliley Act, Pub.L. 106–102, 113 Stat. 1338 (1999), *e.g.,* the Federal Trade Commission definition at 16 CFR § 313.3(h).

As noted *supra* at ¶ 8.01[3][b], "bank" is defined broadly at § 4–105(1) to include "any person engaged in the business of banking, including a savings bank, savings and loan association, credit union or trust company." Revised § 4–104(a)(1) defines also "account" broadly to include "any deposit or credit account with a bank [including] a demand, time, savings, passbook, share draft, or like account, other than an account evidenced by a certificate of deposit." *See generally* Schoenfelder v. Arizona Bank, 165 Ariz. 79, 796 P.2d 881 (Ariz. 1990).

The signature card, account agreement, related customer corporate resolutions, and monthly account statements all form parts of the contract between the payor bank and its customer, and should be reviewed periodically by both parties to assure consistency and that these documents reflect the intended agreement. For example, in Reliance Ins. Co. v. Bank of America Nat'l. Trust & Sav. Ass'n., 43 U.C.C. Rep. Serv.2d 946 (N.D.Ill.2001), the account agreement, customer's corporate resolutions, and monthly statements established 30 days as a reasonable time period for customer examination of the monthly account statements. The parties were bound by this agreement.

118. 472 F.2d 476 (5th Cir.1973), discussed at Bell, The Payor Bank and Its Customer: An Analysis of Recent Cases, 6

agreed to honor certain drafts drawn by Columbian. Columbian did not maintain any funds on deposit and did not have any kind of an account in the normal sense. The court found that the oral arrangements were sufficient to constitute an account within the meaning of Article 4, making Columbian a customer of the bank.

Nonetheless, the definition has certain limits. For example, there must be some contractual nexus between the bank and the customer. And where a particular organization has such a nexus (as where a corporation or partnership has an account),[119] it is only that entity that has the rights of a customer. The individual partners or corporate officers, directors, or shareholders have no rights as customers except as may be derived from the partnership or corporation.[120]

Although the bank-customer relationship is initiated by agreement, it is not necessarily an exclusively contractual relationship.[121] In addition to contract, it may encompass duties that give rise to tort liability for negligence, as well as attributes of a common law relationship based on the status of the parties.[122] Indeed, as noted *infra* at ¶ 9.03 [2], there is even a possibility that the bank's responsibilities may rise to the level of a fiduciary duty in certain circumstances.

[2] Does the Bank Have a Fiduciary or Other Special Duty?

[a] Non-Code Consequences

Traditionally, the bank-customer relationship has been considered that of debtor and creditor, founded on the provisions of the deposit contract (and the rules of Article 4).[123] A debtor-creditor relationship is

---

U. TOL. L. REV. 110, 112–13 (1974). *See also* text and notes *supra* at ¶ 8.01[3][g]. *See also* Parrett v. Platte Valley State Bank & Trust Co., 236 Neb. 139, 459 N.W.2d 371 (Neb. 1990) (corporation president characterized as a bank customer).

119. UCC §§ 1–201(28) and (30) include a partnership as an entity, and indeed, include any legal or commercial entity within the definition of "organization."

120. *See*, however, *supra* note 148 and ¶ 9.02[2][b]. In recent years there have been cases which deal with situations where the organization is merely the alter ego of the primary shareholder. *See, e.g.*, Schoenfelder v. Arizona Bank, 165 Ariz. 79, 796 P.2d 881 (Ariz. 1990); Murdaugh Volkswagen v. First Nat'l Bank of S.C., 801 F.2d 719 (4th Cir. 1986). Other than this, cases like Loucks v. Albuquerque Nat'l Bank, 76 N.M. 735, 418 P.2d 191 (N.M. 1966) (discussed *supra* at ¶ 9.02[2][b]) represent the correct view. *See also supra* ¶ 8.01[3][g], and cases cited in *Schoenfelder*, 796 P.2d at 885.

121. Symons, Jr., The Bank-Customer Relation: Part I, The Relevance of Contract Doctrine, 100 BANKING L.J. 220 (1983). *See also infra* ¶ 9.03[2]. *See, e.g.*, the new privacy rules in the Gramm–Leach–Bliley Act, Pub. L. 106–102, 113 Stat. 1338 (1999), codified in various places by the different banking regulators. The Federal Trade Commission rules are at 16 CFR Pt.313. *See generally*, Symposium on Privacy, 55 CONSUMER FIN. L.Q. REP. 4 (2001).

122. *See, e.g.*, Djowharzedeh v. City Nat'l Bank & Trust Co., 646 P.2d 616 (Okla. Ct. App.1982); Utah v. Thompson, 810 P.2d 415 (Utah 1991) (customers' expectations of privacy); Beshara v. Southern Nat. Bank, 928 P.2d 280 (Okla.1996) (tort liability); *infra* ¶ 9.03[2], and Shaw v. Union Bank & Trust Co., 640 P.2d 953 (Okla. 1981), discussed *supra* this text at note 101. *See also supra* ¶ 9.02[2][b].

123. *See, e.g.*, Brown v. Eastman Nat'l Bank of Newkirk, 291 P.2d 828 (Okla. 1955); Rodgers v. Tecumseh Bank, 756 P.2d 1223 (Okla.1988) (no special obligation of "good faith" in arms-length commercial lending agreement); *supra* Chapter 8 at note 215; *infra* notes 125 and 128–132.

essentially contractual in nature, and by itself does not give rise to any special good faith or fiduciary obligations, save those ordinary obligations to perform in good faith that are a part of every contract.[124] However, there are other aspects of the debtor-creditor relationship that may give rise to fiduciary responsibilities in special circumstances.[125] For example, in *Klein v. First Edina National Bank*,[126] the customer's reliance on the bank's conduct (and the bank's knowledge of that reliance) in connection with a loan to a third party for which the customer pledged stock was held to create an affirmative duty to disclose any material facts that might have a bearing on the transaction. The court found that if the

---

124. *See, e.g.*, Smith, Allis–Chalmers v. Lueck: The United States Supreme Court Rejects Tort Liability for Breach of Good Faith, 43 CONSUMER FIN. L. Q. REP. 258 (1989). *See also supra* note 122, and Copesky v. Superior Court of San Diego County, 229 Cal.App.3d 678, 280 Cal.Rptr. 338 (Cal. App.1991). But a bank remains subject to a duty of good faith in the performance of its contract. *See* Arrow Industries, Inc. v. Zions First National Bank, 767 P.2d 935, 937 (Utah 1988). *See also* the new definition of good faith at § 3–103(a)(4), incorporated into Article 4 at § 4–104(c). However, a bank generally will not have an obligation to advise another bank that a mutual customer may be engaged in check "kiting." *See* Frost Nat'l. Bank v. Midwest Autohaus, Inc., 241 F.3d 862 (7th Cir.2001); Alta Vista State Bank v. Kobliska, 897 F.2d 930 (8th Cir.1990). *But compare infra* ¶ 9.05[3][c][vi] (The Bank Secrecy Act). As noted, this analysis may be affected by the new good faith standard at § 3–104(a)(4). *See, e.g., supra* Chapter 8 at notes 215 and 227.

The higher standard of good faith (including observance of reasonable commercial standards of fair dealing), included at § 3–103(a)(4) as part of the 1990 revisions to the uniform text of Article 3, has begun to be a factor in the case law. Two recent cases illustrate the importance of this in diverse scenarios.

San Tan Irrigation Dist. v. Wells Fargo Bank, 197 Ariz. 193, 3 P.3d 1113 (Ariz.Ct. App. 2000) involved a check that had been deposited with an indorsement forged by one of the plaintiff's employees. When sued for conversion under § 3–420, the depositary bank sought to claim a preclusion against the plaintiff for negligence contributing to the loss, because of the failure of the plaintiff to adequately supervise its employee, under §§ 3–405 and 3–406. But this preclusion is available only if the depositary bank acted in good faith. *See* § 3–405(b), § 3–406(a). In *San Tan*, the plaintiff argued that the bank was careless and therefore did not meet the new standard of good faith at § 3–103(a)(4), and this was sufficient for summary judgement to be awarded against the bank; on appeal this was reversed, the court properly noting that the plaintiff's claim that the bank was careless in taking the items was relevant only to the duty of care, a very different thing from good faith. The case was remanded for a trial on the issue of the bank's good faith, a better though hardly attractive result for the bank.

In Maine Family Federal Credit Union v. Sun Life Assurance Co., 727 A.2d 335 (Me. S.Ct.1999), the court held that the credit union (a "bank" under § 4–105) was not a holder in due course when it took an item for deposit because it did not meet the new standard of good faith at § 3–103(a)(4). The court concluded that the credit union met the former standard of "honesty in fact," and noted that under this traditional standard of good faith depositary banks have routinely qualified as holders in due course of deposited items. But the new standard also requires observance of reasonable commercial standards of fair dealing; illustrating the dangers of this concept, the *Maine Family Credit Union* court allowed the jury to conclude that it was not reasonable for the credit union to allow immediate credit to its depositor for three $40,759.35 checks drawn on a major out-of-state insurance company. The jury concluded it would have been better for the credit union to place a "hold" on the funds in these circumstances, and therefore the credit union failed the good faith test at § 3–103(a)(4) and was not a holder in due course.

125. *See, e.g.*, Peter G. Pierce, III and Alvin C. Harrell, Financiers as Fiduciaries: An Examination of Recent Trends in Lender Liability, 42 OKLA. L. REV. 79 (1989). *See also* Kitchen Krafters v. Eastside Bank, 242 Mont. 155, 789 P.2d 567 (Mont. 1990) (bank acting as escrow agent owed fiduciary duty).

126. 293 Minn. 418, 196 N.W.2d 619 (Minn. 1972). *See also* Spitzmueller v. Burlington Northern R.R. Co., 740 F.Supp. 671 (D.Minn.1990).

bank had disclosed what the loan proceeds were to be used for, the customer might not have entered into the transaction. In another case, a bank that had knowledge that its customer was borrowing money to buy goods from a seller who was in a precarious financial position and who could not deliver the goods was found to have a duty to disclose this before making the loan which would further the fraud being perpetrated by the seller. If the bank is unable to make such a disclosure, the court concluded that the bank should decline to make the loan.[127] Such a duty may exist even in cases where the bank has no more than a prospective debtor-creditor relationship with the other party.[128]

On the other hand, in *Palmer v. Idaho Bank & Trust of Kooskia*[129] a customer claimed that the bank breached its fiduciary duty by failing to disclose that deposits to his account could be subject to an IRS levy without a court judgment. The Idaho Supreme Court upheld summary judgment for the bank on grounds there was no duty on the part of the bank to disclose this information. The customer had received four notices from the IRS indicating that his accounts were subject to levy.

From these cases it seems clear that although a bank generally does not have a fiduciary duty per se as a result of the deposit contract, and while the bank-customer relation remains one of debtor-creditor governed by the deposit contract, because of actions that induce or special knowledge of detrimental reliance on the part of the customer a bank may assume a special status that goes beyond the relationship of mere debtor-creditor. The courts have not always been clear in seeking to articulate exactly what in the way of additional circumstances is necessary in order to convert a contractual relationship into a fiduciary-like duty on the part of the bank. But it is clear that such relationships remain exceptional.

This is vividly illustrated by a non-famous Oklahoma case, *Djowharzadeh v. City National Bank & Trust Co. of Norman*.[130] The bank customer came to the bank requesting a loan to purchase a "bargain priced duplex."[131] As part of the loan application the customer made full disclosure to the bank loan officer of the details of the proposed purchase, as required by the bank. The loan was rejected by the bank and shortly thereafter the duplex was purchased by the wives of the bank's

---

127. Richfield Bank & Trust Co. v. Sjogren, 309 Minn. 362, 244 N.W.2d 648 (Minn. 1976).

128. *See, e.g.*, Dolton v. Capitol Fed. Sav. & Loan Ass'n, 642 P.2d 21 (Colo.App. 1981), involving a loan applicant whose offer to purchase property was not yet accepted; the prospective lender used the information disclosed by the applicant to make a better offer and secure the property for itself. *See also* Djowharzadeh v. City National Bank and Trust, 646 P.2d 616 (Okla. App. 1982), discussed *infra* this text; Pigg v. Robertson, 549 S.W.2d 597 (Mo.Ct.App. 1977); Alvin C. Harrell, The Bank–Customer Relationship: Evolution of a Modern Form?, 11 Okla. City U. L. Rev. 641 (1986), and other commentaries cited *supra* at note 122. These risks are increased somewhat under the new standard of good faith at § 3–103(a)(4), and the new privacy rules. *See generally*, Symposium on Privacy, 55 Consumer Fin. L. Q. Rep. 4 (2001).

129. 100 Idaho 642, 603 P.2d 597 (Idaho 1979).

130. 646 P.2d 616 (Okla. App. 1982). *See also* Jordan v. Shattuck Nat'l Bank, 868 F.2d 383 (10th Cir.1989) and *supra* note 128.

131. *Id.*

president and senior vice-president. It was apparent that bank officials had used the confidential information garnered from the bank customer during the application process to their personal advantage. The Oklahoma Court of Appeals agreed with the customer that such conduct was outrageous, unthinkable, and contrary to common sense and public understanding. In elaborating, however, the court seemed inclined to find in the bank-customer relationship a special status that resulted in some vaguely articulated new duties for the bank. Consider some of the court's language: "Implicit in this policy of fair dealing and even handedness is a requirement that banks not use their favored position to the detriment of their customers, either directly or indirectly...."[132] Absent the special factors that give rise to fiduciary duties in any context, there does not seem to be any statutory or case law basis for such broad, overarching language, although the new definition of good faith at § 3–103(a)(4) may provide some unexpected support for such a view. But *Djowharzadeh* has not been widely followed, in Oklahoma or elsewhere, and probably can be regarded as aberrational or as merely an overstatement of the law. Nonetheless, on its facts it appears correctly decided, and therefore *Djowharzadeh* illustrates the dangers of overreaching in a bank-customer context.

[b] Code Consequences

Those decisions holding that more than a debtor-creditor relationship may exist between a bank and its customer have potential relevance for matters governed by Article 4. Obviously, a non-Code rule invoked through UCC § 1–103 may produce a result that would not be obtained if the Article 4 rules alone were considered. As discussed *supra* at ¶ 9.02, some Article 4 rules (such as § 4–402 governing wrongful dishonor) in conjunction with § 1–106 may displace non-Code rights and remedies. This is also specifically recognized at § 1–103, with the result (noted *supra* at ¶ 9.02) that punitive damages may not be available for wrongful dishonor. But not all Article 4 rules displace other law and some rules outside Article 4 may have an effect on the rights and obligations

---

132. *Id.* at 618–19. *See also supra* notes 123–128, and *infra* ¶ 9.03[4][c]. *See generally* Lawrence A. Young, The Landscape of Privacy, 55 CONSUMER FIN. L.Q. REP. 4 (2001) (noting *Djowharzadeh* and some like cases). It is interesting to note that the *Djowharzadeh* court's language resembles somewhat the language of the new definition of "good faith" in Article 3, which requires "observance of reasonable commercial standards of fair dealing." *See* § 3–103(a)(4). This definition is imputed into Article 4. *See* § 4–104(c), and discussion *supra* Chapter 8 at ¶ 8.04[4]. As noted there, this raises fundamental questions regarding the relative scope of § 1–203 and § 3–103(a)(4), and the Regulation CC good faith provisions at 12 CFR § 229.38(a). *See also infra* ¶ 9.03[2][b] and [c].

In recent years courts generally have declined to recognize a breach of the duty of good faith as an independent cause of action separate from a breach of contract. Illustrative cases include Rodgers v. Tecumseh Bank, 756 P.2d 1223 (Okla.1988); and Frontier Fed. Sav. & Loan Ass'n v. Commercial Bank, N.A., 806 P.2d 1140 (Okla. Ct. App. 1990); *see also* Smith, Allis–Chalmers v. Lueck: The United States Supreme Court Rejects Tort Liability for Breach of Good Faith, 43 CONSUMER FIN. L.Q. REP. 258 (1989). *But see* Beshara v. Southern Nat. Bank, 928 P.2d 280 (Okla.1996) (breach of contract may also give rise to tort action for breach of implied covenant of good faith and fair dealing).

provided in Article 4. For example, in some instances under old Article 4 a bank could receive a stop order before it had paid a check but after the deadline provided by Article 4 and the case law in order for the stop order to be legally effective.[133] As a supplement to the rules governing stop payment orders, the bank is under an obligation of good faith.[134] Did this mean the bank could ignore the order and pay the check, even if it had the capability to honor the customer's order? Or could its customer argue some special duty to the customer from the language in cases like *Djowharzadeh* (which type of duty may now be more implicit in the new definition of good faith)? Or did the bank have a superior duty to the owner of the check who otherwise may be deprived of payment?

Fortunately, in this context the uncertainties are addressed by revised § 4–303(a)(5), permitting the bank to establish a specific "cutoff hour" for stop payment orders and like notices (within enumerated limits); this permits the bank to establish a clear-cut deadline. But since the deadline is for its own benefit, which it thus might waive, the basic issue regarding a bank's good faith and the existence of "fiduciary" duties potentially remains in some scenarios. Some of the cases have further clarified matters somewhat in this area of the law.[135]

One also might argue from these concepts that the customer's duties extend beyond the debtor and creditor relationship and require the customer to use particular care to help the bank protect against loss from the payment of improper items. To some extent this application of the concept (of an affirmative duty of the customer) is codified in Article 4 at § 4–406, as discussed at ¶ 9.03[4]. However, this may not be the exclusive source of a customer's obligations relating to the bank-customer relationship in the cases of errors and unauthorized indorsements not covered by § 4–406; like the bank, the customer remains subject to both statutory and common law duties that also may affect this relationship.[136]

---

133. See old §§ 4–213(1)(c) and (d), 4–303(1)(d); West Side Bank v. Marine Nat'l Exch. Bank, 37 Wis.2d 661, 155 N.W.2d 587 (Wis. 1968); revised §§ 4–403, 4–303; discussion *supra* at ¶¶ 9.01[4][a], [5], and [6].

134. UCC § 1–203. *See also* the new definition of good faith at § 3–103(a)(4).

135. *See, e.g.*, Copesky v. Superior Court of San Diego County, *supra* note 154, and Price v. Wells Fargo Bank, 213 Cal. App.3d 465, 261 Cal.Rptr. 735 (1st Dist. 1989) (holding a bank does not have a fiduciary duty and rejecting Commercial Cotton Co. v. United California Bank, 163 Cal. App.3d 511, 209 Cal.Rptr. 551 (1985), which recognized a fiduciary duty as a matter of law). *See also* Rodgers v. Tecumseh Bank, 756 P.2d 1223 (Okla.1988) (no special duty of good faith in arms-length commercial lending agreement); Frontier Fed. Sav. & Loan Ass'n v. Commercial Bank, N.A., 806 P.2d 1140 (Okla. Ct. App. 1990), *but see* Beshara v. Southern Nat. Bank, 928 P.2d 280 (Okla.1996) (breach of contract may also constitute tort for breach of implied covenant of good faith). *Beshara* is contrary to the trend of authority. *See generally* Smith, Allis–Chalmers v. Lueck: The United States Supreme Court Rejects Tort Liability for Breach of Good Faith, 43 CONSUMER FIN. L.Q. REP. 258 (1989). Note, however, that the new definition of "good faith" in Article 3 imposes a new good faith standard that includes reasonable commercial standards of fair dealing. *See* § 3–103(a)(4), and *supra* Chapter 3. This raises fundamental questions regarding the comparative scope and impact of the differing "good faith" standards at UCC § 1–203 and revised § 3–103(a)(4), not to mention the common law, case law trends noted above, and even the impact of Regulation CC "good faith," at 12 CFR § 229.38(a). *See supra* ¶ 8.04[4].

136. *See, e.g.*, UCC § 1–203 and §§ 3–103(a)(4), 4–104(c), 4–406 (all potentially implicating the duty of good faith),

[c] Regulation of Depositary Services Pricing

On the basis of "good faith" or some other judicially imputed special duty, a few courts have imposed judicial price controls on the fees charged by banks for various depositary services. Affected fees include not only the monthly service charge or per-item charges typically imposed by a bank for maintaining an account, but charges for NSF checks drawn by the customer and fees for charging back to the customer's account items deposited by the customer which subsequently "bounce" and are returned to the depositary unpaid.

Probably the best known case is *Perdue v. Crocker National Bank*.[137] This case is regarded by many as an aberration, and it has not been widely followed. However, at least one other California case[138] followed *Perdue*, and thereafter some legislative proposals and enactments suggested a renewed legislative interest in regulation of deposit account pricing.[139] In addition, there were federal proposals to mandate the availability of basic transaction account services at prescribed prices.[140] For example, it was proposed to require that banks offer a basic bank account to all persons with an annual income of less than $20,000 per year, with a minimum initial balance of $25, and no fees except a monthly maintenance fee which does not exceed the "real, direct, and demonstrable cost" of servicing the account plus a 10% profit.[141] At this writing, mandatory federal legislation on depositary pricing has not been enacted.

These issues are often characterized by an emphasis on "fairness" and economic considerations, rather than traditional legal theories. For example, in the *California Grocers Association*[142] case, the trial court held that a $3.00 charge for NSF checks deposited to the customer's account was too high, and cut it roughly in half. The basis for this decision was the somewhat arbitrary conclusion that the $3.00 charge constituted an unfair business practice, relying on the *Perdue* rationale.

and discussed *infra* at ¶ 9.03[4][c]); *see also* UCC § 4A–304 (customer's duties as sender of a payment order); Critten v. Chemical Nat'l Bank, 171 N.Y. 219, 63 N.E. 969 (N.Y. 1902) (common law duties of customer). *Further see* New York v. Bronx County Trust Co. 261 N.Y. 64, 184 N.E. 495 (1933); and Federal Ins. Co. v. Groveland State Bank, 37 N.Y.2d 252, 372 N.Y.S.2d 18, 333 N.E.2d 334 (1975).

137. 38 Cal. 3d 913, 216 Cal.Rptr. 345, 702 P.2d 503 (1985), *appeal dismissed for want of jurisdiction*, 475 U.S. 1001, 106 S.Ct. 1170, 89 L.Ed.2d 290 (1986). *See also* Lofts, The Perdue Case and Other Litigation Involving Bank Charges, 42 Consumer Fin. L. Q. Rep. 97 (1988). *See also* Best v. U.S. National Bank, 78 Or.App. 1, 714 P.2d 1049 (Ore.App. 1986), *review granted*, Best v. United States National Bank, 301 Or. 165, 719 P.2d 873 (1986), *affirmed*, Best v. United States Nat'l Bank, 303 Or. 557, 739 P.2d 554 (1987)

138. Rebney v. Wells Fargo Bank, N.A. v. Bank of America (joined by) California Grocers Association, 220 Cal.App.3d 1117, 269 Cal.Rptr. 844 (1st Dist.1990), *subsequent hist.*, 232 Cal.App.3d 1344, 284 Cal. Rptr. 113 (1st Dist.1991).

139. By late 1991, legislation to regulate deposit account pricing had been passed or introduced in Illinois, Massachusetts, New York, California, and New Jersey. *See generally* Grace Sterrett, Basic Banking: New York's Attempt to Democratize Banking Services, 49 Consumer Fin. L.Q. Rep. 13 (1995).

140. Senate Bill 543. Without these provisions, the bill became law as the Federal Deposit Insurance Corporation Improvement Act of 1991, P.L. 102–242 (1991).

141. *Id.*

142. *See supra* note 138.

The court concluded that it was justified in reviewing the economic basis for the contract, because of the court's view that there was no competition in the banking industry as regards checking account charges. The court also concluded that the $3.00 charge constituted a 73.4 percent markup above the bank's costs, and that this was unconscionable and violated the bank's duty of good faith and fair dealing.

Also, in 1991, two Tennessee class action lawsuits were filed against 17 financial institutions, alleging that the NSF and returned check charges being imposed by these institutions were unconscionable and constituted a credit transaction violating state usury laws.[143] All of these cases suggested that economic "fairness" would become an important issue in the 1990s with regard to depositary institution fees and transactions. However, the issue seems instead to have receded, with the focus of legislation and litigation shifting to other legal issues.

[3] Modification by Agreement

Generally the parties may modify the effect of the provisions of the UCC by agreement, subject to certain limitations contained in the UCC,[144] in federal law and regulations, in case law, and in public policy. Questions may therefore arise regarding the ability of a bank to insulate itself from potential liabilities resulting from the bank-customer relationship by a disclaimer or other provision in the deposit contract.

Some of the UCC limitations on bank-customer relations are contained at § 1–102. For example, "the obligations of good faith, diligence, reasonableness and care prescribed by this Act may not be disclaimed...."[145] Limitations also are imposed outside Article 4 by Federal Reserve System operating circulars and Regulations J and CC.[146] These duties are not "prescribed by this Act," and therefore are not covered by the provision at § 1–102(3) allowing variation by agreement, even if

---

143. See Wallace v. National Commerce Bancorp., No. 39746–3 T.D. (Cir. Ct. Tenn., 13th Judicial D. at Memphis, filed July 12, 1991); Wright v. Chattanooga TVA Employers Credit Union, No. 91 CV–1444 (Cir. Ct., Hamilton Co., Tenn., 11th Judicial D. at Chattanooga, filed July 16, 1991).

144. UCC § 1–102(3), and § 4–103(a). Article 4 "does not regulate the terms of the bank-customer agreement ..." Section § 4–101, Comment 2. See also supra ¶ 8.01[2], and Jamison v. First Georgia Bank, 193 Ga.App. 219, 387 S.E.2d 375 (Ga.App.1989) (contract between bank and customer to report discrepancies within sixty days controlled). See generally R. David Whitaker, Key Issues and Considerations in Drafting Deposit Agreements and Funds Transfer Services Agreements for Financial Institutions, 50 Consumer Fin. L. Q. Rep. 37 (1996).

The signature card, account agreement, related customer corporate resolutions, and monthly account statements all form parts of the contract between the payor bank and its customer, and should be reviewed periodically by both parties to assure consistency and that these documents reflect the intended agreement. For example, in Reliance Ins. Co. v. Bank of America Nat'l. Trust & Sav. Ass'n., 43 U.C.C. Rep. Serv.2d 946 (N.D.Ill.2001), the account agreement, customer's corporate resolutions, and monthly statements established 30 days as a reasonable time period for customer examination of the monthly account statements. The parties were bound by this agreement. See also Canfield v. Banc One, Texas, N.A., 51 S.W.3d 828 (Tex.App.2001).

145. UCC §§ 1–102(3), 4–103(a).

146. 12 CFR pt. 210, 12 CFR pt. 229. See generally, Sharon A. Sweeney and Jane Anne Schmoker, Federal Reserve Bank and the Payment System: Regulation J, Regulation CC, Operating Circulars, and Other Deposit Account Issues, 51 Consumer Fin. L. Q. Rep. 204 (1997).

state law could control federal rules. However, these rules may be governed by other "variation by agreement" provisions, such as that in Regulation CC at 12 CFR § 229.37, discussed *supra* at ¶ 8.04[4].

Complicating the picture is the fact that Article 4 contains its own variation-by-agreement provision at § 4–103(a). This provision is similar to § 1–102, but is more specific regarding disclaimer of bank duties:

> The effect of the provisions of this Article may be varied by agreement, but the parties to the agreement cannot disclaim a bank's responsibility for its lack of good faith or failure to exercise ordinary care or limit the measure of damages for the lack or failure. However, the parties may determine by agreement the standards by which the bank's responsibility is to be measured if those standards are not manifestly unreasonable.[147]

Federal Reserve System regulations and operating circulars, clearing house rules, and the like, have the effect of agreements under § 4–103(a), whether or not specifically assented to by all parties interested in the items handled.[148] Finally, the UCC is supplemented, unless a UCC provision displaces the rule, by "principles of law and equity, including the law merchant and the law relative to capacity to contract, principal and agent, estoppel, fraud, mistake, bankruptcy, or other validating non-UCC or invalidating cause...."[149] These various provisions and limitations may make it challenging to determine whether and when a bank can modify or even disclaim specific liabilities and duties provided by Article 4.

For example, an interesting question involves the final payment provisions of Article 4.[150] These provisions provide that a payor bank becomes "accountable" for an item if, for example, it fails to return the item or send notice of dishonor before its midnight deadline.[151] Could a bank alter this time period? There is case law indicating that it may be altered by a clearing house rule, at least between banks.[152]

---

147. § 4–103(a).

148. *See* § 4–103(b); Comments 2 and 3 to § 4–103. *See generally* Sweeney and Schmoker, *supra* note 146. The owner of the item may become bound by such agreements on the principle that collecting banks acting as agents have authority to make binding agreements with respect to items being handled. This conclusion was assumed but not flatly decided in Federal Reserve Bank of Richmond v. Malloy, 264 U.S. 160, 44 S.Ct. 296, 68 L.Ed. 617, 31 A.L.R. 1261 (1924). *See* § 4–103, Comment 3. *See also supra* ¶ 8.01[2]. Compare § 3–102(c) which gives greater effect to some operating circulars. *See also* Comment 3 to § 3–102. *But see* discussion *infra* ¶ 9.03[7], as to the impact on other parties to the instrument.

149. UCC § 1–103. *But see* § 1–106.

150. *See* § 4–215; discussion *supra* at ¶ 8.02.

151. *See* §§ 4–215(a)(3), 4–301(a), 4–104(a)(10); discussion *supra* at ¶ 8.02[1][c], ¶ 8.02[2][d], and ¶ 8.02[3].

152. *See, e.g.*, West Side Bank v. Marine Nat'l Exch. Bank, 37 Wis.2d 661, 155 N.W.2d 587 (Wis. 1968). *See also* Merrill Lynch, Pierce, Fenner & Smith, Inc. v. Devon Bank, 654 F.Supp. 506 (N.D.Ill.1987) (clearing house rule established alternative to the Article 4 midnight deadline), *rev'd*, 832 F.2d 1005 (7th Cir.1987); Springhill Bank & Trust Co. v. Citizens Bank & Trust Co., 505 So.2d 867 (La.Ct.App.1987) (midnight deadline excused by agreement between banks); *but see* Lockhart Savings & Loan Association v. RepublicBank Austin, 720 S.W.2d 193 (Tex. Ct. App. 1986) (clearing house rule could not excuse violation of midnight deadline). *See also* discussion *supra* ¶¶ 1.04[4], 8.01[2] and 8.02[6], and *infra* this part and ¶ 9.03[7]. *See also infra* ¶ 9.05.

Section 4–103 prohibits any agreement disclaiming the duty of due care or limiting the measure of damages. *Sun River Cattle Co. v. Miners Bank*[153] held that a course of dealing alone would not alter the midnight deadline rule, and an express clause in the deposit contract could not do so either if the delay would constitute a lack of care, because old § 4–103(1) (revised § 4–103(a)) precludes any disclaimer of liability for a failure to exercise ordinary care. However, since liability under § 4–302 is strict and is not based on a lack of ordinary care, the result could be different. On the other hand, the depositary and intermediary banks are agents of the owner of the item under § 4–201 and owe a duty of care under § 4–202, which cannot be disclaimed (or liability limited) by agreement under § 4–103(a). So an agreement to modify § 4–301 or § 4–302 (the midnight deadline rule) could create liability on the part of collecting banks to other parties who are thereby damaged. The revisions to Article 4 do not alter this analysis. The payment provision at § 4–215 and the accountability provision at § 4–302 are not founded on due care and therefore are not directly subject to the § 4–103 prohibition against variation by agreement. In any event, payment or accountability should not occur if a customer or a person acting for the customer specifically asks the bank to hold and not dishonor the item in the hope that funds will arrive.[154]

Subject only to the duties of good faith and ordinary care, there would seem to be very little in Article 4 that is not subject to variation by an agreement between the parties.[155] Despite this, there have been few cases involving such efforts.[156] An area where that is surprising is that of stop orders. One would think banks would condition such orders

---

153. 164 Mont. 237, 521 P.2d 679 (Mont. 1974), supporting opinion, Sun River Cattle Co. v. Miners' Bank of Montana, 164 Mont. 479, 525 P.2d 19 (1974). *See also* Iverson v. First Bank of Billings, 219 Mont. 283, 712 P.2d 1285 (Mont. 1985); Sunshine v. Bankers Trust Co., 34 N.Y.2d 404, 358 N.Y.S.2d 113, 314 N.E.2d 860 (N.Y.App. 1974), discussed *supra* at ¶ 9.01[6]; Schaller v. Marine National Bank, 131 Wis.2d 389, 388 N.W.2d 645 (Wis. Ct. App. 1986), *on appeal*, 131 Wis.2d 594, 393 N.W.2d 297 (Wis. 1986), discussion *supra* at ¶ 9.02[2][b] and *supra* Chapter 8 ¶ 8.01[2] and 8.02[4].

154. *See* Western Air & Refrig. v. Metro Bank, 599 F.2d 83 (5th Cir.1979); David Graubart, Inc. v. Bank Leumi Trust Co., 48 N.Y.2d 554, 423 N.Y.S.2d 899, 399 N.E.2d 930 (N.Y.1979); Bank of Miami v. Banco Industrial Y Ganadero Del Beni, S.A., 515 So.2d 1038 (Fla.Dist.Ct.App.1987) (checks were delivered to payor with understanding they would be held pending deposit of sufficient funds; this agreement superseded the midnight deadline). *See also supra* ¶ 8.01[2], ¶ 8.02[6], and *infra* ¶ 9.03[7].

155. *See*, Bell, *supra* note 118. Concerning possible limitations on the ability of a bank to unilaterally modify the deposit agreement by mailing the customer "statement stuffers," see Badie v. Bank of America, 67 Cal.App.4th 779, 79 Cal.Rptr.2d 273 (1998), discussed in A. Daniel Woska, Arbitration Clauses in Consumer Retail Installment Sales Contracts After the Green Tree Financial v. Randolph Decision, 55 CONSUMER FIN. L.Q. REP. 107 (2001). *See generally* Whitaker, *supra* note 144; *supra* Chapter 8 ¶ 8.01[2].

156. *Id*. *See also supra* notes 152–154. The signature card, account agreement, related customer corporate resolutions, and monthly account statements all form parts of the contract between the payor bank and its customer. In Reliance Ins. Co. v. Bank of America Nat'l. Trust & Sav. Ass'n., 43 U.C.C. Rep. Serv.2d 946 (N.D.Ill.2001), the account agreement, customer's corporate resolutions, and monthly statements established 30 days as a reasonable time period for customer examination of the monthly account statements. The parties were bound by this agreement. *See supra* Chapter 8 ¶ 8.01[2].

either in the order or in the deposit contract to avoid liability if the order is missed. One would expect customers to contest the clauses. Yet there have been few such cases.

Today, the enhanced standard of good faith at § 3–103(a)(4), which cannot be modified by agreement under § 4–103(a), creates additional hurdles to overcome with respect to such efforts. But other cases suggest that some such efforts may be successful. In one such case, a provision in the signature card, waiving the right to jury trial in any action between the parties, was upheld.[157] In another,[158] a bank was permitted by agreement to define a very short period for the customer to detect forgeries or alterations under § 4–406.[159]

Nonetheless, the emphasis in Article 4 on providing a specific and balanced approach to resolving bank-customer disputes involving such things as stop payment orders, wrongful payment, and wrongful dishonor, together with the duty of ordinary care at § 4–202, the higher standard of good faith at § 3–103(a)(4), and the limits on disclaiming these duties at § 4–103, suggest that a contractual effort to alter significant Article 4 rules in favor of the bank may face judicial scrutiny. Other matters not specified in Article 4, such as the fees charged by a bank for checks returned due to insufficient funds, remain largely within the scope of contract law, so long as the charges are reasonable and not unconscionable.[160]

[4] Customer's Duties Under Section 4–406

[a] Customer's Duty to Examine Checks

Section 4–406 places specific duties on a bank account customer,[161] and raises a preclusion with respect to an unauthorized drawer's signa-

---

157. David v. Manufacturers Hanover Trust Co., 59 Misc.2d 248, 298 N.Y.S.2d 847 (Sup. Ct. 1967).

158. Lawrence Fashions, Inc. v. National Bank of North Am., 8 UCC Rep. Serv. (Callaghan) 729 (N.Y.Sup.Ct.1971).

159. *Id. See also* Reliance Ins. Co. v. Bank of America Nat'l. Trust & Sav. Ass'n., 43 U.C.C. Rep. Serv.2d 946 (N.D.Ill., 2001); Canfield v. Banc One, Texas, N.A., 51 S.W.3d 828 (Tex.App.2001); discussion *supra* in Chapter 8 at ¶ 8.01[2]; *infra* ¶ 9.03[4].

160. *See, e.g., supra* ¶ 9.03[2]; and Lofts, The Perdue Case and Other Litigation Involving Bank Charges, 42 Consumer Fin. L. Q. Rep. 97 (1988); Rodgers v. Tecumseh Bank, 756 P.2d 1223 (Okla.1988) (no special duty or fiduciary relationship in armslength bank-customer transactions). *See also* Comment 3 to § 4–401, Comment 2 to § 4–406 (both citing *Perdue*), and discussion *supra* ¶ 9.03[2][c].

161. Old § 4–406 was held to be applicable to savings as well as checking account customers. *See, e.g.,* Boutros v. Riggs Nat'l Bank, 655 F.2d 1257, 31 UCC Rep. Serv. (Callaghan) 645 (D.C.Cir.1981); Tally v. American Sec. Bank, 35 UCC Rep. Serv. (Callaghan) 215 (D.D.C.1982). The wide scope of revised Article 4 and the broad definition of "item" at § 4–104(a)(9) means that § 4–406 is clearly applicable to savings accounts. *See, e.g.,* § 4–104(a)(1) ("account" defined to include "demand, time, savings, passbook, share draft, or like account," except certificates of deposit); revised § 4–104(a)(5) ("customer" defined as any "person having an account with a bank . . ."); § 4–104(a)(9) (definition of "item"); § 4–105(1) ("bank" defined to include savings banks, savings and loan associations, credit unions, and any other entity "engaged in the business of banking"); § 4–406 (by its terms applicable anytime a "bank . . . sends or makes available to a customer a statement of account"). *See* Shaw v. Union Bank & Trust Co., 640 P.2d 953 (Okla. 1981) (savings withdrawal slip was an "item" under old Article 4; failure to honor withdrawal request was wrongful dishonor

ture (and alterations) premised on negligence. Section 4–406 imposes a duty on the customer of a bank to promptly examine his or her bank statements for forged or altered (or otherwise improper) items and to notify the bank if any are found.[162] Under old Article 4, cases applied a forgery theory to situations where the item had less than the required number of persons who must sign.[163] This is codified in revised Article 4; as noted revised §§ 3–403(b) and 4–104(c) provide that where more than one signature is required as the authorized signature of an organization, if one of the signatures is missing, the signature is deemed to be unauthorized.[164]

Old § 4–406(2) provides that a customer who fails to meet his or her duty under § 4–406 is precluded from raising the unauthorized signature or alteration if the loss results from that failure or, in the case of a series of forgeries or alterations by the same culprit, after a reasonable time not exceeding 14 days. In effect, § 4–406 requires the customer to

---

under § 4–402). *See also* the discussion of Article 4 definitions, *supra* at ¶ 8.01[3].

162. Thus in First Nat'l Bank v. Keshishian, 427 So.2d 313 (Fla.App.1983), where the bank paid a second forged check after the statement covering an earlier forged check was available, the court reversed a summary judgment for the customer against the bank. *See* old § 4–406(1), (2)(b). In Florida Fed. Sav. & Loan Ass'n v. Martin, 400 So.2d 151 (Fla.App.1981), where the items were not returned with the statement nor otherwise made readily available, however, the court held the institution could not avail itself of the protection of old § 4–406 as to forged items. *See also* May–Li Barki, M.D., Inc. v. Liberty Bank and Trust Co., 20 P.3d 135 (Okla.1999) (same). Distinguish Mesnick v. Hempstead Bank, 106 Misc.2d 624, 434 N.Y.S.2d 579 (Sup. Ct. 1980), where the court imposed the customer's duties under § 4–406 even though the account statements were intercepted, saying the basic duty was to avoid losses stemming from an unreasonable lack of concern. Revised § 4–406(a) clearly allows a bank to provide information in lieu of the items, but does not necessarily protect the bank by a § 4–406 preclusion as to information not included on the account statement. *See* May–Li Barki, M.D., Inc. v. Liberty Bank and Trust Co., 20 P.3d 135, 40 U.C.C. Rep. Serv.2d 238 (Okla.1999) (payor bank could not assert preclusion against a drawer-customer whose employee forged indorsements on the customer's payroll tax checks, because the customer had elected to receive her account statements without cancelled checks and therefore could not examine the indorsements). This case was decided under old Article 3, but the court had the benefit of revised § 4–406 and nonetheless stressed the customer's inability to examine indorsements. Still, presumably the result in the case would be different under the comparative negligence standards of the 1990 revisions to the uniform text. As to when a statement is available, *see also* Cooley v. First Nat'l Bank, 276 Ark. 387, 635 S.W.2d 250 (Ark. 1982) (bank authorized to send statements to a post office box).

Section 4–406 establishes a maximum 30 day period for the customer to discover and report items that are not properly payable due to an alteration or lack of customer authorization. This is based on the obvious point that the customer is in the best position to control its agents and employees, and to discover unauthorized items. *See, e.g.,* Reliance Ins. Co. v. Bank of America Nat'l. Trust & Sav. Ass'n., 43 U.C.C. Rep. Serv.2d 946 (N.D.Ill.2001). However, it is possible that this time period and other statutory requirements could be subject to an agreement of the parties. *Id. See supra* ¶ 9.03 [3].

163. *See, e.g.,* Pine Bluff Nat'l Bank v. Kesterson, 257 Ark. 813, 520 S.W.2d 253 (Ark. 1975) (signature card required three signatures; checks had only one signature, albeit an authorized one). *Pine Bluff* held that it is an unauthorized signature where an organization requires multiple signatures and one of those in missing or forged. As noted in the text, this is codified at revised §§ 3–403(b) and 4–104(c). *Contra:* Southern Contract Carpet v. County Nat'l Bank, 528 So.2d 42 (Fla.App.1988); Spears Carpet Mills v. Century Nat'l Bank, 85 B.R. 86 (W.D. Ark. 1988). Revised Articles 3 and 4 adopt the *Pine Bluff* view and reject the *contra* cases. *See* §§ 3–403(b) and 4–104(c), and *infra* this text.

164. *See* §§ 3–403(a),(b), 4–104(c), 4–406(c).

examine each monthly bank statement and to notify the bank of any forgeries or alterations within a reasonable time, not to exceed 14 days, after the statement was available. Revised § 4–406(d) is similar to old Article 4 except that the maximum time period is extended to 30 days. *Winkler v. Commercial National Bank*[165] illustrates the basic principles in the context of old § 4–406(1). There the bank had to take the loss on the first check, but the customer's duty was relevant as to the others that followed.

After one year, there is an absolute preclusion against the customer, regardless of whether either party exercised ordinary care, under § 4–406(f). In *La Sara Grain Co. v. First National Bank*,[166] decided under old Article 4, the bank lost even though the customer delayed examination of the bank statement beyond the one year time period allowed in old § 4–406(4), because the court concluded the bank did not act in good faith in paying checks on only one of two required signatures.[167] This is a questionable application of the good faith doctrine,

---

165. 42 Mich.App. 740, 202 N.W.2d 468 (Mich.App.1972). *See also* First Nat'l Bank v. Keshishian, 427 So.2d 313 (Fla.App. 1983). *See also* Flagship Bank v. Complete Interiors, Inc., 450 So.2d 337 (Fla.Dist.Ct. App.1984) (time period specified for customer to review bank statement under § 4–406 is the outside limit and customer may be held to a shorter time period where reasonable under the circumstances). Revised § 4–406 establishes a maximum 30 day period for a bank customer to discover and report items paid on his or her account that are not obvious; the customer is in the best position to control its agents and employees, and to discover unauthorized items. *See, e.g.,* Reliance Ins. Co. v. Bank of America Nat'l. Trust & Sav. Ass'n. 43 U.C.C. Rep. Serv.2d 946 (N.D.Ill.2001). However, it is possible that this time period and other statutory requirements could be subject to an agreement of the parties. *Id.* See also May–Li Barki, M.D., Inc. v. Liberty Bank and Trust Co., 20 P.3d 135, (Okla.1999) (payor bank could not assert preclusion against a drawer-customer whose employee forged indorsements on the customer's payroll tax checks, because the customer had elected to receive her account statements without cancelled checks and therefore could not examine the indorsements). This case was decided under old Article 3. Presumably this result would be different under the comparative negligence standards of the 1990 revisions to the uniform text.

166. 673 S.W.2d 558, 38 UCC Rep. Serv. (Callaghan) 963 (Tex.1984).

167. *See also,* Annotation, Bank's Liability For Payment or Withdrawal on Less Than Required Number of Signatures, 77 ALR 4th 655 (1981). As noted *supra* this text and notes 198–199, Revised Article 3 treats a signature as being unauthorized when a required signature is missing. *See* Revised § 3–403(b). *See also,* revised § 3–103(a)(7), discussed *infra* at ¶ 9.03[5] ("ordinary care" does not require sight examination of individual items before payment). However, as noted *infra* in this text, there is a higher standard of good faith (including observance of reasonable commercial standards of fair dealing), included at § 3–103(a)(4) as part of the 1990 revisions to the uniform text of Article 3, and this has begun to be a factor in the case law. Two recent cases illustrate the importance of this in diverse scenarios. *See* San Tan Irrigation Dist. v. Wells Fargo Bank, 197 Ariz. 193, 3 P.3d 1113 (Ariz.Ct.App. 2000); Maine Family Federal Credit Union v. Sun Life Assurance Co., 727 A.2d 335 (Me. S.Ct.1999).

San Tan Irrigation Dist. v. Wells Fargo Bank, 197 Ariz. 193, 3 P.3d 1113 (Ariz.Ct. App. 2000) involved a check that had been deposited with an indorsement forged by one of the plaintiff's employees. When sued for conversion under § 3–420, the depositary bank sought to claim a preclusion against the plaintiff for negligence contributing to the loss, because of the failure of the plaintiff to adequately supervise its employee, under §§ 3–405 and 3–406. But this preclusion is available only if the depositary bank acted in good faith. *See* § 3–405(b), § 3–406(a). In *San Tan,* the plaintiff argued that the bank was careless and therefore did not meet the new standard of good faith at § 3–103(a)(4), and this was sufficient for summary judgment to be awarded against the bank; on appeal this was reversed, the court properly noting that the plaintiff's claim that the bank was careless in taking the items was relevant only to the duty of care, a very different thing from good faith.

which is designed to remedy dishonesty rather than innocent mistakes. La Sara may illustrate a seeming propensity to confuse the concepts of good faith and ordinary care, which are very different standards used for different purposes. But the revised definition of good faith at § 3–103(a)(4), incorporating reasonable commercial standards of fair dealing, now looks more similar to the definition of ordinary care at § 3–103(a)(7), which also included observance of reasonable commercial standards. So under revised Articles 3 and 4 the dividing line between good faith and ordinary care is not as clear as it used to be, perhaps suggesting some risk of continuing confusion on these issues. Another odd case is *Commercial Cotton Co. v. United California Bank*,[168] where the customer was excused from compliance with old § 4–406 because the court concluded in essence that payment of a forged check is per se a breach of the bank's duty, in part because the bank owed a special fiduciary duty to its customer.[169] *Commercial Cotton* was later repudiated in California in *Price v. Wells Fargo Bank*;[170] *Commercial Cotton* was also criticized in an *Annual Survey of the Uniform Commercial Code* in *The Business Lawyer*,[171] and was later repudiated in the same appellate district that decided *Commercial Cotton*, in *Copesky v. Superior Court of San Diego County*.[172] Revised § 4–406(e) recognizes the role of ordinary

---

The case was remanded for a trial on the issue of the bank's good faith, a better though hardly satisfactory result for the bank.

In Maine Family Federal Credit Union v. Sun Life Assurance Co., 727 A.2d 335 (Me. S.Ct.1999), the court held that the credit union (a "bank" under § 4–105) was not a holder in due course when it took an item for deposit because it did not meet the new standard of good faith at § 3–103(a)(4). The court concluded that the credit union met the former standard of "honesty in fact," and noted that under this traditional standard of good faith depositary banks have routinely qualified as holders in due course of deposited items. But the new standard also requires observance of reasonable commercial standards of fair dealing; illustrating the dangers of this concept, the *Maine Family Credit Union* court allowed the jury to conclude that it was not reasonable for the credit union to allow immediate credit to its depositor for three $40,759.35 checks drawn on a major out-of-state insurance company. The jury concluded it would have been better for the credit union to place a "hold" on the funds in these circumstances, and therefore the credit union failed the good faith test at § 3–103(a)(4) and was not a holder in due course.

168. 163 Cal.App.3d 511, 209 Cal.Rptr. 551 (1985). *See* Standard Wire & Cable Co. v. Ameritrust Corp., 697 F.Supp. 368 (C.D.Cal.1988); Copesky v. Superior Ct. of San Diego, 229 Cal.App.3d 678, 280 Cal. Rptr. 338 (Cal.App.1991).

169. This entire rationale is spurious and, as noted *infra*, has been almost universally rejected. *See also supra* ¶ 9.03[2]; ¶ 9.05. *Commercial Cotton* is discussed in Kitada, Banking Decisions: Emerging Theories of Bank Liability—The Breach of the Covenant of Good Faith and Fair Dealing, 103 Banking L.J. 80 (1986), and in Harrell, The Bank–Customer Relationship: Evolution of a Modern Form?, 11 Okla. City Univ. L. Rev. 641, 648–651 (1986). *See also infra* text and notes 170–172.

170. 213 Cal.App.3d 465, 261 Cal.Rptr. 735, 740 (Cal.App. 1 Dist.1989) (rejecting *Commercial Cotton* as poorly reasoned).

171. *See* Miller & Ballen, Commercial Paper, Bank Deposits and Collections, and Commercial Electronic Fund Transfers, 41 Bus. Law. 1399, 1421–22 (1986). *See also* Smith, Update on California's Bad Faith Tort, 44 Consumer Fin. L. Q. Rep. 54 (1990); Smith, Allis–Chalmers v. Lueck: The United States Supreme Court Rejects Tort Liability for Breach of Good Faith, 43 Consumer Fin. L. Q. Rep. 258 (1989); *supra* ¶ 9.03[2].

172. 229 Cal.App.3d 678, 280 Cal.Rptr. 338 (Cal.App.1991) (concluding that the bank-customer relation is not "quasi-fiduciary" and characterizing *Commercial Cot-*

care in allocating losses under the new comparative negligence standard in Articles 3 and 4, thereby recognizing the *Commercial Cotton* view that banks have a role to play in detecting forgeries and alterations, even as customer duties under § 4–406 remain the primary line of defense for all concerned. The last sentence of revised § 4–406(e) also gives a nod to *Commercial Cotton* by eliminating the § 4–406(d) customer preclusion if the bank did not pay the item in good faith, and this sentence takes on added importance in view of the expanded definition of good faith at § 3–103(a)(4). Nonetheless, it is clear that *Commercial Cotton* was wrongly decided on its facts and its rationale has been generally rejected by courts and legislatures, *e.g.*, at § 4–406(f) and Comments 4 and 5.

[b] Impact of Revised Section 4–406

Under Article 4, a customer has an obligation to examine his or her bank statements (and/or returned items), and is precluded from asserting alterations or unauthorized drawer's signatures against the bank if the customer fails to comply and the bank complies with § 4–406(a). Section 4–406(a) was completely rewritten in the 1990 revisions, to provide that the bank may either return items that have been paid on the account or make them available to the customer or provide information that reasonably allows their identification.[173] A statement describing the item by number and amount, and the date of payment, is specified to be sufficient. But any preclusion is commensurate with only the information provided.[174] If the items are not returned the bank must retain

---

ton as "misdirected"). The *Commercial Cotton* view has been further undermined by revised §§ 3–103(a)(7) and 4–406. *See* discussion *infra* ¶ 9.03[4][c]; *infra* ¶ 9.05.

173. Whether the items are returned, or only a statement describing the items, is left to the agreement of the parties. *See* § 4–406, Comment 1. In part this is designed to permit check truncation and other technological innovations that may speed the processing of items. *See infra* ¶ 9.03[6]. *But see supra* ¶ 8.01[2]; *infra* ¶ 9.03[3].

174. § 4–406(a) and (c). This information was chosen because it can be obtained by the bank's computer from the check's MICR line without examination of the items involved, and is designed to facilitate the economies that can be achieved through automated processing and truncation. *See* the § 4–406 Comments. Section § 4–406(a) creates an important "safe harbor" that allows banks to supply information obtained by automated means, in lieu of check return, unless there is agreement otherwise. The policy decision was made to accommodate the needs of economical automated processing, rather than imposing large burdens on the entire system just to protect customers who need more information because they do not keep good records.

The door is open for banks to provide more information in the future, as increased use of modern technology leads to advances in systems capabilities, such as image processing or other means. *See* § 4–406 Comments and *infra* ¶ 9.03[6]. Moreover, banks have an incentive to do so as the preclusion in § 4–406(c) is only as extensive as the information provided. *See* May–Li Barki, M.D., Inc. v. Liberty Bank and Trust Co., 20 P.3d 135, 40 U.C.C. Rep. Serv.2d 238 (Okla.1999) (payor bank could not assert preclusion against a drawer-customer whose employee forged indorsements on the customer's payroll tax checks, because the customer had elected to receive her account statements without cancelled checks and therefore could not examine the indorsements). This case was decided under old Article 3. Presumably this result would be different under the comparative negligence standards of the 1990 revisions to the uniform text, as some customer negligence was also apparent.

Section 4–406 establishes a maximum 30 day period for a bank customer to discover and report items paid on his or her account that are not properly payable due to an alteration or lack of customer authorization. This is based on the obvious point

either the items or the capacity to provide legible copies for a period of seven years, and must provide the customer a legible copy within a reasonable time upon request.[175]

The bank must furnish information on the items paid (or the items themselves), pursuant to § 4–406(a), before it can preclude the customer from asserting forgeries and alterations under § 4–406(c).[176] Once the bank has met this burden, the customer must meet the duties imposed by § 4–406(c), by examining the bank statement with "reasonable promptness" in order to identify any forged or altered items. The customer then has a duty to give "prompt" notice to the bank of any "relevant facts" relating to an unauthorized signature of the customer or alteration.[177] Under § 4–406(d), the customer has a maximum period of 30 days (up from 14 days under the old Article 4) in which to discover an unauthorized drawer's signature or alteration and report it to the bank.[178] It should be noted, however, that this is a *maximum* time limit; Article 4 requires "reasonable promptness," and in a given circumstance a court may conclude that an earlier time limit is justified.[179]

If the customer fails to meet this duty the customer is precluded from claiming reimbursement from the bank on grounds of alteration or an unauthorized signature by the same wrongdoer, as to any future items paid by the bank.[180] This is a continuation of prior law, and is based on the theory that had the customer examined the bank statement and reported the discrepancy the bank would have been alerted to more closely inspect subsequent items.[181] In effect the customer's failure to

---

that the customer is in the best position to control its agents and employees, and to discover unauthorized items. However, it is possible that this time period and other statutory requirements could be subject to an agreement of the parties. *See, e.g.,* Reliance Ins. Co. v. Bank of America Nat'l. Trust & Sav. Ass'n., 43 U.C.C. Rep. Serv.2d 946 (N.D.Ill.2001).

175. § 4–406(b). Other law determines the acceptability of the statement as proof of payment. If a customer is concerned with this issue, he or she can contract for the items to be returned or obtain copies before items or copies are eliminated.

176. *See* § 4–406, and Comments.

177. § 4–406(c). As noted *infra*, as to forgeries this applies only to the customer's signature; the customer has no responsibility under § 4–406 to notify the bank of forged indorsements, and the bank has no duty to examine indorsements. *See* § 4–406, Comment 5.

178. The increase from 14 to 30 days reflects the increased volume of check activity since the original Code was finalized in the early 1950s. This recognizes that reconciling large volume bank statements is a time-consuming task that may require up to 30 days. *See* § 4–406 Comments. This is also based on the apparent fact that the customer is in the best position to control its agents and employees, and to discover that unauthorized items have been paid on the account. *See, e.g.,* Reliance Ins. Co. v. Bank of America Nat'l. Trust & Sav. Ass'n., 43 U.C.C. Rep. Serv.2d 946 (N.D.Ill.2001). However, it is possible that this time period could be modified by an agreement of the parties. *Id.*

179. *See supra* note 165.

180. § 4–406(d)(2).

181. § 4–406 Comments. Even banks that process by automated means (*see* § 3–103(a)(7)) normally alter the procedure to check when it is known a problem may exist. The maximum 30 day period for the customer to examine his or her bank statement and notify the bank of forgeries or alterations is based on the obvious point that (regardless of the bank's technology and diligence) the customer is in the best position to discover unauthorized items. The 30 day period is deemed a reasonable maximum for most circumstances, but is subject to modification by agreement. *See, e.g.,* § 4–103; Reliance Ins. Co. v. Bank of America Nat'l. Trust & Sav. Ass'n., 43

examine the bank statement contributed to the loss, so as to preclude the customer from shifting that loss to an equally innocent party (the bank). This is a particularized version of similar preclusion rules at § 3–406, and represents a long standing principle of the common law.[182]

[c] The New Role of Comparative Negligence and Good Faith

Under the old Article 4, the preclusion at § 4–406 did not apply, even if the customer was negligent, if the bank also was negligent.[183] This is changed significantly in revised Article 4. Old § 4–406(3), eliminating the customer preclusion where the bank failed to exercise ordinary care, was deleted. Instead, a new § 4–406(e) provides that where the negligence of the customer and the failure of the bank to exercise ordinary care both contribute to the loss (in the bank's case, the negligence must "substantially contribute"), the loss is allocated between the customer precluded and the bank asserting the preclusion according to the extent to which the failure of each to exercise ordinary care contributed to the loss.[184] As noted, however, the rule precluding the

---

U.C.C. Rep. Serv.2d 946 (N.D.Ill.2001); *supra* ¶ 8.01[2] and ¶ 9.03[3].

182. *See, e.g.,* Price v. Neal, 3 Burr. 1354, 97 Eng. Rep. 871 (K.B. 1762), discussed *supra* Chapter 7.

183. Old § 4–406(3). *See, e.g.,* Hardex–Steubenville Corp. v. Western Pa. Nat'l Bank, 446 Pa. 446, 285 A.2d 874 (Pa. 1971). In Ossip–Harris Ins., Inc. v. Barnett Bank, 428 So.2d 363 (Fla.App.1983), the court held that evidence a trained bank employee had verified each signature and that the president of the corporate customer itself had failed to detect the forgeries on 99 checks as matter of law established that the bank used proper care in the absence of any evidence to the contrary. *Compare* First Nat'l Bank of Cape Canaveral v. Keshishian 427 So.2d 313 (Fla.App.1983) (forgeries not obvious, bank followed customary practice) *with* American Security Bank v. American Motorists Ins. Co., 538 A.2d 736 (D.C.1988) (commercially reasonable standards not followed). The burden to establish a lack of ordinary care of the bank is on the customer. Old § 4–406(3); revised § 4–406(e); *cf.* Federal Ins. Co. v. Bank of New York, 2 UCC Rep. Serv. (Callaghan) 2d 580 (N.Y. Civ. Ct. 1986) (burden erroneously placed on bank). *See also* Travelers Insurance Co. v. Connecticut Bank & Trust Co., 40 Conn. Supp. 70, 481 A.2d 111 (Conn.Super.Ct.1984) (dealing with whether § 4–406 extends to *missing* indorsements). Revised § 4–406 does not deal with indorsements at all. *See* § 4–406(c), and Comment 5. *But see* revised § 4–111. *Cf.* 12 CFR § 229.35 (extensive Regulation CC indorsement standards). *See supra* ¶ 8.04[3][g].

184. § 4–406(e). Note that under § 4–406(d) the customer is precluded from asserting the forgery or alteration upon *any* failure to comply with revised § 4–406(c), subject to a claim that the bank violated its duty of ordinary care under § 4–406(e), and that such bank violation *substantially* contributed to the loss. But the bank loses this preclusion if it did not act in good faith. *See* revised § 4–406(d). In contrast the bank is subject to proportionate loss allocation under revised § 4–406(e) only if "the customer *proves* the bank failed to exercise ordinary care ... *and* that the failure *substantially* contributed to the loss ..." (Emphasis added.) As a result the comparative negligence rule will come into play only if the customer has carried the burden of proving not only that the bank failed to exercise ordinary care, but also that this failure "substantially" contributed to the loss. Neither the statute nor the comments give a clue as to what level of negligence is required, leaving this to be worked out on a case by case basis. *See also* the definition of ordinary care at revised § 3–103(a)(7), discussed *infra* at ¶ 9.03[5].

The new comparative negligence rules in Article 4 follow a trend established by Federal Reserve Regulation CC. *See, e.g.,* 12 CFR § 229.38(c) and the commentary, creating a "pure" comparative negligence standard for liability under Regulation CC, Subpart C (Collection of checks). Other comparative negligence case law may also be relevant in applying the new standards. *See, e.g.,* Boyles v. Oklahoma Natural Gas Co., 619 P.2d 613 (Okla.1980) (explaining

customer from asserting the forgery or alteration (§ 4–406(c), (d)) will not apply if the bank has failed to act in good faith.[185]

In conclusion, if the customer is precluded from asserting the unauthorized drawer's signature or alteration against the bank under § 4–406(d), but seeks to shift some of the loss to the bank on a theory of comparative negligence, the customer must prove "that the bank failed to exercise ordinary care in paying the item and that the failure substantially contributed to [the] loss...."[186] In this event the loss will be allocated between the customer and the bank "according to the extent to which the failure of each to exercise ordinary care contributed to the loss."[187] Note the required elements of this provision: The customer has the burden of proving that the bank failed to exercise "ordinary care" and that this failure "substantially contributed" to the loss. If the customer succeeds, the bank will be liable but only for its proportionate share of the loss, based on the extent to which it contributed to that loss. "Ordinary care" is defined at § 3–103(a)(7); as noted *infra* this text at ¶ 9.03[5], this specifically does not require the bank to subject each item to sight examination.

Oklahoma's comparative negligence doctrine).

185. *See* § 4–406(e) and *supra* ¶ 9.03[4][a], including the discussion of La Sara Grain Co. v. First National Bank, 673 S.W.2d 558, 38 UCC Rep. Serv. (Callaghan) 963 (Tex.1984) and Commercial Cotton Co. v. United California Bank, 163 Cal.App.3d 511, 209 Cal.Rptr. 551 (1985), *supra* ¶ 9.03[4][b]. *See also supra* ¶ 9.01[4][b].

186. § 4–406(e). *See also* § 4–406, Comments, and the Comments to §§ 3–404, 3–405, and 3–406, and *supra* note 183.

187. *Id.* If it is asserted that a bank has violated its duty of care (or other statutory duties) with regard to an item not properly payable, the bank may assert against the claimant a preclusion on grounds the claimant's actions contributed to the loss. Such a preclusion may be asserted under §§ 3–404, 3–405, 3–406, 3–407 or 4–406. If effective, such a preclusion generally means the item will be treated as properly payable, thereby eliminating many grounds for liability on the part of any bank that processed or paid the item. However, in such case the claimant may argue that the bank failed to exercise ordinary care and that this failure substantially contributed to the loss. If this is established, the loss will be apportioned between the parties on the basis of their comparative negligence. The purpose and effect is to encourage settlements where both the bank and claimant contributed to the loss, which often seems to be the case, by making it less likely that either will prevail on a motion for summary judgment and more likely that any trial will result in a roughly equal apportionment of liability.

This is illustrated in the companion cases of Gina Chin & Associates, Inc. v. First Union Bank, 260 Va. 533, 537 S.E.2d 573 (Va. 2000), and Gina Chin & Associates, Inc. v. First Union Bank, 256 Va. 59, 500 S.E.2d 516 (Va. 1998). In these cases, a teller at the depositary bank had conspired with an employee of the drawer, to accept for deposit stolen and forged checks drawn on the drawer's (employer's) account. The employee stole blank checks for the employer's account, forged the employer's signature, and with the help of the teller deposited the checks into an account controlled by one of the conspirators at the depositary bank.

As between the banks involved, the checks were the responsibility of the depositary bank due to the latter's breach of warranty. The depositary bank sued the employer on whose account the checks were drawn, seeking a preclusion under §§ 3–404 and 3–405 for failure to adequately monitor its checkbook and supervise its employee. The employer countered that the depositary bank failed to exercise ordinary care due to its teller's fraud. While a trial court essentially concluded that the teller's fraud was outside the scope of employment and therefore not imputed to the depositary bank, granting summary judgment to the bank, the Supreme Court of Virginia reversed and allowed the case to go forward for trial on the issue of comparative negligence and the scope of the teller's employment.

If, however, the customer proves that the bank did not pay the item in good faith, as defined at § 3–103(a)(4), the customer will not be precluded from asserting the unauthorized signature or alteration against the bank, and the bank will have to recredit the customer's account and will suffer the resulting loss. "Good faith" is defined at § 3–103(a)(4) to include "observance of reasonable commercial standards of fair dealing."[188]

[d] Other Revisions to Section 4–406

Old § 4–406(4) sets an absolute time limit of one year for a customer to assert a forgery or alteration under any circumstances, and also includes forged indorsements, but extends the limit to three years for such indorsements.[189] A bank is prevented under old § 4–406(5) and (as

---

188. *Id. See supra* ¶ 9.01[4][b] and *supra* note 226. The higher standard of good faith (including observance of reasonable commercial standards of fair dealing), included at § 3–103(a)(4) as part of the 1990 revisions to the uniform text of Article 3, has begun to be a factor in the case law. Two recent cases illustrate the importance of this in diverse scenarios.

San Tan Irrigation Dist. v. Wells Fargo Bank, involved a check that had been deposited with an indorsement forged by one of the plaintiff's employees. When sued for conversion under § 3–420, the depositary bank sought to claim a preclusion against the plaintiff for negligence contributing to the loss, because of the failure of the plaintiff to adequately supervise its employee, under §§ 3–405 and 3–406. But this preclusion is available only if the depositary bank acted in good faith. *See* § 3–405(b), § 3–406(a). In *San Tan*, the plaintiff argued that the bank was careless and therefore did not meet the new standard of good faith at § 3–103(a)(4), and this was sufficient for summary judgment to be awarded against the bank; on appeal this was reversed, the court properly noting that the plaintiff's claim that the bank was careless in taking the items was relevant only to the duty of care, a very different thing from good faith. The case was remanded for a trial on the issue of the bank's good faith, a better though hardly desirable result for the bank.

In Maine Family Federal Credit Union v. Sun Life Assurance Co., 727 A.2d 335 (Me. S.Ct. 1999), the court held that the credit union (a "bank" under § 4–105) was not a holder in due course when it took an item for deposit because it did not meet the new standard of good faith at § 3–103(a)(4). The court concluded that the credit union met the former standard of "honesty in fact," and noted that under this traditional standard of good faith depositary banks have routinely qualified as holders in due course of deposited items. But the new standard of good faith also requires observance of reasonable commercial standards of fair dealing; illustrating the dangers of this concept, the *Maine Family Credit Union* court allowed the jury to conclude that it was not reasonable for the credit union to allow immediate credit to its depositor for three $40,759.35 checks drawn on a major out-of-state insurance company. The jury concluded it would have been better for the credit union to place a "hold" on the funds in these circumstances, and therefore the credit union failed the good faith test at § 3–103(a)(4) and was not a holder in due course.

189. *See, e.g.*, Exchange Bank & Trust Co. v. Kidwell Constr. Co., 463 S.W.2d 465 (Tex.Civ.App.1971), *aff'd* 472 S.W.2d 117 (Tex.1971).

A typical example is Sebastian v. D & S Express, Inc., 61 F.Supp. 2d 386 (D.N.J. 1999), where corporate employees (including the President) had issued 87 corporate checks payable to fictitious payees over a seven year period, and cashed them at a local bank after indorsing them in the names of the fictitious payees. The checks were purportedly for maintenance work, which was not performed. When the fraud was discovered, the corporation sued the bank that had cashed the checks. The bank defended that the indorsements were valid under the fictitious payee rule at § 3–404(b), and the corporation countered with a comparative negligence claim on grounds the bank failed to exercise ordinary care under § 3–404(d).

The court held that the corporation's § 3–404(d) comparative negligence claim was barred by the statute of limitations at § 3–118(g) because § 3–404(d) seeks enforcement of a duty; the claims more than three years old were barred. The corpora-

discussed *infra*) revised § 4–406 (f) from waiving a preclusion against its customer and trying to shift the loss instead back up the collection chain to prior parties. Interestingly, there was no comparable provision in the similar preclusion provision of old § 3–406, which seems an undesirable omission.[190] Presumably, under § 4–102(a) the Article 4 provision controls as to bank-customer issues in the event of any such conflict.

Revised § 4–406(f) changes old § 4–406 in several important ways. First, all references to unauthorized indorsements are deleted, including the three year limitation on a customer's right to assert a forged indorsement in an action against the payor bank for wrongful payment. As a result, § 4–406 imposes no duties on the drawer (or payor bank–*see* § 4–406 Comment 5) to look for unauthorized indorsements. The customer still may assert that because of an unauthorized indorsement the item was not properly payable, however, in an action to recover wrongful payment by the payor bank.[191] In that event, § 4–111 provides a three year statute of limitations for the customer's action.[192] The net result is no substantive change from old Article 4, except the new comparative negligence standards.

Second, old § 4–406(5), prohibiting a bank from waiving its defense against a customer in order to assert rights against (and shift the loss to) a collecting bank or other prior party, is deleted. But the substance of

tion's claims for conversion under § 3–420 were also dismissed, on grounds that § 3–420(a) bars such an action by the issuer. The corporation's common law negligence claims were barred as superceded by § 3–404. Thus, the effect of §§ 3–118 and 3–404(b) was to prevent the corporation from shifting its loss (caused by its own president and employees) to the bank, subject to comparative negligence claims asserted within three years under § 3–404(d).

190. *See, e.g.*, Girard Bank v. Mount Holly State Bank, 474 F.Supp. 1225 (D.N.J. 1979); East Gadsden Bank v. First City Nat'l Bank, 50 Ala.App. 576, 281 So.2d 431 (Ala.Civ.App. 1973). On the general difference between §§ 3–406 and 4–406, *see* Hardex-Steubenville Corp. v. Western Pa. Nat'l Bank, 446 Pa. 446, 285 A.2d 874 (Pa. 1971) (§ 3–406 relates to conduct before the wrongful act while § 4–406 relates to conduct afterward). *But see* old § 3–406, Comment 7. *See also* revised §§ 3–417(c) and 4–208(c), discussed *supra* Chapter 7, which now provide a rule similar to old § 4–406(5).

191. *See* old § 4–401(1), revised § 4–401(a), and discussion *supra* ¶ 9.01[3]. If breached, the presentment warranties at § 4–208 allow the payor bank to return an item after the midnight deadline; this may allow the payor bank to recover from the presenting party if the item was not properly payable. The midnight deadline is discussed *supra* at ¶ 8.02. On the Article 4 warranties, *see supra* Chapter 7.

For example, in First National Bank and Trust Co. of the Treasure Coast v. Belmont National Bank, 43 U.C.C. Rep. Serv.2d 666 (Ohio Ct. App. 2001), a check was deposited without the required indorsement of a joint payee. It was sent through the banking system to the payor bank, which gave provisional credit and did not dishonor the item or revoke the credit within its midnight deadline (thereby losing the right to dishonor it under § 4–301 and becoming accountable for the amount of the item under § 4–302).

When the missing indorsement was discovered, the payor bank recredited the drawer's account, returned the item to the depositary bank and revoked the settlement for the item that it had given to the presenting bank, on grounds of breach of warranty. The depositary bank had paid out the funds to its depositor, who was now bankrupt, and the depositary bank sued the payor bank to recover the payment under the midnight deadline rule at § 4–302. The court correctly concluded that recovery under § 4–302 was barred by the payor bank's counter-claim (asserted as a defense) for breach of warranty due to the lack of a required indorsement. Summary judgment for the payor bank was properly affirmed.

192. *See* § 4–111.

that rule is incorporated in revised § 4–406 only in new language at revised § 4–406(f):

> If there is a preclusion under this subsection, (the one year absolute limitation for forged instruments and alterations), the payor bank may not recover for breach of warranty under Section 4–208 with respect to the unauthorized signature or alteration to which the preclusion applies.

As noted in the Comments to revised section 4–406:

> If a drawer has not notified the payor bank of an unauthorized check or material alteration within the one year period, the payor bank may not choose to recredit the drawer's account and pass the loss to the collecting banks on the theory of breach of warranty.[193]

Finally, §§ 4–208(c) and 3–417(c) were added to permit a depositary bank that has been sued for breach of presentment warranty to assert as a defense the right of the payor to seek a preclusion against the customer under §§ 3–406 or 4–406(c) and (d).[194]

Revised Article 3 addresses some related issues in a new § 3–405 ("Employer Responsibility for Fraudulent Indorsement by Employee"). These issues are addressed more specifically *supra* this text in Chapters 6 and 7, but generally § 3–405 makes the employer responsible for any forged indorsement made by an employee charged with responsibility for that instrument. This is consistent with the other UCC provisions precluding any person whose negligence (actual or conclusively presumed) has contributed to a forgery or alteration from asserting that forgery or alteration against an innocent party, subject in most instances to a comparative negligence standard.[195]

[5] Payor Bank's Obligation to Examine Checks

As check processing became increasingly automated, payor banks began to process small dollar amount checks entirely by automated means, without direct examination of the check, including the drawer's signature. While this is essential to the economical processing of large volumes of checks, it led to allegations by some customers that it was not a commercially reasonable practice. For example, in *Rhode Island Hospital Trust National Bank v. Zapata Corp.*,[196] the bank examined all

---

193. § 4–406, Comments. *See also* §§ 3–417(c) and 4–208(c). Otherwise, if breached, the presentment warranties allow the payor bank to return an item after the midnight deadline; this may allow the payor bank to recover from the presenting party and/or depositary bank if the item was not properly payable. The midnight deadline is discussed *supra* at ¶ 8.02. On the Article 4 warranties, *see supra* Chapter 7.

194. *Id.* The provision also extends to §§ 3–404 and 3–405.

195. *See, e.g.*, § 3–404 (impostors and fictitious payees); § 3–406 ("Negligence Contributing to a Forged Signature or Alteration of an Instrument"); § 4–406 (discussed *supra* this text). As discussed *infra* this text, the revisions also introduce a new "comparative negligence" standard to allocate losses where both parties have contributed to the loss. *See, e.g.*, §§ 3–404(d), 3–405(b), 3–406(b) and 4–406(e).

196. 848 F.2d 291 (1st Cir.1988). *See also* Ballen, Baxter, McTaggart, Nyquist & Rubin, Commercial Paper, Bank Deposits and Collections, and Other Payment Systems, 44 Bus. Law. 1515, 1555 (1989); E.S.P., Inc. v. Midway Nat'l Bank, 466

drawers' signatures only as to checks exceeding $1,000 or if there was reason to suspect a problem. Also one percent of the checks between $100 and $1,000 were sight examined on a random basis. Other banks in the area followed similar procedures. It is likely that such dollar amounts have been adjusted upward since the 1980s.

When the customer in the *Rhode Island* case faced a loss under old § 4–406 due to his failure to detect a forgery and notify the bank (as discussed *supra* at ¶ 9.03[4]), the customer argued that the § 4–406 preclusion did not apply because he was relieved of his duty to notify the bank of the forgeries under old § 4–406(3). Old § 4–406(3) relieves the customer of this duty if the bank does not use ordinary care in paying the item, and the customer argued that a failure to examine every item constituted a lack of ordinary care. The court disagreed, finding the bank's practice commercially reasonable; nonetheless, there was contra authority and the specter of similar suits cast uncertainty on the ability of banks to use modern automated processing methods.

The 1990 Article 4 revisions address this at §§ 4–104(c) and 3–103(a)(7) by defining ordinary care at § 3–103(a)(7) as follows:

> (7) "Ordinary care" in the case of a person engaged in business means observance of reasonable commercial standards, prevailing in the area in which the person is located, with respect to the business in which the person is engaged. In the case of a bank that takes an instrument for processing for collection or payment by automated means, reasonable commercial standards do not require the bank to examine the instrument if the failure to examine does not violate the bank's prescribed procedures and the bank's procedures do not vary unreasonably from general banking usage not disapproved by this Article or Article 4.[197]

This codifies the rule of *Rhode Island Hospital Trust National Bank v. Zapata Corp.*[198] and generally permits a bank to rely on automated processing methods without violating its duty of ordinary care. In addition the 1990 Article 4 revisions alter the legal ramifications of a failure to use ordinary care. Under § 4–406(e), if both the customer and the bank fail to exercise ordinary care, then even if the bank's failure substantially contributes to a loss, the loss will be allocated between those parties "according to the extent to which the failure of each to exercise ordinary care contributed to the loss."[199]

N.W.2d 417 (Minn.App.1991); Medford Irrigation Dist. v. Western Bank, 66 Or.App. 589, 676 P.2d 329 (Or.App.1984); Five Towns College v. Citibank, N.A., 108 A.D.2d 420, 489 N.Y.S.2d 338 (1985); Wilder Binding Co. v. Oak Park Trust and Savings Bank, 135 Ill.2d 121, 142 Ill.Dec. 192, 552 N.E.2d 783 (Ill. 1990).

197. § 3–103(a)(7). *See also* discussion *supra* at ¶ 9.01[4][b].

198. 848 F.2d 291 (1st Cir.1988). *See supra* note 194 and accompanying text.

199. *See* § 4–406(e); discussion *supra* ¶ 9.03[4]. *See also* § 3–406(b) (same general rule), § 3–404(d) (same rule in the context of imposter payee problem), § 3–405(b), and discussion *supra* at ¶ 9.03[4][c].

[6] Check Truncation and MICR Encoding

In order to reduce the costs to bank customers associated with the return of canceled checks each month and to expedite check collection, many banks offer checking account services that include check "truncation." Truncation means that physical transportation of the check is stopped (or "truncated") somewhere in the check collection process, thereby saving the costs associated with physical handling of the item from that point on and sending the data electronically and faster than if the check were sent. The physical check is either stored or destroyed after the information contained on the check has been converted into electronic data. Truncation can occur at the payor bank, or even earlier in the collection chain. The earlier that truncation occurs the greater the cost and time savings.[200]

Both the Federal Expedited Funds Availability Act[201] and Federal Reserve System Regulation CC[202] encourage check truncation,[203] but old Articles 3 and 4 contained no provisions relating specifically to truncation and generally were viewed as being neutral on the subject.[204] As a result some cases interpreted old Article 4 in ways that legally impeded truncated processing.[205] The 1990 revisions to Article 4 address this problem in several provisions designed to facilitate check truncation, although as noted *infra* at ¶ 9.03[7] some uncertainties and impediments remain. In addition, as discussed *supra* at ¶ 8.02[6], the 2002 amendments to § 4–301(a)(2) allow a payor bank to dishonor an item by returning an image of the item pursuant to a truncation agreement, and amendments at § 4–301(a)(3) allow dishonor by sending a "record" if the item is unavailable. These 2002 amendments to § 4–301 allow the payor bank to meet its midnight deadline using electronic returns, but do not address related issues affecting liability on the instrument under

---

200. *See generally*, J. Dolan, Uniform Commercial Code §§ 26.4, 26.6 (1991); D. Baker & R. Brandel, The Law of Electronic Fund Transfer Systems § 2.01 (2d ed. 1988); Seibold & Kessler, Credit Unions and Check Truncation, 44 Bus. Law. 1096 (1989).

201. 12 U.S.C.A. §§ 4001–4010. *See also supra* ¶ 8.04.

202. 12 CFR §§ 229.1–229.42, discussed *supra* this text at ¶ 8.04.

203. *See* 12 U.S.C.A. § 4008(b)(2) (requiring the Federal Reserve Board to consider imposing truncation by regulation); 12 U.S.C.A. § 4008(f) (requiring the Federal Reserve Board to study the means of telecommunication to determine ways to "avoid the necessity of actual presentment of the paper instrument"); 12 CFR § 229.36(c) (authorizing truncation and electronic presentment pursuant to an agreement of the parties); and 53 Fed. Reg. 19,490, at 19,-493–95 (1988) (Federal Reserve truncation services).

204. Old Article 4 probably permits truncation by agreement of the parties, pursuant to old § 4–103(1); however, this is a provision of general applicability and does not specifically address issues relating to truncation. Revised Article 4 is more specific in contemplating truncation, but again only pursuant to agreement. As noted *infra* at ¶ 9.03[7], this leaves some issues unresolved.

205. *See, e.g.*, Florida Federal Savings & Loan Association v. Martin, 400 So.2d 151 (Fla.App.1981), holding that a bank was not protected by old § 4–406 as to truncated items, because the physical checks were not forwarded to the customer pursuant to old § 4–406(1). While this decision is questionable under old § 4–406 and a proper agreement, it illustrated the need for revision of Article 4 in order to accommodate truncation issues.

Article 3 if the item is destroyed. *See, e.g.*, the 2002 amendment to § 4–301, Comment 8.

The 1990 revisions to Articles 3 and 4 in no way mandate check truncation, but generally authorize it where the parties so agree. For example, § 3–501(b)(1) specifically permits electronic presentment, and § 4–110 is an entirely new provision recognizing the concept of an "Electronic Presentment" (defined to include by way of an agreement, clearing-house rule, or Federal Reserve regulation or operating circular) and describing the rules applicable to electronic presentment. Under § 4–110, an electronic presentment agreement may provide "procedures governing retention, presentment, payment, dishonor, and other matters concerning items subject to the agreement."[206] "Presentment notice" is defined as "transmission of an image of an item or information describing the item ... rather than delivery of the item itself."[207] An electronic presentment is made when the presentment notice is received by the payor.[208] In such case all references to "check" or "item" in Article 4 will be deemed references to the presentment notice.[209]

Section 4–406 was extensively rewritten in the 1990 revisions,[210] in part to deal with truncation issues, presumably in response to cases like *Florida Federal Savings & Loan Association v. Martin*.[211] Revised § 4–406(a) specifically permits the bank to not return paid items and instead allows the bank to "provide information in the statement of account sufficient to allow the customer to identify the items paid."[212] The same section then provides a "safe harbor" by stipulating that: "[t]he statement of account provides sufficient information if the item is described by item number, amount, and date of payment."[213] The truncated item must either be retained in storage or, if destroyed, there must be a capacity to furnish legible copies for a period of seven years after receipt of the item.[214] During this period the customer is entitled to obtain the item or a legible copy, within a reasonable time, upon request to the payor bank. It should also be noted that these revisions to § 4–406 primarily address truncation issues with regard to paid (not dishonored items). As noted above and discussed *supra* at ¶ 8.02[6], the 2002 amendments to § 4–301(a) fill this gap by authorizing electronic dishonor for purposes of the midnight deadline. However, as suggested in the 2002 amendments to § 4–301 Comment 8, these provisions do not address related issues such as potential liability to the owner of a

---

206. § 4–110(a).
207. *Id.*
208. § 4–110(b).
209. § 4–110(c).
210. *See supra* ¶ 9.03[4].
211. 400 So.2d 151 (Fla.App.1981). *See supra* note 246 and accompanying text.
212. § 4–406(a). Note however that this limits the bank's preclusion under § 4–406(d) to information provided in the statement. *See supra* ¶ 9.03[4].

213. *Id. See supra* notes 173–177 and accompanying text. Note however that this limits the bank's preclusion under § 4–406(d) to information provided in the statement. *See supra* ¶ 9.03[4]. The comments to revised Article 4 also recognize that efforts to accommodate automation and truncation may raise consumer protection issues that can be addressed by other laws. *See, e.g.*, § 4–101, Comment 3.

214. § 4–406(b).

destroyed item if the truncation arrangement adversely affects the rights of that owner as against parties liable on the instrument.

Revised Article 4 also contains a new retention warranty at § 4–209(b), providing that any party who truncates an item (by storing or destroying the item) warrants to subsequent collecting banks and any payor that such truncation is in compliance with the terms of an applicable agreement.

Revised § 4–209 also provides new MICR encoding warranties: Any party who encodes information on an item after issue warrants to any subsequent collecting bank and to any payor that the information is correctly encoded.[215] Unlike the other Article 4 warranties, these encoding and retention warranties are inclusive to Article 4 and have no counterpart in Article 3.[216]

The additional encoding warranty is needed because a misencoding of the MICR data is not an alteration that changes the legal obligation of the drawer, and therefore is not an alteration under § 3–407(a) (or old § 3–407(1)), and therefore is not a breach of warranty under the other Article 3 and 4 warranties.[217] Yet a MICR encoding error by the depositary bank (or a fraud by someone else) might result in a $2,500 check being MICR encoded for $25,000.[218] This check might be paid by automated means (according to the MICR encoding) in the amount of $25,000, yet the payor bank could only charge the drawer's account for the amount of the drawer's obligation ($2,500). Under § 4–209(a), the payor bank will have recourse against the encoding party for breach of warranty, in order to recover any resulting loss, and need not pursue the person paid as a prerequisite to such recourse.[219] Similarly, if a $25,000 check were encoded for $2,500, if the payor cannot recover by a further debit to the drawer's account, it can proceed against the bank that made the encoding error.[220]

As noted, any party who retains an item under a truncation or similar agreement, *e.g.*, in order to allow electronic presentment pursuant to § 4–110, warrants to subsequent collecting banks and to any payor that the retention and presentment comply with the agreement.[221] In each of these instances, any party who took the item in good faith may recover damages for breach of warranty under these provisions, in an amount equal to the loss suffered plus expenses and loss of interest.[222]

---

215. § 4–209(a). "If the customer of a depositary bank encodes, that bank also makes the warranty." *Id.*

216. *Compare* §§ 4–207 and 4–208 *with* §§ 3–416 and 3–417, discussed *supra* Chapter 7. The encoding and retention warranties are "unique to the bank collection process." *See* § 4–209, Comment 1.

217. §§ 3–416, 3–417, 4–207, and 4–208, *See also* § 4–209, Comment 2, which includes the example illustrating a MICR encoding error that is discussed *infra* this text.

218. This is an example noted in § 4–209, Comment 2.

219. *Id.*

220. *Id.*, citing Georgia Railroad Bank & Trust Co. v. First National Bank & Trust Co., 139 Ga.App. 683, 229 S.E.2d 482 (Ga. App.1976), *aff'd*, 238 Ga. 693, 235 S.E.2d 1 (Ga. 1977), and First National Bank of Boston v. Fidelity Bank, National Association, 724 F.Supp. 1168 (E.D.Pa.1989).

221. § 4–209(b).

222. § 4–209(c). Regarding good faith, *see* § 3–103(a)(4); *supra* note 188.

These provisions protect any "subsequent collecting bank" (as well as the payor) and therefore may not be applicable to returned items as opposed to banks in the forward collection process.[223] Regulation CC provides specific warranties governing the return of checks.[224] The Regulation CC warranties are made by each payor and returning bank that handles a check for return after dishonor and receives a settlement or other consideration for it.[225] The Regulation CC warranties are made to the transferee, to any subsequent returning bank, and to the owner of the check, and include a warranty that the check has been returned within the applicable midnight deadline, that the return is authorized, that the check has not been materially altered, and (where a notice is sent in lieu of the check) that the check has not and will not be returned.[226] Damages for breach can include the consideration received by the warrantor, plus finance charges and expenses "related to" the returned check.[227]

[7] Conclusion

Part 4 of Article 4 sets out only a part of the rules that govern the bank-customer relation. These primarily involve deposit accounts on which checks may be drawn. Even then, the complete rules are not contained in Article 4. For example, § 4–401 is supplemented by the deposit contract itself; to a considerable extent the effect of many of the Article 4 rules can be varied by agreement. *See supra* ¶ 8.01[2], ¶ 9.03[3]; *infra* ¶ 9.05. Nonetheless, the 1990 revisions to Article 4 and the 2002 amendments answer many previously unresolved questions in this area of law.

¶ 9.04 NOW and Share Drafts

Under the old version of Article 4, a Negotiable Order of Withdrawal (NOW) drawn on a savings and loan association or a share draft drawn on a credit union perhaps was not a check within the meaning of the Code.[228] Under old Article 4 a NOW or a share draft arguably was not drawn on a bank,[229] and perhaps also was not payable on

---

223. *See* § 4–209(a), (b). *See also* the definition of collecting bank at § 4–105(5). It is also not clear whether the Article 3 and 4 "transfer" warranties apply to items being returned after dishonor. *See* §§ 3–203(a) (definition of "transfer"); *see also* discussion *supra* Chapter 8 at ¶ 8.03 and 8.04[3][c]; *infra* ¶ 9.03[7].

224. *See* 12 CFR § 229.34, discussed *supra* this text at ¶ 8.04 [3][e]. These warranties apply only to checks. *See* 12 CFR § 229.1(b)(3). *See supra* ¶ 8.04[3][c], [e] and [f].

225. 12 CFR § 229.34(a), (b). *See supra* ¶ 8.04[3][c], [e] and [f].

226. 12 CFR § 229.34(a), (b). *See also supra* ¶ 8.04[3][e]. "Alteration" is not defined, but presumably the meaning would be similar to that in § 3–407(a).

227. Regulation CC, 12 CFR § 229.34(c). *Cf.* Article 4 § 4–209(c).

¶ 9.04

228. *See* old § 3–104(2)(b), which requires that the instrument be drawn on a bank and be payable on demand to be a "check."

229. A "bank" was defined in the old Code as an organization engaged in the business of banking. *See* § 1–201(4). This certainly would include a commercial bank. A commercial bank takes deposits and makes loans. So now do savings and loan associations and credit unions, but tradi-

demand.[230]

Even under old Article 3, however, these instruments fit within the broader definition of "draft,"[231] and so Article 3 could govern. Under either version of the Code, they fit within the definition of "item" for purposes of Article 4.[232] Therefore, even under the old version of the Code many provisions of Article 3 and Article 4 will apply, such as old § 3–118 with respect to ambiguous terms and rules of construction, and old § 4–207(1) with respect to warranties made to a payor bank or "other payor." But some provisions of old Article 3 and those provisions of old Article 4 that use the term "bank," such as old § 3–802(1)(a) on discharge of the underlying obligation where a bank is drawer, maker, or acceptor, and old § 4–401(1), which allows a "bank" to charge its customer's account, might not be literally applicable. Little more than semantics would be served, however, if NOW and share drafts were not treated like checks and governed by Articles 3 and 4 for purposes of bank collection and related provisions, and, for the most part, the cases under the old Code have taken that approach. For example, in *In re Estate of McGill*,[233] which involved a sight draft drawn upon a thrift institution, the draft was presented and paid after the drawer's death. The court, consistent with the provisions of old § 4–405 which only applies to banks, held that the drawee could honor the draft. By the same token, the court in *Florida Federal Savings & Loan Association v. Martin*[234] had no trouble applying the rules of old § 4–406, which again only applies to banks.[235] Nonetheless, the issues are important enough[236] that the revised Article 4 contains amendments to clarify the law and make it certain of application.[237]

---

tionally these institutions have had their powers more restricted than commercial banks. *See, e.g.*, J. White, Banking Law 34–44 (1976). Under the old Code it was uncertain whether a court would conclude that the word "bank" in Article 4 includes a savings and loan or a credit union with their new powers. As noted *infra* revised Article 4 resolves this uncertainty in favor of treating thrift institutions, credit unions, and the like as "banks." *See* revised § 4–105(1).

230. This is because of the right to advance notice of withdrawal. *See, e.g.*, American Bankers Ass'n v. Connell, 447 F.Supp. 296 (D.D.C.1978), *vacated* 595 F.2d 887 (D.C.Cir.1979) (share draft on federal credit union); New York State Bankers Ass'n v. Albright, 38 N.Y.2d 430, 381 N.Y.S.2d 17, 343 N.E.2d 735 (Ct.App.1975) (negotiable order of withdrawal); Dime Sav. Bank v. Chase Manhattan Bank, 16 UCC Rep. Serv. (Callaghan) 171 (N.Y.Sup.Ct.1974) (instrument drawing funds from savings account drawn on savings bank). However, the right to demand advance notice would not seem to change the demand nature of the instrument itself.

231. Old §§ 3–104(1), (2)(a).

232. Old § 4–104(1)(g). *Cf.* revised § 4–104(a)(9).

233. 54 Ill.App.3d 533, 13 Ill.Dec. 311, 371 N.E.2d 6 (Ill.App.1977).

234. 400 So.2d 151 (Fla.App.1981).

235. However, the court does not appear to have recognized the issue.

236. For a detailed discussion as to differences dependent upon whether the instrument is treated as a draft or as a check, *see, e.g.*, Leary, Is the UCC Prepared For the Thrifts' NOWs, NINOWs, and Share Drafts?, 30 CATH. U.L. REV. 159 (1981); Wilson, The "New Checks": Thrift Institution Check-like Instruments and the Uniform Commercial Code, 45 MO. L. REV. 199 (1980).

237. For example, in the *McGill* case, the instrument was paid within ten days of death. *In re* Estate of McGill, 54 Ill.App.3d 533, 13 Ill.Dec. 311, 371 N.E.2d 6 (Ill.App. 1977). Ten days is the outside limit for banks with knowledge of death under old § 4–405(2). Under old Article 4 would the court have reached the same result after ten days? Moreover, given the erosion of traditional lines of division between banks

As noted *supra* at ¶ 8.01[3][b], the definition of "bank" at revised § 4–105(1) directly confronts this issue by including within the definition of that term any "person engaged in the business of banking, including a savings bank, savings and loan association, credit union, or trust company."[238] The expanded definition of bank, together with the expanded definition of "item" at revised § 4–104(a)(9) (revised to include any "instrument or a promise or order to pay money handled by a bank for collection or payment," but excluding credit or debit card slips and Article 4A "payment orders"), means that any NOW or share draft will be subject to revised Article 4 and treated as a check for purposes of the Article 4 collection and payment rules.

However, the statute does not deal with whether a NOW or a share draft is payable on demand[239] and therefore check status is not completely clear. The comments to revised § 3–104 make clear, however, that a credit union share draft payable through a bank is within the definition of "check."[240] Thus, these instruments were intended to be treated as checks. It seems appropriate that these instruments be considered as payable "on demand" as that concept is defined at revised § 3–108, although the issue is not directly addressed.

¶ 9.05 The Basic Law of Bank Accounts

[1] *The Traditional Concept and Modern Variations of a "Bank Account"*

This discussion focuses on the basic law of bank accounts, including common law, contractual, statutory, and case law principles. The basic legal foundations for the law governing depositary transactions are discussed, along with some modern variations. There is also discussion of some basic issues relating to the bank-customer relation. Truth in Savings and deposit insurance are also discussed. Finally, there is discussion of some basic operational issues that bankers confront on a regular basis, involving banker's lien, set-off, garnishment, security interests in bank accounts, service charges, and check-kiting.

At common law, courts made no distinction between a deposit and other types of accounts and did not adopt a universal or specialized

---

and other account institutions, the issue now extends beyond even savings and loans and credit unions. *See, e.g.*, Asian Int'l, Ltd. v. Merrill Lynch, Pierce, Fenner & Smith, Inc., 435 So.2d 1058 (La.App.1983). *See* the expanded definition of bank at revised § 4–105(1), and discussion *supra* at ¶ 8.01[3][b]. *See also infra* ¶ 9.05.

238. As a result even nonbank entities that offer certain banking services, such as Merrill Lynch and other providers of cash management accounts accessed by drafts, could be treated as a bank for (some?) purposes under revised Articles 3 and 4. *But see* Merrill Lynch, Pierce, Fenner & Smith, Inc. v. Van Kylen, 98 B.R. 455 (Bankr. W.D.Wis. 1989) (Merrill Lynch cash management account is not a "deposit account" for purposes of the exclusion from old Article 9 at § 9–104(*l*)).

239. *See supra* note 228.

240. *See* revised § 3–104, Comment 4. As noted, a credit union is considered a bank. *See id.*, and revised § 4–105(1). In contrast, a draft drawn on an insurance company is not a check even if it is payable through a bank, because it is not drawn on a bank. *See* revised § 3–104, Comment 4.

definition of the term "deposit."[241] Generally, courts concluded that a deposit occurred when a customer placed money with a banking institution for safekeeping subject to withdrawal on the depositor's demand or pursuant to the deposit contract.[242] A "depositor" was essentially one who loaned money to a bank.[243] At common law, the depository relationship was essentially a contractual, debtor-creditor relationship;[244] as discussed elsewhere, this largely remains the case today, absent unusual circumstances giving rise to a special relationship.

The modern concept of "deposit" is built on these common law foundations, but it is also subject to statutory considerations, though generally these have not altered the contractual basis of the concept. Some statutory definitions are applicable only for a limited purpose. For example, a bank/customer transaction that is not defined as a "deposit account" under UCC Article 9 (old § 9–105(1)(e) or revised § 9–102(a)(29)) nevertheless may be properly classified as an "account" or a "deposit account" pursuant to some other statute, the common law, or the law of contracts. Note that UCC Article 4 uses the term "account" as a substitute for the term "deposit," but Article 9 at §§ 9–102(a)(2) and (29) defines the terms "account" and "deposit account" to mean two different things. In Article 4, an "account" is defined as "any deposit or credit account with a bank, including a demand, time, savings, passbook, share draft, or like account, other than an account evidenced by a certificate of deposit."[245] In revised Article 9, § 9–102(a)(29) defines

---

¶ 9.05

241. Gimbel Bros., Inc. v. White, 256 A.D. 439, 10 N.Y.S.2d 666 (1939). *Cf.* UCC § 4–104(a)(1) (definition of "account" in Article 4 as essentially a deposit account or credit account at a banking institution, other than a certificate of deposit); UCC § 9–102(a)(2) (definition of "account" in revised Article 9 as essentially any right to payment of a monetary obligation in return for an interest in property or services); UCC § 9–102(a)(29) (revised Article 9 definition of "deposit account," to include any account at a bank not evidenced by an instrument).

242. *Id.*; Kalb v. Chemical Bank N.Y. Trust Co., 62 Misc.2d 458, 309 N.Y.S.2d 502 (1969); Board of Educ. of School Dist. No. 148, Cook County, Ill. v. County of Cook, 42 Ill.App.2d 91, 191 N.E.2d 444 (1963). Firstar Eagan Bank, N.A. v. Marquette Bank Minneapolis, N.A., 466 N.W.2d 8 (Minn.Ct. App.1991), held that a dealer escrow account was not a deposit account, since it was not payable on demand. *Cf.* State Bank of Rose Creek v. First Bank of Austin, 320 N.W.2d 723 (Minn.1982). *See also* Woodrum v. Ford Motor Credit Co. (*In re* Dillard Ford, Inc.), 940 F.2d 1507 (11th Cir.1991) (dealer "proceeds withheld" account subject to security interest in inventory and accounts).

243. *Kalb*, 309 N.Y.S.2d at 502.

244. *See generally supra* ¶ 9.03 and *infra* ¶ 9.05.

245. § 4–104(a)(1). "Bank" is defined broadly at revised § 4–105(1) as any "person engaged in the business of banking," including savings and loan associations and credit unions. *See also* the definition of "deposit account" at § 9–102(a)(29). References herein to Article 9 are references to the revised Article 9, 2000 uniform text, unless otherwise stated. A negotiable certificate of deposit is included within the definition of instrument at revised UCC § 3–104(j), and is also defined as an instrument at § 9–102(a)(47), even if not negotiable, so long as it is transferable in the ordinary course of business. As a result a non-negotiable certificate of deposit may be an instrument under Article 9 but not Article 3. Note that if the certificate of deposit is a "promissory note" within the definition at § 9–102(a)(65), a sale of the note will be covered by Article 9 under § 9–109(a)(3). If the note is negotiable in form, such a sale will also be covered by UCC Article 3. As noted *supra*, an instrument is excluded from the Article 9 definition of "deposit account" at UCC § 9–105(1)(e). See *generally* Skiles v. Security State Bank, 1 Neb. App. 360, 494 N.W.2d 355 (Neb.Ct.App.

this as a "deposit account," and the term "account" is defined at § 9–102(a)(2) as something very different.

Federal banking statutes have defined the term "deposit," and the statutory definition of the term may vary according to the purpose of the statute under which it is defined. For example, the Federal Deposit Insurance Act provides that a deposit is "the unpaid balance of money or its equivalent received or held by a bank in the usual course of business and for which it has given or is obligated to give credit, either conditionally or unconditionally to a commercial, checking, savings, time, or thrift account, or which is evidenced by its certificate of deposit, thrift certificate, investment certificate, certificate of indebtedness, or other similar name or a check or draft against a deposit account and certified by the bank, or letter of credit or a traveler's check on which the bank is primarily liable."[246] Federal Reserve Board Regulation D governs reserve requirements of depositary institutions, and adopts a similar definition of "deposit."[247] For purposes of the Federal Truth in Savings Act, the term "account" is subject to yet a different definition.[248] An account is generally not considered to be a security under the federal securities laws.[249]

[2] Common Law Classifications of Deposit Accounts

[a] General and Special Purpose Accounts

A deposit can be classified either as a general or a special deposit. A special deposit is made when the bank and customer agree, either expressly or impliedly, that the money is deposited for a specific purpose.

1992). Bank IV Topeka, N.A. v. Topeka Bank and Trust Co., 15 Kan.App.2d 341, 807 P.2d 686, (Kan.Ct.App.1991), held that a certificate of deposit denoted "nontransferable" was a deposit account for purposes of Article 9 (and was therefore excluded from Article 9 under old § 9–105). *Cf.* revised § 9–109(d)(13). Kansas subsequently amended its version of old § 9–105(1)(i) to change this result. Another case held that a cash management account invested in certificates of deposit was a general intangible under Article 9. Merrill, Lynch, Pierce, Fenner & Smith, Inc. v. Van Kylen (*In re* Van Kylen), 98 B.R. 455 (Bankr.W.D.Wis.1989). However, probably a majority of courts have held that a "nontransferable" certificate of deposit can be transferable and hence an "instrument" under UCC Article 9. *In re* Latin Inv. Corp., 156 B.R. 102 (Bankr.D.D.C.1993). *See generally* Alvin C. Harrell, Security Interests in Deposit Accounts: A Unique Relationship Between the UCC and Other Law, 23 U.C.C. L.J. 153 (1990); *infra* ¶ 9.06.

246. 12 U.S.C. § 1813(1). A letter of credit issued by a bank generally does not meet the definition of "deposit" at 12 U.S.C. § 1813(1). Philadelphia Gear Corp. v. FDIC, 751 F.2d 1131 (10th Cir.1984), *rev'd*, 474 U.S. 918, 106 S.Ct. 245, 88 L.Ed.2d 253 (1985).

247. 12 CFR § 204.2(a)(1).

248. *See* Regulation DD, 12 CFR § 230.2(a).

249. A certificate of deposit is not considered a "security" for purposes of the Securities Exchange Act of 1934, 15 U.S.C. § 78j[b](1981). *See* Marine Bank v. Weaver, 455 U.S. 551, 102 S.Ct. 1220, 71 L.Ed.2d 409 (1982). Similarly a short-term promissory note evidencing a commercial loan is not a "security." *See, e.g.*, American Bank and Trust Co. v. Wallace, 702 F.2d 93 (6th Cir.1983). Certificates of deposit offered by a securities broker representing that the program includes liquidity, possible capital appreciation, and a secondary market are different from ordinary CDs and may be subject to federal securities laws. Gary Plastic Packaging Corp. v. Merrill, Lynch, Pierce, Fenner & Smith, Inc., 756 F.2d 230 (2d Cir.1985). The Truth in Savings Act applies to securities brokers advertising or selling accounts that are subject to the Truth in Savings disclosure requirements.

In contrast, a general account is one that has no special purpose except to be returned or paid (perhaps with interest) upon the customer's direction pursuant to the terms of the deposit contract.[250] All accounts are general accounts, absent a mutual agreement that the account is to be held for a special purpose.

The distinction between general and special accounts is important for three reasons. First, title to the deposited funds is determined by type of account. If funds are deposited in a special account, the customer retains title; if funds are deposited in a general account, title passes to the depositary institution. Second, the legal relationship between the depositary institution and the depositor is determined by the type of account. A special purpose account creates something in the nature of a bailee/bailor relationship; a general account creates a debtor/creditor relationship.[251] Finally, the uses to which the depositary institution may put deposits are determined by the type of account.[252] A special deposit must be segregated, and its use is limited to the agreed purpose;[253] a general deposit becomes part of the bank's general fund[254] and may be commingled with other funds[255] and used in general banking operations.[256] As a result of these distinctions, as noted *infra* at ¶ 9.06, a general account is subject to setoff while a special account is not.

[b] General or Special Purpose

As noted *supra*, an account is classified as general or special on the basis of the intention and understanding of the parties as expressed in

---

250. Mid–City Nat. Bank v. Mar Bldg. Corp., 33 Ill.App.3d 1083, 339 N.E.2d 497 (1975); Rainsville Bank v. Willingham, 485 So.2d 319 (Ala.1986); *infra* notes 251–276. *See also infra* ¶ 9.05[4][c].

251. *See, e.g.*, Soto v. First Gibralter Bank, 868 S.W.2d 400 (Tex. Ct. App. 1993) (party's desire to accumulate funds for daughter's education did not make the account a deposit for a specific special purpose-general funds were available to parents' creditors); Mancuso v. United Bank of Pueblo, 818 P.2d 732 (Colo.1991); Martin v. First State Bank, 490 S.W.2d 208 (Tex.Civ. App.1973), no writ; First Interstate Bank of Idaho v. Gill, 108 Idaho 576, 701 P.2d 196 (Idaho 1985); Tavormina v. Weiner (*In re* Alchar Hardware Co.), 759 F.2d 867 (11th Cir.1985); Capital Serv. v. Dahlinger Pontiac–Cadillac, 10 Kan.App.2d 328, 699 P.2d 549 (Kan.Ct.App.1985); Texas Mtg. Servs. Corp. v. Guadalupe Savings & Loan (*In re* Texas Mortgage Servs. Corp.), 761 F.2d 1068 (5th Cir.1985); American Sec. Bank v. Kaneshiro, 67 Haw. 354, 688 P.2d 254 (Haw.1984). The distinction between general and specific accounts can be significant. For example, a wrongful setoff of a general deposit account cannot be conversion, because title to the funds passed to the bank and the bank cannot convert what it already owns. The bank could still be liable for wrongful dishonor (*see supra*, ¶ 9.02[2]), but absent wrongful dishonor a bank is not liable for damages for wrongful setoff against a general account. *See, e.g., infra* ¶ 9.06; Moore v. State Bank of Burden, 240 Kan. 382, 729 P.2d 1205 (Kan. 1986). *But see* Masi v. Ford City Bank & Trust Co., 779 F.2d 397 (7th Cir.1985), holding that setoff of a special deposit (an IRA account) constituted a violation of the RICO statute.

252. *Mancuso*, 818 P.2d at 732; Bank of West Orange v. Associates Discount Corp., 197 So.2d 858 (Fla.App.1967).

253. McGhee v. Bank of America Nat. Trust & Sav. Ass'n, 60 Cal.App.3d 442, 131 Cal.Rptr. 482 (1976).

254. Mid–City Nat. Bank v. Mar Bldg. Corp., 33 Ill.App.3d 1083, 339 N.E.2d 497 (1975).

255. Hudnall v. Tyler Bank & Trust Co., 448 S.W.2d 503 (Tex.Civ.App.1969), *rev'd on other grounds*, 458 S.W.2d 183 (Tex.1970).

256. McGhee v. Bank of America Nat. Trust & Sav. Assn., 60 Cal.App.3d 442, 131 Cal.Rptr. 482 (1976).

their agreement.[257] Unless the parties expressly agree that an account is to be used for a specified purpose, the courts presume that the account is a general account.[258] Thus, an agreement by a banking institution to accept funds for "safekeeping" does not create a special deposit.[259] In addition, a special account is not necessarily created when a depositor designates a bank as a fiduciary, such as an agent or a trustee.[260]

Purposes for which special accounts have been established include: (1) deposits made under court order to an infant of funds from a negligence action or an inheritance,[261] (2) payments on notes held by a bank that became delinquent,[262] (3) payment of labor and material costs of a building project,[263] (4) payment of principal[264] or interest on bonds,[265] and (5) security for a lease.[266] As another example, a bank may accept and hold funds as an escrow agent to facilitate a real estate or other transaction with or between third parties. The bank becomes a trustee as to the escrow deposit, with a fiduciary obligation to account for the escrowed funds and to disburse them according to the escrow agreement.[267] The common mortgage loan escrow account for taxes, insurance, and the like is also a special account but ordinarily does not create a fiduciary obligation.

[3] The Basic Bank Account Relationship

[a] Creating a Depositary Account

The law does not require a particular procedure in order to establish a depositary account.[268] However, the institution and the customer must mutually assent to creation of the deposit account, either expressly or impliedly.[269] If the parties do not expressly agree to the terms of an

---

257. Martin v. First State Bank, 490 S.W.2d 208 (Tex.Civ.App.1973), no writ. See also Rainsville Bank v. Willingham, 485 So.2d 319 (Ala.1986).

258. First Nat. Bank of Clinton v. Julian, 383 F.2d 329 (8th Cir.1967); Isenhart v. Monty, 161 Colo. 589, 423 P.2d 836 (Colo. 1967); Carpenter v. Suffolk Franklin Sav. Bank, 362 Mass. 770, 291 N.E.2d 609 (Mass. 1973).

259. Mid–City Nat. Bank v. Mar Bldg. Corp., 33 Ill.App.3d 1083, 339 N.E.2d 497 (1975).

260. Denny v. Thompson, 236 Ky. 714, 33 S.W.2d 670 (Ky. 1930); Free v. Elberson, 157 Mont. 424, 486 P.2d 857 (Mont. 1971); Wasserman v. Broderick, 140 Misc. 174, 250 N.Y.S. 84 (1931).

261. Foulkrod v. First Nat. Bank of Waterloo, 70 Misc.2d 616, 334 N.Y.S.2d 285 (1972).

262. First Nat. Bank v. Hargrove, 503 S.W.2d 856 (Tex.Civ.App.1973), no writ.

263. Citizens Nat. Bank of Beaumont v. Francis, 427 S.W.2d 645 (Tex.Civ.App. 1968), writ ref'd n.r.e.

264. In re Interborough Consol. Corp., 288 F. 334 (2d Cir.1923), cert. denied, 262 U.S. 752, 43 S.Ct. 700, 67 L.Ed. 1215 (1923).

265. Northwest Lumber Co. v. Scandinavian–American Bank, 130 Wash. 33, 225 P. 825 (Wash. 1924).

266. Woodhouse v. Crandall, 197 Ill. 104, 64 N.E. 292 (Ill. 1902).

267. See, e.g., DeMello v. Home Escrow, Inc., 4 Haw.App. 41, 659 P.2d 759 (1983); Locks v. North Towne Nat. Bank of Rockford, 115 Ill.App.3d 729, 71 Ill.Dec. 531, 451 N.E.2d 19 (1983).

268. Valley Nat. Bank v. Witter, 58 Ariz. 491, 121 P.2d 414 (Ariz. 1942). See generally supra ¶ 9.03[1] and 9.05[1].

269. Westerly Community Credit Union v. Industrial Nat. Bank, 103 R.I. 662, 240 A.2d 586 (R.I. 1968). See also supra ¶ 8.01[2], 9.03[1], and ¶ 9.05[1]; Paradis v. Greater Providence Deposit Corp., 651 A.2d 738 (R.I.1994) (terms and conditions on signature cards become part of the contract between the parties and the bank). The

account, the law may imply terms based on the usual banking relationship.[270]

The terms that govern checking and savings accounts are generally embodied in a signature card, certificate of deposit, passbook, and/or other deposit agreement that a customer signs when the account is opened, plus any periodic account statements and/or subsequent disclosures sent to the customer.[271] The signature card or other agreement often incorporates by reference the rules of the institution.[272] For example, passbooks or signature cards may include printed rules that (a) release the institution from liability if the institution pays funds to an imposter in possession of the passbook, (b) require presentation of the passbook for withdrawal, (c) delineate requirements for the deposit of checks and other items, and (d) require examination of statements and

---

signature card, account agreement, related customer corporate resolutions, and monthly account statements all form parts of the contract between the payor bank and its customer, and should be reviewed periodically by both parties to assure consistency and that these documents reflect the intended agreement. For example, in Reliance Ins. Co. v. Bank of America Nat'l. Trust & Sav. Ass'n., 43 U.C.C. Rep. Serv.2d 946 (N.D.Ill., 2001), the account agreement, customer's corporate resolutions, and monthly statements established 30 days as a reasonable time period for customer examination of the monthly account statements. The parties were bound by this agreement.

270. Taylor v. Equitable Trust Co., 269 Md. 149, 304 A.2d 838 (Md. 1973). For example, a customer's right to privacy of his or her bank records is governed by the United States Constitution, statutes and case law, as is the right of others to disclosure of those records in certain circumstances. *See* U.S. v. Miller, 425 U.S. 435, 96 S.Ct. 1619, 48 L.Ed.2d 71 (1976). For a more recent case illustrating state law considerations, *see* People v. Jackson, 116 Ill. App.3d 430, 72 Ill.Dec. 153, 452 N.E.2d 85 (1983). *See also* the Bank Secrecy Act and regulations, 31 U.S.C. § 5311 *et. seq.*, 31 CFR Pt. 103 *et. seq.*; the Right of Financial Privacy Act, 12 U.S.C. § 3401 *et. seq.*; and various state financial privacy acts, *e.g.*, Okla. Stat. tit. 6 § 2201 *et. seq.* Developments in this area of law have recently become even more complicated. *See, e.g., Symposium on Privacy*, 55 CONSUMER FIN. L.Q. REP. 4 (2001).

271. *See, e.g., supra* ¶ 9.01[1]; Reliance Ins. Co. v. Bank of America Nat'l Trust & Sav. Ass'n., 43 U.C.C. Rep. Serv.2d 946 (N.D.Ill.2001); Sybert, Adhesion Theory in California: A Suggested Redefinition and its Application to Banking, 11 LOY. L.A. L. REV. 297 (1978). Account disclosures given to the customer, including the Regulation CC disclosures (12 CFR Part 229) and Regulation DD disclosures (12 CFR Part 230), will also be considered part of the deposit contract even if not signed. The bank-customer relation will also be governed by UCC Article 4. *See supra* ¶ 9.03[1], [2]. The deposit agreement is an executory contract subject to modification or termination by either party with minimal notice. Thus, subject to some foundational constraints based on good faith (*see* § 3–103(a)(4)) and a few aberrational cases to the contrary, the deposit agreement can be modified or terminated by either party after notice, *e.g.*, by means of a "statement stuffer" included with a periodic account statement. *See, e.g.*, A. Daniel Woska, Arbitration Clauses in Consumer Retail Installment Sales Contracts After the Green Tree Financial v. Randoph Decision, 55 CONSUMER FIN. L.Q. REP. 107 (2001) (discussing Badie v. Bank of America, 67 Cal.App.4th 779, 79 Cal.Rptr.2d 273 (1998) (statement stuffer was not sufficient notice to change fundamental terms of deposit agreement); Szetela v. Discover Bank, 118 Cal.Rptr.2d 862, 97 Cal.App.4th 1094 (2002) (statement-stuffer is procedurally unconscionable). *Szetela* is criticized in Alan S. Kaplinsky and Mark J. Levin, The Gold Rush of 2002; California Courts Lure Plaintiff Lawyers (but Undermine the Federal Arbitration Act) by Refusing to Enforce "No–Class Action" Clauses in Consumer Arbitration Agreements, 58 Bus. Law. ___ (2003) (in press).

272. In addition, certain disclosures are required under Federal Reserve Board Regulations CC and DD. These rules may also be distributed or made available in a separate brochure.

cancelled checks.[273]

Contractual terms are also included in deposit slips. The customer is bound by the terms appearing on a deposit slip which he or she uses, but is not charged with knowledge of, or assent to, terms that appear only on an institution's copy of the deposit slip.[274] Since the deposit slip generally is part of the contract, extrinsic evidence may not be sufficient to change the terms contained in the deposit slip.[275] The deposit slip is a means to set forth what the parties are required to do.[276]

If the institution and the customer have embodied the terms of their deposit agreement in a written contract (*i.e.*, a signature card or passbook), the contract generally is conclusive as between the customer and the institution. Absent fraud, duress or mistake, a court will be bound by the terms of the agreement, and it should not consider extrinsic evidence of the parties' intent.[277]

As noted earlier in this discussion, the contract is formed when the institution accepts and acknowledges the deposit.[278] Accordingly, the legal relationship is determined at the time the account is established,[279] and the money deposited is consideration for the obligation of the institution to repay the deposit.[280] The contract should be interpreted so as to effectuate the intent of the parties.[281] The relationship is a continuing, or executory contract, and is therefore subject to modification or termination by either party upon reasonable notice.

Generally, the courts will enforce terms that impose limitations upon the institution and/or the customer.[282] The courts, however, will not enforce clauses exculpating the institution from liability for failure to exercise good faith or reasonable care.[283]

---

273. *See also* UCC §§ 3–404, 3–405, 3–406, 4–401, 4–406; *supra* ¶ 9.03.

274. Jiang v. First Nat. City Bank, 65 Misc.2d 150, 317 N.Y.S.2d 635 (1970).

275. Liner v. Commercial Nat. Bank, 85 Ga.App. 278, 69 S.E.2d 119 (Ga.Ct.App. 1952).

276. Citizens Nat. Bank v. Hill, 505 S.W.2d 246 (Tex.1974). *See also* UCC § 4–301; UCC Article 4 Parts 2 and 3, discussed *supra* ¶ 9.02 and ¶ 9.03.

277. *See, e.g.*, First Nat. Bank and Trust v. Kissee, 859 P.2d 502 (Okla.1993); Miller v. American Nat. Bank and Trust Co., 4 F.3d 518 (7th Cir.1993); Bennett v. First Nat. Bank, 443 F.2d 518 (8th Cir. 1971).

278. Gardner v. Warren Bank, 14 Mich. App. 548, 165 N.W.2d 869 (Mich.Ct.App. 1968). *See also supra* notes 269–270.

279. Kos v. Patrons State Bank & Trust Co. (*In re* Estate of Matthews), 208 Kan. 492, 493 P.2d 555 (Kan. 1972). As noted elsewhere in this discussion, this is subject to subsequent modifications by either party upon reasonable notice to the other.

280. Johnson v. Stamets (*In re* Estate of Stamets), 260 Iowa 93, 148 N.W.2d 468 (Iowa 1967).

281. Western Nat. Bank v. Hawkeye–Security Ins., 380 F.Supp. 508 (D.Wyo. 1974).

282. David v. Mfrs. Hanover Trust Co., 59 Misc.2d 248, 298 N.Y.S.2d 847 (1969).

283. *See* UCC § 4–103(a); UCC § 3–103(a)(4); Hy-Grade Oil Co. v. N.J. Bank, 138 N.J.Super. 112, 350 A.2d 279 (App.Div. 1975); Grisinger v. Golden State Bank, 92 Cal.App. 443, 268 P. 425 (Cal.Ct.App.1928); discussion *supra* at ¶ 9.03. *But see* Western Assur. Co. v. Star Financial Bank, 3 F.3d 1129 (7th Cir.1993) (bank excused from violating restrictive indorsement, under deposit contract). The deposit agreement is usually an adhesion contract, but this means only that a heightened judicial sensitivity is appropriate with respect to issues such as good faith and adequate notice. *See, e.g.*, Woska, *supra* note 271.

[b] Nature of the Bank–Customer Relation

The legal relationship between a banking institution and its customer is created by an express or implied contract.[284] If the deposit is a general deposit, title to the money passes to the institution,[285] and a debtor/creditor relationship is created.[286] Thus, the institution assumes an obligation to the depositor to repay the funds, and the funds become the property of the institution.[287] If a deposit is a special deposit, the relationship between the institution and the customer is that of bailor and bailee.[288] The bank has a duty as a bailor to return the deposit to the depositor, and the deposit may not be commingled with the institution's other funds.[289]

[c] Fundamental Duties and Liabilities of the Bank

[i] General Deposits

When title to a general deposit passes to the banking institution, it assumes the risk of loss if the deposit is lost, destroyed, or stolen.[290] Thus, if an institution pays out funds to an imposter on presentment of a lost or stolen passbook, it may suffer the loss and be liable to the account owner for the fraudulently withdrawn funds.[291] Prior to Article

---

284. *Stamets*, 148 N.W.2d at 468. *See also supra* ¶ 9.03. *But see* Shaw v. Union Bank and Trust Co., 640 P.2d 953 (Okla. 1981) (banks have "quaisi-public" status); Banque Arabe Et Intern. D' Inv. v. Maryland Nat. Bank, 819 F.Supp. 1282 (S.D.N.Y. 1993), *aff'd*, 57 F.3d 146 (2d Cir.1995) (bank's superior knowledge created a duty to disclose); Cagle v. Loyd, 617 So.2d 592 (La.App. 3d. Cir.1993) (bank officer with superior knowledge liable to customers who relied on his advice). *Cf.* Gilbreath v. First State Bank of Joplin, 859 S.W.2d 237 (Mo. App. S.D.1993) (no fiduciary duty); cases discussed *infra*, and discussion *supra* at ¶ 9.03.

285. Town Bank & Trust Co. v. Silverman, 3 Mass.App.Ct. 28, 322 N.E.2d 192 (1975). *See also supra* ¶ 9.03 and ¶ 9.05[1].

286. *Id. See, e.g.*, Miller v. American Nat. Bank and Trust Co., 4 F.3d 518 (7th Cir.1993) (bank does not owe a fiduciary duty to its depositors); *Gilbreath*, 859 S.W.2d 237; First Nat. Bank and Trust v. Kissee, 859 P.2d 502 (Okla.1993); Manufacturers Hanover Trust Co. v. Yanakas, 7 F.3d 310 (2d Cir.1993), *motion to vacate denied* 11 F.3d 381 (2d Cir.1993); Aspinall v. U.S., 984 F.2d 355 (10th Cir.1993); Sharpe's Estate v. Metropolitan Nat. Bank, 31 Colo.App. 511, 503 P.2d 1043 (1972); Bank of Marin v. England, 385 U.S. 99, 87 S.Ct. 274, 17 L.Ed.2d 197 (1966); *supra* ¶ 9.03.

287. Meyer v. Idaho First Nat. Bank, 96 Idaho 208, 525 P.2d 990 (Idaho 1974).

288. Citizens Nat. Bank v. Hill, 505 S.W.2d 246 (Tex.1974). *See also supra* ¶ 9.05[2]; *infra* ¶ 9.05[4][c].

289. Rosen v. State Bank, 32 Misc. 231, 65 N.Y.S. 666 (1900); Hager v. Buffalo Sav. Bank, 10 Misc. 455, 31 N.Y.S. 448 (1894). *See also supra* ¶ 9.05[1].

290. Glennan v. Rochester Trust & Safe Deposit Co., 209 N.Y. 12, 102 N.E. 537 (N.Y. 1913). *See also supra* ¶ 9.05[2].

291. UCC § 3–404; discussion *supra* Chapters 6 and 7, and *supra* at ¶ 9.02[3]. *See generally*, John J. Michalik, Annotation, Liability of Savings Bank for Payments to Person Presenting Lost or Stolen Passbook or Savings Account Card, 68 A.L.R.3d 1080 (1976). A depositor may not sue in conversion to recover his deposit but instead must sue for breach of the depository contract. Upper Valley Aviation v. Mercantile Nat. Bank, 656 S.W.2d 952 (Tex.App.1983). *But see, Shaw*, 640 P.2d at 953. If the funds are paid out upon a withdrawal request that is proper under the terms of the deposit agreement, and the withdrawal check is made payable to the account holder, the bank is not responsible for subsequent misuse of the funds, e.g., where an authorized account holder, trustee or corporate officer withdraws funds and then dissipates the money to the detriment of other interested parties. The transferee of such an instrument may be liable, however, for funds paid on an improper indorsement or in an apparent breach of fiduciary duty. *See, e.g.*,

4, absent an agreement limiting the bank's liability, the courts were divided as to the extent of an institution's liability for payments made upon presentment of a lost or stolen passbook.[292] Under Article 4 § 4–103, such an agreement cannot limit the bank's liability for a failure to exercise ordinary care. Generally, courts impose liability only if the fraudulent withdrawal of funds resulted from the institution's failure to exercise ordinary care.[293] If the account holder was negligent and this contributed to the loss, the customer may also be liable under the comparative negligence rules in Article 3, Part 4. Article 3, also qualifies the holdings of some courts that a banking institution breaches its duty of ordinary care if it fails to compare the signature on the signature card with the signature on the withdrawal order.[294] In some cases, where an institution's employee doubts the identity of the person making a withdrawal, it may be under a duty to require identification.[295] Often in such cases there will be fault on both sides (the bank and its customer), resulting in a shared loss allocation under Article 3, *e.g.*, §§ 3–403, 3–404, 3–405, 3–406, 3–407, and/or 4–406.

The duties and liabilities of a banking institution with regard to many deposit account transactions are governed by other provisions of Article 4.[296] Article 4 provides that an institution may be liable for (i) wrongful dishonor,[297] (ii) failure to act properly to dishonor a check or

§§ 3–201, 3–202, 3–307, and 3–420; Article 3 Part 4.

292. *See e.g.*, Ogborn v. Bank of America Nat. Trust & Sav. Ass'n, 28 Cal.App.2d 565, 83 P.2d 44 (1938); Highfield v. First Nat. Bank, 45 Ga.App. 431, 165 S.E. 135 (1932); Polonsky v. Union Fed. Sav. & Loan Ass'n, 334 Mass. 697, 138 N.E.2d 115 (Mass. 1956).

293. *See e.g.*, Gillen v. Maryland Nat. Bank, 274 Md. 96, 333 A.2d 329 (Md. 1975); Kalb v. Chemical Bank N.Y. Trust Co., 62 Misc.2d 458, 309 N.Y.S.2d 502 (1969), *rev'd on other grounds*, 64 Misc.2d 824, 316 N.Y.S.2d 381 (1970). "Ordinary care" is defined in revised UCC Article 3, at § 3–103(a)(7), to mean observance of reasonable commercial standards prevailing in that general geographic area and in that type of business. In the case of checks presented by automated means this does not require sight examination of the drawer's signature.

294. Bulakowski v. Philadelphia Sav. Fund Soc., 270 Pa. 538, 113 A. 553 (1921); Ninoff v. Hazel Green State Bank, 174 Wis. 560, 183 N.W. 673 (1921). *See* UCC § 3–103(a)(7) (definition of ordinary care).

295. Rosen v. State Bank, 32 Misc. 231, 65 N.Y.S. 666 (1900); Hager v. Buffalo Sav. Bank, 10 Misc. 455, 31 N.Y.S. 448 (1894). *See* UCC § 3–501(b)(2). *Cf.* Western Assur. Co. v. Star Financial Bank, 3 F.3d 1129 (7th Cir.1993) (bank's failure to comply with restrictive indorsement excused under deposit contract).

296. *See supra* ¶ 9.01, ¶ 9.02, and ¶ 9.03. Article 4 is not limited to checking accounts. A savings withdrawal order is an "item" governed by Article 4. Shaw v. Union Bank and Trust Co., 640 P.2d 953 (Okla.1981). *See also* the broad definition of "item" at UCC § 4–104(a)(9); *supra* ¶ 8.01 and ¶ 9.01. Application of the UCC does not necessarily preclude a common law action for negligence in the bank's handling of the account, but generally such an action will require egregious circumstances. For example, where a bank advised a customer that a deposited check was "good," the bank was estopped from recovering funds subsequently drawn and paid against that check, even though the deposited check was returned unpaid for insufficient funds. However, the bank was entitled to charge back the returned check to the customer's account, to the extent of funds remaining in the account. *See* First Georgia Bank v. Webster, 168 Ga.App. 307, 308 S.E.2d 579 (Ga.Ct. App.1983); *see also* UCC § 1–103.

297. UCC § 4–402. *See supra* ¶ 9.02. Note that imposing a fee for a noncustomer to cash a check does not constitute dishonor. *See* Moorehouse v. Chase Manhattan Bank, 76 S.W.3d 608 (Tex.Ct.App.2002); Hayes v. First Commerce Corp., 763 So.2d 733 (La.Ct.App.2000); Batten v. Bank One,

other item,[298] (iii) ignoring a stop payment order,[299] or (iv) paying a forged check.[300]

[ii] Special Deposits

A banking institution must exercise reasonable care as bailee of a special deposit.[301] If the institution exercises reasonable care, it will not be held liable for the loss, destruction or theft of the deposit.[302] The loss or theft of a special deposit, however, may raise a presumption that the institution has acted negligently.[303] Thus, the bank may have the burden of proving that it exercised reasonable care.[304] If the institution is acting as a gratuitous bailee, receiving no compensation for holding the special deposit as such, some courts limit liability to actions that are grossly negligent.[305]

[iii] Fiduciary Duty of Disclosure

The law may impose a fiduciary duty of disclosure upon a banking institution in special circumstances.[306] As a general rule, a bank/customer relationship does not create a fiduciary duty of disclosure. However, some courts have held that if an institution assumes a special relationship of trust or confidence with a customer, it assumes a fiduciary duty to disclose material facts.[307] The duty may arise, for example, if the bank

---

N.A., 2000 WL 1364408 (N.D.Ill.2000); Wells Fargo Bank Texas, N.A. v. James, 184 F.Supp.2d 588 (W.D.Tex.2001), aff'd 321 F.3d 488 (5th Cir.2003); Office of the Comptroller of the Currency (OCC) Interpretive Letters 932, 933, and 934 (referencing 12 U.S.C. § 24(7) and 12 CFR § 7.4002).

298. UCC §§ 4–301, 4–302. *See supra* ¶ 9.02. *See also supra* Chapter 8.

299. UCC § 4–403. *See supra* ¶ 9.02. *See also* ¶ 9.01.

300. UCC §§ 4–401, 4–406. *See supra* ¶ 9.01[1], [3]; ¶ 9.03[4]. The deposit contract also may govern these issues. *See, e.g.,* Western Assur. Co. v. Star Financial Bank, 3 F.3d 1129 (7th Cir.1993) (deposit contract excused bank's failure to comply with restrictive indorsement). *See supra* this text ¶ 9.03.

301. Byer v. Canadian Bank of Commerce, 57 P.2d 985 (Cal. Dist. Ct. App. 1936), subsequent opinion, 8 Cal.2d 297, 65 P.2d 67 (Cal. 1937); Friede v. Nat. City Bank, 222 A.D. 645, 227 N.Y.S. 378 (1928), aff'd, 250 N.Y. 288, 165 N.E. 452 (1929). *See also supra* ¶ 9.05[2].

302. Owosso Masonic Temple Ass'n v. State Sav. Bank, 273 Mich. 682, 263 N.W. 771 (Mich. 1935); § 4–202; *supra* ¶ 9.03[7].

303. Minnesota Mut. Life Ins. Co. v. Tagus State Bank, 34 N.D. 566, 158 N.W. 1063 (N.D. 1916); First Nat. Bank v. Graham, 79 Pa. 106, 21 Am. Rep. 49 (1875); Tavormina v. Weiner (*In re* Alchar Hardware Co.), 759 F.2d 867 (11th Cir.1985) (lessee's security deposit under a lease was not a "special fund" protected from the offset); Capital Serv. v. Dahlinger Pontiac-Cadillac, 10 Kan.App.2d 328, 699 P.2d 549 (Kan.Ct.App.1985) (payroll account was a special account not subject to offset). *See also* American Sec. Bank v. Kaneshiro, 67 Haw. 354, 688 P.2d 254 (Haw. 1984); Rainsville Bank v. Willingham, 485 So.2d 319 (Ala.1986). If general funds are commingled into a special account, the account loses its "specialness." *See* Alexander & Jones v. Sovran Bank, 905 F.2d 716 (4th Cir.1990).

304. Trustees of Elon College v. Elon Banking & Trust Co., 182 N.C. 298, 109 S.E. 6 (N.C. 1921).

305. Manhattan Bank v. Walker, 130 U.S. 267, 9 S.Ct. 519, 32 L.Ed. 959 (1889); Pattison v. Syracuse National Bank, 80 N.Y. 82 (1880).

306. *See generally*, Annotation, Existence of Fiduciary Relationship Between Bank and Depositor or Customer so as to Impose Special Duty of Disclosure Upon Bank. 70 A.L.R.3d 1344 (1976); *supra* ¶ 9.03.

307. *Id. See, e.g.,* Tone v. Halsey, Stuart & Co., 286 Ill.App. 169, 3 N.E.2d 142 (1936); First Nat. Bank v. Brown, 181 N.W.2d 178 (Iowa 1970); Bank of Com-

has acted as a personal financial advisor to a depositor for many years, and the depositor has relied upon this advice.[308]

[iv] Duties of the Customer

A depositor owes a banking institution a reciprocal duty of due care in its transactions with the bank.[309] This duty includes a duty (a) to report stolen checks or a stolen passbook, (b) to draft withdrawal instruments carefully and unambiguously, and (c) to otherwise engage in reasonable conduct with respect to the account.[310] The UCC provides that when a bank sends the customer an account statement, the customer has a duty to reasonably and promptly examine the statement and to notify the bank of any alteration or unauthorized signature.[311] A customer's failure to conduct an examination and to notify the bank when required may relieve the bank from liability.[312]

[v] Termination of the Relationship

The relationship between a bank and a customer, absent a contractual provision to the contrary, is an executory contract and is terminable at the will of either party.[313] The bank may terminate the relationship by tendering the full amount of the deposit, though one older case required the bank to give reasonable notice prior to closing the account.[314] A

---

merce & Trust Co. v. Dye, 1 Tenn.App. 486 (1926). "Materiality" is a question of fact to be determined in light of all the circumstances. *Id.*

308. Stewart v. Phoenix Nat. Bank, 49 Ariz. 34, 64 P.2d 101 (Ariz. 1937). A close personal or business relationship is not enough to create a fiduciary duty of disclosure in absence of evidence that the customer placed a special trust or confidence in the banker or relied on the banker's counsel and advice. *See* Baylor v. Jordan, 445 So.2d 254 (Ala.1984). *See also* Miller v. American Nat. Bank and Trust Co., 4 F.3d 518 (7th Cir.1993) (no fiduciary duty); First Nat. Bank and Trust v. Kissee, 859 P.2d 502 (Okla.1993) (same); *supra* ¶ 9.03, ¶ 9.05[2]. In one case a bank officer's oral promise to waive the penalty for early withdrawal from a C.D. was binding. The bank's subsequent failure to waive the penalty ($1,139.98) led to an award of $62,500 punitive damages. City Bank of Alabama v. Eskridge, 521 So.2d 931 (Ala.1988). *See also* Rainsville Bank v. Willingham, 485 So.2d 319 (Ala.1986).

309. *See* Dominion Constr., Inc. v. First Nat. Bank, 271 Md. 154, 315 A.2d 69 (Md. 1974); Park State Bank v. Arena Auto Auction, 59 Ill.App.2d 235, 207 N.E.2d 158 (1965); UCC § 3–103(a)(7). The relation between depositor and depositary bank is that of principal and agent, thereby incorporating the law of agency. *See, e.g.,* § 4–201; *supra* ¶ 9.03.

310. Dominion Constr., Inc. v. First Nat. Bank, 271 Md. 154, 315 A.2d 69 (Md. 1974); George Whalley Co. v. National City Bank of Cleveland, 55 Ohio App.2d 205, 380 N.E.2d 742 (1977). Many of those duties are incorporated in the UCC. *See e.g.,* UCC §§ 4–401, 4–406. *See also* UCC §§ 3–404, 3–405, and 3–406.

311. § 4–406, and discussion *supra* at ¶ 9.03[4].

312. §§ 4–406, 4–407. *See supra* ¶ 9.03[4].

313. Elliott v. Capital City State Bank, 128 Iowa 275, 103 N.W. 777 (Iowa 1905). Generally a bank does not have an obligation to notify other parties that a mutual customer may be engaged in check-kiting, and may protect itself (*e.g.*, by closing the account) without prior notice. *See, e.g.,* Frost Nat'l. Bank v. Midwest Autohaus, Inc., 241 F.3d 862 (7th Cir.2001); Alta Vista State Bank v. Kobliska, 897 F.2d 930 (8th Cir.1990). However, the new higher standard of good faith may affect this analysis, particularly if the bank has assumed a special duty to protect the other party. *See supra* note 95; and *supra* ¶ 9.03.

314. Ambruster v. National Bank, 116 N.J.L. 122, 182 A. 613 (E.&A.1936).

customer generally may terminate the relationship by withdrawing the funds from the account.[315]

[vi] *The Bank Secrecy Act*

The Anti–Drug Abuse Act of 1986 amended the Bank Secrecy Act.[316] Implementing regulations were issued April 6, 1987. The rules require banks to aggregate multiple cash transactions of which they have knowledge, for the purpose of triggering the $10,000 Currency Transaction Report ("CTR") reporting requirement. They also provide procedures for verifying a customer's identity, requiring retention of transaction account records for five years, reducing the reporting period from 30 to 15 days, and clarifying certain exemptions and definitions. Banks must also have procedures for monitoring compliance.[317]

¶ 9.06 Banker's Lien, Setoff, Garnishment and Security Interests in Bank Accounts

In limited circumstances, a banking institution may secure a debt owed by a customer by imposing a banker's lien. In addition, a banking institution may have a right of set-off. A customer's bank account may also be subject to garnishment by another creditor of the customer and under revised Article 9, deposit accounts are directly subject to security interests in non-consumer transactions, as well as the traditional Article 9 proceeds claim. Each of these matters is discussed below.

[1] *Banker's Lien*

The banker's lien has its origins in the common law.[318] It is a lien that gives a banking institution the right to retain possession of securities or other property delivered to the bank in the ordinary course of business by a person to whom the bank has advanced money.[319] A

---

315. F.D.I.C. v. Thompson, 54 Ga.App. 611, 188 S.E. 737 (Ga.Ct.App.1936); Germantown Trust Co. v. Powell, 265 Pa. 71, 108 A. 441 (Pa. 1919); Fisher v. North Penn Bank, 77 Pa.Super. 558 (1921).

316. 12 U.S.C. § 1829b, 12 U.S.C. § 1951 *et. seq.*, 31 U.S.C. § 5311 *et. seq.*

317. The 1986 law did not include a proposed amendment that would have required reporting on all transactions of $3,000 or more. *See* 31 CFR Part 103. The regulatory agencies subsequently adopted a joint rule, effective April 27, 1987, establishing new procedures to assure compliance. Banking institutions generally are required to keep a log of all cash transactions of $3,000 or more, even if such transactions are not reportable. *See* 31 U.S.C. § 5311 *et. seq.*; 31 CFR part 103 *et. seq.*; Pringle & Allen, Currency Transaction Reports, Criminal Referrals, and the Right to Privacy, 46 CONSUMER FIN. L.Q. REP. 33 (1992); Charles W. Blau, The Right to Financial Privacy and the Criminal Referral Process: A Conflict in the Terms and Purpose of the Money Laundering Statutes, 44 CONSUMER FIN. L.Q. REP. 9 (1990). Recent privacy and anti-terrorism legislation has added several new layers to this privacy matrix. *See, e.g.*, Symposium on Privacy, 55 CONSUMER FIN. L.Q. REP. 4 (2001).

¶ 9.06

318. Bank of Jamestown v. Cattaraugus County Bank, 148 Misc. 655, 266 N.Y.S. 622 (1933).

319. Bank of Metropolis v. New England Bank, 42 U.S. (1 How.) 234, 11 L.Ed. 115 (1843); Citizens' Bank of Millerton v. Beeson, 104 Okla. 293, 231 P. 844 (Okla. 1924); First Nat. Bank of Ada v. Jackson, 140 Okla. 282, 283 P. 242 (Okla. 1929); Engleman v. Bank of America Nat. Trust & Sav. Ass'n., 98 Cal.App.2d 327, 219 P.2d 868 (Cal. Dist. Ct. App. 1950). As noted *infra* this text, a banker's lien may arise if

banker's lien may be created by contract,[320] statute,[321] or operation of law.[322] For example, a banker's lien may be created when a loan applicant delivers a deed, abstract of title, or other papers or things of value to a financial institution in conjunction with a loan application, and the papers or other things of value are held by the institution to secure the institution's right to reimbursement for funds expended in processing the loan application.[323]

A banking institution's right to set-off a general deposit against the indebtedness of a depositor is sometimes erroneously referred to as a "banker's lien."[324] However, the right to set-off is not technically a lien, because a banking institution "owns" the funds deposited in a general account and cannot have a lien on its own property.[325] A banker's lien is more correctly viewed as a bundle of rights entirely separate from the right of set-off.

When the parties have not contracted for a lien, the theory underlying the existence of a banker's lien is that a bank performs services for or grants credit to a customer with the implicit understanding that money or property of sufficient value to pay the debt will come into the institution's possession.[326] If special circumstances indicate that this expectation is not justified, no banker's lien arises.[327] For example, no

---

the bank has advanced funds to a third person or performed services at the request or on behalf of a customer or loan applicant.

320. H. Lang & Co. v. Northern Jobbing Co., 22 F.Supp. 688 (D.C.Minn.1938). See also Trust Co. of Columbus v. U.S., 735 F.2d 447 (11th Cir.1984). Cf. U.S. v. Bank of Celina, 721 F.2d 163 (6th Cir.1983) (banker's lien v. federal tax lien). See also, Brown v. Maguire's Real Estate Agency, 343 Mo. 336, 121 S.W.2d 754 (Mo. 1938); Macon Nat. Bank v. Smith, 170 Ga. 332, 153 S.E. 4 (Ga. 1930); Georgia Bank & Trust Co. v. Hadarits, 221 Ga. 125, 143 S.E.2d 627 (Ga. 1965).

321. See, e.g., Engleman v. Bank of America Nat. Trust & Sav. Ass'n., 98 Cal. App.2d 327, 219 P.2d 868 (Cal. Dist. Ct. App. 1950). A credit union may have a special statutory lien. See Witt, Rodeman & Parker, Beyond Setoff: The Credit Union Statutory Lien, 47 CONSUMER FIN. L.Q. REP. 12 (1993).

322. Everglade Cypress Co. v. Tunnicliffe, 107 Fla. 675, 148 So. 192 (Fla. 1933); Spurlock v. Commercial Banking Co., 138 Ga.App. 892, 227 S.E.2d 790 (Ga.Ct.App. 1976), aff'd, 238 Ga. 123, 231 S.E.2d 748 (1977).

323. For example, this would allow an institution to hold a loan applicant's abstract of title to secure its claim against the loan applicant for abstracting expense, or the applicant's deed and/or title insurance policy, where the applicant has withdrawn the loan application after inducing the bank to incur application-related expenses.

324. U.S. v. New York Trust Co., 75 F.Supp. 583 (S.D.N.Y.1946); Aiken v. Bank of Ga., 101 Ga.App. 200, 113 S.E.2d 405 (Ga.Ct.App.1960). For discussion of a bank's right of setoff, see infra ¶ 9.06[2].

325. Gonsalves v. Bank of America Nat. Trust & Sav. Ass'n., 16 Cal.2d 169, 105 P.2d 118 (Cal. 1940); Meyer v. Idaho First Nat. Bank, 96 Idaho 208, 525 P.2d 990 (Idaho 1974); Bonhiver v. State Bank of Clearing, 29 Ill.App.3d 794, 331 N.E.2d 390 (1975); U.S. v. Bank of Celina, 721 F.2d 163 (6th Cir.1983); Kasparek v. Liberty Nat. Bank, 170 Okla. 207, 39 P.2d 127 (Okla. 1934); John P. Roberts, Banker's Right of Set–Off: Overview and Analysis, 47 CONSUMER FIN. L.Q. REP. 173 (1993); Alvin C. Harrell, Security Interests in Deposit Accounts: A Unique Relationship Between the UCC and Other Law, 23 U.C.C. L. J. 153 (1990); TeSelle, Banker's Right of Setoff—Banker Beware, 34 OKLA. L. REV. 40 (1981).

326. Zollmann, the Law of Banks and Banking 72 (perm. ed. 1936).

327. Goggin v. Bank of America Nat. Trust & Sav. Ass'n., 183 F.2d 322 (9th Cir.1950), cert. denied, 340 U.S. 877, 71 S.Ct. 122, 95 L.Ed. 637 (1950), reh. denied, 340 U.S. 898, 71 S.Ct. 237, 95 L.Ed. 651 (1950).

lien is created if the property does not come into possession of the institution in the ordinary course of business,[328] or if the institution knows or should know that the property delivered to the institution is beneficially owned by someone other than the bank's customer,[329] or if the property is deposited for a special purpose.[330] A banker's lien is a possessory lien that does not extend to property outside the institution's possession or control.[331]

The banker's lien may be relinquished by contract[332] or may be lost by waiver[333] or operation of law.[334] In addition, a bank may be estopped from exercising the lien if the banking institution has accepted a deposit for a special purpose or has led a third person to believe that it has no lien, and where that person relies on the institution's assertions to his detriment.[335]

[2] Setoff

[a] Background and Legal Basis

When a depositor is indebted to a banking institution on a matured obligation, the institution has the right, subject to certain limitations, to set-off or reduce the indebtedness by charging the debt to the customer's account.[336] Although many states have authorized the right of setoff by statute,[337] the right exists even without express statutory authority.[338]

---

328. *In re* Dimon's Estate, 32 N.Y.S.2d 239 (1941).

329. Reynes v. Dumont, 130 U.S. 354, 9 S.Ct. 486, 32 L.Ed. 934 (1889); Central National Bank v. Connecticut Mut. Insurance Co., 104 U.S. (14 Otto) 54, 26 L.Ed. 693 (1881).

330. Arkansas v. Pufahl, 52 F.2d 116 (8th Cir.1931); Cassedy v. Johnstown Bank, 246 A.D. 337, 286 N.Y.S. 202 (1936); Gillet v. Bank of America, 160 N.Y. 549, 55 N.E. 292 (1899). *See supra* ¶ 9.05[2].

331. *In re* Greenwald's Estate, 143 N.Y.S.2d 464 (1955); BancoKentucky Co.'s Receiver v. National Bank of Kentucky's Receiver, 281 Ky. 784, 137 S.W.2d 357 (Ky. 1939).

332. *In re* Dimon's Estate, 32 N.Y.S.2d 239 (1941).

333. Wells Fargo Bank & Union Trust Co. v. McDuffie, 71 F.2d 720 (9th Cir.1934), *cert. denied*, 293 U.S. 626, 55 S.Ct. 346, 79 L.Ed. 713 (1934).

334. Mississippi Cottonseed Prod. Co. v. Canal Bank & Trust Co., 172 Miss. 105, 159 So. 404 (Miss. 1935).

335. *In re Dimon's*, 32 N.Y.S. 2d at 339 (lien may be lost by conduct inconsistent with assertion of lien); Custer County v. Walker, 10 S.D. 594, 74 N.W. 1040 (S.D. 1898). *See generally supra* ¶ 9.05[2] (special deposits).

336. *See, e.g.*, Okla. Stat. tit. 42 § 32 (1910); authorities cited *supra* at note 437. *See generally*, Loyd, The Development of Set-off, 64 U. PA. L. REV. 541 (1916); TeSelle, Banker's Right of Setoff—Banker Beware, 34 OKLA. L. REV. 40 (1981); Alvin C. Harrell, Security Interests in Deposit Accounts: A Unique Relationship Between the UCC and Other Law, 23 U.C.C. L.J. 153, 155–165 (1990); John P. Roberts, Banker's Right of Setoff: Overview and Analysis, 47 CONSUMER FIN. L.Q. REP. 173 (1993). The Supreme Court of Iowa has recognized that set-off is a remedy that can be exercised at the option of the creditor, and there is no resulting liability (if setoff was proper) even if the set-off was done in a cavalier or irresponsible manner. Tolander v. Farmers National Bank, 452 N.W.2d 422 (Iowa 1990).

337. *See e.g.*, Cal. Fin. Code § 863 (West Supp. 1982); N.D. Cent. Code § 6–03–67 (1975); N.Y. Debt. & Cred. Law § 151 (McKinney Supp. 1981–1982); *supra* note 336.

338. Skilton, The Secured Party's Rights in a Debtor's Bank Account Under Article 9 of the Uniform Commercial Code, 1977 S. Ill. U. L. J. 120 (1977). As discussed infra at ¶ 9.06[4], revised Article 9 recognizes and awards priority to the set-off rights of the bank where the deposit is maintained, as against other secured par-

The right of set-off is derived from the common law[339] and from the equitable principle that "a man should not be compelled to pay one moment what he will be entitled to recover back the next."[340] Setoff is also based on the theory that the depositor has impliedly consented to the set-off.[341]

In order for a banking institution to exercise a right of setoff, generally three requirements must be met: (1) the account must be deposited with the banking institution without restriction (*i.e.*, it must be a general account–*see supra* ¶ 9.05[2]); (2) the offsetting indebtedness to the bank must be due and owing or mature; and (3) there must be mutuality of obligation between the institution and the depositor and between the debt and the account on deposit.[342] Each of these requirements is discussed further, below.

[b] Maturity of the Debt

Absent a contractual provision to the contrary, a banking institution may not set-off an account against a debt unless the debt is due and payable or mature.[343] A debt is mature at the time the institution opens for business on the date the debt is due.[344]

There are several exceptions to the rule that a banking institution cannot set-off an unmatured debt. First, an institution, in some states,[345]

---

ties claiming security interests in the account (*e.g.*, as proceeds of other collateral). *See* revised § 9–340(a).

339. Faber, Coe & Gregg, Inc. v. First Nat. Bank, 107 Ill.App.2d 204, 246 N.E.2d 96 (1969).

340. Loyd, *supra* note 336. Set-off is not limited to banking institutions, but often arises in this context due to the role of banks as financial intermediaries.

341. Shotwell v. Sioux Falls Sav. Bank, 34 S.D. 109, 147 N.W. 288 (S.D. 1914).

342. That is, the account holder and debtor must be the same person or entity. FDIC v. Pioneer State Bank, 155 N.J.Super. 381, 382 A.2d 958 (Law Div.1977). *See also* Citibank, S.D., N.A. v. Coffey, 281 N.J.Super. 311, 657 A.2d 475 (Law Div.1994) (garnishee bank could not, prior to honoring garnishor's levy on depositor's account, extract an administrative fee attributable to that same levy because no common law right to setoff existed since depositor's debt to garnishee did not exist until after the levy).

343. Bottrell v. American Bank, 237 Mont. 1, 773 P.2d 694 (Mont. 1989); Crocker–Citizens National Bank v. Control Metals Corp., 566 F.2d 631 (9th Cir.1977); Walter v. Nat. City Bank, 42 Ohio St.2d 524, 330 N.E.2d 425 (Ohio 1975); Ingram v. Liberty Nat. Bank & Trust Co. of Oklahoma City, 533 P.2d 975 (Okla.1975). Of course, set-off may occur prior to maturity if the bank acts in good faith and with the debtor's consent. Griffin–Townsend Co. v. First State Bank In Talihina, 191 Okla. 460, 130 P.2d 540 (Okla. 1942).

344. Goldstein v. Jefferson Title & Trust Co., 95 Pa.Super. 167 (1928).

345. Schuler v. Israel, 120 U.S. 506, 7 S.Ct. 648, 30 L.Ed. 707 (1887); Ribaudo v. Citizens Nat. Bank, 261 F.2d 929 (5th Cir. 1958); Kane v. First Nat. Bank, 56 F.2d 534 (5th Cir.1932), *cert. denied*, 287 U.S. 603, 53 S.Ct. 8, 77 L.Ed. 524 (1932); Parker v. First Nat. Bank, 96 Okla. 70, 220 P. 39 (Okla.1923); Friedman v. First Nat'l Bank, 344 Mass. 593, 183 N.E.2d 722 (Mass. 1962) (proof of insolvency required). *Cf.* Harding v. Broadway Nat. Bank, 294 Mass. 13, 200 N.E. 386 (Mass. 1936); Blum Bros., Inc. v. Girard Nat. Bank, 248 Pa. 148, 93 A. 940 (Pa. 1915); McCollum v. Parkdale State Bank, 566 S.W.2d 670 (Tex.Civ.App.1978), no writ; *In re* Moreira, 173 B.R. 965 (Bankr. D.Mass.1994) (credit union's postpetition "freeze" did not violate automatic stay). Regarding set-off in bankruptcy cases, *see* 11 U.S.C. § 553 (effect of bankruptcy on pre-petition set-offs); Citizens Bank v. Strumpf, 516 U.S. 16, 116 S.Ct. 286, 133 L.Ed.2d 258 (1995) (within limits, administrative freeze of deposit account does not violate bankruptcy automatic stay); Alvin C. Harrell and Fred H. Miller, The Law of Personal Property Secured Transactions

may set-off an unmatured debt if the debtor is insolvent and has not filed a bankruptcy petition.[346] If the debtor has died and the estate is insolvent, courts traditionally have held that the bank may set-off unmatured debts of the deceased depositor.[347] However, death of the depositor may not justify set-off of an unmatured debt when the estate is solvent.[348] For purposes of setoff, insolvency is defined as a debtor's failure or refusal to pay his or her debts in the ordinary course of business.[349] Second, if the depositor has acted fraudulently with regard to the debt, the bank is entitled to rescind any agreement as to the time of payment.[350]

Finally, if the debt to be set-off is a demand note, the note matures when the institution makes demand.[351] On non-demand notes, an institution can avoid the inability to set-off a debt due to immaturity by incorporating acceleration provisions in the loan agreement. Such a provision may provide that the institution can accelerate the due date of the note if the borrower defaults in performing any obligations or if the lender deems itself insecure.[352] Acceleration clauses are not per se unconscionable,[353] and generally, are enforceable if the clause is exercised in good faith[354] and is supported by consideration.[355]

[c] *Mutuality of Obligation*

A banking institution has the right to set-off an account only when the institution and the depositor are in a debtor/creditor relationship and there is mutuality of parties.[356] Mutuality of parties exists where the

---

Under the Uniform Commercial Code and Related Laws Ch. 21 (2001).

346. If the debtor is in bankruptcy the institution is subject to the automatic stay and other restrictions. *See* 11 U.S.C. §§ 362(a), 544(a), and 553; *infra* ¶ 9.06[2][f][v].

347. Annotation, Bank's Right to Apply or Setoff Deposit Against Debt of Depositor Not Due at Time of His Death, 7 A.L.R.3d 908 (1966); Roberts, *supra* note 336, at 175.

348. *Annotation, supra* note 347.

349. *McCollum*, 566 S.W.2d at 670.

350. Gilmartin v. Osborne Trust Co., 266 A.D. 1022, 44 N.Y.S.2d 938, *aff'd*, 292 N.Y. 629, 55 N.E.2d 505 (N.Y. 1944); Mann v. Franklin Trust Co., 158 A.D. 491, 143 N.Y.S. 660 (1913).

351. Waller v. Maryland National Bank, 95 Md.App. 197, 620 A.2d 381 (Md. Ct. Spec. App. 1993); Mirax Chemical Products Corp. v. First Interstate Commercial Corp., 950 F.2d 566 (8th Cir.1991); Allied Sheet Metal Fabricators, Inc. v. Peoples Nat. Bank, 10 Wn.App. 530, 518 P.2d 734 (Wash. Ct.App.1974), *cert. denied*, 419 U.S. 967, 95 S.Ct. 231, 42 L.Ed.2d 183 (1974); Marrison v. Hogue, 95 N.E.2d 15 (Ohio Mun. Ct. 1950); UCC §§ 3–501, 3–502. *See generally* Manuel H. Newburger, Acceleration Notices and Demand Letters, 47 CONSUMER FIN. L. Q. REP. 338 (1993).

352. *See, e.g.*, Jensen v. State Bank of Allison, 518 F.2d 1 (8th Cir.1975). Acceleration provisions are specifically approved in the UCC, subject to a duty of good faith, at § 1–208, and are approved at § 3–108(b) as consistent with the concept of negotiability.

353. *See* UCC § 1–208; Greene v. Citizens & Southern Bank, 134 Ga.App. 73, 213 S.E.2d 175 (1975).

354. *See* UCC §§ 1–203, 1–208; Gary D. Spivey, Annotation, What Constitutes "Good Faith" Under Uniform Commercial Code § 1–208 Dealing with "Insecure" or "at Will" Acceleration Clauses, 61 A.L.R.3d 244 (1975). *But see* the newer definition of "good faith" at § 3–103(a)(4) and revised § 9–102(a)(43) (incorporating a standard based on "reasonable commercial standards of fair dealing).

355. P. Pastene & Co. v. First Nat. Bank, 19 Ariz. 493, 172 P. 656 (Ariz. 1918); Bank of Spartanburg v. Mahon, 78 S.C. 408, 59 S.E. 31 (S.C. 1907).

356. Kaufman v. First Nat. Bank, 493 F.2d 1070 (5th Cir.1974); Get It Kwik of

account to be set-off is owned by the same person or entity that owes the debt, and the depositor has opened the account and incurred the debt in the same capacity. Special problems of mutuality occur if the account is in the name of two or more persons, or in the name of an entity such as a corporation, partnership or trust, because it may be difficult to precisely match ownership of the account with the identity of the debtor. Clearly it is improper to set-off the account of one party against the debt of another, and banks considering set-off should exercise caution in this regard.

[d] Absence of Deposit Restrictions

A banking institution has a right to set-off a depositor's account to secure payment of the depositor's indebtedness to the institution only if the account is a general account, *i.e.*, if the account is an account consisting of deposits made in the usual course of business without a restriction that the account be used for a special purpose.[357] Thus, if a deposit is made for a special purpose known to the institution, generally it may not set-off the account.[358] Courts have justified this rule on two grounds. First, because the institution does not take title to a special account,[359] there is no debtor/creditor relationship between the institution and customer; thus, the requirement of mutuality is not met.[360] Second, by accepting a special deposit, the institution has agreed to use the deposit only for the special purposes, and a set-off would violate that agreement.[361]

[e] Competing Claims

The right of setoff of a banking institution may be limited by claims of the depositor's other creditors, including: (1) the holder of an uncashed check drawn on the account subject to setoff, (2) a creditor who garnishes the account, (3) a competing secured creditor claiming an

---

America, Inc. v. First Ala. Bank, 361 So.2d 568 (Ala.Civ.App.1978); Bonhiver v. State Bank, 29 Ill.App.3d 794, 331 N.E.2d 390 (1975).

357. Mancuso v. United Bank of Pueblo, 818 P.2d 732 (Colo.1991); Hall v. Duncan Savings and Loan Ass'n, 820 P.2d 1360 (Okla. Ct. App. 1991); FDIC v. Pioneer State Bank, 155 N.J.Super. 381, 382 A.2d 958 (Law Div.1977); Shull v. Town of Avant, 159 Okla. 271, 15 P.2d 49 (Okla. 1932). *See supra* ¶ 9.05[2] and [4][c].

358. *See e.g.*, Rainsville Bank v. Willingham, 485 So.2d 319 (Ala.1986); First City Nat. Bank v. Long–Lewis Hdwe. Co., 363 So.2d 770 (Ala.1978), *on remand* 363 So.2d 774 (Ala.Civ.App. 1978); Fidelity Nat. Bank of Okla. City v. Copeland, 138 Okla. 19, 280 P. 273 (Okla. 1929); First Nat. Bank & Trust Co. v. Osage Supply Co., 186 Okla. 259, 97 P.2d 3 (Okla. 1939); Security State Bank of Comanche, Okla. v. W.R. Johnston & Co., 204 Okla. 160, 228 P.2d 169 (1951); Roberts, *supra* note 336, at 174. *See also*, Central Bank of Mississippi v. Butler, 517 So.2d 507 (Miss.1987) (statutory trust precludes setoff); Masi v. Ford City Bank & Trust 779 F.2d 397 (7th Cir.1985) (IRA account not subject to setoff); First Nat'l. Bank of Blue Island v. Estate of Philp, 106 Ill.App.3d 360, 62 Ill.Dec. 433, 436 N.E.2d 15 (1982) (IRA not subject to setoff); United States *ex rel.* Crow Creek Sioux Tribe v. Tri–County Bank, 415 F.Supp. 858 (D.S.D. 1976) (payroll account subject to setoff where depositor had unlimited control over the account).

359. *See supra* ¶ 9.05[2] and [4][c].

360. Glenn Justice Mtg. Co. v. First Nat. Bank, 592 F.2d 567 (10th Cir.1979).

361. *Tri-County Bank*, 415 F.Supp. at 858; Martin v. First State Bank, 490 S.W.2d 208 (Tex.Civ.App.1973), no writ. *See also* Smith v. Citizens State Bank of Hugo, 732 P.2d 911 (Okla.Ct.App.1986).

Article 9 security interest in the account, either directly or as proceeds, (4) the Internal Revenue Service, or (5) a trustee in bankruptcy.[362] Each of these is discussed *infra*.

[i] Wrongful Dishonor

Set-off by a bank frequently depletes the customer's account, resulting in dishonor of items drawn on that account. This may raise a question as to whether the bank is liable for wrongful dishonor under UCC § 4–402. Wrongful dishonor is discussed in more detail, *supra* at ¶ 9.02[2]. Generally, if the set-off was proper, any resulting dishonor is proper; but if the set-off was improper, any resulting dishonor is wrongful under § 4–402. In any event, however, the bank may not dishonor any items that were paid before the set-off occurred, as this would violate the finality of payment rules at §§ 4–215, 4–301, 4–302 and 4–303. Under Article 4, set-off is ineffective to prevent payment of an item if it is exercised after the bank has: (1) accepted and certified the item; (2) paid the item in cash; (3) settled without having a right to revoke; or (4) become accountable for the amount of the item under the Article 4 sections dealing with the bank's responsibility for late return of checks.[363] If none of these events has occurred, and set-off is otherwise proper, the customer has no cause of action against the bank for wrongful dishonor.[364] Conversely, however, if a banking institution makes an improper set-off, it is liable to its customer for actual damages due to wrongful dishonor of any items that are subsequently dishonored for insufficient funds as a result of the set-off.[365] In no event, however, does the holder of a dishonored check drawn on the account have a

---

362. See *infra* this text. See *also*, Roberts, *supra* note 336; Whitaker, *supra* note 144; Psencik, Dealing With Daily Operational Issues Concerning Bank Accounts and Deposits, 47 Consumer Fin. L.Q. Rep. 138 (1993), at 146–51; Harrell, Security Interests in Deposit Accounts: A Unique Relationship Between the UCC and Other Law, 23 U.C.C. L.J. 153 (1990); *supra* ¶ 9.06[2][c][iv].

In FDIC v. Golden Imports, Inc., 859 S.W.2d 635 (Tex.App.—Houston [1st Dist.] 1993), a bank exercising set-off was subordinated to the rights of an equitable owner of the funds because the deposit slip provided notice of the owner's claim. See also Rainsville Bank v. Willingham, 485 So.2d 319 (Ala.1986).

363. See §§ 4–303(a), 4–215(a), 4–301(a), 4–302; discussion *supra* Chapter 8. Note that 1990 revisions to Article 4 deleted the "process of posting" as an alternative means of final payment. *Compare* old §§ 4–303(1)(d), 4–213(1)(c).

364. Jensen v. State Bank of Allison, 518 F.2d 1 (8th Cir.1975); Farmers Co-op. Elevator, Inc. v. State Bank, 236 N.W.2d 674 (Iowa 1975); Merchant v. Worley, 79 N.M. 771, 449 P.2d 787 (N.M.Ct.App.1969). Notice that even if the dishonor is wrongful, the bank is liable only to the drawer of the item, the bank's customer, so long as the dishonor is timely under Article 4. See § 3–408, and *supra* ¶ 9.02[2]. The holder of the item has no recourse against the bank unless the bank has paid, accepted or certified the item or otherwise become accountable for it. See §§ 4–215, 4–301, 4–302 and 4–303; and Douglas v. Citizens Bank, 244 Ark. 168, 424 S.W.2d 532 (Ark. 1968). Moreover, the bank's liability to its customer is limited to actual damages, *see* § 4–402; *supra* ¶ 9.02[2].

365. Young v. Mercantile Trust Co., N.A., 552 S.W.2d 247 (Mo.Ct.App.1977); Skov v. Chase Manhattan Bank, 407 F.2d 1318 (3d Cir.1969) (injury to business relationships); First Nat. Bank v. Hubbs, 566 S.W.2d 375 (Tex.Civ.App.1978); Loucks v. Albuquerque Nat'l. Bank, 76 N.M. 735, 418 P.2d 191 (N.M. 1966) (injury to credit record); Northshore Bank v. Palmer, 525 S.W.2d 718 (Tex.Civ.App.1975) (emotional distress). These cases are noted in Roberts, *supra* note 336, at nn. 118–20. *See generally supra* ¶ 9.02[2].

direct cause of action against the bank, under § 3–408 as discussed supra at ¶ 9.02[2].

[ii] *Secured Creditor*

When a depositor has granted a security interest in his or her deposit account to secure a debt, or when the depositor deposits the proceeds of collateral for a security interest in the account, UCC Article 9 may provide the creditor a security interest in the account.[366] If the security interest is in favor of the same bank that holds the account and has the right of setoff, the convergence of these rights should be beneficial to the bank. Under old Article 9, if the security interest runs in favor of a third party it could adversely affect the bank's right of setoff, by raising questions as to whether the banking institution's right to set-off against the account was subordinate to the security interest. If the institution knew that a third person holds a security interest in the account, generally under old Article 9 it could not set-off those funds.[367] If the institution has no actual or constructive knowledge, the courts were divided as to whether the institution could set-off the account. Some courts followed the "legal rule" by which the institution is permitted to set-off an account when it has no actual or constructive knowledge of the security interest.[368] Other courts followed the "equitable rule,"[369] prohibiting the banking institution from exercising its right

---

366. Revised UCC Article 9 allows a creditor to take a security interest in a deposit account as such, in non-consumer cases. *See* § 9–109(a)(1), (d)(13). *See* former UCC § 9–104(*l*). It should be noted "deposit account" is defined at § 9–102(a)(29) to exclude accounts evidenced by an instrument. "Instrument" is defined at § 9–102(a)(47) to include any evidence of a monetary obligation that is transferrable in the ordinary course of business. Therefore a certificate of deposit (CD) may serve as collateral for an Article 9 security interest, either as a deposit account or an instrument, depending on whether the certificate is transferrable in the ordinary course of business. Other bank accounts within the definition of "deposit account" at § 9–102(a)(29) are also subject to an Article 9 security interest, except for consumer transactions, under § 9–109(d)(13). Moreover, Article 9 permits a secured party to trace the proceeds of other collateral into a deposit account and to claim a security interest in that account, subject to limitations. *See* §§ 9–102(a)(12) and (64), 9–203, 9–315, and 9–322. A creditor also may be able to claim a deposit account outside Article 9, pursuant to a common law pledge. *See* Harrell, Security Interests in Deposit Accounts: A Unique Relationship Between the UCC and Other Law, 23 U.C.C. L.J. 153 (1990); Roberts, *supra* note 336, at 176.

367. Commercial Discount Corp. v. Milwaukee Western Bank, 61 Wis.2d 671, 214 N.W.2d 33 (Wis. 1974); First Nat'l Bank & Trust Co. v. Osage Supply Co., 186 Okla. 259, 97 P.2d 3 (Okla. 1939); First Nat'l. Bank v. W.P. Seawell Lumber Co., 135 Okla. 201, 274 P. 873 (Okla. 1928); First Nat'l. Bank v. American Surety Co., 237 Ala. 35, 185 So. 365 (Ala. 1938). As an agent of the bank, an attorney's knowledge of a third party's claim was imputed to the bank, making the setoff wrongful. *See* Insurance Co. of North America v. Northampton Nat. Bank, 708 F.2d 13 (1st Cir.1983). *See also* Rainsville Bank v. Willingham, 485 So.2d 319 (Ala.1986).

368. Brown & Williamson Tobacco Corp. v. First Nat. Bank, 504 F.2d 998 (7th Cir.1974); Skilton, The Secured Party's Rights in a Debtor's Bank Account Under Article 9 of the Uniform Commercial Code, 1977 S. Ill. U. L. J. 120 (1977). This appeared to be the majority view, prior to the effective date of revised Article 9. *See* Roberts, *supra* note 336, at 175.

369. Comment, Conflicts Between a Bank's Common Law Right of Set-off and a Secured Party's Interest in Identifiable Proceeds, 9 Loy. U. Chi. L. J. 454 (1978).

of setoff, even though it had no knowledge, unless the bank had changed its position or otherwise had equities superior to the secured creditor.[370]

All of this was resolved by the Article 9 revisions (enacted in all states and effective July 1, 2001 in all but a few). Under revised § 9–340(a), a bank exercising its right of set-off (or recoupment) against a deposit account maintained at that bank has priority over a competing security interest in the account, unless under § 9–340(c) the competing secured party has obtained "control" of the deposit account by becoming the bank's customer under § 9–104(a)(3). While this reverses prior law in many states, as noted above, it brings the set-off priority rule into conformity with the revised Article 9 rule awarding priority to a security interest of the same bank under §§ 9–104(a)(1) and 9–327, again subject to § 9–104(a)(3).

[iii] *Garnishing Creditor*

When a creditor of the depositor garnishes a bank account and the depositary institution has set-off the account either before or after the writ of garnishment is served, the conflicting rights of the banking institution and the garnishing creditor in the account must be considered. If the institution has set-off the account prior to receiving the writ of garnishment, the depositary institution will prevail because the account is no longer a garnishable asset after the set-off. If set-off occurs after the writ of garnishment has been served, the right of the garnishing creditor to the account is only as great as the rights of the depositor. If the institution could set-off the account as to the depositor, it is of no consequence that the bank has been served with a garnishment summons.[371]

---

370. *Commercial Discount*, 214 N.W.2d at 33; Security State Bank v. W.R. Johnston & Co., 204 Okla. 160, 228 P.2d 169 (Okla. 1951). It generally was not a sufficient change of position for the bank to have cancelled a debt in reliance on the set-off. National Indem. Co. v. Spring Branch State Bank, 162 Tex. 521, 348 S.W.2d 528 (Tex. 1961). However, if the bank extended new credit in reliance on the deposit, that has been treated as sufficient reliance. Brady v. American Nat'l. Bank, 120 Okla. 159, 250 P. 1006 (Okla. 1926). If the bank released collateral in reliance on the set-off, it would seem that detrimental reliance exists and should protect the bank's claim to setoff. *See also*, Murray, Banks Versus Creditors of Their Customers: Set-offs Against Customers' Accounts, 82 COM. L.J. 449 (1977). The right to set-off was recognized in old Article 9 at § 9–104[g], but was not created or otherwise regulated by old Article 9. The effect was to recognize the right of setoff, subject to the Article 9 priority rules, resulting in priority of a perfected security interest (*e.g.*, a proceeds claim) over the right to set-off in many cases. *See, e.g.*, Universal C.I.T. Credit Corp. v. Farmers Bank of Portageville, 358 F.Supp. 317 (E.D. Mo. 1973). In other words, as a general unsecured claim the banker's right of setoff was subordinate to a prior security interest. BBMS, Inc. v. Brown, 251 Ga. 409, 306 S.E.2d 288 (Ga. 1983). *See also* Harrell, Security Interest v. Non–Code Interest: An Analysis of the Ramifications of Utica Nat. Bank and Trust v. Associated Producers, 16 OKLA. CITY U. L. REV. 519 (1981). As noted *infra* this text, this priority rule has been reversed by revised Article 9 § 9–340.

371. *See, e.g.*, Sperry v. Renner, 194 Okla. 285, 149 P.2d 781 (Okla. 1944); Ed Hockaday & Co. v. Randolph, 178 Okla. 234, 62 P.2d 628 (Okla. 1936); First State Bank of Ringling v. Hunt, 77 Okla. 4, 185 P. 1089 (Okla.1919); Farmers' & Merchants' State Bank of Teague v. Setzer, 185 S.W. 596 (Tex.Civ.App.1916), no writ; The President and Directors of the Farmers' and Merchants' Bank of Baltimore v. The Franklin Bank of Baltimore, 31 Md. 404 (1869). *See generally*, Skilton, *supra* notes

Thus, if the debt owed to the depositary institution is matured at the time the writ of garnishment is served, the bank may set-off the account after the writ is received and refuse to turn over the funds to the garnishing creditor.[372] If the debt owed to the depositary institution is unmatured, the institution may refuse to turn over the funds only if it has a security interest or right to set-off under Article 9 or other law, such as an exception to the general rule that an institution may not set-off an unmatured debt.[373]

[iv] Tax Claims and Internal Revenue Service Levies

The Internal Revenue Code ("I.R.C.") provides that the Internal Revenue Service may, subject to certain exceptions, impose a levy on the nonexempt property of a person who owes a debt for taxes.[374] If the depositary institution sets off an account prior to the Internal Revenue Service's levy on that account, the account would no longer be property of the debtor and thus would not be subject to the tax levy.[375] On the other hand, if the tax levy is made prior to the set-off, the tax levy may have priority over the institution's right of set-off.

Traditionally, tax levy has priority over an unexercised right of set-off for several reasons. First, for tax purposes, the account remains the

---

338 and 368; Roberts, *supra* note 336, at 176. In effect the garnisher stands in the shoes of the depositor and is subject to claims of the bank against that depositor. This is consistent with revised Article 9 §§ 9–327 and 9–340.

372. *Id. See also* Bank of Winter Park v. Resolution Trust Corp., 633 So.2d 53 (Fla. Dist.Ct.App.1994); Pennsylvania National Bank & Trust Co. v. CCNB Bank, 446 Pa.Super. 625, 667 A.2d 1151, 1154 (1995), *appeal granted in part limited to another issue*, 544 Pa. 195, 675 A.2d 1209 (1996) (the garnishee bank's right to set-off gives it a right to self-help that takes priority over other creditors claiming the funds on deposit); Barsco, Inc. v. H.W.W., Inc., 346 So.2d 134 (Fla.Dist.Ct.App.1977); Valley National Bank of Arizona v. Hasper, 6 Ariz. App. 376, 432 P.2d 924 (Ariz.App.1967); Messall v. Suburban Trust Company, 244 Md. 502, 224 A.2d 419 (Md. 1966); State National Bank of Decatur v. Towns, 36 Ala.App. 677, 62 So.2d 606 (1952); Levinson v. Home Bank & Trust Co., 337 Ill. 241, 169 N.E. 193 (Ill. 1929); Aarons v. Public Serv. Bldg. & Loan Ass'n., 318 Pa. 113, 178 A. 141 (Pa. 1935).

373. *See* Murray, *supra* note 370. *See also infra* ¶ 9.06[4]; UCC §§ 1–203, 1–208 (acceleration clause permissible if exercised in good faith). The latter may permit acceleration of an unmatured debt for purposes of making a set-off, where the loan agreement contains an acceleration clause.

Revised Article 9 makes it relatively easy for the depositary institution to claim an Article 9 security interest in commercial deposit accounts. *See* §§ 9–109(a)(1) and (d)(13), 9–203(b), 9–312(b)(1), 9–104. Thus in many instances the depositary institutions will have a security interest in the deposit account, as well as a right of set-off, and this security interest will have priority irregardless of whether the debt has matured. *See, e.g.,* §§ 9–201, 9–312(b), 9–317, 9–327, 9–104.

374. I.R.C. § 6331(a), 26 U.S.C. § 6321 *et seq*. The IRS can provisionally levy on a joint bank account for delinquent income taxes owed by either of the joint account holders. This goes only to the procedural right and is not dispositive of ownership rights, which would be determined in a subsequent administrative or judicial hearing. U.S. v. National Bank of Commerce, 472 U.S. 713, 105 S.Ct. 2919, 86 L.Ed.2d 565 (1985); *see also*, Roberts, *supra* note 336, at 177; Psencik, *supra* note 470, at 146–47. In addition, state tax authorities may be entitled to a claim that will be entitled to priority over a bank's right of setoff. *See e.g.*, Okla. Stat. tit. 68 § 812 (1992); Fortune v. City Nat. Bank & Trust Co., 671 P.2d 69 (Okla. Ct. App. 1983). *See generally* Susan Davis, The Tax Man Cometh–Handling Levies, Liens and Summons, 49 Consumer Fin. L. Q. Rep. 196 (1995).

375. *See* U.S. v. Sterling Nat. Bank & Trust Co., 494 F.2d 919 (2d Cir.1974).

property of the debtor until the institution takes some action to set-off and restrict the debtor's use of the account.[376] Thus, the account is within the class of property owned by the debtor that is subject to the tax levy.[377] Second, although the I.R.C. gives priority to secured creditors,[378] the right of set-off does not make the banking institution a secured creditor because the institution's right of setoff is not a consensual right. Note, however, that this analysis may now be changed because revised Article §§ 9–104, 9–109, 9–203, 9–312, and 9–327 make it more likely the depositary institution will have a perfected security interest in the deposit account, with priority under both state and federal law. Finally, (absent an Article 9 security interest) the institution's right to set-off against the deposit account is not established at the time the levy is executed, as required for priority over a tax lien, because the right of set-off creates no lien and, until setoff is made, the depositor is free to deplete the account.[379] Consequently, the depositary institution relying purely on the right of set-off is unlikely to prevail over a federal tax levy unless it exercises its right of set-off before the levy.

[v] *Depositor's Trustee in Bankruptcy*

The Bankruptcy Reform Act of 1978[380] recognizes the right of set-off of a banking institution, but limits this right when exercised with regard

---

376. *Id*; Congress Talcott Corp. v. Gruber, 993 F.2d 315 (3d Cir.1993); U.S. v. Citizens & Southern Nat. Bank, 538 F.2d 1101 (5th Cir.1976). Generally an unexercised right of set-off is not a lien under state law. *Cf.* Bankruptcy Code § 506(a), 11 U.S.C. § 506(a) (contra). Thus, the unexercised right of set-off does not give the bank rights of a lien creditor as against the levy. *But see* Jefferson Bank and Trust v. United States, 894 F.2d 1241 (10th Cir.1990) (right of set-off treated as security interest or common law pledge with priority over tax lien). The same is generally true of the priority of a set-off against a garnishment, and this may give rise to a similar argument in garnishment cases where, however, the results have usually been different. *See supra* ¶ 9.06[2][f][iii]; *infra* ¶ 9.06[3]; *but see also*, Fast Food Systems, Inc. v. Ducotey, 837 P.2d 910 (Okla.1992). As suggested supra, revised Article 9 may change this analysis by: (1) recognizing a security interest in favor of the bank, with priority under § 9–327; and (2) creating a new priority for set-off at § 9–340.

377. *Citizens*, 538 F.2d at 1101.

378. I.R.C. § 6323(a), 12 U.S.C. § 6323(a). This becomes important if the depositary institution has a security interest under revised § 9–203. *See also* §§ 9–104, 9–109, 9–312, and 9–327.

379. I.R.C. § 6323(a); *see also* U.S. By and Through I.R.S. v. McDermott, 507 U.S. 447, 113 S.Ct. 1526, 123 L.Ed.2d 128 (1993) (tax lien prevails over security interest in after-acquired property because the latter is not choate); Congress Talcott Corp. v. Gruber, 993 F.2d 315 (3d Cir.1993); United States v. Euclid Nat. Bank, 510 F.2d 461 (6th Cir.1975); United States v. Trans–World Bank, 382 F.Supp. 1100 (C.D.Cal. 1974). *See generally* Olsen, The Appropriation of Deposits for Debts: Levies, Liens, and Setoffs, 90 BANKING L.J. 827 (1973); Comment, Federal Tax Lien Act of 1966, 2 REAL PROP., PROB. & TR. J. 96 (1967); Plumb, What the Banker Should Know About Federal Tax Liens and Levies—Revisited, 84 BANKING L.J. (1967). As this suggests, the I.R.C. choateness requirement may also be a problem for Article 9 secured parties seeking enforcement of a security interest in the deposit account as against the I.R.S. levy. On the other had, the priority rules at revised §§ 9–201 and 9–317(a)(2) are clear on this point.

380. Bankruptcy Reform Act of 1978, Pub. L. No. 95–598, 92 Stat. 2549 (codified as amended in scattered sections of 11 U.S.C.). The Bankruptcy Reform Act is hereinafter referred to as the Bankruptcy Code and cited as 11 U.S.C. § xxx. *See generally* Freeman, Set-off Under the New Bankruptcy Code: The Effect on Bankers, 97 BANKING L.J. 484 (1980); A. Harrell, F. and Miller, the Law of Personal Property Secured Transactions under the Uniform

to a depositor in bankruptcy.[381] Generally, the institution will prevail over the trustee in bankruptcy if the set-off is valid under state law, and if it occurs 90 days or more prior to the filing of the bankruptcy petition.[382]

If the right of set-off is exercised within 90 days prior to the bankruptcy filing, the setoff may be voidable under Bankruptcy Code § 553. The set-off will be voidable to the extent that the institution has improved its position within the 90–day "preference" period.[383] Improvement of position means that the "insufficiency of the amount by which the debt exceeds the deposit has decreased between the date any insufficiency first occurred during the 90 days prior to the filing of the bankruptcy petition and the date set-off is made."[384]

After a voluntary or involuntary petition in bankruptcy has been filed, an automatic stay is imposed, and the depositary institution may not exercise its right of set-off.[385] The depositary institution may apply to

---

Commercial Code and Related Laws Chs. 20–26 (2001).

381. 11 U.S.C. § 553. *See generally*, Fred H. Miller and Alvin C. Harell, The ABCs of the UCC Related Insolvency Law (Am. Bar Assoc. 2002), 1978 U.S. CODE CONG. & AD. NEWS 578, 584. The Bankruptcy Amendments and Federal Judgeship Act of 1984 further complicated the issue. For example: 11 U.S.C. § 506(a) recognizes a right of set-off as a secured claim (essentially a lien) in bankruptcy; 11 U.S.C. § 553 specifically recognizes a creditor's right of set-off; and 11 U.S.C. § 542(b) exempts property described at § 553 from the order mandating turnover of property to the trustee. But 11 U.S.C. § 362(a)(7) prohibits the bank from making the set-off unless and until the bank can obtain relief from the automatic stay. Also, 11 U.S.C. § 362(a)(3) prohibits creditors from exercising any "control over property of the estate." There were arguments that this precluded even a retention of the debtor's account (*i.e.*, a "freezing" of the account) pending an application to lift the automatic stay. Furthermore, if setting off the account is found to violate the stay, the Bankruptcy Code requires assessment of actual damages. *See* 11 U.S.C. § 362(h). *See also* Harrell and Miller, *supra* note 380, ch. 21; *infra* notes 383–384; Coleman, Garrett & Friedman, *infra* note 385. The U.S. Supreme Court resolved the administrative freeze issue in Citizens Bank v. Strumpf, 516 U.S. 16, 116 S.Ct. 286, 133 L.Ed.2d 258 (1995), holding that an administrative-freeze of the deposit account does not violate the automatic stay. But this does not authorize exercise of the right of set-off during bankruptcy, unless and until the creditor obtains relief from the stay.

382. 11 U.S.C. § 553. *See* Harrell and Miller, *supra* note 380, 762–769.

383. *Id.*; 11 U.S.C. § 553(b); Fred H. Miller and Alvin C. Harrell, The ABCs of the UCC Related Insolvency Law 33–52 (Am. Bar Assoc. 2002). *See generally*, Marquette National Bank v. B.J. Dodge Fiat, 131 Ill.App.3d 356, 86 Ill.Dec. 678, 475 N.E.2d 1057 (Ill.App.1985); Aeronautics & Astronautics Servs. v. First Palm Beach Int'l Bank, 471 So.2d 188 (Fla.App.1985); Brown & Williamson Tobacco Corp. v. First Nat'l Bank of Blue Island, 504 F.2d 998 (7th Cir.1974). *See also* Dillon and Harrell, Anatomy of a Failed Statutory Provision: U.C.C. Section 9–306(4)(d)(ii), 43 CONSUMER FIN. L.Q. REP. 198 (1989). Section 9–306(4)(d)(ii) was repealed as part of the 1998 Article 9 revisions.

384. 11 U.S.C. § 553(b). For a discussion of the improvement of position test, *see generally*, Ahart, Bank Setoff Under the Bankruptcy Reform Act of 1978, 53 AM. BANKR. L.J. 205 (1979).

385. 11 U.S.C. § 362(a)(7). As noted, the United States Supreme Court has authorized depositary institutions to "freeze" prepetition funds in the debtor's account, to the extent of loans due, pending a lifting of the stay or adequate protection. *See* Citizens Bank of Maryland v. Strumpf, 516 U.S. 16, 116 S.Ct. 286, 133 L.Ed.2d 258 (1995). *See also* Heckathorn Const. Co. v. Bass Mechanical Contractors, Inc. (*In re* Bass Mechanical Contractors, Inc.), 84 B.R. 1009 (Bankr.W.D.Ark.1988); *In re* New York City Shoes, Inc., 78 B.R. 426 (Bankr. E.D.Pa.1987); Air Atlanta, Inc. v. National Bank of Georgia, 81 B.R. 724 (N.D.Ga. 1987); *In re* Williams, 61 B.R. 567 (Bankr. N.D.Tex.1986); Bank of America National

have the stay lifted, and may "freeze" the account for a reasonable period pending an application to lift the stay.[386] Trustee may seek to use the deposit account if he or she obtains court approval or if the institution consents.[387] If the trustee uses the deposit account funds, the institution is entitled to "adequate protection" of its interest.[388] "Adequate protection" may include periodic payments to the institution or some other type of security as a substitute for the funds used.[389]

[f] Duty of Set-off

Although a depositary institution may have a right to make a set-off against a deposit account, set-off generally has been characterized as a right that may be waived by the depositary institution.[390] Thus, the depositary institution is not liable to the depositor if the depositary institution fails to set-off the account.[391] The depositary institution is also not liable, in most states, to sureties, indorsers, or other parties secondarily liable on the debt if the depositary institution fails to set-off an account, even though sufficient funds are available in the debtor's deposit account to pay the debt at maturity.[392] In other words, the depositary institution has no obligation to exercise a right of set-off. However, persons secondarily liable may be released from liability on a debt if a banking institution fails to set-off the debtor's deposit account where the account would have been sufficient to satisfy the debt on the date the debt became due.[393] In no event, however, is the institution

---

Trust & Savings Association v. Edgins (*In re* Edgins), 36 B.R. 480 (9th Cir.BAP 1984); *Stann v. Mid American Credit Union,* 39 B.R. 246 (D. Kan. 1984); *In re* Owens–Peterson, 39 B.R. 186 (Bankr.N.D.Ga.1984); *In re* Carpenter, 14 B.R. 405 (Bankr. M.D.Tenn.1981). *See also* Coleman, Garrett & Friedman, Tug of War Over Bank Deposits In Bankruptcy: Debtors Desperation For Cash vs Bank's Demand For Collateral, 47 CONSUMER FIN. L.Q. REP. 156 (1993); *but see*, B.F. Goodrich Employees Fed. Credit Union v. Patterson (*In re* Patterson), 967 F.2d 505 (11th Cir.1992). The *Patterson* view was rejected by the Supreme Court in *Strumpf*, 116 S.Ct. 286. *See also In re* Weisberg, 193 B.R. 916 (9th Cir.BAP (Cal.) 1996), *aff'd in part, rev'd in part on other issues,* 136 F.3d 655 (9th Cir.1998) (a stockbroker or financial institution is not stayed from exercising its right to set-off a claim for a margin payment with securities of the debtor because the broker holds the margin to secure, or settle a securities contract. See 11 U.S.C. § 362(b)(6)).

386. 11 U.S.C. § 362(d); Citizens Bank v. Strumpf, 516 U.S. 16, 116 S.Ct. 286, 133 L.Ed.2d 258 (1995).

387. 11 U.S.C. § 363(b); Harrell and Miller, *supra* note 380, at 395–402.

388. 11 U.S.C. §§ 361, 363(c)(3), 363(*o*). *See also supra* note 387.

389. 11 U.S.C. §§ 361(1), 363. *See generally* Douglas Bacon, *Real Estate Bankruptcies from the Secured Creditor's Standpoint,* 43 CONSUMER FIN. L.Q. REP. 131 (1989).

390. Schultz v. American Nat. Bank & Trust Co., 40 Ill.App.3d 800, 352 N.E.2d 310 (1976); Overland Nat. Bank v. Aurora Co-operative Elevator Co., 184 Neb. 843, 172 N.W.2d 786 (Neb. 1969); Docter v. Riedel, 96 Wis. 158, 71 N.W. 119 (1897).

391. Docter v. Riedel, 96 Wis. 158, 71 N.W. 119 (1897).

392. Bank of America Nat. Trust & Sav. Ass'n. v. Liberty Nat. Bank & Trust Co., 116 F.Supp. 233 (W.D.Okla.), *aff'd*, 218 F.2d 831 (10th Cir.1955); Meredith v. First Nat. Bank, 271 S.W.2d 274 (Ky.Ct.App. 1954). *Cf.* UCC Article 3, § 3–605(e)-(g) (discharge of surety by creditor's impairment of collateral).

393. Bryant v. Williams, 16 F.2d 159 (E.D.N.C.1926); First Nat. Bank v. Peltz, 176 Pa. 513, 35 A. 218 (Pa. 1896).

under a duty to set-off an account belonging to a person secondarily liable on the debt.[394]

[3] *Garnishment*

Garnishment is a proceeding instituted by a creditor to satisfy a debt out of property or credits of the debtor that are possessed or owned by a third person (the "garnishee"). When a customer deposits money in a general deposit account, the banking institution takes title to the property and becomes indebted to the customer.[395] Thus, it is generally recognized that a deposit account is a debt owed to the depositor by the depositary institution, and is subject to garnishment from the time that the depositary institution becomes liable to the depositor for the funds.[396]

A garnishment action may be brought against a depositary institution as garnishee by serving the depositary institution with a writ of garnishment. Although there is some authority to the contrary,[397] generally a writ of garnishment, to be effective against a depositary institution, must be served on the depositary institution's office where the funds are held.[398] Thus, funds held at a depositary institution's main office may be garnished only by serving a writ at the main office, and funds held by a branch office may be garnished only by serving a writ of garnishment at the branch office.[399]

Most courts hold that a joint bank account is garnishable. However, the courts are divided as to the precise extent to which the funds may be garnished.[400] Some courts allow garnishment only to the extent of the

---

394. Bank of America Nat. Trust & Sav. Ass'n. v. Liberty Nat. Bank & Trust Co., 116 F.Supp. 233 (W.D.Okla.), *aff'd*, 218 F.2d 831 (10th Cir.1955).

395. *See* Robison, Creditor's Remedy: Garnishment of the Bank Account, 40 THE ALABAMA LAWYER 438 (1979). *See also supra* ¶ 9.05 and ¶ 9.06[2][f][iii].

396. Savings Bank v. Loewe, 242 U.S. 357, 37 S.Ct. 172, 61 L.Ed. 360 (1917); American Express Co. v. Vella, 94 N.J.Super. 258, 227 A.2d 721 (App.Div.1967); Silsbee State Bank v. French Market Grocery Co., 103 Tex. 629, 132 S.W. 465 (Tex. 1910). *See generally* Susan Davis, The Tax Man Cometh-Handling Levies, Liens and Summons, 49 CONSUMER FIN. L.Q. REP. 196 (1995).

397. Bank of Montreal v. Clark, 108 Ill. App. 163 (1903).

398. *See generally*, Annotation, Attachment and Garnishment of Funds in Branch Bank or Main Office of Bank Having Branch, 12 A.L.R.3d 1088 (1967). *See also* revised Article 9 § 9-304 (law of bank's jurisdiction for purposes of a security interest in a deposit account).

399. *See, e.g.*, United States v. First Nat. City Bank, 321 F.2d 14 (2d Cir.1963);

Shinto Shipping Co. v. Fibrex & Shipping Co., 425 F.Supp. 1088 (N.D.Cal.1976); McCloskey v. Chase Manhattan Bank, 11 N.Y.2d 936, 228 N.Y.S.2d 825, 183 N.E.2d 227 (N.Y. 1962).

400. *See e.g.*, Baker v. Baker, 710 P.2d 129 (Okla. Ct. App. 1985); Walnut Valley State Bank v. Stovall, 223 Kan. 459, 574 P.2d 1382 (Kan. 1978); Barton v. Hudson, 560 S.W.2d 20 (Ky.Ct.App.1977); Musker v. Gil Haskins Auto Leasing, Inc., 18 Ariz. App. 104, 500 P.2d 635 (Ariz.Ct.App.1972); First Nat. Bank v. Hector Supply Co., 236 So.2d 204 (Fla.Dist.Ct.App.1970), *remanded and reh. den.* 254 So.2d 777 (Fla.1971), *vac'd*, 257 So.2d 83 (Fla.App.1972); Olshan v. East N.Y. Sav. Bank, 28 F.Supp. 727 (E.D.N.Y.1939); Park Enterprises, Inc. v. Trach, 233 Minn. 467, 47 N.W.2d 194 (Minn. 1951); Schnellmann v. Southern Commercial & Sav. Bank, 123 Mo.App. 188, 100 S.W. 575 (Mo.Ct.App.1907). *See generally*, Annotation, Joint Bank Account as Subject to Attachment, Garnishment or Execution by Creditor of One of the Joint Depositors, 11 A.L.R.3d 1465 (1967); Whitaker, *supra* note 470, at 172; Psencik, *supra* note 470, at 146; *supra* ¶ 9.06[2][c][i].

debtor's equitable ownership of the account.[401] Other courts allow garnishment to the full amount of the account, regardless of the debtor's equitable interest.[402] Still other courts have prohibited garnishment of a joint deposit account, but these decisions have generally been overruled or disapproved.[403]

[4] Security Interests in Deposit Accounts[404]

Under revised Article 9 § 9–109(a)(1), Article 9 applies to a security interest in any personal property, thus including money.

Money is excluded from the UCC Article 9 definition of general intangibles.[405] Instead, money is within the definition of "goods" at § 9–102(a)(44). However, money is not subject to the perfection rules for most other goods, *e.g.*, § 9–310 permitting perfection by filing. Instead, the exclusive method of perfecting a security interest in money is by possession.[406] But when money is deposited into a deposit account it ceases to be money, insofar as the depositor is concerned. Old Article 9 excluded transfers of interests in deposit accounts from the application of Article 9.[407] A deposit account was defined under the old Article 9 as any deposit, savings passbook, or like account with a bank, savings and loan association, credit union or like organization, excluding an account evidenced by a certificate of deposit.[408] Thus, except for proceeds claims

---

401. Musker v. Gil Haskins Auto Leasing, Inc., 18 Ariz.App. 104, 500 P.2d 635 (Ariz.Ct.App.1972); Miller v. Standard State Bank, 31 Ill.App.2d 189, 176 N.E.2d 639 (1961); Purma v. Stark, 224 Kan. 642, 585 P.2d 991 (Kan. 1978); Beehive State Bank v. Rosquist, 21 Utah 2d 17, 439 P.2d 468 (Utah 1968); *supra* ¶ 9.06[2][c][i].

402. Park Enterprises, Inc. v. Trach, 233 Minn. 467, 47 N.W.2d 194 (Minn. 1951).

403. *See, e.g.*, Comstock v. Morgan Park Trust & Sav. Bank, 319 Ill.App. 253, 48 N.E.2d 980 (1943); Brown, for Use of Buck v. First Nat. Bank, 271 Ill.App. 424 (1933). Both *Comstock* and *Buck* were disapproved in Leaf v. McGowan, 13 Ill.App.2d 58, 141 N.E.2d 67 (1957). *See also supra* ¶ 9.06[2][c][i].

404. *See generally* Roberts, *supra* note 336, at 176 (describing old Article 9). *See generally*, Wilkinson, Third-Party Interests in Deposit Accounts and the Bank's Right of Setoff, 109 BANKING L.J. 247 (1992); Harrell, Security Interests in Deposit Accounts: A Unique Relationship Between the UCC and Other Law, 23 U.C.C. L.J. 163 (1990) (also describing old Article 9). *See also* discussion *supra* at ¶ 9.06[2][f][ii] (security interest vs. garnishment). The discussion here will focus on revised Article 9, which has been enacted in all 50 states and was generally effective July 1, 2001. *See generally* Ben Carpenter, Security Interests in Deposit Accounts and Certificates of Deposit Under Revised Article 9, 55 CONSUMER FIN. L.Q. REP. 123 (2001); John F. Hilson, Bruce A. Markell, Stephen L. Sepinuck and William D. Warren, Report of the Deposit Accounts Task Force to the Article 9 Drafting Committee, 54 CONSUMER FIN. L.Q. REP. 203 (2000) (revised Article 9).

405. UCC § 9–102(a)(42).

406. UCC § 9–312(b)(3) and § 9–313. But, coins of numismatic value are not money and a security interest in such collateral can be perfected by filing. In re Midas Coin Co., 264 F.Supp. 193 (E.D.Mo. 1967). *See* definition of "money" at § 1–201(24).

407. *See* old § 9–104(1). Except as regards proceeds. *See* old § 9–306.

408. Old § 9–105(1)(e). *Cf.* revised § 9–102(a)(29). A cash management account offered by a brokerage firm was held to be a general intangible and not a deposit account, and thus filing was required to perfect the security interest. Merrill, Lynch, Pierce, Fenner & Smith v. Van Kylen (*In re* Kylen), 98 B.R. 455 (Bankr.W.D. Wis. 1989); *see also* Robelen, Creating and Perfecting Security Interests in Investment Accounts, 63 OKLA. BAR. ASS'N. J. 2733 (1992). As noted infra, the definition of "deposit account" at revised § 9–102(a)(29) is similar to old § 9–105(1)(e), except that it excludes accounts evidenced by an instru-

under old § 9–306, old Article 9 largely excluded security interests in deposit accounts from its coverage, although a common law pledge of a deposit account has long been widely recognized as a substitute for an Article 9 security interest.[409] To create a common law pledge, the depositor must deliver the evidence and control of the account to the creditor, or otherwise restrict the pledgor's control of the account.[410] Thus, possession by the creditor of the account passbook[411] or possession of a certificate of deposit[412] would be effective to perfect a common law pledge. Likewise, if the creditor effected a transfer of the deposited funds from the pledgor's deposit account to a deposit account under the sole control of the creditor, the pledge would be effective.[413] Revised Article 9 does not preclude use of a common law pledge as a substitute for or an addition to an Article 9 security interest, though priorities may be affected by revised §§ 9–327 and 9–340. With respect to the priority of a bank's right of set-off versus the common law pledgee of a deposit account, under old Article 9 the pledgee generally would prevail so long as the bank had notice of the pledge.[414] However, revised Article 9

---

ment. "Instrument" is defined at § 9–102(a)(47) as a written obligation to pay that is transferrable in the ordinary course of business. Thus, instead of excluding all CDs from the definition of deposit account, revised § 9–102(a)(29) excludes only CDs that are transferrable in the ordinary course and therefore qualify as instruments under § 9–102(a)(47). As a result, a CD could be either a deposit account (§ 9–102(a)(29)) or an instrument (§ 9–102(a)(47)) depending on its transferability.

A transferable certificate of deposit ("CD") would fall within the definition of "instrument" at old § 9–105(1)(i) or revised § 9–102(a)(47), and would therefore be subject to a possessory security interest under old §§ 9–304 and 9–305, or revised §§ 9–312 and 9–313. See, e.g., Skiles v. Security State Bank, 1 Neb.App. 360, 494 N.W.2d 355 (Neb.Ct. App.1992). Under revised § 9–312(a), instruments are also subject to perfection by filing. There has been some uncertainty about a CD labeled "nontransferable." See Harrell, supra note 362, at 165–68. Courts have held that a CD labeled "nontransferable" can nonetheless be transferred, and hence considered an "instrument" under Article 9. See In re Latin Inv. Corp., 156 B.R. 102 (Bankr.D.C. 1993). Bank IV Topeka, N.A. v. Topeka Bank & Trust Co., 15 Kan.App.2d 341, 807 P.2d 686 (Kan.App.1991), held that a CD denoted "nontransferable" could not qualify as an Article 9 "instrument"; the Kansas legislature subsequently modified Kansas old § 9–105(1)(i) to change this result. Revised Article 9 does not specifically address this, but § 9–102(a)(47) remains consistent with the notion that "non-transferrable" CDs can be transferred. See also revised § 9–406(d), (f); Carpenter, supra note 404.

409. Miller v. Wells Fargo Bank Int'l. Corp., 406 F.Supp. 452 (S.D.N.Y.1975). See generally Congress Talcott Corp. v. Gruber, 993 F.2d 315 (3d Cir.1993) (distinguishing right of set-off from common law pledge); Jamison v. Society National Bank, 66 Ohio St.3d 201, 611 N.E.2d 307 (Ohio 1993) (common law pledge prevailed over "payable on death" beneficiary of nontransferable CD); Hindman v. Community Nat'l. Bank of Pontiac, 14 Mich.App. 746, 165 N.W.2d 894 (Mich.Ct.App.1968) (surviving joint tenant takes subject to common law pledge). Cf. Guilds v. Monroe County Bank, 41 Mich.App. 616, 200 N.W.2d 769 (Mich. Ct.App.1972) (surviving joint tenant has priority over unexercised right of setoff).

410. Id.

411. Walton v. Piqua State Bank, 204 Kan. 741, 466 P.2d 316 (Kan. 1970).

412. Willis v. National Bank of Georgia, 176 Ga.App. 15, 334 S.E.2d 917 (Ga.Ct.App. 1985).

413. Gillman v. Chase Manhattan Bank, 73 N.Y.2d 1, 537 N.Y.S.2d 787, 534 N.E.2d 824 (N.Y. 1988). This would also constitute "control" under revised § 9–104(a)(3), thereby creating the highest level of priority under revised §§ 9–327 and 9–340.

414. First Nat'l Bank in Grand Prairie v. Lone Star Life Ins. Co., 524 S.W.2d 525 (Tex.Civ.App.1975); Guilds v. Monroe County Bank, 41 Mich.App. 616, 200 N.W.2d 769 (Mich.Ct.App.1972) (unexercised right of setoff subject to claim of surviving joint tenant). See also, First Nat.

dramatically changes this result, with revised § 9–340 awarding priority to the depositary institution's right of set-off, unless the pledgee becomes the customer of the bank so as to have "control" under § 9–104(a)(3).

As noted, revised Article 9 § 9–109(a)(1) and (d)(13) permit a direct security interest in a deposit account (as defined at § 9–102(a)(29)), as well as a claim to proceeds of other collateral that can be traced into the depositary account under §§ 9–102(a)(64) and 9–315. In the case of a proceeds claim, perfection as to the original collateral may also constitute perfection as to the proceeds under § 9–315 and the priorities will be governed by § 9–322. However, a direct security interest in the account as such can only be perfected by control, under §§ 9–312(b)(1) and 9–314. Under § 9–104(a)(1), the depositary bank will automatically have control, and under § 9–203(b)(3)(D) the depositary bank can create such a security interest pursuant to a security agreement that need not be authenticated by the debtor. If the depositary bank has such control, it will generally have priority over all competing secured parties under §§ 9–327 and 9–340, unless the competing creditor has achieved "control" by becoming the depositary institution's customer under § 9–104(a)(3).

Bank and Trust Co. of Oklahoma City v. Iowa Beef Processors, Inc., 626 F.2d 764 (10th Cir.1980); *supra* ¶ 9.06[2][f][ii].

In *In re* Collins Securities Corp., 998 F.2d 551 (8th Cir.1993), the FDIC was not liable for a pre-insolvency refusal of the depositary institution to honor an assignment of a deposit account which was reflected on the books of the institution.

Chapter 10

UCC ARTICLE 4A—FUNDS TRANSFERS

Analysis

Para.
- ¶10.01 Introduction and Scope—UCC Article 4A 469
- ¶10.02 Article 4A Definitions and Scope 470
  - [1] Fundamental Concepts 470
  - [2] Scope—Payment Order Must Be Unconditional 472
- ¶10.03 Liability for Errors and Unauthorized Orders 474
  - [1] Authority to Originate 474
  - [2] Security Procedure 475
  - [3] Commercially Reasonable Procedure Required 476
- ¶10.04 Obligations of a Bank Accepting a Payment Order 477
  - [1] In General 477
  - [2] Misdescription of Beneficiary 478
  - [3] Preemption of Other State Law Claims 479
- ¶10.05 Transmitting the Payment Order 482
- ¶10.06 Fees and Settlement 482
- ¶10.07 Payment 483
  - [1] Payment in General 483
  - [2] Payment and Discharge Between Banks 484
  - [3] Obligation of Beneficiary's Bank to Pay Beneficiary 485
  - [4] Payment to the Beneficiary 486
  - [5] Payment and Discharge 486
- ¶10.08 Miscellaneous Article 4A Issues 487
  - [1] Variation by Agreement or Funds—Transfer Rule 487
  - [2] Effect of Creditor Process or Injunction 488
  - [3] The Bank–Customer Relation 489
  - [4] Rate of Interest 489
  - [5] Choice of Law 490
    - [a] U.S. Transactions 490
    - [b] Choice of Law and International Transaction 490
  - [6] Statute of Limitations 492
- ¶10.09 Unauthorized and Erroneous Orders 493
  - [1] Authorized and Unauthorized Orders 493
  - [2] Erroneous Orders 494
  - [3] Beneficiary Misdescription 494
  - [4] Cancellation 495
  - [5] Other 495
- ¶10.10 Summary and Conclusions—Implementing UCC Article 4A 496
  - [1] Summary 496
  - [2] Implementing Article 4A 496

Para.

¶10.11 Regulation J Subpart A: Collection of Checks Through Federal
        Reserve Banks.. 489
¶10.12 Regulation J Subpart B: Fedwire 500
        [1] Scope of Subpart B..................................... 500
        [2] Impact of Subpart B 501
¶10.13 Federal Choice of Law Provisions 503
¶10.14 Wire Transfer Monitoring Rules 504
¶10.15 The U.S. Treasury "Travel Rule" 506
¶10.16 Conclusion 507

¶ 10.01 Introduction and Scope—UCC Article 4A*

Prior to the promulgation of Uniform Commercial Code (UCC) Article 4A (Funds–Transfers) in 1989 there was no clear-cut framework of legal rules governing wholesale wire transfers in the United States. At this writing, Article 4A has been enacted in every American state except South Carolina, an exceptional enactment record that reflects the near universal approval accorded this statute. In addition, the liberal choice of law rule at § 4A–507, the incorporation of Article 4A with slight modification into Federal Reserve Board Regulation J,[1] and the adoption of Article 4A into the rules of several automated clearing-house and related funds-transfer systems,[2] mean that Article 4A is generally applicable to wire transfers and automated clearing house (ACH) transfers worldwide. This is an unparalleled record of success, reflecting the importance of Article 4A in diminishing the legal impediments to funds-transfers.

Article 4A is limited to "wholesale" funds-transfers (including ACH transactions) and does not apply to "retail" consumer electronic "point-of-sale" funds-transfers such as debit and credit card transactions, where there is already extensive federal law coverage.[3] Article 4A is limited to

---

* Portions of this chapter are indebted to: Alvin C. Harrell, UCC Article 4A, 25 OKLA. CITY UNIV. L. REV. 293 (2000); Alvin C. Harrell, Wholesale Funds–Transfers–UCC Article 4A, in Joseph J. Norton, Chris Reed, and Ian Walden, Cross–Border Electronic Banking Ch.8 (1995); Alvin C. Harrell, Payment System Issues–UCC Article 4A, Regulations J, S, and D, 50 CONSUMER FIN. L. Q. REP. 49 (1996); and Fred H. Miller and Alvin C. Harrell, The Law of Modern Payment Systems and Notes Ch. 10 (2nd ed. 1992).

¶ 10.01

1. On choice of law, *see infra* ¶ 10.08 [5]. On Regulation J, *see infra* ¶¶ 10.11 and 10.12. Regulation J is found at 12 CFR Part 210. *See generally* Donmar Enterprises v. Southern Nat'l Bank, 828 F.Supp. 1230 (W.D.N.C.1993), *aff'd*, 64 F.3d 944 (4th Cir. 1995) (Regulation J preempts inconsistent state law remedies).

2. *See, e.g.*, the rules of the New York Clearing House Interbank Payments Systems (CHIPS) and the National Association of Clearing House Associations (NACHA); *infra* notes 31–36 (S.W.I.F.T). *See generally*, Funds-Transfers Under Article 4A: What your Deposit Agreement Should Provide, in 1 Clarks' Bank Dep. and Pymts. No. 12, at 4 (June 1993); Filling Your Wire Transfer Agreements With the Right Stuff–Part 2, *id*. Vol. 2 No. 4 at 3 (Oct. 1993).

3. § 4A–108. *See, e.g.*, Sinclair Oil Corp. v. Sylvan State Bank, 254 Kan. 836, 869 P.2d 675 (Kan.1994); Prefatory Note to Article 4A, "Description of transactions covered by Article 4A," noting coverage of the Electronic Funds–Transfer Act (EFTA), 15 U.S.C. §§ 1693–1693r. *See also* Regulation E, 12 CFR Pt. 205; Abyaneh v. Merchants Bank North, 670 F.Supp. 1298 (M.D.Pa. 1987); Kashanchi v. Texas Commerce Medical Bank, N.A. 703 F.2d 936 (5th Cir.1983);

funds-transfers effectuated through the banking system and does not apply to transfers via nonbank entities such as Western Union.[4] Article 4A generally will apply, either directly or through clearing-house and funds transfer rules, when a paper check is converted to an ACH transfer at the point of sale (in effect the check being used as an Article 4A payment order to originate an ACH transfer).

¶ 10.02   Article 4A Definitions and Scope

[1]   Fundamental Concepts

The concept of a "payment order" is a central focus of Article 4A. "Payment order" is defined as an instruction by a "sender" (transmitted orally, electronically, or in writing) to a bank to pay money to a "beneficiary" within the limitations at § 4A–103(a)(1).[5] "Sender" is the

---

Sinclair Oil Corp. v. Sylvan State Bank, 254 Kan. 836, 869 P.2d 675 (Kan. 1994); *infra* this text Chapter 11.

4.   *See* § 4A–103(a) and Comment 2 to § 4A–104. Except as noted in the next sentence in the text, Article 4A also does not apply to transfers by draft or other "item" as defined in Article 4 § 4–104(a)(9). *See* Continental Airlines, Inc. v. Boatmen's National Bank of St. Louis, 13 F.3d 1254 (8th Cir.1994); *supra* this text ¶ 8.01[1]. Thus, if Article 4A applies, Article 4 does not, and vice versa. *See*, *e.g.*, Brooks v. First Fed. Sav. and Loan Ass'n of Sylacauga, 726 So.2d 640 (Ala.1998).

¶ 10.02

5.   A payment order also must be unconditional. *See* §§ 4A–103(a)(1)(i)-(iii) and 4A–104(a); *infra* this text at notes 16 and 25–27. *But see* Impulse Trading, Inc. v. Norwest Bank Minnesota, N.A., 870 F.Supp. 954 (D.Minn.1994) (application of Article 4A despite lack of a payment order); Centre–Point Merchant Bank Ltd. v. American Express Bank Ltd., 913 F.Supp. 202 (S.D.N.Y. 1996). A check is an instrument governed by UCC Article 3 and is not an Article 4A payment order, but as noted below, and *supra* this text in the preceding paragraph, a check may be used as a payment order to initiate an Article 4A funds transfer. *See* § 4A–104, Official Comment 5. Similarly, an Article 4A payment order is not an "item" under Article 4. *See* UCC § 4–104(a)(9); *supra* this text ¶ 8.01[3][a]; Continental Airlines, 13 F.3d at 1254. As noted *supra* this text, however, a check or other item can be used as a payment order, *e.g.*, at the point of sale. "Bank" is defined broadly at § 4A–105(a)(2) to include savings and loan associations, credit unions, trust companies and any other person or entity engaged in the business of banking.

See also UCC § 4–104(1). Citations herein to UCC Articles 3 and 4 refer to the 1990 uniform text.

A payment order can be oral, electronic or in writing; indeed, in some circumstances it may be transmitted by first class mail. *See* §§ 4A–103(a)(1) and 4A–302(c). Like checks, a payment order is an unconditional (except as to timing) instruction to pay a fixed or determinable amount of money to a beneficiary. § 4A–103(a)(1)(i). Thus an instruction to pay under a letter of credit is not a payment order. § 4A–104, Comment 3. Nor is a check a payment order because a payment order must be transmitted by the sender, not to the payee, but directly to the receiving bank, or to an agent, funds transfer system, or communication system for transmittal to the receiving bank. § 4A–103(a)(1)(iii), Comment 5 to § 4A–104. For the same reason, the concept of payment order excludes payment by credit card. Transfers initiated by debit cards (retail funds transfers) are covered by the federal Electronic Fund Transfer Act. § 4A–108.

Because payment orders must involve banks (§§ 4A–105(a)(2), 4A–103(a)(1)), funds transfers made by Western Union and the like are excluded; they are sufficiently different from the large, commercial transfers that are the subject of Article 4A as to make it inadvisable to employ the same rules. § 4A–104, Comment 2. Credit transfers through automated clearing houses (ACH) are included under Article 4A (including transfers initiated by check), but debit transfers, including those made by ACH, are excluded (§ 4A–103(a)(1)(ii)), again for the reason they involve sufficiently different considerations. § 4A–104, Comment 4. Finally, and as noted above, a funds transfer any part of which is governed by

person giving such an instruction (the initial "sender" is called the "originator"), and the "beneficiary" is the person to be paid.[6] A payment order is initiated when an originator issues such an order to a bank. The receiving bank then "accepts" the order by "executing" it in favor of another receiving bank.[7] This process is repeated until the order is sent to, and accepted by, the beneficiary's bank. Acceptance of a payment order invokes the liability of the receiving bank to comply with the order.[8] Acceptance occurs when the receiving bank executes the payment order by sending payment in accordance with the order or, in the case of the beneficiary's bank, by paying the beneficiary, by notifying the beneficiary that payment has been received, or by receipt of payment by the beneficiary's bank.[9]

The significance of this is illustrated by cases like *Sigmoil Resources, N.V. v. Pan Ocean Oil Corporation (Nigeria)*,[10] where a creditor sought to attach funds in its debtor's bank account after an Article 4A funds-transfer of the funds out of that account had been accepted by the receiving bank. In rejecting this attachment, the court noted that "[a] funds-transfer is complete at the moment the receiving bank receives the credit message, not when the beneficiary acquires the funds...."[11] Once the funds-transfer was complete by reason of the receiving bank's acceptance of the payment order, the sender and originator retained no

---

the federal Electronic Fund Transfer Act, 15 U.S.C. § 1693 *et seq.*, and its implementing Regulation E, 12 CFR pt. 205, which protect consumer rights, is excluded from Article 4A to avoid conflicting rules. § 4A–108. However, a consumer purpose transfer over Fedwire, for example, or a consumer funds transfer excepted from the EFTA such as certain telephone initiated transfers under Regulation E § 205.3(e), could be subject to Article 4A. *See, e.g.*, § 4A–108 and Regulation J, § 210.25(b)(3).

6. *See* § 4A–103(a)(1), (2), (5).

7. *See* §§ 4A–103, 4A–209, and 4A–301 (a); *infra* ¶ 10.04. Under UCC Article 4A, a "funds transfer" (§ 4A–104(a)) is the payment order (§ 4A–103(a)(1)) or series of payment orders by which the originator of the order (§ 4A–104(c)) accomplishes payment to the beneficiary (§ 4A–103(a)(2)) of the originator's order. For example, suppose A wishes to accomplish payment of $1 million to B. A is the originator and B is the beneficiary. A "payment order" is simply an instruction, which can be oral, electronic or written, by the sender (§ 4A–103(a)(5)) to a receiving bank (§§ 4A–103(a)(4) and 4A–105(a)(2)) to pay money to a beneficiary.

8. *See* § 4A–302(a). *See generally* First Security Bank v. Pan American Bank, 215 F.3d 1147 (10th Cir.2000). Thus, once a payment order has been accepted by the beneficiary's bank, ownership of the funds passes to the beneficiary's bank and the transfer cannot be revoked without the consent of the beneficiary. *See* § 4A–404; United States v. BCCI Holdings (Luxembourg), S.A., 956 F.Supp. 5 (D.D.C.1997); United States v. BCCI Holdings (Luxembourg), S.A., 814 F.Supp. 106 (D.D.C.1993). In contrast, if the payment order is not accepted, the funds are not transferred and no legal interest passes to the beneficiary. *See* United States v. BCCI Holdings (Luxembourg), S.A., 977 F.Supp. 20 (D.D.C.1997); United States v. BCCI Holdings (Luxembourg), S.A., 980 F.Supp. 2 (D.D.C.1997). *See also infra* this text at notes 10–12 and 30–33.

9. *See* §§ 4A–209(a), (b), and 4A–301. *See* First Security Bank v. Pan American Bank, 215 F.3d 1147 (10th Cir.2000) (payment to beneficiary may occur upon crediting of beneficiary's account, even without notification to the beneficiary). *See also* § 4A–103(a)(2), (3), (4), (5); *infra* ¶ 10.07[3] and [4].

10. 234 A.D.2d 103, 650 N.Y.S.2d 726 (N.Y.App.Div.1996).

11. 234 A.D. 2d at 104, 650 N.Y.S.2d at 727, citing: § 4A–402; Manufacturas Int'l, LTDA v. Manufacturers Hanover Trust Co., 792 F.Supp. 180, 187 (E.D.N.Y.1992); Sheerbonnet, Ltd. v. American Express Bank, Ltd., 951 F.Supp. 403 (S.D.N.Y.1995). *See also infra* this text note 33.

ownership interest in the funds that would be subject to attachment.[12]

Use of proper terminology is crucial when describing an Article 4A transaction. The "originator" initiates the funds-transfer by giving a "payment order" to the "originator's bank," which "accepts" the payment order by "executing" it, thereby becoming a "sender." The "receiving bank" then likewise "accepts" the order by "executing" it in favor of another "receiving bank." Ultimately it is executed in favor of the "beneficiary's bank," which "accepts" the order by paying the beneficiary or by notifying the "beneficiary" that payment has been received.[13] All "intermediary banks" (those between the originator's bank and the beneficiary's bank) are both a "receiving bank" and a "sender," as they "accept" the order and "execute" it.[14] The essential basis for the obligation of each bank is the underlying contract (the payment order) and the bank's acceptance of that contract pursuant to the rules of Article 4A.[15]

[2] Scope—Payment Order Must Be Unconditional

By definition, an Article 4A payment order must be unconditional.[16] Therefore an important scope issue in determining whether Article 4A applies is whether the payment order in question is or is not conditional. This issue has spawned some important litigation.

In *Grabowski v. Bank of Boston*,[17] an attorney-in-fact made unauthorized funds-transfers to himself out of certain bank accounts in violation

---

12. See id.; see also: §§ 4A–209 (acceptance), 4A–302 and 4A–404; United States v. BCCI Holdings (Luxembourg), S.A., 980 F.Supp. 515, 520–21 (D.D.C.1997) (same, discussing the importance and methods of acceptance), citing Fry, Basic Concepts in Article 4A: Scope and Definitions, 45 Bus. Law. 1401, 1412 (1990). These issues are also discussed in one of several companion BCCI cases, see, e.g., United States v. BCCI Holdings (Luxembourg), S.A., 980 F.Supp. 507, 513 (1997) (same). See also Piedmont Resolution, L.L.C. v. Johnston, Rivlin & Foley, 999 F.Supp. 34, 47 (D.D.C.1998) (discussed infra at ¶ 10.02[2]; BCCI Holdings, 956 F. Supp. at 5; United States v. BCCI Holdings (Luxembourg), S.A., 814 F.Supp. 106 (D.D.C.1993).

13. If the beneficiary's bank receives payment from the sender and takes no action, acceptance occurs at the opening of the bank's next funds-transfer business day. See § 4A–209(b)(3).

14. See definitions at §§ 4A–103, 4A–104, and Article 4A Prefatory Note.

15. Unlike negotiable instruments (notes and drafts—see UCC § 3–104) governed by UCC Article 3, and items governed by Article 4 (see UCC § 4–104), payment orders do not create independent statutory obligations in addition to the underlying agreement. Therefore, the rights and liabilities of the parties to a payment order arise solely under the agreement of the parties in the context of the Article 4A statutory environment. See, e.g., §§ 4A–209 (acceptance) and 4A–212 (nonacceptance); infra ¶ 10.10 (Unauthorized and Erroneous Orders); cf. UCC §§ 3–104, 3–310, 3–412, 3–415, 4–104(a)(9), 4–215, 4–302. As a result, a payment order may be refused without any statutory liability–there is no Article 4A equivalent to the Article 4 wrongful dishonor provision at § 4–402, because payment orders are not like checks where there is a prearranged account with an agreement to honor properly payable items. See § 4A–210 (rejection of payment order). However, the bank rejecting the payment order may be liable if it has separately agreed to honor such orders. See § 4A–305(d).

16. Section 4A–103(a)(1)(i) defines "Payment order" as an instruction to pay money that "does not state a condition to payment to the beneficiary other than time of payment...." See also supra note 5 and accompanying text; infra notes 25–27 and 34–36 and text.

17. 997 F.Supp. 111 (D.Mass.1997) (*Grabowski* I); see also companion case, Grabowski v. Bank of Boston, 997 F.Supp. 130 (D.Mass.1998) (*Grabowsky* II).

of the applicable power-of-attorney. The depositors, owners of the accounts in question, sued the bank to recover the funds. Among the issues confronted by the court were the following Article 4A questions: (1) was the suit barred by the preclusion at § 4A–505 requiring that notice of the customer's objection be given to the bank within one year after the customer received notice of the funds-transfer?;[18] (2) was an agreement requiring the depositors to indemnify the bank for losses due to unauthorized transfers valid under Article 4A?;[19] (3) was a conditional order issued by the attorney-in-fact subject to Article 4A because the condition was not stated in the order?;[20] (4) were the unauthorized payment orders excluded from Article 4A as debit transfers, where the instruction to pay is given by the recipient, because the attorney-in-fact transferred the funds to himself as beneficiary?;[21] and (5) was the indemnity agreement (noted above) a "security procedure" enforceable under Article 4A?[22]

The *Grabowski* I court noted that the one year limitation period at § 4A–505 is not a statute of limitations barring suit after one year, as the bank alleged, but a statute of repose requiring the aggrieved customer to give the bank notice of the customer's objection to the payment order within one year after the customer received notice of the payment.[23] The court also held the indemnity agreement invalid, on grounds that it was not a security procedure under § 4A–202(b) and, therefore, was barred by § 4A–202(f) (enforceability of payment orders are not otherwise subject to variation by agreement).[24]

Another major issue in *Grabowski* I was whether the conditional nature of the power-of-attorney made the payment orders executed pursuant thereto conditional, and therefore outside the scope of Article 4A.[25] The court noted that an Article 4A payment order must be unconditional,[26] and that the power-of-attorney in question included conditions requiring receipt of certain invoices or bank instruments. Had such conditions been included in the payment order to the bank, as required in the power of attorney, the payment order would not have been covered by Article 4A. However, in this case the payment order erroneously omitted the required conditions, and therefore, on its face qualified as an unconditional payment order governed by Article 4A.[27]

The *Grabowski* I court also held that the payment orders were not excluded debit transfers, because the attorney-in-fact was ordering pay-

---

18. See *infra* ¶ 10.08[3].

19. See § 4A–202(b).

20. See § 4A–103(a)(1)(i).

21. See § 4A–103(a)(1)(ii), § 4A–104, Official Comment.

22. See § 4A–202(b). There were 7 additional issues numbered by the court 6 through 12, dealing with enforcement of the terms of the power-of-attorney against the bank and claims for breach of contract and deceit. See *Grabowski* I, 997 F. Supp. at 111.

23. Similar notice periods are found elsewhere in the UCC; *see, e.g.,* Article 4 § 4–406(c), (d), and (f).

24. The purpose is to preserve the loss allocation rules of Article 4A. See *Grabowski* I, 997 F. Supp. at 119–120. See also § 4A–305(f) (same).

25. See § 4A–103(a)(1)(i).

26. See *id*. See also *Grabowski* I, 997 F. Supp. at 121.

27. See *id*.

ment as agent for the account owners and on his own behalf;[28] and the bank was not absolved of liability for the wrongful transfer by its security procedure under § 4A–202(b), because this procedure did not permit the bank to ignore the limitations in the power-of-attorney authorizing the funds-transfers.[29] Accordingly, the bank was deemed to have violated its contractual obligations to the account owners by permitting unauthorized payment orders to withdraw funds from the account.[30]

Another case dealing with the issue of conditional payment orders is *Piedmont Resolution, L.L.C. v. Johnston, Rivlin & Foley*.[31] In *Piedmont*, the bank customer was victimized to the tune of $3 million by a "bank instruments scam" utilizing a funds-transfer through S.W.I.F.T.[32] If this transfer was governed by Article 4A, ownership of the funds would pass to the beneficiary's bank upon acceptance of the order and recourse would largely be limited to the Article 4A loss allocation rules.[33]

However, as noted an Article 4A payment order must be unconditional,[34] and although a funds-transfer by S.W.I.F.T. is normally unconditional (and thus covered by Article 4A), in this case it was not.[35] In *Piedmont*, the court concluded for summary judgment purposes that the funds-transfer could be deemed conditional and therefore outside the scope of Article 4A, despite the use of a S.W.I.F.T. transfer.[36]

¶ 10.03 Liability for Errors and Unauthorized Orders[37]

[1] *Authority to Originate*

The authority of the originator and each sender to initiate or execute the payment order is governed by agency principles.[38] Thus one of the first questions raised by an allegation of unauthorized payment

---

28. *See id.*, at 122.

29. *See id.* at 123. In addition it appears there was no valid security procedure applicable to this case. *Id.*

30. *Id.*, at 124–130. A companion case, Grabowski v. Bank of Boston, 997 F.Supp. 130 (D.Mass.1998) (*Grabowski* II), focuses on the agency issues and is discussed *infra* at ¶ 10.03.

31. 999 F.Supp. 34 (D.D.C.1998).

32. *Id.*, at 43. S.W.I.F.T. is an organization that provides funds transmission services. *See* § 4A–105, Comment 3; *supra* note 2.

33. *See Piedmont*, 999 F. Supp. at 47; *supra* this text at notes 10–12; *infra* ¶¶ 10.03—10.07.

34. *See supra* notes 5, 16, and 25–27 and accompanying text; § 4A–103(a)(1)(i), and discussion *supra*; *Grabowski* I, 997 F. Supp. at 121 ("Such conditions are anathema to Article 4A, which facilitates the low price, high speed, and mechanical nature of funds-transfers.").

35. This conclusion was based on questions of material fact sufficient to defeat a summary judgment motion and was not a definitive judgment on the issues in this case.

36. *Piedmont*, 999 F. Supp. at 48; the court also discussed breach of contract issues, ultimately denying the bank's motion for summary judgment.

¶ 10.03

37. *See also infra* ¶ 10.09 (Unauthorized and Erroneous Orders).

38. *See* § 4A–202(a). *See also* Abyaneh v. Merchants Bank, North, 670 F.Supp. 1298 (M.D.Pa.1987). *Abyaneh*, decided prior to Article 4A, involved an imposter who lacked authority to initiate the subject payment orders, illustrating the authorization problems that can arise in a funds-transfer scenario. *See also* Bradford Trust Co. of Boston v. Texas American Bank–Houston, 790 F.2d 407 (5th Cir.1986); *infra* ¶ 10.09 (Unauthorized and Erroneous Orders).

under Article 4A is whether the payment order was originated by an agent with real or apparent authority.[39] Such authority can be determined under the law of agency and/or by an agreement addressing that authority.[40] For example, in *Grabowski* I the bank's authority to execute payment orders originated by the account owners' attorney-in-fact was governed by the power-of-attorney, which permitted only withdrawals accompanied by corresponding deposits.[41] Therefore, the attorney-in-fact was not authorized to originate the payment orders in question. Article 4A generally imposes strict liability on a bank to refund a payment order wrongfully issued in the name of a customer without an effective authorization.[42]

In *Grabowski* II the court gave more detailed consideration to the bank's argument that under Article 4A a payment order is authorized if it was originated by the person who purportedly sent it.[43] On the facts of that case, the bank argued that the payment order was authorized because it was sent by the identified originator (the attorney-in-fact), not by someone else posing as that person.[44] In this view, whether a payment order was authorized would turn on this type of Article 4A analysis rather than agency principles; however, as the court noted, this view is inconsistent with the text and Official Comments to Article 4A.[45] Thus *Grabowski* II reaffirmed that agency and contract principles determine the authority of an agent to send an Article 4A payment order.[46]

[2] Security Procedure

Even if the order was not authorized under § 4A-202(a) and the law of agency, if the bank has in place a "commercially reasonable security procedure" that had been accepted by the customer, and the bank complied with that procedure in good faith and in accordance with any instructions, the order is treated as having been authorized by the customer.[47] Even without such a security procedure, a bank handling a

---

39. *See* § 4A-202(a); Grabowski v. Bank of Boston, 997 F.Supp. 130 (D.Mass.1998) (*Grabowski* II).

40. *See Grabowski* I, 997 F. Supp. at 123 (citing § 4A-203, Official Comment).

41. *See Grabowski* I, 997 F. Supp. at 128.

42. § 4A-204; *see, e.g.*, Schmidt v. Fleet Bank, 1998 WL 47827 (S.D.N.Y.) (not reported in F. Supp.). This is similar to the rule regarding payment of items not properly payable under UCC Article 4 § 4-401. *But see infra* ¶ 10.03[2] (Security Procedure).

43. *Grabowski* II, 997 F. Supp. at 130-31.

44. *Id.*

45. *Id.*

46. Ironically, the *Grabowski* II court then noted unique facts relating to the separate criminal prosecution of both the principal and agent which might benefit the bank under an agency analysis.

47. § 4A-202(b). *See generally* §§ 4A-201, 4A-202, 4A-203, 4A-204, and 4A-504. *See also* Gatoil (U.S.A.). Inc. v. Forest Hill State Bank, 1 UCC Rep. Serv. 2d 171 (D.Md.1986), which was decided prior to Article 4A, relying on agency principles (and Article 4 by analogy) to determine that the bank used ordinary care in verifying the payment order. The court also concluded that there was no loss because the funds-transfer paid a debt of the customer. *See.* Article 4 § 4-407. The result would likely be the same under Article 4A, though the precise analysis would differ. *See generally infra* ¶ 10.09 (Unauthorized and Erroneous Orders).

payment order is not liable for consequential damages due to delay or other error, unless the bank agreed to assume this risk.[48]

Section 4A–201 defines "Security procedure" as follows:

"Security procedure" means a procedure established by agreement of a customer and a receiving bank for the purpose of (i) verifying that a payment order or communication amending or canceling a payment order is that of the customer, or (ii) detecting error in the transmission or the content of the payment order or communication. A security procedure may require the use of algorithms or other codes, identifying words or numbers, encryption, callback procedures, or similar security devices. Comparison of a signature on a payment order or communication with an authorized specimen signature of the customer is not by itself a security procedure.

Thus if a payment order is determined to be unauthorized under agency and contract principles pursuant to § 4A–202(a), the analysis shifts to § 4A–202(b) to determine whether the receiving bank properly verified the authenticity of the payment order pursuant to a § 4A–201 security procedure. If so, the payment order will be deemed effective even if it was not otherwise authorized.[49] This permits the originator and receiving bank to arrange security procedures adapted to their needs and to the needs of electronic commerce, even if that would not suffice to evidence authority under agency and contract principles.[50]

The security procedure must be "established by agreement" between the customer and bank.[51] A verification procedure unilaterally instituted by the bank does not meet this test, even if implemented for the purpose of verifying payment orders.[52]

[3] *Commercially Reasonable Procedure Required*

Under § 4A–202(b), the implementation of the security procedure is effective in protecting the receiving bank, whether or not the payment order is authorized, only if:

(i) the security procedure is a commercially reasonable method of providing security against unauthorized payment orders; and

---

48. *See* § 4A–305(d). *See also* Hadley v. Baxendale, 156 Eng. Rep. 145 (1854). As noted in Official Comment 2 to § 4A–305, the leading modern case on consequential damages before Article 4A was Evra Corp. v. Swiss Bank Corp., 673 F.2d 951 (7th Cir.1982). In that case a valuable ship charter was lost because a bank failed to properly execute a payment order. The lower court awarded damages of $2.1 million even though the amount of the payment order was only $27,000. The Seventh Circuit U.S. Court of Appeals reversed, partly on the basis of *Hadley v. Baxendale,* and Article 4A confirms this result. *See also infra* ¶ 10.09 (Unauthorized and Erroneous Orders); *infra* ¶¶ 10.04 and 10.07.

49. *See* Hedged Inv. Partners, L.P. v. Norwest Bank Minnesota, N.A., 578 N.W.2d 765, 773 (Minn.Ct.App.1998) (§ 4A–202(a) and (b) "are freestanding alternative methods to ascertaining whether a payment order is authentic.").

50. *Id.*

51. § 4A–201.

52. Skyline Int'l Dev. v. Citibank, F.S.B., 302 Ill.App.3d 79, 83, 236 Ill.Dec. 68, 706 N.E.2d 942, 945 (1998) (failure to follow bank's internal verification system did not violate a security procedure under § 4A–202(b)).

(ii) the bank proves that it accepted the payment order in good faith and in compliance with the security procedure and any written agreement or instruction of the customer restricting acceptance of payment orders issued in the name of the customer.

The term "commercially reasonable" is not defined, but § 4A–202(c) provides that the circumstances of the customer (as known to the bank), alternative security procedures offered, and security procedures "in general use by customers and receiving banks similarly situated" are factors to be used in determining this "question of law." If the customer declines to use a commercially reasonable security procedure that is offered by the bank, and instead opts for a more convenient or less expensive procedure, the customer assumes the risk of a failure of the system.[53]

¶ 10.04 Obligations of a Bank Accepting a Payment Order

[1] In General

Specific Article 4A provisions govern erroneous orders, erroneous execution and duplicate orders, misdescribed beneficiaries, improperly executed orders, and other similar problems.[54] Sections 4A–302 through 4A–305 contain important rules governing the obligations of a bank upon acceptance of a payment order. Generally, if a receiving bank (other than the beneficiary's bank) accepts a payment order, the bank is obligated to issue a payment order on the execution date, following the sender's instruction as to "(i) any intermediary bank or funds-transfer system to be used in carrying out the funds-transfer, or (ii) the means by which payment orders are to be transmitted in the funds-transfer."[55] Under this subsection, the receiving bank is obligated to issue a payment order according to the instruction of the originator if an intermediary bank is involved in the funds-transfer. If the beneficiary's bank does not

---

53. § 4A–202(c), § 4A–203 Comment 4.

¶ 10.04

54. *See, e.g,* §§ 4A–204 to 4A–208 and 4A–302 to 4A–305. *See generally* Sheerbonnet, Ltd. v. American Express Bank, Ltd., 905 F.Supp. 127 (S.D.N.Y.1995) (misdescription of beneficiary under § 4A–207); General Electric Capital Corp. v. Central Bank, 49 F.3d 280 (7th Cir.1995) (inconsistent account number and name under § 4A–207(b)(2)); *infra* ¶ 10.09 (Unauthorized and Erroneous Orders). *See also* First Security Bank v. Pan American Bank, 215 F.3d 1147 (10th Cir.2000), discussed *infra* at note 58 and again at ¶ 10.09.

55. *See* § 4A–302(a)(1). A receiving bank, other than the beneficiary's bank, accepts a payment order if it executes it, that is, if it sends its own order intended to carry out the order it received. *See*

§§ 4A–209(a), 4A–301(a). Note that improper execution, with the exception of too early execution under § 4A–209(d), will be acceptance, but may produce liability. *See* §§ 4A–303, 4A–305. It need not reject those orders it does not accept, unless otherwise provided by agreement or if the receiving bank had sufficient funds of the sender on hand to cover the order. §§ 4A–212, 4A–210(b).

If a funds transfer is not completed by acceptance by the beneficiary's bank of a payment order instructing payment to the beneficiary in accordance with the sender's order, the sender is not obligated to pay for its order, or is entitled to its money back. § 4A–402(c) and (d). *But see* § 4A–402(e). This is known as the "money back guarantee" and is the quid pro quo of protection from consequential damages discussed *infra*.

accept the payment order in accordance with the sender's instructions, the sender is excused from payment and is entitled to recover any payment made.[56] In addition, if a bank erroneously executes a payment order for an amount greater than the payment order from the sender, the bank is entitled to recover the excess from the receiving bank on grounds of restitution.[57]

[2] Misdescription of Beneficiary

The large number of funds-transfers between bank accounts makes it inevitable that errors will be made, directing funds to the wrong beneficiary or account. Article 4A provides rules for allocating losses in such a scenario, and generally these rules preempt alternative state law theories of recovery.

A good illustration of the issues is *Corfan Banco Asuncion Paraguay v. Ocean Bank*.[58] Corfan Banco originated a $72,972 transfer to an

---

56. See § 4A–402 (c) and (d), subject to (e). This is called the "money back guarantee." See infra ¶ 10.09 (Unauthorized and Erroneous Orders). See generally First Security Bank v. Pan American Bank, 215 F.3d 1147 (10th Cir.2000); Grain Traders, Inc. v. Citibank, N.A., 160 F.3d 97 (2d Cir. 1998); infra note 91.

A beneficiary's bank may accept a payment order by paying or notifying the beneficiary. § 4A–209(b)(1). Payment is governed by § 4A–405. Acceptance also may occur when the bank receives payment of the sender's order (an order over Fedwire is paid when received) or by the passage of time if the order is not rejected and the amount of the sender's order is fully paid or covered by a withdrawable credit balance. § 4A–209(b)(2). *See also* UCC § 4A–403(a)(1), and also the balance of subsection (a) and subsection (b); § 4A–209, Comment 6; § 4A–209(b)(3). Acceptance of the order entitles the bank to payment by the sender, and generally obliges it to notify the beneficiary and to pay the amount of the order to the beneficiary. § 4A–402(b); §§ 4A–404 and 4A–405. Failure to pay or to give notice of the receipt of the order may subject the bank to liability. § 4A–404. If the beneficiary's bank accepts the order, generally at this point the debt of the originator to the beneficiary for which the order was issued is discharged. § 4A–406.

57. See § 4A–303; *In re* Calument Farm, Inc., 114 F.3d 1186 (6th Cir.1997) (unpublished); Home Bank, F.S.B. v. Pauer, 1998 WL 78080 (Ohio Ct. App.1998) (not reported in N.E.2d). *See also infra* ¶ 10.09.

58. 715 So.2d 967 (Fla.Dist.Ct.App. 1998). Another recent case on this point involved misappropriation by a deposit broker. In First Security Bank v. Pan American Bank, 215 F.3d 1147 (10th Cir.2000), Article 4A funds transfers were sent to First Security Bank of New Mexico as the beneficiary's bank. The originators thought they were purchasing certificates of deposit at First Security Bank, but instead the funds went into the account of the deposit broker who solicited the investments. The payment order specified the deposit broker's account number at First Security, but named the bank or the originator as beneficiary. The deposit broker apparently dissipated some of the funds in its account, and the originators sued First Security under New Mexico Article 4A § 4A–207(b)(1), alleging that First Security was liable to the originators because it had knowledge that the named beneficiary and designated account number referred to different persons.

The required analysis is fact specific. The district court held that First Security had knowledge of a discrepancy because the payment orders named beneficiaries different from the name on the account designated by number in the payment order; consequently the district court granted summary judgment in favor of the originators. On appeal the Tenth Circuit reversed, noting that the question of actual knowledge is for the fact finder to decide after weighing the conflicting evidence, a determination that is usurped by a summary judgment. In *First Security* there was conflicting evidence as to whether First Security had knowledge of the name discrepancy at the time the funds transfer was accepted and paid to the beneficiary by credit to the account number specified in the order. Thus, the summary judgment was inappropriate and was reversed. The case contains a good discussion of the issues relevant under § 4A–207(b)(1) and (2).

account of its customer (Silva) at Ocean Bank. The payment order named Silva as beneficiary, but erroneously listed a nonexistent account number. Ocean Bank noticed the error and contacted Silva to confirm his correct account number, then accepted the payment order and deposited the funds to this account. Ocean Bank did not, however, notify Corfan Banco or the intermediary bank of the erroneous account number in the payment order or Ocean Bank's correction of that number.

The next day Corfan Banco discovered the error in its previous payment order, and sent a second $72,972 payment order to Silva's correct account. This second transfer was intended as a correction of the prior order, but was not designated as such. This second order was automatically processed at Ocean Bank as a stand-alone payment order and the funds were again deposited in Silva's account, resulting in Silva receiving double payment (which he immediately withdrew).

Corfan Banco brought suit against Ocean Bank to recover the $72,979 overpayment, based on § 4A–207 and an allegation of common law negligence.

Corfan Banco argued that under § 4A–207(a) the nonexistent account number in the first payment order rendered that order invalid and it could not be accepted. Ocean Bank responded that the language should not be given such a "highly technical" reading, on grounds of "commercial and practical considerations and common sense," arguing that the "or" in § 4A–207(a) be given conjunctive rather than disjunctive effect.[59] The Florida District Court of Appeal rejected this "invitation to look behind the plain language of the statute" and required it to be "read as written."[60]

The court noted that this creates an apparent anomaly, in that a payment order payable to an identified beneficiary can be accepted without a designated account number (§ 4A–207(a) being inapplicable), or with an account number of a different person (§ 4A–207(b)), but not with a nonexistent account number, under the plain meaning of § 4A–207(a).[61] Accordingly, the trial court's summary judgment in favor of Ocean Bank on this issue was reversed. A dissenting opinion argued that the statutory language at § 4A–207(a) allows the beneficiary's bank to look to other information ("other information") to confirm the identity of the beneficiary and account and avoid a misdescription invalidating the order under § 4A–207(a).[62]

[3] Preemption of Other State Law Claims

As illustrated by *Corfan Banco*,[63] a recurring issue is whether the Article 4A rules are exclusive, *e.g.*, do they preempt otherwise applicable state law remedies based on contract law or the tort of negligence? While

---

59. 715 So.2d at 969.

60. *Id.*

61. *See id.* at 969 n.4, citing William D. Hawkland & Richard Moreno, Uniform Commercial Code Series § 4A–207:01 (1993). *See also infra* ¶ 10.09[3].

62. *Corfan Banco*, 715 So.2d at 971 (J. Nesbitt, dissenting). *See also* § 4A–207(b), (c), (d); *infra* ¶ 10.09[3].

63. *See Corfan Banco*, 715 So.2d at 967, discussed *supra* at ¶ 10.04[2]. *See also infra* ¶ 10.07[5].

the *Corfan Banco* court specifically "did not reach the issue of whether the adoption of Article 4A of the UCC preempts negligence claims in all cases,"[64] the court cited with approval the Official Comment to § 4A–102, which strongly states that Article 4A preempts inconsistent state law.[65] The *Corfan Banco* court noted that the alleged breach of the duty by Ocean Bank in handling the Silva payment order[66] was "exactly the same duty established and now governed by [Article 4A]."[67] Thus in *Corfan Banco* a negligence claim was inappropriate, as it would create rights, duties and liabilities inconsistent with Article 4A.[68] The Florida appellate court agreed with Ocean Bank that Article 4A preempted the law of negligence in that case, and the trial court's grant of summary judgment was affirmed on this point.

The rule, and result, may be different if the non-Article 4A claim is based on agency or contract law, partly because Article 4A specifically incorporates agency and contract law for some purposes at § 4A–202(a).[69] As noted in *Hedged Investment Partners v. Norwest Bank Minnesota*,[70] "[t]he exclusivity of Article 4A does not prevent application of common law principles specifically provided for within the act or common law actions that do not conflict with the provisions and remedies of Article 4A."[71] Thus, in another case, the common law "discharge for value" rule was applied as being consistent with Article 4A.[72]

Of course, Article 4A is supplemented, and even to some extent potentially preempted, by Federal Reserve System rules, regulations and operating letters, other federal law, and contract-based rules such as clearing house and funds-transfer system agreements.[73] But the nearly unique nature of Article 4A, in terms of setting explicit rules for the

---

64. *Id.* at 971.

65. *Id.*, at 970–71. Similar issues can be confronted with regard to Articles 3 and 4 or even the UCC generally, *e.g.*, pursuant to UCC § 1–103. *See, e.g., supra* this text ¶ 8.01[1], ¶ 8.02[4], and ¶ 9.03[2]. But a temptation to refer to the § 1–103 case law for purposes of Article 4A should be tempered by a recognition that § 1–103 by its terms is slightly more accommodative to other law (*i.e.*, less preemptive) than Article 4A. This view is reinforced by the distinct nature and role of Article 4A. *See, e.g*, § 4A–102, Official Comment.

66. *See* the facts of this case as described *supra* at ¶ 10.04[2].

67. *Corfan Banco*, 715 So.2d at 971.

68. *See id.*, n.5. *See also* Aleo Int'l, Ltd. v. Citibank, N.A., 160 Misc.2d 950, 612 N.Y.S.2d 540 (N.Y.Sup.Ct.1994) (same); Nigerian National Petroleum Corp. v. Citibank, N.A., 1999 WL 558141 (S.D.N.Y. 1999) (same); Banca Commerciale Italiana, New York v. Northern Trust Intern. Banking Corp., 160 F.3d 90 (2d Cir.1998); Grain Traders, Inc. v. Citibank, N.A., 160 F.3d 97 (2d Cir.1998) (same).

69. *See* discussion *supra* at ¶ 10.03[1].

70. 578 N.W.2d 765; *see supra* ¶ 10.03[2] and note 49.

71. *Hedged Investment Partners*, 578 N.W.2d at 765. *See also* Banco De La Provincia De Buenos Aires v. BayBank Boston, N.A., 985 F.Supp. 364 (S.D.N.Y.1997) (Article 4A preempts only inconsistent claims); Impulse Trading, Inc. v. Norwest Bank Minnesota, N.A., 907 F.Supp. 1284 (D.Minn.1995) (same).

72. Banque Worms v. BankAmerica Int'l, 77 N.Y.2d 362, 570 N.E.2d 189, 568 N.Y.S.2d 541 (N.Y. 1991). For a related decision, *see* Banque Worms v. BankAmerica Intern., 928 F.2d 538 (2d Cir.1991). *See also infra* note 113; Grain Traders, Inc. v. Citibank, N.A., 160 F.3d 97 (2d Cir.1998).

73. *Hedged Inv. Partners*, 578 N.W.2d at 771, citing J. J. White & R.S. Summers, Uniform Commercial Code § 22 at 4 (4th ed. 1995). *See also* National Council of Churches of Christ in the USA v. First Union Nat'l Bank of Virginia, 153 F.3d 721, 1998 WL 416744 (4th Cir.) (unpublished) (preemption by Regulation J). *See supra* note 1, and *infra* ¶¶ 10.11 and 10.12.

mechanistic transfer of billions of dollars in relatively anonymous transactions, means that resort to extrinsic and amorphous sources of law must be minimized.

In *Hedged Investment Partners*, the trial court held that Article 4A preempts common law claims to the extent the parties do not have a special relationship, and rejected several contractual defenses on this basis.[74] The Minnesota Court of Appeals took a different view, allowing contractual defenses not in conflict with Article 4A despite the lack of a special relationship.[75] These defenses grew out of the agency contract between the plaintiff (as originator) and the defendant bank (as receiving bank), and therefore in a sense were Article 4A defenses under § 4A–202(a); however, as noted by the Court of Appeals, these defenses involved issues relating to fiduciary obligations that went "well beyond" the Article 4A issues implicated by § 4A–202(a).[76] Accordingly, the court viewed these as non-Article 4A issues that are consistent with Article 4A and, therefore, not excluded by it. In effect, Article 4A does not bar all extraneous claims and defenses between the parties merely because they also made an Article 4A funds-transfer, but merely those claims and defenses that would contradict the Article 4A regime. It is a fine line, but a compelling one.

This principle was also recognized in *Community Bank, FSB v. Stevens Financial Corp.*,[77] where an originator inadvertently sent the payment order to a bank different from the one designated by the beneficiary, but at which the beneficiary had a valid account. The payment order was valid under Article 4A, and the receiving bank (the beneficiary's bank) promptly made a set-off against the funds it deposited into the beneficiary's account. The beneficiary objected, on grounds it had instructed the originator to send the funds to a different bank, but under Article 4A the funds-transfer was valid and had been completed, and could not be cancelled.[78]

The originator then sought to invoke equitable principles of unjust enrichment to compel the beneficiary's bank to return the funds.[79] The court rejected this argument by noting that principles of law and equity extrinsic to Article 4A are applicable only when they are not inconsistent with Article 4A.[80] The setoff of funds received upon acceptance of a

---

74. As reported in the appellate decision, 578 N.W.2d at 771. *See generally supra* ¶ 9.03[1]-[3].

75. 578 N.W.2d at 771.

76. *Id.* Similarly, in a case decided under the New York Uniform Commercial Code Article 4A "money back guarantee" provision, an intermediary bank did not owe a refund to the transferor for failing to release its transfer to $310,000 from the transferor's immediate transferee bank to another bank, where the intermediary was the second bank in a chain of transfers; at best, the transferor could recover only from its immediate transferee. Grain Traders, Inc. v. Citibank, N.A., 960 F.Supp. 784 (S.D.N.Y.1997), *affirmed*, 160 F.3d 97 (2d Cir.1998).

77. 966 F.Supp. 775 (N.D. Ind. 1997).

78. *Id.*, at 783–86; § 4A–211. *See also infra* ¶ 10.09[4].

79. *See Community Bank*, 966 F. Supp. at 787.

80. *Id.*, at 788, citing Centre–Point Merchant Bank Ltd. v. American Express Bank, Ltd., 913 F.Supp. 202, 206 (S.D.N.Y.1996).

payment order is clearly authorized by § 4A–502,[81] and disgorgement of those funds on grounds of unjust enrichment would directly contravene that Article 4A provision. As a result the mistaken payment order, though inadvertent, was valid under Article 4 and could not be cancelled.

¶ 10.05 Transmitting the Payment Order

The means of transmitting the payment order depend upon the sender's instruction, and a stated payment date is valid if the sender's instruction obligates the receiving bank to transmit its payment order "at a time and by a means reasonably necessary to allow payment to the beneficiary on the payment date or as soon thereafter as is feasible."[82] This and other provisions of Article 4A Parts 2 and 3 should be closely reviewed to assure that financial institution staff are familiar with the statutory obligations of a receiving bank with regard to the execution of payment orders.

¶ 10.06 Fees and Settlement

Fees and provisional settlement are important issues to be addressed in the bank-customer agreement. Section 4A–302(d) provides that charges and expenses cannot be deducted nor instructions given for such deduction unless the receiving bank is so "instructed by the sender." The basic rule under Article 4A is that the beneficiary's bank cannot make provisional payment, so the bank (if it accepts an order) takes any credit risk if settlement is not made. Section 4A–405(d) does permit provisional payment to a beneficiary by its bank if statutory criteria are

---

81. See infra ¶ 10.08[2].

¶ 10.05

82. See § 4A–302(a)(2); infra ¶ 10.07[1]. In Central Coordinates, Inc. v. Morgan Guaranty Trust Co., 129 Misc.2d 804, 494 N.Y.S.2d 602, 40 UCC Rep. Serv. 1340 (N.Y.Sup.Ct.1985), the plaintiff, as assignee of Bellmore Investments Limited (Bellmore), sought consequential damages for delay in transmitting a wire transfer. Bellmore had an agreement with Intercare Management Services, Inc. (Intercare) granting Bellmore an option to acquire certain stock. The option agreement allowed Intercare to terminate the agreement in the event Bellmore failed to make any required payment. In order to make the payment due July 14, 1983, Bellmore requested, on July 8, 1983, that its bank, Union Chelsea National Bank (Chelsea), transfer by wire the payment to the New York branch of Barclay's Bank International (Barclay's) to be credited to a specified account, from which Bellmore would withdraw the money and deliver the payment to Intercare. Because Chelsea had no direct correspondent relationship with Barclay's, Chelsea wired the funds by Fedwire on July 11 to Morgan Guaranty to credit the account of Barclay's at Morgan Guaranty for ultimate credit by Barclay's to the account specified by Bellmore. Morgan Guaranty acknowledged receipt of the funds transfer, credited the amount to the account of Barclay's on the same day, but did not timely deliver instructions to Barclay's to credit the account specified by Bellmore.

The court ruled that the common law limited liability to the damages within the contemplation of the parties at the time of contracting, Morgan Guaranty was not informed of Bellmore's purpose in sending the wire, and thus Bellmore's contract action failed. Similarly, Bellmore's tort action failed because the damages requested were not reasonably foreseeable.

Under Article 4A, Morgan Guaranty through Fedwire would have received and accepted, by issuing its own payment instruction (order) to Barclay's, Chelsea's order which executed Bellmore's order. See §§ 4A–209(a), 4A–301(a), 4A–103(a)(1) and Comment 1, Case #3, to § 4A–104. However, it did not properly execute the order. See §§ 4A–302(a)(1), 4–301(b). It thus incurred liability for interest, but not for consequential damages. See § 4A–305(a).

met including: (1) a requirement that the beneficiary, the beneficiary's bank, and the originator's bank agree to be bound by a rule allowing such provisional credit; (2) the rule provides that notice of the provisional nature of the payment be given both to the beneficiary and the originator before the funds-transfer is initiated; and (3) the beneficiary's bank did not receive payment of the order it accepted.[83]

Finally, it should be noted that the Department of Treasury has imposed recordkeeping requirements relating to fund transfers by banks and additional information requests of non-deposit account holders.[84]

¶ 10.07 Payment

[1] Payment in General

Article 4A Part 4 governs payment of the order. The "payment date" is the day on which the amount of the order becomes payable to the beneficiary by the beneficiary's bank.[85] This date is determined by the instructions of the sender, but cannot be earlier than the day of receipt by the beneficiary's bank.[86] In the absence of instructions, the payment date is the day the order is received by the beneficiary's bank.[87]

Each sender has an obligation to pay the receiving bank if the order is accepted by the receiving bank.[88] If the receiving bank is the beneficiary's bank, acceptance of the order obligates the sender to pay on the payment date.[89] In other cases acceptance by the receiving bank obligates the sender to pay on the execution date of the sender's order.[90]

If the payment order is not accepted or completed, the receiving bank is obligated to refund the payment, with interest, to the extent the sender is not obligated to pay.[91] However, if the receiving bank is unable to refund such payment (due to insolvency or other suspension of

---

¶ 10.06

83. *See* § 4A–405(d). *See also supra* note 1, *supra* this text and note 73; and *infra* this text at ¶ 10.07[4] and [5] notes 113. and 119. Consult NACHA and CHIPS rules for variations.

84. *See infra* ¶¶ 10.14 and 10.15.

¶ 10.07

85. *See* § 4A–401; *supra* ¶ 10.05.
86. *Id.*
87. *Id.*
88. § 4A–402.
89. § 4A–402(b). *See also supra* this text at notes 8–11.
90. § 4A–402(c). In such case the sender's obligation is excused if the transfer is not completed by the beneficiary's bank accepting the order. *Id.*
91. § 4A–402(d). As noted *supra* at note 56, this is called the "money back guarantee." *See infra* ¶ 10.09 (Unauthorized and Erroneous Orders). These Article 4 rules generally preempt alternative state law claims. *See supra* ¶ 10.04[3]. For example, the Second Circuit U.S. Court of Appeals held that New York's UCC Article 4 governing the obligation of a receiving bank's refusal to cancel the sender's previously executed payment order when the next transferee suspended payments and the bank determined the next transferee, notwithstanding its debit authorization, had exceeded its credit limitation; such claims would have imposed liability inconsistent with the rights and liabilities expressly created by Article 4A. Grain Traders, Inc. v. Citibank, N.A., 160 F.3d 97, 36 U.C.C. Rep. Serv. 2d (CBC) 1141 (2d Cir.1998). *See also* Nigerian National Petroleum Corp. v. Citibank, N.A., 1999 WL 558141 (S.D.N.Y. 1999) (application of Article 4A precludes competing common law claims).

payments or due to applicable law) and the sender designated that bank, the risk of loss is on the sender.[92]

All of the rules noted above are subject to the provisions of § 4A–303 (on erroneous execution and the right to reimbursement for any excess paid), as well as §§ 4A–205 (erroneous payment orders) and 4A–207 (misdescription of beneficiary).[93] As noted above, the right to be excused from payment and to receive a refund cannot be waived by agreement.[94]

[2] *Payment and Discharge Between Banks*

Article 4A provides rules to govern the finality of payments between banks, similar in some ways to the rules governing final payment of items under UCC Article 4.[95] The sender's obligation to pay the receiving bank may be discharged by:[96]

1. making final settlement through a Federal Reserve Bank;[97]

2. crediting an account of the receiving bank with the sender (payment occurs when that credit is withdrawn or at midnight of the day that the receiving bank learns that the credit is withdrawable);[98] or

3. the receiving bank debiting any account of the sender with the receiving bank (to the extent the debit is covered by a withdrawable credit balance).[99]

If the sender and receiving bank are members of a funds-transfer system that provides for netting mutual obligations, payment will occur

---

92. § 4A–402(e).

93. § 4A–402(a). *See also supra* ¶ 10.04[2] (Misdescription of Beneficiary); *infra* ¶ 10.09 (Unauthorized and Erroneous Orders); First Security Bank v. Pan American Bank, 215 F.3d 1147 (10th Cir.2000).

94. § 4A–402(f).

95. §§ 4A–405, 4A–406. *See also infra* ¶ 10.09 (Unauthorized and Erroneous Orders); *infra* ¶ 10.07[5]. Generally, cancellation of a payment order is effective only if agreed to by the receiving bank, verified pursuant to a security procedure, or received prior to acceptance of the order. *See* § 4A–211(a), (b); *infra* ¶ 10.07[5]. *Cf.* UCC §§ 4–213 to 4–215; *see generally*, *supra* this text ¶ 8.02 and ¶ 8.03; Thomas C. Baxter, Jr., Stephanie A. Heller, and Ana G. Rodriguez, Finality of Payment: Articles 3, 4 and 4A of the Uniform Commercial Code, 51 Consumer Fin. L.Q. Rep. 200 (1997). Section 4A–211(b) rejects the result in pre-Article 4A cases like Mellon Bank, N.A. v. Securities Settlement Co., 710 F.Supp. 991 (D.N.J.1989). *See also infra* notes 113 and 119.

96. *Cf.* UCC § 4–215(a). *See also infra* ¶ 10.07[5].

97. § 4A–403(a)(1).

98. § 4A–403(a)(2). An intermediary bank met its obligations, under the payment order that it accepted, by instructing the next intermediary bank to instruct the receiving bank to deposit $310,000 in the transferee's account and by debiting immediately the previous transferee bank's account by $310,000 and the crediting next bank's account by the same amount, though the intermediary bank froze the next bank's account for other reasons. Grain Traders, Inc. v. Citibank, N.A., 960 F.Supp. 784 (S.D.N.Y.1997), *affirmed*, 160 F.3d 97 (2d Cir.1998).

99. § 4A–403(a)(3); *cf.* UCC Article 4 §§ 4–213 to 4–215. Note, however, if the bank makes payment with actual knowledge of a discrepancy between the named beneficiary and the account holder, the bank may be liable under § 4A–207(b)(2). *See generally* First Security Bank v. Pan American Bank, 215 F.3d 1147 (10th Cir. 2000); *supra* ¶ 10.04[2]; *infra* ¶ 10.09.

when final settlement is received pursuant to the rules of that system.[100] Netting is also allowed, by means of setoff, between banks transmitting offsetting payment orders among themselves pursuant to a netting or settlement agreement.[101] Issues regarding finality of payment not otherwise covered by these rules will be decided according to otherwise applicable law.

[3] Obligation of Beneficiary's Bank to Pay Beneficiary

The beneficiary's bank may accept the payment order by paying or notifying the beneficiary.[102] If the beneficiary's bank accepts a payment order, it is obligated to pay that amount to the beneficiary.[103] This payment will be due on the payment date,[104] unless the order is accepted after the close of the funds-transfer business day, in which case payment is due on the following funds-transfer business day.[105]

If the beneficiary's bank refuses to pay after demand by the beneficiary and notice of specific circumstances that may give rise to consequential damages and their magnitude in the event of nonpayment, the beneficiary may recover consequential damages unless the bank had a reasonable cause to doubt the beneficiary's right to payment.[106]

There are four rules governing the obligation of the beneficiary's bank to give notice to the beneficiary of the payment order:[107]

1. If the payment order instructs payment to an account, the beneficiary's bank is obligated to notify the beneficiary of receipt of the order before midnight of the funds-transfer business day following the payment date.[108]

2. If the payment order does not instruct payment to an account, notice to the beneficiary is required only if the order so provides.

3. Notice may be given by first class mail or any other reasonable means.[109]

4. If the beneficiary's bank fails to provide the required notice, it must pay interest to the beneficiary from the date notice should have been given to the date the beneficiary learned of the payment order's receipt.[110]

---

100. § 4A–403(b).

101. § 4A–403(c).

102. § 4A–209(b)(1). *See also* § 4A–209(b)(2) (acceptance by passage of time). *See* discussion *infra* this part and at ¶ 10.07[4]; *infra* ¶ 10.09. Acceptance of a payment order by the beneficiary's bank generally obliges it to pay the amount of the order to the beneficiary. § 4A–404(a). It also will discharge the obligation the funds transfer was made to pay absent contrary agreement. § 4A–406. Thus, it is extremely important that this payment be final, and Article 4A makes it so. § 4A–405(c).

103. § 4A–404(a).

104. *Id. See also supra* ¶ 10.07[1].

105. § 4A–404(a).

106. *Id. See also* § 4–305(d), and *supra* notes 15, 48, and 54. *Cf.* similar rule for cashier's checks and the like at Article 3 § 3–411.

107. § 4A–404(b).

108. *Cf.* UCC §§ 4–104(a)(10), 4–301, and 4–302 (midnight deadline under UCC Article 4). *See supra* this text ¶ 8.02.

109. *Cf.* UCC § 3–503(b) (means of giving notice under UCC Article 3); UCC § 1–201(27) (notice under UCC Article 1).

110. § 4A–404(b). Reasonable attorney's fees can also be recovered if demand for interest is made and refused before legal action is taken. No other damages can be

The beneficiary's right to payment and the statutory rules governing damages cannot be modified by agreement or funds-transfer rule.[111] The beneficiary's right to receive notice (as described above) may be modified by agreement or funds-transfer rule if the beneficiary is given prior notice.[112]

[4] *Payment to the Beneficiary*

Article 4A provides rules governing the time, method, and finality of payment by the beneficiary's bank to the beneficiary.[113] If the beneficiary's bank credits the beneficiary's account, payment occurs "when and to the extent:" (1) the beneficiary is notified of the right to withdraw the funds; (2) the bank lawfully applies the funds to the beneficiary's debt; or (3) the funds are otherwise made available to the beneficiary.[114]

If payment is made by means other than credit to the beneficiary's account, "the time when payment of the bank's obligation under § 4A-404(a) occurs is governed by principles of law that determine when an obligation is satisfied."[115]

Except as provided at § 4A-405(d) and (e), these rules cannot be modified by agreement, and any contractual condition to payment or agreement to allow the bank to recover payment is unenforceable. As noted *supra*, there is an exception at § 4A-405(d), providing that conditions or provisional payment rules in a funds-transfer system agreement are enforceable under certain circumstances.[116] There is a similar rule nullifying certain payments where the funds-transfer system fails to complete settlements pursuant to its rules.[117]

[5] *Payment and Discharge*

The time and extent of payment as between the originator and the beneficiary may be important as regards discharge of the originator's underlying obligation to the beneficiary. Generally, between the originator and beneficiary payment occurs: (1) when the payment order is accepted by the beneficiary's bank; and (2) in an amount equal to the order accepted by the beneficiary's bank.[118] These rules are subject to other Article 4A provisions governing cancellation or amendment of a payment order,[119] provisional settlement pursuant to a funds-transfer

---

recovered. *Id. See also* § 4A-305(d), and *supra* notes 15, 48, and 54.

111. § 4A-404(c). This is subject to statutory qualifications at § 4A-405, discussed *supra* at ¶ 10.07[2] and *infra* at ¶ 10.07[4].

112. *Id.*

113. *See* § 4A-405; *supra* ¶ 10.04[3]. *See, e.g.*, Impulse Trading, Inc. v. Norwest Bank Minnesota, N.A., 870 F.Supp. 954 (D.Minn.1994). *Cf.* the UCC Article 4 rules governing final payment at § 4-215 and §§ 4-301 and 4-302 (midnight deadline and accountability for late returns), discussed *supra* this text at ¶ 8.02[2].

114. § 4A-405(a). *See* First Security Bank v. Pan American Bank, 215 F.3d 1147 (10th Cir.2000) (payment to beneficiary may occur upon crediting of beneficiary's account, even without notification to the beneficiary).

115. *Id.* § 4A-405(b).

116. *See supra* ¶¶ 10.04 and 10.05.

117. *See* § 4A-405(e).

118. § 4A-406(a).

119. *See* § 4A-211(e). Regarding cancellation or amendment of a payment order, *see* § 4A-211(a), (b); *infra* ¶ 10.04. Generally, a payment order that has been accepted

system agreement,[120] and failure of a funds-transfer system to complete settlement pursuant to its rules.[121]

If the payment is made to satisfy an obligation, the obligation is discharged as if the payment were made in money unless: (1) this method of payment is prohibited by contract; (2) within a reasonable time after receiving notice of the order, the beneficiary notified the originator of his or her refusal to accept payment by such means; (3) the funds were not withdrawn or applied to the credit of the beneficiary; *and* (4) the beneficiary would suffer a loss that could reasonably have been avoided by payment in accordance with the contract.[122] In the absence of discharge the originator is subrogated to the claim of the beneficiary against the beneficiary's bank.[123] The rights of the originator and beneficiary under this section can be modified only by an agreement between those parties.[124]

¶ 10.08 Miscellaneous Article 4A Issues

[1] *Variation by Agreement or Funds—Transfer Rule*

Section 4A–501 provides that unless otherwise provided the rules of Article 4A may be varied by agreement of the parties.[125] Even those rules that cannot be modified by agreement may be subject to variation by funds-transfer system rule.[126] Other provisions specifically are subject to variation by agreement or funds-transfer system rule.[127] "Funds-transfer system rule" is defined as a rule of an association of banks: (1) governing payment orders transmitted through the association's funds-transfer system; or (2) governing the rights and obligations between banks to a funds-transfer via a Federal Reserve Bank.[128] Unless otherwise provided,[129] a funds-transfer system rule will be effective even if it conflicts with Article 4A, and even if it indirectly affects a nonconsenting party.[130]

---

cannot be cancelled without agreement of the parties. See § 4A–211(b). This confirms pre-Article 4A cases like Delbrueck & Co. v. Manufacturers Hanover Trust Co., 609 F.2d 1047 (2d Cir.1979) (funds-transfers were irrevocable once made) and rejects the reasoning in *Mellon Bank*, 710 F.Supp. 991. These and other such cases are discussed *infra* ¶ 10.04. See also *Aleo*, 160 Misc.2d 950, 612 N.Y.S.2d 540, 24 UCC Rep.Serv.2d 164 (no liability in negligence or under § 4A–211 for refusal to cancel a completed payment order). *Cf. Sheerbonnet*, 905 F.Supp. 127 (Article 4A did not bar tort and equity claims). See also supra ¶ 10.04[3].

120. § 4A–405(d). *See supra* ¶ 10.07[4].
121. § 4A–405(e). *See supra* ¶ 10.07[4].
122. § 4A–406(b). *See generally* First Security Bank v. Pan American Bank, 215 F.3d 1147 (10th Cir.2000). *Cf.* the rules governing the impact on the underlying obligation and discharge of payment by negotiable instrument, in UCC Article 3 at § 3–310 and Article 3 Part 6.
123. § 4A–406(b).
124. § 4A–406(d).

¶ 10.08

125. § 4A–501(a). This is a common thread that runs throughout the UCC. *See, e.g.,* §§ 1–102(3), 4–103(a). *See generally supra* ¶ 9.03[3]. *But see* §§ 4A–202(f), 4A–305(d), and (f), 4A–404(c), and 4A–405(c). The latter is subject to § 4–405(d) and (e).
126. *See* § 4A–405(c), (d). *See also supra* ¶ 10.04[3].
127. *See, e.g.,* § 4A–404(e). *See also supra* ¶ 10.04[3].
128. § 4A–501(b).
129. *See* § 4A–404(c).
130. § 4A–501(b). The effect on nonconsenting parties is unusual though not unique. *See, e.g.,* Article 4 § 4–103(b); UCC § 1–102, Official Comment 2; UCC § 1–103; *see also supra* ¶ 9.03[7].

A funds-transfer system rule may also be binding on parties other than participating banks who use the system.[131]

[2] Effect of Creditor Process or Injunction

"Creditor process" is defined in Article 4A to include "levy, attachment, garnishment, notice of lien, sequestration, or similar process issued by or on behalf of a creditor or other claimant with respect to an account."[132] Moreover, § 4A-502 governs the rights and priorities of the respective parties if creditor process is served on a receiving bank while that bank is processing a payment order.[133]

If the receiving bank accepts the payment order, the account balance is deemed to be reduced (and hence unavailable to satisfy the creditor process) to the extent the bank did not otherwise receive payment for the order,[134] unless the creditor process was served "at a time and in a manner affording the bank a reasonable time to act" on the creditor process before accepting the payment order.[135]

If the creditor process is served on the beneficiary's bank, the bank may credit the beneficiary's account *and* set off the funds against any obligation of the beneficiary to the bank, or the funds may be applied to satisfy the creditor process.[136] Alternatively, the bank may credit the account and allow the beneficiary to withdraw the funds, unless the creditor process is served "at a time and in a manner" as will allow the bank to prevent the withdrawal.[137] If the bank has had a reasonable opportunity to act on the creditor process, the bank may not reject the payment order except for reasons unrelated to the creditor process.[138]

Creditor process regarding payment to a beneficiary can only be served on the beneficiary's bank; no other bank is obligated to respond to such process.[139]

An injunction issued for proper cause and in accordance with applicable law may prohibit: (1) issuance of a payment order; (2) execution of a payment order by an originator's bank; or (3) release of funds to the beneficiary by the beneficiary's bank.[140] A court may not otherwise restrain the issuance, payment, receipt, or other processing of a payment order.[141]

---

131. *See* §§ 4A-501(b), 4A-404(c), 4A-405(d), and 4A-507(c); *infra* ¶¶ 10.08[1] and [5].

132. *See* § 4A-502(a).

133. § 4A-502(b).

134. *Id.* This is to prevent the bank from being liable twice, for the payment order and pursuant to the creditor process.

135. *See* § 4A-502(b). This is similar to the timeliness requirements in UCC Article 4 for stop payment orders, legal process, and notices of post-dated checks. *See* Article 4 §§ 4-303, 4-401(c), and 4-403(a); *supra* this text ¶ 9.01[4], 9.01[5], and ¶ 9.02[4].

136. § 4A-502(c)(1).

137. § 4A-502(c)(2). This is also similar to the Article 4 rule. *See supra* note 135.

138. § 4A-502(c)(3).

139. § 4A-502(d).

140. § 4A-503. *Cf.* the adverse claims procedure in UCC Article 3, at § 3-602(b). *See generally* Weston Compagnie De Fin. et D'Investissement v. La Republica Del Ecuador, 1993 WL 267282 (S.D.N.Y.1993).

141. § 4A-503.

[3] The Bank–Customer Relation

The primary source of laws governing the relationship between a banking institution and its deposit customers is UCC Article 4.[142] Once the beneficiary's bank has accepted a payment order and paid the beneficiary by crediting the customer's account, many of the issues relating to that account will be governed by Article 4. Similarly, issues relating to the account of the originator at the originator's bank may be governed by Article 4.[143]

Under § 4A–504, if any receiving bank[144] has received multiple payment orders, and/or other items payable from the sender's account, the bank may charge the sender's account with the orders and/or items in any sequence the bank desires.[145] This is subject to variation by agreement of the parties.[146] In tracing credits into and withdrawals out of an account, Article 4A contemplates that the funds first credited are the ones first withdrawn or otherwise applied.[147]

If a receiving bank has received payment from a customer as sender of a payment order accepted by the bank, and the customer received notice from the bank of payment that identifies the order, the customer cannot seek to recover the payment unless notice of the customer's objection is given to the bank within one year after the customer received notice of the order from the bank.[148] This is in the nature of a statute of repose, to place a time limit on the customer's ability to object to an executed payment order.[149]

[4] Rate of Interest

If a receiving bank is required to pay interest with respect to a payment order,[150] the amount payable may be determined by agreement between the parties, by funds-transfer system rule (if applicable), or by multiplying the applicable daily Federal Funds rate by the number of days for which interest is payable.[151] If a receiving bank is required to refund the amount of an accepted payment order, due to no fault of its own, the interest payable is reduced by a percentage equal to the reserve requirement for deposits at the bank.[152]

---

142. *See generally* UCC §§ 4–401 to 4–407 (Article 4 Part 4); *supra* this text Ch. 9. Another significant applicable law is the federal Expedited Funds Availability Act, 12 U.S.C. §§ 4001–4010 (1987), and Federal Reserve Board Regulation CC, 12 CFR Part 229. *See supra* this text at ¶ 8.04.

143. Some of these have already been mentioned. *See, e.g.,* § 4A–502 and discussion *supra* at ¶ 10.07[2]. *See generally supra* this text Ch. 9.

144. *See* definitions at § 4A–103; *supra* ¶ 10.02.

145. § 4A–504(a). Again, this is consistent with UCC Article 4. *See* § 4–303(b); *supra* this text ¶ 9.02[2].

146. *See* § 4A–504, Official Comment 1; § 4A–501.

147. § 4A–504(b). This also follows the rule in Article 4. *See* § 4–210(b).

148. § 4A–505.

149. *Id.,* Official Comment. *cf.* Article 4 § 4–406, discussed *supra* this text at ¶ 9.03[4]. *See also* Article 3 § 3–118.

150. *See* §§ 4A–204(a), 4A–209(b)(3), 4A–210(b), 4A–305(a), 4A–402(d) and 4A–404(b); § 4A–506, Official Comment 1.

151. § 4A–506(b). "Federal Funds rate" is defined at § 4A–506(b).

152. § 4A–506(b).

[5] Choice of Law

[a] U.S. Transactions

The liberal choice of law rule in Article 4A is one reason that the nationwide implementation of Article 4A was not delayed by the few states that initially did not adopt it. The choice of law rule at § 4A–507(b) allows the parties to a payment order to select any jurisdiction as the source of the applicable law, regardless of whether that choice bears a reasonable relation to the transaction.[153]

This allows parties, in a jurisdiction that has not enacted Article 4A, to contract for application of the law of a state that has enacted Article 4A, and to enforce that choice in any state where constitutional limitations on jurisdiction can be met. Since all major funds-transfer systems have incorporated Article 4A into their system agreements, and the Federal Reserve System likewise has incorporated rules based on Article 4A into Regulation J,[154] Article 4A (or something like it) is applicable to most payment orders in the United States regardless of an individual state's law.[155]

The reason for this approach is the need for a single choice of law rule to govern transactions crossing jurisdictional lines. Since many payment orders cross interstate or even international borders, and may involve a number of jurisdictions, it is essential that there be a clear consensus as to the governing law. Section 4A–507(b) is designed to facilitate and codify that consensus.[156]

More importantly, § 4A–507(c) permits a funds-transfer system to select the law applicable to a payment order processed through the system, and provides that such a selection will be binding on participating banks and the originator, other sender, or a receiving bank with notice.[157] If more than one funds-transfer system is utilized and there is a conflict between the choices made by the two systems, the issue will be governed by the law of that choice that bears the most significant relationship to that issue.[158]

Absent an effective choice, Article 4A provides a hierarchy of statutory choice of law rules, generally referencing the law of the jurisdiction where the respective bank is located.[159]

[b] Choice of Law and International Transactions

Article 4A allows a funds transfer system by rule to select the law of a particular jurisdiction to govern rights and obligations between participating banks and, to the extent they had notice that the system might be

---

153. § 4A–507. *Cf.* UCC § 1–105.
154. 12 CFR Pt. 210. *See also infra* ¶ ¶ 10.11 and 10.12.
155. *See generally infra* ¶ 10.09.
156. *See* § 4A–507, Official Comment 1.
157. § 4A–507(c). However if there is a conflict between the choice of law made by the funds-transfer system and the choice of the parties pursuant to § 4A–507(b), the choice under § 4A–507(b) will prevail. *See* § 4A–507(d).
158. § 4A–507(e).
159. § 4A–507(a). *See also* revised UCC Article 9 § 9–304(b) (2000 Uniform Text) (location of bank for purposes of Article 9).

used and of its choice of law, the rights and obligations of some or all parties to a funds transfer any part of which is carried out by means of the system.[160] The jurisdiction whose law is chosen need not have a relationship to the matter in issue.[161] This reduces the need for individual choice of law agreements.[162] The Federal Reserve Board has acted for Fedwire by selecting the uniform text of Article 4A.[163] So have NACHA and CHIPS.[164]

As pointed out in Comment 2 to UCC § 4A–507, Article 4A can have extra territorial effect only to the extent courts of another jurisdiction are willing to apply it. To the extent Article 4A is chosen by agreement or funds transfer system rule which is recognized by the law, or is widely enacted, this issue diminishes. But in international transactions the issue may well persist for there is less than unanimous agreement among countries as to proper rules to govern international funds transfers.

As of 1992, the United Nations Commission on International Trade Law (UNCITRAL) Working Group on International Payments prepared a Model Law on International Credit Transfers ("Model Law"). The United States Delegation has concerns about the Model Law, particularly with what they perceive as a degree of incompatibility of the model Law with high-speed electronic systems for the transfer of bank credit. They believe that newly developed high-volume, high-speed, and low-cost electronic banking and clearing systems that are now operative cannot operate fully under the Model Law. In fact, the law could impede, rather than facilitate, international commerce. It should be noted, however, that under Article 18 the choice of law of the parties is binding even if there is no nexus between the rule chosen and the transaction or parties, and Article 4A could be selected. However, in the absence of agreement the law of the receiving bank will apply. The United States position advocating a unitary rule based on law applicable to a funds transfer system was not accepted.

To remedy the difficulty if Article 4A is not chosen to govern, the United States Delegation proposed a so-called "two-track" approach. Under this approach, one set of rules governs high-speed, high-volume electronic transfers of credit and another those that do not involve high volume and that are usually initiated with a writing of some kind. This

---

160. § 4A–507(c).

161. *Id.*

162. § 4A–507(b). The agreement will govern whether or not the payment order or the funds transfer bears a reasonable relation to the jurisdiction. Section 4A–507(a) contains choice of law rules where no agreement or funds transfer system rule exists.

163. 12 CFR § 210.25(b). This action makes Article 4A and related other UCC provisions from UCC Article 1, but not the Comments, federal law and not merely a funds transfer system rule. *Id.* § 210.25(a). Thus the federal adoption is not limited as a funds transfer system rule would be. Nonetheless, rights and obligations of parties not directly involved with a Federal Reserve Bank are governed only to the same extent they would be if Regulation J were a funds transfer system rule. *Id.* § 210.25(b)(2)(v). *See also supra* ¶ 9.03[7].

164. Nacha Rules 1.7, 2.1.4, 2.1.5 and 14.1.1, selecting New York law; CHIPS Rule 3 also selecting New York law.

"two-track" approach did not receive support in the Working Group and was abandoned.

Other decisions made by the Working Group, such as those relating to conditional payment orders, do evidence an acceptable approach.

The most significant objections to the Model Law concern four topics. They are: (1) certain duties imposed upon banks concerning notices that are burdensome partly due to the high-volume made possible by EFT (Articles 7 and 9); (2) the liability or possible liability of a bank for breach of a duty under Article 16; (3) provisions that may result in passive acceptance of orders (Articles 6 and 8); and (4) less than full recognition of the right to rely on figures in EDI applications. See Permanent Editorial Board Commentary No. 13, February 16, 1994.

It is necessary therefore to determine whether the Model Law governing international funds transfers is preferable to the less than certain application of Article 4A or law other than Article 4A, and to the extent possible avoid or adjust by agreement differences.

[6] Statute of Limitations

Article 4A provides no statute of limitations,[165] potentially raising the question of the appropriate limitations period where applicable law recognizes more than one period depending on the nature of the cause of action. In *Nigerian National Petroleum Corp. v. Citibank, N.A.*,[166] a bank customer (Vadra) fraudulently induced various parties to improperly wire transfer millions of dollars to the customer's accounts at Citibank, from which the customer transferred the funds to other accounts elsewhere controlled by him. Claiming that the incoming transfers to Citibank were "riddled with inconsistencies and other badges of fraud," the defrauded parties sought to recover from Citibank on various theories. Citibank defended on grounds the claims were barred by the New York three year statute of limitations for statutory claims.[167]

The plaintiff argued that its claims against Citibank were grounded in the common law or had common law antecedents and thus were timely under the longer New York statute of limitations at N.Y. C.P.L.R. § 213(1).[168] In rejecting this argument, the court noted that Article 4A was specifically intended to "correct the perceived inadequacy of 'attempting to define rights and obligations in funds-transfers by general principles of [common law] or by analogy to rights and obligations in negotiable instruments law or the law of check collections.' "[169] The court

---

165. *Cf.* the preclusion at § 4A–505 for failure to give notice of objection within one year, discussed *supra* this text at notes 148–149. *See also* § 3–118.

166. 1999 WL 558141 (S.D.N.Y. 1999).

167. *See id.*, citing N.Y. C.P.L.R. § 214(2). The court had already rejected the plaintiff's claims that Citibank should be estopped from asserting that the plaintiff's negligence and recklessness claims were time-barred under N.Y. C.P.L.R. § 214(4). *See Nigerian National*, 1999 WL 558141.

168. *See id.*.

169. *Id.*, quoting Banque Worms v. BankAmerica Int'l., 77 N.Y.2d 362, 369, 568 N.Y.S.2d 541, 545, 570 N.E.2d 189 (1991) and N.Y. § 4A–102, Official Comment. *See also* Cumis Ins. Soc'y, Inc. v. Munoz, 1996 WL 496982 (D.D.C. 1996) (not reported in

further quoted the Official Comment to Article 4A § 4A–102, noting that Article 4A reflects "a deliberate decision . . . to write on a clean slate and to treat a funds-transfer as a unique method of payment to be governed by unique rules. . . ."[170]

The court further noted that finality of payment was an important policy goal of Article 4A, suggesting that the three-year limitations period for statutory claims is more appropriate than the longer period for common law claims.[171] Though the plaintiff had not specifically identified the Article 4A basis of its UCC claim, neither had it identified any common law basis for that claim; the court concluded that it was an Article 4A claim and that all claims under Article 4A are subject to the three year limitation period.[172]

¶ 10.09 Unauthorized and Erroneous Orders

[1] Authorized and Unauthorized Orders

An authorized payment order properly executed by the receiving bank binds the person identified as the sender.[173] The order may be expressly or impliedly authorized, or the sender may be bound by apparent authority or similar principles,[174] such as in *Gatoil (USA) Inc. v. Forest Hill State Bank*,[175] where the sender benefited by payment of the debt by an unauthorized order.

If the order is not authorized, the receiving bank will have acted improperly in executing the order.[176] However, if an agreed upon commercially reasonable security procedure[177] to verify orders was in place, and the payment order cleared it (that is, the bank accepted the order in good faith and in compliance), and the bank complied with any instructions of the customer as to a proper account to debit ("authorized account")[178] and the like, even an unauthorized order will be effective.[179] Thus the customer will bear the loss of a properly "verified" payment order. There is one exception. Even if an unauthorized order passed an appropriate security procedure, the customer[180] will not bear the loss if the customer proves the order is not attributable to any cause related to the customer's operation.[181] In addition, the bank by agreement can shoulder some or all liability for a verified order.[182]

F. Supp.) (declining to apply UCC Article 3 by analogy to a pre-Article 4A electronic funds-transfer.). *See also supra* note 1; *supra* ¶ 10.04[3].

170. *Nigerian National*, 1999 WL 558141, quoting N.Y. U.C.C. § 4A–102, Official Comment. *See also supra* ¶ 10.04[3].

171. *Nigerian National*, 1999 WL 558141, citing *Banque Worms*, 568 N.Y.S.2d at 547.

172. *Id*. *See also* Banca Commerciale Italiana v. Northern Trust International Banking Corp., 1997 WL 217591 (S.D.N.Y. 1997) (not reported in F. Supp.) (same), *aff'd*, 160 F.3d 90 (2d Cir.1998).

¶ 10.09

173. §§ 4A–202(a), 4A–402(c).

174. § 4A–202, Comment 1.

175. 1 UCC Rep. Serv.2d (Callaghan) 171 (D.Md.1986).

176. § 4A–204(a). *See, e.g.*, Abyaneh v. Merchants Bank, North, 670 F.Supp. 1298 (M.D.Pa.1987).

177. §§ 4A–201, 4A–202(c). *See supra* ¶ 10.03[2], [3].

178. § 4A–105(a)(1).

179. § 4A–202(b). *See supra* ¶ 10.03.

180. §§ 4A–105(a)(3) and 4A–202(d).

181. § 4A–203(a)(2).

If the customer is entitled to a refund, it may lose interest owed on any refundable amounts if it does not use ordinary care after it receives notification of the acceptance of the order to detect any orders not enforceable against it and notify the bank.[183]

[2] Erroneous Orders

If the sender of an order makes an error as to a beneficiary, recipient bank, time, amount, or likewise, or sends duplicate orders, the sender basically is responsible.[184] However, if a security procedure[185] for the detection of the type of error involved was in effect, the error was as to beneficiary or was too large an amount, or involved duplicate orders, and the sender complied with the security procedure but the bank did not, such orders only bind the sender as to the intended beneficiary and amount.[186] The sender has a duty of ordinary care to discover and report an error.[187] A funds transfer or third party communications system (except Fedwire) to which an order is transmitted is the agent of the sender; thus any error made by it is attributed to the sender.[188]

If the error is in the execution of the sender's order and involves an erroneous amount or beneficiary or duplicate orders, the sender is not responsible for the error.[189] The sender nonetheless has a duty of ordinary care to discover and report an error.[190]

[3] Beneficiary Misdescription

Sometimes in fraud schemes or because of mistake, a payment order will identify the beneficiary of the order both by account number and by name, but each refers to a different person.[191] Under Article 4A, the beneficiary's bank is entitled to pay the money to the account if it does not know of the discrepancy.[192] In that case, if the originator is a bank or, unidentifiable person or account, essentially under Article 4A the order miscarries. See § 4A–207(a); supra ¶ 10.04[2].

---

182. § 4A–203(a)(1).

183. § 4A–204.

184. § 4A–205, Comment 1, and § 4A–402. See also First Security Bank v. Pan American Bank, 215 F.3d 1147 (10th Cir.2000), discussed infra at ¶ 10.09[3].

185. § 4A–201. See supra ¶ 10.03[2], [3].

186. § 4A–205(a).

187. § 4A–205(b).

188. § 4A–206.

189. § 4A–303. See Walker v. Texas Commerce Bank, N.A., 635 F.Supp. 678 (S.D.Tex.1986).

190. § 4A–304.

191. See also supra ¶ 10.04[2]; Bradford Trust Co. v. Texas Am. Bank—Houston, 790 F.2d 407 (5th Cir.1986), and Securities Fund Servs., Inc. v. American Nat'l Bank & Trust Co., 542 F.Supp. 323 (N.D.Ill.1982). If the identification refers to a non-existent or

192. § 4A–207(b)(1). In First Security Bank v. Pan American Bank, 215 F.3d 1147 (10th Cir.2000), Article 4A funds transfers were sent to First Security Bank of New Mexico as the beneficiary's bank. The originators thought they were purchasing certificates of deposit at First Security Bank, but instead the funds went into the account of the deposit broker who solicited the investments. The payment order specified the deposit broker's account number at First Security, but named the bank or the originator as beneficiary. The deposit broker apparently dissipated some of the funds in its account, and the originators sued First Security under New Mexico Article 4A § 4A–207(b)(1), alleging that First Security was liable to the originators because it had knowledge that the named beneficiary and designated account number referred to different persons.

if a non-bank originator is involved, if the person received notice that payment might be made by account number even if a name was given, the originator bears the loss unless recovery can be had from the person paid or any crook.[193] If the bank pays the person identified by name or knows of the discrepancy, no person has rights as beneficiary, except the person paid by the beneficiary's bank *if* that person was entitled to payment from the originator.[194] If no person has rights as a beneficiary, acceptance of the order cannot occur,[195] and the money back guaranty applies.[196] Thus the bank must pursue the person paid. Article 4A also contains provisions resolving situations where the beneficiary's bank or an intermediary bank are misdescribed instead of the beneficiary.[197]

[4] Cancellation

UCC Article 4A contains provisions governing cancellation (stop payment) and amendment of payment orders.[198] Basically the ability to cancel or amend ends upon acceptance, although limited exceptions exist if the receiving bank agrees or a funds transfer system rule allows.[199]

[5] Other

UCC Article 4A contains a variety of other provisions governing creditor process served on a receiving bank and set-off by the beneficiary's bank;[200] injunctions prohibiting funds transfers;[201] order of payment of orders and items;[202] preclusion against a customer contesting a payment order made by its bank;[203] and the amount of interest payable.[204] There also is a choice of law provision.

The analysis required in such a case is fact specific. In *First Security*, the district court held that First Security had knowledge of a discrepancy because the payment orders named beneficiaries different from the name on the account designated by number in the payment order; consequently the district court granted summary judgment in favor or the originators. On appeal the Tenth Circuit reversed, noting that the question of actual knowledge is for the factfinder to decide after weighing the conflicting evidence, a determination that is usurped by a summary judgment. In First Security there was conflicting evidence as to whether First Security had knowledge of the name discrepancy at the time the funds transfer was accepted and paid to the beneficiary by credit to the account number specified in the order. Thus, the summary judgment was inappropriate and was reversed. The case contains a good discussion of the issues relevant under § 4A–207(b)(1) and (2).

193. § 4A–207(c) and (d).
194. § 4A–207(b)(2).
195. *Id.*
196. § 4A–402.
197. § 4A–208.
198. § 4A–211.
199. § 4A–211(b) and (c). *See* Mellon Bank, N.A. v. Securities Settlement Corp., 710 F.Supp. 991 (D.N.J.1989); Banque Worms v. Bank America International, 726 F.Supp. 940 (S.D.N.Y.1989), *aff'd*, 928 F.2d 538 (2d Cir.1991); and Delbrueck & Co. v. Manufacturers Hanover Trust Co., 609 F.2d 1047 (2d Cir.1979).
200. § 4A–502. *See supra* ¶ 10.08[2].
201. § 4A–503. *See supra* ¶ 10.08[2].
202. § 4A–504. *See supra* ¶ 10.08[3].
203. § 4A–505.
204. § 4A–506. *See supra* ¶ 10.08[4].

¶ 10.10 Summary and Conclusions—Implementing UCC Article 4A

[1] Summary

Article 4A provides an efficient, comprehensive set of rules to govern funds-transfers that can total billions of dollars over short periods of time. Prior to Article 4A, there was no orderly body of law governing such transactions, and participants in this modern and efficient system of funds-transfers were subject to considerable legal risk and uncertainty.

Article 4A preserves the principle of party autonomy, allowing the parties to a funds-transfer to create a legal environment suitable to their needs. It also provides clear-cut choice of law rules suitable to multi-jurisdictional funds-transfers. It creates a uniform legal foundation for funds-transfers, and provides specific rules governing common issues that are unique to such transactions.[205]

Article 4A also demonstrates the viability of and continuing need for the American uniform law processes, and the importance of state law in preserving and modernizing rational commercial laws for the 21st century.

[2] Implementing Article 4A

NACHA and CHIPS as funds transfer system rules have adopted provisions that make payments made to beneficiaries not final in certain instances.[206] The NACHA rules[207] make payment provisional until receipt of payment by the beneficiary's bank. This also requires a provision in bank agreements because both the originator and the beneficiary must be given notice and the beneficiary must agree to be bound by the rule. The CHIPS rules[208] allow obligations to be netted multilaterally and provide for loss sharing among participants so as to reduce the risk from the insolvency of one participant but ultimately allow unwinding if this process is not sufficient.

¶ 10.10

205. A Model Funds-transfer Services Agreement, designed to assist parties comply with Article 4A, has been made available through the American Bar Association Section of Business Law. Copies may be ordered from the Service Center, American Bar Association, 750 N. Lake Shore Drive, Chicago, ILL 60611 (Phone (312) 988-5522). The cost for ABA members is $39.95 plus $4.95 for handling. The product code is 5070276. *See also* Paul S. Turner, Funds-Transfer Fun and Games, 4 Bus. Law Today No. 3 (Jan./Feb. 1995), at 41.

206. *See* § 4A-405(d) and (e) so allowing.

207. NACHA Rules 2.1.1, 2.1.2, 4.4.6. This lack of finality reflects a risk that will increase as ACH transactions more frequently encompass commercial funds transfers in larger amounts. The risk is that, even with a right to recover payment, if the beneficiary's bank does not receive payment it is exposed to a credit risk for "daylight" or longer "overdrafts." This concern is reflected in the CHIPS rules, which provide for as "additional settlement obligation" if a debtor institution cannot settle (*see* Rule 13(e)), and which limit exposure through bilateral limits (Rule 22) and debit caps (Rule 23). For a discussion of Federal Reserve Board initiatives in these respects, *see, e.g.*, Ballen, Cooper, Davenport, & Nyquist, Commercial Paper, Bank Deposits and Collections, and Other Payment Systems, 43 Bus. Law. 1305, 1309–1312 (1988).

208. CHIPS Rules 2, 12 and 13.

NACHA and CHIPS, as funds transfer system rules, also address certain other matters in relation to UCC Article 4A.[209]

Banks and customers also will wish to revise agreements. Among the points a bank may wish to consider is having a beneficiary either waive notice of the receipt of a funds transfer or agree to a standard for notice in an agreement with the bank.[210]

A bank in all probability will desire to have its customer agree on a proper security procedure for the verification of orders and the detection of errors,[211] and that the authenticity of payment orders will be verified pursuant to that procedure.[212] At the same time, a customer may wish to attempt to persuade the bank to assume a greater share of the risk of loss of unauthorized but verified orders,[213] and to instruct the bank restricting its discretion with respect to the acceptance of orders, such as prohibiting the bank from accepting certain types of payment orders (perhaps those that exceed the balance in specified accounts, or those involving beneficiaries other than those appearing on a list of authorized beneficiaries).[214] The bank in turn will want to contract that valid instructions must be furnished to designated persons and not less than a certain time before the effective date of the instructions.

A bank may wish to consider attempting to regulate when a refund is due[215] so as to avoid a claim, for example, for failure to pay a check written on funds that were due. It also will wish to set a standard as to what constitutes a reasonable time for notification to the bank of an improper order, and to specify in what form it will come.[216] The bank should also agree what the notification that an order was accepted or that the customer's account was debited will contain.[217]

A bank may wish to set the terms under which a payment order may be canceled or amended, including to whom the correction must be transmitted, what is necessary to identify the order, what security for loss and expenses will be necessary if the bank agrees to cancel or amend after acceptance, and so on.[218] Also, as suggested in connection with the *Mellon Bank* case,[219] a bank should agree with its customer about the standard by which to measure its effort to cancel or amend and the consequences of breach of the standard.

Given that a bank becomes liable by acceptance of a payment order, it may wish to set rules by agreement for the procedure to reject an

---

209. See NACHA Rules 2.1.3 and 4.6 on waiver of notice of receipt of an entry (§ 4A–404(b) and (c)), and Rule 12.6 disclaiming agency and allocating responsibility for order discrepancies (§ 4A–206); CHIPS Administrative Procedure No. 12 on funds transfer business day (§§ 4A–105(a)(4) and 4A–106).

210. § 4A–404(b) and (c).

211. § 4A–201.

212. § 4A–202(b).

213. § 4A–203(a)(1).

214. §§ 4A–202(b), 4A–105(a)(1).

215. For example, under § 4A–204(a). However, other provisions present the same issue, for example, § 4A–402(d).

216. §§ 4A–204, 4A–205(b), 4A–304. *See also* 12 CFR § 210.28(c) of Regulation J setting 30 days.

217. Id.

218. § 4A–211.

219. 710 F.Supp. 991, discussed *supra* at note 95.

order, such as what means is reasonable.[220]

A bank may wish to provide in its agreement notice that payment of an order may be made by the beneficiary's bank on the basis of an identifying or bank account number even if the order identifies a person different from the named beneficiary.[221]

In some cases a bank is liable to pay interest; for example, in the case of delay in accordance with § 4A–305. The amount payable may be determined by agreement.[222]

A bank should consider setting a cut-off hour to end a funds transfer business day in order to allow processing of orders, cancellations and amendments. Different cut-off times may be chosen for each of these types of communications, and for categories within each, or categories of senders.[223]

A bank may wish to contract specifically for the ability to recover amounts paid to a beneficiary if it accepts the order prior to the payment date and the order is later canceled or amended, rather than rely on the law of restitution under § 4A–209(d).

A bank may wish to set by agreement a format for a sender to specify, or not specify, instructions as to transmittal of the sender's order, such as the means by which the order is to be carried out, the standard for the bank to determine if a method is reasonable and if the bank has used due care, and the like.[224]

A customer may wish to attempt to obtain the agreement of its bank to accept consequential damages or a share of such damages for a late or improper execution of an order, or for a failure to execute an order.[225]

The bank may wish to place a choice of law clause in its agreements which, if desired, may chose the law of a jurisdiction that bears no relation to the matter at issue.[226]

Finally, as between the originator and the beneficiary, when preparing their contract the parties may wish to address whether payment may be accomplished by funds transfer and, if so, the terms under which discharge of the obligation will occur, including the applicable law.[227]

¶ 10.11 Regulation J Subpart A: Collection of Checks Through Federal Reserve Banks

Regulation J was promulgated by the Board of Governors of the Federal Reserve System to govern the collection of checks and other

---

220. § 4A–210. *Compare* 12 CFR § 210.30(a) of Regulation J.

221. § 4A–207(c)(2). Compare 12 CFR § 210.27(b) of Regulation J. *See also* § 4A–208 and 12 CFR § 210.27(a) of Regulation J.

222. § 4A–506(a). *See* 12 CFR § 210.32(b) of Regulation J.

223. § 4A–106.

224. §§ 4A–301, 4A–302. *Compare* 12 CFR § 210.30(b) and (c) of Regulation J.

225. § 4A–305(c) and (d). *But see* 12 CFR § 210.32(a) of Regulation J.

226. § 4A–507(b). *See* discussion supra at ¶ 10.08[5]. For an overall discussion of selected negotiation issues, see EBS Working Group, Negotiating Agreements for Telephonic and Electronic Funds Transfer Services, Fall 1991 Banking Law Review 10.

227. §§ 4A–406 and 4A–507(b).

items through Federal Reserve Banks.[228] Subpart A provides uniform standards to be followed by Federal Reserve Banks when handling such items, and is also binding on all parties interested in such items.[229] In addition, Subpart B governs funds-transfers through Fedwire.[230]

Subpart A applies to any "item" handled by a Federal Reserve Bank. "Item" means any negotiable or nonnegotiable instrument or other promise or order to pay money, including checks and other drafts as well as other bonds and investment securities that are handled through the Federal Reserve Bank collection system.[231]

By sending an item to a Federal Reserve Bank, either directly or through an intermediary bank, the sender authorizes the Federal Reserve Bank (or intermediary bank) to handle the item pursuant to Subpart A, and warrants its authority to give this authorization. The sender also warrants that the sender is (or is acting on behalf of the person who is) entitled to enforce the instrument and that it has not been subject to any loss or expense sustained (including litigation expense) as a result of handling the item. These warranties are consistent with the 1990 revisions to the uniform text of UCC Article 4.[232]

A Federal Reserve Bank handling such an item acts as the agent or subagent of the owner of the item. The Federal Reserve Bank has a duty of ordinary care and good faith and certain other duties as provided in Regulation CC (12 CFR Part 229). However, Regulation J supersedes the UCC, other state law, and Regulation CC to the extent of any inconsistency.[233]

The bank on which an item is drawn (the "paying bank") becomes accountable for the amount of a cash item received directly or indirectly from a Federal Reserve Bank, at the close of the paying bank's banking day on which it receives the item, if it retains the item beyond the close

---

¶ 10.11

228. 12 CFR Part 210; 45 Fed. Reg. 68634 (Oct. 16, 1980), as amended. Various aspects of Regulation J were amended at: 46 Fed. Reg. 42059 (Aug. 19, 1981); 51 Fed. Reg. 21744 (June 16, 1986); 53 Fed. Reg. 21984 (June 13, 1988); 57 Fed. Reg. 46955 (Oct. 14, 1992); 59 Fed. Reg. 22965 (May 4, 1994); and 62 Fed. Reg. 48171 (Sept. 15, 1997).

229. 12 CFR Pt. 210, Subpart A. *But see supra* ¶ 9.03[7].

230. *Id.* Subpart B. *See infra* ¶ ¶ 10.12. For a general discussion of Fedwire, and a comparison to an alternative automated clearing house (ACH) system, *see* Steven Marjanovic, Risks Seen in Using Clearing House for Big Payments, AM. BANKER, Mar. 20, 1996, at 1.

231. In order to be an "item" for purposes of Subpart A of Regulation J, it must be payable in a Federal Reserve District, sent to a Federal Reserve Bank for handling pursuant to Regulation J, and collectible in funds acceptable to the Reserve Bank. "Item" includes cash and noncash items, and returned checks as well as forward collection items, but does not include Article 4A payment orders (covered in Regulation J Subpart B). Regarding noncash items, *see also* Regulation J, 12 CFR § 210.9(c) (payment). *See* 12 CFR § 210.2(i). This bears similarities to but is not identical to the UCC Article 4 definition at § 4-104(a)(9). *See supra* this text ¶ 8.01[1] and [3][a]. *See also supra* ¶ 10.01 (scope of Article 4A).

232. 12 CFR § 210.5(a). *Cf.* 12 CFR § 210.5(a)(1), *with* UCC § 4-207(a). These warranties cannot be disclaimed. 12 CFR § 210.5(a).

233. 12 CFR § 210.3(f). Again, this is similar to UCC Article 4. *See, e.g.,* UCC Article 4 § 4-202, and *supra* this text ¶ 8.03. On the relationship between UCC Article 4 and Regulation CC, *see generally supra* this text ¶ 8.04.

of that banking day without paying the item. However, such payment may be subsequently rescinded if the item is dishonored and returned within the midnight deadline, or other deadline provided by Regulation CC,[234] or applicable Federal Reserve Bank operating circulars.[235] These deadlines may be shortened, but not extended, by clearinghouse rules. As noted, under 12 CFR § 210.3(f), Regulation J supersedes Article 4, any other state law, or Regulation CC, to the extent of any inconsistency. The paying bank also may return the item in accordance with Regulation J § 210.9(a)-(b) and applicable operating circulars.

A paying bank that receives a check not handled by a Federal Reserve Bank, and decides not to pay such check, may return the check to its Federal Reserve Bank pursuant to Regulation CC Subpart C, the UCC, and applicable operating circulars.[236] In such case, the warranties and other provisions of Regulation J are applicable.[237]

In the event a Federal Reserve Bank handles an item and does not receive payment for that item, the Federal Reserve Bank may recover by chargeback or otherwise collect the amount of such item from any bank from which the item was received,[238] whether or not the item can be returned to such bank.[239] The Federal Reserve Bank has a security interest in such bank's assets, to secure its claims, and this security interest relates back to the time the claim arose for priority purposes.[240]

The time limits imposed under Regulation J may be extended due to disasters or certain other circumstances beyond the control of the bank.[241]

A paying bank that receives presentment from a Federal Reserve Bank and owes settlement to the Federal Reserve Bank may not set-off other claims against that obligation to make settlement. However, such set off is allowed as against private-sector banks.[242]

¶ 10.12   Regulation J Subpart B: Fedwire

[1]   Scope of Subpart B

Regulation J Subpart B applies to funds-transfers through Fedwire.[243] It has the effect of federal law and is not a funds-transfer system rule as defined in UCC Article 4A, although it incorporates the provi-

---

234. 12 CFR Part 229 Subpart C. *See supra* ¶ 8.04[3].

235. *See generally supra* this text ¶ 8.02, and ¶ 8.04; Sharon A. Sweeney and Jane Anne Schmoker, Federal Reserve Bank and the Payment System: Regulation J, Regulation CC, Operating Circulars, and Other Deposit Accoutn Issues, 51 Consumer Fin. L.Q. Rep. 204 (1997).

236. *See supra* this text ¶ 8.04[3]. *See, e.g.*, 12 CFR § 210.12(d), (e).

237. Under 12 CFR § 210.9(f), the Federal Reserve Bank is not liable for a failure of any party to pay an item, except as provided in Regulation CC, 12 CFR § 229.35(b). The Federal Reserve Bank must handle returned items in accordance with Regulation CC Subpart C (and relevant operating circulars).

238. 12 CFR § 210.12(g), (h). *See generally supra* this text ¶ 8.04[3].

239. 12 CFR § 210.12(f), § 210.13.

240. 12 CFR § 210.12(i), and § 210.28; *infra* ¶ 10.12[2].

241. 12 CFR § 210.14.

242. 12 CFR § 210.9(b)(5).

¶ **10.12**

243. See 12 CFR § 210.25.

sions of Article 4A in Appendix B of the Subpart. In the event of a conflict between Subpart B and Article 4A, Subpart B will govern.[244]

Subpart B applies to all parties to a funds-transfer through Fedwire, including the Federal Reserve Banks sending or receiving the payment order, senders and receiving banks that send an order to or receive payment from a Federal Reserve Bank, beneficiaries of such payment orders, and any other party to a funds-transfer that is carried out through Fedwire.[245] Subpart B applies to such a funds-transfer even if a portion of the transfer is governed by the Electronic Fund Transfers Act, although the portion governed by the EFTA is not governed by Subpart B.[246] Similarly, if any portion of the funds-transfer is governed by Regulation CC, for example with regard to the availability of funds, then Subpart B does not apply to that extent.[247]

The potential preemption of Article 4A by Regulation J, in the case of conflict, suggests some possibility that a litigant unhappy with Article 4A might assert such a conflict in order to overcome Article 4A's effects. That is apparently what happened in *Nat'l Council of the Churches of Christ in the USA v. First Union Nat'l Bank of Virginia*,[248] where an allegedly wrongful wire transfer was sent by Fedwire and thus was subject to Regulation J. The plaintiff alleged that its state law negligence claims were not preempted by Article 4A, because Article 4A was itself preempted by Regulation J, which in turn did not apply to (and therefore did not preempt liability for) the defendant's alleged negligence occurring before the Fedwire transfer. The court properly rejected this rather creative argument, noting that Regulation J (like Article 4A) contains standards of care that preempt inconsistent state law claims.[249] Regulation J and Article 4A are intended to work consistently together, not to negate each other. All of the plaintiff's claims arose out of or were related to the Fedwire transfer, and therefore were preempted by Regulation J.

[2] Impact of Subpart B

Each Federal Reserve Bank issues operating circulars to govern the details of Fedwire transfers, including such things as cut-off hours, funds-transfer business days, security procedures, format and media requirements for payment orders, identification of payment orders, and charges for funds-transfer services. Banks must monitor such circulars for compliance with these rules.[250]

The terminology used in Subpart B generally comports with that of UCC Article 4A, with some exceptions. For example, "payment order" has the same meaning as in Article 4A, except that it does not include

---

244. 12 CFR § 210.25(b). Subpart B transactions are also subject to operating circulars. 12 CFR § 210.25(c).

245. *See* 12 CFR § 210.25(b)(2). "Fedwire" is defined at 12 CFR § 210.2(q) and § 210.2b(e).

246. *See id.* at § 210.25(b)(3).

247. 12 CFR § 210.25(b)(4).

248. 153 F.3d 721, 1998 WL 416744, *3–*4 (4th Cir. 1998) (unpublished).

249. *See id,* and *supra* this text ¶ 10.04[3].

250. 12 CFR § 210.25(a).

automated clearing house transfers or communications designated in an operating circular as not being a payment order.[251]

A Federal Reserve Bank may rely on the beneficiary or intermediary bank or beneficiary bank identifying number in the payment order, even if incorrect, and is not required to verify this number or detect any error, so long as it does not know of such error.[252] Therefore, banks must exercise care to assure that any such numbers assigned are correct.

By maintaining or using an account with a Federal Reserve Bank, a bank authorizes the Federal Reserve Bank to obtain payment for payment orders sent by the bank, by charging the bank's account. The bank does not have a right to overdraft this account, and the bank must maintain a balance of collected funds in such account sufficient to cover all obligations to the Federal Reserve Bank, of whatever nature. If such an overdraft is nonetheless created, the Federal Reserve Bank will have a security interest in all of the bank's assets, to be enforced by set-off, realization on any available collateral, or other means allowed by law. In such case the bank will also be liable for overdraft charges.[253]

By sending a payment order to a Federal Reserve Bank, a bank agrees that a reasonable time to notify the Federal Reserve Bank of the relevant facts of an unauthorized or erroneously executed payment order is 30 calendar days after the bank has received notice that the payment order was accepted or executed or that the bank's account was charged for the payment order.[254] If the bank fails to meet this deadline it will be responsible under Article 4A §§ 4A–204(a) and 4A–304, which are incorporated by reference in Regulation J at § 210.28 of Subpart B.[255]

A bank also authorizes the Federal Reserve Bank to credit the bank's account for any payment orders received from the Federal Reserve Bank.[256] Moreover, if the bank is not on-line to the Federal Reserve Bank for Fedwire transfers, it warrants to the Federal Reserve Bank that it does not act as an intermediary bank or a beneficiary's bank for other banks as regards Fedwire transfers, unless it notifies the Federal Reserve Bank in writing that it acts in such capacity.[257]

The bank may not send a payment order to a Federal Reserve Bank unless authorized by the Federal Reserve Bank.[258] The Federal Reserve Bank may reject or impose preconditions on such orders.[259]

If the Federal Reserve Bank accepts a payment order sent by the bank, the Federal Reserve Bank is authorized and directed to execute

---

251. The Subpart B definitions appear at 12 CFR § 210.26. *See generally Donmar Enterprises,* 64 F.3d 944 (*see supra* note 113) (relation between UCC Article 4A and Regulation J Subpart B).

252. 12 CFR § 210.27. *See supra* ¶ 10.04[2] regarding equivalent rule under UCC Article 4A; *see generally supra* ¶ 10.09; First Security Bank v. Pan American Bank, 215 F.3d 1147 (10th Cir.2000).

253. 12 CFR § 210.28. *See also* 12 CFR § 210.12(i); *supra* ¶ 10.11.

254. 12 CFR § 210.28(c).

255. *Id. See also supra* ¶¶ 10.03 and 10.04; 12 CFR § 210.28.

256. *See* 12 CFR § 210.29(a).

257. 12 CFR § 210.29(b).

258. *See* 12 CFR § 210.30(a); *supra* ¶¶ 10.01–10.03.

259. *See id.*

the order through another Federal Reserve Bank.[260] A bank may not send a payment order to the Federal Reserve Bank that requires the Federal Reserve Bank to send the order to an intermediary bank other than another Federal Reserve Bank, unless that intermediary bank is designated in the payment order. A bank may not send to a Federal Reserve Bank a payment order instructing use of a funds-transfer system other than Fedwire, unless the Federal Reserve Bank agrees in writing in advance.[261] A bank may not send to a Federal Reserve Bank a payment order instructing execution on a funds-transfer business day after the day of receipt by the Federal Reserve Bank, unless the Federal Reserve Bank agrees in writing.[262]

A Federal Reserve Bank will not be liable for damages to any party except as provided under UCC Article 4A, and (notwithstanding the above) will not be liable to any sender, receiving bank, beneficiary or other Federal Reserve Bank for consequential damages under Article 4A § 4A–305(d).[263]

¶ 10.13 Federal Choice of Law Provisions

As noted, Regulation J Subpart B incorporates the provisions of Article 4A of the UCC.[264] As a result, the rights and obligations between the sender of a payment order and the receiving bank are governed by the law of the jurisdiction in which the receiving bank is located.[265] The rights and obligations between the beneficiary's bank and the beneficiary are governed by the law of the jurisdiction in which the beneficiary's bank is located.[266] The issue of when payment is made pursuant to a funds-transfer by the originator to the beneficiary is governed by the law of the jurisdiction in which the beneficiary's bank is located.[267]

If the parties have made an agreement selecting the law of a particular jurisdiction to govern rights and obligations between each other, the law of that jurisdiction governs those rights and obligations, whether or not the payment order or the funds-transfer bears a reasonable relation to that jurisdiction.[268]

A funds-transfer system rule may select the law of a particular jurisdiction to govern: (i) rights and obligations between participating banks with respect to payment orders transmitted or processed through the system; or (ii) the rights and obligations of some or all parties to a funds-transfer any part of which is carried out by means of the system. A

---

260. 12 CFR § 229.30(b). *See generally supra* ¶ 10.02[1] and ¶ 10.04.

261. *See id.*

262. 12 CFR § 229.30(c).

263. 12 CFR § 229.32. *See generally supra* ¶¶ 10.02 and 10.03; *supra* note 48; and 12 CFR § 210.32(a). Nothing in Regulation J or any operating circular will be deemed a waiver of a Federal Reserve Bank's right to recover under the law of mistake and restitution. 12 CFR § 210.32(c).

¶ 10.13

264. 12 CFR § 210.25(b).

265. § 4A–507(a)(1). *See supra* ¶ 10.08[5].

266. *See* § 4A–507(a)(2); *see also supra* ¶ 10.08[5].

267. *See* § 4A–507(a)(3). *See generally* revised UCC Article 9 § 9–304 (law of "bank's jurisdiction").

268. *See* § 4A–507(b); *see also supra* ¶ 10.08[5].

choice of law made pursuant to clause (ii) is binding on the originator, other sender, or a receiving bank having notice that the funds-transfer system might be used in the funds-transfer, and of the choice of law by the system when the originator, other sender, or receiving bank issued or accepted a payment order. The beneficiary of a funds-transfer is bound by the choice of law if, when the funds-transfer is initiated, the beneficiary has notice that the funds-transfer system might be used in the funds-transfer, and of the choice of law by the system. The law of a jurisdiction selected pursuant to this subsection may govern, whether or not that law bears a reasonable relation to the matter in issue.[269]

¶ 10.14   Wire Transfer Monitoring Rules

On December 21, 1994, the Financial Crimes Enforcement Network (FinCEN) of the Department of the Treasury and the Board of Governors of the Federal Reserve System approved certain record keeping requirements for wire transfers.[270] After several postponements, the rules became effective May 28, 1996. They cover wire transfers of $3,000 or more. The rules were issued pursuant to the Annunzio–Wylie Anti–Money Laundering Act of 1992. The 31 CFR Part 103 Subpart C record—keeping requirements do not apply to the check processing system; also excluded are funds-transfers governed by the EFTA or made through an automated clearing house, teller machine, or point-of-sale

---

269. *See* § 4A–507(c); *see also supra* ¶ 10.08[5].

¶ 10.14

270. *See* Regulation S, 12 CFR Part 219, Subpart B, as published at 60 Fed. Reg. 233 (Jan. 3, 1995), and amended at 61 Fed. Reg. 58975 (Nov. 20, 1996), implementing 12 U.S.C. § 1829b(b)(2) and (3); 31 CFR Part 103, implementing 12 U.S.C. §§ 1829b and 1951–1959 and 31 U.S.C. §§ 5311–5330; 31 CFR Part 103 was first published at 37 Fed. Reg. 6912 (April 5, 1972), and has been revised some 15 times since 1987. At this writing the most recent revision is at 65 Fed. Reg. 13692 (Mar. 14, 2000). However, additional revisions are likely as part of forthcoming regulations to implement the International Money Laundering Abatement and Anti–Terrorist Financing Act of 2001, Title III of the U.S.A. Patriot Act of 2001, Pub. L. 107–56, 115 Stat. 272 (Oct. 26, 2001). *See generally*, Karen M. Neeley, Third Party Information Sharing Beyond GLB: When is it Okay to Tell All, 55 Consumer Fin. L. Q. Rep. 39 (2001). *See also* Jaret Seiberg, Fed Adopts Wire Transfer Rules to Fight Laundering, Am. Banker, Dec. 22, 1994, at 1; Matt Schulz, New, Wire Transfer Rules Hung Up With Fed and Treasury at Impasse, Am. Banker, Mar. 21, 1996, at 9.

Regulation S was implemented pursuant to the Right to Financial Privacy Act § 1115, 12 U.S.C. § 3415. *See generally* Karen M. Neeley, *id.* The Board of Governors of the Federal Reserve System initially published a rule establishing Regulation S, at 44 Fed. Reg. 55812 (Sept. 28, 1979). Subsequent revisions to Regulation S, creating Subparts A and B of Regulation S, were published at 60 Fed. Reg. 231 (Jan. 3, 1995). A rule delaying the effective date of the proposed changes from Jan. 1, 1996 to April 1, 1996 was published at 60 Fed. Reg. 44144 (Aug. 24, 1995). Proposed revisions were also published, at 60 Fed. Reg. 44146 and 44151 (Aug. 24, 1995). On March 26, 1996 the Federal Reserve System published a rule, effective April, 1996, delaying the effective date to May 28, 1996.

In addition, on December 20, 1995 the Federal Reserve System issued proposed amendments to Subpart A of Regulation S, eliminating unnecessary provisions and updating the schedule of fees and rates that banks may charge for reproduction of records. *See* 60 Fed. Reg. 65599 (Dec. 20, 1995). These changes became effective July 12, 1996. *See* 61 Fed. Reg. 29640 (June 12, 1996).

system.[271]

Beginning May 28, 1996, banks (defined broadly at 31 CFR § 103.11(c) to include savings banks, savings associations, credit unions and other similar institutions) must maintain for five years the following information on the sender of each payment order accepted by the bank. If the originator is an established customer of the bank, the originator's bank must record and retain:

1. The originator's name and address;
2. The amount of the payment order;
3. The date;
4. Payment instructions received with the payment order, including identification of the beneficiary's bank, and the beneficiary's name and address and account number and any other identifier;
5. Other payment instructions, such as the purpose of the funds-transfer and any directions to the beneficiary's bank regarding notification of the beneficiary of receipt of the payment order.
6. The original microfilm, other copy or electronic record of the payment order.[272]

If the originator is not an established customer of the bank, the bank must retain all of the above information and in addition must retain evidence of the following:

1. Verification of the originator's identity (including name and address);
2. Type of identification, and number *(e.g.,* driver's license and number, or alien passport number and country of issue); and
3. A record of the person's tax identification number *(e.g.,* social security or employer identification number) or, if none, alien identification number or number and country of passport or a notation of the lack thereof;
4. If the originator's bank has knowledge that the person placing the order is not the originator, the above information must be obtained and retained with respect to both the originator and the person placing the payment order;
5. If the order is not placed in person, the bank must also retain a copy or record of the method of payment.[273]

Effective May 28, 1996, when the bank acts as a beneficiary's bank in accepting a payment order on behalf of the beneficiary, it must retain for a period of five years the following, for each payment order accepted:

---

271. However, the Subpart B reporting requirements include 12 CFR § 103.29, requiring that records be kept of financial institution sales of cashier's checks and like instruments for $3,000 or more in currency. Subpart B also imposes federal reporting requirements for certain currency transactions. See 12 CFR §§ 103.15–103.29.

272. 31 CFR § 103.33(e)(1).

273. 31 CFR § 103.33 (e)(2).

a copy of each payment order accepted (*e.g.*, the original or a copy of the transmittal order or a microfilm or electronic record).[274]

When the bank acts as a beneficiary's bank in accepting a payment order on behalf of a beneficiary who is not an established customer, it must additionally retain for a period of five years the following, for each payment order accepted:

1. A verification of the identity of the recipient of the funds including name and address, type of identification, and number of the identification document (as above for originators);

2. A copy of the check or other payment instrument and related information such as the name and address of the recipient.[275]

In effect, if the proceeds of the payment order are delivered in person to a beneficiary other than an established customer or representative of such a customer, the bank must verify the identity of the recipient and retain essentially the same information as required by an originator's bank. If proceeds are delivered other than in person, the bank must retain a copy of the check or other instrument used to effect payment, and the name and address of the person to whom it was sent.[276]

All information noted above must be retained for five years and must be readily retrievable.[277] Information required to be verified is subject to verification requirements at 31 CFR § 103.33(e)(5), essentially requiring examination of a photo identification document such as that required to cash checks.

¶ 10.15 The U.S. Treasury "Travel Rule"

When the Board of Governors of the Federal Reserve System and FinCEN of the Treasury Department issued the initial January 3, 1995 rule creating Subparts A and B of Regulation S,[278] requiring financial institutions to collect and retain specified information concerning wire transfers, the Treasury Department also issued a rule (called the "travel rule") requiring that certain of the information collected be included in funds transmittal orders.[279]

This rule generated concerns that the requirements and definitions in the rule conflicted with provisions of UCC Article 4A in the context of international funds-transfers. In response, FinCEN and the Federal Reserve System amended the travel rule to conform the definitions in question to those in Article 4A.[280] In addition, a substantive change to 31 CFR § 103.33(g)(3) allowed institutions to defer inclusion of all required information pending their conversion to the new Fedwire message format, inasmuch as the preconversion format might not accommodate all

---

274. 31 CFR § 103.33(e)(1)(iii).
275. 31 CFR § 103.33(e)(3).
276. *Id.*
277. 31 CFR § 103.33(4).

¶ 10.15
278. 60 Fed. Reg. 231 (Jan. 3, 1995); *see supra* ¶ 10.14.
279. 60 Fed. Reg. 234 (Jan. 3, 1995).
280. 61 Fed. Reg. 14386 (April 1, 1996).

of the required information.[281] The effective date of the travel rule was also postponed until May 28, 1996.[282]

Generally, the travel rule requires that funds-transfer orders executed by the transmittor's financial institution in the amount of $3,000 or more must include:

1. The name of the transmittor and, if payment is ordered from an account, the account number;
2. The address of the transmittor (subject to the exception noted above for orders prior to conversion to the expanded Fedwire format);
3. The amount of the transmittal order;
4. The execution date;
5. The identity of the recipient's financial institution; and
6. Certain other information as received, *e.g.*, the name and/or account number of the recipient or other identifier, and the name, address or numerical identifier of the transmittor's financial institution.[283]

There are similar requirements for intermediary financial institutions.[284]

¶ 10.16 Conclusion

UCC Article 4A provides an optimal legal framework for funds transfers by electronic means. Its success and importance far exceed the limited scope of its direct application. It has been adopted, by rule, agreement, regulation or analogy for many transactions not directly within its scope and, together with other uniform laws and revisions directed in whole or in part toward electronic transactions,[285] provides a comprehensive system of law to govern the new forms of transactions that will be increasingly important in the 21st century. Together these laws also demonstrate once again the superiority of the uniform law process as a means to address and develop new issues and new areas of law.

---

281. *Id.*
282. *Id.*
283. 31 CFR § 103.33(g)(1); 60 Fed. Reg. at 238 (Jan. 3, 1995).
284. 31 CFR § 103.33(g)(2).

¶ 10.16

285. *E.g.*, the Uniform Electronic Transactions Act (UETA), Uniform Computer Information Transaction Act (UCITA), the 1998 revisions to the uniform text of UCC Article 9, and the Electronic Signatures in Global and National Commerce Act. *See generally* Jeremiah S. Buckley and Margo H.K. Tank, Electronic Signatures: Changing the Financial Landscape, 54 CONSUMER FIN. L. Q. REP. 116 (2000); Alvin C. Harrell, UCITA: Opportunity or Obstruction?, 25 OKLA. CITY UNIV. L. REV. 333 (2000).

Chapter 11

NON–UCC PAYMENT SYSTEMS

Analysis

Para.
¶11.01 Introduction 508
¶11.02 The Law of Credit and Debit Cards 516
    [1] Required Federal Disclosures and Documentation 516
    [2] Error Resolution and Wrongful Dishonor 518
        [a] Error Resolution Under Federal Law 518
        [b] Wrongful Dishonor Under Federal and State Law 520
    [3] Consumer Liability for Unauthorized Transfers Under
           Federal Law 521
    [4] Federal Rules on Distribution of Access Devices 524
    [5] State Law 524
    [6] Arbitration Clauses 525
¶11.03 Applicable Law for Selected Other Non–UCC Payment Systems 525
    [1] Smart Cards and Similar Products 525
    [2] E-checks and Similar Products 531

¶ 11.01 Introduction

There are various kinds of payment systems, other than cash, in use today. Some consider letters of credit as a kind of payment system. That view is tenable when one considers a commercial credit that may be used by a seller of goods to obtain payment other than directly from the buyer.[1] However, discussion of the law of letters of credit, even if limited to that contained in UCC Article 5, is beyond the scope of this book. Moreover, as other uses for the credit, such as in the case of a standby credit, are not payment uses, but are more in the nature of an alternative to a guaranty or a secured transaction, the focus in this book is limited to systems for payment (except for the discussion of promissory notes).

Perhaps still the most common system for making payment is the system using drafts and checks. This system is the subject of the previous nine chapters of this book and is governed primarily by the Uniform Commercial Code.

A second kind of payment system in common use, however, is the credit card system. A credit card essentially is a continuing offer by the

---

¶ 11.01

1. *See* UCC § 2–325(2).

card issuer to extend credit to or for the cardholder. This permits the card holder to accept the offer and pay a seller by use of the credit; that is, the card issuer pays the seller on behalf of the cardholder and the cardholder then repays the card issuer on the terms agreed upon between them in the credit card arrangement. For our purposes, there is no difference between a credit card and a charge card. For other purposes there may be; that is, since there is no right to defer payment in a charge card plan (at least not beyond receipt of the statement and the period thereafter allowed for payment), for a number of purposes a charge card, such as American Express, is not treated as a credit card. Of course, a cash advance also may be obtained by a card holder in some kinds of plans, but that process then involves subsequent use of the cash, a subject beyond the scope of this book.

Because the person paid in a two-party (non-bank) credit card situation usually will be the merchant, who both sells the goods or services and issues the card, it is arguable that the two-party card arrangement is not a true payment system. In any event, a three-party credit card arrangement, such as a bank credit card, clearly is a system for making payment. It is a method by which one party may pay another with credit extended by a third party. Today, most credit card transactions are not initiated or completed by the use of paper instruments as opposed to electronically, but paper usually is kept by the merchant and a copy given to the cardholder after the cardholder signs to serve as evidence. This paper may contain a promise or an order to pay, but the language on the paper usually also subjects the promise or order to the credit card agreement, and thus renders it non-negotiable under Article 3,[2] even if it might be an "item" under former Article 4.[3]

A third kind of increasingly common payment system is electronic funds transfer (EFT). This may involve several different methods of transfer. One method involves a payment made using a debit card, such as when one pays for groceries at a store, which may be thought of as a "retail electronic funds transfer." No credit is involved unless there is an overdraft agreement. This kind of transaction is an alternative to using a

---

2. §§ 3–104(a) and 3–106. These paper slips may also often resemble signed pieces of cash register tape or invoices without containing any order or promise to pay. In this instance, for that reason these slips also would not be negotiable instruments.

3. Old § 4–104(1)(g); First United Bank v. Philmont Corp., 533 So.2d 449 (Miss. 1988); Broadway National Bank v. Barton–Russell Corp. 585 N.Y.S.2d 933 (N.Y. Sup. Ct. 1992). The slips, if they are used for more than evidence, normally are truncated at the bank of deposit, and information from them is sent forward to the card issuing bank electronically. In this regard the system essentially is not different than that for truncated checks. Section 4–104(a)(9) now excludes credit card slips from the definition of "item," and thus leaves them to other governing law and system agreements and rules. Note in any credit card transaction, there will be another agreement in addition to the cardholder agreement. Where the credit card is used to purchase or lease goods, for example, it will be a sale or lease subject to UCC Article 2 or Article 2A. In a three party credit card arrangement, such as a bank credit card, there will also be an agreement between the merchant and the card issuing bank or system, often accompanied by elaborate system rules dealing with times of payment, verification of cardholders, charge backs, and a myriad of other matters. These agreements are governed by contract law without any statutory structure, such as exists as a background for the check collection system.

check, and may or may not use a sales slip. If one is used, it is the same as for a credit card, is not negotiable, and is not an "item."[4] As in the case of a credit card, there will be an agreement concerning the underlying transaction, and a merchant/cardholder or system issuer agreement with supplementing rules. NACHA (National Automated Clearing House Association) is an electronic payment system similar to check clearing house arrangements but for electronic payments, and is governed entirely by contractual provisions without statutory basis. A case involving these rules and unauthorized debits from accounts is Security First Network Bank v. C.A.P.S., Inc., 47 UCC Rep.Serv.2d 670 (N.D.Ill.2002); the court in that case held UCC Article 4 did not apply to electronic fund debit transfers as they were not "items," and further that even though the NACHA rules themselves expressly applied the UCC rules to debit entries, that only applied as a "gap filler" and not when a NACHA rule covered the issue, particularly given certain NACHA rules different from UCC rules on check fraud. EFT also encompasses institutional wire transfers like the Clearing House Interbank Payments System (CHIPS), involving billions of dollars. This type of electronic funds transfer, which may be called a "wholesale funds transfer," is the subject of UCC Article 4A discussed in Chapter 10.

Electronic fund transfers largely eliminate paper documentation.[5] Thus even though paper may be generated when a transaction is initiated,[6] or a paper embodiment of the message such as a debit card

---

4. Section 4–104(a)(9) excludes debit card slips from the definition of "item" and thus from Article 4 coverage. *See also* Sinclair Oil Corp. v. Sylvan State Bank, 254 Kan. 836, 869 P.2d 675 (Kan. 1994) (Article 4 does not apply to ACH debit transactions). Since the federal Electronic Fund Transfers Act, 15 U.S.C. § 1693 *et seq.*, covers these transactions (*see* Regulation E, 12 CFR pt. 205, Official Staff Commentary Q2–21.5), this exclusion avoids potential conflict and preemption, which is possible with respect to Article 4 if a paper debit card slip is considered to be an "item." *Also see, infra,* for electronic checks.

5. The paper in the check system, although it still may be involved in the inception of the transaction, increasingly is being "truncated" at an early point and the relevant information is sent forth electronically. *See* the discussion in Chapter 9, *supra.* Thus, truncated checks are practically indistinguishable from an off-line debit system. The remaining differences are likely to continue to be reduced. Nonetheless, as pointed out, *supra,* and *infra,* the federal EFT act does not completely exclude consumer transfers that involve paper. Also Article 4A does not require electronic transmission at all; a payment order may be transmitted orally, electronically, or in writing. § 4A–103(a)(1). In fact, in proper circumstances a payment order may be transmitted by first class mail. § 4A–302(c). However, Regulation E, 12 CFR § 205.2(g), defining "electronic fund transfer," still excludes a transaction originated by check, draft or similar paper instrument, and payments covered by Article 4A are commonly referred to as wire transfers, and usually involve some kind of electronic transmission. § 4A–104, Official Comment 6.

6. *See, e.g.,* Regulation E, 12 CFR § 205.9(a), requiring receipts. On March 28, 2001, the Federal Reserve Board adopted amendments to Regulation E, and Regulation Z as governing aspects of credit cards, to permit the electronic delivery of disclosures and other documents that previously had to be in written form when delivered to the customer, consistent with the federal Electronic Signatures in Global and National Commerce Act, 15 U.S.C. § 7001 *et seq.* (E-sign). *See* 66 Fed. Reg. 17329 (Mar.30, 2001). Regulation E is the regulation under the federal Electronic Fund Transfer Act, 15 U.S.C. § 1693 *et seq.* The federal act specifically excludes transfers generated by paper. Regulation E §§ 205.2(g); 205.3. The March, 2001 rules provided a mandatory compliance date of October 1, 2001, but this was subsequently "lifted." 66 Fed.Reg. 41439 (Aug.8, 2001)

slip or a telex may be involved, the essential nature of the transaction is not paper based. Consequently, whether the transfer is accomplished by the use of a debit card to access an account through a debit card slip or an on-line point-of-sale terminal or an automated teller machine, by a wire transfer, by direct deposit through magnetic tapes, or otherwise, the system serves as another mechanism to provide payment or funds transfer from one party to another.

Both the credit card and the electronic funds transfer systems in the consumer context are subject to extensive federal legislation[7] and regulation.[8] These impose certain disclosures and other requirements designed to protect consumers. In addition, there may be a variety of state statutes and regulations governing the operation of credit card and EFT systems.[9] This matrix of perhaps overlapping, sometimes absent, and sometimes inconsistent legal rules not only raises some difficult questions as to the proper legal rule to apply, but it also invites comparisons among the different approaches to the same problem taken by the separate systems. A purpose of this chapter is to discuss some of these matters in a general way to provide a background for further research.[10]

---

7. *See* 15 U.S.C. §§ 1642–1645 and §§ 1666–1666i in the case of credit cards. *See supra* note 6 as to electronic fund transfers. Some of the credit card rules also have a limited application to business credit cards (*see* 15 U.S.C. § 1645) and to credit cards issued by other generally exempted creditors such as telephone companies. Regulation Z, 12 CFR § 226.3 n. 4.

8. Regulation Z, 12 CFR §§ 226.12 and 226.13 as to credit cards, and Regulation E, 12 CFR pt. 205 as to EFT. Regulation Z, 12 CFR pt. 226, is the regulation under the federal Truth in Lending Act, 15 U.S.C. § 1601 *et seq.* The Truth in Lending disclosure rules for open-end credit in both the statute (essentially 15 U.S.C. § 1637; § 1637a adds additional disclosure for home equity lines which can involve a credit card, but the basic rules are in § 1637), and Regulation Z (12 CFR §§ 226.6, 226.7, 226.8, and 226.9; again §§ 226.5a and 226.5b contain special disclosure rules for credit card applications and solicitations and home equity lines that will not be discussed), also apply to credit card plans. Regulation E has its own disclosure rules. Regulation E, 12 CFR §§ 205.4, 205.7, 205.9.

For this reason, Article 4A is inapplicable to a funds transfer any part of which is governed by the federal law. UCC § 4A–108. A case that discusses this complex interrelationship is American Airlines Employees Federal Credit Union v. Martin, 29 S.W.3d 86, S.W.3d 86, 42 UCC Rep. Serv.2d 359 (Tex.2002).

9. *See, e.g.*, Kan. Stat. Ann. § 16a–3–403 (on claims and defenses assertable against a credit card issuer) and chapter 167B, General Laws of Massachusetts (on EFT). As the statutory law in most states is little developed, or is fragmentary, or is of general applicability, and as there is no uniform law among the states, state law will not be discussed except for isolated references. Nonetheless, state law is important. For example, the matter of wrongful dishonor may involve the general contract law of offer and acceptance and is discussed, *infra*, this chapter. State law may characterize the nature of the transaction and regulate the rate of finance charge and types of fees that a credit card issuer may impose. *See, e.g.*, 14A Okla. Stat. §§ 1–301(9) and (16), 2–104, 2–202, 2–202.2, 2–203(4), 2–207, 3–104, 3–106, 3–202, 3–202.2, 3–203(5), 3–508A. Federal law also may be important in this regard (*see, e.g.*, Marquette Nat'l Bank v. First of Omaha Service Corp., 439 U.S. 299, 99 S.Ct. 540, 58 L.Ed.2d 534 (1978)), but this subject is beyond the scope of this book. *See, e.g.*, B. Clark, The Law of Bank Deposits, Collections and Credit Cards (3d ed. 1990). As the first part of this note indicates, state as well as federal law may regulate the terms of credit card agreements. In relation to EFT, state law may play an important role in defining what sorts of services may be offered at what locations and through what sorts of businesses. Again, this is a matter beyond the scope of this book. *See, e.g.*, B. Clark, The Law of Bank Deposits, Collections and Credit Cards (3d ed. 1990).

10. More detail is not feasible for several reasons. One reason is that to do so would at least double the size of this book.

Beyond the systems described so far, there is continual development, but the use, to date, of other systems is quite limited compared to the systems previously discussed. One generic system in some use employs so-called electronic checks. An electronic check is a paperless, digitally signed negotiable instrument. The term is defined by reference to a negotiable instrument,[11] but reflects that the electronic check is paperless and digitally signed and therefore is not covered by UCC Article 3.[12] The digital signature is an electronically generated numeric code, created using a private key held by the drawer or the drawer's agent and certain cryptographic techniques. The digital signature can be verified using a corresponding public key.

In one scenario, the drawer of an electronic check transfers that electronic check to the payee, the payee (or, less commonly, another third party nonbank transferee) transfers the check to the depositary bank, and the depositary bank, pursuant to rules (the Operating Rules, and Commentary, of the Electronic Check Clearing House Organization—"ECCHO," or through existing banking channels, such as Electronic Check Presentment or ACH networks) transfers the check to the paying bank. Alternatively, the depositary bank may transfer the electronic check to another collecting bank, which would in turn pursuant to the rules transfer that electronic check to the paying bank. The members of ECCHO may decide whether to utilize this scenario for the collection of electronic checks, or may determine to utilize a different scenario that would require ECCHO to develop additional rules.[13]

The presenting bank for an electronic check, if the depositary bank in this scenario will obtain the agreement of its customer that the electronic check is deemed a "negotiable instrument" for purposes of the UCC (and a "check" for purposes of Regulation CC). When the depositary bank accepts an electronic check for deposit from the customer, the depositary bank is thus deemed to be a holder of the check and makes described warranties.[14] In the event the presenting bank is not the depositary bank, the presenting bank warrants that each prior collecting

---

There are other works that already provide needed detail cited in this book. Second, the federal law only deals with certain aspects of the account institution-cardholder relationship. The balance of the picture, if not regulated by spotty state legislation, is left to private agreement and case law, and this does not lend itself to generalized treatment.

11. § 3–104.

12. §§ 3–104(a) and 3–103(a)(6).

13. Other variations exist. For example, Visa ePay electronically links businesses/billers to their customers and, in turn, billers and customers are linked to their financial institutions. Thus a biller sends an invoice directly to the customer, the customer instructs the customer's bank to pay electronically using the biller's Visa ePay biller I.D., and the customer's bank electronically deposits the payment into the biller's account at the biller's bank. The system does not address the applicable law; presumably it relies on agreements and general contract law. Another variation somewhat similar to Visa ePay is the Pay-Now service, which works through the ACH network. Another ACH linked service, but which automatically debits accounts periodically to pay bills, is the Consumer Electronic Payment System from Ameritech.

14. *But see* Sinclair Oil Corp. v. Sylvan State Bank, 254 Kan. 836, 869 P.2d 675 (Kan. 1994) (court noted but did not consider the effect, if any, of the provision in the NACHA rules stating that an ACH debit entry is considered to be an "item" for purposes of UCC Article 4). *See also* the *Security First Network Bank v. C.A.P.S., Inc.* case discussed *supra*.

bank handling the electronic check and the customer of the depositary bank have agreed that the electronic check is a "negotiable instrument" for purposes of the UCC and a "check" for the purposes of Regulation CC. Accordingly, a presenting bank that is not the depositary bank should have an agreement with each collecting bank from which the presenting bank accepts for collection electronic checks. This agreement should appropriately allocate the liability resulting from the warranties/indemnifications and other responsibilities. A paying bank should obtain the agreement of the drawer of the electronic check that the electronic check is deemed a "negotiable instrument" for purposes of the Code, and a "check" for purposes of Regulation CC.

The paying bank must provide the drawer of an electronic check the rights mandated for the drawer in the federal Electronic Fund Transfer Act and Regulation E. The Electronic Fund Transfer Act[15] and Regulation E[16] apply to electronic fund transfers, which are defined as any transfer of funds, other than a transaction originated by check, draft, or similar paper instrument, that is initiated through an electronic terminal, telephone, or computer or magnetic tape for the purpose of ordering, instructing, or authorizing a financial institution to debit or credit an account of a consumer established primarily for personal, family or household purposes.[17] A consumer drawer initiates an electronic check at a computer terminal and that electronic check results in a debit to the consumer drawer's account at the paying bank. Accordingly, it is assumed that an electronic check is an electronic fund transfer subject to Regulation E and, as a result, a consumer drawer of an electronic check must be provided the rights mandated for the consumer drawer under both check law (by agreement, the UCC and Regulation CC) and Regulation E.[18]

Regulation E imposes requirements on the paying bank with respect to, among other things, the following: initial disclosures;[19] error resolution and change in terms notices;[20] periodic statements;[21] limitations on the consumer drawer's liability in the event of an unauthorized electronic fund transfer;[22] and error resolution procedures.[23]

Another generic system that in some forms is in use employs so called "smart cards." The simplest model is that of a single issuer supplying cards for a single use. For example, a card can be purchased that entitles the purchaser to a monetary amount of transportation services or telephone services. Because of the limited range of uses and the fact that the issuer is also the payee, these stored value products involve what are called "closed systems." In contrast, in an "open

---

15. 15 U.S.C. § 1693 *et seq.* The provisions of this act and its implementing regulation are discussed in greater detail, *infra*.

16. 12 CFR Part 205.

17. 12 CFR § 205.2(g).

18. *See* Clarks' Bank Deposits and Payments Monthly, Vol.9, No.10, March 2001, pages 3–5; 66 Fed.Reg.15187 (March 16, 2001).

19. 12 CFR § 205.7.

20. 12 CFR § 205.8.

21. 12 CFR § 205.9.

22. 12 CFR § 205.6.

23. 12 CFR § 205.11

system," a card (or other storage device such as a computer network) can be used for a variety of transactions with different payees.

With a single issuer model, one firm develops and issues the "value" used on the card or other storage device, but may employ other firms to sell the "value" to users. These firms may also accept the "value" accumulated by users and return the excess "value" to the issuing firm. With a multiple issuer model, the issuers adopt a common technology for cards or other access devices, establish a distribution network, and arrange for a mechanism for settlement. Most stored value cards are intended to be used for point-of-sale transactions. On the other hand, "value" stored on a computer network enables a buyer to be at a location remote from the seller and place of sale. Both the cards and computers are different types of storage devices; the computer variation essentially operates like the smart card variation. It differs from the electronic check previously discussed in that the electronic check draws from an asset account while the distinguishing feature of the smart card type of product is that it involves an extension of credit by the users of the product to the issuer of the product from the time a user "pays" for the "value" until the time the purchased "value" is used. For this reason, these new payment products are really obligations of the issuer to pay a monetary amount at a future time.

An example of a smart card system is Mondex. Mondex is one type of smart card product. It is intended primarily for purchases under $20 or "micro-payments" on the Internet. With Mondex, consumers store electronic value on smart cards. They can load their cards with electronic value from public locations such as "cashless" ATMs. Mondex cards can be locked by the cardholder and unlocked by using a personal code. Once locked, the value on the card cannot be spent without re-keying this personal code. Mondex is an off-line system. Shoppers do not need to sign anything when using the card, and there are no authorization calls. To make a purchase, the consumer goes to a merchant that accepts Mondex. The card is inserted in a POS terminal. Electronic value on the card is debited from the consumer's card and added to merchant's electronic storage device. The system depends on agreement under general contract law. For example, the Chase Standalone Smart Card Agreement provides that Chase has no liability to the customer "for smart card usage, for any theft, loss, misuse, malfunction of or damage to the smart card, or for any loss of funds or stored value on the smart card." All warranties are disclaimed; the smart card is provided "as is." In addition, Chase is not responsible "for any other loss, damage or injury, whether caused by the card, the card reader, any automated teller machine or other equipment, nor is Chase responsible for any direct, indirect, special or consequential damages arising in any way out of the use of the card, card reader, any automated teller machine or equipment, except where the law requires a different standard."

Another type of smart card product is Visa Cash. There are two types of Visa Cash cards: disposable and reloadable. Disposable cards are loaded with a pre-determined value, typically in local currency, such as

$10. These cards may be purchased from Card Dispensing Machines which accept various payment methods. Reloadable cards come without a predefined value. Electronic value can be reloaded onto reloadable cards at specialized terminals and ATMs. In order to make a purchase, a consumer selects a merchant that accepts Visa Cash. The card is inserted in a POS terminal. Electronic value on the card is debited from the card and added to the merchant's electronic storage device.

There are a number of other types of products in this category. Another is Visa Travel Money, where the pre-paid value is stored on the system and not on the card. Cyber Coin is a Cyber Cash product that does not involve a card either; rather customers download Cyber Cash's free Wallet software from the Internet to their computer and then transfer funds either from a checking account at one of the participating banks to the Wallet or by charging a credit card. Customers then may use the Wallet to make small payments to participating merchants for services offered over the Internet. The system is based on agreements under general contract law and a disclosure statement in compliance with Regulation E is included in the service agreement that accompanies the software.

This chapter will discuss some of the legal issues raised by these types of products, but again essentially as a beginning place for further research. In many instances, the applicable law is unclear and the proper resolution of issues is even less clear. Moreover, the multiplicity of existing products and the constant evolution of new products complicates matters further, as well as making it unwise to construct a legal regime too early, as that could arrest innovation and development. Two excellent sources of further information are: (1) Task Force on Stored Value Cards, American Bar Association, *A Commercial Lawyer's Take on the Electronic Purse: An Analysis of Commercial Law Issues Associated with Stored–Value Cards and Electronic Money*, 52 Bus. Law 653 (1997), and (2) T. Vartanian, R. Ledig and L. Bruneau, *21st Century Money, Banking & Commerce* (Fried, Frank, Harris, Shriver & Jacobson 1998).

¶ 11.02 The Law of Credit and Debit Cards

With certain exceptions,[24] the federal Electronic Fund Transfer Act governs the electronic transfer of funds to or from any consumer account.[25] Various other provisions of the federal Consumer Credit

---

¶ 11.02

24. The exceptions include nondirect debit and credit check guarantee or authorization services; wire transfers over the networks that are used primarily for business transactions (Fedwire and CHIPS); certain securities and commodity transfers; certain transfers between the institution and the customer (such as crediting interest); and between different accounts of the same customer (such as for a loan payment); telephone transfers not made pursuant to a prearranged plan (*see* Abyaneh v. Merchants Bank, North, 670 F.Supp. 1298 (M.D.Pa.1987)); trust accounts; and preauthorized transfers to small institutions, defined as those having assets of $25 million or less on the preceding December 31. Regulation E, 12 CFR § 205.3.

25. Regulation E, 12 CFR § 205.2(g) defines an "electronic fund transfer" as including transfers originated through an electronic terminal, telephone, computer, or magnetic tape, and excluding transfers originated by check, draft, or similar paper instrument. A consumer "account" is a

Protection Act govern aspects of both consumer and business credit card transactions.[26] In both instances, certain consumer disclosures and documentation are required, limits are placed upon consumer liability for unauthorized use, and error resolution procedures and a prohibition against the unsolicited distribution of access devices are provided, among other protections.[27]

[1] *Required Federal Disclosures and Documentation*

A creditor must furnish certain disclosures to a consumer before the first transaction is made under a credit card plan.[28] These disclosures are designed to permit a consumer to make an informed use of credit and to ascertain the essential terms of the credit plan for which the consumer is contracting. The disclosures cover:

* the circumstances under which a finance charge will be imposed and an explanation of how it will be determined;

* the amount of any other charges for the plan or an explanation of how they will be determined;

* any security interest taken; and

* the billing error rights of the consumer.[29]

A creditor also must make disclosures on or with periodic statements furnished on the account.[30] These disclosures cover, among other

---

checking, savings or other asset account held directly or indirectly by a financial institution and established primarily for personal, family, or household purposes. Regulation E, 12 CFR § 205.2(b). A more extensive treatment of the laws governing electronic fund transfers appears in D. Baker & R. Brandel, The Law of Electronic Fund Transfer Systems (2d ed. 1988).

26. *See, supra,* notes 7 and 8. A more extensive treatment of the laws governing credit cards appears in B. Clark, The Law of Bank Deposits, Collections and Credit Cards (3d ed. 1990); and R. Rohner and F. Miller, Truth in Lending (Am. Bar Ass'n 2000).

27. *See* discussion, *infra,* this chapter. In addition, the federal Electronic Fund Transfer Act specifies financial institution liability for wrongful dishonor (*see infra*), and contains restrictions on compelling the use of electronic fund transfers (15 U.S.C. § 1693k). For a discussion, *see* D. Baker and R. Brandel, The Law of Electronic Fund Transfer Systems, *supra* note 25. Other federal protections that may relate to credit card plans include a requirement to promptly credit payments made (Regulation Z, 12 CFR § 226.12(c)); a provision precluding set off (Regulation Z, 12 CFR § 226.12(e)); a provision that allows merchants to offer discounts for cash and that prohibits tie-in arrangements between card issuers and merchants (Regulation Z, 12 CFR § 226.12(a)); and a right of rescission in connection with a credit plan secured by a lien on a consumer's principal dwelling (Regulation Z, 12 CFR § 226.15). For discussion, *see* R. Rohner and F. Miller, Truth in Lending, *supra* note 26.

28. Regulation Z, 12 CFR § 226.5(b)(1). The Commentary to this provision contains a useful discussion. *See* Commentary ¶ 226.5(b)(1)–1. Certain advance disclosures also are required in credit and charge card applications and solicitations; these include the annual percentage rate, certain fees, any minimum or fixed finance charge, transaction charges, whether or not there is a grace period, and the balance computation method. Regulation Z, 12 CFR § 226.5a(b). If a home equity credit line is involved, yet more detailed advance disclosures must be made. Regulation Z, 12 CFR § 226.5b(d).

29. Regulation Z, 12 CFR § 226.6. In a home equity plan, certain additional disclosures must be made. Regulation Z, 12 CFR § 226.6(e). In order to limit liability for unauthorized use, the creditor also must provide adequate notice of the consumer's potential liability. Regulation Z, 12 CFR § 226.12(b)(2).

30. Regulation Z, 12 CFR § 226.5(b)(2).

matters, account activity during the billing cycle, particularly the identification of transactions on the account and credits to it, and the amount and the periodic and annual rates of the finance charge.[31] Moreover, a creditor who changes a term required to be disclosed when the account is opened generally must give advance written notice of the change in that term to the consumer.[32] Other subsequent disclosures also may be required.[33]

A similar pattern exists for electronic fund transfers. Regulation E requires that a consumer be given certain disclosures at the time she or he contracts for EFT service or before the first transaction.[34] Notice of most changes in the terms of the contract subject to this initial disclosure also must be given to the consumer at least twenty-one days before to the effective date of the change.[35]

Regulation E additionally requires that a periodic statement be sent at certain intervals, usually monthly, to provide account holders a summary of their account activity.[36] These statements must disclose various information, including the amount, date, type, source, and payee of electronic fund transfers to or from the account during the period covered by the statement, the customer's account number, any fees or charges imposed, the beginning and ending account balances, and the address and telephone number to use for error resolution.[37] Passbook and other accounts with only limited electronic funds access are subject to more lenient requirements.[38]

There also is a requirement that a consumer receive a receipt each time an electronic fund transfer transaction at an electronic terminal occurs, detailing the amount of the transfer and any charge, the date, the type of transfer and the account involved, the customer's identification or account number, the location of the terminal, and the name of any third party to whom the transfer is made.[39]

---

31. *Id.* §§ 226.7 and 226.8.

32. *Id.* § 226.9(c).

33. These include statements of billing rights (Regulation Z, 12 CFR § 226.9(a)); disclosures for supplemental devices and additional features (Regulation Z, 12 CFR § 226.9(b)); disclosures upon renewal of the credit card (Regulation Z, 12 CFR § 226.9(e)); and disclosures about changes in credit card account insurance providers (Regulation Z, 12 CFR § 226.9(f)).

34. Regulation E, 12 CFR § 205.7(a). These include a disclosure as to potential liability for unauthorized transfers, of the types of transfers the consumer may make, any applicable limitations on them, of charges to make transfers, of error resolution rights, and of certain rights to documentation of transfers and to stop payment and of the privacy of account information. *See also* Regulation E, 12 CFR §§ 205.14–205.16.

35. *Id.* § 205.8(a). A notice concerning error-resolution procedures also must be given at least annually. Regulation E, 12 CFR § 205.8(b). Alternatively, notice can be included with each of the periodic statements required by Regulation E, 12 CFR § 205.9(b). A similar pattern exists for credit cards. Regulation Z, 12 CFR § 226.9(a).

36. *Id.*, § 205.9(b). Certain exceptions exist in Regulation E, 12 CFR § 205.9(c)(2) (for certain intra-institutional transfers) and (d) (for foreign initiated transfers; this exception also may apply to the receipt requirement noted, *infra*, at note 39).

37. *Id.*

38. *Id.* §§ 205.9(c)(1). Notice of account activity for preauthorized transfers (Regulation E, 12 CFR § 205.2(k)) is regulated in Regulation E, § 205.10. *See also* Regulation E, 12 CFR § 205.9(c) and (d).

39. *Id.* §§ 205.9(a).

[2] Error Resolution and Wrongful Dishonor

[a] Error Resolution Under Federal Law

Both the credit card and the electronic fund transfer systems have elaborate procedures to allow consumers to raise perceived account errors and to force account institutions to resolve asserted errors in the operation of the systems.

A billing error for the purpose of the credit card system is defined as:

* an entry on or with a periodic statement of a transaction not made to the consumer or the consumer's agent;

* an entry on or with a periodic statement of a transaction not properly identified;

* an entry on or with a periodic statement of a transaction where the property or services were not accepted by the consumer or were not delivered as agreed;

* a failure to properly credit the account;

* a computational or similar error;

* an entry on or with a periodic statement for which the consumer requests additional information; or

* a failure to properly deliver a periodic statement.[40]

To assert one of these errors, the consumer must give an appropriate notice within sixty days after the error first appears on a periodic statement.[41] The creditor then must acknowledge the notice and must investigate and resolve the matter, generally within two billing cycles.[42] During this period, the consumer may withhold payment of any disputed amount; the creditor may not try to collect it, and the creditor may not give an adverse credit report because of the dispute.[43]

To resolve the dispute, if the consumer proves to be correct the creditor must correct the error and send notice.[44] If the creditor proves to be correct (or a different error than that asserted is found), the creditor must furnish an explanation, copies of documentary evidence if requested, and, if a different error occurred, correct it.[45] The creditor may then re-establish any debt by giving notice of payment due.[46] If the dispute still continues, the creditor need not go through the process again.[47]

"Error" in the electronic fund transfer context is defined as any unauthorized or incorrect electronic fund transfer, any omission of a transfer from a periodic statement, any computational or bookkeeping error or incorrect amount of money received from an electronic terminal, any transfer not properly identified or documented, or any customer

---

40. Regulation Z, 12 CFR § 226.13(a).
41. *Id.*, § 226.13(b).
42. *Id.*, § 226.13(c).
43. *Id.*, § 226.13(d).
44. *Id.*, § 226.13(e).
45. *Id.*, § 226.13(f).
46. *Id.*, § 226.13(g).
47. *Id.*, § 226.13(h).

request for documentation.[48] The latter, however, does not include a routine inquiry about account balances or a request of data for tax or other record-keeping purposes.[49]

Notice of an error can be given in either oral or written form. The notice must be from the consumer and must be received within sixty days after the institution transmitted the periodic statement that first raised the error or any additional information or clarification. The institution must be able, from the notice, to identify the consumer's name and account number, the type, date, and amount of the error, and the reasons for the consumer's belief that there has been an error.[50]

Following receipt of the error notice, the financial institution must promptly investigate the alleged error and transmit the results of this investigation within thirteen business days.[51] Alternatively, the institution can, within ten business days, recredit the consumer's account in the amount of the alleged error (subject to a $50 exclusion, discussed *infra*), notify the consumer of the recredit within two business days, and then take up to forty-five calendar days to investigate and notify the consumer of the results.[52] During its longer investigation the institution generally must give the consumer full use of the disputed funds and, if it ultimately determines that no error was made, the revocation of the credit can occur only after compliance with a further notice procedure.[53]

The duty to investigate an alleged electronic fund transfer error generally is satisfied by a review of the institution's records if the alleged error concerns a transfer to or from a third party and there is no agreement between the financial institution and the third party regarding the type of electronic fund transfer alleged in the error.[54] If the institution determines that an error did occur, the institution must promptly (within one business day) correct the error, credit any interest due, refund any improper fees or charges, and must give the consumer notice of the correction.[55]

On the other hand, if an institution finds upon investigation that the customer's notice of error is incorrect or inaccurate, the institution must provide the consumer a written explanation after concluding its investigation, including notice of the consumer's right to request further documentation.[56] If the institution has provisionally recredited the account, the institution must notify the consumer of the date and amount of credit revocation and of the fact that the institution must honor checks, drafts, and preauthorized charges against the account for five days after the revocation notice has been transmitted.[57] If the error dispute is not resolved and the consumer subsequently reasserts the

---

48. Regulation E, 12 CFR § 205.11(a).
49. *Id.*, § 205.11(a)(2).
50. *Id.*, § 205.11(b). A written confirmation of oral notice can be required.
51. *Id.* § 205.11(c)(1).
52. *Id.* § 205.11(c)(2). These periods can be extended in certain limited circumstances. *Id.* § 205.11(c)(3).
53. *Id.*, §§ 205.11(c)(2) and (d).
54. *Id.*, § 205.11(c)(4).
55. *Id.*, § 205.11(c)(1) and (2).
56. *Id.*, § 205.11(c) and (d)(1).
57. *Id.*, § 205.11(d)(2).

same error, no further error resolution responsibility is imposed on the institution.[58]

An electronic fund transfer can involve an extension of credit; for example, when the account has an overdraft protection feature. In those cases even though an extension of credit may be involved, the financial institution essentially must comply with Regulation E.[59]

[b] Wrongful Dishonor Under Federal and State Law

What if a financial institution wrongfully refuses or fails to make a credit card or an electronic fund transfer? With the former, liability, if any, would appear to stem only from breach of the cardholder agreement.[60] The case law presumably would deny that the card issuer's failure to complete the transaction gives rise to a wrongful dishonor, as the usual analysis is the credit arrangement is a continuing offer that can be withdrawn at any time.[61] Whether this is a safe harbor can be questioned,[62] but for the most part there seem to be few mistakes that produce litigation since must denials will occur before the transaction without real damage.

The applicability of the UCC also is excluded even in the case of a paper debit card slip,[63] as well as in the case of an on-line transfer.[64] The federal Electronic Fund Transfer Act, however, specifically makes a financial institution liable for wrongful dishonor.[65] A wrongful dishonor

---

58. An assertion of an error based on information received through an earlier error assertion for documentation is excluded from this rule. *Id.*, § 205.11(e).

59. Regulation E, 12 CFR § 205.12(a)(1). However, the unsolicited issuance rules of Regulation Z apply to the addition of a credit feature to an accepted access device or to a credit card that is also an access device. Regulation E, § 205.12(a)(2).

60. Isolated provisions in the federal law may serve to reduce the chance of wrongful dishonor, such as the requirement in Regulation Z, 12 CFR § 226.10 for prompt crediting of payments, and in Regulation Z, 12 CFR § 226.12(e) for prompt credit for refunds, but no provision regulates or imposes liability for wrongful dishonor as such. Note UCC § 4–104(a)(9) excludes credit card slips from the definition of "item," and thus from § 4–402.

61. Jordan v. J. C. Penney Co., 114 Ga. App. 822, 152 S.E.2d 786 (Ga.Ct.App.1966); City Stores Co. v. Henderson, 116 Ga.App. 114, 156 S.E.2d 818 (Ga.Ct.App.1967); Smith v. Federated Dep't Stores, 165 Ga. App. 459, 301 S.E.2d 652 (Ga.Ct.App.1983); and Feder v. Fortunoff, 123 Misc.2d 857, 474 N.Y.S.2d 937 (N.Y.Sup.Ct.1984).

62. In Hill v. American Express Co., 257 S.C. 86, 184 S.E.2d 115 (S.C. 1971), it was suggested there was a breach of contract. Certainly, the decision in the *Smith* case, *supra* note 61, was based on a right to refuse to extend credit at any time provided in the cardholder agreement. Such reservations may raise questions about the characterization of the credit under federal law. See Regulation Z, § 226.2(a)(20), Commentary ¶ 226.2(a)(20)–5. Even within a contract provision that allows a refusal to extend credit without notice, the right may not extend to a consummated transaction. Gray v. American Express Co., 743 F.2d 10 (D.C.Cir.1984).

63. § 4–104(a)(9) excludes debit card slips as "items."

64. Section 4–104(1)(g) requires an "instrument," which everywhere else in the UCC is defined to be a writing. See §§ 3–104 and 3–102(1)(e).

65. The liability is for all damages proximately caused except in the case of a bona fide error, where liability is for actual damages proved. 15 U.S.C. § 1693h(a), (c). Regulation E does not deal with the matter. It is not clear what the difference in the damage measure is intended to be since the "trader rule," as it may have applied under UCC § 4–402, would not seem applicable in a consumer context. Perhaps the intent is to limit damages for mental distress and loss of reputation in a way similar to what

is a failure to make an electronic fund transfer in accordance with the terms and conditions governing the account in the correct amount or in a timely manner when properly instructed by the consumer, unless the failure resulted from an act of God or similar circumstances or a technical malfunction known to the consumer at the time the transfer was initiated.[66] A wrongful dishonor will not result from a failure to make a transfer because there are insufficient funds (except where the insufficiency is due to a failure to properly credit a deposit[67] or to stop payment on a preauthorized transfer); or there is legal process or other encumbrance restricting transfer; or the transfer would exceed a credit limit; or the transfer exceeds the cash available in the ATM.[68]

[3] Consumer Liability for Unauthorized Transfers Under Federal Law

A consumer's[69] liability for the unauthorized use of his or her credit card is severely limited by federal law.[70] Essentially, the consumer incurs no liability for unauthorized use unless the credit card is accepted (a credit card is accepted if it is requested and received, or if it is signed or used, or if it is in substitution for or in renewal of an accepted card); the card issuer has given adequate notice of the consumer's potential liability and how notice of loss or theft of the card may be reported; and the card issuer has provided a means to identify the cardholder.[71] If these conditions are met, then the cardholder is liable for a maximum amount of $50 or, if less, the unauthorized charges incurred prior to notice to the card issuer.[72] The negligence or care of the consumer in relation to the loss is not relevant, except to the extent the $50 exposure induces care or may create a preclusion.

Unauthorized use of a credit card is use without the actual, implied, or apparent authority of the cardholder and from which the cardholder receives no benefit.[73] Thus a cardholder may be able to terminate a

---

exclusion under the "trader rule" would produce.

66. 15 U.S.C. § 1693h(a)(1), (b).

67. Note the provisions of Regulation CC that mandate funds availability may come into play here. Regulation CC, 12 CFR §§ 229.10, 229.12, and 229.13. *See* discussion in Chapter 8.

68. 15 U.S.C. § 1693h(a)(1), (2), (3).

69. Liability for unauthorized use of a business credit card also is dealt with by the federal rule (*see* Regulation Z, 12 CFR § 226.12(b)(5)), and the rules apply to cards involving transactions otherwise excluded from coverage. Regulation Z, 12 CFR § 226.3 n. 4.

70. There also may be limits under state law. If they are more restrictive, they control. Presumably state law generally would not allocate responsibility for an unauthorized credit card use to the customer. *See, e.g.*, Union Oil Co. v. Lull, 220 Or. 412, 349 P.2d 243 (Or. 1960); and Allied Stores v. Funderburke, 52 Misc.2d 872, 277 N.Y.S.2d 8 (N.Y. Civ. Ct. 1967). An enforceable agreement might, however. If the agreement provides additional restriction on liability, it also will govern. Regulation Z, 12 CFR § 226.12(b)(4).

71. Regulation Z, 12 CFR § 226.12(b)(2).

72. *Id.*, § 226.12(b)(1). What constitutes notice is detailed in Regulation Z, § 226.12(b)(3).

73. *Id.*, § 226.12(b)(1) fn.22. Whether the unauthorized user is liable is left to state law. *See, e.g.*, Sears Roebuck & Co. v. Ragucci, 203 N.J.Super. 82, 495 A.2d 923 (Law Div. 1985) (wife not liable for goods purchased using husband's card); Cleveland Trust Co. v. Snyder, 55 Ohio App.2d 168, 380 N.E.2d 354 (Ohio Ct. App. 1978) (same). So too, of course, are the agency issues. *See, e.g.*, Transamerica Ins. Co. v.

user's ability to charge on the card by revoking authority and notifying the card issuer,[74] but he or she normally will be liable for use that merely exceeds the actual authority given the user[75] (but not for use after theft).[76]

A consumer is liable for an unauthorized electronic fund transfer from his or her account only if it results from the use of an "accepted access device,"[77] and if the institution has provided a means of identification of the consumer, a summary of the consumer's potential liability and at its option, the advisability of promptly reporting the loss or theft of the card, and telephone, address, and business days information relevant to making a report of the loss.[78] The consumer's liability, if these conditions are met, is limited to a maximum amount of $50 or, if less, the amount of unauthorized transfers occurring before notice of loss is given to the institution.[79] Negligence (such as putting the personal identification number necessary to initiate a transfer on the card) or care of the cardholder in relation to the loss generally is not relevant, except as the $50 potential liability may prompt care, and except that:

> (1) if the consumer fails to give notice to the financial institution within two business days after learning that the device has been lost or stolen, liability is only limited to the lesser of $500, or the

Standard Oil Co., 325 N.W.2d 210 (N.D. 1982) (changes after company paid for initial unauthorized charges were authorized as apparent authority existed).

74. *In re* Shell Oil Co., (CCH) Consumer Credit Guide [Transfer Binder–Decisions 1974–80] ¶ 97,528, 95 F.T.C. 357 (FTC 1980). On the other hand, in Walker Bank & Trust Co. v. Jones, 672 P.2d 73 (Utah 1983), *cert. den. sub nom.* Harlan v. First Interstate Bank, 466 U.S. 937, 104 S.Ct. 1911, 80 L.Ed.2d 460 (1984), the court refused to find unauthorized use until all credit cards had been surrendered on the ground that until then the asserted unauthorized user, who retained his own card with his name on it, had apparent authority. *Also compare* Oclander v. First Nat'l Bank, 700 S.W.2d 804 (Ky.Ct.App.1985) *with* Cities Serv. Co. v. Pailet, 452 So.2d 319 (La.Ct.App.1984), and Society Nat'l Bank v. Kienzle, 11 Ohio App.3d 178, 463 N.E.2d 1261 (Ohio Ct. App. 1983).

75. *See, e.g.,* Martin v. American Express, 361 So.2d 597 (Ala.Civ.App.1978); Michigan Nat'l Bank v. Olson, 44 Wash. App. 898, 723 P.2d 438 (Wash.Ct.App. 1986); Mastercard v. Town of Newport, 133 Wis.2d 328, 396 N.W.2d 345 (Wis.Ct.App. 1986); Stieger v. Chevy Chase Savings Bank, 666 A.2d 479 (D.C.1995); and Minskoff v. American Express Travel Related Services Co., 98 F.3d 703 (2d Cir.1996) (negligence in failing to discover a fraud by examination of billing statements may preclude denial of apparent authority to use credit card stemming from possession of it and payment of charges). *Cf.* Young v. Bank of America, 141 Cal.App.3d 108, 190 Cal. Rptr. 122 (Cal.Ct.App.1983). It is less than fully clear to what extent lack of care by the card issuer or merchant, as opposed to the cardholder, might be relevant. For example, in the *Olson* case, the credit limit of $1000 was ignored. Under modern commercial law, the negligence of either side generally plays an important role. *See* UCC §§ 3–404, 3–405, 3–406 and 4–406.

76. Vaughn v. United States Nat'l Bank, 79 Or.App. 172, 718 P.2d 769 (Or.Ct. App.1986); Fifth Third Bank/Visa v. Gilbert, 17 Ohio Misc.2d 14, 478 N.E.2d 1324 (Ohio Mun. Ct. 1984).

77. "Access device" is defined as a card, code, or other means of access to the consumer's account for the purpose of making electronic fund transfers. Regulation E, 12 CFR § 205.2(a)(1). An access device is "accepted" when the consumer requests and receives, or signs, or uses, or authorizes use of the device, or requests validation of an unsolicited device, or receives a device in substitution or as renewal of an accepted device. Regulation E, § 205.2(a)(2).

78. *Id.*, § 205.6(a).

79. *Id.*, § 205.6(b). If applicable state law or the agreement provide for a lesser liability, however, that governs. *Id.*, § 205.6(b)(6).

sum of $50 (or the amount of unauthorized transfers within the two days, whichever is less) plus the amount of unauthorized transfers that occur after the two-day period as a result of the consumer's failure to give the required notice;[80] and

(2) if the consumer fails to report an unauthorized transfer within sixty days of receiving a periodic statement showing the unauthorized transfer, the consumer's liability increases to the sum of the lesser of $50 or the amount of unauthorized transfers that appear on the statement or that occur during that 60-day period plus the amount of all unauthorized transfers that occur as a result of the failure to notify after the end of the 60-day period and before notice is given to the institution.[81]

An unauthorized electronic fund transfer is one initiated without actual authority and from which the consumer receives no benefit, but it does not include one initiated by a person who was furnished the access device by the consumer unless the consumer has notified the financial institution the person is no longer an authorized user.[82] In New York, the New York Attorney General in *State by Abrams v. Citibank, N.A.*,[83] brought suit against Citibank on the ground its alleged failure to treat certain electronic fund transfers as unauthorized transfers violated the federal Electronic Fund Transfer Act, and thus the New York law that prohibits unfair, deceptive, and unconscionable business practices. The basis for the suit arose when consumers were tricked into allowing their debit cards to be used by con artists, and the question was whether the cards were "furnished." The suit has been settled without the question being resolved. The Regulation E Commentary has taken the position that an unauthorized transfer includes cases where the access device is furnished as a result of a robbery and where the access device is furnished as the result of a fraud.[84]

Since the exposure of a consumer for and what constitutes unauthorized use may differ between credit card and retail electronic fund transfer transactions, the federal law contains guidance on this matter. Even if an unauthorized electronic fund transfer involves an extension of credit because of an arrangement to cover overdrafts or to maintain a required minimum account balance, the protections of Regulation E control.[85]

---

80. *Id.*, § 205.6(b)(1) and (2).

81. *Id.*, § 205.6(b)(3). *Compare* the *Minskoff* case, *supra* note 75, in the case of credit cards. There is an exception in both cases if the consumer is unable to give notice because of extenuating circumstances such as extended travel. Regulation E, 12 CFR § 205.6(b)(4). As to what constitutes notice, *see* id., § 205.6(b)(5).

82. *Id.*, § 205.2(m). There also are some other exceptions not discussed here.

83. 537 F.Supp. 1192 (S.D.N.Y.1982).

84. Regulation E Official Staff Commentary Q 2–27. However, if the consumer gives the access device to another person with actual limited authority which is exceeded, the consumer is liable for the transfers unless notice revoking authority is given. *Compare* notes 75 and 76, *supra*, with respect to credit cards. But a transfer initiated with fraudulent intent by the consumer or a person acting in concert or by a financial institution or its employee is not unauthorized. Regulation E, 12 CFR § 205.2(m)(2) and (3).

85. Regulation E, 12 CFR § 205.12(a)(1)(iii) and Regulation Z, 12 CFR § 226.12(g).

[4] Federal Rules on Distribution of Access Devices

As a corollary to the rules on limited liability for unauthorized use, generally an access device, whether a credit card, a debit card, or another access device, may be distributed only in response to a consumer request or as a renewal or substitution for an existing device.[86] There is, however, a significant exception in the case of an electronic fund transfer access device. This exception permits the distribution of unsolicited and not validated access devices where they are accompanied by certain required disclosures. These include complete disclosure of the consumer's rights and liabilities and a notice that the device is not validated and will be validated only in response to the consumer's request.[87]

The Regulation E rules govern the issuance of solely electronic fund transfer access devices, the addition of EFT capability to an accepted credit card, and the issuance of an access device that only will allow an overdraft or transfer to maintain a minimum account balance.[88] On the other hand, the Regulation Z rules apply to the issuance of a credit card, the addition of a credit feature to an accepted debit card, and combined debit/credit cards that are not limited to overdraft or minimum account balance arrangements.[89]

[5] State Law

As noted before,[90] state statutory law regulating the operation of credit card or retail electronic fund transfers is both sparse and fragmentary for the most part.[91] There is a paucity of reported cases dealing with credit card and electronic fund transfer issues beyond the federal law.[92]

---

86. Regulation Z, § 226.12(a); Regulation E, § 205.5(a).

87. Regulation E, § 205.5(b). Not only debit cards but unsolicited issuance of PINS (personal identification numbers) for existing debit cards is allowed. Regulation E Official Staff Commentary Q5–4.5. So too a PIN to use with a credit card may be distributed on an unsolicited basis so long as it cannot be used alone. Regulation Z Official Staff Commentary ¶ 226.12(a)(1)–8.

88. Regulation E, 12 CFR § 205.12(a)(i), (ii); Regulation Z, 12 CFR § 226.12(g).

89. Regulation E, 12 CFR § 205.12(a)(2); Regulation Z, 12 CFR § 226.12(g).

90. *See* note 9, *supra*, and the discussion on wrongful dishonor and unauthorized use, *supra*.

91. State statutes that directly regulate consumer EFT transactions are cited in D. Baker & R. Brandel, The Law of Electronic Fund Transfer Systems (2d ed. 1988), and in Fent, Commercial Law: Electronic Funds Transfers: How New U.C.C. Article 4A May Affect Consumers, 43 Okla. L. Rev. 339, 349 (1991).

92. *See, e.g.*, Gaffney v. Community Fed. Sav. & Loan Ass'n, 706 S.W.2d 530 (Mo.Ct.App.1986) (consumer not liable for unauthorized withdrawals under state law regulating the account relationship). *See also* Schorr v. Bank of New York, 5 CCH Consumer Credit Guide ¶ 97,268, 107 Misc.2d 132, 433 N.Y.S.2d 546 (N.Y.City Ct.1980), *rev'd*, 5 CCH Consumer Credit Guide ¶ 96,766, 112 Misc.2d 684, 449 N.Y.S.2d 824 (N.Y. App. Term 1983), where a cardholder asserted his right to raise a defense against the merchant and against the card issuer pursuant to 15 U.S.C. § 1666i. The dispute involved a car repair transaction. The repair shop contested the right of the card issuer to reverse payment to it because of the cardholder's asserted claim. The City Court of New York held that the card issuer should have set a reasonable time limit in its agreement within which to deduct from a merchant's account because of a disputed claim. Because it failed to do this, the court held the provision of the agreement allowing an unlimited right of charge-back was unenforceable. On appeal this decision was reversed, the agreement was held not to be unconscionable, and it was upheld as written.

In many instances this is probably because the parties have anticipated the problems and have resolved them by agreement. But in some situations, the agreement will either be silent or one of the parties will wish to contest the agreement. In this event, and if the money at stake is worth litigation, a reported case may result. Thus it is likely that there will be a slowly accelerating development of the law by cases, but that has not yet occurred to any significant degree.

In the area of commercial electronic fund transfers, the money at stake is enough to prompt litigation and very often transactions proceed without agreement on the issue at dispute because the strength of each party's bargaining power precludes the ability to reach an advance resolution of the issue. There are a growing number of cases as a result. Discussion of these cases and how Article 4A addresses the problems litigated occurs in Chapter 10.

[6] Arbitration Clauses

Arbitration clauses are increasingly used in credit card agreements in particular in an attempt to avoid litigation. The United States Supreme Court[93] has held that such arbitration clauses are generally binding on consumers, and this is so even when involving claims under federal legislation that promotes individual enforcement action as well as allowing class actions, like the Truth in Lending Act. Consequently, any attack on such a clause basically must occur under general provisions of state law, such as unconscionability,[94] the use of deceptive tactics,[95] and whether the clause clearly conveys the consequences asserted for it.[96]

¶ 11.03 Applicable Law for Selected Other Non–UCC Payment Systems

[1] Smart Cards and Similar Products

For the most part, the law that may be applicable to smart card and computer storage type products will be state general contract law. If the

---

93. Green Tree Financial Corp. v. Randolph, 531 U.S. 79, 121 S.Ct. 513, 148 L.Ed.2d 373 (2000). *See also* Johnson v. West Suburban Bank, 225 F.3d 366 (3d Cir.2000), *cert. denied*, 531 U.S. 1145, 121 S.Ct. 1081, 148 L.Ed.2d 957 (2001).

94. *See*, e.g., Brower v. Gateway 2000, Inc., 246 A.D.2d 246, 676 N.Y.S.2d 569 (N.Y.App. Div. 1st Dep't 1998) (term requiring arbitration under rules requiring advance fee of which half was non-refundable even if claimant prevailed was unconscionable); Stirlen v. Supercuts, Inc., 51 Cal.App.4th 1519, 60 Cal.Rptr.2d 138 (1997) (clause which reserved litigation rights to employer only and denied employees rights to exemplary damages, equitable relief, attorneys fees, costs and a shorter statute of limitations, unconscionable); Arnold v. United Cos. Lending Corp., 204 W.Va. 229, 511 S.E.2d 854 (W.Va. 1998) (same); Gonzalez v. Hughes Aircraft Employees Fed. Credit Union, 83 Cal.Rptr. 2d 763 (Cal.App. 1999) (same), *review granted and action deferred*, 85 Cal.Rptr.2d 843, 978 P.2d 1 (1999); Szetela v. Discover Bank, 118 Cal.Rptr.2d 862, 97 Cal.App.4th 1094 (2002) (arbitration clause unconscionable when presented on a "take it or leave it" basis and would only benefit card issuer).

95. *See*, e.g., Engalla v. Permanente Med. Group, Inc., 15 Cal.4th 951, 938 P.2d 903, 64 Cal.Rptr.2d 843 (1997) (fraudulent inducements to agreement to arbitration of disputes).

96. *See, e.g.*, Alamo Rent A Car v. Galarza, 306 N.J.Super. 384, 703 A.2d 961 (1997) (clause that did not clearly include claims of employment discrimination failed to waive employee's statutory rights and remedies).

value is loaded from a consumer account electronically or by use of a credit card, either Regulation E or Regulation Z may be applicable to that extent. Other possibly applicable federal law, such as the Glass–Steagall Act of 1933 regulating what businesses can receive deposits subject to check or to repayment upon presentation of evidence of debt, needs to be considered, as well as a wide range of state laws.[97] However, the discussion here primarily will focus on the commercial law issues and possible applicable law. This law will in most cases be state law, and that law will generally be determined by the agreement of the relevant parties under the law of contract, including limiting principles like unconscionability and good faith. Absent controlling agreement, the common law will normally be applicable, whether that law involves general principles or specific ones perhaps informed by the Uniform Commercial Code. The analysis will be divided into three parts: (1) creation of the stored value obligation, (2) transfer of the stored value obligation, and possible discharge of the underlying obligation, and (3) settlement and discharge of the stored value obligation.

Creation of the obligation. There are several issues regarding when, how, and by whom a stored obligation is created. A stored value obligation will arise from conduct by the issuer, or someone with actual or apparent authority, that is sufficient to create an obligation applying common law contract principles. Absent legislation, there is no statute of frauds. An issue is when will an issuer be liable for obligations created fraudulently by a dishonest employee? One would expect the answer to be there is no liability absent a lack of due care establishing a preclusion.

The identity of the obligor is critical because it is the only way for users of the product to measure the credit risk associated with the product. As previously noted, the obligor is being extended credit. If the issuer/obligor uses an unaffiliated distribution network, the purchaser of a card or other stored value may never know that its credit risk lies with the issuer and not with the other entity that sold the card or other stored value. An innocent user of stored value may look to an entity named on the storage device itself on a number of theories. For example, absent disclosure of the underlying obligor, an entity identified on a card or other access device may be liable to the users of the product as the agent of an undisclosed principal.

Another issue is whether and to what extent an issuer can bind a purchaser or subsequent user of the obligation to terms and conditions on the use of the product. This may depend on legal limitations against variation of certain rights and liabilities by contract, or on the medium and manner of contract formation. The issue in this latter context may involve a debate similar to that in the case of so-called "shrink-wrap" licenses about what terms are a part of the contract,[98] or only additional

¶ 11.03

97. *See* Report of Task Force on Stored Value Cards, 52 Bus. Law 653, at 675–677, 680 (1997). Much of the following discussion is predicated upon that report, and is used with permission.

98. *See, e.g.,* ProCD, Inc. v. Zeidenberg, 86 F.3d 1447 (7th Cir.1996).

proposals to be accepted or rejected.[99] In this regard, for consumer transactions an issuer may be required or encouraged to post the terms of its product conspicuously on a publicly accessible database.[100]

Some of the terms that an issuer may want to include in a contract between itself and the users of the product are relevant in other systems as well. Thus should there be a date after which the issuer's obligation is no longer a valid obligation? This type of rule helps to ensure that lost or stolen access devices have limited uses and that access devices do not become worn or defective over time. This type of rule may also be important if issuers intend to upgrade the access device's technology and security features regularly. But an expired obligation could also mean that the obligations stored on an access device are no longer valid claims against the issuer; moreover, this may raise operational issues, such as how the expiry date of stored value obligations (particularly with reloadable cards) is measured.

Finally, there may be a question as to whether the storage devices associated with the product should be transferable. On the one hand, rendering a device non-transferable may provide the issuer with a defense should it be sued for refusing to honor an obligation where the access device has been used by someone other than the purchaser of the device. On the other hand, by rendering the device non-transferable the issuer may be limiting its right to treat lost storage devices like cash.

Transfer of the obligation. Once a stored value obligation is loaded onto a storage device, the holder of the obligation will want to transfer it, or a part of it, to others. This "divisibility" feature of the product itself involves risk because the obligation may not divide as intended. Suppose A makes ten individual purchases with a smart card containing an original obligation of $100. When all ten of A's purchases are completed, the issuer's obligation to pay A $100 is supposed to be replaced by ten obligations to pay $10 to each seller. But suppose because of some operational problem, when A executes his purchases, the obligation does not divide into ten obligations of $10 but multiplies into ten individual $100 obligations. Who should bear this risk? Does it depend on the cause, the absence of care, other factors? Can agreement effectively allocate this risk since third parties are involved?

When the obligation of the issuer moves from the initial holder of the obligation to a transferee, there may be several other issues. The transfer could be effective when the payor undertakes certain predetermined concrete steps to "send" the stored value to the payee. Or the transfer could be effective only once the obligation is available for use by the recipient. A court's willingness to enforce the transaction between the transferor and transferee will likely depend on whether the method of transfer is commercially reasonable.[101]

---

99. *See, e.g.*, Step–Saver Data Systems Inc. v. Wyse Technology, 939 F.2d 91 (3d Cir.1991).

100. *See, e.g.*, Uniform Computer Information Transactions Act § 114.

101. If the obligation is treated as a general intangible as suggested, *infra*, it will be a payment intangible under UCC Article 9. § 9–102(a)(42) and (61). As such, its transfer (sale), is subject to Article 9

Does an effective transfer of a stored value obligation discharge the underlying obligation of the transferor to pay the transferee? If A effectively transfers $10 to seller to buy goods, seller now has a claim against the issuer of the obligation. What happens if the issuer, however, becomes insolvent before seller can collect? Can seller replevy the goods? Can seller require A to pay for the goods again? If a transferred obligation is treated like cash, the $10 obligation of A to seller is discharged when the stored value obligation is transferred from A to seller. If the rules governing personal checks are the model, the $10 obligation between A and seller is suspended when seller obtains the stored value obligation until the stored value obligation is finally paid. If the issuer fails to honor the stored value obligation, the underlying $10 obligation between A and the seller would be restored. This rule, however, might postpone finality too long and upset transactions, as well as being subject to difficulty in tracing "the" obligation. Acceptance of a stored value obligation could also be treated like the acceptance of a cashier's check. Upon acceptance, A's underlying $10 debt to seller would be discharged. Absent indorsement type liability on the part of A, the seller could only look to the issuer for payment. If issuer refused to or could not honor the stored value obligation, the seller would bear the loss. Willingness to assume this risk clearly would depend upon knowledge of and about the issuer, however. Certainly legal uncertainty about the finality of a transfer may fetter the development of products. To foster certainty, a finality rule should exist by contract between the issuer and users, at least until the matter is settled by the common law. Also, as a practical matter, a rule that renders payment subject to the risk of collection on the issuer's obligation may be of little value if there is no audit trail, and therefore, no practical method to exercise a charge-back right.

Another issue is whether it will be possible for the holder of a stored value obligation to pledge the obligation to a third party. It is likely the products will not be viewed as cash, and will be treated as general intangibles.[102] An interest in a general intangible can only be perfected by filing.[103] Filing may not work well in the context of high-speed electronic transactions where either the stored value obligation is not uniquely identifiable, or where the stored value obligations are designed to be transferred many times, so that a payee must then check with the filing system prior to approving every new transaction. An answer could be to consider the payee as akin to a buyer in the ordinary course of business or a holder in due course (see §§ 9–321(a), 9–330(a)), but for that legislation would be necessary. Practically, it would seem the asset

---

(§ 9–109(a)(3)); *but see* § 9–109(d)(7)), and will require perfection. However, perfection is automatic (§ 9–309(3)) and priority is not subject to later qualification. § 9–322.

102. UCC § 9–102(a)(42). However, inasmuch as that status depends on it not being included in some other collateral category, such as an account (§ 9–102(a)(2)), a deposit account (§ 9–102(a)(29)), or a letter of credit right (§ 9–102(a)(51)), this conclusion is open to discussion. Classification might be driven by the need for perfection, as an unperfected security interest may not prevail over the parties. § 9–317(d).

103. UCC § 9–310(a).

is too small in value to serve as relied upon collateral, and may be virtually impossible to trace, as previously suggested. Thus any claim will no doubt be limited to identifiable proceeds. § 9-315.

Finally, if the transfer fails because the technology needed to effect the transfer does not work, who is liable and what is the measure of damages? Because the effectiveness of a transfer depends on technology, damages should be apportioned to the person whose technology caused the transfer to fail. Thus, an issuer would be liable if equipment malfunctions (e.g., a card reader causes a stored obligation to be erased rather than transferred), or there is a latent defect (e.g., a computer software virus) in the technology provided to all of the users of a product, perhaps subject to extenuating circumstances or an enforceable agreement. Using concepts developed in other areas of commercial law, no one party should be liable when a technological interruption or failure is beyond the control of the party relying on the interruption or the failure to excuse performance, as long as the party exercised such diligence as the circumstances warranted.

As between the transferor and the transferee, damages seemingly should be set "to the end that the aggrieved party may be put in as good a position as if the other party had fully performed ..."[104] The liability of the issuer for malfunctioning equipment should be similarly limited and exclude consequential damages unless the culpable issuer has notice of the particular circumstances giving rise to damages. However, it can be argued, as under Article 4A in the case of low cost fund transfers, that issuers of these products will not be able to offer the product if a $20 transaction can result in unlimited consequential risk. Presumably, a contractual provision to eliminate that risk should be valid.[105]

Discharge and Settlement of the Obligation. Redemption of a stored value obligation occurs when the holder of a stored value obligation presents the storage device (or its information) to the issuer, or to an intermediary, and requests money or deposit credit in exchange. It will be important for all parties to know the status of the credit; that is, whether the credit is final or provisional. If presentation is to the issuer, the credit should be final, perhaps only subject to restitution in certain cases.[106] If presentation is to an intermediary, and if the credit is provisional, it may be charged back to the redeemer if, because of insolvency or some other reason, the intermediary does not receive good value from the issuer.[107]

A problem that may arise when stored value obligations are returned to the issuer is that the issuer may learn about an unanticipated increase in the liability side of the issuer's balance sheet. Whether the problem be one of innocent technological "spawning," or whether it is a problem where a malefactor has found a method of counterfeiting the

---

104. UCC § 1-305.
105. *Compare* UCC § 2-719(3).
106. *Compare* UCC § 3-418.
107. *Compare* UCC § 4-201. Some sort of time frame, however, should exist by contract or, absent contract, a reasonable time, but determining a reasonable time would itself seem quite uncertain.

issuer's obligation (so that it is impossible to distinguish an authentically issued obligation from a counterfeit), the problem is the same. The issuer may face successive problems in this instance. The first problem may be illiquidity; as claimants surface and demand settlement, the issuer may find that the number of claimants exceeds all reasonable projections and it will experience a liquidity problem. Moreover, if the spawning or counterfeiting reaches a specific magnitude, the liquidity problem will degenerate into a solvency problem.

Another discharge issue is who bears the risk of loss if an issuer becomes insolvent after a stored value obligation has been presented to the issuer but before final payment has occurred. If the funds are held in an insured account for the benefit of holders of stored value obligations, the holders will be guaranteed some amount of money or, if held in a trust account, creditors should not be able to reach the funds. Absent an insured or fiduciary account, an intermediary or holder will be a general creditor of an issuer and, may not be able to recover its full investment.

What of spurious stored value obligations? If a product does not permit the users or the issuer to identify a "counterfeit," the issuer may be the best person to bear the loss if there are unauthorized obligations in circulation because the issuer perhaps has the most incentive and the best means to prevent this occurrence. Some payment products, however, may permit the issuer to identify unauthorized obligations. For the reason given, the issuer should bear the loss for counterfeits in these circumstances as well, if the issuer cannot stop the transfer of such counterfeits. Also, if liability for counterfeits is placed on the transferees of the obligations, the first transferee to redeem the obligation will be serendipitously deemed to redeem the true obligation; the remaining holders of identical obligations will, by reason of their position in the cue, hold counterfeits. This rule would assure a race to the issuer if word about the counterfeit fraud leaked out.

Several possible analogies can be used to resolve the question of who bears the risk of loss of a stored value obligation. If a Federal Reserve Note is lost, stolen, or destroyed, the person who lost the note (or from who it was stolen) bears the risk of loss and will not be able to obtain a replacement note. With a cashier's check, however, the holder who has lost possession of the cashier's check can demand payment from the issuer by filing an affidavit of loss (or theft or destruction) that provides reasonable identification of the check and is received in time for the issuer to act.[108] With a personal check, the holder would be able to stop payment on the lost or stolen check if the stop payment order is received by the holder's bank in time to act on it.[109] The holder who has suffered the loss, however, must be able to reasonably identify the stored value obligation; many of the products will not allow a holder to uniquely identify the obligation. Even if the obligation is uniquely identified, the issuer may not be able to stop the transfer of the obligation if the issuer

---

108. UCC § 3–312. *See also* UCC § 3–309.

109. UCC § 4–403.

is unable to notify others using the product at the point of sale or transfer.

[2] E-checks and Similar Products

Like in the case of smart cards and similar stored value devices, for the most part the issues for e-checks and similar products, absent legislation, will be resolved in the first instance by agreements among relevant parties under the general law of contract, including limiting principles such as unconscionability and good faith, and absent controlling agreement, by common law, whether that law involves general principles, or specific ones informed by the Uniform Commercial Code. As has been noted previously, at least some of the products of this type contract for the applicability of the Uniform Commercial Code, specifically Articles 3 and 4. Absent the invalidation of that choice,[110] the provisions of Articles 3 and 4 will apply. If the choice is invalidated, the applicable law would be the general law of contract to the extent of the invalidation or to the extent the agreement did not deal with the matter. There are some problems in that analysis.

One is that Regulation E clearly applies to a number of these products. The Official Staff Commentary to the regulation, as published in the Federal Register[111] and mandatory on January 1, 2002, determines that when a consumer tenders a check to a merchant who scans it at a point of sale terminal but does not otherwise process it further (whether the merchant retains it or not), the funds transfer is subject to Regulation E.[112] Regulation E also will apply if the consumer mails a check to the payee and the payee or a lockbox agent converts the check into an ACH transaction, but not if a check is returned for insufficient funds and subsequently is represented electronically by means of an ACH transaction.[113] Therein lies the problem since arguably the paper check has been issued and constitutes a negotiable instrument under UCC Article 3[114] (and an item under Article 4). Because the Uniform Commercial Code is a commercial statute, it has avoided any overlap with payment systems governed to any degree by federal consumer protection legislation.[115] The

---

110. *But see* Sinclair Oil Corp. v. Sylvan State Bank, 254 Kan. 836, 869 P.2d 675 (Kan.1994), where the court noted but did not consider the effect, if any, of the provision in the NACHA rules stating that an ACH debit entry is considered to be an "item" for purposes of UCC Article 4. *See also* Security First Network Bank v. C.A.P.S., Inc., 47 UCC Rep.Serv.2d 670 (N.D.Ill.2002), discussed *supra*. Nonetheless, unless an applicable rule of law is mandatory (that is, not subject to variance of its effect by agreement), or the agreement attempts to govern the rights or impose liabilities on non-consenting third parties, the agreement should be valid subject to normal contract controls. *Compare* UCC § 4-103(a).

111. 66 Fed. Reg. 15187 (March 16, 2001).

112. However, in such a case the receipt requirement of 12 CFR § 205.9(a) is waived and authorization from the consumer occurs if after notice the consumer completes the funds transfer. The notice may be by sign at the POS, but NACHA rules may require more.

113. Any fee assessed by the payee in connection with representment is covered under Regulation E, however, if the consumer authorized the fee to be electronically debited from the consumer's account.

114. §§ 3-104 and 3-105; *but see* § 3-115 if the check is not completed.

115. §§ 3-103(a)(6) and 3-104 (requiring a writing); § 4-104(a)(9) ("item" ex-

reason is the potential degree of conflict, and the uncertain nature of its outcome.[116] For example, Article 3 allocates the risk of fraudulent instruments in a far different way than does Regulation E. Under Article 3 and Article 4, the purported drawer of a forged check bears no responsibility,[117] but this freedom from liability can be compromised in certain situations of presumed or actual failure to exercise ordinary care.[118] Under Regulation E, the consumer is responsible without regard to fault for a limited amount of an unauthorized electronic fund transfer, but is not responsible for the balance even with fault, except in limited circumstances that do not fully coincide with cases of negligence under the Uniform Commercial Code.[119] Let us assume the consumer mails a check to the payee who converts it into an ACH transaction after raising its amount. The check is paid and a bank statement indicating the transaction is delivered to the consumer, who ignores it. The account agreement provides that any debits to the account must be objected to in 14 days or they are deemed correct. A month later, the consumer mails another check to the same payee, which also is altered and then paid, and again a statement showing the transaction is delivered to the consumer, who now objects to both entries. Under the relevant provision of Article 4 and applicable case law which generally upholds contractual time specifications,[120] the consumer probably is out of luck on the first item.[121] Under Regulation E, the consumer is not out of time[122] unless the account agreement can change the regulatory rule, a dubious proposition.[123]

This alteration example also may serve as an illustration of a second problem, which involves the broad scale imposition by agreement of the provisions of Articles 3 and 4 on transactions that those Articles were never designed for. Assuming Regulation E applies as discussed, *supra*, to an electronic check, and given the application of § 4–406 by agreement, the same issues exist as in the previous example. But a host of other issues now also come more clearly into focus, including is there an alteration if the payee in violation of the agreement with the consumer initiates the ACH transaction in the larger amount,[124] should the altera-

---

cludes credit or debit card slips); § 4A–108 (excluding a funds transfer any part of which is governed by Regulation E).

116. Official Comment to § 4A–108.

117. §§ 3–403, 3–414, 4–401.

118. §§ 3–404—3–406, 4–406.

119. Regulation E, § 205.6.

120. § 4–406(c) and (d); and, *e.g.*, Peak v. Tuscaloosa Commerce Bank, 707 So.2d 59 (La.Ct.App.1997).

121. What if the payee had not altered the check but merely sent the ACH payment through in the larger amount? Arguably § 4–406(c) would not apply, the consumer's account is improperly debited (§ 4–401), and the payor bank may have a claim against the depositary bank or payee, perhaps under or by analogy to § 4–209. But could a common law duty to examine the statement and report the different amount, applicable through UCC § 1–103, exist?

122. Regulation E, 12 CFR § 205.6(b)(3) provides up to 60 days to report an unauthorized electronic fund transfer.

123. *Compare* 1974 Unif. Cons. Credit Code § 1.107; *see also* Buford v. American Fin. Co., 333 F.Supp. 1243 (N.D.Ga.1971) (release executed by consumer for consideration void as against public policy). A further unanswered question is the relation of this analysis to the error correction procedures of Regulation E, 12 CFR §§ 205.11(a)(1) and 205.2(m).

124. *See, e.g.*, Liberty State Bank & Trust v. Hemisphere Development Group, Inc., 98 Mich.App. 285, 296 N.W.2d 241 (Mich.Ct.App.1980) (alteration of loan ledger card not alteration of instrument).

tion discharge the underlying obligation,[125] and is a preclusion possible?[126]

In the end, an intolerable situation may be involved here. The tendency may exist to resolve the issues by further legislation, but, in fact, there probably is too much law now,[127] and given constant product development and change, codification can have serious downsides. Consequently, one key for the present would seem to be (1) better problem recognition and (2) drafting to eliminate as much as possible conflicts and ambiguities. There is another matter to consider as well.

To a large degree, credit card, retail electronic fund transfers, and smart card and electronic check payments presently involve primarily consumer transactions. The Uniform Commercial Code, which governs the negotiable instrument payment system, does not.[128] The federal credit card and retail electronic fund transfer rules focus almost entirely on the consumer-account institution relationship, and do not, except in a few instances, deal with the relationships of the persons through which payment is processed.[129] The UCC, of course, does deal with these other relationships. And, as the discussion indicates, smart card and electronic check payments are governed by little if any specific law, except Regulation E and the UCC rules in Articles 3 and 4 to the extent they apply. Thus, in general, the system involving negotiable instruments and governed by the UCC constitutes a complete set of rules that, though their effect may generally be varied by agreement,[130] provide a "safety net" if there is no agreement on the disputed point. Moreover, the statutory provisions tend to set a standard by which deviations by agreement may be measured for enforceability. Thus, the other payment systems suffer by comparison; they have only part of their operation governed by any legislative guidance, and only aspects of that part. The balance is determined by agreement, including systems rules in some

---

125. Such a sanction imposed by statute is one thing; can an agreement to apply Articles 3 and 4 really be said to contemplate such a sanction and, even if so, is such an agreement one for a penalty that is invalid?

126. For example, what if a security procedure that would have prevented payment of the altered transfer was offered, and refused? *Compare* UCC § 4A–202. A further unanswered question is, what is the relationship of the UCC rules applicable by agreement and the NACHA rules also applicable by authorization. Rationally any agreement should provide an order of priority for rules applicable by agreement with the NACHA rules having priority, but unless a great deal more analysis is completed a general standard of inconsistency would have to control, and that is at best little guidance.

127. At least on the state law level, the admonition against writing more law has been observed. The drafting committee to make amendments to UCC Articles 3 and 4 eschewed drafting to cover electronic checks, and the study committee on electronic payments of the National Conference of Commissioners on Uniform State Laws has yet to recommend any additional product in this area.

128. Article 4A, which governs commercial electronic funds transfers and is discussed in Chapter 10 with minor exceptions also does not cover consumer payments. § 4A–108, Official Comment; Article 4A, Prefatory Note: Description of transaction covered by Article 4A. Of course, a consumer transfer accomplished over Fedwire or otherwise not within the federal Electronic Fund Transfer Act may end up being covered under Article 4A. This is discussed, *supra*, in Chapter 10, and in greater detail in Fent, Commercial Law: Electronic Funds Transfers: How New U.C.C. Article 4A May Affect Consumers, 43 Okla.L.Rev. 339, 349 (1990).

129. *See* the discussion of the *Schorr* case, *supra*, at note 92.

130. UCC §§ 1–302(a), 4–103(a).

cases, and on a case-by-case development of the law which may not uphold the agreement on any particular point, and which supplies rules for lapses in or in the absence of agreements with little legislative guidance.[131]

This is not to conclude that the UCC, even given the update of Articles 3 and 4, represents an entirely rational state of the law, nor is it to conclude that different sources of law and rules to govern payment systems do or do not make good sense. The point here is not necessarily to argue that the rules for the different systems, which vary markedly, perhaps should not. Rather, since further reconciliation of those rules presently is unlikely, given the experience with the New Payments Code,[132] it is to recognize that the attorney advising his or her clients must struggle with the differences, as those differences may influence the choice of system use, and certainly will impact on rights and responsibilities for a consummated transaction.

However in the long run as time passes and payment systems beyond checks continue to develop and come into even broader use, the differences among them will become increasingly evident. As a result, even long-established rules eventually may come into question through the comparison.

---

131. This state of affairs in the context of commercial funds transfers was precisely the motivating force for Article 4A. As the district court in its opinion in Bradford Trust Co. v. Texas Am. Bank–Houston, 790 F.2d 407 (5th Cir.1986), lamented in that context: "The district courts find themselves adrift in a sea of unsettled questions...." On the other hand, as note 127, *supra*, suggests, there is not several hundred years of legal development to improve upon as in the case of checks, nor the magnitude of amounts involved and the consequential system risk as in the case of commercial funds transfers.

132. Miller, Report on the New Payments Code, 41 BUS. LAW. 1007 (1986).

Appendix

RESEARCHING THE LAW OF MODERN PAYMENT SYSTEMS AND NOTES

1. Introduction
2. Westlaw Databases
3. Retrieving a Document with a Citation: Find and Hypertext Links
    3.1 Find
    3.2 Hypertext Links
4. Searching with Natural Language
    4.1 Natural Language Search
    4.2 Browsing Search Results
    4.3 Next 20 documents
5. Searching with Terms and Connectors
    5.1 Terms
    5.2 Alternative Terms
    5.3 Connectors
    5.4 Field Restrictions
    5.5 Date Restrictions
    5.6 KeySearch™
6. Searching with Topic and Key Numbers
    6.1 Custom Digest
7. Verifying Your Research with Citation Research Services
    7.1 KeyCite® for cases
    7.2 KeyCite for Statutes and Federal Regulations
    7.3 KeyCite for Administrative Materials
    7.4 KeyCite Alert
8. Researching with Westlaw—Examples
    8.1 Retrieving Law Review Articles
    8.2 Retrieving Case Law
    8.3 Retrieving Statutes and Regulations
    8.4 Using KeyCite
    8.5 Following Recent Developments

Section 1. Introduction

Law of Modern Payment Systems and Notes provides a strong base for analyzing even the most complex problem involving issues related to modern payment systems and notes. Whether your research requires examination of case law, statutes, expert commentary, or other materials, West books and Westlaw are excellent sources of information.

To keep you informed of current developments, Westlaw provides frequently updated databases. With Westlaw, you have unparalleled legal research resources at your fingertips.

Additional Resources

If you have not previously used Westlaw or have questions not covered in this appendix, call the West Reference Attorneys at 1–800–REF–ATTY (1–800–733–2889). The West Reference Attorneys are trained, licensed attorneys, available 24 hours a day to assist you with your Westlaw search questions. To subscribe to Westlaw, call 1–800–344–5008 or visit westlaw.com at **www.westlaw.com**.

Section 2. Westlaw Databases

Each database on Westlaw is assigned an abbreviation called an *identifier*, which you use to access the database. You can find identifiers for all databases in the online Westlaw Directory and in the printed *Westlaw Database Directory*. When you need to know more detailed information about a database, use Scope. Scope contains coverage information, lists of related databases, and valuable search tips.

The following chart lists Westlaw databases that contain information pertaining to commercial law and contracts, including issues relating to negotiable instruments. For a complete list of commercial law databases, see the online Westlaw Directory or the printed *Westlaw Database Directory*. Because new information is continually being added to Westlaw, you should also check the tabbed Westlaw page and the online Westlaw Directory for new database information.

Selected Commercial Law and Contracts and Related Databases on Westlaw

Database	Identifier	Coverage
Federal and State Case Law Combined		
Federal and State Case Law	ALLCASES	Begins with 1945
Federal and State Case Law–Before 1945	ALLCASES–OLD	1789–1944
Uniform Commercial Code Cases	UCC–CS	Begins with 1898
Uniform Commercial Code Cases Plus	UCC–CS+	Begins with 1898
State Case Law		
Multistate Commercial Law and Contracts Cases	MCML–CS	Varies by state
Individual State Commercial Law and Contracts Cases	XXCML–CS (where XX is a state's two-letter postal abbreviation)	Varies by state

APPENDIX

Database	Identifier	Coverage
Federal Case Law		
Federal Commercial Law and Contracts–Cases	FCML–CS	Varies by court
Federal Commercial Law and Contracts–Supreme Court Cases	FCML–SCT	Begins with 1790
Federal Commercial Law and Contracts–Courts of Appeals Cases	FCML–CTA	Begins with 1891
Federal Commercial Law and Contracts–District Courts Cases	FCML–DCT	Begins with 1789
State Statutes and Regulations		
State Statutes–Annotated	ST–ANN–ALL	Current data
Individual State Statutes–Annotated	XX–ST–ANN (where XX is a state's two-letter postal abbreviation)	Current data
State Administrative Code Multibase	ADC–ALL	Current data
Individual State Administrative Code	XX–ADC (where XX is a state's two-letter postal abbreviation)	Current data
Federal Statutes and Regulations		
Federal Commercial Law and Contracts–U.S. Code Annotated	FCML–USCA	Current data
Federal Commercial Law and Contracts–Code of Federal Regulations	FCML–CFR	Current data
Federal Commercial Law and Contracts–Federal Register	FCML–FR	Current data
Uniform Commercial Code and Related Materials		
Uniform Commercial Code Official Text	UCC–TEXT	Current data
Uniform Commercial Code Official National Forms	UCC–ART9FM	Current data
Uniform Commercial Code Permanent Edi-	UCC–PEB	Current data

Database	Identifier	Coverage
torial Board Commentary		
Uniform Commercial Code–Revised Article 9. Secured Transactions	**UCC-SECTR**	Current data
Uniform Commercial Code State Variation Service	**UCC-VAR**	Current data
Uniform Commercial Code Records–Combined	UCC-ALL	Current data
Uniform Commercial Code Records–Individual State	UCC-XX (where XX is a state's two-letter postal abbreviation)	Current data

Legal Texts, Periodicals, and Practice Materials

Database	Identifier	Coverage
Commercial Law and Contracts–Law Reviews, Texts, and Bar Journals	CML–TP	Varies by publication
Anderson on the Uniform Commercial Code	ANDR–UCC	Current data
Asset–Based Lending	PLIREF–LEND	Current data
Commercial Law Journal	COMLJ	Begins with 1991 (Vol. 96)
Law of Suretyship and Guaranty	SURETY	Current data
PLI Commercial Law and Practice Course Handbook Series	PLI–COMM	Begins with 1984
Structured Finance	PLIREF–STRFIN	Current data
Uniform Commercial Code Series (Hawkland)	HAWKLAND	Current data
West's® McKinney's® Forms–Uniform Commercial Code	MCF–UCC	Current data
White and Summers' Uniform Commercial Code	WS–UCC	Current data

News and Information

Database	Identifier	Coverage
ABA Banking Journal	ABABKJ	Begins with January 1989
American Banker	AMBKR	Begins with January 1985

Database	Identifier	Coverage
Commercial Finance Newsletter	COMFINNL	Begins with August 2002
Finance and Banking News	FINNEWS	Varies by publication
Uniform Commercial Code Law Letter	UCCLAWLET	Begins with January 2002

Directories

West Legal Directory®– Commercial	WLD–CML	Current data

Section 3. Retrieving a Document with a Citation: Find and Hypertext Links

3.1 Find

Find is a Westlaw service that allows you to retrieve a document by entering its citation. Find allows you to retrieve documents from anywhere in Westlaw without accessing or changing databases. Find is available for many documents, including case law (state and federal), the *United States Code Annotated*®, state statutes, administrative materials, and texts and periodicals.

To use Find, simply type the citation in the *Find this document by citation* text box on the tabbed Westlaw page and click **GO**. The following list provides some examples:

To Find This Document	Access Find and Type
John Hancock Financial Services, Inc. v. Old Kent Bank 185 F. Supp. 2d 771 (E.D.Mich. 2002)	**185 fsupp2d 771**
National Title Ins. Corp. Agency v. First Union Nat. Bank 47 U.C.C. Rep. Serv.2d 318 (Va. 2002)	**47 uccrepserv2d 318**
Uniform Commercial Code § 3–302	**ucc s 3–302**
California Commercial Code § 3503	**ca coml s 3503**

For a complete list of publications that can be retrieved with Find and their abbreviations, click **Find** on the toolbar and then click **Publications List**.

3.2 Hypertext Links

Use hypertext links to move from one location to another on Westlaw. For example, use hypertext links to go directly from the statute, case, or law review article you are viewing to a cited statute, case, or article; from a headnote to the corresponding text in the opinion; or from an entry in a statutes index database to the full text of the statute.

Section 4. Searching with Natural Language

Overview: With Natural Language, you can retrieve documents by simply describing your issue in plain English. If you are a relatively new Westlaw user, Natural Language searching can make it easier for you to retrieve cases that are on point. If you are an experienced Westlaw user, Natural Language gives you a valuable alternative search method.

When you enter a Natural Language description, Westlaw automatically identifies legal phrases, removes common words, and generates variations of terms in your description. Westlaw then searches for the concepts in your description. Concepts may include significant terms, phrases, legal citations, or topic and key numbers. Westlaw retrieves the 20 documents that most closely match your description, beginning with the document most likely to match.

4.1 Natural Language Search

Access a database, such as Journals and Law Reviews (JLR). In the *Natural Language description* text box, type a description such as the following:

> can a negotiable instrument be created electronically

4.2 Browsing Search Results

Best Mode: To display the best portion (the portion that most closely matches your description) of each document in a Natural Language search result, click the **Best** arrow at the bottom of the page.

Term Mode: Click the **Term** arrow at the bottom of the page to display portions of the document that contain search terms.

Previous/Next Document: Click the left or right **Doc** arrow to view the previous or the next document in the search result.

Citations List: The citations list in the left frame lists the documents retrieved by the search. Click a hypertext link to display a document in the right frame.

4.3 Next 20 Documents

Westlaw displays the 20 documents that most closely match your description, beginning with the document most likely to match. If you want to view an additional 20 documents, click the right arrow in the left frame.

Section 5. Searching with Terms and Connectors

Overview: With Terms and Connectors searching, you enter a query, which consists of key terms from your issue and connectors specifying the relationship between these terms.

Terms and Connectors searching is useful when you want to retrieve a document for which you know specific details, such as the title or the fact situation. Terms and Connectors searching is also useful when you want to retrieve documents relating to a specific issue.

5.1 Terms

Plurals and Possessives: Plurals are automatically retrieved when you enter the singular form of a term. This is true for both regular and irregular plurals (e.g., **child** retrieves *children*). If you enter the plural form of a term, you will not retrieve the singular form.

If you enter the nonpossessive form of a term, Westlaw automatically retrieves the possessive form as well. However, if you enter the possessive form, only the possessive form is retrieved.

Compound Words, Abbreviations, and Acronyms: When a compound word is one of your search terms, use a hyphen to retrieve all forms of the word. For example, the term **along-side** retrieves *along-side, alongside,* and *along side.*

When using an abbreviation or acronym as a search term, place a period after each of the letters to retrieve any of its forms. For example, the term **u.c.c.** retrieves *UCC, U.C.C., U C C,* and *U. C. C.* Note: The abbreviation does *not* retrieve *Uniform Commercial Code,* so remember to add additional alternative terms to your query such as "**uniform commercial code**".

The Root Expander and the Universal Character: When you use the Terms and Connectors search method, placing the root expander (!) at the end of a root term generates all other terms with that root. For example, adding the ! to the root *negotiat* in the query

> **negotiat! /s paper /s bearer**

instructs Westlaw to retrieve such terms as *negotiate, negotiated, negotiable,* and *negotiating.*

The universal character (*) stands for one character and can be inserted in the middle or at the end of a term. For example, the term

> **withdr*w**

will retrieve *withdraw* and *withdrew.* Adding three asterisks to the root *elect*

> **elect* * ***

instructs Westlaw to retrieve all forms of the root with up to three additional characters. Terms such as *elected* or *election* are retrieved by this query. However, terms with more than three letters following the root, such as *electronic,* are not retrieved. Plurals are always retrieved, even if more than three letters follow the root.

Phrase Searching: To search for an exact phrase, place it within quotation marks. For example, to search for references to *holder in due course,* type "**holder in due course**". When you are using the Terms and Connectors search method, you should use phrase searching only if you are certain that the terms in the phrase will not appear in any other order.

5.2 Alternative Terms

After selecting the terms for your query, consider which alternative terms are necessary. For example, if you are searching for the term *bank*, you might also want to search for the terms *"financial institution"* or *"credit union."* You should consider both synonyms and antonyms as alternative terms. You can also use the Westlaw thesaurus to add alternative terms to your query.

5.3 Connectors

After selecting terms and alternative terms for your query, use connectors to specify the relationship that should exist between search terms in your retrieved documents. The connectors are described below:

Use:	To retrieve documents with:	Example:
& (and)	both terms	**maker & "promissory note"**
or (space)	either term or both terms	**u.c.c. "uniform commercial code"**
/p	search terms in the same paragraph	**signature /p valid! invalid!**
/s	search terms in the same sentence	**payment /s drawee pay*r**
+s	the first search term preceding the second within the same sentence	**present! +s note instrument**
/n	search terms within *n* terms of each other (where *n* is a number)	**wrongful! /5 dishonor!**
+n	the first search term preceding the second by *n* terms (where *n* is a number)	**bearer +5 instrument paper**
" "	search terms appearing in the same order as in the quotation marks	**"negotiable instrument"**

Use:	To exclude documents with:	Example:
% (but not)	search terms following the % symbol	**check %examin! inspect!**

5.4 Field Restrictions

Overview: Documents in each Westlaw database consist of several segments, or fields. One field may contain the citation, another the title, another the synopsis, and so forth. Not all databases contain the same fields. Also depending on the database, fields with the same name may contain different types of information.

To view a list of fields for a specific database and their contents, see Scope for that database. Note that in some databases not every field is available for every document.

To retrieve only those documents containing your search terms in a specific field, restrict your search to that field. To restrict your search to a specific field, type the field name or abbreviation followed by your search terms enclosed in parentheses. For example, to retrieve a U.S. Supreme Court case titled *Securities Industry Association v. Board of Governors of the Federal Reserve System,* access the U.S. Supreme Court Cases database (SCT) and search for your terms in the title field (ti).

ti(securities & "federal reserve")

The fields discussed below are available in Westlaw case law databases you might use for researching issues related to payment and notes.

Digest and Synopsis Fields: The digest (di) and synopsis (sy) fields, added to case law databases by West's attorney-editors, summarize the main points of a case. The synopsis field contains a brief description of a case. The digest field contains the topic and headnote fields and includes the complete hierarchy of concepts used by West's editors to classify the headnotes to specific West digest topic and key numbers. Restricting your search to the synopsis and digest fields limits your result to cases in which your terms are related to a major issue in the case.

Consider restricting your search to one or both of these fields if

- you are searching for common terms or terms with more than one meaning, and you need to narrow your search; or

- you cannot narrow your search by using a smaller database.

For example, to retrieve state cases that discuss the requirement that documents state a sum certain to qualify as a negotiable instrument, access the Multistate Commercial Law and Contracts Cases database (MCML–CS) and type the following query:

sy,di(instrument /s negotiable /p "sum certain")

Headnote Field: The headnote field (he) is part of the digest field but does not contain topic numbers, hierarchical classification information, or key numbers. The headnote field contains a one-sentence summary for each point of law in a case and any supporting citations given by the author of the opinion. A headnote field restriction is useful when you are searching for specific statutory sections or rule numbers. For example, to retrieve headnotes from Florida cases that cite Florida statute § 673.4021, access the Florida Commercial Law and Contracts Cases database (FLCML–CS) and type the following query:

he(673.4021)

Topic Field: The topic field (to) is also part of the digest field. It contains hierarchical classification information, including the West digest topic names and numbers and the key numbers. You should restrict search terms to the topic field in a case law database if

- a digest field search retrieves too many documents; or
- you want to retrieve cases with digest paragraphs classified under more than one topic.

For example, the topic Bills and Notes has the topic number 56. To retrieve state cases that discuss forged signatures on promissory notes, access the Multistate Commercial Law and Contracts Cases database (MCML–CS) and type a query like the following:

to(56) /p forg! /s signature /s "promissory note"

For a complete list of West digest topics and their corresponding topic numbers, access the Custom Digest by choosing **Key Numbers and Digest** from the *More* drop-down list.

> *Note*: Slip opinions and cases from topical services do not contain the digest, headnote, and topic fields.

Prelim and Caption Fields: When searching in a database containing statutes, rules, or regulations, restrict your search to the prelim (pr) and caption (ca) fields to retrieve documents in which your terms are important enough to appear in a section name or heading. For example, to retrieve Ohio statutes regarding notice of dishonor, access the Ohio Statutes–Annotated database (OH–ST–ANN) and type the following:

pr,ca(notice & dishonor)

5.5 Date Restrictions

You can use Westlaw to retrieve documents *decided* or *issued* before, after, or on a specified date, as well as within a range of dates. The following sample queries contain date restrictions:

da(2002) & wrongful! /s dishonor! /s damages
da(aft 1998) & bank /s liab! /s forg! /s signature
da(10/2/2000) & negotiat! /s bearer /s deliver!

You can also search for documents *added to a database* on or after a specified date, as well as within a range of dates. The following sample queries contain added-date restrictions:

ad(aft 1999) & "midnight deadline" /p settl!
ad(aft 12/31/2000 & bef 6/1/2002) & "payor bank" /p payment /s stop!

Section 6. Searching with Topic and Key Numbers

To retrieve cases that address a specific point of law, use topic and key numbers as your search terms. If you have an on-point case, run a search using the topic and key number from the relevant headnote in an appropriate database to find other cases containing headnotes classified to that topic and key number. For example, to search for state and federal cases containing headnotes classified under topic 56 (Bills and Notes) and key number 158 (Interest), access the Federal and State Case Law database (ALLCASES) and enter the following query:

56k158

For a complete list of West digest topics and their corresponding topic numbers, access the Custom Digest by choosing **Key Numbers and Digest** from the *More* drop-down list.

> *Note*: Slip opinions and cases from topical services do not contain West topic and key numbers.

Section 6.1   Custom Digest

The Custom Digest contains the complete topic and key number outline used by West attorney-editors to classify headnotes. You can use the Custom Digest to obtain a single document containing the case law headnotes that are related to your legal issue from a particular jurisdiction.

Access the Custom Digest by choosing **Key Numbers and Digest** from the *More* drop-down list on the toolbar. Select up to 10 topics and key numbers from the easy-to-browse outline and click **GO**. Then follow the on-screen instructions.

For example, to research issues involving negotiable instruments, scroll down the Custom Digest page until topic 56, *Bills and Notes*, is displayed. Click the plus symbol (+) to display key number information. Select the check box next to each key number you want to include in your search, then click **GO**. Select the jurisdiction from which you want to retrieve headnotes and, if desired, select a date restriction and type additional search terms. Click **Search**.

Section 6.2   KeySearch

KeySearch is a research tool that helps you find cases and secondary sources in a specific area of the law. KeySearch guides you through the selection of terms from a classification system based on the West Key Number System® and then uses the key numbers and their underlying concepts to formulate a query for you. To access KeySearch, click **KeySearch** on the toolbar. Then browse the list of topics and subtopics and select a topic or subtopic to search by clicking the hypertext links. For example, to search for cases that discuss an issue related to a holder in due course, click **Negotiable Instruments** below *Commercial Law and Contracts* at the first KeySearch page. Then click **Holder in due course** on the next page.

Section 7. Verifying Your Research with Citation Research Services

Overview: A citation research service, such as they KeyCite service, is a tool that helps you ensure that your cases are good law; helps you retrieve cases, legislation, or articles that cite a case, rule, or statute; and helps you verify that the spelling and format of your citations are correct.

7.1 KeyCite for Cases

KeyCite for cases covers case law on Westlaw, including unpublished opinions. KeyCite for cases provides

- direct appellate history of a case, including related references, which are opinions involving the same parties and facts but resolving different issues
- negative indirect history of a case, which consists of cases outside the direct appellate line that may have a negative impact on its precedential value
- the title, parallel citations, court of decision, docket number, and filing date of a case
- citations to cases, administrative decisions, and secondary sources on Westlaw that have cited a case
- complete integration with the West Key Number System so you can track legal issues discussed in a case

7.2 KeyCite for Statutes and Federal Regulations

KeyCite for statutes and federal regulations covers the *United States Code Annotated* (USCA®), the *Code of Federal Regulations* (CFR), and statutes from all 50 states. KeyCite for statutes provides

- links to session laws amending or repealing a statute
- statutory credits and historical notes
- citations to pending legislation affecting a federal statute or a statute from California or New York
- citations to cases, administrative decisions, and secondary sources that have cited a statute

7.3 KeyCite for Administrative Materials

KeyCite for administrative materials includes

- National Labor Relations Board decisions beginning with 1935
- Board of Contract Appeals decisions (varies by agency)
- Board of Immigration Appeals decisions beginning with 1940
- Comptroller General decisions beginning with 1921
- Environmental Protection Agency decisions beginning with 1974
- Federal Communications Commission decisions beginning with 1960

- Federal Energy Regulatory Commission (Federal Power Commission) decisions beginning with 1931 (history only)
- Internal Revenue Service revenue rulings beginning with 1954
- Internal Revenue Service revenue procedures beginning with 1954
- Internal Revenue Service private letter rulings beginning with 1954
- Internal Revenue Service technical advice memoranda beginning with 1954
- Public Utilities Reports beginning with 1974 (history only)
- U.S. Merit Systems Protection Board decisions beginning with 1979
- U.S. Patent and Trademark Office decisions beginning with 1987
- U.S. Tax Court (Board of Tax Appeals) decisions beginning with 1924
- U.S. patents beginning with 1976

7.4 KeyCite Alert

KeyCite Alert monitors the status of your cases or statutes and automatically sends you updates at the frequency you specify when their KeyCite information changes.

Section 8. Researching with Westlaw—Examples

8.1 Retrieving Law Review Articles

Recent law review articles are often a good place to begin researching a legal issue because law review articles serve 1) as an excellent introduction to a new topic or review for a stale one, providing terminology to help you formulate a query; 2) as a finding tool for pertinent primary authority, such as rules, statutes, and cases; and 3) in some instances, as persuasive secondary authority.

Suppose you need to gain background information on the relevance of negotiable instruments to modern payment systems.

Solution

- To retrieve recent law review articles relevant to your issue, access the Journals and Law Reviews database (JLR). Using the Natural Language search method, enter a description like the following:

    relevance of negotiable instruments law to modern payment systems

- If you have a citation to an article in a specific publication, use Find to retrieve it. For more information on Find, see Section 3.1 of this appendix. For example, to retrieve the article found at 44 UCLA L. Rev. 951, access Find and type

    44 ucla l rev 951

- If you know the title of an article but not which journal it appeared in, access the Journals and Law Reviews database (JLR) and search for key terms using the title field. For example, to retrieve the article

"The Holder in Due Course Doctrine As a Default Rule," type the following Terms and Connectors query:

ti(holder & doctrine & "default rule")

8.2 Retrieving Case Law

Suppose you need to retrieve state cases discussing bank liability for dishonoring a cashier's check.

Solution

- Access the Multistate Commercial Law and Contracts Cases database (MCML–CS). Type a Natural Language description such as the following:

bank liability for dishonoring cashier's check

- When you know the citation for a specific case, use Find to retrieve it. For more information on Find, see Section 3.1 of this appendix. For example, to retrieve *Flatiron Linen, Inc. v. First American State Bank*, 23 P.3d 1209 (Colo. 2001), access Find and type

23 p3d 1209

- If you find a topic and key number that is on point, run a search using that topic and key number to retrieve additional cases discussing that point of law. For example, to retrieve New York state cases containing headnotes classified under topic 56 (Bills and Notes) and key number 279 (Indorsement Unauthorized, Procured by Fraud, or Forged), access the New York Commercial Law and Contracts Cases database (NYCML–CS) and type the following query:

56k279

- To retrieve cases written by a particular judge, add a judge field (ju) restriction to your query. For example, to retrieve cases written by Judge Politz that contain headnotes classified under topic 56 (Bills and Notes), type the following query:

ju(politz) & to(56)

- You can also use KeySearch and the Custom Digest to help you retrieve cases and headnotes that discuss the issue you are researching.

8.3 Retrieving Statutes and Regulations

Suppose you need to retrieve Iowa statutes addressing stop-payment orders on checks.

Solution

- Access the Iowa Statutes–Annotated database(IA–ST–ANN). Search for your terms in the prelim and caption fields using the Terms and Connectors search method:

APPENDIX

pr,ca(stop! & payment)

- When you know the citation for a specific statute, regulation, or code section, use Find to retrieve it. For example, to retrieve North Carolina General Statute § 25–4–301, access Find and type

nc st s 25-4-301

- To look at surrounding sections, use the Table of Contents service. Click the **TOC** tab in the left frame. To display a section listed in the Table of Contents, click its hypertext link. You can also use Documents in Sequence to retrieve the section following section 25–4–301 even if that subsequent section was not retrieved with your search or Find request. Select **Docs in Seq** from the drop-down list at the bottom of the right frame and click **GO**.

- When you retrieve a statute on Westlaw, it will contain a message if legislation amending or repealing it is available online. To display this legislation, click the *KeyCite* link in the message.

> Because slip copy versions of laws are added to Westlaw before they contain full editorial enhancements, they are not retrieved with the update feature. To retrieve slip copy versions of laws, access the United States Public Laws database (US-PL) or a state's legislative service database (XX-LEGIS, where XX is the state's two-letter postal abbreviation). Then type **ci(slip)** and descriptive terms, e.g., **ci(slip) & "negotiable instrument"**. Slip copy documents are replaced by the editorially enhanced versions within a few working days. The update feature also does not retrieve legislation that enacts a new statute or covers a topic that will not be incorporated into the statutes. To retrieve this legislation, access US-PL or a legislative service database and enter a query containing terms that describe the new legislation.

8.4 Using KeyCite

Suppose one of the cases you retrieve in your case law research is *Menichini v. Grant*, 995 F.2d 1224 (3d Cir. 1993). You want to determine whether this case is good law and to find other cases or sources that have cited this case.

Solution

- Use KeyCite to retrieve direct and negative indirect history for *Menichini v. Grant*.
- Use KeyCite to display citing references for *Menichini v. Grant*.

8.5 Following Recent Developments

If you are researching issues related to modern payment systems, notes, or other commercial law issues, it is important to keep up with recent developments. How can you do this efficiently?

Solution

One of the easiest ways to follow recent developments in commercial law is to access the Westlaw Topical Highlights–Commercial Law database (WTH–CML). The WTH–CML database contains summaries of recent legal developments, including court decisions, legislation, and materials released by administrative agencies in the area of commercial law. Some summaries also contain suggested queries that combine the proven power of West's topic and key numbers and West's case headnotes to retrieve additional pertinent cases. When you access WTH–CML, you automatically retrieve a list of documents added to the database in the last two weeks.

You can also use the WestClip® clipping service to stay informed of recent developments of interest to you. WestClip will run your Terms and Connectors queries on a regular basis and deliver the results to you automatically. You can run WestClip queries in legal and news and information databases. More information about WestClip is available at **www.westgroup.com/documentation**.

Table of Cases

A

A. Alport & Son, Inc. v. Hotel Evans, Inc., 65 Misc.2d 374, 317 N.Y.S.2d 937 (N.Y.Sup.1970)—¶ **2.02, n. 205.**

Aarons v. Public Service Building & Loan Ass'n, 318 Pa. 113, 178 A. 141 (Pa. 1935)—¶ **9.06, n. 372.**

Abby Financial Corp. v. Margrove Mfg. Co., Inc., 5 UCC Rep. Serv. 1088 (N.Y.Sup. 1968)—¶ **4.02, n. 9.**

Abby Financial Corp. v. Weydig Auto Supplies Unlimited, Inc., 4 UCC Rep. Serv. 858 (N.Y.Sup.1967)—¶ **6.03, n. 281.**

Abilities, Inc. v. Citibank, N.A., 87 A.D.2d 831, 449 N.Y.S.2d 242 (N.Y.A.D. 2 Dept. 1982)—¶ **4.04, n. 169;** ¶ **9.01, n. 68.**

Abyaneh v. Merchants Bank, North, 670 F.Supp. 1298 (M.D.Pa.1987)—¶ **10.01, n. 3;** ¶ **10.03, n. 38;** ¶ **10.09, n. 176;** ¶ **11.02, n. 24.**

A.C. Davenport & Son Co. v. United States, 538 F.Supp. 730 (N.D.Ill.1982)—¶ **1.03, n. 158;** ¶ **3.03;** ¶ **3.03, n. 211, 279.**

A/C Elec. Co. v. Aetna Ins. Co., 251 Md. 410, 247 A.2d 708 (Md.1968)—¶ **5.01, n. 5.**

Ackmann v. Merchants Mortg. & Trust Corp., 659 P.2d 697 (Colo.App.1982)—¶ **3.03;** ¶ **3.03, n. 274, 281.**

Adamar of New Jersey, Inc. v. Chase Lincoln First Bank, N.A., 201 A.D.2d 174, 615 N.Y.S.2d 550 (N.Y.A.D. 4 Dept. 1994)—¶ **3.03, n. 269, 289;** ¶ **4.04, n. 169.**

Adam Intern. Trading Ltd. v. Manufacturers Hanover Trust Co., 150 A.D.2d 294, 542 N.Y.S.2d 1 (N.Y.A.D. 1 Dept.1989)—¶ **8.01, n. 67.**

Aeronautics and Astronautics Services v. First Palm Beach Intern. Bank, 471 So.2d 188 (Fla.App. 3 Dist.1985)—¶ **9.06, n. 383.**

Aetna Cas. & Sur. Co. v. Bank of New York, 22 UCC Rep. Serv.2d 813 (N.Y.Sup. 1993)—¶ **7.03, n. 175.**

Aetna Cas. & Sur. Co. v. Hepler State Bank, 6 Kan.App.2d 543, 630 P.2d 721 (Kan. App.1981)—¶ **4.02;** ¶ **4.02, n. 33.**

Agaliotis v. Agaliotis, 38 N.C.App. 42, 247 S.E.2d 28 (N.C.App.1978)—¶ **3.02, n. 122.**

Agfa–Gevaert, Inc. v. Bueding, 11 UCC Rep. Serv. 794 (Md. Dist.1972)—¶ **3.02;** ¶ **3.02, n. 127;** ¶ **5.02, n. 30.**

A.G. King Tree Surgeons v. Deeb, 140 N.J.Super. 346, 356 A.2d 87 (N.J.Dist. Ct.1976)—¶ **2.02, n. 160;** ¶ **7.01, n. 32.**

AgriStor Credit Corp. v. Lewellen, 472 F.Supp. 46 (N.D.Miss.1979)—¶ **6.02, n. 53.**

Ahmann v. American Federal Sav. and Loan Ass'n, 235 Mont. 184, 766 P.2d 853 (Mont.1988)—¶ **8.03, n. 224.**

Aiken v. Bank of Ga., 101 Ga.App. 200, 113 S.E.2d 405 (Ga.App.1960)—¶ **9.06, n. 324.**

Aimco Imports, Ltd. v. Industrial Valley Bank & Trust Co., 291 Pa.Super. 233, 435 A.2d 884 (Pa.Super.1981)—¶ **4.02, n. 12.**

Air Atlanta, Inc. v. National Bank of Georgia, Inc., 81 B.R. 724 (N.D.Ga.1987)—¶ **9.06, n. 385.**

Air Van Lines, Inc. v. Buster, 673 P.2d 774 (Alaska 1983)—¶ **7.01, n. 38.**

A.I. Trade Finance, Inc. v. Laminaciones de Lesaca, S.A., 41 F.3d 830 (2nd Cir. 1994)—¶ **3.03, n. 208.**

A.J. Armstrong Co. v. Janburt Embroidery Corp., 97 N.J.Super. 246, 234 A.2d 737 (N.J.Super.L.1967)—¶ **5.02, n. 50.**

Akin v. Dahl, 661 S.W.2d 914 (Tex.1983)—¶ **2.02, n. 179.**

Akron Auto Finance Co. v. Stonebraker, 66 Ohio App. 507, 35 N.E.2d 585 (Ohio App. 9 Dist.1941)—¶ **2.02, n. 71.**

Alamo Rent A Car v. Galarza, 306 N.J.Super. 384, 703 A.2d 961 (N.J.Super.A.D.1997)—¶ **11.02, n. 96.**

Alcoa Credit Co. v. Nickerson, 5 UCC Rep. Serv. 152 (Mass.App.Div.1968)—¶ **3.04, n. 422.**

Alcock, In re, 50 F.3d 1456 (9th Cir.1995)—¶ **6.03, n. 272.**

Aldens, Inc. v. Ryan, 571 F.2d 1159 (10th Cir.1978)—¶ **1.03, n. 108.**

Aleo Intern., Ltd. v. Citibank, N.A., 160 Misc.2d 950, 612 N.Y.S.2d 540 (N.Y.Sup. 1994)—¶ **10.04, n. 68.**

Alexander & Jones v. Sovran Bank, 905 F.2d 716 (4th Cir.1990)—¶ **9.05, n. 303.**

A.L. Jackson Chevrolet, Inc. v. Oxley, 564 P.2d 633 (Okla.1977)—¶ **5.03, n. 98, 100.**

TABLE OF CASES

All American Finance Co. v. Pugh Shows, Inc., 30 Ohio St.3d 130, 507 N.E.2d 1134 (Ohio 1987)—¶ **3.01, n. 25.**

Allen v. Crocker Nat. Bank, 733 F.2d 642 (9th Cir.1984)—¶ **1.03, n. 122.**

Allen Sales & Servicenter, Inc. v. Ryan, 525 S.W.2d 863 (Tex.1975)—¶ **4.05, n. 195.**

Allied Color Corp. v. Manufacturers Hanover Trust Co., 484 F.Supp. 881 (S.D.N.Y. 1980)—¶ **9.01, n. 5, 13; ¶ 9.02, n. 112.**

Allied Concord Financial Corp. v. Bank of America Nat. Trust & Sav. Ass'n, 275 Cal.App.2d 1, 80 Cal.Rptr. 622 (Cal.App. 2 Dist.1969)—¶ **7.03, n. 150.**

Allied Ins. Center, Inc. v. Wauwatosa Sav. and Loan Ass'n, 200 Wis.2d 369, 546 N.W.2d 544 (Wis.App.1996)—¶ **4.02, n. 34; ¶ 7.03, n. 145.**

Allied Sheet Metal Fabricators, Inc. v. Peoples Nat. Bank, 10 Wash.App. 530, 518 P.2d 734 (Wash.App. Div. 1 1974)—¶ **1.04, n. 217; ¶ 9.06, n. 351.**

Allied Stores v. Funderburke, 52 Misc.2d 872, 277 N.Y.S.2d 8 (N.Y.City Civ.Ct. 1967)—¶ **11.02, n. 70.**

All Lease Co. v. Bowen, 20 UCC Rep. Serv. 790 (Md.Cir.Ct.1975)—¶ **2.02, n. 75, 89.**

All Service Exportacao, Importacao Comercio, S.A. v. Banco Bamerindus Do Brazil, S.A., 921 F.2d 32 (2nd Cir.1990)—¶ **3.01, n. 32.**

Allyn–Mason, Inc. v. Kuehl, 10 UCC Rep. Serv. 675 (N.Y.Sup.1972)—¶ **4.06, n. 209.**

Alta Vista State Bank v. Kobliska, 897 F.2d 930 (8th Cir.1990)—¶ **3.03, n. 262; ¶ 8.01, n. 54; ¶ 9.03, n. 124; ¶ 9.05, n. 313.**

Alves v. Baldaia, 14 Ohio App.3d 187, 470 N.E.2d 459 (Ohio App. 6 Dist.1984)—¶ **2.02, n. 162.**

Amarillo Nat. Bank v. Dilday, 693 S.W.2d 38 (Tex.App.-Amarillo 1985)—¶ **2.01, n. 10.**

Ambassador Financial Services, Inc. v. Indiana Nat. Bank, 605 N.E.2d 746 (Ind. 1992)—¶ **7.03, n. 152.**

Ambassador Financial Services, Inc. v. Indiana Nat. Bank, 591 N.E.2d 1061 (Ind.App. 4 Dist.1992)—¶ **2.02, n. 262.**

Ambruster v. National Bank of Westfield, 182 A. 613 (N.J.Err. & App.1936)—¶ **9.05, n. 314.**

American Airlines Employees Federal Credit Union v. Martin, 29 S.W.3d 86 (Tex. 2002)—¶ **11.01, n. 8.**

Americana State Bank v. Jensen, 353 N.W.2d 652 (Minn.App.1984)—¶ **6.03, n. 275.**

American Bank & Trust Co. v. Sunbelt Environmental Systems, Inc., 451 So.2d 1111 (La.App. 1 Cir.1984)—¶ **3.03, n. 209.**

American Bank & Trust Co. v. Wallace, 702 F.2d 93 (6th Cir.1983)—¶ **9.05, n. 249.**

American Bankers Ass'n v. Connell, 447 F.Supp. 296 (D.D.C.1978)—¶ **9.04, n. 230.**

American Discount Corp. v. Glover, 391 So.2d 853 (La.App. 3 Cir.1980)—¶ **6.03, n. 268.**

American Exchange Bank, Collinsville, Okl. v. Cessna, 386 F.Supp. 494 (N.D.Okla. 1974)—¶ **3.03, n. 241; ¶ 5.03, n. 98.**

American Exp. Co. v. Vella, 94 N.J.Super. 258, 227 A.2d 721 (N.J.Super.A.D.1967)—¶ **9.06, n. 396.**

American Exp. Intern. Banking Corp. v. Sabet, 512 F.Supp. 463 (S.D.N.Y.1980)—¶ **6.03, n. 249.**

American Federal Sav. and Loan Ass'n v. Madison Valley Properties Inc., 288 Mont. 365, 958 P.2d 57 (Mont.1998)—¶ **7.01, n. 25.**

American Mach. Tool Distributors Ass'n v. National Permanent Federal Sav. and Loan Ass'n, 464 A.2d 907 (D.C.1983)—¶ **4.02, n. 34.**

American Nat. Bank in St. Louis v. Seidel, 622 S.W.2d 19 (Mo.App. E.D.1981)—¶ **3.02, n. 71, 107; ¶ 7.03, n. 154.**

American Nat. Bank & Trust Co. v. St. Joseph Valley Bank, 180 Ind.App. 546, 389 N.E.2d 379 (Ind.App. 4 Dist.1979)—¶ **3.02; ¶ 3.02, n. 62, 79.**

American Nat. Bank & Trust Co. of Chicago v. Scenic Stage Lines of Savanna, Inc., 2 Ill.App.3d 446, 276 N.E.2d 420 (Ill.App. 2 Dist.1971)—¶ **3.02, n. 72.**

American Nat. Ins. Co. v. Fidelity Bank, N. A., 691 F.2d 464 (10th Cir.1982)—¶ **4.02, n. 34.**

American Parkinson Disease Ass'n, Inc. v. First Nat. Bank of Northfield, 584 N.W.2d 437 (Minn.App.1998)—¶ **7.02, n. 67; ¶ 7.03, n. 143, 145.**

American Sec. Bank v. Kaneshiro, 67 Haw. 354, 688 P.2d 254 (Hawai'i 1984)—¶ **9.05, n. 251, 303.**

American Sec. Bank, N.A. v. American Motorists Ins. Co., 538 A.2d 736 (D.C. 1988)—¶ **9.03, n. 183.**

American State Bank v. Richendifer, 36 Or. App. 199, 584 P.2d 323 (Or.App.1978)—¶ **3.03, n. 202.**

American State Bank of Pierre v. Northwest South Dakota Production Credit Ass'n, 404 N.W.2d 517 (S.D.1987)—¶ **3.03, n. 240; ¶ 8.02, n. 169.**

American Title Ins. Co. v. Shawmut Bank of Rhode Island, N.A., 812 F.Supp. 301 (D.R.I.1993)—¶ **7.03, n. 178.**

American Travel Corp. v. Central Carolina Bank & Trust Co., 57 N.C.App. 437, 291 S.E.2d 892 (N.C.App.1982)—¶ **4.02, n. 18.**

American Underwriting Corp. v. Rhode Island Hospital Trust Co., 111 R.I. 415, 303 A.2d 121 (R.I.1973)—¶ **1.04, n. 231;**

¶ 2.02; ¶ 2.02, n. 171; ¶ 6.03; ¶ 6.03, n. 149.
American Viking Contractors, Inc. v. Scribner Equipment Co., Inc., 745 F.2d 1365 (11th Cir.1984)—¶ 5.02, n. 42.
Ameritrust Co., N.A. v. White, 73 F.3d 1553 (11th Cir.1996)—¶ 2.02, n. 75.
Amex–Protein Development Corp., In re, 504 F.2d 1056 (9th Cir.1974)—¶ 2.02, n. 87.
Ampex Corp. v. Appel Media, Inc., 374 F.Supp. 1114 (W.D.Pa.1974)—¶ 1.04, n. 230; ¶ 6.03, n. 153; ¶ 7.01, n. 32.
Anderson v. Consolidated Auto Wholesalers, Inc., 4 UCC Rep. Serv. 205 (N.Y.Sup.1967)—¶ 2.02, n. 141.
Anderson, Clayton & Co. v. Farmers Nat. Bank of Cordell, 624 F.2d 105 (10th Cir.1980)—¶ 4.04; ¶ 4.04, n. 170.
Anderson, Clayton & Co. v. First American Bank of Erick, 614 P.2d 1091 (Okla. 1980)—¶ 8.02, n. 104.
Andrew D. Taylor Trust v. Security Trust Federal Sav. and Loan Ass'n, 844 F.2d 337 (6th Cir.1988)—¶ 1.03, n. 133.
Anna Nat. Bank v. Wingate, 63 Ill.App.3d 676, 21 Ill.Dec. 84, 381 N.E.2d 19 (Ill. App. 5 Dist.1978)—¶ 5.01, n. 3; ¶ 5.02, n. 60.
Antweil, In re, 931 F.2d 689 (10th Cir. 1991)—¶ 9.01, n. 81.
Any Kind Checks Cashed, Inc. v. Talcott, 830 So.2d 160 (Fla.App.2002)—¶ 3.03, n. 253.
Apcoa, Inc. v. Fidelity Nat. Bank, 906 F.2d 610 (11th Cir.1990)—¶ 7.03, n. 189.
Appliance Buyers Credit Corp. v. Prospect Nat. Bank of Peoria, 708 F.2d 290 (7th Cir.1983)—¶ 3.02, n. 156; ¶ 8.01, n. 57; ¶ 8.03, n. 200, 207, 217; ¶ 8.04, n. 396, 491.
Arcanum Nat. Bank v. Hessler, 69 Ohio St.2d 549, 433 N.E.2d 204 (Ohio 1982)—¶ 3.04, n. 412.
Arkansas v. Pufahl, 52 F.2d 116 (8th Cir. 1931)—¶ 9.06, n. 330.
Arnd v. Aylesworth, 145 Iowa 185, 123 N.W. 1000 (Iowa 1909)—¶ 3.03; ¶ 3.03, n. 328.
Arnold v. United Companies Lending Corp., 204 W.Va. 229, 511 S.E.2d 854 (W.Va. 1998)—¶ 11.02, n. 94.
Arrow Industries, Inc. v. Zions First Nat. Bank, 767 P.2d 935 (Utah 1988)—¶ 8.01, n. 25; ¶ 9.03, n. 124.
Artistic Greetings, Inc. v. Sholom Greeting Card Co., 36 A.D.2d 68, 318 N.Y.S.2d 623 (N.Y.A.D. 3 Dept.1971)—¶ 6.03, n. 305.
Ashford v. Thos. Cook & Son (Bankers) Limited, 52 Haw. 113, 471 P.2d 530 (Hawai'i 1970)—¶ 2.01, n. 29.
Ashley–Hall Interiors, Ltd., Inc. v. Bank of New Orleans, 389 So.2d 850 (La.App. 4 Cir.1980)—¶ 4.02, n. 24.

Asian Intern., Ltd. v. Merrill Lynch, Pierce, Fenner and Smith, Inc., 435 So.2d 1058 (La.App. 1 Cir.1983)—¶ 1.01, n. 27; ¶ 3.01, n. 34; ¶ 8.01, n. 48; ¶ 9.04, n. 237.
Aspinall v. United States, 984 F.2d 355 (10th Cir.1993)—¶ 9.05, n. 286.
Associated Carriages, Inc. v. International Bank of Commerce, 37 S.W.3d 69 (Tex. App.-San Antonio 2000)—¶ 4.04, n. 169, 177; ¶ 7.01, n. 26; ¶ 9.01, n. 62, 65, 68.
Associates Home Equity Services, Inc. v. Troup, 343 N.J.Super. 254, 778 A.2d 529 (App.Div.2001)—¶ 3.04, n. 425.
Atherton v. Federal Deposit Ins. Corporation, 519 U.S. 213, 117 S.Ct. 666, 136 L.Ed.2d 656 (1997)—¶ 1.03, n. 142.
Atlantic Bank of New York v. Israel Discount Bank Ltd., 108 Misc.2d 342, 441 N.Y.S.2d 315 (N.Y.Sup.App.Term 1981)—¶ 7.03, n. 152.
Atlantic Cement Co., Inc. v. South Shore Bank, 730 F.2d 831 (1st Cir.1984)—¶ 4.04, n. 144.
Atlantic Mut. Ins. Co. v. The Provident Bank, 79 Ohio Misc.2d 5, 669 N.E.2d 901 (Ohio Mun.1996)—¶ 4.02, n. 24.
Atlas Steel Corp. v. Steel Fabricators & Erectors, Inc., 12 UCC Rep. Serv. 910 (Mass.App.Div.1973)—¶ 2.02, n. 45.
Available Iron & Metal Co. v. First Nat. Bank of Blue Island, 56 Ill.App.3d 516, 13 Ill.Dec. 940, 371 N.E.2d 1032 (Ill. App. 1 Dist.1977)—¶ 4.03; ¶ 4.03, n. 113.
Averon v. First Nat. City Bank, 23 UCC Rep. Serv. 402 (N.Y.Sup.1978)—¶ 7.03, n. 146.

B

Badie v. Bank of America, 79 Cal.Rptr.2d 273 (Cal.App. 1 Dist.1998)—¶ 8.01, n. 46; ¶ 9.03, n. 155; ¶ 9.05, n. 271.
Bagby v. Merrill Lynch, Pierce, Fenner & Smith, Inc., 491 F.2d 192 (8th Cir. 1974)—¶ 4.02, n. 27.
Baker v. Baker, 710 P.2d 129 (Okla.App. Div. 2 1985)—¶ 9.06, n. 400.
Ballengee v. New Mexico Federal Sav. & Loan Ass'n, 109 N.M. 423, 786 P.2d 37 (N.M.1990)—¶ 3.01, n. 11.
Bamberg v. Griffin, 76 Ill.App.3d 138, 31 Ill.Dec. 708, 394 N.E.2d 910 (Ill.App. 2 Dist.1979)—¶ 3.03; ¶ 3.03, n. 231.
Banca Commerciale Italiana, New York Branch v. Northern Trust Intern. Banking Corp., 160 F.3d 90 (2nd Cir.1998)—¶ 10.04, n. 68.
Banca Commerciale Italianan, New York Branch v. Northern Trust Intern. Banking Corp., 1997 WL 217591 (S.D.N.Y. 1997)—¶ 10.08, n. 172.

TABLE OF CASES

Banco De La Provincia De Buenos Aires v. BayBank Boston N.A., 985 F.Supp. 364 (S.D.N.Y.1997)—¶ **10.04, n. 71.**

Banco Ganadero Y Agricola, S.A. v. Society Nat. Bank, 418 F.Supp. 520 (N.D.Ohio 1976)—¶ **2.04, n. 271.**

BancoKentucky Co.'s Receiver v. National Bank of Kentucky's Receiver, 281 Ky. 784, 137 S.W.2d 357 (Ky.1939)—¶ **9.06, n. 331.**

Banco Mercantil De Sao Paulo S.A. v. Nava, 120 Misc.2d 517, 466 N.Y.S.2d 198 (N.Y.Sup.1983)—¶ **7.02, n. 95.**

Bankers Trust Co. v. Javeri, 105 A.D.2d 638, 481 N.Y.S.2d 362 (N.Y.A.D. 1 Dept. 1984)—¶ **5.03, n. 86.**

Bankers Trust Co. v. Litton Systems, Inc., 599 F.2d 488 (2nd Cir.1979)—¶ **6.02; ¶ 6.02, n. 52.**

Bankers Trust Co., United States v., 17 UCC Rep. Serv. 136 (E.D.N.Y.1975)—¶ **4.02, n. 32.**

Bankers Trust Co. of Western New York v. Crawford, 781 F.2d 39 (3rd Cir.1986)—¶ **3.04, n. 412.**

Bankers Trust (Delaware) v. 236 Beltway Inv., 865 F.Supp. 1186 (E.D.Va.1994)—¶ **2.01, n. 10; ¶ 3.04, n. 390.**

Bank IV Topeka, N.A. v. Topeka Bank & Trust Co., 15 Kan.App.2d 341, 807 P.2d 686 (Kan.App.1991)—¶ **9.05, n. 245; ¶ 9.06, n. 408.**

Bank Leumi Trust Co. of New York v. Bally's Park Place, Inc., 528 F.Supp. 349 (S.D.N.Y.1981)—¶ **8.02; ¶ 8.02, n. 113, 161, 167.**

Bank of America v. Superior Court, 4 Cal. App.3d 435, 84 Cal.Rptr. 421 (Cal.App. 4 Dist.1970)—¶ **5.02, n. 15.**

Bank of America Nat. Trust & Sav. Ass'n v. Edgins (Edgins, In re), 36 B.R. 480 (9th Cir.1984)—¶ **9.06, n. 385.**

Bank of America Nat. Trust & Sav. Ass'n v. Liberty Nat. Bank & Trust Co., 116 F.Supp. 233 (W.D.Okla.1953)—¶ **9.06, n. 392, 394.**

Bank of America Nat. Trust & Sav. Ass'n v. Security Pacific Nat. Bank, 23 Cal. App.3d 638, 100 Cal.Rptr. 438 (Cal.App. 5 Dist.1972)—¶ **1.04, n. 226; ¶ 4.04, n. 151.**

Bank of America Nat. Trust & Sav. Ass'n v. United States, 552 F.2d 302 (9th Cir. 1977)—¶ **1.03; ¶ 1.03, n. 156.**

Bank of America Nat. Trust & Sav. Ass'n, United States v., 438 F.2d 1213 (9th Cir.1971)—¶ **1.03, n. 127.**

Bank of Celina, United States v., 721 F.2d 163 (6th Cir.1983)—¶ **9.06, n. 320, 325.**

Bank of Commerce & Trust Co. v. Dye, 1 Tenn.App. 486 (Tenn.Ct.App.1926)—¶ **9.05, n. 307.**

Bank of Glen Burnie v. Loyola Federal Sav. Bank, 336 Md. 331, 648 A.2d 453 (Md. 1994)—¶ **7.02, n. 95.**

Bank of Jamestown v. Cattaraugus County Bank, 148 Misc. 655, 266 N.Y.S. 622 (N.Y.Sup.1933)—¶ **9.06, n. 318.**

Bank of Marin v. England, 385 U.S. 99, 87 S.Ct. 274, 17 L.Ed.2d 197 (1966)—¶ **9.01; ¶ 9.01, n. 77; ¶ 9.05, n. 286.**

Bank of Metropolis v. New England Bank, 42 U.S. 234, 1 How. 234, 11 L.Ed. 115 (1843)—¶ **9.06, n. 319.**

Bank of Miami v. Banco Indus. Y Ganadero Del Beni, S.A., 515 So.2d 1038 (Fla.App. 3 Dist.1987)—¶ **4.03, n. 59; ¶ 8.02, n. 134; ¶ 9.03, n. 154.**

Bank of Miami v. Florida City Express, Inc., 367 So.2d 683 (Fla.App. 3 Dist.1979)—¶ **6.03, n. 206.**

Bank of Montreal v. Clark, 108 Ill.App. 163 (Ill.App. 1 Dist.1903)—¶ **9.06, n. 397.**

Bank of New Effington v. Thompson, 502 P.2d 978 (Colo.App.1972)—¶ **6.03, n. 133, 306.**

Bank of New York v. Bersani, 90 A.D.2d 302, 457 N.Y.S.2d 142 (N.Y.A.D. 4 Dept. 1982)—¶ **6.03, n. 298.**

Bank of New York v. Welz, 118 Misc.2d 645, 460 N.Y.S.2d 867 (N.Y.Sup.1983)—¶ **4.04, n. 179; ¶ 6.03, n. 222.**

Bank of Southern Maryland v. Robertson's Crab House, Inc., 39 Md.App. 707, 389 A.2d 388 (Md.App.1978)—¶ **7.03, n. 118.**

Bank of Spartanburg v. Mahon, 78 S.C. 408, 59 S.E. 31 (S.C.1907)—¶ **9.06, n. 355.**

Bank of Statesville v. Blackwelder Furniture Co., 11 N.C.App. 530, 181 S.E.2d 785 (N.C.App.1971)—¶ **3.03, n. 322.**

Bank of St. Helens v. Clayton Bank, 502 S.W.2d 449 (Mo.App.1973)—¶ **7.02, n. 100.**

Bank of Suffolk County v. Kite, 427 N.Y.S.2d 782, 404 N.E.2d 1323 (N.Y. 1980)—¶ **2.02, n. 176; ¶ 6.01, n. 26.**

Bank of Viola v. Nestrick, 72 Ill.App.3d 276, 28 Ill.Dec. 469, 390 N.E.2d 636 (Ill.App. 3 Dist.1979)—¶ **2.02, n. 186.**

Bank of Waverly v. City Bank & Trust Co., 600 S.W.2d 630 (Mo.App. W.D.1980)—¶ **3.01; ¶ 3.01, n. 7, 52.**

Bank of West Orange v. Associates Discount Corp., 197 So.2d 858 (Fla.App. 4 Dist. 1967)—¶ **9.05, n. 252.**

Bank of Winter Park v. Resolution Trust Corp., 633 So.2d 53 (Fla.App. 5 Dist. 1994)—¶ **9.06, n. 372.**

Bank of Wyandotte v. Woodrow, 394 F.Supp. 550 (W.D.Mo.1975)—¶ **4.03, n. 108; ¶ 6.03, n. 91.**

Bank One, Merrillville, NA v. Northern Trust Bank/DuPage, 775 F.Supp. 266 (N.D.Ill.1991)—¶ **4.04, n. 169.**

Bank One of Columbus, NA v. Myers, 14 Ohio App.3d 196, 470 N.E.2d 485 (Ohio App. 10 Dist.1984)—¶ **3.04, n. 418.**

TABLE OF CASES

Bank Polska Kasa Opieki, S.A. v. Pamrapo Sav. Bank, S.L.A., 909 F.Supp. 948 (D.N.J.1995)—¶ **7.03, n. 123, 134.**

Banque Arabe Et Internationale D'Investissement v. Maryland Nat. Bank, 819 F.Supp. 1282 (S.D.N.Y.1993)—¶ **9.05, n. 284.**

Banque Worms v. BankAmerica Intern., 928 F.2d 538 (2nd Cir.1991)—¶ **10.04, n. 72.**

Banque Worms v. BankAmerica Intern., 568 N.Y.S.2d 541, 570 N.E.2d 189 (N.Y. 1991)—¶ **10.04, n. 72;** ¶ **10.08, n. 169.**

Banque Worms v. Bank America Intern., 726 F.Supp. 940 (S.D.N.Y.1989)—¶ **10.09, n. 199.**

Barber v. United States Nat. Bank of Oregon, 90 Or.App. 68, 750 P.2d 1183 (Or. App.1988)—¶ **3.01, n. 36;** ¶ **4.04, n. 144;** ¶ **7.02, n. 104.**

Barber v. White, 46 N.C.App. 110, 264 S.E.2d 385 (N.C.App.1980)—¶ **7.01, n. 39.**

Barclays Bank of New York, N.A., State v., 561 N.Y.S.2d 697, 563 N.E.2d 11 (N.Y. 1990)—¶ **7.03, n. 134.**

Barclays Discount Bank Ltd. v. Levy, 743 F.2d 722 (9th Cir.1984)—¶ **1.03, n. 117.**

Barden & Robeson Corp. v. Ferrusi, 52 A.D.2d 1061, 384 N.Y.S.2d 596 (N.Y.A.D. 4 Dept.1976)—¶ **2.02, n. 168.**

Barden & Robeson Corp. v. Tompkins County Trust Co., 67 Misc.2d 587, 324 N.Y.S.2d 543 (N.Y.Sup.1971)—¶ **3.02, n. 104.**

Barnhill v. Johnson, 503 U.S. 393, 112 S.Ct. 1386, 118 L.Ed.2d 39 (1992)—¶ **4.04, n. 145;** ¶ **7.01, n. 4;** ¶ **9.01, n. 81.**

Bar–Ram Irr. Products v. Phenix–Girard Bank, 779 F.2d 1501 (11th Cir.1986)—¶ **8.03, n. 196.**

Barsco, Inc. v. H.W.W., Inc., 346 So.2d 134 (Fla.App. 1 Dist.1977)—¶ **9.06, n. 372.**

Barton v. Hudson, 560 S.W.2d 20 (Ky.App. 1977)—¶ **9.06, n. 400.**

Barton v. Scott Hudgens Realty & Mortg., Inc., 136 Ga.App. 565, 222 S.E.2d 126 (Ga.App.1975)—¶ **2.02, n. 234.**

Bartoni–Corsi Produce, Inc., In re, 130 F.3d 857 (9th Cir.1997)—¶ **7.02, n. 67.**

Basse Truck Line, Inc. v. First State Bank, Bandera, Texas, 949 S.W.2d 17 (Tex. App.-San Antonio 1997)—¶ **7.03, n. 177.**

Batchelder v. Granite Trust Co., 339 Mass. 20, 157 N.E.2d 540 (Mass.1959)—¶ **4.03, n. 89.**

Bates v. City of New York, 10 UCC Rep. Serv. 151 (N.Y.Sup.1971)—¶ **3.02, n. 118.**

Batten v. Bank One, N.A., 2000 WL 1364408 (N.D.Ill.2000)—¶ **9.01, n. 29;** ¶ **9.02, n. 95;** ¶ **9.05, n. 297.**

Baumann v. Savers Federal Sav. & Loan Ass'n, 934 F.2d 1506 (11th Cir.1991)—¶ **1.03, n. 134.**

Baylor v. Jordan, 445 So.2d 254 (Ala. 1984)—¶ **9.05, n. 308.**

BBMS, Inc. v. Brown, 251 Ga. 409, 306 S.E.2d 288 (Ga.1983)—¶ **9.06, n. 370.**

BCCI Holdings (Luxembourg), S.A., United States v., 977 F.Supp. 20 (D.D.C.1997)—¶ **10.02, n. 8.**

BCCI Holdings (Luxembourg), S.A., United States v., 980 F.Supp. 2 (D.D.C.1997)—¶ **10.02, n. 8.**

BCCI Holdings (Luxembourg), S.A., United States v., 980 F.Supp. 515 (D.D.C. 1997)—¶ **10.02, n. 12.**

BCCI Holdings (Luxembourg), S.A., United States v., 980 F.Supp. 507 (D.D.C. 1997)—¶ **10.02, n. 12.**

BCCI Holdings (Luxembourg) S.A., United States v., 956 F.Supp. 5 (D.D.C.1997)—¶ **10.02, n. 8.**

BCCI Holdings (Luxembourg), S.A., United States v., 814 F.Supp. 106 (D.D.C. 1993)—¶ **10.02, n. 8, 12.**

B & C Enterprises v. Utter, 88 Nev. 433, 498 P.2d 1327 (Nev.1972)—¶ **2.02, n. 57.**

Beal Bank, S.S.B. v. Caddo Parish–Villas South, Ltd., 218 B.R. 851 (N.D.Tex. 1998)—¶ **3.01, n. 19.**

Becker v. National Bank & Trust Co., 222 Va. 716, 284 S.E.2d 793 (Va.1981)—¶ **3.01, n. 24;** ¶ **3.02, n. 88.**

Beehive State Bank v. Rosquist, 21 Utah 2d 17, 439 P.2d 468 (Utah 1968)—¶ **9.06, n. 401.**

Behavioral Health and Wellness, Inc. v. FDIC, 802 So.2d 374 (Fla.Dist.Ct.App. 2001)—¶ **8.01, n. 65;** ¶ **9.01, n. 62, 65, 68.**

Beighley v. Federal Deposit Ins. Corporation, 868 F.2d 776 (5th Cir.1989)—¶ **1.03, n. 133.**

Belknap, Inc., In re, 909 F.2d 879 (6th Cir.1990)—¶ **9.01, n. 81.**

Bell & Murphy and Associates v. Interfirst Bank Gateway, N.A., 894 F.2d 750 (5th Cir.1990)—¶ **1.03, n. 130, 155.**

Beneficial Finance Co. of Jamestown v. Lawrence, 301 N.W.2d 114 (N.D.1980)—¶ **6.03, n. 274.**

Beneficial Finance Co. of New York, Inc. v. Husner, 82 Misc.2d 550, 369 N.Y.S.2d 975 (N.Y.Sup.1975)—¶ **6.03, n. 264.**

Bennett v. Cannon, 114 Ga.App. 479, 151 S.E.2d 828 (Ga.App.1966)—¶ **3.02, n. 117.**

Bennett v. First Nat. Bank of Humboldt, Iowa, 443 F.2d 518 (8th Cir.1971)—¶ **9.05, n. 277.**

Bergren v. Davis, 287 F.Supp. 52 (D.Conn. 1968)—¶ **2.03, n. 268.**

Berman v. United States Nat. Bank, 197 Neb. 268, 249 N.W.2d 187 (Neb.1976)—¶ **2.04, n. 292.**

Berryfast, Inc. v. Zeinfeld, 714 F.2d 826 (8th Cir.1983)—¶ **5.03, n. 103.**

TABLE OF CASES

Beshara v. Southern Nat. Bank, 928 P.2d 280 (Okla.1996)—¶ **9.03, n. 122, 132, 135.**

Best v. United States Nat. Bank of Oregon, 78 Or.App. 1, 714 P.2d 1049 (Or.App. 1986)—¶ **9.03, n. 137.**

Best Fertilizers of Arizona, Inc. v. Burns, 117 Ariz. 178, 571 P.2d 675 (Ariz.App. Div. 2 1977)—¶ **6.03**; ¶ **6.03, n. 189.**

B.F. Goodrich Employees (Patterson, In re), 967 F.2d 505 (11th Cir.1992)—¶ **9.06, n. 385.**

Bidwell & Co. v. National Union Fire Ins. Co. of Pittsburgh, PA., 44 UCC Rep. Serv. 2d 221 (D.Or.2001)—¶ **7.02, n. 61.**

Bigger v. Fremont Nat. Bank & Trust Co., 215 Neb. 580, 340 N.W.2d 142 (Neb. 1983)—¶ **4.04, n. 144.**

Bijlani v. Nationsbank of Florida, N.A., 25 UCC Rep. Serv. 2d 1165 (Fla.Cir.Ct. 1995)—¶ **2.02, n. 262.**

Billingsley v. Kelly, 261 Md. 116, 274 A.2d 113 (Md.1971)—¶ **3.01, n. 11.**

Bisson v. Eck, 430 Mass. 406, 720 N.E.2d 784 (Mass.1999)—¶ **3.03, n. 347.**

Black v. Hart, 301 So.2d 787 (Fla.App. 3 Dist.1974)—¶ **9.01, n. 84.**

Blake v. Coates, 292 Ala. 351, 294 So.2d 433 (Ala.1974)—¶ **6.03**; ¶ **6.03, n. 158.**

Blake v. Woodford Bank & Trust Co., 555 S.W.2d 589 (Ky.App.1977)—¶ **8.03**; ¶ **8.03, n. 222.**

Blottner, Derrico, Weiss & Hoffman, P.C. v. Fier, 101 Misc.2d 371, 420 N.Y.S.2d 999 (N.Y.City Civ.Ct.1979)—¶ **7.01, n. 37.**

Bluffestone v. Abrahams, 125 Ariz. 42, 607 P.2d 25 (Ariz.App. Div. 2 1979)—¶ **6.02**; ¶ **6.02, n. 79**; ¶ **6.03**; ¶ **6.03, n. 158.**

Blum Bros. v. Girard Nat. Bank, 248 Pa. 148, 93 A. 940 (Pa.1915)—¶ **9.06, n. 345.**

Board of Ed. of School Dist. No. 148, Cook County v. County of Cook, 42 Ill.App.2d 91, 191 N.E.2d 444 (Ill.App. 1 Dist. 1963)—¶ **9.05, n. 242.**

Boardwalk Marketplace Securities Litigation, In re, 849 F.2d 89 (2nd Cir.1988)—¶ **2.02, n. 232.**

Bobby D. Associates v. DiMarcantonio, 751 A.2d 673 (Pa.Super.2000)—¶ **3.01, n. 19.**

Bon Bon Productions, Ltd. v. Xanadu Productions, Inc., 1981 WL 138017 (D.Mass. 1981)—¶ **8.02, n. 142.**

Bonhiver v. State Bank of Clearing, 29 Ill. App.3d 794, 331 N.E.2d 390 (Ill.App. 1 Dist.1975)—¶ **9.06, n. 325, 356.**

Bottrell v. American Bank, 237 Mont. 1, 773 P.2d 694 (Mont.1989)—¶ **9.06, n. 343.**

Boutros v. Riggs Nat. Bank, D. C., 655 F.2d 1257 (D.C.Cir.1981)—¶ **9.03, n. 161.**

Bowen v. Danna, 276 Ark. 528, 637 S.W.2d 560 (Ark.1982)—¶ **2.02, n. 152.**

Bowen v. Federal Deposit Ins. Corporation, 915 F.2d 1013 (5th Cir.1990)—¶ **1.03, n. 133.**

Bowles v. City Nat. Bank & Trust Co. of Oklahoma City, 537 P.2d 1219 (Okla. App. Div. 2 1975)—¶ **6.03, n. 241.**

Bowling Green, Inc. v. State St. Bank & Trust Co., 425 F.2d 81 (1st Cir.1970)—¶ **1.04**; ¶ **1.04, n. 223**; ¶ **3.01**; ¶ **3.01, n. 31**; ¶ **3.02**; ¶ **3.02, n. 77**; ¶ **3.03**; ¶ **3.03, n. 281, 354**; ¶ **8.01**; ¶ **8.01, n. 9, 10.**

Boyles v. Oklahoma Natural Gas Co., 619 P.2d 613 (Okla.1980)—¶ **8.04, n. 482**; ¶ **9.03, n. 184.**

Braden Corp. v. Citizens Nat. Bank of Evansville, 661 N.E.2d 838 (Ind.App. 1996)—¶ **5.03, n. 98.**

Bradford Trust Co. v. Texas American Bank–Houston, 790 F.2d 407 (5th Cir. 1986)—¶ **2.02, n. 64**; ¶ **10.03, n. 38**; ¶ **10.09, n. 191**; ¶ **11.03, n. 131.**

Brady v. American Nat. Bank, 120 Okla. 159, 250 P. 1006 (Okla.1926)—¶ **9.06, n. 370.**

Brames v. Crates, 399 N.E.2d 437 (Ind.App. 3 Dist.1980)—¶ **6.01, n. 33.**

Branch Banking and Trust Co. v. Creasy, 44 N.C.App. 289, 260 S.E.2d 782 (N.C.App.1979)—¶ **3.03**; ¶ **3.03, n. 272.**

Brandywine Associates, In re, 30 UCC Rep. Serv. 1369 (Bkrtcy.E.D.Pa.1980)—¶ **9.02**; ¶ **9.02, n. 124.**

Brannon v. Langston, 375 So.2d 231 (Miss. 1979)—¶ **6.03, n. 247.**

Braun v. C. E. P. C. Distributors, Inc., 77 A.D.2d 358, 433 N.Y.S.2d 447 (N.Y.A.D. 1 Dept.1980)—¶ **7.01, n. 34.**

Breslin v. New Jersey Investors, Inc., 70 N.J. 466, 361 A.2d 1 (N.J.1976)—¶ **3.03, n. 253.**

Briand v. Wild, 110 N.H. 373, 268 A.2d 896 (N.H.1970)—¶ **3.03, n. 308**; ¶ **6.03**; ¶ **6.03, n. 150.**

Brighton, Inc. v. Colonial First Nat. Bank, 176 N.J.Super. 101, 422 A.2d 433 (N.J.Super.A.D.1980)—¶ **1.04**; ¶ **1.04, n. 224**; ¶ **7.03, n. 122.**

Brite Lite Lamps Corp. v. Manufacturers Hanover Trust Co., 34 UCC Rep. Serv. 1221 (N.Y.Sup.1982)—¶ **4.02, n. 32**; ¶ **7.03, n. 136.**

Broadview Lumber Co., Inc., In re, 118 F.3d 1246 (8th Cir.1997)—¶ **3.03, n. 295, 302.**

Broadway Management Corp. v. Briggs, 30 Ill.App.3d 403, 332 N.E.2d 131 (Ill.App. 4 Dist.1975)—¶ **2.02, n. 107, 230.**

Broadway Nat. Bank v. Barton–Russell Corp., 154 Misc.2d 181, 585 N.Y.S.2d 933 (N.Y.Sup.1992)—¶ **11.01, n. 3.**

Brock v. Adams, 79 N.M. 17, 439 P.2d 234 (N.M.1968)—¶ **2.02, n. 163.**

Brooks v. First Federal Sav. and Loan Ass'n of Sylacauga, 726 So.2d 640 (Ala.1998)—¶ **10.01, n. 4.**

TABLE OF CASES

Brooks v. McCorkle, 174 Ga.App. 132, 329 S.E.2d 214 (Ga.App.1985)—¶ **2.02, n. 178.**

Brower v. Franklin Nat. Bank, 311 F.Supp. 675 (S.D.N.Y.1970)—¶ **4.04, n. 187.**

Brower v. Gateway 2000, Inc., 246 A.D.2d 246, 676 N.Y.S.2d 569 (N.Y.A.D. 1 Dept. 1998)—¶ **11.02, n. 94.**

Brown v. Arcuri, 43 A.D.2d 993, 352 N.Y.S.2d 254 (N.Y.A.D. 3 Dept.1974)—¶ **5.02; ¶ 5.02, n. 65.**

Brown v. Eastman Nat. Bank of Newkirk, 291 P.2d 828 (Okla.1955)—¶ **9.03, n. 123.**

Brown v. Maguire's Real Estate Agency, 343 Mo. 336, 121 S.W.2d 754 (Mo. 1938)—¶ **9.06, n. 320.**

Brown v. South Shore Nat. Bank of Chicago, 1 Ill.App.3d 136, 273 N.E.2d 671 (Ill.App. 1 Dist.1971)—¶ **4.04, n. 142.**

Brown, for Use of Buck v. First Nat. Bank, 271 Ill.App. 424 (Ill.App. 1 Dist.1933)—¶ **9.06, n. 403.**

Brown & Williamson Tobacco Corp. v. First Nat. Bank, 504 F.2d 998 (7th Cir. 1974)—¶ **9.06, n. 368, 383.**

Bruer v. Sanford Atlantic Nat. Bank, 247 So.2d 764 (Fla.App. 4 Dist.1971)—¶ **5.02, n. 61.**

Brunswick Corp. v. Briscoe, 523 S.W.2d 115 (Mo.App.1975)—¶ **3.01, n. 19; ¶ 6.03, n. 247.**

Bryan v. Bartlett, 435 F.2d 28 (8th Cir. 1970)—¶ **2.05, n. 303.**

Bryant v. Williams, 16 F.2d 159 (E.D.N.C. 1926)—¶ **9.06, n. 393.**

Bryant Heating & Air Conditioning Co., Inc. v. United States Nat. Bank of Omaha, 216 Neb. 107, 342 N.W.2d 191 (Neb. 1983)—¶ **7.03, n. 132.**

Buckeye Fed. S. & L. Assn. v. Guirlinger, 62 Ohio St.3d 312, 581 N.E.2d 1352 (Ohio 1991)—¶ **2.02, n. 194; ¶ 6.03, n. 265.**

Buckley v. Trenton Saving Fund Soc., 111 N.J. 355, 544 A.2d 857 (N.J.1988)—¶ **9.02, n. 101.**

Buford v. American Finance Co., 333 F.Supp. 1243 (N.D.Ga.1971)—¶ **11.03, n. 123.**

Bulakowski v. Philadelphia Sav. Fund Soc., 270 Pa. 538, 113 A. 553 (Pa.1921)—¶ **9.05, n. 294.**

Burke v. Burke, 89 Ill.App.3d 826, 45 Ill. Dec. 71, 412 N.E.2d 204 (Ill.App. 2 Dist. 1980)—¶ **5.02, n. 42.**

Burkett v. Finger Lake Development Corp., 32 Ill.App.3d 396, 336 N.E.2d 628 (Ill. App. 5 Dist.1975)—¶ **2.02, n. 56.**

Burrus v. Farmers Bank of Nicholasville, 938 S.W.2d 889 (Ky.App.1997)—¶ **5.03, n. 85.**

Bursey v. CFX Bank, 145 N.H. 126, 756 A.2d 1001 (N.H.2000)—¶ **7.03, n. 131, 152; ¶ 8.03, n. 232; ¶ 9.02, n. 100.**

Byer v. Canadian Bank of Commerce, 57 P.2d 985 (Cal.App. 2 Dist.1936)—¶ **9.05, n. 301.**

C

Cagle v. Loyd, 617 So.2d 592 (La.App. 3 Cir.1993)—¶ **9.05, n. 284.**

Cairo Co-op. Exchange v. First Nat. Bank of Cunningham, 228 Kan. 613, 620 P.2d 805 (Kan.1980)—¶ **3.02; ¶ 3.02, n. 170.**

Calfo v. D.C. Stewart Co., 717 P.2d 697 (Utah 1986)—¶ **2.02, n. 121.**

C.A.L., Inc. v. Worth, 813 S.W.2d 12 (Mo. App. W.D.1991)—¶ **7.03, n. 134.**

Calumet Farm, Inc., In re, 114 F.3d 1186 (6th Cir.1997)—¶ **10.04, n. 57.**

Calvert Credit Corp. v. Humble, 249 A.2d 518 (D.C.App.1969)—¶ **6.01; ¶ 6.01, n. 7.**

Campbell Leasing, Inc. v. Federal Deposit Ins. Corporation, 901 F.2d 1244 (5th Cir.1990)—¶ **1.03, n. 130, 142, 152.**

Campion v. Wynn, 486 N.E.2d 543 (Ind. App. 4 Dist.1985)—¶ **5.03, n. 84.**

Canadian Imperial Bank of Commerce v. Federal Reserve Bank, 64 Misc.2d 959, 316 N.Y.S.2d 507 (N.Y.Sup.1970)—¶ **7.02, n. 104.**

Canal–Randolph Anaheim, Inc. v. Wilkoski, 78 Cal.App.3d 477, 144 Cal.Rptr. 474 (Cal.App. 4 Dist.1978)—¶ **7.01, n. 9.**

Canal–Randolph Anaheim, Inc. v. Wilkoski, 78 Cal.App.3d 477, 143 Cal.Rptr. 789 (Cal.App. 4 Dist.1978)—¶ **4.03, n. 135.**

Canfield v. Banc One, Texas, N.A., 51 S.W.2d 828 (Tex.App.2001)—¶ **8.01, n. 30; ¶ 9.03, n. 144, 159.**

Cantonwine v. Fehling, 582 P.2d 592 (Wyo. 1978)—¶ **6.03, n. 244.**

Capital Bank and Trust Co. v. Lacey, 393 So.2d 668 (La.1980)—¶ **3.04, n. 425.**

Capital City First Nat. Bank v. Lewis State Bank, 341 So.2d 1025 (Fla.App. 1 Dist. 1977)—¶ **4.03, n. 88, 93.**

Capital Investors Co. v. Executors of Morrison's Estate, 484 F.2d 1157 (4th Cir. 1973)—¶ **3.03, n. 354; ¶ 6.03, n. 94.**

Capital Services v. Dahlinger Pontiac–Cadillac, Inc., 10 Kan.App.2d 328, 699 P.2d 549 (Kan.App.1985)—¶ **9.05, n. 251, 303.**

Carelli v. Hall, 279 Mont. 202, 926 P.2d 756 (Mont.1996)—¶ **4.02, n. 3.**

Carnival Leisure Industries, Ltd. v. Aubin, 830 F.Supp. 371 (S.D.Tex.1993)—¶ **2.04, n. 300; ¶ 2.05, n. 310; ¶ 3.03, n. 333; ¶ 6.02, n. 54; ¶ 6.03, n. 133.**

Carpenter, In re, 14 B.R. 405 (Bkrtcy. M.D.Tenn.1981)—¶ **9.06, n. 385.**

Carpenter v. Payette Valley Co-op., Inc., 99 Idaho 143, 578 P.2d 1074 (Idaho 1978)—¶ **4.02, n. 40.**

Carpenter v. Suffolk Franklin Sav. Bank, 362 Mass. 770, 291 N.E.2d 609 (Mass. 1973)—¶ **9.05, n. 258.**

Carroll v. Twin City Pontiac Used Cars, Inc., 397 So.2d 42 (La.App. 2 Cir.1981)— ¶ **4.04, n. 144.**

Carter v. DeJarnatt, 523 S.W.2d 88 (Tex. Civ.App.-Texarkana 1975)—¶ **3.01;** ¶ **3.01, n. 45.**

Carter & Grimsley v. Omni Trading, Inc., 306 Ill.App.3d 1127, 240 Ill.Dec. 187, 716 N.E.2d 320 (Ill.App. 3 Dist.1999)— ¶ **3.03, n. 225.**

Caruth v. United States, 411 F.Supp. 604 (N.D.Tex.1976)—¶ **2.02, n. 231.**

Cassedy v. Johnstown Bank, 246 A.D. 337, 286 N.Y.S. 202 (N.Y.A.D. 3 Dept.1936)— ¶ **9.06, n. 330.**

Cassello v. Allegiant Bank and Royal Bank of Missouri, 288 F.3d 339 (8th Cir. 2002)—¶ **7.02, n. 79;** ¶ **7.03, n. 123;** ¶ **8.01, n. 46.**

Catalina Yachts v. Old Colony Bank and Trust Co. of Middlesex County, 497 F.Supp. 1227 (D.Mass.1980)—¶ **4.03, n. 93;** ¶ **8.02, n. 142.**

Cayer, In re, 6 UCC Rep. Serv. 869 (Bkrtcy. D.Me.1969)—¶ **1.03, n. 108.**

Central Bank v. Kaiperm Santa Clara Fed. Credit Union, 191 Cal.App.3d 186, 236 Cal.Rptr. 262 (Cal.App. 6 Dist.1987)— ¶ **2.02, n. 38;** ¶ **8.01, n. 53, 64.**

Central Bank of Alabama, N.A. v. Peoples Nat. Bank of Huntsville, 401 So.2d 14 (Ala.1981)—¶ **4.03, n. 93;** ¶ **8.02;** ¶ **8.02, n. 143.**

Central Bank of Mississippi v. Butler, 517 So.2d 507 (Miss.1987)—¶ **9.06, n. 358.**

Central Bank & Trust Co. v. First Northwest Bank, 332 F.Supp. 1166 (E.D.Mo. 1971)—¶ **3.03, n. 260.**

Central Coordinates, Inc. v. Morgan Guar. Trust Co., 129 Misc.2d 804, 494 N.Y.S.2d 602 (N.Y.Sup.1985)—¶ **10.05, n. 82.**

Central Home Trust. Co. of Elizabeth v. Lippincott, 392 So.2d 931 (Fla.App. 5 Dist.1980)—¶ **6.03, n. 308.**

Central Nat. Bank v. Connecticut Mut. Life Ins. Co., 104 U.S. 54, 14 Otto 54, 26 L.Ed. 693 (1881)—¶ **9.06, n. 329.**

Central State Bank v. Baccara Restaurant, Inc., 9 UCC Rep. Serv. 488 (N.Y.City Civ.Ct.1971)—¶ **4.06, n. 209.**

Central State Bank v. Kilroy, 57 A.D.2d 940, 395 N.Y.S.2d 78 (N.Y.A.D. 2 Dept. 1977)—¶ **3.03, n. 317.**

Centre Le Corbusier v. Nabis Fine Arts, Inc., 13 UCC Rep. Serv. 500 (N.Y.Sup. 1973)—¶ **3.02, n. 101.**

Centre–Point Merchant Bank Ltd. v. American Exp. Bank Ltd., 913 F.Supp. 202 (S.D.N.Y.1996)—¶ **10.02, n. 5;** ¶ **10.04, n. 80.**

Champion Intern. Corp. v. Union Nat. Bank, 73 N.C.App. 147, 325 S.E.2d 656 (N.C.App.1985)—¶ **6.03, n. 204.**

Chancellor, Inc. v. Hamilton Appliance Co., Inc., 175 N.J.Super. 345, 418 A.2d 1326 (N.J.Dist.Ct.1980)—¶ **7.01, n. 38.**

Chandler Motors, Inc. v. Dunham, 127 N.J.Super. 320, 317 A.2d 386 (N.J.Super.A.D.1974)—¶ **7.01, n. 17.**

Channel Equipment Co., Inc. v. Community State Bank, 996 S.W.2d 374 (Tex.Ct. App.1999)—¶ **8.02, n. 151, 155, 169.**

Chaplin v. Milne, 555 S.W.2d 161 (Tex.Civ. App.-El Paso 1977)—¶ **6.01, n. 39.**

Chase Manhattan Bank v. Equibank, 394 F.Supp. 352 (W.D.Pa.1975)—¶ **2.02, n. 64.**

Cheltenham Nat. Bank v. Snelling, 230 Pa.Super. 498, 326 A.2d 557 (Pa.Super.1974)—¶ **3.03, n. 336.**

Chemical Bank v. PIC Motors Corp., 87 A.D.2d 447, 452 N.Y.S.2d 41 (N.Y.A.D. 1 Dept.1982)—¶ **5.02, n. 16.**

Chemical Bank v. Valentini, 84 A.D.2d 801, 444 N.Y.S.2d 154 (N.Y.A.D. 2 Dept. 1981)—¶ **6.03, n. 271.**

Chemical Bank New York Trust Co. v. Brand, 6 UCC Rep. Serv. 1078 (N.Y.Sup. 1969)—¶ **3.02, n. 149.**

Chemical Bank of Rochester v. Haskell, 432 N.Y.S.2d 478, 411 N.E.2d 1339 (N.Y. 1980)—¶ **3.03, n. 292.**

Chemical Bank of Rochester v. Haskell, 68 A.D.2d 347, 417 N.Y.S.2d 541 (N.Y.A.D. 4 Dept.1979)—¶ **6.03, n. 105, 151.**

Chenowith v. Bank of Dardanelle, 243 Ark. 310, 419 S.W.2d 792 (Ark.1967)—¶ **3.01;** ¶ **3.01, n. 49;** ¶ **6.03, n. 207.**

Chera v. The Shores, 145 N.J.Super. 19, 366 A.2d 994 (N.J.Super.A.D.1976)— ¶ **6.01, n. 35.**

Cheshire Commercial Corp. v. Messier, 6 Conn.Cir.Ct. 542, 278 A.2d 413 (Conn. Cir.A.D.1971)—¶ **3.02, n. 68.**

Chicago City Bank & Trust Co. v. Davidson, 42 Ill.App.3d 386, 1 Ill.Dec. 128, 356 N.E.2d 128 (Ill.App. 1 Dist.1976)— ¶ **3.03, n. 338.**

Chicago Heights Currency Exchange, Inc. v. Par Steel Products and Service Co., Inc., 123 Ill.App.3d 1054, 79 Ill.Dec. 275, 463 N.E.2d 829 (Ill.App. 1 Dist.1984)— ¶ **4.02, n. 22.**

Chicago Title & Trust Co. v. Walsh, 34 Ill.App.3d 458, 340 N.E.2d 106 (Ill.App. 1 Dist.1975)—¶ **3.03, n. 205, 240;** ¶ **3.04;** ¶ **3.04, n. 400.**

Chilson v. Capital Bank of Miami, Florida, 10 Kan.App.2d 111, 692 P.2d 406 (Kan. App.1984)—¶ **8.04, n. 451.**

Chitty v. Bank One, N.A., 42 UCC Rep. Serv. 2d 799 (Ohio App. 9 Dist.2000)— ¶ **8.03, n. 197, 240.**

TABLE OF CASES

Christensen Aviation, Inc. v. State Bank, N.A., 20 P.3d 170 (Okla.Civ.App. Div. 2 2001)—¶ **7.02, n. 59;** ¶ **8.02, n. 127.**

Chrysler Credit Corp. v. First Nat. Bank and Trust Co. of Washington, 582 F.Supp. 1436 (W.D.Pa.1984)—¶ **4.03, n. 93;** ¶ **8.01, n. 60;** ¶ **8.02, n. 143.**

C.H. Sanders Const. Co., Inc. v. Bankers Trust Co., 123 A.D.2d 251, 506 N.Y.S.2d 58 (N.Y.A.D. 1 Dept.1986)—¶ **3.02, n. 98.**

Cipra v. Seeger, 215 Kan. 951, 529 P.2d 130 (Kan.1974)—¶ **6.03;** ¶ **6.03, n. 202, 240.**

Circle v. Jim Walter Homes, Inc., 535 F.2d 583 (10th Cir.1976)—¶ **2.02, n. 210;** ¶ **3.04, n. 423.**

Cissna Park State Bank v. Johnson, 21 Ill. App.3d 445, 315 N.E.2d 675 (Ill.App. 4 Dist.1974)—¶ **6.01, n. 9.**

Citibank, South Dakota, N.A. v. Coffey, 281 N.J.Super. 311, 657 A.2d 475 (N.J.Super.L.1994)—¶ **9.06, n. 342.**

Cities Service Co. v. Pailet, 452 So.2d 319 (La.App. 4 Cir.1984)—¶ **11.02, n. 74.**

Citizens and Southern Nat. Bank, United States v., 538 F.2d 1101 (5th Cir.1976)—¶ **9.06, n. 376.**

Citizens Bank v. Strumpf, 516 U.S. 16, 116 S.Ct. 286, 133 L.Ed.2d 258 (1995)—¶ **9.01, n. 80;** ¶ **9.06, n. 345, 381, 385, 386.**

Citizens Bank of Maryland v. Maryland Indus. Finishing Co. Inc., 338 Md. 448, 659 A.2d 313 (Md.1995)—¶ **3.02, n. 167;** ¶ **7.02, n. 67, 92.**

Citizens' Bank of Millerton v. Beeson, 104 Okla. 293, 231 P. 844 (Okla.1924)—¶ **9.06, n. 319.**

Citizens Bank of Smithville v. Lair, 687 S.W.2d 268 (Mo.App. W.D.1985)—¶ **6.03, n. 281.**

Citizens Fidelity Bank & Trust Co. v. Stark, 431 S.W.2d 722 (Ky.1968)—¶ **6.03, n. 234.**

Citizens Nat. Bank v. Bornstein, 374 So.2d 6 (Fla.1979)—¶ **2.02, n. 122.**

Citizens Nat. Bank v. First Nat. Bank, 347 So.2d 964 (Miss.1977)—¶ **3.03, n. 262.**

Citizens Nat. Bank v. Fort Lee Sav. & Loan Ass'n, 89 N.J.Super. 43, 213 A.2d 315 (N.J.Super.L.1965)—¶ **2.01, n. 13;** ¶ **3.01;** ¶ **3.01, n. 43;** ¶ **3.02, n. 158;** ¶ **3.03, n. 224;** ¶ **8.02, n. 114.**

Citizens Nat. Bank v. Hill, 505 S.W.2d 246 (Tex.1974)—¶ **9.05, n. 276, 288.**

Citizens Nat. Bank of Beaumont v. Francis, 427 S.W.2d 645 (Tex.Civ.App.-Beaumont 1968)—¶ **9.05, n. 263.**

Citizens Nat. Bank of Quitman v. Brazil, 141 Ga.App. 388, 233 S.E.2d 482 (Ga.App.1977)—¶ **6.02, n. 60;** ¶ **6.03, n. 112.**

Citizens State Bank v. Beermann Bros. Dehy., 188 Neb. 597, 198 N.W.2d 458 (Neb.1972)—¶ **2.04, n. 280.**

City Bank of Alabama v. Eskridge, 521 So.2d 931 (Ala.1988)—¶ **9.05, n. 308.**

City Bank of Honolulu v. Tenn, 52 Haw. 51, 469 P.2d 816 (Hawai'i 1970)—¶ **9.01, n. 48.**

City Bank & Trust Co. v. White, 434 So.2d 1299 (La.App. 3 Cir.1983)—¶ **5.03, n. 84.**

City Check Cashing, Inc. v. Jul–Ame Const. Co., 326 N.J.Super. 505, 742 A.2d 141 (N.J.Super.A.D.1999)—¶ **4.02, n. 29.**

City Check Cashing, Inc. v. Manufacturers Hanover Trust Co., 166 N.J. 49, 764 A.2d 411 (N.J.2001)—¶ **7.03, n. 123.**

City Nat. Bank of Miami, N. A. v. Wernick, 368 So.2d 934 (Fla.App. 3 Dist.1979)—¶ **7.03, n. 147.**

City of (see name of city)

City Stores Co. v. Henderson, 116 Ga.App. 114, 156 S.E.2d 818 (Ga.App.1967)—¶ **11.02, n. 61.**

Clawson v. Berklund, 188 Mont. 48, 610 P.2d 1168 (Mont.1980)—¶ **2.02;** ¶ **2.02, n. 130.**

Clearfield Trust Co. v. United States, 318 U.S. 363, 318 U.S. 744, 63 S.Ct. 573, 87 L.Ed. 838 (1943)—¶ **1.03, n. 122.**

Clemens v. First Nat. Bank of Berryville, 286 Ark. 290, 692 S.W.2d 222 (Ark.1985)—¶ **7.03, n. 152.**

Cleveland Trust Co. v. Snyder, 55 Ohio App.2d 168, 380 N.E.2d 354 (Ohio App. 8 Dist.1978)—¶ **11.02, n. 73.**

Collection Control Bureau v. Weiss, 50 Cal. App.3d 865, 123 Cal.Rptr. 625 (Cal.App. 2 Dist.1975)—¶ **6.03, n. 211.**

Collins Securities Corp., In re, 998 F.2d 551 (8th Cir.1993)—¶ **9.06, n. 414.**

Colonial Baking Co. of Des Moines v. Dowie, 330 N.W.2d 279 (Iowa 1983)—¶ **5.03, n. 98.**

Colonial Cadillac, Inc. v. Shawmut Merchants Bank, N.A., 488 F.Supp. 283 (D.Mass.1980)—¶ **8.01, n. 42, 54.**

Colorado Nat. Bank v. First Nat. Bank & Trust Co., 459 F.Supp. 1366 (W.D.Mich.1978)—¶ **8.01;** ¶ **8.01, n. 33.**

Columbian Peanut Co. v. Frosteg, 472 F.2d 476 (5th Cir.1973)—¶ **3.02, n. 181;** ¶ **6.03;** ¶ **6.03, n. 187;** ¶ **9.03;** ¶ **9.03, n. 118.**

Commonwealth v. _____ (see opposing party)

Comerica Bank v. Michigan Nat. Bank, 211 Mich.App. 534, 536 N.W.2d 298 (Mich.App.1995)—¶ **7.02, n. 61.**

Comet Check Cashing Service, Inc. v. Hanover Ins. Group, 5 UCC Rep. Serv. 852 (N.Y.City Civ.Ct.1968)—¶ **1.02, n. 50.**

Commerce Bank, N.A. v. Rickett, 329 N.J.Super. 379, 748 A.2d 111 (N.J.Super.A.D.2000)—¶ **2.04, n. 300;** ¶ **3.03, n. 313.**

Commerce Union Bank v. Davis, 581 S.W.2d 142 (Tenn.Ct.App.1978)—¶ 4.05, n. 194; ¶ 5.02, n. 36; ¶ 6.03, n. 277.

Commerce Union Bank v. May, 503 S.W.2d 112 (Tenn.1973)—¶ 6.03, n. 277.

Commercial Cotton Co. v. United California Bank, 163 Cal.App.3d 511, 209 Cal.Rptr. 551 (Cal.App. 4 Dist.1985)—¶ 9.03; ¶ 9.03, n. 135, 168, 185.

Commercial Credit Equipment Corp. v. First Alabama Bank of Montgomery, N.A., 636 F.2d 1051 (5th Cir.1981)— ¶ 4.02, n. 24.

Commercial Discount Corp. v. Milwaukee Western Bank, 61 Wis.2d 671, 214 N.W.2d 33 (Wis.1974)—¶ 3.03, n. 353; ¶ 9.06, n. 367.

Commonwealth Bank & Trust Co. v. Plotkin, 371 Mass. 218, 355 N.E.2d 917 (Mass.1976)—¶ 6.03, n. 89.

Commonwealth ex rel. v. ———— (see opposing party and relator)

Commonwealth Federal Sav. & Loan Ass'n v. First Nat. Bank of New Jersey, 513 F.Supp. 296 (E.D.Pa.1979)— ¶ 3.02, n. 72; ¶ 7.03, n. 131.

Common Wealth Ins. Systems, Inc. v. Kersten, 40 Cal.App.3d 1014, 115 Cal.Rptr. 653 (Cal.App. 4 Dist.1974)—¶ 5.02, n. 36.

Commonwealth of Virginia v. Wills, 27 UCC Rep. Serv. 2d 926 (Va. Cir. Ct.1995)— ¶ 7.01, n. 42.

Community Bank v. Federal Reserve Bank, 500 F.2d 282 (9th Cir.1974)—¶ 1.03, n. 163; ¶ 8.01, n. 41, 42; ¶ 8.02, n. 93.

Community Bank, FSB v. Stevens Financial Corp., 966 F.Supp. 775 (N.D.Ind.1997)— ¶ 10.04; ¶ 10.04, n. 77.

Community Nat. Bank v. Channelview Bank, 814 S.W.2d 424 (Tex.App.-Hous. (1 Dist.) 1991)—¶ 4.02, n. 2.

Community Nat. Bank v. Dawes, 369 Mass. 550, 340 N.E.2d 877 (Mass.1976)— ¶ 2.02, n. 102.

Community Nat. Bank and Trust Co. v. Gold, 45 A.D.2d 947, 359 N.Y.S.2d 118 (N.Y.A.D. 1 Dept.1974)—¶ 6.03, n. 245.

Comstock v. Morgan Park Trust & Savings Bank, 319 Ill.App. 253, 48 N.E.2d 980 (Ill.App. 1 Dist.1943)—¶ 9.06, n. 403.

Congress Talcott Corp. v. Gruber, 993 F.2d 315 (3rd Cir.1993)—¶ 9.06, n. 376, 379, 409.

Continental Airlines, Inc. v. Boatmen's Nat. Bank, 13 F.3d 1254 (8th Cir.1994)— ¶ 2.01, n. 25; ¶ 3.02, n. 167; ¶ 7.02, n. 92; ¶ 7.03, n. 140; ¶ 10.01, n. 4.

Continental Bank v. Fitting, 114 Ariz. 98, 559 P.2d 218 (Ariz.App. Div. 1 1977)— ¶ 9.01, n. 47.

Continental Bank v. Wa–Ho Truck Brokerage, 122 Ariz. 414, 595 P.2d 206 (Ariz. App. Div. 1 1979)—¶ 4.02, n. 32.

Continental Bankers Life Ins. Co. v. Bank of Alamo, 578 S.W.2d 625 (Tenn.1979)— ¶ 1.02, n. 48.

Continental Cas. Co. v. Huron Valley Nat. Bank, 85 Mich.App. 319, 271 N.W.2d 218 (Mich.App.1978)—¶ 7.03, n. 130.

Continental State Bank, Boyd v. Miles General Contractors, Inc., 661 S.W.2d 770 (Tex.App.-Fort Worth 1983)—¶ 4.02, n. 34.

Cooley v. First Nat. Bank of Little Rock, 276 Ark. 387, 635 S.W.2d 250 (Ark. 1982)—¶ 9.03, n. 162.

Cooper v. Emery and Sons, 829 S.W.2d 642 (Mo.App. W.D.1992)—¶ 5.03, n. 98.

Cooper v. Stock Yards Bank of Oklahoma City, Okl., 644 P.2d 123 (Okla.App. Div. 2 1981)—¶ 9.02; ¶ 9.02, n. 110.

Cooper v. Union Bank, 107 Cal.Rptr. 1, 507 P.2d 609 (Cal.1973)— ¶ 4.02, n. 22; ¶ 6.03, n. 209; ¶ 7.03; ¶ 7.03, n. 146; ¶ 9.02, n. 100, 107.

Copesky v. Superior Court, 229 Cal.App.3d 678, 280 Cal.Rptr. 338 (Cal.App. 4 Dist. 1991)—¶ 9.03; ¶ 9.03, n. 124, 168, 172.

Coplan Pipe & Supply Co. v. Ben–Frieda Corp., 256 So.2d 218 (Fla.App. 3 Dist. 1972)—¶ 3.04; ¶ 3.04, n. 399.

Copple v. Boatmen's First Nat. Bank of Oklahoma, 958 P.2d 820 (Okla.Civ.App. Div. 2 1998)—¶ 8.02; ¶ 8.02, n. 115, 127, 190.

Corbin Deposit & Trust Co. v. Mullins Enterprises, Inc., 641 S.W.2d 760 (Ky.App. 1982)—¶ 2.02, n. 229.

Corfan Banco Asuncion Paraguay v. Ocean Bank, 715 So.2d 967 (Fla.App. 3 Dist. 1998)—¶ 10.04; ¶ 10.04, n. 58.

Corporacion Venezolana de Fomento v. Vintero Sales Corp., 452 F.Supp. 1108 (S.D.N.Y.1978)—¶ 3.02; ¶ 3.02, n. 64.

Cosmopolitan Financial Corp. v. Runnels, 2 Haw.App. 33, 625 P.2d 390 (Hawai'i App.1981)—¶ 2.02, n. 175; ¶ 6.01, n. 27.

Coulter Electronics, Inc. v. Commercial Bank of Cobb County, 727 F.2d 1078 (11th Cir.1984)—¶ 7.03, n. 137.

Country Club Casuals, Inc., In re, 1 B.R. 274 (Bkrtcy.S.D.Fla.1979)—¶ 1.04, n. 232.

County Concrete Corp. v. Smith, 317 N.J.Super. 50, 721 A.2d 34 (N.J.Super.A.D.1998)—¶ 3.02, n. 106; ¶ 7.03, n. 152.

County Trust Co. v. Pascack Valley Bank & Trust Co., 93 N.J.Super. 252, 225 A.2d 605 (N.J.Super.A.D.1966)—¶ 3.03, n. 316.

Courtesy Financial Services, Inc. v. Hughes, 424 So.2d 1172 (La.App. 1 Cir.1982)— ¶ 3.04, n. 417.

Coussement, Ex parte, 412 So.2d 783 (Ala. 1982)—¶ 5.03; ¶ 5.03, n. 100.

TABLE OF CASES 561

Covington v. Penn Square Nat. Bank, 545 P.2d 824 (Okla.App. Div. 1 1975)—¶ 7.03, n. 164.

Cox v. First Nat. Bank of Cincinnati, 633 F.Supp. 236 (S.D.Ohio 1986)—¶ 3.04, n. 432.

Crest Finance Co. v. First State Bank of Westmont, 37 Ill.2d 243, 226 N.E.2d 369 (Ill.1967)—¶ 3.03; ¶ 3.03, n. 236.

Crimmins v. Lowry, 691 S.W.2d 582 (Tex. 1985)—¶ 6.03, n. 249.

Criterion Ins. Co. v. Fulgham, 219 Va. 294, 247 S.E.2d 404 (Va.1978)—¶ 6.03, n. 167; ¶ 7.01; ¶ 7.01, n. 1.

Critten v. Chemical Nat. Bank, 171 N.Y. 219, 63 N.E. 969 (N.Y.1902)—¶ 9.03, n. 136.

Crocker–Citizens Nat. Bank v. Control Metals Corp., 566 F.2d 631 (9th Cir.1977)—¶ 9.06, n. 343.

Crow Creek Sioux Tribe, United States ex rel. v. Tri–County Bank of Chamberlain, S. D., 415 F.Supp. 858 (D.S.D.1976)—¶ 9.06, n. 358.

Crown Mortg. Corp. v. Tarantino, 606 So.2d 29 (La.App. 5 Cir.1992)—¶ 2.02, n. 229.

Crunk v. State Farm Fire & Cas. Co., 106 Wash.2d 23, 719 P.2d 1338 (Wash. 1986)—¶ 9.01, n. 58, 68.

Crystaplex Plastics, Ltd. v. Redevelopment Agency, 92 Cal.Rptr.2d 197 (Cal.App. 4 Dist.2000)—¶ 3.01, n. 8; ¶ 7.01, n. 4, 14.

Cuchine v. H.O. Bell, Inc., 210 Mont. 312, 682 P.2d 723 (Mont.1984)—¶ 3.04, n. 432.

Cullotta v. Kemper Corp., 78 Ill.2d 25, 34 Ill.Dec. 306, 397 N.E.2d 1372 (Ill. 1979)—¶ 7.01; ¶ 7.01, n. 11, 23.

Cumis Ins. Soc., Inc. v. Girard Bank, 522 F.Supp. 414 (E.D.Pa.1981)—¶ 4.02, n. 12; ¶ 9.01; ¶ 9.01, n. 3.

Cumis Ins. Soc., Inc. v. Munoz, 1996 WL 496982 (D.D.C.1996)—¶ 10.08, n. 169.

Cusick v. Ifshin, 70 Misc.2d 564, 334 N.Y.S.2d 106 (N.Y.City Civ.Ct.1972)—¶ 5.02, n. 22.

Cusimano v. First Maryland Sav. and Loan, Inc., 639 A.2d 553 (D.C.1994)—¶ 5.02, n. 20.

Custer County v. Walker, 10 S.D. 594, 74 N.W. 1040 (S.D.1898)—¶ 9.06, n. 335.

C & Z, Inc. v. Oklahoma Tax Commission, 459 P.2d 601 (Okla.1969)—¶ 2.02, n. 229.

D

Dalton & Marberry, P.C. v. NationsBank, N.A., 982 S.W.2d 231 (Mo.1998)—¶ 7.03, n. 123.

Daly v. Del E. Webb Corp., 96 Nev. 359, 609 P.2d 319 (Nev.1980)—¶ 2.02, n. 180.

D'Andrea v. Feinberg, 45 Misc.2d 270, 256 N.Y.S.2d 504 (N.Y.Sup.1965)—¶ 2.02, n. 143.

Danje Fabrics Division of Kingspoint Intern. Corp. v. Morgan Guaranty Trust Co., 96 Misc.2d 746, 409 N.Y.S.2d 565 (N.Y.Sup.1978)—¶ 7.03, n. 175.

D'Annolfo v. D'Annolfo Const. Co., Inc., 39 Mass.App.Ct. 189, 654 N.E.2d 82 (Mass. App.Ct.1995)—¶ 5.02, n. 17.

Darden v. Harrison, 511 S.W.2d 925 (Tex. 1974)—¶ 5.02, n. 38, 53, 56.

Daric Const. Corp. v. Radice Const. Corp., 4 UCC Rep. Serv. 763 (N.Y.Sup.1967)—¶ 3.03, n. 324.

Da Silva v. Sanders, 38 UCC Rep. Serv. 270 (D.D.C.1984)—¶ 3.01, n. 7.

David v. Manufacturers Hanover Trust Co., 59 Misc.2d 248, 298 N.Y.S.2d 847 (N.Y.Sup.App.Term 1969)—¶ 9.03, n. 157; ¶ 9.05, n. 282.

David Graubart, Inc. v. Bank Leumi Trust Co., 423 N.Y.S.2d 899, 399 N.E.2d 930 (N.Y.1979)—¶ 7.01, n. 14; ¶ 8.01; ¶ 8.01, n. 26, 46; ¶ 8.02, n. 134; ¶ 9.03, n. 154.

Davidson Oil Country Supply, Inc. v. Klockner, Inc., 908 F.2d 1238 (5th Cir.1990)—¶ 1.03, n. 105.

Davis v. Committee for First Home Owners, Inc., 180 Misc.2d 425, 692 N.Y.S.2d 882 (N.Y.City Civ.Ct.1997)—¶ 7.03, n. 127.

Davis v. Davis, 838 S.W.2d 415 (Ky.App. 1992)—¶ 2.02, n. 239.

Davis v. Timeshare Travel Intern., 489 So.2d 47 (Fla.App. 2 Dist.1986)—¶ 2.02, n. 128.

Davis Aircraft Products Co. v. Bankers Trust Co., 36 A.D.2d 705, 319 N.Y.S.2d 379 (N.Y.A.D. 1 Dept.1971)—¶ 7.02, n. 83.

Dayton, Price & Co., Ltd. v. First Nat. City Bank, 64 A.D.2d 563, 406 N.Y.S.2d 823 (N.Y.A.D. 1 Dept.1978)—¶ 7.03, n. 173.

Decibel Credit Union v. Pueblo Bank & Trust Co., 996 P.2d 784 (Colo.App. 2000)—¶ 8.02, n. 127, 165; ¶ 8.04, n. 416.

Deep South Services, Inc. v. Wade, 248 Ga. 80, 281 S.E.2d 561 (Ga.1981)—¶ 5.02, n. 42; ¶ 6.03; ¶ 6.03, n. 162.

Deerfield Beach, City of v. Florida Nat. Bank, 428 So.2d 779 (Fla.App. 4 Dist. 1983)—¶ 2.02, n. 121; ¶ 7.01, n. 35; ¶ 9.01; ¶ 9.01, n. 6.

Deese v. Mobley, 392 So.2d 364 (Fla.App. 1 Dist.1981)—¶ 6.03, n. 180.

Delano v. Putnam Trust Co., 33 UCC Rep. Serv. 635 (Conn.Super.1981)—¶ 9.01, n. 23.

Delbrueck & Co. v. Manufacturers Hanover Trust Co., 609 F.2d 1047 (2nd Cir. 1979)—¶ 2.02, n. 64; ¶ 10.07, n. 119; ¶ 10.09, n. 199.

Delmar Bank of University City v. Fidelity & Deposit Co. of Md., 428 F.2d 32 (8th Cir.1970)—¶ **7.03, n. 163, 174.**

DeLuca v. BancOhio Natl. Bank, 74 Ohio App.3d 233, 598 N.E.2d 781 (Ohio App. 10 Dist.1991)—¶ **3.01, n. 2.**

Demaio v. Theriot, 343 So.2d 1143 (La.App. 3 Cir.1977)—¶ **2.02, n. 161.**

DeMello v. Home Escrow, Inc., 4 Haw.App. 41, 659 P.2d 759 (Hawai'i App.1983)— ¶ **9.05, n. 267.**

Denn v. First State Bank of Spring Lake Park, 316 N.W.2d 532 (Minn.1982)— ¶ **7.03, n. 137.**

Dennis Joslin Co. v. Robinson Broadcasting Corp., 977 F.Supp. 491 (D.D.C.1997)— ¶ **1.03, n. 155;** ¶ **3.01, n. 19;** ¶ **7.01, n. 14;** ¶ **9.01, n. 69.**

Denny v. Thompson, 236 Ky. 714, 33 S.W.2d 670 (Ky.1930)—¶ **9.05, n. 260.**

DH Cattle Holdings Co. v. Reinoso, 176 A.D.2d 1057, 575 N.Y.S.2d 203 (N.Y.A.D. 3 Dept.1991)—¶ **2.02;** ¶ **2.02, n. 206.**

DH Cattle Holdings Co. v. Reno, 196 A.D.2d 670, 601 N.Y.S.2d 714 (N.Y.A.D. 3 Dept. 1993)—¶ **2.02, n. 145.**

DH Cattle Holdings Co. v. Smith, 195 A.D.2d 202, 607 N.Y.S.2d 227 (N.Y.A.D. 1 Dept.1994)—¶ **3.03, n. 269.**

Dhiman v. Rockford Industries, Inc., 42 UCC Rep. Serv. 2d 767 (N.D.Ill.2000)— ¶ **3.03, n. 257;** ¶ **7.01, n. 42.**

Diaz v. Manufacturer's Hanover Trust Co., 92 Misc.2d 802, 401 N.Y.S.2d 952 (1977)—¶ **9.01, n. 68.**

Dillard Ford, Inc., In re, 940 F.2d 1507 (11th Cir.1991)—¶ **9.05, n. 242.**

Dime Sav. Bank of New York v. Chase Manhattan Bank, 16 UCC Rep. Serv. 171 (N.Y.Sup.1974)—¶ **7.02;** ¶ **7.02, n. 82;** ¶ **9.04, n. 230.**

Dimonda v. Freedom Federal Sav., 1981 Mass.App.Div. 148 (Mass.App.Div. 1981)—¶ **7.03, n. 134.**

DiMonda v. Freedom Federal Sav. & Loan Ass'n, 385 Mass. 1012, 434 N.E.2d 210 (Mass.1982)—¶ **3.01, n. 9.**

Dimon's Estate, In re, 32 N.Y.S.2d 239 (N.Y.Sur.1941)—¶ **9.06, n. 328, 332.**

Directors Guild of America v. Harmony Pictures, Inc., 32 F.Supp.2d 1184 (C.D.Cal. 1998)—¶ **7.01, n. 38.**

Di Roma v. Merchants Bank of New York, 92 A.D.2d 42, 459 N.Y.S.2d 592 (N.Y.A.D. 1 Dept.1983)—¶ **4.04, n. 171.**

Discount Purchasing Co. v. Porch, 12 UCC Rep. Serv. 600 (Tenn.Ct.App.1973)— ¶ **2.02, n. 76, 88, 94.**

DiVall Insured Income Fund Ltd. Partnership v. Boatmen's First Nat. Bank, 69 F.3d 1398 (8th Cir.1995)—¶ **1.03, n. 133.**

Djowharzadeh v. City Nat. Bank and Trust Co. of Norman, 646 P.2d 616 (Okla.App. Div. 2 1982)—¶ **9.03;** ¶ **9.03, n. 122, 128, 130.**

Dluge v. Robinson, 204 Pa.Super. 404, 204 A.2d 279 (Pa.Super.1964)—¶ **4.06, n. 238;** ¶ **6.03, n. 230.**

D. Nelsen & Sons, Inc. v. General Am. Development Corp., 6 Ill.App.3d 6, 284 N.E.2d 478 (Ill.App. 1 Dist.1972)— ¶ **3.03, n. 357.**

DNI Nevada, Inc. v. Medi-Peth Medical Lab, Inc., 337 N.J.Super. 313, 766 A.2d 1197 (N.J.Sup.Ct.2001)—¶ **8.03, n. 207, 230.**

Dobbs–Maynard Co., Inc. v. Jumper, 388 So.2d 879 (Miss.1980)—¶ **3.03, n. 206.**

Docter v. Riedel, 96 Wis. 158, 71 N.W. 119 (Wis.1897)—¶ **9.06, n. 390, 391.**

Dodd v. Citizens Bank of Costa Mesa, 222 Cal.App.3d 1624, 272 Cal.Rptr. 623 (Cal. App. 4 Dist.1990)—¶ **8.01, n. 53.**

D'Oench, Duhme & Co. v. Federal Deposit Ins. Corporation, 315 U.S. 447, 62 S.Ct. 676, 86 L.Ed. 956 (1942)—¶ **1.03;** ¶ **1.03, n. 122, 131;** ¶ **6.01, n. 27.**

Dolton v. Capitol Federal Sav. and Loan Ass'n, 642 P.2d 21 (Colo.App.1981)— ¶ **9.03, n. 128.**

Dominion Bank, N.A. v. Household Bank, F.S.B., 827 F.Supp. 463 (S.D.Ohio 1993)—¶ **7.03, n. 168.**

Dominion Const., Inc. v. First Nat. Bank, 271 Md. 154, 315 A.2d 69 (Md.1974)— ¶ **4.02, n. 26;** ¶ **9.05, n. 309, 310.**

Don E. Williams Co. v. Commissioner, 527 F.2d 649 (7th Cir.1975)—¶ **2.04, n. 297.**

Donmar Enterprises v. Southern Nat. Bank, 828 F.Supp. 1230 (W.D.N.C. 1993)—¶ **10.01, n. 1.**

Douglas v. Citizens Bank, 244 Ark. 168, 424 S.W.2d 532 (Ark.1968)—¶ **9.01, n. 90;** ¶ **9.06, n. 364.**

Doyle v. Resolution Trust Corp., 999 F.2d 469 (10th Cir.1993)—¶ **3.03, n. 269, 289.**

Doyle v. Trinity Sav. and Loan Ass'n, 869 F.2d 558 (10th Cir.1989)—¶ **2.01, n. 10.**

Dozier v. First Alabama Bank of Montgomery, N.A., 363 So.2d 781 (Ala.Civ.App. 1978)—¶ **4.06;** ¶ **4.06, n. 241;** ¶ **7.02, n. 52.**

DRP, Inc. v. Burgess, 730 So.2d 474 (La. App. 4 Cir.1999)—¶ **4.04, n. 181;** ¶ **7.01, n. 26.**

Drug House, Inc. v. Keystone Bank, 272 Pa.Super. 130, 414 A.2d 704 (Pa.Super.1979)—¶ **7.03, n. 131, 134.**

Dubin v. Hudson County Probation Dept., 267 N.J.Super. 202, 630 A.2d 1207 (N.J.Super.L.1993)—¶ **4.02, n. 21.**

Duggan v. State Bank of Antioch, 184 Ill. App.3d 699, 133 Ill.Dec. 245, 540 N.E.2d 1111 (Ill.App. 2 Dist.1989)—¶ **8.01, n. 67.**

Duilio v. Senechal, 7 UCC Rep. Serv. 222 (Mass.App.Div.1969)—¶ **6.03, n. 203.**

TABLE OF CASES

Dunnigan v. First Bank, 217 Conn. 205, 585 A.2d 659 (Conn.1991)—¶ **9.01, n. 40.**

Duxbury v. Roberts, 388 Mass. 385, 446 N.E.2d 401 (Mass.1983)—¶ **3.03, n. 358;** ¶ **6.03, n. 99.**

Dykstra v. National Bank of South Dakota, 328 N.W.2d 862 (S.D.1983)—¶ **7.03, n. 185.**

Dynamic Homes, Inc. v. Rogers, 331 So.2d 326 (Fla.App. 4 Dist.1976)—¶ **4.02, n. 3.**

Dynamite Enterprises, Inc. v. Eagle Nat. Bank of Miami, 517 So.2d 112 (Fla.App. 3 Dist.1987)—¶ **9.01, n. 28.**

Dziurak v. Chase Manhattan Bank, N. A., 58 A.D.2d 103, 396 N.Y.S.2d 414 (N.Y.A.D. 2 Dept.1977)—¶ **9.01, n. 55.**

E

East Gadsden Bank v. First City Nat. Bank of Gadsden, 50 Ala.App. 576, 281 So.2d 431 (Ala.Civ.App.1973)—¶ **4.02, n. 28;** ¶ **7.02;** ¶ **7.02, n. 97;** ¶ **9.03, n. 190.**

Eatinger v. First Nat. Bank of Lewistown, 199 Mont. 377, 649 P.2d 1253 (Mont. 1982)—¶ **7.03, n. 152.**

E. Bierhaus & Sons, Inc. v. Bowling, 486 N.E.2d 598 (Ind.App. 1 Dist.1985)— ¶ **3.03, n. 259.**

Eder v. Yvette B. Gervey Interiors, Inc., 407 So.2d 312 (Fla.App. 4 Dist.1981)— ¶ **7.01, n. 34.**

Ed Hockaday & Co. v. Randolph, 178 Okla. 234, 62 P.2d 628 (Okla.1936)—¶ **9.06, n. 371.**

Ed Stinn Chevrolet, Inc. v. National City Bank, 28 Ohio St.3d 221, 503 N.E.2d 524 (Ohio 1986)—¶ **4.02, n. 27.**

Educational Beneficial, Inc. v. Reynolds, 67 Misc.2d 739, 324 N.Y.S.2d 813 (N.Y.City Civ.Ct.1971)—¶ **3.04, n. 419.**

Edward A. Kemmler Memorial Found. v. 691/733 East Dublin–Granville Road Co., 62 Ohio St.3d 494, 584 N.E.2d 695 (Ohio 1992)—¶ **5.03, n. 79.**

Edward Fineman Co. v. Superior Court, 78 Cal.Rptr.2d 478 (Cal.App. 2 Dist.1998)— ¶ **5.03, n. 68.**

E.F. Hutton & Co. v. City National Bank, 149 Cal.App.3d 60, 196 Cal.Rptr. 614 (Cal.App. 2 Dist.1983)—¶ **7.03, n. 185.**

E.F. Hutton & Co. v. Manufacturers Nat. Bank, 259 F.Supp. 513 (E.D.Mich. 1966)—¶ **1.03;** ¶ **1.03, n. 94.**

Eggleston v. George Braun Packing Co., 470 S.W.2d 69 (Tex.Civ.App.-San Antonio 1971)—¶ **4.02, n. 42.**

Eikel v. Bristow Corp., 529 S.W.2d 795 (Tex.Civ.App.-Hous. (1 Dist.) 1975)— ¶ **3.01, n. 25;** ¶ **3.02, n. 180.**

Eisenberg v. Wachovia Bank, N.A., 301 F.3d 220 (4th Cir.2002)—¶ **7.03, n. 114.**

Eldon's Super Fresh Stores, Inc. v. Merrill Lynch, Pierce, Fenner & Smith, Inc., 296 Minn. 130, 207 N.W.2d 282 (Minn. 1973)—¶ **3.01, n. 8;** ¶ **3.03;** ¶ **3.03, n. 213, 300, 356;** ¶ **3.04;** ¶ **3.04, n. 405.**

Elizarraras v. Bank of El Paso, 631 F.2d 366 (5th Cir.1980)—¶ **9.02, n. 100.**

Elliott v. Capital City State Bank, 128 Iowa 275, 103 N.W. 777 (Iowa 1905)—¶ **9.05, n. 313.**

Emerson v. Zagurski, 3 Neb.App. 658, 531 N.W.2d 237 (Neb.App.1995)—¶ **6.03, n. 286.**

Emery–Waterhouse Co. v. Rhode Island Hosp. Trust Nat. Bank, 757 F.2d 399 (1st Cir.1985)—¶ **3.03, n. 206.**

Employers Ins. of Wausau v. Chemical Bank, 117 Misc.2d 601, 459 N.Y.S.2d 238 (N.Y.City Civ.Ct.1983)—¶ **8.01, n. 13.**

Engalla v. Permanente Medical Group, Inc., 64 Cal.Rptr.2d 843, 938 P.2d 903 (Cal. 1997)—¶ **11.02, n. 95.**

Engine Parts, Inc. v. Citizens Bank of Clovis, 92 N.M. 37, 582 P.2d 809 (N.M. 1978)—¶ **4.03, n. 57.**

Engleman v. Bank of America Nat. Trust & Savings Ass'n, 98 Cal.App.2d 327, 219 P.2d 868 (Cal.App. 2 Dist.1950)—¶ **9.06, n. 319, 321.**

Environics, Inc. v. Pratt, 50 A.D.2d 552, 376 N.Y.S.2d 510 (N.Y.A.D. 1 Dept.1975)— ¶ **2.02, n. 226;** ¶ **6.03, n. 295.**

Epstein v. Paskow & Epstein, 4 UCC Rep. Serv. 1066 (N.Y.Sup.1968)—¶ **6.03;** ¶ **6.03, n. 123.**

Equitable Discount Corp. v. Fischer, 12 Pa. D. & C.2d 326 (Pa.Com.Pl.1957)— ¶ **6.02;** ¶ **6.02, n. 63.**

E.S.P., Inc. v. Midway Nat. Bank of St. Paul, 466 N.W.2d 417 (Minn.App. 1991)—¶ **9.03, n. 196.**

E.S.P., Inc. v. Midway Nat. Bank of St. Paul, 447 N.W.2d 882 (Minn.1989)— ¶ **6.03, n. 292;** ¶ **7.02, n. 61.**

Estate of (see name of party)

Estrada v. River Oaks Bank & Trust Co., 550 S.W.2d 719 (Tex.Civ.App.-Hous. (14 Dist.) 1977)—¶ **3.02;** ¶ **3.02, n. 85.**

Eton Furniture Co., In re, 286 F.2d 93 (3rd Cir.1961)—¶ **4.02, n. 7.**

Euclid Nat. Bank, United States v., 510 F.2d 461 (6th Cir.1975)—¶ **9.06, n. 379.**

European American Bank & Trust Co. v. Starcrete Intern. Ind., Inc., 613 F.2d 564 (5th Cir.1980)—¶ **1.03, n. 74.**

Eutsler v. First Nat. Bank, Pawhuska, 639 P.2d 1245 (Okla.1982)—¶ **4.02, n. 40;** ¶ **9.01, n. 11.**

Evans v. Harry Robinson Pontiac–Buick, Inc., 336 Ark. 155, 983 S.W.2d 946 (1999)—¶ **8.01, n. 24.**

Evenson v. Hlebechuk, 305 N.W.2d 13 (N.D.1981)—¶ **2.02, n. 178;** ¶ **3.03, n. 203.**

Everglade Cypress Co. v. Tunnicliffe, 107 Fla. 675, 148 So. 192 (Fla.1933)—¶ **9.06, n. 322.**

Evra Corp. v. Swiss Bank Corp., 673 F.2d 951 (7th Cir.1982)—¶ **1.01, n. 6; ¶ 2.02, n. 64; ¶ 10.03, n. 48.**

Exchange Bank & Trust Co. v. Kidwell Const. Co., 463 S.W.2d 465 (Tex.Civ. App.-Tyler 1971)—¶ **9.03, n. 189.**

Exchange Intern. Leasing Corp v. Consolidated Business Forms Co., Inc., 462 F.Supp. 626 (W.D.Pa.1978)—¶ **6.02, n. 65.**

Executive Bank of Ft. Lauderdale, Fla. v. Tighe, 66 A.D.2d 70, 411 N.Y.S.2d 939 (N.Y.A.D. 2 Dept.1978)—¶ **6.03, n. 283.**

Ex parte (see name of party)

Expresso Roma Corp. v. Bank of America, N.A., 100 Cal.App.4th 525, 124 Cal. Rptr.2d 549 (2002)—¶ **7.03, n. 114.**

F

Faber, Coe & Gregg, Inc. v. First Nat. Bank, 107 Ill.App.2d 204, 246 N.E.2d 96 (Ill.App. 1 Dist.1969)—¶ **9.06, n. 339.**

Factors & Note Buyers, Inc. v. Green Lane, Inc., 102 N.J.Super. 43, 245 A.2d 223 (N.J.Super.L.1968)—¶ **5.03, n. 102; ¶ 6.01, n. 40.**

Fairfax Bank & Trust Co. v. Crestar Bank, 247 Va. 356, 442 S.E.2d 651 (Va.1994)—¶ **3.02, n. 147.**

Fairfield County Trust Co. v. Steinbrecher, 5 Conn.Cir.Ct. 405, 255 A.2d 144 (Conn. Cir.A.D.1968)—¶ **6.03, n. 135.**

Fairfield Credit Corp. v. Donnelly, 158 Conn. 543, 264 A.2d 547 (Conn.1969)—¶ **2.01, n. 29.**

Fair Park Nat. Bank v. Southwestern Inv. Co., 541 S.W.2d 266 (Tex.Civ.App.-Dallas 1976)—¶ **7.03; ¶ 7.03, n. 165.**

Falk v. Northern Trust Co., 327 Ill.App.3d 101, 261 Ill.Dec. 410, 763 N.E.2d 380 (2001)—¶ **7.03, n. 114.**

Fallimento C.Op.M.A. v. Fischer Crane Co., 995 F.2d 789 (7th Cir.1993)—¶ **6.03, n. 287; ¶ 7.01, n. 3.**

Fall River Sav. Bank v. Lebel, 1982 Mass. App.Div. 20 (Mass.App.Div.1982)—¶ **6.03, n. 180.**

Falls Church Bank v. Wesley Heights Realty, Inc., 256 A.2d 915 (D.C.App.1969)—¶ **3.03; ¶ 3.03, n. 223.**

Family Bank of Hallandale, State v., 623 So.2d 464 (Fla.1993)—¶ **1.03, n. 129.**

Family Provisioners, Inc. v. Columbia Acceptance Co., 274 Or. 303, 545 P.2d 1379 (Or.1976)—¶ **6.03, n. 272.**

Farmers and Merchants State Bank v. Lloyd, 99 Idaho 416, 582 P.2d 1094 (Idaho 1978)—¶ **6.03, n. 231.**

Farmers & Merchants State Bank v. Western Bank, 841 F.2d 1433 (9th Cir. 1987)—¶ **3.03, n. 262; ¶ 9.01, n. 40, 67, 68.**

Farmers' & Merchants' Bank of Baltimore v. Franklin Bank of Baltimore, 31 Md. 404 (Md.1869)—¶ **9.06, n. 371.**

Farmers' & Merchants' State Bank of Teague v. Setzer, 185 S.W. 596 (Tex.Civ. App.-Dallas 1916)—¶ **9.06, n. 371.**

Farmers Co-op. Elevator, Inc., Duncombe v. State Bank, 236 N.W.2d 674 (Iowa 1975)—¶ **9.06, n. 364.**

Farmers State Bank of Hart v. Ray, 565 S.W.2d 103 (Tex.Civ.App.-Amarillo 1978)—¶ **6.02; ¶ 6.02, n. 82.**

Farmington Nat. Bank v. Basin Plastics, Inc., 94 N.M. 668, 615 P.2d 985 (N.M. 1980)—¶ **2.02, n. 178; ¶ 6.01, n. 40.**

Farner v. Farner, 480 N.E.2d 251 (Ind.App. 1 Dist.1985)—¶ **6.03, n. 226.**

Farrington, United States v., 172 F.Supp. 797 (D.Mass.1959)—¶ **2.02, n. 147.**

Far West Citrus, Inc. v. Bank of America, 91 Cal.App.3d 913, 154 Cal.Rptr. 464 (Cal.App. 2 Dist.1979)—¶ **5.03, n. 68.**

Fast Food Systems, Inc. v. Ducotey, 837 P.2d 910 (Okla.1992)—¶ **9.06, n. 376.**

Favors v. Yaffe, 605 S.W.2d 342 (Tex.Civ. App.-Hous. (14 Dist.) 1980)—¶ **3.03, n. 318, 327; ¶ 6.01, n. 12.**

FDIC/Manager Fund v. Larsen, 793 S.W.2d 37 (Tex.App.-Dallas 1990)—¶ **1.03, n. 152.**

Feder v. Fortunoff, 123 Misc.2d 857, 474 N.Y.S.2d 937 (N.Y.Sup.1984)—¶ **11.02, n. 61.**

Federal Deposit Ins. Corp. v. Blue Rock Shopping Center, Inc., 766 F.2d 744 (3rd Cir.1985)—¶ **1.03, n. 130.**

Federal Deposit Ins. Corp. v. Borne, 599 F.Supp. 891 (E.D.N.Y.1984)—¶ **2.02, n. 178.**

Federal Deposit Ins. Corp. v. Bracero & Rivera, Inc., 895 F.2d 824 (1st Cir. 1990)—¶ **1.03, n. 153.**

Federal Deposit Ins. Corp. v. Byrne, 736 F.Supp. 727 (N.D.Tex.1990)—¶ **1.03, n. 152.**

Federal Deposit Ins. Corp. v. Cremona Co., 832 F.2d 959 (6th Cir.1987)—¶ **1.03, n. 142.**

Federal Deposit Ins. Corp. v. Deglau, 207 F.3d 153 (3rd Cir.2000)—¶ **1.03, n. 133.**

Federal Deposit Ins. Corp. v. Galloway, 856 F.2d 112 (10th Cir.1988)—¶ **1.03, n. 149.**

Federal Deposit Ins. Corp. v. Golden Imports, Inc., 859 S.W.2d 635 (Tex.App.-Hous. (1 Dist.) 1993)—¶ **9.06, n. 362.**

Federal Deposit Ins. Corp. v. Gulf Life Ins. Co., 737 F.2d 1513 (11th Cir.1984)—¶ **1.03, n. 149.**

Federal Deposit Ins. Corp. v. Kirkland, 272 S.C. 310, 251 S.E.2d 750 (S.C.1979)—¶ **6.03, n. 265.**

Federal Deposit Ins. Corp. v. Kratz, 898 F.2d 669 (8th Cir.1990)—¶ **1.03, n. 149.**
Federal Deposit Ins. Corp. v. Leach, 772 F.2d 1262 (6th Cir.1985)—¶ **1.03, n. 142.**
Federal Deposit Ins. Corp. v. Linn, 671 F.Supp. 547 (N.D.Ill.1987)—¶ **3.01, n. 11; ¶ 3.02, n. 65.**
Federal Deposit Ins. Corp. v. Manatt, 688 F.Supp. 1327 (E.D.Ark.1988)—¶ **1.03, n. 151.**
Federal Deposit Ins. Corp. v. Marine Nat. Bank of Jacksonville, 431 F.2d 341 (5th Cir.1970)—¶ **7.03; ¶ 7.03, n. 131, 141.**
Federal Deposit Ins. Corp. v. McKnight, 769 F.2d 658 (10th Cir.1985)—¶ **7.02, n. 81; ¶ 8.04, n. 310.**
Federal Deposit Ins. Corp. v. Merchants Nat. Bank of Mobile, 725 F.2d 634 (11th Cir.1984)—¶ **1.03, n. 152.**
Federal Deposit Ins. Corp. v. Moore, 448 F.Supp. 493 (D.S.C.1978)—¶ **6.03; ¶ 6.03, n. 100, 222.**
Federal Deposit Ins. Corp. v. Nemecek, 641 F.Supp. 740 (D.Kan.1986)—¶ **1.03, n. 150.**
Federal Deposit Ins. Corp. v. Newhart, 713 F.Supp. 320 (W.D.Mo.1989)—¶ **1.03, n. 155.**
Federal Deposit Ins. Corp. v. Percival, 752 F.Supp. 313 (D.Neb.1990)—¶ **1.03, n. 149.**
Federal Deposit Ins. Corp. v. Pioneer State Bank, 155 N.J.Super. 381, 382 A.2d 958 (N.J.Super.L.1977)—¶ **9.06, n. 342, 357.**
Federal Deposit Ins. Corp. v. Prann, 694 F.Supp. 1027 (D.Puerto Rico 1988)—¶ **1.03, n. 152.**
Federal Deposit Ins. Corp. v. Rockelman, 460 F.Supp. 999 (E.D.Wis.1978)—¶ **1.03; ¶ 1.03, n. 137.**
Federal Deposit Ins. Corp. v. Thompson, 54 Ga.App. 611, 188 S.E. 737 (Ga.App. 1936)—¶ **9.05, n. 315.**
Federal Deposit Ins. Corp. v. Trans Pacific Industries, Inc., 14 F.3d 10 (5th Cir. 1994)—¶ **5.03, n. 84.**
Federal Deposit Ins. Corp. v. Turner, 869 F.2d 270 (6th Cir.1989)—¶ **1.03, n. 152.**
Federal Deposit Ins. Corp. v. Vara, 1979 Mass.App.Div. 434 (Mass.App.Div. 1979)—¶ **6.03, n. 255.**
Federal Deposit Ins. Corp. v. Virginia Crossings Partnership, 909 F.2d 306 (8th Cir.1990)—¶ **1.03, n. 135.**
Federal Deposit Ins. Corp. v. Webb, 464 F.Supp. 520 (E.D.Tenn.1978)—¶ **3.01, n. 24; ¶ 3.04, n. 390.**
Federal Deposit Ins. Corp. v. West, 244 Ga. 396, 260 S.E.2d 89 (Ga.1979)—¶ **3.01, n. 25.**
Federal Deposit Ins. Corp. v. Wood, 758 F.2d 156 (6th Cir.1985)—¶ **1.03, n. 142.**

Federal Deposit Ins. Corp. v. Woodside Const., Inc., 979 F.2d 172 (9th Cir. 1992)—¶ **5.03, n. 79.**
Federal Deposit Ins. Corp. Liquidators of Northeast Bank v. Manning, 608 S.W.2d 270 (Tex.Civ.App.-Hous. (14 Dist.) 1980)—¶ **6.03, n. 181.**
Federal Factors, Inc. v. Wellbanke, 241 Ark. 44, 406 S.W.2d 712 (Ark.1966)—¶ **2.02, n. 140.**
Federal Ins. Co. v. Bank of New York, 1986 WL 213403 (N.Y.City Civ.Ct.1986)—¶ **9.03, n. 183.**
Federal Ins. Co. v. First Nat. Bank of Boston, 633 F.2d 978 (1st Cir.1980)—¶ **3.03, n. 303; ¶ 7.02, n. 92.**
Federal Ins. Co. v. Groveland State Bank, 372 N.Y.S.2d 18, 333 N.E.2d 334 (N.Y. 1975)—¶ **7.02, n. 92; ¶ 9.03, n. 136.**
Federal Ins. Co. v. NCNB Nat. Bank of North Carolina, 958 F.2d 1544 (11th Cir. 1992)—¶ **4.02, n. 12; ¶ 7.02, n. 67.**
Federal Reserve Bank of Richmond v. Malloy, 264 U.S. 160, 44 S.Ct. 296, 68 L.Ed. 617 (1924)—¶ **8.01, n. 36; ¶ 9.03, n. 148.**
Federal Sav. and Loan Ins. Corp. v. Port Allen Development Corp., 684 F.Supp. 439 (M.D.La.1988)—¶ **1.03, n. 151.**
Federal Sav. and Loan Ins. Corp. v. T.F. Stone-Liberty Land Associates, 787 S.W.2d 475 (Tex.App.-Dallas 1990)—¶ **1.03, n. 152.**
Fehling v. Cantonwine, 522 F.2d 604 (10th Cir.1975)—¶ **2.02, n. 261.**
Feldman Constr. Co. v. Union Bank, 28 Cal.App.3d 731, 104 Cal.Rptr. 912 (Cal. App. 2 Dist.1972)—¶ **3.02; ¶ 3.02, n. 103; ¶ 6.03, n. 208.**
Ferguson Pontiac-GMC, Inc. v. Henson, 892 P.2d 657 (Okla.App. Div. 1 1994)—¶ **2.01, n. 27.**
Fewox v. Tallahassee Bank & Trust Co., 249 So.2d 55 (Fla.App. 1 Dist.1971)—¶ **2.02, n. 167; ¶ 5.02, n. 16.**
Fidelity & Cas. Co. of New York v. Constitution Nat. Bank, 167 Conn. 478, 356 A.2d 117 (Conn.1975)—¶ **4.02, n. 28.**
Fidelity & Deposit Co. of Md. v. Chemical Bank New York Trust Co., 65 Misc.2d 619, 318 N.Y.S.2d 957 (N.Y.Sup.App. Term 1970)—¶ **4.02, n. 26.**
Fidelity & Deposit Co. of Md. v. First Nat. Bank of Kenosha, 98 Wis.2d 474, 297 N.W.2d 46 (Wis.App.1980)—¶ **4.02, n. 23.**
Fidelity Nat. Bank v. Reid, 180 Ga.App. 428, 348 S.E.2d 913 (Ga.App.1986)—¶ **6.03, n. 246.**
Fidelity Nat. Bank of Oklahoma City v. Copeland, 138 Okla. 19, 280 P. 273 (Okla.1929)—¶ **9.06, n. 358.**
Fifth Third Bank/Visa v. Gilbert, 17 Ohio Misc.2d 14, 478 N.E.2d 1324 (Ohio Mun. 1984)—¶ **11.02, n. 76.**

Financial Associates v. Impact Marketing Inc., 90 Misc.2d 545, 394 N.Y.S.2d 814 (N.Y.City Civ.Ct.1977)—¶ **3.03, n. 306**; ¶ **5.03, n. 98**.

Fireman's Fund Ins. Co. v. Security Pacific Nat. Bank, 85 Cal.App.3d 797, 149 Cal. Rptr. 883 (Cal.App. 2 Dist.1978)— ¶ **2.02, n. 264**; ¶ **7.02, n. 92**; ¶ **7.03, n. 118**.

Firemen's Ins. Co. of Newark, New Jersey v. Chase Manhattan Bank, N.A., 102 Misc.2d 613, 424 N.Y.S.2d 83 (N.Y.Sup. 1979)—¶ **7.03, n. 175**.

First Alabama Bank of Guntersville v. Hunt, 402 So.2d 992 (Ala.Civ.App. 1981)—¶ **3.04, n. 390**.

First American Nat. Bank of Nashville v. Commerce Union Bank of White County, 692 S.W.2d 642 (Tenn.Ct.App. 1985)—¶ **9.02, n. 103**.

Firstar Eagan Bank, N.A. v. Marquette Bank Minneapolis, N.A., 466 N.W.2d 8 (Minn.App.1991)—¶ **9.05, n. 242**.

First Bank & Trust Co., Palatine v. Post, 10 Ill.App.3d 127, 293 N.E.2d 907 (Ill.App. 1 Dist.1973)—¶ **5.03**; ¶ **5.03, n. 90**; ¶ **6.03**; ¶ **6.03, n. 282**.

First City Nat. Bank v. Federal Deposit Ins. Co., 730 F.Supp. 501 (E.D.N.Y.1990)— ¶ **1.03, n. 154**.

First City Nat. Bank v. Long–Lewis Hardware Co., 363 So.2d 770 (Ala.1978)— ¶ **9.06, n. 358**.

First Galesburg Nat. Bank & Trust Co. v. Martin, 58 Ill.App.3d 113, 15 Ill.Dec. 603, 373 N.E.2d 1075 (Ill.App. 3 Dist. 1978)—¶ **6.03, n. 235**.

First Georgia Bank v. Webster, 168 Ga.App. 307, 308 S.E.2d 579 (Ga.App.1983)— ¶ **4.04, n. 144**; ¶ **8.03, n. 231**; ¶ **9.05, n. 296**.

FirsTier Bank, N.A. v. Triplett, 242 Neb. 614, 497 N.W.2d 339 (Neb.1993)— ¶ **6.03, n. 230**.

First Intern. Bank of Israel, Ltd. v. L. Blankstein & Son, Inc., 465 N.Y.S.2d 888, 452 N.E.2d 1216 (N.Y.1983)— ¶ **3.03, n. 324, 326**.

First Intern. Bank of Israel, Ltd. v. L. Blankstein & Son, Inc., 88 A.D.2d 501, 449 N.Y.S.2d 737 (N.Y.A.D. 1 Dept. 1982)—¶ **6.03**; ¶ **6.03, n. 152**.

First Interstate Bank of Idaho v. Gill, 108 Idaho 576, 701 P.2d 196 (Idaho 1985)— ¶ **9.05, n. 251**.

First Israel Bank & Trust Co. of New York v. Franklin Nat. Bank, 9 UCC Rep. Serv. 861 (N.Y.Sup.1971)—¶ **3.03, n. 379**; ¶ **7.02, n. 95**.

First Nat. Bank v. American Sur. Co., 237 Ala. 35, 185 So. 365 (Ala.1938)—¶ **9.06, n. 367**.

First Nat. Bank v. Brown, 181 N.W.2d 178 (Iowa 1970)—¶ **9.05, n. 307**.

First Nat. Bank v. Duncan Sav. and Loan Ass'n, 656 F.Supp. 358 (W.D.Okla. 1987)—¶ **2.01, n. 10**; ¶ **8.01, n. 47, 64, 67**.

First Nat. Bank v. Graham, 79 Pa. 106 (Pa.1875)—¶ **9.05, n. 303**.

First Nat. Bank v. Hargrove, 503 S.W.2d 856 (Tex.Civ.App.-Texarkana 1973)— ¶ **6.03, n. 249**; ¶ **9.05, n. 262**.

First Nat. Bank v. Hector Supply Co., 236 So.2d 204 (Fla.App. 3 Dist.1970)— ¶ **9.06, n. 400**.

First Nat. Bank v. Hubbs, 566 S.W.2d 375 (Tex.Civ.App.-Hous. (1Dist.) 1978)— ¶ **9.06, n. 365**.

First Nat. Bank v. Hull, 189 Neb. 581, 204 N.W.2d 90 (Neb.1973)—¶ **1.03**; ¶ **1.03, n. 72**.

First Nat. Bank v. Jackson, 140 Okla. 282, 283 P. 242 (Okla.1929)—¶ **9.06, n. 319**.

First Nat. Bank v. Jefferson Sales & Distributors, Inc., 341 F.Supp. 659 (S.D.Miss.1971)—¶ **1.03**; ¶ **1.03, n. 112**.

First Nat. Bank v. North Adams Hoosac Sav. Bank, 7 Mass.App.Ct. 790, 391 N.E.2d 689 (Mass.App.Ct.1979)—¶ **2.02, n. 144**.

First Nat. Bank v. Peltz, 176 Pa. 513, 35 A. 218 (Pa.1896)—¶ **9.06, n. 393**.

First Nat. Bank v. Twombly, 213 Mont. 66, 689 P.2d 1226 (Mont.1984)—¶ **1.04, n. 217**; ¶ **2.02, n. 152**.

First Nat. Bank v. Whaley, 168 W.Va. 327, 284 S.E.2d 618 (W.Va.1981)—¶ **1.03, n. 108**.

First Nat. Bank v. W.P. Seawell Lumber Co., 135 Okla. 201, 274 P. 873 (Okla. 1928)—¶ **9.06, n. 367**.

First Nat. Bank & Trust Co. v. Cutright, 189 Neb. 805, 205 N.W.2d 542 (Neb. 1973)—¶ **4.02, n. 21**.

First Nat. Bank and Trust Co. of Oklahoma City v. Iowa Beef Processors, Inc., 626 F.2d 764 (10th Cir.1980)—¶ **9.06, n. 414**.

First Nat. Bank & Trust Co. v. Osage Supply Co., 186 Okla. 259, 97 P.2d 3 (Okla. 1939)—¶ **9.06, n. 358, 367**.

First Nat. Bank and Trust Co. of Treasure Coast v. Belmont Nat. Bank, 43 UCC Rep. Serv. 2d 666 (Ohio App. 7 Dist. 2001)—¶ **8.02**; ¶ **8.02, n. 112, 115, 127, 165, 189**; ¶ **8.04, n. 416**; ¶ **9.01, n. 42**; ¶ **9.03, n. 191**.

First Nat. Bank and Trust Co. v. Kissee, 859 P.2d 502 (Okla.1993)—¶ **9.05, n. 277, 286, 308**.

First Nat. Bank, Giddings v. Helwig, 464 S.W.2d 953 (Tex.Civ.App.-Austin 1971)—¶ **6.03, n. 265**.

First Nat. Bank in Albuquerque v. Allison, 85 N.M. 511, 514 P.2d 30 (N.M.1973)— ¶ **6.03**; ¶ **6.03, n. 299**.

First Nat. Bank In Eureka v. Giles, 225 Mont. 467, 733 P.2d 357 (Mont.1987)—¶ 8.01, n. 53.
First Nat. Bank in Grand Prairie v. Lone Star Life Ins. Co., 524 S.W.2d 525 (Tex. Civ.App.-Dallas 1975)—¶ 9.06, n. 414.
First Nat. Bank in Harvey v. Colonial Bank, 898 F.Supp. 1220 (N.D.Ill.1995)—¶ 3.03; ¶ 8.02, n. 169.
First Nat. Bank in Lenox v. Creston Livestock Auction, Inc., 447 N.W.2d 132 (Iowa 1989)—¶ 3.03, n. 205, 211.
First Nat. Bank in Marlinton v. Blackhurst, 176 W.Va. 472, 345 S.E.2d 567 (W.Va. 1986)—¶ 5.03, n. 86.
First Nat. Bank of Arizona v. Continental Bank, 138 Ariz. 194, 673 P.2d 938 (Ariz. App. Div. 1 1983)—¶ 9.01, n. 21.
First Nat. Bank of Atlanta v. C. & S. Concrete Structures, Inc., 128 Ga.App. 330, 196 S.E.2d 473 (Ga.App.1973)—¶ 5.03, n. 80.
First Nat. Bank of Blue Island v. Estate of Philp, 106 Ill.App.3d 360, 62 Ill.Dec. 433, 436 N.E.2d 15 (Ill.App. 1 Dist. 1982)—¶ 9.06, n. 358.
First Nat. Bank of Boston v. Fidelity Bank, Nat. Ass'n, 724 F.Supp. 1168 (E.D.Pa. 1989)—¶ 9.03, n. 220.
First Nat. Bank of Cape Canaveral v. Keshishian, 427 So.2d 313 (Fla.App. 5 Dist. 1983)—¶ 9.03, n. 162, 165, 183.
First Nat. Bank of Clinton v. Julian, 383 F.2d 329 (8th Cir.1967)—¶ 9.05, n. 258.
First Nat. Bank of Commerce v. Anderson Ford–Lincoln–Mercury, Inc., 704 S.W.2d 83 (Tex.App.-Dallas 1985)—¶ 4.04, n. 144.
First Nat. Bank of Fort Worth v. United States, 41 UCC Rep. Serv. 1583 (Cl.Ct. 1985)—¶ 4.04, n. 173; ¶ 9.01, n. 68.
First Nat. Bank of Gatlinburg v. RepublicBank Dallas, N.A., 676 F.Supp. 128 (N.D.Tex.1987)—¶ 8.01, n. 31.
First Nat. Bank of Gwinnett v. Barrett, 141 Ga.App. 161, 233 S.E.2d 24 (Ga.App. 1977)—¶ 3.01, n. 39; ¶ 3.02, n. 71.
First Nat. Bank of Layton v. Egbert, 663 P.2d 85 (Utah 1983)—¶ 6.03, n. 255.
First Nat. Bank of Lewisville, Ark. v. First Nat. Bank of Clinton, Ky., 258 F.3d 727 (8th Cir.2001)—¶ 8.01, n. 23.
First Nat. Bank of Linton v. Otto Huber & Sons, Inc., 394 F.Supp. 1284 (D.S.D. 1975)—¶ 3.03; ¶ 3.03, n. 290.
First Nat. Bank of Martinsville v. Cobler, 215 Va. 852, 213 S.E.2d 800 (Va.1975)—¶ 6.03, n. 243.
First Nat. Bank of Mexico v. Munns, 602 S.W.2d 910 (Mo.App. E.D.1980)—¶ 3.03, n. 295.
First Nat. Bank of Neenah v. Security Nat. Bank of Springfield, 32 UCC Rep. Serv. 926 (D.Mass.1981)—¶ 7.03, n. 178.
First Nat. Bank of Odessa v. Fazzari, 223 N.Y.S.2d 483, 179 N.E.2d 493 (N.Y. 1961)—¶ 3.03, n. 244; ¶ 6.02, n. 61.
First Nat. Bank & Trust Co. in Macon v. Thompson, 240 Ga. 494, 241 S.E.2d 253 (Ga.1978)—¶ 6.01; ¶ 6.01, n. 29.
First Nat. Bank, United States v., 263 F.Supp. 298 (D.Mass.1967)—¶ 1.03, n. 157.
First Nat. City Bank v. American Broadcasting Co., 68 Misc.2d 861, 328 N.Y.S.2d 326 (N.Y.Sup.1971)—¶ 2.05, n. 309; ¶ 6.03, n. 143.
First Nat. City Bank v. Metal Trading Co., Ltd., 71 F.R.D. 363 (S.D.Fla.1976)—¶ 2.02; ¶ 2.02, n. 173; ¶ 6.01, n. 25, 28.
First Nat. City Bank, United States v., 321 F.2d 14 (2nd Cir.1963)—¶ 9.06, n. 399.
First New Haven Nat. Bank v. Tirkot, 25 UCC Rep. Serv. 795 (Conn.Super.1978)—¶ 6.03, n. 283.
First Pennsylvania Banking & Trust Co. v. De Lise, 186 Pa.Super. 398, 142 A.2d 401 (Pa.Super.1958)—¶ 4.06, n. 219.
First Pennsylvania Bank, N. A. v. Triester, 251 Pa.Super. 372, 380 A.2d 826 (Pa.Super.1977)—¶ 6.03, n. 202.
First RepublicBank Fort Worth v. Norglass, 751 F.Supp. 1224 (N.D.Tex.1990)—¶ 1.03, n. 152.
First Rome Bank v. Reese Oil Co., Inc., 206 Ga.App. 667, 426 S.E.2d 384 (Ga.App. 1992)—¶ 4.02, n. 10; ¶ 7.02, n. 67.
First Sec. Bank v. Goddard, 181 Mont. 407, 593 P.2d 1040 (Mont.1979)—¶ 3.01, n. 6.
First Sec. Bank v. Pan American Bank, 215 F.3d 1147 (10th Cir.2000)—¶ 10.02, n. 8, 9; ¶ 10.04, n. 54, 56, 58; ¶ 10.07, n. 93, 99, 114, 122; ¶ 10.09, n. 184, 192; ¶ 10.12, n. 252.
First Sec. Bank of Utah, N.A. v. Ezra C. Lundahl, Inc., 22 Utah 2d 433, 454 P.2d 886 (Utah 1969)—¶ 8.03; ¶ 8.03, n. 201, 214.
First State Bank v. Clark, 91 N.M. 117, 570 P.2d 1144 (N.M.1977)—¶ 2.01, n. 10; ¶ 2.02, n. 238.
First State Bank v. Hunt, 77 Okla. 4, 185 P. 1089 (Okla.1919)—¶ 9.06, n. 371.
First Stroudsburg Nat. Bank v. Nixon, 53 Pa. D. & C.2d 672 (Pa.Com.Pl.1971)—¶ 4.03, n. 110.
First Union National Bank v. Bank One, 47 UCC Rep.Serv.2d 645 (E.D.Pa.2002)—¶ 7.02, n. 45; ¶ 8.03, n. 197.
First United Bank v. Philmont Corp., 533 So.2d 449 (Miss.1988)—¶ 11.01, n. 3.
First Western Bank & Trust Co. v. Bookasta, 267 Cal.App.2d 910, 73 Cal.Rptr. 657 (Cal.App. 2 Dist.1968)—¶ 4.02, n. 1.
First Wyoming Bank v. Cabinet Craft Distributors, Inc., 624 P.2d 227 (Wyo. 1981)—¶ 8.03, n. 222.

Fisher v. First Citizens Bank, 302 Mont. 473, 14 P.3d 1228 (Mont.2000)—¶ **6.03, n. 287.**

Fisher v. North Penn Bank, 77 Pa.Super. 558 (Pa.Super.1921)—¶ **9.05, n. 315.**

Fithian v. Jamar, 286 Md. 161, 410 A.2d 569 (Md.1979)—¶ **5.02, n. 66;** ¶ **6.03, n. 177.**

Five Towns College v. Citibank, N.A., 108 A.D.2d 420, 489 N.Y.S.2d 338 (N.Y.A.D. 2 Dept.1985)—¶ **9.03, n. 196.**

Flagship Bank of Seminole v. Complete Interiors, Inc., 450 So.2d 337 (Fla.App. 5 Dist.1984)—¶ **9.03, n. 165.**

Flatiron Linen, Inc. v. First American State Bank, 23 P.3d 1209 (Colo.2001)—¶ **7.01, n. 26.**

Flatiron Linen, Inc. v. First American State Bank, 1 P.3d 244 (Colo.App.1999)—¶ **4.04, n. 169.**

Fleet Real Estate Funding Corp. v. Frampton, 812 P.2d 416 (Okla.App. Div. 3 1991)—¶ **6.03, n. 228.**

Florida Bar v. Allstate Ins. Co., 391 So.2d 238 (Fla.App. 3 Dist.1980)—¶ **4.02, n. 23.**

Florida Federal Sav. & Loan Ass'n v. Martin, 400 So.2d 151 (Fla.App. 2 Dist. 1981)—¶ **9.03;** ¶ **9.03, n. 162, 205, 211;** ¶ **9.04;** ¶ **9.04, n. 234.**

Florida Frozen Foods, Inc. v. National Commercial Bank & Trust Co., 81 A.D.2d 978, 439 N.Y.S.2d 771 (N.Y.A.D. 3 Dept. 1981)—¶ **4.04;** ¶ **4.04, n. 172.**

Flushing Nat. Bank v. Brightside Mfg. Inc., 59 Misc.2d 108, 298 N.Y.S.2d 197 (N.Y.Sup.1969)—¶ **6.03, n. 141.**

Ford Motor Credit Co. v. Morgan, 404 Mass. 537, 536 N.E.2d 587 (Mass. 1989)—¶ **3.04, n. 432.**

Ford Motor Credit Co. v. United Services Automobile Assn., 11 UCC Rep. Serv. 361 (N.Y.City Civ.Ct.1972)—¶ **3.02, n. 98.**

Fore v. Bles, 149 Ariz. 603, 721 P.2d 151 (Ariz.App. Div. 1 1986)—¶ **3.01, n. 25;** ¶ **3.02, n. 65.**

Foreman v. Melrod, 257 Md. 435, 263 A.2d 559 (Md.1970)—¶ **2.02, n. 177.**

Foremost Ins. Co. v. First City Sav. & Loan Ass'n of Lucedale, 374 So.2d 840 (Miss. 1979)—¶ **3.03, n. 322.**

Fortune v. City Nat. Bank & Trust Co., 671 P.2d 69 (Okla.App. Div. 2 1983)—¶ **9.06, n. 374.**

Foulkrod v. First Nat. Bank of Waterloo, 70 Misc.2d 616, 334 N.Y.S.2d 285 (N.Y.Co. Ct.1972)—¶ **9.05, n. 261.**

Fourth St. Nat. Bank v. Yardley, 165 U.S. 634, 17 S.Ct. 439, 41 L.Ed. 855 (1897)—¶ **4.04, n. 147.**

France v. Ford Motor Credit Co., 323 Ark. 167, 913 S.W.2d 770 (Ark.1996)—¶ **2.04, n. 273.**

Franklin v. Safeco Ins. Co. of America, 303 Or. 376, 737 P.2d 1231 (Or.1987)—¶ **7.03, n. 131.**

Franklin Nat. Bank v. Eurez Const. Corp., 60 Misc.2d 499, 301 N.Y.S.2d 845 (N.Y.Sup.1969)—¶ **1.04, n. 228;** ¶ **6.03;** ¶ **6.03, n. 161.**

Franklin Nat. Bank v. Shapiro, 7 UCC Rep. Serv. 317 (N.Y.Sup.1970)—¶ **7.03, n. 164.**

Franklin Nat. Bank v. Sidney Gotowner, Inc., 4 UCC Rep. Serv. 953 (N.Y.Sup. 1967)—¶ **6.01, n. 20;** ¶ **6.03, n. 146.**

Frantz v. First Nat. Bank of Anchorage, 584 P.2d 1125 (Alaska 1978)—¶ **3.03, n. 276.**

Fred Meyer, Inc. v. Temco Metal Products Co., 267 Or. 230, 516 P.2d 80 (Or. 1973)—¶ **4.02, n. 21.**

Fred Shearer & Sons, Inc. v. Prendergast, 152 Or.App. 657, 955 P.2d 324 (Or.App. 1998)—¶ **4.03, n. 131;** ¶ **5.03, n. 79.**

Free v. Elberson, 157 Mont. 424, 486 P.2d 857 (Mont.1971)—¶ **9.05, n. 260.**

Fremarek v. John Hancock Mut. Life Ins. Co., 272 Ill.App.3d 1067, 209 Ill.Dec. 423, 651 N.E.2d 601 (Ill.App. 1 Dist. 1995)—¶ **7.01, n. 42.**

Friede v. National City Bank of New York, 222 A.D. 645, 227 N.Y.S. 378 (N.Y.A.D. 1 Dept.1928)—¶ **9.05, n. 301.**

Friedman v. First Nat. Bank, 344 Mass. 593, 183 N.E.2d 722 (Mass.1962)—¶ **9.06, n. 345.**

Frontier Federal Sav. and Loan Ass'n v. Commercial Bank, N.A., 806 P.2d 1140 (Okla.App. Div. 3 1990)—¶ **9.03, n. 132, 135.**

Frost Nat. Bank v. Midwest Autohaus, Inc., 241 F.3d 862 (7th Cir.2001)—¶ **3.03;** ¶ **4.03, n. 110;** ¶ **9.03, n. 124;** ¶ **9.05, n. 313.**

Frost Nat. Bank v. Nicholas & Barrera, 500 S.W.2d 906 (Tex.Civ.App.-San Antonio 1973)—¶ **2.02;** ¶ **2.02, n. 250, 264.**

Frye v. Farmers and Merchants Bank of Cape Girardeau, 561 S.W.2d 392 (Mo. App.1977)—¶ **3.03, n. 252.**

Fulka v. Florida Commercial Banks, Inc., 371 So.2d 521 (Fla.App. 3 Dist.1979)—¶ **7.03.**

Fulton Nat. Bank v. Delco Corp., 128 Ga. App. 16, 195 S.E.2d 455 (Ga.App. 1973)—¶ **3.03;** ¶ **3.03, n. 358, 365;** ¶ **4.04, n. 180;** ¶ **6.03, n. 93, 99, 219;** ¶ **9.01, n. 55.**

Funding Consultants, Inc. v. Aetna Cas. and Sur. Co., 187 Conn. 637, 447 A.2d 1163 (Conn.1982)—¶ **3.03, n. 254, 329.**

Fur Funtastic, Ltd. v. Kearns, 104 Misc.2d 1030, 430 N.Y.S.2d 27 (N.Y.City Civ.Ct. 1980)—¶ **4.04, n. 178;** ¶ **6.03, n. 220.**

G

Gabovitch v. Coolidge Bank & Trust Co., 1980 Mass.App.Div. 64 (Mass.App.Div. 1980)—¶ **7.02, n. 92.**

Gaetani v. Goss–Golden West Sheet Metal Profit Sharing Plan, 101 Cal.Rptr.2d 432 (Cal.App. 1 Dist.2000)—¶ **3.02, n. 129;** ¶ **4.06, n. 206.**

Gaffney v. Community Federal Sav. and Loan Ass'n, 706 S.W.2d 530 (Mo.App. E.D.1986)—¶ **11.02, n. 92.**

Galatia Community State Bank v. Kindy, 307 Ark. 467, 821 S.W.2d 765 (Ark. 1991)—¶ **3.03, n. 250.**

Galaxy Boat Mfg. Co. v. East End State Bank, 641 S.W.2d 584 (Tex.App.-Hous. (14 Dist.) 1982)—¶ **4.04, n. 144.**

Gallagher v. Santa Fe Federal Employees Federal Credit Union, 132 N.M. 552, 52 P.3d 412, 48 UCC Rep.Serv.2d 655 (App. 2002)—¶ **7.03, n. 123, 152.**

Gallant Ins. Co. v. Amaizo Federal Credit Union, 726 N.E.2d 860 (Ind.App.2000)—¶ **7.01, n. 4.**

Gallinaro v. Fitzpatrick, 359 Mass. 6, 267 N.E.2d 649 (Mass.1971)—¶ **4.03, n. 74.**

Garden Check Cashing Service, Inc. v. First Nat. City Bank, 25 A.D.2d 137, 267 N.Y.S.2d 698 (N.Y.A.D. 1 Dept.1966)—¶ **1.01, n. 23;** ¶ **2.02, n. 52;** ¶ **4.04, n. 154;** ¶ **8.01, n. 67.**

Gardner v. Warren Bank, 14 Mich.App. 548, 165 N.W.2d 869 (Mich.App.1968)—¶ **9.05, n. 278.**

Gary Plastic Packaging Corp. v. Merrill Lynch, Pierce, Fenner & Smith, Inc., 756 F.2d 230 (2nd Cir.1985)—¶ **9.05, n. 249.**

Gas Reclamation, Inc. Securities Litigation, In re, 741 F.Supp. 1094 (S.D.N.Y. 1990)—¶ **2.01, n. 10.**

Gatoil (U.S.A.), Inc. v. Forest Hill State Bank, 1 UCC Rep. Serv. 2d 171 (D.Md. 1986)—¶ **9.02, n. 111;** ¶ **10.03, n. 47;** ¶ **10.09;** ¶ **10.09, n. 175.**

G.E. Capital Mortg. Services, Inc. v. Neely, 135 N.C.App. 187, 519 S.E.2d 553 (N.C.App.1999)—¶ **6.03, n. 230.**

Gehrig v. Ray, 332 So.2d 703 (Fla.App. 1 Dist.1976)—¶ **5.02;** ¶ **5.02, n. 35.**

Geiger Finance Co. v. Graham, 123 Ga.App. 771, 182 S.E.2d 521 (Ga.App.1971)—¶ **2.02;** ¶ **2.02, n. 80, 82, 86, 89.**

General Elec. Capital Corp. v. Central Bank, 49 F.3d 280 (7th Cir.1995)—¶ **10.04, n. 54.**

General Elec. Credit Corp. v. R.A. Heintz Const. Co., 302 F.Supp. 958 (D.Or. 1969)—¶ **1.03, n. 125.**

General Inv. Corp. v. Angelini, 58 N.J. 396, 278 A.2d 193 (N.J.1971)—¶ **3.03;** ¶ **3.03, n. 263.**

Gensplit Finance Corp. v. Link Power & Machinery Corp., 36 UCC Rep. Serv. 588 (S.D.N.Y.1983)—¶ **2.02, n. 162.**

Gentner and Co. v. Wells Fargo Bank, 90 Cal.Rptr.2d 904 (Cal.App. 2 Dist.1999)—¶ **3.03, n. 208, 373;** ¶ **4.04, n. 173, 175;** ¶ **7.02, n. 82;** ¶ **8.02;** ¶ **8.02, n. 129, 132, 169, 191;** ¶ **9.01, n. 52, 67, 69.**

George, In re, 85 B.R. 133 (Bkrtcy.D.Kan. 1988)—¶ **2.02, n. 116.**

George Whalley Co. v. National City Bank of Cleveland, 55 Ohio App.2d 205, 380 N.E.2d 742 (Ohio App. 8 Dist.1977)—¶ **9.05, n. 310.**

Georgia Bank & Trust Co. v. Hadarits, 221 Ga. 125, 143 S.E.2d 627 (Ga.1965)—¶ **9.06, n. 320.**

Georgia R.R. Bank & Trust Co. v. First Nat. Bank & Trust Co. of Augusta, 139 Ga. App. 683, 229 S.E.2d 482 (Ga.App. 1976)—¶ **8.02, n. 112;** ¶ **9.03, n. 220.**

Germantown Trust Co. v. Powell, 265 Pa. 71, 108 A. 441 (Pa.1919)—¶ **9.05, n. 315.**

Get It Kwik of America, Inc. v. First Alabama Bank, 361 So.2d 568 (Ala.Civ.App. 1978)—¶ **9.06, n. 356.**

Getty Petroleum Corp. v. American Exp. Travel Related Services Co., Inc., 660 N.Y.S.2d 689, 683 N.E.2d 311 (N.Y. 1997)—¶ **7.03, n. 173.**

Ghitter v. Edge, 118 Ga.App. 750, 165 S.E.2d 598 (Ga.App.1968)—¶ **2.04, n. 278.**

Gibraltar Sav. Ass'n v. Watson, 624 S.W.2d 650 (Tex.App.-Hous. (14 Dist.) 1981)—¶ **6.03;** ¶ **6.03, n. 235.**

Gilbreath v. First State Bank of Joplin, 859 S.W.2d 237 (Mo.App. S.D.1993)—¶ **9.05, n. 284.**

Gillen v. Maryland Nat. Bank, 274 Md. 96, 333 A.2d 329 (Md.1975)—¶ **9.05, n. 293.**

Gillespie v. Riley Management Corp., 59 Ill.2d 211, 319 N.E.2d 753 (Ill.1974)—¶ **3.01;** ¶ **3.01, n. 9.**

Gillet v. Bank of America, 160 N.Y. 549, 55 N.E. 292 (N.Y.1899)—¶ **9.06, n. 330.**

Gillman v. Chase Manhattan Bank, N.A., 537 N.Y.S.2d 787, 534 N.E.2d 824 (N.Y. 1988)—¶ **9.06, n. 413.**

Gilmartin v. Osborne Trust Co., 266 A.D. 1022, 44 N.Y.S.2d 938 (N.Y.A.D. 2 Dept. 1943)—¶ **9.06, n. 350.**

Gimbel Bros. v. White, 256 A.D. 439, 10 N.Y.S.2d 666 (N.Y.A.D. 3 Dept.1939)—¶ **9.05, n. 241.**

Gimby v. Frost, 84 A.D.2d 806, 444 N.Y.S.2d 143 (N.Y.A.D. 2 Dept.1981)—¶ **7.01, n. 34.**

Gina Chin & Associates, Inc. v. First Union Bank, 256 Va. 59, 500 S.E.2d 516 (Va. 1998)—¶ **8.03, n. 195, 227;** ¶ **9.03, n. 187.**

Gina Chin & Associates, Inc. v. First Union Bank, 260 Va. 533, 537 S.E.2d 573 (Va.

2000)—¶ **8.03, n. 195, 227**; ¶ **9.03, n. 187.**

Girard Bank v. Mount Holly State Bank, 474 F.Supp. 1225 (D.N.J.1979)—¶ **7.03, n. 119, 129, 175;** ¶ **9.03, n. 190.**

Glennan v. Rochester Trust & Safe Deposit Co., 209 N.Y. 12, 102 N.E. 537 (N.Y. 1913)—¶ **9.05, n. 290.**

Glenn Justice Mortg. Co., Inc. v. First Nat. Bank, 592 F.2d 567 (10th Cir.1979)—¶ **9.06, n. 360.**

Global Distribution Network, Inc. v. Star Expansion Co., 949 F.2d 910 (7th Cir. 1991)—¶ **9.01, n. 81.**

Godat v. Mercantile Bank of Northwest County, 884 S.W.2d 1 (Mo.App. E.D. 1994)—¶ **3.03, n. 230, 323;** ¶ **4.04, n. 177;** ¶ **6.01, n. 11;** ¶ **7.01, n. 26.**

Godfrey State Bank v. Mundy, 90 Ill.App.3d 142, 45 Ill.Dec. 549, 412 N.E.2d 1131 (Ill.App. 4 Dist.1980)—¶ **6.03, n. 249, 267.**

Goggin v. Bank of America Nat. Trust & Sav. Ass'n, 183 F.2d 322 (9th Cir. 1950)—¶ **9.06, n. 327.**

Goldberg v. Rothman, 66 Misc.2d 981, 322 N.Y.S.2d 931 (N.Y.City Civ.Ct.1971)—¶ **3.03;** ¶ **3.03, n. 345.**

Goldstein v. Jefferson Title & Trust Co., 95 Pa.Super. 167 (Pa.Super.1928)—¶ **9.06, n. 344.**

Gonsalves v. Bank of America Nat. Trust & Savings Ass'n, 16 Cal.2d 169, 105 P.2d 118 (Cal.1940)—¶ **9.06, n. 325.**

Gonzalez v. Hughes Aircraft Employees Fed. Credit Union, 83 Cal.Rptr.2d 763 (Cal.App. 2 Dist.1999)—¶ **11.02, n. 94.**

Gonzalez v. Old Kent Mortgage Company and Quality Builders, Inc., 2000 WL 1469313 (E.D.Pa.2000)—¶ **3.04, n. 425.**

Good v. Good, 72 N.C.App. 312, 324 S.E.2d 43 (N.C.App.1985)—¶ **3.01, n. 21, 45.**

Goodwin v. Robarts, 10 Ex. 76 (Ex Ct 1875)—¶ **1.03, n. 76;** ¶ **2.01;** ¶ **2.01, n. 28.**

Gordon v. State St. Bank & Trust Co., 361 Mass. 258, 280 N.E.2d 152 (Mass. 1972)—¶ **3.02;** ¶ **3.02, n. 106;** ¶ **7.03;** ¶ **7.03, n. 152, 170.**

Gorham v. John F. Kennedy College, Inc., 191 Neb. 790, 217 N.W.2d 919 (Neb. 1974)—¶ **6.03, n. 242.**

Goss v. Trinity Sav. & Loan Ass'n, 813 P.2d 492 (Okla.1991)—¶ **2.01, n. 10.**

Govoni & Sons Const. Co., Inc. v. Mechanics Bank, 51 Mass.App.Ct. 35, 742 N.E.2d 1094 (Mass.App.Ct.2001)—¶ **2.02, n. 264;** ¶ **3.03, n. 303;** ¶ **7.02, n. 92;** ¶ **7.03, n. 118;** ¶ **8.03, n. 215, 232.**

Grabowski v. Bank of Boston, 997 F.Supp. 130 (D.Mass.1998)—¶ **10.02, n. 17, 30;** ¶ **10.03, n. 39.**

Grabowski v. Bank of Boston, 997 F.Supp. 111 (D.Mass.1997)—¶ **10.02;** ¶ **10.02, n. 17.**

Grain Traders, Inc. v. Citibank, N.A., 160 F.3d 97 (2nd Cir.1998)—¶ **10.04, n. 56, 68, 72;** ¶ **10.07, n. 91.**

Grain Traders, Inc. v. Citibank, N.A., 960 F.Supp. 784 (S.D.N.Y.1997)—¶ **10.04, n. 76;** ¶ **10.07, n. 98.**

Gray v. American Exp. Co., 743 F.2d 10 (D.C.Cir.1984)—¶ **11.02, n. 62.**

Gray v. American Exp. Co., 34 N.C.App. 714, 239 S.E.2d 621 (N.C.App.1977)—¶ **2.05, n. 305, 316;** ¶ **3.01, n. 4.**

G & R Corp. v. American Sec. & Trust Co., 523 F.2d 1164 (D.C.Cir.1975)—¶ **9.01, n. 14.**

Great Western Bank v. Steve James Ford, Inc., 915 F.Supp. 392 (S.D.Ga.1996)—¶ **2.04, n. 292, 297.**

Greene v. Citizens and Southern Bank of Cobb County, 134 Ga.App. 73, 213 S.E.2d 175 (Ga.App.1975)—¶ **9.06, n. 353.**

Greene v. Cotton, 457 S.W.2d 493 (Ky. 1970)—¶ **6.03, n. 244.**

Green Property Corp. v. O'Callaghan, Saunders & Stumm, P.C., 177 Ga.App. 686, 340 S.E.2d 652 (Ga.App.1986)—¶ **4.04, n. 144;** ¶ **9.02, n. 103.**

Green Tree Financial Corp. v. Randolph, 531 U.S. 79, 121 S.Ct. 513, 148 L.Ed.2d 373 (2000)—¶ **8.01, n. 46;** ¶ **11.02, n. 93.**

Greenwald's Estate, In re, 143 N.Y.S.2d 464 (N.Y.Sur.1955)—¶ **9.06, n. 331.**

Gregoire v. Lowndes Bank, 176 W.Va. 296, 342 S.E.2d 264 (W.Va.1986)—¶ **1.03, n. 148;** ¶ **2.02, n. 128.**

Griffin v. Ellinger, 538 S.W.2d 97 (Tex. 1976)—¶ **3.02, n. 128;** ¶ **5.03, n. 98.**

Griffin–Townsend Co. v. First State Bank in Talihina, 191 Okla. 460, 130 P.2d 540 (Okla.1942)—¶ **9.06, n. 343.**

Griffith v. Griffith, 250 Ark. 845, 467 S.W.2d 737 (Ark.1971)—¶ **6.03, n. 213.**

Grimes v. Grimes, 47 N.C.App. 353, 267 S.E.2d 372 (N.C.App.1980)—¶ **2.04, n. 278.**

Grisinger v. Golden State Bank, 92 Cal.App. 443, 268 P. 425 (Cal.App. 2 Dist.1928)—¶ **9.05, n. 283.**

Grist v. Osgood, 90 Nev. 165, 521 P.2d 368 (Nev.1974)—¶ **4.03, n. 121.**

Grotz v. Jerutis, 13 Ill.App.3d 543, 301 N.E.2d 60 (Ill.App. 1 Dist.1973)—¶ **5.03, n. 79.**

Grubb v. Federal Deposit Ins. Corp., 868 F.2d 1151 (10th Cir.1989)—¶ **1.03, n. 152.**

Guaranty Bank & Trust Co. v. Federal Reserve Bank of Kansas City, 454 F.Supp. 488 (W.D.Okla.1977)—¶ **4.02, n. 40;** ¶ **8.04, n. 467;** ¶ **9.01, n. 11.**

Guaranty Federal Sav. Bank v. Horseshoe Operating Co., 793 S.W.2d 652 (Tex. 1990)—¶ **4.04, n. 176.**

TABLE OF CASES

Guaranty Federal Sav. & Loan Ass'n v. Horseshoe Operating Co., 748 S.W.2d 519 (Tex.App.-Dallas 1988)—¶ **4.04, n. 169, 176.**

Guardian Life Ins. Co. of America v. Chemical Bank, 705 N.Y.S.2d 553, 727 N.E.2d 111 (N.Y.2000)—¶ **7.03, n. 174.**

Guardian Life Ins. Co. of America v. Weisman, 223 F.3d 229 (3rd Cir.2000)— ¶ **4.02, n. 14; ¶ 7.02, n. 65; ¶ 7.03, n. 178.**

Guardian Life Ins. Co. of America v. Weisman, 30 F.Supp.2d 720 (D.N.J.1998)— ¶ **7.03, n. 178.**

Guild v. Meredith Village Sav. Bank, 639 F.2d 25 (1st Cir.1980)—¶ **6.03, n. 284, 286.**

Guilds v. Monroe County Bank, 41 Mich. App. 616, 200 N.W.2d 769 (Mich.App. 1972)—¶ **9.06, n. 409, 414.**

Gullette v. Federal Deposit Ins. Corp., 231 Va. 486, 344 S.E.2d 920 (Va.1986)— ¶ **6.03, n. 241.**

Gunter v. Hutcheson, 674 F.2d 862 (11th Cir.1982)—¶ **1.03, n. 142.**

Guttman v. National Westminster Bank, U.S.A., 146 Misc.2d 391, 550 N.Y.S.2d 812 (N.Y.Sup.1990)—¶ **7.01, n. 14; ¶ 9.01, n. 68.**

H

Hadley v. Baxendale, 156 Eng. Rep. 145 (Ex Ct 1854)—¶ **10.03, n. 48.**

Hager v. Buffalo Sav. Bank, 10 Misc. 455, 31 N.Y.S. 448 (N.Y.Super.1894)—¶ **9.05, n. 289, 295.**

Halifax Corp. v. First Union Nat. Bank, 262 Va. 91, 546 S.E.2d 696 (Va.2001)— ¶ **7.03, n. 123.**

Halifax Corp. v. Wachovia Bank, N.A., 2000 WL 1434123 (Va. Cir. Ct.2000)—¶ **7.03, n. 114.**

Hall v. Duncan Sav. & Loan Ass'n, 820 P.2d 1360 (Okla.App. Div. 3 1991)—¶ **9.06, n. 357.**

Hall v. Fuller, 5 B & C 750, 198 Eng. Rep. 179 (K.B.1826)—¶ **9.01.**

Hall v. Mid–Century Ins. Co., Inc., 248 Kan. 847, 811 P.2d 855 (Kan.1991)—¶ **7.03, n. 152.**

Halla v. Norwest Bank Minnesota, N.A., 601 N.W.2d 449 (Minn.App.1999)— ¶ **3.03, n. 251; ¶ 4.02, n. 14, 32.**

Hall-Mark Electronics Corp. v. Sims (Lee, In re), 179 B.R. 149 (9th Cir.1995)— ¶ **4.04, n. 145; ¶ 7.01, n. 4.**

Halpin v. Frankenberger, 231 Kan. 344, 644 P.2d 452 (Kan.1982)—¶ **5.01, n. 5.**

Handel v. Manufactureres Hanover Trust Co., 16 UCC Rep. Serv. 762 (N.Y.Sup. 1975)—¶ **3.02, n. 137; ¶ 7.03; ¶ 7.03, n. 143.**

Hane v. Exten, 255 Md. 668, 259 A.2d 290 (Md.1969)—¶ **3.03, n. 313.**

Hansman v. Imlay City State Bank, 121 Mich.App. 424, 328 N.W.2d 653 (Mich. App.1982)—¶ **4.04, n. 144; ¶ 9.02, n. 106.**

Hanson v. Cheek, 251 Ark. 897, 475 S.W.2d 526 (Ark.1972)—¶ **5.02, n. 36.**

Happy Cattle Feeders, Inc. v. First Nat. Bank in Canyon, 618 S.W.2d 424 (Tex. Civ.App.-Amarillo 1981)—¶ **4.04, n. 144.**

Hardeman v. Wheels, Inc., 56 Ohio App.3d 142, 565 N.E.2d 849 (Ohio App. 12 Dist. 1988)—¶ **3.04, n. 432.**

Hardex–Steubenville Corp. v. Western Pennsylvania Nat. Bank, 446 Pa. 446, 285 A.2d 874 (Pa.1971)—¶ **9.03, n. 183, 190.**

Harding v. Broadway Nat. Bank of Chelsea, 294 Mass. 13, 200 N.E. 386 (Mass. 1936)—¶ **9.06, n. 345.**

Hardison v. Jackson, 45 Ark.App. 49, 871 S.W.2d 410 (Ark.App.1994)—¶ **7.01, n. 32, 37.**

Hardy v. Brookhart, 259 Md. 317, 270 A.2d 119 (Md.1970)—¶ **6.03, n. 172.**

Harper v. K & W Trucking Co., 725 P.2d 1066 (Alaska 1986)—¶ **8.03, n. 193.**

Harris v. Reitz, 649 S.W.2d 228 (Mo.App. E.D.1983)—¶ **5.03, n. 79.**

Harris & Harris v. Tabler, 232 Va. 75, 348 S.E.2d 241 (Va.1986)—¶ **6.03, n. 293.**

Harrison v. Wahatoyas, 253 F.3d 552 (10th Cir.2001)—¶ **1.03, n. 133.**

Hartford Acc. & Indem. Co. v. American Exp. Co., 544 N.Y.S.2d 573, 542 N.E.2d 1090 (N.Y.1989)—¶ **3.03, n. 301.**

Hartford Acc. and Indem. Co. v. Dean's Shop–Rite, Inc., 48 N.C.App. 615, 269 S.E.2d 282 (N.C.App.1980)—¶ **4.02, n. 22, 34.**

Hartford Acc. & Indem. Co. v. First Pennsylvania Bank, N.A., 859 F.2d 295 (3rd Cir.1988)—¶ **7.02, n. 96; ¶ 9.01; ¶ 9.01, n. 38, 40.**

Hartford Acc. & Indem. Co. v. South Windsor Bank & Trust Co., 171 Conn. 63, 368 A.2d 76 (Conn.1976)—¶ **5.03, n. 74.**

Hartford Fire Ins. Co. v. Cavallo, 27 UCC Rep. Serv. 2d 35 (N.Y.Sup.1995)— ¶ **7.03, n. 123.**

Hartford Fire Ins. Co. v. Maryland Nat. Bank, N.A., 341 Md. 408, 671 A.2d 22 (Md.1996)—¶ **7.02, n. 67, 79; ¶ 7.03, n. 128, 134, 136.**

Hartford Life Ins. Co. v. Title Guarantee Co., 520 F.2d 1170 (D.C.Cir.1975)— ¶ **7.02, n. 70.**

Harvey v. Casebeer, 531 S.W.2d 206 (Tex. Civ.App.-Tyler 1975)—¶ **3.01; ¶ 3.01, n. 55; ¶ 3.02; ¶ 3.02, n. 174.**

Hayes v. First Commerce Corp., 763 So.2d 733 (La.App. 4 Cir.2000)—¶ **9.01, n. 29; ¶ 9.02, n. 95; ¶ 9.05, n. 297.**

Hayman, In re, 6 UCC Rep. Serv. 928 (W.D.Okla.1969)—¶ 7.01, n. 15.

Hays v. Friendly Nat. Bank, 591 P.2d 1274 (Okla.App. Div. 1 1979)—¶ 3.02, n. 70.

Hearst Corp. v. Lauerer, Markin & Gibbs, Inc., 37 Ohio App.3d 87, 524 N.E.2d 193 (Ohio App. 6 Dist.1987)—¶ 7.01, n. 39.

Hebel v. Ebersole, 543 F.2d 14 (7th Cir. 1976)—¶ 4.03; ¶ 4.03, n. 140.

Heche v. Chase Manhatten Bank, 45 UCC Rep.Serv.2d 549 (Conn.Sup.Ct.2001)—¶ 7.03, n. 123; ¶ 8.01, n. 46.

Hechter v. New York Life Ins. Co., 412 N.Y.S.2d 812, 385 N.E.2d 551 (N.Y. 1978)—¶ 7.03, n. 130.

Heckathorn Const. Co. v. Bass Mechanical Contractors (Bass Mechanical Contractors, Inc., In re), 84 B.R. 1009 (Bkrtcy. W.D.Ark.1988)—¶ 9.06, n. 385.

Hecker v. Ravenna Bank, 237 Neb. 810, 468 N.W.2d 88 (Neb.1991)—¶ 7.03, n. 131.

Hedged Inv. Partners v. Norwest Bank Minnesota, N.A., 578 N.W.2d 765 (Minn. App.1998)—¶ 10.03, n. 49; ¶ 10.04; ¶ 10.04, n. 70.

Heilig Trust and Beneficiaries v. First Interstate Bank of Washington, 93 Wash. App. 514, 969 P.2d 1082 (Wash.App. Div. 2 1998)—¶ 3.03, n. 297.

Hein, In re, 20 UCC Rep. Serv. 745 (Bkrtcy. W.D.Wis.1976)—¶ 1.03; ¶ 1.03, n. 73.

Hennesy Equipment Sales Co. v. Valley Nat. Bank, 25 Ariz.App. 285, 543 P.2d 123 (Ariz.App. Div. 1 1975)—¶ 4.02, n. 38.

Henrickson, In re, 14 B.R. 474 (Bkrtcy. D.Minn.1981)—¶ 4.04, n. 173.

Henry v. Cobb Bank & Trust Co., 151 Ga. App. 725, 261 S.E.2d 459 (Ga.App. 1979)—¶ 2.01, n. 10.

Herdman v. First Nat. City Bank, 30 UCC Rep. Serv. 628 (N.Y.Sup.App.Term 1966)—¶ 2.05, n. 317.

Heritage Bank v. Lovett, 613 N.W.2d 652 (Iowa 2000)—¶ 8.01, n. 3, 47.

Herzog Contracting Corp. v. McGowen Corp., 976 F.2d 1062 (7th Cir.1992)—¶ 2.05, n. 314.

Hibernia Nat. Bank, United States v., 841 F.2d 592 (5th Cir.1988)—¶ 2.04; ¶ 2.04, n. 288.

Highfield v. First Nat. Bank, 45 Ga.App. 431, 165 S.E. 135 (Ga.App.1932)—¶ 9.05, n. 292.

Hildebrandt v. Anderson, 180 Or.App. 192, 42 P.3d 355 (2002)—¶ 2.02, n. 175.

Hill v. American Exp. Co., 257 S.C. 86, 184 S.E.2d 115 (S.C.1971)—¶ 11.02, n. 62.

Hill v. Mayall, 886 P.2d 1188 (Wyo.1994)—¶ 6.03, n. 286.

Hill v. Mercantile First Nat. Bank of Doniphan, 693 S.W.2d 285 (Mo.App. S.D. 1985)—¶ 4.04, n. 173; ¶ 8.02, n. 129; ¶ 9.01, n. 68.

Hill v. St. Paul Federal Bank, 329 Ill.App.3d 705, 263 Ill.Dec. 562, 768 N.E.2d 322 (2002)—¶ 8.02, n. 140; ¶ 9.01, n. 14.

Hinckley v. Eggers, 587 S.W.2d 448 (Tex. Civ.App.-Dallas 1979)—¶ 2.02; ¶ 2.02, n. 185, 207.

Hindman v. Community Nat. Bank of Pontiac, 14 Mich.App. 746, 165 N.W.2d 894 (Mich.App.1968)—¶ 9.06, n. 409.

H. Lang & Co. v. Northern Jobbing Co., 22 F.Supp. 688 (D.Minn.1938)—¶ 9.06, n. 320.

Hoffman v. Security Pacific Nat. Bank, 121 Cal.App.3d 964, 176 Cal.Rptr. 14 (Cal. App. 2 Dist.1981)—¶ 9.01, n. 48.

Holcomb State Bank v. Adamson, 107 Ill. App.3d 908, 63 Ill.Dec. 704, 438 N.E.2d 635 (Ill.App. 2 Dist.1982)—¶ 2.04, n. 282; ¶ 6.03, n. 281.

Holland v. First Nat. Bank, 597 S.W.2d 406 (Tex.Civ.App.-Dallas 1980)—¶ 2.02, n. 54.

Holley v. Coggin Pontiac, Inc., 43 N.C.App. 229, 259 S.E.2d 1 (N.C.App.1979)—¶ 7.01, n. 33.

Holliday v. Anderson, 428 S.W.2d 479 (Tex. Civ.App.-Waco 1968)—¶ 2.02, n. 223; ¶ 6.03, n. 119, 124.

Holloway v. Bristol–Myers Corp., 485 F.2d 986 (D.C.Cir.1973)—¶ 3.04, n. 425.

Holly Hill Acres, Ltd. v. Charter Bank, 314 So.2d 209 (Fla.App. 2 Dist.1975)—¶ 2.02; ¶ 2.02, n. 148.

Holm v. Woodworth, 271 So.2d 167 (Fla. App. 4 Dist.1972)—¶ 6.03, n. 155.

Home Bank F.S.B. v. Pauer, 1998 WL 78080 (Ohio App. 8 Dist.1998)—¶ 10.04, n. 57.

Hooper v. Bank of New Jersey, 30 UCC Rep. (Callaghan) 1369 (Bankr.E.D.Pa. 1980)—¶ 9.02, n. 104.

Horney v. Covington County Bank, 716 F.2d 335 (5th Cir.1983)—¶ 2.04, n. 292; ¶ 4.03, n. 94; ¶ 8.03, n. 205.

Horn Waterproofing Corp. v. Bushwick Iron & Steel Co., Inc., 497 N.Y.S.2d 310, 488 N.E.2d 56 (N.Y.1985)—¶ 7.01, n. 33.

Hoss v. Fabacher, 578 S.W.2d 454 (Tex.Civ. App.-Hous. (1 Dist.) 1979)—¶ 2.05, n. 304; ¶ 6.03, n. 132.

Hotel Riviera, Inc. v. First Nat. Bank and Trust Co. of Oklahoma City, Okl., 768 F.2d 1201 (10th Cir.1985)—¶ 4.04, n. 173; ¶ 7.01, n. 26; ¶ 9.01, n. 68.

Household Finance Co. v. Watson, 522 S.W.2d 111 (Mo.App.1975)—¶ 2.02, n. 54.

Houston Contracting Co. v. Chase Manhattan Bank, 539 F.Supp. 247 (S.D.N.Y. 1982)—¶ 2.02, n. 64.

Howell v. Continental Credit Corp., 655 F.2d 743 (7th Cir.1981)—¶ 1.03, n. 152.

HSBC Bank U.S.A. v. F & M Bank Northern Virginia, 246 F.3d 335 (4th Cir. 2001)—¶ 4.02, n. 20; ¶ 6.02, n. 81.

H. Schultz & Sons, Inc. v. Bank of Suffolk County, 439 F.Supp. 1137 (E.D.N.Y. 1977)—¶ **9.01, n. 90.**

Hudnall v. Tyler Bank & Trust Co., 448 S.W.2d 503 (Tex.Civ.App.-Tyler 1969)—¶ **9.05, n. 255.**

Humberto Decorators, Inc. v. Plaza Nat. Bank, 180 N.J.Super. 170, 434 A.2d 618 (N.J.Super.A.D.1981)—¶ **3.01, n. 8; ¶ 7.03, n. 134.**

Humble Oil & Refining Co. v. Copley, 213 Va. 449, 192 S.E.2d 735 (Va.1972)—¶ **7.01, n. 3.**

Hunt v. Clark, 41 UCC Rep. Serv. 2d 541 (Mass.Super.2000)—¶ **7.02, n. 67.**

Hunter v. McLelland, 143 Ga.App. 746, 240 S.E.2d 153 (Ga.App.1977)—¶ **2.02, n. 164.**

Husker News Co. v. Mahaska State Bank, 460 N.W.2d 476 (Iowa 1990)—¶ **6.03, n. 292.**

Hutcheson v. Herron, 131 Ill.App.2d 409, 266 N.E.2d 449 (Ill.App. 1 Dist.1970)—¶ **6.03, n. 127.**

Hutzler v. Hertz Corp., 383 N.Y.S.2d 266, 347 N.E.2d 627 (N.Y.1976)—¶ **4.02, n. 23.**

Hydroflo Corp. v. First Nat. Bank of Omaha, 217 Neb. 20, 349 N.W.2d 615 (Neb. 1984)—¶ **7.03, n. 137.**

Hy–Grade Oil Co. v. New Jersey Bank, 138 N.J.Super. 112, 350 A.2d 279 (N.J.Super.A.D.1975)—¶ **9.05, n. 283.**

I

Ickes v. Bache Halsey Stuart Shields, Inc., 133 Ariz. 300, 650 P.2d 1282 (Ariz.App. Div. 1 1982)—¶ **7.03, n. 139.**

Idah–Best, Inc. v. First Sec. Bank of Idaho, N. A., Hailey Branch, 101 Idaho 402, 614 P.2d 425 (Idaho 1980)—¶ **4.03, n. 93.**

Idah–Best, Inc. v. First Sec. Bank of Idaho, N.A., Hailey Branch, 99 Idaho 517, 584 P.2d 1242 (Idaho 1978)—¶ **8.02; ¶ 8.02, n. 141.**

Idaho Forest Industries, Inc. v. Minden Exchange Bank & Trust Co., 212 Neb. 820, 326 N.W.2d 176 (Neb.1982)—¶ **8.02, n. 134.**

IFCO of South Carolina, Inc. v. Southern Nat. Bank of North Carolina, 42 N.C.App. 499, 256 S.E.2d 825 (N.C.App. 1979)—¶ **4.02, n. 11.**

Illinois State Bank v. Yates, 678 S.W.2d 819 (Mo.App. E.D.1984)—¶ **3.01, n. 25; ¶ 3.02, n. 69.**

Illinois Valley Acceptance Corp. v. Woodard, 159 Ind.App. 50, 304 N.E.2d 859 (Ind. App. 1 Dist.1973)—¶ **3.03, n. 339; ¶ 6.03, n. 170.**

Impulse Trading, Inc. v. Norwest Bank Minnesota, 907 F.Supp. 1284 (D.Minn. 1995)—¶ **10.04, n. 71.**

Impulse Trading, Inc. v. Norwest Bank Minnesota, N.A., 870 F.Supp. 954 (D.Minn.1994)—¶ **10.02, n. 5; ¶ 10.07, n. 113.**

Indianapolis Morris Plan Corp. v. Karlen, 319 N.Y.S.2d 831, 268 N.E.2d 632 (N.Y. 1971)—¶ **6.03, n. 281.**

Ingram v. Liberty Nat. Bank & Trust Co. of Oklahoma City, 533 P.2d 975 (Okla. 1975)—¶ **9.06, n. 343.**

Inn Foods, Inc. v. Equitable Co-op. Bank, 45 F.3d 594 (1st Cir.1995)—¶ **4.02, n. 12; ¶ 7.02, n. 67.**

In re (see name of party)

Insurance Agency Managers v. Gonzales, 578 S.W.2d 803 (Tex.Civ.App.-Hous. (1 Dist.) 1979)—¶ **2.02, n. 86, 91.**

Insurance Co. of North America v. Atlas Supply Co., 121 Ga.App. 1, 172 S.E.2d 632 (Ga.App.1970)—¶ **7.02, n. 93, 102.**

Insurance Co. of North America v. Manufacturers Bank of Southfield, N.A., 127 Mich.App. 278, 338 N.W.2d 214 (Mich. App.1983)—¶ **7.03, n. 130.**

Insurance Co. of North America v. Northampton Nat. Bank, 708 F.2d 13 (1st Cir.1983)—¶ **9.06, n. 367.**

Insurance Co. of State of Pa. v. Citibank (Delaware), 145 A.D.2d 218, 537 N.Y.S.2d 519 (N.Y.A.D. 1 Dept.1989)—¶ **7.03, n. 127.**

Intelogic Trace Texcom Group, Inc. v. Merchants Nat. Bank, 626 N.E.2d 839 (Ind. App. 2 Dist.1993)—¶ **7.03, n. 168.**

Interborough Consol. Corp., In re, 288 F. 334 (2nd Cir.1923)—¶ **9.05, n. 264.**

Interfirst Bank Carrollton v. Northpark Nat. Bank, 671 S.W.2d 100 (Tex.App.-El Paso 1984)—¶ **2.02, n. 52; ¶ 4.04, n. 154.**

International Finance Bank v. COFO Financial Group, Case No. 98-30116 CA09 (Fla.Cir.Ct.2002)—¶ **3.03.**

International Industries, Inc. v. Island State Bank, 348 F.Supp. 886 (S.D.Tex. 1971)—¶ **7.03, n. 150.**

International Minerals and Chemical Corp. v. Matthews, 71 N.C.App. 209, 321 S.E.2d 545 (N.C.App.1984)—¶ **2.02, n. 148.**

Investment Service Co. v. Martin Bros. Container & Timber Products Corp., 255 Or. 192, 465 P.2d 868 (Or.1970)—¶ **3.01, n. 50.**

Isenhart v. Monty, 161 Colo. 589, 423 P.2d 836 (Colo.1967)—¶ **9.05, n. 258.**

Isolano v. Chase Manhattan Bank, N.A., 25 UCC Rep. Serv. 2d 1174 (N.Y.Sup. 1995)—¶ **3.03, n. 224.**

Israel Discount Bank Ltd. v. Rosen, 465 N.Y.S.2d 885, 452 N.E.2d 1213 (N.Y. 1983)—¶ **1.03, n. 117.**

Iverson v. First Bank of Billings, 219 Mont. 283, 712 P.2d 1285 (Mont.1985)—¶ 8.01, n. 29; ¶ 9.03, n. 153.

J

Jackson, People v., 116 Ill.App.3d 430, 72 Ill.Dec. 153, 452 N.E.2d 85 (Ill.App. 1 Dist.1983)—¶ 9.05, n. 270.

Jackson Vitrified China Co. v. People's American Nat. Bank of North Miami, 388 So.2d 1059 (Fla.App. 3 Dist.1980)—¶ 7.03, n. 137.

Jacoby Transport Systems, Inc. v. Continental Bank, 277 Pa.Super. 440, 419 A.2d 1227 (Pa.Super.1980)—¶ 2.02, n. 52.

Jaeger & Branch, Inc. v. Pappas, 20 Utah 2d 100, 433 P.2d 605 (Utah 1967)—¶ 3.03, n. 260.

Jamaica Tobacco & Sales Corp. v. Ortner, 70 Misc.2d 388, 333 N.Y.S.2d 669 (N.Y.City Civ.Ct.1972)—¶ 4.06, n. 216.

James Pair, Inc. v. Gentry, 134 Ga.App. 734, 215 S.E.2d 707 (Ga.App.1975)—¶ 3.03, n. 207; ¶ 3.04; ¶ 3.04, n. 398, 409.

James Talcott, Inc. v. Fred Ratowsky Associates, Inc., 2 UCC Rep. Serv. 1134 (Pa.Com.Pl.1965)—¶ 3.01, n. 17; ¶ 5.02, n. 40.

Jamison v. First Georgia Bank, 193 Ga.App. 219, 387 S.E.2d 375 (Ga.App.1989)—¶ 9.03, n. 144.

Jamison v. Society Natl. Bank, 66 Ohio St.3d 201, 611 N.E.2d 307 (Ohio 1993)—¶ 9.06, n. 409.

Jefferson v. Mitchell Select Furniture Co., Inc., 56 Ala.App. 259, 321 So.2d 216 (Ala.Civ.App.1975)—¶ 1.04; ¶ 1.04, n. 211.

Jefferson Bank and Trust v. United States, 894 F.2d 1241 (10th Cir.1990)—¶ 9.06, n. 376.

Jenkins v. Evans, 31 A.D.2d 597, 295 N.Y.S.2d 226 (N.Y.A.D. 3 Dept.1968)—¶ 5.03, n. 97.

Jenkins v. Karlton, 329 Md. 510, 620 A.2d 894 (Md.1993)—¶ 6.03, n. 286, 295.

Jennings v. United States Fidelity & Guaranty Co., 294 U.S. 216, 55 S.Ct. 394, 79 L.Ed. 869 (1935)—¶ 8.01, n. 74.

Jensen v. State Bank of Allison, 518 F.2d 1 (8th Cir.1975)—¶ 9.06, n. 352, 364.

J. Gordon Neely Enterprises, Inc. v. American Nat. Bank, 403 So.2d 887 (Ala. 1981)—¶ 2.02, n. 264; ¶ 3.03; ¶ 3.03, n. 289; ¶ 7.03, n. 145.

Jiang v. First Nat. City Bank, 65 Misc.2d 150, 317 N.Y.S.2d 635 (N.Y.City Civ.Ct. 1970)—¶ 9.05, n. 274.

Joe Morgan, Inc., In re, 985 F.2d 1554 (11th Cir.1993)—¶ 3.03; ¶ 3.03, n. 261.

Joffe v. United California Bank, 141 Cal. App.3d 541, 190 Cal.Rptr. 443 (Cal.App. 2 Dist.1983)—¶ 2.02, n. 250; ¶ 3.02, n. 98, 112.

John Grier Const. Co. v. Jones Welding & Repair, Inc., 238 Va. 270, 383 S.E.2d 719 (Va.1989)—¶ 7.01, n. 40.

Johnson, Matter of, 552 F.2d 1072 (4th Cir.1977)—¶ 3.03; ¶ 3.03, n. 346.

Johnson v. Grant Square Bank & Trust Co., 634 P.2d 1324 (Okla.App. Div. 1 1981)—¶ 9.02, n. 98.

Johnson v. Stamets (Stamets' Estate, In re), 260 Iowa 93, 148 N.W.2d 468 (Iowa 1967)—¶ 9.05, n. 280.

Johnson v. West Suburban Bank, 225 F.3d 366 (3rd Cir.2000)—¶ 11.02, n. 93.

Johnstown School Emp. Federal Credit Union v. Mock, 47 Pa. D. & C.2d 703 (Pa. Com.Pl.1969)—¶ 4.02, n. 13.

Jones v. Approved Bancredit Corp., 256 A.2d 739 (Del.Supr.1969)—¶ 3.04, n. 418.

Jones v. Phillips, 237 Ga.App. 24, 513 S.E.2d 241 (Ga.App.1999)—¶ 2.05, n. 314; ¶ 3.01, n. 2; ¶ 6.03, n. 142.

Jones v. United Sav. & Loan Ass'n, 515 S.W.2d 869 (Mo.App.1974)—¶ 1.03, n. 91; ¶ 2.02, n. 253.

Jonwilco, Inc. v. C.I.T. Financial Services, 662 S.W.2d 664 (Tex.App.-Hous. (14 Dist.) 1983)—¶ 3.03, n. 320, 324.

Jordan v. J.C. Penney Co., 114 Ga.App. 822, 152 S.E.2d 786 (Ga.App.1966)—¶ 11.02, n. 61.

Jordan v. Shattuck Nat. Bank, 868 F.2d 383 (10th Cir.1989)—¶ 9.03, n. 130.

Joseph v. United of America Bank, 131 Ill.App.2d 434, 266 N.E.2d 438 (Ill.App. 1 Dist.1970)—¶ 4.03, n. 60.

J.R. Simplot, Inc. v. Knight, 93 Wash.App. 369, 973 P.2d 472 (Wash.App. Div. 3 1998)—¶ 2.02, n. 262.

Justus Co., Inc. v. Gary Wheaton Bank, 509 F.Supp. 103 (N.D.Ill.1981)—¶ 7.03, n. 146, 150.

K

Kalb v. Chemical Bank New York Trust Co., 62 Misc.2d 458, 309 N.Y.S.2d 502 (N.Y.City Civ.Ct.1969)—¶ 9.05, n. 242, 293.

KAM, Inc. v. White, 675 S.W.2d 459 (Mo. App. S.D.1984)—¶ 6.03, n. 231.

Kane v. American Nat. Bank & Trust Co., 21 Ill.App.3d 1046, 316 N.E.2d 177 (Ill. App. 2 Dist.1974)—¶ 1.03, n. 167; ¶ 8.01, n. 43.

Kane v. First Nat. Bank, 56 F.2d 534 (5th Cir.1932)—¶ 9.06, n. 345.

Kane v. Kroll, 196 Wis.2d 389, 538 N.W.2d 605 (Wis.App.1995)—¶ 3.03, n. 210.

Kansas Bankers Sur. Co. v. Bank of Odessa, 386 F.Supp. 555 (W.D.Mo.1974)—¶ **7.03, n. 169.**

Kanterman, In re, 108 B.R. 432 (S.D.N.Y. 1989)—¶ **1.03, n. 133.**

Karlton v. Jenkins, 86 Md.App. 556, 587 A.2d 580 (Md.App.1991)—¶ **6.03, n. 286.**

Karmin Door Co. v. BankBoston, N.A., 41 UCC Rep. Serv. 2d 1191 (Mass.Super.2000)—¶ **4.02, n. 14.**

Karner v. Willis, 238 Kan. 246, 710 P.2d 21 (Kan.1985)—¶ **2.02, n. 152.**

Karr v. Baumann, 3 UCC Rep. Serv. 180 (N.Y.Sup.1966)—¶ **5.03, n. 81.**

Kashanchi v. Texas Commerce Medical Bank, N.A., 703 F.2d 936 (5th Cir. 1983)—¶ **10.01, n. 3.**

Kasparek v. Liberty Nat. Bank, 170 Okla. 207, 39 P.2d 127 (Okla.1934)—¶ **9.06, n. 325.**

Katski v. Boehm, 249 Md. 568, 241 A.2d 129 (Md.1968)—¶ **6.02; ¶ 6.02, n. 45.**

Kaufman v. First Nat. Bank, 493 F.2d 1070 (5th Cir.1974)—¶ **9.06, n. 356.**

Kaw Valley State Bank & Trust Co. v. Riddle, 219 Kan. 550, 549 P.2d 927 (Kan.1976)—¶ **3.03, n. 269, 308; ¶ 3.04, n. 416.**

Kedzie and 103rd Currency Exchange, Inc. v. Hodge, 156 Ill.2d 112, 189 Ill.Dec. 31, 619 N.E.2d 732 (Ill.1993)—¶ **3.03, n. 333; ¶ 6.02, n. 53.**

Kellerman, United States v., 729 F.2d 281 (4th Cir.1984)—¶ **3.03, n. 337.**

Kelley v. Carson, 120 Ga.App. 450, 171 S.E.2d 150 (Ga.App.1969)—¶ **6.01, n. 33.**

Kelly v. Kowalsky, 186 Conn. 618, 442 A.2d 1355 (Conn.1982)—¶ **7.01, n. 32.**

Kemper, In re, 263 B.R. 773 (Bankr. E.D.Tex.2001)—¶ **8.01, n. 24.**

Kenerson v. Federal Deposit Ins. Corporation, 44 F.3d 19 (1st Cir.1995)—¶ **2.02, n. 262; ¶ 6.03, n. 208.**

Kennard v. Reliance, Inc., 257 Md. 654, 264 A.2d 832 (Md.1970)—¶ **3.04, n. 421.**

Kerney v. Kerney, 120 R.I. 209, 386 A.2d 1100 (R.I.1978)—¶ **5.02, n. 27.**

Ketchian v. Concannon, 435 So.2d 394 (Fla. App. 5 Dist.1983)—¶ **2.02, n. 179.**

Kilander v. Blickle Co., 280 Or. 425, 571 P.2d 503 (Or.1977)—¶ **7.01, n. 32.**

Kimball, Matter of, 16 B.R. 201 (Bkrtcy. M.D.Fla.1981)—¶ **4.04, n. 146.**

Kimbell Foods, Inc., United States v., 440 U.S. 715, 99 S.Ct. 1448, 59 L.Ed.2d 711 (1979)—¶ **1.03, n. 122.**

Kimberly A. Allen Trust v. Firstbank of Lakewood, N.A., 989 P.2d 203 (Colo. App.1999)—¶ **8.02, n. 110, 127, 165.**

King v. White, 265 Kan. 627, 962 P.2d 475 (Kan.1998)—¶ **7.03, n. 168.**

Kings Premium Service Corp. v. Manufacturers Hanover Trust Co., 115 A.D.2d 707, 496 N.Y.S.2d 524 (N.Y.A.D. 2 Dept. 1985)—¶ **7.03, n. 148.**

Kinzig v. First Fidelity Bank, N.A., 277 N.J.Super. 255, 649 A.2d 634 (N.J.Super.L.1994)—¶ **2.02, n. 262.**

Kirby v. Bergfield, 186 Neb. 242, 182 N.W.2d 205 (Neb.1970)—¶ **4.03, n. 87; ¶ 7.01; ¶ 7.01, n. 8.**

Kirby v. First and Merchants Nat. Bank, 210 Va. 88, 168 S.E.2d 273 (Va.1969)—¶ **7.02, n. 72; ¶ 8.02; ¶ 8.02, n. 130, 158; ¶ 9.01, n. 90.**

Kitchen Krafters, Inc. v. Eastside Bank of Montana, 242 Mont. 155, 789 P.2d 567 (Mont.1990)—¶ **9.03, n. 125.**

Kitzer v. Kitzer, 20 Ill.App.3d 54, 312 N.E.2d 699 (Ill.App. 2 Dist.1974)—¶ **2.02, n. 188.**

K & K Mfg., Inc. v. Union Bank, 129 Ariz. 7, 628 P.2d 44 (Ariz.App. Div. 2 1981)—¶ **4.02, n. 24.**

Klein v. First Edina Nat. Bank, 293 Minn. 418, 196 N.W.2d 619 (Minn.1972)—¶ **9.03; ¶ 9.03, n. 126.**

Klein v. Tabatchnick, 418 F.Supp. 1368 (S.D.N.Y.1976)—¶ **4.03, n. 133.**

Klomann v. Sol K. Graff and Sons, 22 Ill. App.3d 572, 317 N.E.2d 608 (Ill.App. 1 Dist.1974)—¶ **3.03; ¶ 3.03, n. 368.**

Knesz v. Central Jersey Bank and Trust Co. of Freehold, 97 N.J. 1, 477 A.2d 806 (N.J.1984)—¶ **7.03; ¶ 7.03, n. 138, 144.**

Knight Pub. Co., Inc. v. Chase Manhattan Bank, N.A., 125 N.C.App. 1, 479 S.E.2d 478 (N.C.App.1997)—¶ **7.03, n. 176, 180.**

Knox v. Columbia Banking Fed. Sav. & Loan Ass'n, 488 N.Y.S.2d 146, 477 N.E.2d 448 (N.Y.1985)—¶ **3.03, n. 295.**

Koerner & Lambert v. Allstate Ins. Co., 374 So.2d 179 (La.App. 4 Cir.1979)—¶ **4.02, n. 23.**

Koger v. East First Nat. Bank, 443 So.2d 141 (Fla.App. 2 Dist.1983)—¶ **9.02, n. 103.**

Kohlenberg v. American Plumbing Supply Co., 82 Wis.2d 384, 263 N.W.2d 496 (Wis.1978)—¶ **6.03, n. 227.**

Kohlhepp's Estate v. Mason, 25 Utah 2d 155, 478 P.2d 339 (Utah 1970)—¶ **4.03, n. 52.**

Kordick v. Merchants Nat. Bank & Trust Co., 496 N.E.2d 119 (Ind.App. 4 Dist. 1986)—¶ **2.02, n. 128.**

Korzenik v. Supreme Radio, Inc., 347 Mass. 309, 197 N.E.2d 702 (Mass.1964)—¶ **3.03; ¶ 3.03, n. 235.**

Kos v. Patrons State Bank & Trust (Matthews' Estate, In re), 208 Kan. 492, 493 P.2d 555 (Kan.1972)—¶ **9.05, n. 279.**

Kosic v. Marine Midland Bank, 76 A.D.2d 89, 430 N.Y.S.2d 175 (N.Y.A.D. 4 Dept. 1980)—¶ **7.03, n. 152.**

Kovash v. McCloskey, 386 N.W.2d 32 (N.D. 1986)—¶ **3.03, n. 206.**

TABLE OF CASES

Kraftsman Container Corp. v. United Counties Trust Co., 169 N.J.Super. 488, 404 A.2d 1288 (N.J.Super.L.1979)—¶ **7.03, n. 181, 184.**

Krajcir v. Egidi, 305 Ill.App.3d 613, 238 Ill.Dec. 813, 712 N.E.2d 917 (Ill.App. 1 Dist.1999)—¶ **2.02, n. 234.**

Kroll v. Crest Plastics, Inc., 142 Mich.App. 284, 369 N.W.2d 487 (Mich.App.1985)—¶ **5.03, n. 79.**

Krom v. Chemical Bank New York Trust Co., 38 A.D.2d 871, 329 N.Y.S.2d 91 (N.Y.A.D. 3 Dept.1972)—¶ **2.02, n. 52;** ¶ **4.04, n. 154.**

K. & S. Intern., Inc. v. Howard, 249 Ark. 901, 462 S.W.2d 458 (Ark.1971)—¶ **6.03, n. 239.**

Kunkel v. First Nat. Bank of Devils Lake, 393 N.W.2d 265 (N.D.1986)—¶ **9.01, n. 23.**

Kupersmith v. Manufacturers Hanover Trust Co., 15 UCC Rep. Serv. 696 (N.Y.City Civ.Ct.1974)—¶ **2.04, n. 296.**

L

Lakeshore Commercial Finance Corp. v. Bradford Arms Corp., 45 Wis.2d 313, 173 N.W.2d 165 (Wis.1970)—¶ **3.03, n. 363.**

Lamb v. Opelika Production Credit Ass'n, 367 So.2d 957 (Ala.1979)—¶ **3.01, n. 11;** ¶ **3.02;** ¶ **3.02, n. 67.**

Lambert v. Barker, 232 Va. 21, 348 S.E.2d 214 (Va.1986)—¶ **6.03, n. 204.**

Lamson v. Commercial Credit Corp., 187 Colo. 382, 531 P.2d 966 (Colo.1975)—¶ **3.01, n. 28.**

Landreth v. First Nat. Bank of Cleburne County, 45 F.3d 267 (8th Cir.1995)—¶ **6.03, n. 291.**

Landscape Design & Const., Inc. v. Warren, 598 S.W.2d 38 (Tex.Civ.App.-Texarkana 1980)—¶ **6.03, n. 97.**

Lange–Finn Const. Co., Inc. v. Albany Steel & Iron Supply Co., Inc., 94 Misc.2d 15, 403 N.Y.S.2d 1012 (N.Y.Sup.1978)—¶ **7.01, n. 36.**

Langeveld v. L.R.Z.H. Corp., 74 N.J. 45, 376 A.2d 931 (N.J.1977)—¶ **6.03, n. 263.**

Langley v. Federal Deposit Ins. Corp., 484 U.S. 86, 108 S.Ct. 396, 98 L.Ed.2d 340 (1987)—¶ **1.03, n. 135.**

Larstone Corrugated Carton Co. v. First Seneca Bank & Trust Co., 39 UCC Rep. Serv. 1397 (Pa.Com.Pl.1984)—¶ **9.02, n. 101, 106.**

La Sara Grain Co. v. First Nat. Bank of Mercedes, 673 S.W.2d 558 (Tex.1984)—¶ **9.03;** ¶ **9.03, n. 166, 185.**

Latin Inv. Corp., In re, 156 B.R. 102 (Bkrtcy.D.Dist.Col.1993)—¶ **9.05, n. 245;** ¶ **9.06, n. 408.**

Laubach v. Morgan, 588 P.2d 1071 (Okla. 1978)—¶ **8.04, n. 482.**

Laurel Bank & Trust Co. v. City Nat. Bank of Connecticut, 33 Conn.Supp. 641, 365 A.2d 1222 (Conn.Super.App.1976)—¶ **4.04, n. 169.**

Laurel Bank & Trust Co. v. Sahadi, 32 Conn.Supp. 172, 345 A.2d 53 (Conn. Com.Pl.1975)—¶ **3.01, n. 19;** ¶ **4.06, n. 208.**

Lausen v. Federman, 9 UCC Rep. Serv. 866 (N.Y.Sup.1971)—¶ **2.02, n. 218.**

LaVoie v. Celli, 61 Misc.2d 126, 304 N.Y.S.2d 671 (N.Y.Sup.1969)—¶ **6.01;** ¶ **6.01, n. 32, 38.**

Lawrence v. Central Plaza Bank and Trust Co., 469 So.2d 201 (Fla.App. 2 Dist. 1985)—¶ **7.03, n. 134.**

Lawrence Fashions, Inc. v. National Bank of North America, 8 UCC Rep. Serv. 729 (N.Y.Sup.1971)—¶ **9.03, n. 158.**

Lawson v. Finance America Private Brands, Inc., 537 S.W.2d 483 (Tex.Civ.App.-El Paso 1976)—¶ **3.01, n. 40.**

Lawson v. Gibbs, 591 S.W.2d 292 (Tex.Civ. App.-Hous. (14 Dist.) 1979)—¶ **3.01, n. 11.**

Lawyers' Fund for Client Protection of State v. Bank Leumi Trust Co. of New York, 706 N.Y.S.2d 66, 727 N.E.2d 563 (N.Y.2000)—¶ **7.03, n. 132.**

Lawyers' Fund for Client Protection of State v. Gateway State Bank, 273 A.D.2d 565, 709 N.Y.S.2d 243 (N.Y.A.D. 3 Dept.2000)—¶ **8.02, n. 112;** ¶ **8.03, n. 232;** ¶ **9.02, n. 100.**

Lawyers Title Ins. Corp. v. United American Bank of Memphis, 21 F.Supp.2d 785 (W.D.Tenn.1998)—¶ **3.03.**

Lazere Financial Corp. v. Crystal Mart, Inc., 78 Misc.2d 379, 357 N.Y.S.2d 973 (N.Y.City Civ.Ct.1974)—¶ **3.03;** ¶ **3.03, n. 245.**

L.B. Smith, Inc. v. Bankers Trust Co. of Western N. Y., 80 A.D.2d 496, 439 N.Y.S.2d 543 (N.Y.A.D. 4 Dept.1981)—¶ **3.02, n. 102.**

Leaf v. McGowan, 13 Ill.App.2d 58, 141 N.E.2d 67 (Ill.App. 1 Dist.1957)—¶ **9.06, n. 403.**

Leahy v. McManus, 237 Md. 450, 206 A.2d 688 (Md.1965)—¶ **5.03;** ¶ **5.03, n. 105.**

Lee Federal Credit Union v. Gussie, 542 F.2d 887 (4th Cir.1976)—¶ **5.02;** ¶ **5.02, n. 34;** ¶ **6.03, n. 254.**

Lee Newman, M.D., Inc. v. Wells Fargo Bank, 104 Cal.Rptr.2d 310 (Cal.App. 2 Dist.2001)—¶ **7.02, n. 57;** ¶ **8.01, n. 46.**

Lee & Ota, In re, 108 F.3d 239 (9th Cir. 1997)—¶ **4.04, n. 145.**

Legg v. Kelly, 412 So.2d 1202 (Ala.1982)—¶ **5.03, n. 103.**

Leinert v. Sabine Nat. Bank, 541 S.W.2d 872 (Tex.Civ.App.-Beaumont 1976)—¶ **3.02;** ¶ **3.02, n. 99.**

TABLE OF CASES

Lenders Collection Corp. v. Harris, 900 P.2d 1022 (Okla.App. Div. 1 1995)—¶ **6.03, n. 286.**

Leopold v. Halleck, 106 Ill.App.3d 386, 62 Ill.Dec. 447, 436 N.E.2d 29 (Ill.App. 1 Dist.1982)—¶ **2.02, n. 58;** ¶ **3.01, n. 7;** ¶ **3.03, n. 202, 322.**

Levinson v. Home Bank & Trust Co., 337 Ill. 241, 169 N.E. 193 (Ill.1929)—¶ **9.06, n. 372.**

Lewis v. Citizens and Southern Nat. Bank, 139 Ga.App. 855, 229 S.E.2d 765 (Ga. App.1976)—¶ **6.01, n. 28.**

Lewittes Furniture Enterprises, Inc. v. Peoples Nat. Bank of Long Island, 82 Misc.2d 1013, 372 N.Y.S.2d 830 (N.Y.Dist.Ct.1975)—¶ **7.03, n. 137.**

L.H. Wagener, Inc. v. Kendall, 278 N.W.2d 18 (Iowa 1979)—¶ **3.02, n. 173;** ¶ **5.02, n. 44;** ¶ **6.03, n. 232.**

Lialios v. Home Ins. Companies, 87 Ill. App.3d 740, 43 Ill.Dec. 193, 410 N.E.2d 193 (Ill.App. 1 Dist.1980)—¶ **2.02, n. 133.**

Liberty Nat. Bank & Trust Co. of Savannah v. Interstate Motel Developers, Inc., 346 F.Supp. 888 (S.D.Ga.1972)—¶ **6.03, n. 269.**

Liberty State Bank & Trust v. Hemisphere Development Group, Inc., 98 Mich.App. 285, 296 N.W.2d 241 (Mich.App.1980)—¶ **6.02, n. 86;** ¶ **6.03, n. 121;** ¶ **11.03, n. 124.**

Lichtenstein v. Kidder, Peabody & Co. Inc., 840 F.Supp. 374 (W.D.Pa.1993)—¶ **4.02, n. 31;** ¶ **6.02, n. 82.**

Ligran, Inc. v. Medlawtel, Inc., 86 N.J. 583, 432 A.2d 502 (N.J.1981)—¶ **6.03, n. 296.**

Lindenbaum's, Inc., In re, 2 UCC Rep. Serv. 495 (Bkrtcy.E.D.Pa.1964)—¶ **4.03, n. 78.**

Liner v. Commercial Nat. Bank, 85 Ga.App. 278, 69 S.E.2d 119 (Ga.App.1952)—¶ **9.05, n. 275.**

Lipkowitz & Plaut v. Affrunti, 95 Misc.2d 849, 407 N.Y.S.2d 1010 (N.Y.Sup. 1978)—¶ **3.01, n. 28.**

Littky & Mallon v. Michigan Nat. Bank, 94 Mich.App. 29, 287 N.W.2d 359 (Mich. App.1979)—¶ **2.02;** ¶ **2.02, n. 51.**

Litwin v. Barrier, 6 Kan.App.2d 128, 626 P.2d 1232 (Kan.App.1981)—¶ **6.03, n. 178.**

Livingston Industries, Inc. v. Walker Bank & Trust Co., 565 P.2d 1117 (Utah 1977)—¶ **7.03, n. 121.**

Lloyd v. Lawrence, 472 F.2d 313 (5th Cir. 1973)—¶ **3.01, n. 46.**

Locke v. Aetna Acceptance Corp., 309 So.2d 43 (Fla.App. 1 Dist.1975)—¶ **2.02, n. 253.**

Lockhart Sav. & Loan Ass'n v. Republic-Bank Austin, 720 S.W.2d 193 (Tex.App.-Austin 1986)—¶ **8.01, n. 32;** ¶ **8.02, n. 134;** ¶ **9.03, n. 152.**

Locks v. North Towne Nat. Bank, 115 Ill. App.3d 729, 71 Ill.Dec. 531, 451 N.E.2d 19 (Ill.App. 2 Dist.1983)—¶ **3.01, n. 7;** ¶ **9.05, n. 267.**

London Leasing Corp. v. Interfina, Inc., 53 Misc.2d 657, 279 N.Y.S.2d 209 (N.Y.Sup. 1967)—¶ **6.03, n. 250.**

Longhorn Securities Litigation, In re, 573 F.Supp. 278 (W.D.Okla.1983)—¶ **1.03, n. 133.**

Long Island Trust Co. v. International Institute for Packaging Ed., Ltd., 381 N.Y.S.2d 445, 344 N.E.2d 377 (N.Y. 1976)—¶ **6.01, n. 33;** ¶ **6.03, n. 151.**

Los Angeles National Bank v. Bank of Canton, 37 Cal.Rptr.2d 389 (Cal.App. 2 Dist. 1995)—¶ **4.03, n. 93.**

Loucks v. Albuquerque Nat. Bank, 76 N.M. 735, 418 P.2d 191 (N.M.1966)—¶ **8.01, n. 53;** ¶ **9.01, n. 16;** ¶ **9.03, n. 120;** ¶ **9.06, n. 365.**

Lou Levy & Sons Fashions, Inc., In re, 988 F.2d 311 (2nd Cir.1993)—¶ **4.02, n. 17;** ¶ **7.03, n. 145.**

Lucas' Estate v. Whiteley, 550 S.W.2d 767 (Tex.Civ.App.-Amarillo 1977)—¶ **3.04;** ¶ **3.04, n. 397;** ¶ **6.02, n. 46;** ¶ **6.03, n. 109.**

Lufthansa German Airlines v. Bank of America Nat. Trust and Sav. Ass'n, 478 F.Supp. 1195 (N.D.Cal.1979)—¶ **4.03, n. 105;** ¶ **8.01, n. 57;** ¶ **8.02, n. 134, 181;** ¶ **8.03, n. 206, 210, 212.**

Lund v. Chemical Bank, 665 F.Supp. 218 (S.D.N.Y.1987)—¶ **7.03, n. 134.**

Lynric Associates, Inc. v. Moroh, 3 UCC Rep. Serv. 181 (N.Y.Sup.1966)—¶ **6.02, n. 65.**

M

Maber, Inc. v. Factor Cab Corp., 19 A.D.2d 500, 244 N.Y.S.2d 768 (N.Y.A.D. 1 Dept. 1963)—¶ **3.03, n. 294.**

Macon Nat. Bank v. Smith, 170 Ga. 332, 153 S.E. 4 (Ga.1930)—¶ **9.06, n. 320.**

Main Bank v. Baker, 86 Ill.2d 188, 56 Ill. Dec. 14, 427 N.E.2d 94 (Ill.1981)—¶ **2.02, n. 178;** ¶ **6.01;** ¶ **6.01, n. 36.**

Maine Family Federal Credit Union v. Sun Life Assur. Co., 727 A.2d 335 (Me. 1999)—¶ **2.01, n. 13;** ¶ **3.03, n. 224, 323, 336;** ¶ **8.03, n. 215, 232;** ¶ **8.04;** ¶ **8.04, n. 498;** ¶ **9.01, n. 40;** ¶ **9.03, n. 124, 167, 188.**

Maine Gas & Appliances, Inc. v. Siegel, 438 A.2d 888 (Me.1981)—¶ **5.03, n. 87.**

Makel Textiles, Inc. v. Dolly Originals, Inc., 4 UCC Rep. Serv. 95 (N.Y.Sup.1967)—¶ **4.06, n. 252.**

Maley v. East Side Bank, 361 F.2d 393 (7th Cir.1966)—¶ **3.03, n. 295;** ¶ **7.03;** ¶ **7.03, n. 115.**

Malphrus v. Home Sav. Bank of City of Albany, 44 Misc.2d 705, 254 N.Y.S.2d 980 (N.Y.Co.Ct.1965)—¶ **9.01, n. 55.**

Mammoth Cave Production Credit Ass'n v. Geralds, 551 S.W.2d 5 (Ky.App.1977)—¶ **2.02, n. 214.**

Mancuso v. United Bank of Pueblo, 818 P.2d 732 (Colo.1991)—¶ **9.05, n. 251;** ¶ **9.06, n. 357.**

Mandelbaum v. P & D Printing Corp., 279 N.J.Super. 427, 652 A.2d 1266 (N.J.Super.A.D.1995)—¶ **7.02, n. 65.**

Mandolfo v. Chudy, 253 Neb. 927, 573 N.W.2d 135 (Neb.1998)—¶ **3.01, n. 24.**

Manhattan Bank v. Walker, 130 U.S. 267, 9 S.Ct. 519, 32 L.Ed. 959 (1889)—¶ **9.05, n. 305.**

Mann v. Franklin Trust Co., 158 A.D. 491, 143 N.Y.S. 660 (N.Y.A.D. 2 Dept.1913)—¶ **9.06, n. 350.**

Mansion Carpets, Inc. v. Marinoff, 24 A.D.2d 947, 265 N.Y.S.2d 298 (N.Y.A.D. 1 Dept.1965)—¶ **3.03, n. 206.**

Manufacturas Intern., Ltda v. Manufacturers Hanover Trust Co., 792 F.Supp. 180 (E.D.N.Y.1992)—¶ **10.02, n. 11.**

Manufacturers Hanover Trust Co. v. Robinson, 157 Misc.2d 651, 597 N.Y.S.2d 986 (N.Y.Sup.1993)—¶ **3.01, n. 25.**

Manufacturers Hanover Trust Co. v. Yanakas, 7 F.3d 310 (2nd Cir.1993)—¶ **9.05, n. 286.**

Manufacturers Nat. Bank v. Sutherland, 16 Mich.App. 286, 167 N.W.2d 894 (Mich. App.1969)—¶ **2.04, n. 293.**

Manufacturers & Traders Trust Co. v. Murphy, 369 F.Supp. 11 (W.D.Pa.1974)—¶ **3.03, n. 318.**

Maplewood Bank & Trust Co. v. F. I. B., Inc., 142 N.J.Super. 480, 362 A.2d 44 (N.J.Super.A.D.1976)—¶ **3.02;** ¶ **3.02, n. 116;** ¶ **3.03;** ¶ **3.03, n. 384.**

Marcoux v. Mid–States Livestock, Inc., 429 F.Supp. 155 (N.D.Iowa 1977)—¶ **1.04, n. 220.**

Marcoux v. Van Wyk, 572 F.2d 651 (8th Cir.1978)—¶ **8.04, n. 491.**

Marek Interior Systems, Inc. v. White, 230 Ga.App. 518, 496 S.E.2d 749 (Ga.App. 1998)—¶ **5.03, n. 79.**

Marengo State Bank v. Meyers, 89 Ill. App.2d 421, 232 N.E.2d 75 (Ill.App. 2 Dist.1967)—¶ **2.02, n. 108.**

Marine Bank v. Weaver, 455 U.S. 551, 102 S.Ct. 1220, 71 L.Ed.2d 409 (1982)—¶ **9.05, n. 249.**

Marine Midland Bank, N.A. v. Price, Miller, Evans & Flowers, 455 N.Y.S.2d 565, 441 N.E.2d 1083 (N.Y.1982)—¶ **3.01, n. 35;** ¶ **3.02, n. 71, 167.**

Marine Midland Bank, N. A. v. Price, Miller, Evans & Flowers, 85 A.D.2d 903, 446 N.Y.S.2d 797 (N.Y.A.D. 4 Dept. 1981)—¶ **3.01, n. 36;** ¶ **8.01, n. 11.**

Marine Midland Bank–New York v. Graybar Elec. Co., Inc., 395 N.Y.S.2d 403, 363 N.E.2d 1139 (N.Y.1977)—¶ **3.01, n. 44;** ¶ **6.03, n. 305.**

Mark Twain Bank–Kansas City, United States v., 771 F.2d 361 (8th Cir.1985)—¶ **3.03, n. 215.**

Marques, People v., 184 Colo. 262, 520 P.2d 113 (Colo.1974)—¶ **7.02, n. 44.**

Marquette Nat. Bank v. B.J. Dodge Fiat, Inc., 131 Ill.App.3d 356, 86 Ill.Dec. 678, 475 N.E.2d 1057 (Ill.App. 2 Dist.1985)—¶ **9.06, n. 383.**

Marquette Nat. Bank v. First of Omaha Service Corp., 439 U.S. 299, 99 S.Ct. 540, 58 L.Ed.2d 534 (1978)—¶ **1.03, n. 108;** ¶ **11.01, n. 9.**

Marrison v. Hogue, 95 N.E.2d 15 (Ohio Mun.1950)—¶ **9.06, n. 351.**

Martin v. American Express, Inc., 361 So.2d 597 (Ala.Civ.App.1978)—¶ **11.02, n. 75.**

Martin v. First State Bank, 490 S.W.2d 208 (Tex.Civ.App.-Amarillo 1973)—¶ **9.05, n. 251, 257;** ¶ **9.06, n. 361.**

Martin Glennon, Inc. v. First Fidelity Bank, N.A., 279 N.J.Super. 48, 652 A.2d 199 (N.J.Super.A.D.1995)—¶ **4.02, n. 34, 36;** ¶ **7.03, n. 145.**

Martin Management Corp. v. Farner, 124 Ga.App. 552, 184 S.E.2d 597 (Ga.App. 1971)—¶ **3.03;** ¶ **3.03, n. 341.**

Masi v. Ford City Bank and Trust Co., 779 F.2d 397 (7th Cir.1985)—¶ **9.05, n. 251;** ¶ **9.06, n. 358.**

Mastercard v. Town of Newport, 133 Wis.2d 328, 396 N.W.2d 345 (Wis.App.1986)—¶ **11.02, n. 75.**

Matco Tools Corp. v. Pontiac State Bank, 614 F.Supp. 1059 (E.D.Mich.1985)—¶ **4.02, n. 32.**

Matter of (see name of party)

Matthews v. Saleen, 812 P.2d 1186 (Colo. App.1991)—¶ **6.03, n. 178.**

May Dept. Stores Co. v. Pittsburgh Nat. Bank, 374 F.2d 109 (3rd Cir.1967)—¶ **7.03, n. 174.**

May–Li Barki, M.D., Inc. v. Liberty Bank and Trust Co., 20 P.3d 135 (Okla. 1999)—¶ **9.03, n. 162, 165, 174.**

Mazer v. Williams Bros. Co., 461 Pa. 587, 337 A.2d 559 (Pa.1975)—¶ **1.03, n. 96;** ¶ **3.01, n. 21;** ¶ **3.04, n. 388.**

McAdam v. Dean Witter Reynolds, Inc., 896 F.2d 750 (3rd Cir.1990)—¶ **7.03, n. 174, 182.**

McCarthy v. Kasperak, 3 Ohio App.3d 206, 444 N.E.2d 472 (Ohio App. 8 Dist. 1981)—¶ **3.03;** ¶ **3.03, n. 255.**

McCarthy, Kenney & Reidy, P.C. v. First Nat. Bank of Boston, 402 Mass. 630, 524 N.E.2d 390 (Mass.1988)—¶ **7.03, n. 183.**

McCloskey v. Chase Manhattan Bank, 228 N.Y.S.2d 825, 183 N.E.2d 227 (N.Y. 1962)—¶ **9.06, n. 399.**

McCollum v. Parkdale State Bank, 566 S.W.2d 670 (Tex.Civ.App.-Corpus Christi 1978)—¶ **9.06, n. 345.**

McCollum v. Steitz, 261 Cal.App.2d 76, 67 Cal.Rptr. 703 (Cal.App. 5 Dist.1968)—¶ **2.02, n. 44.**

McConnico v. Third Nat. Bank in Nashville, 499 S.W.2d 874 (Tenn.1973)—¶ **3.03, n. 297;** ¶ **7.03, n. 173.**

McCook County Nat. Bank v. Compton, 558 F.2d 871 (8th Cir.1977)—¶ **3.03, n. 240, 260.**

McCormick, In re, 5 B.R. 726 (Bkrtcy. N.D.Ohio 1980)—¶ **9.01, n. 89.**

McCusker v. Fascione, 117 R.I. 478, 368 A.2d 1220 (R.I.1977)—¶ **2.02, n. 57.**

McGhee v. Bank of America, 60 Cal.App.3d 442, 131 Cal.Rptr. 482 (Cal.App. 1 Dist. 1976)—¶ **9.05, n. 253, 256.**

McGill's Estate, Matter of, 54 Ill.App.3d 533, 13 Ill.Dec. 311, 371 N.E.2d 6 (Ill. App. 2 Dist.1977)—¶ **9.04;** ¶ **9.04, n. 233, 237.**

McLaughlin v. Franklin Soc. Federal Sav. & Loan Assn., 6 UCC Rep. Serv. 1183 (N.Y.City Civ.Ct.1969)—¶ **8.01, n. 67.**

McMahon Food Corp. v. Burger Dairy Co., 103 F.3d 1307 (7th Cir.1996)—¶ **7.01, n. 40, 42.**

McMullen Oil Co., In re, 251 B.R. 558 (Bkrtcy.C.D.Cal.2000)—¶ **4.02, n. 14;** ¶ **7.02, n. 67;** ¶ **8.03, n. 232.**

McNall v. Tatham, 676 F.Supp. 987 (C.D.Cal.1987)—¶ **1.03, n. 117.**

McNeal Const. Co. v. Wilson, 271 Ga. 540, 522 S.E.2d 222 (Ga.1999)—¶ **6.03, n. 286.**

McPherson v. Longview United Pentecostal Church, Inc., 540 S.W.2d 424 (Tex.Civ. App.-Tyler 1976)—¶ **2.02, n. 167.**

Meador v. Ranchmart State Bank, 213 Kan. 372, 517 P.2d 123 (Kan.1973)—¶ **2.02, n. 142;** ¶ **5.03, n. 73.**

Mecham v. United Bank of Ariz., 107 Ariz. 437, 489 P.2d 247 (Ariz.1971)—¶ **2.02, n. 198;** ¶ **6.03, n. 168.**

Mechanics Nat. Bank v. Shear, 7 Mass.App. Ct. 255, 386 N.E.2d 1299 (Mass.App.Ct. 1979)—¶ **2.02, n. 54;** ¶ **6.03, n. 179.**

Mechanics Nat. Bank of Worcester v. Killeen, 377 Mass. 100, 384 N.E.2d 1231 (Mass.1979)—¶ **6.03, n. 309.**

Medford Irr. Dist. v. Western Bank, 66 Or. App. 589, 676 P.2d 329 (Or.App.1984)—¶ **4.02, n. 14;** ¶ **9.03, n. 196.**

Medi–Fi Two Inc. v. Riordan, 71 Ill.App.3d 491, 28 Ill.Dec. 19, 390 N.E.2d 1 (Ill. App. 1 Dist.1979)—¶ **6.01, n. 5.**

Mellon Bank, N.A. v. Securities Settlement Corp., 710 F.Supp. 991 (D.N.J.1989)—¶ **10.07, n. 95;** ¶ **10.09, n. 199.**

Mellon Nat. Bank & Trust Co. v. Merchants Bank of New York, 15 UCC Rep. Serv. 691 (S.D.N.Y.1972)—¶ **7.02, n. 104.**

Menichini v. Grant, 995 F.2d 1224 (3rd Cir.1993)—¶ **6.03, n. 292;** ¶ **7.03, n. 130.**

Menke v. Board of Ed., 211 N.W.2d 601 (Iowa 1973)—¶ **2.02, n. 50.**

Merchant v. Worley, 79 N.M. 771, 449 P.2d 787 (N.M.App.1969)—¶ **9.06, n. 364.**

Merchants Nat. Bank v. Professional Men's Ass'n, 409 F.2d 600 (5th Cir.1969)—¶ **2.02, n. 158.**

Merchants Nat. Bank of Fort Smith v. Blass, 282 Ark. 497, 669 S.W.2d 195 (Ark.1984)—¶ **6.03, n. 237.**

Merchants Nat. Bank & Trust Co. of Indianapolis v. United States, 202 Ct.Cl. 343 (Ct.Cl.1973)—¶ **3.03;** ¶ **3.03, n. 298.**

Meredith v. First Nat. Bank, 271 S.W.2d 274 (Ky.1954)—¶ **9.06, n. 392.**

Meritor v. Duke, 31 Va. Cir. 183 (Va. Cir. Ct.1993)—¶ **4.04, n. 169.**

Merrill Lynch, Pierce, Fenner and Smith, Inc. v. Devon Bank, 832 F.2d 1005 (7th Cir.1987)—¶ **8.02, n. 123, 134.**

Merrill Lynch, Pierce, Fenner and Smith, Inc. v. Devon Bank, 654 F.Supp. 506 (N.D.Ill.1987)—¶ **9.03, n. 152.**

Merrill Lynch, Pierce, Fenner & Smith, Inc. v. Chemical Bank, 456 N.Y.S.2d 742, 442 N.E.2d 1253 (N.Y.1982)—¶ **1.04, n. 225;** ¶ **7.03, n. 126, 183.**

Merrill Lynch, Pierce, Fenner & Smith, Inc. v. Chemical Bank, 82 A.D.2d 772, 440 N.Y.S.2d 643 (N.Y.A.D. 1 Dept.1981)—¶ **7.03, n. 125.**

Merrill Lynch, Pierce, Fenner & Smith, Inc. v. Van Kylen, 98 B.R. 455 (Bkrtcy. W.D.Wis.1989)—¶ **8.01, n. 48;** ¶ **9.04, n. 238;** ¶ **9.05, n. 245;** ¶ **9.06, n. 408.**

Merriman v. Sandeen, 267 N.W.2d 714 (Minn.1978)—¶ **4.03, n. 60;** ¶ **7.01;** ¶ **7.01, n. 12.**

Mesnick v. Hempstead Bank, 106 Misc.2d 624, 434 N.Y.S.2d 579 (N.Y.Sup.1980)—¶ **9.03, n. 162.**

Messall v. Suburban Trust Co., 244 Md. 502, 224 A.2d 419 (Md.1966)—¶ **9.06, n. 372.**

Messing v. Bank of America, 143 Md.App. 1, 792 A.2d 312 (Md.Ct. Spec.App.2002)—¶ **4.03, n. 60;** ¶ **4.04, n. 151.**

Metalcraft, Inc. v. Pratt, 65 Md.App. 281, 500 A.2d 329 (Md.App.1985)—¶ **2.02, n. 154.**

Meyer v. Idaho First Nat. Bank, 96 Idaho 208, 525 P.2d 990 (Idaho 1974)—¶ **9.05, n. 287;** ¶ **9.06, n. 325.**

M.G. Sales, Inc. v. Chemical Bank, 161 A.D.2d 148, 554 N.Y.S.2d 863 (N.Y.A.D. 1 Dept.1990)—¶ **3.02, n. 133.**

Michaeli v. Greater New York Sav. Bank, 129 Misc.2d 1096, 498 N.Y.S.2d 90

(N.Y.Sup.App.Term 1985)—¶ **4.02, n. 21.**

Michelin Tires (Canada) Ltd. v. First Nat. Bank of Boston, 666 F.2d 673 (1st Cir. 1981)—¶ **3.03, n. 349.**

Michigan Att'y Gen. Op. No. 5947, 33 UCC Rep. Serv. 1445 (Mich. Atty. Gen. 1981)—¶ **9.01, n. 29.**

Michigan Nat. Bank v. Olson, 44 Wash.App. 898, 723 P.2d 438 (Wash.App. Div. 3 1986)—¶ **11.02, n. 75.**

Mid–America Real Estate & Inv. Corp. v. Lund, 353 N.W.2d 286 (N.D.1984)—¶ **5.03, n. 84.**

Midas Coin Co., In re, 264 F.Supp. 193 (E.D.Mo.1967)—¶ **9.06, n. 406.**

Mid–City Nat. Bank v. Mar Bldg. Corp., 33 Ill.App.3d 1083, 339 N.E.2d 497 (Ill.App. 1 Dist.1975)—¶ **9.05, n. 250, 254, 259.**

Mid–Continent Cas. Co. v. Jenkins, 431 P.2d 349 (Okla.1967)—¶ **7.03, n. 113.**

Mid–Continent Nat. Bank v. Bank of Independence, 523 S.W.2d 569 (Mo.App. 1975)—¶ **3.03; ¶ 3.03, n. 246, 262.**

Middle States Leasing Corp. v. Manufacturers Hanover Trust Co., 62 A.D.2d 273, 404 N.Y.S.2d 846 (N.Y.A.D. 1 Dept. 1978)—¶ **3.02, n. 111.**

Midfirst Bank, SSB v. C.W. Haynes & Co., Inc., 893 F.Supp. 1304 (D.S.C.1994)—¶ **3.01, n. 11; ¶ 3.04, n. 390.**

Midwest Indus. Funding v. First Nat. Bank, 973 F.2d 534 (7th Cir.1992)—¶ **2.02, n. 262; ¶ 7.03, n. 124.**

Milgram Food Stores, Inc. v. Gelco Corp., 550 F.Supp. 992 (W.D.Mo.1982)—¶ **7.01, n. 38.**

Milgrim v. Moses, 19 UCC Rep. Serv. 541 (N.Y.Sup.1976)—¶ **6.03, n. 305.**

Military Circle Pet Center No. 94, Inc., In re, 181 B.R. 282 (Bkrtcy.E.D.Va.1994)—¶ **3.03, n. 269.**

Miller v. American Nat. Bank and Trust Co., 4 F.3d 518 (7th Cir.1993)—¶ **9.05, n. 277, 286, 308.**

Miller v. Jung, 361 So.2d 788 (Fla.App. 2 Dist.1978)—¶ **7.01, n. 34.**

Miller v. Race, 1 Burr. 452, 97 Eng.Rep. 398 (K.B.1758)—¶ **2.01, n. 3.**

Miller v. Standard State Bank, 31 Ill.App.2d 189, 176 N.E.2d 639 (Ill.App. 1 Dist. 1961)—¶ **9.06, n. 401.**

Miller, United States v., 425 U.S. 435, 96 S.Ct. 1619, 48 L.Ed.2d 71 (1976)—¶ **9.05, n. 270.**

Miller v. Wells Fargo Bank Intern. Corp., 406 F.Supp. 452 (S.D.N.Y.1975)—¶ **9.06, n. 409.**

Milligan v. Gilmore Meyer Inc., 775 F.Supp. 400 (S.D.Ga.1991)—¶ **1.03, n. 130.**

Millman v. State Nat. Bank, 323 A.2d 723 (D.C.1974)—¶ **2.02; ¶ 2.02, n. 157; ¶ 3.03, n. 248.**

Milwaukee Petroleum Co. v. Glembin, 89 Wis.2d 174, 278 N.W.2d 471 (Wis.App. 1979)—¶ **2.05, n. 311.**

Minneapolis Sash & Door Co. v. Metropolitan Bank, 76 Minn. 136, 78 N.W. 980 (Minn.1899)—¶ **4.03, n. 86.**

Minnesota Mut. Life Ins. Co. v. Tagus State Bank, 34 N.D. 566, 158 N.W. 1063 (N.D. 1916)—¶ **9.05, n. 303.**

Minskoff v. American Exp. Travel Related Services Co., Inc., 98 F.3d 703 (2nd Cir. 1996)—¶ **11.02, n. 75.**

Minster State Bank v. Baybank Middlesex, 414 Mass. 831, 611 N.E.2d 200 (Mass. 1993)—¶ **7.03, n. 168.**

Mirax Chemical Products Corp. v. First Interstate Commercial Corp., 950 F.2d 566 (8th Cir.1991)—¶ **9.06, n. 351.**

Mississippi Cottonseed Products Co. v. Canal Bank & Trust Co., 172 Miss. 105, 159 So. 404 (Miss.1935)—¶ **9.06, n. 334.**

Mitchell v. Ringson, 169 Ga.App. 88, 311 S.E.2d 516 (Ga.App.1983)—¶ **6.03, n. 275.**

Mitchell Buick & Oldsmobile Sales, Inc. v. McHenry Sav. Bank, 235 Ill.App.3d 978, 176 Ill.Dec. 662, 601 N.E.2d 1360 (Ill. App. 2 Dist.1992)—¶ **4.04, n. 144.**

MJZ Corp. v. Gulfstream First Bank & Trust, N. A., 420 So.2d 396 (Fla.App. 4 Dist.1982)—¶ **9.01, n. 49.**

Modern Free and Accepted Masons of World v. Cliff M. Averett, Inc., 118 Ga. App. 641, 165 S.E.2d 166 (Ga.App. 1968)—¶ **5.03, n. 77.**

Moncrief v. Williston Basin Interstate Pipeline Co., 880 F.Supp. 1495 (D.Wyo. 1995)—¶ **7.01, n. 43.**

Money Mart Check Cashing Center, Inc. v. Epicycle Corp., 667 P.2d 1372 (Colo. 1983)—¶ **3.03, n. 259.**

Moody Nat. Bank v. Texas City Development, Ltd. Co., 46 S.W.3d 373 (Tex.Ct. App.2001)—¶ **8.01, n. 46.**

Moore v. State Bank of Burden, 240 Kan. 382, 729 P.2d 1205 (Kan.1986)—¶ **9.05, n. 251.**

Moore v. Travelers Indem. Ins. Co., 408 A.2d 298 (Del.Super.1979)—¶ **7.01, n. 18.**

Moore v. White, 603 P.2d 1119 (Okla. 1979)—¶ **5.03, n. 95.**

Moorehouse v. Chase Manhattan Bank, 76 S.W.3d 608 (Tex.Ct.App.2002)—¶ **4.03, n. 60; ¶ 9.02, n. 95; ¶ 9.05, n. 297.**

Moreira, In re, 173 B.R. 965 (Bkrtcy. D.Mass.1994)—¶ **9.06, n. 345.**

Morgan Guar. Trust Co. of New York v. American Sav. and Loan Ass'n, 804 F.2d 1487 (9th Cir.1986)—¶ **8.02, n. 161.**

Morgan Guar. Trust Co. of N.Y. v. Chase Manhattan Bank, N.A., 36 UCC Rep. Serv. 584 (N.Y.Sup.1983)—¶ **3.02, n. 80.**

Morrow v. First Interstate Bank of Oregon, N.A., 118 Or.App. 164, 847 P.2d 411 (Or.App.1993)—¶ **7.03, n. 131.**

Morse v. Mutual Federal Sav. & Loan Ass'n of Whitman, 536 F.Supp. 1271 (D.Mass. 1982)—¶ **9.02, n. 101, 106.**

Mortgage Associates v. Siverhus, 63 Wis.2d 650, 218 N.W.2d 266 (Wis.1974)—¶ **2.02, n. 210.**

Motley v. Motley, 60 F.Supp.2d 380 (D.N.J. 1999)—¶ **6.03, n. 286.**

Mountain Stone Co. v. H. W. Hammond Co., 39 Colo.App. 58, 564 P.2d 958 (Colo. App.1977)—¶ **7.01; ¶ 7.01, n. 16.**

Mozingo v. North Carolina Nat. Bank, 31 N.C.App. 157, 229 S.E.2d 57 (N.C.App. 1976)—¶ **2.02, n. 225; ¶ 6.01, n. 37.**

Munson v. American Nat. Bank & Trust Co., 484 F.2d 620 (7th Cir.1973)—¶ **3.01, n. 14; ¶ 6.03, n. 90.**

Murdaugh Volkswagen, Inc. v. First Nat. Bank of South Carolina, 801 F.2d 719 (4th Cir.1986)—¶ **9.03, n. 120.**

Murphy v. Bank of Dahlonega, 151 Ga.App. 264, 259 S.E.2d 670 (Ga.App.1979)—¶ **5.02, n. 18.**

Murphy v. Federal Deposit Ins. Corporation, 61 F.3d 34 (D.C.Cir.1995)—¶ **1.03, n. 133.**

Murray Hill Investments, Inc. v. Adas Yereim, Inc., 205 A.D.2d 512, 612 N.Y.S.2d 679 (N.Y.A.D. 2 Dept.1994)—¶ **7.03, n. 164.**

Musker v. Gil Haskins Auto Leasing, Inc., 18 Ariz.App. 104, 500 P.2d 635 (Ariz. App. Div. 1 1972)—¶ **9.06, n. 400, 401.**

Mustin v. Citizens & Southern Nat. Bank, 168 Ga.App. 549, 309 S.E.2d 822 (Ga. App.1983)—¶ **3.01, n. 25.**

Mutual Finance Co. v. Martin, 63 So.2d 649 (Fla.1953)—¶ **3.04, n. 414.**

Mutual Home Dealers Corp. v. Alves, 23 A.D.2d 791, 258 N.Y.S.2d 786 (N.Y.A.D. 2 Dept.1965)—¶ **3.03, n. 252.**

Mutual Service Cas. Co. v. Elizabeth State Bank, 265 F.3d 601 (7th Cir.2001)—¶ **8.01, n. 46.**

N

NAB Asset Venture II v. Lenertz, Inc., 36 UCC Rep. Serv. 2d 474 (Minn.App. 1998)—¶ **3.01, n. 19.**

Nashville City Bank and Trust Co. v. Massey, 540 F.Supp. 566 (M.D.Ga.1982)—¶ **3.03, n. 295.**

National Bank of Canada v. Artex Industries, Inc., 627 F.Supp. 610 (S.D.N.Y. 1986)—¶ **8.02, n. 161.**

National Bank of Commerce, United States v., 472 U.S. 713, 105 S.Ct. 2919, 86 L.Ed.2d 565 (1985)—¶ **9.06, n. 374.**

National Bank of Detroit v. Alford, 65 Mich. App. 634, 237 N.W.2d 592 (Mich.App. 1975)—¶ **6.03, n. 248.**

National Bank of North America v. Around the Clock Truck Service, 58 Misc.2d 660, 296 N.Y.S.2d 606 (N.Y.Sup.1968)—¶ **2.02, n. 214.**

National Bank of North America v. Beinhorn, 10 UCC Rep. Serv. 847 (N.Y.Sup. 1972)—¶ **5.02, n. 43.**

National Bank of North America v. Flushing Nat. Bank, 72 A.D.2d 538, 421 N.Y.S.2d 65 (N.Y.A.D. 1 Dept.1979)—¶ **3.02, n. 69.**

National Bank & Trust Co. of Central Pennsylvania, Commonwealth v., 469 Pa. 188, 364 A.2d 1331 (Pa.1976)—¶ **4.02, n. 28; ¶ 7.02, n. 102.**

National Council of Churches of Christ in USA v. First Union National Bank of Virginia, 153 F.3d 721 (4th Cir.1998)—¶ **10.04, n. 73; ¶ 10.12; ¶ 10.12, n. 248.**

National Credit Union Admin. v. Michigan Nat. Bank of Detroit, 771 F.2d 154 (6th Cir.1985)—¶ **7.02, n. 95.**

National Equipment, Ltd. v. David Jones Sales, Trucking Division, Inc., 268 S.C. 551, 235 S.E.2d 125 (S.C.1977)—¶ **6.01; ¶ 6.01, n. 4.**

National Indem. Co. v. Spring Branch State Bank, 162 Tex. 521, 348 S.W.2d 528 (Tex.1961)—¶ **9.06, n. 370.**

National Loan Investors, L.P. v. Martin, 488 N.W.2d 163 (Iowa 1992)—¶ **6.03, n. 135.**

National Sav. and Trust Co. v. Park Corp., 722 F.2d 1303 (6th Cir.1983)—¶ **8.02; ¶ 8.02, n. 129, 158, 161, 163, 166; ¶ 8.03, n. 222.**

National Shawmut Bank v. International Yarn Corp., 322 F.Supp. 116 (S.D.N.Y. 1970)—¶ **1.03; ¶ 1.03, n. 114; ¶ 3.01, n. 18; ¶ 7.01, n. 14.**

National State Bank of Elizabeth, N.J. v. Kleinberg, 4 UCC Rep. Serv. 100 (N.Y.Sup.1967)—¶ **3.03; ¶ 3.03, n. 288; ¶ 6.03; ¶ 6.03, n. 126, 146.**

National Sur. Corp. v. Citizens State Bank, 41 Colo.App. 580, 593 P.2d 362 (Colo. App.1978)—¶ **7.02, n. 101.**

National Title Ins. Corp. Agency v. First Union Nat. Bank, 263 Va. 355, 559 S.E.2d 668 (2002)—¶ **8.01, n. 30.**

National Union Fire Ins. Co. v. Alexander, 728 F.Supp. 192 (S.D.N.Y.1989)—¶ **2.02, n. 199.**

Nationsbank of Virginia, N.A. v. Cookies, Inc., 31 Va. Cir. 320 (Va. Cir. Ct.1993)—¶ **3.03, n. 224.**

Nation-Wide Check Corp. v. Banks, 260 A.2d 367 (D.C.App.1969)—¶ **1.02, n. 51.**

Nawas v. Holmes, 541 S.W.2d 283 (Tex.Civ. App.-Waco 1976)—¶ **3.03; ¶ 3.03, n. 367; ¶ 6.01, n. 33.**

TABLE OF CASES

NCNB Texas Nat. Bank v. Campise, 788 S.W.2d 115 (Tex.App.-Hous. (14 Dist.) 1990)—¶ **1.03, n. 142, 155.**

Ness v. Greater Arizona Realty, Inc., 21 Ariz.App. 231, 517 P.2d 1278 (Ariz.App. Div. 2 1974)—¶ **4.02, n. 3.**

Nester v. O'Donnell, 301 N.J.Super. 198, 693 A.2d 1214 (N.J.Super.A.D.1997)—¶ **5.02, n. 18.**

Nevada State Bank v. Fischer, 93 Nev. 317, 565 P.2d 332 (Nev.1977)—¶ **4.06;** ¶ **4.06, n. 233.**

Neve-Welch Enters. v. Twelves, 27 UCC Rep. Serv. 1071 (Bkrtcy.D.Utah 1979)—¶ **7.01, n. 25.**

New Amsterdam Cas. Co. v. First Pennsylvania Banking & Trust Co., 451 F.2d 892 (3rd Cir.1971)—¶ **7.03, n. 176.**

Newby v. Armour Agr. Chemical Co., 119 Ga.App. 650, 168 S.E.2d 652 (Ga.App. 1969)—¶ **6.01;** ¶ **6.01, n. 8;** ¶ **6.03;** ¶ **6.03, n. 140.**

New England Sav. Bank v. Bedford Realty Corp., 238 Conn. 745, 680 A.2d 301 (Conn.1996)—¶ **3.01, n. 19.**

New Hampshire Boring, Inc. v. Adirondack Environmental Associates, Inc., 145 N.H. 397, 762 A.2d 1036 (N.H.2000)—¶ **7.01, n. 32.**

New Jersey Mortg. & Inv. Corp. v. Berenyi, 140 N.J.Super. 406, 356 A.2d 421 (N.J.Super.A.D.1976)—¶ **6.02, n. 55.**

New Jersey Steel Corp. v. Warburton, 139 N.J. 536, 655 A.2d 1382 (N.J.1995)—¶ **4.02, n. 20.**

New Jersey Title Ins. Co. v. Caputo, 163 N.J. 143, 748 A.2d 507 (N.J.2000)—¶ **3.03, n. 297.**

New Waterford Bank v. Morrison Buick, Inc., 3 UCC Rep. Serv. 426 (Pa.Com.Pl. 1965)—¶ **3.03;** ¶ **3.03, n. 287.**

New York, City of v. Bronx County Trust Co., 261 N.Y. 64, 184 N.E. 495 (N.Y. 1933)—¶ **9.03, n. 136.**

New York City Shoes, Inc., In re, 78 B.R. 426 (Bkrtcy.E.D.Pa.1987)—¶ **9.06, n. 385.**

New York State Bankers Ass'n v. Albright, 381 N.Y.S.2d 17, 343 N.E.2d 735 (N.Y. 1975)—¶ **9.04, n. 230.**

New York Trust Co., United States v., 75 F.Supp. 583 (S.D.N.Y.1946)—¶ **9.06, n. 324.**

Nguyen v. State of Nevada, 14 P.3d 515 (2000)—¶ **8.01, n. 3.**

Nicklaus v. Peoples Bank & Trust Co., Russellville, Ark., 258 F.Supp. 482 (E.D.Ark. 1965)—¶ **3.03;** ¶ **3.03, n. 280.**

Nida v. Michael, 34 Mich.App. 290, 191 N.W.2d 151 (Mich.App.1971)—¶ **3.03, n. 215;** ¶ **7.02, n. 102.**

Niebergall v. A.B.A. Contracting & Supply Co., 24 A.D.2d 799, 263 N.Y.S.2d 589 (N.Y.A.D. 3 Dept.1965)—¶ **4.06, n. 257.**

Nigerian Nat. Petroleum Corp. v. Citibank, N.A., 1999 WL 558141 (S.D.N.Y.1999)—¶ **10.04, n. 68;** ¶ **10.07, n. 91;** ¶ **10.08;** ¶ **10.08, n. 166.**

Ninoff v. Hazel Green State Bank, 174 Wis. 560, 183 N.W. 673 (Wis.1921)—¶ **9.05, n. 294.**

Norman v. World Wide Distributors, Inc., 202 Pa.Super. 53, 195 A.2d 115 (Pa.Super.1963)—¶ **3.03;** ¶ **3.03, n. 265.**

Norris' Estate, In re, 532 P.2d 981 (Colo. App.1974)—¶ **2.05, n. 307.**

North Bank v. Circle Inv. Co., 104 Ill. App.3d 363, 60 Ill.Dec. 105, 432 N.E.2d 1004 (Ill.App. 1 Dist.1982)—¶ **6.03, n. 255.**

North Carolina Nat. Bank v. McCarley & Co., Inc., 34 N.C.App. 689, 239 S.E.2d 583 (N.C.App.1977)—¶ **4.04, n. 144.**

North Central Kansas Production Credit Ass'n v. Boese, 19 UCC Rep. Serv. 179 (D.Kan.1976)—¶ **6.02, n. 54.**

Northern Helex Co. v. United States, 197 Ct.Cl. 118, 455 F.2d 546 (Ct.Cl.1972)—¶ **7.01, n. 33.**

Northern Plumbing Supply, Inc. v. Gates, 196 N.W.2d 70 (N.D.1972)—¶ **6.03, n. 169.**

Northpark Nat. Bank v. Bankers Trust Co., 572 F.Supp. 524 (S.D.N.Y.1983)—¶ **8.03, n. 231.**

Northshore Bank v. Palmer, 525 S.W.2d 718 (Tex.Civ.App.-Hous. (14 Dist.) 1975)—¶ **9.06, n. 365.**

Northside Bank of Tampa v. Investors Acceptance Corp., 278 F.Supp. 191 (W.D.Pa.1968)—¶ **6.01, n. 12.**

North Side State Bank v. Board of County Com'rs of Tulsa County, 894 P.2d 1046 (Okla.1994)—¶ **7.03, n. 168.**

Northwestern Bank v. Neal, 271 S.C. 544, 248 S.E.2d 585 (S.C.1978)—¶ **2.02, n. 115.**

Northwestern Nat. Ins. Co. v. Maggio, 976 F.2d 320 (7th Cir.1992)—¶ **3.03, n. 253.**

Northwestern Nat. Ins. Co. of Milwaukee v. Midland Nat. Bank., 96 Wis.2d 155, 292 N.W.2d 591 (Wis.1980)—¶ **8.01, n. 34;** ¶ **8.02, n. 112, 114, 163, 179.**

Northwest Lumber Co. v. Scandinavian–American Bank, 130 Wash. 33, 225 P. 825 (Wash.1924)—¶ **9.05, n. 265.**

O

Oak Brook Bank v. Northern Trust Co., 256 F.3d 638 (7th Cir.2001)—¶ **4.03, n. 79;** ¶ **8.01, n. 38, 55;** ¶ **8.02, n. 100;** ¶ **8.04, n. 332, 333, 334, 343, 345, 347, 349, 462, 465.**

Oak Park Currency Exchange, Inc. v. Maropoulos, 48 Ill.App.3d 437, 6 Ill.Dec. 525, 363 N.E.2d 54 (Ill.App. 1 Dist.1977)—¶ **5.02, n. 36;** ¶ **7.02, n. 47.**

Ocean First Nat. Bank of Fort Lauderdale v. Baird, 9 UCC Rep. Serv. 1092 (N.Y.Sup.1971)—¶ **3.03, n. 307.**
Oclander v. First Nat. Bank, 700 S.W.2d 804 (Ky.App.1985)—¶ **11.02, n. 74.**
Ogborn v. Bank of America Nat. Trust & Savings Ass'n, 28 Cal.App.2d 565, 83 P.2d 44 (Cal.App. 1 Dist.1938)—¶ **9.05, n. 292.**
O'Grady v. First Union Nat. Bank, 296 N.C. 212, 250 S.E.2d 587 (N.C.1978)—¶ **4.06;** ¶ **4.06, n. 212.**
Oki Semiconductor Co. v. Wells Fargo Bank, N.A., 298 F.3d 768 (9th Cir. 2002)—¶ **7.03, n. 124.**
Oklahoma Brick Corp. v. McCall, 497 P.2d 215 (Okla.1972)—¶ **6.03, n. 307.**
Oklahoma Nat. Bank v. Equitable Credit Finance Co., 489 P.2d 1331 (Okla. 1971)—¶ **3.03, n. 278.**
Oklahoma Preferred Finance & Loan Corp. v. Morrow, 497 P.2d 221 (Okla.1972)— ¶ **2.02, n. 202.**
Olean Area Camp Fire Council, Inc. v. Olean Dresser Clark Federal Credit Union, 142 Misc.2d 1049, 538 N.Y.S.2d 905 (N.Y.Sup.1989)—¶ **7.03, n. 127.**
Olshan v. East New York Sav Bank, 28 F.Supp. 727 (E.D.N.Y.1939)—¶ **9.06, n. 400.**
O'Neill v. Steppat, 270 N.W.2d 375 (S.D. 1978)—¶ **7.01, n. 3.**
O.P. Ganjo, Inc. v. Tri–Urban Realty Co., 108 N.J.Super. 517, 261 A.2d 722 (N.J.Super.L.1969)—¶ **3.03;** ¶ **3.03, n. 232, 327.**
Opinion of Atty Gen. of Iowa, 3 UCC Rep. Serv. 183 (Iowa Atty. Gen.1965)— ¶ **2.02, n. 152.**
Opinion of Comptroller General of United States, 4 UCC Rep. Serv. 1176 (U.S. 1968)—¶ **2.02, n. 121.**
Orrico v. Beverly Bank, 109 Ill.App.3d 102, 64 Ill.Dec. 701, 440 N.E.2d 253 (Ill.App. 1 Dist.1982)—¶ **8.01, n. 13.**
Oscar Gruss and Son v. First State Bank of Eldorado, 582 F.2d 424 (7th Cir.1978)— ¶ **3.02, n. 60.**
Ossip–Harris Ins., Inc. v. Barnett Bank of South Florida, N.A., 428 So.2d 363 (Fla. App. 3 Dist.1983)—¶ **9.03, n. 183.**
Outdoor Technologies, Inc. v. Allfirst Financial, Inc., 44 UCC Rep. Serv. 2d 801 (Del.Super.2001)—¶ **4.04, n. 144;** ¶ **7.03, n. 111.**
Overland Nat. Bank v. Aurora Co-op. Elevator Co., 184 Neb. 843, 172 N.W.2d 786 (Neb.1969)—¶ **9.06, n. 390.**
Overton v. Tyler, 3 Pa. 346 (Pa.1846)— ¶ **2.01, n. 2;** ¶ **2.02, n. 67.**
Owensboro Nat. Bank v. Crisp, 608 S.W.2d 51 (Ky.1980)—¶ **4.02, n. 20, 31;** ¶ **6.02;** ¶ **6.02, n. 83;** ¶ **6.03;** ¶ **6.03, n. 120.**
Owens–Peterson, In re, 39 B.R. 186 (Bkrtcy.N.D.Ga.1984)—¶ **9.06, n. 385.**
Owosso Masonic Temple Ass'n v. State Sav. Bank, 273 Mich. 682, 263 N.W. 771 (Mich.1935)—¶ **9.05, n. 302.**

P

Pacific Finance Loans v. Goodwin, 41 Ohio App.2d 141, 324 N.E.2d 578 (Ohio App. 8 Dist.1974)—¶ **2.02;** ¶ **2.02, n. 79.**
Pacific Nat. Bank v. Hernreich, 240 Ark. 114, 398 S.W.2d 221 (Ark.1966)—¶ **6.02, n. 57.**
Pain v. Packard, 13 Johns. 174 (N.Y.Sup. 1816)—¶ **5.02, n. 48.**
Palmer v. Idaho Bank & Trust, 100 Idaho 642, 603 P.2d 597 (Idaho 1979)—¶ **9.03;** ¶ **9.03, n. 129.**
Palmetto Leasing Co. v. Chiles, 235 Ill. App.3d 986, 176 Ill.Dec. 770, 602 N.E.2d 77 (Ill.App. 2 Dist.1992)—¶ **3.03, n. 269.**
Pancoast v. Century Homes, Inc., 8 UCC Rep. Serv. 1289 (Okla.App.1971)— ¶ **3.01, n. 27.**
Pandol Bros., Inc. v. NCNB Nat. Bank of Florida, 450 So.2d 592 (Fla.App. 4 Dist. 1984)—¶ **8.03, n. 231.**
Paradis v. Greater Providence Deposit Corp., 651 A.2d 738 (R.I.1994)—¶ **9.05, n. 269.**
Paragon Buying Service, Inc. v. Sylbay Realty Corp., 3 UCC Rep. Serv. 67 (N.Y.Sup.1966)—¶ **4.06, n. 207.**
Pargas, Inc. v. Taylor's Estate, 416 So.2d 1358 (La.App. 3 Cir.1982)—¶ **4.02, n. 34.**
Park Enterprises v. Trach, 233 Minn. 467, 47 N.W.2d 194 (Minn.1951)—¶ **9.06, n. 400, 402.**
Parker v. First Nat. Bank, 96 Okla. 70, 220 P. 39 (Okla.1923)—¶ **9.06, n. 345.**
Park State Bank v. Arena Auto Auction, Inc., 59 Ill.App.2d 235, 207 N.E.2d 158 (Ill.App. 2 Dist.1965)—¶ **4.02, n. 23;** ¶ **9.05, n. 309.**
Parkwood, Inc., In re, 461 F.2d 158 (D.C.Cir.1971)—¶ **3.03;** ¶ **3.03, n. 271.**
Parr v. Security Nat. Bank, 680 P.2d 648 (Okla.App. Div. 1 1984)—¶ **9.01, n. 23.**
Parrett v. Platte Valley State Bank & Trust Co., 236 Neb. 139, 459 N.W.2d 371 (Neb. 1990)—¶ **9.03, n. 118.**
Participating Parts Associates, Inc. v. Pylant, 460 So.2d 1299 (Ala.Civ.App. 1984)—¶ **2.02, n. 179.**
Patterson v. Federal Deposit Ins. Corporation, 918 F.2d 540 (5th Cir.1990)— ¶ **1.03, n. 147.**
Patterson v. First Nat. Bank of Huntsville, 47 Ala.App. 98, 251 So.2d 230 (Ala.Civ. App.1971)—¶ **3.03, n. 324.**
Pattison v. Syracuse Nat. Bank, 80 N.Y. 82 (N.Y.1880)—¶ **9.05, n. 305.**

Payne v. Mundaca Inv. Corp., 562 N.E.2d 51 (Ind.App. 1 Dist.1990)—¶ **1.03, n. 130.**

Pazol v. Citizens Nat. Bank of Sandy Springs, 110 Ga.App. 319, 138 S.E.2d 442 (Ga.App.1964)—¶ **3.02, n. 167.**

Peak v. Tuscaloosa Commerce Bank, 96 1258 La.App. 1 Cir. 12/29/9, 707 So.2d 59 (La.App. 1 Cir.1997)—¶ **11.03, n. 120.**

Peerless Ins. Co. v. Texas Commerce Bank–New Braunfels, N.A., 791 F.2d 1177 (5th Cir.1986)—¶ **7.03, n. 138.**

Penagos v. Capital Bank, 766 So.2d 1089 (Fla.App. 3 Dist.2000)—¶ **6.03, n. 291.**

Pennsylvania Nat. Bank & Trust Co. v. CCNB Bank, 446 Pa.Super. 625, 667 A.2d 1151 (Pa.Super.1995)—¶ **9.06, n. 372.**

People v. _____ (see opposing party)

People ex rel. v. _____ (see opposing party and relator)

Peoples Bank of Aurora v. Haar, 421 P.2d 817 (Okla.1966)—¶ **3.03, n. 318, 327;** ¶ **6.01, n. 6, 12.**

Peoria Sav. and Loan Ass'n v. Jefferson Trust and Sav. Bank of Peoria, 81 Ill.2d 461, 43 Ill.Dec. 712, 410 N.E.2d 845 (Ill.1980)—¶ **3.03, n. 230.**

Peppers v. Citizens and Southern Nat. Bank, 127 Ga.App. 16, 192 S.E.2d 409 (Ga.App.1972)—¶ **6.03, n. 114.**

Peppertree Apartments, Ltd. v. Peppertree Apartments, 631 So.2d 873 (Ala.1993)—¶ **2.02, n. 183.**

Perdue v. Crocker National Bank, 216 Cal. Rptr. 345, 702 P.2d 503 (Cal.1985)—¶ **9.03;** ¶ **9.03, n. 137.**

Perfect Picture Frames, Inc. v. Consolidated Fine Arts, Ltd., 9 UCC Rep. Serv. 283 (N.Y.Sup.1971)—¶ **5.02, n. 45;** ¶ **6.01, n. 26.**

Perini Corp. v. First Nat. Bank of Habersham County, Georgia, 553 F.2d 398 (5th Cir.1977)—¶ **3.03, n. 379, 380;** ¶ **4.02, n. 12;** ¶ **7.02, n. 95;** ¶ **7.03, n. 157;** ¶ **8.01, n. 10;** ¶ **9.01, n. 4.**

Perkins State Bank v. Connolly, 632 F.2d 1306 (5th Cir.1980)—¶ **7.02, n. 59.**

Perley v. Glastonbury Bank & Trust Co., 170 Conn. 691, 368 A.2d 149 (Conn. 1976)—¶ **3.02, n. 105;** ¶ **7.02, n. 99;** ¶ **7.03;** ¶ **7.03, n. 172.**

Perry v. Cain, 581 P.2d 891 (Okla.1978)—¶ **2.02, n. 156.**

Perry & Greer, Inc. v. Manning, 282 Or. 25, 576 P.2d 791 (Or.1978)—¶ **3.01, n. 28;** ¶ **3.03, n. 202.**

Peterson v. Crown Financial Corp., 661 F.2d 287 (3rd Cir.1981)—¶ **6.03;** ¶ **6.03, n. 236.**

Peterson v. Crown Financial Corp., 476 F.Supp. 1155 (E.D.Pa.1979)—¶ **7.01, n. 33.**

Phenix Girard Bank v. Cannon, 414 So.2d 926 (Ala.1982)—¶ **5.03, n. 87.**

Philadelphia Bond & Mortg. Co. v. Highland Crest Homes, Inc., 235 Pa.Super. 252, 340 A.2d 476 (Pa.Super.1975)—¶ **4.05, n. 191;** ¶ **5.02, n. 48.**

Philadelphia Bond & Mortg. Co. v. Highland Crest Homes, Inc., 221 Pa.Super. 89, 288 A.2d 916 (Pa.Super.1972)—¶ **5.02, n. 45.**

Philadelphia Gear Corp. v. Federal Deposit Ins. Corp., 751 F.2d 1131 (10th Cir. 1984)—¶ **9.05, n. 246.**

Philadelphia Nat. Bank, United States v., 304 F.Supp. 955 (E.D.Pa.1969)—¶ **1.03;** ¶ **1.03, n. 128.**

Philadelphia Title Ins. Co. v. Fidelity–Philadelphia Trust Co., 419 Pa. 78, 212 A.2d 222 (Pa.1965)—¶ **7.03;** ¶ **7.03, n. 167.**

Philco Finance Co. v. Patton, 248 Or. 310, 432 P.2d 686 (Or.1967)—¶ **6.03, n. 256.**

Phoenix Assur. Co. v. Davis, 126 N.J.Super. 379, 314 A.2d 615 (N.J.Super.L.1974)—¶ **7.03, n. 158.**

Phoenix, City of v. Great Western Bank & Trust, 148 Ariz. 53, 712 P.2d 966 (Ariz. App. Div. 1 1985)—¶ **7.03, n. 183, 189.**

Piatt v. Medford Highlands, LLC, 173 Or. App. 409, 22 P.3d 767 (Or.App.2001)—¶ **2.02, n. 262.**

Pickard, Matter of Estate of, 97 A.D.2d 61, 468 N.Y.S.2d 264 (N.Y.A.D. 4 Dept. 1983)—¶ **6.03, n. 126.**

Piedmont Resolution, L.L.C. v. Johnston, Rivlin & Foley, 999 F.Supp. 34 (D.D.C. 1998)—¶ **10.02;** ¶ **10.02, n. 12, 31.**

Pigg v. Robertson, 549 S.W.2d 597 (Mo.App. 1977)—¶ **9.03, n. 128.**

Pine Bluff Nat. Bank v. Kesterson, 257 Ark. 813, 520 S.W.2d 253 (Ark.1975)—¶ **5.03, n. 68;** ¶ **9.03, n. 163.**

Piper v. Goodwin, 20 F.3d 216 (6th Cir. 1994)—¶ **3.01, n. 19.**

Pittsburgh Nat. Bank v. United States, 657 F.2d 36 (3rd Cir.1981)—¶ **9.01, n. 89.**

Placido v. Citizens Bank & Trust Co. of Maryland, 38 Md.App. 33, 379 A.2d 773 (Md.App.1977)—¶ **6.03, n. 124.**

Pollin v. Mindy Mfg. Co., 211 Pa.Super. 87, 236 A.2d 542 (Pa.Super.1967)—¶ **2.02;** ¶ **2.02, n. 49;** ¶ **5.03, n. 97.**

Polonsky v. Union Federal Sav. & Loan Ass'n, 334 Mass. 697, 138 N.E.2d 115 (Mass.1956)—¶ **9.05, n. 292.**

Port City State Bank v. American Nat. Bank, 486 F.2d 196 (10th Cir.1973)—¶ **2.04, n. 287;** ¶ **8.03;** ¶ **8.03, n. 223.**

Poullier v. Nacua Motors, Inc., 108 Misc.2d 913, 439 N.Y.S.2d 85 (N.Y.Sup.1981)—¶ **9.01, n. 23.**

Powers v. American Exp. Financial Advisors, Inc., 82 F.Supp.2d 448 (D.Md. 2000)—¶ **4.02, n. 5.**

TABLE OF CASES

P. Pastene & Co. v. First Nat. Bank, 19 Ariz. 493, 172 P. 656 (Ariz.1918)—¶ 9.06, n. 355.

Pracht v. Oklahoma State Bank, 592 P.2d 976 (Okla.1979)—¶ 8.02; ¶ 8.02, n. 133, 139.

Premier Capital, Inc. v. Doucette, 797 A.2d 32, 47 UCC Rep.Serv.2d 1409 (Me. 2002)—¶ 6.03, n. 309.

Premier Capital, Inc. v. Gallagher, 144 N.H. 284, 740 A.2d 1047 (N.H.1999)—¶ 6.03, n. 286.

Pribus v. Bush, 118 Cal.App.3d 1003, 173 Cal.Rptr. 747 (Cal.App. 4 Dist.1981)—¶ 3.02, n. 83.

Price v. Neal, 97 Eng. Rep. 871 (Unknown Court 1762)—¶ 3.03; ¶ 3.03, n. 375; ¶ 7.02; ¶ 7.02, n. 46, 80; ¶ 9.03, n. 182.

Price v. Wells Fargo Bank, 213 Cal.App.3d 465, 261 Cal.Rptr. 735 (Cal.App. 1 Dist. 1989)—¶ 9.03; ¶ 9.03, n. 135, 170.

ProCD, Inc. v. Zeidenberg, 86 F.3d 1447 (7th Cir.1996)—¶ 11.03, n. 98.

Program Aids Co., Inc. v. W. R. Bean & Son, Inc., 4 UCC Rep. Serv. 210 (N.Y.Sup.1967)—¶ 4.04, n. 160.

Prudential–Bache Securities, Inc. v. Citibank, N.A., 539 N.Y.S.2d 699, 536 N.E.2d 1118 (N.Y.1989)—¶ 7.03, n. 174.

Prudential–Bache Securities, Inc. v. Citibank, N.A., 4 UCC Rep. Serv. 2d 533 (N.Y.Sup.1987)—¶ 7.03, n. 183.

Prudential Ins. Co. of America v. Marine Nat. Exchange Bank, 371 F.Supp. 1002 (E.D.Wis.1974)—¶ 7.03, n. 182.

Prudential Ins. Co. of America v. Marine Nat. Exchange Bank, 55 F.R.D. 436 (E.D.Wis.1972)—¶ 4.02, n. 28.

Prudential Ins. Co. of America v. Marine Nat. Exchange Bank, 315 F.Supp. 520 (E.D.Wis.1970)—¶ 7.03, n. 150.

Pugh v. First Nat. Bank, 130 Ga.App. 627, 204 S.E.2d 370 (Ga.App.1974)—¶ 2.02; ¶ 2.02, n. 165; ¶ 4.05, n. 192.

Pulaski Chase Co-op. v. Kellogg–Citizens Nat. Bank, 130 Wis.2d 200, 386 N.W.2d 510 (Wis.App.1986)—¶ 4.04, n. 175; ¶ 9.01, n. 67.

Pulaski State Bank v. Kalbe, 122 Wis.2d 663, 364 N.W.2d 162 (Wis.App.1985)—¶ 8.02, n. 169.

Purma v. Stark, 224 Kan. 642, 585 P.2d 991 (Kan.1978)—¶ 9.06, n. 401.

Q

Qatar, State of v. First American Bank of Virginia, 885 F.Supp. 849 (E.D.Va. 1995)—¶ 7.03, n. 136, 173.

Qatar, State of v. First American Bank of Virginia, 880 F.Supp. 463 (E.D.Va. 1995)—¶ 3.02, n. 167; ¶ 7.03, n. 173.

Quantum Development Corp., In re, 397 F.Supp. 329 (D.Virgin Islands 1975)—¶ 3.02; ¶ 3.02, n. 143.

Quazzo v. Quazzo, 136 Vt. 107, 386 A.2d 638 (Vt.1978)—¶ 6.02, n. 48; ¶ 6.03, n. 173.

Quigley v. Acker, 288 Mont. 190, 955 P.2d 1377 (Mont.1998)—¶ 7.01, n. 4.

Quistgaard v. EAB European American Bank and Trust Co., 182 A.D.2d 510, 583 N.Y.S.2d 210 (N.Y.A.D. 1 Dept. 1992)—¶ 4.03, n. 52, 73; ¶ 4.04, n. 156, 159, 169.

R

Rago v. Cosmopolitan Nat. Bank, 89 Ill. App.2d 12, 232 N.E.2d 88 (Ill.App. 1 Dist.1967)—¶ 6.03; ¶ 6.03, n. 166.

Rahall v. Tweel, 186 W.Va. 136, 411 S.E.2d 461 (W.Va.1991)—¶ 4.06, n. 204; ¶ 5.01, n. 1.

Rainsville Bank v. Willingham, 485 So.2d 319 (Ala.1986)—¶ 9.05, n. 250, 257, 303, 308; ¶ 9.06, n. 358, 362, 367.

Ralls v. First Federal Sav. and Loan Ass'n of Andalusia, 422 So.2d 764 (Ala.1982)—¶ 6.02, n. 48.

Rapp v. Dime Sav. Bank of New York, 421 N.Y.S.2d 347, 396 N.E.2d 740 (N.Y. 1979)—¶ 8.02, n. 175.

Rapp v. Dime Sav. Bank of New York, 64 A.D.2d 964, 408 N.Y.S.2d 540 (N.Y.A.D. 2 Dept.1978)—¶ 8.04, n. 457.

Rassette v. Jacobson, 39 Mich.App. 172, 197 N.W.2d 330 (Mich.App.1972)—¶ 5.02, n. 48.

Rebney v. Wells Fargo Bank, 220 Cal. App.3d 1117, 269 Cal.Rptr. 844 (Cal. App. 1 Dist.1990)—¶ 9.03, n. 138.

Reese v. First Missouri Bank & Trust Co. of Creve Coeur, 664 S.W.2d 530 (Mo.App. E.D.1983)—¶ 2.02, n. 229.

Regent Corp. U.S.A. v. Azmat Bangladesh, Ltd., 32 UCC Rep. Serv. 2d 900 (N.Y.Sup.1997)—¶ 2.02, n. 234.

Reid v. Key Bank, Inc., 821 F.2d 9 (1st Cir.1987)—¶ 1.04, n. 217.

Reliance Ins. Co. v. Bank of America Nat. Trust & Sav. Ass'n, 43 UCC Rep. Serv. 2d 946 (N.D.Ill.2001)—¶ 9.01, n. 2; ¶ 9.03, n. 117, 144, 156, 159, 162, 165, 174, 178, 181; ¶ 9.05, n. 269, 271.

Republic of Texas Sav. Ass'n v. First Republic Life Ins. Co., 417 So.2d 1251 (La. App. 1 Cir.1982)—¶ 3.03, n. 262.

Residential Indus. Loan Co. v. Brown, 559 F.2d 438 (5th Cir.1977)—¶ 6.03, n. 270.

Resolution Trust Corp. v. Gill, 960 F.2d 336 (3rd Cir.1992)—¶ 3.03, n. 299, 306.

Resolution Trust Corp. v. Juergens, 965 F.2d 149 (7th Cir.1992)—¶ 3.02, n. 66, 185.

Resolution Trust Corp. v. Oaks Apartments Joint Venture, 966 F.2d 995 (5th Cir. 1992)—¶ **2.02, n. 197.**

Resolution Trust Corp. v. 1601 Partners, Ltd., 796 F.Supp. 238 (N.D.Tex.1992)— ¶ **1.03, n. 133.**

Rex Smith Propane, Inc. v. National Bank of Commerce, 372 F.Supp. 499 (N.D.Tex. 1974)—¶ **3.01;** ¶ **3.01, n. 6;** ¶ **4.04, n. 145.**

Reynes v. Dumont, 130 U.S. 354, 9 S.Ct. 486, 32 L.Ed. 934 (1889)—¶ **9.06, n. 329.**

Reynolds–Wilson Lumber Co. v. Peoples Nat. Bank, 699 P.2d 146 (Okla.1985)— ¶ **2.04, n. 292;** ¶ **4.03, n. 137;** ¶ **8.01, n. 33, 52;** ¶ **8.02, n. 138;** ¶ **8.03, n. 193, 205.**

Rezapolvi v. First Nat. Bank of Maryland, 296 Md. 1, 459 A.2d 183 (Md.1983)— ¶ **4.04, n. 175.**

Rhode Island Depositors Economic Protection Corp. v. Ryan, 697 A.2d 1087 (R.I. 1997)—¶ **1.03, n. 130.**

Rhode Island Hosp. Trust Nat. Bank v. Zapata Corp., 848 F.2d 291 (1st Cir. 1988)—¶ **9.03;** ¶ **9.03, n. 196, 198.**

Ribaudo v. Citizens Nat. Bank of Orlando, 261 F.2d 929 (5th Cir.1958)—¶ **9.06, n. 345.**

Rich v. Franklin Sav. Bank of New York, 18 UCC Rep. Serv. 451 (N.Y.Sup.1975)— ¶ **4.03, n. 130.**

Richfield Bank & Trust Co. v. Sjogren, 309 Minn. 362, 244 N.W.2d 648 (Minn. 1976)—¶ **9.03, n. 127.**

Ridings v. Motor Vessel Effort, 387 F.2d 888 (2nd Cir.1968)—¶ **5.02, n. 53.**

Riedel v. First Nat. Bank of Oregon, 287 Or. 285, 598 P.2d 302 (Or.1979)—¶ **8.04, n. 467.**

Riegler v. Riegler, 244 Ark. 483, 426 S.W.2d 789 (Ark.1968)—¶ **5.02, n. 36.**

Riley v. First State Bank, Spearman, 469 S.W.2d 812 (Tex.Civ.App.-Amarillo 1971)—¶ **3.03, n. 253;** ¶ **4.05, n. 202.**

Rimberg v. Union Trust Co. of the District of Columbia, 12 UCC Rep. Serv. 527 (D.C. Super.1973)—¶ **9.01;** ¶ **9.01, n. 26.**

Ritz v. Karstenson, 39 Ill.App.3d 877, 350 N.E.2d 870 (Ill.App. 2 Dist.1976)— ¶ **3.03, n. 320.**

Riverside Park Realty Co. v. Federal Deposit Ins. Corp., 465 F.Supp. 305 (M.D.Tenn.1978)—¶ **1.03, n. 152.**

Roark v. Hicks, 234 Va. 470, 362 S.E.2d 711 (Va.1987)—¶ **6.03, n. 178.**

Roberts Fertilizer, Inc. v. Steinmeier, 748 S.W.2d 883 (Mo.App. W.D.1988)— ¶ **8.01, n. 61.**

Robinson Bros. Drilling, Inc., In re (ABB Vecto Gray, Inc. v. First National Bank of Bethany), 9 F.3d 871 (10th Cir. 1993)—¶ **5.01, n. 1.**

Rockland Trust Co. v. South Shore Nat. Bank, 366 Mass. 74, 314 N.E.2d 438 (Mass.1974)—¶ **3.03;** ¶ **3.03, n. 386;** ¶ **4.03, n. 68;** ¶ **4.04, n. 184;** ¶ **8.01;** ¶ **8.01, n. 8.**

Rodgers v. Tecumseh Bank, 756 P.2d 1223 (Okla.1988)—¶ **1.04, n. 217;** ¶ **9.03, n. 123, 132, 135, 160.**

Roehrich, In re, 107 B.R. 675 (Bkrtcy. D.N.D.1989)—¶ **4.04, n. 146.**

Roland v. Republic Nat. Bank, 463 S.W.2d 747 (Tex.Civ.App.-Waco 1971)—¶ **2.02, n. 46.**

Rosen v. State Bank, 32 Misc. 231, 65 N.Y.S. 666 (N.Y.City Ct.1900)—¶ **9.05, n. 289, 295.**

Roswell Bank v. Atlanta Utility Works, Inc., 149 Ga.App. 660, 255 S.E.2d 124 (Ga. App.1979)—¶ **3.02, n. 181.**

Rothenberg v. Mellow Music, Inc., 291 So.2d 234 (Fla.App. 3 Dist.1974)— ¶ **2.02, n. 186.**

Rotuba Extruders, Inc. v. Ceppos, 413 N.Y.S.2d 141, 385 N.E.2d 1068 (N.Y. 1978)—¶ **5.03, n. 102.**

Rourke v. Angelis, 12 UCC Rep. Serv. 526 (N.Y.Sup.1973)—¶ **4.06, n. 250.**

Royal Bank of Canada v. Federal Deposit Ins. Corporation, 733 F.Supp. 1091 (N.D.Tex.1990)—¶ **1.03, n. 154.**

Royal Trust Bank of Orlando v. All Florida Fleets, Inc., 431 So.2d 1043 (Fla.App. 5 Dist.1983)—¶ **8.03, n. 228.**

RSR Properties, Inc. v. Federal Deposit Ins. Corporation, 706 F.Supp. 524 (W.D.Tex. 1989)—¶ **1.03, n. 154.**

Russell v. Maxson Sales Co., 591 P.2d 703 (Okla.1979)—¶ **3.01, n. 46;** ¶ **3.02, n. 67;** ¶ **6.03, n. 199.**

Rutherford v. Darwin, 95 N.M. 340, 622 P.2d 245 (N.M.App.1980)—¶ **3.02, n. 171.**

Ryan v. Ryan, 298 A.2d 343 (Del.Super.1972)—¶ **6.02, n. 44;** ¶ **6.03, n. 142.**

S

Saale v. Interstate Steel Co., 27 A.D.2d 1, 275 N.Y.S.2d 532 (N.Y.A.D. 1 Dept. 1966)—¶ **3.03;** ¶ **3.03, n. 249.**

Sabin Meyer Regional Sales Corp. v. Citizens Bank, 502 F.Supp. 557 (N.D.Ga. 1980)—¶ **4.02, n. 8;** ¶ **4.04, n. 144.**

Saka v. Mann Theatres, 94 Nev. 137, 575 P.2d 1335 (Nev.1978)—¶ **3.03;** ¶ **3.03, n. 234.**

Saka v. Sahara–Nevada Corp., 92 Nev. 703, 558 P.2d 535 (Nev.1976)—¶ **3.03;** ¶ **3.03, n. 212, 311.**

Saloga v. Central Kansas Credit Union, 245 Kan. 668, 783 P.2d 339 (Kan.1989)— ¶ **3.01, n. 7.**

TABLE OF CASES 587

Salsman v. National Community Bank, 105 N.J.Super. 164, 251 A.2d 460 (N.J.Super.A.D.1969)—¶ **3.02;** ¶ **3.02, n. 166.**

Salsman v. National Community Bank of Rutherford, 102 N.J.Super. 482, 246 A.2d 162 (N.J.Super.L.1968)—¶ **1.04, n. 227.**

Salter v. AmSouth Bank, N.A., 487 So.2d 927 (Ala.Civ.App.1985)—¶ **6.03, n. 268.**

Salter v. Vanotti, 42 Colo.App. 448, 599 P.2d 962 (Colo.App.1979)—¶ **3.03, n. 308.**

Sandler v. Eighth Judicial Dist. Court In and For Clark County, 96 Nev. 622, 614 P.2d 10 (Nev.1980)—¶ **6.02, n. 56.**

Sanitary and Improvement Dist. No. 32 of Sarpy County v. Continental Western Corp., 215 Neb. 843, 343 N.W.2d 314 (Neb.1983)—¶ **1.03, n. 90.**

San Tan Irr. Dist. v. Wells Fargo Bank, 197 Ariz. 193, 3 P.3d 1113 (Ariz.App. Div. 1 2000)—¶ **3.03, n. 251;** ¶ **8.03, n. 215, 232;** ¶ **9.03, n. 124, 167.**

Santos v. First Nat. State Bank, 186 N.J.Super. 52, 451 A.2d 401 (N.J.Super.A.D.1982)—¶ **3.01, n. 19;** ¶ **9.01, n. 68.**

Sass Trucking, Inc. v. Security Bank and Trust Co., 737 P.2d 113 (Okla.1987)—¶ **8.01, n. 60;** ¶ **8.02, n. 141;** ¶ **8.04, n. 474.**

Savemart, Inc. v. Bowery Sav. Bank, 117 Misc.2d 947, 461 N.Y.S.2d 144 (N.Y.Sup. App.Term 1982)—¶ **4.02, n. 21.**

Savings Bank v. Loewe, 242 U.S. 357, 37 S.Ct. 172, 61 L.Ed. 360 (1917)—¶ **9.06, n. 396.**

Savings Banks Trust Co. v. Federal Reserve Bank of New York, 738 F.2d 573 (2nd Cir.1984)—¶ **7.02, n. 104.**

Sayan v. Riggs Nat. Bank of Washington, D.C., 544 A.2d 267 (D.C.1988)—¶ **8.02, n. 168.**

Scafidi v. Johnson, 420 So.2d 1113 (La. 1982)—¶ **2.02, n. 179;** ¶ **6.01, n. 37.**

SCCI, Inc. v. United States Nat. Bank of Oregon, 78 Or.App. 176, 714 P.2d 1113 (Or.App.1986)—¶ **7.03, n. 132.**

Schaeffer v. United Bank & Trust Co. of Maryland, 32 Md.App. 339, 360 A.2d 461 (Md.App.1976)—¶ **5.02, n. 31, 45.**

Schaller v. Marine Nat. Bank of Neenah, 131 Wis.2d 389, 388 N.W.2d 645 (Wis. App.1986)—¶ **4.04, n. 144;** ¶ **9.03, n. 153.**

Schauss v. Garner, 590 P.2d 1316 (Wyo. 1979)—¶ **6.03, n. 274.**

Schenck's Estate, In re, 63 Misc.2d 721, 313 N.Y.S.2d 277 (N.Y.Sur.1970)—¶ **4.04, n. 147.**

Schenectady Trust Co. v. Sciocchetti's Estate, 82 Misc.2d 1075, 371 N.Y.S.2d 36 (N.Y.Sup.1975)—¶ **4.06, n. 252.**

Schmidt v. Fleet Bank, 1998 WL 47827 (S.D.N.Y.1998)—¶ **10.03, n. 42.**

Schneider Fuel & Supply Co. v. West Allis State Bank, 70 Wis.2d 1041, 236 N.W.2d 266 (Wis.1975)—¶ **3.03;** ¶ **3.03, n. 270;** ¶ **6.03, n. 198.**

Schnellmann v. Southern Commercial & Savings Bank, 123 Mo.App. 188, 100 S.W. 575 (Mo.App.1907)—¶ **9.06, n. 400.**

Schoenfelder v. Arizona Bank, 165 Ariz. 79, 796 P.2d 881 (Ariz.1990)—¶ **8.01, n. 53;** ¶ **9.03, n. 117, 120.**

Scholl v. Tallman, 247 N.W.2d 490 (S.D. 1976)—¶ **7.01, n. 38;** ¶ **9.01, n. 8.**

Schoonmaker v. Merchants Nat. Bank & Trust Co. of Syracuse, 81 Misc.2d 967, 365 N.Y.S.2d 103 (N.Y.Co.Ct.1974)—¶ **3.02;** ¶ **3.02, n. 186.**

Schorr v. Bank of New York, 107 Misc.2d 132, 433 N.Y.S.2d 546 (N.Y.City Ct.1980)—¶ **11.02, n. 92.**

Schranz v. I.L. Grossman, Inc., 90 Ill. App.3d 507, 45 Ill.Dec. 654, 412 N.E.2d 1378 (Ill.App. 1 Dist.1980)—¶ **3.03, n. 237.**

Schuler v. Israel, 120 U.S. 506, 7 S.Ct. 648, 30 L.Ed. 707 (1887)—¶ **9.06, n. 345.**

Schultz v. American Nat. Bank & Trust Co., 40 Ill.App.3d 800, 352 N.E.2d 310 (Ill.App. 2 Dist.1976)—¶ **9.06, n. 390.**

Schwartz v. Disneyland Vista Records, 383 So.2d 1117 (Fla.App. 4 Dist.1980)—¶ **5.03, n. 84.**

Scott v. Wall, 55 Wash.App. 404, 777 P.2d 581 (Wash.App. Div. 1 1989)—¶ **2.02, n. 179;** ¶ **3.03, n. 203.**

Sears Roebuck & Co. v. Ragucci, 203 N.J.Super. 82, 495 A.2d 923 (N.J.Super.L.1985)—¶ **11.02, n. 73.**

Seattle–First Nat. Bank v. Pacific Nat. Bank of Washington, 22 Wash.App. 46, 587 P.2d 617 (Wash.App. Div. 1 1978)—¶ **7.03, n. 178.**

Seattle–First Nat. Bank v. Schriber, 282 Or. 625, 580 P.2d 1012 (Or.1978)—¶ **2.02, n. 229.**

Sebastian v. D & S Exp., Inc., 61 F.Supp.2d 386 (D.N.J.1999)—¶ **8.03, n. 227;** ¶ **9.02, n. 111;** ¶ **9.03, n. 189.**

Second Nat. Bank of North Miami, United States v., 502 F.2d 535 (5th Cir.1974)—¶ **3.03, n. 205;** ¶ **6.03, n. 171.**

Securities Fund Services, Inc. v. American Nat. Bank and Trust Co. of Chicago, 542 F.Supp. 323 (N.D.Ill.1982)—¶ **10.09, n. 191.**

Security Bank & Trust Co. v. Federal Nat. Bank & Trust Co. of Shawnee, 1976 OK CIV APP 24, 554 P.2d 119 (Okla.App. Div. 2 1976)—¶ **8.01, n. 32.**

Security First Network Bank v. C.A.P.S., Inc., 47 UCC Rep.Serv.2d 670 (N.D.Ill. 2002)—¶ **11.01;** ¶ **11.03, n. 110.**

Security Pacific Nat. Bank v. Chess, 58 Cal.App.3d 555, 129 Cal.Rptr. 852 (Cal. App. 2 Dist.1976)—¶ **2.02, n. 246;**

¶ 3.01, n. 30; ¶ 3.02; ¶ 3.02, n. 75; ¶ 4.02, n. 3; ¶ 5.03, n. 96.
Security State Bank v. W.R. Johnston & Co., 204 Okla. 160, 228 P.2d 169 (Okla. 1951)—¶ 9.06, n. 358, 370.
Security State Bank of Aitkin v. Morlock, 355 N.W.2d 441 (Minn.App.1984)—¶ 9.01, n. 69.
Security Trust Co. of New York v. First Nat. Bank of Rochester, 79 Misc.2d 523, 358 N.Y.S.2d 943 (N.Y.Sup.1974)—¶ 4.03, n. 109.
Seifert v. Seifert, 708 S.W.2d 150 (Mo.App. E.D.1985)—¶ 6.03, n. 295.
Seigel v. Merrill Lynch, Pierce, Fenner & Smith, Inc., 745 A.2d 301 (D.C.2000)—¶ 3.03, n. 319.
Seinfeld v. Commercial Bank & Trust Co., 405 So.2d 1039 (Fla.App. 3 Dist.1981)—¶ 3.03; ¶ 3.03, n. 224, 282.
Senate Motors, Inc. v. Industrial Bank of Washington, 9 UCC Rep. Serv. 387 (D.C. Super.1971)—¶ 5.03, n. 75.
Sequoyah State Bank v. Union Nat. Bank, 274 Ark. 1, 621 S.W.2d 683 (Ark.1981)—¶ 1.01, n. 24; ¶ 2.02, n. 52; ¶ 4.04, n. 154; ¶ 8.01, n. 67.
Serna v. Milanese, Inc., 643 So.2d 36 (Fla. App. 3 Dist.1994)—¶ 5.03, n. 98.
Shaffer v. Brooklyn Park Garden Apartments, 311 Minn. 452, 250 N.W.2d 172 (Minn.1977)—¶ 2.02, n. 120; ¶ 3.03; ¶ 3.03, n. 277.
Sharpe's Estate v. Metropolitan Nat. Bank, 31 Colo.App. 511, 503 P.2d 1043 (Colo. App.1972)—¶ 9.05, n. 286.
Shatz v. Dunn, 18 Ill.App.3d 390, 309 N.E.2d 702 (Ill.App. 5 Dist.1974)—¶ 2.02, n. 110.
Shaw v. Union Bank and Trust Co., 640 P.2d 953 (Okla.1981)—¶ 8.01, n. 3, 47; ¶ 9.01, n. 2; ¶ 9.02, n. 101; ¶ 9.03, n. 122, 161; ¶ 9.05, n. 284, 296.
Shearson Lehman Bros., Inc. v. Wasatch Bank, 788 F.Supp. 1184 (D.Utah 1992)—¶ 7.03, n. 173.
Sheerbonnet, Ltd. v. American Exp. Bank, Ltd., 905 F.Supp. 127 (S.D.N.Y.1995)—¶ 10.04, n. 54.
Sheerbonnet, Ltd. v. American Exp. Bank, Ltd., 951 F.Supp. 403 (S.D.N.Y.1995)—¶ 10.02, n. 11.
Sheiman v. Lafayette Bank & Trust Co., 4 Conn.App. 39, 492 A.2d 219 (Conn.App. 1985)—¶ 3.01, n. 7.
Shell Oil Co., In re, (CCH) Consumer Credit Guide [Transfer Binder-Decisions 1974-80] ¶ 978,528, 95 F.T.C. 357 (FTC 1980)—¶ 11.02, n. 74.
Shelley v. AmSouth Bank, 2000 WL 1121778 (S.D.Ala.2000)—¶ 8.02, n. 140.
Shepherd Mall State Bank v. Johnson, 603 P.2d 1115 (Okla.1979)—¶ 2.02, n. 194; ¶ 3.02, n. 83.

Sherrill v. Frank Morris Pontiac–Buick–GMC, Inc., 366 So.2d 251 (Ala.1978)—¶ 3.03, n. 217; ¶ 9.01; ¶ 9.01, n. 25.
Shields v. Prendergast, 36 N.C.App. 633, 244 S.E.2d 475 (N.C.App.1978)—¶ 2.02, n. 226.
Shinto Shipping Co. v. Fibrex & Shipping Co., Inc., 425 F.Supp. 1088 (N.D.Cal. 1976)—¶ 9.06, n. 399.
Shipp v. First Alabama Bank of Gadsden, N.A., 473 So.2d 1014 (Ala.1985)—¶ 5.03, n. 84.
Shotwell v. Sioux Falls Savings Bank, 34 S.D. 109, 147 N.W. 288 (S.D.1914)—¶ 9.06, n. 341.
Shube v. Cheng, 157 Misc.2d 255, 596 N.Y.S.2d 335 (N.Y.Sup.1993)—¶ 7.03, n. 164.
Shull v. Town of Avant, 159 Okla. 271, 15 P.2d 49 (Okla.1932)—¶ 9.06, n. 357.
Siegel v. New England Merchants Nat. Bank, 386 Mass. 672, 437 N.E.2d 218 (Mass.1982)—¶ 9.01, n. 5, 13; ¶ 9.02, n. 112.
Siegler v. Ginther, 680 S.W.2d 886 (Tex. App.-Hous. (1 Dist.) 1984)—¶ 6.03, n. 178.
Sigmoil Resources, N.V. v. Pan Ocean Oil Corp. (Nigeria), 234 A.D.2d 103, 650 N.Y.S.2d 726 (N.Y.A.D. 1 Dept.1996)—¶ 10.02; ¶ 10.02, n. 10.
Silk v. Merrill Lynch, Pierce, Fenner & Smith, Inc., 437 So.2d 112 (Ala.1983)—¶ 6.03, n. 298.
Silsbee State Bank v. French Market Grocery Co., 103 Tex. 629, 132 S.W. 465 (Tex.1910)—¶ 9.06, n. 396.
Silver Creations, Ltd. v. United Parcel Service, 133 N.J.Super. 543, 337 A.2d 641 (N.J.Super.L.1975)—¶ 2.02, n. 224.
Silverglit v. Borsil Realty Corp., 2 UCC Rep. Serv. 408 (N.Y.Sup.1965)—¶ 6.03, n. 144.
Silvia v. Industrial Nat. Bank of Rhode Island, 121 R.I. 810, 403 A.2d 1075 (R.I. 1979)—¶ 6.03; ¶ 6.03, n. 118.
Simcoe & Erie General Ins. Co. v. Chemical Bank, 770 F.Supp. 149 (S.D.N.Y.1991)—¶ 4.02, n. 14, 20.
Simmons v. Lennon, 139 Md.App. 15, 773 A.2d 1064 (Md.App.2001)—¶ 7.02, n. 88.
Simson v. Bilderbeck, Inc., 76 N.M. 667, 417 P.2d 803 (N.M.1966)—¶ 6.03, n. 214.
Sinclair Oil Corp. v. Sylvan State Bank, 254 Kan. 836, 869 P.2d 675 (Kan.1994)—¶ 10.01, n. 3; ¶ 11.01, n. 4, 14; ¶ 11.03, n. 110.
626 Joint Venture v. Spinks, 873 S.W.2d 73 (Tex.App.-Austin 1993)—¶ 4.02, n. 3.
Skiles v. Security State Bank, 1 Neb.App. 360, 494 N.W.2d 355 (Neb.App.1992)—¶ 9.05, n. 245; ¶ 9.06, n. 408.

TABLE OF CASES

Skov v. Chase Manhattan Bank, 407 F.2d 1318 (3rd Cir.1969)—¶ **9.06, n. 365.**

Skyline Intern. Development v. Citibank, F.S.B., 302 Ill.App.3d 79, 236 Ill.Dec. 68, 706 N.E.2d 942 (Ill.App. 1 Dist.1998)—¶ **10.03, n. 52.**

Slavenburg Corp. v. Kenli Corp., 36 UCC Rep. Serv. 8 (E.D.Pa.1983)—¶ **7.01, n. 40.**

Smart v. Woo, 20 UCC Rep. Serv. 2d 1288 (Va. Cir. Ct.1993)—¶ **3.01, n. 2; ¶ 4.04, n. 145; ¶ 7.01, n. 4.**

Smiley v. Wheeler, 602 P.2d 209 (Okla. 1979)—¶ **6.03, n. 278.**

Smith v. Citizens State Bank of Hugo, 732 P.2d 911 (Okla.App.1986)—¶ **9.02, n. 106; ¶ 9.06, n. 361.**

Smith v. Federated Dept. Stores, 165 Ga. App. 459, 301 S.E.2d 652 (Ga.App. 1983)—¶ **11.02, n. 61.**

Smith v. General Cas. Co. of Wisconsin, 75 Ill.App.3d 971, 31 Ill.Dec. 602, 394 N.E.2d 804 (Ill.App. 3 Dist.1979)—¶ **7.03, n. 132.**

Smith v. Gentilotti, 371 Mass. 839, 359 N.E.2d 953 (Mass.1977)—¶ **2.02; ¶ 2.02, n. 235.**

Smith v. Haran, 273 Ill.App.3d 866, 210 Ill.Dec. 191, 652 N.E.2d 1167 (Ill.App. 1 Dist.1995)—¶ **1.02, n. 43; ¶ 1.03, n. 70.**

Smith v. Mark Twain Nat. Bank, 805 F.2d 278 (8th Cir.1986)—¶ **8.01, n. 9.**

Smith v. Olympic Bank, 103 Wash.2d 418, 693 P.2d 92 (Wash.1985)—¶ **3.03, n. 295.**

Smith v. Singleton, 124 Ga.App. 394, 184 S.E.2d 26 (Ga.App.1971)—¶ **5.01; ¶ 5.01, n. 2.**

Smith v. Union State Bank, 452 N.E.2d 1059 (Ind.App. 2 Dist.1983)—¶ **2.02, n. 152.**

SMS Financial, Ltd. Liability Co. v. ABCO Homes, Inc., 167 F.3d 235 (5th Cir. 1999)—¶ **6.03, n. 286.**

Snug Harbor Realty Co. v. First Nat. Bank of Toms River, N. J., 105 N.J.Super. 572, 253 A.2d 581 (N.J.Super.A.D.1969)—¶ **7.03, n. 175.**

Snyder v. Town Hill Motors, Inc., 193 Pa.Super. 578, 165 A.2d 293 (Pa.Super.1960)—¶ **3.02; ¶ 3.02, n. 179; ¶ 3.04; ¶ 3.04, n. 403.**

Society Natl. Bank v. Kienzle, 11 Ohio App.3d 178, 463 N.E.2d 1261 (Ohio App. 8 Dist.1983)—¶ **11.02, n. 74.**

Society Natl. Bank v. Security Fed. S. & L., 71 Ohio St.3d 321, 643 N.E.2d 1090 (Ohio 1994)—¶ **3.02, n. 167, 171.**

Sony Corp. of America v. American Exp. Co., 115 Misc.2d 1060, 455 N.Y.S.2d 227 (N.Y.City Civ.Ct.1982)—¶ **7.03, n. 134.**

SOS Oil Corp. v. Norstar Bank of Long Island, 561 N.Y.S.2d 887, 563 N.E.2d 258 (N.Y.1990)—¶ **8.01, n. 26; ¶ 8.02, n. 135.**

Soto v. First Gibraltar Bank, 868 S.W.2d 400 (Tex.App.-San Antonio 1993)—¶ **9.05, n. 251.**

Southeastern Mun. Supply Co., Inc. v. Citizens First Nat. Bank of Citrus County, 432 So.2d 753 (Fla.App. 5 Dist.1983)—¶ **3.02, n. 80.**

Southeast Investments, Inc. v. Clade, 40 UCC Rep. Serv. 2d 255 (N.D.Tex. 1999)—¶ **3.01, n. 19.**

Southern Cal. Permanente Medical Group v. Bozinovski, 148 Cal.App.3d 503, 196 Cal.Rptr. 150 (Cal.App. 2 Dist.1983)—¶ **7.03, n. 132.**

Southern Contract Carpet, Inc. v. County Nat. Bank of South Florida, 528 So.2d 42 (Fla.App. 3 Dist.1988)—¶ **9.03, n. 163.**

Southern Cotton Oil Co., Inc. v. Merchants Nat. Bank, 670 F.2d 548 (5th Cir. 1982)—¶ **2.04, n. 292; ¶ 8.03, n. 193, 205, 218.**

Southern Oxygen Supply Co. v. de Golian, 230 Ga. 405, 197 S.E.2d 374 (Ga.1973)—¶ **5.03, n. 86.**

South Rayne Water Corp. v. Bank of Commerce & Trust Co., 619 So.2d 158 (La. App. 3 Cir.1993)—¶ **7.02, n. 92.**

South Sound Nat. Bank v. First Interstate Bank, 65 Or.App. 553, 672 P.2d 1194 (Or.App.1983)—¶ **4.03, n. 93.**

Southwest Bank v. Information Support Concepts, Inc., 48 UCC Rep.Serv.2d 675, 85 S.W.2d 462 (Tex.Ct.App.2002)—¶ **7.02, n. 92.**

Spear Ins. Co., Ltd. v. Bank of America, N.A., 40 UCC Rep. Serv. 2d 807 (N.D.Ill. 2000)—¶ **4.02, n. 12; ¶ 7.02, n. 67, 81.**

Spears Carpet Mills, Inc. v. Century Nat. Bank of New Orleans, 85 B.R. 86 (W.D.Ark.1988)—¶ **9.03, n. 163.**

Speer v. Friedland, 276 So.2d 84 (Fla.App. 2 Dist.1973)—¶ **5.03, n. 99.**

Spencer Companies, Inc. v. Chase Manhattan Bank, N.A., 81 B.R. 194 (D.Mass. 1987)—¶ **4.04, n. 144.**

Sperry v. Renner, 194 Okla. 285, 149 P.2d 781 (Okla.1944)—¶ **9.06, n. 371.**

Spielman v. Manufacturers Hanover Trust Co., 469 N.Y.S.2d 69, 456 N.E.2d 1192 (N.Y.1983)—¶ **4.02, n. 32; ¶ 7.03, n. 180.**

Spitzmueller v. Burlington Northern R. Co., 740 F.Supp. 671 (D.Minn.1990)—¶ **9.03, n. 126.**

Sportsco, Inc., In re, 12 B.R. 34 (Bkrtcy. D.Ariz.1981)—¶ **4.04, n. 146.**

Springhill Bank & Trust Co. v. Citizens Bank & Trust Co., 505 So.2d 867 (La. App. 2 Cir.1987)—¶ **8.02, n. 134; ¶ 9.03, n. 152.**

Spurlock v. Commercial Banking Co., 151 Ga.App. 649, 260 S.E.2d 912 (Ga.App. 1979)—¶ **2.02, n. 54.**

Spurlock v. Commercial Banking Co., 138 Ga.App. 892, 227 S.E.2d 790 (Ga.App. 1976)—¶ **9.06, n. 322.**

Staff Builders of Philadelphia, Inc. v. Koschitzki, 989 F.2d 692 (3rd Cir.1993)—¶ **4.04, n. 145;** ¶ **7.01, n. 4.**

Staff Builders of Philadelphia, Inc. v. Koschitzki, 18 UCC Rep. Serv. 2d 228 (E.D.Pa.1992)—¶ **2.04, n. 300;** ¶ **4.04, n. 145.**

Standard Federal Sav. & Loan Ass'n v. Citizens Ins. Co., 99 Mich.App. 338, 297 N.W.2d 656 (Mich.App.1980)—¶ **2.02, n. 133.**

Standard Premium Plan Corp. v. Hirschhorn, 56 Misc.2d 687, 290 N.Y.S.2d 226 (N.Y.City Civ.Ct.1968)—¶ **2.02, n. 74;** ¶ **4.06, n. 216.**

Standard Wire & Cable Co. v. AmeriTrust Corp., 697 F.Supp. 368 (C.D.Cal.1988)—¶ **9.03, n. 168.**

Stanley v. Ames, 378 Mass. 364, 391 N.E.2d 908 (Mass.1979)—¶ **6.03, n. 251.**

Stann v. Mid American Credit Union, 39 B.R. 246 (D.Kan.1984)—¶ **9.06, n. 385.**

Stapleton v. First Sec. Bank, 219 Mont. 323, 711 P.2d 1364 (Mont.1985)—¶ **7.03, n. 132.**

Starcraft Co., A Div. of Bangor Punta Operations, Inc. v. C.J. Heck Co. of Texas, Inc., 748 F.2d 982 (5th Cir.1984)—¶ **8.02, n. 163, 169.**

Starkey Const., Inc. v. Elcon, Inc., 248 Ark. 958, 248 Ark. 978A, 457 S.W.2d 509 (Ark.1970)—¶ **3.02;** ¶ **3.02, n. 109;** ¶ **4.02, n. 40.**

State v. _____ (see opposing party)

State and Sav. Bank of Monticello, Ind. v. Meeker, 469 N.E.2d 55 (Ind.App. 1 Dist. 1984)—¶ **8.02, n. 163, 169.**

State Bank of Greeley v. Owens, 31 Colo. App. 351, 502 P.2d 965 (Colo.App. 1972)—¶ **5.02, n. 55.**

State Bank of Rose Creek v. First Bank of Austin, 320 N.W.2d 723 (Minn.1982)—¶ **9.05, n. 242.**

State Bank of Southern Utah v. Stallings, 19 Utah 2d 146, 427 P.2d 744 (Utah 1967)—¶ **4.04, n. 146;** ¶ **7.03, n. 112.**

State Bank & Trust v. First State Bank of Texas, 242 F.3d 390 (10th Cir.2000)—¶ **1.01, n. 7;** ¶ **7.01, n. 26;** ¶ **7.02, n. 59;** ¶ **8.01, n. 52.**

State Bank & Trust, N.A. v. First State Bank of Texas, 39 UCC Rep. Serv. 191 (N.D.Okla.1999)—¶ **4.02, n. 40.**

State by Abrams v. Citibank, N.A., 537 F.Supp. 1192 (S.D.N.Y.1982)—¶ **11.02;** ¶ **11.02, n. 83.**

State ex rel. v. _____ (see opposing party and relator)

State Nat. Bank of Decatur v. Towns, 36 Ala.App. 677, 62 So.2d 606 (Ala.App. 1952)—¶ **9.06, n. 372.**

State of (see name of state)

St. Croix Engineering Corp. v. McLay, 304 N.W.2d 912 (Minn.1981)—¶ **5.03;** ¶ **5.03, n. 101.**

Steinroe Income Trust v. Continental Bank N.A., 238 Ill.App.3d 660, 179 Ill.Dec. 671, 606 N.E.2d 503 (Ill.App. 1 Dist. 1992)—¶ **7.02, n. 79.**

Stella v. Dean Witter Reynolds, Inc., 241 N.J.Super. 55, 574 A.2d 468 (N.J.Super.A.D.1990)—¶ **4.02, n. 40;** ¶ **7.03.**

Step–Saver Data Systems, Inc. v. Wyse Technology, 939 F.2d 91 (3rd Cir. 1991)—¶ **11.03, n. 99.**

Sterling Nat. Bank & Trust Co. v. Fidelity Mortg. Investors, 510 F.2d 870 (2nd Cir. 1975)—¶ **6.03, n. 122.**

Sterling Nat. Bank & Trust Co. of New York, United States v., 494 F.2d 919 (2nd Cir.1974)—¶ **9.06, n. 375.**

Stevens v. Bowie Nat. Bank, 517 S.W.2d 686 (Tex.Civ.App.-Fort Worth 1974)—¶ **3.01;** ¶ **3.01, n. 25.**

Stewart v. Credithrift of America Consumer Discount Co., 93 B.R. 878 (Bkrtcy. E.D.Pa.1988)—¶ **3.04, n. 432.**

Stewart v. Phoenix Nat. Bank, 49 Ariz. 34, 64 P.2d 101 (Ariz.1937)—¶ **9.05, n. 308.**

Stewart Office Suppliers, Inc. v. First Union Nat. Bank, 97 N.C.App. 353, 388 S.E.2d 599 (N.C.App.1990)—¶ **3.02, n. 149, 171;** ¶ **7.03, n. 128.**

Stewart Office Suppliers, Inc. v. Southern Nat. Bank of N.C., 328 N.C. 83, 399 S.E.2d 108 (N.C.1991)—¶ **7.03, n. 128.**

Stieger v. Chevy Chase Sav. Bank, F.S.B., 666 A.2d 479 (D.C.1995)—¶ **11.02, n. 75.**

Still v. Citizens Bank of Drumright, 6 UCC Rep. Serv. 813 (Okla.App.1969)—¶ **5.02;** ¶ **5.02, n. 47;** ¶ **6.03, n. 264.**

Still v. Plaza Marina Commercial Corp., 21 Cal.App.3d 378, 98 Cal.Rptr. 414 (Cal. App. 5 Dist.1971)—¶ **6.03, n. 226.**

Stirlen v. Supercuts, Inc., 60 Cal.Rptr.2d 138 (Cal.App. 1 Dist.1997)—¶ **11.02, n. 94.**

St. James v. Diversified Commercial Finance Corp., 102 Nev. 23, 714 P.2d 179 (Nev.1986)—¶ **3.04, n. 412.**

St. Nicholas Bank v. State Nat. Bank, 128 N.Y. 26, 27 N.E. 849 (N.Y.1891)—¶ **8.01, n. 22.**

Stockton v. Gristedes Supermarkets, Inc., 177 A.D.2d 425, 576 N.Y.S.2d 267 (N.Y.A.D. 1 Dept.1991)—¶ **7.03, n. 134.**

Stockwell v. Bloomfield State Bank, 174 Ind.App. 307, 367 N.E.2d 42 (Ind.App. 1 Dist.1977)—¶ **6.03, n. 226.**

Stoerger v. Ivesdale Co-op. Grain Co., 15 Ill.App.3d 313, 304 N.E.2d 300 (Ill.App. 4 Dist.1973)—¶ **1.03, n. 99.**

Stone Mfg. Co. v. NCNB of South Carolina, 308 S.C. 287, 417 S.E.2d 628 (S.C.App. 1992)—¶ **7.03, n. 173.**

Stone & Webster Engineering Corp. v. First Nat. Bank & Trust Co. of Greenfield, 345 Mass. 1, 184 N.E.2d 358 (Mass. 1962)—¶ **7.03, n. 147, 148, 149.**

Story Road Flea Market, Inc. v. Wells Fargo Bank, 50 Cal.Rptr.2d 524 (Cal.App. 6 Dist.1996)—¶ **4.02, n. 14.**

Stowell v. Cloquet Co-op Credit Union, 557 N.W.2d 567 (Minn.1997)—¶ **4.02, n. 14;** ¶ **7.03, n. 114.**

St. Paul Fire and Marine Ins. Co. v. State Bank of Salem, 412 N.E.2d 103 (Ind. App. 1 Dist.1980)—¶ **3.03, n. 230.**

Stratton v. Equitable Bank, N.A., 104 B.R. 713 (D.Md.1989)—¶ **3.02, n. 71.**

St. Regis Paper Co. v. Wicklund, 93 Wash.2d 497, 610 P.2d 903 (Wash. 1980)—¶ **1.04, n. 232;** ¶ **5.03;** ¶ **5.03, n. 91.**

Strickland v. Kafko Mfg., Inc., 512 So.2d 714 (Ala.1987)—¶ **3.03, n. 259.**

Strickler v. Marx, 246 Va. 384, 436 S.E.2d 447 (Va.1993)—¶ **3.01, n. 19.**

Sumiton Bank v. Funding Systems Leasing Corp., 512 F.2d 774 (5th Cir.1975)—¶ **3.02, n. 132.**

Sun Bank/Miami, N.A. v. First Nat. Bank of Maryland, 698 F.Supp. 1298 (D.Md. 1988)—¶ **4.03, n. 104.**

Sunbelt Factors, Inc. v. Bank of Gonzales, 481 So.2d 648 (La.App. 1 Cir.1985)—¶ **7.03, n. 148.**

Sunbelt Sav., FSB, Dallas, Texas v. Amrecorp Realty Corp., 742 F.Supp. 370 (N.D.Tex.1990)—¶ **1.03, n. 142, 153.**

Sunbelt Sav., FSB, Dallas, Texas v. Cashin Const. Co., Inc., 737 F.Supp. 41 (E.D.Tex.1990)—¶ **1.03, n. 155.**

Sunbelt Sav., FSB Dallas, Texas v. Montross, 923 F.2d 353 (5th Cir.1991)—¶ **1.03, n. 149.**

Sun Forest Corp. v. Shvili, 152 F.Supp.2d 367 (S.D.N.Y.2001)—¶ **8.01, n. 24.**

Sun 'n Sand, Inc. v. United California Bank, 148 Cal.Rptr. 329, 582 P.2d 920 (Cal.1978)—¶ **7.02, n. 57, 79, 92, 102;** ¶ **7.03, n. 118, 147, 149, 150.**

Sun River Cattle Co. v. Miners Bank, 164 Mont. 237, 521 P.2d 679 (Mont.1974)—¶ **1.04, n. 218;** ¶ **8.01;** ¶ **8.01, n. 29;** ¶ **9.03;** ¶ **9.03, n. 153.**

Sun River Cattle Co. v. Miners' Bank of Montana, 164 Mont. 479, 525 P.2d 19 (Mont.1974)—¶ **9.03, n. 186.**

Sunshine v. Bankers Trust Co., 358 N.Y.S.2d 113, 314 N.E.2d 860 (N.Y. 1974)—¶ **8.01;** ¶ **8.01, n. 44;** ¶ **9.01;** ¶ **9.01, n. 86;** ¶ **9.03, n. 153.**

Swiss Baco Skyline Logging, Inc. v. Haliewicz, 18 Wash.App. 21, 567 P.2d 1141 (Wash.App. Div. 2 1977)—¶ **3.02, n. 104;** ¶ **3.03, n. 295.**

Swiss Credit Bank v. Chemical Bank, 422 F.Supp. 1305 (S.D.N.Y.1976)—¶ **4.02, n. 13.**

Sybedon Corp. v. Bank Leumi Trust Co. of New York, 224 A.D.2d 320, 638 N.Y.S.2d 50 (N.Y.A.D. 1 Dept.1996)—¶ **7.03, n. 173.**

Sylvester v. Watkins, 538 S.W.2d 827 (Tex. Civ.App.-Amarillo 1976)—¶ **4.05, n. 197.**

Szetela v. Discover Bank, 97 Cal.App.4th 1094, 118 Cal.Rptr.2d 862 (2002)—¶ **11.02, n. 94;** ¶ **9.05, n. 271.**

T

Taines v. Capital City First Nat. Bank, 344 So.2d 273 (Fla.App. 1 Dist.1977)—¶ **2.04, n. 283;** ¶ **6.03, n. 225.**

Tally v. American Sec. Bank, 35 UCC Rep. Serv. 215 (D.D.C.1982)—¶ **8.01, n. 3, 47;** ¶ **9.03, n. 161.**

Tampa Bay Bank v. Loveday, 526 S.W.2d 480 (Tenn.Ct.App.1974)—¶ **4.06, n. 211.**

Tampa Bay Economic Development Corp. v. Edman, 598 So.2d 172 (Fla.App. 2 Dist. 1992)—¶ **5.03, n. 84.**

Tanenbaum v. Agri–Capital, Inc., 885 F.2d 464 (8th Cir.1989)—¶ **2.01, n. 10;** ¶ **2.02, n. 195.**

Tatum v. Bank of Cumming, 135 Ga.App. 675, 218 S.E.2d 677 (Ga.App.1975)—¶ **6.01, n. 34.**

Tavormina v. Weiner (Alchar Hardware Co., Inc., In re), 759 F.2d 867 (11th Cir.1985)—¶ **9.05, n. 251, 303.**

Taylor v. Equitable Trust Co., 269 Md. 149, 304 A.2d 838 (Md.1973)—¶ **9.05, n. 270.**

Taylor v. Quality Hyundai, Inc., 150 F.3d 689 (7th Cir.1998)—¶ **3.04, n. 432.**

Taylor v. Roeder, 234 Va. 99, 360 S.E.2d 191 (Va.1987)—¶ **2.01, n. 10.**

TeleRecovery of Louisiana, Inc. v. Gaulon, 738 So.2d 662 (La.App. 5 Cir.1999)—¶ **2.02, n. 64, 70, 145.**

Tennant v. Satterfield, 158 W.Va. 917, 216 S.E.2d 229 (W.Va.1975)—¶ **7.01, n. 31.**

Tepper By and Through Michelson v. Citizens Federal Sav. and Loan Ass'n, 448 So.2d 1138 (Fla.App. 3 Dist.1984)—¶ **6.03, n. 295.**

Teratron General v. Institutional Investors Trust, 18 Wash.App. 481, 569 P.2d 1198 (Wash.App. Div. 1 1977)—¶ **6.02, n. 78.**

Terry v. Kemper Ins. Co., 390 Mass. 450, 456 N.E.2d 465 (Mass.1983)—¶ **1.04, n. 226;** ¶ **4.02, n. 23.**

Tette v. Marine Midland Bank, 78 A.D.2d 383, 435 N.Y.S.2d 413 (N.Y.A.D. 4 Dept. 1981)—¶ **7.03, n. 154.**

Texas Export Development Corp. v. Schleder, 519 S.W.2d 134 (Tex.Civ.App.-Dallas 1974)—¶ **6.01, n. 37.**

Texas Mortg. Services Corp. v. Guadalupe Savings & Loan (In re Mortgage Servs. Corp.), 761 F.2d 1068 (5th Cir.1985)—¶ **9.05, n. 251.**

Texas Stadium Corp. v. Savings of America, 933 S.W.2d 616 (Tex.App.-Dallas 1996)—¶ **7.03, n. 175.**

Texas State Bank v. Sharp, 506 S.W.2d 761 (Tex.Civ.App.-Austin 1974)—¶ **2.02, n. 159.**

The Bank/First Citizens Bank v. Citizens and Associates, 82 S.W.3d 259 (Tenn. 2002)—¶ **7.03, n. 174.**

The Bank/First Citizens Bank v. Citizens and Associates, 44 UCC Rep. Serv. 2d 1072 (Tenn.Ct.App.2001)—¶ **4.02, n. 31;** ¶ **7.03, n. 114, 139.**

Thermo Contracting Corp. v. Bank of New Jersey, 69 N.J. 352, 354 A.2d 291 (N.J. 1976)—¶ **4.02, n. 41.**

Thiele v. Security State Bank of New Salem, 396 N.W.2d 295 (N.D.1986)—¶ **4.04, n. 144.**

Thieme v. Seattle–First Nat. Bank, 7 Wash. App. 845, 502 P.2d 1240 (Wash.App. Div. 3 1972)—¶ **7.02, n. 92.**

Third Century Recycling, Inc. v. Bank of Baroda, 704 F.Supp. 417 (S.D.N.Y. 1989)—¶ **8.02, n. 139.**

Third Nat. Bank v. Hardi–Gardens Supply, Inc., 380 F.Supp. 930 (M.D.Tenn. 1974)—¶ **3.01, n. 21;** ¶ **3.04, n. 391.**

Thomas v. Estate of Eubanks, 358 So.2d 709 (Miss.1978)—¶ **2.02, n. 261.**

Thomas v. Marine Midland Tinkers Nat. Bank, 86 Misc.2d 284, 381 N.Y.S.2d 797 (N.Y.City Civ.Ct.1976)—¶ **9.01;** ¶ **9.01, n. 24.**

Thomas v. McNeill, 448 N.W.2d 231 (S.D. 1989)—¶ **5.03, n. 84.**

Thompson v. Lake County Nat. Bank, 47 Ohio App.2d 249, 353 N.E.2d 895 (Ohio App. 11 Dist.1975)—¶ **4.02, n. 32.**

Thompson, State v., 810 P.2d 415 (Utah 1991)—¶ **9.03, n. 122.**

Thompson Maple Products, Inc. v. Citizens Nat. Bank of Corry, 211 Pa.Super. 42, 234 A.2d 32 (Pa.Super.1967)—¶ **4.02, n. 28.**

Thornton & Co., Inc. v. Gwinnett Bank & Trust Co., 151 Ga.App. 641, 260 S.E.2d 765 (Ga.App.1979)—¶ **7.03, n. 132.**

Thurman v. Federal Deposit Ins. Corporation, 889 F.2d 1441 (5th Cir.1989)—¶ **1.03, n. 152.**

Tifton Bank & Trust Co. v. Knight's Furniture Co., Inc., 215 Ga.App. 471, 452 S.E.2d 219 (Ga.App.1994)—¶ **7.02, n. 67.**

Timeplan Corp. of Oklahoma City, Inc. v. Fuxa, 9 UCC Rep. Serv. 262 (Okla.App. 1971)—¶ **3.04, n. 417.**

Titan Air Conditioning Corp. v. Chase Manhattan Bank, N.A., 61 A.D.2d 764, 402 N.Y.S.2d 12 (N.Y.A.D. 1 Dept.1978)—¶ **7.03, n. 117.**

Title Ins. Co. v. Comerica Bank - California, 32 Cal.Rptr.2d 735 (Cal.App. 6 Dist. 1994)—¶ **7.03, n. 168.**

Tolander v. Farmers Nat. Bank, 452 N.W.2d 422 (Iowa 1990)—¶ **9.06, n. 336.**

Tone v. Halsey, Stuart & Co., 286 Ill.App. 169, 3 N.E.2d 142 (Ill.App. 1 Dist. 1936)—¶ **9.05, n. 307.**

Torino Const. Corp. of Nevada v. Ensign Federal Credit Union, 111 Nev. 1515, 908 P.2d 702 (Nev.1995)—¶ **7.03, n. 142.**

Tormo v. Yormark, 398 F.Supp. 1159 (D.N.J.1975)—¶ **7.02, n. 92.**

Tormo v. Yormark, 14 UCC Rep. Serv. 962 (D.N.J.1974)—¶ **4.02, n. 23.**

T.O. Stanley Boot Co., Inc. v. Bank of El Paso, 847 S.W.2d 218 (Tex.1992)—¶ **2.02, n. 194;** ¶ **6.03, n. 248.**

Total Aviation Services, Inc. v. United Jersey Bank, 39 UCC Rep. Serv. 969 (E.D.N.Y.1984)—¶ **3.01, n. 34;** ¶ **4.04, n. 144.**

Town Bank & Trust Co. v. Silverman, 3 Mass.App.Ct. 28, 322 N.E.2d 192 (Mass. App.Ct.1975)—¶ **9.05, n. 285.**

Town North Nat. Bank v. Broaddus, 569 S.W.2d 489 (Tex.1978)—¶ **6.01;** ¶ **6.01, n. 30.**

TPO Inc. v. Federal Deposit Ins. Corp., 487 F.2d 131 (3rd Cir.1973)—¶ **9.01;** ¶ **9.01, n. 66.**

Transamerica Commercial Finance Corp. v. Naef, 842 P.2d 539 (Wyo.1992)—¶ **6.03, n. 178.**

Transamerica Ins. Co. v. Standard Oil Co., 325 N.W.2d 210 (N.D.1982)—¶ **11.02, n. 73.**

Trans–World Bank, United States v., 382 F.Supp. 1100 (C.D.Cal.1974)—¶ **9.06, n. 379.**

Travco Corp. v. Citizens Federal Sav. & Loan Ass'n of Port Huron, 42 Mich.App. 291, 201 N.W.2d 675 (Mich.App.1972)—¶ **7.03, n. 180.**

Travelers Indem. Co. v. American Exp. Co., 559 F.Supp. 452 (S.D.N.Y.1983)—¶ **3.03, n. 209;** ¶ **3.04, n. 410.**

Travelers Indem. Co. v. Stedman, 910 F.Supp. 203 (E.D.Pa.1995)—¶ **4.02, n. 14.**

Travelers Indem. Co. v. Stedman, 895 F.Supp. 742 (E.D.Pa.1995)—¶ **7.02, n. 95.**

Travelers Ins. Co. v. Connecticut Bank and Trust Co., 40 Conn.Supp. 70, 481 A.2d 111 (Conn.Super.1984)—¶ **9.03, n. 183.**

Travelers Ins. Co. v. Jefferson Nat. Bank at Kendall, 404 So.2d 1131 (Fla.App. 3 Dist.1981)—¶ **4.02, n. 30;** ¶ **7.03, n. 142.**

Travis v. La Junta State Bank, 694 P.2d 350 (Colo.App.1984)—¶ **3.02, n. 167.**

Trenton Trust Co. v. Western Sur. Co., 599 S.W.2d 481 (Mo.1980)—¶ **3.03, n. 295;** ¶ **6.02;** ¶ **6.02, n. 43.**

TABLE OF CASES

Tri-County Bank, United States ex rel. Crow Creek Sioux Tribe v., 415 F.Supp. 858 (D.S.D.1976)—¶ **9.06, n. 358.**

Triffin v. Bridge View Bank, 330 N.J.Super. 473, 750 A.2d 136 (N.J.Super.A.D.2000)—¶ **9.01, n. 69.**

Triffin v. Dillabough, 448 Pa.Super. 72, 670 A.2d 684 (Pa.Super.1996)—¶ **2.02, n. 132.**

True v. Fleet Bank-NH, 138 N.H. 679, 645 A.2d 671 (N.H.1994)—¶ **2.02, n. 262;** ¶ **7.02, n. 67;** ¶ **7.03, n. 123.**

Trueheart v. Braselton, 875 S.W.2d 412 (Tex.App.-Corpus Christi 1994)—¶ **3.03, n. 347;** ¶ **6.01, n. 14.**

Trust Co. of Columbus v. Refrigeration Supplies, Inc., 241 Ga. 406, 246 S.E.2d 282 (Ga.1978)—¶ **3.02;** ¶ **3.02, n. 110.**

Trust Co. of Columbus v. United States, 735 F.2d 447 (11th Cir.1984)—¶ **9.06, n. 320.**

Trust Co. of Georgia Bank of Savannah, N. A. v. Port Terminal & Warehousing Co., 153 Ga.App. 735, 266 S.E.2d 254 (Ga. App.1980)—¶ **4.02;** ¶ **4.02, n. 17.**

Trustees of Elon College v. Elon Banking & Trust Co., 182 N.C. 298, 109 S.E. 6 (N.C.1921)—¶ **9.05, n. 304.**

Tufi, United States v., 536 F.2d 855 (9th Cir.1976)—¶ **3.02, n. 81;** ¶ **4.06;** ¶ **4.06, n. 215.**

Turner, In re, 49 B.R. 231 (Bkrtcy.D.Mass. 1985)—¶ **5.03, n. 98.**

Turney v. Seale, 473 So.2d 855 (La.App. 1 Cir.1985)—¶ **3.03, n. 209.**

Tusso v. Security Nat. Bank, 76 Misc.2d 12, 349 N.Y.S.2d 914 (N.Y.Dist.Ct.1973)—¶ **9.01, n. 22.**

Tuttle v. Rose, 102 Ill.App.3d 865, 58 Ill. Dec. 414, 430 N.E.2d 356 (Ill.App. 1 Dist.1981)—¶ **2.02, n. 58;** ¶ **3.01, n. 7;** ¶ **3.03, n. 202, 322.**

Twellman v. Lindell Trust Co., 534 S.W.2d 83 (Mo.App.1976)—¶ **4.02, n. 38;** ¶ **7.03, n. 178.**

Twin City Bank v. Isaacs, 283 Ark. 127, 672 S.W.2d 651 (Ark.1984)—¶ **9.02, n. 101, 106.**

T.W. Sommer Co. v. Modern Door & Lumber Co., 293 Minn. 264, 198 N.W.2d 278 (Minn.1972)—¶ **5.02;** ¶ **5.02, n. 54, 56.**

U

UMLIC-TEN Corp. v. Jones, 41 UCC Rep. Serv. 2d 1187 (Conn.Super.2000)—¶ **3.03, n. 351.**

Unadilla Nat. Bank v. McQueer, 27 A.D.2d 778, 277 N.Y.S.2d 221 (N.Y.A.D. 3 Dept. 1967)—¶ **3.03, n. 316.**

Underpinning & Foundation Constructors, Inc. v. Chase Manhattan Bank, N.A., 414 N.Y.S.2d 298, 386 N.E.2d 1319 (N.Y. 1979)—¶ **3.02;** ¶ **3.02, n. 168;** ¶ **7.03;** ¶ **7.03, n. 127, 136, 140, 180.**

Unger v. NCNB Nat. Bank, 540 So.2d 246 (Fla.App. 4 Dist.1989)—¶ **8.01, n. 67.**

Unico v. Owen, 50 N.J. 101, 232 A.2d 405 (N.J.1967)—¶ **1.03, n. 144;** ¶ **2.01, n. 29;** ¶ **3.04;** ¶ **3.04, n. 413.**

Union Bank v. Wolas, 502 U.S. 151, 112 S.Ct. 527, 116 L.Ed.2d 514 (1991)—¶ **9.01, n. 81.**

Union Bank of Benton v. First Nat. Bank of Mt. Pleasant, 621 F.2d 790 (5th Cir. 1980)—¶ **8.02, n. 169.**

Union Const. Co., Inc. v. Beneficial Standard Mortg. Investors, 125 Ariz. 433, 610 P.2d 67 (Ariz.App. Div. 1 1980)—¶ **2.04, n. 280.**

Union Nat. Bank of Little Rock v. Daneshvar, 33 Ark.App. 171, 803 S.W.2d 567 (Ark.App.1991)—¶ **4.02, n. 22.**

Union Oil Co. of Cal. v. Lull, 220 Or. 412, 349 P.2d 243 (Or.1960)—¶ **11.02, n. 70.**

Union Planters Bank, N.A. v. Watson, 2001 WL 336055 (Ala.2001)—¶ **8.02, n. 140.**

United Bank v. Mesa N. O. Nelson Co., Inc., 121 Ariz. 438, 590 P.2d 1384 (Ariz. 1979)—¶ **4.02, n. 28, 36.**

United Bank Ltd. v. Cambridge Sporting Goods Corp., 392 N.Y.S.2d 265, 360 N.E.2d 943 (N.Y.1976)—¶ **1.03, n. 75;** ¶ **3.01, n. 32;** ¶ **3.03, n. 320, 324.**

United Bank of Crete-Steger v. Gainer Bank, N.A., 874 F.2d 475 (7th Cir. 1989)—¶ **8.01, n. 55.**

United Bank & Trust Co. of Maryland v. Schaeffer, 280 Md. 10, 370 A.2d 1138 (Md.1977)—¶ **6.02;** ¶ **6.02, n. 64.**

United Burner Service, Inc. v. George Peters & Sons, Inc., 3 UCC Rep. Serv. 180 (N.Y.Sup.1968)—¶ **5.03, n. 84, 88.**

United Credit Corp. v. Necamp, 19 UCC Rep. Serv. 1197 (Pa.Com.Pl.1976)—¶ **3.02;** ¶ **3.02, n. 185.**

United East Coast Corp., In re, 6 UCC Rep. Serv. 449 (E.D.N.Y.1969)—¶ **1.03, n. 111;** ¶ **3.01;** ¶ **3.01, n. 51.**

United Kentucky Bank, Inc. v. Eagle Mach. Co., Inc., 644 S.W.2d 649 (Ky.App. 1983)—¶ **8.03, n. 205, 228.**

United Nat. Bank v. Airport Plaza Ltd., 537 So.2d 608 (Fla.App. 3 Dist.1988)—¶ **2.02;** ¶ **2.02, n. 125, 185.**

United Overseas Bank v. Veneers, Inc., 375 F.Supp. 596 (D.Md.1973)—¶ **1.03, n. 116;** ¶ **3.01, n. 35;** ¶ **3.03, n. 241;** ¶ **8.01, n. 11.**

United States v. _____ (see opposing party)

United States By and Through I.R.S. v. McDermott, 507 U.S. 447, 113 S.Ct. 1526, 123 L.Ed.2d 128 (1993)—¶ **9.06, n. 379.**

United States ex rel. v. _____ (see opposing party and relator)

United States Fidelity and Guar. Co. v. Federal Reserve Bank of New York, 620 F.Supp. 361 (S.D.N.Y.1985)—¶ **8.03, n. 233.**

United States Fidelity and Guar. Co. v. Federal Reserve Bank of New York, 590 F.Supp. 486 (S.D.N.Y.1984)—¶ **8.03, n. 233.**

United States Finance Co. v. Jones, 285 Ala. 105, 229 So.2d 495 (Ala.1969)— ¶ **3.04, n. 415.**

United States for Use and Benefit of D'Agostino Excavators, Inc. v. Heyward–Robinson Co., 430 F.2d 1077 (2nd Cir. 1970)—¶ **7.01, n. 22.**

United States Trust Co. of New York v. McSweeney, 91 A.D.2d 7, 457 N.Y.S.2d 276 (N.Y.A.D. 1 Dept.1982)—¶ **9.01, n. 48.**

Universal C.I.T. Credit Corp. v. Farmers Bank of Portageville, 358 F.Supp. 317 (E.D.Mo.1973)—¶ **8.01, n. 42;** ¶ **8.02;** ¶ **8.02, n. 104;** ¶ **9.06, n. 370.**

Universal C.I.T. Credit Corp. v. Ingel, 347 Mass. 119, 196 N.E.2d 847 (Mass. 1964)—¶ **2.02;** ¶ **2.02, n. 91, 199;** ¶ **2.04;** ¶ **2.04, n. 274.**

Universal Metals & Machinery, Inc. v. Bohart, 539 S.W.2d 874 (Tex.1976)— ¶ **5.02, n. 50.**

Universal Premium Acceptance Corp. v. York Bank & Trust Co., 69 F.3d 695 (3rd Cir.1995)—¶ **1.02, n. 53.**

Unruh v. Nevada Nat. Bank, 88 Nev. 427, 498 P.2d 1349 (Nev.1972)—¶ **6.03, n. 173.**

Upper Valley Aviation v. Mercantile Nat. Bank, 656 S.W.2d 952 (Tex.App.-Dallas 1983)—¶ **9.05, n. 291.**

Uptown Federal Sav. and Loan Ass'n v. Collins, 105 Ill.App.2d 459, 245 N.E.2d 521 (Ill.App. 1 Dist.1969)—¶ **5.03, n. 108.**

U.S. Bank National Ass'n v. First Security Bank, 44 UCC Rep.Serv.2d 1088 (D.Utah 2001)—¶ **7.02, n. 45.**

V

Valley Bank v. Monarch Inv. Co., 118 Idaho 747, 800 P.2d 634 (Idaho 1990)—¶ **7.03, n. 168.**

Valley Bank of Nevada v. JER Management Corp., 149 Ariz. 415, 719 P.2d 301 (Ariz. App. Div. 1 1986)—¶ **8.02, n. 169.**

Valley Bank & Trust Co. v. First Sec. Bank of Utah, N. A., 538 P.2d 298 (Utah 1975)—¶ **4.03;** ¶ **4.03, n. 122.**

Valley Nat. Bank v. Hasper, 6 Ariz.App. 376, 432 P.2d 924 (Ariz.App.1967)— ¶ **9.06, n. 372.**

Valley Nat. Bank v. Porter, 705 F.2d 1027 (8th Cir.1983)—¶ **3.03, n. 299.**

Valley Nat. Bank v. Tang, 18 Ariz.App. 40, 499 P.2d 991 (Ariz.App. Div. 1 1972)— ¶ **8.01, n. 13.**

Valley Nat. Bank v. Witter, 58 Ariz. 491, 121 P.2d 414 (Ariz.1942)—¶ **9.05, n. 268.**

Valley Nat. Bank, Sunnymead v. Cook, 136 Ariz. 232, 665 P.2d 576 (Ariz.App. Div. 1 1983)—¶ **5.03, n. 97.**

Valmont Credit Corp. v. McIlravy, 344 N.W.2d 691 (S.D.1984)—¶ **3.04, n. 412.**

Van Balen v. Peoples Bank & Trust Co., 3 Ark.App. 243, 626 S.W.2d 205 (Ark.App. 1981)—¶ **6.03, n. 263.**

Vasquez v. Superior Court, 94 Cal.Rptr. 796, 484 P.2d 964 (Cal.1971)—¶ **3.04, n. 417.**

Vaughn v. United States Nat. Bank, 79 Or.App. 172, 718 P.2d 769 (Or.App. 1986)—¶ **11.02, n. 76.**

Vectra Bank of Englewood v. Bank Western, 890 P.2d 259 (Colo.App.1995)— ¶ **4.02, n. 29;** ¶ **7.02, n. 59.**

Vedder v. Spellman, 78 Wash.2d 834, 480 P.2d 207 (Wash.1971)—¶ **1.04;** ¶ **1.04, n. 216;** ¶ **6.02, n. 53;** ¶ **7.01, n. 2.**

Venners v. Goldberg, 133 Md.App. 428, 758 A.2d 567 (Md.App.2000)—¶ **2.03, n. 268;** ¶ **6.03, n. 154.**

Ventures, Inc. v. Jones, 101 Idaho 837, 623 P.2d 145 (Idaho 1981)—¶ **3.03, n. 203;** ¶ **6.03, n. 147.**

Verde America, Inc. v. Bank of New York, 24 UCC Rep. Serv. 2d 154 (N.Y.Sup. 1994)—¶ **7.03, n. 175.**

Victory Nat. Bank v. Oklahoma State Bank, 520 P.2d 675 (Okla.1973)—¶ **1.03;** ¶ **1.03, n. 89.**

Vietnam Veterans of America, Inc. v. Guerdon Industries, Inc., 644 F.Supp. 951 (D.Del.1986)—¶ **3.04, n. 432.**

Village Motors, Inc. v. American Federal Sav. and Loan Ass'n, 231 Va. 408, 345 S.E.2d 288 (Va.1986)—¶ **3.03, n. 208.**

Vinick v. Fourth Nat. Bank, 531 P.2d 327 (Okla.1974)—¶ **2.02, n. 73, 101.**

Virginia Nat. Bank v. Holt, 216 Va. 500, 219 S.E.2d 881 (Va.1975)—¶ **2.02, n. 56.**

Vitols v. Citizens Banking Co., 10 F.3d 1227 (6th Cir.1993)—¶ **3.04, n. 414.**

Voelker, Estate of, 252 N.W.2d 400 (Iowa 1977)—¶ **6.03, n. 273.**

Voight's Estate, In re, 95 N.M. 625, 624 P.2d 1022 (N.M.App.1981)— ¶ **1.03;** ¶ **1.03, n. 110.**

von Frank v. Hershey Nat. Bank, 269 Md. 138, 306 A.2d 207 (Md.1973)—¶ **1.03;** ¶ **1.03, n. 69;** ¶ **2.02, n. 109.**

W

Walcott v. Manufacturers Hanover Trust, 133 Misc.2d 725, 507 N.Y.S.2d 961 (N.Y.City Civ.Ct.1986)—¶ **3.02, n. 164.**

Waldron v. Delffs, 988 S.W.2d 182 (Tenn. Ct.App.1998)—¶ **2.02, n. 239.**

Walker v. Community Bank, 596 So.2d 886 (Ala.1992)—¶ **3.01, n. 6.**

Walker v. Texas Commerce Bank, N.A., 635 F.Supp. 678 (S.D.Tex.1986)—¶ **10.09, n. 189.**

Walker v. Wallace Auto Sales, Inc., 155 F.3d 927 (7th Cir.1998)—¶ **3.04, n. 432.**

Walker Bank & Trust Co. v. Jones, 672 P.2d 73 (Utah 1983)—¶ **11.02, n. 74.**

Wallace v. National Commerce Bancorp., No. 39746-3 T.D. (Cir.Ct.Tenn., 13th Jud.D. at Memphis, filed July 12, 1991)—¶ **9.03, n. 143.**

Wallach Sons, Inc. v. Bankers Trust Co., 62 Misc.2d 19, 307 N.Y.S.2d 297 (N.Y.City Civ.Ct.1970)—¶ **4.04; ¶ 4.04, n. 166, 189; ¶ 6.02; ¶ 6.02, n. 77.**

Waller v. Maryland Nat. Bank, 95 Md.App. 197, 620 A.2d 381 (Md.App.1993)— ¶ **9.06, n. 351.**

Walls v. Morris Chevrolet, Inc., 515 P.2d 1405 (Okla.App. Div. 1 1973)—¶ **2.02, n. 210.**

Walnut Valley State Bank v. Stovall, 223 Kan. 459, 574 P.2d 1382 (Kan.1978)— ¶ **9.06, n. 400.**

Walter v. National City Bank, 42 Ohio St.2d 524, 330 N.E.2d 425 (Ohio 1975)— ¶ **9.06, n. 343.**

Walton v. Piqua State Bank, 204 Kan. 741, 466 P.2d 316 (Kan.1970)—¶ **9.06, n. 411.**

WAMCO, III, Ltd. v. First Piedmont Mortg. Corp., 856 F.Supp. 1076 (E.D.Va.1994)— ¶ **3.01, n. 25; ¶ 6.03, n. 287.**

Warner–Lambert Pharmaceutical Co. v. Sylk, 471 F.2d 1137 (3rd Cir.1972)— ¶ **5.02, n. 49.**

Warren v. Washington Trust Bank, 92 Wash.2d 381, 598 P.2d 701 (Wash. 1979)—¶ **6.03, n. 190.**

Warren v. Washington Trust Bank, 19 Wash.App. 348, 575 P.2d 1077 (Wash. App. Div. 3 1978)—¶ **5.02, n. 44.**

Warren Finance, Inc. v. Barnett Bank of Jacksonville, N.A., 552 So.2d 194 (Fla. 1989)—¶ **4.04, n. 178.**

Wasserman v. Broderick, 140 Misc. 174, 250 N.Y.S. 84 (N.Y.Sup.1931)—¶ **9.05, n. 260.**

Waterbury Sav. Bank v. Jaroszewski, 4 Conn.Cir.Ct. 620, 238 A.2d 446 (Conn. Cir.Ct.1967)—¶ **3.04, n. 419.**

Waters v. Waters, 498 S.W.2d 236 (Tex.Civ. App.-Tyler 1973)—¶ **3.01; ¶ 3.01, n. 38.**

Watertown Federal Sav. & Loan Ass'n v. Spanks, 346 Mass. 398, 193 N.E.2d 333 (Mass.1963)—¶ **2.02, n. 48; ¶ 3.02; ¶ 3.02, n. 73.**

Watkins v. Sheriff of Clark County, 85 Nev. 246, 453 P.2d 611 (Nev.1969)—¶ **3.03, n. 352.**

WDT–Winchester v. Nilsson, 32 Cal.Rptr.2d 511 (Cal.App. 6 Dist.1994)—¶ **4.03, n. 135.**

Wear v. Farmers & Merchants Bank, 605 P.2d 27 (Alaska 1980)—¶ **3.01, n. 11.**

Webb Business Promotions, Inc. v. American Electronics & Entertainment Corp., 617 N.W.2d 67 (Minn.2000)—¶ **7.01, n. 42.**

Webb Carter Const. Co., Inc. v. Louisiana Cent. Bank, 922 F.2d 1197 (5th Cir. 1991)—¶ **4.02, n. 20.**

Webb & Sons, Inc. v. Hamilton, 30 A.D.2d 597, 290 N.Y.S.2d 122 (N.Y.A.D. 3 Dept. 1968)—¶ **2.02, n. 184.**

Wegematic Corp., United States v., 360 F.2d 674 (2nd Cir.1966)—¶ **1.03; ¶ 1.03, n. 123, 124.**

Wegener, In re, 186 B.R. 692 (Bkrtcy. D.Neb.1995)—¶ **2.05, n. 311, 317.**

Weisberg, In re, 193 B.R. 916 (9th Cir. 1996)—¶ **9.06, n. 385.**

Weissman v. Banque De Bruxelles, 254 N.Y. 488, 173 N.E. 835 (N.Y.1930)—¶ **8.01, n. 22.**

Wells Fargo Bank v. Hartford Nat. Bank and Trust Co., 484 F.Supp. 817 (D.Conn. 1980)—¶ **4.03, n. 111; ¶ 8.01, n. 32, 57; ¶ 8.02, n. 102, 181, 184; ¶ 8.03, n. 210.**

Wells Fargo Bank Texas, N.A. v. James, 184 F.Supp.2d 588 (W.D.Tex.2001)—¶ **9.02, n. 95; ¶ 9.05, n. 297.**

Wells Fargo Bank & Union Trust Co. v. McDuffie, 71 F.2d 720 (9th Cir.1934)— ¶ **9.06, n. 333.**

Wellston, City of v. Jackson, 965 S.W.2d 867 (Mo.Ct.App.1998)—¶ **7.03, n. 123.**

Wenke v. Norton, 120 Ga.App. 70, 169 S.E.2d 663 (Ga.App.1969)—¶ **4.02, n. 9.**

Wertling v. Manufacturers Hanover Trust Co., 118 Misc.2d 722, 461 N.Y.S.2d 157 (N.Y.City Civ.Ct.1983)—¶ **8.03, n. 228.**

Wertz v. Richardson Heights Bank and Trust, 495 S.W.2d 572 (Tex.1973)— ¶ **4.04, n. 169; ¶ 9.01, n. 68.**

West v. Turchioe, 144 N.H. 509, 761 A.2d 382 (N.H.1999)—¶ **2.02, n. 164.**

Westerly Community Credit Union v. Industrial Nat. Bank, 103 R.I. 662, 240 A.2d 586 (R.I.1968)—¶ **9.05, n. 269.**

Western Air and Refrigeration, Inc. v. Metro Bank of Dallas, 599 F.2d 83 (5th Cir.1979)—¶ **4.03, n. 59; ¶ 8.02; ¶ 8.02, n. 134, 138; ¶ 9.03, n. 154.**

Western Assur. Co. v. Star Financial Bank of Indianapolis, 3 F.3d 1129 (7th Cir. 1993)—¶ **7.02, n. 67; ¶ 9.05, n. 283, 295, 300.**

Western Auto Supply Co. v. Craig, 30 UCC Rep. Serv. 1206(S.D.Ala.1981)—¶ **1.03; ¶ 1.03, n. 107.**

Western Cas. & Sur. Co. v. Citizens Bank of Las Cruces, 676 F.2d 1344 (10th Cir. 1982)—¶ **7.03; ¶ 7.03, n. 177, 183.**

Western Iowa Farms Co., In re, 135 F.3d 1257 (8th Cir.1998)—¶ **7.03, n. 169.**

Western Nat. Bank v. Hawkeye–Sec. Ins. Co., 380 F.Supp. 508 (D.Wyo.1974)—¶ **9.05, n. 281.**

Western Nat. Bank v. Rives, 927 S.W.2d 681 (Tex.App.-Amarillo 1996)—¶ **3.01, n. 19.**

Western Union Tel. Co. v. Peoples Nat. Bank, 169 N.J.Super. 272, 404 A.2d 1178 (N.J.Super.A.D.1979)—¶ **2.04;** ¶ **2.04, n. 286.**

West Greeley Nat. Bank v. Wygant, 650 P.2d 1339 (Colo.App.1982)—¶ **1.02, n. 42;** ¶ **2.02;** ¶ **2.02, n. 123.**

Weston Compagnie De Finance et D'Investissement v. La Republica Del Ecuador, 1993 WL 267282 (S.D.N.Y.1993)—¶ **10.08, n. 140.**

West Penn Administration, Inc. v. Union Nat. Bank, 233 Pa.Super. 311, 335 A.2d 725 (Pa.Super.1975)—¶ **2.02, n. 264;** ¶ **4.02, n. 25;** ¶ **7.03, n. 135.**

West Side Bank v. Marine Nat. Exchange Bank, 37 Wis.2d 661, 155 N.W.2d 587 (Wis.1968)—¶ **8.01, n. 31;** ¶ **8.02, n. 134;** ¶ **9.01, n. 90;** ¶ **9.03, n. 133, 152.**

Wetmore's Estate, Matter of, 36 Ill.App.3d 96, 343 N.E.2d 224 (Ill.App. 5 Dist. 1976)—¶ **6.03, n. 164.**

Whalen v. Chase Manhattan Bank, N.A., 43 UCC Rep. Serv. 2d 614 (S.D.N.Y.2000)—¶ **7.03, n. 131, 146.**

Whalen & Sons Grain Co. v. Missouri Delta Bank, 496 F.Supp. 211 (E.D.Mo.1980)—¶ **8.02, n. 185.**

White v. Gilliam, 244 Va. 113, 419 S.E.2d 247 (Va.1992)—¶ **3.04, n. 414, 417.**

White County Bank v. Noland Co., 214 Ga. App. 780, 449 S.E.2d 325 (Ga.App. 1994)—¶ **7.02, n. 92.**

Whitehall Packing Co., Inc. v. First Nat. City Bank, 55 A.D.2d 675, 390 N.Y.S.2d 189 (N.Y.A.D. 2 Dept.1976)—¶ **2.04, n. 295.**

White Sands Forest Products, Inc. v. First Nat. Bank of Alamogordo, 132 N.M. 453, 50 P.3d 202 (N.M.App.2002)—¶ **4.02, n. 25;** ¶ **7.03, n. 123;** ¶ **8.01, n. 46.**

Whiteside v. Douglas County Bank, 145 Ga. App. 775, 245 S.E.2d 2 (Ga.App.1978)—¶ **2.02, n. 178.**

Wickman v. Kane, 136 Md.App. 554, 766 A.2d 241 (Md.App.2001)—¶ **7.01, n. 32.**

Wickware v. National Mortg. Corp., 570 P.2d 330 (Okla.1977)—¶ **2.02, n. 83, 94.**

Wilcox Press, Inc. v. Beauty Fashion, Inc., 73 A.D.2d 988, 423 N.Y.S.2d 565 (N.Y.A.D. 3 Dept.1980)—¶ **7.01, n. 35.**

Wilder Binding Co. v. Oak Park Trust and Sav. Bank, 135 Ill.2d 121, 142 Ill.Dec. 192, 552 N.E.2d 783 (Ill.1990)—¶ **9.03, n. 196.**

Wiley v. Manufacturers Hanover Trust Co., 6 UCC Rep. Serv. 1083 (N.Y.Sup.1969)—¶ **4.02, n. 10.**

Wiley, Tate & Irby v. Peoples Bank & Trust Co., 438 F.2d 513 (5th Cir.1971)—¶ **2.02, n. 63.**

Willey v. Mayer, 876 P.2d 1260 (Colo. 1994)—¶ **4.02, n. 11;** ¶ **5.03, n. 67;** ¶ **6.03, n. 140.**

Williams v. Cooper, 504 S.W.2d 564 (Tex. Civ.App.-Eastland 1973)—¶ **2.02, n. 227.**

Williams v. Cullen Center Bank & Trust, 685 S.W.2d 311 (Tex.1985)—¶ **9.01, n. 11.**

Williams, Estate of, 109 Ill.App.3d 828, 65 Ill.Dec. 499, 441 N.E.2d 412 (Ill.App. 3 Dist.1982)—¶ **6.03, n. 202, 235.**

Williams, In re, 61 B.R. 567 (Bkrtcy. N.D.Tex.1986)—¶ **9.06, n. 385.**

Williamson v. Bertino, 685 So.2d 93 (Fla. App. 4 Dist.1997)—¶ **5.03, n. 82, 85.**

Willis v. National Bank of Georgia, 176 Ga.App. 15, 334 S.E.2d 917 (Ga.App. 1985)—¶ **9.06, n. 412.**

Willis v. Willis, 30 UCC Rep. Serv. 1332 (D.D.C.1980)—¶ **6.02, n. 86;** ¶ **6.03; ¶ 6.03, n. 129.**

Wills, Commonwealth of Virginia v., 27 UCC Rep.Serv. 2d 926 (Va. Cir. Ct.1995)—¶ **7.01, n. 42.**

Wilmington Trust Co. v. Phoenix Steel Corp., 273 A.2d 266 (Del.Supr.1971)—¶ **4.02, n. 12.**

Wilson Supply Co. v. West Artesia Transmission Co., 505 S.W.2d 312 (Tex.Civ. App.-San Antonio 1974)—¶ **3.03, n. 230.**

Winkel v. Erpelding, 526 N.W.2d 316 (Iowa 1995)—¶ **6.03, n. 230.**

Winkie, Inc. v. Heritage Bank of Whitefish Bay, 99 Wis.2d 616, 299 N.W.2d 829 (Wis.1981)—¶ **7.02, n. 95.**

Winkler v. Commercial Nat. Bank of L'Anse, 42 Mich.App. 740, 202 N.W.2d 468 (Mich.App.1972)—¶ **9.03;** ¶ **9.03, n. 165.**

Winn v. First Bank, 581 S.W.2d 21 (Ky.App. 1978)—¶ **3.01, n. 7.**

Witten Productions, Inc. v. Republic Bank and Trust Co., 102 N.C.App. 88, 401 S.E.2d 388 (N.C.App.1991)—¶ **7.03, n. 174.**

Wohlhuter v. St. Charles Lumber & Fuel Co., 62 Ill.2d 16, 338 N.E.2d 179 (Ill. 1975)—¶ **5.02, n. 28.**

Wohlhuter v. St. Charles Lumber & Fuel Co., 25 Ill.App.3d 812, 323 N.E.2d 134 (Ill.App. 2 Dist.1975)—¶ **5.01, n. 6;** ¶ **6.03, n. 258.**

Wohlrabe v. Pownell, 307 N.W.2d 478 (Minn.1981)—¶ **3.03;** ¶ **3.03, n. 275, 325.**

Wolfe v. University Nat. Bank, 270 Md. 70, 310 A.2d 558 (Md.1973)—¶ **2.02, n. 43.**

TABLE OF CASES

Wolfram v. Halloway, 46 Ill.App.3d 1045, 5 Ill.Dec. 264, 361 N.E.2d 587 (Ill.App. 1 Dist.1977)—¶ **4.06, n. 206**; ¶ **5.03, n. 96.**

Wolverton Farmers Elevator v. First American Bank of Rugby, 851 F.2d 223 (8th Cir.1988)—¶ **8.01, n. 27, 32**; ¶ **8.02, n. 134.**

Wood v. Willman, 423 P.2d 82 (Wyo.1967)—¶ **3.04**; ¶ **3.04, n. 394**; ¶ **6.03, n. 201.**

Woodhouse v. Crandall, 197 Ill. 104, 64 N.E. 292 (Ill.1902)—¶ **9.05, n. 266.**

Woods v. Bank of New York, 806 F.2d 368 (2nd Cir.1986)—¶ **8.01, n. 25.**

Wool v. NationsBank of Virginia, N.A., 248 Va. 384, 448 S.E.2d 613 (Va.1994)—¶ **6.03, n. 286.**

Wooldridge v. Groos Nat. Bank, 603 S.W.2d 335 (Tex.Civ.App.-Waco 1980)—¶ **2.02, n. 176**; ¶ **6.01**; ¶ **6.01, n. 31.**

Woolridge v. J.F.L. Electric, Inc., 96 Cal. App.4th Supp. 52, 117 Cal.Rptr.2d 771 (Super.Ct.2002)—¶ **3.03, n. 257.**

W.R. Grimshaw Co. v. First Nat. Bank & Trust Co. of Tulsa, 563 P.2d 117 (Okla. 1977)—¶ **4.02, n. 10**; ¶ **5.03, n. 75.**

Wright v. Chattanooga TVA Employers Credit Union, No. 91 CV-1444 (Cir.Ct. Hamilton Co. Tenn., 11th Jud.D. at Chattanooga, filed July 16, 1991)—¶ **9.03, n. 143.**

Wright v. Commercial and Sav. Bank, 297 Md. 148, 464 A.2d 1080 (Md.1983)—¶ **9.02, n. 98.**

Wurzburg Bros., Inc. v. Coleman, 404 So.2d 334 (Ala.1981)—¶ **5.03, n. 86.**

Wyatt v. Mount Airy Cemetery, 209 Pa.Super. 250, 224 A.2d 787 (Pa.Super.1966)—¶ **3.04, n. 389.**

Wymore State Bank v. Johnson Intern. Co., 873 F.2d 1082 (8th Cir.1989)—¶ **7.03, n. 134, 150.**

Y

Yacht Club Sales and Service, Inc. v. First Nat. Bank of North Idaho, 29 UCC Rep. Serv. 1340 (Idaho 1979)—¶ **9.02**; ¶ **9.02, n. 100.**

Yahn & McDonnell, Inc. v. Farmers Bank of State of Del., 708 F.2d 104 (3rd Cir. 1983)—¶ **3.03, n. 313.**

Yandell v. White City Amusement Park, Inc., 232 F.Supp. 582 (D.Mass.1964)—¶ **9.01**; ¶ **9.01, n. 93.**

Yanoff v. Muncy, 676 N.E.2d 765 (Ind.App. 1997)—¶ **3.01, n. 19.**

Yeager & Sullivan, Inc. v. Farmers Bank, 162 Ind.App. 15, 317 N.E.2d 792 (Ind. App. 2 Dist.1974)—¶ **7.03, n. 130.**

Yeomans v. Coleman, Meadows, Pate Drug Co., 167 Ga.App. 646, 307 S.E.2d 121 (Ga.App.1983)—¶ **5.03, n. 86.**

Yin v. Society Nat. Bank Indiana, 665 N.E.2d 58 (Ind.App.1996)—¶ **2.02**; ¶ **2.02, n. 196.**

Yoder v. Cromwell State Bank, 478 N.E.2d 131 (Ind.App. 3 Dist.1985)—¶ **8.02, n. 181**; ¶ **8.03, n. 210.**

Young v. Bank of America, 141 Cal.App.3d 108, 190 Cal.Rptr. 122 (Cal.App. 1 Dist. 1983)—¶ **11.02, n. 75.**

Young v. Mercantile Trust Co., 552 S.W.2d 247 (Mo.App.1977)—¶ **9.06, n. 365.**

Your Style Publications, Inc. v. Mid Town Bank and Trust Co. of Chicago, 150 Ill. App.3d 421, 103 Ill.Dec. 488, 501 N.E.2d 805 (Ill.App. 1 Dist.1986)—¶ **4.03, n. 60.**

Yukon Nat. Bank v. Modern Builders Supply, Inc., 686 P.2d 307 (Okla.App. Div. 1 1984)—¶ **4.04, n. 169**; ¶ **9.01, n. 68.**

YYY Corp. v. Gazda, 145 N.H. 53, 761 A.2d 395 (N.H.2000)—¶ **3.01, n. 19.**

Z

Zagoria v. Dubose Enterprises, Inc., 163 Ga.App. 880, 296 S.E.2d 353 (Ga.App. 1982)—¶ **5.03, n. 79.**

Zambia Nat. Commercial Bank Ltd. v. Fidelity Intern. Bank, 855 F.Supp. 1377 (S.D.N.Y.1994)—¶ **4.02, n. 21**; ¶ **7.03, n. 174.**

Zapp Nat. Bank v. Metropolitan Planning and Redevelopment Corp., 308 Minn. 309, 242 N.W.2d 96 (Minn.1976)—¶ **4.06, n. 256**; ¶ **5.02**; ¶ **5.02, n. 64.**

Zara Cont. Co., Inc. v. De Lillo Const. Co., Inc., 2 UCC Rep. Serv. 277 (N.Y.Sup. 1964)—¶ **6.03, n. 125.**

Zener v. Velde, 135 Idaho 352, 17 P.3d 296 (Idaho App.2000)—¶ **3.03, n. 351.**

Table of Statutes

UNITED STATES

UNITED STATES CONSTITUTION

Art.	This Work Par.	Note
I, § 8	9.01	79

Amend.		
14	9.06	

UNITED STATES CODE ANNOTATED

9 U.S.C.A.—Arbitration

Sec.	This Work Par.	Note
2	8.01	46

11 U.S.C.A.—Bankruptcy

Sec.	This Work Par.	Note
361	9.06	388
361(1)	9.06	389
362	9.01	78
362	9.01	80
362(a)	9.06	346
362(a)(3)	9.06	381
362(a)(7)	9.06	381
362(a)(7)	9.06	385
362(b)(6)	9.06	385
362(d)	9.06	386
362(h)	9.06	381
363	9.06	389
363(b)	9.06	387
363(c)(3)	9.06	388
363(o)	9.06	388
506(a)	9.06	376
506(a)	9.06	381
541	9.01	78
542(b)	9.06	381
542(c)	9.01	80
544(a)	9.06	346
547	4.04	145
547(c)(2)	4.04	146
547(c)(2)	9.01	81
549(b)	9.01	81
553	9.06	
553	9.06	345
553	9.06	346
553	9.06	381
553	9.06	382
553(b)	9.06	383

UNITED STATES CODE ANNOTATED
11 U.S.C.A.—Bankruptcy

Sec.	This Work Par.	Note
553(b)	9.06	384

12 U.S.C.A.—Banks and Banking

Sec.	This Work Par.	Note
24(7)	9.02	95
24(7)	9.05	297
1787(p)(2)	1.03	134
1787(p)(2)	1.03	146
1813(1)	9.05	246
1823	1.03	
1823(e)	1.03	
1823(e)	1.03	134
1823(e)	1.03	146
1823(e)	1.03	147
1829b	9.05	316
1829b	10.14	270
1829b(b)(2)	10.14	270
1829b(b)(3)	10.14	270
1951—1959	10.14	270
1951 et seq.	9.05	316
3401 et seq.	9.05	270
3415	10.14	270
4001—4010	8.04	253
4001—4010	8.04	309
4001—4010	9.03	201
4001—4010	10.08	142
4001 et seq.	1.01	21
4001 et seq.	1.03	159
4001 et seq.	1.04	181
4008(b)(2)	8.04	434
4008(b)(2)	9.03	203
4008(c)	1.03	164
4008(c)(1)	8.04	310
4008(f)	8.04	434
4008(f)	9.03	203
6323(a)	9.06	378

15 U.S.C.A.—Commerce and Trade

Sec.	This Work Par.	Note
45	3.04	425
78j(b)	9.05	249
1601 et seq.	1.03	168
1601 et seq.	2.01	9
1601 et seq.	3.04	427
1601 et seq.	11.01	8

TABLE OF STATUTES

UNITED STATES CODE ANNOTATED

15 U.S.C.A.—Commerce and Trade

Sec.	Par. (This Work)	Note
1637	11.01	8
1637a	11.01	8
1642—1645	11.01	7
1643	1.03	169
1643(a)(1)(B)	1.03	173
1645	11.01	7
1666—1666i	11.01	7
1666i	1.03	145
1666i	3.04	420
1666i	11.02	92
1691—1691f	3.02	107
1691 et seq.	7.03	171
1692f(4)	8.01	17
1693—1693r	10.01	3
1693 et seq.	1.01	4
1693 et seq.	1.01	31
1693 et seq.	10.02	5
1693 et seq.	11.01	4
1693 et seq.	11.01	6
1693 et seq.	11.01	15
1693h(a)	11.02	65
1693h(a)(1)	11.02	66
1693h(a)(1)	11.02	68
1693h(a)(2)	11.02	68
1693h(a)(3)	11.02	68
1693h(b)	11.02	66
1693h(c)	11.02	65
1693k	11.02	27
7001 et seq.	11.01	6
7003(a)(3)	1.01	12

18 U.S.C.A.—Crimes and Criminal Procedure

Sec.	Par. (This Work)	Note
2113(b)	8.02	168

26 U.S.C.A.—Internal Revenue Code

Sec.	Par. (This Work)	Note
6321 et seq.	9.06	374
6323(a)	9.06	378
6323(a)	9.06	379
6331(a)	9.06	374

31 U.S.C.A.—Money and Finance

Sec.	Par. (This Work)	Note
5101 et seq.	1.03	79
5311—5330	10.14	270
5311 et seq.	9.05	270
5311 et seq.	9.05	316
5311 et seq.	9.05	317

42 U.S.C.A.—The Public Health and Welfare

Sec.	Par. (This Work)	Note
4001 et seq.	8.01	37

STATUTES AT LARGE

Year	Par. (This Work)	Note
1978, P.L. 95–598	9.06	380
1991, P.L. 102–242	9.03	140
1999, P.L. 106–102	8.01	53
1999, P.L. 106–102	9.03	117
1999, P.L. 106–102	9.03	121
2001, P.L. 107–56	10.14	270

POPULAR NAME ACTS

BANKRUPTCY ACT

Sec.	Par. (This Work)	Note
70a	9.01	78

EXPEDITED FUNDS AVAILABILITY ACT

Sec.	Par. (This Work)	Note
609(c)	1.03	164

FAIR CREDIT BILLING ACT

Sec.	Par. (This Work)	Note
170	3.04	420

FEDERAL TRADE COMMISSION ACT

Sec.	Par. (This Work)	Note
5	3.04	425

GARN–ST. GERMAIN DEPOSITORY INSTITUTIONS ACT

Sec.	Par. (This Work)	Note
327	9.05	

RIGHT TO FINANCIAL PRIVACY ACT

Sec.	Par. (This Work)	Note
1115	10.14	270

STATE STATUTES

WEST'S ANNOTATED CALIFORNIA CIVIL CODE

Sec.	Par. (This Work)	Note
1526(a)	7.01	38

TABLE OF STATUTES

WEST'S ANNOTATED CALIFORNIA FINANCIAL CODE

Sec.	This Work Par.	Note
863	9.06	337
866—866.9	8.02	177

KANSAS STATUTES ANNOTATED

Sec.	This Work Par.	Note
16a–3–403	11.01	9

MASSACHUSETTS GENERAL LAWS ANNOTATED

Ch.	This Work Par.	Note
167B	11.01	9

NEW YORK, MCKINNEY'S BANKING LAW

Sec.	This Work Par.	Note
14–3	8.02	177

NEW YORK, MCKINNEY'S CIVIL PRACTICE LAW AND RULES

Sec.	This Work Par.	Note
213(1)	10.08	
214(2)	10.08	167
214(4)	10.08	167

NEW YORK, MCKINNEY'S DEBTOR AND CREDITOR LAW

Sec.	This Work Par.	Note
151	9.06	337

NEW YORK, MCKINNEY'S UNIFORM COMMERCIAL CODE

Sec.	This Work Par.	Note
4A–102, Comment	10.08	169
4A–102, Comment	10.08	170

NORTH DAKOTA CENTURY CODE

Sec.	This Work Par.	Note
6–03–67	9.06	337

OKLAHOMA STATUTES ANNOTATED

Tit.	This Work Par.	Note
6, § 2201 et seq.	9.05	270

OKLAHOMA STATUTES ANNOTATED

Tit.	This Work Par.	Note
14A, § 1–301(9)	11.01	9
14A, § 1–301(16)	11.01	9
14A, § 2–104	11.01	9
14A, § 2–202	11.01	9
14A, § 2–202.2	11.01	9
14A, § 2–203(4)	11.01	9
14A, § 2–207	11.01	9
14A, § 2–403	3.04	424
14A, § 2–404	3.04	420
14A, § 3–104	11.01	9
14A, § 3–106	11.01	9
14A, § 3–202	11.01	9
14A, § 3–203(5)	11.01	9
14A, § 3–508A	11.01	9
21, § 1541.3	9.01	49
21, § 1541.4	9.01	49
25, § 26	2.02	42
42, § 32	9.06	336
68, § 812	9.06	374

UNIFORM COMMERCIAL CODE

Sec.	This Work Par.	Note
Art. 1	1.01	1
Art. 1	1.03	
Art. 1	1.04	
Art. 1	1.04	175
Art. 1	1.04	213
Art. 1	1.04	217
Art. 1	1.04	221
Art. 1	4.02	18
Art. 1	7.01	
Art. 1	7.03	123
Art. 1	8.01	24
Art. 1	8.02	
Art. 1	8.04	
Art. 1	8.04	484
Art. 1	9.01	36
Art. 1	10.07	109
Art. 1	10.08	163
1–102	9.03	
1–102(1)	1.04	
1–102(1)	8.01	4
1–102(2)	8.01	4
1–102(3)	4.04	187
1–102(3)	8.04	484
1–102(3)	8.04	486
1–102(3)	8.04	503
1–102(3)	9.03	
1–102(3)	9.03	144
1–102(3)	9.03	145
1–102(3)	10.08	125
1–102, Comment 2	10.08	130
1–103	2.02	
1–103	6.03	208
1–103	7.03	123
1–103	8.01	
1–103	8.02	
1–103	8.02	113
1–103	8.02	150

TABLE OF STATUTES

UNIFORM COMMERCIAL CODE

Sec.	Par.	Note
1–103	9.02	101
1–103	9.03	
1–103	9.03	149
1–103	9.05	296
1–103	10.04	65
1–103	10.08	130
1–103	11.03	121
1–103(a)	1.03	
1–103(a)	1.04	
1–103(a)	1.04	221
1–103(a)	2.01	19
1–103(b)	1.04	
1–103(b)	2.02	
1–103(b)	3.03	336
1–103(b)	4.02	11
1–103(b)	4.04	165
1–103(b)	5.02	39
1–103(b)	6.01	19
1–103(b)	6.03	
1–103(b)	6.03	284
1–103(b)	6.03	286
1–103(b)	7.01	14
1–103(b)	7.02	79
1–103(b)	7.03	106
1–103, Comment 2	1.04	221
1–103, Comment 2	7.03	123
1–105	1.03	108
1–105	8.01	24
1–105	10.08	153
1–105(1)	1.03	
1–105, Comment	1.03	108
1–105, Comment 2	1.03	
1–105, Comment 3	1.03	
1–105, Comment 3	1.03	105
1–106	9.02	
1–106	9.03	
1–106	9.03	149
1–106(1)	9.02	
1–106(1)	9.02	101
1–106, Comment 3	4.04	177
1–201(3)	8.01	28
1–201(3)	8.01	30
1–201(4)	1.04	178
1–201(4)	9.04	229
1–201(19)	1.04	
1–201(19)	8.04	
1–201(19)	8.04	499
1–201(20)	8.02	
1–201(20)	9.03	
1–201(24)	9.06	406
1–201(27)	10.07	109
1–201(28)	9.03	119
1–201(30)	8.01	
1–201(30)	9.03	119
1–201(38)	8.02	
1–201(38)	8.03	210
1–201(a)(5)	3.02	59
1–201(a)(15)	3.01	2
1–201(a)(15)	3.01	3
1–201(a)(21)(A)	3.01	10
1–201(a)(21)(A)	3.01	11
1–201(a)(21)(A)	3.01	17

UNIFORM COMMERCIAL CODE

Sec.	Par.	Note
1–201(a)(21)(A)	3.03	198
1–201(a)(24)	2.02	216
1–201(a)(25)	2.02	263
1–201(a)(27)	2.02	263
1–201(b)(3)	7.01	30
1–201(b)(4)	7.01	24
1–201(b)(8)	3.03	320
1–201(b)(11)	1.03	106
1–201(b)(15)	3.03	192
1–201(b)(16)	1.03	81
1–201(b)(20)	1.04	214
1–201(b)(20)	2.02	152
1–201(b)(20)	3.03	
1–201(b)(20)	3.03	251
1–201(b)(20)	7.03	182
1–201(b)(24)	1.03	77
1–201(b)(31)	6.03	247
1–201(b)(31)	9.01	36
1–201(b)(33)	5.01	10
1–201(b)(33)	5.03	67
1–201(b)(36)	8.02	
1–201(b)(37)	2.02	40
1–201(b)(37)	4.04	153
1–201(b)(37)	6.03	229
1–201(b)(39)	5.01	4
1–201(b)(41)	1.04	227
1–201(b)(41)	2.02	57
1–201(b)(41)	4.02	35
1–201(b)(41)	7.02	92
1–201(b)(43)	2.02	37
1–201, Comment 37	2.02	41
1–202	3.03	243
1–202	3.03	247
1–202	4.03	111
1–202(a)(1)	3.03	267
1–202(a)(2)	3.03	267
1–202(a)(3)	3.03	268
1–202(b)	3.03	292
1–203	4.02	18
1–203	6.03	
1–203	8.02	113
1–203	8.03	220
1–203	8.04	
1–203	8.04	499
1–203	9.01	44
1–203	9.01	85
1–203	9.03	132
1–203	9.03	134
1–203	9.03	135
1–203	9.03	136
1–203	9.06	354
1–203	9.06	373
1–204	3.03	218
1–205	1.04	
1–205	8.01	28
1–207	1.04	
1–207	7.01	
1–207	9.01	
1–207	9.01	8
1–208	9.06	352
1–208	9.06	353
1–208	9.06	354

TABLE OF STATUTES

UNIFORM COMMERCIAL CODE

Sec.	Par.	This Work Note
1–208	9.06	373
1–210(b)(3)	2.02	
1–301	1.03	
1–301	8.01	24
1–301	1.03	105
1–301(a)(1)	1.03	106
1–301(a)(2)	1.03	106
1–301(c)(1)	1.03	106
1–301(c)(2)	1.03	106
1–301(d)	1.03	
1–301(d)	1.03	109
1–301(e)	1.03	105
1–301(e)	1.03	106
1–301(f)	1.03	106
1–301(g)	1.03	106
1–301(g)(3)	1.03	105
1–301, Comment 1	1.03	108
1–302	2.01	23
1–302	4.04	184
1–302	4.05	192
1–302	7.02	81
1–302(a)	3.02	89
1–302(a)	4.04	188
1–302(a)	11.03	130
1–302(b)	2.02	132
1–302(b)	7.02	81
1–302, Comment 1	2.01	27
1–302, Comment 1	3.02	90
1–303	1.04	
1–304	1.04	214
1–304	4.02	18
1–304	4.02	30
1–304	6.03	
1–304	7.03	182
1–305	4.04	177
1–305	11.03	104
1–308(a)	7.01	
1–308(b)	7.01	
1–308(b)	7.01	41
1–309	2.02	
1–309	2.02	152
1–309	2.02	230
Art. 2	3.03	229
Art. 2	7.02	
Art. 2	7.02	62
Art. 2	11.01	3
2–105(1)	1.03	81
2–203	6.03	165
2–275	6.03	287
2–302, Comment 1	6.02	49
2–312	7.02	
2–312, Comment 1	7.02	66
2–316	7.02	
2–318, Comment 1	7.02	64
2–325	1.01	8
2–325(2)	1.01	
2–325(2)	11.01	1
2–506	1.01	9
2–719	7.02	
2–719(3)	11.03	105
2–725	6.03	287
2–725, Comment	6.03	286

UNIFORM COMMERCIAL CODE

Sec.	Par.	This Work Note
Art. 2A	7.02	
Art. 2A	7.02	62
Art. 2A	11.01	3
2A–216	7.02	64
2A–407(3)	2.01	33
Art. 3	1.01	
Art. 3	1.01	1
Art. 3	1.01	11
Art. 3	1.01	22
Art. 3	1.01	29
Art. 3	1.01	30
Art. 3	1.02	
Art. 3	1.02	46
Art. 3	1.02	47
Art. 3	1.02	53
Art. 3	1.03	
Art. 3	1.03	68
Art. 3	1.03	71
Art. 3	1.03	76
Art. 3	1.03	93
Art. 3	1.03	104
Art. 3	1.03	105
Art. 3	1.03	129
Art. 3	1.03	164
Art. 3	1.04	
Art. 3	1.04	174
Art. 3	1.04	178
Art. 3	1.04	212
Art. 3	1.04	213
Art. 3	1.04	217
Art. 3	1.04	226
Art. 3	1.04	232
Art. 3	2.01	
Art. 3	2.01	10
Art. 3	2.01	13
Art. 3	2.01	17
Art. 3	2.01	20
Art. 3	2.01	26
Art. 3	2.01	27
Art. 3	2.01	34
Art. 3	2.02	
Art. 3	2.02	38
Art. 3	2.02	64
Art. 3	2.02	113
Art. 3	2.02	114
Art. 3	2.02	115
Art. 3	2.02	116
Art. 3	2.02	121
Art. 3	2.02	134
Art. 3	2.02	138
Art. 3	2.02	139
Art. 3	2.02	152
Art. 3	2.02	167
Art. 3	2.02	170
Art. 3	2.02	172
Art. 3	2.02	174
Art. 3	2.02	175
Art. 3	2.02	195
Art. 3	2.02	217
Art. 3	2.02	218
Art. 3	2.02	224
Art. 3	2.02	225

TABLE OF STATUTES

UNIFORM COMMERCIAL CODE

Sec.	Par.	This Work Note
Art. 3	2.02	238
Art. 3	2.02	249
Art. 3	2.02	264
Art. 3	2.03	
Art. 3	2.03	268
Art. 3	2.04	
Art. 3	2.04	269
Art. 3	2.04	272
Art. 3	2.04	279
Art. 3	2.04	281
Art. 3	2.04	298
Art. 3	2.04	302
Art. 3	2.05	
Art. 3	3.01	
Art. 3	3.01	5
Art. 3	3.01	12
Art. 3	3.01	25
Art. 3	3.02	
Art. 3	3.02	83
Art. 3	3.02	84
Art. 3	3.02	115
Art. 3	3.02	175
Art. 3	3.03	193
Art. 3	3.03	196
Art. 3	3.03	199
Art. 3	3.03	233
Art. 3	3.03	247
Art. 3	3.03	262
Art. 3	3.03	275
Art. 3	3.03	286
Art. 3	3.03	295
Art. 3	3.03	304
Art. 3	3.03	313
Art. 3	3.03	322
Art. 3	3.03	332
Art. 3	3.03	336
Art. 3	3.03	357
Art. 3	3.03	362
Art. 3	3.03	366
Art. 3	3.03	378
Art. 3	3.04	
Art. 3	3.04	406
Art. 3	3.04	425
Art. 3	4.02	
Art. 3	4.02	2
Art. 3	4.02	18
Art. 3	4.02	25
Art. 3	4.02	29
Art. 3	4.02	34
Art. 3	4.03	
Art. 3	4.03	60
Art. 3	4.03	64
Art. 3	4.03	72
Art. 3	4.03	98
Art. 3	4.03	102
Art. 3	4.03	106
Art. 3	4.03	115
Art. 3	4.03	127
Art. 3	4.03	128
Art. 3	4.03	137
Art. 3	4.04	
Art. 3	4.04	154

UNIFORM COMMERCIAL CODE

Sec.	Par.	This Work Note
Art. 3	4.04	174
Art. 3	4.04	175
Art. 3	4.04	186
Art. 3	4.05	193
Art. 3	4.05	199
Art. 3	4.06	
Art. 3	4.06	210
Art. 3	4.06	225
Art. 3	4.06	232
Art. 3	4.06	245
Art. 3	4.06	249
Art. 3	5.01	5
Art. 3	5.02	
Art. 3	5.02	16
Art. 3	5.02	18
Art. 3	5.02	23
Art. 3	5.02	39
Art. 3	5.02	58
Art. 3	5.02	61
Art. 3	5.02	62
Art. 3	5.03	
Art. 3	5.03	68
Art. 3	5.03	69
Art. 3	6.01	
Art. 3	6.01	14
Art. 3	6.01	15
Art. 3	6.01	16
Art. 3	6.01	17
Art. 3	6.02	
Art. 3	6.03	
Art. 3	6.03	88
Art. 3	6.03	91
Art. 3	6.03	110
Art. 3	6.03	115
Art. 3	6.03	175
Art. 3	6.03	183
Art. 3	6.03	192
Art. 3	6.03	218
Art. 3	6.03	225
Art. 3	6.03	229
Art. 3	6.03	248
Art. 3	6.03	249
Art. 3	6.03	251
Art. 3	6.03	256
Art. 3	6.03	276
Art. 3	6.03	281
Art. 3	6.03	286
Art. 3	6.03	287
Art. 3	6.03	288
Art. 3	6.03	298
Art. 3	7.01	
Art. 3	7.01	7
Art. 3	7.01	14
Art. 3	7.01	26
Art. 3	7.01	30
Art. 3	7.01	34
Art. 3	7.01	38
Art. 3	7.02	
Art. 3	7.02	45
Art. 3	7.02	90
Art. 3	7.02	104
Art. 3	7.03	

TABLE OF STATUTES 605

UNIFORM COMMERCIAL CODE

Sec.	Par.	Note
Art. 3	7.03	120
Art. 3	7.03	127
Art. 3	7.03	128
Art. 3	7.03	130
Art. 3	7.03	131
Art. 3	7.03	133
Art. 3	7.03	134
Art. 3	7.03	137
Art. 3	7.03	139
Art. 3	7.03	147
Art. 3	7.03	155
Art. 3	7.03	157
Art. 3	7.03	173
Art. 3	7.03	174
Art. 3	8.01	
Art. 3	8.01	1
Art. 3	8.01	3
Art. 3	8.01	47
Art. 3	8.01	50
Art. 3	8.01	52
Art. 3	8.02	
Art. 3	8.02	113
Art. 3	8.02	114
Art. 3	8.02	119
Art. 3	8.02	156
Art. 3	8.02	169
Art. 3	8.03	
Art. 3	8.03	215
Art. 3	8.03	232
Art. 3	8.04	
Art. 3	8.04	401
Art. 3	8.04	479
Art. 3	8.04	498
Art. 3	9.01	
Art. 3	9.01	1
Art. 3	9.01	2
Art. 3	9.01	4
Art. 3	9.01	36
Art. 3	9.01	54
Art. 3	9.01	57
Art. 3	9.01	68
Art. 3	9.03	
Art. 3	9.03	124
Art. 3	9.03	132
Art. 3	9.03	135
Art. 3	9.03	162
Art. 3	9.03	163
Art. 3	9.03	165
Art. 3	9.03	167
Art. 3	9.03	174
Art. 3	9.03	184
Art. 3	9.03	188
Art. 3	9.03	223
Art. 3	9.04	
Art. 3	9.04	238
Art. 3	9.05	
Art. 3	9.05	245
Art. 3	9.05	293
Art. 3	9.06	392
Art. 3	10.02	5
Art. 3	10.02	15
Art. 3	10.04	65

UNIFORM COMMERCIAL CODE

Sec.	Par.	Note
Art. 3	10.07	109
Art. 3	10.07	122
Art. 3	10.08	169
Art. 3	11.01	
Art. 3	11.03	
Art. 3	11.03	125
Art. 3	11.03	127
Art. 3	11.03	
3–102(1)(a)	3.01	5
3–102(1)(d)	2.04	281
3–102(1)(d)	4.03	53
3–102(1)(d)	4.05	193
3–102(1)(d)	4.06	210
3–102(1)(e)	11.02	64
3–102(a)	1.01	10
3–102(a)	1.01	30
3–102(a)	1.03	59
3–102(a)	1.03	78
3–102(a)	1.03	86
3–102(a)	1.03	104
3–102(a)	2.01	26
3–102(a)	2.02	64
3–102(a)	8.01	3
3–102(b)	1.04	179
3–102(b)	1.04	209
3–102(b)	1.04	210
3–102(b)	3.01	32
3–102(c)	4.03	108
3–102(c)	9.03	148
3–102, Comment 2	1.01	10
3–102, Comment 2	1.01	33
3–102, Comment 2	1.03	82
3–102, Comment 2	1.03	85
3–102, Comment 2	1.03	88
3–102, Comment 2	2.02	62
3–102, Comment 2	8.01	3
3–102, Comment 3	2.02	258
3–102, Comment 3	9.03	148
3–103	8.01	6
3–103	8.01	50
3–103(a)	2.01	18
3–103(a)	2.02	35
3–103(a)	8.01	64
3–103(a)(1)	4.02	47
3–103(a)(2)	1.01	13
3–103(a)(2)	1.04	192
3–103(a)(2)	4.02	46
3–103(a)(2)	7.02	46
3–103(a)(3)	1.01	13
3–103(a)(3)	3.01	1
3–103(a)(3)	4.02	43
3–103(a)(3)	4.03	50
3–103(a)(4)	1.04	214
3–103(a)(4)	2.02	152
3–103(a)(4)	3.03	224
3–103(a)(4)	3.03	251
3–103(a)(4)	4.02	18
3–103(a)(4)	4.02	30
3–103(a)(4)	7.03	182
3–103(a)(4)	8.02	114
3–103(a)(4)	8.03	215
3–103(a)(4)	8.03	232

TABLE OF STATUTES

UNIFORM COMMERCIAL CODE

Sec.	Par.	This Work Note
3–103(a)(4)	8.04	
3–103(a)(4)	8.04	460
3–103(a)(4)	8.04	498
3–103(a)(4)	9.01	
3–103(a)(4)	9.01	29
3–103(a)(4)	9.01	40
3–103(a)(4)	9.01	43
3–103(a)(4)	9.01	44
3–103(a)(4)	9.01	85
3–103(a)(4)	9.03	
3–103(a)(4)	9.03	124
3–103(a)(4)	9.03	128
3–103(a)(4)	9.03	132
3–103(a)(4)	9.03	134
3–103(a)(4)	9.03	135
3–103(a)(4)	9.03	136
3–103(a)(4)	9.03	167
3–103(a)(4)	9.03	184
3–103(a)(4)	9.03	188
3–103(a)(4)	9.03	222
3–103(a)(4)	9.05	271
3–103(a)(4)	9.05	283
3–103(a)(4)	9.06	354
3–103(a)(5)	1.01	15
3–103(a)(5)	3.01	1
3–103(a)(5)	4.02	48
3–103(a)(6)	1.01	13
3–103(a)(6)	1.02	34
3–103(a)(6)	1.02	35
3–103(a)(6)	2.01	1
3–103(a)(6)	2.01	6
3–103(a)(6)	2.02	36
3–103(a)(6)	2.02	38
3–103(a)(6)	2.02	61
3–103(a)(6)	2.02	116
3–103(a)(6)	2.02	117
3–103(a)(6)	2.02	215
3–103(a)(6)	2.02	258
3–103(a)(6)	3.01	1
3–103(a)(6)	11.01	12
3–103(a)(6)	11.03	115
3–103(a)(7)	4.02	14
3–103(a)(7)	4.02	30
3–103(a)(7)	7.02	81
3–103(a)(7)	7.03	114
3–103(a)(7)	7.03	128
3–103(a)(7)	8.01	28
3–103(a)(7)	9.01	
3–103(a)(7)	9.03	
3–103(a)(7)	9.03	167
3–103(a)(7)	9.03	172
3–103(a)(7)	9.03	181
3–103(a)(7)	9.03	184
3–103(a)(7)	9.03	194
3–103(a)(7)	9.05	293
3–103(a)(7)	9.05	294
3–103(a)(7)	9.05	309
3–103(a)(9)	1.01	15
3–103(a)(9)	1.02	34
3–103(a)(9)	1.02	35
3–103(a)(9)	1.03	60
3–103(a)(9)	2.01	1

UNIFORM COMMERCIAL CODE

Sec.	Par.	This Work Note
3–103(a)(9)	2.01	6
3–103(a)(9)	2.02	36
3–103(a)(9)	2.02	38
3–103(a)(9)	2.02	65
3–103(a)(9)	2.02	116
3–103(a)(9)	2.02	117
3–103(a)(9)	2.02	215
3–103(a)(9)	3.01	1
3–103(a)(11)	3.01	5
3–103(a)(11)	6.03	279
3–103(a)(11)	7.03	134
3–103(a)(11)	9.01	53
3–103(a)(14)	6.03	247
3–103(a)(14)	9.01	36
3–103(a)(16)	7.02	46
3–103(a)(17)	5.02	16
3–103(a)(17)	6.03	249
3–103(b)	8.01	64
3–103(c)	1.01	27
3–103(c)	1.04	178
3–103(c)	4.03	52
3–103(d)	7.01	24
3–103(d)	1.04	213
3–103(d)	6.03	229
3–103, Comment 2	9.01	57
3–103, Comment 3	2.02	66
3–103, Comment 3	6.03	249
3–103, Comment 4	1.02	55
3–103, Comment 4	3.03	
3–103, Comment 4	3.03	251
3–103, Comment 4	9.01	
3–104	1.01	10
3–104	1.01	31
3–104	1.02	52
3–104	1.03	
3–104	1.03	67
3–104	1.04	
3–104	1.04	191
3–104	2.01	
3–104	2.01	13
3–104	2.02	
3–104	2.02	52
3–104	2.02	113
3–104	2.05	
3–104	3.03	193
3–104	8.01	
3–104	8.01	3
3–104	8.01	47
3–104	8.03	215
3–104	9.01	52
3–104	9.01	55
3–104	9.04	
3–104	10.02	15
3–104	11.01	11
3–104	11.02	64
3–104	11.03	114
3–104	11.03	115
3–104(1)	2.01	
3–104(1)	9.04	231
3–104(2)(a)	1.04	178
3–104(2)(a)	9.04	231
3–104(2)(b)	1.04	178

TABLE OF STATUTES 607

UNIFORM COMMERCIAL CODE

Sec.	Par.	Note
3–104(2)(b)	9.04	228
3–104(a)	1.01	2
3–104(a)	1.01	13
3–104(a)	1.01	15
3–104(a)	1.02	34
3–104(a)	1.02	35
3–104(a)	1.02	37
3–104(a)	1.02	41
3–104(a)	1.03	60
3–104(a)	1.03	80
3–104(a)	2.01	
3–104(a)	2.01	1
3–104(a)	2.01	4
3–104(a)	2.01	6
3–104(a)	2.01	11
3–104(a)	2.01	18
3–104(a)	2.01	26
3–104(a)	2.02	
3–104(a)	2.02	35
3–104(a)	2.02	36
3–104(a)	2.02	38
3–104(a)	2.02	59
3–104(a)	2.02	92
3–104(a)	2.02	116
3–104(a)	2.02	117
3–104(a)	2.02	189
3–104(a)	2.02	194
3–104(a)	2.02	195
3–104(a)	2.02	203
3–104(a)	2.02	206
3–104(a)	2.02	211
3–104(a)	2.02	215
3–104(a)	2.02	225
3–104(a)	3.01	1
3–104(a)	3.03	193
3–104(a)	6.01	17
3–104(a)	8.01	3
3–104(a)	8.01	64
3–104(a)	11.01	2
3–104(a)	11.01	12
3–104(a)(1)	1.02	39
3–104(a)(1)	2.01	1
3–104(a)(1)	2.02	78
3–104(a)(1)	2.02	238
3–104(a)(1)	2.02	254
3–104(a)(2)	1.02	38
3–104(a)(2)	2.01	5
3–104(a)(2)	2.02	221
3–104(a)(2)	2.04	275
3–104(a)(3)	1.02	40
3–104(a)(3)	2.01	2
3–104(a)(3)	2.02	
3–104(a)(3)	2.02	68
3–104(a)(3)	2.02	78
3–104(a)(3)	2.02	90
3–104(a)(3)(i)	2.02	72
3–104(a)(3)(i)	2.02	84
3–104(a)(3)(i)—(a)(3)(iii)	2.02	69
3–104(a)(3)(ii)	2.02	72
3–104(a)(3)(ii)	2.02	106
3–104(a)(3)(iii)	2.02	95

UNIFORM COMMERCIAL CODE

Sec.	Par.	Note
3–104(a)(3)(iii)	2.02	100
3–104(a)(4)	9.03	124
3–104(b)	1.02	41
3–104(b)	3.01	4
3–104(b)	8.01	3
3–104(c)	1.01	14
3–104(c)	1.01	18
3–104(c)	1.02	
3–104(c)	1.02	39
3–104(c)	1.02	57
3–104(c)	1.03	
3–104(c)	2.02	78
3–104(c)	2.02	238
3–104(c)	2.02	254
3–104(c)	3.03	193
3–104(c)	8.04	459
3–104(d)	1.01	18
3–104(d)	1.02	58
3–104(d)	1.03	
3–104(d)	2.01	10
3–104(e)	1.01	13
3–104(e)	1.01	15
3–104(e)	1.03	60
3–104(e)	2.02	60
3–104(e)	2.04	270
3–104(e)	6.03	294
3–104(f)	1.01	14
3–104(f)	1.01	19
3–104(f)	1.01	25
3–104(f)	1.01	26
3–104(f)	1.04	178
3–104(f)	4.03	51
3–104(f)	6.03	294
3–104(f)	8.01	64
3–104(f)	8.01	66
3–104(f)	9.01	54
3–104(f)—(h)	9.01	54
3–104(f)(i)	1.01	28
3–104(f)(i)	1.03	60
3–104(f)(ii)	1.01	26
3–104(g)	1.01	5
3–104(g)	1.01	26
3–104(g)	4.02	43
3–104(g)	7.01	28
3–104(g)	8.01	61
3–104(g)	9.01	56
3–104(g)	9.01	60
3–104(h)	1.01	5
3–104(h)	1.01	26
3–104(h)	7.01	29
3–104(h)	8.01	61
3–104(h)	9.01	
3–104(h)	9.01	56
3–104(h)	9.01	60
3–104(i)	1.01	26
3–104(i)	8.01	62
3–104(j)	1.01	16
3–104(j)	1.03	60
3–104(j)	4.05	199
3–104(j)	9.05	245
3–104, Comment 1	1.03	76
3–104, Comment 1	2.01	

TABLE OF STATUTES

UNIFORM COMMERCIAL CODE

Sec.	Par.	This Work Note
3–104, Comment 1	2.02	69
3–104, Comment 1	2.02	216
3–104, Comment 1	8.01	3
3–104, Comment 2	1.02	49
3–104, Comment 2	1.02	53
3–104, Comment 2	1.02	56
3–104, Comment 2	1.03	
3–104, Comment 2	1.03	76
3–104, Comment 2	2.01	
3–104, Comment 2	2.01	30
3–104, Comment 2	2.02	78
3–104, Comment 2	2.02	97
3–104, Comment 3	4.02	30
3–104, Comment 4	1.01	25
3–104, Comment 4	1.01	26
3–104, Comment 4	1.01	27
3–104, Comment 4	2.02	52
3–104, Comment 4	9.04	240
3–105	2.01	17
3–105	2.05	314
3–105	6.03	142
3–105	11.03	114
3–105(1)	2.02	119
3–105(1)(b)	2.02	
3–105(1)(b)	2.02	135
3–105(1)(c)	2.02	134
3–105(1)(c)	2.02	137
3–105(1)(d)	2.02	138
3–105(1)(e)	2.02	139
3–105(1)(g)	2.02	187
3–105(1)(h)	2.02	187
3–105(2)(b)	2.02	126
3–105(2)(b)	2.02	183
3–105(a)	1.04	
3–105(a)	3.01	2
3–105(a)	3.01	5
3–105(a)	3.01	8
3–105(a)	3.01	9
3–105(a)	7.03	134
3–105(b)	2.05	314
3–105(b)	3.01	2
3–105(b)	3.01	4
3–105(b)	3.03	191
3–105(b)	6.03	143
3–105(b)	6.03	146
3–105(c)	3.01	5
3–105, Comment	3.01	5
3–105, Comment 1	6.03	142
3–105, Comment 2	6.03	142
3–105, Comment 3	2.02	153
3–105, Comment 7	2.02	187
3–106	2.01	11
3–106	2.02	92
3–106	11.01	2
3–106—3–109	2.01	17
3–106(1)(b)	2.02	92
3–106(1)(d)	2.02	211
3–106(1)(e)	2.02	211
3–106(2)	2.02	114
3–106(a)	1.01	2
3–106(a)	2.02	70
3–106(a)	2.02	119

UNIFORM COMMERCIAL CODE

Sec.	Par.	This Work Note
3–106(a)	2.02	135
3–106(a)	2.02	137
3–106(a)	2.02	208
3–106(a)(i)	1.04	222
3–106(a)(i)	2.02	77
3–106(a)(i)	2.02	115
3–106(a)(i)	2.02	118
3–106(a)(ii)	2.02	146
3–106(a)(iii)	2.02	146
3–106(b)(i)	2.02	
3–106(b)(i)	2.02	134
3–106(b)(ii)	2.02	
3–106(b)(ii)	2.02	126
3–106(b)(ii)	2.02	189
3–106(b)(ii)	2.02	225
3–106(c)	2.02	192
3–106(c)	8.01	62
3–106(d)	2.01	10
3–106(d)	2.02	193
3–106, Comment	2.02	193
3–106, Comment 1	2.02	70
3–106, Comment 1	2.02	120
3–106, Comment 1	2.02	135
3–106, Comment 1	2.02	137
3–106, Comment 1	2.02	150
3–106, Comment 1	2.02	151
3–106, Comment 1	2.02	153
3–106, Comment 1	2.02	190
3–106, Comment 1	2.02	204
3–106, Comment 2	2.02	192
3–106, Comment 3	2.01	10
3–106, Comment 3	2.02	119
3–106, Comment 5	2.02	213
3–107	2.02	
3–107	2.02	219
3–107(2)	2.02	218
3–107, Comment 1	2.02	217
3–108	1.03	
3–108	2.02	
3–108	2.02	124
3–108	2.02	221
3–108	9.04	
3–108(a)	2.02	222
3–108(a)	6.03	294
3–108(b)	2.02	129
3–108(b)	2.02	226
3–108(b)	2.02	228
3–108(b)	2.02	232
3–108(b)	2.04	275
3–108(b)	9.06	352
3–108(b)(ii)	2.02	85
3–108(c)	2.02	229
3–109(a)	2.02	
3–109(a)	2.02	239
3–109(a)	3.02	59
3–109(a)(2)	2.02	239
3–109(b)	2.02	
3–109(b)	2.02	251
3–109(b)	2.02	252
3–109(b)	2.02	255
3–109(b)	2.02	257
3–109(b)	2.02	259

TABLE OF STATUTES 609

UNIFORM COMMERCIAL CODE			UNIFORM COMMERCIAL CODE		
		This Work			This Work
Sec.	Par.	Note	Sec.	Par.	Note
3–109(b)	2.02	260	3–112(1)(a)	2.04	299
3–109(b)	3.02	61	3–112(1)(b)	2.02	
3–109(c)	2.02	244	3–112(1)(d)	2.02	
3–109(c)	2.02	246	3–112(1)(f)	2.02	111
3–109, Comment 1	2.02	233	3–112(1)(g)	2.02	113
3–109, Comment 2	2.02	239	3–112(2)	2.02	114
3–109, Comment 2	2.02	240	3–112(a)	2.02	195
3–109, Comment 2	2.02	247	3–112(b)	2.02	
3–109, Comment 2	2.02	248	3–112(b)	2.02	195
3–109, Comment 2	2.02	249	3–112(b)	2.02	200
3–109, Comment 3	2.04	301	3–112(b)	2.02	217
3–110	2.02	264	3–112, Comment 2	2.02	195
3–110	3.02	136	3–112, Comment 2	2.02	212
3–110	7.03		3–112, Comment 5	2.02	113
3–110	9.01	4	3–113	2.03	268
3–110(1)	2.02	257	3–113	2.04	300
3–110(1)(a)	2.02	260	3–113(a)	2.02	224
3–110(1)(b)	2.02	260	3–113(a)	2.04	300
3–110(1)(c)	2.02	260	3–113(a)	9.01	13
3–110(1)(e)	2.02		3–113(a)	9.02	
3–110(1)(e)	2.02	250	3–113(b)	2.04	300
3–110(2)	2.02	255	3–113, Comment	2.02	224
3–110(3)	2.02	249	3–114	2.02	209
3–110(a)	2.02	260	3–114	2.04	
3–110(a)	2.02	264	3–114	2.04	273
3–110(c)	2.02	264	3–114	2.04	284
3–110(c)	3.02	119	3–114	9.02	
3–110(c)(1)	2.02	251	3–114(1)	2.02	224
3–110(c)(1)	2.02	264	3–114(1)	2.04	300
3–110(c)(1)	3.02	112	3–114, Comment 2	2.04	301
3–110(c)(2)(i)	2.02	262	3–115	1.02	36
3–110(c)(2)(i)	2.02	264	3–115	1.03	
3–110(c)(2)(i)	3.02	113	3–115	1.03	60
3–110(c)(2)(i)	3.02	118	3–115	2.02	
3–110(c)(2)(ii)	2.02	265	3–115	2.02	239
3–110(c)(2)(ii)	3.02	114	3–115	2.05	311
3–110(c)(2)(ii)	3.02	115	3–115	4.04	149
3–110(c)(2)(ii)	3.02	117	3–115	4.04	159
3–110(c)(2)(iii)	2.02	264	3–115	4.05	
3–110(c)(2)(iii)	3.02	113	3–115	11.03	114
3–110(c)(2)(iv)	2.02	265	3–115(a)	2.05	311
3–110(c)(2)(iv)	3.02	114	3–115(a)	2.05	314
3–110(d)	2.02	261	3–115(a)	6.03	131
3–110(d)	2.02	262	3–115(b)	2.05	311
3–110(d)	2.04	289	3–115(b)	2.05	312
3–110(d)	3.02	94	3–115(b)	4.03	52
3–110(d)	3.02	95	3–115(b)	6.03	131
3–110(d)	3.02	98	3–115(b)	6.03	132
3–110(d)	6.03	208	3–115(b)	6.03	133
3–110, Comment 1	3.02	120	3–115(c)	2.05	315
3–110, Comment 3	2.02	266	3–115(c)	6.03	130
3–110, Comment 4	3.02	97	3–115(d)	2.05	311
3–110, Comment 5	2.02	256	3–115(d)	6.03	139
3–111	2.04	289	3–115, Comment	2.05	310
3–111	4.03	91	3–115, Comment 2	2.02	237
3–111	4.03	93	3–115, Comment 2	2.02	239
3–111, Comment	2.04	289	3–115, Comment 2	2.02	247
3–112	2.02	92	3–115, Comment 2	2.05	304
3–112	2.02	194	3–115, Comment 2	2.05	308
3–112	2.02	203	3–115, Comment 2	2.05	313
3–112	2.02	206	3–115, Comment 2	2.05	316
3–112	2.04	276	3–115, Comment 2	6.03	124

UNIFORM COMMERCIAL CODE

Sec.	Par.	This Work Note
3–115, Comment 2	6.03	132
3–115, Comment 3	2.05	304
3–115, Comment 3	2.05	307
3–115, Comment 3	6.03	132
3–115, Comment 4	6.03	130
3–115, Comment 5	6.03	138
3–116	4.06	253
3–116	4.06	255
3–116	5.01	5
3–116	5.02	51
3–116	5.02	52
3–116	5.02	66
3–116(a)	2.04	277
3–116(a)	4.06	255
3–116(a)	5.02	63
3–116(b)	2.04	277
3–116(b)	2.04	278
3–116(b)	6.03	178
3–116(c)	2.04	277
3–116(c)	6.03	178
3–116, Comment	3.02	96
3–116, Comment	3.02	100
3–117	2.02	
3–117	2.02	154
3–117	2.02	155
3–117	2.02	156
3–117	2.02	162
3–117	2.02	170
3–117	2.02	175
3–117	2.02	264
3–117	5.02	45
3–117	6.01	
3–117	6.01	19
3–117	6.01	24
3–117(c)	2.02	264
3–117(c)	3.02	119
3–117, Comment 1	2.02	174
3–117, Comment 1	3.02	115
3–117, Comment 1	6.01	24
3–117, Comment 1	6.01	27
3–117, Comment 1	6.01	33
3–117, Comment 2	1.03	132
3–117, Comment 2	2.02	174
3–117, Comment 2	2.02	175
3–117, Comment 2	2.02	180
3–117, Comment 2	6.01	
3–117, Comment 2	6.01	24
3–117, Comment 2	6.01	27
3–117, Comment 3	3.02	115
3–118	2.02	172
3–118	2.03	268
3–118	2.04	269
3–118	6.03	
3–118	6.03	88
3–118	6.03	286
3–118	6.03	288
3–118	6.03	297
3–118	7.01	3
3–118	8.03	227
3–118	9.01	57
3–118	9.02	111
3–118	9.03	189

UNIFORM COMMERCIAL CODE

Sec.	Par.	This Work Note
3–118	9.04	
3–118	10.08	149
3–118	10.08	165
3–118(a)	2.04	
3–118(a)	6.03	
3–118(a)	6.03	287
3–118(a)	6.03	304
3–118(a)	6.03	309
3–118(b)	6.03	287
3–118(b)	6.03	295
3–118(c)	6.03	288
3–118(c)	6.03	298
3–118(c)	6.03	303
3–118(c)	6.03	304
3–118(d)	2.02	
3–118(d)	6.03	289
3–118(d)	6.03	294
3–118(d)	6.03	295
3–118(d)	6.03	302
3–118(e)	2.04	277
3–118(e)	6.03	291
3–118(e)	6.03	297
3–118(e)	6.03	302
3–118(f)	2.04	
3–118(f)	6.03	225
3–118(f)	6.03	290
3–118(f)	6.03	294
3–118(f)(i)	6.03	304
3–118(g)	1.04	226
3–118(g)	6.03	292
3–118(g)	8.03	227
3–118(g)	9.02	111
3–118(g)	9.03	
3–118(g)	9.03	189
3–118(g)(i)	7.03	130
3–118(g)(ii)	7.02	61
3–118, Comment 1	2.04	269
3–118, Comment 1	6.03	286
3–118, Comment 2	6.03	298
3–118, Comment 3	6.03	303
3–118, Comment 4	6.03	303
3–119	2.02	162
3–119	2.02	175
3–119	4.02	2
3–119	7.02	100
3–119	8.04	
3–119(1)	2.02	
3–119(1)	2.02	162
3–119(1)	6.01	24
3–119(2)	2.02	115
3–119(2)	2.02	208
3–119, Comment 1	2.02	175
3–119, Comment 3	2.02	166
3–122	6.03	297
3–122(1)	6.03	285
3–122(1)(a)	6.03	304
3–122(1)(b)	6.03	295
3–122(2)	6.03	285
3–122(2)	6.03	297
3–122(2)	6.03	301
3–122(3)	6.03	285
3–122(3)	6.03	298

TABLE OF STATUTES

UNIFORM COMMERCIAL CODE

Sec.	Par.	This Work Note
3–122(4)	6.03	285
3–201	3.01	
3–201	3.01	17
3–201	3.01	19
3–201	3.01	28
3–201	3.01	30
3–201	3.01	41
3–201	3.01	53
3–201	3.02	66
3–201	6.03	
3–201	8.03	215
3–201	9.01	
3–201	9.03	
3–201	9.05	291
3–201—3–206	8.04	479
3–201(a)	3.01	21
3–201(a)	3.01	22
3–201(a)	3.02	58
3–201(a)	3.02	87
3–201(a)	3.02	92
3–201(b)	1.03	64
3–201(b)	2.02	241
3–201(b)	3.02	60
3–201(b)	3.02	62
3–201(b)	3.02	66
3–201(b)	3.02	91
3–201(b)	3.02	131
3–201(b)	3.02	135
3–201(b)	6.03	104
3–201(b)	7.02	49
3–201(b)	8.04	446
3–201, Comment 1	3.02	63
3–201, Comment 1	3.02	65
3–201, Comment 2	3.02	66
3–201, Comment 2	3.03	358
3–202	3.01	54
3–202	3.02	172
3–202	3.03	358
3–202	9.05	291
3–202(1)	8.01	
3–202(4)	3.02	84
3–202(b)	3.02	177
3–202, Comment 2	3.02	175
3–202, Comment 2	3.02	176
3–202, Comment 3	3.02	86
3–202, Comment 3	3.02	173
3–202, Comment 3	3.02	178
3–203	3.01	41
3–203	3.01	53
3–203	6.03	210
3–203	6.03	212
3–203	7.02	92
3–203	8.02	
3–203	9.01	
3–203	9.01	69
3–203(a)	3.01	22
3–203(a)	3.01	24
3–203(a)	3.02	57
3–203(a)	3.03	192
3–203(a)	7.02	51
3–203(a)	8.04	414
3–203(a)	9.03	223

UNIFORM COMMERCIAL CODE

Sec.	Par.	This Work Note
3–203(b)	2.02	156
3–203(b)	3.01	
3–203(b)	3.01	19
3–203(b)	3.01	24
3–203(b)	3.01	25
3–203(b)	3.01	28
3–203(b)	3.02	67
3–203(b)	3.03	192
3–203(b)	3.03	204
3–203(b)	3.03	321
3–203(b)	3.03	335
3–203(b)	3.04	
3–203(b)	3.04	392
3–203(b)	7.01	14
3–203(b)	7.03	107
3–203(b)	8.04	414
3–203(c)	8.04	414
3–203(d)	3.01	25
3–203(d)	3.02	84
3–203, Comment 1	3.01	22
3–203, Comment 1	3.01	24
3–203, Comment 1	3.02	57
3–203, Comment 2	3.01	40
3–203, Comment 3	3.01	26
3–203, Comment 3	3.02	68
3–203, Comment 4	3.01	25
3–204	5.03	79
3–204(a)	2.04	289
3–204(a)	3.02	81
3–204(a)	3.02	82
3–204(a)	3.02	83
3–204(a)	3.02	84
3–204(a)	3.02	91
3–204(a)	3.02	126
3–204(a)	3.02	129
3–204(a)	4.06	204
3–204(a)	4.06	214
3–204(a)	6.03	104
3–204(a)(iii)	5.01	9
3–204(a)(iii)	5.02	14
3–204(b)	4.02	44
3–204(b)	4.06	203
3–204(b)	4.06	204
3–204(c)	3.01	25
3–204(d)	3.02	121
3–204(d)	3.02	123
3–204(d)	7.02	92
3–204, Comment 1	3.02	82
3–204, Comment 1	3.02	83
3–204, Comment 1	4.06	213
3–204, Comment 1	8.04	581
3–204, Comment 2	3.01	25
3–205	3.02	136
3–205	7.02	49
3–205	9.03	
3–205—3–206	8.04	446
3–205(a)	2.02	243
3–205(a)	2.02	244
3–205(a)	3.02	61
3–205(a)	3.02	135
3–205(a)	3.02	136
3–205(a)	5.01	7

611

TABLE OF STATUTES

UNIFORM COMMERCIAL CODE

Sec.	Par.	This Work Note
3–205(b)	2.02	245
3–205(b)	2.02	246
3–205(b)	3.02	59
3–205(b)	3.02	130
3–205(b)	3.02	132
3–205(b)	5.01	7
3–205(c)	3.02	134
3–205(d)	3.02	126
3–205(d)	5.01	8
3–205(d)	5.01	9
3–205(d)	5.02	29
3–205(d)	9.03	
3–205, Comment 2	3.02	130
3–205, Comment 2	3.02	136
3–205, Comment 2	3.02	138
3–206	7.03	130
3–206	8.01	25
3–206	8.04	
3–206	9.03	
3–206(a)	3.02	139
3–206(a)	3.02	146
3–206(a)	3.02	160
3–206(a)	8.04	
3–206(b)	3.02	147
3–206(b)	3.02	148
3–206(b)	3.02	162
3–206(c)	3.02	149
3–206(c)	3.02	162
3–206(c)	8.04	
3–206(c)(1)	3.02	164
3–206(c)(1)—(c)(3)	3.03	217
3–206(c)(2)	3.02	164
3–206(c)(2)	7.03	128
3–206(c)(3)	3.02	164
3–206(c)(4)	3.02	161
3–206(c)(4)	3.02	163
3–206(c)(4)	3.02	165
3–206(c)(i)	3.02	152
3–206(d)	3.02	142
3–206(d)	3.02	146
3–206(d)	3.02	161
3–206(d)	3.02	163
3–206(d)(1)	3.03	217
3–206(d)(2)	3.02	146
3–206(e)	3.02	146
3–206(e)	3.02	162
3–206(e)	8.04	
3–206(f)	3.02	146
3–206, Comment	3.02	164
3–206, Comment 2	3.02	141
3–206, Comment 2	3.02	148
3–206, Comment 3	3.02	171
3–206, Comment 4	3.02	144
3–207	3.02	
3–207	3.02	66
3–207	3.02	180
3–207	3.02	181
3–207	3.02	182
3–207	3.02	184
3–207	3.02	187
3–207	3.03	
3–207	3.03	334

UNIFORM COMMERCIAL CODE

Sec.	Par.	This Work Note
3–207	6.03	183
3–207	6.03	184
3–207	6.03	190
3–207	6.03	197
3–207	9.03	
3–207, Comment	3.02	66
3–207, Comment	3.02	180
3–207, Comment	3.02	183
3–207, Comment	6.03	186
3–208	3.02	
3–208	6.03	
3–208, Comment	3.02	182
3–301	3.01	
3–301	3.01	12
3–301	3.01	13
3–301	3.01	14
3–301	3.01	24
3–301	3.01	42
3–301	3.01	50
3–301	3.02	158
3–301	3.02	187
3–301	3.03	188
3–301	3.03	202
3–301	4.04	168
3–301	5.02	40
3–301	6.03	104
3–301	6.03	204
3–301	8.04	446
3–301	9.03	
3–301(i)	3.01	
3–301(i)	3.01	12
3–301(i)	3.01	47
3–301(ii)	3.01	
3–301(ii)	3.01	24
3–301(ii)	3.01	37
3–301(ii)	3.02	67
3–301(iii)	3.01	
3–301(iii)	3.01	18
3–301(iii)	3.01	23
3–301(iii)	3.02	67
3–301, Comment	3.01	12
3–301, Comment	3.01	41
3–302	1.03	
3–302	3.03	205
3–302	3.04	
3–302	8.01	11
3–302	9.01	
3–302	9.03	
3–302—3–305	8.03	215
3–302—3–308	8.04	458
3–302(1)	7.02	84
3–302(2)	3.03	205
3–302(2)	3.04	406
3–302(a)	3.02	159
3–302(a)	3.03	200
3–302(a)	3.03	224
3–302(a)—(c)	3.03	284
3–302(a)(1)	3.03	239
3–302(a)(1)	3.03	285
3–302(a)(1)	3.03	291
3–302(a)(1)	6.03	130
3–302(a)(2)	3.03	239

TABLE OF STATUTES

UNIFORM COMMERCIAL CODE

Sec.	Par.	This Work Note
3-302(a)(2)	8.02	169
3-302(a)(2)	8.04	
3-302(a)(2)(i)	3.03	217
3-302(a)(2)(ii)	3.03	238
3-302(a)(2)(iii)	3.03	312
3-302(a)(2)(iii)	3.03	314
3-302(a)(2)(iii)	6.03	
3-302(a)(2)(iv)	3.03	323
3-302(b)	3.02	183
3-302(b)	3.03	286
3-302(b)	3.03	299
3-302(b)	3.03	334
3-302(b)	6.01	22
3-302(b)	6.02	69
3-302(b)	6.03	174
3-302(b)	6.03	233
3-302(c)	1.03	97
3-302(c)(i)	3.01	21
3-302(c)(i)	3.04	388
3-302(c)(ii)	1.03	140
3-302(c)(ii)	3.04	390
3-302(c)(iii)	3.04	389
3-302(d)	3.03	
3-302(d)	3.03	233
3-302(e)	3.02	159
3-302(e)	3.04	393
3-302(f)	3.03	242
3-302(f)	3.03	284
3-302(g)	1.04	212
3-302(g)	2.02	81
3-302(g)	3.04	412
3-302(g)	3.04	414
3-302(g)	3.04	424
3-302(g)	3.04	425
3-302, Comment 1	3.03	285
3-302, Comment 1	3.03	291
3-302, Comment 2	3.03	
3-302, Comment 2	3.03	323
3-302, Comment 2	3.04	404
3-302, Comment 2	3.04	407
3-302, Comment 3	3.03	334
3-302, Comment 4	3.03	
3-302, Comment 4	3.03	205
3-302, Comment 4	3.03	206
3-302, Comment 4	3.03	208
3-302, Comment 4	3.03	209
3-302, Comment 4	3.03	212
3-302, Comment 4	3.03	213
3-302, Comment 4	3.03	216
3-302, Comment 5	1.03	140
3-302, Comment 5	3.04	390
3-302, Comment 5	3.04	392
3-302, Comment 6	3.03	233
3-302, Comment 6	3.04	395
3-302, Comment 7	3.04	414
3-303	6.03	156
3-303	8.01	
3-303	8.01	9
3-303	8.02	114
3-303(a)	3.03	219
3-303(a)(1)	3.03	225
3-303(a)(2)	3.03	225

UNIFORM COMMERCIAL CODE

Sec.	Par.	This Work Note
3-303(a)(3)	3.03	226
3-303(a)(3)	6.03	156
3-303(a)(4)	3.03	227
3-303(a)(5)	3.03	227
3-303(b)	3.03	
3-303(b)	3.03	191
3-303(b)	5.02	42
3-303(b)	6.03	154
3-303(b)	6.03	155
3-303(b)	6.03	156
3-303(b)	6.03	162
3-303(b)	6.03	163
3-303, Comment 1	6.03	156
3-303, Comment 1	6.03	168
3-303, Comment 1	6.03	172
3-303, Comment 2	3.03	220
3-303, Comment 2	3.03	229
3-303, Comment 2	6.03	171
3-303, Comment 3	3.03	237
3-303, Comment 4	6.03	159
3-303, Comment 5	3.03	237
3-304	7.03	139
3-304(1)	3.03	
3-304(1)(a)	3.03	285
3-304(1)(a)	7.03	179
3-304(1)(b)	3.03	286
3-304(1)(b)	6.02	
3-304(2)	3.03	
3-304(2)	3.04	406
3-304(3)	3.03	
3-304(3)(a)	3.03	313
3-304(3)(c)	3.03	316
3-304(3)(c)	8.02	169
3-304(4)	3.03	
3-304(4)(a)	3.03	305
3-304(4)(b)	3.03	264
3-304(4)(b)	3.03	305
3-304(4)(c)	3.03	309
3-304(4)(d)	3.03	310
3-304(5)	3.03	
3-304(a)	3.03	316
3-304(a)(2)	8.02	169
3-304(b)	3.03	284
3-304(b)(1)	3.03	313
3-304(b)(2)	3.03	313
3-304(b)(3)	3.03	315
3-304(c)	3.03	317
3-304, Comment 1	3.03	316
3-304, Comment 4	6.02	70
3-304, Comment 12	3.03	242
3-305	1.03	67
3-305	3.03	
3-305	3.04	
3-305	3.04	412
3-305	3.04	425
3-305	5.01	5
3-305	6.01	14
3-305	6.01	15
3-305	6.03	169
3-305	9.03	
3-305(1)	3.03	
3-305(1)	3.03	357

614 TABLE OF STATUTES

UNIFORM COMMERCIAL CODE

Sec.	This Work Par.	Note
3–305(1)	3.04	402
3–305(1)	3.04	410
3–305(2)	3.03	
3–305(2)	3.03	207
3–305(2)	3.03	214
3–305(2)	3.04	396
3–305(2)	3.04	410
3–305(2)(e)	3.03	286
3–305(2)(e)	6.02	68
3–305(a)	3.03	197
3–305(a)	6.01	10
3–305(a)(1)	1.04	
3–305(a)(1)	3.02	
3–305(a)(1)	3.03	333
3–305(a)(1)	6.01	16
3–305(a)(1)	6.01	22
3–305(a)(1)	6.01	23
3–305(a)(1)(i)	6.02	41
3–305(a)(1)(ii)	6.02	41
3–305(a)(1)(ii)	6.02	47
3–305(a)(1)(ii)	6.02	50
3–305(a)(1)(ii)	6.03	109
3–305(a)(1)(ii)	7.03	108
3–305(a)(1)(iii)	6.02	58
3–305(a)(1)(iii)	6.03	108
3–305(a)(1)(iv)	3.03	334
3–305(a)(1)(iv)	6.01	15
3–305(a)(1)(iv)	6.02	66
3–305(a)(1)(iv)	6.03	174
3–305(a)(2)	3.01	2
3–305(a)(2)	3.03	191
3–305(a)(2)	3.03	337
3–305(a)(2)	6.03	
3–305(a)(2)	6.03	88
3–305(a)(2)	7.03	109
3–305(a)(3)	3.03	191
3–305(a)(3)	3.03	337
3–305(a)(3)	3.03	340
3–305(a)(3)	3.03	349
3–305(a)(3)	6.03	91
3–305(a)(3)	6.03	95
3–305(b)	1.03	141
3–305(b)	2.01	
3–305(b)	3.02	159
3–305(b)	3.03	193
3–305(b)	3.03	197
3–305(b)	3.03	209
3–305(b)	4.03	139
3–305(b)	4.04	173
3–305(b)	6.01	10
3–305(b)	6.01	13
3–305(b)	6.02	41
3–305(b)	6.02	47
3–305(b)	6.02	50
3–305(b)	6.02	58
3–305(b)	6.02	66
3–305(b)	6.03	
3–305(b)	9.01	
3–305(c)	3.03	197
3–305(c)	3.03	323
3–305(c)	3.03	359
3–305(c)	3.03	360

UNIFORM COMMERCIAL CODE

Sec.	This Work Par.	Note
3–305(c)	3.03	361
3–305(c)	3.03	363
3–305(c)	3.03	369
3–305(c)	4.04	
3–305(c)	4.04	182
3–305(c)	6.03	
3–305(c)	6.03	101
3–305(c)	6.03	224
3–305(c)	8.02	
3–305(c)	8.02	132
3–305(c)	8.02	169
3–305(c)	9.01	
3–305(c)	9.01	69
3–305(c)	9.01	70
3–305(d)	3.03	197
3–305(d)	3.03	362
3–305(d)	5.01	5
3–305(d)	5.02	50
3–305(d)	6.03	88
3–305(d)	6.03	98
3–305(d)	6.03	102
3–305(d)	9.01	
3–305(d)	9.01	70
3–305(e)	1.04	212
3–305(e)	2.02	10
3–305(e)	2.02	81
3–305(e)	2.02	93
3–305(e)	3.04	425
3–305(f)	1.04	212
3–305(f)	2.02	81
3–305(f)	2.02	93
3–305(f)	3.04	424
3–305(f)	3.04	425
3–305, Comment 1	6.02	42
3–305, Comment 1	6.02	44
3–305, Comment 1	6.02	46
3–305, Comment 1	6.02	48
3–305, Comment 1	6.02	51
3–305, Comment 1	6.02	59
3–305, Comment 1	6.02	61
3–305, Comment 1	6.03	108
3–305, Comment 1	6.03	111
3–305, Comment 2	3.03	206
3–305, Comment 2	3.03	208
3–305, Comment 2	3.03	209
3–305, Comment 2	3.03	337
3–305, Comment 2	6.03	88
3–305, Comment 2	6.03	143
3–305, Comment 2	6.03	146
3–305, Comment 2	6.03	148
3–305, Comment 2	6.03	153
3–305, Comment 3	3.03	209
3–305, Comment 3	3.03	348
3–305, Comment 3	3.03	350
3–305, Comment 3	3.03	358
3–305, Comment 3	6.01	14
3–305, Comment 3	6.03	91
3–305, Comment 3	6.03	169
3–305, Comment 3	6.03	170
3–305, Comment 4	3.03	358
3–305, Comment 4	6.03	99
3–305, Comment 5	3.03	362

TABLE OF STATUTES

UNIFORM COMMERCIAL CODE

Sec.	Par.	This Work Note
3–305, Comment 8	6.02	67
3–305, Comment 9	6.02	70
3–306	1.03	67
3–306	3.02	
3–306	3.02	159
3–306	3.02	178
3–306	3.03	193
3–306	3.03	197
3–306	3.03	216
3–306	3.03	331
3–306	3.03	336
3–306	3.03	355
3–306	3.03	357
3–306	3.03	363
3–306	4.04	173
3–306	6.01	13
3–306	6.01	14
3–306	6.01	15
3–306	6.03	92
3–306	6.03	95
3–306	6.03	154
3–306	9.03	
3–306(a)	3.03	357
3–306(c)	6.03	
3–306(d)	3.03	361
3–306(d)	4.04	180
3–306(d)	6.03	
3–306(d)	6.03	102
3–306(d)	6.03	105
3–306(d)	9.01	
3–306(d)	9.01	69
3–306(d)	9.01	70
3–306, Comment	3.03	358
3–306, Comment	6.03	95
3–306, Comment 4	6.03	148
3–306, Comment 5	6.03	96
3–307	1.02	46
3–307	1.03	
3–307	2.02	
3–307	3.01	32
3–307	3.02	146
3–307	3.03	
3–307	3.03	284
3–307	4.02	14
3–307	6.03	
3–307	6.03	154
3–307	7.02	92
3–307	7.03	139
3–307	9.03	
3–307	9.05	291
3–307(1)(b)	3.02	74
3–307(a)	3.03	295
3–307(b)	3.03	
3–307(b)	3.03	293
3–307(b)	3.03	296
3–307(b)(2)	3.03	295
3–307(b)(2)(iii)	3.03	295
3–307(b)(3)	3.03	297
3–307(b)(4)	3.03	209
3–307(b)(4)	3.03	303
3–307(b)(4)	3.04	406
3–307(b)(4)	7.02	92

UNIFORM COMMERCIAL CODE

Sec.	Par.	This Work Note
3–307, Comment 2	3.03	
3–307, Comment 2	3.03	303
3–307, Comments 2—5	3.03	247
3–307, Comment 3	3.03	295
3–307, Comment 5	3.03	
3–307, Comment 5	3.03	209
3–307, Comment 5	3.03	303
3–308	1.03	62
3–308	2.02	47
3–308	3.01	32
3–308	3.03	324
3–308	6.03	
3–308	7.02	92
3–308	9.01	
3–308	9.01	64
3–308	9.03	
3–308(a)	2.02	53
3–308(a)	2.02	55
3–308(a)	3.02	74
3–308(a)	3.03	323
3–308(a)	5.03	77
3–308(a)	5.03	78
3–308(a)	6.01	3
3–308(b)	2.02	58
3–308(b)	3.01	19
3–308(b)	3.01	40
3–308(b)	3.01	46
3–308(b)	3.01	47
3–308(b)	3.03	201
3–308(b)	3.03	323
3–308(b)	4.03	138
3–308(b)	6.01	2
3–308(b)	6.01	6
3–308(b)	6.01	11
3–308(b)	6.01	20
3–308, Comment 1	3.03	323
3–308, Comment 2	3.03	202
3–309	1.03	155
3–309	3.01	
3–309	3.01	19
3–309	7.01	14
3–309	7.01	26
3–309	7.03	133
3–309	8.02	187
3–309	9.01	
3–309	9.01	68
3–309	9.02	107
3–309	9.03	
3–309	11.03	108
3–309(a)	3.01	18
3–309(a)	3.01	19
3–309(a)	7.01	14
3–309(a)(1)(b)	3.01	19
3–309(a)(i)	7.01	14
3–309(a)(i)	9.03	236
3–309(a)(iii)	7.01	14
3–309, Comments	3.01	19
3–309, Comment 2	3.01	19
3–309, Comment 3	3.01	19
3–309, Comment 3	7.01	14
3–309(b)	3.01	19
3–310	2.01	

615

UNIFORM COMMERCIAL CODE

Sec.	This Work Par.	Note
3–310	4.02	7
3–310	6.03	288
3–310	7.02	56
3–310	7.03	133
3–310	8.02	
3–310	8.02	129
3–310	8.02	132
3–310	8.02	169
3–310	8.03	225
3–310	8.03	229
3–310	9.02	107
3–310	9.03	
3–310	10.02	15
3–310	10.07	122
3–310(a)	7.01	4
3–310(a)	7.01	25
3–310(a)	9.01	58
3–310(a)	9.01	72
3–310(b)	1.04	206
3–310(b)	4.04	145
3–310(b)	7.01	3
3–310(b)	7.01	4
3–310(b)	7.01	17
3–310(b)	7.01	20
3–310(b)(1)	7.01	17
3–310(b)(2)	7.01	17
3–310(b)(3)	7.01	13
3–310(b)(3)	7.01	14
3–310(b)(3)	7.01	17
3–310(b)(3)	7.03	133
3–310(b)(4)	7.01	13
3–310(b)(4)	7.01	14
3–310(b)(4)	7.03	133
3–310(b)(4)	9.03	
3–310(c)(i)	7.01	4
3–310(c)(i)	7.01	25
3–310(c)(ii)	7.01	4
3–310(c)(ii)	7.01	17
3–310(c)(ii)	7.01	20
3–310, Comment 3	7.01	13
3–310, Comment 3	7.01	14
3–310, Comment 3	7.01	17
3–310, Comment 4	7.01	14
3–310, Comment 4	7.03	133
3–311	2.02	112
3–311	7.01	42
3–311	9.01	
3–311(a)	7.01	41
3–311(b)	7.01	41
3–311(b)	9.01	9
3–311(c)(1)	7.01	42
3–311(c)(1)	9.01	10
3–311(c)(2)	7.01	43
3–311(c)(2)	9.01	10
3–311(d)	7.01	42
3–311(d)	7.01	43
3–311, Comment 1	7.01	
3–311, Comment 3	7.01	
3–311, Comment 4	3.03	
3–311, Comment 4	7.01	32
3–312	2.02	
3–312	3.01	19

UNIFORM COMMERCIAL CODE

Sec.	This Work Par.	Note
3–312	7.01	26
3–312	7.03	134
3–312	8.01	61
3–312	9.01	
3–312	9.01	68
3–312	11.03	108
3–312(a)(3)	9.01	
3–312(b)	9.01	
3–312(b)(1)	9.01	
3–312(b)(2)	9.01	
3–312(b)(4)	9.01	
3–312(c)	9.01	
3–312(d)	9.01	
Art. 3, Pt. 4	8.02	
Art. 3, Pt. 4	9.05	
Art. 3, Pt. 4	9.05	291
3–401	3.03	190
3–401(a)	1.02	35
3–401(a)	2.02	39
3–401(a)	3.03	190
3–401(a)	4.02	1
3–401(a)	4.04	143
3–401(a)	5.01	12
3–401(a)	5.03	70
3–401(a)	6.01	1
3–401(a)	6.01	21
3–401(a)	6.02	72
3–401(a)	7.03	110
3–401(a)(ii)	2.02	39
3–401(a)(ii)	4.02	2
3–401(a)(ii)	6.02	72
3–401(b)	2.02	41
3–401(b)	4.02	2
3–401, Comment 2	4.02	2
3–402	2.01	
3–402	4.02	10
3–402	5.03	84
3–402(a)	2.02	39
3–402(a)	5.01	12
3–402(a)	5.03	72
3–402(a)	5.03	84
3–402(a)	7.03	110
3–402(b)(1)	5.01	11
3–402(b)(1)	5.03	79
3–402(b)(2)	2.02	169
3–402(b)(2)	5.01	13
3–402(b)(2)	5.03	79
3–402(b)(2)	5.03	83
3–402(b)(2)	5.03	84
3–402(b)(2)	5.03	85
3–402(b)(2)	5.03	86
3–402(b)(2)	5.03	95
3–402(b)(2)	5.03	100
3–402(b)(2)	5.03	109
3–402(c)	5.03	93
3–402, Comment	4.06	213
3–402, Comment 1	2.02	39
3–402, Comment 1	4.02	2
3–402, Comment 2	5.03	79
3–402, Comment 2	5.03	80
3–402, Comment 2	5.03	82
3–402, Comment 2	5.03	84

TABLE OF STATUTES

UNIFORM COMMERCIAL CODE

Sec.	Par.	Note
3–402, Comment 2	5.03	92
3–402, Comment 2	5.03	94
3–402, Comment 2	5.03	106
3–403	1.02	46
3–403	4.02	13
3–403	6.01	1
3–403	9.05	
3–403	11.03	117
3–403(a)	3.02	
3–403(a)	3.02	87
3–403(a)	3.03	333
3–403(a)	4.02	4
3–403(a)	4.02	11
3–403(a)	4.02	13
3–403(a)	4.02	35
3–403(a)	5.01	13
3–403(a)	5.03	69
3–403(a)	5.03	71
3–403(a)	6.01	21
3–403(a)	6.02	71
3–403(a)	6.02	73
3–403(a)	6.03	104
3–403(a)	7.03	110
3–403(a)	9.03	164
3–403(b)	5.03	68
3–403(b)	9.03	
3–403(b)	9.03	163
3–403(b)	9.03	164
3–403(b)	9.03	167
3–403(c)	4.02	38
3–403(c)	4.02	39
3–403(c)	7.03	162
3–403, Comment 1	4.02	11
3–403, Comment 1	5.03	68
3–403, Comment 1	5.03	76
3–403, Comment 2	4.02	2
3–403, Comment 3	4.02	37
3–403, Comment 3	5.03	82
3–404	1.03	74
3–404	2.02	240
3–404	3.02	108
3–404	3.02	167
3–404	3.03	380
3–404	4.02	
3–404	4.02	16
3–404	4.02	18
3–404	7.02	92
3–404	7.02	98
3–404	7.03	
3–404	7.03	114
3–404	7.03	182
3–404	8.03	195
3–404	8.03	227
3–404	8.04	483
3–404	9.02	111
3–404	9.03	187
3–404	9.03	189
3–404	9.03	194
3–404	9.03	195
3–404	9.05	
3–404	9.05	273
3–404	9.05	291

UNIFORM COMMERCIAL CODE

Sec.	Par.	Note
3–404	9.05	310
3–404	11.02	75
3–404—3–406	7.02	67
3–404—3–406	9.03	
3–404—3–406	11.03	118
3–404(1)	4.02	11
3–404(1)	4.02	13
3–404(1)	4.02	18
3–404(a)	7.03	155
3–404(a)	7.03	156
3–404(a)	7.03	164
3–404(b)	2.02	242
3–404(b)	2.02	264
3–404(b)	7.02	95
3–404(b)	7.03	158
3–404(b)	7.03	169
3–404(b)	8.03	227
3–404(b)	9.01	4
3–404(b)	9.02	111
3–404(b)	9.03	189
3–404(b)(i)	7.03	158
3–404(b)(ii)	7.03	158
3–404(c)	7.03	
3–404(c)	7.03	118
3–404(c)	7.03	181
3–404(d)	4.02	25
3–404(d)	7.02	95
3–404(d)	7.03	
3–404(d)	7.03	117
3–404(d)	7.03	118
3–404(d)	7.03	128
3–404(d)	7.03	173
3–404(d)	8.03	227
3–404(d)	8.03	232
3–404(d)	8.04	482
3–404(d)	9.01	4
3–404(d)	9.02	111
3–404(d)	9.03	189
3–404(d)	9.03	195
3–404(d)	9.03	199
3–404, Comments	9.03	186
3–404, Comment 1	7.02	92
3–404, Comment 1	7.03	155
3–404, Comment 1	7.03	173
3–404, Comment 2	4.02	12
3–404, Comment 2	7.02	95
3–404, Comment 2	7.03	123
3–404, Comment 2	7.03	157
3–404, Comment 2	7.03	158
3–404, Comment 2	7.03	164
3–404, Comment 3	7.02	81
3–404, Comment 3	7.02	94
3–404, Comment 3	7.03	120
3–404, Comment 3	7.03	189
3–404, Comment 4	4.02	11
3–404, Comment 4	4.02	13
3–405	1.03	
3–405	1.04	225
3–405	3.02	
3–405	3.02	108
3–405	4.02	16
3–405	7.02	57

617

618   TABLE OF STATUTES

UNIFORM COMMERCIAL CODE

Sec.	Par.	This Work Note
3–405	7.02	92
3–405	7.02	98
3–405	7.03	
3–405	7.03	114
3–405	7.03	139
3–405	7.03	163
3–405	7.03	175
3–405	7.03	176
3–405	7.03	182
3–405	7.03	185
3–405	8.01	46
3–405	8.03	195
3–405	8.03	215
3–405	8.03	227
3–405	8.04	481
3–405	8.04	483
3–405	9.03	
3–405	9.03	124
3–405	9.03	167
3–405	9.03	187
3–405	9.03	188
3–405	9.03	194
3–405	9.05	
3–405	9.05	273
3–405	9.05	310
3–405	11.02	75
3–405(1)	7.03	159
3–405(1)(a)	7.03	156
3–405(1)(a)	7.03	164
3–405(1)(b)	7.03	157
3–405(1)(b)	7.03	158
3–405(1)(b)	7.03	169
3–405(1)(c)	3.02	
3–405(1)(c)	7.03	174
3–405(a)(1)	7.03	176
3–405(a)(3)	4.02	23
3–405(a)(3)	7.03	176
3–405(b)	4.02	25
3–405(b)	6.03	209
3–405(b)	7.03	
3–405(b)	7.03	116
3–405(b)	7.03	117
3–405(b)	7.03	118
3–405(b)	7.03	126
3–405(b)	7.03	128
3–405(b)	7.03	159
3–405(b)	7.03	160
3–405(b)	7.03	174
3–405(b)	7.03	174
3–405(b)	8.03	215
3–405(b)	8.03	232
3–405(b)	8.04	482
3–405(b)	9.01	4
3–405(b)	9.03	124
3–405(b)	9.03	167
3–405(b)	9.03	188
3–405(b)	9.03	195
3–405(b)	9.03	199
3–405(c)	7.03	
3–405(c)	7.03	118
3–405, Comments	9.03	186
3–405, Comment 1	7.03	166

UNIFORM COMMERCIAL CODE

Sec.	Par.	This Work Note
3–405, Comment 2	7.03	124
3–405, Comment 3	7.03	118
3–405, Comment 3	7.03	174
3–405, Comment 3	7.03	175
3–405, Comment 3	7.03	176
3–405, Comment 4	7.03	161
3–405, Comment 4	7.03	174
3–405, Comment 4	7.03	189
3–406	1.03	171
3–406	1.03	173
3–406	3.02	98
3–406	3.03	371
3–406	4.02	
3–406	4.02	11
3–406	4.02	13
3–406	4.02	16
3–406	4.02	20
3–406	4.02	34
3–406	6.02	80
3–406	6.03	106
3–406	6.03	137
3–406	7.02	65
3–406	7.02	92
3–406	7.02	98
3–406	7.02	104
3–406	7.03	
3–406	7.03	114
3–406	7.03	175
3–406	7.03	188
3–406	8.03	215
3–406	8.03	227
3–406	8.03	232
3–406	8.04	401
3–406	8.04	481
3–406	8.04	483
3–406	9.01	4
3–406	9.03	
3–406	9.03	124
3–406	9.03	167
3–406	9.03	184
3–406	9.03	187
3–406	9.03	188
3–406	9.03	190
3–406	9.03	195
3–406	9.05	
3–406	9.05	273
3–406	9.05	310
3–406	11.02	75
3–406(a)	6.02	74
3–406(a)	8.03	215
3–406(a)	9.03	124
3–406(a)	9.03	167
3–406(a)	9.03	188
3–406(b)	4.02	30
3–406(b)	4.02	34
3–406(b)	6.02	
3–406(b)	6.02	74
3–406(b)	7.02	81
3–406(b)	7.03	174
3–406(b)	8.03	232
3–406(b)	8.04	482
3–406(b)	9.03	195

TABLE OF STATUTES

UNIFORM COMMERCIAL CODE

Sec.	Par.	This Work Note
3–406(b)	9.03	199
3–406, Comments	9.03	186
3–406, Comment 1	4.02	16
3–406, Comment 1	4.02	20
3–406, Comment 1	4.02	25
3–406, Comment 1	6.02	81
3–406, Comment 2	4.02	15
3–406, Comment 2	4.02	23
3–406, Comment 2	4.02	29
3–406, Comment 2	6.03	137
3–406, Comment 3	3.02	120
3–406, Comment 3	4.02	12
3–406, Comment 3	4.02	20
3–406, Comment 3	4.02	21
3–406, Comment 3	4.02	23
3–406, Comment 3	6.02	81
3–406, Comment 4	7.03	189
3–406, Comment 7	9.03	190
3–407	1.02	46
3–407	1.03	
3–407	2.01	
3–407	6.02	85
3–407	6.03	137
3–407	7.02	68
3–407	8.03	227
3–407	8.04	401
3–407	9.01	41
3–407	9.02	
3–407	9.02	107
3–407	9.02	109
3–407	9.03	187
3–407	9.05	
3–407(1)	6.02	85
3–407(1)	6.03	
3–407(1)	6.03	115
3–407(1)	9.03	
3–407(1)(a)	6.03	117
3–407(1)(c)	6.03	117
3–407(2)(a)	6.02	85
3–407(2)(b)	6.03	133
3–407(a)	6.02	85
3–407(a)	6.03	115
3–407(a)	9.03	
3–407(a)	9.03	226
3–407(a)(i)	6.03	117
3–407(a)(ii)	6.03	117
3–407(a)(ii)	6.03	130
3–407(b)	6.01	15
3–407(b)	6.02	76
3–407(b)	6.02	78
3–407(b)	6.02	80
3–407(b)	6.02	86
3–407(b)	6.02	87
3–407(b)	6.03	110
3–407(b)	6.03	114
3–407(b)	6.03	126
3–407(b)	6.03	130
3–407(b)	6.03	133
3–407(b)	6.03	134
3–407(c)	2.05	315
3–407(c)	3.03	333
3–407(c)	6.01	15

UNIFORM COMMERCIAL CODE

Sec.	Par.	This Work Note
3–407(c)	6.01	21
3–407(c)	6.02	76
3–407(c)	6.02	87
3–407(c)	6.03	130
3–407(c)(ii)	6.03	134
3–407(c)(ii)	6.03	136
3–407, Comment 1	6.02	85
3–407, Comment 1	6.02	86
3–407, Comment 1	6.02	87
3–407, Comment 1	6.03	114
3–407, Comment 1	6.03	115
3–407, Comment 1	6.03	116
3–407, Comment 2	6.02	87
3–407, Comment 2	6.03	138
3–407, Comment 4	6.03	136
3–407, Comment 4	6.03	137
3–408	1.04	
3–408	4.02	47
3–408	4.04	142
3–408	4.04	144
3–408	4.04	145
3–408	4.04	148
3–408	6.03	160
3–408	7.03	111
3–408	9.01	54
3–408	9.01	81
3–408	9.02	98
3–408	9.06	
3–408	9.06	364
3–408, Comment	4.04	144
3–408, Comment 2	6.03	157
3–408, Comment 3	6.03	165
3–409	4.04	144
3–409	9.01	
3–409—3–414	9.01	
3–409(1)	9.01	81
3–409(2)	4.04	144
3–409(2)	7.03	121
3–409(a)	3.01	2
3–409(a)	3.03	372
3–409(a)	4.04	144
3–409(a)	4.04	150
3–409(a)	4.04	151
3–409(a)	4.04	152
3–409(a)	4.04	158
3–409(a)	8.01	63
3–409(a)	8.02	
3–409(a)	9.01	
3–409(b)	4.04	159
3–409(c)	4.04	157
3–409(c)	4.04	159
3–409(d)	1.01	5
3–409(d)	3.03	372
3–409(d)	4.03	73
3–409(d)	4.03	74
3–409(d)	4.04	155
3–409(d)	8.01	63
3–409(d)	8.02	
3–409(d)	9.01	
3–409, Comment 2	4.04	156
3–410(1)	6.03	294
3–410(a)	4.03	66

UNIFORM COMMERCIAL CODE

Sec.	Par.	This Work Note
3–410(b)	4.03	69
3–410(c)	4.03	66
3–410, Comment 1	4.03	67
3–411	2.04	272
3–411	3.03	208
3–411	4.04	
3–411	4.04	166
3–411	4.04	177
3–411	6.03	218
3–411	7.01	26
3–411	7.02	82
3–411	8.01	61
3–411	8.02	150
3–411	9.01	
3–411	9.01	68
3–411	10.07	106
3–411(1)	9.01	72
3–411(b)	7.01	26
3–411(b)	9.01	
3–411(c)	9.01	
3–411(c)(ii)	7.01	26
3–411(c)(iii)	4.04	181
3–411(c)(iv)	4.04	181
3–411, Comment 1	9.01	55
3–411, Comment 3	9.01	
3–412	1.01	26
3–412	1.03	60
3–412	1.03	61
3–412	3.01	1
3–412	3.03	189
3–412	4.02	43
3–412	4.02	48
3–412	4.03	55
3–412	4.03	70
3–412	4.05	191
3–412	4.05	193
3–412	4.05	199
3–412	6.03	104
3–412	6.03	286
3–412	6.03	294
3–412	8.01	61
3–412	8.02	132
3–412	9.01	
3–412	9.01	54
3–412	9.01	55
3–412	9.01	56
3–412	9.01	57
3–412	9.01	58
3–412	9.01	63
3–412	9.01	64
3–412	9.01	68
3–412	10.02	15
3–412—3–415	3.01	37
3–412—3–415	6.03	196
3–412, Comment 1	4.05	191
3–413	3.01	2
3–413	3.03	189
3–413	4.02	47
3–413	4.03	52
3–413	4.04	148
3–413	4.04	149
3–413	4.04	165

UNIFORM COMMERCIAL CODE

Sec.	Par.	This Work Note
3–413	4.04	187
3–413	4.04	190
3–413	6.03	294
3–413	9.01	
3–413(1)	4.04	
3–413(1)	4.04	187
3–413(2)	4.03	102
3–413(2)	4.03	115
3–413(2)	6.03	298
3–413(3)	3.02	175
3–413(3)	4.04	165
3–413(3)	7.03	158
3–413(a)	4.04	168
3–413(a)	6.03	104
3–413(a)(i)	4.04	
3–413(a)(i)	4.04	149
3–413(a)(i)	4.04	184
3–413(a)(i)	4.04	188
3–413(b)	4.04	
3–413(b)	4.04	149
3–413(b)	4.04	168
3–413, Comment 3	4.03	52
3–414	1.02	46
3–414	3.01	1
3–414	3.03	189
3–414	4.02	43
3–414	4.03	52
3–414	4.04	190
3–414	4.06	206
3–414	6.03	298
3–414	8.03	225
3–414	9.01	57
3–414	9.03	
3–414	11.03	117
3–414(1)	4.06	208
3–414(1)	6.03	298
3–414(2)	4.06	253
3–414(2)	5.02	62
3–414(a)	1.01	26
3–414(a)	1.03	61
3–414(a)	4.03	55
3–414(a)	4.03	118
3–414(a)	4.05	191
3–414(b)	1.03	61
3–414(b)	4.03	52
3–414(b)	4.03	55
3–414(b)	4.03	70
3–414(b)	4.03	71
3–414(b)	4.03	80
3–414(b)	4.03	83
3–414(b)	4.03	103
3–414(b)	4.03	118
3–414(b)	6.03	104
3–414(b)	7.03	133
3–414(b)	9.01	63
3–414(b)	9.03	
3–414(c)	4.03	52
3–414(c)	4.03	102
3–414(c)	4.03	118
3–414(c)	4.04	161
3–414(c)	4.04	163
3–414(c)	7.01	17

TABLE OF STATUTES 621

UNIFORM COMMERCIAL CODE

Sec.	Par.	This Work Note
3–414(c)	7.01	26
3–414(c)	7.01	27
3–414(c)	9.01	72
3–414(d)	4.03	55
3–414(d)	4.03	70
3–414(d)	4.03	83
3–414(d)	4.03	102
3–414(d)	4.03	118
3–414(d)	4.06	203
3–414(d)	4.06	243
3–414(d)	6.03	
3–414(e)	4.03	51
3–414(e)	4.06	237
3–414(f)	2.02	131
3–414(f)	4.03	78
3–414(f)	4.03	84
3–414(f)	4.03	119
3–414(f)	4.03	121
3–414(f)	4.05	199
3–414(f)	4.05	200
3–414(f)	4.06	235
3–414(f)	4.06	236
3–414, Comment 2	4.06	210
3–414, Comment 3	4.03	102
3–414, Comment 3	4.04	161
3–414, Comment 3	4.06	207
3–414, Comment 3	7.01	27
3–414, Comment 4	4.06	254
3–414, Comment 6	4.03	121
3–415	1.02	46
3–415	1.03	66
3–415	2.01	
3–415	3.01	16
3–415	3.03	189
3–415	4.02	45
3–415	4.05	199
3–415	4.06	208
3–415	4.06	253
3–415	5.01	1
3–415	5.01	5
3–415	6.03	298
3–415	8.02	
3–415	8.03	
3–415	8.03	214
3–415	8.03	225
3–415	9.03	
3–415	10.02	15
3–415(3)	5.02	18
3–415(3)	5.02	32
3–415(5)	4.06	257
3–415(5)	6.03	
3–415(5)	6.03	211
3–415(a)	3.02	
3–415(a)	3.02	173
3–415(a)	4.03	83
3–415(a)	4.06	204
3–415(a)	4.06	207
3–415(a)	4.06	208
3–415(a)	4.06	217
3–415(a)	4.06	222
3–415(a)	6.03	104
3–415(a)	6.03	249

UNIFORM COMMERCIAL CODE

Sec.	Par.	This Work Note
3–415(a)	8.03	
3–415(a)	9.03	
3–415(b)	3.02	129
3–415(b)	3.02	173
3–415(b)	4.06	206
3–415(b)	7.02	45
3–415(b)	7.02	54
3–415(c)	4.03	102
3–415(c)	4.03	103
3–415(c)	4.03	106
3–415(c)	4.06	220
3–415(c)	4.06	223
3–415(c)	8.03	
3–415(c)	8.03	229
3–415(d)	4.04	162
3–415(d)	7.01	17
3–415(d)	7.01	26
3–415(d)	9.01	72
3–415(e)	4.03	78
3–415(e)	4.03	84
3–415(e)	4.04	190
3–415(e)	4.05	199
3–415(e)	4.05	200
3–415(e)	4.06	225
3–415(e)	4.06	235
3–415(e)	4.06	239
3–415(e)	4.06	240
3–415, Comment 1	4.06	253
3–415, Comment 1	5.01	5
3–415, Comment 1	5.02	62
3–415, Comment 3	5.02	39
3–415, Comment 4	4.06	238
3–416	1.03	66
3–416	2.01	
3–416	6.03	298
3–416	7.02	45
3–416	7.02	46
3–416	7.02	47
3–416	7.02	53
3–416	7.02	55
3–416	7.02	70
3–416	7.02	77
3–416	7.02	81
3–416	8.02	
3–416	8.02	127
3–416	8.03	195
3–416	8.04	401
3–416	8.04	413
3–416	8.04	415
3–416	8.04	418
3–416	8.04	423
3–416	9.03	
3–416	9.03	216
3–416	9.03	217
3–416(4)	5.02	23
3–416(4)	5.02	23
3–416(5)	4.03	127
3–416(5)	5.02	24
3–416(a)	7.02	48
3–416(a)	7.02	49
3–416(a)	7.02	52
3–416(a)(1)	7.02	65

TABLE OF STATUTES

UNIFORM COMMERCIAL CODE

Sec.	Par.	This Work Note
3–416(a)(2)	7.02	51
3–416(a)(2)	7.02	67
3–416(a)(3)	7.02	68
3–416(a)(4)	3.03	228
3–416(a)(4)	7.02	70
3–416(a)(5)	7.02	71
3–416(a)(6)	3.03	378
3–416(a)(6)	7.02	46
3–416(a)(6)	7.02	67
3–416(b)	7.02	48
3–416(b)	7.02	58
3–416(b)	8.04	430
3–416(b)	9.03	
3–416(c)	7.02	55
3–416(c)	7.02	62
3–416(d)	7.02	61
3–416, Comment	5.02	26
3–416, Comment 1	7.02	49
3–416, Comment 3	7.02	55
3–416, Comment 3	7.02	66
3–416, Comment 3	7.02	70
3–416, Comment 3	7.02	73
3–416, Comment 5	7.02	62
3–416, Comment 5	7.02	63
3–416, Comment 5	7.02	64
3–416, Comment 6	7.02	59
3–416, Comment 6	8.04	430
3–416, Comment 6	8.04	467
3–416, Comment 8	7.02	46
3–416, Comment 8	7.02	81
3–417	3.03	
3–417	3.03	371
3–417	4.04	164
3–417	4.04	185
3–417	7.02	
3–417	7.02	45
3–417	7.02	46
3–417	7.02	50
3–417	7.02	53
3–417	7.02	77
3–417	7.02	81
3–417	7.02	87
3–417	7.02	91
3–417	7.02	102
3–417	7.03	150
3–417	8.02	127
3–417	9.01	42
3–417	9.03	216
3–417	9.03	217
3–417(1)	3.03	371
3–417(1)	7.02	52
3–417(1)(a)	7.02	74
3–417(1)(a)	7.02	88
3–417(1)(b)	7.02	75
3–417(1)(b)	7.02	78
3–417(1)(b)	7.02	79
3–417(1)(b)	7.02	84
3–417(1)(b)(i)	7.02	85
3–417(1)(b)(ii)	7.02	86
3–417(1)(b)(iii)	7.02	87
3–417(1)(c)	7.02	76
3–417(1)(c)	7.02	78

UNIFORM COMMERCIAL CODE

Sec.	Par.	This Work Note
3–417(1)(c)	7.02	89
3–417(1)(c)(i)	7.02	91
3–417(1)(c)(i)	7.02	105
3–417(1)(c)(ii)	7.02	91
3–417(1)(c)(ii)	7.02	105
3–417(1)(c)(iii)	7.02	91
3–417(1)(c)(iv)	7.02	91
3–417(1)(c)(iv)	7.02	105
3–417(2)	7.02	49
3–417(3)	7.02	55
3–417(3)	7.02	70
3–417(4)	7.02	47
3–417(a)	7.02	78
3–417(a)(1)	3.03	377
3–417(a)(1)	3.03	378
3–417(a)(1)	7.02	65
3–417(a)(1)	7.02	88
3–417(a)(1)	7.02	96
3–417(a)(1)	7.02	101
3–417(a)(1)	7.03	123
3–417(a)(2)	3.03	377
3–417(a)(2)	3.03	378
3–417(a)(2)	7.02	
3–417(a)(2)	7.02	68
3–417(a)(2)	7.02	89
3–417(a)(2)	7.02	103
3–417(a)(3)	3.03	378
3–417(a)(3)	7.02	51
3–417(a)(3)	7.02	67
3–417(a)(3)	7.02	79
3–417(a)(4)	7.02	46
3–417(a)(4)	7.02	67
3–417(a)(4)	7.02	78
3–417(b)	7.02	58
3–417(b)	7.02	65
3–417(b)	7.02	96
3–417(b)	7.02	104
3–417(c)	7.02	98
3–417(c)	7.02	104
3–417(c)	9.03	
3–417(c)	9.03	190
3–417(c)	9.03	193
3–417(d)	4.04	186
3–417(d)	7.02	
3–417(d)	7.02	78
3–417(d)	7.02	96
3–417(d)	7.02	101
3–417(d)(1)	7.02	102
3–417(d)(2)	7.02	58
3–417(e)	7.02	55
3–417(e)	7.02	62
3–417(f)	7.02	61
3–417, Comment 1	7.02	
3–417, Comment 1	7.02	57
3–417, Comment 1	7.02	60
3–417, Comment 1	7.02	63
3–417, Comment 2	7.02	79
3–417, Comment 2	7.02	93
3–417, Comment 2	7.02	102
3–417, Comment 2	7.03	150
3–417, Comment 3	7.02	81
3–417, Comment 4	4.04	186

TABLE OF STATUTES

UNIFORM COMMERCIAL CODE

Sec.	Par.	This Work Note
3–417, Comment 4	7.02	81
3–417, Comment 4	7.02	84
3–417, Comment 4	7.02	87
3–417, Comment 4	7.02	91
3–417, Comment 5	7.02	59
3–417, Comment 5	7.02	65
3–417, Comment 5	9.01	46
3–417, Comment 7	7.02	62
3–418	1.03	
3–418	1.04	232
3–418	3.03	
3–418	3.03	208
3–418	3.03	324
3–418	3.03	378
3–418	4.04	159
3–418	4.04	164
3–418	4.04	165
3–418	4.04	168
3–418	4.04	176
3–418	4.04	185
3–418	7.01	26
3–418	7.02	
3–418	7.02	82
3–418	7.02	96
3–418	8.02	
3–418	8.02	113
3–418	8.02	114
3–418	8.02	129
3–418	8.02	131
3–418	8.02	132
3–418	8.02	150
3–418	8.02	154
3–418	8.02	156
3–418	8.02	169
3–418	8.02	171
3–418	8.04	319
3–418	9.01	31
3–418	9.01	69
3–418	9.03	
3–418	11.03	106
3–418(a)	3.03	
3–418(a)	4.04	173
3–418(a)	8.02	
3–418(a)(i)	7.02	104
3–418(a)(ii)	7.02	83
3–418(b)	3.03	
3–418(b)	3.03	385
3–418(b)	3.03	387
3–418(b)	8.02	
3–418(c)	3.03	201
3–418(c)	3.03	370
3–418(c)	3.03	373
3–418(c)	4.04	186
3–418(c)	8.02	
3–418(c)	8.02	111
3–418(c)	8.02	132
3–418(c)	8.02	169
3–418(c)	8.02	171
3–418(d)	3.01	23
3–418(d)	3.02	67
3–418(d)	3.03	370
3–418(d)	8.02	

UNIFORM COMMERCIAL CODE

Sec.	Par.	This Work Note
3–418(d)	9.03	
3–418, Comment 1	3.03	
3–418, Comment 1	3.03	374
3–418, Comment 1	3.03	383
3–418, Comment 1	7.02	81
3–418, Comment 1	8.02	113
3–418, Comment 2	3.03	374
3–418, Comment 2	3.03	381
3–418, Comment 2	4.04	173
3–418, Comment 2	8.02	
3–418, Comment 2	8.02	129
3–418, Comment 3	3.03	382
3–419	1.04	
3–419	2.01	
3–419	2.02	105
3–419	3.01	16
3–419	3.03	189
3–419	5.01	1
3–419	5.01	5
3–419	5.03	79
3–419	7.02	92
3–419	7.03	139
3–419	8.03	232
3–419	9.02	100
3–419(1)(a)	7.03	131
3–419(1)(b)	7.03	131
3–419(2)	7.03	132
3–419(3)	4.02	34
3–419(3)	7.03	
3–419(3)	7.03	137
3–419(a)	5.01	1
3–419(a)	5.02	14
3–419(a)	5.02	36
3–419(b)	4.03	127
3–419(b)	5.01	6
3–419(b)	5.02	17
3–419(b)	5.02	20
3–419(b)	5.02	25
3–419(b)	5.02	37
3–419(b)	5.02	38
3–419(b)	5.02	41
3–419(b)	5.02	42
3–419(b)	5.02	43
3–419(b)	5.02	52
3–419(b)	6.03	154
3–419(b)	6.03	156
3–419(b)	6.03	160
3–419(b)	6.03	162
3–419(b)	6.03	173
3–419(c)	3.02	126
3–419(c)	4.03	127
3–419(c)	5.01	4
3–419(c)	5.02	19
3–419(c)	5.02	23
3–419(c)	5.02	28
3–419(c)	5.02	29
3–419(c)	5.02	32
3–419(c)	5.02	56
3–419(c)	5.03	
3–419(d)	4.06	204
3–419(d)	4.06	253
3–419(d)	5.01	4

TABLE OF STATUTES

UNIFORM COMMERCIAL CODE		
Sec.	This Work Par.	Note
3–419(d)	5.02	19
3–419(d)	5.02	21
3–419(d)	5.02	22
3–419(d)	5.02	46
3–419(e)	5.01	4
3–419(e)	6.03	178
3–419(f)	4.06	204
3–419(f)	4.06	253
3–419(f)	4.06	255
3–419(f)	4.06	257
3–419(e)	5.02	19
3–419(e)	5.02	20
3–419(e)	5.02	22
3–419(e)	5.02	48
3–419(f)	5.02	51
3–419(f)	5.02	57
3–419(f)	5.02	58
3–419(f)	5.02	59
3–419(f)	6.03	
3–419(f)	6.03	178
3–419(f)	6.03	190
3–419(f)	6.03	210
3–419(f)	6.03	238
3–419, Comment 1	5.01	1
3–419, Comment 1	5.02	36
3–419, Comment 2	5.02	37
3–419, Comment 2	6.03	160
3–419, Comment 2	6.03	173
3–419, Comment 2	7.02	44
3–419, Comment 2	7.03	131
3–419, Comment 2	7.03	132
3–419, Comment 3	7.03	131
3–419, Comment 4	5.01	4
3–419, Comment 4	5.02	25
3–419, Comment 4	7.03	132
3–419, Comment 5	5.02	59
3–420	7.02	92
3–420	7.03	123
3–420	7.03	131
3–420	8.01	46
3–420	8.02	94
3–420	8.03	215
3–420	8.03	227
3–420	9.02	100
3–420	9.02	107
3–420	9.02	111
3–420	9.03	
3–420	9.03	124
3–420	9.03	167
3–420	9.03	188
3–420	9.03	189
3–420	9.05	291
3–420(a)	1.04	226
3–420(a)	1.04	227
3–420(a)	3.01	8
3–420(a)	7.03	130
3–420(a)	7.03	131
3–420(a)	7.03	134
3–420(a)	8.03	227
3–420(a)	9.02	111
3–420(a)	9.03	189
3–420(a)(i)	7.03	123

UNIFORM COMMERCIAL CODE		
Sec.	This Work Par.	Note
3–420(a)(i)	7.03	128
3–420(a)(i)	7.03	147
3–420(a)(i)	7.03	151
3–420(a)(ii)	7.03	134
3–420(b)	7.03	132
3–420(b)	8.02	95
3–420(c)	7.03	
3–420(c)	7.03	138
3–420(c)	8.03	232
3–420, Comment 1	3.01	2
3–420, Comment 1	3.01	8
3–420, Comment 1	3.01	12
3–420, Comment 1	4.04	151
3–420, Comment 1	7.02	79
3–420, Comment 1	7.03	128
3–420, Comment 1	7.03	131
3–420, Comment 1	7.03	134
3–420, Comment 1	7.03	151
3–420, Comment 2	7.03	132
3–420, Comment 3	7.03	138
3–420, Comment 3	7.03	144
Art. 3, Pt. 5	2.02	103
Art. 3, Pt. 5	4.03	101
Art. 3, Pt. 5	4.05	200
Art. 3, Pt. 5	8.02	
Art. 3, Pt. 5	8.02	90
Art. 3, Pt. 5	9.01	63
Art. 3, Pt. 5	9.03	
3–501	4.06	226
3–501	8.02	137
3–501	8.03	225
3–501	8.04	380
3–501	8.04	433
3–501	9.06	351
3–501(1)(a)	4.06	222
3–501(1)(c)	4.05	199
3–501(2)(b)	4.03	102
3–501(2)(b)	4.03	106
3–501(3)	4.03	115
3–501(3)	4.06	224
3–501(4)	4.06	225
3–501(a)	4.03	56
3–501(a)	4.03	94
3–501(a)	4.04	190
3–501(a)	4.05	199
3–501(a)	8.02	144
3–501(b)	4.03	75
3–501(b)(1)	4.03	87
3–501(b)(1)	4.03	88
3–501(b)(1)	4.03	89
3–501(b)(1)	4.03	91
3–501(b)(1)	4.03	92
3–501(b)(1)	4.03	93
3–501(b)(1)	4.03	94
3–501(b)(1)	4.03	95
3–501(b)(1)	8.04	435
3–501(b)(1)	9.03	
3–501(b)(2)	4.03	97
3–501(b)(2)	9.02	107
3–501(b)(2)	9.05	295
3–501(b)(3)	4.03	97
3–501(b)(3)	9.02	107

TABLE OF STATUTES 625

UNIFORM COMMERCIAL CODE		
Sec.	This Work Par.	Note
3–501(b)(3)(i)	3.01	34
3–501(b)(3)(i)	4.03	63
3–501(b)(4)	4.03	79
3–501(b)(4)	4.03	99
3–501, Comment	4.03	97
3–501, Comment	4.03	98
3–501, Comment	4.03	101
3–501, Comment 4	4.05	198
3–501, Comment 6	4.03	115
3–501, Comment 6	4.03	124
3–502	4.03	
3–502	4.03	60
3–502	4.03	81
3–502	4.03	82
3–502	4.03	101
3–502	4.06	218
3–502	4.06	222
3–502	4.06	225
3–502	4.06	228
3–502	8.02	156
3–502	8.03	214
3–502	8.03	229
3–502	9.06	351
3–502(1)	6.03	300
3–502(1)(a)	7.01	17
3–502(1)(b)	4.03	106
3–502(a)	1.01	17
3–502(a)	4.03	77
3–502(a)	4.05	195
3–502(a)	4.05	199
3–502(a)(1)	4.03	60
3–502(a)(2)	4.03	60
3–502(a)(3)	4.03	60
3–502(b)	1.01	17
3–502(b)	4.03	55
3–502(b)	4.03	60
3–502(b)	4.03	71
3–502(b)	4.03	74
3–502(b)	4.03	77
3–502(b)	8.02	185
3–502(b)(1)	4.03	101
3–502(b)(1)	8.02	
3–502(b)(3)	4.03	72
3–502(b)(4)	4.03	72
3–502(c)	1.01	17
3–502(c)	4.03	60
3–502(c)	4.03	77
3–502(c)	4.03	100
3–502(d)	4.03	55
3–502(d)	4.03	60
3–502(d)	4.03	77
3–502(d)	4.04	190
3–502(e)	4.03	62
3–502(e)	4.03	77
3–502(e)	4.06	219
3–502(e)	7.01	14
3–502(e)	7.03	133
3–502(f)	4.03	77
3–502(f)	4.03	100
3–502(f)	4.03	137
3–502, Comments	4.03	60
3–502, Comment 2	4.03	76

UNIFORM COMMERCIAL CODE		
Sec.	This Work Par.	Note
3–502, Comment 2	4.05	194
3–502, Comment 2	4.05	197
3–502, Comment 2	4.06	244
3–502, Comment 3	4.03	76
3–502, Comment 4	4.03	72
3–502, Comment 4	7.01	19
3–502, Comment 4	8.02	126
3–502, Comment 4	8.02	151
3–502, Comment 4	8.02	156
3–502, Comment 4	8.02	171
3–503	4.03	
3–503	4.03	111
3–503	4.06	243
3–503	8.02	
3–503	8.02	185
3–503	8.03	
3–503	8.03	214
3–503	8.03	229
3–503(2)	1.01	17
3–503(2)	6.03	300
3–503(a)	4.03	102
3–503(a)	4.03	103
3–503(a)	4.03	104
3–503(a)	4.03	106
3–503(a)	4.03	118
3–503(a)	4.06	220
3–503(a)	4.06	221
3–503(a)	4.06	223
3–503(a)	4.06	234
3–503(a)	8.03	
3–503(b)	4.03	104
3–503(b)	4.03	107
3–503(b)	4.03	108
3–503(b)	4.03	109
3–503(b)	4.03	111
3–503(b)	4.03	114
3–503(b)	4.06	229
3–503(b)	4.06	230
3–503(b)	8.02	183
3–503(b)	8.02	186
3–503(b)	8.03	210
3–503(b)	10.07	109
3–503(c)	4.03	118
3–503(c)	4.06	229
3–503(c)	4.06	234
3–503(c)	4.06	242
3–503(c)	8.01	52
3–503(c)	8.02	
3–503(c)	8.03	
3–503(c)	8.03	194
3–503(c)(i)	4.03	105
3–503(c)(i)	4.06	231
3–503(c)(ii)	4.03	106
3–503(c)(ii)	4.06	231
3–503(d)(ii)	8.01	52
3–504	4.03	
3–504	4.03	61
3–504	4.03	64
3–504	4.03	128
3–504	4.03	132
3–504	4.05	
3–504	4.06	247

UNIFORM COMMERCIAL CODE

Sec.	Par.	This Work Note
3–504	4.06	249
3–504	8.02	
3–504	8.03	214
3–504	8.03	225
3–504	8.03	229
3–504(2)(c)	4.03	127
3–504(a)	7.01	9
3–504(a)	8.02	
3–504(a)(i)	4.03	136
3–504(a)(i)	7.01	14
3–504(a)(i)	7.03	133
3–504(a)(ii)	4.03	133
3–504(a)(ii)	4.03	134
3–504(a)(iii)	4.03	134
3–504(a)(iv)	4.03	131
3–504(a)(iv)	4.03	133
3–504(a)(iv)	4.05	201
3–504(a)(iv)	4.06	248
3–504(a)(iv)	4.06	251
3–504(a)(v)	4.03	133
3–504(b)	4.03	132
3–504(b)	4.03	133
3–504(b)	4.03	136
3–504(b)(i)	4.03	134
3–504(b)(ii)	4.03	131
3–504(b)(ii)	4.05	201
3–504(b)(ii)	4.06	248
3–504(c)	4.03	130
3–504(c)	8.02	
3–504, Comment	4.03	128
3–505	4.03	123
3–505(2)	4.03	98
3–505(a)	4.06	246
3–505(a)(1)	4.03	124
3–505(a)(2)	4.03	110
3–505(a)(2)	4.03	114
3–505(a)(2)	4.03	125
3–505(a)(3)	4.03	126
3–505(b)	4.03	116
3–505, Comment	4.03	115
3–505, Comment	4.03	132
3–505, Comment	4.06	220
3–505, Comment 2	4.03	96
3–508(1)	4.03	102
3–508(1)	4.03	104
3–508(2)	4.06	242
3–508(3)	4.03	111
3–508(4)	4.03	111
3–508(6)	4.03	104
3–508(7)	4.03	104
3–508, Comment 2	4.06	232
3–509(4)	4.03	117
3–510	4.03	125
3–510, Comment 2	4.03	125
3–511	8.02	
3–511(1)	4.03	128
3–511(2)(b)	4.06	251
3–511(2)(b)	7.01	9
3–511(2)(b)	8.02	
3–511(2)(c)	8.02	
3–511(4)	8.02	
3–511(6)	4.03	132

UNIFORM COMMERCIAL CODE

Sec.	Par.	This Work Note
3–511(6)	4.06	249
3–511(6)	6.03	281
3–511, Comment 2	4.03	129
Art. 3, Pt. 6	1.02	46
Art. 3, Pt. 6	3.01	41
Art. 3, Pt. 6	10.07	122
3–601	6.03	197
3–601	8.02	
3–601	9.03	
3–601(1)	6.03	175
3–601(3)	6.03	
3–601(3)	6.03	183
3–601(3)(a)	6.03	190
3–601(a)	6.03	175
3–601(a)	6.03	176
3–601(a)	6.03	200
3–601(a)	6.03	246
3–601(b)	3.02	183
3–601(b)	3.03	286
3–601(b)	3.03	334
3–601(b)	6.01	15
3–601(b)	6.02	69
3–601(b)	6.03	107
3–601(b)	6.03	174
3–601(b)	6.03	205
3–601(b)	6.03	233
3–601, Comment	3.03	334
3–601, Comment	6.03	186
3–601, Comment 2	6.03	182
3–602	1.03	85
3–602	3.01	50
3–602	3.02	146
3–602	3.03	
3–602	3.03	286
3–602	3.03	364
3–602	3.04	412
3–602	4.04	183
3–602	6.02	
3–602	6.03	210
3–602	6.03	224
3–602	7.02	66
3–602	8.02	
3–602	9.01	
3–602	9.01	50
3–602	9.03	
3–602(a)	3.01	48
3–602(a)	3.03	363
3–602(a)	4.04	183
3–602(a)	6.03	104
3–602(a)	6.03	197
3–602(a)	6.03	200
3–602(a)	6.03	204
3–602(a)	7.03	133
3–602(b)	3.01	48
3–602(b)	10.08	140
3–602(b)(1)	3.01	50
3–602(c)	3.01	48
3–602(c)	6.03	216
3–602(c)	6.03	219
3–602(d)	3.01	48
3–602(d)	3.03	334
3–602(d)	6.02	69

TABLE OF STATUTES 627

UNIFORM COMMERCIAL CODE

Sec.	Par.	This Work Note
3–602(e)	7.01	26
3–602(e)(1)	6.03	218
3–602(e)(1)(i)	4.04	
3–602(e)(1)(i)	4.04	183
3–602(e)(1)(ii)	6.03	
3–602(e)(2)	4.04	180
3–602(e)(2)	4.04	183
3–602(e)(2)	6.03	223
3–602(f)	2.02	40
3–602(f)	4.02	2
3–602, Comment	6.02	70
3–602, Comment	6.03	218
3–603	2.04	283
3–603	3.01	50
3–603(1)	6.03	200
3–603(1)	7.03	133
3–603(1)(b)	6.03	224
3–603(2)	3.01	25
3–603(2)	5.02	61
3–603(2)	6.03	
3–603(2)	6.03	210
3–603(2)	6.03	211
3–603(a)	6.03	225
3–603(b)	6.03	225
3–603(c)	6.03	226
3–603(c)	6.03	228
3–603, Comment 3	6.03	215
3–604	6.03	229
3–604	9.03	
3–604(a)	3.02	183
3–604(a)	6.02	
3–604(a)	6.03	229
3–604(a)(i)	6.03	190
3–604(a)(i)	6.03	230
3–604(a)(ii)	6.03	231
3–604(b)	6.03	233
3–604(c)	2.02	40
3–605	2.01	
3–605	2.02	103
3–605	5.02	50
3–605	6.03	
3–605	6.03	88
3–605	6.03	114
3–605	6.03	185
3–605	6.03	197
3–605	6.03	249
3–605	6.03	251
3–605	6.03	256
3–605	6.03	276
3–605	9.03	
3–605(1)(a)	6.03	190
3–605(a)	6.03	
3–605(a)	6.03	178
3–605(a)	6.03	180
3–605(a)	6.03	248
3–605(a)	6.03	253
3–605(a)(3)	6.03	257
3–605(b)	5.01	5
3–605(b)	6.03	
3–605(b)	6.03	114
3–605(b)	6.03	178
3–605(b)	6.03	180

UNIFORM COMMERCIAL CODE

Sec.	Par.	This Work Note
3–605(b)	6.03	185
3–605(b)	6.03	248
3–605(b)	6.03	253
3–605(b)	6.03	255
3–605(b)(2)	6.03	257
3–605(c)	6.03	
3–605(c)	6.03	248
3–605(c)	6.03	252
3–605(c)	6.03	259
3–605(c)	6.03	260
3–605(c)	7.01	26
3–605(d)	6.03	261
3–605(d)	6.03	262
3–605(d)	6.03	263
3–605(d)	6.03	264
3–605(d)	6.03	265
3–605(d)	6.03	266
3–605(d)	6.03	274
3–605(d)	6.03	275
3–605(e)	5.02	32
3–605(e)	6.03	258
3–605(e)—(g)	9.06	392
3–605(f)	6.03	250
3–605(f)	6.03	280
3–605(f)	6.03	281
3–605(g)	6.03	251
3–605(g)(i)	6.03	
3–605(h)	6.03	252
3–605(h)	6.03	257
3–605(h)	6.03	263
3–605(i)	6.03	252
3–605(i)	6.03	257
3–605(i)	6.03	263
3–605, Comment 2	5.02	16
3–605, Comment 2	6.03	248
3–605, Comment 2	6.03	279
3–605, Comment 3	5.02	16
3–605, Comment 3	6.03	178
3–605, Comment 3	6.03	185
3–605, Comment 3	6.03	276
3–605, Comment 4	6.03	178
3–605, Comment 4	6.03	185
3–605, Comment 4	6.03	251
3–605, Comment 4	6.03	252
3–605, Comment 4	6.03	257
3–605, Comment 5	5.02	61
3–605, Comment 5	6.03	251
3–605, Comment 5	6.03	252
3–605, Comment 5	6.03	257
3–605, Comment 6	6.03	190
3–605, Comment 7	6.03	261
3–605, Comment 9	6.03	250
3–605, Comment 9	6.03	281
3–606	1.03	130
3–606	5.01	5
3–606	6.03	178
3–606	6.03	249
3–606	6.03	259
3–606(1)(a)	5.01	5
3–606(1)(a)	6.03	248
3–606(1)(a)	6.03	256
3–606, Comment 3	6.03	252

TABLE OF STATUTES

UNIFORM COMMERCIAL CODE

Sec.	Par.	This Work Note
Art. 3, Pt. 7	4.04	147
3–701(2)	4.04	147
3–701, Comment 2	4.04	147
3–801	2.02	113
3–801	6.03	191
3–801	6.03	192
3–801(1)	6.03	193
3–801(2)	6.03	193
3–801(3)	6.03	194
3–801(4)	6.03	195
3–801, Comment 3	2.02	113
3–802	7.01	9
3–802	7.03	133
3–802(1)	7.01	30
3–802(1)(a)	7.01	30
3–802(1)(a)	9.01	72
3–802(1)(a)	9.04	
3–802(1)(b)	7.01	17
3–802(2)	7.01	7
3–802, Comment 2	7.01	21
3–802, Comment 3	7.01	5
3–802, Comment 3	7.01	10
3–804	1.03	
3–804	3.01	
3–804	7.01	14
3–804	7.03	133
3–805	1.02	
3–805	1.02	44
3–805	1.02	53
3–805	1.03	
3–805	1.03	68
3–805	2.01	17
3–805	2.01	21
3–805	2.01	26
3–805	2.02	238
3–805	3.03	193
3–805, Comment	1.02	46
3–805, Comment	1.03	63
3–805, Comment	1.03	65
3–805, Comment	1.03	70
3–805, Comment	2.01	34
Art. 4	1.01	
Art. 4	1.01	1
Art. 4	1.01	11
Art. 4	1.01	22
Art. 4	1.01	30
Art. 4	1.01	33
Art. 4	1.02	
Art. 4	1.03	
Art. 4	1.03	105
Art. 4	1.03	164
Art. 4	1.04	
Art. 4	1.04	177
Art. 4	1.04	189
Art. 4	1.04	210
Art. 4	1.04	218
Art. 4	2.02	
Art. 4	2.02	64
Art. 4	2.02	172
Art. 4	2.03	268
Art. 4	2.04	289
Art. 4	3.02	156

UNIFORM COMMERCIAL CODE

Sec.	Par.	This Work Note
Art. 4	3.03	
Art. 4	3.03	371
Art. 4	3.04	425
Art. 4	4.02	2
Art. 4	4.03	
Art. 4	4.03	77
Art. 4	4.03	101
Art. 4	4.04	186
Art. 4	5.03	69
Art. 4	7.01	30
Art. 4	7.02	
Art. 4	7.02	45
Art. 4	7.02	46
Art. 4	7.02	51
Art. 4	7.02	77
Art. 4	7.02	90
Art. 4	7.02	104
Art. 4	7.03	
Art. 4	7.03	120
Art. 4	7.03	139
Art. 4	8.01	
Art. 4	8.01	1
Art. 4	8.01	3
Art. 4	8.01	7
Art. 4	8.01	9
Art. 4	8.01	15
Art. 4	8.01	21
Art. 4	8.01	46
Art. 4	8.01	47
Art. 4	8.01	53
Art. 4	8.01	64
Art. 4	8.01	67
Art. 4	8.01	70
Art. 4	8.01	82
Art. 4	8.02	
Art. 4	8.02	96
Art. 4	8.02	99
Art. 4	8.02	100
Art. 4	8.02	108
Art. 4	8.02	113
Art. 4	8.02	114
Art. 4	8.02	115
Art. 4	8.02	119
Art. 4	8.02	145
Art. 4	8.02	147
Art. 4	8.02	164
Art. 4	8.02	174
Art. 4	8.02	177
Art. 4	8.02	179
Art. 4	8.02	181
Art. 4	8.02	185
Art. 4	8.02	187
Art. 4	8.03	
Art. 4	8.03	194
Art. 4	8.03	197
Art. 4	8.03	200
Art. 4	8.03	240
Art. 4	8.03	241
Art. 4	8.03	251
Art. 4	8.03	252
Art. 4	8.04	
Art. 4	8.04	259

TABLE OF STATUTES

UNIFORM COMMERCIAL CODE		
		This Work
Sec.	Par.	Note
Art. 4	8.04	284
Art. 4	8.04	292
Art. 4	8.04	312
Art. 4	8.04	315
Art. 4	8.04	319
Art. 4	8.04	320
Art. 4	8.04	334
Art. 4	8.04	344
Art. 4	8.04	345
Art. 4	8.04	350
Art. 4	8.04	354
Art. 4	8.04	357
Art. 4	8.04	366
Art. 4	8.04	367
Art. 4	8.04	371
Art. 4	8.04	373
Art. 4	8.04	378
Art. 4	8.04	385
Art. 4	8.04	386
Art. 4	8.04	391
Art. 4	8.04	393
Art. 4	8.04	396
Art. 4	8.04	398
Art. 4	8.04	399
Art. 4	8.04	401
Art. 4	8.04	406
Art. 4	8.04	411
Art. 4	8.04	414
Art. 4	8.04	416
Art. 4	8.04	418
Art. 4	8.04	419
Art. 4	8.04	420
Art. 4	8.04	429
Art. 4	8.04	439
Art. 4	8.04	453
Art. 4	8.04	462
Art. 4	8.04	470
Art. 4	8.04	484
Art. 4	8.04	485
Art. 4	8.04	488
Art. 4	8.04	491
Art. 4	8.04	494
Art. 4	8.04	496
Art. 4	8.04	498
Art. 4	8.04	499
Art. 4	8.05	
Art. 4	9.01	
Art. 4	9.01	1
Art. 4	9.01	4
Art. 4	9.01	27
Art. 4	9.01	43
Art. 4	9.01	45
Art. 4	9.01	48
Art. 4	9.01	54
Art. 4	9.01	74
Art. 4	9.01	75
Art. 4	9.01	80
Art. 4	9.01	89
Art. 4	9.02	
Art. 4	9.02	101
Art. 4	9.02	107
Art. 4	9.03	

UNIFORM COMMERCIAL CODE		
		This Work
Sec.	Par.	Note
Art. 4	9.03	117
Art. 4	9.03	124
Art. 4	9.03	132
Art. 4	9.03	144
Art. 4	9.03	152
Art. 4	9.03	161
Art. 4	9.03	163
Art. 4	9.03	184
Art. 4	9.03	191
Art. 4	9.03	193
Art. 4	9.03	204
Art. 4	9.03	205
Art. 4	9.03	213
Art. 4	9.03	223
Art. 4	9.03	227
Art. 4	9.04	
Art. 4	9.04	229
Art. 4	9.04	237
Art. 4	9.04	238
Art. 4	9.05	
Art. 4	9.05	271
Art. 4	9.05	296
Art. 4	9.06	363
Art. 4	9.06	364
Art. 4	10.01	4
Art. 4	10.02	5
Art. 4	10.02	15
Art. 4	10.03	42
Art. 4	10.03	47
Art. 4	10.04	65
Art. 4	10.07	
Art. 4	10.07	91
Art. 4	10.07	99
Art. 4	10.07	108
Art. 4	10.07	113
Art. 4	10.08	
Art. 4	10.08	135
Art. 4	10.08	137
Art. 4	10.08	145
Art. 4	10.08	147
Art. 4	10.11	
Art. 4	10.11	231
Art. 4	10.11	233
Art. 4	11.01	
Art. 4	11.01	4
Art. 4	11.01	14
Art. 4	11.03	
Art. 4	11.03	110
Art. 4	11.03	125
Art. 4	11.03	127
Art. 4	11.03	
4–101	8.01	
4–101, Comment 2	9.03	144
4–101, Comment 3	8.01	14
4–101, Comment 3	8.01	16
4–101, Comment 3	8.01	17
4–101, Comment 3	8.01	69
4–101, Comment 3	9.03	213
4–102	9.01	
4–102(a)	1.04	179
4–102(a)	3.01	32
4–102(a)	4.03	

629

UNIFORM COMMERCIAL CODE

Sec.	This Work Par.	Note
4-102(a)	8.01	7
4-102(a)	8.02	94
4-102(a)	9.03	
4-102(b)	1.03	105
4-102(b)	8.01	
4-102(b)	8.01	19
4-102, Comment 1	8.01	7
4-102, Comment 1	8.01	12
4-102, Comment 1	8.01	15
4-102, Comment 1	8.01	39
4-102, Comment 1	8.01	47
4-102, Comment 1	8.02	108
4-102, Comment 1	8.02	119
4-102, Comment 1	8.04	258
4-102, Comment 1	8.04	313
4-102, Comment 2	8.01	
4-102, Comment 2	8.01	20
4-102, Comment 2	8.01	21
4-102, Comment 2	8.01	22
4-102, Comment 2	8.01	23
4-102, Comment 2	8.01	24
4-103	8.01	
4-103	8.01	6
4-103	8.01	13
4-103	8.01	36
4-103	8.02	107
4-103	8.03	
4-103	8.03	195
4-103	8.03	200
4-103	8.03	203
4-103	8.03	207
4-103	8.03	236
4-103	8.04	
4-103	8.04	486
4-103	8.04	487
4-103	8.04	634
4-103	9.02	
4-103	9.03	
4-103	9.03	
4-103	9.03	181
4-103	9.05	
4-103	9.05	
4-103(1)	1.03	165
4-103(1)	8.01	
4-103(1)	8.03	227
4-103(1)	8.04	485
4-103(1)	9.03	
4-103(1)	9.03	204
4-103(2)	8.01	
4-103(5)	8.03	200
4-103(5)	8.03	227
4-103(5)	8.04	494
4-103(a)	1.03	165
4-103(a)	7.02	81
4-103(a)	8.01	
4-103(a)	8.01	24
4-103(a)	8.01	25
4-103(a)	8.03	220
4-103(a)	8.03	227
4-103(a)	8.04	
4-103(a)	8.04	484
4-103(a)	8.04	485

UNIFORM COMMERCIAL CODE

Sec.	This Work Par.	Note
4-103(a)	8.04	503
4-103(a)	9.01	4
4-103(a)	9.03	
4-103(a)	9.03	144
4-103(a)	9.03	145
4-103(a)	9.03	147
4-103(a)	9.05	283
4-103(a)	10.08	125
4-103(a)	11.03	110
4-103(a)	11.03	130
4-103(a)—(e)	8.01	21
4-103(a)(3)	8.01	6
4-103(b)	1.03	166
4-103(b)	8.01	
4-103(b)	8.01	31
4-103(b)	9.03	148
4-103(b)	10.08	130
4-103(c)	8.01	28
4-103(e)	8.01	52
4-103(e)	8.03	
4-103(e)	8.03	226
4-103(e)	8.03	227
4-103(e)	8.03	230
4-103(e)	8.04	396
4-103(e)	8.04	420
4-103(e)	8.04	491
4-103(e)	8.04	494
4-103(e)	8.04	499
4-103, Comment 2	8.01	30
4-103, Comment 2	8.01	36
4-103, Comment 2	9.03	148
4-103, Comment 3	8.01	36
4-103, Comment 3	8.04	258
4-103, Comment 3	8.04	313
4-103, Comment 3	9.03	148
4-103, Comment 6	8.03	227
4-103, Comment 6	8.03	228
4-104	8.01	2
4-104	8.01	53
4-104	8.02	
4-104	9.01	
4-104	9.03	117
4-104	10.02	15
4-104(1)	10.02	5
4-104(1)(e)	9.01	
4-104(1)(g)	1.01	33
4-104(1)(g)	1.02	54
4-104(1)(g)	1.04	191
4-104(1)(g)	2.01	17
4-104(1)(g)	8.01	3
4-104(1)(g)	8.01	47
4-104(1)(g)	9.04	232
4-104(1)(g)	11.01	3
4-104(1)(g)	11.02	64
4-104(1)(h)	8.02	134
4-104(1)(i)	9.01	
4-104(1)(j)	8.01	58
4-104(1)(j)	8.02	
4-104(a)(1)	1.04	178
4-104(a)(1)	9.01	
4-104(a)(1)	9.03	117
4-104(a)(1)	9.03	161

TABLE OF STATUTES

UNIFORM COMMERCIAL CODE

Sec.	Par.	This Work Note
4–104(a)(1)	9.05	241
4–104(a)(1)	9.05	245
4–104(a)(3)	4.03	79
4–104(a)(3)	8.01	55
4–104(a)(3)	8.04	427
4–104(a)(5)	8.01	53
4–104(a)(5)	8.04	414
4–104(a)(5)	9.01	16
4–104(a)(5)	9.01	59
4–104(a)(5)	9.02	
4–104(a)(5)	9.02	102
4–104(a)(5)	9.03	117
4–104(a)(5)	9.03	161
4–104(a)(6)	8.03	
4–104(a)(8)	8.01	50
4–104(a)(9)	1.01	3
4–104(a)(9)	1.01	30
4–104(a)(9)	1.01	31
4–104(a)(9)	1.02	54
4–104(a)(9)	1.03	104
4–104(a)(9)	1.04	191
4–104(a)(9)	2.02	64
4–104(a)(9)	7.02	45
4–104(a)(9)	8.01	
4–104(a)(9)	8.01	3
4–104(a)(9)	8.01	47
4–104(a)(9)	9.03	161
4–104(a)(9)	9.04	
4–104(a)(9)	9.04	232
4–104(a)(9)	9.05	
4–104(a)(9)	9.05	296
4–104(a)(9)	10.01	4
4–104(a)(9)	10.02	5
4–104(a)(9)	10.02	15
4–104(a)(9)	10.11	231
4–104(a)(9)	11.01	3
4–104(a)(9)	11.01	4
4–104(a)(9)	11.02	60
4–104(a)(9)	11.02	63
4–104(a)(9)	11.03	115
4–104(a)(10)	8.01	56
4–104(a)(10)	8.01	57
4–104(a)(10)	8.02	
4–104(a)(10)	8.02	132
4–104(a)(10)	8.03	202
4–104(a)(10)	8.03	230
4–104(a)(10)	8.04	427
4–104(a)(10)	9.03	151
4–104(a)(10)	10.07	108
4–104(a)(11)	8.01	58
4–104(a)(11)	8.02	
4–104(a)(11)	8.02	91
4–104(a)(11)	8.02	108
4–104(a)(11)	8.03	198
4–104(a)(12)	8.01	75
4–104(c)	3.03	251
4–104(c)	7.02	46
4–104(c)	8.01	50
4–104(c)	8.01	61
4–104(c)	8.01	63
4–104(c)	8.04	498
4–104(c)	9.01	43

UNIFORM COMMERCIAL CODE

Sec.	Par.	This Work Note
4–104(c)	9.01	45
4–104(c)	9.01	85
4–104(c)	9.03	
4–104(c)	9.03	124
4–104(c)	9.03	132
4–104(c)	9.03	136
4–104(c)	9.03	163
4–104(c)	9.03	164
4–104(d)	7.01	24
4–105	8.01	2
4–105	8.02	
4–105	8.02	89
4–105	8.03	215
4–105	8.04	345
4–105	8.04	512
4–105	9.03	124
4–105	9.03	167
4–105	9.03	231
4–105(1)	1.01	27
4–105(1)	1.04	178
4–105(1)	3.01	34
4–105(1)	4.03	52
4–105(1)	8.01	
4–105(1)	8.01	48
4–105(1)	8.04	259
4–105(1)	8.04	398
4–105(1)	8.04	428
4–105(1)	9.03	117
4–105(1)	9.03	161
4–105(1)	9.04	
4–105(1)	9.04	229
4–105(1)	9.04	237
4–105(1)	9.04	240
4–105(1)	9.05	245
4–105(2)	1.04	194
4–105(2)	3.02	150
4–105(2)	8.01	49
4–105(2)	8.03	
4–105(2)	8.04	378
4–105(3)	1.04	192
4–105(3)	3.02	153
4–105(3)	8.01	50
4–105(3)	8.04	315
4–105(3)	8.04	398
4–105(4)	3.02	151
4–105(4)	8.01	51
4–105(4)	8.03	
4–105(4)	8.04	344
4–105(5)	8.01	52
4–105(5)	8.03	
4–105(5)	8.04	344
4–105(5)	8.04	414
4–105(5)	8.04	428
4–105(5)	9.03	223
4–105(6)	8.01	51
4–105(a)	8.01	49
4–105(b)	8.01	50
4–105, Comment 4	8.01	50
4–105, Comment 5	8.01	51
4–106	2.04	
4–106	8.01	
4–106	8.01	54

TABLE OF STATUTES

UNIFORM COMMERCIAL CODE

Sec.	Par.	This Work Note
4–106	8.01	59
4–106	8.03	
4–106	8.03	193
4–106	8.04	473
4–106(a)	2.04	290
4–106(a)	2.04	291
4–106(a)	4.03	58
4–106(a)	8.03	205
4–106(b)	2.04	
4–106(b)	2.04	289
4–106(b)	2.04	294
4–106(c)	2.04	292
4–106(d)	8.01	52
4–106, Comment 1	2.04	290
4–107	8.01	59
4–107, Comment 3	8.01	59
4–107, Comment 4	8.01	59
4–107, Comment 5	8.01	59
4–108	4.03	79
4–108	8.01	6
4–108	8.01	55
4–108	8.01	56
4–108	8.03	
4–108	8.04	
4–108	8.04	385
4–108	9.01	
4–108	9.01	71
4–108(1)	8.03	
4–108(2)	8.03	
4–109	8.01	6
4–109	8.02	
4–109	8.02	145
4–109	8.03	195
4–109	8.03	203
4–109	8.03	205
4–109	8.03	207
4–109	8.04	487
4–109	9.01	74
4–109	9.03	
4–109(a)	4.03	101
4–109(a)	8.02	134
4–109(a)	8.03	
4–109(b)	8.02	
4–109(b)	8.03	
4–109(b)	8.03	219
4–109(b)	8.03	223
4–109(b)	8.04	292
4–109(e)	8.02	
4–109, Comment 1	8.03	220
4–109, Comment 3	8.03	219
4–109, Comment 3	8.03	223
4–109, Comments	8.03	
4–110	4.03	90
4–110	4.03	97
4–110	7.02	81
4–110	8.01	
4–110	8.01	6
4–110	8.04	433
4–110	8.04	435
4–110	8.04	477
4–110	9.03	
4–110(a)	8.01	68

UNIFORM COMMERCIAL CODE

Sec.	Par.	This Work Note
4–110(a)	9.03	206
4–110(b)	9.03	208
4–110(c)	9.03	209
4–110, Comment 2	8.01	70
4–111	7.03	187
4–111	9.03	
4–111	9.03	183
4–111	9.03	192
Art. 4, Pt. 2	8.02	
Art. 4, Pt. 2	8.03	223
Art. 4, Pt. 2	8.03	226
Art. 4, Pt. 2	8.03	291
Art. 4, Pt. 2	9.05	276
4–201	3.01	
4–201	3.01	33
4–201	3.02	154
4–201	8.01	
4–201	8.01	21
4–201	8.03	203
4–201	8.04	354
4–201	8.04	368
4–201	8.04	373
4–201	8.04	391
4–201	8.04	438
4–201	8.04	442
4–201	8.04	469
4–201	9.03	
4–201	9.05	309
4–201	11.03	107
4–201—4–214	8.03	240
4–201(1)	8.03	203
4–201(2)	3.01	28
4–201(a)	3.01	44
4–201(a)	8.01	36
4–201(a)	8.01	54
4–201(a)	8.03	
4–201(a)	8.03	194
4–201(a)	8.03	199
4–201(a)	8.03	203
4–201(a)	8.04	351
4–201(a)	8.04	367
4–201(a)	8.04	441
4–201(a)	8.04	444
4–201(b)	3.01	23
4–201(b)	3.01	28
4–201(b)	3.02	149
4–201(b)	3.02	152
4–201(b)(1)	3.02	158
4–201(b)(1)	3.02	184
4–201(b)(2)	3.02	158
4–201, Comment	8.04	367
4–201, Comments 2—4	8.01	54
4–201, Comment 3	8.03	194
4–201, Comment 3	8.04	354
4–201, Comment 4	8.02	108
4–201, Comment 4	8.02	121
4–201, Comment 4	8.03	199
4–201, Comment 4	8.04	354
4–201, Comment 4	8.04	367
4–201, Comment 4	8.04	369
4–201, Comment 4	8.04	371
4–201, Comment 4	8.04	441

TABLE OF STATUTES 633

UNIFORM COMMERCIAL CODE

Sec.	Par.	This Work Note
4–201, Comment 4	8.04	442
4–202	1.04	
4–202	1.04	219
4–202	4.03	115
4–202	8.01	
4–202	8.01	6
4–202	8.01	52
4–202	8.03	
4–202	8.03	194
4–202	8.03	195
4–202	8.03	200
4–202	8.03	205
4–202	8.03	207
4–202	8.03	216
4–202	8.03	220
4–202	8.03	226
4–202	8.04	
4–202	8.04	353
4–202	8.04	354
4–202	8.04	373
4–202	8.04	396
4–202	8.04	420
4–202	8.04	438
4–202	8.04	444
4–202	8.04	495
4–202	9.03	
4–202	9.05	302
4–202	10.11	233
4–202(1)	8.04	487
4–202(1)(b)	8.03	
4–202(1)(b)	8.03	202
4–202(1)(d)	4.03	115
4–202(2)	8.03	
4–202(2)	8.03	202
4–202(2)	8.04	487
4–202(a)	8.01	21
4–202(a)	8.03	
4–202(a)	8.03	217
4–202(a)	8.04	
4–202(a)	8.04	420
4–202(a)	8.04	487
4–202(a)(1)	4.03	86
4–202(a)(1)	8.02	89
4–202(a)(2)	4.03	104
4–202(a)(2)	8.03	
4–202(a)(2)	8.03	202
4–202(a)(2)	8.03	209
4–202(a)(2)	8.04	357
4–202(b)	4.03	105
4–202(b)	8.02	
4–202(b)	8.02	89
4–202(b)	8.03	
4–202(b)	8.03	202
4–202(b)	8.03	231
4–202(b)	8.04	344
4–202(b)	8.04	350
4–202(b)	8.04	360
4–202(b)	8.04	420
4–202(b)	8.04	462
4–202(b)	8.04	487
4–202(c)	8.01	54
4–202(c)	8.02	89

UNIFORM COMMERCIAL CODE

Sec.	Par.	This Work Note
4–202, Comment 4	8.01	54
4–202, Comment 4	8.03	194
4–202, Comment 4	8.03	205
4–202, Comment 4	8.04	354
4–203	8.01	25
4–203	8.03	195
4–203	8.03	200
4–203	8.03	203
4–203	8.03	207
4–203	8.03	217
4–203	8.04	
4–204	8.02	89
4–204	8.03	194
4–204	8.03	195
4–204	8.03	200
4–204	8.03	205
4–204	8.03	207
4–204	8.03	217
4–204	8.04	
4–204(3)	8.01	60
4–204(b)(1)	4.03	86
4–204(c)	4.03	93
4–204(c)	8.01	60
4–204(c)	8.02	
4–204(c)	8.04	475
4–204, Comment 4	4.03	90
4–204, Comment 4	8.02	89
4–204, Comment 4	8.03	194
4–205	3.01	
4–205	3.01	33
4–205	3.01	34
4–205	3.02	
4–205	4.02	14
4–205	4.04	144
4–205	7.02	104
4–205	8.01	
4–205	8.01	11
4–205	8.03	215
4–205	8.04	446
4–205(1)	3.01	
4–205(1)	3.01	36
4–205(1)	3.02	167
4–205(1)	8.01	11
4–205(1)	8.01	48
4–205(1)	8.04	
4–205(2)	3.01	36
4–205(a)	8.01	
4–206	3.02	130
4–206	8.04	446
4–206	8.04	479
4–207	7.02	45
4–207	7.02	46
4–207	7.02	49
4–207	7.02	53
4–207	7.02	59
4–207	7.02	67
4–207	7.02	77
4–207	7.02	81
4–207	7.02	84
4–207	8.02	
4–207	8.02	112
4–207	8.04	

TABLE OF STATUTES

UNIFORM COMMERCIAL CODE

Sec.	Par.	This Work Note
4–207	8.04	413
4–207	8.04	415
4–207	8.04	416
4–207	8.04	418
4–207	8.04	423
4–207	8.04	446
4–207	9.03	
4–207	9.03	216
4–207	9.03	217
4–207(1)	8.01	53
4–207(1)	9.04	
4–207(1)(a)	7.02	74
4–207(1)(a)	7.02	88
4–207(1)(b)	7.02	75
4–207(1)(b)	7.02	78
4–207(1)(b)	7.02	79
4–207(1)(b)(i)	7.02	85
4–207(1)(b)(ii)	7.02	86
4–207(1)(b)(iii)	7.02	87
4–207(1)(c)	7.02	76
4–207(1)(c)	7.02	78
4–207(1)(c)	7.02	89
4–207(1)(c)(i)	7.02	91
4–207(1)(c)(i)	7.02	105
4–207(1)(c)(ii)	7.02	91
4–207(1)(c)(ii)	7.02	105
4–207(1)(c)(iv)	7.02	91
4–207(1)(c)(iv)	7.02	105
4–207(2)	7.02	49
4–207(a)	4.06	208
4–207(a)	7.02	52
4–207(a)	8.02	
4–207(a)	8.02	112
4–207(a)	10.11	232
4–207(a)(1)	7.02	65
4–207(a)(2)	7.02	67
4–207(a)(3)	7.02	68
4–207(a)(3)	7.02	69
4–207(a)(3)	8.04	401
4–207(a)(4)	7.02	70
4–207(a)(5)	7.02	71
4–207(a)(6)	7.02	46
4–207(b)	3.02	130
4–207(b)	4.06	208
4–207(b)	7.02	45
4–207(c)	7.02	58
4–207(c)	8.01	21
4–207(c)	8.02	127
4–207(c)	8.04	411
4–207(c)	8.04	430
4–207(c)	8.04	467
4–207(d)	7.02	55
4–207(d)	7.02	62
4–207(e)	7.02	61
4–207, Comment 5	8.04	467
4–208	3.03	371
4–208	7.02	45
4–208	7.02	46
4–208	7.02	53
4–208	7.02	59
4–208	7.02	67
4–208	7.02	77

UNIFORM COMMERCIAL CODE

Sec.	Par.	This Work Note
4–208	7.02	81
4–208	7.02	82
4–208	7.02	91
4–208	7.02	102
4–208	8.01	9
4–208	8.02	
4–208	8.02	112
4–208	8.02	165
4–208	8.04	
4–208	8.04	416
4–208	8.04	418
4–208	8.04	446
4–208	9.01	42
4–208	9.03	
4–208	9.03	191
4–208	9.03	216
4–208	9.03	217
4–208(1)	8.01	
4–208(a)	7.02	78
4–208(a)	8.01	21
4–208(a)	8.02	112
4–208(a)(1)	7.02	88
4–208(a)(1)	7.02	96
4–208(a)(1)	7.02	101
4–208(a)(1)	8.04	451
4–208(a)(2)	7.02	
4–208(a)(2)	7.02	89
4–208(a)(2)	7.02	103
4–208(a)(2)	9.01	41
4–208(a)(3)	7.02	79
4–208(a)(3)	8.02	171
4–208(a)(4)	7.02	46
4–208(b)	7.02	58
4–208(b)	7.02	96
4–208(b)	7.02	104
4–208(b)	9.01	
4–208(c)	7.02	98
4–208(c)	7.02	104
4–208(c)	9.03	
4–208(c)	9.03	190
4–208(c)	9.03	193
4–208(d)	4.04	186
4–208(d)	7.02	
4–208(d)	7.02	58
4–208(d)	7.02	78
4–208(d)	7.02	96
4–208(d)	7.02	101
4–208(d)	7.02	102
4–208(d)	8.02	127
4–208(e)	7.02	55
4–208(e)	7.02	62
4–208(e)	8.02	217
4–208(f)	7.02	61
4–209	2.04	
4–209	7.02	45
4–209	7.02	46
4–209	8.02	112
4–209	8.04	
4–209	9.03	
4–209	11.03	121
4–209(a)	8.04	
4–209(a)	8.04	362

TABLE OF STATUTES

UNIFORM COMMERCIAL CODE

Sec.	Par.	This Work Note
4–209(a)	9.03	
4–209(a)	9.03	215
4–209(a)	9.03	223
4–209(b)	9.03	
4–209(b)	9.03	221
4–209(b)	9.03	223
4–209(c)	9.03	222
4–209(c)	9.03	227
4–209, Comment 1	9.03	216
4–209, Comment 2	9.03	217
4–209, Comment 2	9.03	218
4–210	3.03	379
4–210	8.01	9
4–210	8.02	
4–210	8.02	116
4–210	8.02	181
4–210	8.03	211
4–210	8.03	215
4–210	9.03	
4–210(a)	1.04	208
4–210(a)	8.01	9
4–210(a)(1)	3.03	222
4–210(a)(2)	3.03	222
4–210(a)(3)	3.03	222
4–210(b)	3.03	222
4–210(b)	10.08	147
4–210(c)	1.04	208
4–210(c)	1.04	210
4–210(c)	3.03	222
4–210(c)	8.01	
4–211	3.02	159
4–211	3.03	221
4–211	3.03	379
4–211	8.02	116
4–211	8.02	181
4–211	8.03	211
4–211	8.03	215
4–211	8.03	234
4–211	9.03	
4–211(1)	8.03	
4–211(1)	8.03	235
4–211(1)(a)	8.04	386
4–211(1)(b)	8.04	386
4–211(2)	8.03	235
4–211(2)	8.03	240
4–211(2)	8.03	242
4–211(3)	8.03	240
4–211(3)	8.03	242
4–211(3)(c)	8.03	241
4–212	4.03	89
4–212	4.03	101
4–212	8.01	
4–212	8.03	
4–212	8.03	194
4–212	8.03	203
4–212	8.04	428
4–212(1)	4.03	105
4–212(1)	8.03	
4–212(1)	8.03	202
4–212(1)	8.03	203
4–212(2)	8.02	
4–212(2)	8.04	350

UNIFORM COMMERCIAL CODE

Sec.	Par.	This Work Note
4–212(2)	8.04	470
4–212(2)	8.04	471
4–212(4)	8.03	
4–212(4)(b)	8.03	
4–212(4)(b)	8.03	203
4–213	8.02	
4–213	8.02	91
4–213	8.02	108
4–213	8.02	154
4–213	8.03	
4–213	8.03	194
4–213	8.03	203
4–213	8.03	234
4–213	8.03	242
4–213	8.04	367
4–213	8.04	368
4–213	8.04	386
4–213	8.04	391
4–213	8.04	488
4–213	9.01	75
4–213—4–215	10.07	95
4–213—4–215	10.07	99
4–213(1)	8.02	
4–213(1)	8.02	115
4–213(1)	8.02	124
4–213(1)	8.02	162
4–213(1)(a)	8.02	120
4–213(1)(a)	8.02	129
4–213(1)(a)	9.01	90
4–213(1)(b)	8.02	
4–213(1)(b)	8.02	117
4–213(1)(b)	8.02	118
4–213(1)(b)	8.02	121
4–213(1)(b)	9.01	90
4–213(1)(c)	8.02	
4–213(1)(c)	8.02	122
4–213(1)(c)	9.01	90
4–213(1)(c)	9.03	133
4–213(1)(c)	9.06	363
4–213(1)(d)	8.02	123
4–213(1)(d)	9.01	90
4–213(1)(d)	9.03	133
4–213(4)(a)	8.02	
4–213(a)	8.02	107
4–213(a)	8.02	129
4–213(a)	8.02	132
4–213(a)	8.03	
4–213(a)	8.03	235
4–213(a)	8.03	236
4–213(a)	8.04	367
4–213(a)	8.04	386
4–213(a)(1)	4.04	173
4–213(a)(1)	8.03	237
4–213(a)(2)	8.03	
4–213(a)(2)	8.03	245
4–213(b)	8.03	235
4–213(b)	8.03	238
4–213(b)	8.04	386
4–213(c)	4.04	173
4–213(c)	8.02	
4–213(c)	8.02	129
4–213(c)	8.02	132

TABLE OF STATUTES

UNIFORM COMMERCIAL CODE

Sec.	This Work Par.	Note
4–213(c)	8.04	386
4–213(c)(1)	8.02	
4–213(c)(1)	8.03	
4–213(c)(1)	8.03	240
4–213(c)(2)	8.02	
4–213(c)(2)	8.03	241
4–213(d)	8.03	243
4–213, Comment 1	8.03	236
4–213, Comment 1	8.03	237
4–213, Comment 1	8.03	239
4–213, Comment 2	8.03	240
4–213, Comment 3	8.03	242
4–213, Comment 3	8.03	244
4–213, Comment 3	8.04	386
4–214	3.02	156
4–214	4.03	105
4–214	4.06	208
4–214	8.01	
4–214	8.01	52
4–214	8.01	83
4–214	8.02	
4–214	8.03	
4–214	8.03	194
4–214	8.03	203
4–214	8.03	207
4–214	8.03	216
4–214	8.03	226
4–214	8.04	
4–214	8.04	352
4–214	8.04	354
4–214	8.04	367
4–214	8.04	368
4–214	8.04	373
4–214	8.04	391
4–214	8.04	396
4–214	8.04	462
4–214	8.04	483
4–214	8.04	487
4–214	9.03	
4–214(1)	8.01	84
4–214(2)	8.01	85
4–214(3)	8.01	86
4–214(4)	8.01	87
4–214(a)	3.02	156
4–214(a)	4.03	105
4–214(a)	4.06	231
4–214(a)	8.02	
4–214(a)	8.02	154
4–214(a)	8.02	181
4–214(a)	8.03	
4–214(a)	8.03	194
4–214(a)	8.03	200
4–214(a)	8.03	202
4–214(a)	8.03	203
4–214(a)	8.03	206
4–214(a)	8.03	209
4–214(a)	8.03	217
4–214(a)	8.03	230
4–214(a)	8.04	350
4–214(a)	8.04	393
4–214(a)	9.03	
4–214(b)	8.02	

UNIFORM COMMERCIAL CODE

Sec.	This Work Par.	Note
4–214(b)	8.04	
4–214(b)	8.04	319
4–214(b)	8.04	324
4–214(b)	8.04	350
4–214(b)	8.04	442
4–214(b)	8.04	471
4–214, Comment 2	8.03	197
4–214, Comment 2	8.03	199
4–214, Comment 3	8.03	217
4–214, Comment 3	8.03	218
4–214, Comment 4	8.02	174
4–214, Comment 4	8.03	251
4–214, Comment 4	8.04	354
4–214, Comment 4	8.04	393
4–214, Comment 4	8.04	442
4–214, Comment 4	8.04	471
4–214, Comment 5	8.03	217
4–214, Comment 5	8.03	218
4–214, Comment 5	8.03	233
4–214, Comment 6	8.03	217
4–214, Comment 6	8.03	218
4–215	3.03	371
4–215	7.01	19
4–215	8.01	5
4–215	8.01	6
4–215	8.02	
4–215	8.02	91
4–215	8.02	92
4–215	8.02	115
4–215	8.02	119
4–215	8.02	124
4–215	8.02	127
4–215	8.02	131
4–215	8.02	132
4–215	8.02	156
4–215	8.02	169
4–215	8.03	203
4–215	8.04	
4–215	8.04	319
4–215	8.04	368
4–215	8.04	373
4–215	8.04	438
4–215	8.04	462
4–215	8.04	469
4–215	8.04	488
4–215	8.04	495
4–215	9.01	
4–215	9.01	15
4–215	9.01	31
4–215	9.02	
4–215	9.03	
4–215	9.03	150
4–215	9.06	
4–215	9.06	364
4–215	10.02	15
4–215	10.07	113
4–215(a)	8.02	
4–215(a)	8.02	108
4–215(a)	8.02	110
4–215(a)	8.02	115
4–215(a)	8.02	122
4–215(a)	8.02	124

TABLE OF STATUTES

UNIFORM COMMERCIAL CODE

Sec.	Par.	This Work Note
4–215(a)	8.02	135
4–215(a)	8.02	156
4–215(a)	8.02	162
4–215(a)	9.01	74
4–215(a)	9.01	75
4–215(a)	9.01	90
4–215(a)	9.06	363
4–215(a)	10.07	96
4–215(a)(1)	4.04	173
4–215(a)(1)	8.02	120
4–215(a)(1)	8.02	129
4–215(a)(1)	8.02	156
4–215(a)(1)	9.01	90
4–215(a)(2)	4.04	173
4–215(a)(2)	8.02	
4–215(a)(2)	8.02	116
4–215(a)(2)	8.02	117
4–215(a)(2)	8.02	118
4–215(a)(2)	8.02	121
4–215(a)(2)	8.02	129
4–215(a)(2)	8.02	132
4–215(a)(2)	8.02	156
4–215(a)(2)	9.01	90
4–215(a)(3)	4.03	112
4–215(a)(3)	8.02	
4–215(a)(3)	8.02	123
4–215(a)(3)	8.02	150
4–215(a)(3)	8.02	171
4–215(a)(3)	8.03	
4–215(a)(3)	8.04	427
4–215(a)(3)	9.03	151
4–215(b)	8.02	
4–215(b)	8.02	110
4–215(b)	8.02	150
4–215(c)	8.02	
4–215(c)	8.02	153
4–215(d)	8.02	
4–215(d)	8.02	154
4–215(d)	8.03	
4–215(e)	1.03	161
4–215(e)	1.04	185
4–215(e)	8.02	
4–215(e)	8.02	154
4–215(e)	8.04	258
4–215(e)(1)	8.02	173
4–215(e)(2)	8.02	172
4–215(f)	1.03	161
4–215(f)	1.04	185
4–215(f)	8.02	172
4–215(f)	8.04	258
4–215(f)	8.04	260
4–215(f)	8.04	261
4–215, Comment 1	8.02	119
4–215, Comment 3	4.04	173
4–215, Comment 3	8.02	119
4–215, Comment 3	8.02	129
4–215, Comment 4	8.02	108
4–215, Comment 4	8.02	119
4–215, Comment 4	8.02	129
4–215, Comment 4	8.02	148
4–215, Comment 4	8.02	174
4–215, Comment 5	9.01	74

UNIFORM COMMERCIAL CODE

Sec.	Par.	This Work Note
4–215, Comment 6	8.02	124
4–215, Comment 6	8.02	127
4–215, Comment 6	9.01	75
4–215, Comments 6—10	8.02	110
4–215, Comment 7	8.02	128
4–215, Comment 7	8.02	134
4–215, Comment 7	8.02	149
4–215, Comment 7	8.02	151
4–215, Comment 7	8.02	152
4–215, Comment 8	4.04	173
4–215, Comment 8	8.02	
4–215, Comment 8	8.02	88
4–215, Comment 8	8.02	129
4–215, Comment 8	8.02	131
4–215, Comment 8	8.02	132
4–215, Comment 8	8.02	150
4–215, Comment 8	8.02	152
4–215, Comment 8	8.02	156
4–215, Comments 9—11	8.02	154
4–215, Comment 11	8.04	258
4–216	4.03	134
4–216	8.01	
4–216	8.01	71
4–216	8.01	83
4–216(a)	8.01	75
4–216(a)	8.01	84
4–216(b)	8.01	85
4–216(c)	8.01	78
4–216(c)	8.01	86
4–216(d)	8.01	79
4–216(d)	8.01	87
4–216, Comment	8.01	
4–216, Comment 2	8.01	72
4–216, Comment 2	8.01	73
4–216, Comment 3	8.01	74
4–301	3.03	371
4–301	4.03	
4–301	4.03	60
4–301	4.03	105
4–301	4.03	112
4–301	8.01	5
4–301	8.01	6
4–301	8.01	52
4–301	8.02	
4–301	8.02	98
4–301	8.02	113
4–301	8.02	117
4–301	8.02	127
4–301	8.02	129
4–301	8.02	131
4–301	8.02	156
4–301	8.02	165
4–301	8.02	181
4–301	8.03	
4–301	8.04	
4–301	8.04	319
4–301	8.04	337
4–301	8.04	373
4–301	8.04	416
4–301	8.04	427
4–301	8.04	462
4–301	8.04	469

TABLE OF STATUTES

UNIFORM COMMERCIAL CODE

Sec.	Par.	This Work Note
4–301	8.04	488
4–301	8.04	495
4–301	9.01	
4–301	9.01	15
4–301	9.03	
4–301	9.03	191
4–301	9.05	276
4–301	9.05	298
4–301	9.06	
4–301	9.06	364
4–301	10.07	108
4–301	10.07	113
4–301(1)	8.02	
4–301(1)(b)	8.02	179
4–301(a)	4.03	112
4–301(a)	4.04	173
4–301(a)	8.02	
4–301(a)	8.02	92
4–301(a)	8.02	109
4–301(a)	8.02	117
4–301(a)	8.02	129
4–301(a)	8.02	131
4–301(a)	8.02	132
4–301(a)	8.02	135
4–301(a)	8.02	156
4–301(a)	8.02	178
4–301(a)	8.03	208
4–301(a)	8.04	319
4–301(a)	9.03	
4–301(a)	9.03	151
4–301(a)	9.06	363
4–301(a)(1)	8.02	
4–301(a)(2)	8.02	
4–301(a)(2)	8.02	179
4–301(a)(2)	8.02	182
4–301(a)(2)	8.02	184
4–301(a)(2)	9.03	
4–301(a)(3)	8.02	184
4–301(a)(3)	9.03	
4–301(b)	8.02	
4–301(b)	8.02	92
4–301(b)	8.02	117
4–301(b)	8.02	135
4–301(b)	10.05	82
4–301(d)	8.02	
4–301(d)	8.04	319
4–301(d)(1)	8.02	188
4–301(d)(2)	8.02	188
4–301, Comment 2	8.02	92
4–301, Comment 2	8.02	101
4–301, Comment 2	8.02	129
4–301, Comment 2	8.02	131
4–301, Comment 2	8.02	136
4–301, Comment 2	8.02	179
4–301, Comment 2	8.02	186
4–301, Comment 3	8.02	110
4–301, Comment 3	8.02	152
4–301, Comment 4	8.02	135
4–301, Comment 7	8.02	111
4–301, Comment 7	8.02	129
4–301, Comment 7	8.02	131
4–301, Comment 7	8.02	165

UNIFORM COMMERCIAL CODE

Sec.	Par.	This Work Note
4–301, Comment 7	8.02	166
4–301, Comment 8	8.02	180
4–301, Comment 8	9.03	
4–302	1.04	
4–302	1.04	218
4–302	2.04	292
4–302	4.03	60
4–302	4.03	112
4–302	4.04	144
4–302	8.01	
4–302	8.01	5
4–302	8.01	6
4–302	8.01	52
4–302	8.02	
4–302	8.02	88
4–302	8.02	94
4–302	8.02	98
4–302	8.02	113
4–302	8.02	115
4–302	8.02	124
4–302	8.02	127
4–302	8.02	135
4–302	8.02	156
4–302	8.02	163
4–302	8.02	164
4–302	8.02	165
4–302	8.02	169
4–302	8.02	171
4–302	8.02	185
4–302	8.03	
4–302	8.03	205
4–302	8.03	220
4–302	8.04	
4–302	8.04	319
4–302	8.04	373
4–302	8.04	416
4–302	8.04	427
4–302	8.04	462
4–302	8.04	483
4–302	8.04	488
4–302	8.04	495
4–302	9.01	
4–302	9.01	14
4–302	9.01	15
4–302	9.01	75
4–302	9.01	90
4–302	9.02	
4–302	9.03	
4–302	9.03	191
4–302	9.03	193
4–302	9.05	298
4–302	9.06	
4–302	9.06	363
4–302	9.06	364
4–302	10.02	15
4–302	10.07	108
4–302	10.07	113
4–302(a)	8.02	
4–302(a)	8.02	95
4–302(a)	8.02	155
4–302(a)	8.02	156
4–302(a)	8.02	171

TABLE OF STATUTES 639

UNIFORM COMMERCIAL CODE

Sec.	Par.	This Work Note
4–302(a)	8.02	178
4–302(a)(1)	8.02	
4–302(a)(1)	8.02	92
4–302(a)(1)	8.02	124
4–302(a)(1)	8.03	224
4–302(b)	8.02	
4–302(b)	8.02	95
4–302(b)	8.02	111
4–302(b)	8.02	112
4–302(b)	8.02	113
4–302(b)	8.02	117
4–302(b)	8.02	127
4–302(b)	8.02	129
4–302(b)	8.02	131
4–302(b)	8.02	150
4–302(b)	8.02	155
4–302(b)	8.02	156
4–302(b)	8.02	168
4–302(b)	8.02	171
4–302(b)	8.03	224
4–302(b)	9.03	
4–302, Comment 1	8.02	108
4–302, Comment 1	8.02	121
4–302, Comment 2	8.02	110
4–302, Comment 2	8.02	155
4–302, Comment 3	8.02	111
4–302, Comment 3	8.02	124
4–302, Comment 3	8.02	155
4–302, Comment 3	8.02	168
4–302, Comment 3	9.01	75
4–302, Comment 5	9.01	75
4–303	9.01	
4–303	9.01	89
4–303	9.01	90
4–303	9.03	133
4–303	9.06	
4–303	9.06	364
4–303	10.08	135
4–303(1)(a)	3.01	32
4–303(1)(d)	9.01	
4–303(1)(d)	9.01	74
4–303(1)(d)	9.01	94
4–303(1)(d)	9.03	133
4–303(1)(d)	9.06	363
4–303(2)	8.02	
4–303(2)	9.02	
4–303(a)	9.01	
4–303(a)	9.01	21
4–303(a)	9.01	75
4–303(a)	9.02	
4–303(a)	9.06	363
4–303(a)(1)	3.01	32
4–303(a)(1)	4.04	167
4–303(a)(4)	9.01	75
4–303(a)(5)	9.01	
4–303(a)(5)	9.01	21
4–303(a)(5)	9.01	71
4–303(a)(5)	9.01	91
4–303(a)(5)	9.03	
4–303(b)	8.02	
4–303(b)	9.01	14
4–303(b)	9.02	

UNIFORM COMMERCIAL CODE

Sec.	Par.	This Work Note
4–303(b)	10.08	145
4–303, Comment 2	9.01	80
4–303, Comment 3	9.01	94
4–303, Comment 4	9.01	71
4–303, Comment 4	9.01	74
4–303, Comment 7	8.02	140
4–303, Comment 7	9.01	14
4–305(d)	10.07	106
4–310, Comment 7	8.02	131
4–320(d)	9.02	100
Art. 4, Pt. 4	10.08	142
4–401	1.03	170
4–401	3.03	376
4–401	6.03	188
4–401	7.02	83
4–401	7.02	99
4–401	8.03	
4–401	9.01	
4–401	9.01	1
4–401	9.02	
4–401	9.03	
4–401	9.05	273
4–401	9.05	300
4–401	9.05	310
4–401	10.03	42
4–401	11.03	117
4–401	11.03	121
4–401—4–407	10.08	142
4–401(1)	9.02	
4–401(1)	9.03	191
4–401(1)	9.04	
4–401(2)	9.02	109
4–401(2)(a)	9.01	7
4–401(a)	4.02	5
4–401(a)	6.02	
4–401(a)	8.02	111
4–401(a)	8.03	225
4–401(a)	9.01	
4–401(a)	9.01	14
4–401(a)	9.01	48
4–401(a)	9.02	107
4–401(a)	9.03	191
4–401(b)	9.01	1
4–401(b)	9.01	48
4–401(c)	2.02	224
4–401(c)	8.01	
4–401(c)	8.01	16
4–401(c)	8.01	18
4–401(c)	9.01	
4–401(c)	9.01	5
4–401(c)	9.01	13
4–401(c)	9.01	15
4–401(c)	9.02	
4–401(c)	9.02	107
4–401(c)	9.02	113
4–401(c)	10.08	135
4–401(d)	9.01	7
4–401(d)	9.02	
4–401(d)	9.02	109
4–401(d)(1)	4.04	186
4–401(d)(1)	6.02	
4–401(d)(1)	9.02	107

TABLE OF STATUTES

UNIFORM COMMERCIAL CODE

Sec.	Par.	This Work Note
4–401, Comment 1	9.01	48
4–401, Comment 2	9.01	1
4–401, Comment 3	9.01	
4–401, Comment 3	9.01	29
4–401, Comment 3	9.03	160
4–401, Comment 4	9.02	109
4–402	4.04	141
4–402	8.01	3
4–402	8.04	494
4–402	9.01	
4–402	9.02	
4–402	9.02	101
4–402	9.02	107
4–402	9.03	
4–402	9.03	161
4–402	9.05	297
4–402	9.06	
4–402	9.06	364
4–402	10.02	15
4–402	10.04	54
4–402	11.02	60
4–402	11.02	65
4–402(a)	9.02	
4–402(b)	8.02	
4–402(b)	9.02	
4–402(b)	9.02	96
4–402(c)	8.02	178
4–402(c)	9.02	
4–402, Comment 1	9.02	
4–402, Comment 1	9.02	95
4–402, Comment 1	9.02	97
4–402, Comment 1	9.02	99
4–402, Comment 2	9.02	98
4–402, Comment 2	9.02	105
4–402, Comment 3	9.02	97
4–402, Comment 4	8.02	105
4–402, Comment 5	8.01	53
4–402, Comment 5	9.02	103
4–403	8.01	66
4–403	8.04	494
4–403	9.01	
4–403	9.01	54
4–403	9.01	61
4–403	9.01	68
4–403	9.01	73
4–403	9.02	
4–403	9.03	133
4–403	9.05	299
4–403	11.03	109
4–403(1)	9.01	
4–403(3)	9.02	
4–403(a)	4.04	167
4–403(a)	7.01	26
4–403(a)	9.01	
4–403(a)	9.01	13
4–403(a)	9.01	17
4–403(a)	9.01	18
4–403(a)	9.01	21
4–403(a)	9.01	32
4–403(a)	9.01	33
4–403(a)	10.08	135
4–403(b)	9.01	

UNIFORM COMMERCIAL CODE

Sec.	Par.	This Work Note
4–403(b)	9.01	27
4–403(b)	9.01	35
4–403(b)	9.02	
4–403(c)	9.01	
4–403(c)	9.01	30
4–403(c)	9.01	39
4–403(c)	9.02	
4–403(c)	9.02	105
4–403(c)	9.02	107
4–403, Comment	9.01	73
4–403, Comment	9.02	
4–403, Comment 1	9.01	
4–403, Comment 2	9.01	16
4–403, Comment 4	9.01	51
4–403, Comment 4	9.01	60
4–403, Comment 5	9.01	
4–403, Comment 6	9.01	37
4–403, Comment 7	9.01	
4–403, Comment 7	9.01	31
4–403, Comment 7	9.01	41
4–403, Comment 7	9.02	
4–404	9.01	44
4–405	2.02	236
4–405	3.01	2
4–405	9.01	
4–405	9.04	
4–405(2)	9.04	237
4–405(a)	9.01	82
4–405(b)	9.01	83
4–405(d)	10.08	125
4–405(e)	10.08	125
4–405, Comment 2	9.01	84
4–405, Comment 2	9.01	85
4–405, Comment 3	9.01	84
4–405, Comment 3	9.01	85
4–406	4.02	16
4–406	6.02	80
4–406	6.03	106
4–406	7.02	98
4–406	7.03	
4–406	7.03	114
4–406	7.03	188
4–406	8.01	3
4–406	8.01	30
4–406	8.03	227
4–406	8.04	477
4–406	8.04	481
4–406	8.04	483
4–406	9.01	
4–406	9.01	41
4–406	9.01	44
4–406	9.01	46
4–406	9.03	
4–406	9.03	136
4–406	9.03	161
4–406	9.03	162
4–406	9.03	165
4–406	9.03	172
4–406	9.03	174
4–406	9.03	176
4–406	9.03	177
4–406	9.03	183

TABLE OF STATUTES 641

UNIFORM COMMERCIAL CODE		
		This Work
Sec.	Par.	Note
4–406	9.03	187
4–406	9.03	190
4–406	9.03	195
4–406	9.03	205
4–406	9.04	
4–406	9.05	
4–406	9.05	273
4–406	9.05	300
4–406	9.05	310
4–406	9.05	311
4–406	9.05	312
4–406	10.08	149
4–406	11.02	75
4–406	11.03	
4–406	11.03	118
4–406(1)	9.03	
4–406(1)	9.03	162
4–406(1)	9.03	205
4–406(2)	9.03	
4–406(2)(b)	9.03	162
4–406(3)	9.03	
4–406(3)	9.03	183
4–406(4)	7.03	
4–406(4)	9.03	
4–406(5)	7.02	104
4–406(5)	9.03	
4–406(5)	9.03	190
4–406(a)	9.03	
4–406(a)	9.03	162
4–406(a)	9.03	174
4–406(a)	9.03	212
4–406(b)	9.03	175
4–406(b)	9.03	214
4–406(c)	7.03	114
4–406(c)	9.03	
4–406(c)	9.03	164
4–406(c)	9.03	174
4–406(c)	9.03	177
4–406(c)	9.03	183
4–406(c)	9.03	184
4–406(c)	10.02	23
4–406(c)	11.03	120
4–406(c)	11.03	121
4–406(d)	7.03	114
4–406(d)	9.03	
4–406(d)	9.03	184
4–406(d)	9.03	212
4–406(d)	9.03	213
4–406(d)	10.02	23
4–406(d)	11.03	120
4–406(d)(2)	9.03	180
4–406(e)	7.03	114
4–406(e)	8.03	232
4–406(e)	8.04	482
4–406(e)	8.04	499
4–406(e)	9.01	44
4–406(e)	9.01	45
4–406(e)	9.03	
4–406(e)	9.03	183
4–406(e)	9.03	184
4–406(e)	9.03	185
4–406(e)	9.03	186

UNIFORM COMMERCIAL CODE		
		This Work
Sec.	Par.	Note
4–406(e)	9.03	195
4–406(e)	9.03	199
4–406(f)	7.03	114
4–406(f)	7.03	123
4–406(f)	7.03	187
4–406(f)	9.03	
4–406(f)	10.02	23
4–406, Comment	9.03	219
4–406, Comments	9.03	
4–406, Comments	9.03	174
4–406, Comments	9.03	176
4–406, Comments	9.03	178
4–406, Comments	9.03	181
4–406, Comments	9.03	186
4–406, Comments	9.03	193
4–406, Comment 1	9.03	173
4–406, Comment 2	9.03	160
4–406, Comment 4	9.03	
4–406, Comment 5	7.03	187
4–406, Comment 5	9.03	
4–406, Comment 5	9.03	
4–406, Comment 5	9.03	177
4–406, Comment 5	9.03	183
4–407	3.03	371
4–407	3.03	376
4–407	3.03	381
4–407	4.04	175
4–407	8.02	
4–407	8.02	111
4–407	8.02	129
4–407	8.02	132
4–407	8.02	169
4–407	8.03	225
4–407	9.01	
4–407	9.01	41
4–407	9.01	52
4–407	9.01	67
4–407	9.01	69
4–407	9.01	87
4–407	9.02	
4–407	9.02	107
4–407	9.02	112
4–407	9.02	115
4–407	9.05	312
4–407	10.03	47
4–407(1)	8.02	169
4–407(2)	8.02	169
4–407, Comment 5	8.02	170
Art. 4, Pt. 5	8.01	
Art. 4, Pt. 5	8.03	222
Art. 4, Pt. 5	8.04	473
4–501	4.03	105
4–501—4–504	8.03	
4–502	4.03	101
4–503(2)	8.01	54
Art. 4A	1.01	
Art. 4A	1.01	30
Art. 4A	1.01	31
Art. 4A	1.03	
Art. 4A	1.03	102
Art. 4A	1.03	103
Art. 4A	1.03	104

TABLE OF STATUTES

UNIFORM COMMERCIAL CODE

Sec.	Par.	This Work Note
Art. 4A	1.03	121
Art. 4A	1.03	164
Art. 4A	1.04	185
Art. 4A	1.04	189
Art. 4A	1.04	232
Art. 4A	2.02	64
Art. 4A	8.01	
Art. 4A	8.01	3
Art. 4A	8.01	46
Art. 4A	8.01	47
Art. 4A	8.03	
Art. 4A	9.02	105
Art. 4A	9.02	108
Art. 4A	9.04	
Art. 4A	10.01	
Art. 4A	10.01	3
Art. 4A	10.01	4
Art. 4A	10.02	
Art. 4A	10.02	5
Art. 4A	10.02	7
Art. 4A	10.02	14
Art. 4A	10.02	15
Art. 4A	10.02	24
Art. 4A	10.03	
Art. 4A	10.03	38
Art. 4A	10.03	47
Art. 4A	10.03	48
Art. 4A	10.04	
Art. 4A	10.04	58
Art. 4A	10.04	65
Art. 4A	10.04	71
Art. 4A	10.05	82
Art. 4A	10.07	
Art. 4A	10.07	91
Art. 4A	10.07	102
Art. 4A	10.07	119
Art. 4A	10.08	
Art. 4A	10.08	163
Art. 4A	10.08	169
Art. 4A	10.09	
Art. 4A	10.09	191
Art. 4A	10.09	192
Art. 4A	10.10	
Art. 4A	10.10	205
Art. 4A	10.11	231
Art. 4A	10.12	
Art. 4A	10.12	251
Art. 4A	10.12	252
Art. 4A	10.13	
Art. 4A	10.15	
Art. 4A	10.16	
Art. 4A	11.01	
Art. 4A	11.01	5
Art. 4A	11.02	
Art. 4A	11.03	128
Art. 4A	11.03	131
4A–102, Comment	10.04	
4A–102, Comment	10.04	65
4A–102, Comment	10.08	
4A–103	10.02	7
4A–103	10.02	14
4A–103	10.08	144

UNIFORM COMMERCIAL CODE

Sec.	Par.	This Work Note
4A–103(a)	10.01	4
4A–103(a)(1)	1.01	31
4A–103(a)(1)	1.03	102
4A–103(a)(1)	10.02	
4A–103(a)(1)	10.02	5
4A–103(a)(1)	10.02	6
4A–103(a)(1)	10.02	7
4A–103(a)(1)	10.05	82
4A–103(a)(1)	11.01	5
4A–103(a)(1)(i)	10.02	5
4A–103(a)(1)(i)	10.02	16
4A–103(a)(1)(i)	10.02	20
4A–103(a)(1)(i)	10.02	25
4A–103(a)(1)(i)	10.02	34
4A–103(a)(1)(i)—(a)(1)(iii)	10.02	5
4A–103(a)(1)(ii)	10.02	5
4A–103(a)(1)(ii)	10.02	21
4A–103(a)(1)(iii)	1.01	30
4A–103(a)(1)(iii)	10.02	5
4A–103(a)(2)	10.02	6
4A–103(a)(2)	10.02	7
4A–103(a)(2)	10.02	9
4A–103(a)(3)	10.02	9
4A–103(a)(4)	10.02	7
4A–103(a)(4)	10.02	9
4A–103(a)(5)	10.02	6
4A–103(a)(5)	10.02	7
4A–103(a)(5)	10.02	9
4A–103, Comment 5	1.01	30
4A–104	10.02	14
4A–104(a)	10.02	5
4A–104(a)	10.02	7
4A–104(c)	10.02	7
4A–104, Comment	10.02	21
4A–104, Comment 1	10.05	82
4A–104, Comment 2	1.03	102
4A–104, Comment 2	10.01	4
4A–104, Comment 2	10.02	5
4A–104, Comment 3	2.02	120
4A–104, Comment 3	10.02	5
4A–104, Comment 4	10.02	5
4A–104, Comment 5	1.01	31
4A–104, Comment 5	1.03	104
4A–104, Comment 5	10.02	5
4A–104, Comment 6	11.01	5
4A–105(a)(1)	10.09	178
4A–105(a)(1)	10.10	214
4A–105(a)(2)	10.02	5
4A–105(a)(2)	10.02	7
4A–105(a)(3)	10.09	180
4A–105(a)(4)	10.10	209
4A–105, Comment 3	10.02	32
4A–106	10.10	209
4A–106	10.10	223
4A–108	1.01	31
4A–108	1.03	104
4A–108	10.01	3
4A–108	10.02	5
4A–108	11.03	115
4A–108, Comment	11.03	116
4A–108, Comment	11.03	128

TABLE OF STATUTES

UNIFORM COMMERCIAL CODE

Sec.	This Work Par.	Note
Art. 4A, Pt. 2	10.05	
4A–201	10.03	
4A–201	10.03	47
4A–201	10.03	51
4A–201	10.09	177
4A–201	10.09	185
4A–201	10.10	211
4A–202	10.03	47
4A–202	11.03	126
4A–202(a)	10.03	
4A–202(a)	10.03	38
4A–202(a)	10.03	39
4A–202(a)	10.03	49
4A–202(a)	10.04	
4A–202(a)	10.09	173
4A–202(b)	10.02	
4A–202(b)	10.02	19
4A–202(b)	10.02	22
4A–202(b)	10.03	
4A–202(b)	10.03	49
4A–202(b)	10.03	52
4A–202(b)	10.09	179
4A–202(b)	10.10	212
4A–202(b)	10.10	214
4A–202(c)	10.03	
4A–202(c)	10.03	53
4A–202(c)	10.09	177
4A–202(d)	10.09	180
4A–202(f)	10.02	
4A–202(f)	10.08	125
4A–202, Comment 1	10.09	174
4A–203	10.03	47
4A–203(a)(1)	10.09	182
4A–203(a)(1)	10.10	213
4A–203(a)(2)	10.09	181
4A–203, Comment	10.03	40
4A–203, Comment 4	10.03	53
4A–204	10.03	42
4A–204	10.03	47
4A–204	10.09	183
4A–204	10.10	216
4A–204—4A–208	10.04	54
4A–204(a)	10.08	150
4A–204(a)	10.09	176
4A–204(a)	10.10	215
4A–204(a)	10.12	
4A–205	10.07	
4A–205(a)	10.09	186
4A–205(b)	10.09	187
4A–205(b)	10.10	216
4A–205, Comment 1	10.09	184
4A–206	10.09	188
4A–206	10.10	209
4A–207	2.04	285
4A–207	10.04	
4A–207	10.04	54
4A–207	10.07	
4A–207(a)	10.04	
4A–207(a)	10.09	191
4A–207(b)	10.04	
4A–207(b)	10.04	62
4A–207(b)(1)	10.04	58

UNIFORM COMMERCIAL CODE

Sec.	This Work Par.	Note
4A–207(b)(1)	10.09	192
4A–207(b)(2)	10.04	54
4A–207(b)(2)	10.04	58
4A–207(b)(2)	10.07	99
4A–207(b)(2)	10.09	192
4A–207(b)(2)	10.09	194
4A–207(c)	10.04	62
4A–207(c)	10.09	193
4A–207(c)(2)	10.10	221
4A–207(d)	1.04	232
4A–207(d)	10.04	62
4A–207(d)	10.09	193
4A–208	10.09	197
4A–208	10.10	221
4A–209	10.02	7
4A–209	10.02	12
4A–209	10.02	15
4A–209(a)	10.02	9
4A–209(a)	10.04	55
4A–209(a)	10.05	82
4A–209(b)	10.02	9
4A–209(b)(1)	10.04	56
4A–209(b)(1)	10.07	102
4A–209(b)(2)	10.04	56
4A–209(b)(2)	10.07	102
4A–209(b)(3)	10.02	13
4A–209(b)(3)	10.04	56
4A–209(b)(3)	10.08	150
4A–209(d)	10.04	55
4A–209(d)	10.10	
4A–209, Comment 6	10.04	56
4A–210	10.02	15
4A–210	10.10	220
4A–210(b)	10.04	55
4A–210(b)	10.08	150
4A–211	10.04	78
4A–211	10.07	119
4A–211	10.09	198
4A–211	10.10	218
4A–211(a)	10.07	95
4A–211(a)	10.07	119
4A–211(b)	10.07	95
4A–211(b)	10.07	119
4A–211(b)	10.09	199
4A–211(c)	10.09	199
4A–211(e)	10.07	119
4A–212	1.01	32
4A–212	10.02	15
4A–212	10.04	55
Art. 4A, Pt. 3	10.05	
4A–301	10.02	9
4A–301	10.10	224
4A–301(a)	10.02	7
4A–301(a)	10.04	55
4A–301(a)	10.05	82
4A–302	10.02	12
4A–302	10.10	224
4A–302—4A–305	10.04	
4A–302—4A–305	10.04	54
4A–302(a)	10.02	8
4A–302(a)(1)	10.04	55
4A–302(a)(1)	10.05	82

TABLE OF STATUTES

UNIFORM COMMERCIAL CODE		
Sec.	This Work Par.	Note
4A–302(a)(2)	10.05	82
4A–302(c)	10.02	5
4A–302(c)	11.01	5
4A–303	10.04	57
4A–303	10.07	
4A–303(a)	10.09	189
4A–304	9.03	136
4A–304	10.09	190
4A–304	10.10	216
4A–304	10.12	
4A–305	10.04	54
4A–305	10.04	55
4A–305	10.10	
4A–305(a)	10.05	82
4A–305(a)	10.08	150
4A–305(c)	10.10	225
4A–305(d)	10.02	15
4A–305(d)	10.03	48
4A–305(d)	10.07	110
4A–305(d)	10.08	125
4A–305(d)	10.10	225
4A–305(d)	10.12	
4A–305(f)	10.02	24
4A–305(f)	10.08	125
4A–305, Comment 2	10.03	48
Art. 4A, Pt. 4	10.07	
4A–401	10.07	85
4A–402	10.02	11
4A–402	10.07	88
4A–402	10.09	184
4A–402	10.09	196
4A–402(a)	10.07	93
4A–402(b)	10.04	56
4A–402(b)	10.07	89
4A–402(c)	10.04	56
4A–402(c)	10.07	90
4A–402(c)	10.09	173
4A–402(d)	10.04	55
4A–402(d)	10.04	56
4A–402(d)	10.07	91
4A–402(d)	10.08	150
4A–402(d)	10.10	215
4A–402(e)	10.04	55
4A–402(e)	10.04	56
4A–402(e)	10.07	92
4A–402(f)	10.07	94
4A–403(a)	10.04	56
4A–403(a)(1)	10.04	56
4A–403(a)(1)	10.07	97
4A–403(a)(2)	10.07	98
4A–403(a)(3)	10.07	99
4A–403(b)	10.04	56
4A–403(b)	10.07	100
4A–403(c)	10.07	101
4A–404	1.03	161
4A–404	1.04	185
4A–404	10.02	8
4A–404	10.02	12
4A–404	10.04	56
4A–404(a)	10.07	102
4A–404(a)	10.07	103
4A–404(a)	10.07	105

UNIFORM COMMERCIAL CODE		
Sec.	This Work Par.	Note
4A–404(b)	10.07	107
4A–404(b)	10.07	110
4A–404(b)	10.08	150
4A–404(b)	10.10	209
4A–404(b)	10.10	210
4A–404(c)	10.07	111
4A–404(c)	10.08	125
4A–404(c)	10.08	129
4A–404(c)	10.08	131
4A–404(c)	10.10	209
4A–404(c)	10.10	210
4A–404(e)	10.08	127
4A–405	10.04	56
4A–405	10.07	95
4A–405	10.07	111
4A–405	10.07	113
4A–405(a)	10.07	114
4A–405(b)	10.07	115
4A–405(c)	10.07	102
4A–405(c)	10.08	125
4A–405(c)	10.08	126
4A–405(d)	10.06	83
4A–405(d)	10.07	
4A–405(d)	10.07	120
4A–405(d)	10.08	126
4A–405(d)	10.08	131
4A–405(d)	10.10	206
4A–405(e)	10.07	
4A–405(e)	10.07	117
4A–405(e)	10.07	121
4A–405(e)	10.10	206
4A–406	10.04	56
4A–406	10.07	95
4A–406	10.07	102
4A–406	10.10	227
4A–406(a)	8.03	
4A–406(a)	10.07	118
4A–406(b)	10.07	122
4A–406(b)	10.07	123
4A–406(d)	10.07	124
4A–501	10.08	
4A–501	10.08	146
4A–501(a)	10.08	125
4A–501(b)	10.08	128
4A–501(b)	10.08	130
4A–501(b)	10.08	131
4A–502	9.01	76
4A–502	9.02	108
4A–502	10.04	
4A–502	10.08	
4A–502	10.08	143
4A–502	10.09	200
4A–502(a)	10.08	132
4A–502(b)	10.08	133
4A–502(b)	10.08	135
4A–502(c)(1)	10.08	136
4A–502(c)(2)	10.08	137
4A–502(c)(3)	10.08	138
4A–502(d)	10.08	139
4A–503	9.01	76
4A–503	10.08	140
4A–503	10.08	141

TABLE OF STATUTES

UNIFORM COMMERCIAL CODE

Sec.	Par.	This Work Note
4A–503	10.09	201
4A–504	9.01	76
4A–504	9.02	108
4A–504	10.03	47
4A–504	10.08	
4A–504	10.09	202
4A–504(a)	10.08	145
4A–504(b)	10.08	147
4A–504, Comment 1	10.08	146
4A–505	10.02	
4A–505	10.08	148
4A–505	10.08	165
4A–505	10.09	203
4A–505, Comment	10.08	149
4A–506	10.09	204
4A–506(a)	10.10	222
4A–506(b)	8.04	430
4A–506(b)	10.08	151
4A–506(b)	10.08	152
4A–506, Comment 1	10.08	150
4A–507	10.01	
4A–507	10.08	153
4A–507(a)	10.08	159
4A–507(a)	10.08	162
4A–507(a)(1)	10.13	265
4A–507(a)(2)	10.13	266
4A–507(a)(3)	10.13	267
4A–507(b)	10.08	
4A–507(b)	10.08	157
4A–507(b)	10.08	162
4A–507(b)	10.10	226
4A–507(b)	10.10	227
4A–507(b)	10.13	268
4A–507(c)	10.08	
4A–507(c)	10.08	131
4A–507(c)	10.08	157
4A–507(c)	10.08	160
4A–507(c)	10.13	269
4A–507(d)	10.08	157
4A–507(e)	10.08	158
4A–507, Comment 1	10.08	156
4A–507, Comment 2	10.08	
Art. 5	1.03	
Art. 5	3.01	32
Art. 5	8.01	
Art. 5	11.01	
5–102, Comment 11	1.04	213
5–108	1.01	
5–108	3.01	32
5–108	4.03	60
5–108	4.03	100
5–109	3.01	32
5–109(a)(1)	1.03	
5–114	3.01	32
5–114(2)	3.01	32
5–114(2)(a)	1.03	
5–116(d)	3.01	32
5–116(d)	4.03	60
5–116(d)	4.03	100
5–116, Comment 4	3.01	32
Art. 7	2.01	
Art. 7	8.01	

UNIFORM COMMERCIAL CODE

Sec.	Par.	This Work Note
7–104(1)	2.01	31
7–502	2.01	31
7–504	2.01	31
Art. 8	1.01	
Art. 8	1.01	10
Art. 8	1.03	
Art. 8	1.03	93
Art. 8	2.01	
Art. 8	4.02	5
Art. 8	8.01	
Art. 8	8.01	3
Art. 8	8.01	7
Art. 8	8.01	47
8–102	8.01	3
8–102(a)(4)	2.01	32
8–102(a)(13)	1.03	90
8–102, Comment 15	1.03	92
8–103(d)	1.01	10
8–103(d)	1.03	83
8–103(d)	1.03	87
8–103, Comment 5	1.03	93
8–105	1.03	93
8–107	4.02	5
8–206(a)(1)	1.03	100
8–207	1.03	85
8–301	2.01	32
8–303	2.01	32
8–303	7.02	100
8–507	4.02	5
Art. 9	1.02	
Art. 9	1.04	
Art. 9	1.04	176
Art. 9	1.04	207
Art. 9	1.04	208
Art. 9	2.01	
Art. 9	3.03	222
Art. 9	3.03	338
Art. 9	3.04	425
Art. 9	6.03	266
Art. 9	6.03	281
Art. 9	8.01	
Art. 9	8.01	3
Art. 9	8.01	9
Art. 9	8.01	19
Art. 9	8.01	21
Art. 9	8.01	47
Art. 9	8.01	48
Art. 9	8.01	59
Art. 9	9.01	20
Art. 9	9.01	89
Art. 9	9.04	238
Art. 9	9.05	
Art. 9	9.05	241
Art. 9	9.05	245
Art. 9	9.06	
Art. 9	9.06	338
Art. 9	9.06	366
Art. 9	9.06	368
Art. 9	9.06	370
Art. 9	9.06	371
Art. 9	9.06	373
Art. 9	9.06	376

TABLE OF STATUTES

UNIFORM COMMERCIAL CODE

Sec.	Par.	This Work Note
Art. 9	9.06	379
Art. 9	9.06	383
Art. 9	9.06	398
Art. 9	9.06	404
Art. 9	9.06	408
Art. 9	10.08	159
Art. 9	10.13	267
Art. 9	10.16	285
Art. 9	11.03	101
9–102(a)(2)	9.01	20
9–102(a)(2)	9.05	
9–102(a)(2)	9.05	241
9–102(a)(2)	11.03	102
9–102(a)(3)	3.04	425
9–102(a)(8)	8.01	48
9–102(a)(12)	9.06	366
9–102(a)(29)	8.01	48
9–102(a)(29)	9.05	
9–102(a)(29)	9.05	241
9–102(a)(29)	9.05	245
9–102(a)(29)	9.06	
9–102(a)(29)	9.06	366
9–102(a)(29)	9.06	408
9–102(a)(29)	11.03	102
9–102(a)(42)	9.06	405
9–102(a)(42)	11.03	101
9–102(a)(42)	11.03	102
9–102(a)(43)	9.06	354
9–102(a)(44)	9.06	
9–102(a)(47)	1.02	52
9–102(a)(47)	2.01	17
9–102(a)(47)	8.01	
9–102(a)(47)	8.01	3
9–102(a)(47)	8.01	47
9–102(a)(47)	9.05	245
9–102(a)(47)	9.06	366
9–102(a)(47)	9.06	408
9–102(a)(51)	11.03	102
9–102(a)(59)	2.02	105
9–102(a)(61)	11.03	101
9–102(a)(64)	8.01	9
9–102(a)(64)	9.06	
9–102(a)(64)	9.06	366
9–102(a)(65)	1.04	207
9–102(a)(65)	9.05	245
9–104	8.01	9
9–104	9.01	89
9–104	9.06	
9–104	9.06	373
9–104	9.06	378
9–104(1)	9.06	407
9–104(a)(1)	9.06	
9–104(a)(3)	9.06	
9–104(a)(3)	9.06	413
9–104(g)	9.06	370
9–104(l)	8.01	9
9–104(l)	9.04	238
9–104(l)	9.06	366
9–105	9.05	245
9–105(1)(e)	8.01	48
9–105(1)(e)	9.05	
9–105(1)(e)	9.05	245

UNIFORM COMMERCIAL CODE

Sec.	Par.	This Work Note
9–105(1)(e)	9.06	408
9–105(1)(i)	9.05	245
9–105(1)(i)	9.06	408
9–109	9.06	
9–109	9.06	378
9–109(a)(1)	9.06	
9–109(a)(1)	9.06	366
9–109(a)(1)	9.06	373
9–109(a)(3)	1.04	207
9–109(a)(3)	3.02	65
9–109(a)(3)	9.05	245
9–109(a)(3)	11.03	101
9–109(a)(6)	1.04	208
9–109(b)	1.04	209
9–109(d)(7)	11.03	101
9–109(d)(10)	9.01	89
9–109(d)(13)	8.01	9
9–109(d)(13)	9.05	245
9–109(d)(13)	9.06	
9–109(d)(13)	9.06	366
9–109(d)(13)	9.06	373
9–109, Comment 5	3.01	19
9–109, Comment 5	7.01	14
9–201	1.04	
9–201	9.06	373
9–201	9.06	379
9–203	1.04	
9–203	9.01	89
9–203	9.06	
9–203	9.06	366
9–203	9.06	378
9–203(1)	8.01	12
9–203(1)(a)	8.01	9
9–203(b)	9.06	373
9–203(b)(3)	8.01	9
9–203(b)(3)(D)	8.01	9
9–203(b)(3)(D)	9.06	
9–203(c)	3.03	222
9–203(f)	8.01	9
9–206	1.04	
9–304	8.01	9
9–304	8.01	19
9–304	8.01	21
9–304	8.01	59
9–304	9.06	398
9–304	9.06	408
9–304	10.13	267
9–304(b)	10.08	159
9–305	8.01	9
9–305	9.06	408
9–306	9.06	
9–306	9.06	574
9–306(4)(d)(ii)	9.06	383
9–308	8.01	9
9–309	8.01	9
9–309(3)	11.03	101
9–309(7)	3.03	222
9–310	9.06	
9–310(a)	11.03	103
9–312	8.01	9
9–312	9.06	
9–312	9.06	378

TABLE OF STATUTES

UNIFORM COMMERCIAL CODE

Sec.	Par. (This Work)	Note
9–312	9.06	408
9–312(1)	8.01	12
9–312(a)	9.06	408
9–312(b)	9.06	373
9–312(b)(1)	9.06	
9–312(b)(1)	9.06	373
9–312(b)(3)	9.06	406
9–313	8.01	9
9–313	9.06	406
9–313	9.06	408
9–314	8.01	9
9–314	9.06	
9–315	8.01	9
9–315	9.06	
9–315	9.06	366
9–315	11.03	
9–317	9.06	373
9–317(a)(2)	9.06	379
9–317(d)	11.03	102
9–321(a)	11.03	
9–322	9.06	
9–322	9.06	366
9–322	11.03	101
9–327	8.01	9
9–327	9.01	89
9–327	9.06	
9–327	9.06	371
9–327	9.06	373
9–327	9.06	376
9–327	9.06	378
9–327	9.06	413
9–330	8.01	9
9–330(a)	11.03	
9–331	3.03	299
9–331	8.01	9
9–331(c)	3.03	
9–331, Comment 5	1.04	214
9–331, Comment 5	3.03	
9–331, Comment 5	3.03	253
9–332	8.01	9
9–340	9.01	89
9–340	9.06	
9–340	9.06	370
9–340	9.06	371
9–340	9.06	376
9–340	9.06	413
9–340(a)	9.06	
9–340(a)	9.06	338
9–340(c)	9.06	
9–402(1)	6.03	273
9–403	1.04	
9–403	2.01	33
9–403	2.02	93
9–403	3.03	338
9–403(b)	3.03	330
9–404	2.02	93
9–404	3.03	338
9–404—9–406	3.04	425
9–404(b)	3.03	349
9–406(a)	6.03	204
9–406(d)	9.06	408
9–406(f)	9.06	408

UNIFORM COMMERCIAL CODE

Sec.	Par. (This Work)	Note
9–602	2.02	105
9–602	6.03	281
9–602, Comment 4	6.03	281
9–604, Comment 4	2.02	105

UNIFORM COMPUTER INFORMATION TRANSACTIONS ACT

Sec.	Par. (This Work)	Note
209	11.03	100

UNIFORM CONSUMER CREDIT CODE

Sec.	Par. (This Work)	Note
1.107	11.03	123
1.201	1.03	108
1.201(8)	8.01	24
1.301(12)	3.04	412
1.301(15)	3.04	412
2.502	2.02	89
2.507	2.02	214
2.510	2.02	94
3.204	3.04	412
3.301—3.303	2.02	83
3.306	2.02	106
3.307	1.03	144
3.307	2.02	93
3.307	3.04	423
3.309	3.03	266
3.403—3.405	1.03	144
3.404	2.02	93
3.404	3.04	
3.404	3.04	420
3.404	3.04	423
5.201	1.03	144

UNIFORM ELECTRONIC TRANSACTIONS ACT

Sec.	Par. (This Work)	Note
2(13)	9.01	36
3(b)(2)	1.01	12
3(b)(2)	4.02	2
9	4.02	12
16	1.02	34
16	2.02	36
16	2.02	37
16	3.02	65
103(a)(3)	1.01	29
103(a)(3)	2.02	36

CODE OF FEDERAL REGULATIONS

Tit.	Par. (This Work)	Note
12, § 7.4002	9.02	95
12, § 7.4002	9.05	297

TABLE OF STATUTES

CODE OF FEDERAL REGULATIONS

Tit.	Par.	This Work Note
12, Pt. 34, Subpt. B	2.02	195
12, § 34.7	2.02	195
12, §§ 103.15—103.29	10.14	271
12, § 103.29	10.14	271
12, Pt. 202	3.02	107
12, § 202.7(d)	3.02	107
12, § 202.7(d)	7.03	171
12, § 202.7(d)(1)	6.03	178
12, § 204.2(a)(1)	9.05	247
12, Pt. 205	1.01	4
12, Pt. 205	1.01	31
12, Pt. 205	10.01	3
12, Pt. 205	10.02	5
12, Pt. 205	11.01	4
12, Pt. 205	11.01	8
12, Pt. 205	11.01	16
12, § 205.2(a)(1)	11.02	77
12, § 205.2(a)(2)	11.02	77
12, § 205.2(b)	11.02	25
12, § 205.2(g)	1.01	31
12, § 205.2(g)	11.01	5
12, § 205.2(g)	11.01	6
12, § 205.2(g)	11.01	17
12, § 205.2(g)	11.02	25
12, § 205.2(k)	11.02	38
12, § 205.2(m)	11.02	82
12, § 205.2(m)	11.03	123
12, § 205.2(m)(2)	11.02	84
12, § 205.2(m)(3)	11.02	84
12, § 205.3	11.01	6
12, § 205.3	11.02	24
12, § 205.3(c)(1)	1.01	4
12, § 205.3(e)	10.02	5
12, § 205.4	11.01	8
12, § 205.5(a)	11.02	86
12, § 205.5(b)	11.02	87
12, § 205.6	11.01	22
12, § 205.6	11.03	119
12, § 205.6(a)	11.02	78
12, § 205.6(a)	11.04	134
12, § 205.6(b)	11.02	79
12, § 205.6(b)(1)	11.02	80
12, § 205.6(b)(2)	11.02	80
12, § 205.6(b)(3)	11.02	81
12, § 205.6(b)(3)	11.03	122
12, § 205.6(b)(4)	11.02	81
12, § 205.6(b)(5)	11.02	81
12, § 205.6(b)(6)	11.02	79
12, § 205.7	11.01	8
12, § 205.7	11.01	19
12, § 205.7(a)	11.02	34
12, § 205.8	11.01	20
12, § 205.8(a)	11.02	35
12, § 205.8(b)	11.02	35
12, § 205.9	11.01	8
12, § 205.9	11.01	21
12, § 205.9(a)	11.01	6
12, § 205.9(a)	11.02	39
12, § 205.9(a)	11.03	112
12, § 205.9(b)	11.02	35
12, § 205.9(b)	11.02	36
12, § 205.9(c)	11.02	38

CODE OF FEDERAL REGULATIONS

Tit.	Par.	This Work Note
12, § 205.9(c)(1)	11.02	38
12, § 205.9(c)(2)	11.02	36
12, § 205.9(d)	11.02	36
12, § 205.9(d)	11.02	38
12, § 205.10	11.02	38
12, § 205.11	11.01	23
12, § 205.11(a)	11.02	48
12, § 205.11(a)(1)	11.03	123
12, § 205.11(a)(2)	11.02	49
12, § 205.11(b)	11.02	50
12, § 205.11(c)	11.02	56
12, § 205.11(c)(1)	11.02	51
12, § 205.11(c)(1)	11.02	55
12, § 205.11(c)(2)	11.02	52
12, § 205.11(c)(2)	11.02	53
12, § 205.11(c)(2)	11.02	55
12, § 205.11(c)(3)	11.02	52
12, § 205.11(c)(4)	11.02	54
12, § 205.11(d)	11.02	53
12, § 205.11(d)(1)	11.02	56
12, § 205.11(d)(2)	11.02	57
12, § 205.11(e)	11.02	58
12, § 205.12(a)(1)	11.02	59
12, § 205.12(a)(1)(iii)	11.02	85
12, § 205.12(a)(2)	11.02	59
12, § 205.12(a)(2)	11.02	89
12, § 205.12(a)(i)	11.02	88
12, § 205.12(a)(ii)	11.02	88
12, §§ 205.14—205.16	11.02	34
12, Pt. 210	8.01	40
12, Pt. 210	8.04	314
12, Pt. 210	8.04	320
12, Pt. 210	8.04	453
12, Pt. 210	9.03	146
12, Pt. 210	10.01	1
12, Pt. 210	10.08	154
12, Pt. 210	10.11	228
12, Pt. 210, Subpt. A	10.11	229
12, Pt. 210, Subpt. B	10.11	230
12, § 210.1	8.01	41
12, § 210.1	8.04	425
12, § 210.2(g)	1.03	164
12, § 210.2(i)	10.11	231
12, § 210.2(q)	10.12	245
12, § 210.2b(e)	10.12	245
12, § 210.3	8.01	41
12, § 210.3(a)	8.01	31
12, § 210.3(b)	1.03	164
12, § 210.3(b)	8.01	31
12, § 210.3(c)	10.10	224
12, § 210.3(f)	10.11	
12, § 210.3(f)	10.11	233
12, § 210.5(a)	8.01	31
12, § 210.5(a)	10.11	232
12, § 210.5(a)(1)	10.11	232
12, § 210.5(a)(2)	7.02	68
12, § 210.6(a)	8.01	54
12, § 210.6(a)(1)	8.01	31
12, § 210.6(a)(1)	8.03	194
12, § 210.6(b)	7.02	68
12, § 210.9(a)	8.02	93
12, § 210.9(a)—(b)	10.11	

TABLE OF STATUTES

CODE OF FEDERAL REGULATIONS

Tit.	Par.	This Work Note
12, § 210.9(b)(5)	10.11	242
12, § 210.9(c)	10.11	231
12, § 210.9(f)	10.11	237
12, § 210.12	8.04	
12, § 210.12	8.04	427
12, § 210.12(a)	8.01	42
12, § 210.12(a)	8.02	93
12, § 210.12(a)	8.04	399
12, § 210.12(a)	8.04	406
12, § 210.12(a)—(c)	8.04	429
12, § 210.12(c)	8.04	424
12, § 210.12(d)	10.11	236
12, § 210.12(e)	10.11	236
12, § 210.12(f)	10.11	239
12, § 210.12(g)	10.11	238
12, § 210.12(h)	10.11	238
12, § 210.12(i)	10.11	240
12, § 210.12(i)	10.12	253
12, § 210.13	10.11	239
12, § 210.14	10.11	241
12, § 210.25	1.03	164
12, § 210.25	10.12	243
12, § 210.25(a)	10.08	163
12, § 210.25(a)	10.12	250
12, § 210.25(b)	10.08	163
12, § 210.25(b)	10.12	244
12, § 210.25(b)	10.13	264
12, § 210.25(b)(2)	10.12	245
12, § 210.25(b)(2)(v)	10.08	163
12, § 210.25(b)(3)	10.02	5
12, § 210.25(b)(3)	10.12	246
12, § 210.25(b)(4)	10.12	247
12, § 210.25(c)	10.12	244
12, § 210.26	10.12	251
12, § 210.26(c)	1.03	164
12, § 210.27	10.12	252
12, § 210.27(a)	10.10	221
12, § 210.27(b)	1.03	164
12, § 210.27(b)	10.10	221
12, § 210.28	10.02	8
12, § 210.28	10.11	240
12, § 210.28	10.12	
12, § 210.28	10.12	253
12, § 210.28	10.12	255
12, § 210.28(c)	10.10	216
12, § 210.28(c)	10.12	254
12, § 210.29(a)	10.12	256
12, § 210.29(b)	10.12	257
12, § 210.30(a)	10.10	220
12, § 210.30(a)	10.12	258
12, § 210.30(b)	10.10	224
12, § 210.32(a)	10.10	225
12, § 210.32(a)	10.12	263
12, § 210.32(b)	10.10	222
12, § 210.32(c)	10.12	263
12, Pt. 219, Subpt. B	10.14	270
12, Pt. 22	1.03	168
12, Pt. 226	11.01	8
12, § 226.2(a)(20)	11.02	62
12, § 226.3	11.01	7
12, § 226.3	11.02	69
12, § 226.5(b)(1)	11.02	28

CODE OF FEDERAL REGULATIONS

Tit.	Par.	This Work Note
12, § 226.5(b)(2)	11.02	30
12, § 226.5a	11.01	8
12, § 226.5a(b)	11.02	28
12, § 226.5b	11.01	8
12, § 226.5b(d)	11.02	28
12, § 226.6	11.01	8
12, § 226.6	11.02	29
12, § 226.6(e)	11.02	29
12, § 226.7	11.01	8
12, § 226.7	11.02	31
12, § 226.8	11.01	8
12, § 226.8	11.02	31
12, § 226.9	11.01	8
12, § 226.9(a)	11.02	33
12, § 226.9(a)	11.02	35
12, § 226.9(b)	11.02	33
12, § 226.9(c)	11.02	32
12, § 226.9(e)	11.02	33
12, § 226.9(f)	11.02	33
12, § 226.10	11.02	60
12, § 226.12	11.01	8
12, § 226.12(a)	11.02	27
12, § 226.12(a)	11.02	86
12, § 226.12(b)(1)	11.02	72
12, § 226.12(b)(1)	11.02	73
12, § 226.12(b)(2)	11.02	29
12, § 226.12(b)(2)	11.02	71
12, § 226.12(b)(3)	11.02	72
12, § 226.12(b)(4)	1.03	172
12, § 226.12(b)(4)	11.02	70
12, § 226.12(b)(5)	11.02	69
12, § 226.12(c)	11.02	27
12, § 226.12(e)	11.02	27
12, § 226.12(e)	11.02	60
12, § 226.12(g)	11.02	85
12, § 226.12(g)	11.02	88
12, § 226.12(g)	11.02	89
12, § 226.13	11.01	8
12, § 226.13(a)	11.02	40
12, § 226.13(b)	11.02	41
12, § 226.13(c)	11.02	42
12, § 226.13(d)	11.02	43
12, § 226.13(e)	11.02	44
12, § 226.13(f)	11.02	45
12, § 226.13(g)	11.02	46
12, § 226.13(h)	11.02	47
12, § 226.15	11.02	27
12, § 226.19(b)	2.02	195
12, § 226.36(d)	8.03	194
12, Pt. 22	1.01	20
12, Pt. 229	1.03	160
12, Pt. 229	1.04	180
12, Pt. 229	2.01	13
12, Pt. 229	3.02	155
12, Pt. 229	3.03	224
12, Pt. 229	4.03	60
12, Pt. 229	4.03	65
12, Pt. 229	8.04	254
12, Pt. 229	8.04	312
12, Pt. 229	9.03	146
12, Pt. 229	9.05	271
12, Pt. 229	10.08	142

CODE OF FEDERAL REGULATIONS

Tit.	Par.	This Work Note
12, Pt. 229	10.11	
12, Pt. 229, Subpt. C	10.11	234
12, §§ 229.1—229.42	8.01	37
12, §§ 229.1—229.42	9.03	202
12, § 229.1(b)(3)	8.01	41
12, § 229.1(b)(3)	8.03	200
12, § 229.1(b)(3)	8.03	248
12, § 229.1(b)(3)	8.04	426
12, § 229.1(b)(3)	9.03	224
12, § 229.2	8.04	269
12, § 229.2(a)	1.04	183
12, § 229.2(e)	1.04	182
12, § 229.2(e)	8.04	259
12, § 229.2(e)	8.04	398
12, § 229.2(e)	8.04	426
12, § 229.2(f)	4.03	79
12, § 229.2(g)	4.03	79
12, § 229.2(k)	1.01	19
12, § 229.2(k)	1.04	191
12, § 229.2(k)	8.04	439
12, § 229.2(o)	1.04	194
12, § 229.2(o)	8.04	378
12, § 229.2(q)	8.04	323
12, § 229.2(r)	8.04	269
12, § 229.2(r)	8.04	272
12, § 229.2(s)	8.04	269
12, § 229.2(s)	8.04	272
12, § 229.2(u)	1.04	191
12, § 229.2(u)	4.03	59
12, § 229.2(u)	4.03	65
12, § 229.2(v)	8.04	272
12, § 229.2(w)	8.04	272
12, § 229.2(z)	1.04	192
12, § 229.2(z)	8.01	85
12, § 229.2(z)	8.04	315
12, § 229.2(z)	8.04	398
12, § 229.2(z)	8.04	426
12, § 229.2(z)(2)	8.04	618
12, § 229.2(bb)	8.04	327
12, § 229.2(cc)	1.04	193
12, § 229.2(cc)	8.03	200
12, § 229.2(cc)	8.04	343
12, § 229.2(cc)	8.04	344
12, § 229.2(cc)	8.04	426
12, § 229.2(nn)	8.04	
12, § 229.2(nn)	8.04	492
12, § 229.2(nn)	8.04	500
12, § 229.10	1.04	184
12, § 229.10	11.02	67
12, §§ 229.10—229.13	3.02	157
12, §§ 229.10—229.21	8.02	174
12, § 229.10(a)	8.04	
12, § 229.10(a)	8.04	261
12, § 229.10(b)	8.04	
12, § 229.10(b)	8.04	261
12, § 229.10(c)	8.04	
12, § 229.10(c)	8.04	273
12, § 229.10(c)(1)(i)	8.04	262
12, § 229.10(c)(1)(i)—(c)(1)(v)	8.04	
12, § 229.10(c)(1)(ii)	8.04	263
12, § 229.10(c)(1)(ii)	8.04	268

CODE OF FEDERAL REGULATIONS

Tit.	Par.	This Work Note
12, § 229.10(c)(1)(iii)	8.04	263
12, § 229.10(c)(1)(iii)	8.04	268
12, § 229.10(c)(1)(iv)	8.04	264
12, § 229.10(c)(1)(iv)	8.04	268
12, § 229.10(c)(1)(v)	8.04	265
12, § 229.10(c)(1)(v)	8.04	268
12, § 229.10(c)(1)(vi)	8.04	
12, § 229.10(c)(1)(vi)	8.04	266
12, § 229.10(c)(1)(vii)	8.04	
12, § 229.10(c)(1)(vii)	8.04	267
12, § 229.10(c)(2)	8.04	
12, § 229.10(c)(2)	8.04	268
12, § 229.10(c)(3)	8.04	265
12, § 229.11	8.04	
12, § 229.11 (repealed)	8.04	270
12, § 2	1.04	184
12, § 229.12	8.04	
12, § 229.12	8.04	455
12, § 229.12	8.04	463
12, § 229.12	11.02	67
12, § 229.12(b)	8.04	269
12, § 229.12(b)	8.04	456
12, § 229.12(c)	8.04	271
12, § 229.12(c)	8.04	456
12, § 229.12(c)(1)(i)	8.04	272
12, § 229.12(c)(1)(ii)	8.04	273
12, § 229.13	1.04	186
12, § 229.13	8.04	275
12, § 229.13	11.02	67
12, § 229.13(a)(1)(i)	8.04	277
12, § 229.13(a)(1)(ii)	8.04	279
12, § 229.13(a)(1)(iii)	8.04	281
12, § 229.13(a)(2)	8.04	276
12, § 229.13(b)	8.04	282
12, § 229.13(c)	4.03	65
12, § 229.13(c)	8.04	284
12, § 229.13(c)(1)	8.04	285
12, § 229.13(c)(2)	8.04	285
12, § 229.13(d)	8.04	286
12, § 229.13(d)(1)	8.04	287
12, § 229.13(d)(2)	8.04	287
12, § 229.13(e)	2.02	
12, § 229.13(e)(1)	8.04	288
12, § 229.13(e)(2)	8.04	291
12, § 229.13(f)	8.04	292
12, § 229.13(g)	8.04	290
12, § 229.13(g)(1)	8.04	293
12, § 229.13(g)(2)	8.04	294
12, § 229.13(g)(3)	8.04	296
12, § 229.13(h)(1)	8.04	297
12, § 229.13(h)(4)	8.04	298
12, § 229.14	1.04	187
12, §§ 229.15—229.18	1.04	188
12, § 229.15(a)	8.04	300
12, § 229.15(a)	8.04	301
12, § 229.16(a)	8.04	300
12, § 229.17(a)	8.04	301
12, § 229.17(b)	8.04	301
12, § 229.18(a)	8.04	302
12, § 229.18(b)	8.04	302
12, § 229.18(c)	8.04	303
12, § 229.18(d)	8.04	303

TABLE OF STATUTES

CODE OF FEDERAL REGULATIONS

Tit.	Par.	This Work Note
12, § 229.18(e)	8.04	304
12, § 2	1.04	184
12, § 229.19(c)(2)	8.04	394
12, § 229.19(c)(2)(ii)	8.04	393
12, § 229.20	1.04	189
12, § 229.21	1.04	190
12, § 229.21	8.02	185
12, § 229.21(a)(1)	8.04	305
12, § 229.21(a)(2)	8.04	305
12, § 229.21(a)(3)	8.04	306
12, § 229.21(c)	8.04	307
12, § 229.21(e)	8.04	307
12, § 229.30	8.02	88
12, § 229.30	8.02	92
12, § 229.30	8.02	98
12, § 229.30	8.02	108
12, § 229.30	8.02	109
12, § 229.30	8.02	119
12, § 229.30	8.02	128
12, § 229.30	8.02	149
12, § 229.30	8.02	157
12, § 229.30	8.04	
12, § 229.30	8.04	373
12, § 229.30	8.04	457
12, § 229.30	8.04	461
12, § 229.30	8.04	463
12, §§ 229.30—229.42	8.04	308
12, § 229.30(a)	8.02	96
12, § 229.30(a)	8.02	100
12, § 229.30(a)	8.04	
12, § 229.30(a)	8.04	312
12, § 229.30(a)	8.04	316
12, § 229.30(a)	8.04	318
12, § 229.30(a)	8.04	319
12, § 229.30(a)	8.04	320
12, § 229.30(a)	8.04	328
12, § 229.30(a)	8.04	350
12, § 229.30(a)	8.04	355
12, § 229.30(a)	8.04	370
12, § 229.30(a)	8.04	373
12, § 229.30(a)	8.04	404
12, § 229.30(a)	8.04	406
12, § 229.30(a)	8.04	426
12, § 229.30(a)	8.04	470
12, § 229.30(a)—(c)	8.04	319
12, § 229.30(a)(1)	8.04	317
12, § 229.30(a)(1)	8.04	321
12, § 229.30(a)(2)	8.04	317
12, § 229.30(a)(2)	8.04	319
12, § 229.30(a)(2)	8.04	322
12, § 229.30(a)(2)	8.04	326
12, § 229.30(a)(2)	8.04	327
12, § 229.30(a)(2)	8.04	328
12, § 229.30(b)	8.04	320
12, § 229.30(b)	8.04	328
12, § 229.30(b)	10.12	260
12, § 229.30(c)	8.01	15
12, § 229.30(c)	8.02	98
12, § 229.30(c)	8.02	134
12, § 229.30(c)	8.02	136
12, § 229.30(c)	8.04	
12, § 229.30(c)	8.04	314

CODE OF FEDERAL REGULATIONS

Tit.	Par.	This Work Note
12, § 229.30(c)	8.04	319
12, § 229.30(c)	8.04	320
12, § 229.30(c)	8.04	332
12, § 229.30(c)	8.04	373
12, § 229.30(c)	8.04	404
12, § 229.30(c)	8.04	406
12, § 229.30(c)	8.04	419
12, § 229.30(c)	8.04	465
12, § 229.30(c)	10.12	262
12, § 229.30(c)(1)	8.04	333
12, § 229.30(c)(1)	8.04	334
12, § 229.30(d)	3.03	
12, § 229.30(d)	4.03	110
12, § 229.30(d)	8.04	335
12, § 229.30(e)	8.04	328
12, § 229.30(f)	8.02	179
12, § 229.30(f)	8.02	187
12, § 229.30(f)	8.04	336
12, § 229.30(f)	8.04	337
12, § 229.31	8.02	119
12, § 229.31	8.03	194
12, § 229.31	8.03	204
12, § 229.31	8.03	207
12, § 229.31	8.03	210
12, § 229.31	8.03	217
12, § 229.31	8.03	226
12, § 229.31	8.04	
12, § 229.31	8.04	316
12, § 229.31	8.04	364
12, § 229.31	8.04	461
12, § 229.31	8.04	463
12, § 229.31	8.04	471
12, § 229.31(a)	8.04	
12, § 229.31(a)	8.04	312
12, § 229.31(a)	8.04	346
12, § 229.31(a)	8.04	349
12, § 229.31(a)	8.04	350
12, § 229.31(a)	8.04	355
12, § 229.31(a)	8.04	357
12, § 229.31(a)	8.04	358
12, § 229.31(a)	8.04	359
12, § 229.31(a)	8.04	360
12, § 229.31(a)	8.04	363
12, § 229.31(a)	8.04	370
12, § 229.31(a)	8.04	397
12, § 229.31(a)	8.04	404
12, § 229.31(a)	8.04	426
12, § 229.31(a)(1)	8.04	346
12, § 229.31(a)(2)	8.04	346
12, § 229.31(a)(2)	8.04	347
12, § 229.31(b)	8.04	328
12, § 229.31(c)	8.02	90
12, § 229.31(c)	8.02	91
12, § 229.31(c)	8.02	108
12, § 229.31(c)	8.02	109
12, § 229.31(c)	8.02	119
12, § 229.31(c)	8.03	197
12, § 229.31(c)	8.03	199
12, § 229.31(c)	8.03	200
12, § 229.31(c)	8.03	234
12, § 229.31(c)	8.03	247
12, § 229.31(c)	8.03	249

TABLE OF STATUTES

CODE OF FEDERAL REGULATIONS

Tit.	Par.	This Work Note
12, § 229.31(c)	8.03	251
12, § 229.31(c)	8.03	252
12, § 229.31(c)	8.04	257
12, § 229.31(c)	8.04	350
12, § 229.31(c)	8.04	354
12, § 229.31(c)	8.04	365
12, § 229.31(c)	8.04	367
12, § 229.31(c)	8.04	371
12, § 229.31(c)	8.04	372
12, § 229.31(c)	8.04	373
12, § 229.31(c)	8.04	392
12, § 229.31(c)	8.04	468
12, § 229.31(d)	8.04	357
12, § 229.31(d)	8.04	375
12, § 229.31(d)	8.04	395
12, § 229.31(f)	8.02	103
12, § 229.31(f)	8.02	136
12, § 229.31(f)	8.03	209
12, § 229.31(f)	8.03	212
12, § 229.31(f)	8.04	376
12, § 229.31(g)	8.04	376
12, § 229.32	1.04	195
12, § 229.32	8.03	207
12, § 229.32	8.03	217
12, § 229.32	8.03	226
12, § 229.32	8.04	
12, § 229.32	8.04	373
12, § 229.32	8.04	377
12, § 229.32	10.12	263
12, § 229.32(a)	8.01	59
12, § 229.32(a)	8.04	
12, § 229.32(a)	8.04	317
12, § 229.32(a)	8.04	321
12, § 229.32(a)	8.04	333
12, § 229.32(a)	8.04	338
12, § 229.32(a)	8.04	356
12, § 229.32(a)(1)	8.04	380
12, § 229.32(a)(2)	8.04	
12, § 229.32(a)(2)	8.04	384
12, § 229.32(a)(2)(i)	8.04	381
12, § 229.32(a)(2)(i)	8.04	382
12, § 229.32(a)(2)(ii)	8.04	383
12, § 229.32(a)(2)(iii)	8.04	383
12, § 229.32(a)(2)(iv)	8.04	383
12, § 229.32(b)	3.02	155
12, § 229.32(b)	8.02	108
12, § 229.32(b)	8.02	109
12, § 229.32(b)	8.02	119
12, § 229.32(b)	8.03	197
12, § 229.32(b)	8.03	199
12, § 229.32(b)	8.03	200
12, § 229.32(b)	8.03	234
12, § 229.32(b)	8.03	247
12, § 229.32(b)	8.04	
12, § 229.32(b)	8.04	257
12, § 229.32(b)	8.04	354
12, § 229.32(b)	8.04	367
12, § 229.32(b)	8.04	371
12, § 229.32(b)	8.04	373
12, § 229.32(b)	8.04	385
12, § 229.32(b)	8.04	386
12, § 229.32(b)	8.04	387

CODE OF FEDERAL REGULATIONS

Tit.	Par.	This Work Note
12, § 229.32(b)	8.04	389
12, § 229.32(b)	8.04	390
12, § 229.32(b)	8.04	391
12, § 229.32(b)	8.04	392
12, § 229.32(b)	8.04	393
12, § 229.32(b)	8.04	468
12, § 229.32(b)(1)—(b)(4)	8.04	386
12, § 229.32(c)	8.04	397
12, § 229.32(d)	8.04	395
12, § 229.33	1.04	196
12, § 229.33	8.01	57
12, § 229.33	8.02	
12, § 229.33	8.02	102
12, § 229.33	8.02	103
12, § 229.33	8.02	136
12, § 229.33	8.02	176
12, § 229.33	8.02	179
12, § 229.33	8.02	181
12, § 229.33	8.03	212
12, § 229.33	8.03	217
12, § 229.33	8.04	
12, § 229.33	8.04	373
12, § 229.33	8.04	419
12, § 229.33	8.04	464
12, § 229.33(a)	8.04	339
12, § 229.33(a)	8.04	412
12, § 229.33(b)	8.04	
12, § 229.33(b)(8)	3.03	
12, § 229.33(c)	8.01	59
12, § 229.33(d)	8.03	200
12, § 229.33(d)	8.03	202
12, § 229.33(d)	8.03	204
12, § 229.33(d)	8.03	207
12, § 229.33(d)	8.03	217
12, § 229.33(d)	8.03	226
12, § 229.33(d)	8.03	230
12, § 229.33(d)	8.04	377
12, § 229.33(d)	8.04	393
12, § 229.33(d)	8.04	396
12, § 229.34	1.04	197
12, § 229.34	8.04	
12, § 229.34	8.04	415
12, § 229.34	8.04	427
12, § 229.34	8.04	430
12, § 229.34	9.03	224
12, § 229.34(a)	8.04	
12, § 229.34(a)	8.04	399
12, § 229.34(a)	8.04	403
12, § 229.34(a)	8.04	404
12, § 229.34(a)	8.04	406
12, § 229.34(a)	8.04	418
12, § 229.34(a)	8.04	419
12, § 229.34(a)	8.04	428
12, § 229.34(a)	8.04	466
12, § 229.34(a)	9.03	225
12, § 229.34(a)	9.03	226
12, § 229.34(a)(1)	8.04	399
12, § 229.34(a)(1)	8.04	419
12, § 229.34(a)(2)	8.04	400
12, § 229.34(a)(2)	8.04	417
12, § 229.34(a)(2)	8.04	421

TABLE OF STATUTES

CODE OF FEDERAL REGULATIONS

Tit.	Par.	This Work Note
12, § 229.34(a)(3)	8.04	401
12, § 229.34(a)(3)	8.04	417
12, § 229.34(a)(4)	8.04	402
12, § 229.34(a)(4)	8.04	422
12, § 229.34(b)	8.04	
12, § 229.34(b)	8.04	406
12, § 229.34(b)	8.04	409
12, § 229.34(b)	8.04	412
12, § 229.34(b)	8.04	418
12, § 229.34(b)	8.04	419
12, § 229.34(b)	9.03	225
12, § 229.34(b)	9.03	226
12, § 229.34(b)(1)	8.04	406
12, § 229.34(b)(1)	8.04	419
12, § 229.34(b)(2)	8.04	407
12, § 229.34(b)(2)	8.04	417
12, § 229.34(b)(2)	8.04	421
12, § 229.34(b)(3)	8.04	408
12, § 229.34(b)(3)	8.04	417
12, § 229.34(c)	8.04	404
12, § 229.34(c)	8.04	410
12, § 229.34(c)	8.04	411
12, § 229.34(c)	8.04	420
12, § 229.34(c)	8.04	467
12, § 229.34(c)	8.04	483
12, § 229.34(c)	9.03	227
12, § 229.34(d)	8.04	
12, § 229.34(d)	8.04	430
12, § 229.35	1.01	22
12, § 229.35	1.04	198
12, § 229.35	8.04	
12, § 229.35	8.04	382
12, § 229.35	9.03	183
12, § 229.35(a)	8.04	446
12, § 229.35(a)	8.04	448
12, § 229.35(a)	8.04	449
12, § 229.35(a)	8.04	450
12, § 229.35(a)	8.04	451
12, § 229.35(a)	8.04	478
12, § 229.35(b)	4.06	205
12, § 229.35(b)	8.01	82
12, § 229.35(b)	8.04	
12, § 229.35(b)	8.04	374
12, § 229.35(b)	10.11	237
12, § 229.35(c)	3.02	152
12, § 229.36	1.04	199
12, § 229.36	8.02	90
12, § 229.36	8.02	137
12, § 229.36(a)	8.04	
12, § 229.36(a)	8.04	472
12, § 229.36(b)	4.03	93
12, § 229.36(b)	8.01	59
12, § 229.36(b)	8.01	60
12, § 229.36(b)	8.02	89
12, § 229.36(b)	8.02	146
12, § 229.36(b)	8.02	147
12, § 229.36(b)	8.03	194
12, § 229.36(b)	8.04	475
12, § 229.36(b)–1	8.01	60
12, § 229.36(c)	4.03	90
12, § 229.36(c)	8.01	70
12, § 229.36(c)	8.04	433

CODE OF FEDERAL REGULATIONS

Tit.	Par.	This Work Note
12, § 229.36(c)	8.04	434
12, § 229.36(c)	8.04	436
12, § 229.36(c)	8.04	476
12, § 229.36(c)	9.03	203
12, § 229.36(d)	3.02	155
12, § 229.36(d)	8.01	15
12, § 229.36(d)	8.01	54
12, § 229.36(d)	8.02	103
12, § 229.36(d)	8.02	108
12, § 229.36(d)	8.02	109
12, § 229.36(d)	8.02	119
12, § 229.36(d)	8.03	194
12, § 229.36(d)	8.03	197
12, § 229.36(d)	8.03	199
12, § 229.36(d)	8.03	200
12, § 229.36(d)	8.03	205
12, § 229.36(d)	8.03	247
12, § 229.36(d)	8.04	
12, § 229.36(d)	8.04	257
12, § 229.36(d)	8.04	354
12, § 229.36(d)	8.04	367
12, § 229.36(d)	8.04	371
12, § 229.36(d)	8.04	392
12, § 229.36(d)	8.04	439
12, § 229.36(d)	8.04	440
12, § 229.36(d)	8.04	441
12, § 229.36(d)	8.04	444
12, § 229.36(d)	8.04	468
12, § 229.36(d)	8.04	469
12, § 229.36(f)	8.04	
12, § 229.37	1.04	201
12, § 229.37	8.03	227
12, § 229.37	8.03	248
12, § 229.37	8.04	485
12, § 229.37	8.04	486
12, § 229.37	8.04	503
12, § 229.37	9.03	
12, § 229.37(a)	8.03	264
12, § 229.38	1.04	200
12, § 229.38	8.02	88
12, § 229.38	8.02	119
12, § 229.38	8.02	128
12, § 229.38	8.02	149
12, § 229.38	8.02	157
12, § 229.38	8.04	
12, § 229.38	8.04	361
12, § 229.38	8.04	404
12, § 229.38	8.04	419
12, § 229.38(a)	8.02	99
12, § 229.38(a)	8.02	147
12, § 229.38(a)	8.02	185
12, § 229.38(a)	8.03	204
12, § 229.38(a)	8.03	205
12, § 229.38(a)	8.03	207
12, § 229.38(a)	8.03	226
12, § 229.38(a)	8.03	227
12, § 229.38(a)	8.03	228
12, § 229.38(a)	8.03	230
12, § 229.38(a)	8.04	
12, § 229.38(a)	8.04	358
12, § 229.38(a)	8.04	373
12, § 229.38(a)	8.04	396

TABLE OF STATUTES

CODE OF FEDERAL REGULATIONS

Tit.	Par.	This Work Note
12, § 229.38(a)	8.04	431
12, § 229.38(a)	8.04	445
12, § 229.38(a)	8.04	488
12, § 229.38(a)	8.04	489
12, § 229.38(a)	8.04	490
12, § 229.38(a)	8.04	491
12, § 229.38(a)	8.04	492
12, § 229.38(a)	8.04	493
12, § 229.38(a)	8.04	494
12, § 229.38(a)	8.04	496
12, § 229.38(a)	8.04	497
12, § 229.38(a)	8.04	500
12, § 229.38(a)	8.04	503
12, § 229.38(a)	8.04	504
12, § 229.38(a)	9.01	45
12, § 229.38(a)	9.03	132
12, § 229.38(a)	9.03	135
12, § 229.38(b)	8.02	99
12, § 229.38(b)	8.02	100
12, § 229.38(b)	8.03	204
12, § 229.38(b)	8.03	227
12, § 229.38(b)	8.03	230
12, § 229.38(b)	8.04	320
12, § 229.38(b)	8.04	328
12, § 229.38(b)	8.04	373
12, § 229.38(b)	8.04	432
12, § 229.38(b)	8.04	445
12, § 229.38(b)	8.04	496
12, § 229.38(b)	8.04	504
12, § 229.38(c)	8.02	99
12, § 229.38(c)	8.03	227
12, § 229.38(c)	8.03	230
12, § 229.38(c)	8.03	232
12, § 229.38(c)	8.04	396
12, § 229.38(c)	8.04	480
12, § 229.38(c)	8.04	483
12, § 229.38(c)	9.03	184
12, § 229.38(d)	8.02	98
12, § 229.38(e)	8.03	219
12, § 229.39	1.04	202
12, § 229.39	8.01	82
12, § 229.39	8.01	83
12, § 229.39	8.04	374
12, § 229.39(a)	8.01	84
12, § 229.39(b)	8.01	85
12, § 229.39(c)	8.01	86
12, § 229.39(d)	8.01	87
12, § 229.40	1.04	203
12, § 229.41	1.04	205
12, § 229.41	8.01	38
12, § 229.41	8.02	89
12, § 229.41	8.02	97
12, § 229.41	8.03	248
12, § 229.41	8.04	311
12, § 229.41	8.04	454
12, § 229.42	1.04	204
12, Pt. 230	9.05	271
12, § 230.2(a)	9.05	248
12, § 330.1(b)	9.05	317
16, § 310.3(a)(3)	7.02	67
16, Pt. 313	9.03	121
16, § 313.3(h)	8.01	53

CODE OF FEDERAL REGULATIONS

Tit.	Par.	This Work Note
16, § 313.3(h)	9.03	117
16, Pt. 433	1.03	145
16, Pt. 433	2.02	93
16, Pt. 433	3.04	426
16, § 433.1(d)	3.04	427
16, § 433.1(i)	3.04	431
16, § 433.1(j)	3.04	430
16, § 433.2(a)	3.04	432
16, § 433.2(b)	3.04	431
16, § 444.1	2.02	83
16, § 444.2(a)(1)	2.02	106
16, § 444.2(a)(2)	2.02	104
16, § 444.2(a)(4)	2.02	83
16, § 444.4	2.02	89
31, Pt. 103	9.05	317
31, Pt. 103	10.14	270
31, Pt. 10et seq.	9.05	270
31, Pt. 10et. seq.	9.05	317
31, Pt. 103, Subch. C	10.14	
31, § 103.11(c)	10.14	
31, § 103.33(4)	10.14	277
31, § 103.33(e)(1)	10.14	272
31, § 103.33(e)(1)(iii)	10.14	274
31, § 103.33(e)(2)	10.14	273
31, § 103.33(e)(3)	10.14	275
31, § 103.33(e)(5)	10.14	
31, § 103.33(g)(1)	10.15	283
31, § 103.33(g)(2)	10.15	284
31, § 103.33(g)(3)	10.15	

FEDERAL REGISTER

Vol.	Par.	This Work Note
37, p. 6912	10.14	270
44, p. 55812	10.14	270
44, p. 65771	3.04	426
45, p. 68634	10.11	228
46, p. 42059	10.11	228
51, p. 21744	10.11	228
53, p. 19490	9.03	203
53, p. 21984	8.01	31
53, p. 21984	10.11	228
53, p. 44456	3.04	426
57, p. 46955	10.11	228
59, p. 22965	10.11	228
60, p. 220	10.01	1
60, p. 231	10.14	270
60, p. 231	10.15	278
60, p. 233	10.14	270
60, p. 234	10.15	279
60, p. 238	10.15	283
60, p. 44144	10.14	270
60, p. 44146	10.14	270
60, p. 44151	10.14	270
60, p. 65599	10.14	270
61, p. 14386	10.15	280
61, p. 29640	10.14	270
61, p. 58975	10.14	270
62, p. 48171	10.11	228
65, p. 13692	10.14	270

FEDERAL REGISTER

Vol.	Par.	This Work Note
66, p. 15187	11.01	18
66, p. 15187	11.03	111

FEDERAL REGISTER

Vol.	Par.	This Work Note
66, p. 17329	11.01	6
66, p. 41439	11.01	6

*

Subject Index

(Most subjects are listed alphabetically both under their UCC Article heading and separately)

References are to Paragraph Number

Absence of liability as drawee, 4.04[1]
Acceptance and certification, 4.04[2][a]
Acceptance by and duties of beneficiary's bank of payment order, 10.04[1]
Acceptance by and duties of receiving bank of payment order, 10.04[1]
Acceptance by depositary bank of returned checks under Regulation CC, 8.04[3][d][i]
Acceptance, consequences, 4.04[2][b]
Acceptor liability, 4.04[2]
Acceptor or payor, warranties made to, 7.02[3]
Accommodation parties, 5.02
Accord and satisfaction, 7.01[3]
"Account", definition for stop payment orders, 9.01[4][a]
Accountability and final payment under Article 4, 8.02[3]
Adverse claims, 6.03[6][b][iii]
Agent liability alone, 5.03[3]
Agents, 5.03
Alteration defense, 6.02[7]
Alteration, warranty concerning, 7.02[3][c]
Alternatives to stopping payment, 9.01[4][c]
Ambiguities and omissions in instruments, 2.04
Arbitration clauses, 11.02[6]
Article 3 [see also particular headings]
   Acceptance and certification, 4.04[2][a]
   Acceptance, consequences, 4.04[2][b]
   Acceptor liability, 4.04[2]
   Acceptor or payor, warranties made to, 7.02[3]
   Accommodation parties, 5.02
   Accord and satisfaction, 7.01[3]
   Adverse claims, 6.03[6][b][iii]
   Agents, 5.03
   Alteration defense, 6.02[7]
   Alteration, warranty concerning, 7.02[3][c]
   Ambiguities and omissions in instruments, 2.04
   Authorized complete instruments, 2.05[2]
   Authorized signatures, creating principal but not agent liability, 5.03[2]

Article 3 [see also particular headings] —Cont'd
   Bad faith, holder in due course, 3.03[2][b][ii]
   Basis for liability and rights—negligence, conversion, etc., 7.03
   Basis for liability on instrument, 4.02
   Blank indorsements, 3.02[3][c][i]
   Burden of proof, holder in due course, 3.03[2][c]
   By analogy, application of 1.03[1][b]
   Cancellation and renunciation, 6.03[6][c]
   Capacity and liability, 4.02[3]
   Certificate of deposit, 1.01[4][b]
   Certification and acceptance, 4.04[2][a]
   Checks, when is payment required, permitted, or prohibited, 9.01
   Choice of law, 1.03[3]
   Claims and defenses, 6.02, 6.03
   Claims and defenses, freedom of holder in due course, 3.03[3][a]
   Collateral, provisions relating to, 2.02[3][a][ii][A]
   Complete instruments, authorized and unauthorized, 2.05[2]
   Conditions impacting on negotiability, 2.02[3]
   Consequences of acceptance, 4.04[2][b]
   Contract law, applicability of, 1.03[1][a]
   Conversion, 7.03[3]
   "Counterparts" of real defenses, 6.03[2]
   Creation of liability on instrument, 2.02[2][a], 4.02
   Defenses and claims, 6.02, 6.03
   Defenses and claims, freedom of holder in due course, 3.03[3][a]
   Defenses and liability, relation between, 6.01[1]
   Definitional exclusions from Article 3, 1.03[1]
   Definitions, 1.01, 1.01 [4], 2.02
   Delivery (transfer), requirements of, 3.02[1], [3][a]
   Discharge of liability, 4.03[d][i], 4.06[2][b], 6.02[5], 6.03[6]
   Discharge, personal defense of, 6.02[6]
   Discharge, real defense of, 6.02[5]

658 INDEX

Article 3 [see also particular headings] —Cont'd
　Dishonor by drawer, 4.03[2][a]
　Dishonor, condition of indorser contract, 4.06[2][a]
　Dishonor of a cashier's check, bank liability for, 9.01[4][d][iii]
　Dishonor or payment of the instrument, effect on underlying transaction, 7.01[1][c]
　Drawee liability, absence of, 4.04[1]
　Drawer liability, 4.03[1]
　Duress, 6.02[2]
　Effects of various types of indorsements, 3.02[3][c]
　Elements of taking as holder in due course, 3.03[2]
　Employer's forged indorsements, 7.03[3][c][ii]
　Enforcement, rights of holder, 3.01[4][b]
　Erosion of negotiable status, 2.01[2][a], 3.03[1][a], 3.04
　Evidence of liability, 4.03[2][d][ii], 4.06[2][b], 5.02[1], 5.03[3]
　Excessive luggage encumbering the promise or order, 2.02[3][a][ii]
　Exclusion from Article 3, 1.01[4][d], 1.02[2], 1.03[2]
　Excuse of liability, 4.03[2][d][iii], 4.06[2][b], 6.03[6][d]
　Failure or want of consideration, 6.03[5]
　Federal law, 1.03[3][d]
　Fictitious payee cases, 7.03[3][c][ii]
　Foreign money, instruments payable in, 2.02[5][b]
　Forged or unauthorized signature, 4.02[1], 7.02[3][a]
　Fraud, 6.02[4], 6.03[2]
　Freedom from claims and defenses, holder in due course, 3.03[3][a]
　Good faith, 3.03[2][b][iii], 8.04[4][l], 9.01[4][b], 9.03[4][c]
　History of negotiable instrument law form requirements, 2.01[1]
　Holder, concept of, 3.01[2]
　Holder in due course, 3.03, 3.04
　Illegality, 6.02[3]
　Impact of Regulation CC on UCC Articles 3 and 4, 8.04[4]
　Impairment of recourse and collateral, 6.03[6][d][i] and [ii]
　Impairment of recourse and collateral, waiver of defense, 6.03[6][d][iii]
　Imposter cases, 7.03[3][c][ii]
　Inadequacy of form, 2.01[2][b]
　Incomplete instruments, 2.05
　Indorsement, 3.02[3], 4.06, 8.04[3][g], [4][h]
　Indorser's liability, 4.06
　Infancy and other incapacity, 6.02[1]
　Informal instruments, 2.02[3][a][i]
　Instrument in relation to underlying transaction, 2.02[3][b], 7.01[1]

Article 3 [see also particular headings] —Cont'd
　Instrument on which a bank is liable and underlying transaction, 7.01[2]
　Instruments, 1.01, 2.02, 4.02
　Issuance and rights created on negotiable instrument, 3.01
　Jus tertii (third party defenses), 6.03[1][b]
　Knowledge of agent relevant to holding in due course, 3.03[2][b][ii]
　Lack of notice, element of holder in due course, 3.03[2][b]
　Liability and defenses, relation between, 6.01[1]
　Liability and rights with respect to the underlying transaction, 7.01
　Liability for dishonor of a cashier's check, 9.01[4][d][iii], [iv]
　Liability other than on the instrument, Chapter 7
　Liability to and of party accommodated, 5.02[3]
　Liability to taker of instrument of accommodation party, 5.02[2]
　Limitations on holder in due course status, 3.04
　Limitations on source of payment, impact on negotiability, 2.02[3][c]
　Limited and unconditional promise or order, impact on negotiability, 2.02[3]
　Lost, destroyed, and stolen cashier's, tellers or certified checks, 9.01[4][d][v]
　Maker's liability, 4.05
　Misrepresentation, 6.02[4], 6.03[2]
　Money order, 1.01[4][c]
　Nature of promise or order, 2.02[3][a]
　Nature of warranty obligations, 7.02[1][a]
　Negligence as a basis for liability and rights, 7.03[2]
　Negotiation, 3.02[2], [3]
　No alterations, warranty, 7.02[2], [3][c]
　No forged indorsements, warranty, 7.02[2], [3][b]
　No unauthorized signature, warranty, 7.02[2], [3][a]
　Nondelivery, defense, 6.03[4]
　Nonperformance of a condition precedent, defense, 6.03[4]
　Non-possessors, rights of, 3.01[3][a]
　Notes and certificates of deposit, 1.01[4][b]
　Notice, holder in due course, 3.03[2][b][iv]
　Notice of dishonor, 4.03[2][b], 4.06[2][a], 8.02[6]
　Omissions in instruments, 2.04
　Oral parol evidence, 2.02[3][b][iii]
　Order of liability of indorsers, 4.06[3]

Article 3 [see also particular headings]
—Cont'd
Order paper, drafts and checks, 1.01[4][a]
Other agreements affecting the instrument, 2.02[3][b][ii]
Owner's basis for suit in conversion, 7.03[3][a]
Padded payroll cases, 7.03[3][c][ii]
Parity of rights and liabilities on instrument and obligation, 7.01[1][a]
Parol evidence, 6.01[2]
Payable on demand or definite time as requirement for negotiability, 2.02[6]
Payable to order or bearer as requirement for negotiability, 2.02[7]
Payee as holder in due course, 3.03[1][b]
Payment of the instrument or dishonor, effect of, 6.03[6][b], 7.01[1][c]
Payment or satisfaction and tender of payment, 6.03[6][b]
Payment or satisfaction to the holder, 6.03[6][b][ii]
Payor or acceptor, warranties made to, 7.02[3]
Personal and real defenses, 6.01[1][b], 6.02, 6.03
Popular name instruments, 1.01[4][c]
Preclusion, 4.02[2][a]
Presentment as a condition of dishonor, 4.03[2][a][i]
Principal but not agent liability, 5.03[2]
Procedural considerations in relation to defenses, 6.01[1][a]
Promissory note, 1.01[4][b]
Protest of dishonor, generally, 4.03[2][c]
Protest of dishonor, indorser, 4.06[2][a]
Ratification, 4.02[2][b]
Real defenses, 6.02
Reasons for form requirements of negotiable instruments, 2.01[1]
References not permitted, 2.02[3][b][i][B]
References permitted, 2.02[3][b][i][A]
References verses incorporation, 2.02[3][b][i]
Refusal to pay and dishonor of a cashier's or similar check, measure of liability, 9.01[4][d][iii], [iv]
Relation between the instrument and the transaction in general, 7.01[1]
Relevant time for meeting requirements of holder in due course, 3.03[2][b][i]
Remedies and limitations of warranties, 7.02[1][b]
Remitters, rights of, 3.01[3][a]
Renunciation and cancellation, 6.03[6][c]
Requirements for "promise" for negotiability, 2.02[3][a]
Requirements of transfer and delivery, 3.02[3][a]
Reacquisition, 3.02[4][b]

Article 3 [see also particular headings]
—Cont'd
Rescission of final payment on restitutionary grounds, 3.03[3][b], 8.02[4]
Rescission of negotiation, 3.02[4][a]
Restrictive indorsements, types and effects, 3.02[3][c][iii]
Right of enforcement, 3.01[4][b]
Right of discharge, 3.01[4][b]
Right to transfer or negotiate instrument, 3.01[4][c]
Rights and liability with respect to the underlying transaction, 7.01
Rights created on instrument, 3.01
Rights, holder of an instrument, 3.01[4]
Rules to forestall ambiguities, 2.04[1]
Satisfaction or payment and tender of payment, 6.03[6][b]
Satisfaction or payment to the holder, 6.03[6][b][ii]
Scope of Articles 3 and 4, 1.02[1]
Seals, 2.03
Shelter rights, 3.01[3][b]
Signature as basis for liability, 4.02[1]
Signing requirement, 2.02[2]
Special indorsements, 3.02[3][c][ii]
Specific notice provisions and holder in due course, 3.03[2][b][v]
Status of holder in due course, 3.03[3]
Statute of limitations, 6.03[7]
Sum certain, amount ascertainable from instrument, 2.02[4][a]
Sum certain provisions not creating uncertainty, 2.02[4][b]
Sum payable in money, 2.02[5]
Supplementary governing law, 1.04
Suspension of the underlying obligation, 7.01[1][b]
Takers, rights of, 3.01[3][a]
Teller's checks, 1.01[4][c]
Tender of payment and satisfaction or payment, 6.03[6][b]
Third party defenses (Jus tertii), 6.03[1][b]
Time of presentment, 4.03[2][a][ii]
Transaction and the instrument, relation between, 7.01[1]
Transferees, rights of, 3.01[3][b]
Transferor, warranties made by, 7.02[2]
Transfer, 3.02[1]
Traveler's checks, 1.01[4][c]
Unauthorized complete instruments, 2.05[2]
Unauthorized completion, 6.03[3]
Unauthorized indorsers of instruments, 3.02[3][b][iv], 7.03[3][b]
Unauthorized signature, 4.02, 5.03[1], 7.02[3][a]
Underlying obligation, suspension of, 7.01[1][b]
Underlying transaction, rights and liability with respect to, 7.01

Article 3 [see also particular headings]
—Cont'd
  Use of parol evidence to show defense, 6.01[2]
  Uses of instruments, 1.01[2], [3]
  Value, element of taking as holder in due course, 3.03[2][a]
  Variation by agreement, 2.01[3], 8.01[2], 8.04[4][j], 9.01[4][b]
  Waiver of defense, impairment of recourse and collateral, 6.03[6][d][iii]
  Want or failure of consideration, 6.03[5]
  Warranties made by transferor, 7.02[2]
  Warranties made to an acceptor or payor, 7.02[3]
  Who may indorse instruments payable to estates, offices and the like, 3.02[3][b][iii]
  Who may indorse instruments payable to more than one person, 3.02[3][b][ii]
  Written instrument requirement, 2.02[1]
Article 4 [see also particular headings]
  Ability to stop payment, 9.01[4][a][d][i], [ii]
  Accountability and final payment under Article 4, 8.02[3]
  Alteration, warranty concerning, 7.02[3][c]
  Availability of funds and time of deposit, 8.04[2][d]
  Avoidance of payment on restitutionary grounds, 8.02[4]
  Bank accounts, law of, 9.05
  Bank deposits and collections, 1.04[1], Chapters 8 and 9
  Banker's lien, set off, garnishment, security interests, 9.06
  Check collection and return, 8.02, 8.03, 8.04, [3]
  Check truncation and MICR encoding, 9.03[6]
  Checks, when is payment required, permitted or prohibited, 9.01
  Choice of law, 8.01[1][b]
  Comparative negligence and good faith, 9.03[4][c]
  Consequences of wrongful payment and wrongful dishonor, 9.02
  Creditor process, 9.01[5], 9.06, 10.08[2]
  Customer relationship, generally, 9.03[1]
  "Cutoff" hour for bank, 9.01[7]
  Death or incompetence of the drawer, 9.01[6]
  Definitions, 8.01[3],
  Drawer, incompetence or death of, 9.01[6]
  Duties of customer under Section 4–406, 9.03[4]
  Excuses for failure to meet the midnight deadline, 8.03[3]
  Excuses for failure to send timely notice of dishonor, 8.02[7]

Article 4 [see also particular headings]
—Cont'd
  Final and provisional payment, 8.02, 8.03
  Final payment, the "four legals" and the bank's "cutoff" hour, 9.01[7]
  Final settlement and accountability, 8.02, [3]
  "Four legals", 9.01[7]
  Funds availability under Article 4, Regulation CC, 8.02[5], 8.04[2]
  Good faith, 3.03[2][b][iii], 8.04[4][l], 9.01[4][b], 9.03[4][c]
  Impact of Regulation CC on UCC Articles 3 and 4, 8.04[4]
  Impact of revised Section 4–406 on customer's duties, 9.03[4][b]
  Incompetence or death of drawer, 9.01[6]
  Initial settlement, 8.02[1][a]
  Insolvency, 8.01[4]
  Legal process, receipt of, 9.01[5]
  Liability for dishonor of a cashier's check, 9.01[4][d][iii]
  Liability and subrogation after wrongful payment, 9.02[3]
  Limitations of liability for wrongful dishonor, 9.02[2][b]
  Measure of liability when bank misses its midnight deadline, 8.02[3], 8.03[4]
  Methods of making final payment, 8.02[2]
  MICR encoding and check truncation, 9.03[6]
  "Midnight deadline", 8.01[3][j], 8.02[2][c], 8.03, 8.04[4][b]
  Midnight deadline, when it runs, 8.02[2][c], 8.03
  Modification by agreement and preemption by federal rule of Article 4, 8.01[2]
  Modification of bank customer relationship by agreement, 9.03[3]
  Nature of warranty obligations, 7.02[1][a]
  No alterations, warranty, 7.02[2], [3][c]
  No forged indorsements, warranty, 7.02[2], [3][b]
  No unauthorized signature, warranty, 7.02[2], [3][a]
  Now and Share drafts, 9.04
  Obligation of payor bank to examine checks and of customer to examine statement, 9.03[4], 9.03[5]
  Oral notice as means of dishonor, 8.02[6]
  Overdrafts, 9.01[2]
  Payment, finality of, 8.02[1][c], [2], 8.03
  Payment, methods of, 8.02[2]
  Payment of a customer's check required, 9.01
  Payment of an altered item over a stop order, 9.01[4][b]

INDEX

Article 4 [see also particular headings]
—Cont'd
Payor bank, provisional settlement versus final payment, 8.02[1][b]
Payor bank's obligation to examine checks, 9.03[5]
Payor or acceptor, warranties made to, 7.02[3]
Permitting payment of customer's check, 9.01
Postdated checks, 9.01[2], 9.02[4]
Preemption by federal rule and modification by agreement of Article 4 provisions, 8.01[2]
Presentment of checks and truncation, 8.02, 8.03, 8.04[3][f], [4][c], [e], [g]
Prohibiting payment of customer's check, 9.01
"Properly payable," concept of, 9.01[1], [3]
Provisional and final payment, 8.02, 8.03, 8.04
Receipt of legal process, 9.01[5]
Remedies and limitations of warranties, 7.02[1][b]
Remote data processing centers, 8.04[4][f]
Requiring payment of customer's check, 9.01
Rescission of final payment on restitutionary grounds, 3.03[3][b], 8.02[4]
Reserving the right to revoke settlement, 8.02[2][b]
Restitutionary grounds for avoidance of payment, 3.03[3][b], 8.02[4]
Return of the item and notice of dishonor, 8.02[6]
Right to subrogation after wrongful payment, 9.02[3]
Rights and obligations of bank customers, 9.03
Rights to stop payment, 9.01[4]
Scope of Article 4, 8.01[1][a]
Settlement, 8.01[3][k], 8.02[1], [3]; 8.03[2], 8.04[3][c][iv], [f][iii], [4][c]
Stop payment, 9.01[4]
Subrogation, right to after wrongful payment, 9.02[3]
Transferor, warranties made by, 7.02[2]
Truncation, 8.01[3][n], 8.04[3][f], 8.04[4][g], 9.03[7]
Warranties made by transferor, 7.02[2]
Warranties made to an acceptor or payor, 7.02[3]
Warranties under Regulation CC, 8.04[3][e]
Wrongful dishonor, limitation of liability, 9.02[2][b]
Wrongful dishonor, 9.02[2]
Wrongful payment, 9.02[3]
Article 4A [see also particular headings]

Article 4A [see also particular headings]
—Cont'd
Authorized and unauthorized payment orders, 10.03, 10.09
Authority to originate, 10.03[1]
Bank-customer relation, 10.08[3]
Beneficiary misdescription in payment order, 10.09[3]
Beneficiary's bank, duties of and acceptance of payment order, 10.04[1]
Cancellation, 10.09[4]
Choice of law, 10.08[5], 10.13
Consumer transactions, exclusion from Article 4A, 10.01
Creditor process, 10.08[2]
Definitions, 10.02
Discharge, 10.07[2], 10.07[5]
Duties of and acceptance by beneficiary's bank of payment order, 10.04
Duties of and acceptance by receiving bank of payment order, 10.04
Erroneous and unauthorized payment orders, 10.09
Fees, 10.06
Finality of payment in funds transfers, 10.07
Fundamental concepts, 10.02[1]
Funds transfer, 10.01, 10.02[1]
Improperly executed payment orders, 10.09
Interest, 10.08[4]
Liability for errors and orders, 10.03, 10.09
Limitations, statute of, 10.08[6]
Misdescription, 10.04[2], 10.09[3]
Nature of payment order, 10.02[2]
Obligations of banks, 10.4, 10.7[3]
Orders improperly executed, 10.04[1], 10.05, 10.09[2]
Payment, 10.07
Payment, finality of, 10.07[2]
Payment order, 10.02, 10.04[1]
Payment order, definition, 10.02[1]
Payment order, nature of, 10.02[1]
Payment orders and stop payment, 10.09[4]
Preemption of other state law claims, 10.04[3]
Receiving banks, duties and acceptance of payment orders, 10.04
Regulation J Subparts A and B, 10.11, 10.12
Rights to stop payment, 10.09[4]
Scope, 10.01, 10.02
Security procedure, 10.03[2], [3]
Stop payment, 10.09[4]
Transmitting payment orders, 10.05
Treasury "Travel Rule", 10.15
Unauthorized and erroneous orders, 10.09
Variation by agreement or rule, 10.08[1]
"Wholesale funds transfer", 10.01
Wire transfer, 10.01

Article 4A [see also particular headings]
—Cont'd
Wire transfer monitoring rule, 10.14
Authorized complete instruments, 2.05[2]
Authorized signatures, creating principal but not agent liability, 5.03[2]
Automated Clearing Houses (ACH), 10.01, 11.01, 11.03
Automated tellers (ATM), 11.01, 11.02[2][b]
Availability of funds and time of deposit, 8.04[2]
Avoidance of payment on restitutionary grounds, 8.02[4]
Bad faith, holder in due course, 3.03[2][b][ii]
Bank
  Accounts, 9.05
  Ability to stop payment, 9.01[4][d][ii]
  Comparative negligence and good faith, role of, 9.03[4][c]
  Customer relationship, 9.03[1], 10.08[3]
  Customers, rights and obligations of, 9.03, 10.03, 10.09
  "Cutoff" hour, 9.01[7]
  Fiduciary or other special duty, 9.03[2]
  Indorsements, 8.04[3][g]
  Insolvency, 8.01[4]
  Liability and subrogation after wrongful payment, 9.02[3]
  Liability for dishonor of a cashier's check, 9.01[4][d][iii]
  Liability on instruments, 7.01[2]
  Savings & loan and credit union instruments, 1.01[4][c], 9.04
Bank Accounts
  Agreements, 9.05[1]
  Automated tellers (ATM), 11.01, 11.02[2][b]
  Bank Secrecy Act, 9.05[3][c][vi]
  Branches, 8.01[3][l]
  General or special purpose accounts, 9.05[2][a], [b], [3][c][i], [ii]
  Interest rates, 9.05[3][b], 10.08[4]
  Joint accounts, 9.06[2][c]
  Law of, 9.05
  Money Market accounts, 9.05[3][a]
  Security interest, 9.06[4]
  Termination, 9.05[3][c][v]
  Trust accounts, 9.05[3][c], 9.06[2][c]
Bank Secrecy Act, 9.05[3][c][vi]
Bankers lien, 9.06[1]
Basis for liability and rights—negligence, conversion, etc., 7.03
Basis for liability on instrument, 4.02
Beneficiary misdescription in payment order, 10.04[2], 10.09[3]
Beneficiary's bank, duties of and acceptance of payment order, 10.04[1]
Bill of exchange, 1.01[4][a]
Blank indorsements, 3.02[3][c][i]
Branches, 8.01[3][l]
Burden of proof, holder in due course, 3.03[2][c]
Cancellation of payment order, 10.09[4]

Cancellation and renunciation, 6.03[6][c]
Capacity and liability, 4.02[3]
Cashier's check
  Bank liability for dishonor of, 9.01[4][d][iii]
  Generally, 1.01[4][c], 8.01[3][m]
  Rights in, 3.01[3]
  Stopping payment, 9.01[4][d]
Certificate of deposit, 1.01[4][b]
Certification and acceptance, 4.04[2][a], 9.01[4][e]
Charges, settlement, and other notices, 8.04[3][c][iv]
Check cashing fees, 4.03[2][a][i]
Check collection and return, 8.02, 8.03, 8.04, [3]
Check guarantee cards, 1.03[3][d][ii]
Check truncation and MICR encoding, 9.03[6]
Check truncation, issuance and presentment of checks, 8.04[3][f]
Checks, when is payment required, permitted, or prohibited, 9.01
CHIPS, 10.10[2], 11.01
Choice of law, 1.03[3], 8.01[1][b], 10.08[5], 10.13
Civil liability, disclosure, 8.04[2][c], 11.02[1]
Claims and defenses, 6.02, 6.03
Claims and defenses, freedom of holder in due course, 3.03[3][a]
"Close-connectedness doctrine", 3.04[2]
Code consequences of bank's fiduciary or other special duty, 9.03[2][b]
Collateral, provisions relating to, 2.02[3][a][ii][A]
Collection of checks, Subpart C of Regulation CC, 8.04[3]
Commercial funds transfers, 10.01
Commercial transactions, use of instruments in, 1.01[3][b]
Comparative negligence and good faith, 7.03[2], 8.04[4][i], 9.03[4][c]
Comparison of consumer payment systems, 11.04
Comparison with UCC Article 4, the return process under Reg. CC, 8.04[3][c][iii]
Complete instruments, authorized and unauthorized, 2.05[2]
Conditions impacting on negotiability, 2.02[3]
Concept of "properly payable", 9.01[1]
Consequences of acceptance, 4.04[2][b]
Consequences of wrongful payment and wrongful dishonor, 9.02
Constructive possession, 3.02[2]
Consumer Credit Protection Act, 10.01, 11.01, 11.02, 11.03
Consumer liability for unauthorized transfers under federal law, 11.02[3]
Consumer payment systems, comparison of, 11.04
Consumer transactions, exclusion from Article 4A, 10.01

Consumer transactions, use of instruments in, 1.01[3][a]
Contract law, applicability of, 1.03[1][a]
Conversion, 7.03[3]
"Counterparts" of real defenses, 6.03[2]
Creation of liability on instrument, 2.02[2][a], 4.02
Credit cards, 11.02
Creditor process, 9.01[5], 9.06, 10.08[2]
Creditors, rights of against instrument, 3.01[3][a]
Customer
  Ability to stop payment, 9.01[4][d][i]
  Checks, when is payment required, permitted, or prohibited, 9.01
  Definition for stop-payment orders, 9.01[4][a]
  Duties under Section 4–406, 9.03[4]
  Overdrafts, post-dated checks, 9.01[2]
Customer-bank relationship, 9.03[1]
"Cutoff" hour for bank, 9.01[7]
Cyber Coin, 11.01
Death or incompetence of the drawer, 9.01[6]
Debit and credit cards, overview, 11.02
Debit card, 11.01
Defenses and claims, 6.02, 6.03
Defenses and claims, freedom of holder in due course, 3.03[3][a]
Defenses and liability, relation between, 6.01[1]
Defenses to action based on a forged indorsement, 7.03[3][b]
Definitional exclusions from Article 3, 1.03[1]
Definitions
  Acceptor, 4.04[2][a]
  Accommodation, 5.02[1][a]
  Agency, 8.01[3][h]
  Bank, 8.01[3][b]
  Banking Day, 8.01[3][i]
  Beneficiary, 10.02[1]
  Branch, 8.01[3][1]
  Check, 1.01[4][a]
  Collecting Bank, 8.01[3][f]
  Customer, 8.01[3][g]
  Depositary Bank, 8.01[3][c]
  Drawee, 1.01[4][a], 4.04
  Drawer, 1.01[4][a], 4.03
  Electronic presentment, 8.01[3][n]
  Funds transfer, 10.01
  Intermediary Bank, 8.01[3][e], 10.02[1]
  Item, 8.02[3][a]
  Maker, 1.01[4][b], 4.05
  Midnight Deadline, 8.01[3][j]
  Negotiable Instrument, 1.01[4]
  Payee, 1.01[4][a], [b]
  Payment order, 10.02[1]
  Payor bank, 8.01[3][d]
  Security procedure, 10.03[2]
  Sender, 10.02[1]
  Settle, 8.01[3][k]
  Signed, 2.02[2][b], 4.02[1]
  Stop-payment order, 9.01[4][a]

Definitions—Cont'd
  Types of checks, 1.01[4][c], 8.01[3][m]
Delivery for a special purpose, 6.03[4]
Delivery (transfer), requirements of, 3.02[1], [3][a]
Demand draft, 2.02[6][a]
Determination of accommodation status, 5.02[1][b]
Direct return of dishonored items, 8.04[4][d]
Discharge of liability, 4.03[d][i], 4.06[2][b], 6.02[5], 6.03[6]
Discharge, personal defense of, 6.02[6]
Discharge, real defense of, 6.02[5]
Disclosure and documentation, 8.04[2][c], 9.05[3][c][iii], 11.02[1], 11.04[3][b]
Disclosure requirements of Reg. CC, 8.04[2][c]
Dishonor by drawer, 4.03[2][a]
Dishonor, condition of indorser contract, 4.06[2][a]
Dishonor of a cashier's check, bank liability for, 9.01[4][d][iii]
Dishonor or payment of the instrument, effect on underlying transaction, 7.01[1][c]
Distribution of access devices, federal rules on, 11.02[4]
Documents of title, 1.03[2][b]
D'Oench Duhme doctrine, 1.03[3][d]
Draft, 1.01[4][a]
Drawee liability, absence of, 4.04[1]
Drawer liability, 4.03[1]
Drawer, incompetence or death of, 9.01[6]
Due care, need for, 4.02[2], 7.03[2], 7.03[3][c][B], 8.04[4][k], 9.01[4][b], 9.03[4][c]
Duress, 6.02[2]
Duties of and acceptance by bank of payment order, 10.04
Duties of customer under Section 4–406, 9.03[4]
Duties of depositary bank under Article 4 and Regulation CC, 8.03, 8.04[3][d], [g]
Duties of returning banks under Regulation CC, 8.04[3][c]
ECCHO, 11.01
E–Checks, 11.01, 11.03[2]
Effect of indorsements by banks and restrictive or missing indorsements, 3.02[3][c][iii], 7.02, 7.03, 8.04[3][g]
Effects of various types of indorsements, 3.02[3][c]
Electronic Funds Transfer Act, 11.02
Electronic payment systems, 11.01
Elements of taking as holder in due course, 3.03[2]
Emergency conditions, exceptions for funds availability, 8.04[2]b]
Employer's forgedindorsements, 7.03[3][c]ii]
Enforcement, rights of holder, 3.01[4][b]

Erosion of negotiable status, 2.01[2][a], 3.03[1][a], 3.04
Erroneous and unauthorized payment orders, 10.09
Error resolution and wrongful dishonor, federal law, 11.02[2]
Error resolution and wrongful dishonor, systems comparison, 11.04[3][a]
Evidence of debt, methods of, 1.01[2]
Evidence of liability, 4.03[2][d][ii], 4.06[2][b], 5.02[1], 5.03[3]
Excessive luggage encumbering the promise or order, 2.02[3][a][ii]
Exclusion from Article 3, 1.01[4][d], 1.02[2], 1.03[2]
Excuse of liability, 4.03[2][d][iii], 4.06[2][b], 6.03[6][d][iii]
Excuses for failure to meet the midnight deadline, 8.03[3]
Excuses for failure to send timely notice of dishonor, 8.02[7]
Expedited Funds Availability Act, 1.03[3][d][ii], 8.04
Expeditious return of dishonored checks, 8.04[3][a], [c][ii]
Failure or want of consideration, 6.03[5]
Failure to follow reasonable commercial standards, effect of, 7.03[3][b][i]
Federal law, 1.03[3][d], 8.04, 10.11, 10.12, 10.15, 11.02
Fictitious payee cases, 7.03[3][c][ii]
Fiduciary duties, 3.03[2][b][v], 9.03[2], 9.05[3][c][iii]
Final and provisional payment, 8.02, 8.03
Final payment, the "four legals" and the bank's "cutoff" hour, 9.01[7]
Final settlement and accountability, 8.02, [3]
Finality of payment in funds transfers, 10.07
Foreign law, choice of and exclusions, 1.03[3][b], [c], 10.08[5][b]
Foreign money, instruments payable in, 2.02[5][b]
Forged indorsements, 7.02[3][b], 7.03[3][b], [c]
Forged or unauthorized signature, 4.02[1], 7.02[3][a]
Forward collection settlements deemed final, under Regulation CC, impact on Article 4, 8.04[3][f][iii]
"Forward collection" test, 8.04[3][a][ii], [c][ii]
"Four legals", 9.01[7]
Fraud, 6.02[4], 6.03[2]
Freedom from claims and defenses, holder in due course, 3.03[3][a]
Funds availability
    Article 4, 8.02[5]
    Regulation CC, 8.04[2]
Funds transfers, definition, 10.01
Garnishment, 9.06[3], 10.08[2]
Good faith

Good faith—Cont'd
    Element in taking as holder in due course, 3.03[2][b][iii]
    New role, 9.03[4][c]
    Ordinary care distinguished, 3.03[2][b], 9.01[4][b]
    Regulation CC, 8.04[4][l]
History of negotiable instrument law form requirements, 2.01[1]
Holder, concept of, 3.01[2]
Holder in due course
    Burden of proof, 3.03[2][c]
    Case law limitations on, 3.04[2]
    Federal rule on, 3.04[4]
    Payee as, 3.03[1][b]
    Rationale and need, 3.03[1][a]
    State legislation, 3.04[3]
    Status of for freeedom from claims and defenses, finality of payment, 3.03[3]
    UCC limitations on, 3.04[1]
Identification of returned checks and notice of return, duties of payor bank, 8.04[3][b]
Identifying the depositary bank, notice of nonpayment, 8.04[3][b][ii]
Illegality, 6.02[3]
Impact of Regulation CC on UCC Article 4 midnight deadline, 8.04[4][b]
Impact of Regulation CC on UCC Articles 3 and 4, 8.04[4]
Impact of revised Section 4–406 on customer's duties, 9.03[4][b]
Impairment of recourse and collateral, 6.03[6][d][i] and [ii]
Impairment of recourse and collateral, waiver of defense, 6.03[6][d][iii]
Imposter cases, 7.03[3][c][ii]
Improperly executed payment orders, 10.09
Inability to invoke Article 3 by agreement, 2.01[3][a]
Inadequacy of form of instrument, 2.01[2][b]
Incompetence or death of drawer, 9.01[6]
Incomplete instruments, 2.05
Indirectly obtaining benefits of Article 3, 2.01[3]
Indorsement, 3.02[3], 4.06, 8.04[3][g], [4][h]
Indorsement of instruments payable to more than one person, 3.02[3][b][ii]
Indorsement, requirements of, 3.02[3][a]
Indorsements and indorsement standards under Regulation CC, 8.04[3][g]
Indorsements by banks and restrictive or missing indorsements, effect of, 3.02[3][c][iii], 7.03[3][c][ii][B], 8.04[3][g]
Indorsements of instruments payable to estates, offices and the like, 3.02[3][b][iii]
Indorser's liability, 4.06
Infancy and other incapacity, 6.02[1]
Informal instruments, 2.02[3][a][i]
Initial settlement, 8.02[1][a]

Instrument in relation to underlying transaction, 2.02[3][b], 7.01[1]
Instrument on which a bank is liable and underlying transaction, 7.01[2]
Instruments
    Accommodation indorsers, 3.02[3][b][iv], 4.06
    Definition of, 1.01[4]
    Interest (sum certain), 2.02[4]
    Liability on, 4.02, 4.03, 4.04, 4.05, 4.06
    Limited or Unconditional, 2.02[3]
    Misspelled names, 3.02[3][b][iv]
    Payable on demand or at definite time, 2.02[6]
    Payable to order or to bearer, 2.02[7]
    Unauthorized indorsers, 3.02[3][b][iv]
International transactions and choice of law, 1.03[3][c], 10.08[5][b]
Investment securities, 1.03[2][c]
Irrelevant forged indorsements, 7.03[3][c]
Issuance and presentment of checks and truncation, 8.04[3][f], [4][g], 9.03[6]
Issuance and rights created on negotiable instrument, 3.01
Jus tertii (third party defenses), 6.03[1][b]
Knowledge of agent relevant to holding in due course, 3.03[2][b][ii]
Lack of notice, element of holder in due course, 3.03[2][b]
Legal process, receipt of to stop payment, 9.01[5]
Length of delay, exceptions for funds availability, 8.04[2][b]
Liability and defenses, relation between, 6.01[1]
Liability and rights with respect to the underlying transaction, 7.01
Liability for dishonor of a cashier's check, 9.01[4][d][iii], [iv]
Liability other than on the instrument, Chapter 7
Liability for failure to use ordinary care, 7.03[2]
Liability for nonconforming indorsements, Reg. CC, 8.04[3][g]
Liability for unauthorized funds transfers, 10.03, 11.02[3]
Liability to and of party accommodated, 5.02[3]
Liability to taker of instrument of accommodation party, 5.02[2]
Limitations of liability for wrongful dishonor, 9.02[2][b]
Limitations on holder in due course status, 3.04
Limitations on source of payment, impact on negotiability, 2.02[3][c]
Limited and unconditional promise or order, impact on negotiability, 2.02[3]
Lost, destroyed, and stolen cashier's, tellers or certified checks, 9.01[4][d][v]
Maker's liability, 4.05
Mandatory funds availability rules and the depositary bank, 8.04[4][a]

Manner of presentment, 4.03[2][a][iii], 8.01[3][n], 8.02
Measure of liability when bank misses its midnight deadline, 8.02[3], 8.03[4]
Methods of making final payment, 8.02[2]
MICR encoding and check truncation, 9.03[6]
"Midnight deadline", 8.01[3][j], 8.02[2][c], 8.03, 8.04[4][b]
Midnight deadline, when it runs, 8.02[2][c], 8.03
Misrepresentation, 6.02[4], 6.03[2]
Missing indorsements, indorsements by banks and restrictive indorsements, effect of, 3.02[3], 7.02, 7.03[3], 8.04[3][g]
Model Law on International Credit Transfers, 10.08[5][b]
Modern critique of negotiability requirements, 2.01[2]
Modification by agreement and preemption by federal rule of Article 4, 8.01[2]
Modification of bank customer relationship by agreement, 9.03[3]
Mondex ("smart card"), 11.01
Money excluded as negotiable instrument, instrument payable in, 1.03[2][a], 2.02[5]
Money order, 1.01[4][c]
NACHA, 10.10[2], 11.01
Nature of payment order, 10.02[2]
Nature of promise or order, 2.02[3][a]
Nature of warranty obligations, 7.02[1][a]
Negligence, 4.02[2], 7.03[2], 7.03[3][c][B], 8.04[4][k]
Negligence as basis for liability and rights, 7.03[2]
Negotiable instruments, use of; definition of, 1.01[3], [4]
Negotiable orders of withdrawal (NOW), 1.01[4][c], 9.04
Negotiation, 3.02
    Bearer instrument, 3.02[2]
    Order instrument, 3.02[3]
    Rescission and requisition, 3.02[4]
New account exceptions for funds availability, 8.04[2][b]
No alterations, warranty, 7.02[2], [3][c]
No forged indorsements, warranty, 7.02[2], [3][b]
No unauthorized signature, warranty, 7.02[2], [3][a]
Non–Code consequences of bank's fiduciary or other special duty, 9.03[2][a]
Non-possessors, rights of, 3.01[3][a]
Nondelivery, defense, 6.03[4]
Nonperformance of a condition precedent, defense, 6.03[4]
Notes, 1.01[2], [4][b]
Notes and certificates of deposit, 1.01[4][b]
Notice, holder in due course, 3.03[2][b][iv]
Notice of dishonor, 4.03[2][b], 4.06[2][a], 8.02[6]

Notice of exceptions for funds availability, 8.04[2]
Notice of nonpayment, and dishonor, identifying depositary banks, 8.02[6], 8.04[3][b][ii]
Notice of return and identification of returned checks, duties of payor bank, 8.04[3][b]
Notice to customer of returned items, 8.04[3][d][iii]
Now and Share drafts, 9.04
Obligation of payor bank to examine checks, with respect to funds transfers, and of customer to examine statement, 9.03[4], 9.03[5], 10.4, 10.7[3]
Obligations and rights of bank customers, 9.03
Omissions in instruments, 2.04
Oral notice as means of dishonor, 8.02[6]
Oral parol evidence, 2.02[3][b][iii]
Order of liability of indorsers, 4.06[3]
Order paper, drafts and checks, 1.01[4][a]
Orders improperly executed, 10.04[1], 10.05, 10.09[2]
Other agreements affecting the instrument, 2.02[3][b][ii]
Overdrafts, 9.01[2]
Overview of the law of credit and debit cards, 11.02
Owner's basis for suit in conversion, 7.03[3][a]
Padded payroll cases, 7.03[3][c][ii]
Parity of rights and liabilities on instrument and obligation, 7.01[1][a]
Parol evidence
   Evidence of conditions, 6.01[2][c]
   Evidence the instrument is not to be binding, 6.01[2][b]
   Use of evidence to show defenses, 6.01[2]
Payable on demand or definite time as requirement for negotiability, 2.02[6]
Payable through and at drafts, documentary drafts, Regulation CC, 8.04, [4][e]
Payable through or at checks and truncation, 8.04[3][f]
Payable to order or bearer as requirement for negotiability, 2.02[7]
Payee as holder in due course, 3.03[1][b]
Paying and returning banks, warranties of, 8.04[3][e]
Payment, finality of, 8.02[1][c], [2], 8.03, 10.07[2], [3]
Payment for returned items, 8.04[3][d][ii]
Payment in cash, 8.02[2][a]
Payment, methods of, 1.01[2], 8.02[2]
Payment of a customer's check required, 9.01
Payment of an altered item over a stop order, 9.01[4][b]
Payment of the instrument or dishonor, effect of, 6.03[6][b], 7.01[1][c]
Payment or satisfaction and tender of payment, 6.03[6]b]

Payment or satisfaction to the holder, 6.03[6][b][ii]
Payment order, definition, 10.02[1]
Payment order, nature of, 10.02[1]
Payment orders excluded from Article 3, 1.03[2][d]
Payment orders and stop payment (cancellation), 10.09[4]
Payor bank, provisional settlement versus final payment, 8.02[1][b]
Payor bank, Regulation CC and impact on Article 4, 8.04[3][a][iii]
Payor bank's obligation to examine checks, 9.03[5]
Payor or acceptor, warranties made to, 7.02[3]
Permitting payment of customer's check, 9.01
Personal and real defenses, 6.01[1][b], 6.02, 6.03
Personal defenses, 6.03
Point of sale terminal (POS), 11.01
Popular name instruments, 1.01[4][c]
Positive pay, 7.02[3][a]
Postdated checks, 9.01[2], 9.02[4]
Preclusion, 4.02[2][a]
Preemption by federal rule and modification by agreement of Article 4 provisions, 8.01[2]
Presentment of checks and truncation, 8.02, 8.03, 8.04[3][f], [4][c], [e], [g]
Presentment as a condition of dishonor, 4.03[2][a][i]
Principal but not agent liability, 5.03[2]
Procedural considerations in relation to defenses, 6.01[1][a]
Proceeds correctly paid, defense to action for forged indorsement, 7.03[3][c][i]
Proceeds remaining, effect of in relation to action for forged indorsement, 7.03[3][b][ii]
Prohibiting payment of customer's check, 9.01
Promissory note, 1.01[4][b]
"Properly payable," concept of, 9.01[1], [3]
Protest of dishonor, generally, 4.03[2][c]
Protest of dishonor, indorser, 4.06[2][a]
Provisional and final payment, 8.02, 8.03, 8.04
Provisional settlement, 8.02[1][b], 8.03[2], 8.04[4][c]
Provisional versus final settlement and payment, 8.02[1][b]
Ratification, 4.02[2][b]
Real defenses, 6.02
Reasonable cause to doubt collectability, exceptions for funds availability, 8.04[2][b]
Reasons for form requirements of negotiable instruments, 2.01[1]
Receipt of legal process, 9.01[5]
Receiving banks, duties and acceptance of payment orders, 10.04
Redeposited checks, exceptions for funds availability, 8.04[2][b]

INDEX

References not permitted, 2.02[3][b][i][B]
References permitted, 2.02[3][b][i][A]
References verses incorporation, 2.02[3][b][i]
Refusal to pay and dishonor of a cashier's or similar check, measure of liability, 9.01[4][d][iii], [iv]
Regulation CC (see also Expedited Funds Availability Act), 1.04[2], 8.04
   Duties of returning and depositary banks, 8.04[3][c], [d]
   Expeditious return, 8.04[3][a], [c][ii]
   Payor bank impact, 8.04[3][a][iii]
   Return process, comparison with UCC, 8.04[3][c][iii]
Regulation DD, 11.04[3][b]
Regulation E, 10.01, 11.01, 11.02, 11.03[2], 11.04
Regulation J, Subpart B, 10.12
Regulation J, Subpart A, collection of checks, 10.11
Regulation of depository services pricing, 9.03[2][c]
Relation between liability and defenses, 6.01[1]
Relation between the instrument and the transaction in general, 7.01[1]
Relevant time for meeting requirements of holder in due course, 3.03[2][b][i]
Remedies and limitations of warranties, 7.02[1][b]
Remitters, rights of, 3.01[3][a]
Remote data processing centers, 8.04[4][f]
Renunciation and cancellation, 6.03[6][c]
Repeated overdrafts, exception for funds availability, 8.04[2][b]
Requirements for "promise" for negotiability, 2.02[3][a]
Requirements of transfer and delivery, 3.02[3][a]
Requiring payment of customer's check, 9.01
Reacquisition, 3.02[4][b]
Rescission of final payment on restitutionary grounds, 3.03[3][b], 8.02[4]
Rescission of negotiation, 3.02[4][a]
Reserving the right to revoke settlement, 8.02[2][b]
Restitutionary grounds for avoidance of payment, 3.03[3][b], 8.02[4]
Restrictive indorsements, missing indorsements, and indorsements by banks, effect of, 3.02[3][c][iii], 7.03[3][c][ii][B], 8.04[3][g]
Restrictive indorsements, types and effects, 3.02[3][c][iii]
Return of the item and notice of dishonor, 8.02[6]
Return process, comparison to UCC Article 4, 8.04[3][c][iii]
Returning banks, duties of under Regulation CC, 8.04[3][c]
Right of enforcement, 3.01[4][b]
Right of discharge, 3.01[4][b]

Right to transfer or negotiate instrument, 3.01[4][c]
Right to subrogation after wrongful payment, 9.02[3]
Rights and liability with respect to the underlying transaction, 7.01
Rights and obligations of bank customers, 9.03
Rights created on instrument, 3.01
Rights, holder of an instrument, 3.01[4]
Rights to stop payment (or cancel), 9.01[4], 10.09[4]
Rules to forestall ambiguities, 2.04[1]
Satisfaction or payment and tender of payment, 6.03[6][b]
Satisfaction or payment to the holder, 6.03[6][b][ii]
Scope of Article 4, 8.01[1][a]
Scope of Article 4A, 10.01
Scope of Regulation CC, 8.04[1]
Seals, 2.03
Security procedure, 10.03[2]
Set off
   Absence of restrictions, 9.06[2][d]
   Competing claims, 9.06[2][e]
   Duty, 9.06[2][g], 10.08[2]
   Maturity of debt, 9.06[2][b]
   Mutuality of obligation, 9.06[2][c]
Settlement, 8.01[3][k], 8.02[1], [3]; 8.03[2], 8.04[3][c][iv], [f][iii], [4][c]
Settlement, charges and other notices, 8.04[3][c][iv]
Share drafts, 1.01[4][c], 9.04
Shelter rights, 3.01[3][b]
Signature as basis for liability, 4.02[1]
Signing requirement, 2.02[2]
Smart cards, 11.03[1]
Special indorsements, 3.02[3][c][ii]
Specific notice provisions and holder in due course, 3.03[2][b][v]
Standard of care and measure of damages under Regulation CC, 8.04[4][k]
State law in relation to credit and debit cards, 11.02[5]
State law, choice of law for negotiable instruments, 1.03[3][a]
Status of holder in due course, 3.03[3]
Statute of limitations, 6.03[7]
Stop payment
   Alternatives to, 9.01[4][c]
   Bank's ability to, 9.01[4][d][ii]
   Cashier's check, 9.01[4][d]
   Customer's ability to, 9.01[4][d][i]
   Orders, 9.01[4][a]
   Payment orders, cancellation, 10.09[4]
Stored value, 11.01, 11.03[1]
Subrogation, right to after wrongful payment, 9.02[3]
Sum certain, amount ascertainable from instrument, 2.02[4][a]
Sum certain provisions not creating uncertainty, 2.02[4][b]
Sum payable in money, 2.02[5]
Supplementary governing law, 1.04

Suspension of the underlying obligation, 7.01[1][b]
Takers, rights of, 3.01[3][a]
Teller's checks, 1.01[4][c]
Tender of payment and satisfaction or payment, 6.03[6][b]
Third party defenses (Jus tertii), 6.03[1][b]
Time of deposit and availability of funds, 8.02[5], 8.04[2]
Time of presentment, 4.03[2][a][ii]
Transaction and the instrument, relation between, 7.01[1]
Transferees, rights of, 3.01[3][b]
Transferor, warranties made by, 7.02[2]
Transfer, 3.02[1]
Traveler's checks, 1.01[4][c]
Treasury "Travel Rule", 10.15
Truncation, 8.01[3][n], 8.04[3][f], 8.04[4][g], 9.03[6]
Trust account, 9.05[3][c], 9.06[2][c]
Truth in Lending Act, 11.02, 11.04
Truth in Savings, 11.04[3][b]
"Two-day/Four-day" test of Regulation CC, 8.04[3][a][i]
UCC Article 1, general provisions, 1.04[4]
UCC Article 1, Section 1–103(b), general provisions outside the UCC, 1.04[5]
Unauthorized and erroneous orders, 10.09
Unauthorized complete instruments, 2.05[2]
Unauthorized completion, 6.03[3]
Unauthorized indorsers of instruments, 3.02[3][b][iv], 7.03[3][a]
Unauthorized signature, 4.02, 5.03[1], 7.02[3][a]
Unauthorized transfers, consumer liability under federal law, 11.02[3], 11.04[2]
Underlying obligation, suspension of, 7.01[1][b]

Underlying transaction, rights and liability with respect to, 7.01
United Nations Convention on Bills of Exchange and International Promissory Notes, 1.03[3][c]
Use of parol evidence to show defense, 6.01[2]
Uses of instruments, 1.01[2], [3]
Value, element of taking as holder in due course, 3.03[2][a]
Variation by agreement, 2.01[3], 8.01[2], 8.04[4][j], 9.01[4][b]
Visa cash, 11.01
Visa Travel Money, 11.01
Waiver of defense, impairment of recourse and collateral, 6.03[6][d][iii]
"Waiver of defenses" clause, 2.01[3][b]
Want or failure of consideration, 6.03[5]
Warranties made by transferor, 7.02[2]
Warranties made to an acceptor or payor, 7.02[3]
Warranties of paying and returning banks under Regulation CC, 8.04[3][e]
Warranty, in general, 7.02
Warranty obligations, nature of, 7.02[1][a]
Who may indorse instruments payable to estates, offices and the like, 3.02[3][b][iii]
Who may indorse instruments payable to more than one person, 3.02[3][b][ii]
"Wholesale funds transfer", 10.01
Wire transfer, 10.01
Written instrument requirement, 2.02[1]
Wrongful dishonor and error resolution, state and federal law, 11.02[2]
Wrongful dishonor, limitation of liability, 9.02[2][b]
Wrongful dishonor, 9.02[2]
Wrongful payment, 9.02[3]